# THE LEGAL, ETHICAL, AND REGULATORY ENVIRONMENT OF BUSINESS

*Eighth Edition*

BRUCE D. FISHER
*University of Tennessee*

MICHAEL J. PHILLIPS

THOMSON
™
SOUTH-WESTERN
WEST

Australia · Canada · Mexico · Singapore · Spain · United Kingdom · United States

**THOMSON**

**SOUTH-WESTERN**

**WEST**

*The Legal, Ethical, and Regulatory Environment of Business,* Eighth Edition
by Bruce D. Fisher and Michael J. Phillips

**Editor-in-Chief:**
Mike Roche

**Senior Acquisitions Editor:**
Rob Dewey

**Senior Developmental Editor:**
Susanna C. Smart

**Marketing Manager:**
Steve Silverstein

**Production Editor:**
Tammy E. Moore

**Senior Media Technology Editor:**
Vicky True

**Media Developmental Editor:**
Peggy Buskey

**Manufacturing Coordinator:**
Rhonda Utley

**Production House/Compositor:**
DPS Associates, Inc.

**Printer:**
Phoenix Color
Hagerstown, Maryland

**Design Project Manager:**
Bethany Casey

**Internal Designer:**
Jennifer Lambert, Jen2 Design

**Cover Design:**
Bethany Casey

**Cover Photography:**
PhotoDisc, Inc.

**Cover Illustration:**
Bethany Casey

For permission to use material from
this text or product, contact us by
Tel (800) 730-2214
Fax (800) 730-2215
http://www.thomsonrights.com

Library of Congress Control
Number: 2002116006

ISBN: 0-324-15474-7
(core text with InfoTrac)

ISBN: 0-324-27482-3
(core text only)

dedicated to Yves
Patron Saint of Lawyers
(1235 circa to 1303)
the late Marvin R. Wollin
and Beatrice M. Wollin

# BRIEF CONTENTS

# CONTENTS

## MODULE 1
## LEGAL AND BUSINESS ETHICS, OVERVIEW, AND FINDING THE LAW

## MODULE 2
## BUSINESS AND LEGAL SYSTEMS: COURTS, LEGISLATURES, ADMINISTRATIVE AGENCIES, CONSTITUTIONAL AND INTERNAL LAW AFFECTING REGULATION

---

## MODULE 3
## PRIVATE LAW AFFECTING ENTREPRENEURS

## MODULE 4
## LAW AFFECTING THE BUSINESS HUMAN RESOURCES DEPARTMENT

## MODULE 5
# LAW AFFECTING BUSINESS FINANCING

## 18 Business Organizations  478

## 19 Securities Regulation  517

## MODULE 6
# LAW AFFECTING THE MARKETING DEPARTMENT

# MODULE 7
# LAW AFFECTING THE MANUFACTURING DEPARTMENT

## 24  Environmental Law  685

# TABLE OF CASES

Principal cases in this text are listed below. References are to chapter and page numbers.

# PREFACE

## OUR PHILOSOPHY AND APPROACH

The eighth edition of *The Legal, Ethical, and Regulatory Environment of Business* reflects several events since the seventh edition that have cast new light on the way we look at the legal, ethical, and regulatory environment of business.

### ETHICS

The first of these events is the corporate and accounting scandals, which raise both positive law and ethical issues. Included are instances of high level corporate corruption in the form of outright positive law violations, for example, insider trading, "pump and dump" schemes, and other violations of securities and other laws. Of course, accusations are merely that. Just as we recoil when the poor and disadvantaged are deprived of their due process, so we must remember that everyone, even the rich and powerful, is innocent until proven guilty. Thus we should be wary of extrapolating from what appear to be the actions of a few to a conclusion that the entire market and corporate system is corrupt.

To address corporate illegality and ethics, we have included a new case in Chapter 1 dealing with a corrupt executive who persuades his auditors to sign off on questionable accounting. Sound familiar? Also, the eighth edition includes new material in Chapter 7 on the Sarbanes–Oxley Act's *financial expert* "mandate" for public companies' boards, a new proposed regulation implementing this mandate (*financial literacy*, education, experience, and other factors), actual public comments from experts on who financial experts are, whether the SEC proposed regulation should be modified, and suggestions to students on how they can use the Internet to locate the final *promulgated* SEC regulation (when it appears) on who possesses the qualifications to be a financial expert for the board.

The corporate corruption and ethics issue is dealt with again in Chapter 19 that outlines major provisions of the Sarbanes–Oxley Act, the new federal legislation aimed at curtailing corporate and accounting abuses. Additionally, we retain cases on insider trading and various other forms—new and old—of securities fraud (Chapter 19) so these important assemblers of business information can be aware of basic liabilities to their clients and third parties.

Other ethical concerns raised by corporate and accounting improprieties are treated in a number of ways. First, the whole question of whether use of the corporate form is a proper way to avoid debts is raised in a new case in Chapter 18. Of course, ethical considerations in various contexts remain as the central theme in Chapter 1. Additionally, each chapter begins with a Positive Law Ethical Problem(s) which anticipates actual cases in the chapter. Because most of the cases are set in a business context, ethical and legal issues are repeatedly raised. Also, at the conclusion of each chapter is a Manager's Ethical Dilemma, some of which are open-ended, others are actual cases, although even they are, to some extent, open-ended. Ethical questions after various cases throughout the text ask students to recall ethical considerations raised in Chapter 1.

Finally, to dispel the cynicism that the corporate and accounting scandals have bred, Chapter 1 begins on an optimistic note with the story of Oseola McCarty, an 87-year-old cleaning lady, who gave her entire life savings to a university so others could obtain the college education she never enjoyed. Ms. McCarty's story leads into the new inclusion of the important ethical topic of *virtue ethics*. New text presents levels of *giving* at the national as well as corporate and individual levels.

## SECURITY

The tragic events of September 11, 2001 will live in our memories forever. These horrors show how distorted ideas can lead to the need for enhanced security. Security is dealt with directly in a new case in Chapter 14 discussing an employer's liability when a guard kills a person on company property.

Security is present also in privacy matters. Chapter 10 presents the matter of whether a corporation enjoys the common law right of privacy. Consumer privacy is presented in Chapter 22 with discussion of the Gramm–Leach–Bliley Act's privacy provisions. Two other new cases in the government regulation chapters (6 and 7) present privacy issues under FERPA (the Family Educational Rights and Privacy Act) and the matter of when Social Security numbers may not be suppressed under the Federal Privacy Act and other federal privacy laws.

A diagram in Chapter 6 shows the newly created Department of Homeland Security, which is charged with maintaining and improving domestic security in the United States.

Finally, on the security/privacy front, there is a new administrative search-and-seizure case in the context of an EEOC "random" investigation of whether a company is complying with affirmative action.

Security for employees often takes the form of health insurance. Chapter 15 contains new text which explains COBRA. The considerable limits on COBRA may cause many employees to wonder if it really provides any health security at all.

## INTELLECTUAL PROPERTY

Even though the dot-com/telecom bubble has burst, the need for business coverage of intellectual property remains strong. This edition contains expanded coverage of copyright and trademark law. Types of copyright infringement are discussed, including vicarious and contributory infringement along with new cases. Trademark coverage includes updated materials on cybersquatting and nominative use.

## INTERNATIONAL TOPICS

The internationalization of the U.S. economy is old news. However, the two chapters on this important topic include new text on *Comparative Advantage*, the theoretical basis for international trade, and the *Kyoto Treaty*, a document the U.S. has refused to sign. A new chart depicts recent comparative international manufacturing costs. Chapter 2 contains a case dealing with smuggling money out of the United States, which takes on significance when funding of international terrorism is a concern.

# PROVOCATIVE NEW CASES

Approximately 20 percent of the cases in the eighth edition are new. Almost every chapter in this edition has at least one new principal case in the body of the chapter. However, classic cases such as the *Erie Railroad v. Tompkins*, *Riggs v. Palmer*, and *Palsgraf v. Long Island Railroad Co.* remain. Other case changes reflect new legal approaches or applications.

New cases throughout the text include the following:

- *In the Matter of the Estate of Marshall Gardiner* in Chapter 1 deals with the topic of diversity in the context of whether or not to recognize a male-to-female transsexual as a woman with a right to inherit under her late husband's will.
- *U.S. v. Bajakajian* in Chapter 2 explores penalties for smuggling currency out of the U.S.
- *Bush v. Gore* in Chapter 3 examines which cases are appropriate for legal as opposed to political disposition.
- A new case deals with an attorney's ethical duties to a client in Chapter 4.
- Four new cases deal with constitutional law (one on the commerce clause, a second on commercial speech, a third on preemption, and a fourth on takings) in Chapter 5.
- *In re Crawford* in Chapter 6 presents the problem of a professional bankruptcy petition preparer's requirement to include his Social Security number on petitions he drafts.
- *Gonzaga v. Doe* (also Chapter 6) explores a recent U.S. Supreme Court interpretation of FERPA in which a college student sued a professor for making accusations of sexual immorality preventing the student from obtaining a teaching certificate.
- *Beverly Enterprises v. Herman* in Chapter 7 shows a business challenging the EEOC's random searches of businesses for compliance purposes.
- *Felsher v. University of Evansville* in Chapter 10 considers whether corporations should have a common law right of privacy.
- A new statute of frauds case appears in Chapter 11 covering contracts.
- A new landlord/tenant case appears in Chapter 12 on property.
- Several new intellectual property cases in Chapter 13 include the *Napster* case, *Sporty's Farm v. Sportsman's Market* (dealing with cybersquatting), and *Playboy Enterprises v. Welles* (concerning a former Playmate's right to use Playboy Enterprise's trademarks on her Web site).
- *Ruiz v. Belk Masonry* is a new case in Chapter 14 dealing with whether illegal aliens are covered by an employer's worker's compensation insurance.
- A new case in Chapter 15 deals with an employer's liability for FICA and FUTA contributions for "leased" employees when the leasing employer has paid the leasor employer for such payments and the lessor fails to remit them to the government.
- Cases in Chapter 16 on employment discrimination include a "voluntary" Title VII reverse discrimination case (an application of *Steelworkers v. Webber*), a new same-sex sexual harassment case, and a new 2002 U.S. Supreme Court case concerning the Americans with Disabilities Act.
- *Bloedon v. Francisco Foods*, a new case in Chapter 17 on labor law, discusses successor employer's liability for a prior employer's union contracts.
- *Agway v. Brooks*, a new case in Chapter 18, presents the question of whether shareholders are ever liable for corporate debts.

- *SEC v. Zandford*, a new U.S. Supreme Court case in Chapter 19, examines the scope of fraud in connection with the purchase or sale of any security.
- The *Microsoft* case as well as a new Clayton Act horizontal merger case which includes an application of the Herfindahl-Hirschmann Index appears in Chapter 20.
- A newly organized section on Section 5 of the FTC Act as well as a 2002 U.S. Supreme Court decision on the Lanham Act are included in Chapter 21.
- A new case on the Truth-in-Lending Act plus discussion of the Gramm–Leach–Bliley Act are in Chapter 22.
- Three new cases (one on implied warranty of fitness, a second on negligence/strict liability with a terrorism angle, and a third that covers UCC remedy limitations) are included in Chapter 23.
- Two new cases (one on environmental racism and a second on the NPDES permit system under the Clean Water Act) are in Chapter 24.
- An update on developments under the Nuclear Waste Policy Act and subsequent legislation dealing with siting of nuclear waste are also included.

## RETAINED EMPHASES

We continue to place a prime emphasis on American Assembly of Collegiate Schools of Business (AACSB) suggestions on appropriate legal coverage for business students. The AACSB sets the accreditation standards for schools and colleges of business nationwide. Coverage should include: ethical and global issues; the influence of political, social, legal and regulatory, environmental, and technological issues; and the impact of demographic diversity on organizations.

Thus, environmental coverage has been expanded, not only in the environmental law chapters, but elsewhere if appropriate. The continued emphasis in the business arena of international business issues has resulted in increased and updated international law coverage, as well as employment law coverage.

Issues concerning ethics continue to be an important part of business dealings globally. Clearly, there is no more important ethic than the positive law—the constitution, treaties, statutes, and regulations on the books—with which the business community must contend on a daily basis. Further, it is essential that business be aware of the social, political, and demographic context that has shaped positive law, particularly positive law that regulates business. By being familiar with these forces, businesses—and citizens in general—can understand why the law is as it is today. This edition also addresses the recent developments that promise to shape our national and international legal, regulatory, and ethical environment for years to come.

## TEXT FEATURES

### INTERNET FEATURES IN EACH CHAPTER

The eighth edition continues to utilize Internet addresses in textual margin notations so inquisitive students can have easy access to topical areas peripheral to chapter content, or in more depth than the chapter content. Given the volatility of this rapidly changing area of technology, the Internet addresses in the text are updated periodically on the text's Web site at **http://fisher.westbuslaw.com**.

New to this edition are *InfoTrac Keywords* at the end of each chapter. The keywords direct students to articles relevant to chapter topics through the InfoTrac® library at **http://www.infotrac-college.com**. An access card with passcode is provided at no additional cost with every new textbook.

## CLOSED-LOOP APPROACH TO ETHICAL PEDAGOGY IN EVERY CHAPTER

Each chapter starts with a Positive Law Ethical Problem and concludes with a Manager's Ethical Dilemma. This forces students to take note of ethical considerations when they start each chapter and to apply their skills to another ethical problem at the end of each chapter. The introductory ethical problem in each chapter is answered either by chapter cases or discussion. The Manager's Ethical Dilemma is open-ended.

## MANAGER'S ETHICAL DILEMMAS

Unlike the positive law ethical problems, at least one of which starts each chapter, a Manager's Ethical Dilemma concludes each chapter. In contrast to positive law ethical problems, the Manager's Ethical Dilemma is more open-ended. This is in keeping with the managerial focus of this text, where some actual ethical problems are presented that managers either have faced or are likely to encounter in their roles. These segments—placed near the end of the chapter—are suitable for class discussion. Some are based on actual cases while others present hypothetical situations. The Manager's Ethical Dilemma deals with topics raised by or as an extension of the chapter's material.

## CHAPTER SUMMARIES

The chapter summary at the conclusion of each chapter enables the student to briefly review the material studied. Key points in the chapter are summarized. Students who are vague on key concepts can return to the full text and reread problem segments.

## COURSE SUPPORT MATERIALS

- The *Instructor's Manual with Test Bank* has been revised by Professor Hamilton Peterson of American University, and contains case briefs, answers to end-of-case questions, solutions to end-of-chapter problems, and Internet exercises, as well as an expanded test bank.
- *ExamView, Computerized Testing Software* contains all of the questions in the printed test bank. This program is an easy-to-use test creation software compatible with Microsoft Windows. Instructors can add or edit questions, instructions, and answers, and select questions by previewing them on the screen and selecting them randomly or selecting them by number. Instructors can also create and administer quizzes online, whether over the Internet, a local area network (LAN), or a wide area network (WAN).

- *PowerPoint Lecture Slides*, prepared by Jimidene Murphy of South Plains College, are available on the text Web site to both instructors—to serve as a lecture aid—and students—to aid in note-taking and study.
- *Online Quizzes*, prepared by William E. Dellinger of the University of Missouri at Columbia, provide practice questions for students to test their understanding of each chapter with immediate feedback so students will know what topics they need to study more carefully.
- The text Web site at *http://fisher.westbuslaw.com* contains Internet Updates, Case Updates by legal topics, the PowerPoint slides, Online Quizzes, links to the West Business Law Faculty Center and its many teaching resources, and the Student Center with links to news, legal, and government links, InfoTrac College Edition, and much more.
- *Westlaw.* Ten complimentary hours of Westlaw are available to qualified adopters from West's premier legal research system.
- *Infotrac® College Edition* is an online library containing hundreds of scholarly and popular periodicals, including *American Business Law Journal*, *Journal of International Business Studies*, *Environmental Law*, and *Ethics*. It offers a database updated daily, full-length articles, and keyword searches that quickly and efficiently scan the entire database. *InfoTrac® College Edition* is packaged with all new copies of this text at no additional cost to instructors or students.
- The *West Legal Studies Video Library* is available to qualified adopters of this text. You may be eligible to access the entire library of West videos, a vast selection covering most business law and legal environment issues. There are some restrictions, and if you have questions, please contact your local Thomson Learning/West Legal Studies sales representative or visit **http://www. Westbuslaw.com/video_library.html**.
- A *Handbook of Basic Law Terms* (*Black's Dictionary* Series) may be shrink-wrapped with the text at a discounted price. A *Handbook of Basic Law Terms* is a guide to the most important and most common words and phrases used in the law today. Students can keep this comprehensive and helpful dictionary for both their professional and personal lives.

## ACKNOWLEDGMENTS

The authors wish to acknowledge their editors' efforts in preparing this edition, and thanks go to Rob Dewey, Susanna Smart, Tamborah Moore, Steve Silverstein, and Crystal Chapin. We also wish to thank the following reviewers for their contributions to this and previous editions:

A. David Austill, Union University
Robert B. Bennett, Butler University
Linda Christiansen, Indiana University, Southeast
Novella Clevenger, Washburn University
Vince Enslein, Clinton Community College
Jay Erstling, University of St. Thomas
Joan T. A. Gabel, Georgia State University
Paula S. Hearn, University of Tennessee–Martin
David I. Kapelner, Merrimack College
David Kent, Plymouth State College

Kurtis P. Klumb, University of Wisconsin–Milwaukee
Paul J. Krazeise, Jr., Bellarmine College
E. Bruce Mather, Emory University
Ann C. Morales, University of Miami
David W. Murphy, Madisonville Community College–University of Kentucky
Hamilton Peterson, American University
James T. Poindexter, Duquesne University
Roger W. Reinsch, Emporia State University
James G. Rittenbaum, St. Louis University
Richard D. Sambuco, West Virginia Northern Community College
Leo J. Stevenson, Western Michigan University
William H. Volz, Wayne State University
Michael G. Walsh, Villanova University
Pamela Poole Weber, Seminole Community College

We also thank Marshall Ramsey, award-winning cartoonist for the Clarion Ledger of Madison, Mississippi, one of three nominees for a Pulitzer Prize for editorial cartooning. Marshall's cartoons are found in several chapters. His wit, wisdom, and, at times, sardonic perspective all add an extra dimension to the chapters.

# LEGAL AND BUSINESS ETHICS, OVERVIEW, AND FINDING THE LAW

**CHAPTER 1**

The Law, and Legal and
Business Ethics

**CHAPTER 2**

Overview and Finding the Law

# THE LAW, AND LEGAL AND BUSINESS ETHICS

## POSITIVE LAW ETHICAL PROBLEMS

Oseola McCarty was an 87-year-old cleaning lady. She had no family and always lived alone. She had spent her entire life in her hometown of Hattiesburg, Mississippi. One day she called the University of Southern Mississippi in Hattiesburg and set up an appointment to see the university's president. On the given day, Miss McCarty was ushered into the president's office.

"It's a pleasure to meet you, Miss McCarty. Please sit down," said the president. "To what do I owe the honor of this visit?"

"Mr. President, I want to give the University of Southern Mississippi my entire life savings of $150,000," she replied.

The president was taken aback. "Miss McCarty, I am overwhelmed by your generosity. Why do you want to do this? You are not an alumna." What the president did not say was that the university did not even admit African-Americans until the 1960s, long after Miss McCarty would have attended.

"I am giving it away so that the children won't have to work so hard like I did," she said.

Miss McCarty did, in fact, give her entire life savings to the University of Southern Mississippi. Following public announcement of her gift, Miss McCarty became a national celebrity at the age of eighty-seven. She was honored at the University of Southern Mississippi, the United Nations, met President Clinton, and received an honorary Harvard degree. When she traveled, she stayed in a hotel for the first time, where she made her own bed because she was unaware that guests were spared this chore.

What ethical values are at work in the true story recited above?

"They don't believe me!" exclaimed Wilson Ford, after he had been dismissed by his employer, A&P grocery store.

"But why should they?" asked a friend. "You failed a lie detector test. You said that you deposited A&P's cash into the night depository slot at NCNB Bank. But the bank did not find the deposit bag the next morning when it looked, so your employer, A&P, assumed that you lied about depositing the money in the bank. They fired you when you failed a lie detector test about the matter."

Should an employee's failing a lie detector test be conclusive as to a person's trust worthiness?

"Eric, I am not going to pay you the contract amount of $5,107.40 for building the swimming pool for my trailer park," said Dorothy Powell to an astounded Eric Rushing.

"But, why, Ms. Powell?" asked Eric. "The pool works fine and it looks great in your trailer park."

Dorothy replied, "Well, Eric, I have learned that you don't have a swimming pool contractor's license, and the law says that your contracts to build swimming pools are invalid."

Eric thought this was legal mumbo-jumbo, "Look, Ms. Powell, people today are relying too much on the law to determine what is right or wrong. You came to me and asked me to bid on your swimming pool, which I did. I was the low bidder. I built the pool, and it works fine. The licensing law does not say you may not pay me; it only says that you *legally* do not have to pay me. Rise above the law. Do the *morally* right thing: Pay me."

"We can't sign off on your books, Mr. Roth," said Mr. Simon, an accountant with the Lybrand, Ross Brothers and Montgomery Accounting firm.
 "Why is that?" asked Harold Roth, the president of Continental Vending Corporation, which had hired the Lybrand firm for several years to audit Continental's books.
 "Because we have found that you have been improperly borrowing corporate funds through an intermediary company and cannot repay the loan. This entire situation 'smells bad,' and, as ethical accountants, we cannot sign off on your books," replied Mr. Simon.
 "You signed off on my books last year, and I was doing the same thing. If you don't sign off this year I'll sue you on behalf of Continental, claiming that you were negligent in your prior years' audits. Now go back to your office and think that over," said Mr. Roth.
 What should an ethical accountant do—admit a past mistake and be sued for negligence, or compromise his ethics and try to cover up a past error?

The preceding stories challenge and often trouble us because of their many conflicting ideas about proper conduct. Determining appropriate conduct in a given situation is what ethics is about. This chapter introduces the topic of ethics in the following way: first, a general discussion of the meaning, nature, and limits of ethics is presented. Second, the ethic of positive law is explained. Third, **jurisprudence**—the study of legal ethics—is discussed and defined along with a brief discussion of various recognized beliefs about ethical values associated with law. Fourth comes an examination of **business ethics**—values that the business community uses to determine proper conduct. By the time one considers the many various aspects of ethics, the very notion of what *is* ethical conduct can become confusing. To help alleviate some of that confusion, our discussion concludes with a strategy for managers to follow when confronting situations involving ethical issues.

## THE MEANING, NATURE, AND LIMITS OF ETHICS

**Ethics** (also called **deontology**) refers to the study of conduct that is right, good, or moral in a given set of circumstances. Said another way, ethics involves the study of clashes of moral values. In other words, ethical problems exist because we have choices. For example, should a rich person offer money to a beggar who asks for it on the street? The rich person might ponder the situation and conclude that giving a small amount is "a good thing" because doing so will enable the beggar to buy food and thereby survive. On the other hand, the rich person might think that giving money to panhandlers will encourage begging rather than working, which is the socially preferable means of acquiring money. Thus, ethics assumes a person has several choices in a situation. Most situations do, in fact, offer several choices of conduct.
 Consider another example. A businessperson might not want to pay income taxes. In such a situation one might say that the businessperson has no choice but to pay because the law requires it. However, the business could cease to operate; then it would owe no taxes. This choice might seem absurd when survival is an ethic that most recognize, but the decision to continue in business is a choice. Another choice would be to lie about one's income, claiming that no taxable income exists. Here, the choice involves violating the law (or positive law, as we

shall soon define it) or obeying it. The study of ethics does not necessarily assume that the positive law must in all circumstances be obeyed.

One often hears of ethical codes for accountants, lawyers, doctors, architects, engineers, and other professions. These codes attempt to establish in advance what professionals should do in situations involving clashes of values. For example, an accountant might face an ethical dilemma when a client insists on following a risky tax strategy that the accountant knows has been questioned in the past by the tax authorities. The accountant is supposed to observe the law if it is certain, but the client is paying the accountant's salary, and the law might not be that definite. A professional code of ethics may help to address this matter.

## NATURE (A PRIORI) AND LIMITS TO ETHICS (ETHICAL AMBIGUITY)

*A Priori.* Several points emerge from the study of ethics. First, ethics are by their nature ultimate values. That is, we attribute a moral value to something because we value that thing. Because ethics are ultimate values, they self-justify. Said another way, ethics are *a priori*, meaning that they are assumed valuable with no further need for justification. If one says *justice* is an ethic or ultimate value, further explanation is seldom needed because most people readily understand the desirability of justice.

*Ethical Ambiguity.* Ethics or ultimate values sometimes conflict, and one ethic can even justify opposite sides of the same issue. When this type of conflict occurs, we have ethical ambiguity. Each of the stories at the start of this chapter contains ethical ambiguity. For another example, consider a law allowing the death penalty. A believer in the ethic of justice might argue that capital punishment laws are unjust and invalid because society is doing the very thing it condemns (murder) by intentionally taking the life of the murderer. The supporter of the capital punishment law, on the other hand, might argue that justice demands the death penalty as a deterrent to would-be murderers, and also cite the Bible's "eye for an eye" proposition that if one person deprives another of her life, the murderer should give up his life. Who is right about capital punishment? Both sides have strong ethical arguments. Ethical arguments do not necessarily result in *one* correct answer. Hence, we have what is called an *ethical ambiguity*, or ethical dilemma.

How do we resolve ethical dilemmas? We make a decision. We do something. Although ethical dilemmas may, at times, confuse us, their value lies in helping us make informed decisions. We are taking all relevant factors into account in making our decisions. Also, ethical knowledge makes us more articulate. The more articulate we are in justifying projects or positions, the more power we give to those positions and their potential acceptance by others.

One approach to dealing with ethical ambiguity in our daily lives is the manager's ethical decision model. The next section of this chapter examines this model.

## MANAGER'S ETHICAL DECISION MODEL

### STRATEGY FOR MANAGERS CONFRONTING AN ETHICAL PROBLEM

As we shall see throughout this chapter, businesspeople confront many situations in which they must ask, "What should I do? What is the proper, ethical conduct in this matter?" The following *ethical manager's strategy* is suggested:[1]

1. State the problem. This statement may be modified as additional facts appear.
2. Choose your goals or objectives in dealing with the problem.
3. Determine the facts and other contextual factors in the situation, which is often difficult if some or all of the parties have an interest in concealing or misrepresenting key facts. Contextual factors include:
   a. Identifying the stakeholders
   b. Learning the stakeholders' demands and expectations
   c. Ascertaining what resources are available to satisfy stakeholders and whether those resources are available to the decision makers
   d. Noting the relevant institutional framework (Is this a matter within a company, or does it involve community matters such as positive law issues?)
   e. Learning the customary practices in settling such matters
   f. Identifying major social trends or movements that could affect the problem
4. Identify *all possible courses of action* you could take to deal with the problem. This involves *brainstorming* (creative, uninhibited thinking).
5. Project the probable outcomes for each course of action, and select the course that conforms to positive law as well as has the highest likelihood of achieving your goal with the least adverse impact on stakeholders while affording the greatest benefits.

## CAVEATS IN APPLYING THE MANAGER'S ETHICAL DECISION MODEL

Managers should keep several warnings in mind in applying the manager's ethical decision model. First, this model is an approach to finding an ethical course of action; it does not guarantee the "correctness" of the decision itself. Second, sometimes a manager might want to change the order of the steps, for example, when a manager wants to do fact-finding *before* trying to state the problem. The model even suggests that the statement of the problem may have to be modified in light of later developed facts.

Lastly, this decision model requires that persons using it exercise judgment. Judgment refers to the ability to see relationships, distinguish alternatives, and make reasonable decisions in light of those relationships and alternatives.

If the manager's ethical decision model seems too complex, there is another practical way to be ethical: Follow the positive law. The next section discusses the positive law and why it can be an ethic.

## THE ETHIC OF POSITIVE LAW

### POSITIVE LAW DEFINED

Upon exiting the trial of former aid John Poindexter, former President Ronald Reagan reportedly said, "I followed the law." In so doing, Mr. Reagan was implicitly saying that a person who follows the law is ethical.

---

[1] The authors acknowledge Professors Mayo and Jones's Basic Decision Model in devising this decision approach.

When most people use the word *law* they are referring to **positive law**.[2] An Englishman named John Austin, writing in the nineteenth century, is credited with developing the idea of positive law as we know it today. Austin said that positive law consists of three parts:

1. a rule
2. from a political superior to a political inferior that the inferior habitually obeys
3. with sanctions imposed if the rule is broken.

## SOME POSITIVE LAW CHARACTERISTICS

*Command Element of Positive Law.* One aspect of positive law is that it commands us to do certain things, such as drive no more than 25 miles per hour or pay income taxes. In other words, positive law often imposes a duty or obligation on us.

Sometimes positive law does not command but merely permits us to do something. For example, the positive law might say that 18-year-olds may make contracts, but it does not require 18-year-olds to make contracts.

*No Requirements on the Type of Ruler.* Positive law supports lawful authority and does not question how the ruler got its authority. Thus, a king, a dictator, the U.S. Supreme Court, a U.S. president, the local city council, and state judges are all positive lawmakers. Note that some of these lawmakers are elected and others are not.

In the United States, with its strong democratic tradition, persons with authority to make law generally are elected and thus receive their authority from the people they rule. Being democratically elected confers legitimacy on a ruler. By legitimacy, we mean that people are not as likely to question something's origin. If people question the rules democratically elected rulers make, voters face the challenge, "Well, you elected them. If you do not like what the rulers have done, vote them out at the next election."

However, positive law theorists generally do not require that the rulers be elected, nor do they say anything about how the lawmaker is selected. Thus, according to positive law theorists, tyrants such as Hitler and Stalin were rulers even if they were not democratically elected.

*Classical Positive Law Expects Habitual Obedience to the Rules.* Some positive law advocates say that both citizens and rulers must obey the law. (Actually John Austin, an early legal positivist, believed that the ruler was above the law and did not have to obey it, but other legal positivists do not take such an extreme position.) Perhaps the strongest aspect of positive law is the **rule of law**, which states that all citizens—the president, governors, members of the Supreme Court, star athletes, and average citizens—must obey the rules. However, modern positive law theory also requires that rulers obey their own system's procedures and rules for passing laws.

---

[2]The terms *positive law* and *analytical positivism* are used interchangeably here. Positive law is actually a broader term than analytical positivism. John Austin's command definition is a recognized positive law definition although Professor Hart has outlined four other definitions of legal positivism: (1) the separation of law and morality; (2) noncognitivism, the idea that law represents choices among competing values that are a priori or presumptively good, such as "family values;" (3) the "mechanical view" that law is a logically contained system and that judges therefore mechanically apply the rules to specific cases; and (4) that people should obey law even if it is unjust. Analytical positivists would fall into the "mechanical" school of legal positivism.

Although talk shows and other media highlight legal controversies such as mercy killings and same-sex marriages, making it seem that the U.S. legal system is in turmoil, most people agree with the vast majority of laws on the books in the United States that deal with such mundane matters as contracts, property transfers, and traffic regulation.

*Positive Law Generally Advances Constructive Goals.* Virtually all positive law tries to promote constructive goals. For example, the rules forbidding fraud, murder, environmental degradation, and many other antisocial activities are the result of positive law.

*Positive Law Can Be Moral, Amoral, or Immoral.* Suppose a country tried to control population growth by limiting couples to one child, killing all children beyond the firstborn. Would positive law say that such a law is valid? If such a law is passed according to that country's legal procedures and conforms to all of its laws, then positive law theorists would say that an infanticide (baby killing) law is valid.

The preceding example leads to another point about positive law: Positive law theory does not require that the positive law be moral or fair. In fact, some legal positivists agree that questions of law and morality are separate issues in the sense that if positive law settles a matter, it settles the legal matter only but not the moral issue. That is, just because a law is immoral does not make it invalid. Also, moral conduct is not necessarily legal conduct.

Of course, positive laws that most of us encounter in our daily lives have some rational basis, and thus we consider them fair or moral. For example, most people would say that it is wrong to misrepresent facts in our business dealings with others, and so does positive law when it forbids fraud. Thus positive law and morality frequently overlap as a practical matter.

However, in Hitler's Germany, it was against the law for a Jew to have a driver's license, attend certain universities, or hold certain jobs. Should these restrictions be so simply because of one's religion or ethnic background? Even a legal positivist would say that if Hitler's laws are legally valid, they do not resolve the separate moral question, "Should I obey this law?" Thus, legal positivists recognize that morality exists. Also, legal positivists know that morality and positive law can overlap, and often they reach the same conclusion on an issue. For example, both moralists and legal positivists would probably agree that arson should be illegal.

The following case presents the issue of whether the positive law should be followed when obeying it would arguably produce an unjust result. Ask yourself whether positive law or fairness (which we shall see later in this chapter refers to *natural law*) wins out.

## Rushing v. Powell
California Court of Appeal (5th Dist.)
130 Cal. Rptr. 110 (1976)

### Background and Facts

Dorothy Powell hired Eric Rushing to build a swimming pool for her trailer park for $5,107.40. Eric had an individual California concrete contractor's license. However, he did not have a California swimming pool contractor's license. California law forbids persons from doing work for which they are unlicensed.

Junior Ray Anderson had a California swimming pool contractor's license. Eric used Junior to get a swimming pool contractor's license so he could build Dorothy Powell's pool. Eric and Junior got a joint swimming pool contractor's license under the name "Stardust Pools." Because Junior already had such a license, the California licensing officials waived Eric from taking and passing the licensing exam or showing fitness to be a swimming pool contractor. Eric gave Junior equipment worth $6,000 for helping him get the license. Junior never actually did any swimming pool construction with Eric.

Eric built Dorothy Powell's pool, but she refused to pay. She claimed that Eric did not follow the plans. Eric sued Dorothy for breach of contract. Dorothy defended by arguing that Eric had not complied with California's fictitious business name statute or California's contractor licensing law. The trial court awarded Eric $5,107.40 (the contract amount) plus $198.73 for extras beyond the contract. Dorothy appealed.

## Issue

May a contractor recover for work if he or she does not have the proper contractor's license and has not complied with the fictitious name statute?

## Decision

A contractor may not recover for work if he or she is unlicensed. The contractor's licensing law is intended to protect the public against

dishonesty and incompetence and deter would-be violators. The unlicensed contractor may not collect the $5,107.40 contract amount. However, the contractor may recover $198.73 for extras that were not part of the contract.

The contractor (Eric) complied with the fictitious name statute by filing a certificate showing that he was doing business as an individual.

## Questions

1. Which prevailed in the *Rushing v. Powell* case, the "rules on the books," that is, positive law, or justice?
2. Is it necessarily unjust for a person such as Ms. Powell to avail herself of a rule to excuse performance of an otherwise legally owing debt? But was the debt *legally* owing?
3. If the purpose of the licensing law—one of the rules at issue in *Rushing v. Powell*—is to protect the public against dishonesty and incompetence, how was Ms. Powell cheated or harmed by incompetence? Could it be argued that Ms. Powell, as the person whom the licensing law was attempting to protect, was the wrongdoer in this instance?

---

*Possible Weaknesses of Positive Law.* Positive law is open to several other weaknesses. It can be vague, causing people to wonder what is legal or illegal. For example, the **Robinson-Patman Act** is an antitrust law making the selling of goods at unreasonably low prices a criminal act. Many businesspeople ask, "What is an unreasonably low price?" If they guess incorrectly, they could be criminally charged.

Positive law is, as a practical matter, vast and unknowable. Consider the following: A motorist from New York drives to Tennessee where it is raining and rams another car. The police officer issues the New Yorker a ticket for driving without her headlights on during a rainstorm. The New Yorker argues that she is ignorant of Tennessee's traffic laws and that because it was daylight, she had no reason to put on her headlights. Ignorance of the law is no excuse. We are held responsible for obeying (and knowing) the positive laws of every jurisdiction into which we venture.

We can understand why ignorance should not be a defense, because one could literally get away with murder (the first time, at least) by arguing ignorance of murder laws when charged with murdering one's spouse. Therefore, ignorance is *not* a defense, and people are expected to know the positive law even though, as a practical matter, complete knowledge is impossible. For an extreme example of this requirement, read the *Federal Crop Insurance v. Merrill* case in Chapter 7 in which a farmer was expected to know the requirements of crop regulations contained in the *Federal Register,* which typically has over 50,000 pages each year.

Finally, the positive law might not address specific matters of what is right or wrong. For example, as of this writing, leveraged buyouts (LBOs) are not generally illegal, according to the positive law, even though they often destroy companies, cause workers to lose their jobs, and disrupt communities where the destroyed employers used to operate. Should LBOs be made illegal? This issue is repeatedly debated by financial, economic, legal, and other experts, with positive law providing few definite answers. Often, in areas where there previously has been no positive law, courts (one positive lawmaker) speak out on a matter, followed by the legislature's (another type of positive lawmaker) actions if a general social consensus develops. If no consensus develops, the courts can either leave the matter unregulated or deal with the situation on a piecemeal basis.

## DEMOCRATIC, CONSTITUTIONAL, EMPIRICALLY BASED POSITIVE LAW: THE ETHIC OF OUR TIME

This book follows the view that democratic (small "d," thus covering Republicans as well as Democrats), constitutional, empirically based positive law is the ethic of our time. First, let us point out *the* major difference between traditional positive law and modern democratic, constitutional positive law. As already discussed, traditional positive law does not require that the law be moral or immoral, but democratic, constitutional positive law *does* have a moral element in several senses. First, it is moral in that the lawmaker derives its authority from the people. In a democracy, the people either make the law or elect those who do. People have the right to vote and thus share to some extent in the lawmaking. Democracy gives legitimacy and hence confers morality on the law.

Second, constitutionality confers morality on positive law because a constitution limits what positive law can do according to general principles that have a moral element. For example, the U.S. Constitution's Bill of Rights contains many limits on positive law based on fairness—the right to express oneself freely, the right to due process (such as notice and hearing before one can be punished), the privilege against self-incrimination, and the protection against cruel and unusual punishment, to name but a few.

Third, positive law intrudes into the lives of individuals and businesses as never before. We are told to clean up toxic waste dumps, which can cost billions. People rightly ask to see the science behind such positive law demands. What harm do small amounts of asbestos cause? If the answer is "serious harm," then, of course, positive law regulations should stand. The use of data, facts, and empirical evidence as the basis for positive law commands is called **philosophical positivism**. It differs from positive law, which is the law on the books. If the regulation is based merely on a "hunch" or intuition, the "feeling" that asbestos harms people, a philosophical positivist would say that no positive law should regulate asbestos until facts establish that it is harmful.

## WHY DEMOCRATIC, CONSTITUTIONAL, EMPIRICALLY BASED LAW IS THE ETHIC OF OUR TIME

Today, more than ever, democratic, constitutional, empirically based positive law is the dominant ethic in U.S. society. In other words, when people try to determine what is the proper course of conduct, they ask, "What does the law require?" For several reasons, the authors of this book adopt the view that democratic, constitutional, empirically based positive law is the guide to ethical (proper) conduct.

*The Lack of Trust in Society.* Today, a decline in trust in U.S. society, and, perhaps, in the world generally, is evident. We need only read the newspapers to learn of stories in which high-placed government or corporate officials have lied to us. The average person thinks, "Why should I trust people who lie?"

People tend to think that the pain of perjury punishment will cause people to be more honest in their claims under oath and in their dealings. However, even

U.S. presidents can lie under oath. Of course, one must raise the further judgmental question, "Is what a person lies about important, or is it a trivial matter unrelated to the larger question of a person's fitness to do the job and, if so, do we overlook what he or she lies about?" For example, one might ask a presidential candidate, "Do you wear false teeth?" If the person does, in fact, wear false teeth but answers "No," we might dismiss this untruth as the result of vanity and elect that candidate anyway. To claim that small lies can lead to big lies is to overextrapolate and tends to lead to moral zealotry: "If he lies about false teeth, he'll lie about Social Security." The logic of this proposition does not always hold true.

To ascertain truth, one might subject individuals thought to be lying to polygraph (lie detector) tests. However, lie detector tests are not foolproof. They can register truth when a person is lying; likewise, they can indicate that a truthful person is lying and therefore not trustworthy. The following case illustrates the unreliability of lie detectors as a measure of trust.

## Ford v. NCNB Corporation
Court of Appeals of North Carolina
104 N.C. App.172 (1991)

### Background and Facts

On August 19, 1987, Wilson Ford sued NCNB Corporation (a bank) to recover damages that allegedly resulted from the bank's losing, for about two years, $5,000.15 that Ford placed in one of defendant bank's night depositories for his employer, A&P. The only theory of liability initially alleged was the breach of a special bailment in regard to the deposit. The complaint alleged that the bank's negligent failure to have the depository properly searched caused plaintiff to lose his job and suffer loss of earnings, emotional anguish, humiliation, scorn, and derision. The bank searched the depository for the missing bag but did not disassemble it. Prior to dismissing Ford, A&P questioned him and had him submit to a polygraph test at the store's request. After the test indicated some of his answers were deceptive, A&P terminated plaintiff's employment on October 9, 1984, and so advised the bank a few days later.

During the first few months following his dismissal in trying to obtain employment elsewhere Ford truthfully told prospective employers what had happened at A&P and was not hired. After he stopped listing A&P as a former employer he immediately obtained employment at minimum wages and within a few months thereafter earned more than what he had received at the A&P.

Before the deposit bag was lost Ford enjoyed a good reputation among A&P employees and was outgoing and sociable, helped to support his mother and three younger brothers, and was paying for a new car on the installment plan. After being discharged he became withdrawn and lost sleep and weight. When his "friends" either avoided him or teased him for refusing to share the "lost" money with them, he was embarrassed and depressed and would sit in his room for hours wondering what could have happened to the deposit bag. His new car was repossessed when he could not make payments and his good credit rating was ruined.

On June 19, 1986—about two years later—the lock on the NCNB Bank's night deposit was serviced to correct another customer's misuse of the night depository. The service technician heard a scraping sound in the depository and upon removing the head of the depository found the missing deposit bag. After learning that the "lost" deposit had been found, A&P's store manager offered Ford his job back, which Ford declined. Ford then sued NCNB for negligent failure to have the depository properly searched. A jury found NCNB's negligence damaged Ford in the amount of $100,000, and judgment was entered for that amount. NCNB appealed.

### Issue

Was NCNB's negligence the "proximate" or close cause of A&P's dismissing Ford?

### Decision

Yes. When the bank reported that it had not received the deposit, this caused A&P to distrust Ford. NCNB caused A&P to investigate, administer the polygraph test, and fire Ford when he failed the test. Thus, NCNB's act of negligently investigating and not finding the bag that was in fact there, set in motion the events that led up to the polygraph test. Thus NCNB's negligence was the "close" or proximate cause of Ford's dismissal.

### Questions

1. What evidence was there that Ford lied?
2. What could have been done to avoid the problem the Ford case presents?

*Cultural Pluralism.* A further reason for the shift of positive law to moral status is the rise of cultural pluralism. The United States has always been a nation of diversity. Consider the inscription on our money: *E pluribus unum*, which means "From many, one," or from many peoples, we form one nation.

People from all parts of the world have come to the United States in search of freedom and economic prosperity. These people have brought with them different religions, different values, and differing life styles—in short, different cultures. The positive law—our constitution and laws enacted, as well as those passed by each state—have been the melding force for this diversity. One might see current diversity or dissension over issues ranging from legalized abortion, to legalization of gay marriages, to the appropriate role of women in society, to questions of what is a family, as reflections of this diverse thought. Like it or not, the traditional U.S. approach to settling controversial issues involving cultural clashes is by passing a law, which leads to the next manifestation of the shift of law to moral status. The *In Re Estate of Gardiner* case illustrates a problem of cultural pluralism in a very practical setting: Should a man who became a woman (a transsexual) who later married a man be able to inherit from "her" husband?

## In Re Estate of Gardiner
Supreme Court of Kansas
42 P.3d 120 (2002)

### Background and Facts

J'Noel was born in Green Bay, Wisconsin. J'Noel's original birth certificate indicated J'Noel was born a male. The record shows that after sex reassignment surgery, J'Noel's birth certificate was amended in Wisconsin, pursuant to Wisconsin statutes, to state that she was female. J'Noel argued that the order drafted by a Wisconsin court directing the Department of Health and Social Services in Wisconsin to prepare a new birth record must be given full faith and credit in Kansas.

Marshall Gardiner was a businessman in northeast Kansas who had accumulated some wealth. He had one son, Joe, from whom he was estranged. Marshall's wife had died some time before he met J'Noel. There is no evidence that Marshall was not competent. Indeed, both Marshall and J'Noel possessed intelligence and real world experience. J'Noel had a Ph.D. in finance and was a teacher at Park College.

J'Noel met Marshall while on the faculty at Park College in May 1998. Marshall was a donor to the school. After the third or fourth date, J'Noel testified that Marshall brought up marriage. J'Noel wanted to get to know Marshall better, so they went to Utah for a trip. When asked about when they became sexually intimate, J'Noel testified that on this trip, Marshall had an orgasm. J'Noel stated that sometime in July 1998, Marshall was told about J'Noel's prior history as a male. The two were married in Kansas on September 25, 1998.

There is no evidence in the record to support Joe's suggestion that Marshall did not know about J'Noel's sex reassignment. It had been completed years before Marshall and J'Noel met. Nor is there any evidence that Marshall and J'Noel were not compatible.

Both parties agreed that J'Noel has gender dysphoria or is a transsexual. J'Noel agrees that she was born with male genitalia. In a deposition, J'Noel testified that she was born with a "birth defect"—a penis and testicles. J'Noel stated that she thought something was "wrong" even pre-puberty and that she viewed herself as a girl but had a penis and testicles.

J'Noel's journey from perceiving herself as one sex to the sex her brain suggests she was, deserves to be detailed. In 1991 and 1992, J'Noel began electrolysis and then thermolysis to remove body hair on the face, neck, and chest. J'Noel was married at the time and was married for 5 years. Also beginning in 1992, J'Noel began taking hormones, and in 1993, she had a tracheal shave. A tracheal shave is a surgery to the throat to change the voice. All the while, J'Noel was receiving therapy and counseling.

In February 1994, J'Noel had a bilateral orchietomy to remove the testicles. J'Noel also had a forehead/eyebrow lift at this time and rhinoplasty. Rhinoplasty refers to plastic surgery to alter one's nose. In July 1994, J'Noel consulted with a psychiatrist, who opined that there were no signs of thought disorder or major affective disorder, that J'Noel fully understood the nature of the process of transsexual change, and that her life history was consistent with a diagnosis of transsexualism. The psychiatrist recommended to J'Noel that total sex reassignment was the next appropriate step in her treatment. In August 1994, J'Noel underwent further sex reassignment surgery.

After the surgery in 1994, J'Noel petitioned the Circuit Court of Outagamie County, Wisconsin, for a new birth certificate which would reflect her new name as J'Noel Ball and sex as a female. The court issued a report ordering the state registrar to make these changes and issue a new birth certificate. A new birth certificate was issued on September 26, 1994. The birth certificate indicated the child's name as J'Noel Ball and sex as a female. J'Noel also has had her driver's license, passport, and health documents changed to reflect her new sex designation.

Before meeting Marshall, J'Noel was married to S.P., a female. J'Noel and S.P. met and began living together in 1980, while J'Noel was in college. They married in 1988. J'Noel testified she and S.P. engaged in heterosexual relations during their relationship. J'Noel believed she was capable of fathering children, and the couple used birth control so S.P. would not become pregnant. J'Noel and S.P. divorced in May 1994.

J'Noel Ball and Marshall Gardiner were married in Kansas in September 1998. Marshall died intestate (without a will) in August 1999. Joe, Marshall's son from his prior marriage, filed a petition for letters of administration, alleging that J'Noel had waived any rights to Marshall's estate. J'Noel filed an objection and asked that letters of administration be issued to her. The court appointed a special administrator. Joe amended his petition, alleging that he was the sole heir in that the marriage between J'Noel and Marshall was void since J'Noel was born a man. J'Noel argues that she is a biological female and was at the time of her marriage to Marshall. There is no dispute that J'Noel is a transsexual. The district court found for Joe, the son. The court of appeals affirmed. J'Noel appealed to the Supreme Court of Kansas.

## Issue

Was the marriage between a male and a post-operative male-to-female transsexual void under Kansas law thereby preventing the transsexual "spouse" from receiving a spousal share of her deceased "husband's" estate?

## Decision

The Supreme Court of Kansas said that the marriage was void.

. . . The words "sex," "male," and "female" in everyday understanding do not encompass transsexuals. The plain, ordinary meaning of "persons of the opposite sex" contemplates a biological man and a biological woman and not persons who are experiencing gender dysphoria. A male-to-female post-operative transsexual does not fit the definition of a female. The male organs have been removed, but the ability to "produce ova and bear offspring" does not and never did exist. . . . J'Noel does not fit the common meaning of female.

The interpretation of [Ed.: state statutes] . . . is supported by the legislative history of the statute. That legislative history is set out in the Court of Appeals decision: "The amendment to 23-101 limiting marriage to two parties of the opposite sex began its legislative history in 1975. The minutes of the Senate Committee on Judiciary for January 21, 1976, state that the amendment would 'affirm the traditional view of marriage.' The proposed amendment was finally enacted in 1980.

"K.S.A. 23-101 was again amended in 1996 when language was added, stating: 'All other marriages are declared to be contrary to the public policy of this state and are void.' This sentence was inserted immediately after the sentence limiting marriage to two persons of the opposite sex.

"In 1996, K.S.A. 23-115 was amended, with language added stating: 'It is the strong public policy of this state only to recognize as valid marriages from other states that are between a man and a woman.'". . .

The court of appeals then noted:

"The legislative history contains discussions about gays and lesbians, but nowhere is there any testimony that specifically states that marriage should be prohibited by two parties if one is a post-operative male-to-female or female-to-male transsexual. Thus the question remains: Was J'Noel a female at the time the license was issued for the purpose of the statute?". . .

As we have previously noted, the legislature clearly viewed "opposite sex" in the narrow traditional sense. The legislature has declared that the public policy of this state is to recognize only the traditional marriage between "two persons who are of the opposite sex," and all other marriages are against public policy and void. Our responsibility is to interpret K.S.A. . . . 23-101, and not to rewrite it. That is for the legislature to do if it so desires. If the legislature wishes to change public policy, it is free to do so; we are not.

Finally, we recognize that J'Noel has traveled a long and difficult road. J'Noel has undergone electrolysis, thermolysis, tracheal shave, hormone injections, extensive counseling, and reassignment surgery. Unfortunately, after all that, J'Noel remains a transsexual, and a male for purposes of marriage under [Ed.: state statutes]. We are not blind to the stress and pain experienced by one who is born a male but perceives oneself as a female. We recognize that there are people who do not fit neatly into the commonly recognized category of male or female, and to many life becomes an ordeal. However, the validity of J'Noel's marriage to Marshall is a question of public policy to be addressed by the legislature and not by this court. . . .

## Questions

1. Would you describe the Kansas Supreme Court's approach to sanctioning the marriage of a male and a male-to-female transsexual as avant-garde or traditional?
2. What public policy reasons can be advanced to support Kansas' position on a fundamental matter such as who should be allowed to marry?
3. Had the Kansas legislature ever considered the matter of gay or lesbian marriages? How had it decided the matter? Had it addressed transsexual marriages?
4. What public policy reasons can be advanced to support Kansas' position on a fundamental matter such as who should be allowed to marry? Do you accept the Supreme Court of Kansas' statement that courts do not decide matters of policy? When a court decides that male-on-male sexual harassment is covered by Title VII (as did the U.S. Supreme Court in a virtual unanimous decision 8-0-1 in Oncale in 1998), is it not making public policy?
5. Much is said about "individual freedom" and the desire to permit individuals to "self-actualize." How does the Kansas decision score on that score?

*The Trend Toward Legalizing All Areas of Society.* Since the early 1960s, positive law has expanded at an unprecedented pace in the United States. Laws regulate more and more areas of human endeavor, and for justifiable reasons. For example, no one wants water or air pollution, discrimination based on race, religion, or sex, or mistreatment of employees. Thus, the U.S. legal system has witnessed the civil rights revolution, the explosion of employer/employee laws, the consumer movement and its accompanying laws, and environmentalism with its lengthy statutes and regulations, to name four prominent issues within the positive law explosion.

Among the positive laws reaching the books since the mid-1960s are the Civil Rights Act of 1964, the Clean Air Act Amendments of 1970, 1977, and 1990, the Federal Water Pollution Control Act of 1972 (later renamed the Clean Water Act), the National Environmental Policy Act (1970), the Occupational Safety and Health Act (1970), the Fair Credit Reporting Act (1970), the Federal Noise Control Act of 1972, the Endangered Species Act (1973), the Safe Drinking Water Act (1974), the Employee Retirement Income Security Act (1974), the Equal Credit Opportunity Act (1974), the Federal Privacy Act (1974), the Fair Credit Billing Act (1975), the Resource Conservation and Recovery Act (1976), the Toxic Substances Control Act (1976), the Electronic Fund Transfer Act (1978), the Bankruptcy Reform Act (1978), the Nuclear Waste Policy Act (1982), the Clean Water Act amendments of 1986, and the Glass Ceiling Act of 1991, the Americans with Disabilities Act (1990), and Gramm, Leach, Bliley Act and Sarbanes-Oxley Act of 2002 (on corporate governance reforms), to name some of the federal laws falling into this category. In addition, most of these statutes have pages of implementing regulations that micromanage how businesses and each of us must act. States and municipalities also have been busy during the same period, passing economically and socially aggressive laws and regulations.

Given the onslaught of positive laws that impose many costly, burdensome (in terms of paperwork) responsibilities on businesses, public institutions, and other segments of society, people in the United States are inclined to say, "If I have done all that the law requires, I am ethical." These enacted regulations are not a *limit* on the responsibilities we may take. For example, one could contribute to the United Way even though no positive law requires it. However, this book takes the position that, given the extensive and expensive burdens that today's positive law places upon us, businesspeople or anyone can justifiably say that they are ethical if they follow the positive law. Further, one could argue that by extending positive law into areas formerly left for private morality (civil rights laws, for example), the positive law is merging with natural law. In other words, what *is* commanded (the positive law) is becoming what *ought* (natural law) to be done. Thus, following the positive law today involves doing far more than it did a generation ago.

*Massive Noncompliance with Positive Law and Resort to the Courts as the Way to Achieve Justice.* The number of lawsuits—criminal and civil—in one year in the early 1990s was 98 million! Although this figure does include minor traffic violations, it suggests that resorting to the legal process is necessary to determine what is right. The United States has the highest incarceration rate of any nation in the world; approximately 1.4 million people are in jail or in prison (roughly one in every 250 people), indicating that a significant number of people do not comply with the criminal law.

*Failure to Keep Our Promises.* Further evidence that following the law on the books is the most that some individuals can do is supported by the failure of so many to keep their promises. For example, in 1999 more than 1.3 million bankruptcies were filed in the United States, which means that people who had made contracts, or legally binding promises, were not keeping them. People were not paying their bills on time or conforming to contracts and contract law. For such people, contracts and contract law are a ceiling—the most they could do—not a floor. Of course, on the positive side we should not lose sight of the fact that more people were keeping their contractual promises than breaking them.

A further disturbing example of not keeping one's promises is the divorce rate. The United States has the world's highest divorce rate; half the marriages end in divorce, indicating failure to observe the marital promise.

*Greed.* One of the overriding values of modern society appears to be greed. Just as the fictional character Gordon Gekko in the movie *Wall Street* shouts that "Greed is good," many real-life persons seemingly follow the same philosophy. When federal district court judge John M. Walker, Jr., sentenced hotel entrepreneur and millionairess Leona Helmsley to a four-year prison term and fined her $7.1 million for tax fraud, the judge remarked, "Unlike many defendants who come before this court, you were not driven to this crime by financial need. Rather, your conduct was the product of naked greed." (Ms. Helmsley's conviction was upheld on appeal. She has since been released from federal prison.) Similarly, stockbroker Michael Milken's pleading guilty in 1990 to six felony counts in connection with his security dealings also illustrates greed. Because Milken was a millionaire before committing the acts for which he pleaded guilty, one can logically conclude that greed drove him to violate the positive law in pursuit of even more money. Dr. Sam Waksal, ex-ImClone CEO, pled guilty in 2002 to securities fraud, perjury, and obstruction of justice. Waksal was a wealthy man prior to committing these crimes, which, again, evidences greed. So, also, was Michael Kopper, ex-Enron executive, who pled guilty to conspiracy to commit wire fraud and money laundering while at Enron.

Consider the outrageous pay to top U.S. executives, which is a multiple of more than 500 times that of the average workers in the same firm. Why should such executives overpay themselves while refusing to recognize the contributions of average workers? Why should executives encourage their workers to invest all of their pension money in company stock at the very time they (the executives) are selling that stock? Greed. On a worldwide level, consider the refusal of wealthy nations to forgive debts owed to them by developing nations. Rich nations are being asked by persons such as the pope to "forgive debt" to very poor nations where the per capita gross national product is under $1,000 per year. Sometimes this is done, but often it is not. Why? One answer is greed.

Given the abundant evidence of greed, obedience to the positive law is realistically what society can expect of us.

*Lack of Personal Responsibility.* The perception today is that personal responsibility has fallen to new lows in the United States. An area that supports this notion is in credit card use, coupled with the increasing use of the positive law of bankruptcy to pay off one's debts. In today's consumer society, persons purchase items using credit cards. The *U.S. Statistical Abstract* (2001) reports that there will be 166 million credit card holders in the United States by the year 2005. That same source reports that in 2005, more than 1.565 billion credit cards will be in use in the United States, and it projects credit card debt for that year at $860 billion. Approximately 26 percent of credit card holders hardly ever pay off the entire balance owed. Undoubtedly, failure to pay off one's credit card debt with high interest rates for unpaid balances is a contributor to the large number of bankruptcies in the United States. Many of the more than one million people who file for bankruptcy in the United States each year are using the positive law of bankruptcy to avoid their otherwise legally owed debts. If people assert that "the law allows it," they show their agreement that positive law is setting the level for the most that one can be expected to do. Said another way, the positive law of bankruptcy has become an *ethic*.

The high number of bankruptcies, while showing evidence of a decline in personal responsibility, can be attributed to other factors as well. For instance, many persons enter bankruptcy for reasons beyond their control unrelated to credit card use—unexpected job loss, overwhelming medical expenses, and death of a family breadwinner.

*The Rewards for Winning Stimulate Cheating.* In today's society, winning is the name of the game. People idolize the honor student, the prominent and successful businessperson, the champion athlete, and anyone who has "made it." You are what you have done. Statistics show that better-educated people, prominent athletes, and professional people do make significantly higher incomes than the general population. Businesses are judged by the bottom line—how much money have they made, what their market share is. Salespeople are judged on how much they sell, not on the techniques used to make sales. The desire to succeed, unfortunately, too often causes otherwise good people to cut corners to succeed. The "corners" in society are the positive law. An example of the high stakes in business would be multimillion-dollar U.S. Defense Department contracts. Contracts for missiles, ships, or planes can mean millions—even billions—of dollars for a company and also help the local and state economies. With such large amounts of money at stake, it is understandable that military procurement fraud occurs. Such high stakes increase the incentive to obtain a competitive advantage, even though violating the positive law. Unfortunately, violation of the law today is occurring with alarming frequency.

*The Tendency to Resolve Problems by Passing Laws.* Legislators want to be reelected. And when voters take their problems to their legislators and demand solutions, legislators can show their concern with voters' problems by enacting positive laws that purport to solve them. Often, well-intentioned laws are worthless. For example, low-income workers claim that they need more money to live on, so they urge Congress to increase the federal minimum wage law. The idea is to increase the pay of low-income workers. What actually may happen is that low-income jobs are lost to Third World countries or eliminated entirely because low-income workers are paid low wages for a good reason: They are worth only what they are being paid. Thus, passing a law forcing employers to pay an artificially higher minimum wage to *help* low-income workers could end up *hurting* such workers if their jobs are lost. What has been gained by passing such a law?

## JURISPRUDENCE: THE STUDY OF OTHER ETHICS (VALUES) INFLUENCING POSITIVE LAW

The search for proper or ethical conduct has led to many answers in addition to the view that positive law determines what is right. The next section surveys a number of these views and offers several other values that can either support or challenge the positive law for ethical supremacy.

**Jurisprudence** is an area of study that examines the values or ethics associated with positive law. The word *jurisprudence* is derived from the Latin words *juris* meaning "the law" and *prudens* meaning "wisdom." Thus, by studying jurisprudence we are going beyond just learning the rules (positive law). We are trying to learn what values the rules attempt to impart to society. The next subsections explore the ethic of justice, the ethic of power, the ethic of custom, the ethic of conduct, the ethic of civilization, the ethic of reality, and the ethic of utility.

## THE ETHIC OF JUSTICE

Justice is a highly important legal ethic. Every legal system, no matter how good or bad, has claimed to promote justice. The **natural law** school of jurisprudence defines law in terms of justice. Natural law ideas have a long history, reaching at least from the time of the Stoics in ancient Greece. Natural law thinkers include medieval philosophers such as St. Thomas Aquinas, the eighteenth century English jurist Sir William Blackstone, and modern egalitarian philosophers such as John Rawls. Natural law thinkers such as Blackstone say, "An unjust law is not law and should not be obeyed." The *Riggs v. Palmer* case on page 18 illustrates the concept of natural law.

*Due Process.* Another example of natural law (the justice ethic) is due process. Due process refers to the right to a notice and a fair hearing before the law imposes sanctions on us. Due process gives all people in the United States rights, including the right to jury trials in cases where their rights are substantially affected. Thus, if businesspeople are accused of violating the Sherman Antitrust Act by price fixing, they have a jury trial right, and the crime must be proved before they can be punished.

*Equity Courts.* Equity courts and equitable remedies also show how the justice ethic influences positive law. The word *equity* means "fairness." Equity courts originated in England when law courts became inflexible in remedying wrongs.

*Advantage of the Justice Ethic.* The legal ethic of justice has broad appeal. Who can be against it as a general idea? But closer analysis reveals its major weakness.

*Disadvantages of the Justice Ethic.* The main weakness in the justice ethic is that one person's idea of justice is not necessarily the same as another's, which might be called the **multiple-conscience problem**. In other words, we all might agree to be fair, but we might disagree about what fairness means in a legal matter.

In many, if not most, instances, people agree on what justice is in a particular case. For example, most of us would probably agree that the law forbidding murder is fair and just. But we might disagree on the punishment for murderers: Some believe in the death penalty, and some do not.

*Should the Law Be "Moral"?* Natural law deals with whether the positive law is "right," which leads to the question of whether the positive law should be moral. One scholar who has tackled this question is former Harvard Law School Professor Lon Fuller. Fuller developed what he called the **internal morality of law (IML)**. According to Fuller, positive law must meet eight tests to be considered internally moral. These eight tests are as follows:

1. *There should be law; that is, rules should exist.* This point seems obvious, except when one considers the alternative: Law made by a particular person. Without rules, a mayor responsible for setting speed limits could set *different* speed limits every time a different person was charged with speeding. This randomness would destroy uniformity and could lead to different rules for different people, depending on whether the mayor liked or disliked the individual charged. Clearly, such a situation would deny people a cherished right guaranteed by the U.S. Constitution—*equal* protection of the laws.

2. *The rules should be promulgated.* The idea here is that the rules should be made publicly available so they can be followed. Said another way, the rules must be knowable. When rules are promulgated, citizens are protected because they can conduct themselves knowing what is allowed and forbidden. If the rules are not publicly available, citizens could be arrested for violations of laws they never knew existed. Secret laws were once part of the Nazi legal system in Germany.

3. *The rules must be clear.* An income tax law that tells citizens to "pay their fair share" of the taxes is vague. Is a fair share 10 percent, 20 percent, or 50 percent of one's income? If this determination is left up to the Internal Revenue Service, it might be 50 percent, but to each taxpayer what is fair would likely be much lower. One reason for the clarity requirement is to have laws the citizens can reasonably obey. As we shall learn later in this text, the idea that laws should be clear is required by the U.S. Constitution's due process clause.

4. *The rules should be retroactive as seldom as possible.* Suppose you go fishing on Monday and catch a 10-inch bass, which is then allowed. If on Tuesday the legislature passes a statute making catching bass less than 12 inches in length illegal *anytime during the previous week*, you have broken the law. You cannot avoid breaking this law because you caught the 10-inch bass before the law was passed. Retroactive laws are thought to be unfair when they punish a person for committing an act that was legal when it was done. The U.S. Constitution forbids *ex post facto* laws, which are retroactive criminal laws that work to the disadvantage of the accused. Two other parts of the U.S. Constitution—the Fifth Amendment and the Fourteenth Amendment—generally forbid retroactive laws, whether civil or criminal. Occasionally in the United States, certain rules, such as tax laws, apply to events that have already occurred. For example, under the 1993 Federal Budget Reform Act, certain parts of that statute were applied to taxable events occurring prior to that law's passage.

5. *The rules should be noncontradictory.* If one rule says, "Dump toxic wastes in your backyard" and another law forbids such dumping, citizens scratch their heads and wonder what to do. Rules should be consistent so people can act legally.

   All states except Virginia have legalized auto radar detectors (devices that help drivers violate the speed limits and evade the police). One wonders why a state would pass a law setting speed limits and later enact another statute enabling people to violate that same law.

6. *The rules should not require the impossible.* The Clean Water Act declared in 1972 that by 1985 no pollutants should be discharged into U.S. waters. This result was not achieved in 1985, nor is it likely ever to be achieved. What the law demands should be doable. A law or set of laws that seeks the impossible makes the legal system appear foolish and undercuts public respect for law.

7. *The rules should not change often.* Learning the law can be difficult. Learning the law and then seeing it change the next week and then change again the

following week is confusing and frustrating. Why bother learning rules that will only change? Fortunately, many rules are stable. Property law, contract law, and many areas of commercial law seldom change. Tax law, criminal law, environmental law, and employer/employee relations law have changed frequently in recent years.

8. *There should be congruence between official conduct and the rules.* Said another way, rulemakers and those in charge should obey the rules just as much as the average citizen. If a mayor, congressperson, senator, or president makes speeches condemning illegal drug use, tax evasion, or other crimes, and then is caught committing those crimes, people correctly call the official a hypocrite. Citizens like to see their leaders follow the rules. When the average person observes the mayor commit tax evasion, individuals might wonder why they should follow the rules the leading citizen in town does not follow.

*A Natural Law Concept of John Rawls: The Original Position.* A leading twentieth-century philosopher named John Rawls developed several natural law ideas including the *original position.* According to this idea, if each of us did not know what position we would start from in society—that is, whether we would be rich or poor, smart or stupid, male or female, black or white, gay or straight, handicapped or not handicapped, of Asian or African or European extraction, and all of the other possible characteristics—what would we want the rules to be? Rawls called this starting point the original position. It is helpful in justifying laws protective of classes of persons who have traditionally been discriminated against, such as women and racial minorities.

*A Final Natural Law Concept: Kant's Categorical Imperative.* The philosopher Immanuel Kant, who lived in the eighteenth century, suggested an ethic called the **categorical imperative**. This idea has natural law roots and says we should act in the same way we would want the law to be. In other words, if we would want the law to prohibit stealing, we as individuals should not steal. This ethic follows the same principle as the golden rule, which says, "Do unto others as you would have them do unto you."

How would the categorical imperative deal with tax fraud? Would you want others to cheat on their taxes? Most would say that taxpayers should pay all that they legally owe the government; thus, the categorical imperative tells each of us to be honest in paying our taxes.

## Riggs v. Palmer
New York Court of Appeals
115 N.Y. 509 (1889)

### Background and Facts

On August 13, 1880, Francis Palmer, a wealthy farmer, made his will, which gave the bulk of his estate to his grandson, Elmer Palmer. Francis was a widower, and in March 1882 he married Mrs. Bresee, with whom he entered a prenuptial agreement in which it was agreed that instead of giving Mrs. Bresee a claim on Francis' estate if she survived him, she would be given a claim on Francis' farm for her support.

When Francis executed his will, Elmer lived with Francis as a member of his family, and at Francis' death, Elmer was 16 years old. Elmer knew of the provisions of Francis' will and that Francis had shown some intent to change the will so Elmer would take less. To prevent his grandfather from modifying his will and get speedy enjoyment and immediate possession of his will expectancy, Elmer murdered Francis by poisoning him.

Elmer was convicted of murder, but nonetheless claimed his inheritance under his grandfather's will. Mr. Francis Palmer's two daughters, Mrs. Riggs and Mrs. Preston, sued Elmer arguing that they, not Elmer, should take Francis' estate because to give it to Elmer would allow him to profit from his wrong. Elmer argued that the will gave the bulk of the estate to him and that the statute governing wills literally would require that the property go to him.

## Issue

Could Elmer recover under the valid will of the grandfather even though Elmer had murdered his grandfather to accelerate his inheritance?

## Decision

No, a beneficiary who murders his testator (person who makes a will) cannot take under the testator's will. Even though the statutes regulating the making, proof, and effect of wills, if literally read, would give the property to the murderer, in some cases the letter of a statute is restrained by an equitable construction. The objective is to imagine what the legislators if present meant or would do if they had seen a similar situation when they wrote the statute.

Blackstone, the great English jurisprudent, stated that if absurd consequences manifestly contradictory to common reason would arise by reading the statute literally, judges are, in decency, to conclude the legislature did not foresee such consequences. In such a case judges are free to read the statute by equity (general fairness). All laws may be controlled in their operation and effect by general, fundamental maxims of the common law. No one shall be permitted to profit by his own fraud, or to take advantage of his own wrong, or to found any claim upon his own iniquity, or to acquire property by his own crime. These maxims are dictated by public policy and have their foundation in universal law administered in all civilized countries, and have nowhere been superseded by statutes.

The New York Court of Appeals held that Elmer took no property from Francis and that the will was ineffective to pass ownership to Elmer because Elmer murdered Francis. Francis's two daughters were declared to be the owner of his estate subject to Francis's widow's claim.

## Questions

1. Who was arguing for natural law, Elmer or the deceased's daughters? Why?
2. If a statute literally covers a situation, and a court (judge) departs from the meaning of the statute to achieve "justice," what, if any, dangers does this situation present?

## THE ETHIC OF POWER

Power is a basic ethic. Plato recognized this in his book, *The Republic*, when, through the character Thrasymachus he said, "Justice is the will of the stronger."[3] Another way of expressing this idea is "Might makes right."

Power is essential for positive law, because positive law assumes that a political superior exists. Some suggest that positivists are merely power worshippers. One gets and keeps political superiority by being powerful. Furthermore, power is needed to provide positive law's sanctions.

Power can take several forms. It can be military might. It can also take the form of economic power. The ability to cut off someone's budget or benefits or job is economic power. The power of an idea is, in many ways, the most long-lasting form of power.

Rent controls are a contemporary example of the power ethic's influence on positive law. Many municipalities throughout the United States have passed rent control ordinances that stop landlords from raising rent more than a specified amount each year. These controls are controversial laws that show the power ethic of tenants in the municipal population. These people use their electoral power to force city councils to pass rent control laws. Such ordinances are politically popular because there are more tenants than landlords. However, rent control laws could be unwise economically. New rental housing will not be built because landlords

---

[3]Some will argue that Plato himself did not believe power as an ethic, given the ensuing discussion among Socrates, Thrasymachus, and others in this segment of *The Republic*.

will not get a fair return on their investment if rent cannot be raised to reflect the property's market value. Rent controls actually are a legal attempt to repeal an economic "law," the law of supply and demand, which sets prices. The power ethic can legally control rents, but it jeopardizes the supply of future rental housing. Whatever the wisdom of rent control laws, they illustrate the power ethic.

*Advantages of the Power Ethic.* Order is a major advantage of the power ethic. Whoever has power can, by force or threat of force, bring law and order to a society. Order when based on sound economics can bring long-run stability, which encourages people to make investments and long-range commitments of resources that work to the betterment of society. Investments in plant, equipment, and people (by training and education) improve a society's quality of life, but a long time frame is needed to realize benefits from investments. People and companies are willing to invest only where long-run order and stability make gains from investments likely. Gains are not likely to be realized where the government constantly changes its rules. (Consider the economic decline of modern Italy, which, at last count, has had more than forty governments since World War II.) Order and stability exist because of the power ethic.

*Disadvantages of the Power Ethic.* Power can be abused. For example, many years ago the railroads charged farmers and small businesses higher rates for hauling freight than they did certain large customers. This unfair rate discrimination led to regulation of common carriers by the Interstate Commerce Commission (ICC).

Another abuse of power can occur when businesses hire or promote people because of race, religion, sex, national origin, or age. A reward system should be based on productivity and not on the employer's dislike of, for example, Catholics, blacks, and women (or men).

*United States v. Simon* illustrates how knowledge about a CPA firm's alleged mistake in auditing a client can confer leverage or power over the accountants. Read the case to see if the corporate executive's power over the accountants led them to compromise their ethics by attempting to "cover up" their past error.

## United States v. Simon
U.S. Court of Appeals (2nd Cir.)
425 F.2d 796 (1969)

### Background and Facts

Continental Vending Corporation hired Lybrand, Ross Brothers, and Montgomery, an independent public accounting firm, to audit its books. The auditors discovered that Roth, Continental's president, was using company money to play the stock market (probably embezzlement).

Roth tried to hide his improper use of Continental's funds by "laundering" the money (loaning it to Valley, an affiliated company Roth managed), which then loaned it to Roth. Roth's activities raised doubts about Continental's solvency. Lybrand (the auditors) discovered Roth's activities, but Roth threatened them with a malpractice suit (for not detecting his wrongdoing in previous years) unless they gave a favorable opinion on Continental's financial statements in the current year.

The auditors (Lybrand) gave Continental a "clean" (favorable) opinion on its financial statements but hedged somewhat. The auditor put a footnote in the financial statement that incompletely and vaguely pointed out what they (the auditors) knew about Roth.

Continental later went bankrupt. The United States government prosecuted the Lybrand accounting firm partner supervising the audit (Simon) and two other associates of the auditing firm for criminally violating the 1934 Securities Exchange Act. The firm defended on the grounds that professional auditing standards did not require auditors of Continental to know what Valley did with the money it had borrowed from Continental and loaned to Roth. Several prominent members of the accounting profession corroborated the defendants on this point.

The U.S. prosecutor gave Roth immunity from prosecution (from possible securities law violations and embezzlement) in exchange for his (Roth's) testimony against his former auditors (Lybrand). This evidence proved irresistible to the jury and they convicted the auditors. The accountant/auditors appealed.

### Issue

Did the independent auditors commit a federal crime by giving favorable opinions on false financial reports filed with the Securities and Exchange Commission?

### Decision

Yes. Even though auditing standards did not require auditors of Continental to know that Valley loaned funds it borrowed from Continental to Roth, accountants have a duty to disclose facts they actually know if nondisclosure makes the financial reports materially false. Since the auditors knew about Roth's improper activities, failure to disclose these activities in the SEC financial reports made the reports materially false. Failure to disclose was a federal crime.

### Questions

1. How might knowledge by a client of potentially embarrassing or negligent conduct of someone in a professional position confer power on the client? In the case of such a role reversal, does the client become the dominant party?
2. Can negligence by a professional or allegations of negligent practices ever be a tool to control someone or influence someone's conduct?
3. Can any sort of indiscretion or alleged misconduct by anyone— professional, subordinate or superior—be a control device? Can you think of any recent incidents involving high-level politicians, government officials, clergy, or business leaders where alleged legal indiscretions might lead such individuals to compromise their actions as officials? Is anyone perfect?

## THE ETHIC OF CUSTOM

*Custom* refers to longstanding conduct. How people have acted and continue to act is an ethic influencing positive law. Savigny, a German writing in the early nineteenth century, helped develop the historical school of law. It says that positive law reflects longstanding custom.

Many examples demonstrate how custom influences positive law. Consider wills, the documents we customarily use to transfer property when we die. A will takes effect only when a person dies, but the testator (or testatrix, if a woman) is no longer with us.[4] In effect, a dead person is telling the living what to do with resources such as money and other property that are left. Transferring property by will is a longstanding custom recognized by positive law.

---

[4] A person who makes a will.

Owning private property—the idea that one person can own a house or car—is another longstanding custom recognized by positive law. The definition of private property occasionally changes. At one time in the United States, slaves were property that could be bought and sold. Perhaps one day planets will be considered property capable of ownership.

Contracts are a third example of how the legal ethic of custom can affect positive law. Contracts are agreements voluntarily entered between private individuals or between groups and are enforceable in court. A graduating student who agrees to work for IBM for $35,000 per year has made a contract. Contracts have long been enforceable in the United States. People can change their lives by entering contracts. Which job offer should one accept? Should one buy a house or raw land that might have oil under it?

To appreciate the control over your life that freedom of contract gives you, contrast it with feudal society, wherein a person's status was set by birth. If you were lucky enough to be born a noble, you remained a noble. If you were born a serf, you generally stayed a serf. In medieval society, contract in its modern form did not exist. Later, with the development of the merchant class, private agreements were made and enforced in merchant courts. Trade custom, recognized in settling contract disagreements, was called the law merchant. Contracts themselves, as well as the **law merchant**, came to be recognized by society's law and equity courts. Thus, the ethic of custom is deeply embedded in commercial law. An example of a longstanding custom that has found its way into positive law is that of an employer who may fire an employee any time for any reason in an at-will employment relationship.

*Geary v. U.S. Steel Corporation* provides an example of the custom ethic.

## Geary v. U.S. Steel Corporation
Supreme Court Pennsylvania
318 A.2d 174 (1974)

### Background and Facts

George B. Geary was continuously employed by appellee, U.S. Steel Corporation (hereinafter "company"), from 1953 until July 13, 1967, when he was dismissed from his position. Geary's duties involved the sale of tubular products to the oil and gas industry. His employment was at-will. The dismissal is said to have stemmed from a disagreement concerning one of the company's new products, a tubular casing designed for use under high pressure. Geary alleges that he believed the product had not been adequately tested and constituted a serious danger to anyone who used it; that he voiced his misgivings to his superiors and was ordered to "follow directions," which he agreed to do; that he nevertheless continued to express his reservations, taking his case to a vice-president in charge of sale of the product; that as a result of his efforts the product was reevaluated and withdrawn from the market; that he at all times performed his duties to the best of his ability and always acted with the best interests of the company and the general public in mind; and that because of these events he was summarily discharged without notice. Geary asserts that the company's conduct in so acting was "wrongful, malicious and abusive," resulting in injury to his reputation in the industry, mental anguish, and direct financial harm, for which he seeks both punitive and compensatory damages. . . .

No court in this Commonwealth has ever recognized a nonstatutory cause of action for an employer's termination of an at-will employment relationship.

The Pennsylvania law is in accordance with the weight of authority elsewhere. Absent a statutory or contractual provision to the contrary, the law has taken for granted the power for either party to terminate an employment relationship for any or no reason. . . .

Appellant's final argument is an appeal to considerations of public policy. Geary asserts in his complaint that he was acting in the best interests of the general public, as well as of his employer, in opposing the marketing of a product which he believed to be defective.

The praiseworthiness of Geary's motives does not detract from the company's legitimate interest in preserving its normal operational procedures from disruption.

We hold only that where the complaint itself discloses a plausible and legitimate reason for terminating an at-will employment relationship and no clear mandate of public policy is violated thereby, an employee at-will has no right of action against his employer for wrongful discharge.

**Issue**

Did the employer have the right to dismiss Geary even though he pointed out a defect in a company product?

**Decision**

The Supreme Court of Pennsylvania said that the whistleblower was not wrongfully dismissed by his employer. Geary recovered nothing from his former employer.[5]

**Questions**

1. What evidence supported the whistleblower's claim that the company's product was defective?
2. What legal ethic supports the company's firing the whistleblower?

---

*Advantages of Custom.* Because customs are longstanding, they are known and observed by most people. People implicitly are saying that they agree with a custom when they follow it. Hence, custom provides stability to society. Also, customs help people plan because they know the custom seldom changes.

*Disadvantages of Custom.* Custom can be backward, oppressive, or simply wrong. Racial prejudice has been a longstanding custom in the United States. Sexism has also been a longstanding custom in the United States, especially in the job market. An effect of sexism and racism is that until recently, the U.S. job market has been dominated by white males. Title VII of the Civil Rights Act of 1964 has to some extent changed the customs of white male dominance. But customs are slow to change. Passage of such positive laws as the Civil Rights Act is an attempt to change custom. Some other longstanding customs such as sexual harassment are illegal today.

## THE ETHIC OF NORMS OF CONDUCT

Norms of conduct, which refer to how most people act, are another ethic influencing positive law. Norms are like customs, except they are not as longstanding. Eugen Ehrlich's sociological school of law has conduct as its ethic, or value. Some groups' norms of conduct include sexual promiscuity, drunkenness, marijuana smoking, price fixing, and bid rigging, which have a negative image. But these norms of conduct are not necessarily illegal (in the positive law sense). For example, all types of drunkenness and sexual promiscuity are not illegal, although public drunkenness, drunken driving, and certain sexual practices often are. Thus, norms that some groups in society would question on grounds of morality are not necessarily illegal. On the other hand, marijuana smoking, bid rigging, and price fixing are generally illegal in the positive law sense, even though these activities could be the norm of conduct for certain sectors of society. As we can see, norms could be above or below the positive law and still be questioned, based on various other values such as public health or morality.

*Advantages of Norms of Conduct.* The ethic of conduct is an advantage because it is how, by definition, people act. We could solve the problem of lawbreaking

---

[5]The *Geary* case has *not*, as of this writing, been reversed by the Pennsylvania Supreme Court. However, exceptions (loopholes) in the *Geary* result exist. See Chapter 14 under the topic "Employment At-Will" for a discussion of exceptions to the at-will rule.

simply by changing positive law so that it agrees with social conduct. If positive law and conduct were the same, law enforcement would be easier and cheaper.

*Disadvantages of Norms of Conduct.* Conduct, such as murder, arson, rape, price fixing, drug taking, and cheating on one's income tax can also be socially undesirable. Positive law should help society improve. If positive law were to be relaxed to allow the worst conduct, civilization would be endangered. People would no longer be safe; they could not believe what others say; and property could be stolen without fear of punishment.

Positive law and the ethic of conduct are often at odds because positive law encourages ideal conduct. Norms of conduct attempt to lower positive law's ideal by claiming it sets unrealistically high standards.

## THE ETHIC OF CIVILIZATION

Civilization is an ethic influencing positive law. Psychoanalyst Sigmund Freud said that law shows the ethic of civilization because it frustrates (tries to stop) instincts such as the desires to lie, cheat, and steal. The more we as individuals and as a society frustrate our base instincts, the more civilized we become.

Law helps us to be civilized because it states rules telling us what we may or may not do. We may not misrepresent the mileage on our car when we sell it because this could be fraud. We may not cheat our business partner because this would violate our fiduciary duty, our duty of loyalty. We may not dump untreated chemicals into a stream because this would violate the Clean Water Act. We may not drive our car above the speed limit. We may not fail to turn over part of our income to the government as taxes. In employment, we may not discriminate based on age. These and other laws frustrate our base instincts. However, they do not totally restrict us, because many activities we enjoy doing do not arise from our base instincts—for example, working, studying, and helping others.

*Advantages of the Civilization Ethic.* The advantage of civilization is practical freedom from harm. Under civilization, people, business, and government are under control and are modulated, and everyone gets a taste of freedom's good life.

*Disadvantages of the Civilization Ethic.* The civilization ethic also has its disadvantages or costs. Civilization causes frustrations, and people must direct their hostilities and aggressions inward, which can cause ulcers, heart attacks, high blood pressure, allergies, and psychosomatic illnesses.

*Regina v. Dudley and Stephens* illustrates the civilization ethic.

## Regina v. Dudley and Stephens
### Queens Bench
### L.R., Q.B. 61 (1884)

### Background and Facts

On July 25, 1884, three seamen and a young boy drifted in a small boat in the ocean. They were 1,000 miles off the African coast, had no fresh water, and had not eaten for eight days, with no signs of rescue. They had been floating for twenty days after their yacht was wrecked in a storm. The three men argued quietly among themselves about sacrificing one of them so that the others could be saved. The three knew they meant the boy would be the one killed. They said nothing to the boy. On the nineteenth day, two of the three men wanted to draw lots to decide who would die so the others could eat. One man refused to draw. On the twentieth day, one man with the other's consent (the third man disagreeing) went to the boy, told him what was going to happen, put a knife to the boy's throat, and killed him. The boy did not agree to be murdered. All three men ate the boy and survived four more days until their rescue.

The two men who agreed to sacrifice the boy were later tried in England for murder. They raised the defense of necessity.

## Issue

Is the deliberate killing of an unoffending and unresisting boy murder if the killing is necessary to permit others to survive?

## Decision

Yes, it was murder. The English court held that it was not a case of necessity. The court said that morality and law are not always the same but should be the same as often as possible. Separating law from morality would be a mistake, which would happen if necessity were a defense to murder in this case. Dudley and Stephens were convicted of murder. (The death sentence was commuted to six months' imprisonment.)

## Questions

1. What argument did the sailors make to justify their cannibalism?
2. Did the court's decision support or undercut the civilization ethic?

## THE ETHIC OF REALITY

Have you ever thought that, even though a positive law rule requires a certain result, the result would never happen because of human factors, such as a jury or a judge's liking or disliking one of the parties? Do you also think that definitions of law ignoring human factors are inadequate? If so, you think like a legal realist.

One prominent legal realist was Jerome Frank, a former federal judge and University of Chicago Law School professor who wrote in the 1930s. He thought how law was applied in court cases was as important as, if not more important than, the law in the books, and that an ethic of realism is at work when trial juries and judges decide cases. In other words, what trial judges and juries do in fact, even if the positive law rule differs, is the ethic of realism. Legal realism can also be present in legal matters outside the courtroom.

For examples of how courts act in fact, visit *http://www.courttv.com*

Why do judges and juries sometimes disregard positive law in deciding cases? They usually *do* obey positive law, but sometimes do not, and this makes a difference. For example, in one case, some high-level certified public accountants were prosecuted criminally for violating the federal securities laws. The CPAs wanted another professional—the judge—to act as the jury (fact trier). The prosecutor wanted a jury made up of average people to decide fact issues. Why the concern? Who would be more sympathetic to high-level CPAs: another professional such as a judge, or a group of jurors, the majority of whom seldom are professionals but rather people from socioeconomic circumstances different from CPAs? The prosecutor won the point, and the jurors ended up convicting the CPAs. That the CPAs' wealth and status worked against them is not certain, but it is possible. If it did, it supports the legal realists.

*Advantage of Reality.* At times, extreme circumstances justify not following positive law. Cases have occurred in which physicians have permanently put to sleep deathly ill patients who were in great pain and beyond saving. When such physicians were criminally charged with manslaughter, juries sometimes refused to convict. Such a refusal is based on the jury's belief that the law is unfair, reflecting the legal ethic of realism in a good way.

*Disadvantage of Reality.* Prejudice is undesirable in legal proceedings. We have trials to hear legal arguments and prove facts so that we can make judgments. The ideal is to avoid prejudging people based on their wealth, race, color, national origin, sex, religion, or other irrelevant factors. When such prejudice occurs, the objective of jury trials is defeated.

Do you think the following case shows the advantage or disadvantage of legal realism?

## Delaware Tire v. Fox
### Delaware Supreme Court
### 411 A.2d 606 (1980)

### Background and Facts

On April 13, 1973, Earl A. Fox, Jr. suffered an injury at work and subsequently recovered workers' compensation. He continued to have pain from the injury and in 1975 attempted suicide unsuccessfully. In February 1977, Fox's doctor referred him to a psychologist to help him overcome pain and hold a job. The psychologist said the 1973 injury caused an emotional disorder (depression) due to pain. On June 8, 1977, Fox killed himself. His wife filed a claim for workers' compensation death benefits. Such claims must be job-related to allow recovery. The state workers' compensation statute (Delaware's) specifically did not allow recovery for deaths of "wilful intention."

### Issue

Could Mrs. Fox recover under the workers' compensation statute for her husband's suicide?

### Decision

The Delaware Supreme Court held that Mrs. Fox could recover. The court reasoned that Earl's suicide was caused by severe pain and despair, which proximately resulted from a compensable accident. Furthermore, the pain and despair were so great that they overcame normal, rational judgment. Therefore, there was no "wilful intention" to take his life.

### Questions

1. What factor made the plaintiff's (Mrs. Fox's) claim sympathetic?
2. Was the law ambiguous, thereby, permitting the court to take account of Mrs. Fox's personal situation?

## THE ETHIC OF UTILITY

For a site providing economic information, go to
http://www.dismal.com.

English jurist and philosopher Jeremy Bentham wrote in the late 1700s and early 1800s of the need to promote the greatest good for the greatest number, also known as the **ethic of utilitarianism**. The basic idea of utilitarianism is to maximize the happiness of society. Happiness has come to mean utility (satisfaction). Modern economics is based on Bentham's ideas of utility because economics says that society's resources are limited and, therefore, we should use them to maximize their utility.

Hence, persons who use the ethic of utilitarianism as their guide to proper conduct try to maximize utility. In so doing they are constantly weighing one course of action against others, in effect, balancing alternatives to see which produces the greatest good for the greatest number.

The utility ethic is often reflected in the positive law. The lawmaker (a court or legislature) often balances competing arguments or claims to decide what is the proper rule for the conduct of society. Balancing is a form of utilitarian reasoning. For example, suppose O owns a diamond ring. T, a thief, steals the ring and sells it to G, a good-faith purchaser for value, who believes that T owns the ring. O later learns that G has the ring and sues G to get it back. (T cannot be found.) On the one hand, G will argue that she bought the ring in good faith for value without notice that T did not own it. G will also argue that people should be able to buy goods from persons who appear to own them, which promotes the value of freedom of contract and encourages business. O, on the other hand, will argue that she has a property right (owns) the ring, which a thief should not be able to destroy by selling it to a good-faith purchaser. The judge in this case must choose between the values of property (promoting stability of property ownership) and promoting business (by encouraging people to enter contracts). (In the United States, most judges would decide that O would win over G.)

Utilitarianism has been refined to include two different ideas: **rule utilitarianism** and **act utilitarianism**. Rule utilitarians try to maximize society's happiness within the rules (the positive law). Act utilitarians try to maximize society's utility even if it means breaking the positive law. The difference between rule and act utilitarianism can be understood by considering illegal drug use. Assume a positive law forbids the use of drugs unless one has a physician's approval. A rule utilitarian would not use such drugs without a physician's approval, even if doing so would *temporarily* make her feel better. An act utilitarian, on the other hand, might use illegal drugs if they made her more relaxed. This reasoning follows because act utilitarians ignore positive law when they try to maximize utility. A rule utilitarian who wanted to relax might exercise vigorously for twenty minutes. Exercising does not violate any positive law and it generates endorphin betas, a natural type of painkiller, which naturally and legally relaxes one. Thus, when you see joggers, you most likely are observing rule utilitarians!

*Advantages of the Utilitarian Ethic.* Weighing competing claims causes people to think and consider alternatives before they act, which is clearly desirable. When a court or legislature makes a law and uses the utilitarian ethic as a guide, the weightier value (in the eyes of the lawmaker) will prevail.

Cites to historic Supreme Court cases can be found at **http://supct.law. cornell.edu/supct/cases/ historic.htm**

The earth faces a reality: scarce resources and more people all over the world wanting to improve their living standard. Utilitarians place a high value on maximizing total social utility. Thus utilitarians play an important role in setting positive law today, because the rules should be written to maximize social utility given the increasingly scarce resources.

A third advantage of the utilitarian ethic is that it emphasizes the market as the way to ration scarce resources. The market—as distinct from governments—is more efficient than most bureaucracies. The market is currently being looked at as a mechanism for health care delivery, rather than government regulators, given the need for efficiency in this important area.

The utilitarian ethic provides a fourth advantage, which in a sense repeats something implicit in the first three strengths just noted, but which is so important that it deserves special mention: Utilitarianism provides a way to limit in a rational way the positive law. Today the law and economics (another way of saying utilitarianism) movement is an important analytical tool in devising positive law. The reason is that people demand rights, but fail to see that such demands have associated costs. The law and economics movement, by imposing the cost/benefit discipline on positive law, has the potential of making positive law (and the public) more sensitive to the fact that giving people rights imposes costs. Costs of positive laws should not exceed their benefits. If they do, the positive law fails the test of utilitarianism.

*Disadvantages of the Utilitarian Ethic.* Using utility as a guide to ethical conduct has several disadvantages. First, utilitarianism gives the decision maker (you, the judge, or the legislature, for instance) too much power, because competing claims always exist when any decision is made. Judges can slant their opinions to favor one competing claim over another by making the strongest arguments for the favored claim and only weak arguments for the disfavored competing claim. For example, in the O and G case involving who had the greater right to the ring, legal systems of some European countries would allow G to win. If we are intellectually honest, we must admit that when judges decide cases, sometimes—maybe often—strong arguments exist for the opposite result.

A second criticism of utilitarianism is that it is amoral if not immoral. Consider the following example: Dr. Swan is a wife beater. He also is a creative research scientist who is on the brink of discovering a cure for cancer. His work is unique and cannot be pursued by anyone else. You are the head of the laboratory that employs Dr. Swan. Dr. Swan's wife has just called you asking that you intervene on her behalf and urge that Dr. Swan see a psychiatrist. You know that Dr. Swan is temperamental and that even discussing his personal life with him would result in his ceasing his research, setting back the development of a cancer cure for years. You also learn that Mrs. Swan has never been beaten so severely that her life has been threatened. Because thousands are dying and suffering from cancer, if you follow utilitarian dictates you might well reason that the harm done to Mrs. Swan is not as great as the relief that will be enjoyed by the cancer victims when his cure is forthcoming. Thus, you would sympathize with Mrs. Swan but point out why it is more important that Dr. Swan continue his research, which could save many lives, rather than attend to her, which, after all, is the nonlife-threatening plight of one person.

A third criticism of utilitarianism is that it often involves a market analysis, which uses supply and demand curves. Supply and demand curves are aggregates, representing mythical "average" consumers and "average" suppliers. In effect, by concentrating on averages, everyone is reduced to a clone of everyone else. Is everyone, in fact, identical? No, but by treating everyone as identical, market analysis denies individuality.

A fourth criticism of utilitarianism is that consumers—you and I—are sovereign, the most important people in society. What could be wrong with treating consumers as important? The answer is that some consumers are undiscerning: Some may prefer hog-calling contests, for example, over symphony orchestras. An answer to this criticism is, "That is freedom. People can choose what means the most to them as individuals. Who is to say what is best way to maximize utility from our incomes?" But if people buy and eat potato chips instead of salads, their behavior affects national health care costs, so freedom is not without social costs.

A fifth criticism of utilitarianism is the assumption that all things have a dollar value. Said another way, "Can every decision be reduced to a question of dollars and cents?" Loved ones take care of aged or sick relatives without concern for the economic cost, as do parents of a sick child. The parent never looks at the child and says, "Honey, here's your breakfast. That'll be $1.95."

What claims did the court have to balance in the *Baby M* case?

## In the Matter of BABY M, a pseudonym for an actual person
Supreme Court of New Jersey
109 N.J. 396, 537 A.2d 1227 (1988)

### Background and Facts

In February 1985, William Stern and Mary Beth Whitehead entered into a surrogacy contract. It recited that Stern's wife, Elizabeth, was infertile, that they wanted a child, and that Mrs. Whitehead as the mother was willing to provide that child with Mr. Stern as the father.

The contract provided that through artificial insemination using Mr. Stern's sperm, Mrs. Whitehead would become pregnant, carry the child to term, bear it, deliver it to the Sterns, and thereafter do whatever was necessary to terminate her maternal rights so that Mrs. Stern could thereafter adopt the child. Mrs. Whitehead's husband, Richard, was also a party to the contract; Mrs. Stern was not. Mr. Whitehead promised to do all acts necessary to rebut the presumption of paternity under the Parentage Act. . . . Although Mrs. Stern was not a party to the surrogacy agreement, the contract gave her sole custody of the child in the event of Mr. Stern's death. Mrs. Stern's status as a nonparty to the surrogate parenting agreement presumably was to avoid the application of the baby-selling statute to this agreement.

Mr. Stern, on his part, agreed to attempt the artificial insemination and to pay Mrs. Whitehead $10,000 after the child's birth, on its delivery to him. In a separate contract, Mr. Stern agreed to pay $7,500 to the Infertility Center of New York ("ICNY"). The Center's advertising campaigns solicit surrogate mothers and encourage infertile couples to consider surrogacy. ICNY arranged for the surrogacy contract by bringing the parties together, explaining the process to them, furnishing the contractual form, and providing legal counsel.

Mrs. Whitehead was artificially inseminated with Mr. Stern's sperm, became pregnant, had her baby, "bonded" with it, and after initially relinquishing it to the Sterns, went to them and convinced them to turn Baby M over to her for "a week." Mrs. Whitehead kept the baby for several months, however, despite the Sterns' pleas for the child's return. Mr. Stern filed a lawsuit in which he tried to enforce the surrogacy contract against Mrs. Whitehead. A lower court enforced the surrogacy contract, and the Sterns took custody of the child. Mrs. Whitehead then appealed the result to the New Jersey Supreme Court.

## Issue

Is a surrogacy contract, under which a married couple unable to have children pays money to a surrogate mother who is artificially inseminated with the natural father's sperm, valid?

## Decision

No, the contract here was invalid. "We invalidate the surrogacy contract because it conflicts with the law and public policy of this State. While we recognize the depth of the yearning of infertile couples to have their own children, we find the payment of money to a 'surrogate' mother illegal, perhaps criminal, and potentially degrading to women. Although in this case we grant custody to the natural father, the evidence having clearly proved such custody to be in the best interests of the infant, we void both the termination of the surrogate mother's parental rights and the adoption of the child by the wife/stepparent. We thus restore the 'surrogate' as the mother of the child. We remand the issue of the natural mother's visitation rights to the trial court, since that issue was not reached below and the record before us is not sufficient to permit us to decide it de novo.

"We find no offense to our present laws where a woman voluntarily and without payment agrees to act as a 'surrogate' mother, provided that she is not subject to a binding agreement to surrender her child. Moreover, our holding today does not preclude the Legislature from altering the current statutory scheme, within constitutional limits, so as to permit surrogacy contracts. Under current law, however, the surrogacy agreement before us is illegal and invalid."

## Questions

1. Did the Sterns or Mrs. Whitehead assert the ethic or value of freedom of contract? Does the result in the "Baby M" case uphold the principle of complete freedom of contract? What was peculiar about this contract that made it an extremely unattractive case for application of the freedom of contract ethic?

2. What claim or value did Mrs. Whitehead, the natural mother, make to recover "her" child? Was Mr. Stern the natural father? Are we absolutely certain of this?

3. The "Baby M" case holds that certain surrogacy contracts are invalid. Does this result support or undercut the concept of regulation?

4. In focusing on the Sterns and Mrs. Whitehead, are we forgetting the most important party, Baby M? Who does the court focus on in deciding to void the surrogacy contract but in granting Mr. Stern custody rights subject to Mrs. Whitehead's parental rights? If a court ultimately gives custody to one natural parent (which it did, to Mr. Stern) and visitation rights to the other natural parent (which it did, to Mrs. Whitehead), what does this do to Baby M's perception of her parents when she is a child?

## ETHICS SUMMARY

You should be familiar with (1) the names of the theories of law that represent the various ethics examined, (2) a philosopher representing each value, and (3) some advantages and disadvantages of each ethic. You should also be able to give an example of each ethic.

## FURTHER POINTS ABOUT LEGAL ETHICS

## ETHICAL UNITY

The ethics in positive law we have examined do not represent all of the possible values influencing positive law. Recall that we discussed legal ethics by first seeing what positive law (the rules on the books) requires of us. All other legal values (norms of conduct, longstanding customs, reality, and justice) may point toward the same result as the positive law rule. In this case, we have what is called **ethical unity**, which means that all ethics or ethical values are in agreement on a particular matter.

An example of a positive law with probable ethical unity is the rule forbidding murder. Such a positive law is just and represents a longstanding custom. Murder is contrary to society's accepted norm of conduct. The rule forbidding murder certainly promotes civilization, because it inhibits violence. Finally, juries often follow the law in murder cases so that positive law and realism do not conflict.

## WHICH ETHIC IS "RIGHT"?

The cornered accountant and fired employee cases earlier in this chapter indicate that different legal ethics can lead to opposite conclusions. The same ethic (justice or utility) can even lead to opposite conclusions about what is "right." For example, in the seamen case, society viewed the killing as murder while the seamen saw what they did as right because of the need to survive. What, then, is the value of ethics? Should people simply give up and conclude that ethics only confuse an already difficult problem? Four points can be made.

*Positive Law: Society's Ethical Floor and Sometimes, Its Ethical Ceiling.* First, positive law represents the basic social ethic on a matter. In other words, positive law is society's ethical floor because society (via the government) has ordered or prohibited certain conduct and will punish violators. If people do not follow positive law, they should be prepared to be punished.

*Other Ethics: No Defense to Positive Law.* Second, other legal ethics may lead an individual to break the positive law, although these other ethics provide no defense to the charge of violating positive law. They represent a personal defense or rejection of society's rules. If enough people agree that the positive law is wrong, society can change or eliminate the positive law; but once individuals start selectively obeying and disobeying positive law, civilization is threatened. Every time positive law is broken, a minirevolution breaks out. Also, violating positive law can work against individual interests. Many positive laws, such as the U.S. Constitution's Bill of Rights, protect individuals, and one presumes that individual lawbreakers want government officials to respect these laws. If individuals and government officials can exempt themselves from one positive law, they break the delicate social contract that holds civilization together.

*Ethics that Raise Conduct Above Positive Law.* Third, if positive law is an ethical floor, other legal ethics should rarely be used to justify conduct below that floor. However, other ethics could justify raising conduct above positive law requirements. For example, in the United States a swimmer usually has no positive law duty to save a drowning person, even if rescue presents little or no danger to the swimmer. Justice, utility, and balancing competing claims are ethics that suggest rescue is proper even though not required.

*Ethics that Lower or Limit Positive Law Demands.* Today positive law places demands on all sectors of society, but especially on business, so great that ways are being sought to limit or lower such requirements. The law and economics movement—based on utilitarianism—is today an important device used to question and, perhaps, lower certain positive law requirements such as protective labor laws (minimum wage laws, plant closure laws) and environmental laws. The idea is, if benefits from such laws are less than their costs, such laws should be eliminated or modified until benefits exceed costs.

Further, you and I as consumers economically veto U.S. positive laws when we buy cheap, but good quality, foreign-made goods, which are less costly than comparable U.S. goods because they lack the "social overhead" of U.S. positive laws related to employee and environmental protection. It is a known fact that many nations' positive laws—or, more importantly, their enforcement—are a joke. Korea, Japan, and Mexico are notorious environmental abusers. So, too, are they sexist societies, depriving women of the equal employment opportunity women have in the United States. By not having effective positive laws regarding environmental and employee protections, these nations are able to cut costs for their manufacturers, thereby undercutting U.S. manufacturers' prices. When U.S. consumers purchase such foreign goods, consumers economically veto U.S. positive laws providing those same protections. Ethical consumers have a duty to support, via their purchasing patterns, businesses subject to positive laws from which the consumer receives substantial benefits from or with which the consumer philosophically agrees. To do otherwise is to act in a manner lower than the U.S. positive law.

*Positive Law Changes.* Fourth, positive law and legal ethics are a process, not always a hard-and-fast rule. Government must be flexible and wise enough to realize that times change. For positive law to survive, it must reflect shifts in the various legal ethics.

## COMMUNITARIANISM

Several philosophers, including Professor Amitai Etzioni, have recently advanced the idea of communitarianism. *Communitarianism* refers to the need for community values—commonly shared values—that bind us as a multicultural society. These values are often independent of the positive law, and thus could be seen as social values or norms. They hold a society together and include concern about community peace, tranquillity, and mutual respect, as well as a recognition that each of us has community duties as well as rights.

Communitarianism can be shown in many ways from actions as simple as not ridiculing others because of their dress or lifestyles to efforts to not deface or destroy public parks. Communitarianism also stresses recognition of responsibilities as well as rights. Too often today, sectors of society are eager to demand rights without recognizing that every right places a burden on someone else.

Communitarianism has elements of natural law, positive law, utilitarianism, and the sociological school of jurisprudence. The natural law dimension occurs due to communitarianism's implicit ideas of fairness. Communitarianism has positive law aspects because it recognizes the legal correlatives of right and duty. The utilitarianism can be seen in the maximizing of human happiness resulting from the active practice of communitarian principles. Sociological jurisprudence is evident from the emphasis communitarianism places on conduct.

## BENEFICENCE

**Beneficence** refers to doing good deeds. It is also called *virtue ethics*. When one engages in charitable work, she does so with little or no thought of direct, immediate financial or other gain. Giving money to the United Fund, the Salvation Army, one's school, college, or house of worship are all examples of beneficence. Miss McCarty's very generous gift to the University of Southern Mississippi discussed at the outset of this chapter would be an outstanding example of beneficence. When one agrees to contribute to a charity, the charity gives no equivalent value in return, which makes the contribution beneficent.

There is substantial empirical evidence of beneficence in society today. On the international level, nations give foreign aid to other countries whose populations are in need. In terms of the absolute amount given, Japan leads with more than $15 billion per year while the United States is second with more than $9 billion. As a percentage of gross domestic product, the nation that gives the most is Denmark, which gives almost one percent per year. The United States is not among the top twenty-four nations by this measure.

In terms of domestic giving, the U.S. population shows up quite favorably, having given or volunteered $1,339 per household in 1998. This represented about 2.5 percent of household income. Total private philanthropy in the United States in 2000 was $203.5 billion. Of this, individuals gave $152.1 billion, foundations gave $24.5 billion, corporations gave $10.3 billion, and charitable bequests totaled $16.1 billion. The beneficiaries of this giving were religious organizations ($74.3 billion), education ($28.2 billion), health organizations ($18.8 billion), arts and cultural organizations ($11.5 billion), and environmental/wildlife organizations ($6.2 billion).

Beneficence conflicts with the utilitarian ethic because, arguably, donors would perform a cost/benefit analysis prior to contributing resources to another. The U.S. positive law supports beneficence to the extent that it allows a tax deduction for charitable contributions in calculating one's income taxes.

Critics of virtue ethics point to it as ethical "cover" that cynical businesses use to show their sensitivity at the very moment they plan harmful acts. An example would be a firm's making donations to a local museum to show community support while simultaneously laying off workers and moving local plants to third-world nations.

## BUSINESS ETHICS

### DEFINITION OF BUSINESS ETHICS

Recall from our earlier discussion that ethics refer to values. Business ethics refer to values that a business follows in conducting its affairs. Businesses express values more accurately by actions than by words, which does not mean that any business necessarily lies about its ethics.

Rather, a business does not always have the time or objectivity to perceive correctly the significance of what it is doing when it is making or selling a product. Also, business, as does everyone, tries to put the best face on what it does by making public statements with an eye to promoting positive public relations (PR). By watching what a business does, however, one can get a clearer picture of that business's ethics than by merely reading its press releases.

*Examples of Business Ethics.* Some positive ethical values that a business can promote in its operations include (1) making a profit, (2) delivering the best products and services to consumers, (3) providing workers with jobs, (4) giving stockholders a good return on their investment, and (5) being a good community citizen. We shall examine each of these in greater detail.

- *Making a profit.* Business has profit making as its prime objective. In other words, selling goods or services for more than it costs to make and distribute them is the primary ethic of business. Even though this motivation sounds selfish, at least three factors make it a positive selfishness. First, consumers voluntarily decide to buy from one particular seller; no one forces them to spend their money. Thus, the consumers maximize their utility by voluntarily purchasing what they want. Second, by having fair tariffs and antitrust laws that promote an open market, competition should keep prices as low as possible. Furthermore, competitors will have the incentive of profit to enter the market, which will insure that consumers will be supplied. Third, businesses that make a profit in the face of competition are both keeping costs under control and producing what consumers want. In other words, they maximize society's utility and make efficient use of scarce resources.

- *Delivering the best products and services to consumers.* Because sellers want to make a profit, and they generally face competition, businesses have an incentive to deliver products and services that will outsell those of competitors. To win sales over competitors, businesses attempt to make products and services perceived as superior to those of competitors.

  Also, today's consumers are knowledgeable about goods and services as a result of increasing consumer education levels as well as availability of consumer buying guides on every topic from autos to can openers. Such information increases the pressure on business to produce the highest quality products and services.

- *Providing workers with jobs.* Businesses employ workers and so provide them with a means of financial support. It has been said that a job is the best welfare system that people can have. This statement asserts that jobs not only contribute to workers' economic well-being but also give their lives meaning and a sense of purpose, thereby contributing to workers' self-esteem.

  Perhaps one of the most disturbing aspects of the current employment environment is the trend toward *contingent employment* where many are "temps"—temporary workers. There are self-esteem as well as economic issues for temps.

  The contingent employment aspect of the U.S. job market can be seen as an outgrowth of the *internationalization* of the U.S. economy, where U.S. manufacturers are willing to export jobs to reduce costs. Obviously, the willingness of U.S. workers to compromise on wages, hours, and working conditions reduces the incentive of U.S. manufacturers to relocate in lower-cost nations, where worker productivity is often lower.

- *Giving owners a good return on their investment.* Closely related to earning a profit is the ethic of giving the business owners (stockholders in the case of a corporation) a good return on their investment. A difference between a business's earning a profit and giving the owners a handsome return lies in whether profit can be kept in the business for expansion and improvement of operations. On the other hand, when profits are distributed to the business's owners, such earnings are taken out of the business and can be used by the owners for whatever purpose they desire, which often has nothing to do with improving or developing the firm.

• *Being a good citizen.* Businesses can be good citizens by paying taxes that support community schools, hospitals, and other governmental services. Also, by following laws that promote environmental and consumer protection, equal employment, product quality, and other such concerns, the business community acts as a good citizen.

Business efforts at good citizenship, however, extend beyond merely following the positive law. Many businesses support charities such as the United Way, contribute to community development by donating property for parks and playgrounds, make financial contributions to colleges, art museums, symphony orchestras, ballets, sporting teams, and scout troops, and make many other efforts to enhance community life. Also, employees contribute their time by serving on school boards, as members of charity drives, and as coaches of Little League ball clubs. Businesspeople engage in these civic-minded activities because they believe such contributions make their communities a more appealing place to live, which, in turn provides an incentive for qualified employees to remain in the community even when job opportunities appear elsewhere.

***Making Business Ethics Mutually Compatible with Each Other.*** Businesses can sometimes make decisions that satisfy all business ethics. For example, a decision to dump toxic wastes in a properly prepared site will promote long-term profits by preventing huge future lawsuits from not following proper dumping practices. Also, proper dumping can provide the business owners with a long-run return on their investment by ensuring that they will still be in business if and when their dumping is challenged. Further, by remaining in business, the ethic of providing employees with a job will be accomplished. The ethic of providing consumers with excellent products and services also comes into play because a product or service cannot be judged excellent if it is made under conditions that ruin the human environment. Finally, following safe and proper dumping practices is good citizenship because environmental problems such as contaminated water supplies are avoided.

***Dealing with Conflicting Business Ethics.*** If the business ethic of making a profit is viewed in the short run, it can, and too often does, conflict with other business ethics. For example, a corporation with many plants in the United States may feel great pressure to close down a marginally profitable plant that is not making profits at the level desired for the corporation as a whole. But what if the plant is the sole economic base of a small community and closure threatens the livelihood of the community? In this case, being a good citizen and providing the workers with jobs might conflict with making a profit or giving the shareholders a fair return on their investment. Also, one could ask whether the business is giving the consumer the desired product or service if a particular plant is only marginally profitable. (It is simplistic to ask such a question when many considerations of intrafirm resource allocation, such as marketing and product development, are involved in assessing the performance of one plant in a multiplant operation.) Nonetheless, the business ethics in such a case do not necessarily all point toward one "right" answer.

## HOW BUSINESS ETHICS RELATE TO LEGAL ETHICS

*Ethical Floor.* A business decision involving ethics is generally assumed to follow the positive law. In other words, the legal ethic of positive law is an ethical floor for business. Thus, a business should not have to ask whether it should follow laws regulating accuracy of financial reports, occupational health and safety, dumping of toxic wastes, equal employment opportunity, insider trading, or any of the thousands of other laws regulating business. It is assumed that businesses follow the positive law ethic.

*Business Ethics Above Positive Law Requirements.* Even though positive law often is assumed to dictate proper ethical conduct for business, it often falls short of this expectation. Businesses often realize this shortfall and engage in desirable ethical conduct *before* positive law mandates it. For example, some businesses, in an effort to hasten the arrival of a racially integrated workforce, voluntarily instituted affirmative action plans beyond that required by positive law. On occasion, though, this policy has resulted in a business being sued for discriminating against white males. (However, in *United Steelworkers v. Weber* the white males lost their suit for reverse discrimination.)

*Business Ethics Conflicting with and Falling Below Positive Law.* Sometimes businesses, in their effort to make profits and provide workers with jobs, violate the positive law. In November 1989 the former president of Beech-Nut Nutrition Corporation pleaded guilty to ten felony counts for violating the Food, Drug, and Cosmetic Act. Under a plea bargain, this person was fined $100,000 and given five years probation and six consecutive months of full-time community service. Federal Judge Thomas Platt accepted the plea bargain to end the case, which had been going on for three years. The defendant stated, "I did not intend to defraud, but I do plead guilty of intent to mislead the public. I did it knowingly." After the plea agreement was approved by the judge, the U.S. Attorney remarked, "This case has probably cost Nestlé, the corporate parent of Beech-Nut, in fines and legal fees, many times the few millions they saved in passing off this bogus apple juice to the public."

Beech-Nut Corp. had earlier pleaded guilty to 215 counts of violating the Food, Drug, and Cosmetic Act and was fined $2 million. The product in question was misrepresented as apple juice even though it consisted of sugar, corn syrup, and various other ingredients but little, if any, apple juice. After the company's then chief executive learned of the misrepresented product, he relied at least partially on attorneys' opinions and continued to sell the product. Had sales not continued, the company would have lost money, the prosecutor alleged. Here is a clear case in which the business ethic of making a profit (in the short run, at least) conflicted with the legal ethic of the positive law. The business ethic of keeping the company workers employed arguably might have prompted this positive law violation. With regard to the business ethic of giving the consumer the best product, the prosecution did not prove that the juice was harmful. However, few would claim that sugar water with possibly small amounts of apple juice is as healthy or healthier than pure apple juice.

In more recent times, the Enron Corporation's suspension of its ethics code was a forewarning of impropriety. Enron's auditor—Arthur Andersen, LLP—is a convicted felon as of this writing, as is the Andersen partner formerly in charge of the Enron audit. While Enron's legal fate remains in doubt as of this writing, its financial future is glum given its bankruptcy filing. Perhaps the greatest lesson from Enron is that taking short-term measures to "cook the books" undermines the trust of supporters: shareholders, employees, the community, suppliers, and customers. Lying is a formula for failure in the long run.

## OBJECTIVES OF LAW

Six key objectives of law are justice, speed, economy, flexibility, stability, and knowability. Law has more than six objectives, but the six chosen represent major legal goals and to some extent complement our earlier discussion of legal ethics.

### JUSTICE, SPEED, AND ECONOMY

One legal rule that expressly requires the three objectives of justice, speed, and economy is Rule 1 of the Federal Rules of Civil Procedure, which tells how to conduct civil trials. That law says the rules for running federal trials should promote the "just, speedy, and inexpensive determination of every action."

The justice, speed, and economic objectives do not always agree, however. An example is the rule concerning jury size. With a smaller jury (six instead of twelve), an agreement can generally be reached faster. Small juries have fewer jurors to be paid; however, smaller juries might not represent the community as well. For example, the smaller the jury, the less likely are minorities to be on them. On the other hand, extremely large juries are costly, slow, and perhaps unjust, because justice delayed is justice denied.

### FLEXIBILITY

Laws should be flexible to take into account differences among people. For example, real estate taxes are generally higher on large houses than on small ones. But too much flexibility can unnecessarily complicate the law. Federal income tax laws are an example. They take into account such factors as the taxpayer's age, marital status, stock portfolio, childcare arrangements, and whether the taxpayer pays a mortgage.

Great flexibility can also make law enforcement too difficult. An extreme case might be different speed limits for motorists depending on their age, reaction time, and condition of their cars. Under such a law, different speed limits would be needed for each of us, which is clearly impractical.

### STABILITY AND KNOWABILITY

Stable law is desirable because people find it easy to plan if the law does not change. Also, legal training costs are lower, because once a person knows the law, the need to know about changes occurs infrequently. When law is knowable, people can obey it more easily and take greater interest in it because they can learn what it is.

Special interest groups sometimes see knowability of the law as a disadvantage because they have a legal advantage that they want to hide. For example, in some states, learning the salaries of public officials or school budgets is difficult. Such secrecy is sometimes defended on privacy grounds. When public agencies such as schools are involved, however, the general rule should be one of disclosure (knowability).

## WHY STUDY LAW?

The reasons for studying law are many, but in business three are paramount. First, law (technically, positive law) is the cutting edge of society, telling us what we must do and what we cannot do. Students in general and business students in particular should be adequately informed about the legal system's mandates.

Second, the business environment today is increasingly legalized. Rules, often with criminal *and* civil sanctions, outlaw conduct that at first may seem perfectly harmless. For example, corporate directors who buy or sell stock in their company because of information not available to the public are engaging in conduct that is illegal. A corporation (or anyone) that dumps untreated pollutants into a stream is acting illegally. Dumping something into a stream or buying stock might seem harmless to the average person. However, laws regulate these and many other activities.

Third, future businesspeople should practice preventive law. That is, business should take steps to stop or reduce the potentially adverse impact of law on them while law is being made. For example, by knowing the steps in making administrative regulations, business can point out weaknesses in agency proposals *before* they become law. This knowledge can reduce the cost of complying with proposed regulations before millions of dollars have to be spent.

## WHAT IS THE LEGAL ENVIRONMENT?

Figure 1.1 shows law covered in the legal environment of business and is a modern way of classifying law. Its focus is on problems or situations. We see a problem or situation and then look at clusters of rules that try to solve or cope with the problem or situation. For example, product liability shown in Figure 1.1 deals with products that do not work. The figure groups together legal theories that help people recover if a defective product injures them or their property.

Constitutional law appears in the figure. Such law is above all other law because it limits what other laws can do. The remainder of this book looks at all of the legal areas presented in Figure 1.1.

## CHAPTER SUMMARY

Ethics refer to desirable conduct. Determining what is desirable conduct in a given situation depends on what values one follows. The value that the authors of this book recommend to guide managers and, indeed, everyone is positive law.

Jurisprudence is the study of values concerning law and legal systems. Schools of jurisprudence present different values for judging whether positive law is appropriate ethical conduct.

This chapter has examined the ethic of justice. Natural law is what each person thinks is fair, just, or right even though it might be different from positive law. In considering justice, the matter of morality was discussed. Lon Fuller's internal morality of law (IML) lays out eight characteristics of moral positive law. John Rawls's original position is a type of natural law. Kant's categorical imperative expresses a natural law concept similar to the golden rule.

**Figure 1.1 Legal Environment of Business**

Justice (natural law) often, but not always, agrees with positive law.

Power is an ethic that shapes positive law. Unless power supports positive law, the positive law will not last.

Custom (historical jurisprudence) is a value or ethic that refers to repeated conduct over a long period of time. Many positive laws, such as contract law and those creating private property, reflect custom. A German, Savigny, espoused the ethic of custom.

Eugen Ehrlich's sociological school of jurisprudence emphasizes the ethic of norms of conduct. How the average person acts is an ethic.

The ethic of civilization refers to frustration of our base instincts, such as the desire to steal. Sigmund Freud espoused this idea.

Legal realism refers to what trial court judges and juries do in fact, regardless of what the positive law requires. This ethic of reality was developed by Jerome Frank.

Jeremy Bentham advocated the ethic of utilitarianism. This ethic says that appropriate conduct is determined by trying to promote the greatest good for the greatest number.

Business ethics focus on appropriate conduct for business to follow. Business ethics can focus on stakeholders affected by business decisions. Stakeholders include stockholders, customers, employees, the community in which the business operates, and society in general. Beneficence, or virtue ethics, is the idea that one should do good deeds irrespective of the lack of immediate payoff to the donor.

Business ethics relate to legal ethics in several ways. The ethic of positive law sets an ethical floor. If business ethics conflict with or do less than the positive law requires, persons following business ethics should be prepared to be punished.

Some objectives of positive law are the promotion of justice, speed, and economy. Positive law should be flexible, yet stable and knowable.

The Manager's Ethical Decision Model provides a step-by-step process that can assist persons confronting ethical issues.

---

## ■ MANAGER'S ETHICAL DILEMMA

Jean was nearing retirement. She lived in a house that was too large for her, so she planned to sell it and move into a condominium that would be more manageable. She was not knowledgeable about property values, so, thinking her house was worth $100,000, she listed it with a realtor for that amount. The fair market value for her property was actually closer to $140,000. Given the low price, several persons called and told her they would give her the asking price. Jean orally accepted the first buyer's offer, but put nothing in writing.

That evening she had dinner with Bob, a friend who was a lawyer. She told Bob that she had sold her house for $100,000. Bob was shocked at how low the price was and told Jean that she should have gotten at least $140,000 to $150,000. Bob then asked Jean if she had signed any document yet. When Jean replied "No," Bob told her that a statute called the Statute of Frauds requires all contracts for the sale of an interest in realty to be written and signed by the seller to bind the seller.

Bob: Jean, I advise you to call the buyer and tell him that you have changed your mind.

Jean: But, Bob, I gave the seller my word to sell it to him for $100,000. It wouldn't be morally right to back out now.

Bob: Jean, this is a matter of money, $40,000 or $50,000 to be specific. You are going to retire soon and you will need that money to supplement your pension.

What ethical conflicts are present in this scenario? If you were Jean, what would you do?

## Discussion Questions

1. A movement on in certain sectors of the United States supports a no-consumption day. In other words, some persons believe that excessive consumerism exploits the environment at unsustainable levels as well as devaluing time spent with families and friends on matters unrelated to wealth accumulation (such as having a family picnic or going fishing). What philosophies discussed in this chapter are implicit in no-consumption days? What approach should a clothing manufacturer take when confronted with a petition circulated in the community urging citizens to participate in a no-buy day?

2. A surrogate mother was implanted with the zygote (fertilized genetic matter) of a married man and woman (the commissioning parents), who desired to have their "own child." The commissioning parents were of different races; the mother was Filipina and the father Caucasian. They entered a contract with a surrogate mother, who was African-American, who agreed to be implanted with the commissioning couple's zygote and carry it to term. The surrogate mother was paid for this service and was also to renounce any parental claim to the child. Prior to giving birth, the surrogate mother repudiated the surrogacy contract and sued for custody of "her" child. How is this case different from the *Baby M* case presented in this chapter? [*Johnson v. Calvert*, 19 Cal. Rptr. 2d 494 (1993)].

3. You are president of BMA, a company that makes computers that it sells worldwide. The company sells to a largely upscale market with particular emphasis on business and professional clients. As part of the marketing strategy, BMA has sponsored on national TV the Professional Golf Championship, an event that draws the best golfers worldwide. The event is scheduled to be played next year at Pleasant Hills Country Club, which has an internationally famous golf course that has hosted several world-class golf tournaments in the past. The club receives about $250,000 in net income from TV sponsors, the sale of food, tickets, and other concessions operating during the tournament. Also, the club gains enormous prestige from hosting such highly visible events. The club also does not accept women, minorities, or Jews as members. This fact has come to light, as you are in the final stages of confirming arrangements for next year's tournament. You fear that the national media will learn of this fact. Several contestants in the tournament are African Americans and some others are Jewish. What business ethics occur to you in deciding what course of conduct to take? Are any other values (ethics) discussed in this chapter relevant to resolving the matter?

4. Guy Burgess was the manager of Mother's Home Cooking Shops. Guy held traditional values and emphasized them when instructing his employees and conducting his business, a chain of restaurants and grocery stores catering to motorists on U.S. interstate highways in the southeastern United States. Guy determined that two waitresses and a male cook were homosexual. He immediately fired them, although the sexual preference of each was not apparent to any customers or other workers. Guy sent a memo to all 9,000 company employees saying that homosexual employees would be dismissed because "Mother's Home Cooking Shops were founded on concepts of traditional American values. Employment of persons whose sexual preference fails to demonstrate normal heterosexual values which have been the foundation of families in our society is inconsistent with perceived values of our customer base."

   You are Guy Burgess's immediate superior and must review this policy that Guy has drafted. What action should you take, based on business ethics? On other ethics discussed in this chapter?

5. The U.S. Secretary of Transportation announced a zero tolerance program for enforcing U.S. drug laws. Under the program ships and vehicles carrying *any* amount of illegal drugs are subject to confiscation by the U.S. Coast Guard. A boat seized under the zero tolerance program will be returned to its owners only when allegations of illegal drugs on board turn out to be false. If the allegations are true, the boat is turned over to the U.S. Customs Service to be auctioned off. Under the zero tolerance program, the Coast Guard seized a $2.5 million, 133-foot yacht that contained a teaspoon of marijuana. Only the crew of six, not the owners or other passengers, were on board at the time of seizure. Discuss the legal ethics involved in the zero tolerance program that permit such a result.

6. The Railway Labor Executives Association, an unincorporated association representing all crafts of railroad workers in the United States, sued the U.S. Secretary of Transportation over regulations requiring that blood and urine samples be taken from all crew members of a train involved in various events. Among the events giving rise to the blood and urine testing are major train accidents involving a fatality, release of hazardous material with either evacuation or injury, or $500,000 damage to railroad property; impact accidents involving a reportable injury or damage to railroad property of $50,000; and fatal accidents involving the death of an on-duty railroad employee. The blood samples are to be taken at independent medical facilities by qualified medical professionals or technicians. Refusal to provide the sample results in a nine-month period of disqualification. The

regulations authorize railroads to require covered employees to submit to breath or urine tests when a supervisor has a reasonable suspicion that an employee is under the influence or impaired by alcohol or drugs. To require a urine test, two supervisors must have reasonable suspicion, and, if drug use is suspected, one of them must have been trained in spotting drug use.

This case had no factual disputes except the extent of alcohol and drug abuse in the railroad industry and the number of accidents involving either substance. The record shows that between 1975 and 1984, 37 of 791 fatalities caused by railroad employees (or 4.7 percent) resulted from accidents or incidents involving drug use. The Federal Railroad Administration (FRA) contended that the problem was more serious than 4.7 percent would indicate because of underreporting by the railroad industry of alcohol and drug involvement, because of the increased dangers involved in railroad transport of hazardous materials, and because drug and alcohol abuse has become more pervasive in recent years. The federal district court upheld the FRA regulations.

On appeal, the U.S. Court of Appeals for the Ninth Circuit analyzed the case in the following terms: "On the one side of the balance are the railroad employees' reasonable expectations of privacy and on the other side is the governmental interest in the safe and efficient operation of the railroads for the benefit of railroad employees and the public affected by that operation." The court of appeals then proceeded to invalidate the regulations on grounds that they violated the U.S. Constitution's prohibition of unreasonable searches and seizures under the Fourth Amendment. The U.S. Supreme Court ultimately upheld the regulations. What legal ethics are present in this decision? What business ethics are involved? [*Skinner v. Railway Labor Executives' Ass'n*, 489 U.S. 602 (1989)].

7. In some countries, notably France and Italy, the reputed practice of businesspeople is to keep two sets of books: one for the tax assessor, which understates income, and the other for themselves, which accurately reflects business earnings. How would the various legal ethics view this situation? Would they all condemn this conduct?

8. Larry Wieland audited the Falconer Company's books. During the audit, Larry discovered that a company clerk was embezzling on a regular basis. He reported his findings to Falconer's president, Harvey Slater, who asked the amount of the embezzlement. Upon being told the employee was stealing $3,000 per year, Slater replied, "Don't say anything. The clerk is worth $18,000, his salary is $10,000, and he's stealing $3,000, so the company is coming out

ahead." What legal ethics does Slater's remark reflect? What legal ethics does it ignore?

9. The economy was in a recession. The United Motor Manufacturing Company had to lay off 30 percent of its workforce because of low demand for its cars. Because the most recently hired employees were minorities and women, the layoffs would fall most heavily on them. Suppose no positive law requires any order for layoffs. Devise a layoff scheme that will promote the natural law ethic, the utility ethic, and the ethic of custom.

10. Diane Wentworth was a 30-year-old MBA who worked for a Fortune 500 company. Diane performed her job well and socialized extensively with the company president, John Dough. After Diane worked for the firm for eighteen months, Mr. Dough promoted her to a vice-president's position over several more experienced people. Are any legal ethics involved here? If so, what are they?

11. The Foreign Corrupt Practices Act of 1977 makes it a crime for a U.S. corporation or its agent to offer a bribe to an official of a foreign government to obtain business. The act does not forbid paying small amounts (called grease payments) to low-level foreign officials who do minor clerical jobs that speed up the flow of work. The act does not outlaw paying money that foreign officials extort from U.S. business. (In extortion, the demand for money comes from the other person, not the individual paying.) Discuss the act in light of the following legal ethics: positive law, natural law, and sociological jurisprudence.

12. In 1965 Adolpho Perez, an uninsured motorist, had an auto accident in Tucson, Arizona. Perez injured Miss Pinkerton in the mishap. She sued Perez and won a judgment of $2,425.98. Perez immediately went bankrupt to escape paying his debts, which included the $2,425.98 now owed to his accident victim. The state of Arizona has a statute that suspends the driver's license of anyone filing bankruptcy to escape debts resulting from auto accidents. Was this Arizona statute valid, resulting in Perez having to pay Miss Pinkerton to get his driver's license back, or did this statute violate the U.S. Constitution? What does this case tell you about positive law? If Perez escaped paying, how would natural law evaluate it? Is it possible to balance of bankruptcy laws and the right of a creditor to be paid? [*Perez v. Campbell*, 402 U.S. 637 (1971)].

13. Booker ran a migrant agricultural camp in Johnson County, North Carolina. Two of his lieutenants, Rollins and Gibson, brought Gary Walters and two others to the camp from Florida, having promised them free transportation and steady work. But Walters and the others discovered that employment was only occasional, that they would be charged

both for their meals while idle and for their transportation from Florida, and that Booker withheld their wages and made them buy everything they needed at the camp. They were also not allowed to leave the camp until they had paid Booker any debts allegedly owed to him. Booker repeatedly threatened workers at the camp with death or serious injury if they tried to leave without paying their debts. He backed up his threats with severe beatings and assaults with firearms. Prosecutors charged Booker and his lieutenants with violating the U.S. Constitution's Thirteenth Amendment and antislavery statutes. Booker argued that it was not formal slavery but merely a work camp. What was the result? What legal philosophies would find Booker guilty? Innocent? [*United States v. Booker*, 655 F.2d 562 (4th Cir. 1981)].

14. Give an example of a positive law that violates natural law principles.

15. Can a positive law ever be illegal? How?

16. Farouk Al Attar and Rima Al Attar were husband and wife and also business partners in the Apollo Paint and Body Shop. One of their employees, Janet Brunner, told Farouk that she would be volunteering her free time on Saturdays and Sundays and in the evenings with the AIDS Foundation. Brunner promised that her volunteer work would not interfere with her position at Apollo. She told Farouk that the employees at Apollo Paint & Body were not in danger of contracting AIDS because Brunner could not catch AIDS from the patients' touching, sneezing, or breathing on her. Brunner further informed Farouk that his customers did not have to know about her volunteer work.

   Farouk thought about what Brunner had said. On the one hand, Brunner had been a good worker, and, in a way, Farouk admired her community spiritedness and compassion for persons afflicted with AIDS. On the other hand, he did not want to place himself, his family, and the other office workers in jeopardy. He urged Brunner to resign from her volunteer work. She refused. Should Farouk fire her, retain her, or do something else? [*Brunner v. Al Attar*, 786 S.W.2d 784 (Tex. App.— Houston 1st Dist. 1990)].

17. "But he's the star quarterback. The team will lose every game if we lose him," said William Winn, head coach of Kallikak State University. Charges had been brought against Ron Guy, the star football player on Kallikak's team after Guy had been caught by police in an opened appliance store window at 2 A.M. with a television in his hands. The athletic department hired Mack E. Velli, famed criminal lawyer, to represent Guy.

The case came to trial and Mack made the following argument to the court: "What would happen to gate receipts at Kallikak University, to say nothing of the community's restaurant, motel, and retail store receipts, if Kallikak's football team started losing games because its star was locked up?"

Mack then put Guy on the stand and asked him this question: "What was in your mind when the police caught you?"

Guy responded, "I realized just before the police arrived that what I was doing was wrong, and I was *entering*, not exiting, the store to *return* the TV."

The judge looked down at Guy and said, "You are accused of larceny. The law defines larceny as taking away another's property with intent to deprive the owner of it permanently. Obviously, because you recognized the error of your ways and were in the act returning the property when the police arrived, you did not have the intent to deprive the owner of the television. Charges dismissed!"

What legal philosophies are implicit in this case?

## INFOTRAC KEYWORDS

**Use your InfoTrac password to look up articles on http://www.infotrac-college.com**

Keywords: *Business ethics.*
Look up business ethics for articles on ethical issues in business, including "Scandal 101: Lessons from Ken Lay."

For suggested readings, please visit this book's Web site at **http://fisher.westbuslaw.com** (click on "Internet Applications").

# OVERVIEW AND FINDING THE LAW

---

## POSITIVE LAW ETHICAL PROBLEM

"This isn't logical. I was convicted for violating federal law requiring the reporting of more than $10,000 being taken out of the United States and was fined $5,000. Then the 'feds' also claimed that I should forfeit all of the money I was secretly trying to take out of the U.S.," shouted Hosep Bajakajian to his lawyer.

"Well, Mr. Bajakajian, you are a currency smuggler. The U.S. Code allows for forfeiture of any property involved in the offense. How much are they trying to get you to forfeit?" asked Bajakajian's lawyer.

"Over $357,000," he replied.

"Requiring you to forfeit that much when the criminal fine was only $5,000 seems like an excessive fine under the 'excessive fines clause' of the U.S. Constitution," said his lawyer.

Was the lawyer correct?

---

This chapter provides an overview of law. We examine forms that law takes and then look at several legal classifications. The chapter also gives some idea of how to find the law. Because this book contains legal cases, the chapter tells how to analyze, or brief, a legal case.

*"I WILL NOT SAY WITH LORD HALE, THAT 'THE LAW WILL ADMIT NO RIVAL' . . . BUT I WILL SAY THAT IT IS A JEALOUS MISTRESS, AND REQUIRES A LONG AND CONSTANT COURTSHIP. IT IS NOT TO BE WON BY TRIFLING FAVORS BUT BY LAVISH HOMAGE."*

—JOSEPH STORY
INAUGURAL
ADDRESS AS DANE
PROFESSOR OF LAW
AT HARVARD
UNIVERSITY (1829)

## FORMS OF LAW

Law comes in many forms, including constitutions, statutes, administrative regulations, and municipal ordinances (see Figure 2.1).

### CONSTITUTIONS

A constitution is the skeleton for a legal system. It sets out the form and basic principles by which the government will operate. It covers matters such as the number of branches of government and the powers given to each. In the Western world, constitutions, such as the U.S. Constitution's Bill of Rights, create individual protections. Constitutions generally are written, although those of some nations, notably Great Britain, are not. They tend to be vague, broad statements that leave to statutes, judges, and administrative agencies the job of making specific rules that govern society. Since constitutions are enduring statements of principle, they are designed so that changing them is difficult.

**FIGURE 2.1 DIAGRAM OF THE FORMS OF LAW**

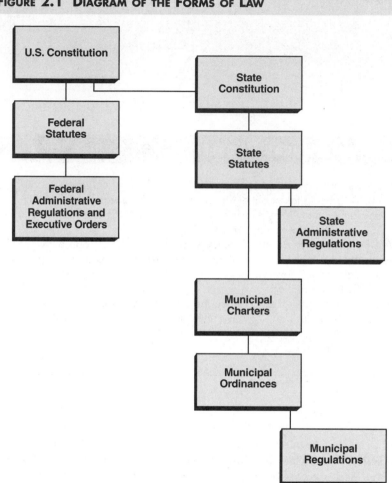

## STATUTES

Statutes are enactments by national and state legislatures. Laws passed by city governments are referred to as **ordinances**, not statutes, even though they represent efforts by city councils, which are legislative bodies. States and the national government are separate sovereigns according to the dual sovereignty notion that is the basis for federalism. However, cities, being mere creations of the states in which they are located, are not on the same level politically with either national or state governments.

All states pass many statutes regulating business. With fifty sovereign states, fifty different rules could regulate the same thing. For example, each state could have a different rule on when a contract exists. Wide differences in legal rules on the same matter are generally undesirable for the many firms doing business in several states. Business generally favors uniformity and simplicity in order to promote efficiency. Consider the problem of the Michigan salesperson who may think she has a million-dollar contract made in Louisiana in the bag, only to learn that Louisiana law would not enforce the deal even though the deal would be enforceable if subject to Michigan law.

To help states make laws regulating business more uniform, a private group of legal scholars and business lawyers called the **National Conference of Commissioners on Uniform State Laws** was formed in the 1800s. It drafted **model statutes** to provide the needed regulation in the most effective, efficient way. The model statutes were actually not *laws* at all because the commissioners had no lawmaking authority. The commissioners would present their model statutes to each state's legislature and urge passage of the particular model act.

Over the years, state legislatures have reacted favorably to the model statutes and have passed many into law. This practice has tended to reduce variation in many rules regulating multistate businesses. Among the more important model statutes that have been passed are the Uniform Commercial Code (UCC), the Uniform Partnership Act, and the Uniform Bills of Lading Act. The most significant of the uniform acts is the UCC. It lays down rules for contracts dealing with goods, negotiable instruments, bank deposits and collections, letters of credit, bulk transfers, investment securities, and secured transactions.

## FEDERAL ADMINISTRATIVE REGULATIONS AND EXECUTIVE ORDERS

Federal administrative regulations are rules made by federal administrative agencies. (See Chapter 7 for further discussion of this topic.) Executive orders refer to rules made by the president to interpret, promote, or put into operation some statute, treaty, or constitutional provision.

## CLASSIFICATIONS OF LAW

Law can be classified in a number of ways. Two of the main classifications are substantive-procedural and civil-criminal.

### SUBSTANTIVE LAW AND PROCEDURAL LAW

**Substantive law** refers to rules that govern people's relations with one another in their daily lives. Some examples are a rule of contract law that an acceptance takes effect when sent, the rule of environmental law that a person must have an NPDES[1] permit to discharge into U.S. waters, and the consumer law rule that lets homeowners escape contracts with door-to-door salespeople within three days after the contract is made. Such rules determine what people can do in society.

Contrast substantive law with **procedural law**. Procedural laws are rules of legal administration. Statutes of limitations, for instance, are usually procedural laws that tell us that a suit against someone must be filed within a specified time period. The rule setting the number of people on a jury is procedural because it deals with an administrative matter. Unlike substantive law, it does not tell people how to act in their everyday lives.

### CIVIL LAW AND CRIMINAL LAW

Law can be divided into civil law and criminal law. Figure 2.2 shows civil law and criminal law and many of their subcategories.

---

[1] The National Pollutant Discharge Elimination System is a permit system to control water pollution. It was established by the Clean Water Act.

# Figure 2.2 Overview of Civil and Criminal Law

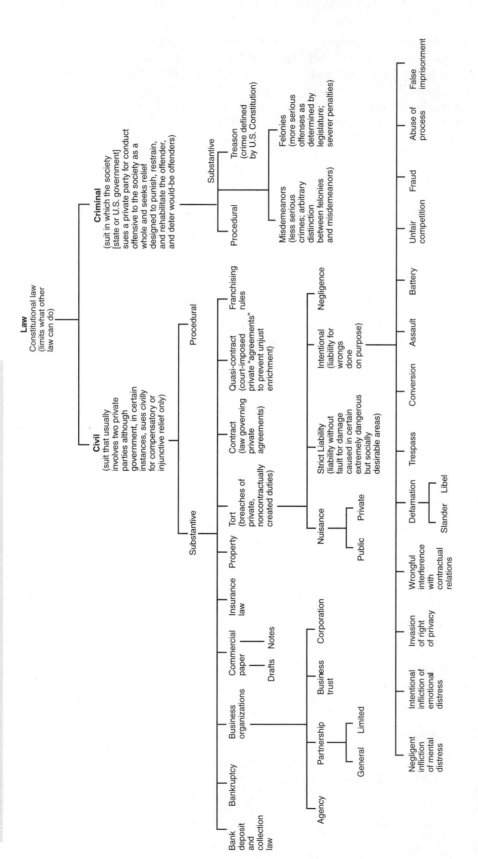

**Note:** These definitions do not purport to be complete but are merely indications of the nature of the various areas of the law.

**Civil law** refers to several things. For our purposes, it refers principally to rules that determine rights and duties between and among private individuals—for example, rules involving tort, contract, and property law. Civil law also has another meaning: The law of certain European and other countries relies on codes (lengthy statutes) to a greater extent than the discretionary power of a judge (common law) to make rules. France is a civil law country because it relies on a code for the source of its rules. But the important definition of civil law for our purposes is the establishment of legal relations between private parties.

**Criminal law** refers to the rules designed to protect and vindicate society's interest with respect to individuals. For example, in a murder, even though only one member of society is killed, society is deemed to be harmed. Such outrageous, antisocial conduct threatens the tacit bond of restraint that distinguishes civilization from the jungle.

## DIFFERENCES BETWEEN CIVIL AND CRIMINAL LAW

*Civil Law Objectives.* Several differences distinguish civil from criminal law. First, each has a different objective. Civil law is generally **compensatory**, whereas criminal law is generally **punitive**. For example, when one person sues another for breaking a contract, the party suing (the plaintiff) hopes to recover damages sustained as a result of the other person's (the defendant's) breach of the plaintiff's rights. Even though the damage recovery (called **compensatory damages**) is taken from the defendant and turned over to the plaintiff, this action is not considered punishment of the defendant. The reasoning is that the defendant is only paying for harm that has been caused, which agrees with basic natural law concepts of fairness. It also follows historical jurisprudence, which requires wrongdoers to compensate their victims, and is a longstanding community custom.

Contrast compensatory damages with a second type of recovery sometimes awarded in civil law: **punitive damages**. As the word *punitive* suggests, punitive damages are designed to punish wrongdoers, not to compensate victims for harm sustained. Punitive damages represent an exception to the general rule that civil law does not punish. Because punitive damages *do* punish, they are awarded when the defendant's conduct is particularly reprehensible. Punitive damages are most commonly awarded in intentional **tort** cases—cases in which the defendant often intends to harm someone. For example, spitting in someone's face is the intentional tort of battery (unauthorized touching of another) and might not result in any compensatory damages, although punitive damages are appropriate owing to the offensive, outrageous character of the spitting. Punitive damages are not awarded in all or even most successful intentional tort suits, because not all intentional torts involve reprehensible conduct.

Sometimes civil and criminal law objectives overlap. For example, one objective of criminal law is to punish violators. Generally civil law aims only to "make the victim whole" by awarding compensatory damages. However, occasionally civil law assesses punitive damages—that is, damages designed to punish the wrongdoer—against someone who intentionally harms another.

**Nominal damages** are a final type of damage awarded in civil law. Nominal damages, as the name suggests, involve a nominal amount of money—one dollar or six cents, for example. This recovery is given to the plaintiff to indicate that the plaintiff's rights have been broken but that no actual damages have been sustained. For example, if the defendant who agreed to buy a car from the plaintiff for $400 broke the contract, and if the plaintiff then sold the car to another person for $500 but sued the defendant for breach of contract, then clearly, the plaintiff had a right breached but sustained no actual damages.

*Equitable Remedies.* In addition to the three types of damages—compensatory, punitive, and nominal—civil law remedies include the equitable remedies of an **injunction** (a court order to do or not do something) and **specific performance** (a court order to do what one has by contract agreed to do). **Equitable remedies** arose in ancient England when litigants who had lost their cases in law court went to the king's minister to tell him their troubles. The king's minister was called the chancellor and was known as the king's conscience. Occasionally, the chancellor was convinced that the litigant in the law court lost because the strict common law rules were formulated without anticipation of this person's unusual situation. If he believed the loser had been ill-treated by the common law courts, the chancellor issued an injunction against the sheriff executing the law court's judgment. Other losers in law courts heard about the chancellor's injunctions against unfair common law court judgments and rushed to the chancellor to convince him of the injustice of the law courts' handling of their cases. Soon a court developed around the person of the chancellor to handle all such cases. This court became known as the **equity** (or chancery) **court**; *equity* means "fairness," which the chancellor supposedly dispensed.

The law court judges, hearing about how the chancellor in effect overruled or nullified law court judgments, took the matter to the king. The king settled the matter of which court prevailed when the law court judges and chancellor clashed by dividing the jurisdiction between law and equity courts so that the average case would be decided by a law court. Equity courts were given jurisdiction to settle cases only in which legal remedies (typically, the award of money damages) were inadequate. This situation can occur when one contracts to buy a unique item (an antique, a rare gem, or land) but the seller refuses to carry out the contract. A rare gem or any piece of the earth's surface is unique, and money is inadequate to procure it because only one person has claim to the item.

## CRIMINAL LAW OBJECTIVES

Thus far, we have discussed the objectives of civil law. Now we briefly turn our attention to criminal law objectives. One most frequently mentioned objective is punishment of those who break society's criminal laws. This objective is sometimes referred to as **retribution**, which occurs by imprisonment, imposition of fines, or a combination of the two. The death penalty also effects the retribution goal.

The punitive aspect of criminal law is but one of four ends of that branch of the law. Others frequently mentioned include **restraint**, **deterrence**, and **rehabilitation**. Restraint occurs when people are convicted and imprisoned so that they cannot repeat—at least not immediately—the sort of antisocial activity that landed them in prison. Deterrence occurs when one person's punishment by the criminal law system serves to inhibit or stop other would-be criminals from committing crimes. This justification is commonly given for the death penalty. The rehabilitation objective of criminal law is usually more a hope than a reality. Too often, the result is that people who are sent to prison for several years are counseled by various prison officials but housed with other felons, after which they emerge several years later as persons skilled in effecting more sophisticated crimes. Perhaps this point is an overstatement, but the restraint, vengeance, and deterrent objectives of imprisonment are more obviously served by the criminal justice system as it now exists. Rehabilitation seems better achieved by probation so that a person can learn a skill as well as resist the social pressures to commit crimes. Probation, on the other hand, has short-run social costs, such as subjecting other members of society to the criminal's **recidivism**.

*Plaintiffs.* Aside from their objectives, other differences exist between civil and criminal law. The plaintiff in criminal cases is always a national, state, or municipal government. The official who represents the government as attorney is usually called the **prosecutor**, **district attorney**, or **attorney general**. In civil cases, the plaintiff is usually a private party, such as a business or an individual.

*Burden of Proof.* One final distinction between civil and criminal law lies in the different burdens of proof the respective plaintiffs must satisfy in each type of case. In civil cases, plaintiffs must generally prove their case by a **preponderance of the evidence**. In a criminal case, the government (the plaintiff) must prove its case **beyond a reasonable doubt**, a heavier burden than that which the civil plaintiff must satisfy. The objective of the heavier criminal burden on the government is not to promote crime in the streets but to effect the presumption of innocence long recognized in Anglo-American jurisprudence. One is not a criminal until adjudged to be such in a court of law. Anglo-American jurisprudence has followed the philosophy, "Better to let a hundred criminals go free than convict one innocent person."

## POSSIBLE OVERLAP OF CIVIL AND CRIMINAL LAW

*Legal Effect of Drunk Driving.* Civil and criminal law may overlap because a fact situation could give rise to both a criminal lawsuit and a civil lawsuit. For example, if a person gets drunk, drives a car carelessly, and kills another person, the prosecutor could sue the drunk driver for manslaughter (a criminal lawsuit), and the surviving family of the person killed could sue the drunk driver for wrongful death (a civil lawsuit). In other words, two lawsuits may arise from the same basic fact pattern.

*Legal Effect of Sherman Act Violation.* Another example of the possible civil-criminal overlap occurs when a Sherman Act Section 1 case is brought by both the federal government suing criminally and a private party suing civilly for damages (which are tripled under the Sherman Act to encourage private parties' enforcement of this act) sustained as a result of others' violating Section 1 of the Sherman Act. Diagrammatically, the resulting lawsuits would appear as follows:

Not all wrongful acts give rise to both civil and criminal lawsuits against the same individual. The Sherman Act does allow both types of suits to be brought for having done the same act. Why is facing both civil and criminal proceedings for the same act not a violation of the constitutional principle that no person may be put in jeopardy twice for the same crime? The answer is apparent when one considers the nature of the two suits being brought against one person for the same act: That person is not being tried twice criminally but only once criminally; the other suit is civil, not criminal. The double jeopardy prohibition prohibits only being tried *criminally* more than once for the same act by the same sovereign, that is, the federal government or a particular state.

Incidentally, no law dictates a particular order in which civil or criminal suits must be brought when two such suits arise from the same general facts. However, because the government usually has more resources to develop evidence, because such evidence is a matter of public record if introduced in the criminal case, and because a criminal conviction is usually harder to get, a civil plaintiff often waits to sue until after the government has sued criminally on the matter.

Sometimes a criminal suit is brought, a person convicted of a property crime, and that person is fined or imprisoned or both. Then another civil suit follows in which the "guilty" property (called *in rem*) is proceeded against in a forfeiture action by the government. Occasionally these are challenged as violating the *double jeopardy* clause on grounds they constitute punishment *twice* for the same offense. (The Manager's Ethical Dilemma at the end of this chapter deals with such a case.) A slightly different situation arises, however, when a criminal case is brought, the defendant is convicted of a crime and fined, and also, as part of the *same* criminal action, forfeits the "guilty" property as part of the criminal punishment. Does such "double punishment" violate any part of the U.S. Constitution? The *U.S. v. Bajakajian* case provides an answer.

## United States v. Bajakajian
### 524 U.S. 321 (1998)

### Background and Facts

On June 9, 1994, Bajakajian, his wife, and two daughters were waiting at Los Angeles International Airport to board a flight to Italy. Their final destination was Cyprus. Using dogs trained to detect currency by its smell, customs inspectors discovered some $230,000 in cash in the Bajakajians' checked baggage. A customs inspector approached Bajakajian and his wife and told them that they were required to report all money in excess of $10,000 in their possession or in their baggage. Bajakajian said that he had $8,000 and that his wife had another $7,000, but that the family had no additional currency to declare. A search of their carry-on bags, purse, and wallet revealed more cash; in all, customs inspectors found $357,144. The currency was seized and Bajakajian was arrested.

A federal grand jury indicted Bajakajian on three counts. Count One charged him with failing to report, as required by [Ed.: the U.S. Code], that he was transporting more than $10,000 outside the United States, and was doing so "willfully," in violation of § 5322(a).

Count Two charged him with making a false material statement to the United States Customs Service, in violation of [Ed.: the U.S. Code]. Count Three sought forfeiture of the $357,144 pursuant to [Ed.: the U.S. Code], which provides:

"The court, in imposing sentence on a person convicted of an offense in violation of section . . . 5316, . . . shall order that the person forfeit to the United States any property, real or personal, involved in such offense, or any property traceable to such property."

Bajakajian pleaded guilty to the failure to report in Count One; the Government agreed to dismiss the false statement charge in Count Two; and Bajakajian elected to have a bench trial on the forfeiture in Count Three. After the bench trial, the District Court found that the entire $357,144 was subject to forfeiture because it was "involved in" the offense. The court also found that the funds were not connected to any other crime and that Bajakajian was transporting the money to repay a lawful debt. The District Court further found that Bajakajian had failed to report that he was taking the currency out of the United States because of fear stemming from "cultural differences": Bajakajian, who had grown up as a member of the Armenian minority in Syria, had a "distrust for the Government."

Although § 982(a)(1) directs sentencing courts to impose full forfeiture, the District Court concluded that such forfeiture would be "extraordinarily harsh" and "grossly disproportionate to the offense in question," and that it would therefore violate the Excessive Fines Clause. The court instead ordered forfeiture of $15,000, in addition to a sentence of three years of probation and a fine of $5,000—the maximum fine under the Sentencing Guidelines—because the court believed that the maximum Guidelines fine was "too little" and that a $15,000 forfeiture would "make up for what I think a reasonable fine should be."

The United States appealed, seeking full forfeiture of Bajakajian's currency as provided in § 982(a)(1). The Court of Appeals for the Ninth Circuit affirmed. Applying Circuit precedent, the Court held that, to satisfy the Excessive Fines Clause, a forfeiture must fulfill two conditions: The property forfeited must be an "instrumentality" of the crime committed, and the value of the property must be proportional to the culpability of the owner. A majority of the panel determined that the currency was not an "instrumentality" of the crime of failure to report because "'the crime in a currency reporting offense is the withholding of information, . . . not the possession or the transportation of the money.'" The majority therefore held that § 982(a)(1) could never satisfy the Excessive Fines Clause in cases involving forfeitures of currency and that it was unnecessary to apply the "proportionality" prong of the test. Although the panel majority concluded that the Excessive Fines Clause did not permit forfeiture of *any* of the unreported currency, it held that it lacked jurisdiction to set the $15,000 forfeiture aside because Bajakajian had not cross-appealed to challenge that forfeiture.

Because the Court of Appeals holding—that the forfeiture ordered by § 982(a)(1) was per se unconstitutional in cases of currency forfeiture—invalidated a portion of an Act of Congress, the U.S. Supreme Court granted certiorari.

## Body of Opinion

**Justice Thomas.** The Eighth Amendment provides: "Excessive bail shall not be required, nor excessive fines imposed, nor cruel and unusual punishments inflicted.". . . This Court has had little occasion to interpret, and has never actually applied, the Excessive Fines Clause. We have, however, explained that at the time the Constitution was adopted, "the word 'fine' was understood to mean a payment to a sovereign as punishment for some offense.". . . The Excessive Fines Clause thus "limits the government's power to extract payments, whether in cash or in kind, 'as punishment for some offense.'". . . Forfeitures—payments in kind—are thus "fines" if they constitute punishment for an offense.

We have little trouble concluding that the forfeiture of currency ordered by § 982(a)(1) constitutes punishment. . . .

The United States argues, however, that the forfeiture of currency under § 982(a)(1) "also serves important remedial purposes.". . . The Government asserts that it has "an overriding sovereign interest in controlling what property leaves and enters the country.". . . It claims that full forfeiture of unreported currency supports that interest by serving to "deter illicit movements of cash" and aiding in providing the Government with "valuable information to investigate and detect criminal activities associated with that cash.". . .

The Government specifically contends that the forfeiture of respondent's currency is constitutional because it involves an "instrumentality" of respondent's crime. According to the Government, the unreported cash is an instrumentality because it "does not merely facilitate a violation of law," but is "'the very sine qua non of the crime.'". . . The Government reasons that "there would be no violation at all without the exportation (or attempted exportation) of the cash.". . .

Acceptance of the Government's argument would require us to expand the traditional understanding of instrumentality forfeitures. This we decline to do. Instrumentalities historically have been treated as a form of "guilty property" that can be forfeited in civil in rem proceedings. In this case, however, the Government has sought to punish respondent by proceeding against him criminally, in personam, rather than proceeding in rem against the currency. It is therefore irrelevant whether respondent's currency is an instrumentality; the forfeiture is punitive, and the test for the excessiveness of a punitive forfeiture involves solely a proportionality determination. . . .

Because the forfeiture of respondent's currency constitutes punishment and is thus a "fine" within the meaning of the Excessive Fines Clause, we now turn to the question whether it is "excessive."

The touchstone of the constitutional inquiry under the Excessive Fines Clause is the principle of proportionality: The amount of the forfeiture must bear some relationship to the gravity of the offense that it is designed to punish. . . . We now hold that a punitive forfeiture violates the Excessive Fines Clause if it is grossly disproportional to the gravity of a defendant's offense. . . .

Under this standard, the forfeiture of respondent's entire $357,144 would violate the Excessive Fines Clause. Respondent's crime was solely a reporting offense. It was permissible to transport the currency out of the country so long as he reported it. . . . Whatever his other vices, respondent does not fit into the class of persons for whom the statute was principally designed: He is not a money launderer, a drug trafficker, or a tax evader. . . .

The harm that respondent caused was also minimal. Failure to report his currency affected only one party, the Government, and in a relatively minor way. There was no fraud on the United States, and respondent caused no loss to the public fisc. Had his crime gone undetected, the Government would have been deprived only of the information that $357,144 had left the country. . . .

## Judgment and Result

The U.S. Supreme Court affirmed the Court of Appeals decision. Full forfeiture of Bajakajian's $357,144 was improper.

## Questions

1. How did the Eighth Amendment to the U.S. Constitution come into play in the above case?
2. Does the Supreme Court ever admit that the dividing line between "civil" and "criminal" punishments to some extent "bleed into each other" in the Bajakajian case? In *Bajakajian* the fact that the forfeiture occurred in the criminal case and not in a separate civil case (as sometimes occurs) seemed to make a difference in the court's analysis that this was an Excessive Fines case and not a double jeopardy case (where two separate suits and criminal punishments are for the same wrong).
3. Are "sniffer dogs" used only to catch drug smugglers? Does "smuggling" occur only when one is trying to bring property *into* the United States? Why did Bajakajian not report the currency export to U.S. authorities as required by the U.S. Code?
4. What ethical considerations noted in Chapter 1 might be at work in justifying the *Bajakajian* result?
5. Do you think that after 9/11, the Government's need to know about money leaving the country (possibly bound to support terrorists) might be greater than it was when the *Bajakajian* case was decided?

## DIAGRAMS OF CIVIL AND CRIMINAL LAW

Figure 2.2 is a traditional way of looking at law. The two broad categories of civil law and criminal law are broken down into substantive and procedural rules. There are civil procedural laws, such as a statute of limitations for breach of contract, and criminal procedural laws, such as a statute of limitations for the crime of federal income tax evasion. Civil substantive laws include tort law, which deals with broad classes of breaches of noncontractual duties that do not arise by contract; specific examples of torts are fraud and negligence. An example of criminal substantive laws is the law forbidding arson. Figure 2.2 looks detailed but is by no means complete. Many legal theories are not shown here.

## FINDING THE LAW

### FINDING NATIONAL AND STATE CONSTITUTIONS

*U.S. Code.* The national and state governments are legally separate sovereigns with lawmaking authority. The national government and each of the fifty states have a set of law books, called a *code*, which usually contains the constitution of the applicable government unit. The U.S. Constitution is also in the books containing the U.S. Code Annotated. Technically, the Constitution has not been codified; however, it is contained in the same books as the U.S. Code Annotated. When the code contains reference to cases interpreting it, it is called the annotated code. The **unannotated** version is legislative law without reference to case interpretations.

*State Code.* Each state has a constitution, and, similarly, each state has a code that contains a copy of the state constitution. Again, state constitutions are usually not part of the state code in a legal sense but are contained in the same books as the state code. Also, state codes come in **annotated** versions as well as unannotated versions. Annotated codes have footnotes referring to cases interpreting particular code words. Because of this feature, annotated codes are considered more helpful than unannotated codes. A state code could have the word *code* in its name, such as Tennessee Code Annotated or Iowa Code Annotated, but could be known by other names, such as New Mexico Statutes Annotated, Michigan Compiled Laws, or New York Consolidated Laws.

## FINDING LEGISLATIVE ENACTMENTS

The reason this section has been called "Finding Legislative Enactments" instead of "Finding Statutes" requires a bit of explanation. When a legislator drops a proposed law into the hopper in the state or national legislature, this proposed statute is technically called a bill. If the bill is passed by the legislature and signed into law by the chief executive or becomes law over an executive veto, the bill then becomes an act (also called a statute or **session law**). If the matter ended there, the legislatures would wind up producing a series of acts or statutes unrelated in subject matter and not easily accessible, because legislatures obviously do not pass laws in alphabetical order (e.g., with Adoptions first and Zoning last).

## CODES ORGANIZE STATUTES BY SUBJECT

The solution to the disorganized, uncompiled law problem associated with acts, statutes, or session laws is the code. A **code** is a set of law books that contain the public statutes passed by Congress or by a state legislature. It is organized by subject matter, such as by taxation, domestic law, recording laws, and criminal law. No magic determines how the topics for a code are organized. The selection of topics is to some extent arbitrary and reflects recognized legal subject matters that cover wide areas. For example, criminal law is a more likely general topic than murder. Subject indexes to the codes help identify specific topics. Although municipal (city) codes contain municipal ordinances, only national and state codes are discussed here.

*Updating Codes.* Copies of the U.S. Code are available in most public libraries and so, most likely, is the state code. Codes are periodically, usually annually, updated by the insertion of **pocket parts** in the back of each of the bound volumes of the code.

*Meaning of Codification.* A law or statute that has been put into a national or state code is said to have been codified. Codes are arranged according to subject matter called *titles* (general areas of the law such as commercial law, domestic law, and probate law). Each title contains a number of subcategories called sections, which, in turn, are subdivided into subsections. Thus, referring to a particular part of a code is done in the following manner. The title is given first, then the particular code, followed by the section or sections of the title. For example, Title 5 of the U.S. Code, Section 552 is how one refers to a particular part of the U.S. Code. This reference is usually shortened to 5 U.S.C. § 552, which is known as a cite to a part of the U.S. Code. The date of the code edition is usually included. A similar process takes place when one refers to part of a state code.

## FINDING FEDERAL ADMINISTRATIVE REGULATIONS

*Code of Federal Regulations.* The Securities and Exchange Commission (SEC), Environmental Protection Agency (EPA), Interstate Commerce Commission (ICC), and various other agencies make law by issuing regulations. At the federal level, most agency regulations are contained in a set of law books called the *Code of Federal Regulations*, abbreviated *C.F.R.* The *Code of Federal Regulations* is arranged according to titles and sections in much the same way as statutory codes. A customary practice in referring to a *C.F.R.* section is to use the *C.F.R.* cite.

An example of a *C.F.R.* cite is 40 C.F.R. § 124.2 (2001), the 40 being the title, *C.F.R.* being the series of books containing federal regulations, and 124.2 being the section. The book's date is usually included, too.

*The Federal Register.* When a federal agency first promulgates regulations, the regulations are published in the *Federal Register*, a type of official newspaper and notice giver of the federal government. The *C.F.R.* is revised annually so that those federal regulations made by the agencies since publication of the last annual *C.F.R.* can update the preceding edition of the *C.F.R.*

Between annual publications of the *C.F.R.*, the agencies will be revising their regulations and making new regulations. To find those regs (as regulations are informally but respectfully called) issued after publication of the last *C.F.R.* and before publication of the next *C.F.R.*, it is necessary to consult the *Federal Register*. This process is somewhat tedious, because the *Federal Register* is issued every federal agency business day, Monday through Friday, but *Federal Register* indexes are published periodically for affected *C.F.R.* sections.

States are increasingly developing state register systems to help people find state administrative law.

## FINDING INFORMATION ABOUT FEDERAL AGENCIES

Occasionally a person must find the address, phone number, regional office location nearest him, or some other feature of a federal agency. The *U.S. Government Manual*, published annually, provides this and much more information. Any public library should have a copy. Also, copies can be purchased from the U.S. Government Printing Office for a nominal amount.

## FINDING COMMON LAW

*Only Written Opinions Count.* A final source of legal authority is common law, which is law made by judges who settle disputes brought to them by litigants (people who are parties to lawsuits). A judge may announce a decision and provide no opinion or rationale as to why one party prevails over the other. One reason for giving no opinion is a lack of time brought on by the need to settle many cases. Another reason was succinctly stated by Louis Brandeis before his appointment to the U.S. Supreme Court: "I do not wish to argue the matter; therefore, I give no reasons for my decision." Most judges, however, do at least announce orally the reasons they decide a case one way or the other. Yet, such decisions amount to nothing for nonparties to the suit because they are not written down as precedent. Hence, the opinions that are of significance to future litigants in other lawsuits and that function as guideposts for society because they announce rules or the law are found in *written* opinions of judges pursuant to settling a dispute. Written judicial opinions are discussed here.

*Courts that Do Not Write Opinions.* Most trial court judges do not write opinions in cases they decide because they simply are not required to do so. Traffic court judges, probate court judges, juvenile court judges, small claims court judges, and judges in most state trial courts of general jurisdiction do not write opinions. All of these judges are excused from the task of writing opinions largely because of the need to speed up decision making. The value of having a written opinion is outweighed by the slowdown in decision making created by written opinions and by the need for more judges to handle the extra work that would be brought on by such a requirement.

*Courts that Write Opinions.* A number of courts do write opinions that are a source of legal authority. Federal district courts, federal courts of appeal, the U.S. Supreme Court, state courts of last resort (usually referred to as state supreme courts, except in New York), and state appellate courts above the trial court level all write opinions.

## REPORTERS

*Reporters Contain Common Law.* An intricate set of books (called **reporters**) has been established to compile the written opinions of the courts issuing written opinions. (The reporter system is not to be confused with individuals called court reporters, who transcribe comments made in the open courtroom and at depositions.) The books known as reporters look like sets of encyclopedias. Each reporter is made up of many books. A different reporter is established for each different court system. The U.S. Supreme Court opinions are reported in three different sets of reporters: *United States Reports* (the official government-published reporter), the *Supreme Court Reporter*, and *Lawyers Edition*. U.S. courts of appeals opinions are reported in the *Federal Reporter*, and federal district courts are reported in the *Federal Supplement*. In the state of New York, where the highest state court is called the court of appeals, the reporter covering that court is *New York Appellate Reports*. Thus, separate sets of books called reporters cover the different states' appellate courts and all federal courts. Regional reporters (privately published by West Publishing Company) also publish state appellate opinions for states within a particular geographic region. The seven regional reporters are Pacific, North Western, South Western, North Eastern, Atlantic, South Eastern, and Southern.

*Case Cites Help Find Cases.* The following discussion uses the case of *Hynes v. New York Central Railroad* to explain how to locate a case in a reporter. Cases have cites, which are used to find the case in the law library. Most cases contained in law texts are shortened to remove material irrelevant to its teaching purpose and to simplify case reading considerably for students. However, if students want to read the full opinion and they have an extensive law library nearby (which usually occurs only if a law school or state or federal court law library is available), the cite enables them to do so. Assuming you have the cite to the *Hynes* case, which is 231 N.Y. 229, you can now find the case in the law library.

The numbers and letters that make up the case cite mean the following: The 231 refers to the volume number in a series of books called the reporter, the N.Y. tells what reporter the case appears in—here, the New York Reports—and the 229 refers to the page number in volume 231 of the New York Reports on which the *Hynes* opinion starts. Much the same system is used for the West Regional Reporters, in which most state cases are also found.

Printed in Figure 2.3 is a portion of the Hynes opinion. It is used to illustrate case parts.

## USING COMPUTERS TO FIND THE LAW

Legal research has become computerized. The two major computerized legal research systems are Westlaw and Lexis. Westlaw was developed by the West

**FIGURE 2.3 CASE PARTS ILLUSTRATED**

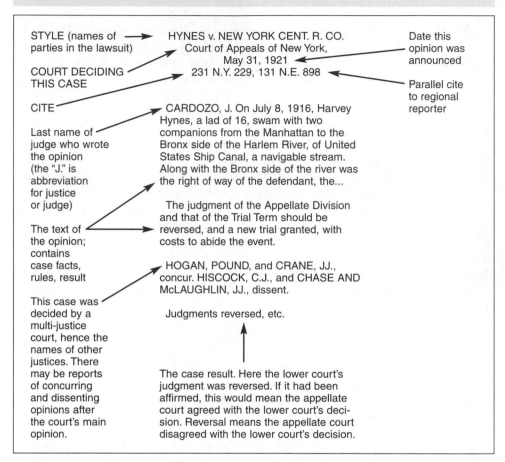

Publishing Company of St. Paul, Minnesota, the nation's largest law publisher. Lexis was developed by Mead Data Corporation. Both are nongovernmental publishers.

Both Westlaw and Lexis use video monitors, computer keyboards, and phone lines to access constitutions, treaties, codes, session laws, cases, regulations, and some bar journals and law reviews that make up the databases of these respective companies. The databases of Lexis and Westlaw differ somewhat, so it is possible that a researcher might find on one what she or he cannot find on the other.

Essentially both Westlaw and Lexis use symbols, key words, and phrases as ways to access legal authority in the database. A key word or phrase is punched into the keyboard, sent off, and in a matter of seconds the computer "reads" literally thousands or even millions of pages of statutes and casebooks for a match to the key word or phrase the researcher plugged into the research request. The computer reports back the cases, statutes, or whatever was requested, or reports that nothing was found. Usually the researchers modify their requests until they find what they are looking for.

*Advantages of Computerized Legal Research.* The advantages of computerized legal research are apparent: Time is saved when a computer scans hundreds of books in seconds and reports the results immediately. Also, it permits individually tailored research formats not readily available through traditional, noncomputerized legal research. In particular, computers allow research based on fact patterns, whereas law books are organized around legal theories, not facts.

*Disadvantages of Computerized Legal Research.* Certain disadvantages, however, limit computerized legal research. First, the years in the database may be limited. For example, if the database goes back only a certain number of years, cases and statutes and other laws passed or occurring *before* that date would be missed by the research. It is possible that a key decision helpful to the researcher might be found in those missing years. Second, the laws covered in the database may be limited. Some computer databases do not cover all regulations or repealed regulations, or legislative reports giving background on statutes or bills pending in Congress or state legislatures. Third, some systems are not user friendly; they have rigid ways of framing research requests and, unless the researcher can come within these request protocols, the request will fail. Finally, computerized research can be costly. The cost of the computerized research systems is usually measured by a monthly rental. The cost for a private attorney to use a law school Westlaw system is often measured in terms of dollars per minute. The rate for Westlaw varies with time used, but it can be costly unless one has a fixed-cost subscription—often a monthly charge. However, when the cost of hiring someone to conduct this research by hand is compared with an efficient computer operator, the cost of computer research may be lower. Of course, not everyone is competent to use computerized legal research efficiently; to place sophisticated research tools in the hands of the unskilled can be wasteful.

## INTERNET SEARCHES TO FIND THE LAW

The Internet can also assist in finding the law. If you have a computer with a modem, you, as a practical matter, have a law library.

*The Library of Congress Web site:*
***http://thomas.loc.gov***

   You should obtain a legally based Internet address so that you can access the law that you want. One Internet address (among many) valid for locating the U.S. Constitution as well as other legal materials is http://thomas.loc.gov (the Library of Congress Web site), which gives access to statutes.

## HOW TO ANALYZE A CASE

### DEFINITION OF A JUDICIAL OPINION

A judicial opinion contained in a reporter is a story of how one person allegedly breached another's legal rights. The opinion contains a statement of the relevant facts, a discussion of rules competing for application to these facts, and a judicial resolution of this conflict. Issues or problems, both legal and factual, are presented in an opinion of a case. For example, in a breach-of-contract case a legal issue might be, "Can a breach of contract occur before the date of contract performance is due?" A factual issue would be, "Did defendant sign the document that purports to be a contract?"

### MANY ISSUES IN A CASE

A case could have many issues—legal and factual, procedural and substantive. Generally, by the time a case reaches an appellate court, the issues are reduced to a few, and they almost always are legal, not factual, because either a jury or trial judge will decide fact questions at the trial court level. Appellate courts do not have juries or other fact finders.

## The Purpose of Cases in Texts

A textbook presents a case to teach at least one legal principle. Assuming the case is reasonably well selected and introduced in a casebook, the problem confronting the student is to reduce the puffy, cotton-candy language of the case opinion into a one-line legal rule.

A rule derived from a judicial decision is called a *ratio decidendi*, which is Latin for "reasoning which flows from the decision." A simpler way of expressing it is to say, "rule of the case." Note that there are many ways of stating a case's *ratio decidendi*. Because of this, studying cases is analogous to examining modern art. Just as many meanings can be found in a Picasso portrait, many interpretations can be drawn from a case. This is not to say that a given case means whatever one wants it to mean. Rather, a *ratio decidendi* is limited to a case's facts. A *ratio decidendi* beyond a case's facts is invalid as a *ratio decidendi*. Thus, in the *Bajakajian* case earlier in this chapter, one could develop a broad *ratio decidendi*, such as a criminal suit by the federal government against a person, followed by a civil forfeiture by the same sovereign against the same person, violates the U.S. Constitution's excessive fines clause. A narrow *ratio decidendi* of *Bajakajian* might be where there is a federal, criminal suit resulting in a conviction and fine for violating a currency reporting law, the government may not then also seize the currency at issue if it is far beyond the criminal fine. To do so violates the U.S. Constitution's excessive fines clause. An invalid or overly broad *ratio decidendi* would be a state criminal suit followed by a federal criminal suit based on essentially the same facts that does not violate the double jeopardy clause. This last *ratio decidendi* is invalid for *Bajakajian* because no state criminal prosecution was brought in *Bajakajian*. Some other case will have to support the last offered *ratio decidendi*.

## The Meaning of Briefing

We brief cases to analyze them. *Brief*, like so many words, has at least two meanings when used in a legal context. One meaning of *brief* is a set of written legal arguments an attorney draws up to support a client's legal position in a court case. That is not the sense in which the word brief is used here. **Brief**, as described here, means the result of a student's analyzing a case by dividing the case into five parts:

1. The **case style** includes the parties suing and being sued, along with the case cite and date of the case's decision.
2. The crucial case *facts* must be succinctly stated. One way to tell whether a fact is crucial is to ask if the result would have been different had the fact not been present; if so, the fact is crucial.
3. The *issue* must be stated as precisely as possible. Legal, not factual, issues are important because the legal issue states in question form a possible legal rule presented by the case (e.g., "Do all contracts have to be written to be enforceable?"). However, separating fact from law issues is often difficult because no single way is always best to state a legal issue. An issue can be stated in as many ways as there are staters of the issue. It can also be stated narrowly or

broadly (e.g., "Do all contracts have to be written to be enforceable?" versus "Do all contracts for the sale of land have to be written to be enforceable?").

4. The *holding* is a yes or no answer to the question presented by the issue.
5. The *rationale* is the reason for the holding. For example, why do some contracts have to be evidenced by a signed writing to be enforceable, whereas others do not? The reasons could run the gamut from historical (it has always been the rule that has been followed) to policy considerations (to prevent fraud).

The following is a possible way of briefing the *Carroll v. Exxon* case.

---

*Facts:*
Single, working woman applied for Exxon credit card in August 1976.

- Exxon denied her credit card application on 9/14/76. No reason was given for credit denial.
- Applicant sends Exxon letter on 9/28/76 asking reason for credit denial.
- Exxon sends applicant undated response indicating credit bureau did not give adverse information about application but could not get enough information about her credit history.
- Neither letter from Exxon to applicant gave investigating credit bureau's name.
- Applicant sued Exxon on 10/26/76 claiming violation of Fair Credit Reporting Act.
- Exxon sends applicant name and address of investigating credit bureau on 11/2/76.

*Issue 1:*
Did Exxon's conduct violate the Fair Credit Reporting Act (FCRA)?

*Holding:*
Yes

*Issue 2:*
Was Exxon's conduct willful, entitling plaintiff to punitive damages?

*Holding:*
Yes

*Rationale:*
The court found Exxon's violations willful. Exxon did not immediately and voluntarily furnish the credit reporting agency's name and address.

The court rejected the Exxon defenses:
- That it did not deny credit based on the credit bureau's report
- That it gave plaintiff the name of the credit reporting agency
- That Exxon had reasonable procedures to assure compliance with the FCRA

*Notes*
Students usually brief cases before class and reserve this half of the page for modifications, additions, and other notes from class.

---

Aside from providing the holding(s), which means answering a specific legal or fact question that must be answered to settle the case, judges will often include "might have been" situations in their opinions. These situations are similar to but different enough from the case at hand that the judge believes a different result would be justified. Such remarks, not essential to resolution of the case, are referred to as **dicta** or **obiter dicta**.

Students can add a number of embellishments to a brief but should not forget that the more complex and detailed the brief, the harder it is for students to remember. The purpose of the brief is to simplify complex cases and make life easy for students. The brief is just a tool to help distill a few rules from a case, enable quick review of those rules for exams, and help students when their professors ask about cases in class.

## CHAPTER SUMMARY

Law (positive law) is found in the form of constitutions, statutes, administrative regulations, and executive orders.

Classifications of law include substantive and procedural as well as civil and criminal, with some overlap between civil and criminal law.

Positive law is found in several places, including session laws as well as federal and state codes. Codes organize session laws alphabetically by topic. Annotated codes contain footnote references to case interpretations of words in codes.

Federal administrative regulations are found in the *Federal Register* and in the *Code of Federal Regulations*. The *Federal Register* publishes regulations chronologically in no particular order. The *Code of Federal Regulations* organizes regulations by agency. The *Federal Register* is now available on the Internet.

Computer systems such as Westlaw and Lexis can help find the law. Persons having a computer equipped with a modem have a cyberspace law library.

Briefing a case is an analytical tool that divides a case into facts, issues, holding, and rationale.

## DISCUSSION QUESTIONS

1. A New Yorker, Bernhard H. Goetz, was allegedly assaulted on a New York City subway. In defending himself, Goetz shot and paralyzed one of his perceived assailants. Goetz, the original victim of the alleged assault and robbery, was then tried criminally but was acquitted for crimes based on self-defense. Then, one of his original assailants whom Goetz paralyzed by use of a gun sued Goetz civilly in a New York court. A Bronx jury awarded Darrell Cabgey, one of the four young men originally trying to rob Goetz, $43 million—$18 million for past and future pain and suffering and $25 million for punitive damages. Do you think that Goetz was being "twice put in jeopardy" in violation of the Fifth Amendment's double jeopardy prohibition?

2. Guilt in criminal cases and liability in civil cases can be the result of race. Racial overtones were part of the Goetz case in the previous question—the four young men trying to rob Goetz are black and Goetz is white. This fact gives rise to the question of whose legal philosophies are used in analyzing this series of cases related to Goetz.

3. Describe the function of a cite. Which of the following have cites?
   a. cases
   b. statutes
   c. regulations

4. The Clean Water Act makes illegal the dumping of pollutants into U.S. waters without a permit. People who break this law can be subject to civil damages and can be punished criminally by fines or imprisonment or both for certain offenses. The objectives of the Clean Water Act include making the nation's waters swimmable and fishable by 1983 and having zero discharges of pollutants by 1985. Given these objectives, could they best be achieved by civil law, criminal law, or a combination of both? Does the risk presented by water pollution justify the imposition of criminal sanctions? What are some consequences of making something both a civil and criminal offense? (As we shall see throughout this book, a number of federal statutes set up regulatory schemes imposing both civil and criminal liability.)

5. Why should some acts be criminal offenses, others only civil wrongs, and still others be completely legal? For example, is there anything inherently wrong with one person's talking to another? What if they are talking about dividing markets and bid rigging in violation of the Sherman Antitrust Act?

6. Do civil and criminal law have any common objectives? What are they? In what way do they differ?

7. A major distinction in law is that of rights and remedies. Rights are sometimes known as **primary rights** and remedies are called **secondary rights**. Laws telling us what we can and cannot do in society are generally primary rights. For example, agency law allows people to hire employees, while the Civil Rights Act of 1964 makes it illegal to discriminate in hiring based on race or religion. Both agency law and the Civil Rights Act create primary rights. If W discriminates illegally against B, W breaks B's primary rights. B can seek a remedy, such as damages (money) or an order directing W to hire B. Remedies are not the same for all primary rights. Secondary rights are usually proportional to the primary right to which they attach. For example, society's remedy if someone commits murder could be life imprisonment. (Because murder is a serious

## ■ MANAGER'S ETHICAL DILEMMA

The Michigan police found marijuana growing adjacent to Guy Usery's house, and discovered marijuana seeds, stems, stalks, and a growlight within the house. The United States instituted civil forfeiture proceedings against the house, alleging that the property was subject to forfeiture under a federal forfeiture statute because it had been used for several years to facilitate the unlawful processing and distribution of a controlled substance. Usery ultimately paid the United States $13,250 to settle the forfeiture claim in full. Shortly before the settlement, Usery was indicted for manufacturing marijuana in violation of another section of the U.S. Code. A jury found him guilty, and he was sentenced to prison for 63 months.

The Court of Appeals for the Sixth Circuit by a divided vote reversed Usery's criminal conviction, holding that the conviction violated the Double Jeopardy Clause of the Fifth Amendment of

the U.S. Constitution. The Sixth Circuit read Supreme Court decisions *U.S. v. Halper* and *Austin v. United States*, as saying that any civil forfeiture under U.S. Code Section 881 (a)(7) was punishment under the Fifth Amendment's Double Jeopardy Clause. Usery, in the Sixth Circuit's view, had therefore been "punished" in the forfeiture proceeding against his property, and could not later be criminally tried in violation of U.S. Code Section 841 (a)(1). The Supreme Court granted the federal petition for certiorari (a way to appeal a case to a higher court). Do you believe the second trial for essentially the "same offense" is double jeopardy? Although businesspeople typically do not grow marijuana, they do engage in conduct where civil and criminal penalties are possible for the same act. As a matter of public policy, do you believe that businesses should support or condemn successive civil and criminal punishments for essentially the same act?

---

offense, a severe punishment such as life imprisonment seems appropriate.)

The idea that the primary and secondary rights should be proportional is sometimes expressed as "Let the punishment fit the crime." This statement is true for criminal law, but civil law speaks in terms of remedies, usually not of punishment. What are some examples of secondary rights—remedies or punishments—that are not proportional to the attached primary rights? Would imposing the death penalty on someone who jaywalks be an example?

8. Sarah Romberg owned a clothing store that obtained 95 percent of its business through mail orders. A selling point for her business was her payment of all shipping costs (usually using the U.S. Postal Service). Sarah learned that the U.S. Postal Service had recently published a regulation requiring that

packages be double wrapped. She wanted to read the regulation to determine its exact requirements. Where would she obtain this information? Assume she is in a town of 15,000 people.

### INFOTRAC KEYWORDS

**Use your InfoTrac password to look up articles on http://www.infotrac-college.com**

Keywords: *Civil v. criminal law.*
Read articles on civil versus criminal law issues.

For suggested readings, please visit this book's Web site at **http://fisher.westbuslaw.com** (click on "Internet Applications").

# MODULE 2

# BUSINESS AND LEGAL SYSTEMS: COURTS, LEGISLATURES, ADMINISTRATIVE AGENCIES, CONSTITUTIONAL AND INTERNATIONAL LAW AFFECTING REGULATION

**CHAPTER 3**
Sources of Law: Political and Institutional

**CHAPTER 4**
Settling Legal Disputes: Alternative Dispute Resolution and Civil Lawsuits

**CHAPTER 5**
Business and the Constitution

**CHAPTER 6**
Government Regulation: Overview

**CHAPTER 7**
Government Regulation: Anatomy and Enforcement of a Regulation

**CHAPTER 8**
International Business:  Public Law

**CHAPTER 9**
Private Business Dealings in International Contexts

# SOURCES OF LAW: POLITICAL AND INSTITUTIONAL

## POSITIVE LAW ETHICAL PROBLEMS

Rehnquist: "I think we should put an end to the repetitive vote-counting in Florida."

Stevens: "On what grounds? It is a "states' rights" matter. You have always been in favor of states' rights."

Rehnquist: "But we have to bring closure to this presidential election."

Stevens: "But the state officials can do that. It is up to Florida officials to count the Florida votes."

Should the U.S. Supreme Court stop a state from repeatedly recounting votes in a federal election? Is this a legal suit for the courts or a political question best left to political officials?

"No judge can reduce what a jury says a plaintiff is entitled to. It violates my constitutional right to a jury trial," declared Bob Anderson. A jury had just declared that Anderson was entitled to $2 million in compensatory damages and $3.5 million in punitive damages when Conwood Co. used Anderson's private credit information in litigation in violation of the Fair Credit Reporting Act.

What bothered Anderson was that the trial judge wanted to reduce his jury verdict by millions of dollars to a mere $50,000 in compensatory damages and totally nullify the jury's $3.5 million punitive damage award. Is this change legally possible?

"The statute is unfair because it is vague," shouted Mr. McBoyle, after being criminally convicted of transporting a stolen airplane interstate. The statute he was convicted under made it illegal to transport a stolen "motor vehicle" interstate. Lower courts held that the statute applied to airplanes. Did the U.S. Supreme Court agree?

*"POWER TENDS TO CORRUPT; ABSOLUTE POWER CORRUPTS ABSOLUTELY."*

—LORD ACTON
LETTER TO
BISHOP MANDELL
CREIGHTON (1887)

In Chapters 1 and 2 we saw what law is and examined some legal and business ethics. This chapter focuses on sources of law in the United States. A wide variety of approaches can be taken in the study of legal sources. One can consider law as the product of political, institutional, historical, economic, or anthropological sources. Chapter 3 is limited to political and institutional sources.

## POLITICAL SOURCES OF LAW

The discussion of the political sources of law refers to the number of people involved in the rule-making process.

### MONARCHY

An efficient way to make a legal rule is to have as few people as possible involved in developing it. One person who has absolute power to govern is known as a monarch. The monarch spends no time consulting various groups to learn what laws the groups desire. **Monarchy** probably is most workable when the people ruled are uneducated, tractable, and indifferent to how their lives are managed. Because the ruler answers to no one, the monarch is not politically accountable. Such an arrangement creates considerable potential for rulers to abuse their law-making power. Individuals and businesses might have no right to criticize the monarch for excessive taxes or absurd laws. Various freedoms (speech, press, and religion) and rights (such as trial by jury) that U.S. citizens take for granted would probably not exist under a monarchy.

## OLIGARCHY

In an **oligarchy**, a small group makes the rules. An oligarchy's characteristics are similar to those of a dictatorship. Greater continuity of rule exists in an oligarchy, however, because, unlike a dictatorship, if one member of the ruling clique should die, others in the group can continue to carry on the functions of government. Selection to membership in the oligarchy is usually thought to result from the oligarchy's decision rather than the wishes of the general population.

## DEMOCRACY

In a **democracy**, the ruled make the rules. In a technical sense, democratic government includes all of the people. However, practical as well as policy considerations result in, for example, denying suffrage to a one-year-old child, a convicted criminal, people who have recently moved, and foreign exchange students.

An effective democracy requires an educated, informed **body politic**. Given the unwieldiness and impracticability of getting an entire population together every time a new law is proposed, having people represent the population has developed. Such **representative democracy** gives rise to potential distortion of the popular will and promotes popular apathy regarding public matters. Pressure groups, coupled with soaring campaign costs, further accentuate the potential for representatives to distort the popular will.

The major positive factors of a democracy are responsiveness of leaders to the desires of the governed and political stability born of political equality.

## ANARCHY

**Anarchy** exists when no one has legal authority to make rules binding others. In other words, anarchy exists when no government exists. Every person must govern himself or herself. In Chapter 1 we learned that Sigmund Freud saw civilization as the step individuals make when they join together collectively and replace individual will with group will. When anarchy exists, no civilization exists because no law restrains people. Anarchy sometimes is referred to as the **state of nature**, meaning people in a prebody politic or unorganized state without a legally recognized lawmaker (government).

## THE SOCIAL COMPACT (GOVERNMENT)

Two philosophers who provided theories about the organization of the body politic are Thomas Hobbes and John Locke, Englishmen who wrote in the seventeenth century. The body politic is simply society in an organized state, meaning it has a government. Because they have sufficient cultural, philosophical, and geographic factors in common, as well as common needs, people decide they should organize politically and name someone or some group to make rules.

The state of nature vanished when people joined to form the body politic, which had a government making rules binding on all. Both Hobbes and Locke then introduced another concept: the **social compact** or **social contract**, or the agreement among people who lived in a state of nature to form an organized society with a government. The government would have authority to make rules binding on all persons in the body politic. The document that comes closest to representing the social compact, or social contract, is a government's **constitution**. A constitution usually establishes the government's organizational framework and announces which rule-making power the government has or does not have, what governmental institutions have lawmaking authority, and the extent of the government's authority.

## HOBBESIAN AND LOCKEAN SOCIAL COMPACTS

A main difference between the Hobbesian social compact and the Lockean compact lies in the extent to which individuals surrender their rights to the state or government when the social compact is formed. Hobbes, being a strong positive law advocate who stressed the need for stability and order in society, said that people relinquish all of their rights to the state, which he called the Leviathan, when the social compact is formed. In so doing, Hobbes provided a theoretical justification for a dictatorship or totalitarian government. Unlike many modern totalitarians, however, Hobbes wanted repressive rule because it could provide the social benefit of order and stability. One reason for his view was the civil unrest that characterized the period in which Hobbes wrote. He was disturbed by the social costs of disorder and violence. When viewed in this context, Hobbes's desire for order is understandable.

Locke, on the other hand, saw the dangers of oppressive government that could result from giving up all rights to government. According to his view of the social compact, people relinquish some but not all of their rights when they form the social compact (government). Those rights retained by individuals were so-called inalienable rights—rights that, according to Locke, could not be relinquished. The rights to life, liberty, and property were the basic inalienable rights recognized by Locke. Locke's notion of inalienable rights is recognized in the Fifth and Fourteenth Amendments to the U.S. Constitution. These clauses state that no person may be deprived of life, liberty, or property *without due process of law*. Chapter 6 further develops the due process concept.

## THE U.S. SOCIAL COMPACT

Many cases on "Court TV" that are of current public interest can be found at http://www.courttv.com

The United States has followed the social compact of John Locke. The U.S. Constitution is the basic social compact establishing who or what institutions have lawmaking authority and to what extent. The important Lockean idea of limited government has been followed in the U.S. legal system. It is evident in the Bill of Rights (the first ten amendments to the U.S. Constitution), which sets out areas of freedom whereby the national government may not make any law that would limit these freedoms. For example, the First Amendment right to freedom of speech limits the lawmaking authority of the federal government when it tries to control or limit free speech.

## FEDERALISM

**Federalism**, another example of limited government in the United States, means that lawmaking authority is divided between dual sovereigns. Given the word **sovereign**, meaning supreme lawmaker, one might wonder how dual sovereigns could be within the same country. The United States resolved this problem in its social compact, or Constitution, by the *division of powers* concept. According to this concept, the national government has authority to make law in enumerated areas (areas listed in the Constitution), and the regional or state governments have authority to make laws in the reserved areas.

When one of the dual sovereigns of the federal system attempts to make law outside its area of lawmaking authority, such attempted exercise violates the social compact and is invalid as unconstitutional if challenged in court. The power marble diagram in Figure 3.1 illustrates federalism's division of lawmaking power.

The concept of a limited national government in domestic lawmaking was well stated in *Carter v. Carter Coal Co.*, 298 U.S. 238 (1936), where the U.S. Supreme Court noted that "the proposition often advanced and as often discredited, that the power of the federal government inherently extends to purposes affecting the nation as a whole with which the states severally cannot deal or cannot adequately deal, and the related notion that Congress, entirely apart from those powers delegated by the Constitution, may enact laws to promote the general welfare, have never been accepted but always definitely rejected by this court." As early as 1816, Mr. Justice Story laid down the cardinal rule that has since been followed—that the national government "can claim no powers which are not granted to it by the Constitution, and the powers actually granted, must be such as are expressly given, or given by necessary implication."

Interestingly, the U.S. government has no federalism principle with respect to foreign affairs. In foreign affairs, governmental power is consolidated solely in

### FIGURE 3.1 FEDERALISM'S DIVISION OF LAWMAKING POWER

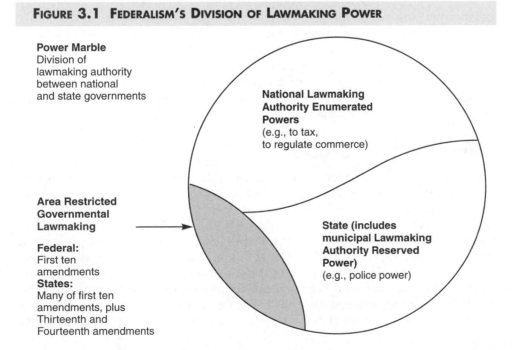

**Power Marble**
Division of lawmaking authority between national and state governments

**Area Restricted Governmental Lawmaking**

**Federal:**
First ten amendments
**States:**
Many of first ten amendments, plus Thirteenth and Fourteenth amendments

**National Lawmaking Authority Enumerated Powers**
(e.g., to tax, to regulate commerce)

**State (includes municipal Lawmaking Authority Reserved Power)**
(e.g., police power)

the national government. The individual states have no power in foreign affairs. The state of New York may not make a treaty with Israel, nor may South Dakota make a treaty with Saudi Arabia. Only the national government may make treaties with foreign governments. We deal with the strength of unlimited power in foreign affairs.

## FEDERALISM TODAY

Federalism at the year 2004 has some characteristics of earlier years: Federal statutes such as the Clean Water Act, the Clean Air Act, and OSHA set national standards, but these laws allow states to administer federal standards if states show they have adequate funding and legal authority.

Budget crunches for the federal government in the 1990s led the George H.W. Bush administration to push more matters formerly handled by the federal government to the states. Then President Clinton, a former governor, assumed power. He understood that states lack the money to pay for federal mandates and are reluctant to assume financial responsibility for them. President George W. Bush, also a former governor, is, as of this writing, so involved in the war on terrorism that he has yet to take a definite position in the ongoing federalism/funding debate. One would think that his conservative credentials would tilt him toward states' rights, but budgetary matters sometimes lead political leaders to take unexpected positions. Also, even under federalism there is a tendency for state governments to shove funding responsibilities from the states to the municipalities. Mayors fear that if federal money accompanies federal program mandates, cash-starved governors will skim federal money for the state treasury, even though it was intended for city governments.

## INSTITUTIONAL SOURCES OF LAW: COURTS AND LEGISLATURES

Institutional sources of law refer to governmental bodies empowered to make law. Ask for institutional sources of law, and the average person will probably name courts and legislatures. However, before exploring courts and legislatures and the limits of their lawmaking authority, note the major governmental institutional source of rules in our society today: the **administrative agency**. An administrative agency is any nonlegislative, nonjudicial, governmental law maker. Later chapters discuss these law makers in detail.

## COURTS AND COURT SYSTEMS

Courts (meaning judges) are a major source of law in the United States. Judge-made law is called **common law**. The United States has two major **court systems**: the federal court system and the state court system. Several reasons exist for having two court systems when one would seem to be enough. First, we have dual sovereigns (i.e., the federal and state governments), and each sovereign wants its own court system. When the U.S. Constitution was set up, many resisted a federal court system. They argued that federal courts unnecessarily duplicate state courts. Also, they feared a strong national government. Others, realizing how provincial the individual states and their citizens were, saw a need for a more neutral court when out-of-staters are sued. Federal courts, with judges appointed for life, are more neutral than elected state court judges. Many also felt that federal judges would be more knowledgeable about national laws and would interpret them more sympathetically than would state courts. Thus, Article III of the U.S. Constitution established the U.S. Supreme Court and gave Congress the power to create other federal courts.

*State Courts.* The Tenth Amendment to the U.S. Constitution reserves to the states powers not delegated to the national government or prohibited to the states. This amendment, among other things, lets states set up their own court systems. Each state has done so in its constitution or its statutes. In effect, the United States has fifty-one separate court systems (the fifty separate state court systems, plus the one federal court system, with at least one federal district court in every state).

Most lawsuits in the United States take place in state courts. Figure 3.2 diagrams the typical state court system. Keep in mind, however, that the fifty states' court structures do differ.

## FIGURE 3.2 STATE JUDICIAL SYSTEM

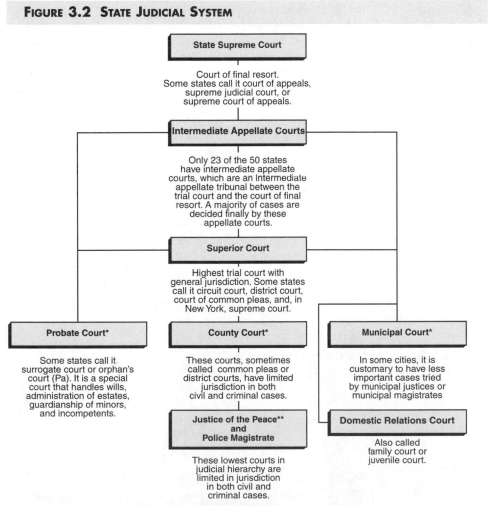

**State Supreme Court**

Court of final resort.
Some states call it court of appeals,
supreme judicial court, or
supreme court of appeals.

**Intermediate Appellate Courts**

Only 23 of the 50 states
have intermediate appellate
courts, which are an intermediate
appellate tribunal between the
trial court and the court of final
resort. A majority of cases are
decided finally by these
appellate courts.

**Superior Court**

Highest trial court with
general jurisdiction. Some states
call it circuit court, district court,
court of common pleas, and, in
New York, supreme court.

**Probate Court***

Some states call it
surrogate court or orphan's
court (Pa). It is a special
court that handles wills,
administration of estates,
guardianship of minors,
and incompetents.

**County Court***

These courts, sometimes
called common pleas or
district courts, have limited
jurisdiction in both
civil and criminal cases.

**Municipal Court***

In some cities, it is
customary to have less
important cases tried
by municipal justices or
municipal magistrates

**Justice of the Peace****
and
Police Magistrate**

These lowest courts in
judicial hierarchy are
limited in jurisdiction
in both civil and
criminal cases.

**Domestic Relations Court**

Also called
family court or
juvenile court.

**Note:** The names of courts are illustrative. Other names are used.

*Courts of special jurisdiction, such as probate, family, or juvenile, and the so-called inferior courts, such as common pleas or municipal courts, may be separate courts or may be part of the trial court of general jurisdiction.
**Not all states have justices of the peace. Their jurisdictions vary greatly from state to state when they do exist.

*Where Cases Start: Courts of Original Jurisdiction.* Note in Figure 3.2 the eight kinds of courts. The court where a case starts is called a **court of original jurisdiction**. A case that deals with juvenile delinquency or divorce, for example, starts in a **domestic relations court**. If someone's father dies and leaves a will disposing of his property, that person (or the person's lawyer) would take the will to a **probate court** (called a surrogate court, or orphan's court in some states). Probate courts deal with estate administration, which involves collecting dead people's assets, paying off their debts, and distributing any remaining assets according to the will or the **statute of descent** (a legislatively drafted will). **County courts** hear cases involving relatively small civil matters, such as a homeowner breaking a contract with a painter, or criminal matters, such as a bank teller embezzling $1,500. Such courts are also called **common pleas courts** or **district courts** in a number of states. County courts typically have jurisdiction up to a certain dollar amount, such as $3,000.

Some, but not all, states have **justice of the peace courts**, often called J.P. courts. Along with **police magistrates**, these courts deal with minor legal violations—traffic violations, for example—of both a civil and a criminal nature.

In a number of states, the **municipal courts** also deal with minor civil and criminal offenses. You may be wondering why so many types of low-level courts have overlapping, or concurrent, jurisdiction. This duplication is sometimes justified on the basis of specializing to create judicial expertise. In less populous areas, one court, such as the county court, may do the job of several different types of low-level state courts, such as domestic relations courts, J.P. courts, and municipal courts.

The courts in the diagram in Figure 3.2 that are lower than the superior court (those already described) are not courts of record, which means that no court stenographer makes a record of the proceedings. Not having a record saves society money. If a litigant in such a court wishes to appeal the result to the superior court, the case is retried from beginning to end, a so-called **de novo trial**, because no lower court record of witnesses' testimony is available for review. Economy is also promoted by not having juries in courts below the superior court level. The judge in such courts fills the jury fact-finder role as well as presides over the proceedings and rules on legal issues.

*Where Jury Trials Occur.* The basic trial-level courts are called **superior** or **circuit courts**. (In New York state they are called supreme courts.) Because they are courts of record, a court stenographer makes a record of the proceedings so that, if the matter is appealed, all comments made by any witness or attorney or by the judge will be available for the appellate court to consider. The presence of the stenographer taking a record of the proceedings tends to make all persons in the courtroom—including the judge—more careful about their remarks. Juries are available, if requested, for most types of cases. Superior courts can usually hear civil or criminal cases. In larger cities, superior courts are sometimes separated into civil and criminal courts.

*Law and Equity Courts.* Occasionally, one hears the terms **law courts** and **equity courts**. (Recall that we discussed these terms in Chapter 1 under the legal ethic of justice.) The distinction between law and equity is historical, not logical. It is the result of the way the United States patterned its legal system after that of England. The English law court judges could give remedies only *in rem* (in a thing), which meant that if wrongs occurred and a remedy could not be given in a thing—for example, where money damages were not satisfactory—then the injured person had no remedy. This system frustrated some injured people. They went to one of the English king's advisors, the **chancellor**, and asked for an order directing the wrongdoer to do or not do something. If the chancellor thought the person had an inadequate legal remedy, an order called an *injunction* or other equitable remedy might be given. The chancellor intervened in this way often enough that a court arose about him called the **chancery** or **equity court**. Persons could get their cases into equity courts only if the legal remedies were inadequate. Legal remedies included such things as money, land, or other property. (Refer to the law-equity discussion under the justice ethic in Chapter 1 for an example of when legal remedies are inadequate.) Equity courts are civil, not criminal. No right to a jury exists in equity courts. Chancellors sometimes appoint advisory juries in equity cases. Early settlers in the United States brought the English law and equity courts with them. By the mid-twentieth century, the law and equity court functions had been combined in most states as well as in the federal courts.

*Correcting Judges' Mistakes.* What happens if a state judge makes a mistake in a case? The person who thinks an error has occurred may appeal to a higher court. Generally, cases decided by a lower court can be appealed to the next higher court in Figure 3.2. For example, a matter decided by a probate court can be appealed to the superior court and from there to the intermediate state appellate court. If a person is still not satisfied, the case can be appealed to the state supreme court. If it involves a federal constitutional, federal statutory, or federal treaty issue, the U.S. Supreme Court might hear the case.

*State Courts of Appeal.* A few points should be noted about state intermediate appellate and supreme courts. First, no juries or witnesses appear in them—only lawyers, who argue law, not usually facts. Generally, the facts in a dispute are decided by the trial court. Appellate courts accept the trial court facts unless they are clearly erroneous. Second, every state has at least one appellate court level. Many have two levels of appellate courts, such as in the state court diagram in Figure 3.2. All states have a highest-level appellate court called the state supreme court (except in New York, where it is called the court of appeals). Third, appellate courts above the superior court level have several judges, called justices, at the highest level. The idea is that several heads are better than one, particularly if the legal issue is complex or politically sensitive.

*Wrong Court.* The state court system is complex. What happens if people take their cases to the wrong court? First, people should hire attorneys to prevent this problem from occurring. However, if a layperson insists on acting *pro se* (as one's own attorney) and starts the case in the wrong court, it will be dismissed (thrown out without a trial). One basic reason for having a case in the wrong court is lack of jurisdiction, which means that for some reason the court does not have the power to hear and try the case.

*Court's Power to Hear Cases: Jurisdiction.* **Jurisdiction** has several aspects: subject matter, territorial, in rem, quasi in rem, and in personam. **Subject matter jurisdiction** refers to the court's power to hear the type of lawsuit in question. Some courts, such as probate courts, have limited subject matter jurisdiction and hear only certain kinds of cases. Probate courts cannot, for example, try murder cases. Other courts, such as superior courts, have **general jurisdiction** and can try any kind of case. Subject matter jurisdiction must always be present for a court to hear a case. In a civil action, one of the other types of jurisdiction (in rem, in personam, quasi in rem) must also exist. *In rem* **jurisdiction** refers to power over things and is based on the physical presence of property in the state. If a case in an Indiana court involves Nevada land, the Indiana court has no *in rem* jurisdiction because that land is in another state.

*In personam* **jurisdiction** refers to power over a person and is commonly based on one of the following: (1) physical presence within the state, (2) state citizenship, (3) consent to the state's jurisdiction (e.g., by coming into the state to defend), (4) sufficient contacts with the state (e.g., a sales office in the state), or (5) commission of a tort (civil wrong) within the state. If, for example, the owner of the Nevada land is served with process while in Indiana, the Indiana court has *in personam* jurisdiction over the Nevada landowner. If a Nevadan is not served with process in Indiana but owns a vacation cottage in Indiana, Indiana courts have **quasi *in rem*** (literally, like in a thing) **jurisdiction** over the Nevadan to the extent of the Indiana land. In other words, the Indiana land is like (or personifies) the Nevadan in Indiana. Therefore, someone can sue the Nevadan in Indiana and collect a judgment against the Nevadan in Indiana up to the value of the Indiana land (but only if the claim giving rise to the lawsuit relates to the Indiana land, such as a trespass to the land).

The *Kopycinski v. Aserkoff* case illustrates an increasingly common feature of the U.S. legal system: A screening tribunal of experts can make it more difficult for plaintiffs to pursue certain types of claims (here medical malpractice) before such claim can go to a jury trial. In Massachusetts if the tribunal rules that the plaintiff's claim is spurious, the plaintiff may, nonetheless pursue the claim by going to court only after posting a bond payable to the defendant for costs if plaintiff loses at a jury trial.

The idea behind such screening tribunals is to discourage ridiculous claims from going to a jury. Just the threat of a jury trial—even one based on spurious grounds—can induce some defendants to settle even if they think the claim is groundless because the attorney cost of defending such claims, the prejudice against the wealthy, and the time spent to defend weigh in the balance. Such screening tribunals are controversial. On the one hand, they can reduce claims and thus control insurance and other litigation costs. On the other hand, they can reduce access to jury trial, which is a constitutionally protected right, although it has never been an absolute right. Judges, for example, have generally had the power to reduce (called a *remittitur*) or increase (called an *additur*) jury awards.

*Kopycinski v. Aserkoff* shows some problems that can arise with such screening panels. The *Anderson v. Conwood* case following *Kopycinski* deals with controlling jury verdicts by use of remittiturs.

---

## Kopycinski v. Aserkoff
Supreme Judicial Court of Massachusetts
573 N.E.2d 961 (1991)

### Background and Facts

Catherine Kopycinski's claim arises from the treatment of her late husband Joseph V. Kopycinski, while he was a patient at Massachusetts General Hospital (MGH). On December 31, 1986, Joseph went to MGH's emergency ward complaining of vomiting, inability to eat, and excessive weight loss. He was examined by defendant, Dr. Hopkins, who admitted Joseph to the hospital. Thereafter, Dr. Hopkins consulted with Dr. Aserkoff, also a defendant, as to Joseph's treatment. Dr. Aserkoff's notes concerning the decedent appear throughout the medical records. Dr. Aserkoff ordered a number of tests, including an abdominal CT-Scan, to determine the causes of Joseph's condition. Although the CT-Scan showed evidence of an inguinal hernia, the defendant physicians allegedly failed to determine that the hernia was the cause of the decedent's medical problems.

On January 6, 1987, less than 24 hours before his death, the defendant doctors obtained a surgical consultation from Dr. Carter. Dr. Carter recommended an exploratory laparotomy after the decedent's condition was stabilized. On January 7, 1987, the decedent died while an inpatient at MGH.

On November 20, 1989, the plaintiff, Catherine Kopycinski, filed a complaint for medical malpractice against the defendants. The complaint alleged that the defendants had failed to properly identify and treat the decedent's medical condition, and that the decedent suffered damages as a result of this failure. On March 26, 1990, a medical malpractice tribunal convened as required by state law to review the plaintiff's offer of proof (to show she had a meritorious, not a spurious, claim). The tribunal consisted of a physician, an attorney, and a judge of the Superior court (a trial court). The attorney and the physician found in favor of each defendant. The judge, however, overruled the majority, stating that, as a matter of law, the plaintiff's offer of proof was sufficient and her claim should

go to trial. The defendants appealed to Court of Appeals and eventually the case reached the Massachusetts Supreme Judicial Court.

### Body of Opinion

**Justice Nolan.** We are faced with the question whether the decision of a medical malpractice tribunal as to the sufficiency of a plaintiff's offer of proof must conform to the conclusion of the tribunal's judicial member, in spite of the contrary views of the medical and legal members. . . .

General Laws . . . provides for the screening claims of medical malpractice by a tribunal. The statute states, in part, that "[e]very action for malpractice, error or mistake against a provider of health care shall be heard by a tribunal consisting of a single justice of the superior court, a physician licensed to practice medicine in the commonwealth . . . and an attorney authorized to practice law in the commonwealth, at which hearing the plaintiff shall present an offer of proof and said tribunal shall determine if the evidence presented if properly substantiated is sufficient to raise a legitimate question of liability appropriate for judicial inquiry or whether the plaintiff's case is merely an unfortunate medical result." The statute provides that, if the tribunal finds for the defendant, the plaintiff may pursue the claim through the regular judicial process, but only upon filing a bond in the amount of $6,000.

The plaintiff argues that the question which the tribunal is ultimately asked to resolve is a legal one and, thus, solely within the purview of the judicial member of the tribunal. The defendants rely on our decision in *Paro v. Longwood Hospital* . . . arguing that the question for the tribunal is not a legal question and should be decided by the majority vote of the tribunal. We agree with defendants. The question to be decided ultimately by the tribunal is a factual one. The plain meaning of the statute, and the legislative guidelines for interpreting statutes which involve tribunals, make it clear that the Legislature intended that a majority vote of the tribunal would determine whether a plaintiff's offer of proof is sufficient.

The words of the statute themselves suggest that the tribunal's decision is a factual and not a legal determination. Words such as *legitimate* and *appropriate*, which are used to describe the standard of proof, suggest determinations of fact. Moreover, the statute repeatedly refers to the "finding" of the tribunal, once again suggesting that the task of the tribunal is a fact-finding mission. Perhaps most telling is the "either," "or" language used in the framing of the tribunal's task. The tribunal determines whether the evidence is "sufficient to raise a legitimate question of liability appropriate for judicial inquiry OR whether the plaintiff's case is merely an unfortunate medical result" [emphasis supplied]. Surely the determination whether a medical result is merely "unfortunate" is not a legal determination. The plain meaning of the words used within the statute suggests that the task of the tribunal is fact-finding, for which the judicial member is no better equipped than the legal or medical member. . . .

The plain meaning of the language "said tribunal shall determine" says that the tribunal as a whole, and not one particular member, shall make the determination. When the legislature intended for the judicial member to have specific powers with regard to the tribunal, it said so explicitly. For instance, [the statute] . . . provides that the judge is to select the health service professional and the attorney who are to serve as co-members of the tribunal; the section also provides that the judicial member may increase or decrease the amount of the bond to be filed.

We note that the judicial member of the tribunal would certainly be solely responsible for deciding purely legal issues. In *Paro v. Longwood Hospital* . . . we rejected the . . . argument that the tribunal statute violated . . . the Massachusetts Declaration of Rights because it allows the two lay panel members to override the judge in the decision of legal issues. The *Paro* court stated that "[t]he lawyer and the health service representative are placed on the panel because of their expertise in relevant fields. This expertise is useful in deciding *the primary question* faced by the tribunal— whether the plaintiff has presented a legally sufficient claim. As to the determination of *this issue*, the tribunal decision is a collective one, with all three panel members participating equally. The responsibility for deciding purely legal questions, however, is left

solely with the judge-member of the tribunal, and thus no interference with his function occurs."

[In determining the standard the tribunal is to use to judge the plaintiff's offer of proof the Massachusetts Supreme Judicial Court held it was] comparable to a trial judge's function in ruling on a motion for a directed verdict. . . .

Moreover, our decision in *Broadard v. Hubbard Regional Hospital* . . . supports our determination that the tribunal must come to a decision as a whole. In *Broadard*, the judicial member felt that it was clear that the offer of proof would be sufficient to raise a legitimate question of liability appropriate for judicial inquiry, and that he intended to find for the plaintiff. Therefore, the judge did not convene the tribunal, seeing it as a "needless exercise." We reversed the judge's decision stating that, even though the judge was certain, the statute called for an interplay among the judicial, legal, and medical members. . . . Here we determine that . . . [the statute] not only requires a convening of the tribunal, but also an interplay in which all three members play an equal role in determining the outcome.

## Judgment and Result

The Massachusetts Supreme Court decided that the decision of a majority of the tribunal shall determine the finding of the tribunal. Therefore, the judge sitting as a member of the tribunal was without power to rule that the plaintiff's offer of proof was sufficient to raise a legitimate question of liability appropriate for judicial inquiry. However because the matter was fully before the state supreme court, it decided that plaintiff's offer of proof was sufficient and that the plaintiff should have been allowed to proceed without posting bond. Therefore, it affirmed.

## Questions

1. Does the tribunal have the power to bar totally a plaintiff from going to a jury trial?
2. Why should there be three distinct experts on the screening tribunal? May they act alone, or must they act together? Why?
3. If a clear legal question arises, who decides? Who decides if something is a legal question, as opposed to a fact question? Does this procedure represent a weakness in the court's opinion?

---

Motions can be made prior to, during, and after a verdict and judgment have been entered. One type of motion that occurs after a jury verdict is for either an additur or a remittitur. Generally, if credible evidence supports a jury's verdict, a court (judge) will not change it. In the case of the motion for an additur, the plaintiff's attorney claims that the jury has been "too stingy" in the amount it has awarded plaintiff. The *Elena DeZavala* judgment in Chapter 4 is an example of a judge raising a jury's verdict to a higher amount. The following case of *Anderson v. Conwood* illustrates a remittitur where the court reduces the jury's verdict because it is too high.

# Anderson v. Conwood Co.
U.S. District Court (W.D. Tennessee)
34 F.Supp.2d 650 (1999)

## Background and Facts

Plaintiffs filed suit against the defendants for violations of the Fair Credit Reporting Act (FCRA). The plaintiffs complained that their credit reports were improperly acquired by defendant Conwood on May 25, 1994. The credit reports provided by Equifax, were to be used by the defendants in civil litigation against the plaintiffs. Equifax's contractual agreement prohibited its subscribers from accessing the consumer credit information if the intended use was for employment or judicial/litigation purposes. Additionally, plaintiffs claimed that the subsequent sharing, dissemination, and usage of their credit reports by the defendants violated provisions of the FCRA.

Plaintiffs sought damages on the basis of pecuniary loss, emotional distress, and other related claims. After an August 1998 trial on the merits, in which the plaintiffs presented minimal evidence of damages and made no precise demand in the presence of the jury, the jury awarded each plaintiff compensatory damages in the amount of $2,000,000. The jury also awarded plaintiffs punitive damages in the amount of $3,500,000.

## Body of Opinion

**District Judge Donald.** Judicial review of the size of punitive damages has been a safeguard against excessive verdicts for as long as punitive damages awards have been awarded . . . . Punitive damages are not compensation for injury . . . . Instead, they are private fines levied by civil juries to punish reprehensible conduct, and deter its future occurrence. . . .

Case law from the U.S. Supreme Court, recognizes that "the Constitution imposes a substantive limit on the size of punitive damages awards. . . . Although the cases fail to draw a mechanical bright line between the constitutionally acceptable and the constitutionally unacceptable, "a majority of the Justices agree that the Due Process Clause imposes a limit on punitive damages awards.... The Supreme Court has repeatedly expressed its concern about punitive damages that "run wild.". . .

The Sixth Circuit's general rule governing the remission of compensatory damages is that the jury's verdict should not be reduced "unless it is beyond the maximum damages that the jury reasonably could find to be compensatory for a party's loss.". . . The *Farber* court held that a trial court is within its discretion in remitting a verdict only when "after reviewing all evidence in the light most favorable to the awardee," it is convinced that the verdict is clearly excessive, or the result of bias, prejudice, or passion. . . . A trial court has the authority to reduce a verdict that is so excessive or inadequate, it shocks the judicial conscience of the court. . . . In appropriate cases, reductions in awards may well be justified even when the amount in controversy does not necessarily "shock the conscience," but rather leaves us with "the definite and firm conviction that a mistake has been committed," resulting in a plain injustice. . . .

If there is any credible evidence to support a verdict, it should not be set aside. . . . The trial court may not substitute its judgment, or credibility determinations, for those of the jury. . . .

When a defect in a jury's award is readily identified and measured, remittitur is more appropriate than a new trial. . . . District courts should grant a motion for remittitur only if the award clearly exceeds "the amount which, under the evidence in the case was the maximum that a jury could reasonably find to be compensatory" for the plaintiff's loss. . . . Unless the award is beyond the range supportable by proof, the court must let the award stand. . . .

Conwood avers that opposing counsel's comments regarding the financial condition of the defendants, and how they spent time "at country clubs," had a prejudicial effect on the jury. . . . Moreover, counsel for the plaintiffs described himself as a representative of "little people," and commented on how his clients were bearing the heat of the day while defendants spent time at their clubs. . . . Conwood argues that such remarks were intended to prejudice the jury, and draw attention to class distinctions and social positions. . . .

Conwood argues that the verdict of the jury, regarding both compensatory and punitive damages, is so outrageous, enormous and shocking as to indicate passion and prejudice by this sympathetic jury. . . . Conwood claims that unaccountable caprice was definitely prevalent given the extremely meager evidence of damages proximately caused by the defendants. . . . Conwood contends that the verdict of the jury should be set aside, because it was arbitrary, capricious and the result of passion and/or prejudice. . . . On this point, the Court concurs. Conwood states that the information contained within the credit reports was admittedly public information. . . . Conwood further avers that the plaintiffs' lives did not change as a result of their credit reports being acquired. . . . The record supports this fact.

In the instant case the Court finds that the verdict was clearly excessive. The record is void of any proof of damages beyond plaintiffs' testimony of worry, stress, anxiety, loss of sleep and expense in bringing litigation. Indeed, plaintiffs failed to present any demand for a monetary amount of damages as evidenced by the jury's first question, "What amount of damages did the plaintiffs ask for?" Thus, the jury's verdict lacks an evidentiary foundation.

Based upon the lack of evidence showing actual damage to the plaintiffs, the jury's compensatory damage awards must be remitted, as they are clearly excessive. . . . The inescapable conclusion is that rational thought was vacated by the jury, and replaced with their own passion and prejudices. . . .

Notwithstanding the jury's sentiments that punitive damages were justified and warranted in the present case, the Court finds that there was no proof of any action on the part of defendants which warranted the imposition of punitive damages. Therefore the court will vacate the award of punitive damages against the defendants. . . .

## Judgment and Result

The district court granted a remittitur reducing Anderson's jury award for compensatory damages from $2,000,000 to $50,000; plaintiff's $3,500,000 punitive damages award is vacated totally. Plaintiffs are awarded reasonable attorney fees. The jury verdict was clearly excessive because it lacked an evidentiary foundation.

## Questions

1. What was the amount of the remittitur in the *Anderson* case? Who makes a remittitur?

2. What might make a remittitur objectionable? Who would most likely object to a remittitur—plaintiff or defendant?
3. Given the tendency of some juries to award huge punitive damage amounts, why do you suppose the trial judges do not employ remittiturs more often?
4. Whose legal philosophies mentioned in Chapter 1 are in evidence in this case?

## FEDERAL COURTS

*Federal District Courts: Where Cases Start.* The federal district courts are those courts where most lawsuits begin in the federal court system. The federal court system, diagrammed in Figure 3.3, has 89 federal district courts in the 50 states, one in the District of Columbia, and another in Puerto Rico, bringing the total number of federal districts to 91. With 91 federal districts, one might expect 91 federal district judges, but this is not the case. There are from 2 to 27 federal judges in each district, depending on the population and amount of litigation in the district. Where more than one federal district judge presides in a district, the district is divided into divisions. The 50 states contain 541 permanent federal district judgeships, 15 more in the District of Columbia, and 7 more in Puerto Rico. Also, temporary federal judgeships may be created by Congress to last only for the life of the person appointed to fill them.

Federal district judges perform the function of a law court judge and equity court chancellor. They also have subject matter jurisdiction to hear either civil or criminal cases. However, federal courts are courts of limited jurisdiction. That is, not all civil or criminal lawsuits may be heard there. Basically, two types of civil cases may be brought into federal district courts: **diversity of citizenship** cases, which are cases involving lawsuits brought by a person from one state against a person from a different state, and **federal question** cases in which a federal constitutional or statutory right is at issue. A $75,000 jurisdictional limit in diversity cases was also designed to keep out small disputes better handled in state courts. Such a limit no longer exists in federal question cases.

*Administrative Quasi-Judicial Agencies.* The **administrative quasi-judicial agencies** in Figure 3.3 refer to nonjudicial, nonlegislative government entities having rule-making authority. As such, these agencies are not even courts in a strict sense, although their rules and adjudications may often be appealed directly to the federal courts of appeal, thus bypassing the trial-level federal district courts. Two reasons for no retrial of administrative adjudications from scratch in district courts are to defer to the expertise of administrative law judges and to be expedient; it saves money not to have to redevelop in district court evidence already produced at the administrative level.

*Other Federal Courts.* The U.S. Court of International Trade. (formerly the U.S. Customs Court) is a federal court with exclusive jurisdiction over civil actions

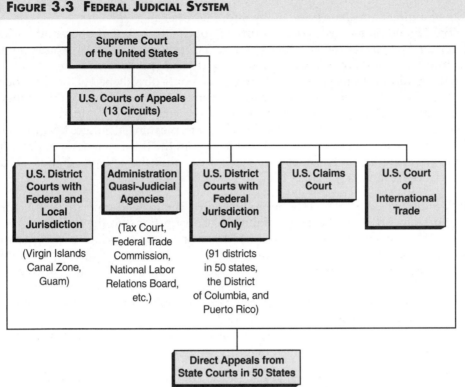

FIGURE 3.3 FEDERAL JUDICIAL SYSTEM

arising under the U.S. tariff laws in such matters as appraised value or classification of imported goods. It tries cases without juries and has appellate authority from customs officers under the Anti-Dumping Act of 1921. The **U.S. Court of Appeals** for the Federal Circuit, created in 1982, hears cases appealed from the U.S. Patent Office (such as validity of trademarks and patents), the U.S. Court of International Trade, and the U.S. Claims Court. The **U.S. Claims Court** came into existence on October 1, 1982. It takes over the trial court functions of the defunct Court of Claims, which are basically those of a limited jurisdictional trial court where a person may sue the federal government on a claim arising from the U.S. Constitution, any congressional statute, any executive department regulation, any expressed or implied contract to which the U.S. government is an obligor, and any liquidated or unliquidated nontort damages. Matters such as federal income tax refund claims, suits on supply or construction contracts with the federal government, back-pay claims for civilian and military government employees are handled by the U.S. Claims Court.

*U.S. Courts of Appeals.* Most **U.S. courts of appeals** (formerly called U.S. circuit courts of appeals) were established in 1891 to ease the burden on the Supreme Court. Appeals from U.S. district courts formerly went directly to the Supreme Court. Generally, appeals from federal trial-level courts must go to one of the thirteen U.S. courts of appeals before they can be considered by the U.S. Supreme Court. Two exceptions, where the U.S. courts of appeals are bypassed and appeal is directly to the U.S. Supreme Court, are (1) when a three-judge district court issues injunctions against state court proceedings in particular cases in which congressional statutes are held unconstitutional and (2) when a few criminal cases follow a direct appellate route to the Supreme Court.

The United States has thirteen courts of appeals including the recently created Court of Appeals for the Federal Circuit in D.C. (refer to Figure 3.3). Cases do not start in U.S. courts of appeals. Cases in courts of appeals come from one of the courts or administrative agencies shown in the boxes directly below the U.S. courts of appeals. Each court of appeals hears cases in divisions made up of three judges. Currently, each U.S. court of appeals has from four to twenty-three judges. In important cases, U.S. courts of appeals sit *en banc*, meaning all judges hear the case.

Figure 3.4 shows the states contained in each of the thirteen federal judicial circuits covering the fifty states and territories, plus the federal circuits in the District of Columbia.

*U.S. Supreme Court.* The U.S. Supreme Court was formed on February 2, 1790, pursuant to Article III, Section 1 of the U.S. Constitution and the Judiciary Act of 1789. The Court now consists of a Chief Justice and eight associate justices. At various times as many as ten and as few as six justices have presided. Supreme Court justices assume office after presidential nomination and U.S. Senate confirmation. No legal requirement exists stating that a Supreme Court nominee must be an attorney although, as a practical matter, Senate confirmation would probably be impossible for someone not legally trained.

The Supreme Court has the power to hear cases pursuant to Article III, Section 2, of the U.S. Constitution, which notes:

> The judicial power shall extend to all Cases, in Law and Equity, arising under this constitution, the Laws of the United States, and Treaties made, or which shall be made, under their Authority;—to all Cases affecting Ambassadors, other public Ministers and Consuls;—to all Cases of admiralty and maritime Jurisdiction;—to Controversies to which the United States shall be a Party;—to Controversies between two or more States;—between a State and Citizens of another State;—between Citizens of different States;—between Citizens of the same State claiming Lands under Grants of different States, and between a State, or the Citizens thereof, and foreign States, Citizens or Subjects.
>
> In all cases affecting Ambassadors, other public Ministers and Consuls, and those in which a State shall be Party, the Supreme Court shall have original jurisdiction. In all other cases before mentioned, the Supreme Court shall have appellate jurisdiction, both as to Law and Fact, with such Exceptions, and under such Regulations as the Congress shall make.

As the prior language illustrates, some, but not all, of the Supreme Court's authority to hear cases comes from the Constitution. Other authority to hear cases comes from congressional statutes. Such statutory jurisdiction generates many of the cases the Supreme Court decides. Congress has some power to remove the Supreme Court's jurisdiction to hear particular types of cases if the Congress originally gave the Court that jurisdiction. This power is a potent check on Supreme Court decisions, and threats of its use are frequent when decisions are handed down that are unpopular with some members of Congress. The extent of congressional power to cut federal court jurisdiction is uncertain and controversial.

## IN WHICH COURT SYSTEM SHOULD I SUE?

When a federal court hears a diversity case, it sits as a state court but presumably without the local prejudice of the state court judge. But what is the limit on federal

**FIGURE 3.4 THE THIRTEEN FEDERAL JUDICIAL CIRCUITS**

judges' lawmaking authority when they sit in a diversity case? What if the state court had ruled one way on an issue? Could the federal court in another later case involving similar facts in the same state make a contrary rule? In *Erie Railroad Co. v. Tompkins*, Harry Tompkins lost an arm and learned that federal judges have no power to make common law in nonenumerated areas (areas reserved to the states by the U.S. Constitution). This means federal judges must follow state law when they decide diversity cases and the case involves a reserved power matter (that is, most property, contract, and tort civil wrongs such as slander and negligence covered by state law—areas *reserved* for state lawmaking).

## Erie Railroad Co. v. Tompkins
U.S. Supreme Court
304 U.S. 64 (1938)

### Background and Facts

Tompkins, a citizen of Pennsylvania, was injured on a dark night by a passing freight train of the Erie Railroad Company while walking along its right of way at Hughestown in that state. He claimed that the accident occurred through negligence in the operation, or maintenance, of the train; that he was rightfully on the premises as licensee because on a commonly used, beaten footpath which ran for a short distance alongside the tracks; and that he was struck by something which looked like a door projecting from one of the moving cars. To enforce that claim he brought an action in the federal court for southern New York, which had jurisdiction because the company is a corporation of that State. It denied liability and the case was tried by a jury.

Erie insisted that its duty to Tompkins was no greater than that owed to a trespasser. It contended, among other things, that its duty to Tompkins, and hence its liability, should be determined in accordance with the Pennsylvania law; that under the law of Pennsylvania, as declared by its highest court, persons who use pathways along the railroad right of way—that is, a longitudinal pathway as distinguished from a crossing—are to be deemed trespassers; and that the railroad is not liable for injuries to undiscovered trespassers resulting from its negligence, unless it be wanton or willful. Tompkins denied that any such rule had been established by the decision of the Pennsylvania courts and contended that, since there was no statute of the State on the subject, the railroad's duty and liability is to be determined in federal courts as a matter of general law.

The trial judge refused to rule that the applicable law precluded recovery. The jury brought in a verdict of $30,000; and the judgment entered thereon was affirmed by the Circuit Court of Appeals, which held, . . . that it was unnecessary to consider whether the law of Pennsylvania was as contended because the question was one not of local, but of general law and that "upon questions of general law the federal courts are free, in the absence of local statute, to exercise their independent judgment as to what the law is; and it is well settled that the question of the responsibility of a railroad for injuries caused by its servants is one of general law. . . . Where the public has made open and notorious use of a railroad right of way for a long period

of time and without objection, the company owes to persons on such permissive pathway a duty of care in the operation of the trains. . . . It is likewise generally recognized law that a jury may find that negligence exists toward a pedestrian using a permissive path on the railroad right of way if he is hit by some object projecting from the side of the train."

### Body of Opinion

**Justice Brandeis.** The Erie had contended that application of the Pennsylvania rule was required, among other things, by § 34 of the Federal Judiciary Act of September 24, 1789, c. 20, 28 U.S.C. § 725, which provides:

> The laws of the several States, except where the Constitution, treaties, or statutes of the United States otherwise require or provide, shall be regarded as rules of decision in trials at common law, in the courts of the United States, in cases where they apply.

Because of the importance of the question whether the federal court was free to disregard the alleged rule of the Pennsylvania common law, we granted certiorari.

First, *Swift v. Tyson* . . . held that federal courts exercising jurisdiction on the ground of diversity of citizenship need not, in matters of general jurisprudence, apply the unwritten law of the State as declared by its highest court; that they are free to exercise an independent judgment as to what the common law of the State is—or should be. . . .

Experience in applying the doctrine of *Swift v. Tyson* had revealed its defects, political and social; and the benefits expected to flow from the rule did not accrue. . . .

Diversity of citizenship jurisdiction was conferred in order to prevent apprehended discrimination in state courts against those not citizens of the State. *Swift v. Tyson* introduced grave discrimination by non-citizens against citizens. It made rights enjoyed under the unwritten "general law" vary according to whether enforcement was sought in the state or in the federal court; and the privilege of selecting the court in which the right should be determined was conferred upon the non-citizen. Thus, the doctrine rendered impossible equal protection of the law. In attempting to promote uniformity of law throughout the United States, the doctrine had prevented uniformity in the administration of the law of the State. The discrimination resulting became in practice far-reaching. This resulted in part from the broad provision accorded to the so-called "general law" as to which federal courts exercised an independent judgment. In addition to questions of purely commercial law, "general law" was held to include the obligations under contracts entered into and to be performed within the State, the extent to which a carrier operating within a State may stipulate for exemption from liability for his own negligence or that of his employee; the liability for torts committed within the State upon persons resident or property located there, even where the question of liability depended upon the scope of a property right conferred by the State; and the right to exemplary or punitive damages. Furthermore, state decisions construing local deeds, mineral conveyances, and even devises of real estate were disregarded.

In part the discrimination resulted from the wide range of persons held entitled to avail themselves of the federal rule by resort to the diversity of citizenship jurisdiction. Through this jurisdiction individual citizens willing to remove from their own State and become citizens of another might avail themselves of the federal rule. And without even change of residence, a corporate citizen of the State could avail itself of the federal rule by re-incorporating under the laws of another State, as was done in the Taxicab case.

The injustice and confusion incident to the doctrine of *Swift v. Tyson* have been repeatedly urged as reasons for abolishing or limiting diversity of citizenship jurisdiction. Other legislative relief has been proposed. If only a question of statutory construction were involved, we should not be prepared to abandon a doctrine so widely applied throughout nearly a century. But the unconstitutionality of the course pursued has now been made clear and compels us to do so. The fallacy underlying the rule declared in *Swift v. Tyson* is made clear by Mr. Justice Holmes. The doctrine rests upon the assumption that there is a "transcendental body of law outside of any particular State but obligatory within it unless and until changed by statute," that federal courts have the power to use their judgment as to what the rules of common law are; and that in the federal courts "the parties are entitled to an independent judgment on matters of general law":

"But law in the sense in which courts speak of it today does not exist without some definite authority behind it. The common law so far as it is enforced in a State, whether called common law or not, is not the common law generally but the law of that State existing by the authority of that State without regard to what it may have been in England or anywhere else. . . .

"The authority and only authority is the State, and if that be so, the voice adopted by the State as its own (whether it be of its Legislature or of its Supreme Court) should utter the last word."

Thus the doctrine of *Swift v. Tyson* is, as Mr. Justice Holmes said, "an unconstitutional assumption of powers by courts of the United States which no lapse of time or respectable array of opinion should make us hesitate to correct." In disapproving that doctrine we do not hold unconstitutional § 34 of the Federal Judiciary Act of 1789 or any other Act of Congress. We merely declare that in applying the doctrine this Court and the lower courts have invaded the rights which, in our opinion are reserved by the Constitution to the several States. . . .

### Judgment and Result

The U.S. Supreme Court decided the case in favor of the railroad. Tompkins lost. The Supreme Court said federal courts deciding a diversity case must apply state substantive law where the *federal* government has *no enumerated power*. In this case, rules dealing with landowners' liability to people on their land fall into the *states' reserved* area of lawmaking, *not* the *federal enumerated area* of lawmaking. (Refer to the power marble in Figure 3.1.) Thus, in this case, the New York federal district court should have applied the Pennsylvania rule, which would have denied Tompkins recovery because he was a trespasser on the railroad property.

## LEGISLATURES AND LEGISLATIVE FORMS

Legislatures are public bodies of elected officials who make law by passing statutes. The national legislature is called the Congress of the United States, which comprises the House and Senate. Each state also has a legislature. This section focuses on how a bill becomes a statute, some ways to influence legislation, and differences between courts and legislatures. The work of the U.S. Congress starts with a proposal taking one of the following four forms: a **bill**, a **joint resolution**, a **concurrent resolution**, or a **simple resolution**. Only bills will be discussed here.

*Bills.* Most federal legislation takes the form of a bill when proposed. A bill becomes an act or **session law** when it is passed by both houses of Congress and is signed by the president, when two-thirds of each House overrides a presidential veto, or when the president fails to return it with his objections to the originating house within ten days while Congress is

*The Web site to the Library of Congress is* **http://thomas.loc.gov**

in session. Federal bills can start in either the House or Senate, except for revenue-raising or general appropriation bills (tax bills), which must originate in the House of Representatives. A bill originating in the House is designated H.R. (for House of Representatives) followed by a number, such as H.R. 2070, which it keeps all during its parliamentary stages. Senate bills are similarly designated S (for Senate), followed by a number, such as S.7.

Figure 3.5 indicates some major steps by which a **bill** becomes a statute. A proposed statute introduced by a member of Congress is called a **bill**. If the bill survives and becomes law, it is called an act, statute, or session law. Acts can be private acts (a law passed to deal with nonrecurring, private matters, such as a law to pay a farmer when a military jet crashes into and destroys the farmer's barn) or public acts (laws having general social impact).

*Statutory Construction.* One role the judiciary must play is that of gap filler. The gaps arise when legislatures pass statutes that do not address all possible situations arising under a statute and such an unanticipated situation arises in an actual lawsuit. Judicial gap filling is commonly referred to as **interstitial lawmaking** or **statutory construction**.

A number of rules and maxims of statutory construction have been developed by judges over at least two centuries of deciding reported cases in the United States. They are not binding rules because the maxims themselves are not always consistent with one another. For example, one maxim is that "a statute will be read to give it a rational rather than arbitrary meaning." Yet another maxim says that nonlegal words and phrases will be interpreted in their ordinary sense. Thus, the U.S. Supreme Court, in one of its less-publicized opinions, has held that "tomatoes are vegetables." What makes this decision notable is that it offends botany, since tomatoes are technically fruit. Arguably, then, this decision observes the ordinary sense rule but violates the rational rather than arbitrary meaning rule.

Despite such peculiarities, some of the more common maxims of statutory construction worth listing include the following:

1. Words of plain meaning will not be extended to mean something different or additional to that plain meaning.
2. The purpose of statutory interpretation (by judges) is to determine legislative intent.

## FIGURE 3.5  HOW A BILL BECOMES AN ACT

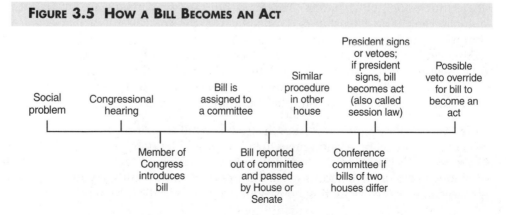

3. Penal statutes are to be strictly construed in favor of the accused.
4. Statutes in derogation of the common law are to be strictly construed to reverse or modify the common law rules as little as possible.
5. Where words are omitted from a statute by inadvertence or clerical error and the legislative intent is clear, the court will insert the missing words.
6. *Expressio unius, exclusio alterius* (what is expressed implies exclusion of other matters).
7. When general words follow particular classes, the *ejusdem generis* principle is applied (limiting words to same class as were named).
8. *Reddendo singula singulis* (each word or phase in a statute will be applied to its appropriate referent).
9. Legislative history will be used only when the statute, to which the legislative history relates, is unclear.

Many other maxims and rules of statutory construction exist. Those maxims just listed are used frequently by courts. Some are obvious rules of common sense or, at least, good sense, such as the maxim that where words are omitted from a statute by inadvertence or clerical error and the rule that where legislative intent is clear, the court will insert the missing words. Other of the maxims deserve some elaboration. Penal (criminal) statutes are construed strictly in the accused's favor because criminal punishment is meted out in limited portions, particularly when prison is possible. Also, the presumption of innocence attributed by the U.S. legal system to each defendant and the procedural due process notice requirement as to what is criminal support construction of criminal statutes in the accused's favor.

Statutes in derogation of the common law, such as **survival statutes** or **statutes of limitations** are strictly construed to preserve the common law rules, thereby promoting legal stability. Such rules have been developed over many years and are relied on by many in planning their affairs.

The maxim that "when general words follow particular classes, the *ejusdem generis* principle is applied," can be best explained by example. If a statute read, "Whoever operates a restaurant, bar, . . . or other place of public accommodation shall obtain a license," would the statute require a license for a dentist's office? According to *ejusdem generis*, the answer is, "No," because this maxim limits general words to the same class as named by the preceding specific words.

Likewise, *reddendo singula singulis* is best explained by illustration. The statute commands: "Go to London by rail and by steamer." The *reddendo* maxim would not be applied so that the command would be read to require one to go to London once using one mode (rail) and go to London again using another mode (steamer). Rather, one would be required to go to London once, using both modes on appropriate land and water segments to make one trip.

Legislative history is sometimes a problem for those engaging in statutory construction. Courts are supposed to follow the intent of the legislatures. Usually, intent is clear from reading the statute. Legislative history is usually used only when the statute is unclear on its face. It will not be used to read language out of the statute or to thwart legislative intent—usually. However, if statutory language is unclear or an advocate can convince a judge that statutory language is unclear, whether it in fact is unclear, legislative history will be used to clear up the uncertainty. A problem with consulting legislative history to clear up statutory ambiguities is that it, too, is often ambiguous, because any member of Congress may testify before the congressional committee or subcommittee responsible for drafting a bill. Members of Congress may also stand up on the floor of Congress during final deliberations on a bill and state his or her interpretation of a controversial section. Even though such a personal interpretation is probably not so persuasive of true legislative intent as the committee report, all individual remarks made at committee hearings during the drafting of a bill and floor remarks during debate are part of the legislative history of an act. Given that members of Congress are highly individualistic, one can frequently find "rebel" statements in the legislative history that are contrary to the intent of most members of Congress. Such statements are available for an effective advocate to use to induce or mislead a judge into construing a statute to a client's advantage. It is up to the good judgment of the court, aided by opposing counsel, to resist atypical interpretations and instead accurately perceive legislative intent.

The following case shows a problem of statutory construction. There, a federal statute punished whoever transported in interstate commerce a motor vehicle knowing it to have been stolen. The statute defined "motor vehicle" to include many things, but it did not include airplanes. The question then became, "Did the statute cover airplanes?" Read *McBoyle v. United States* to learn the answer.

## McBoyle v. United States
U.S. Supreme Court
283 U.S. 25 (1931)

### Background and Facts

McBoyle was convicted of transporting from Ottawa, Illinois, to Guymon, Oklahoma, an airplane that he knew to have been stolen, and was sentenced to serve three years' imprisonment and to pay a fine of $2,000. The judgment was affirmed by the Circuit Court of Appeals for the Tenth Circuit. The Supreme Court granted a writ of certiorari so it could hear McBoyle's case on the question of whether the National Motor Vehicle Theft Act applies to aircraft.

### Body of Opinion

**Justice Holmes.** The [National Motor Vehicle Theft] Act provides: "Sec. 2. That when used in this Act: (a) The term 'motor vehicle' shall include an automobile, automobile truck, automobile wagon, motor cycle, or any other self-propelled vehicle not designed for running on rails; . . . Sec. 3. That whoever shall transport or cause to be transported in interstate or foreign commerce a motor vehicle, knowing the same to have been stolen, shall be punished by a fine of not more than $5,000, or by imprisonment of not more than five years, or both."

Section 2 defines motor vehicles of which the transportation in interstate commerce is punished in § 3. The question is the meaning of the word *vehicle* in the phrase "any other self-propelled vehicle not designed for running on rails." No doubt etymologically it is possible to use the word to signify a conveyance working on land, water or air, and sometimes legislation extends the use in that direc-

tion, e.g., land and air, water being separately provided for, in the Tariff Act. . . . But in everyday speech "vehicle" calls up the picture of a thing moving on land. Thus in Rev. Stats. § 4, intended, the Government suggests, rather to enlarge than to restrict the definition, vehicle includes every contrivance capable of being used "as a means of transportation on land." And this is repeated, expressly excluding aircraft, in the Tariff Act. . . . So here, the phrase under discussion calls up the popular picture. For after including automobile truck, automobile wagon and motor cycle, the words "any other self-propelled vehicle not designed for running on rails" still indicate that a vehicle in the popular sense, that is a vehicle running on land, is the theme. It is a vehicle that runs, not something not commonly called a vehicle, that flies. Airplanes were well known in 1919, when this statute was passed; but it is admitted that they were not mentioned in the reports or in the debates in Congress. It is impossible to read words that so carefully enumerate the different forms of motor vehicles and have no reference of any kind to aircraft, as including airplanes under a term that usage more and more precisely confines to a different class. The counsel for the petitioner have shown that the phraseology of the statute as to motor vehicles follows that of earlier statutes of Connecticut, Delaware, Ohio, Michigan, and Missouri, not to mention the late Regulations of Traffic for the District of Columbia . . . none of which can be supposed to leave the earth.

Although it is not likely that a criminal will carefully consider the text of the law before he murders or steals, it is reasonable that a fair warning should be given to the world in language that the common world will understand, of what the law intends to do if a certain line is passed. To make the warning fair, so far as possible the line should be clear. When a rule of conduct is laid down in words that evoke in the common mind only the picture of vehicles moving on land, the statute should not be extended to aircraft, simply because it may seems to us that a similar policy applies, or upon the speculation that, if the legislature had thought of it, very likely broader words would have been used.

### Judgment and Result

Judgment of the Court of Appeals was reversed. The expression "motor vehicle" as used in the National Motor Vehicle Theft Act does not cover airplanes.

### Questions

1. Were "airplanes" known to exist when Congress wrote the statute in the *McBoyle* case? If so, what does the exclusion of "airplanes" suggest? Did Justice Holmes rely on the *ejusdem generis* principle, the *expressio unius* doctrine of statutory construction, the "penal statutes are to be strictly construed in favor of the accused" doctrine, or the "plain [no pun intended] meaning" rule? Or could some or all be used implicitly if not explicitly?
2. Is it likely that the accused here, Mr. McBoyle, ever read the act in question before flying a plane interstate? How, then, could he be said to be prejudiced by the ambiguity in the statute?
3. Why are rules of statutory construction necessary? Because the legislature did its job well or poorly? How could the problem here have been corrected?

## DIFFERENCES BETWEEN COURTS AND LEGISLATURES

The following differences exist between courts and legislatures as lawmakers:

1. Courts and legislatures make law in different *form*.
2. Courts mete out *commutative* justice, whereas legislatures dispense *distributive* justice.
3. Courts are *passive* lawmakers, while legislatures are *self-animating* lawmakers.
4. The *procedural due process protections* afforded litigants when courts make law are greater than the procedural due process protection afforded people when legislatures make law.
5. Courts deal with *legal* questions, while legislatures deal with *political* questions.

*Form.* Judge-made law is common law. The form in which courts make law includes decisions in cases in which no opinion is rendered, decisions in cases in which an opinion is rendered, and situations in which various court orders are entered. For practical purposes and for purposes of cases other than the case in which a rule is made, the instance in which a court makes a rule and renders an opinion is most important because these rules serve as precedents for future cases.

Generally speaking, judge-made law having precedential effect is found in state appellate court opinions and all federal court decisions resulting in a majority opinion. State trial court opinions usually are not significant for other cases because they are seldom written, due to time constraints and the pressure of other work. Also, state trial court opinions bind only the court that gives them, not other trial courts, so they would only be persuasive, not binding, precedent for other trial courts. One might ask why the same reasoning does not hold for federal trial-level courts (federal district courts). Federal courts are generally regarded as more powerful and prestigious than state courts; they are fewer in number than state courts; they write opinions more frequently than do state courts; and they are courts of limited jurisdiction and hence involve fewer and generally more significant legal issues, often presenting problems having nationwide interest.

Legislatures, contrary to courts, issue their laws in the form of statutes or acts. As discussed earlier, when a proposed law is introduced into the legislature, it is called a *bill*. Once it is signed into law by the president or governor or passes the legislature over a veto, it becomes an act, statute, or a session law.

*Commutative versus Distributive Justice.* Justice handed out by judges when they settle lawsuits is referred to as commutative justice. It is usually designed to correct a past wrong between specific parties. Justice meted out by legislatures is referred to as distributive justice. It is designed to address broad, societal problems and usually to take effect in the future.

*Passive versus Self-Animating Lawmakers.* Judges are, by nature, passive lawmakers. Millions of wrongs may be committed in society, but a judge will not lift an official finger to correct any situation unless someone refers the matter to court in a lawsuit. The litigation will examine the alleged breach of the alleged right to see whether a legally recognized right has been broken and, if so, the extent of the damage sustained. It is up to people claiming their rights have been broken to prove it. The judge just sits in court, listens to the assertions made, and presides over the proceedings. The judge has no duty to collect the evidence for either party.

Legislatures, on the other hand, are active, self-animating lawmakers. If they think wrongs are being committed, they can pass laws forbidding such conduct and attach criminal penalties to them. Usually, legislative hearings are held in which members of the public may point out the need for statutes in a particular area. Nonetheless, the legislature need not wait for a wrong to occur before doing something to improve a social situation. Also, an attorney does not have to be hired to generate legislation.

*Greater Procedural Due Process Protections in Courts than in Legislatures.* Procedural due process refers to the constitutional requirement that a person be given notice and a fair hearing. This requirement applies in general to both courts when they make law in deciding a lawsuit and to legislatures when they pass laws. However, the degree to which procedural due process must be provided or observed is considerably greater in courts than in legislatures partly because court disputes involve particular parties, not everyone in society. Also, in 99 percent of the cases the matters that courts are called upon to decide have occurred before the lawsuit. Additionally, courts are called upon to take something (usually money or property) from one party and turn it over to the other party in civil cases. In criminal cases, courts may fine, imprison, or even take a person's life. Legislatures, on the other hand, usually act upon the population as a whole. Their mandates take effect at some time in the future (generally not in the past); and legislative enactments that involve extracting money or property from someone often have broad impact (such as to increase income tax rates). In such cases of generalized extractions on the population, a general public legislative hearing or a public discussion of the proposed statute with juries, cross-examination, counsel, and many of the other trappings of procedural due process would be uneconomical.

*Courts Deal with Legal Issues, and Legislatures Deal with Political Issues.* One of the basic dogmas of our system is that courts decide legal questions, whereas legislatures decide political questions. But what does this mean? Is not a legislature making a law when it passes a statute imposing higher income tax rates for single people than for families with one wage earner? Here, the legislature is not applying this law to a specific case. Also, the decision to tax one group at rates higher than other groups is essentially a matter of political strength, the will of the stronger. Because married voters with one income outnumber single taxpayers, married people support laws imposing higher taxes on singles. Matters decided by *power* tend to be political, and matters determined by *logic* tend to be legal. The courts must determine the many unanticipated matters not addressed by the statute. For example, a court must determine if a wage earner who marries during the tax year is treated as single for tax purposes for the entire year, or is treated as single for that part of the year the wage earner was single and as married for the remainder of the year. Such court clarifications of statutes are known as interstitial lawmaking.

In *Baker v. Carr*, 369 U.S. 186 (1962), the U.S. Supreme Court tried to state the difference between a legal issue (suitable for courts to decide) and a political issue (suitable for legislatures):

> Prominent on the surface of any case held to involve a political question is found a textually demonstrable constitutional commitment of the issue to a coordinate political department; or a lack of judicially discoverable and manageable standards for resolving it; or the impossibility of deciding without an initial policy determination of a kind clearly for nonjudicial discretion; or the impossibility of a court's undertaking independent resolution without expressing lack of the respect due coordinate branches of government; or an unusual need for unquestioning adherence to a political decision already made; or the potentiality of embarrassment from multifarious pronouncements by various departments on one question.

The Supreme Court's statement would prompt the following kinds of questions:

1. Has the Constitution expressly said the legislature, and not the courts, is to decide the matter?
2. Is there a way for a court to settle the dispute?
3. Does settling the dispute require a policy decision that should be made by an elected official?
4. If the Supreme Court decides the matter, will its decision show disrespect for the president or Congress?
5. Has another branch of government (the president or Congress) already decided the matter, and does a need exist to stick to this decision?

The answers to these questions help the U.S. Supreme Court decide whether a matter is political or legal. Is busing to achieve racial balance in public schools legal or political? (Because courts decide this issue, it must be a legal one.) What about abortion? (Courts have decided this question, so it, too, must be a legal issue.) Yet, busing and abortion seem like political matters when using the *Baker v. Carr* factors just listed. The previous examples indicate that the modern U.S. Supreme Court is a *political* actor, which tells you that deciding whether something is political or legal is not always predictable.

Read the *Bush v. Gore* case to see if you think the matter decided there was a legal or political question.

## Bush v. Gore
U.S. Supreme Court
531 U.S. 98 (2000)

## Background and Facts

On December 8, 2000, the Florida Supreme Court ordered, among other things, that manual recounts of ballots for the recent presidential election were required in all Florida counties where so-called "undervotes" had not been subject to manual tabulation, and that the manual recounts should begin at once. Noting the closeness of the election, the Florida Supreme Court explained that, on the record before it, there could be no question that there were uncounted "legal votes"—that is, those in which there was a clear indication of the voter's intent—sufficient to place the results of the election in doubt. Petitioners, the Republican candidates for president and vice president who had been certified as the winners in Florida, filed an emergency application for a stay of this mandate. On December 9, this Court granted the stay application, treated it as a petition for a writ of certiorari, and granted certiorari. . . .

## Body of Opinion

**Per Curiam.** . . . The petition presents the following questions: whether the Florida Supreme Court established new standards for resolving presidential election contests, thereby violating Art. II, § 1, cl. 2, of the United States Constitution and failing to comply with 3 U.S.C. § 5, and whether the use of standardless manual recounts violates the Equal Protection and Due Process Clauses. With respect to the equal protection question, we find a violation of the Equal Protection Clause. . . .

The individual citizen has no federal constitutional right to vote for electors for the President of the United States unless and until the state legislature chooses a statewide election as the means to implement its power to appoint members of the Electoral College. This is the source for the statement . . . that the state legislature's power to select the manner for appointing electors is plenary; it may, if it chooses, select the electors itself, which indeed was the manner used by state legislatures in several States for many years after the framing of our Constitution. . . . History has now favored the voter, and in each of the several States the citizens themselves vote for presidential electors. . . .

The right to vote is protected in more than the initial allocation of the franchise. Equal protection applies as well to the manner of its exercise. Having once granted the right to vote on equal terms, the State may not, by later arbitrary and disparate treatment, value one person's vote over that of another. . . .

There is no difference between the two sides of the present controversy on these basic propositions. Respondents say that the very purpose of vindicating the right to vote justifies the recount procedures now at issue. The question before us, however, is whether the recount procedures the Florida Supreme Court has adopted are consistent with its obligation to avoid arbitrary and disparate treatment of the members of its electorate.

Much of the controversy seems to revolve around ballot cards designed to be perforated by a stylus but which, either through error or deliberate omission, have not been perforated with sufficient precision for a machine to register the perforations. In some cases, a piece of the card—a chad—is hanging, say, by two corners. In other cases there is no separation at all, just an indentation.

The Florida Supreme Court has ordered that the intent of the voter be discerned from such ballots. For purposes of resolving the equal protection challenge, it is not necessary to decide whether the Florida Supreme Court had the authority under the legislative scheme for resolving election disputes to define what a legal vote is and to mandate a manual recount implementing that definition. The recount mechanisms implemented in response to the decisions of the Florida Supreme Court do not satisfy the minimum requirement for nonarbitrary treatment of voters necessary to secure the fundamental right. Florida's basic command for the count of legally cast votes is to consider the "intent of the voter.". . . This is objectionable as an abstract proposition and a starting principle. The problem inheres in the absence of specific standards to ensure its equal application. The formulation of uniform rules to determine intent based on these recurring circumstances is practicable and, we conclude, necessary.

The law does not refrain from searching for the intent of the actor in a multitude of circumstances; and in some cases the general command to ascertain intent is not susceptible to much further refinement. In this instance, however, the question is not whether to believe a witness but how to interpret the marks or holes or scratches on an inanimate object, a piece of cardboard or paper which, it is said, might not have registered as a vote during the machine count. The factfinder confronts a thing, not a person. The search for intent can be confined by specific rules designed to ensure uniform treatment.

The want of those rules here has led to unequal evaluation of ballots in various respects. . . . ("Should a county canvassing board count or not count a 'dimpled chad' where the voter is able to successfully dislodge the chad in every other contest on that ballot? Here, the county canvassing boards disagree.") As seems to have been acknowledged at oral argument, the standards for accepting or rejecting contested ballots might vary not only from county to county but indeed within a single county from one recount team to another. . . .

The State Supreme Court ratified this uneven treatment. It mandated that the recount totals from two counties, Miami-Dade and Palm Beach, be included in the certified total. . . . Yet each of the counties used varying standards to determine what was a legal vote. Broward County used a more forgiving standard than Palm Beach

County, and uncovered almost three times as many new votes, a result markedly disproportionate to the difference in population between the counties.

In addition, the recounts in these three counties were not limited to so-called undervotes but extended to all of the ballots. The distinction has real consequences. A manual recount of all ballots identifies not only those ballots which show no vote but also those which contain more than one, the so-called overvotes. Neither category will be counted by the machine. This is *not* a trivial concern. At oral argument, respondents estimated there are as many as 110,000 overvotes statewide. As a result, the citizen whose ballot was not read by a machine because he failed to vote for a candidate in a way readable by a machine may still have his vote counted in a manual recount; on the other hand, the citizen who marks two candidates in a way discernible by the machine will not have the same opportunity to have his vote count, even if a manual examination of the ballot would reveal the requisite indicia of intent. Furthermore, the citizen who marks two candidates, only one of which is discernible by the machine, will have his vote counted even though it should have been read as an invalid ballot. The State Supreme Court's inclusion of vote counts based on these variant standards exemplifies concerns with the remedial processes that were under way. . . .

Seven Justices of the Court agree that there are constitutional problems with the recount ordered by the Florida Supreme Court that demand a remedy. . . . The only disagreement is as to the remedy. Because the Florida Supreme Court has said that the Florida Legislature intended to obtain the safe-harbor benefits of 3 U.S.C. § 5, Justice Breyer's proposed remedy—remanding to the Florida Supreme Court for its ordering of a constitutionally proper contest until December 18—contemplates action in violation of the Florida Election Code and, hence could not be part of an "appropriate" order authorized by [Ed.: Florida law]. . . .

None are more conscious of the vital limits on judicial authority than are the Members of this Court, and none stand more in admiration of the Constitution's design to leave the selection of the president to the people, through their legislatures, and to the political sphere. When contending parties invoke the process of the courts, however, it becomes our unsought responsibility to resolve the federal and constitutional issues the judicial system has been forced to confront.

## Judgment and Result

The judgment of the Supreme Court of Florida is reversed, and the case is remanded for further proceedings not inconsistent with this opinion.

## Dissenting Opinion

Justice Stevens with whom Justice Ginsburg and Justice Breyer join, dissenting.

The Constitution assigns to the States the primary responsibility for determining the manner of selecting the presidential electors. . . . When questions arise about the meaning of state laws, including election laws, it is our settled practice to accept the opinions of the highest courts of the States as providing the final answers. On rare occasions, however, either federal statutes or the Federal Constitution may require federal judicial intervention in state elections. This is not such an occasion. . . .

It hardly needs stating that Congress, pursuant to 2 U.S.C. § 5, did not impose any affirmative duties upon the States that their governmental branches could "violate." Rather, § 5 provides a safe harbor for States to select electors in contested elections "by judicial or other methods" established by laws prior to the election day. Section 5, like Article II, assumes the involvement of the state judiciary in interpreting state election laws and resolving election disputes under those laws. Neither § 5 nor Article II grants federal judges any special authority to substitute their views for those of the state judiciary on matters of state law. . . .

What must underlie petitioners' entire federal assault on the Florida election procedures is an unstated lack of confidence in the impartiality and capacity of the state judges who would make the critical decisions if the vote count were to proceed. Otherwise, their position is wholly without merit. The endorsement of that position by the majority of this Court can only lend credence to the most cynical appraisal of the work of judges throughout the land. It is confidence in the men and women who administer the judicial system that is the true backbone of the rule of law. Time will one day heal the wound to that confidence that will be inflicted by today's decision. One thing, however, is certain. Although we may never know with complete certainty the identity of the winner of this year's presidential election, the identity of the loser is perfectly clear. It is the Nation's confidence in the judge as an impartial guardian of the rule of law.

## Questions

1. Was the matter which the Supreme Court's majority decided a "legal" or "political" matter? One immediately can see how one area bleeds into the other, particularly in a close election.
2. Did the majority decision respect states' rights or undercut states' rights? Is there not a certain irony in the fact that the justices who sided with the majority opinion were states righters even though their decision arguably undercut a state judiciary and state legislature?
3. Following the *Bush v. Gore* decision, separate organizations reviewed the ballots and found that if there had been a recount in the counties Gore had wanted recounted, Bush would still have prevailed. The studies also showed that a statewide recount—which Gore did not ask for—would have favored Gore.

*Relationship between Legislative Law and Court Law.* As noted previously, both courts and legislatures make law. Courts (federal and state) may make law in any area subject to constitutional limits. Court lawmaking is generally subordinate to legislatively made law. Judges may have spent years developing an elaborate rule in thousands of cases, only to see it reversed by legislative passage of one statute. For example, judges decided thousands of cases over many years that said workers injured on the job could recover from their employer only if the employer were at fault. But in the early twentieth century, state legislatures passed workers' compensation statutes. These laws eliminated fault as the basis for worker recovery from employers. In effect, legislatures repealed judge-made law simply by passing a statute, indicating that legislatively made law is usually superior to judge-made law. The exception occurs when legislatures pass statutes that courts later declare unconstitutional.

## Chapter Summary

Political sources of law include monarchy, oligarchy, and democracy. Democracy can be organized into a federal system. Federalism means dual sovereigns. Do not confuse federal government (one of the sovereigns in federalism) with federalism (government with two sovereigns).

Law also comes from institutions such as courts and legislatures. Each sovereign in a federal system has a court system; thus, along with a federal court system, each state has its own court system.

Law made by courts is called common law. Laws made by Congress are called statutes, acts, or resolutions.

Rules of statutory construction help judges clear up problems created by poorly drafted statutes.

## Manager's Ethical Dilemma

Monica Long was the product liability manager for the Cotter Ladder Company. One of Monica's major headaches was liability exposure brought on by the product they made: Stepladders. Every year the Cotter Ladder Company was sued by individuals after falls from Cotter-built ladders that resulted in serious injury or even death.

One aspect of her legal environment that baffled Monica was that a consumer in California and a consumer in Florida could each fall off a Cotter ladder, sustain the same injuries, and yet the rules that governed whether they recovered or not were significantly different. It seemed unfair to both the injured consumers and to the Cotter Ladder Company. Why should it make a difference whether the consumer were injured in one state instead of another with respect to the consumer's ability to recover? Also, the crazy quilt of different state liability laws made it difficult for the Cotter Ladder Company to predict its liability exposure. Monica had heard that a federal product liability bill had been introduced in Congress. If passed, this bill would wipe out the different state product liability laws and replace them with uniform product liability standards in all states. Thus, consumers injured in exactly the same way in different states would stand a good chance of having the same result in their cases. This law seemed like equal justice to Monica. Should she support the federal product liability law?

## DISCUSSION QUESTIONS

1. Some private, "rebel" organizations—often "hate" groups—have established their own courts in which they kidnap people and try such individuals for violating the rebel groups' laws. These groups hand out punishment—often killing offenders. How can these groups claim to be legitimate courts? How do such courts differ from those established by alternative dispute resolution (ADR)? Should a hate group have the same rights as a bank or stockbroker to establish ADR?

2. If a manufacturing company sells its products in all fifty states, would it prefer regulation by state law or by federal law?

3. The two ideas of federalism and separation of powers are cornerstones in the U.S. government. Separation of powers refers to the idea that, at a particular level of government, lawmaking power is separated among the executive, judicial, and legislative branches. Each branch acts as a check on the other, thereby preventing any one branch from abusing its power. What is the idea behind federalism? Does a similarity exist between federalism and separation of powers? Do improved communications and mobility of the U.S. population bring into question the continued validity of federalism? Did the U.S. Supreme Court, in telling President Nixon to turn over the White House tapes to government authorities, illustrate federalism or separation of powers?

4. Several times in recent years, Congress has attempted to cut back on federal court jurisdiction, largely in response to federal court decisions that some legislators disagreed with, such as enlarging the rights of the criminally accused, desegregating schools, busing students to achieve racial balance, and prohibiting prayer in public schools. What were the original reasons federal courts were set up? To make popular decisions? Which branch of government caters to popularity: courts or legislatures?

5. Must a country have courts? The Appellate Division of the New York Supreme Court said, "It is a fundamental obligation of every civilized government to provide a system of impartial courts which can fairly adjudicate disputes involving its citizens." The case involved a suit by the country of Iran against the former Empress of Iran for alleged wrongs she committed against the people of Iran while in Iran [*Islamic Republic of Iran v. Pahlavi*, 94 A.D. 2d 374, 464 N.Y.S.2d 487 (1983)].

## INFOTRAC KEYWORDS

**Use your InfoTrac password to look up articles on http://www.infotrac-college.com**

Keywords: *monarchy, oligarchy, anarchy, federalism.*

For suggested readings, please visit this book's Web site at **http://fisher.westbuslaw.com** (click on "Internet Applications").

# SETTLING LEGAL DISPUTES: ALTERNATIVE DISPUTE RESOLUTION AND CIVIL LAWSUITS

*"LAWSUIT: A MACHINE YOU GO INTO AS A PIG AND COME OUT AS A SAUSAGE."*

— **AMBROSE BIERCE,** THE DEVIL'S DICTIONARY

Abraham Lincoln, a lawyer at one point in his career, once said, "Avoid lawsuits." Lincoln's advice is sound for businesses and all types of people because lawsuits are often expensive, slow, and emotionally draining. They may cause long-lasting bad will and yet not end the way the parties desire. But people do have disputes about contracts, auto accidents, and many other matters that need resolution. This chapter is organized on the theme that a lawsuit should only be used as a last resort to settle disputes. Thus, the first topic is alternative dispute resolution followed by selection of a lawyer, a discussion of attorney fees, and a survey of civil lawsuits.

## ALTERNATIVE DISPUTE RESOLUTION

Courts are the usual means of settling legal disputes. **Alternative dispute resolution (ADR)** refers to any means of settling legal disputes without using courts. The several types of ADR include conciliation, mediation, and arbitration.

### CONCILIATION

**Conciliation** means that the two disputants get together and work things out between themselves without having anyone else present. This form of ADR generally works when the parties really want to end the dispute. Conciliation is private and minimizes publicity.

## MEDIATION

**Mediation** involves using a neutral third party, called a mediator, to hear both sides of the dispute and to communicate between the disputants and reach a compromise. Mediators do not have to be lawyers (although many are) or be trained in the law, for their advice and decisions are nonbinding. *Nonbinding* means the parties do not have to follow the mediator's suggestion. Mediation can be used in most types of disputes *if* both disputants agree to it. In the international arena, for example, Pope John Paul II acted as a mediator between two South American countries. If a mediator has prestige and unquestioned goodwill, the disputants and public tend to attach great significance to the mediator's suggestions.

## ARBITRATION

**Arbitration** is the formal submission of a dispute to a nonjudicial third person. Arbitration can be nonbinding or binding, although typically it is binding. *Binding* means the parties must do what the arbitrator requires.

*The Web site of the American Arbitration Association is found at* **http://www.adr.org**

People are usually not forced to arbitrate their disputes unless they have, by contract, agreed to do so or if a statute requires it. Agreements to arbitrate can be made anytime, even after the dispute occurs.

In effect, an arbitrator is a privately hired judge. Sometimes more than one arbitrator is used. Arbitrators do not have to be lawyers, although some are. They follow their own procedures and rules of evidence, which are usually more relaxed than those used in courts. Arbitrators can also make up their own rules of substantive law, within limits. Arbitrators give decisions, called **awards**, which bind the parties. Courts will enforce an arbitrator's decision just as though it were a court's judgment, even though the arbitrator did not follow the rules of law a court would have applied. Arbitrators also do not have to give reasons for their opinions, although they usually do. A period follows the filing in court of an arbitrator's award during which a party can raise an objection. However, courts give only limited review to an arbitrator's decisions and will overturn these decisions for only a few reasons: if arbitrator fraud or misconduct exists (such as the taking of a bribe); if a decision is given on an issue not submitted for arbitration; or if arbitrators go beyond their powers in fashioning an award.

## ADVANTAGES OF ADR

ADR is usually faster, cheaper, and less emotionally draining than a lawsuit in court because no jury is needed to settle fact issues. Although no judge who is a governmental employee presides, ADR usually involves using a neutral third party who serves as both judge and jury. Some forms of ADR, such as "Rent-a-Judge" programs (usually a form of arbitration), use neutral third parties called judges, who in actuality are not publicly employed judges, to settle the case. Such individuals usually work on an hourly rate.

Litigation costs can be lower with ADR than for conventional lawsuits, which can be a major consideration when attorney fees run more than $100 per hour.

Such matters as discovery, pretrial hearings, legal research, and brief writing are part of an attorney's services and costs.

One major advantage of ADR is its privacy. The parties' "dirty laundry" is not publicly exposed. Competitors (other than the parties themselves) and others cannot, therefore, obtain information that would damage or embarrass the parties. This privacy can be particularly important in commercial matters involving trade secrets or other intellectual property.

ADR also does not establish a precedent as do published judicial decisions, which is either an advantage or disadvantage, depending on whether the decision is favorable or unfavorable to one's interests.

## DISADVANTAGES OF ADR

ADR has several drawbacks. First, it is an attack on the jury system. Juries are a time-honored way of determining facts: Did the doctor sew the sponge into the plaintiff's stomach? Did the stockbroker churn the client's account? Juries are asked to resolve these sorts of fact questions. None of the ADR methods covered here uses a jury. Insurance companies, physicians accused of medical malpractice, and other defendants frequently lambaste lawyers and courts in media ads complaining about million-dollar verdicts. Such ads seldom mention, though, that it is juries, not lawyers or judges, that render these verdicts. Juries, average men and women drawn from the community, hear the facts under rules of evidence, subject to the right of cross examination and rebuttal, and then award a plaintiff damages. By complaining about jury verdicts, are critics really saying that plaintiffs should not be able to recover fully as judged by a jury of their peers? Also, for every horror story about runaway juries, many more stories can be told of skeptical juries that give plaintiffs little or nothing. Consider the *Elena DeZavala* case in this chapter to see what a Tennessee jury awarded a nine-year-old, orphaned when a driver killed her father in an auto accident. This is a more typical result than the million-dollar verdict.

A second ADR weakness is that it substitutes amateurs for professionals when it displaces lawyers and judges with mediators or arbitrators who often are not lawyers. Crucial problems in settling disputes may be ignored; questionable evidence is admitted because rules of evidence are not followed; and careless, amateurish conduct of the process is the order of the day.

Third, arbitration agreements (a form of ADR) often appear to favor one of the disputants over the other. This lack of objectivity is often due to how the arbitrator is selected. For example, in the *Shearson/American Express* case, a customer had to select arbitrators from securities industry sources (the National Association of Securities Dealers in New York or American Stock Exchange arbitrators) instead of independent arbitrators. Such arbitrators often favor brokers.

A fourth drawback to ADR settlements is that they can always be challenged in court. This means that arbitration, for instance, may not be faster and cheaper than suing in court. The parties can refuse to obey the arbitrator's award, which forces the other party to court to enforce the award. Even though court review of arbitrators' awards is not *de novo* (is not "from scratch," where every bit of evidence is reintroduced) but is limited, court review takes time and adds costs. In effect, arbitration merely adds another layer of dispute settlement overhead to the court system.

Fifth, arbitration "agreements" are not knowingly entered; that is, people often do not realize they are agreeing to arbitration when they sign complicated contracts for something else, such as hiring a stockbroker. The agreement to arbitrate is often buried in the fine print and is never read by the client. ADR should be permitted, but such agreements should also be knowingly entered by *both* parties with a full understanding of what they mean.

## TYPES OF DISPUTES FOR ADR SETTLEMENT

ADR can be used to settle most types of legal disputes, such as breach of contract matters, divorce, international disputes between multinational businesses, and labor disputes. Tort disputes seem less likely ADR candidates because plaintiffs prefer juries rather than arbitrators to assess their damages.

## ADR UNDER THE FEDERAL ARBITRATION ACT OF 1925[1]

ADR is not new. It was recognized in 1925 when Congress enacted the Federal Arbitration Act. This act required courts to enforce arbitration agreements, just as they would any other contract. This law thus encouraged and established a federal policy promoting arbitration as a form of ADR. The Federal Arbitration Act was a legislative attempt to reverse common law (judicial) hostility to arbitrators.

## HOSTILITY TO ADR IN BROKERAGE DISPUTES: *WILKO V. SWAN*

Stockbrokers soon recognized possible advantages of ADR. By putting arbitration provisions in customers' brokerage contracts (when the brokerage contract was opened) and controlling who were the arbitrators, brokers could, in effect, "stack the deck" against customers and thereby minimize customer claims against the brokers. However, in 1953 the Supreme Court decided in *Wilko v. Swan* that broker-customer predispute arbitration agreements were invalid because they deprived customers of their right to select a court instead of arbitration. The Supreme Court in *Wilko* was skeptical of arbitrators' ability to protect investors' rights under federal securities laws.

## SUPREME COURT REASSESSMENT OF ARBITRATION

In the 1980s, several U.S. Supreme Court cases upheld arbitration provisions in contracts. In *Southland v. Keating* (1983) the Court enforced a franchise agreement arbitration clause. Support for arbitration was again forthcoming in *Mitsubishi Motors v. Soler Chrysler-Plymouth*. In this 1985 decision the Supreme Court stated that it was "well past the time when judicial suspicion of the desirability of arbitration and of the competence of arbitration tribunals inhibited the development of arbitration as an alternative means of dispute resolution."

The *Mitsubishi* and *Southland* cases dealt with arbitration in areas other than brokerage contracts. *The Shearson/American Express v. McMahon* case in 1987 resulted in the Supreme Court's upholding a predispute brokerage arbitration agreement regarding customer claims under the Securities Exchange Act of 1934. This decision was made even in the presence of considerable evidence of brokers' abuse of customers' accounts and a vigorous dissent by Justice Blackmun.

---

[1] The authors acknowledge reliance on Bedell & Bosch, "The Rodriguez Decision: A New Tradition in the Arbitration of Securities Disputes," 18 Securities *Regulation Law Journal* 53 (1990).

Another predispute arbitration agreement—this time under the Securities Act of 1933—was at issue in *Rodriguez de Quijas v. Shearson/American Express, Inc.* In this case the Supreme Court upheld such predispute arbitration agreements in 1989 and expressly overruled *Wilko v. Swan.*

In recent years employers and businesses such as retailers and banks have routinely placed arbitration clauses in employment contracts as well as contracts for the sale of goods and services. Then, if the consumer has a dispute with the employer, retailer, or bank, they must go to arbitration instead of going to court to settle the matter.

Courts generally uphold arbitration clauses in contracts when challenged on grounds of unconscionability if such clauses meet both procedural and substantive fairness tests. Although drawing the line between procedural and substantive fairness is not always easy, procedural fairness involves an examination of the setting when the contract was entered: Did the parties have a chance to think about what they were doing? Were high pressure tactics used to "close" the deal? Did the agreement have a lot of fine print? How balanced was the parties' bargaining power? Generally, did both parties have a meaningful choice?

Substantive fairness involves an examination of the rules in the arbitration itself; matters such as independence of the arbitrator from the parties, convenience of the location and timing of the arbitration, even-handedness of the duty to arbitrate (some arbitration agreements require consumers or employees but not business sellers or employers to arbitrate), what remedies the arbitrator can award, and whether the arbitration requires excessive fees of the parties as a condition to arbitrate. Various consumer and employer groups are currently trying to articulate standards for fair arbitration, but as of this writing, no universal standards are in place.

A strong public policy favors arbitration. Recently, however, in California and New York, where many U.S. legal developments tend to originate, courts have invalidated some arbitration agreements and allowed the plaintiff (usually the consumer or employee) to go directly to court, bypassing arbitration, or have modified the arbitration to make it fairer. The grounds for invalidation or modification include adhesion contracts, unconscionability, or the lack of consent (no "meeting of the minds" of the parties on the matter). Courts examining the unconscionability of arbitration agreements focus on both procedural and substantive fairness issues. In *Brower v. Gateway 2000*, a court rewrote an arbitration agreement on grounds it was unconscionable.

## Brower v. Gateway 2000
Appellate Division of New York Supreme Court
676 N.Y.S.2d 569 (1998)

### Background and Facts

Brower and other consumers purchased consumers and software products from defendant Gateway 2000 through a direct sales system, by phone and mail order. As of July 3, 1995, it was Gateways practice to include, along with the merchandise, a copy of its Standard Terms and Conditions Agreement and any relevant warranties for the products in the shipment. The Agreement begins with a "NOTE TO CUSTOMER," which provides, in slightly larger print than the remainder of the document, in a box that spans the width of the page: "This document contains Gateway 2000s Standard Terms and Conditions. By keeping your Gateway 2000 computer system beyond thirty (30) days after the date of delivery, you accept these Terms and Conditions." This document consists of 16 paragraphs, and, as is relevant to this appeal, paragraph 10 of the agreement entitled "DISPUTE RESOLUTION," reads as follows:

"Any dispute or controversy arising out of or relating to this Agreement or its interpretation shall be settled exclusively and finally by arbitration. The arbitration shall be conducted in accordance with the Rules of Conciliation and Arbitration of the International Chamber of Commerce. The arbitration shall be conducted in Chicago, Illinois, U.S.A. before a sole arbitrator. Any award rendered in any such arbitration proceeding shall be final and binding on each of the parties, and judgment may be entered thereon in a court of competent jurisdiction."

Plaintiffs brought this action on behalf of themselves and others similarly situated for compensatory and punitive damages, alleging deceptive sales practices in seven causes of action, including breach of warranty, breach of contract, fraud, and unfair trade practices. In particular, the allegations focused on Gateways representations and advertising that promised "service when you need it," including around-the-clock free technical support, free software technical support, and certain on-site services. According to plaintiffs, not only were they unable to avail themselves of this offer because it was virtually impossible to get through to a technician, but also Gateway continued to advertise this claim notwithstanding numerous complaints and reports about the problem.

Insofar as is relevant to Brower and the other plaintiffs, who purchased their computers after July 3, 1995, Gateway moved to dismiss the complaint based on the arbitration clause in the Agreement. Brower and other plaintiffs argued that the arbitration clause is unconscionable under UCC 2-302 and an unenforceable contract of adhesion. Specifically, they claimed that the provision was obscure; that a customer could not reasonably be expected to appreciate or investigate its meaning and effect; that the International Chamber of Commerce (ICC) was not a forum commonly used for consumer matters; and that because ICC headquarters were in France, it was particularly difficult to locate the organization and its rules. To illustrate just how inaccessible the forum was, Brower advised the court that the ICC was not registered with the Secretary of State, that efforts to locate and contact the ICC had been unsuccessful, and that apparently the only way to attempt to contact the ICC was through the U.S. Council for International Business, with which the ICC maintained some sort of relationship.

In support of their arguments, Brower and other plaintiffs submitted a copy of the ICCs Rules of Conciliation and Arbitration and contended that the cost of ICC arbitration was prohibitive, particularly given the amount of the typical consumer claim involved. For example, a claim of less than $50,000 required advance fees of $4,000 (more than the cost of most Gateway products), of which the $2,000 registration fee was nonrefundable even if the consumer prevailed at the arbitration. Consumers would also incur travel expenses disproportionate to the damages sought, which plaintiffs counsel estimated would not exceed $1,000 per customer in this action, as well as bear the cost of Gateways legal fees if the consumer did not prevail at the arbitration; in this respect, the ICC rules follow the "loser pays" rule used in England. Also, although Chicago was designated as the site of the actual arbitration, all correspondence must be sent to ICC headquarters in France.

The IAS court dismissed the complaint as to plaintiff/appellants based on the arbitration clause in the Agreements delivered with their computers.

## Body of Opinion

**Justice Milonas.** . . . With respect to plaintiff/appellants claim that the arbitration claim is unenforceable as a contract of adhesion, in that it involved no choice or negotiation on the part of the consumer but was a "take it or leave it" proposition . . . we find that this argument, too, was properly rejected by the IAS court.

Although the parties clearly do not possess equal bargaining power, this factor alone does not invalidate the contract as one of adhesion. As the IAS court observed, with the ability to make the purchase elsewhere and the express option to return the goods, the consumer is not in a "take it or leave it" position at all; if any term of the agreement is unacceptable to the consumer, he or she can easily buy a competitors product instead—either from a retailer or directly from the manufacturer—and reject Gateways agreement by returning the merchandise. . . . The consumer has thirty days to make that decision. Within that time, the consumer can inspect the goods and examine and seek clarification of the terms of the agreement: until those thirty days have elapsed, the consumer has the unqualified right to return the merchandise, because the goods or terms are unsatisfactory or for no reason at all.

. . . That a consumer does not read the agreement or thereafter claims he or she failed to understand or appreciate some term therein does not invalidate the contract any more than such claim would undo a contract formed under other circumstances. . . .

Finally, we turn to appellant/plaintiffs argument that the IAS court should have declared the contract unenforceable, pursuant to UCC 2-302, on the ground that the arbitration clause is unconscionable due to the unduly burdensome procedure and cost for the individual consumer. The IAS court found that while a class action lawsuit such as the one herein, may be a less costly alternative to the arbitration (which is generally less costly than litigation), that does not alter the binding effect of the arbitration clause contained in the agreement. . . .

As a general matter, under New York law, unconscionability requires a showing that a contract is "both procedurally and substantively unconscionable when made." . . . That is, there must be "some showing of an absence of meaningful choice on the part of one of the parties together with contract terms which are unreasonably favorable to the other party." . . . The Acco court (in another case) took pains to note, however, that the purpose of this doctrine is not to redress the inequality between the parties but simply to insure that the more powerful party cannot "surprise the other party with some overly oppressive term." . . .

As to the procedural element, a court will look to the contract formation process to determine if in fact one party lacked any meaningful choice in entering into the contract taking into consideration such factors as the setting of the transaction, the experience and education of the party claiming unconscionability, whether the contract contained "fine print," whether the seller used "high pressure tactics" and any disparity in the parties bargaining power. . . . None of these factors supports plaintiff/appellants claims here. . . . The Agreement itself, which is entitled in large print "STANDARD TERMS AND CONDITIONS AGREEMENT," consists of only three pages and 16 paragraphs, all of which appear in the same size print. Moreover, despite appellant/plaintiffs claims to the contrary, the arbitration clause is in no way "hidden" or "tucked away" within a complex document of inordinate length, nor is the option of returning the merchandise, to avoid the contract, somehow a "precarious" one. . . .

With respect to the substantive element . . . we do not find that the possible inconvenience of the chosen site (Chicago) alone rises to the level of unconscionability. We do find, however, that the excessive cost factor that is necessarily entailed in arbitrating before the ICC is unreasonable and surely serves to deter the individual consumer from invoking the process. . . . Barred from resorting to the courts by the arbitration clause in the first instance, the designation of a financially prohibitive forum effectively bars consumers from this forum as well; consumers are thus left with no forum at all in which to resolve a dispute. . . .

Gateways brief includes the text of a new arbitration agreement that it claims has been extended to all customers, past, present, and future. . . . The new arbitration agreement provides for the consumers choice of the AAA [American Arbitration Association] or the ICC as the arbitral body and the designation of any location for the arbitration by agreement of the parties, which "shall not be unreasonably withheld." It also provides telephone numbers for information regarding the "organizations and their procedures."

As noted, however, plaintiff/appellants complain that the AAA fees are also excessive and thus in no way have they accepted defendants offer . . . because they make the same claim as to the ICC, the issue of unconscionability is not rendered moot, as defendant suggests. We cannot determine on this record whether the AAA process and costs would be so "egregiously oppressive" that they, too, would be unconscionable. . . .

## Judgment and Result

The New York Supreme Court order dismissing plaintiff/appellants complaint on the ground that a valid agreement to arbitrate had been entered was modified by the New York Supreme Court, Appellate Division. The appellate court vacated the part of the trial court order requiring arbitration before the International Chamber of Commerce and left the parties to seek appointment of a substitute arbitrator under the Federal Arbitration Act.

## Questions

1. When and under what circumstances does a customer enter an arbitration agreement with the seller of a computer?
2. Why did the appellate court refuse to hold that the arbitration provision was an adhesion contract?
3. Was the arbitration contract in *Brower v. Gateway* unconscionable? Was the arbitration provision procedurally or substantively unconscionable?
4. If the arbitration provision was substantively unconscionable, why did the court end up ordering arbitration?

## SEC Rules Regarding Arbitration

Concern about the fairness of predispute arbitration clauses in customer brokerage agreements following the *McMahon* case led the SEC to regulate such forms of ADR. Here are two regulated matters. Introductory language in customer agreements must explain the effect of the arbitration clause; that is, brokers' customers give up the right to sue their broker in court, accept that arbitration is final, accept that the arbitrator does not have to give reasons for its award or make fact findings, and accept that the arbitration panel usually will have some persons who have been stockbrokers. Second, these disclosures must be conspicuous in the customer's agreement, and another warning must appear above the signature line pointing out where the arbitration provision is in the brokerage contract. Also, the SEC refuses to allow arbitration agreements to deprive customers of remedies they could have gotten in court. For example, if punitive damages are possible in court, the arbitration clause may not prevent the stock buyer from obtaining them. One matter the SEC regs do not require is that customers, when they open an account, be given an option to sue brokers in court or seek arbitration.

Keep in mind that the *McMahon* and *Rodriguez* cases expressly uphold arbitration of Securities Exchange Act or Securities Act claims against brokers—not against other businesses. However, these cases, coupled with the 1925 Federal Arbitration Act and the *Southland* and *Mitsubishi* cases, clearly do signal greater Supreme Court approval of arbitration (ADR) in many contexts.

## THE ATTORNEY'S ROLE IN THE LEGAL SYSTEM

Three objectives of law are justice, speed, and economy. They can be achieved by having professionals, called *attorneys* or *lawyers*, advocate others' claims.

### THE REASON FOR ATTORNEYS

The social justification for attorneys' existence occurs when they raise appropriate, persuasive arguments on behalf of their client. These arguments expose judges to better ideas, which can lead to sound rules of law and reasonable precedent for future cases. Also, because attorneys are familiar with court procedures, speed is potentially promoted. The qualifying word *potentially* is added because attorneys may also use their skills to delay matters to benefit their clients.

For information about the American Bar Association and its members, go to **http://www.abanet.org**

### ATTORNEY FEES

A sensitive issue concerning attorneys is the manner and amount of payment for their professional services. In civil cases, attorneys can be paid by fixed or contingent fees. Under the fixed-fee arrangement attorneys tell the client how much the service will cost before it is given. The fixed fee is used for much nonlitigation legal work, such as drafting contracts, wills, trusts, and organizing partnerships and corporations. Attorney ethics only allow fixed fees—not contingent fees—for criminal cases.

**Contingent fees** mean that one's attorney gets a fee only after winning the lawsuit or a settlement acceptable to the client. One advantage of contingent fees is that a poor person with a potentially large claim could get the best lawyer in town. A contingent-fee option is available only in those cases in which one can win money. Thus, such fees are possible for plaintiffs but not for defendants, unless they bring counterclaims.

In the United States, the *American rule* is that each party pays its own attorney fees no matter who wins the case, unless a statute or contract provides otherwise. This rule is to be contrasted with the *English rule,* under which the loser pays the winner's attorney fees. In effect, the English rule discourages litigation.

*Some Aspects of Attorney Fees.*  The economics of the practice of law are not well understood by the general public. TV programs and movies would have you believe that all attorneys drive BMWs, live in swanky houses or condos, wear $1,000 suits, and work in fancy offices. The reality is different.

Types of law practice include corporate, tax, trial, family law, poverty law, environmental law, general practice, and many others. Income expectations can vary widely, depending on what type of law one practices and where one practices it. One hears about $1 million judgments and concludes that all lawyers must be experiencing such success. However, consider that most lawsuits end with a winner and a loser. In such a case, the attorneys for one party will get no fee, assuming the matter is handled on a contingency basis.

Also, consider that attorneys who are in private practice have overhead expenses associated with running a law office, such as paying rent for an office, plus the costs for heating, lighting, secretarial help, a law library, bar association dues, Social Security taxes, income taxes, and health insurance for the attorney and office staff. Also, many law office personnel want child-care allowances, vacation pay, retirement plans, and flex time. All of these benefits cost money. Thus, when one hears of an attorney winning a $100,000 judgment for a client and asking the client for $33,333 (one-third of the fee), it is *not* all profit. This fee must pay for the expenses of the law firm.

Some argue that the 25 percent or 33 $^1/_3$ percent contingency fees are too high. However, consider the following: A Wall Street financial firm several years ago found that the amount paid to workers' compensation beneficiaries as a percentage of premium dollar going to insurance was 59 percent, meaning that the workers' compensation insurers had a 41 percent overhead—several percentage points higher than the contingent fees of attorneys. Also consider another fact: Most major universities in the United States impose an overhead charge of 40 to 60 percent on grants received by professors from the government or private foundations, a much higher overhead charge than attorneys. These examples suggest, though perhaps not conclusively, that the impression that attorneys are scalping the public is untrue. No doubt some are earning high incomes, but others make far more modest incomes.

## ATTORNEY-CLIENT CONTROL OF THE CASE

Most civil lawsuits are settled out of court when the plaintiff and defendant agree on an outcome and drop the suit at some point in the proceedings, often before trial. Settlement of a case can result in the plaintiff's attorney getting a lower fee either because fewer billable hours are spent on the client's behalf or because contingent fees often give the attorney a lower percentage of the settlement when the case does not go to trial.

A related issue concerns an attorney's duty to keep a client informed about the progress of a civil case, explain matters to clients so they can make informed decisions about the course the wish to follow (for example, accept a settlement offer or "roll the dice" and go for a larger jury verdict), and follow the client's wishes as to whether to accept a settlement offer. In *Re Disciplinary Action Against Crary* discusses duties attorneys owe their clients.

---

## In Re Disciplinary Action Against Crary
### Supreme Court of North Dakota
### 638 S.W.2d 23 (2002)

### Background and Facts

**Body of Opinion.** Paul Crary has been admitted to practice law in North Dakota since 1965. In 1997, Crary's wife became acquainted with 85-year-old Mary Harris. In August 1997, Harris asked to meet with Crary to prepare a new will. Crary drafted a will for Harris, and Harris also signed documents giving Crary power of attorney. Although Harris was not related to the Crarys, over the next two-and-one-half years Crary and his wife provided general assistance to Harris, including bringing her meals, taking her to medical appointments, and visiting her regularly.

In December 1997, Crary drafted a codicil [modification] to Harris's will. The codicil provided that Crary's wife would receive one-half of any funds which Harris's estate received from insurance companies, including annuities, life insurance policies, and other benefits. Crary's wife also was to receive a grandfather clock under the codicil to Harris's will.

Harris also asked Crary to help with her investments. In September 1997, Crary assisted Harris in purchasing a $42,000 annuity from the Independent Order of Foresters (IOF). In December 1997, Crary had Harris purchase a $10,000 annuity from IOF. In January 1998, Crary assisted Harris in cashing out an existing $100,000 annuity she had purchased just over a year earlier from Bankers Life and Casualty. Harris received approximately $92,000 in proceeds from the Bankers Life annuity, and used those funds to purchase a $90,000 annuity from IOF. Throughout this series of transactions Crary never told Harris he was an agent for IOF and received commissions on the annuities she purchased.

In September 1998, Harris gave Crary a check for $3,500. A note on the memo line of the check indicated it was a loan to Crary. Harris testified Crary promised to repay the loan within six months with 8 percent interest. Crary never repaid the $3,500 to Harris.

The relationship between Harris and the Crarys eventually soured, and in January 2000 Harris terminated Crary's legal representation. In October 2000, disciplinary counsel filed a petition for discipline. Following a hearing, the hearing panel concluded that: (1) the $3,500 payment to Crary was a loan which constituted a prohibited transaction in violation of N.D.R. Prof. Conduct 1.8(a); (2) the annuity purchases upon which Crary received commissions were prohibited transactions under N.D.R. Prof. Conduct 1.8(b); and (3) Crary's drafting of the codicil devising property to his wife was a prohibited transaction under N.D.R. Prof. Conduct 1.8(c). The hearing panel recommended that Crary be disbarred and ordered to pay restitution.

## Per curiam

The hearing panel found that Harris loaned $3,500 to Crary, that Crary failed to advise Harris she could consult another attorney about the transaction, and that Crary never repaid the $3.500. The panel concluded this transaction violated . . . 1.8(a), which provides:

(a) Except for standard commercial transactions involving products or services that the client generally markets to others, a lawyer shall not enter into a business, financial or property transaction with a client unless:
  1) The transaction is fair and reasonable to the client, and
  2) After consultation, including advice to seek independent counsel, the client consents to the transaction.

Harris testified that Crary asked to borrow the money and said he would pay it back within six months with 8 percent interest. She also testified he did not advise her to consult another attorney about the transaction. The check bears the notation "Lone (sic) to Paul Crary" on the memo line, and Harris testified she wrote that notation.

When Crary was asked at the hearing whether he advised Harris to seek independent counsel when he received the $3,500, he replied:

A. I don't recall telling her to seek another attorney about the $3,500. I told—do recall telling her to seek another attorney about anything that I was doing, you know.
Q. Okay. So then—
A. I mean, I recall telling her that she could seek another attorney if she wanted to. I don't remember how many times I said this, but—
Q. Okay. But specifically, in regard to this $3,500, which she indicates on the check is a loan, you did not tell her before she gives you this money she should go talk to another attorney?
A. Well, I don't recall telling her that, no.

At the hearing, Crary admitted that he asked Harris for the $3,500. When asked whether the $3,500 was a loan, Crary responded:

A. Well, at the—I don't remember at the time exactly how I looked at it, but when I started looking at my out-of-pocket expenses on the thing, I could see where it couldn't have been a loan, because I had out-of-pocket expenses of several thousand dollars on this deal.

Crary's response suggests that, in hindsight, he believed he was entitled to keep the $3,500 as compensation for the personal services and expenses he and his wife had provided to Harris. Although it is clear from the record that Crary and his wife did provide personal services to Harris, the record is equally clear that there was no agreement, express or implied, for payment for those services. Nor did Crary argue the $3,500 was for legal services or expenses he had provided.

On this record, we agree with the hearing panel's finding that the $3,500 was a loan to Crary at his request, that Crary did not advise Harris to seek independent counsel before entering into the transaction, and that Crary never repaid the loan. Crary's conduct violated . . . 1.8(a).

The hearing panel found that Crary, while acting as Harris's lawyer and with power of attorney, had Harris cash in other annuities and investments to purchase annuities from IOF without advising Harris that he was an agent for IOF and would receive commissions on those transactions, and without advising her to seek independent legal advice about the transactions. . . . N.D.R. Prof. Conduct 1.8(b) provides:

(b) Except as permitted or required in Rules 1.6 and 3.3, a lawyer shall not use information relating to representation of a client to the disadvantage of the client for purposes of furthering either the lawyer's or another person's interest unless after consultation, including advice to seek independent counsel, the client consents. . . .

Crary's assertion that Harris "must have known" he was an agent of IOF and receiving commissions merely because he procured the applications and assisted Harris in filling them out is not plausible. It would be commonplace for a person acting as counsel, and with power of attorney, to provide such assistance without being an agent of the company from which the annuities were being purchased. We agree with the hearing panel's findings that Crary did not advise Harris he was an agent of IOF, did not advise her he received commissions on the transactions, and did not advise her to seek independent counsel. Crary's conduct violated . . . 1.8(b). . . .

There was no dispute that Crary drafted the codicil, and that the Crarys were not related to Harris. The codicil to Harris will created a testamentary gift to Crary's wife of one-half of the value of "all moneys and funds which my estate shall receive from all insurance companies, including, but not limited to, annuities, life insurance policies and any other benefits." Crary's wife was also to receive a "large Grandfather's Clock." At various times after Harris signed the codicil the values of her annuities ranged between $130,000 and $180,000. . . .

At the hearing Crary suggested the codicil was prepared at Harris's request. When asked whether he told her she could consult another attorney, he responded, "I think I told her she could talk to someone else."

Unlike prohibitions in . . . 1.8(a) and (b), Rule 1.8(c) creates a bright-line rule. . . . Courts interpreting other states' adoptions of Rule 1.8(c) . . . have held that the rule creates a strict and explicit prohibition against attorneys drafting documents which result in a substantial gift to the attorney or the attorney's parent, child, sibling, or spouse. . . . Noting that Rule 1.8(c) "flatly prohibits a lawyer from preparing an instrument giving the lawyer a testamentary gift from a client" and "does not include any disclosure or fairness provisions," . . . the Supreme Court of Washington concluded:

. . . Nevertheless, the fact remains that the RPC explicitly prohibit exactly what Gillingham did, whether or not it was according to Liebel's instructions. Unlike the other rules governing conflicts of interest, the prohibition on testamentary gifts which are drafted by the lawyer-beneficiary does not include an exception when the client gives informed consent. . . .

We conclude Crary's conduct violated . . . 1.8(c).

## Judgment and Result

The Supreme Court of North Dakota disbarred Crary and ordered restitution to Harris of the loan and that Crary pay costs of the disciplinary proceedings.

## Questions

1. What is a "conflict of interest"?
2. Does the *Crary* case say that attorneys may not EVER sell annuities to their clients? How about clients making loans to their attorneys? How about drafting wills leaving items to their attorney even if the client consents?
3. What remedy does a client have when her attorney is dishonest?
4. Where did the clients go to complain about the poor service they had received from their attorney? Note that the client filed a grievance with the Disciplinary Commission several months after hiring Samai based on her inability to contact him. Does this claim undermine Samai's assertion that he could not find his client?
5. How might a client confer authority on an attorney to settle claims or sign legal documents without the client's actually knowing about such actions? What is a "power of attorney"?

## FINDING A LAWYER—ATTORNEY ADVERTISING

Until recently various rules (mainly state bar association ethical rules) outlawed attorney advertising. This rule actually discouraged many laypeople from seeking professional help from an attorney because they were unsure about the charge for an initial contact as well as other potential fees. Often people would ask a realtor, accountant, or insurance agent for legal help when they should have been asking a legal expert.

In 1977, the U.S. Supreme Court decided *Bates v. State Bar of Arizona*. This case held that states may *not* prevent truthful attorney ads concerning the availability and terms of routine legal services. Since the *Bates* case broke the ice, attorney ads in various media (TV, radio, and newspapers) are now common, and the public is better informed about fee basics. But the effect of this decision should not be exaggerated. It is highly unlikely that the president of IBM would thumb through the want ads to find a cheap lawyer to handle an antitrust case. Big users of legal services (corporations, unions, large organizations, and wealthy individuals) are largely unaffected by this decision.

In 1995 the U.S. Supreme Court took another look at attorney advertising. This time the case involved the propriety of truthful but possibly offensive contacting of accident victims or their immediate families immediately following an injury. The Florida Bar had imposed a thirty-day blackout period during which attorneys were forbidden to send targeted, direct-mail attorney solicitations to such persons. *Florida Bar v. Went For It* presents the Supreme Court's view on the legality of such restrictions on attorney advertising.

| **Florida Bar v. Went For It, Inc.** |
| :---: |
| U.S. Supreme Court |
| 115 S.Ct. 2371 (1995) |

## Background and Facts

In 1989, the Florida Bar completed a two-year study of the effects of lawyer advertising on public opinion. After conducting hearings, commissioning surveys, and reviewing extensive public commentary, the Bar determined that several changes to its advertising rules were in order. In late 1990, the Florida Supreme Court adopted the Bar's proposed amendments with some modifications. . . . Two of those amendments are at issue in this case. Rule 4-7.4 (b)(1) provides that "[a] lawyer shall not send, or knowingly permit to be sent, . . . a written communication to a prospective client for the purpose of obtaining professional employment if: (A) the written communication concerns an action for personal injury or wrongful death or otherwise relates to an accident or disaster involving the person to whom the communication addressed or a relative of that person, unless the accident or disaster occurred more than thirty days prior to the mailing of the communication." Rule 4-7.8(a) states that "[a] lawyer shall not accept referrals from a lawyer referral service unless the service: (1) engages in no communication with the public and in no direct contact with prospective clients in a manner that would violate the Rules of Professional Conduct if the communication or contact were made by the lawyer." Together, these rules create a brief thirty-day blackout period after an accident during which lawyers may not, directly or indirectly, single out accident victims or their relatives in order to solicit their business.

In March 1992, G. Stewart McHenry and his wholly owned lawyer referral service, Went For It, Inc., filed this action for declaratory and injunctive relief in the U.S. District Court challenging Rules 4-7.4(b)(1) and 4-7.8 as violative of the First and Fourteenth Amendments of the Constitution. McHenry alleged that he routinely sent targeted solicitations to accident victims or their survivors within 30 days after accidents and that he wished to continue doing so in the future. In October 1992 McHenry was disbarred for reasons unrelated to this suit and another Florida lawyer, John Blakely, was substituted.

The District Court rejected a Magistrate Judge's report and recommendations and entered judgment for plaintiffs relying on *Bates v. State Bar of Arizona*. The Eleventh Circuit affirmed on similar grounds. The Supreme Court granted certiorari.

## Body of Opinion

**Justice O'Connor.** Constitutional protection for attorney advertising, and for commercial speech generally, is of recent vintage. Until the mid-1970s, we adhered to the broad rule laid out in *Valentine v. Chrestensen* . . . (1942), that, while First Amendment guards against government restriction of speech in most contexts, "the Constitution imposes no such restraint on government as respects purely commercial advertising." In 1976, the Court

changed course. In *Virginia State Bd. of Pharmacy v. Virginia Citizens Consumer Council, Inc* . . . we invalidated a state statute barring pharmacists from advertising prescription drug prices. . . .

In *Virginia State Board*, the Court limited its holding to advertising by pharmacists. . . . One year later, however, the Court applied the Virginia State Board principles to invalidate a state rule prohibiting lawyers from advertising in newspapers and other media. In *Bates v. State Bar of Arizona* . . . the Court struck a ban on price advertising for what it deemed "routine" legal services. . . .

Nearly two decades of cases have built upon the foundation laid by *Bates*. It is now well established that lawyer advertising is commercial speech and, as such, is accorded a measure of First Amendment protection. . . . Such First Amendment protection is, of course, not absolute. . . . We have always been careful to distinguish commercial speech from speech at the First Amendment's core. "'Commercial speech [enjoys] a limited measure of protection, commensurate with its subordinate position in the scale of First Amendment values', and is subject to 'modes of regulation that might be impermissible in the realm of noncommercial expression.'" . . .

Mindful of these concerns, we engage in "intermediate" scrutiny of restrictions on commercial speech, analyzing them in the framework set forth in *Central Hudson Gas & Electric Corp. v. Public Service Comm'n. of N.Y.* (1980). Under *Central Hudson*, the government may freely regulate commercial speech that concerns unlawful activity or is misleading. . . . Commercial speech that falls into neither of those categories, like the advertising at issue here, may be regulated if the government satisfies a test consisting of three related prongs: first, the government must assert a substantial interest in support of its regulation; second, the government must demonstrate that the restriction on commercial speech directly and materially advances that interest; and third, the regulation must be "narrowly drawn. . . ."

We have little trouble crediting the Bar's interest as substantial. . . . Under *Central Hudson*'s second prong, the State must demonstrate that the challenged regulation "advances the Government's interest 'in a direct and material way.'" . . . That burden, we have explained, "is not satisfied by mere speculation and conjecture; rather, a governmental body seeking to sustain a restriction on commercial speech must demonstrate that the harms it recites are real and that its restriction will in fact alleviate them to a material degree.'" . . .

The direct mail solicitation regulation before us does not suffer from such infirmities. The Florida Bar submitted a 106-page summary of its two-year study of lawyer advertising and solicitation to the District Court. That summary contains data—both statistical and anecdotal—supporting the Bar's contentions that the Florida public views direct-mail solicitations in the immediate wake of accidents as an intrusion on privacy that reflects poorly upon the profession. As of June 1989, lawyers mailed 700,000 direct solicitations in Florida annually, 40 percent of which were aimed at accident victims or their survivors. . . . Significantly, 27 percent of direct-mail recipients reported that their regard for the legal profession and for the judicial process as a whole was "lower" as a result of receiving the direct mail. . . .

The anecdotal record mustered by the Bar is noteworthy for its breadth and detail. . . . The study summary also includes page upon page of excerpts from complaints of direct-mail recipients. . . . For example, a Florida citizen described how he was "'appalled and angered by the brazen attempt'" of a law firm to solicit him by letter shortly after he was injured and his fiance was killed in an auto accident. . . . Still another described as "'beyond comprehension'" a letter his nephew's family received the day of the nephew's funeral. . . . One citizen wrote, "'I consider the unsolicited contact from you after my child's accident to be of the rankest form of ambulance chasing and in incredibly poor taste. . . . I cannot begin to express with my limited vocabulary the utter contempt in which I hold you and your kind.'"

In light of this showing . . . we conclude that the Bar has satisfied the second prong of the *Central Hudson* test. . . .

Passing to *Central Hudson*'s third prong, we examine the relationship between the Florida Bar's interests and the means chosen to serve them . . . . Respondents' second point would have force if the Bar's rule were not limited to a brief period and if there were not many other ways for injured Floridians to learn about the availability of legal representation during that time . . . Florida permits lawyers to advertise on prime-time television and radio as well as in newspapers and other media. They may rent space on billboards. They may send untargeted letters to the general population, or to discrete segments thereof. There are, of course, pages upon pages devoted to lawyers in the Yellow Pages of Florida telephone directories. . . . We see no defect in Florida's regulation. . . .

## Judgment and Result

The judgment of the U.S. Court of Appeals was reversed. The Florida bar rules prohibiting lawyers from using direct mail to solicit personal injury clients within thirty days of an accident were valid.

## Questions

1. U.S. Supreme Court decisions starting with *Bates* have generally supported attorneys' rights to advertise truthful, nondeceptive services. Does this case impose a limit on attorney advertising? Why?
2. Could Florida attorneys contact accident victims during the thirty-day period immediately following an accident using less intrusive means such as billboards and television advertising? Are billboards and TV ads "targeted" or aimed at a "general" audience? Does their ruling suggest that the Supreme Court was bothered by the "targeted" aspect of the ads in *Went For It*?
3. Was the advertising in *Went For It* untruthful? Deceptive? Distasteful and degrading to the practice of a "great" profession?
4. What are the prongs of the *Central Hudson* test on regulation of nondeceptive, legal activity? Did the Court apply that test in *Went For It*?
5. Is the practice of law a profession or a business? What does the *Bates* decision suggest? How about the *Went For It* case?
6. Note that the *Went For It* decision was decided 5 to 4. What does this result indicate about the strength of the arguments competing for dominance in this case? How important was the empirical evidence? Does it suggest a link between positive law and philosophical positivism discussed in Chapter 1?

## ATTORNEYS AND THE MIDDLE CLASS

Today the public and the legal profession find themselves in an awkward situation: An oversupply of well-trained, capable attorneys to serve the public where the middle class must do without legal help because it cannot afford the price of counsel. The rich can afford to hire attorneys, and the poor qualify for legal aid, but the middle class is often underserved by the legal profession. The law of supply and demand seems to work for most types of professional compensation except for the legal profession's fee schedules, which remain fixed. In part, the high fees are due to the high costs of being an attorney, such as office rent, costs of maintaining a law library and office staff, and phone bills, to say nothing of regaining a return on the high costs and opportunity costs of a legal education.

*Judicare.* Whether relaxing regulations on attorney advertising will resolve the dual problem of the oversupply of attorneys and the legal underrepresentation of large segments of the population remains an imponderable issue. Two avenues seem worth exploring as ways to solve this middle-class underrepresentation problem: judicare and small claims courts with pro se litigants.

**Judicare** is a similar to the Medicare concept used to provide medical care for certain members of society, but judicare could help provide *legal* services for all segments of the population.

Many ways of implementing judicare exist. For example, everyone could be given an opportunity to receive a fixed-dollar amount of legal service each year. Under judicare, the government would provide a person with a voucher entitling that person to go to any lawyer and receive legal services up to the amount of the voucher. The attorney would then turn in the vouchers and receive payment from the government for services rendered. Judicare could also be implemented by a federal tax deduction or tax credit for expenditures for legal services during the tax year. Possibly, too, the state or federal government could establish large legal aid societies to render socialized legal services for all people or for those earning less than a certain income. The principal problem is whether society is willing to allocate its scarce resources for legal services rather than for other goods or services.

One answer to the problem of providing legal services to the middle class has come from the American Express Company. For a small monthly charge, a customer qualifies for a legal services plan. Some issues concerning these plans are what services are covered and not covered? What are the provider's qualifications? Are these services really needed? (It should be noted that most liability insurance policies provide attorney services if you are sued.)

*Pro se Litigants.* Another possible solution to the problem of the legally underrepresented lies in expansion of small claims courts where only **pro se litigants** are allowed. *Pro se* means "through oneself," and pro se litigants are people involved in lawsuits who act as their own attorneys.

*Small Claims Courts.* Small claims courts have been established in a number of states to allow people with small-dollar claims a forum to collect them without high court costs and attorney fees to deter the suit. Consider the plight of the newspaper carrier who has a customer with an unpaid bill of $25. This amount is hardly worth suing for in a conventional court because the fee to file a complaint is often $10 or $12, to say nothing of attorney fees necessary to get the complaint properly drafted and filed in the appropriate court. If conventional courts were to deal with such a matter, the newspaper carrier would be without remedy for all practical purposes.

Small claims courts, however, have simplified procedures. Litigants may not have attorneys, court costs are low, and the courts do provide a realistic solution to the problem of satisfying the needs of small claimants. But small claims courts are not problem free. A provision usually allows appeal of small claims court judgments to courts of record, so a recalcitrant defendant might effectively undercut many of the advantages of small claims courts simply by appealing the judgment to the higher court. This appeal could prompt the plaintiff to drop the matter.

## OVERVIEW OF CIVIL LAWSUITS

This part of the chapter deals with civil procedure or civil adjective law, which is law designed to guide a legal dispute through the civil justice system. The usual objective of civil lawsuits is compensatory, either to obtain money for wrongs done to one or to force someone to do or not do something.

Figure 4.1 shows some of the steps in a civil lawsuit. Each of these steps is discussed in the following paragraphs.

## WHO MAY SUE: THE STANDING ISSUE

*Standing* is a concept that limits who may sue to correct a legal wrong. In the usual civil case, the standing concept means that a person directly and tangibly injured by another may bring suit. For example, if B punches C in the nose, C is said to have standing to sue B for committing the legal wrong (here, battery) against C.

*Discussions of U.S. Supreme Court cases and justices can be found at http://oyez.nwu.edu*

One reason for the standing rule is to control the amount of litigation arising from a wrong by letting the injured party, but no one else, sue for recovery. The legal system does not exist to facilitate or encourage endless arguments, but rather to settle them. The belief is that the injured party (or the party allegedly injured)—not a stranger—is in the best position to determine whether to seek legal rectification of the wrong. Also, in federal courts, standing provides the possibility that the party in the lawsuit has something to lose and hence will argue and present issues with an intensity and vigor not found by a disinterested litigant who has no personal stake in the case outcome.

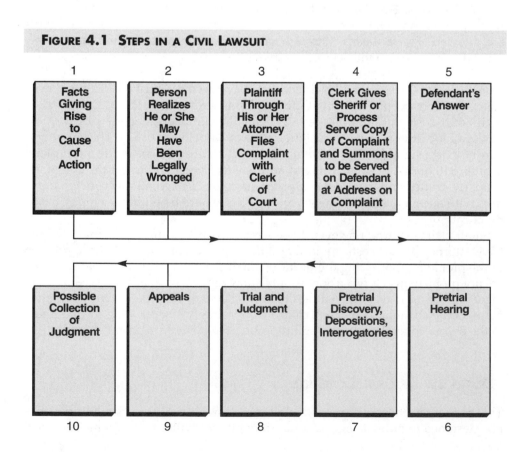

**FIGURE 4.1 STEPS IN A CIVIL LAWSUIT**

| 1 | 2 | 3 | 4 | 5 |
|---|---|---|---|---|
| Facts Giving Rise to Cause of Action | Person Realizes He or She May Have Been Legally Wronged | Plaintiff Through His or Her Attorney Files Complaint with Clerk of Court | Clerk Gives Sheriff or Process Server Copy of Complaint and Summons to be Served on Defendant at Address on Complaint | Defendant's Answer |

| 10 | 9 | 8 | 7 | 6 |
|---|---|---|---|---|
| Possible Collection of Judgment | Appeals | Trial and Judgment | Pretrial Discovery, Depositions, Interrogatories | Pretrial Hearing |

Standing issues usually do not arise in the average suit in which one private party sues another private party for breaking a contract or a leg. Rather, standing problems occur in lawsuits involving public law, such as where taxpayers sue the government to stop the spending of their tax dollars on programs with which the taxpayers disagree. Such suits are now usually tolerated, but at one time were barred by the standing rule.

Today, standing issues are prominent in environmental lawsuits. A case in point would arise where an environmental group such as the Wilderness Society sues an agency of the federal government or the secretary of the U.S. Department of Interior to halt construction of the trans-Alaska pipeline. In such a case, if the Wilderness Society owned no land or other interests that could possibly be harmed by construction of the pipeline, the argument could be made that the society is meddling by sticking its unwanted nose into someone else's business. Along this line, one case held that consumer advocate Ralph Nader lacked standing to sue to stop the merger of an insurance company with the International Telephone and Telegraph Company.

A basic question involved in standing is, "Does the plaintiff have some legal, potential loss that is close enough to someone else's wrong to justify holding the wrongdoer liable?" Certainly the potential loss of money would amount to sufficient interest to give a plaintiff standing to sue. Other potential losses were noted by the *U.S. Supreme Court in Association of Data Processing Service Organizations, Inc. v. Camp*, 397 U.S. 150 (1970), when it observed:

> The question of standing concerns, apart from the *case* or *controversy* test, the question whether the interest sought to be protected by the complainant is arguably within the zone of interests to be protected or regulated by the statute or constitutional guarantee in question. Thus the Administrative Procedure Act grants standing to a person "aggrieved by agency action within the meaning of a relevant statute." That interest, at times, may reflect *aesthetic, conservational, and recreational* as well as *economic values*. A person or a family may have a spiritual stake in First Amendment value sufficient to give him standing to raise issues concerning the Establishment Clause and the Free Exercise Clause. We mention these noneconomic values to emphasize that standing may stem from them as well as from the economic injury on which petitioner relies here. Certainly he who is "likely to be *financially*" injured may be a reliable attorney general to litigate the issues of public interest in the present case.

The private attorneys general mentioned in the quote are private parties, such as Ralph Nader and the National Resources Defense Council, who, though not official public organizations, sue to vindicate public rights.

In summary, litigants today are deemed to have standing to sue if they are tangibly injured and a sufficient connection exists between the broken duty and the harm. Furthermore, in federal courts where private parties sue to vindicate rights under a federal statute or the federal constitution, the standing requirement is satisfied if they are actually injured and "arguably within the zone of interests" designed to be protected by the statute or constitution.

## CLASS ACTIONS

Modern rules of civil procedural law allow people to sue others not only on behalf of themselves but also on behalf of all other people similarly situated and injured by the same defendant in what is called a *class action*. The justification for the class action becomes clear when we consider what might be called the social-ized wrong—that is, a small wrong inflicted upon many people by one person. Class actions make suits against social wrongdoers economically feasible in cases in which suits brought by individual litigants would be uneconomical.

Consider an example. A consumer, X, who buys stock on the New York Stock Exchange (NYSE), might well be charged the same commission irrespective of the broker used. X might claim that the commission paid was $70 too high due to price fixing, a violation of the Sherman Act. Hiring an attorney, incurring court costs, and taking the time and trouble of going to court is not worth possibly recovering $70 in alleged commission overcharge (or $210 due to trebled damages under the Sherman Act if the case is proved). Yet, if each of the thousands of pur-chasers of securities through brokers is damaged about the same amount as X, the total amount of all of their injuries would be huge.

Basically, the class action works as follows. A person injured by a small amount hires an attorney, who files a complaint on behalf of the client and all the people injured by the same defendant. The attorney then estimates the number of transactions, multiplies the amount of damage each person probably sus-tained by the wrong (here, the price fixing), and sues the defendant (the broker or NYSE or both) on behalf of all such consumers, even though they do not actu-ally authorize or in person join the suit. The class action can be used in environ-mental cases, consumer cases, corporate shareholder **derivative suits**, and cases in which small, fragmented injury exists among many. The class action device allows attorneys enough of a financial incentive to offer their services to such class action clients.

The greatest advantage of the class action is that people have a legal vehicle enabling them to recover for injuries caused by another in cases in which this recovery would not have been available through the conventional lawsuit where each plaintiff sues separately. Society benefits in at least two ways from the class action. First, the social interest is promoted in seeing that wrongdoers are held accountable for the harm they cause. Second, class actions are a substitute for the ongoing government regulation that would otherwise be needed to protect the individual's interests. In class actions, attorneys eager to collect their fee get relief for their clients quickly, something for which government regulatory agencies are not noted. Once judgments against the social wrongdoers are collected and dis-tributed to all members of the class, the attorneys disappear until needed again.

*Many landmark cases are listed at http://www.nytimes.com/library/politics/scotus/court-major-cases.html*

The class action sounds like a cure-all promoting consumerism and corporate responsibility and ending bureaucratic government. However, some recent U.S. Supreme Court cases have cut back on the class action device in federal courts by requiring that each individual member of the class meet the jurisdictional amount to sue in federal courts ($75,000) and that the plaintiff starting the suit give actual notice to all people who are members of the class. As an economic matter, the costs of giving actual notice to all class members is prohibitive, and the identifi-cation of all class members, while possible, is difficult. The limits on class actions do not apply to class actions brought in state courts. Here, though, the problem is either that state rules of civil procedure do not allow class actions in the first place or that rules forbidding attorney solicitation of clients inhibit such actions. Nonetheless, federal legislation could reverse the Supreme Court rulings inhibit-ing class suits, and state legislatures could enact laws allowing such devices.

Probably the greatest deterrent to such legal reform is the fear that some aggressive attorney will do such an effective selling job to a jury that it will bring in a huge verdict to bankrupt large U.S. corporations. (Class action claims and recoveries can be tremendous.) The ripple effects are not to be underestimated: loss of jobs for employees, loss of the value of stock for stockholders, loss of pensions for retired individuals whose retirement income is tied to the income-generating capacity of the corporation's stock, and elimination of orders to suppliers, with resultant reduced demand for their products and further layoffs of employees.

## CAUSE OF ACTION

The term **cause of action** has a special legal meaning. It refers to facts that indicate that someone has been *legally wronged* by someone else and is entitled to have a court provide relief or a remedy.

But some legal wrongs are easier to recognize than others. For example, if one's rights are broken abruptly by another, one might have a good legal case against such a person. Thus, having one's nose punched will usually give rise to the civil action of battery. Even though laypeople do not know the legal theory that should be used to recover for damages, they intuitively know a wrong has been committed and that a visit to an attorney is in order.

But some wrongs are subtler, or the circumstances of their occurrence might lead the victim to doubt whether any wrong has been committed. For example, if a person bought stock in a company relying on financial statements audited by an accountant, and the stock later proved worthless because the statement of financial position (balance sheet) greatly overstated the inventory, the stock purchaser may just philosophically accept this loss, never realizing legal recourse was available against the accountant who did the audit. Then, a few months later, the "victim" contacts a lawyer, relates the stock loss story, and asks what to do. Assuming the attorney is reasonably familiar with federal Securities Act of 1933, the lawyer would explain that a possible avenue of recovery exists against the accountant.

Note that the failure of people to realize that they have been legally wronged is not unusual. Many people are simply ignorant of their legal rights. Another factor that to some extent reduces the number of lawsuits is the set of legal and ethical rules governing attorneys.

## STATUTE OF LIMITATIONS

Assuming that people do realize they have been wronged and seek out an attorney, a next major hurdle awaits: the statute of limitations.

A statute of limitations is a law that bars a plaintiff's lawsuit because the complaint is filed too long after the wrong occurred. The objective of the statute of limitations is repose—community peace. Also, evidence is lost and witnesses move away or die as time passes. The statute of limitations implies to a potential plaintiff, "Sue promptly, or you lose." Note that a statute of limitations means that people who wait too long to sue after they were wronged lose the lawsuit even if they clearly were wronged. In effect, a statute of limitations takes away someone's right to be restored after being wronged.

Many statutes of limitations exist—not just one. They vary in length, and different statutes of limitations apply to different theories of recovery. For example, torts[2] generally have statutes of limitations of one year, whereas contract matters often have longer statute of limitations periods, such as six years. Some property matters have even longer periods ranging up to twenty years or more. The length of the time period reflects the importance of the right under challenge. For example, in the statutes of limitations periods already mentioned, one can conclude that property rights are more important than contract rights, which in turn are more crucial than rights attached to recovery for injuries to the person (torts).

Note that statutes of limitations do not require that a lawsuit be completed before the statute of limitations period expires. It is only necessary to *start* the suit (file the complaint) before the statutory period ends. Sometimes the statute of limitations is *tolled*, meaning that time is not considered to run, because of war or other extraordinary event. Finally, note that it is the defendant who seeks to raise the statute of limitations, because the statute of limitations stops lawsuits. It does not create rights.

## BURDEN OF PROOF

Burden of proof is not an exciting concept, yet it is probably the single largest reason people lose lawsuits. The burden of proof in a civil case is generally said to rest on the person who wants the legal system to do something for him or her. This person is usually the plaintiff—the party suing. However, if the defendant files what is called a **counterclaim**, the burden of proof with respect to matters asserted in the counterclaim falls on the defendant. A counterclaim arises when the plaintiff sues the defendant and the defendant sues the plaintiff in return, claiming the plaintiff did something wrong to the defendant. An example is a case in which a merchant sells a toaster to a consumer on an installment plan, the toaster does not work, the consumer stops payment on the toaster, the merchant sues the consumer for the installment payments, and the consumer counterclaims against the merchant for breach of warranty because the toaster does not work.

After establishing who has the burden of proof, the next matter to determine is what one has to prove. Generally, all elements of the legal theory that the moving party (usually the plaintiff) must establish must be proved to induce the legal system to force the defendant to pay something or do something for the plaintiff. The amount of proof a moving party must present to win a civil lawsuit is generally said to be a preponderance of the evidence.

## JURISDICTION

Jurisdiction connotes power or authority over something. When used in reference to courts, it refers to the power to hear and try a case. Jurisdiction has both personal and subject matter aspects.

Subject matter jurisdiction refers to a court's power to deal with a particular type of case. A number of courts have jurisdiction over only a limited sort of case. For example, probate courts deal only with determining the validity of wills. Thus, a murder case could not be brought in a probate court because it has no subject matter jurisdiction over criminal matters. Subject matter jurisdiction is in part a result of history and in part recognition of the large case load that no single court could bear.

---

[2] Torts or civil wrongs are those branches of civil duties that do not arise by contract, such as the duty not to slander another.

*In personam* **jurisdiction** refers to a court's power over people. State courts generally have *in personam* jurisdiction over people physically within their borders who are served with process, which refers to delivering a summons and complaint to the defendant personally or to the defendant's residence. **Long-arm statutes** let a state get *in personam* jurisdiction over out-of-staters for certain wrongs occurring within the state (usually in such incidents as auto accidents). For example, if an Oregonian injured a Californian in San Francisco and hurried back to Oregon before process could be served on him, and if California had a long-arm statute covering auto accidents, the Californian could get *in personam* jurisdiction over the Oregonian *in California*. Mechanically, the Californian sends the process to a state official (usually the state's secretary of state), who sends it to the Oregonian. If the Oregonian does not answer, the plaintiff wins a default judgment for the amount sued for. This judgment can then be taken to the defendant's home state and enforced against the defendant just as if the case had been tried there.

## Starting Lawsuits: The Complaint

A person does not start a lawsuit by walking into the courthouse, finding the nearest judge, and stating the problem to the judge. Procedural due process requires that all sorts of legal niceties be observed to protect defendants, who presumably do not yet know they are about to be sued. Assuming the plaintiff does *not* act *pro se* but instead hires an attorney to present the claim against the defendant, the plaintiff's attorney drafts a **complaint**. The complaint is designed to notify the defendant of the suit and the reasons for the suit—breach of contract or slanderous remarks, for example.

In the complaint in Figure 4.2, the injured victim (the little girl suing through her grandfather) tries to state a cause of action in the complaint. Note paragraph VI of the complaint. The plaintiff points out several laws she claims the defendants violated when Betty Hobbs killed the plaintiff's father.

The complaint and two copies are taken to the clerk of the court, who puts a stamp on the complaint, indicating the time and date the complaint is filed. (The sample complaint in Figure 4.2 has a time stamp in the right center of the first page.) The complaint is put in a file folder that the clerk starts for the case, a copy is given to the plaintiff, and another copy is given along with a summons to an official process server, such as a deputy sheriff or some other person employed to perform this task. The summons directs the defendant to appear in court to answer the complaint. The process server takes a copy of the complaint and the summons to the address the plaintiff put on the complaint and hands them to the defendant or leaves them at the address indicated if the defendant is not there.

## Defendant's Response: The Answer

Upon receiving the complaint, the defendant will realize s/he has just been sued, possibly for more money than s/he has or ever expects to have. Once the defendant recovers from the shock of having been sued, s/he will probably hire an attorney to draft an **answer**. The answer is a piece of paper the defendant must file with the clerk of court where the plaintiff sued. The answer must be filed within a short time after the defendant has received a copy of the complaint—usually 30 days.

**FIGURE 4.2 EXAMPLE OF A COMPLAINT**

IN THE UNITED STATES DISTRICT COURT
FOR THE EASTERN DISTRICT OF TENNESSEE,
NORTHERN DIVISION

ELENA DeZAVALA a minor who sues by
next friend and grandfather,
LOUIS B. DeZAVALA, citizens and
residents of Linn County, Iowa,
and of no other place, <u>PLAINTIFFS</u>

vs.

BETTY J. HOBBS AND
JAMES B. HOBBS,
126 South Purdue Avenue,
Oak Ridge, Anderson County,
Tennessee, <u>DEFENDENTS</u>

NO. _3-75-125_

<u>COMPLAINT</u>

The plaintiff, Elena DeZavala, is a minor, nine years of
age, who sues by next friend and grandfather, Louis B.
DeZavala, both of whom are citizens and residents of Linn
County, Iowa, and of no other place, and further aver that
said plaintiff, Elena DeZavala, is the sole surviving child
and lineal descendant and next of kin of Louis Victor
DeZavala who died in Sullivan County, Tennessee on May 2,
1975. Said plaintiffs complain of the defendants, Betty J.
Hobbs and James B. Hobbs, of 126 South Purdue Avenue, Oak
Ridge, Tennessee, who are citizens and residents of
Anderson County, Tennessee, and of no other place and
State.

Said plaintiff, Elena DeZavala, brings this suit by her
grandfather and next friend, Louis B. DeZavala, by reason
of the wrongful death of her father, Louis Victor DeZavala,
who was divorced from the mother of the plaintiff, said
mother having remarried.

I

Plaintiff avers that the amount in controversy exceeds
the sum of Ten Thousand Dollars ($10,000)* exclusive of
interest and costs, and that a complete diversity of citizenship exists between the plaintiff and the defendants,
and jurisdiction of this Honorable Court is based on Title
28 U. S. Code Section 1332(a).

II

Plaintiff avers that on May 2, 1975, at approximately
11:00 a.m., that the plaintiff's intestate-father was
operating his vehicle in a southwardly direction along
Interstate Highway 81, approximately one mile south of the
intersection of said Interstate 81 with Tennessee highway
137. Plaintiff avers that said vehicle of Louis Victor
DeZavala was being operated in a southwardly direction in a
proper and lawful manner upon its right hand side of said
Interstate which at that point was a two lane two-way highway.

**FIGURE 4.2 CONTINUED**

### III

Plaintiff avers that said highway was plainly marked every thousand feet as a two-way highway for more than six miles in each direction from the location aforedescribed.

### IV

Plaintiff avers that at said time and place as plaintiff's intestate and deceased father, Louis Victor DeZavala, was operating his said vehicle in a southwardly direction along said highway in a proper and lawful manner and upon its right hand side of the highway in broad daylight, that the defendant, Betty J. Hobbs, operating a vehicle within the purview of the Family Purpose Doctrine, which said vehicle was the property of her husband, James B. Hobbs, in a northwardly direction along said highway, meeting the automobile of the plaintiff's intestate father. That the said defendant, Betty J. Hobbs, while operating her automobile at a high, reckless, wrongful and negligent rate of speed, and without keeping her said vehicle under control, and without keeping a lookout ahead, undertook to overtake and pass a truck traveling northwardly along said highway, and drove her said vehicle from its right hand or proper side of the highway to its left hand or improper side of the highway in an effort to overtake and pass said tractor-trailer traveling in the same direction in which she was traveling and drove her said vehicle in the manner and under the conditions aforedescribed into a violent head-on collision with the vehicle operated by the plaintiff's intestate and father.

### V

Plaintiff avers that as the direct and proximate result of the negligence of the defendent as aforedescribed, operating her vehicle upon the highway upon the business of the defendant, James B. Hobbs, and within the purview of the Family Purpose Doctrine, that the plaintiff's intestate was crushed and mangled in a horrible manner sustaining such comprehensive, mangling and horrible injuries that as a direct and proximate result thereof after suffering a large amount of pain and mental anguish, that said plaintiff's intestate died, as a result of said injuries and as a proximate result of the negligence of the defendants as aforedescribed.

### VI

Plaintiff avers that the defendants by the negligence as aforedescribed violated the following sections of the 1956 Tennessee Code Annotated, and that such violations on their part were the proximate contributing cause to the collision heretofore described and the death of plaintiff's intestate and the destruction of the automobile belonging to him at the time and place complained of:

Section 59-815
Driving on right side of roadway.

**FIGURE 4.2 CONTINUED**

Section 59-819
Limitations on overtaking on the left.

Section 59-820
Further limitations on driving to the left of center of
roadway. (1)

Section 59-821
No passing zones.

Section 59-823
Driving on roadways laned for traffic (a).

Section 59-852
Speed limit (a).

Section 59-858
Reckless driving (a).

VII

Plaintiff avers that the death of plaintiff's
intestate resulted solely from the negligence of the defendants
as aforedescribed and that the plaintiff's
intestate was a young and healthy man, 30 years of age.
Plaintiff was the intestate's only child.  Plaintiff has
further been put to the expense of the funeral bills and
medical expenses, and the destruction of the automobile
being occupied by the plaintiff's intestate at the time and
place complained of.

WHEREFORE, plaintiff respectfully prays judgment against
the defendants and each of them in the sum of Six Hundred
Thousand Dollars ($600,000) and respectfully demands a jury
to try the issues joined.

KENNERLY, MONTGOMERY, HOWARD & FINLEY

By _George D. Montgomery_
George D. Montgomery,
Attorneys for Plaintiff
12th Floor Bank of Knoxville Building
Post Office Box 442
Knoxville, Tennessee  37901

COST BOND

We do hereby acknowledge ourselves as
surety for the costs in this cause in an amount
not to exceed Two Hundred Fifty Dollars
(250.00).

KENNERLY, MONTGOMERY,
HOWARD & FINLEY

By _George D. Montgomery_

The answer will explain the defendant's version of the incident the plaintiff mentioned in the complaint. It may also state defenses the defendant relies on to escape liability. If the defendant does not file an answer, the plaintiff wins without even having to go to trial, barring unusual circumstances, through a **default judgment**. Figure 4.3 is the answer filed in response to the sample complaint. The complaint and answer together are referred to as the **pleadings**.

The defendants in their answer admit certain things (for instance, diversity jurisdiction in paragraph 2) and set up certain defenses (in paragraphs 5, 6, 7, and 8). Note that in paragraph 6, the defendants claim the plaintiff's father died instantly. If this claim is true, it would mean the plaintiff's father sustained no pain and suffering. (Note paragraph V of the complaint: "plaintiff's intestate [her father] was crushed and mangled in a horrible manner . . . after suffering a large amount of pain and mental anguish." Damages for pain and suffering can sometimes be recovered.)

## PRETRIAL DISCOVERY AND PRETRIAL CONFERENCES

Pretrial discovery permits a party to find out what sort of evidence the other party has that relates to the suit at hand, although certain privileged matters are not subject to discovery. Both parties also attempt to gather evidence in support of their contentions. To gather certain evidence, procedural rules permit the taking of **depositions**, sworn statements by someone on a matter relating to the suit at hand. Depositions are solicited by one of the parties to buttress his or her case; they add to the cost of a lawsuit; and they are usually made to preserve testimony of witnesses who will be unavailable for trial or to preserve witnesses' reactions to evidence while it is still fresh in their minds.

Pretrial conferences are simply meetings at which the opposing attorneys get together with the judge before the actual trial to state the heart of their case and how they intend to prove it. This meeting, coupled with pretrial discovery, reduces trial time and the gamesmanship element that formerly existed when opposing lawyers would delay trials with spurious arguments or conceal their evidence and theories until the last moments of the trial to surprise their opponent and win the case. Movies often have courtroom scenes of an attorney producing a key witness who, in the final moments, wins the case with the disclosure of some devastating fact. Such histrionics are unlikely in a modern procedural system with effective pretrial discovery and conferences.

## MOTIONS

During the various stages of a suit, the parties may make several types of motions. After the pleadings are completed, for example, the defendant may decide that the plaintiff's claim can easily be defeated. The device the defendant uses to achieve this end is called the **motion to dismiss**. A motion to dismiss can be based on a wide variety of grounds. For instance, the defendant may claim that the court has no jurisdiction over the case.

The most important type of motion to dismiss, though, is the motion to dismiss for failure to state a claim upon which relief can be granted, often called the *demurrer*. This motion hypothetically assumes the truth of all the facts stated in the plaintiff's complaint—just for purposes of the motion. It asserts that even if all these facts are true, the plaintiff cannot win because no legal theory will support a recovery on those facts. In effect the demurrer says, "So what?" to the factual allegations

## FIGURE 4.3 EXAMPLE OF AN ANSWER

IN THE UNITED STATES DISTRICT COURT
FOR THE EASTERN DISTRICT OF TENNESSEE,
NORTHERN DIVISION

ELENA DeZAVALA b/n/f
LOUIS B. DeZAVALA, <u>PLAINTIFFS</u>
          VS.
BETTY J. HOBBS
and
JAMES B. HOBBS, <u>DEFENDENTS</u>          NO. 3-75-125

FILED
JUN 18 1975

<u>ANSWERS</u>

The defendants, Betty J. Hobbs and James B. Hobbs, for answer to the complaint filed against them in this cause, say as follows:

1. They admit that they are citizens of Tennessee and that Louis Victor DeZavala died in Sullivan County, Tennessee, on May 2, 1975, but they have no knowledge as to the other allegations in the first and second paragraphs of the complaint so they neither admit nor deny such allegations and demand strict proof thereof.

2. They admit that this Court has jurisdiction of this action, provided there is diversity of citizenship, as alleged.

3. They admit that the defendant, Betty J. Hobbs, was driving the automobile which collided with the automobile driven by the deceased, Louis Victor DeZavala at or about the time and place alleged.

4. They admit that the defendant, James B. Hobbs, was the owner of the automobile being driven by his wife, Betty J. Hobbs, at the time of this accident, and that the family purpose doctrine is applicable.

5. They deny all allegations of negligence and statutory violations on the part of the defendant, Betty J. Hobbs.

6. They admit that the deceased, Louis Victor DeZavala, died as a result of injuries in this accident, but they aver that his death was instantaneous.

7. For lack of knowledge, they neither admit nor deny the allegations in paragraph VII of the complaint, and demand strict proof thereof.

8. They plead proximate or remote contributory negligence on the part of the deceased.

AND NOW HAVING ANSWERED, the defendants pray to be hence dismissed with their costs and demand a jury to try this cause.

Fred H. Cagle, Jr.
P. O. Box 39
Knoxville, Tennessee  37901

Attorney for Defendants
FRANTZ, McCONNELL & SEYMOUR

CERTIFICATION OF SERVICE

I certify that an exact copy the the forgoing document has been served upon counsel for all parties to the litigation to which it pertains, either by hand delivery of a copy thereof to the officer of said counsel, or by mailing a copy to said counsel in a properly addressed and stamped envelope regularly deposited in the United States Mail.

This 17 day of July , 19 75

Fred H. Cagle, Jr.

For FRANTZ, McCONNELL & SEYMOUR

in the complaint. Suppose, to take an extreme example, that A sues B on a theory of aesthetic pollution because B's ugliness constitutes an affront to civilized people. Such a claim, even if amply bolstered by descriptions of B's ugliness, will fail because no legal rules exist that impose civil liability simply for being ugly.

## THE TRIAL, VERDICT, AND JUDGMENT

The function of the trial is to settle disputes without resorting to violence. A trial is a civilized substitute for jungle law, where the stronger prevails. It gives litigants an opportunity to have their day in court to publicly present their evidence and legal theories of recovery. Aside from the litigants and their attorneys, the judge and jury are the principal actors in a trial. The judge's function is to ensure that only proper evidence and legal arguments are presented for the fact trier's consideration. When a case reaches the trial stage, some conflict inevitably arises in what the parties claim are the facts. The jury's function is to resolve fact disputes, unless a jury trial is waived, in which case the judge assumes the jury's function. Jury selection involves questioning prospective jurors to reveal competence, bias, prejudice, or conflicts of interest. Such questioning is the *voir dire*.

Once each party's case has been presented, the fact trier decides who is telling the truth by announcing its verdict (Latin derivation, *vera dicta*, meaning "say what is true"). The court usually then pronounces judgment in accordance with the jury's verdict. The judgment is a court declaration that the plaintiff recovers or that his or her action be dismissed. A court's judgment does not have to follow what the jury has decreed as its verdict. If, for example, the jury has returned a verdict completely at odds with the evidence (motivated, for instance, by sympathy for one of the parties), the other party can ask the court for **judgment notwithstanding the verdict**. This motion is a jury control device. Much the same is true of the **directed verdict**, which is a motion a party's counsel makes during the actual trial, asking, in effect, that the judge stop the trial and direct or order what the verdict should be. This motion is made on the premise that the evidence presented up to that point is fatal to the other party's case so that nothing subsequently introduced could reverse the inevitable result. Figure 4.4 contains an example of a judgment.

Motions can be made prior to, during, and after a verdict and judgment have been entered. One type of motion that occurs after a jury verdict is for either an additur or a remittitur. Generally, if credible evidence supports a jury's verdict, a court judge will not change it. In the case of the motion for an additur, the plaintiff's attorney claims that the jury has been "too stingy" in the amount it has awarded plaintiff. The Elena DeZavala judgment illustrates a judge's raising a jury's verdict to a higher amount, whereas *Anderson v. Conwood Co.*, presented in Chapter 3, illustrates a remittitur where the court reduces the jury's verdict because it is too high.

## RES JUDICATA

Parties to a dispute do have a right to have their case tried, but only once, given normal circumstances, under the *res judicata* principle. If this rule were not available, disputes would never be settled. The losing party would return to court asking for a retrial of the case until a more sympathetic judge or jury granted the relief requested. At that point, the other party would follow the same procedure until receiving a favorable judgment—again. The legal process would thus be interminable, and the legal system's objective of settling disputes would be lost.

**FIGURE 4.4 EXAMPLE OF A JUDGMENT**

# United States District Court

FOR THE

EASTERN DISTRICT OF TENNESSEE, NORTHERN DIVISION

ELENA DeZAVALA, b/n/f/
and grandfather
LOUIS B. DeZavala

vs.

BETTY J. HOBBS &
JAMES HOBBS

CIVIL ACTION FILE NO. 3-75-125

} **JUDGMENT**

   This action came on trial before the Court and a jury, Honorable Robert L. Taylor, United States District Judge, presiding, and the issues having been duly tried and the jury having duly rendered its verdict;

   It is Ordered and Adjudged that the Plaintiffs, Elena DeZavala, b/n/f and grandfather, Louis B. DeZavala, recover of the defendents Betty J. Hobbs and James Hobbs, the sum of Twenty-Five Thousand ($25,000)* Dollars, plus property damage in the amount of Three Hundred ($300) Dollars, with interest thereon at the rate of six percent as provided by law, and their costs of action.

Dated at Knoxville, Tennessee, this 25th day of August, 1975.

Filed _25_ day of _Aug_ 19 _75_
Ent'd _____ Order Book _71_, p. _326_
   KARL D. SAULPAW, JR., CLERK
by _Jean Medlock_ Dep.Clerk

KARL D. SAULPAW, JR.
Clerk of Court

By _Jean Medlock_

---

*Later raised to $50,000 by an additur.

## APPEALS

The finality objective of the *res judicata* rule has one escape valve: the appeal. A party dissatisfied with the trial court's disposition of the case may appeal to a higher court on the theory that the trial court made a mistake at some point. An appeal is usually pursued after a motion for a new trial has been made in the trial court, wherein the loser asks the trial judge to correct mistakes that resulted in the unfavorable judgment. A new trial, not surprisingly, seldom happens.

Because most trial courts are **courts of record** (meaning that a clerk keeps a transcript of the courtroom proceedings), the evidence and witnesses are not reintroduced at the appellate level. Instead, the justices consult the record, accepting the conclusions of the fact trier at the lower level unless a blatant error appears to have been made. The appellate court's main function is to ensure that the proper legal rules were recognized and correctly applied in disposing of the case in the lower court. If an error of law or if an outrageous determination affecting the outcome was made, the appellate court returns the case to the lower court and directs a retrial to apply the correct principles.

## COLLECTING JUDGMENT

Suppose a civil lawsuit and all appeals have ended in the defendant's favor. Assuming no counterclaim was filed by defendant in the case, the matter would end with no order of payment of money from the defendant to the plaintiff.

If, on the other hand, the plaintiff has won the lawsuit, prevailed on any appeals, and been awarded a money judgment, the plaintiff becomes a **judgment creditor**. The losing defendant becomes a **judgment debtor** in such a case. If the world were perfect from the judgment creditor's standpoint, the judgment debtor would pull out his wallet, peel off cash in the amount of the judgment, and turn it over to the judgment creditor. The dispute would then end.

Successful plaintiffs in civil lawsuits seldom see this happen, of course. Often, defendant's liability insurance pays the judgment fully, which ends the matter. Other times, the defendant proves **judgment proof**, meaning that the defendant is so poor that any attempt to collect would be futile. However, judgments last for a number of years and can be renewed. Therefore, a judgment creditor may have a number of years to collect from a judgment debtor. Thus, one should not quickly give up hope of collecting the judgment. Also, a judgment that has not been paid by the defendant can be sold by the judgment creditor (for a fraction of the judgment's face value) to a third party who was not involved in the original suit.

*Judgment Debtor's Property.* Assume the judgment creditor tries to collect the judgment from the judgment debtor's assets. The first question that arises concerns what property of the debtor is available to pay the creditor's claims. The general rule is that all of the debtor's property currently owned or possibly acquired at some future date may be seized by the judgment creditor unless it is exempt.[3] For example, the debtor's car, house, personal belongings, club memberships (to the extent they have commercial value), stocks, bonds, notes receivable

---

[3] The authors wish to acknowledge the article by William T. Vukowich, "Debtors' Exemption Rights," 62 *Georgetown Law Journal* (1974), from which many ideas and much information for this chapter were obtained.

from third parties, money market accounts, and proprietary interests in a sole proprietorship or partnership business may all be seized and sold to pay amounts owed to a judgment creditor unless they are exempt.

*Exempt Property.* Exempt property results from state and federal laws designed to protect the debtor's ability to survive by allowing the retention of bare necessities required to survive. The theory of state exemption laws is that, while a debtor should pay legal debts, the debtor should not be cast naked and penniless on welfare with no place to live or without clothes or basic household goods. Nor should that punitive relic from Charles Dickens's era—the debtor's prison—be revived.

Having examined the theory of exemption laws, what specific items fall into the category of exempt property that may not be seized to pay his or her debts? The answer is complex because exemption laws are both state and federal, and a variance exists among the states as to items exempted. Most states give a debtor a **homestead exemption,** which, as the name suggests, refers to the house in which the debtor lives, although the exemption is often limited to a low dollar figure (which may or may not be enough to protect debtor's home equity). All states exempt life insurance policies to some extent. The earnings or wages of the debtor are generally not exempt under exemption laws, but state and federal garnishment limitations, discussed later, do limit a creditor's ability to take a debtor's wages. It would seem incredible to allow a judgment creditor to seize a debtor's welfare payments, given the live-and-let-live philosophy of exemption laws, yet about half of the states do not exempt welfare payments. Generally, amounts of money debtors receive from retirement programs—both public and private—are exempt from creditor's claims, although some private plans are exempt only up to a specific dollar amount. Usually alimony and child support payments are not exempt—another peculiar anomaly, given the philosophy of exemption laws. Certain household and personal items, such as furniture, stoves, refrigerators, beds, and televisions, are exempt, again on the theory that they are essential for the debtor's survival. Professor Vukowich has assembled a picturesque list of miscellaneous exempted property that includes wedding rings, Bibles, family pictures, books, guns, historical and scientific collections, and cemetery lots.

*Exemption Waivers.* Two final points about exemptions warrant discussion: They may be waived, and certain debts may be collected even from property that would otherwise be exempt. The **waiver** idea is easily understood when one considers someone who buys a house and finances it by borrowing the bulk of the purchase price from a local savings and loan association. If the homeowner does not repay the loan and the lending institution sues for the money loaned, winning a judgment against the defaulting house buyer, it would be ludicrous to let the homeowner assert that the homestead exemption prevented the lender from selling the house to recover the amount loaned to buy it. Sellers of exempt property would require cash and would not risk selling on credit to avoid the risk of default and noncollection due to the exemption.

A need exists for credit transactions in many property items receiving exemptions under state law, particularly high-priced items such as houses, where people seldom have the entire purchase price at the time of purchase. The problem of extending credit to buy exempt property is handled by getting borrowers to waive their exemption. Thus, if a savings and loan association loans money to a person to purchase a house, the lending institution will not make the loan unless the homeowner-borrower waives (usually in the borrowing contract) the homestead exemption.

The second concluding point about exemptions is that they do not apply to situations in which the judgment debtor owes certain types of debts. For example, exemptions may not be asserted against claims for child support and alimony.

*Writs of Execution and Garnishment.* As the prior discussion illustrates, much potential property of the judgment debtor is available to pay off a judgment obtained by the successful plaintiff. The next inquiry is, "What legal devices are available to enable the judgment creditor to obtain such property?" Generally speaking, a judgment creditor may not simply walk onto a judgment debtor's property and take whatever property can be found that appears valuable enough to pay off the judgment debt. Rather, the judgment creditor must again return to the legal system and bring what, in many states, are ancillary actions (in effect, sue again, though technically it is part of the same suit) to collect the judgment. After-judgment legal devices the judgment creditor may use to obtain the judgment debtor's property include writs of execution and garnishment, which are state law remedies and thus vary in detail from state to state.

A **writ of execution** is a form the judgment creditor gets from the court clerk that tells a court official, such as the sheriff, to go to the judgment debtor's property and take nonexempt assets. After the official seizes the property, he conducts a public auction to sell it and turns over the money received to the judgment creditor. Any amount greater than the judgment debt is returned to the judgment debtor. If the amount received is insufficient to pay the judgment, more nonexempt property of the judgment debtor may be seized and sold in like manner.

If the writ of execution results in the seizure and sale of all the debtor's nonexempt property and it is still not enough to pay off the judgment debt, **garnishment** is another legal method available to the judgment creditor to obtain payment of the judgment. One could well ask what value garnishment has if the writ of execution has already resulted in the sale of all of the debtor's nonexempt property. The answer is that writs of execution are used only to take property directly from the judgment debtor. However, many times other people (called *garnishees* if a creditor goes after the debtor's property in their hands) owe the judgment debtor money. An employer, for example, could owe the judgment debtor salary or wages. Also, debtors may own property that is not in their possession. A writ of execution cannot reach such property. The garnishment order may be obtained from the clerk of court to reach assets of the sorts described. However, it usually may not be obtained until after a writ of execution fails to produce enough property to satisfy the judgment.

*Prejudgment Attachment and Garnishment.* The execution process just described sometimes proves unsatisfactory from the judgment creditor's standpoint because the creditor is forced to wait until the case has slowly dragged through the courts before collecting the claim. How nice it would be if the plaintiff could seize the defendant's property *before* the suit even reached the trial stage of the proceedings to prevent such unethical defendant practices as running away, plundering the property, or giving the property to friends or relatives so that the plaintiff cannot have any debtor property to satisfy the judgment the plaintiff *might* get in the lawsuit.

For hundreds of years, in some instances, the legal system provided at least two ways in which the plaintiff in a lawsuit could obtain a defendant's property *before* winning a full-blown lawsuit. Neither of these devices observed the defendant's due process protections of notice and full and fair hearing on the matter sued over. The devices are known as prejudgment attachment and garnishment.

**Prejudgment attachment** lets a plaintiff seize a defendant's property at the start of the lawsuit before it is even determined that the plaintiff has won the suit. The violation of procedural due process created by such a process is obvious: The defendant has had property taken from him or her without a trial. The *protection* given to defendant in such case flows from the requirement that the plaintiff is required to post a bond (similar to an insurance policy) that supposedly covers the defendant's opportunity cost of being deprived of her own property until the matter can be fully litigated in court. Certain limits on availability of the attachment devices vary somewhat from state to state. Some of the limits on attachment are found in circumstances that must exist before attachment's issuance: the defendant's absconding, or absenting himself or herself; the defendant's nonresidence in the state; the defendant's fraudulent transfer or disposition of property; the defendant's removing or concealing property; and various other miscellaneous grounds, such as impairment of security (the defendant's tearing up or abusing property in which the plaintiff has a security interest).

**Prejudgment garnishment** is a serious violation of a person's procedural due process rights. It allows the taking of a person's wages directly from his employer *before* trial is held to determine if any debt is owed. A defendant could be put on welfare if this were allowed. Postjudgment garnishment is a recognized, legitimate creditor remedy not violative of a defendant's procedural due process rights since it is not forthcoming until *after* notice and trial have been held on the validity of a plaintiff's claim and a determination has been made that the plaintiff has a valid claim against the defendant.

*Constitutionality of Prejudgment Creditor Remedies.* The constitutionality of prejudgment creditor remedies is open to question today. This conclusion follows from the apparently conflicting U.S. Supreme Court decisions on the subject in the past several years, plus the fact that each state's prejudgment garnishment and attachment vary as to the extent of their applicability. In 1969, the Supreme Court held that prejudgment wage garnishment without notice and a hearing before such garnishment violates procedural due process.[4] In a similar vein, the Supreme Court held in 1972 that prejudgment seizure of goods that the seller sold and retained a security interest without a hearing or notice to the defendant debtor, by *ex parte* proceeding (only plaintiff is at and knows about the proceeding) violates the due process clause of the Fourteenth Amendment.[5] Only two years later, however, the Supreme Court said that Louisiana's prejudgment remedy, allowing the creditor-plaintiff to take the defendant-debtor's property that had an unpaid balance and on which the plaintiff-creditor had a lien, satisfied due process requirements if the plaintiff filed a bond.[6] Due process was satisfied even though the seizure was authorized ex parte without notice to or hearing before the taking of the defendant's property. However, *ex parte* prejudgment garnishments, as opposed to attachments where no notice or hearing is provided to the defendant, do still appear to be unconstitutional.

---

[4] *Sniadach v. Family Finance Corp.*, 395 U.S. 337 (1969).
[5] *Fuentes v. Shevin*, 407 U.S. 67 (1972).
[6] *Mitchell v. W.T. Grant Co.*, 416 U.S. 600 (1974).

*Consumer Credit Protection Act.* In 1968 the Consumer Credit Protection Act became federal law. One of its many accomplishments was to set limits on the amount of a person's earnings that could be garnished by a creditor to pay amounts owed to the creditor. These limits are 25 percent of the debtor's weekly disposable income (take-home pay, after income taxes and Social Security have been deducted) or the amount by which the person's weekly take-home pay exceeds thirty times the existing federal minimum hourly wage. Which alternative is taken depends on which amount is the smaller, the smaller figure being the one that is required to be taken. In other words, an objective of this federal law is to limit the amount that can be taken from a person's earnings by garnishment so that the debtor will not have to go on welfare.

The Federal Consumer Credit Protection Act applies to all states. Because employers do not enjoy having employees' earnings garnished because of the added bookkeeping expense and harassment that results, frequently they would fire employees whose earnings were garnished. The federal law now allows states to prohibit firing employees for this reason. Also, states *may* totally eliminate the garnishment process now available to creditors in most states. As the title of this act indicates, it is a *Consumer* Credit Protection Act, designed to enlarge debtors' rights and reduce creditor's rights.

*Uniform Consumer Credit Code.* Another model or suggested law, the Uniform Consumer Credit Code (UCCC) enacted in some states, exempts more of a debtor's earned income from garnishment than does the federal law, which the federal law allows individual states to do. It makes the alternatives available for garnishment the lesser of 25 percent of weekly take-home pay or the amount by which disposable income is greater than forty times the federal minimum hourly wage per week (instead of thirty). Thus, the UCCC provides a greater protection from garnishment to defaulting consumer judgment debtors than does federal law.

*Bankruptcy.* Two final devices are available to judgment debtors to escape paying judgments obtained against them: voluntary bankruptcy and transferring ownership of their property to noncreditor relatives or friends to hold for the debtor's benefit. The power to allow a person, business, or other entity to go bankrupt is exclusively a federal—not a state—power. Basically, any natural person, partnership, or corporation may go bankrupt. The objective of the Bankruptcy Code is to allow people or business organizations hopelessly in debt to turn over all their nonexempt assets to a court-appointed official or trustee, who distributes them among the creditors. Secured creditors (lenders with claims against specific assets such as a house or a car) may generally have their claims paid before those of unsecured creditors, primarily because mortgaged property or property subject to a timely **perfected security interest** is not considered part of the bankrupt's estate.

Assuming that here we are examining bankruptcy as a device to escape paying judgment debts, attention must turn to the limits on a person's ability to go bankrupt. The two ways of going bankrupt are voluntarily and involuntarily. In the first case, because debtors *want* to go bankrupt to rid themselves of overwhelming debts, they voluntarily start bankruptcy proceedings. In the second case— involuntary bankruptcy—at least three creditors from among at least twelve or more creditors in all with claims totaling $5,000 or more against the debtor must petition the federal district court (the *only* court where bankruptcy proceedings start) for such action. If the debtor has fewer than twelve creditors, only one creditor having $5,000 or more in claims may put the debtor into bankruptcy.

Limits have been placed on who may petition a federal bankruptcy court to go through voluntary bankruptcy. The debtor alone is petitioning in a voluntary bankruptcy, but the nature of the debtor is first determined. Any natural person, partnership, or corporation may go bankrupt voluntarily with a few exceptions: Banks, railroads, municipalities, savings and loan associations, and insurance companies may not go bankrupt voluntarily; however, municipalities may now "adjust their debts." Most of these same institutions that affect the public interest may *not* go bankrupt *in*voluntarily, either. Second, it is not essential that a voluntary bankrupt be insolvent (not paying debts as they come due in the ordinary course of business or being unable to do so); but it is necessary that a voluntary bankrupt owe debts. Also, the limit on receiving a straight bankruptcy discharge is *once every six years*, and certain obligations may not be escaped (so-called nondischargeable debts) by going bankrupt. These include judgments for the commission of intentional torts, alimony, and child support. **Negligence** judgments, however, are dischargeable in bankruptcy.

*Fraudulent Transfers.*  A property transfer is another possible way to escape judgment debts. The debtor transfers title to a friend or relative who will hold the property voluntarily with the understanding that it will remain the debtor's property, although on paper title and possession will reside with the friend. Then, when the judgment creditor seeks a writ of attachment against the judgment debtor's property, the judgment debtor will be execution-proof with no property to seize.

The law that deals with this problem is called the Uniform Fraudulent Conveyance Act. This act does not allow creditors to go to *all* third parties and reclaim property that their debtor has ever transferred to them, but it does permit reclamation where a fraudulent conveyance has occurred. The term **fraudulent conveyance** refers to a transfer of property by a debtor to third parties with the purpose of depriving creditors of the debtor's property that they could otherwise seize to repay amounts the debtor owes them. A transfer by a debtor is presumed fraudulent when the debtor is insolvent. Insolvency in this context means debtors are unable to pay their debts as they come due. The debtor may challenge this presumption in court, but if a transfer of property by a debtor is determined to be a fraudulent transfer under the Uniform Fraudulent Conveyance Act, the transfer may be set aside. In such a case the property held by the debtor's friend may be reclaimed, again put in the debtor's estate, and be available so that creditors may seize it.

## CONCLUSION

As you can see from this look at the anatomy of a civil lawsuit, lawsuits have a to-and-fro motion, a battle of forms filed with court officials by the respective litigants. The complexity of this process, which was only alluded to here, is, at least in part, the result of forces designed to refine justice by spelling out specific rules for the many different situations that can arise in a lawsuit. This increased complexity of the legal process creates two problems: The average person will not understand the process, and the process will become too lengthy and expensive.

## CHAPTER SUMMARY

Alternative dispute resolution (ADR) refers to settling disputes without resort to lawsuits. Conciliation, mediation, and arbitration are forms of ADR. The U.S. Supreme Court has approved the use of ADR to settle investor complaints against stockbrokers.

Attorneys represent persons involved in legal disputes. Attorneys can be paid on a fixed or contingency basis. Provisions in attorney-client contracts requiring clients to give up control of the right to settle their suits are generally void. Attorneys may advertise their fees and services in routine legal matters provided the ads are truthful and not misleading. Companies such as American Express, unions, and some law firms have legal plans that entitle consumers to certain legal services for a year at a set fee. Also, many liability insurance policies provide free legal assistance as part of the policy's coverage.

It is legal for a person who is not an attorney to plead his or her own case. Such a person is called a pro se litigant. The steps in civil lawsuits may include the facts giving rise to the cause of action, the realization that one has a cause of action, filing of the complaint, serving of the complaint and process on the defendant, the defendant's filing an answer, the pretrial hearing, pretrial discovery, depositions, and interrogatories, the trial and judgment, appeals, and collection of the judgment.

### ■ MANAGER'S ETHICAL DILEMMA

Petitioners are individuals who invested about $400,000 in securities. They signed a standard customer agreement with the broker, which included a clause stating that the parties agreed to settle any controversies "relating to [the] accounts" through binding arbitration that complies with specified procedures. The agreement to arbitrate these controversies is unqualified, unless it is found to be unenforceable under federal or state law. . . . The investments turned sour, and petitioners eventually sued respondent and its broker-agent in charge of the accounts, alleging that their money was lost in unauthorized and fraudulent transactions. In their complaint they pleaded various violations of federal and state law, including claims under §12(2) of the Securities Act of 1933 . . . and claims under three sections of the Securities Exchange Act of 1934.

The District Court ordered all the claims to be submitted to arbitration except for those raised under § 12(2) of the Securities Act. It held that the latter claims must proceed in the court action under our clear holding on the point in *Wilko v. Swan*. . . (1953). The District Court reaffirmed its ruling upon reconsideration, and also entered a default judgment against the broker, who is no longer in the case. The Court of Appeals reversed, concluding that the arbitration agreement is enforceable because this Court's subsequent decisions have reduced Wilko to "obsolescence." . . . The U.S. Supreme Court granted certiorari.

What arguments can a securities firm make before the U.S. Supreme Court in favor of upholding its arbitration agreement with its customers? Do you think that public policy reasons justify striking down or upholding this arbitration agreement?

## Discussion Questions

1. Recently states have reached multi-billion-dollar settlement of lawsuits brought against tobacco companies for contributions to Medicare and other government programs that have paid out benefits to cigarette smokers for various ailments. Several states—notably Texas and Florida—were represented by private attorneys against the tobacco companies. These attorneys were successful on the states' behalf, winning several billion dollars in settlement (a reported $15.3 billion for the state of Texas alone). The attorney fees for Texas were reportedly $2.3 billion. Then Governor George Bush of Texas stated that such attorney fees were "outrageous." What public policy arguments can you adduce both to support and to challenge such high attorney fees?

2. What are some public policy considerations behind the following legal subjects?
   a. standing
   b. class actions
   c. statutes of limitations

3. In the past, attorney advertising was legally prohibited. What arguments can be made supporting such a ban? Does advertising promote consumer knowledge or mislead consumers? Is a little knowledge always a dangerous thing? Sometimes? Do we ever know everything about a subject?

4. Rule 4 of the Missouri Supreme Court regulates lawyer advertising. The rule says a lawyer may include ten categories of information in a published ad: name, address, and phone number; areas of practice; date and place of birth; schools attended; foreign language ability; office hours; fee for initial consultation; availability of a fee schedule; credit arrangements; and the fixed fee to be charged for certain routine legal services. The Missouri Supreme Court interpreted Rule 4 as allowing release of *only* these ten categories of information. The Missouri Advisory Committee charged R. M. J., an unidentified lawyer practicing in St. Louis, with violating Rule 4. R. M. J. allegedly published ads listing areas of practice in words other than what Rule 4 allowed. R. M. J. also listed courts where R. M. J. was admitted to practice, although this information was not included among the ten categories of information that Rule 4 authorized. Also, R. M. J. allegedly mailed announcements of R. M. J.'s law practice to people other than what Rule 4 allowed. R. M. J. argued that Rule 4 violated the First and Fourteenth Amendments. The Missouri Supreme Court said Rule 4 was constitutional and reprimanded R. M. J. who then appealed the judgment to the U.S. Supreme Court. What was the result? [*Matter of R. M. J.*, 455 U.S. 191 (1982)].

5. Why should an attorney not have the exclusive power to settle a client's civil case? What policy arguments favor giving the client the right to settle?

## INFOTRAC KEYWORDS

**Use your InfoTrac password to look up articles on http://www.infotrac-college.com**

Keywords: *Alternative dispute resolution, civil lawsuits, legal complaint, Uniform Credit Protection Act.*

For suggested readings, please visit this book's Web site at **http://fisher.westbuslaw.com** (click on "Internet Applications").

# BUSINESS AND THE CONSTITUTION

*"[W]E MUST NEVER FORGET THAT IT IS A **CONSTITUTION** WE ARE EXPOUNDING . . . A CONSTITUTION INTENDED TO ENDURE FOR AGES TO COME, AND, CONSEQUENTLY, TO BE ADAPTED TO THE VARIOUS CRISES OF HUMAN AFFAIRS."*

—CHIEF JUSTICE JOHN MARSHALL IN *MCCULLOCH V. MARYLAND,* 4 WHEAT. 316 (1819).

A constitution is the fundamental law of the society it governs. In the American system, the U.S. Constitution and state constitutions serve two broad purposes. First, they set up the basic structure of government. This includes establishing the various branches of the central government and the powers granted and denied to each, as well as defining the power relations between the central government and subordinate units of government. For example, the U.S. Constitution states what the different branches of the federal government can do, what the states can do, and what happens when state and federal laws conflict. Second, constitutions limit the power of government. In part, they do so by the way they state the powers given to, and withheld from, the various branches and subunits. In addition, constitutions specifically block certain government actions. For example, constitutions forbid government behavior that deprives people of certain rights. The most important example is the Bill of Rights in the U.S. Constitution. Finally, to promote these two general purposes, constitutions must be supreme—the last word—on legal questions. All of these generalizations are true of the U.S. Constitution.

## THE UNITED STATES CONSTITUTION: AN OVERVIEW

This chapter does not discuss all areas of U.S. constitutional law. Instead, it examines only the most important constitutional doctrines affecting government regulation of business. To see how those doctrines fit within the Constitution's larger scheme, and to learn something about that scheme, we begin with a brief overview of the Constitution.

Article I of the Constitution gives Congress the sole power to *legislate* at the federal level. It also sets out rules for the passage of legislation, including the presidential veto and Congress's ability to override a veto by a two-thirds vote of each House. Section 8 of Article I states a long list of federal legislative powers: the specific ways in which Congress is allowed to legislate. Most important here are the commerce, taxing, and spending powers discussed later in the chapter. Article I, Section 9 states a brief list of specific powers that Congress is *not* allowed to exercise. Article I, Section 10 declares that the states cannot exercise certain powers. One example, the states' inability to impair the obligations of contracts, is discussed later in the chapter.

Article II begins by placing the *executive power* (the power to execute the laws passed by Congress) in the president. Article II also lists the president's powers, which include the role of commander-in-chief of the armed forces and the ability to make treaties, which must also be approved by two-thirds of the Senate. But Article II's list of presidential powers understates the practical importance of the presidency in our scheme of government today.

Article III of the Constitution deals with the *judicial power* of the federal government. It establishes the United States Supreme Court and gives Congress the power to create other federal courts, a power Congress has exercised. Article III also describes the types of cases the federal courts can hear.

Article IV of the Constitution sets out a number of rules governing relationships among the states. It provides, for instance, that each state must give "Full Faith and Credit" to the laws and legal proceedings of other states.

Article V sets out the procedures for amending the Constitution.

Article VI contains the supremacy clause, which makes federal law supreme over state law in case of a clash between them. This is the basis for the doctrine of *federal preemption* discussed toward the end of the chapter.

The U.S. Constitution has twenty-six amendments. The first ten are the Bill of Rights. This chapter discusses three important Bill of Rights provisions: the Fifth Amendment's due process and "takings" clauses and the First Amendment's guarantee of free speech. Originally, the Bill of Rights applied only to the activities of the federal government. But due to the *incorporation* doctrine examined later in this chapter, most of these constitutional protections now limit the states as well. This chapter also examines two provisions of the Constitution's Fourteenth Amendment: its due process and equal protection clauses. The former is worded like the Fifth Amendment's due process clause, but applies to the states. The latter, which now applies both to the states and the federal government, forbids many kinds of discriminatory lawmaking.

## THE NATURE OF CONSTITUTIONAL DECISION MAKING

People often make confident statements about what the U.S. Constitution means. These people apparently assume that the Constitution's provisions are clear and unchanging. They also seem to think that courts deciding constitutional cases simply follow the Constitution's literal language and the historical materials accompanying its enactment.

Like it or not, the beliefs just described generally are incorrect. Some constitutional provisions are anything but clear. Often, moreover, courts do not passively interpret constitutional language. Instead, they frequently *create* constitutional law. As a result, some constitutional provisions now mean something different from what they once meant, and the Constitution as a whole evolves rather than remains stable.

### WHY THE CONSTITUTION'S MEANING CHANGES

Why does the meaning of constitutional provisions change over time? For one thing, some of those provisions lacked a clear meaning in the first place. Often their language is obscure. For example, such imprecise terms as "due process of law" and "equal protection of the laws" can be—and have been—interpreted in many ways. In addition, the debates and other history surrounding the enactment of constitutional provisions often do not cure their ambiguity. Thus, courts must fill in the blanks where the language and history of a constitutional provision are unclear.

Probably the most important reason for constitutional change, however, is social change. For better or worse, new social conditions and values sometimes lead judges to alter constitutional doctrine to reflect such changes. As the old saying goes, the Supreme Court's decisions tend to follow the election returns. The Constitution's adaptability also might reflect the wishes of the Founders, who may have used broad and flexible language to make future change possible. In addition, it probably reflects the wishes of most Americans, who might like the idea of a fixed and certain constitution in the abstract, but would be unhappy if they had to live under one.

### THE SUPREME COURT'S POWER AND ITS LIMITS

For the reasons just discussed, the Supreme Court (and other courts) play a major role in determining the Constitution's practical meaning. Charles Evans Hughes, U.S. chief justice from 1930 to 1941, said, "the Constitution not only is, but ought to be, what the judges say it is."[1] Theoretically, constitutional change can be achieved through the Constitution's formal amendment process, but this process is difficult to use. For better or worse, therefore, the Supreme Court has been the Constitution's principal amender.

From the points just made, it follows that the Supreme Court exercises political power. Under the doctrine of **judicial review**, the Court (and courts in general) can declare the actions of other government bodies unconstitutional. If the Court exercised judicial review under clear constitutional provisions whose meaning it passively followed, no one would regard it as especially powerful. In fact, however, the Court sometimes invalidates federal and state laws under ambiguous provisions whose meaning it largely determines. These discretionary exercises of power resemble legislative or administrative policy making. This means that the

---

[1] L.J. Peters, *Peter's Quotations* (New York: Wm Morrow and Company, 1980), p. 117.

values, judicial philosophies, and political beliefs of judges are important factors in determining how the United States is governed. That is why the nomination of Supreme Court justices often involves so much political controversy.

The Supreme Court's political power creates a problem. In theory, such power is supposed to be exercised only by democratically elected bodies such as legislatures. The Supreme Court and other courts are not democratically elected bodies. Thus, when courts declare a statute unconstitutional, they basically are telling the people's elected representatives that they cannot govern the country as they like. This might be permissible if, when doing so, the Court was passively following clear constitutional provisions to which the people theoretically have consented. But as we have seen, this is not the case. Thus, there is a clash between majority rule and the power exercised by the modern judiciary.

Due to this clash, the Supreme Court and other courts do not have a completely free hand when they decide constitutional cases. In other words, they do not push their power as far as they can by interpreting the Constitution as loosely as they might. One reason is that many judges genuinely believe in majority rule. Another is the courts' potential political vulnerability. Courts are dependent on the executive branch of government to enforce their decisions. Moreover, legislatures usually have the power to impeach judges, and also may determine their compensation. Thus, courts often are reluctant to engage in direct power struggles with the other branches of government. If courts do engage in such a struggle, their ability to prevail may depend on how much their decisions reflect, if not general public sentiment, at least the wishes of important groups. It may also depend on their ability to convince the public that they are being faithful to "the Constitution," and are not merely enacting their own political views.

Another restraint on the courts concerns the Constitution's language. Although constitutional language often is indefinite, it almost always has some meaning. In fact, certain constitutional provisions—for example, those governing the ages of senators and representatives—are perfectly clear on their face. Even the constitution's indefinite provisions express general values whose moral authority has continued over time. A broad phrase like *equal protection of the laws*, for example, at least suggests that the government cannot make completely arbitrary and irrational distinctions in its lawmaking. And the term *due process of law* at least implies that government should use fair procedures before depriving someone of life, liberty, or property.

## ENUMERATED POWERS AND INDEPENDENT CONSTITUTIONAL CHECKS AT THE FEDERAL LEVEL

This chapter discusses constitutional doctrines that determine government's ability to regulate the economy. The constitutionality of government regulation involves two general questions. First, did the government act pursuant to a *constitutionally granted power* when it enacted the law in question? Second, even if it did act pursuant to such a power, did its exercise of this power collide with an *independent constitutional check* contained elsewhere in the Constitution? If the first question is answered in the negative, the law in question is unconstitutional. And regardless of how the first question is answered, a positive answer to the second question also means that the law is unconstitutional. Figure 5.1 summarizes these points as they apply at the federal level.

**FIGURE 5.1   ENUMERATED POWERS AND INDEPENDENT CONSTITUTIONAL CHECKS AT THE FEDERAL LEVEL**

## ENUMERATED POWERS

One of the U.S. Constitution's main aims is to limit government power, and the two questions posed above represent two distinct ways of doing so. First, the Constitution limits congressional power by specifically listing or enumerating the areas in which Congress can make law, and by tacitly saying that it can exercise those powers and no others. Article I, Section 8 of the Constitution and a few other constitutional provisions give Congress a lengthy, but not unlimited, collection of powers. Under the long-settled doctrine of **enumerated powers**, Congress only can do those things listed or enumerated in the Constitution, and cannot exercise any powers other than those specifically granted it by the Constitution.

In reality, however, congressional regulatory power now greatly exceeds anything you would expect after reading the specific powers enumerated in the Constitution. Extensive federal regulation of the economy has been a fact of life since at least the 1930s. During most of that period, the enumerated powers doctrine has not been a major obstacle to such regulation, because the Supreme Court has interpreted many of Congress's enumerated powers broadly. The following discussion of the commerce, tax, and spending powers provides examples. But as that discussion also reveals, the enumerated powers doctrine has shown signs of renewed life in recent years.

## INDEPENDENT CONSTITUTIONAL CHECKS

Due to the way Congress's enumerated powers have been interpreted over the past several decades, the main constitutional restrictions on federal regulation of the economy now lie outside the enumerated power on which a regulation is based. We call these external restrictions **independent constitutional checks**. Independent constitutional checks create protected zones into which government regulation cannot reach. A regulation intruding into one of these zones is unconstitutional even if it is based on an enumerated power. For example,

Congress has the power to regulate commerce among the states. By itself, this power might enable Congress to pass a statute prohibiting women from conducting business in interstate commerce. But such a law would be unconstitutional under one of the Constitution's independent checks—the equal protection clause discussed later in the chapter.

## An Introduction to the Remainder of the Chapter

This chapter is organized around the concepts just discussed. After briefly discussing state legislative authority, it examines three important enumerated powers that enable Congress to regulate social and economic matters: its commerce, tax, and spending powers. Later, attention turns to three of the most significant independent checks on federal and state power to regulate: due process, equal protection, and the First Amendment's free speech guarantee. Understanding these three independent checks requires that we discuss three other notions: the incorporation doctrine, state action, and means-ends scrutiny. The chapter also considers three independent checks—the contract clause, the burden-on-commerce doctrine, and federal preemption—that only limit state regulatory power. The chapter concludes by examining a provision—the Fifth Amendment's takings clause—that both recognizes a governmental power and contains its own limits on that power's exercise.

## State Power to Regulate the Economy

Strictly speaking, the enumerated powers doctrine only applies to Congress. In other words, the U.S. Constitution does not list or enumerate specific powers that the states may exercise.[2] However, state constitutions may do so. The most important state regulatory power is the **police power**. This is a broad state power to regulate to advance the public health, safety, morals, and welfare. Of course, exercises of the police power and other powers granted by state constitutions are subject to whatever independent checks state constitutions impose. They also are subject to the federal independent checks discussed later. In particular, state laws may be unconstitutional because they are *preempted* by federal regulation of the same subject.

## Three Enumerated Congressional Powers

### The Commerce Power

Article I, Section 8 of the Constitution gives Congress the power "[t]o regulate Commerce . . . among the several States." This **commerce clause** has two main thrusts: One represents its purpose and one reflects its language. The framers

---

[2] However, the U.S. Constitution does say that certain powers—for example, creating currency and taxing imports—may be exercised only by Congress. In most other areas, Congress and the state legislatures have *concurrent powers*; in these areas, both can make law.

put the commerce clause in the Constitution to promote national commercial activity by preventing the states from engaging in the economic protectionism that was common after the Revolution. In line with this purpose, the clause is an independent check on state lawmaking that hinders or burdens interstate commerce. We discuss this use of the commerce clause later in the chapter. Here, our concern is the scope of Congress's enumerated power to regulate interstate commerce.

The language of the commerce clause seems limited to business or commercial matters. Perhaps more importantly, the clause only appears to reach *interstate* commerce (commerce among the states) and not *intrastate* matters (things happening within a state). By the mid-twentieth century, however, the commerce clause had become an all-purpose federal police power with great intrastate reach. That is, the clause enabled Congress to legislate on a wide range of subjects and to reach deep within the states while doing so. This happened because it came to be accepted that Congress could regulate intrastate matters if such matters had a sufficient effect on interstate commerce. In 1914, for example, the Court let Congress regulate railroad rates within Texas (an intrastate matter) because of the economic impact those rates had on an interstate subject Congress obviously could regulate: rail traffic between Texas and Louisiana.

In that 1914 case, Congress was regulating for broadly commercial reasons, and not for "police power" purposes such as the public health, safety, morals, and welfare. Eventually, though, the "affecting commerce" doctrine was used to justify federal regulation of noneconomic matters within the states. In 1964, for instance, the Court considered whether the 1964 Civil Rights Act's ban on racial discrimination by restaurants applied to Ollie's Barbecue, a 220-seat family-owned establishment in Birmingham, Alabama whose business was almost totally local. In fact, there was no claim that interstate travelers ever visited Ollie's. Nonetheless, the Court found that Ollie's racial discrimination was within the commerce power because it affected interstate commerce. For one thing, such discrimination restricted interstate travel by black people. Furthermore, Ollie's discrimination meant that it did less business and therefore reduced its interstate meat purchases. The Court conceded that, due to Ollie's small size, each of these effects on interstate commerce was insignificant taken by itself. But the aggregate effect of racial discrimination by all similarly situated restaurants was significant, and this was enough to justify federal regulation of Ollie's.

Due to such decisions, it used to be widely believed that there are few, if any, limits to Congress's regulatory power under the commerce clause. To be sure, an effect on interstate commerce had to be shown if Congress was to regulate intrastate activities. But in the complex, interconnected social and economic life of modern America, some such effect usually could be found if a court wanted to find it. In addition, courts often would defer to congressional statements that the necessary effect on interstate commerce exists.

In 1995, however, the Court breathed new life into the enumerated powers doctrine when it decided *United States v. Lopez*. In that case, the Court struck down a federal statute forbidding the knowing possession of a firearm within a school zone because the forbidden behavior lacked a *substantial* effect on interstate commerce. The following *Morrison* case, which was decided by a 5-4 vote, continues this new trend.

## United States v. Morrison
U.S. Supreme Court
529 U.S. 598 (2000)

### Background and Facts

In 1994, a female student at Virginia Polytechnic Institute allegedly was raped by two Virginia Tech football players. She claimed that after the rape one of the players told her: "You better not have any [expletive deleted] diseases." Later, in a dormitory dining room, the same player allegedly said that he liked to get women drunk and have sex with them.

The female student (the petitioner below) sued the two players and the university in federal district court under Section 13981 of the federal Violence Against Women Act of 1994, which provided a civil remedy for crimes of violence motivated by gender. Such crimes included those "due, at least in part, to an animus based on the victim's gender." The players moved to dismiss the claim on the basis that the relevant provisions of the act were an unconstitutional assertion of Congressional power. The district court agreed, dismissing the student's claim. After a full panel of the Fourth Circuit Court of Appeals affirmed this decision, the case came before the United States Supreme Court.

### Body of Opinion

**Chief Justice Rehnquist.** Every law enacted by Congress must be based on one or more of its powers enumerated in the Constitution. The powers of the legislature are defined and limited; and [so] that those limits may not be mistaken or forgotten, the Constitution is written. Congress explicitly identified the sources of federal authority on which it relied in enacting Section 13981. It said that a "federal civil rights cause of action" is established "[p]ursuant to the affirmative power of Congress . . . under . . . Section 8 of Article I of the Constitution. . . . " [The petitioner relies] upon the third clause of the Article, which gives Congress power "[t]o regulate Commerce with foreign Nations, and among the several States, and with the Indian Tribes."

As we discussed at length in *Lopez*, our interpretation of the commerce clause has changed as our nation has developed. . . . In the years since 1937, Congress has had considerably greater latitude in regulating conduct and transactions under the commerce clause than our previous case law permitted. . . .

[Petitioner seeks] to sustain Section 13981 as a regulation of activity that substantially affects interstate commerce. . . . Section 13981 is supported by numerous findings regarding the serious impact that gender-motivated violence has on victims and their families. But the existence of Congressional findings is not sufficient, by itself, to sustain the constitutionality of commerce clause legislation. As we stated in *Lopez*, simply because Congress may conclude that a particular activity substantially affects interstate commerce does not necessarily make it so. . . .

Congress's findings are substantially weakened by the fact that they rely so heavily on a method of reasoning that we have already rejected as unworkable if we are to maintain the constitution's enumeration of powers. Congress found that gender-motivated violence affects interstate commerce:

> By deterring potential victims from traveling interstate, from engaging in employment in interstate business, and from transacting with business, and in places, involved in interstate commerce; . . . by diminishing national productivity, increasing medical and other costs, and decreasing the supply of and the demand for interstate products.

Given these findings and petitioner's arguments, the concern that we expressed in *Lopez* that Congress might use the commerce clause to completely obliterate the constitution's distinction between national and local authority seems well-founded. The reasoning that petitioner advances seeks to follow the but-for causal chain from the initial occurrence of violent crime . . . to every attenuated effect upon interstate commerce. . . . Petitioner's reasoning, moreover, will not limit Congress to regulating violence, but may . . . be applied equally as well to family law and other areas of traditional state regulation, since the aggregate effect of marriage, divorce, and childrearing on the national economy is undoubtedly significant. . . .

We accordingly reject the argument that Congress may regulate noneconomic, violent criminal conduct based solely on that conduct's aggregate effect on interstate commerce. The Constitution requires a distinction between what is truly national and what is truly local. In recognizing this fact we preserve one of the few principles that has been consistent since the [commerce] clause was adopted. The regulation and punishment of intrastate violence that is not directed at the instrumentalities, channels, or goods involved in interstate commerce has always been the province of the states. Indeed, we can think of no better example of the police power, which the Founders denied the national government and reposed in the states, than the suppression of violent crimes and vindication of its victims.

### Judgment and Result

Court of appeals decision affirmed; the female student's claim under the Violence Against Women Act fails.

### Questions

1. Why was the language used by one of the players important for the plaintiff's claim under the Violence Against Women Act?
2. Does the Supreme Court's decision leave the female student without any claim against the players or the university?

3. Suppose that the players had raped the student on a train bound from Virginia to North Carolina. Suppose further that the Violence Against Women Act had included a provision providing civil remedies for crimes against women committed on trains bound from one state to another. Would that provision have been an unconstitutional assertion of the commerce power?

4. Did Chief Justice Rehnquist show that gender-motivated violence has *no* effect on interstate commerce? If not, how did he argue?

## THE TAXING POWER

Article I, Section 8 gives Congress "Power To lay and collect Taxes, Duties, Imposts and Excises." The purpose behind this language is to let Congress raise revenue for the operations of government.[3] But our concern here is with the use of this **taxing power** to regulate. Taxation can regulate because it tends to discourage the activity taxed. The power to tax, it is said, is the power to destroy.

Since the 1930s, the courts usually have upheld Congress's use of the taxing power for regulatory purposes unrelated to the raising of revenue. In recent years, few cases have explored the limits of Congress's regulatory authority under the taxing power. To some extent, this reflects the broad reach of the commerce power and the inefficiencies involved with using taxation to regulate, both of which make the commerce power the preferred basis for federal regulation of the economy. But even though its outer limits are uncertain, the taxing power is still a very sweeping source of congressional regulatory authority.

## THE SPENDING POWER

Immediately after stating the taxing power, Article I, Section 8 goes on to give Congress the power "to pay the Debts and provide for the common Defence and general Welfare of the United States." This language has been read as giving Congress broad authority to spend for the public welfare. The **spending power** is an important source of federal authority to regulate. This is accomplished by conditioning federal appropriations on compliance with a specified course of behavior. Just as the taxing power is a stick compelling chosen conduct through fear of financial loss, the spending power is a carrot inducing favored behavior through the promise of economic reward.

Although the spending power can be employed for a wide range of purposes, there are some limits on its use. The constitutional language quoted above limits federal spending to the promotion of general purposes, and this requirement could block conditional grant programs that serve special interests. Also, the Supreme Court has declared that if Congress wishes to put a condition on the receipt of federal money, it must do so clearly. Moreover, the Court has said that the condition must be reasonably related to the purpose behind the federal expenditure. For example, Congress might run into constitutional problems if it tries to condition the receipt of federal health care money on a state's elimination of highway billboards. Finally, note that, in theory, the would-be recipient of a conditional federal grant can avoid the condition by doing without federal money.

---

[3] The Constitution places certain restrictions on the use of taxation to raise revenue, but these restrictions are beyond the scope of this text.

## INDEPENDENT CHECKS APPLYING TO BOTH CONGRESS AND THE STATES

This portion of the chapter examines certain constitutional limitations that apply to both the federal government and the states. The provisions we discuss are the due process guarantees contained in the Fifth and Fourteenth Amendments, the First Amendment's guarantee of free speech, and the Fourteenth Amendment's equal protection clause. Each has its business applications, and our discussion is largely limited to those applications. Before examining them, however, we must consider some preliminary matters.

### INCORPORATION

The Fifth Amendment applies only to the federal government and the Fourteenth Amendment only to the states. Because each amendment contains a due process clause, due process applies at both the federal and state levels. The First Amendment, however, only restricts the federal government. Its application to the states, which first occurred early in this century, happened because of its incorporation within the liberty protected by the Fourteenth Amendment's due process clause. By now, most other Bill of Rights provisions also have been incorporated within Fourteenth Amendment due process liberty and thus apply to the states. This process was reversed in the case of the Fourteenth Amendment's equal protection clause. The Fourteenth Amendment applies only to the states, but its equal protection guarantee has been incorporated within the Fifth Amendment's due process clause and thus applies to the federal government. Figure 5.2 summarizes the points made in this and the preceding paragraph.

### MEANS-ENDS TESTS

Means-ends tests are used when laws are challenged under the constitution's individual rights provisions. They exist because no constitutional right is absolute in the sense that it can never be restricted by the government. Thus, such tests try to strike a balance between individual rights and the needs of society. They do so by (1) stating how important a challenged law's ends must be in order for that law to be constitutional, and (2) stating how effectively the challenged law must advance those ends in order for the law to be constitutional.

### FIGURE 5.2 THE APPLICATION OF INDEPENDENT CHECKS TO THE FEDERAL GOVERNMENT AND THE STATES

|  | Federal Government | States |
|---|---|---|
| Due Process | Fifth Amendment | Fourteenth Amendment |
| Free Speech | First Amendment | Incorporation within Fourteenth Amendment |
| Equal Protection | Incorporation within Fifth Amendment | Fourteenth Amendment |

Because courts regard some rights as more important than others and therefore require more justification for favored rights to be restricted, means-ends tests come in many forms. Here, we oversimplify by identifying three different kinds of means-ends scrutiny:

1. *Full strict scrutiny.* This very tough test of constitutionality is reserved for rights of special importance. A court employing full strict scrutiny might say that, to be constitutional, a challenged law must be *necessary* to the achievement of a *compelling* government purpose.
2. *Intermediate scrutiny.* This fairly tough test of constitutionality comes in many different forms. One example discussed later in the chapter is the test applied to laws that discriminate on the basis of gender. This test says that such laws must be *substantially* related to the promotion of an *important* government purpose.
3. *The rational basis test.* A typical formulation of this lenient test of constitutionality says that a challenged law must be *rationally* related to a *legitimate* government purpose in order to be constitutional. The rational basis test is the basic constitutional standard under the equal protection clause.

## STATE ACTION

Most of the Constitution's individual rights protections only protect people against government activity. Such activity typically is described as **government action** or **state action**. Thus, the Constitution's individual rights provisions usually do not protect people when their rights are infringed by private actors.[4] However, state and federal statutes often provide such protection.

The Supreme Court's attempts to draw the line between government activity and private activity have created great confusion. In part, this is because the Court has drawn the line differently at different times. Before World War II, state action was limited to the activities of formally governmental bodies such as legislatures, administrative agencies, courts, municipalities, and state universities. Beginning in the late 1940s, however, the definition of *state action* expanded considerably, with all sorts of formally private activities being subjected to constitutional restrictions.

In a 1948 case, the Supreme Court found that a private agreement among white property owners forbidding the transfer of their land to nonwhites was unconstitutional state action because the state of Missouri enforced it in court. Two years earlier, the Court applied the First Amendment to a company town owned by a private corporation, because the town performed all the functions of a regular municipality. This **public function doctrine** reached its high point in 1968, when it was extended to cover a private shopping center.

During the 1960s and early 1970s, courts considered various other factors when making government action determinations. Among the considerations leading courts to find state action were extensive government *regulation* of a private activity, substantial government *funding* of such activity, and *public-private cooperation* (or *symbiosis*) of the sort found in the defense industry.

---

[4] One exception is the Thirteenth Amendment, which flatly says that neither slavery nor involuntary servitude shall exist within the United States, except as punishment for crimes. Also, some state constitutions do not have a government action requirement.

Why did state action expand so dramatically in the twenty-five years following World War II? One reason is that for much of that time, the Supreme Court was dominated by justices who were anxious to protect certain individual rights and concerned about the way private bodies might infringe those rights. "Constitutionalizing" private bodies through an expansion of state action was a way to prevent them from discriminating and from threatening personal liberty.

Beginning in the early 1970s, however, the Court's composition began to change. The result was a contraction in the reach of government action. To be sure, state action has not yet returned to its narrow pre-World War II definition, and the cases expanding the doctrine have not been overruled. Nonetheless, constitutional challenges to formally private activity are less likely to succeed today than they were twenty or thirty years ago. The public function doctrine, for instance, is now limited to situations where a private entity exercises powers, such as police protection, that have *traditionally* been *exclusively* reserved to government. Even private activity that is extensively regulated and/or publicly funded is not necessarily state action. Recent state action cases have stated that, for a state action to be present, the government must be *responsible* for the activity challenged as unconstitutional by directly compelling or encouraging it.

In 2001, however, the Court arguably expanded the scope of state action under what may be a new theory: *entwinement* between the government and a formally private body. The private body in question was the Tennessee Secondary School Athletic Association, which regulates interscholastic sports among the state's public and private high schools. By a 5-4 vote, the Court found the Association a government actor due to its entwinement with the state. It did so for the following reasons, among others: (1) most of the state's public high schools were Association members and they comprised 84 percent of the Association's membership; (2) within the Association, each school was represented by a principal or faculty member who voted to select the Association's governing body, which itself was composed of school administrators; (3) because athletics are an important function of high schools, all these people acted in their official capacity when they performed services for the Association; (4) state Board of Education personnel sat as nonvoting members of the Association's governing body; and (5) Association employees participated in the state's retirement system.

## BUSINESS AND THE FIRST AMENDMENT

Under the First Amendment's free speech guarantee, many kinds of expression receive a very high degree of constitutional protection. Laws restricting such expression receive something like the full strict scrutiny described earlier. The most common justification for this protection is the social interest in the free competition of ideas. "[T]he best test of truth," Justice Oliver Wendell Holmes once wrote, "is the power of the thought to get itself accepted in the competition of the market."[5] If government can exclude speech from the marketplace of ideas, many believe, our ability to separate truth from falsehood would suffer.

Most of the issues raised by the First Amendment's free speech guarantee are beyond the scope of this text, as are the special problems of the communications media and of corporate political financing. Here, we limit ourselves to two First Amendment doctrines affecting government's ability to regulate speech by

---

[5] *Abrams v. United States*, 250 U.S. 616 (1919) (Holmes, J., dissenting).

corporations and other business entities. In each case, the "marketplace" argument for free speech is the basis for the First Amendment protection business receives.

*Corporate Political Speech.* In *First National Bank of Boston v. Bellotti* (1978), the Supreme Court struck down a state law forbidding corporate expenditures to influence a public vote on a matter not involving the property or business of the affected corporation. In the process, *Bellotti* established a corporation's First Amendment right to express itself on public issues unrelated to its direct economic interests. In 1980, the Court used this right to strike down a state public service commission's refusal to allow a utility to include inserts promoting nuclear power in the bills it sent to its customers. And in 1986 it invalidated a state utility commission order compelling a regulated private utility to periodically include the comments of a rate reform group in its billing envelopes.

The policy behind *Bellotti's* protection of corporate political speech is the social interest in the free competition of ideas—an interest that would be frustrated by arbitrarily removing corporations from the political marketplace of ideas. Therefore, laws restricting the right of corporate political speech receive strict scrutiny. Critics of business, however, have attacked *Bellotti* as an unjustified assist to corporate power. The assets and communications skills possessed by large corporations, these critics argue, enable corporations to distort the free market of ideas in favor of their own interests.

*Commercial Speech.* Commercial speech might be defined as expression proposing a commercial transaction. The main example is commercial advertising. Drawing the line between commercial speech and other forms of protected First Amendment speech can be difficult. In a 1983 case, for example, a corporation's marketing campaign for condoms included the mass mailing of "informational pamphlets" discussing the usefulness of condoms (especially the corporation's own brand) for preventing venereal disease and aiding family planning. Individually, the fact that the pamphlets were advertisements, their reference to a specific product, and the corporation's economic motivation for mailing them were not enough to convince the Supreme Court that they should be regarded as commercial speech. The combination of all these characteristics, however, made the pamphlets commercial speech.

In 1942, the Supreme Court held that commercial speech is not entitled to First Amendment protection. During the 1970s, however, the Court concluded that commercial speech is covered by the First Amendment, but that it receives an intermediate level of constitutional protection. The specific test, which comes from *Central Hudson Gas & Electric Corporation v. Public Service Commission* (1980), is stated in the following *Lorillard* case.

The main reason for protecting commercial speech is to increase the flow of consumer information, and thus to promote free competition and economic efficiency. This purpose arguably was achieved in some Supreme Court decisions striking down state restrictions on advertising by professionals such as lawyers and pharmacists. These restrictions probably limited competition for such professionals' products and services and allowed them to charge inflated prices. However, some laws restricting commercial speech help consumers make informed, rational choices and thus promote competition and efficiency. Examples include measures that regulate deceptive, misleading, or overaggressive advertising, or that require firms to disclose information useful to consumers. Laws of this kind get only light First Amendment scrutiny.

## Lorillard Tobacco Co. v. Reilly
### 533 U.S. 525 (2001)
### U.S. Supreme Court

## Background and Facts

In 1999, the Attorney General of Massachusetts promulgated comprehensive regulations governing the advertising and sale of cigarettes, smokeless tobacco, and cigars. Among these regulations were: (1) a ban on smokeless tobacco and cigar advertising within a 1,000-foot radius of a school or playground; (2) a point-of-sale regulation stating that advertising for smokeless tobacco and cigars could not be placed lower than five feet from the floor of any retail establishment located within a 1,000-foot radius of a school or playground; and (3) other miscellaneous regulations that restricted certain sales practices by sellers of cigarettes, smokeless tobacco, and cigars.

Various tobacco manufacturers and retailers challenged these regulations and others promulgated by the Attorney General in federal district court. Among other constitutional claims, they argued that the regulations violated the First Amendment. After the parties moved for summary judgment, the district court upheld the ban on outdoor advertising and the sales practices regulations, but struck down the point-of-sale rule. The First Circuit Court of Appeals affirmed the district court on the first two points, but reversed its decision to strike down the point-of-sale rule. The plaintiffs (petitioners below) then appealed to the United States Supreme Court.

## Body of Opinion

**Justice O'Connor.** For over 25 years, the Court has recognized that commercial speech does not fall outside the purview of the First Amendment. Instead, the Court has afforded commercial speech a measure of First Amendment protection commensurate with its position in relation to other constitutionally guaranteed expression. . . . The analysis contains four elements:

[1] At the outset, we must determine whether the expression is protected by the First Amendment. For commercial speech to come within that provision, it at least must concern lawful activity and not be misleading. [2] Next, we ask whether the asserted government interest is substantial. If both inquiries yield positive answers, we must determine [3] whether the regulation directly advances the governmental interest asserted, and [4] whether it is not more extensive than is necessary to serve that interest. *Central Hudson Gas & Electric Corp v. Public Service Commission* (1980).

Only the last two steps of *Central Hudson's* four-part analysis are at issue here. The Attorney General has assumed that petitioners' speech is entitled to First Amendment protection. With respect to the second step, none of the petitioners contests the importance of the state's interest in preventing the use of tobacco products by minors. The third step of *Central Hudson* concerns the relationship between the harm that underlies the state's interest and the means identified by the state to advance that interest. It requires that the speech restriction directly and materially advance the asserted governmental interest. . . . The last step of the *Central Hudson* analysis complements the third step, asking whether the speech restriction is not more extensive than necessary to serve the interests that support it. [Here,] . . . the case law requires a reasonable fit between the legislature's ends and the means chosen to accomplish those ends, a means narrowly tailored to achieve the desired objective.

The outdoor advertising regulations prohibit smokeless tobacco or cigar advertising within a 1,000-foot radius of a school or playground. . . . Whatever the strength of the Attorney General's evidence to justify the outdoor advertising regulations, we conclude that the regulations do not satisfy the fourth step of the *Central Hudson* analysis, [which] . . . requires a reasonable fit between the means and ends of the regulatory scheme. . . . The broad sweep of the regulations indicates that the Attorney General did not carefully calculate the costs and benefits associated with the burden on speech imposed by the regulations. . . . In the district court, petitioners maintained that this prohibition would prevent advertising in 87 to 91 percent of Boston, Worcester, and Springfield. The 87 to 91 percent figure appears to include not only the effect of the regulations, but also the limitations imposed by other generally applicable zoning regulations. The Attorney General disputed petitioners' figures but conceded that the reach of the regulations is substantial. . . . The substantial geographical reach of the Attorney General's outdoor advertising regulations is compounded by other factors. "Outdoor" advertising includes not only advertising located outside an establishment, but also advertising inside a store if that advertising is visible from outside the store. The regulations restrict advertisements of any size and the term "advertisement" also includes oral statements. In some geographical areas, these regulations would constitute nearly a complete ban on the communication of truthful information about smokeless tobacco and cigars to adult consumers. . . .

Massachusetts has also restricted indoor, point-of-sale advertising for smokeless tobacco and cigars. Advertising cannot be placed lower than five feet from the floor of any retail establishment which is located within a 1,000-foot radius of any school or playground. . . . We conclude that [these] regulations fail both the third and fourth steps of the *Central Hudson* analysis. A regulation cannot be sustained if it provides only ineffective or remote support for the government's purpose, or if there is little chance that the restriction will advance the state's goal. As outlined above, the state's goal is to prevent minors from using tobacco products and to curb demand for that activity by limiting youth exposure to advertising. The five-foot rule does not seem to advance that goal. Not all children are less than five feet tall, and those who are certainly have the ability to look up and take in their surroundings. . . .

The Attorney General also promulgated a number of regulations that restrict sales practices by cigarette, smokeless tobacco, and cigar manufacturers and retailers. Among other restrictions, the regulations bar the use of self-service displays and require that tobacco products be placed out of the reach of all consumers in a location accessible only to salespersons. . . .

The district court concluded that these restrictions implicate no cognizable speech interest, but the court of appeals did not fully adopt that reasoning. . . . [Even] assuming that petitioners have a cognizable speech interest in a particular means of displaying their products, these regulations withstand First Amendment scrutiny. . . . Unattended displays of tobacco products present an opportunity for access without the proper age verification required by law. Thus, the state prohibits self-service and other displays that would allow an individual to obtain tobacco products without direct contact with a salesperson. It is clear that the regulations leave open ample channels of communication. The regulations do not significantly impede adult access to tobacco products. Moreover, retailers have other means of exercising any cognizable speech interest in the presentation of their products. We presume that vendors may place empty tobacco packaging on open display, and display actual tobacco products so long as that display is only accessible to sales personnel. . . . We conclude that the sales practices regulations withstand First Amendment scrutiny. The means chosen by the state are narrowly tailored to prevent access to tobacco products by minors, are unrelated to expression, and leave open alternative avenues for vendors to convey information about products and for would-be customers to inspect products before purchase.

## Judgment and Result

On the First Amendment questions, the Supreme Court upheld the court of appeals' judgment in part and reversed it in part. Specifically, the Supreme Court struck down the ban on outdoor advertising and the point-of-sale regulation, but upheld the sales practices regulations. The case was remanded for further proceedings consistent with the Court's opinion.

## Questions

1. Why were the first two elements of the *Central Hudson* test not at issue in this case?
2. What is the difference between the third and fourth elements of the *Central Hudson* test?
3. In the portion of the Court's opinion discussing the ban on outdoor advertising, we omitted several pages discussing many studies which purported to show that cigar and smokeless tobacco use by minors has become a fairly serious national problem, and that advertising for such products contributes to the problem. Why did these studies not matter to the Court's decision to strike down the outdoor advertising ban?
4. In the last paragraph of the opinion, note the claim that the sales practices regulations "implicate no cognizable speech interest." This probably means that these regulations did not really restrict speech at all. Did the Court agree with this argument? If not, how did it treat the question of whether the sales practices regulations restrict speech?

## DUE PROCESS

The Fifth and Fourteenth Amendments prevent the federal government and the states from depriving any person of life, liberty, or property without due process of law. For a violation of these provisions to occur, there must be: (1) a deprivation of life, liberty, or property; (2) by government (the state action requirement discussed earlier); (3) without due process of law. The due process guarantee has both *procedural* and *substantive* dimensions. Rules of substantive law establish rights, duties, and standards of behavior governing individuals as they act in society. Procedural rules concern the legal machinery through which substantive rules are enforced. For example, the law of contract is substantive. But the legal rules detailing the steps through which a court must proceed in a suit for breach of contract are procedural. When due process is substantive, it involves a constitutional attack on the fairness of substantive rules. When it is procedural, it involves a constitutional attack on the fairness of procedural rules. In each case, the relevant notions of fairness are quite different.

*Procedural Due Process.* The traditional definition of due process is procedural. The central theme of this **procedural due process** is that people are entitled to both reasonable notice of the charges to be brought against them and a fair trial

*Check out the actual text of the Fifth and Fourteenth Amendments' due process clauses at* **http://www. law.cornell.edu/** *under "Constitutions and Codes."*

or hearing before government can deprive them of life, liberty, or property. Historically, procedural due process probably has been most important in criminal cases. But it can apply any time that either a state or the federal government deprives a person of life, liberty, or property.

In order for there to be a violation of due process, the claimant must have been deprived of either liberty or property. Procedural due process liberty is very broadly defined, and it is difficult to specify its scope with any precision. Procedural due process property interests, on the other hand, usually are created by state law. For someone to have such an interest, moreover, the person must have an actual, legitimate claim of entitlement to it, rather than some abstract need or desire for it. The range of protected property interests is broad. Examples include a horse trainer's license, utility service, disability benefits, welfare benefits, government employment, and a driver's license.

The typical procedural due process claim arises when the government deprives a person of life, liberty, or property, and the person claims that the deprivation occurred without constitutionally adequate procedural safeguards. What procedural standards is government required to meet in such cases? As we saw earlier, the central requirements are reasonable notice and some fair trial or hearing. But the actual standards courts apply inevitably vary from situation to situation. Someone who loses welfare benefits, for instance, is not entitled to the same procedural due process as a defendant in a murder case. The following case discusses some factors that courts examine when determining what process is due.

## Gilbert v. Homar
United States Supreme Court
520 U.S. 924 (1997)

## Background and Facts

On August 26, 1992, while employed as a policeman at East Stroudsburg University (ESU), a state institution, Richard Homar was arrested by the state police and charged with a drug felony. ESU officials then suspended Homar without notice or a hearing pending their own investigation. This suspension was without pay. Although the criminal charges were dismissed on September 1, Homar's suspension remained in effect. On September 18, he finally was provided the opportunity to tell his side of the story to ESU officials. Subsequently, he was demoted to groundskeeper. He then filed suit under a federal civil rights statute, claiming that university officials' failure to provide him with notice and a hearing before suspending him without pay violated due process. The federal district court granted ESU summary judgment, but the court of appeals reversed. ESU appealed to the U.S. Supreme Court.

## Body of Opinion

**Justice Scalia.** The protections of the due process clause apply to government deprivation of those perquisites of government employment in which the employee has a constitutionally protected property interest. Although we have previously held that public employees who can be discharged only for cause have a constitutionally protected property interest in their tenure and cannot be fired without due process, we have not had occasion to decide whether the protections of the due process clause extend to discipline of tenured public employees short of termination. ESU, however, does not contest this preliminary point, and so without deciding it we will, like the district court, assume that the suspension infringed a protected property interest, and turn at once to ESU's contention that Homar received all the process he was due.

In *Cleveland Board of Education v. Loudermill* (1985), we concluded that a public employee dismissible only for cause was entitled to a very limited hearing prior to his termination, to be followed by a more comprehensive post-termination hearing. Stressing that the pre-termination hearing should be an initial check against mistaken decisions—essentially, a determination of whether there are reasonable grounds to believe that the charges against the employee are true and support the proposed action, we held that pre-termination process need only include oral or written notice of the charges, an explanation of the employer's evidence, and an opportunity for the employee to tell his side of the story. . . .

It is by now well established that due process, unlike some legal rules, is not a technical conception with a fixed content unrelated to time, place and circumstances. Due process is flexible and calls for such procedural protections as the particular situation demands. This Court has recognized, on many occasions, that where a state must act quickly, or where it would be impractical to provide pre-deprivation process, post-deprivation process satisfies the requirements of the due process clause. . . .

To determine what process is constitutionally due, we have generally balanced three distinct factors: first, the private interest that will be affected by the official action; second, the risk of an erroneous deprivation of such interest through the procedures used, and the probable value, if any, of additional or substitute procedural safeguards; and finally, the government's interest. Homar contends that he has a significant private interest in the uninterrupted receipt of his paycheck. But while our opinions have recognized the severity of depriving someone of the means of his livelihood, they have also emphasized that in determining what process is due, account must be taken of the length and finality of the deprivation. Unlike the employee in *Loudermill*, who faced termination, Homar faced only a temporary suspension without pay. So long as the suspended employee receives a sufficiently prompt post-suspension hearing, the lost income is relatively insubstantial (compared with termination), and fringe benefits such as health and life insurance are often not affected at all.

On the other side of the balance, the state has a significant interest in immediately suspending, when felony charges are filed against them, employees who occupy positions of great public trust and high public visibility, such as police officers. Homar contends that this interest in maintaining public confidence could have been accommodated by suspending him with pay until he had a hearing. We think, however, that the government does not have to give an employee charged with a felony a paid leave at taxpayer expense. If his services to the government are no longer useful once the felony charge has been filed, the Constitution does not require the government to bear the added expense of hiring a replacement while still paying him. . . .

The last factor in the balancing, and the factor most important to resolution of this case, is the risk of erroneous deprivation and the likely value of any additional procedures. . . . We noted in *Loudermill* that the purpose of a pre-termination hearing is to determine whether there are reasonable grounds to believe the charges

against the employee are true and support the proposed action. By parity of reasoning, the purpose of any pre-*suspension* hearing would be to assure that there are reasonable grounds to support the suspension without pay. But here that has already been assured by the arrest and the filing of charges. . . . They serve to assure that the state employer's decision to suspend the employee is not baseless or unwarranted, in that an independent third party has determined that there is probable cause to believe the employee committed a serious crime. . . .

Whether Homar was provided an adequately prompt *post*-suspension hearing in the present case is a separate question. Although the charges against Homar were dropped on September 1 . . . , he did not receive any sort of hearing until September 18. Once the charges were dropped, the risk of erroneous deprivation increased substantially, and, as petitioners conceded at oral argument, there was likely value in holding a prompt hearing.

Because neither the Court of Appeals nor the District Court addressed whether, under the particular facts of this case, ESU violated due process by failing to provide a sufficiently prompt post-suspension hearing, we will not consider this issue in the first instance, but remand for consideration by the Court of Appeals.

## Judgment and Result

The Court held that ESU's failure to give Homar notice and a hearing before suspending him without pay did not violate due process. The failure to give Homar a prompt *post*-suspension hearing, however, might have violated due process. The court of appeals' decision was reversed and the case was returned to the court of appeals for it to consider whether Homar should have received a post-deprivation hearing.

## Questions

1. Did ESU deprive Homar of a property interest? How did the Court deal with this question?
2. Of the three factors the Court considered, which favored ESU and which favored Homar?
3. Why did the Court not decide whether Homar should have received a post-deprivation hearing?

*Substantive Due Process.* On occasion, the Supreme Court has given due process a substantive meaning by deciding whether a deprivation of liberty or property is justified as a matter of sound public policy. Here, the Court is looking at the reasonableness of a rule for the governance of social life, and not at the procedural machinery through which such a substantive rule is enforced. In its various forms, this **substantive due process** usually involves two steps: (1) choosing certain preferred rights and including them within the liberty or property protected by the Fifth and Fourteenth Amendments, and (2) giving such liberty or property interests substantive protection by applying some kind of means-ends scrutiny to laws that deprive people of those interests.

From the 1890s through the 1930s, the Supreme Court created the doctrine now known as *economic substantive due process*. It did so by including various economic freedoms among the liberty and property rights protected by the Fifth and Fourteenth Amendments, and by requiring laws restricting these freedoms to meet some means-ends test or other test of constitutionality. In *Lochner v. New York* (1905), for example, it required that for freedom of contract to be restricted by government, there had to be a real and substantial relationship between the restriction and a valid governmental purpose. Then it used this test to strike down a New York statute setting maximum hours of work for bakery employees. It concluded that this law, which obviously restricted freedom of contract, did not have a sufficiently close relationship to valid public purposes such as protecting worker health.

As the previous example indicates, the old economic form of substantive due process sometimes was a threat to laws regulating working conditions and to other kinds of government regulations. Still, most social and economic regulations challenged on substantive due process grounds in the first part of this century survived the attack. After 1937, moreover, the doctrine ceased to be a serious threat to government regulation of social and economic matters. Since then, such regulations have usually been tested under a weak rational basis test when they are challenged on substantive due process grounds. Thus, they have virtually always survived the challenge.

But substantive due process lives on in noneconomic areas of life. The main example consists of several fundamental "privacy" rights that receive an extremely high degree of constitutional protection. Recently, the Supreme Court has said that these include the rights to marry, have children, direct their education and upbringing, enjoy marital privacy, use contraception, and have an abortion. Laws restricting these rights, it continued, must be narrowly tailored to meet a compelling government purpose. Laws that restrict nonfundamental rights, however, get some kind of rational basis review.

The following case presents two distinct substantive due process claims. The first is an economic substantive due process argument based on the right to pursue the trade, profession, or occupation of one's choice. The second is a privacy claim based on a woman's right to choose how she shall give birth to a child.

## Lange-Kessler v. Department of Education
### United States Courts of Appeals for Second Circuit
### 109 F.3d 137 (1997)

### Background and Facts

New York's Professional Midwifery Practice Act (PMPA) limits the practice of midwifery. One provision of the act requires that midwifery must be practiced in accordance with a written practice agreement between the midwife and: (1) a board- certified obstetrician-gynecologist; (2) a licensed physician who practices obstetrics; or (3) a hospital that provides obstetric services. Another PMPA provision basically requires that all applicants for a professional midwifery license meet educational requirements for both the practice of nursing and the practice of midwifery.

Julia Lange-Kessler was a direct-entry midwife. A direct-entry midwife trains through apprenticeship with other midwives rather than through formal education. Because Lange-Kessler could not be licensed under the PMPA, she sued in federal district court, claiming that the act deprived her of the ability to earn a living in her chosen profession, in violation of the Fourteenth Amendment's due process clause. Joining Lange-Kessler's lawsuit were three women of child-bearing age who had previously used Lange-Kessler's home-birthing services and who wished to do so again. These women claimed that, by restricting their right to choose a birthing style and a qualified attendant of their choice, the PMPA violated their right to privacy under Fourteenth Amendment due process.

The state then moved for summary judgment. In support of its motion, the state submitted an affidavit from Mary Applegate, who was Medical Director for Reproductive and Perinatal Health at the New York State Department of Health, and was responsible for reviewing the credentials and practice arrangements of nurse-midwives applying for practice in New York State. Dr. Applegate asserted that direct-entry midwives are not qualified to handle the physical complications that may arise during pregnancy and childbirth. In response, the plaintiffs filed approximately twenty-eight affidavits from consumers of direct-entry midwives' services, various midwives, and physicians. Collectively, those affidavits contended that home births supervised by direct-entry midwives are just as safe as births performed by doctors or nurse-midwives. In addition, the affidavits of the licensed nurse-midwives claimed that licensed obstetricians refused to enter into practice agreements with them, thus preventing the midwives from performing home births.

The district court granted the state's motion for summary judgment, and the plaintiffs appealed.

## Body of Opinion

**Judge Parker.** This action presents a substantive due process challenge to the Professional Midwifery Practice Act. There are principally two issues on appeal: (1) whether the district court erred when it determined that the PMPA is rationally related to a legitimate state interest; and (2) whether the district court erred when it determined that the right to privacy does not encompass the right to choose a direct-entry midwife to assist with childbirth. We affirm the district court on both issues. . . .

The right to follow a chosen profession is a property interest protected by the Fifth and Fourteenth Amendments. State-imposed restrictions on this right must be rationally related to a legitimate state interest. A statute regulating a profession is presumed to have a rational basis unless the plaintiff shows that the legislative facts upon which the statute is apparently based could not reasonably be conceived to be true by the governmental decisionmaker. To defeat this challenge, the state is not required to come forth with empirical evidence tending to show that the facts underlying the restrictions are true. Rather, a statute withstands a substantive due process challenge if it might be thought that enacting the statute was a rational way to further a legitimate interest.

In the instant case, the state has identified an interest in protecting the health and welfare of mothers and infants. In *Roe v. Wade*, the Supreme Court specifically categorized those same interests as "important and legitimate" ones. Therefore, as long as the restrictions that the PMPA places on the practice of midwifery are rationally related to protecting the health and welfare of mothers and infants, those restrictions must be upheld. Put another way, the relevant question is whether the legislature might have thought that an applicant with (1) a formal education and (2) a written practice agreement with a licensed physician or hospital is more fit to practice midwifery than

is an applicant without these qualifications. This question must be answered in the affirmative.

The affidavit of Dr. Applegate describes two conditions that may arise during pregnancy: pregnancy-induced hypertension and gestational diabetes mellitus. According to Dr. Applegate, if left untreated, these conditions may result in the death of mother and fetus. In addition, Dr. Applegate describes several potentially fatal complications that may arise during the birthing process, including fetal distress, failure to progress, postpartum hemorrhaging, and ruptured uterus. . . . In light of these risks, the legislature could reasonably have believed that midwives who have completed a nursing program, and who are affiliated with a medical professional, are more fit than direct-entry midwives to practice midwifery. Moreover, insuring the fitness of midwives is rationally related to the state's legitimate interest in protecting the health and welfare of mothers and infants. Plaintiffs argue, however, that genuine issues of material fact exist as to whether direct-entry midwives are less capable than other professionals of diagnosing and treating the various complications associated with pregnancy and childbirth. For example, they argue that because their own experts contested Dr. Applegate's assertions that direct-entry midwives exhibit poor judgment while attending home births, summary judgment was improper as the district court could not conclude, as a matter of law, that the state legislature could reasonably rely on the facts asserted in her affidavit. Plaintiffs' argument, in and of itself, demonstrates the futility of their constitutional challenge: If reasonable minds could differ on the issue of a direct-entry midwife's competence, then it is wholly conceivable that the legislature took the view that direct-entry midwives are not likely to be sufficiently competent. Accordingly, we affirm the district court on this issue.

In *Griswold v. Connecticut* (1965), the Supreme Court established that the Constitution guarantees the fundamental right to privacy. Since that time, the right to privacy has been interpreted to protect freedom of choice in certain matters related to childbearing [such as the purchase and use of contraceptives, as well as abortion]. Whenever it is determined that legislation significantly interferes with the exercise of a fundamental right, a court must review the legislation with strict judicial scrutiny. Under this heightened standard of review, the state must demonstrate that the statute serves a compelling state interest and that the state's objectives could not be achieved by any less restrictive measures. We are unable to conclude, however, that the PMPA significantly interferes with the exercise of a fundamental right. In the abortion context, the Supreme Court has not interpreted the right to privacy so broadly that it encompasses the right to choose a particular healthcare provider. . . . [Thus,] we hold that the right to privacy does not encompass the right to choose a direct-entry midwife to assist with childbirth. Therefore, the appropriate standard of review is whether the challenged provisions bear a rational relationship to a legitimate state purpose. As we concluded in the previous section, insuring the fitness of midwives is rationally related to the state's legitimate interest in protecting the health and welfare of mothers and infants. Therefore, we affirm the district court on this issue.

## Judgment and Result

The decision of the district court granting the state's motion for summary judgment was affirmed.

## Questions

1. In your opinion, how convincing are Dr. Applegate's justifications of the PMPA? In any event, do you think that arguments like these motivated the legislature when it passed the act? Who benefits from the PMPA? Who loses out? Which of these groups probably has the most political power?

2. The rights to purchase and use contraceptives and to have an abortion are fundamental, and laws restricting these rights get full strict scrutiny. Why is the right the choose a midwife to assist with childbirth not fundamental, too? What makes it less important than these other rights?

3. Lange-Kessler's claim involves a right that occasionally got considerable substantive protection during the first third of this century: the right to pursue the trade, calling, or profession of one's choice. Based on this case, how much protection does it get today? Why is *this* right not fundamental? That is, what makes occupational freedom less important than, say, the rights to buy and use contraceptives, or to have an abortion?

## EQUAL PROTECTION

*For another discussion of equal protection doctrine, see http://www. law.cornell.edu/ under "law about, the Constitution."*

The Fourteenth Amendment's equal protection guarantee says that the states cannot deny people the "equal protection of the laws." As we have seen, equal protection standards now apply to the federal government as well. The equal protection clause was added to the Constitution shortly after the Civil War. Some historians argue that it originally was intended to apply only to discrimination against blacks. By the beginning of the twentieth century, however, the equal protection guarantee had become a general check against arbitrary and unjustified governmental distinctions of all sorts.

Law-making inevitably requires that government *discriminate* by creating distinctions and classifications. Some individuals, groups, or activities are subjected to burdens or given advantages, and some are not. Equal protection sets the standards for the constitutionality of such distinctions and classifications. For example, if State X legislates so as to subject A to a disadvantage or give A a benefit, but does not do the same for B, equal protection requires that there be a *reason* for the distinction. The reasons that might justify governmental classifications vary from situation to situation. In other words, the tests imposed by the equal protection clause vary depending on the type of discrimination at issue.

*The Rational Basis Test.* The basic equal protection standard—and the equal protection standard applied to social and economic regulation—is the **rational basis test** described earlier in the chapter. As the *Stanglin* case on the next page suggests, the rational basis test usually is not a significant obstacle to government regulation of social and economic matters. Under this standard, courts typically defer to the government's judgment. Usually, only the most arbitrary classifications are endangered by rational basis review.

*Stricter Scrutiny.* Due to changes in approach that mainly began during the 1960s and 1970s, the courts now apply more rigorous equal protection standards when examining two general types of classifications: (1) those creating unequal enjoyment of certain **fundamental rights**, and (2) those discriminating on the basis of

## City of Dallas v. Stanglin
U.S. Supreme Court
490 U.S. 19 (1989)

### Background and Facts

In 1985, the city of Dallas passed an ordinance stating that only those age 14 through 18 could be admitted to so-called "Class E" dance halls. However, the ordinance did not apply to other places where teenagers might congregate, such as roller skating rinks. Charles Stanglin operated the Twilight Skating Rink, a combined roller skating rink and Class E dance hall. To achieve this combination, Stanglin divided the floor of his rink into two sections by using movable plastic cones or pylons. On one side, those between the ages of 14 and 18 would dance, while on the other side people of all ages would skate to the same music.

Apparently becoming fed up with this arrangement, Stanglin challenged the ordinance's constitutionality in the Texas courts. After a Texas appellate court struck down the ordinance's time limitation, the city appealed to the U.S. Supreme Court.

### Body of Opinion

**Chief Justice Rehnquist.** The Dallas ordinance . . . implicates no suspect class and impinges upon no constitutionally protected right. The question remaining is whether the classification engaged in by the city survives rational basis scrutiny under the equal protection clause. The city has chosen to impose a rule that separates 14- to 18-year-olds from what may be the corrupting influences of older teenagers and young adults. Ray Couch, an urban planner for the city, testified:

> [O]lder kids [whom the ordinance prohibits from entering Class E dance halls] can access drugs and alcohol, and they have more mature sexual attitudes, more liberal sexual attitudes in general. . . . And we're concerned about mixing up these [older] individuals with youngsters that [sic] have not fully matured. . . .

Stanglin claims that this restriction has no real connection with the city's stated interests and objectives. Except for saloons and teenage dance halls, he argues, teenagers and adults in Dallas may associate with each other, including at the skating area of the Twilight Skating rink. . . .

We think Stanglin's arguments misapprehend the nature of rational basis scrutiny, which is the most relaxed and tolerant form of judicial scrutiny under the equal protection clause. . . . [I]n the local economic sphere, it is only the invidious discrimination, the wholly arbitrary act, which cannot stand consistently with the Fourteenth Amendment. The city could reasonably conclude, as Couch stated, that teenagers might be susceptible to corrupting influences if permitted to frequent a dance hall with older persons. . . . The city could properly conclude that limiting dance-hall contacts between juveniles and adults would make less likely illicit or undesirable juvenile involvement with alcohol, illegal drugs, and promiscuous sex. It is true that the city allows teenagers and adults to roller-skate together, but skating involves less physical contact than dancing. The differences between the two activities may not be striking, but differentiation need not be striking in order to survive rational basis scrutiny.

### Judgment and Result

Texas appellate court decision reversed; the ordinance is constitutional and Stanglin loses.

### Questions

1. In equal protection cases, the claimant is challenging a governmental *classification*. What precisely was the challenged classification in this case? How did the Supreme Court justify the classification under the rational basis test?
2. What level of scrutiny would the Court have applied if the ordinance had required that black teenagers dance in one area of a dance hall, and white teenagers in another? Examine the discussion of strict scrutiny immediately following this case.
3. Would the Dallas ordinance have survived full strict scrutiny? Intermediate scrutiny?

a **suspect classification**. Table 5.1 summarizes the degree of equal protection scrutiny received by the various kinds of governmental classifications.

In equal protection cases involving fundamental rights, the challenged law discriminates by, in effect, giving one class of people less of a fundamental right than other classes of people. The rights deemed fundamental for equal protection purposes are not completely clear and are not necessarily the same as the rights deemed fundamental for substantive due process purposes. Included, however, are the rights to vote, to travel interstate, and to enjoy certain procedural protections in criminal cases. Laws creating unequal enjoyment of such

## TABLE 5.1 EQUAL PROTECTION SCRUTINY

|  | Very Strict | Fairly Strict | Rational Basis |
|---|:---:|:---:|:---:|
| Social and economic regulation that does not implicate fundamental rights or suspect classifications |  |  | X |
| Discrimination regarding fundamental rights | X |  |  |
| Racial discrimination | X |  |  |
| Most discrimination against aliens |  | X |  |
| Sex discrimination |  | X |  |
| Discrimination against illegitimates |  | X |  |

rights generally receive quite strict scrutiny. For example, a state statute restricting voting in school district elections to parents of schoolchildren and to property owners within the district was held unconstitutional in a 1969 case. Also, the idea that the right to vote is fundamental for equal protection purposes played a major role in the Supreme Court's controversial decision striking down the Florida Supreme Court's construction of Florida election law after the 2000 presidential election.

Suspect classification cases involve a claim that the challenged law unconstitutionally discriminates on the basis of personal traits that rarely, if ever, afford legitimate grounds for differentiating people. The traits in question—the "suspect" bases of classification—are race (including national origin), alienage (status as an alien), sex (or gender), and illegitimacy. The degree of scrutiny applied to laws distinguishing people on these grounds varies from suspect classification to suspect classification.

1. Racial classifications that expressly disadvantage African-Americans and other racial or national minorities receive full strict scrutiny. The same is true for discrimination that favors such groups and disadvantages whites. This full strict scrutiny now applies regardless of whether a state or the federal government has enacted the challenged classification. In recent years, many of the cases presenting equal protection challenges to government action favoring racial minorities have involved school admissions and public contracting. The results in these cases have been mixed.

2. Laws discriminating against aliens usually receive strict scrutiny. However, it is doubtful whether this scrutiny is as rigorous as the scrutiny applied in race discrimination cases. Nonetheless, laws expressly classifying to the disadvantage of aliens often are found unconstitutional. For example, the Supreme Court has struck down state laws denying aliens welfare benefits and the right to practice law.

Not all laws disadvantaging aliens, however, get strict scrutiny. Under the "political function" exception, measures blocking aliens from employment in positions that are intimately related to democratic self-government are tested under rational basis standards and usually are upheld. This exception has been read broadly to allow the Supreme Court to uphold laws preventing aliens from being state troopers, public school teachers, and probation officers.

3. As the Court declared in a 1996 case, gender-based discrimination requires an "exceedingly persuasive" justification. The usual test is that laws discriminating on the basis of sex must be substantially related to the furtherance of an important government purpose. This is a fairly strict form of intermediate scrutiny. Although this test is less strict than the test used for laws that disadvantage racial minorities, it is tough enough to strike down almost all government action disadvantaging women. The Supreme Court has said that the same test applies to discrimination against men. In 1981, however, the Supreme Court found the draft registration system constitutional, even though it did not include women, and also upheld a California law making statutory rape a crime for men but not for women.

4. Discrimination on the basis of illegitimacy receives a degree of scrutiny that is fairly strict, but that does not approach the full strict scrutiny applied to laws discriminating against racial minorities. For example, the Supreme Court has struck down laws denying illegitimate children wrongful death benefits and workers' compensation recoveries for the death of a parent.

## INDEPENDENT CONSTITUTIONAL CHECKS APPLYING ONLY TO THE STATES

### THE CONTRACT CLAUSE

Article I, Section 10 of the Constitution says that "No State shall . . . pass any . . . Law impairing the Obligation of Contracts." This **contract clause** was included in the Constitution to protect contract creditors against the many debtor relief statutes passed by the states after the Revolution. These laws erased contract-based debts and thus impaired the obligations of contracts. In the famous cases of *Fletcher v. Peck* (1810) and *Dartmouth College v. Woodward* (1819), the Supreme Court extended the contract clause to governmental contracts, grants, and charters, and not just to private contractual obligations. In 1827, moreover, the Court made it clear that the clause is retroactive or retrospective in operation. That is, it only poses a constitutional obstacle to state laws impairing contracts formed before these laws were passed, and not to prospective state regulation of contracts. Thus, for example, the contract clause would prevent a state debtor relief law from canceling debts created before the law's enactment, but would not prevent it from canceling debts arising after its passage.

The contract clause probably was the most important constitutional check on state regulation of the economy during the nineteenth century. By the mid-twentieth century, however, it was common to regard the contract clause as a constitutional dead letter. The reason is that throughout most of this century, the courts have subordinated contract clause claims to the states' exercise of their police powers. For example, a state prohibition law was held constitutional even though it impaired contracts for the sale of beer, a law forbidding lotteries was upheld even though it invalidated existing lottery tickets, and a workers' compensation law was valid even though it changed the terms of contracts between employers and employees.

However, in *United States Trust Company v. New Jersey* (1977) the Supreme Court breathed new life into the contract clause. In this case, the Court announced a tough new test for state laws impairing the obligations of their own contracts: that laws restricting such *governmental* contracts must be "reasonable and necessary to serve an important public purpose." This test seems to significantly restrict the states' ability to impair their own contract obligations.

For the most part, however, the Court has continued to defer to the states when regulation impairing *private* contracts is at issue. For example, in *Exxon Corporation v. Eagerton* (1983), it upheld an Alabama law preventing oil and gas producers from passing on a severance tax increase to their customers. This law impaired Exxon's contracts with its customers—contracts that required the customers to reimburse Exxon for the severance taxes Exxon paid on the gas and oil it sold them. The Court's justification for upholding the Alabama statute was that, like prohibition laws, laws banning lotteries, and workers' compensation, it was a generally applicable measure designed to advance a broad social interest: protecting consumers from excessive gas and oil prices. In particular, the Alabama statute applied to all oil and gas producers, regardless of whether they had made any contracts permitting them to pass increased severance taxes on to their customers. A law aimed only at parties with existing contracts, the Court suggested, might be unconstitutional under the contract clause.

## STATE REGULATION OF INTERSTATE COMMERCE

Recall from earlier in the chapter that the original purpose behind the commerce clause was to nationalize trade by restricting state economic favoritism and protectionism. Article I, Section 8, however, merely gives Congress the power to regulate interstate commerce. It says nothing about the states' ability or inability to do so. If Congress chooses to regulate commerce among the states, inconsistent state laws are invalid under the Constitution's supremacy clause. But what about the constitutionality of state laws that affect interstate commerce but do not conflict with federal law? Here, Congress and the state legislatures have concurrent law-making powers, with the state law subject to commerce clause checks. In such cases, courts examine the state law in light of the purposes behind the commerce clause. That is, they inquire whether the state regulation unduly hinders, burdens, or discriminates against interstate commerce. This involves use of the commerce clause as an implicit check on state law-making. As has been said, this is a matter of negative implication arising from one of the "great silences" of the Constitution.[6]

The tests employed by the Supreme Court in cases involving state restrictions on interstate commerce have varied over time. In a 1994 case, the Court said that state laws that discriminate against interstate commerce must satisfy the strictest scrutiny in order to be constitutional and rarely survive this test. By *discrimination*, the Court meant any different treatment of in-state and out-of-state economic interests that significantly benefits the former and burdens the latter. The following *Wyoming* case involves a state law that expressly discriminates against interstate

---

[6] *H.P. Hood & Sons, Inc. v. Du Mond*, 336 U.S. 525 (1949) (Jackson, J.).

commerce. But state laws that have a discriminatory effect may be unconstitutional even though they are neutral on their face. For example, state pure-food laws setting standards for the sale of certain food products will face constitutional problems if (1) they favor local food producers while disadvantaging out-of-state producers, and (2) do not clearly advance important state interests.

On the other hand, nondiscriminatory regulations that have only incidental effects on interstate commerce are constitutional unless the burden they impose on interstate commerce clearly exceeds their local benefits. In such cases, the courts must balance the state law's bad effects on interstate commerce against its local benefits. In a 1981 case, the Supreme Court struck down an Iowa statute imposing complicated limitations on the length of the trucks that could pass through the state. It did so mainly because the law's burden on interstate commerce exceeded its local benefits. Because other states had different standards, Iowa's unusual truck-length limits imposed significant additional costs on trucking firms. Because the trucks that Iowa allowed were scarcely safer than those it banned, moreover, the measure did little to serve legitimate state interests.

The Court also has said that laws that directly regulate interstate commerce usually are unconstitutional. In a 1986 case, for instance, the New York State Liquor Authority attempted to revoke a liquor seller's license under a state law allowing revocation if the prices the licensee charged in other states were lower than those it charged in New York. The Supreme Court found the law unconstitutional because its practical effect was to control the prices at which liquor could be sold in other states.

## Wyoming v. Oklahoma
### U.S. Supreme Court
### 502 U.S. 437 (1992)

### Background and Facts

From 1981 to 1986, Wyoming mines provided virtually all the coal purchased by four Oklahoma electric utilities. In 1986, the Oklahoma legislature enacted a statute requiring Oklahoma coal-fired electric generating plants producing power for sale in Oklahoma to burn at least 10 percent Oklahoma-mined coal. This caused the state of Wyoming to lose severance tax revenues it otherwise would have received. Thus, Wyoming sued Oklahoma under the Supreme Court's original jurisdiction, seeking a declaratory judgment that the Oklahoma statute violated the commerce clause and a permanent injunction against its enforcement.

### Body of Opinion

**Justice White.** While a literal reading [of the commerce clause] evinces a grant of power to Congress, the commerce clause also directly limits the power of the states to discriminate against interstate commerce. This "negative" aspect of the commerce clause prohibits economic protectionism—that is, regulatory measures designed to benefit in-state economic interests by burdening out-of-state competitors. When a state statute clearly discriminates against interstate commerce, it will be struck down unless the discrimination is demonstrably

justified by a valid factor unrelated to economic protectionism. Indeed, when the state statute amounts to simple economic protectionism, a virtual per se rule of invalidity has applied. . . .

[T]he act . . . discriminates against interstate commerce. Section 939 of the act expressly reserves a segment of the Oklahoma coal market for Oklahoma-mined coal, to the exclusion of coal mined in other states. Such a preference for coal from domestic sources cannot be characterized as anything other than protectionist and discriminatory. . . .

Oklahoma . . . emphasize[s] that the act sets aside only a small portion of the Oklahoma coal market, without placing an overall burden on out-of-state coal producers doing business in Oklahoma. [But] the volume of commerce affected measures only the *extent* of the discrimination; it is of no relevance to the determination whether a state has discriminated against interstate commerce. . . .

Because the act discriminates, . . . the burden falls on Oklahoma to justify it. . . . At a minimum such facial discrimination invokes the strictest scrutiny of any purported legitimate local purpose. . . . Oklahoma has not met its burden in this respect. In this Court, Oklahoma argues quite briefly that the act's discrimination against out-of-state coal is justified because sustaining the

Oklahoma coal-mining industry lessens the state's reliance on a single source of coal delivered over a single rail line. This justification . . . is foreclosed by the Court's reasoning in [two previous cases], cases that the state's brief ignores. . . . The state embellishes this argument somewhat when suggesting that, by requiring the utilities to supply 10 percent of their needs for fuel from Oklahoma coal, which because of its higher sulfur content cannot be the primary source of supply, the state thereby conserves Wyoming's cleaner coal for future use. We have no reason to doubt Wyoming's unrebutted factual response to this argument: reserves of low-sulfur, clean-burning sub-bituminous coal from the Powder River Basin are estimated to be in excess of 110 billion tons, thus providing Wyoming coal for several hundred years at current rates of extraction.

## Judgment and Result

Judgment for Wyoming; permanent injunction against enforcement of the Oklahoma statute issued.

## Questions

1. Who benefits economically from the Oklahoma statute?
2. As a matter of general policy, what's bad about protectionist statutes like this one?
3. How would the Court have approached the case if, instead of passing the law at issue above, Oklahoma had commanded Oklahoma utilities to burn a particular type of coal that is readily available in Oklahoma, but not in Wyoming?

## FEDERAL PREEMPTION

Article VI of the Constitution provides that the Constitution, laws, and treaties of the United States "shall be the Supreme Law of the Land . . . , any Thing in the Constitution or Laws of any State to the Contrary notwithstanding." This provision is called the **supremacy clause**, and it establishes the principle of **federal supremacy**. According to this principle, the U.S. Constitution, treaties, and other federal laws defeat inconsistent state law. Where a state law is declared unconstitutional under the supremacy clause because it conflicts with a federal statute, it is said to be *preempted* by federal law. Preemption questions are decided on a case-by-case basis. However, a few general preemption principles have emerged over time. A state law normally is preempted (and therefore is unconstitutional) when any one of the following occurs:

1. The state law conflicts on its face with a valid federal measure and there is no way to follow both rules simultaneously.
2. The federal statute explicitly declares that state law is to be preempted in certain areas, and the challenged state law falls within one of those areas.
3. The federal regulation is so pervasive or comprehensive that it is reasonable to conclude that Congress did not want the states to regulate the area. This conclusion may result from the fact that Congress has regulated some subject in great breadth and/or considerable detail, or has given an administrative agency broad powers to deal with the subject.
4. The challenged state law conflicts with the goals or purposes of the federal law. In defining these goals or purposes, courts generally look to the federal statute's legislative history.

The following *Egelhoff* case involves an express preemption provision in a federal statute (point 2 above). To interpret that provision, the Court relied on the purposes of the federal statute (point 4). It also made an argument that sometimes appears in preemption cases: the need for uniform national interpretation and administration of federal statutes.

## Egelhoff v. Egelhoff
532 U.S. 141 (2001)
U.S. Supreme Court

### Background and Facts

At one time, Donna Rae Egelhoff was married to David Egelhoff, who then worked for the Boeing Company. Boeing provided David with a pension plan and a life insurance policy, each of which made Donna the beneficiary. Both plans are governed by the federal Employee Retirement Income Security Act (ERISA). Shortly after the Egelhoffs were divorced in 1994, David died intestate following an automobile accident. Donna Rae remained the beneficiary on both plans, and David's children by a previous marriage sued her in Washington state court to recover the benefits. They relied on a Washington statute which provided that the designation of a spouse as the beneficiary of a nonprobate asset is revoked automatically upon divorce. Without a designated beneficiary for this money, their argument continued, it should pass to them as David's heirs. The trial court held for Donna Rae on the theory that ERISA preempted the Washington statute, but a state intermediate appellate court reversed and the Supreme Court of Washington affirmed that reversal. Donna Rae (the petitioner below) appealed to the U.S. Supreme Court.

### Body of Opinion

**Justice Thomas.** Petitioner argues that the Washington statute falls within the terms of ERISA's express preemption provision and that it is preempted by ERISA under traditional principles of conflict preemption. Because we conclude that the statute is expressly preempted by ERISA, we address only the first argument. ERISA's preemption provision states that ERISA "shall supersede any and all State laws insofar as they may now or hereafter relate to any employee benefit plan" covered by ERISA. We have observed repeatedly that this broadly worded provision is clearly expansive. But at the same time, we have recognized that the term "relate to" cannot be taken to extend to the furthest stretch of its indeterminacy, or else for all practical purposes preemption would never run its course.

We have held that a state law relates to an ERISA plan if it has a connection with or reference to such a plan. Petitioner focuses on the "connection with" part of this inquiry. . . . [T]o determine whether a state law has the forbidden connection, we look to both the objectives of the ERISA statute as a guide to the scope of the state law that Congress understood would survive, as well as to the nature of the effect of the state law on ERISA plans. Applying this framework, petitioner argues that the Washington statute has an impermissible connection with ERISA plans. We agree. The statute binds ERISA plan administrators to a particular choice of rules for determining beneficiary status. The administrators must pay benefits to the beneficiaries chosen by state law, rather than to those identified in the plan documents. The statute thus implicates an area of core ERISA concern. In particular, it runs counter to ERISA's

commands that a plan "shall specify the basis on which payments are made to and from the plan," and that the fiduciary shall administer the plan "in accordance with the documents and instruments governing the plan," making payments to a "beneficiary" who is "designated by a participant, or by the terms of [the] plan" [quoting ERISA]. In other words, unlike generally applicable laws regulating areas where ERISA has nothing to say, which we have upheld notwithstanding their incidental effect on ERISA plans, this statute governs the payment of benefits, a central matter of plan administration.

The Washington statute also has a prohibited connection with ERISA plans because it interferes with nationally uniform plan administration. One of the principal goals of ERISA is to enable employers to establish a uniform administrative scheme, which provides a set of standard procedures to guide processing of claims and disbursement of benefits. Uniformity is impossible, however, if plans are subject to different legal obligations in different states. The Washington statute at issue here poses precisely that threat. Plan administrators cannot make payments simply by identifying the beneficiary specified by the plan documents. Instead, they must familiarize themselves with state statutes so that they can determine whether the named beneficiary's status has been revoked by operation of law. And in this context the burden is exacerbated by the choice-of-law problems that may confront an administrator when the employer is located in one state, the plan participant lives in another, and the participant's former spouse lives in a third. In such a situation, administrators might find that plan payments are subject to conflicting legal obligations. . . .

### Judgment and Result

The judgment of the Washington Supreme Court was reversed, and the case was returned to the Washington courts for proceedings not inconsistent with the U.S. Supreme Court's opinion. Donna Rae's preemption attack on the Washington statute was successful.

### Questions

1. In this case, what would have been the result if ERISA had flatly invalidated all state laws revoking the designation of a spouse as the beneficiary of a nonprobate asset?
2. What did Justice Thomas mean when he said that "the term 'relate to' cannot be taken to extend to the furthest stretch of its indeterminacy, or else for all practical purposes preemption would never run its course?"
3. Suppose the Supreme Court had concluded that ERISA's express preemption provision did not block the Washington statute. Would this have meant that no preemption attack on the statute could succeed?

## The Takings Clause

The Fifth Amendment states that "[p]rivate property [shall not] be taken for public use, without just compensation." Although the Fifth Amendment applies only to the federal government, this **takings clause** has been incorporated within Fourteenth Amendment due process and thus applies to the states as well. The takings clause recognizes government's power to condemn or otherwise appropriate private property, but also limits government's exercise of that power. That is, a governmental *taking* of *property* is unconstitutional unless it is for a *public use* and the property owner receives *just compensation*. Figure 5.3 outlines how takings clause cases should be analyzed.

### Taking

There has long been considerable uncertainty about when a taking occurs. Nevertheless, some generalizations are possible.

1. The takings clause obviously applies when the government takes property by formally condemning it through the power of eminent domain.
2. A taking also occurs when the government physically occupies private property or authorizes a private party to do so. This is true no matter how minimal the occupation. In a 1982 case, for example, a New York law requiring landlords to let cable companies place cable facilities in the landlords'

### Figure 5.3 Analyzing Takings Clause Cases

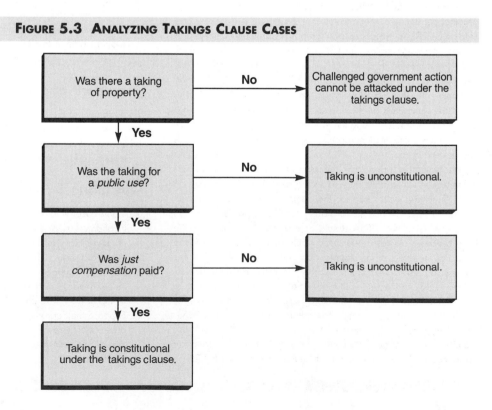

apartment buildings was held to be a taking. This was true even though the cable facilities occupied no more than one and one-half cubic feet of the landlords' property.

3.  At least since the Court's 1922 decision in *Pennsylvania Coal Co. v. Mahon*, it has been recognized that government regulation may sometimes constitute a taking. Just when this happens, however, is most unclear. Not every government regulation can be a taking, or else the government's power to regulate would be severely crippled by the need to compensate property owners. Traditionally, general police measures that apply to a wide range of properties usually have not been takings. For example, even though zoning laws obviously restrict the uses to which private property can be put, they normally are safe from takings clause attacks.

    So when might government regulation create a taking? A regulation definitely will be a taking if it deprives the owner of all, or virtually all, economically beneficial uses of his land. In other cases, various factors come into play. One of these is the economic impact of the regulation on the landowner; the greater this impact, the more likely the regulation will be deemed a taking. This is especially true where the regulation interferes with the owner's definite expectations regarding the future use of her property, and the owner has made investments to advance those expectations. Finally, sometimes courts also look at the purposes served by the regulation and the degree to which it advances them. In a 1987 case, for example, the Supreme Court said that land use regulation does not effect a taking if it substantially advances legitimate state interests.

## PROPERTY

The takings clause potentially has a wide reach, for it could apply to all kinds of government regulation. Another reason for the clause's broad potential scope is the range of property interests it covers. Obviously, land and interests in land are property for takings clause purposes, as is tangible personal property. In a 1984 case, moreover, the Supreme Court stated that valid contracts, various kinds of liens, and trade secrets also qualify as property. Many other kinds of personal property may enjoy protection as well.

## PUBLIC USE

Once there has been a taking of property, that taking is unconstitutional if it is not for a public use. Today the public use test is very easy to meet. For example, courts have said that the challenged taking need only be rationally related to a conceivable public purpose to meet the test.

## JUST COMPENSATION

Even if a taking of property is for a public use, it still is unconstitutional unless the owner receives just compensation. Usually, just compensation is the fair market value of the property that has been taken. Where the effect of the taking is merely to diminish property values, the standard for compensation often is the difference between the fair market value of the property before the taking and its fair market value after the taking.

*You can find a summary of the Palazzolo case in the U.S. Supreme Court Center of* **http://www.megalaw.com** *under "2000 term opinions."*

As you might expect, takings cases sometimes involve politically charged issues. The following *Palazzolo* case, for example, was a 5-4 decision in which the Court's conservatives were in the majority. The cases raises an interesting issue: Can there be a valid takings claim where the challenged government regulation was enacted *before* the property owner acquired title?

## Palazzolo v. Rhode Island
### 533 U.S. 606 (2001)
### U.S. Supreme Court

## Background and Facts

In 1959, Anthony Palazzolo purchased a parcel of waterfront land in the town of Westerly, Rhode Island. He did so through a corporation in which he eventually became the sole shareholder. In 1971, the Rhode Island legislature created the Rhode Island Coastal Resources Management Council (the Council), and empowered it to protect the state's coastal properties. Some time thereafter, but before 1978, the Council enacted regulations under which the property owned by Palazzolo's corporation became a protected coastal wetland. In 1978, the corporation had its charter revoked for failure to pay corporate income taxes, and title to the waterfront property passed to Palazzolo. In 1985, Palazzolo applied to the council for permission to build a private beach club on his property. The Council denied the application, after which Palazzolo challenged that denial as a regulatory taking in the Rhode Island courts. Eventually, the Rhode Island Supreme Court rejected Palazollo's claim.

Palazollo had made two main arguments in support of his claim that the Council's decision was a regulatory taking. First, he asserted that the decision deprived him of all economically beneficial use of his land. The Rhode Island Supreme Court rejected this claim because Palazzolo had $200,000 in development value remaining on an upland portion of his property. In addition, the court ruled that Palazzolo had no right to challenge regulations predating 1978, the year when he acquired personal ownership of the property. This also was the court's reason for denying Palazzolo's other claim, which was based on the U.S. Supreme Court's 1978 decision in *Penn Central Transportation Co v. New York City*. This basically was a claim that the Council's decision interfered with his reasonable investment-backed expectations regarding the property.

## Body of Opinion

**Justice Kennedy.** The takings clause of the Fifth Amendment, applicable to the states through the Fourteenth Amendment, prohibits the government from taking private property for public use without just compensation. The clearest sort of taking occurs when the government encroaches upon or occupies private land for its own proposed use. Our cases establish that even a minimal permanent physical occupation of real property requires compensation under the clause. In *Pennsylvania Coal Co. v. Mahon* (1922), the Court recognized that there will be instances when government actions do not encroach upon or occupy the property yet still affect and limit its use to such an extent that a taking occurs. In Justice Holmes's well-known, if less than self-defining, formulation, "while property may be regulated to a certain extent, if a regulation goes too far it will be recognized as a taking."

Since *Mahon*, we have given some, but not too specific, guidance to courts confronted with deciding whether a particular government action goes too far and effects a regulatory taking. First, we have observed . . . that a regulation which denies all economically beneficial or productive use of land will require compensation under the takings clause. Where a regulation places limitations on land that fall short of eliminating all economically beneficial use, a taking nonetheless may have occurred, depending on a complex of factors including the regulation's economic effect on the landowner, the extent to which the regulation interferes with reasonable investment-backed expectations, and the character of the government action [citing *Penn Central*]. These inquiries are informed by the purpose of the takings clause, which is to prevent the government from forcing some people alone to bear public burdens which, in all fairness and justice, should be borne by the public as a whole. . . .

When the Council promulgated its wetlands regulations, the disputed parcel was owned not by petitioner [Palazzolo], but by the corporation of which he was sole shareholder. When title was transferred to petitioner by operation of law, the wetlands regulations were in force. The state court held the post-regulation acquisition of title was fatal to the claim of [deprivation of] all economic use, and to the *Penn Central* claim. . . . [T]he two holdings together amount to a single, sweeping rule: a purchaser or a successive title holder like petitioner is deemed to have notice of an earlier-enacted restriction and is barred from claiming that it effects a taking.

The theory underlying the argument that post-enactment purchasers cannot challenge a regulation under the takings clause seems to run on these lines: Property rights are created by the state. So, the argument goes, by prospective legislation the state can shape and define property rights and reasonable investment-backed expectations, and subsequent owners cannot claim any injury from lost value. After all, they purchased or took title with notice of the limitation.

The state may not put so potent a Hobbesian stick into the Lockeian bundle. The right to improve property, of course, is subject to the reasonable exercise of state authority, including the enforcement of valid zoning and land-use restrictions. The takings clause, however, in certain circumstances allows a landowner to assert that a particular exercise of the state's regulatory power is so unreasonable or onerous as to compel compensation. Just as a prospective enactment, such as a new zoning ordinance, can limit the value of land without effecting a taking because it can be understood as reasonable by all concerned, other enactments are unreasonable and do not become less so through passage of time or title. Were we to accept the state's rule, the post-enactment transfer of title would absolve the state of its obligation to defend any action restricting land use, no matter how extreme or unreasonable. A state would be allowed, in effect, to put an expiration date on the takings clause. This ought not to be the rule. Future generations, too, have a right to challenge unreasonable limitations on the use and value of land. . . .

We have no occasion to consider the precise circumstances when a legislative enactment can be deemed a [reasonable] background principle of state law or whether those circumstances are present here. It suffices to say that a regulation that otherwise would be unconstitutional absent compensation is not transformed into a background principle of the state's law by mere virtue of the passage of title. . . . For reasons we discuss next, the state court will not find it necessary to explore these matters on remand in connection with the claim that all economic use was deprived; it must address, however, the merits of petitioner's claim under *Penn Central*. That claim is not barred by the mere fact that title was acquired after the effective date of the state-imposed restriction. . . .

[Since] the date of transfer of title does not bar petitioner's takings claim, we have before us the alternative ground relied upon by the Rhode Island Supreme Court in ruling upon the merits of the takings claims. It held that all economically beneficial use was not deprived because the uplands portion of the property can still be improved. On this point, we agree with the court's decision. . . .

[T]he state supreme court erred in . . . ruling that acquisition of title after the effective date of the regulations barred the takings claims. The court did not err in finding that petitioner failed to establish a deprivation of all economic value, for it is undisputed that the parcel retains significant worth. . . . [But] the claims under the *Penn Central* analysis were not examined, and for this purpose the case should be remanded.

## Judgment and Result

The decision of the Rhode Island Supreme Court was affirmed in part and reversed in part. The case was returned to the Rhode Island courts for further proceedings not inconsistent with the U.S. Supreme Court's opinion. This means that the state court would have to examine Palazzolo's *Penn Central* claim, which asserted that the Council's decision deprived him of his reasonable investment-backed expectations regarding the property.

## Questions

1. Suppose that Palazzolo had always held title to the property in his own name, rather than through a corporation. How would this fact have changed the Rhode Island Supreme Court's decision against him?
2. On remand, why did the Rhode Island courts have to consider Palazzolo's *Penn Central* claim, but not have to consider his claim that he was deprived of all economically beneficial use of the property?
3. Did the Supreme Court give much guidance for determining when regulations that occur before the acquisition of title do or do not constitute a taking?

## CHAPTER SUMMARY

Constitutions usually limit government power, and the U.S. Constitution does so in two general ways. First, the Constitution limits Congress to those powers it specifically enumerates. Second, it imposes various independent constitutional checks on both Congress and the state legislatures.

The Constitution gives Congress the power to regulate interstate commerce. Although it has recently been limited by the Supreme Court, this commerce power remains a wide-ranging federal police power that can reach almost all intrastate matters. In addition, Congress can regulate by using its enumerated taxing power to discourage disfavored activities by taxing them. Congressional spending power regulation works in the opposite fashion. Here Congress regulates by telling its would-be recipient that it will not receive the money unless it follows a certain course of conduct. Both the taxing and the spending power have few inherent limits.

But even though Congress's enumerated powers and the states' police powers have few innate limits, they are subject to certain independent constitutional checks. These checks fall into two broad classes. Some apply both to the federal government and to the states, while others apply to the states alone. For these checks to apply, there must be government action. In determining whether a particular regulation really violates a particular independent check, courts often use means-ends tests of constitutionality.

The most important business-related independent checks that apply to both the federal government and the states are the First Amendment's free speech guarantee, the due process clauses of the Fifth and Fourteenth Amendments, and the Fourteenth Amendment's equal protection clause. The First Amendment applies to the states because it has been incorporated within Fourteenth Amendment due process, and the equal protection clause applies to the federal government because it has been incorporated within Fifth Amendment due process. The First Amendment's most important business-related application is the obstacle it poses to government regulation of commercial speech such as commercial advertising. An intermediate test of constitutionality applies to such regulations.

Due process comes in two forms—procedural and substantive. In each case, a person must have been deprived of life, liberty, or property before due process standards apply. Substantive due process concerns the actual policy merits of government action, while procedural due process concerns the fairness of the machinery through which substantive laws are enforced. The central elements of procedural due process are fair notice of the action to be taken, and some sort of fair trial or hearing before that action can occur. Over time, substantive due process has assumed many forms. Once it was an important check on government regulation of the economy, but today it most often is significant when personal rights are at issue.

Equal protection law determines the constitutionality of governmental distinctions or classifications. Most such classifications—including those created when government regulates business—are tested under the lenient rational basis test. However, governmental distinctions that involve certain fundamental rights or suspect classifications are subjected to stricter scrutiny by the courts. The "suspect" bases of classification are race or national origin, gender, alienage, and illegitimacy.

At least three important constitutional provisions check state regulation of business. The contract clause puts some restrictions on laws that impair the obligations of existing contracts, both private and governmental. In addition to giving Congress the power to regulate interstate commerce, the commerce clause restricts state laws that unduly burden such commerce. Finally, federal regulation may preempt state law in certain cases. Whether this occurs essentially is a matter of statutory interpretation.

The U.S. Constitution's takings clause both recognizes a government power possessed by Congress and the state legislatures, and puts some restrictions on its use. The power in question is the power to "take" private property. The main restrictions on this power are the requirements that the taking be for a public use, and that government pay just compensation for property taken. Today the public use requirement is very easily met. Before these requirements come into play, however, there first must be a "taking," and the law on this subject is very complex.

### ■ MANAGER'S ETHICAL DILEMMA ■

You are the owner and operator of a teenage dance hall in a major American urban area. Your business has been terrific for some time. The reason that business has been so great, however, is that your dance hall has become a major center for the distribution of illegal drugs to teenagers. Right now, the drug trade at your establishment is limited to marijuana, but that might change.

Of course, you most likely can stop the distribution of drugs at your dance hall by notifying the police, but doing so probably would ruin your business. Unfortunately, many of your patrons want to do drugs, and if they can't get them at your establishment, they'll get them somewhere else. Also, if the police action becomes public knowledge, the straight kids might well stay away, too. Because the users and their suppliers simply will move elsewhere, you are also beginning to wonder whether tipping the police really would accomplish anything. Why should you suffer to achieve little or nothing? Also, it's not as if *you* are dealing the drugs—isn't there a moral difference between actively causing harm and merely permitting it to happen? (By the way, your lawyer thinks that if you keep your mouth shut and play dumb, you probably won't have any *legal* problems either.) Finally, just how much harm is being caused, anyhow? So far, only marijuana is being sold at your place. How bad is it?

Despite all this, the drug trade at your dance hall is still bothering you. What should you do? Why?

### DISCUSSION QUESTIONS

1. This chapter's discussion of the commerce, tax, and spending powers paid little attention to the principle of *federalism*, under which the federal government is supposed to respect state sovereignty in certain spheres. Yet the U.S. Constitution's Tenth Amendment plainly says that "[t]he powers not delegated to the United States by the Constitution, nor prohibited by it to the States, are reserved to the States respectively, or to the people." How have courts managed to get around Tenth Amendment arguments when considering Congress's authority under the commerce, tax, and spending powers? *Hint*: Pay close attention to the first eleven words of the language quoted above.

2. One valid generalization about the post-1937 Supreme Court is that it abandoned its earlier role as a protector of economic rights in favor of a new role as promoter of personal liberties. Based on the materials in this chapter, what is the most important example of the Court's earlier role? Although this chapter does not focus on personal rights, what examples of the Court's later role does it provide? Over the past fifteen to twenty years, the Court has given somewhat greater constitutional protection to economic rights. Based on this chapter, provide as many examples as you can.

3. The Supreme Court has had a hard time articulating reasons why some due process rights are fundamental and others are not. The dominant test asks whether the right in question is "deeply rooted in this nation's history and tradition" and "implicit in the concept of ordered liberty." But traditions are living things, and this raises the question of whether the Court should be looking at our tradition's past manifestations or its more recent manifestations. Why does this question matter in determining whether economic rights ought to be fundamental?

   The other approach for determining which rights are fundamental asks questions such as whether the right in question is central to one's life, one's self-definition, and one's personal development. How do economic rights fare under this test?

   How do the two substantive due process rights asserted in the *Lange-Kessler* case fare under each our tests? What does this whole exercise suggest to you about the Supreme Court's choice of fundamental rights?

4. Review this chapter's discussion of constitutional means-ends tests. This chapter has provided you with many examples of such tests. From the materials in this chapter, identify as many of these constitutional tests as you can. Then try to classify them according to their "strictness." *Hint*: You might use categories like "very strict," "somewhat strict," and "lenient." Do you think that laws restricting the various rights to which these tests apply really should get the degree of scrutiny that they actually do get? Should they receive stricter or less strict review by the courts?

5. In the 2001 government action case involving Tennessee high school athletics, discussed in the text, the Supreme Court said that one reason for the state action requirement is to "preserve an area of individual freedom by limiting the reach of federal law." What did the Court mean? What would life be like if the Constitution's individual rights guarantees applied to all private actors?

6. Why is it so difficult for the Supreme Court to come up with precise standards in areas such as the burden-on-commerce doctrine and federal preemption?

7. Prior to the 1970s, there were few cases challenging laws that discriminated against women, and in these cases the challenged law was usually upheld. Today, of course, laws discriminating against women almost always are unconstitutional. The change began early in the 1970s and was completed by the end of that decade. What do you think best explains the change? What does this tell you about constitutional interpretation and about the way the Supreme Court sometimes decides cases? What does it do to the idea that we live under a fixed, unchanging Constitution?

8. In *Romer v. Evans* (1996), the Supreme Court struck down a Colorado constitutional amendment, passed in a statewide referendum, that forbade all action by any level of state or local government to protect against discrimination on the basis of sexual orientation or give homosexuals any "quota preferences." The amendment apparently was a response to Aspen, Boulder, and Denver ordinances forbidding various kinds of discrimination on the basis of sexual orientation. The amendment, the Court concluded, violated equal protection because it lacked a rational basis. One strand in the Court's reasoning was that the amendment made it more difficult for one group of citizens (in this case, gay people) to seek protection from the government. Another was that the amendment originated in animosity toward gays, and that such motives could never serve as a rational basis for lawmaking. For its part, the state of Colorado argued that the amendment was rationally related to a legitimate state objective: protecting the freedom of association of landlords or employers who object to homosexuality. So far as the rational basis test is concerned, who has the better argument? Is the Court really engaging in something other than rational basis review?

   Interestingly, *Romer v. Evans* did not consider another possible argument for its result. This is the idea that sexual orientation should be a suspect basis of classification under the equal protection clause. This would mean that laws classifying people on the basis of their sexual orientation would receive some kind of stricter scrutiny. Perhaps it would mean that laws classifying people on the basis of their sexual behavior also would receive stricter scrutiny. Over time, courts and commentators have suggested criteria for determining whether particular personal traits should be "suspect." They include: (1) a history of discrimination and disapproval that makes those possessing the trait a "discrete and insular minority"; (2) the fact that the trait is not voluntarily acquired and cannot be voluntarily eliminated; and (3) the fact that the trait bears no relation to the individual's ability to contribute fully to society. Based on these criteria, should sexual orientation join race, national origin, gender, alienage, and illegitimacy as a suspect classification?

9. Suppose that a local government passes an ordinance regulating trailer parks. The ordinance says that the owner must give his tenants a permanent lease and that he can terminate the lease only for good cause; in addition, it establishes a system of rent control. Two stereotypes sometimes are used to describe laws of this kind. On the one hand, such laws may be regarded as enlightened, compassionate efforts to protect society's victims against those who would oppress them through superior economic power. On the other hand, such laws can be depicted as abuses of the democratic process in which politicians attract the votes of society's unproductive losers by passing laws enabling them to take wealth from society's achievers. As applied to our ordinance, which of these two stereotypes generally seems more accurate to you?

10. The text discussed the Supreme Court's 1905 substantive due process decision in *Lochner v. New York*, where the Court struck down a state maximum-hours law because it restricted freedom of contract and did not have a real and substantial relationship to the promotion of worker health. Why would it be difficult for such a law to be challenged under the contract clause? Assume that the employment contract at issue in *Lochner* occurred after the state maximum-hours law was passed.

## INFOTRAC KEYWORDS

**Use your InfoTrac password to look up articles on http://www.infotrac-college.com**

Keywords: *constitutional checks, First Amend-ment, procedural due process, contract clause, federal preemption.*

For suggested readings, please visit this book's Web site at **http://fisher.westbuslaw.com** (click on "Internet Applications").

# GOVERNMENT REGULATION:
## OVERVIEW

*"THE RISE OF ADMINISTRATIVE BODIES PROBABLY HAS BEEN THE MOST SIGNIFICANT LEGAL TREND OF THE LAST CENTURY."*

—JUSTICE JACKSON
DISSENTING IN
*FTC V. RUBEROID
CO., 343 U.S. 470
(1952)*

This chapter presents a survey of administrative law that consists of several parts. First we present some basic definitions of administrative law and administrative agencies. We then examine the purposes of administrative agencies. Finally, we discuss controls on administrative agencies.

Administrative law, also known as generic regulation making and enforcement, takes place in the United States in an environment that could fairly be characterized as schizophrenic: Americans are philosophically conservative, and hence, are against "big government" usually associated with government regulation; at the same time they are functionally liberal, demanding public protections against unsafe airlines, uncooked hamburgers, and blood tainted with HIV virus. It is in such a philosophically splintered environment that regulators in the United States must operate.

## ADMINISTRATIVE LAW AND ADMINISTRATIVE AGENCIES

Broadly defined, **administrative law** is all law concerning administrative agencies, including statutes, rules, and regulations, and court and agency interpretations. Narrowly defined, administrative law means court review of what administrative agencies have done. This chapter follows the broad definition.

An **administrative agency** is any nonlegislative, nonjudicial governmental law-maker. This definition excludes rules made by private business corporations. An administrative agency could be a person or an institution clothed with governmental authority. It has no single official label and need not have the word *agency* in its name. It could be called the Environmental Protection Agency, the Federal Trade Commission, the Police Department of Portland, Maine, or the Department of Public Health of the State of Tennessee. As these names suggest, administrative agencies exist at the federal, state, and municipal levels of government.

Agencies are usually created by a statute called the agency's organic act. In an agency's organic act, the legislature recognizes that a problem exists, creates an agency to deal with the problem, and delegates legislative authority to the agency to make appropriate regulations to cope with the problem. The **organic act** also gives judicial authority for the agency to hear cases dealing with the agency's subject matter. Finally, the organic act confers executive authority, which allows the agency to investigate and administer its subject matter.

The number of administrative agencies at the federal level runs into the hundreds. The SEC, ICC, FDA, EPA, OMB, and many more acronyms identify different federal agencies. Tables 6.1 and 6.2 dramatize the dynamic nature and extent of federal agencies and distinguish between executive departments and independent agencies. This difference is based on executive agency inclusion within the executive branch of the government; independent agencies are not. Because of this difference, the president's control over executive agencies is greater than that over independent agencies.

## ORIGIN AND PURPOSE OF ADMINISTRATIVE AGENCIES

Executive orders create a few administrative agencies, but most federal agencies are created by federal statutes. As such, Congress can legally dissolve these agencies. For instance, Congress could eliminate all statutorily created federal administrative agencies merely by passing another law. Although Congress will probably never take this action, the example shows the extent of congressional power over federal agencies.

*Expertise.* Administrative agencies have arisen for several reasons. First, legislatures and courts do not have the technical expertise to deal with the many complicated problems the United States currently faces. For example, the technical problems associated with toxic waste disposal require the skills of specialists, not courts or legislatures.

*Oversight of Socialized Harm.* Second, a need exists for ongoing supervision in areas in which the potential for harm is small on an individual level but great on a collective level. For example, the harm from air pollution on a single person is small, but over time such pollution could cause skin cancer, destroy crops, and cause other damage.

*Protect the Weak.* Third, administrative agencies are designed to help the weak and poor fight corporate giants. For example, farmers in the Midwest in the late 1800s were victims of discriminatory railroad rates. They took their case against the railroads to Congress, and the Interstate Commerce Commission was created to regulate railroad rates, among other things. Ironically, the ICC has since been captured by the powerful organized interests it was originally designed to regulate.

## TABLE 6.1 FEDERAL CIVILIAN EMPLOYMENT BY BRANCH AND AGENCY: 1990 TO 2000

[For fiscal year ending in year shown: excludes Central Intelligence Agency, National Security Agency; and, as of November 1984, the Defense Intelligence Agency; and, as of October 1996, the National Imagery and Mapping Agency]

| Agency | 1990 | 1999 | 2000 | Percent change, 1999–00 |
|---|---|---|---|---|
| **Total, all agencies** | **3,128,267** | **2,749,239** | **2,708,101** | **−1.5** |
| Legislative Branch, total | 37,495 | 30,353 | 31,157 | 2.6 |
| Judicial Branch | 23,605 | 32,196 | 32,186 | − |
| Executive Branch, total | 3,067,167 | 2,686,690 | 2,644,758 | −1.6 |
| Executive Departments | 2,065,542 | 1,614,097 | 1,592,200 | −1.4 |
| State | 25,288 | 25,892 | 27,983 | 8.1 |
| Treasury | 158,655 | 143,088 | 143,508 | 0.3 |
| Defense | 1,034,152 | 690,706 | 676,268 | −2.1 |
| Justice | 83,932 | 124,885 | 125,970 | 0.9 |
| Interior | 77,679 | 72,541 | 73,818 | 1.8 |
| Agriculture | 122,594 | 104,661 | 104,466 | −0.2 |
| Commerce | 69,920 | 60,765 | 47,652 | −21.6 |
| Labor | 17,727 | 15,913 | 16,040 | 0.8 |
| Health & Human Services | 123,959 | 61,403 | 62,605 | 2.0 |
| Housing & Urban Development | 13,596 | 10,273 | 10,319 | 0.4 |
| Transportation | 67,364 | 64,135 | 63,598 | −0.8 |
| Energy | 17,731 | 15,820 | 15,692 | −0.8 |
| Education | 4,771 | 4,770 | 4,734 | −0.8 |
| Veterans Affairs[1] | 248,174 | 219,245 | 219,547 | 0.1 |
| Independent Agencies: | | | | |
| Armed Forces Retirement Home | 966 | 801 | 765 | −4.5 |
| Board of Gov Fed Reserve System | 1,525 | 1,688 | 1,644 | −2.6 |
| Commodity Futures Trading Comm | 542 | 574 | 574 | − |
| Consumer Product Safety Comm | 520 | 483 | 479 | −0.8 |
| Environmental Protection Agency | 17,123 | 18,590 | 18,036 | −3.0 |
| Equal Employment Opportunity Comm | 2,880 | 2,945 | 2,780 | −5.6 |
| Federal Communications Commission | 1,778 | 1,978 | 1,965 | −0.7 |
| Federal Deposit Insurance Corporation | 17,641 | 7,492 | 6,958 | −7.1 |
| Fed Emergency Managmt Agency | 3,137 | 5,521 | 4,813 | −12.8 |
| Federal Trade Commission | 988 | 982 | 1,019 | 3.8 |
| General Services Administration | 20,277 | 14,199 | 14,334 | 1.0 |
| In Boun & Wat Comm (U.S. & Mexico) | 260 | 286 | 268 | −6.3 |
| National Archives & Recds Admin | 3,120 | 2,612 | 2,702 | 3.4 |
| National Aeronautics & Space Admin | 24,872 | 18,647 | 18,819 | 0.9 |
| Natl Labor Relations Board | 2,263 | 1,897 | 2,054 | 8.3 |
| Natl Science Foundation | 1,318 | 1,271 | 1,247 | −1.9 |
| Nuclear Regulatory Commission | 3,353 | 2,862 | 2,858 | −0.1 |
| Office of Personnel Management | 6,636 | 3,689 | 3,780 | 2.5 |
| Panama Canal Commission | 8,240 | 9,060 | 6 | −99.9 |
| Peace Corps | 1,178 | 1,097 | 1,065 | −2.9 |
| Railroad Retirement Board | 1,772 | 1,252 | 1,176 | −6.1 |
| Securities & Exchange Comm. | 2,302 | 2,866 | 2,955 | 3.1 |
| Small Business Administration | 5,128 | 4,575 | 4,150 | −9.3 |
| Smithsonian Institution, summary | 5,092 | 5,271 | 5,065 | −3.9 |
| Social Security Admin | [2](X) | 64,008 | 64,474 | 0.7 |
| Tennessee Valley Authority | 28,392 | 13,321 | 13,145 | −1.3 |
| U.S. Information Agency | 8,555 | 6,318 | 2,436 | −61.4 |
| U.S. Postal Service | 816,886 | 866,342 | 860,726 | −0.6 |

− Represents zero.    X Not applicable.    [1]Formerly Veterans Administration    [2]Included with HHS

**Source:** U.S. Office of Personnel Management, *Federal Civilian Workforce Statistics—Employment and Trends*, bimonthly.

## TABLE 6.2 THE SHAPE OF A DOMESTIC SECURITY DEPARTMENT

| Department of Homeland Security | The agencies and departments that will be moved to the main divisions of the Department of Homeland Security under the legislation passed yesterday: | Department or agency they are now under: | From President Bush's budget for the 2003 fiscal year: | |
|---|---|---|---|---|
| | | | Budget request, in millions: | Estimated number of employees: |
| **Border and Trans- portation Security** | Immigration and Naturalization Service enforcement functions* | Justice Dept. | $ 6,416 | 39,459 |
| | Transportation Security Administration | Transportation Dept. | 4,800 | 41,300 |
| | Customs Service | Treasury Dept. | 3,796 | 21,743 |
| | Federal Protective Services | General Services Administration | 418 | 1,408 |
| | Animal and Plant Health Inspection Service (parts) | Agriculture Dept. | 402 | 3,974 |
| **Emergency Preparedness and Response** | Federal Emergency Management Agency | (*Independent agency*) | $ 6,174 | 5,135 |
| | Chemical, biological, radiological, and nuclear response units | Health and Human Services Dept. | 2,104 | 150 |
| | Nuclear incident response teams | Energy Dept. | 91 | † |
| | National Domestic Preparedness Office | F.B.I. | 2 | 15 |
| | Office of Domestic Preparedness | Justice Dept. | § | § |
| | Domestic Support Teams | (*From various depts. and agencies*) | *Not applicable* | *Not applicable* |
| **Science and Technology** | Civilian biodefense research programs | Health and Human Services Dept. | $ 1,993 | 150 |
| | National Biological Warfare Defense Analysis Center | (*Proposed in fiscal 2003 budget*) | 420 | *Not available* |
| | Plum Island Animal Disease Center | Agriculture Dept. | 25 | 124 |
| | Lawrence Livermore National Laboratory (parts) | Energy Dept. | *Not available* | *Not available* |
| **Information Analysis and Infrastructure Protection** | National Communications System | Defense Dept. | $    155 | 91 |
| | National Infrastructure Protection Center | F.B.I. | 151 | 795 |
| | Critical Infrastructure Assurance Office | Commerce Dept. | 27 | 65 |
| | National Infrastructure Simulation and Analysis Center | Energy Dept. | 20 | 2 |
| | Federal Computer Incident Response Center | General Services Administration | 11 | 23 |
| **Secret Service** | Secret Service, including presidential protection units | Treasury Dept. | $ 1,248 | 6,111 |
| **Coast Guard** | Coast Guard | Transportation Dept. | $ 7,274 | 43,639 |
| | | **Total** | **$35,527** | **164,184** |

*Immigration services will be a separate bureau within the department.    †Classified.    § Included in FEMA budget request.

**Source:** The White House.

*Speed and Economy.* Fourth, the growth of administrative agencies also occurred because of the need for speed and economy in running the government. For example, having court proceedings to license a barber is wasteful.

*Class Struggle.* Finally, some people see the administrative agency as a way to solve social roadblocks put up by judges. In the late nineteenth century, workers who tried to form labor unions were brought before courts and tried for criminal conspiracy. Judges at that time often saw unions as threats to the individual right to manage one's own business. Labor leaders, on the other hand, viewed labor as part of the production process. They tried to get the judges to legalize unions. In the short run, they failed. Later, a combination of events legalized the labor union: the removal of much federal court jurisdiction to stop union activity and the establishment of a federal administrative agency—the National Labor Relations Board (NLRB)—to deal with labor matters such as union recognition. The NLRB is probably the most prominent example of an administrative agency created to get around the judiciary. The creation of the NLRB strengthened the political power of organized labor compared with business.

## LEGISLATIVE DELEGATIONS TO AGENCIES: ENABLING ACTS

A statute is a law passed by a federal or state legislature. Statutes are important in administrative law because agencies have the power to make legally binding regulations, or rules only if the legislature gives them the power.[1] Legislatures give agencies power through what is called *legislative delegation*. Statutes delegating legislative power to make regulations are called **enabling statutes**.

Administrative agencies have the power to make laws, which are called **regulations** (regs) or **rules**. The two general types of regulations are interpretative and substantive, sometimes called legislative. *Substantive regulations* are given the force and effect of law by courts; they are legally binding. They must be made in what is called *rulemaking*, or *regulation making*, as set forth by the federal Administrative Procedure Act (APA).

*Interpretative rules*, general agency policy statements, or rules of agency procedure, practice, or organization are not given the effect of law by courts. Interpretative rules are generally effective as soon as the federal agency announces their existence.

## SOME IMPORTANT FEDERAL ADMINISTRATIVE STATUTES

### THE FEDERAL REGISTER ACT

A little known but important federal law is the Federal Register Act, passed in 1935. The act provides a way to get up-to-date information about an agency and its regulations. This function is done by the **Federal Register system**, created by the Federal Register Act.

---

[1] The words *rules* and *regulations* (regs) are used interchangeably here. Professor Kenneth Culp Davis considers them synonymous, though some authorities do not.

***The Federal Register System.*** The Federal Register system has three parts: the federal *Government Manual* (formerly called the *Government Organization Manual*), the *Federal Register*, and the *Code of Federal Regulations*.

To access the Government Manual go to ***http://ww1. access.gpo.gov/nara/ nara001.html***

- *Government Manual.* The *Government Manual* lists the names and addresses of all U.S. government agencies and provides additional information about each agency. A new edition of this book is published each year and can be purchased from the U.S. Government Printing Office.

- *Federal Register.* The *Federal Register* resembles a small newspaper and is published by the federal government every business day, Monday through Friday. Among the more important items it contains are presidential proclamations, notices of federal agency public meetings, proposed federal regulations, and promulgated federal regulations. A federal agency's substantive regulation is usually not the law unless it is promulgated in the *Federal Register*. The function of the *Federal Register* is to give public notice of federal agencies' official acts. The *Federal Register* is available in most large libraries. Also, thanks to the Internet, anyone with access to a computer and modem has the *Federal Register* at his or her fingertips. An Internet address to the *Federal Register* is provided in the Internet exercises at the end of this chapter.

To research items within the Federal Register, go to ***http://www.gpo.gov/ su_docs.aces/aces140.html***

The Web site for Code of Federal Regulations can be found at ***http://ww1.access.gpo.gov/ nara/cfr/index.html***

- *Code of Federal Regulations.* The *Code of Federal Regulations* (C.F.R.) is the third part of the Federal Register system. It arranges all currently effective federal agency regulations by agency. (Regulations promulgated in the *Federal Register* are not arranged in this way.) A regulation appears when the agency delivers a regulation to the *Federal Register* office. The *C.F.R.* is a multivolume set of paperbound books, and each book usually contains all current regulations of federal agencies.

***Need to Read the Federal Register.*** Is the average citizen bound by what appears in the *Federal Register* daily editions and the *C.F.R.*? In *Federal Crop Ins. Corp. v. Merrill*, an Idaho farmer learned the hard way about his duty to read the *Federal Register*.

## Federal Crops Insurance Corp. v. Merrill
U.S. Supreme Court
332 U.S. 380 (1947)

### Background and Facts

Merrill applied for crop insurance with the Federal Crop Insurance Corporation to insure a wheat crop in Idaho. Because part of the crop was reseeded, Merrill asked the government employee if his crop was insurable. The government official said it was, so Merrill bought crop insurance. When his crops were later destroyed by drought, Merrill filed a claim under his crop insurance. The government agency refused to pay because a regulation said that reseeded crops were not insurable. Merrill said he did not know of the regulation and claimed that the agency official had said his crop was insurable.

The trial jury and judge said Merrill could recover. The Idaho Supreme Court agreed. The Federal Crop Insurance Corporation appealed to the U.S. Supreme Court.

### Body of Opinion

**Justice Frankfurter.** The case no doubt presents phases of hardship. We take for granted that, on the basis of what they were told by the Corporation's local agent, the respondents reasonably believed that their entire crop was covered by petitioner's insurance. And so we assume that recovery could be had against a private insurance company. But the Corporation is not a private insurance company. . . . Whatever the form in which the Government functions, anyone entering into an arrangement with the Government takes the risk of having accurately ascertained that he who purports to act for the Government stays within the bounds of his authority. The scope of this authority may be explicitly defined by Congress or be limited by delegated legislation, properly exercised through the rule-making power. And this is so even though, as here, the agent himself may have been unaware of the limitations upon his authority. . . .

If the Federal Crop Insurance Act had by explicit language prohibited the insurance of spring wheat which is reseeded on winter wheat acreage, the ignorance of such a restriction, either by the respondents or the Corporation's agent, would be immaterial and recovery could not be had against the Corporation for loss of such reseeded wheat. Congress could hardly define the multitudinous details appropriate for the business of crop insurance when the Government entered it. Inevitably, the "terms and conditions" upon which valid governmental insurance can be had must be defined by the agency acting for the Government. And so Congress has legislated in this instance, as in modern regulatory enactments it so often does, by conferring the rule-making power upon the agency created for carrying out its policy. Just as everyone is charged with knowledge of the United States Statutes at Large, Congress has provided that the appearance of rules and regulations in the *Federal Register* gives legal notice of their contents.

Accordingly, the Wheat Crop Insurance Regulations were binding on all who sought to come within the Federal Crop Insurance Act, regardless of actual knowledge of what is in the Regulations or of the hardship resulting from innocent ignorance. The oft-quoted observation in *Rock Island, Arkansas & Louisiana Railroad Co. v. United States*, 254 U.S. 141, that "Men must turn square corners when they deal with the Government," does not reflect a callous outlook. It merely expresses the duty of all courts to observe the conditions defined by Congress for charging the public treasury. The "terms and conditions" defined by the Corporation, under authority of Congress, for creating liability on the part of the Government preclude recovery for the loss of the reseeded wheat no matter with what good reason the respondents thought they had obtained from the Government. Indeed, not only do the Wheat Regulations limit the liability of the Government as if they had been enacted by Congress directly, but they were in fact incorporated by reference in the application, as specifically required by the Regulations.

We have thus far assumed, as did the parties here and the courts below, that the controlling regulation in fact precluded insurance coverage for spring wheat reseeded on winter wheat acreage. It explicitly states that the term "wheat crop shall not include . . . winter wheat in the 1945 crop year, and spring wheat which has been reseeded on winter wheat acreage in the 1945 crop year." . . . The circumstances of this case tempt one to read the regulation, since it is for us to read it, with charitable laxity. But not even the temptations of a hard case can elude the clear meaning of the regulation. It precludes recovery for "spring wheat which has been reseeded on winter wheat acreage in the 1945 crop year." Concerning the validity of the

regulation, as "not inconsistent with the provisions" of the Federal Crop Insurance Act, no question has been raised.

The judgment is reversed and the cause remanded for further proceedings not inconsistent with this opinion.

## Judgment and Result

The farmer lost.

Mr. Justice Black and Mr. Justice Rutledge dissent. [Dissents do not count, since they represent a minority of the justices. However, sometimes they make more sense than the majority opinion.]

**Mr. Justice Jackson, dissenting.** I would affirm the decision of the court below. If crop insurance contracts made by agencies of the United States Government are to be judged by the law of the State in which they are written, I find no error in the court below. If, however, we are to hold them subject only to federal law and to declare what that law is, I can see no reason why we should not adopt a rule which recognizes the practicalities of the business.

It was early discovered that fair dealing in the insurance business required that the entire contract between the policyholder and the insurance company be embodied in the writings which passed between the parties, namely, the written application, if any, and the policy issued. It may be well enough to make some types of contracts with the Government subject to long and involved regulations published in the *Federal Register*. To my mind, it is an absurdity to hold that every farmer who insures his crop knows what the *Federal Register* contains or even knows that there is such a publication. If he were to peruse this voluminous and dull publication as it is issued from time to time in order to make sure whether anything has been promulgated that affects his rights, he would never need crop insurance, for he would never get time to plant any crops. Nor am I convinced that a reading of technically-worded regulations would enlighten him much in any event. . . .

It is very well to say that those who deal with the government should turn square corners. But there is no reason why the square corners should constitute a one-way street. . . .

Mr. Justice Douglas joins in this opinion.

## Questions

1. The dissenting opinion does not count in the preceding case. A dissent is a way for a Supreme Court justice to blow off steam by telling why he or she thinks the majority opinion is wrong. Which opinion is more persuasive to you: Frankfurter's majority or Jackson's dissent? Why?
2. Which opinion represents positive law? Natural law?
3. Does the majority opinion encourage or discourage reading the *Federal Register*?
4. Does the majority opinion encourage or discourage relying on government employees' interpretations of federal regulations?

## Administrative Procedure Act (APA)

Even though the 1930s saw the creation of many new administrative agencies at the federal level, the Administration Procedure Act (APA) was not passed until 1946. It was enacted because of widespread concern with the lack of regularized procedures for agency actions. For example, before the APA was created some federal agencies decided cases after hearing only the government's evidence.

Administrative agencies make rules. They decide cases by applying agency rules. The APA sets the requirements (structure) for conducting rulemakings and adjudications.

The APA has been amended several times since its original passage in 1946. Among the more important APA amendments are the Freedom of Information Act, the Federal Privacy Act of 1974, and the Government in the Sunshine Act.

## Freedom of Information Act

The Freedom of Information Act (FOIA) was passed in 1966. Its main purpose is to disclose information that federal agencies have in their possession. The information might include pictures, studies, files, letters, and many other tangible bits of information.

A brief letter directed to the particular agency's FOIA office is usually sufficient to make an FOIA request. An **FOIA request** must have a reasonable description of the records one wants, which helps the agency locate the material. For example, a request for all information the Federal Trade Commission has about price discrimination is too broad, but a request for the FTC study of the life insurance industry in the late 1970s would probably be specific enough. The request must be made in accordance with an agency's rules about the time, place, fees, and procedures to be followed. An agency must make records promptly available after an FOIA request has been made. An agency usually has ten business days to decide whether to honor an FOIA request.

The federal FOIA has nine exemptions, meaning that certain types of information falling within any one of the nine exemptions do not have to be disclosed, even if the public requests this information. However, the **FOIA exemptions** do not allow agencies to withhold information from Congress. The nine FOIA exemptions cover the following:

1. National defense or foreign policy matters
2. Internal personnel rules and practices of an agency
3. Other statutes specifically allowing nondisclosure
4. Trade secrets and commercial or financial information obtained from a person and privileged or confidential
5. Interagency or intra-agency memoranda or letters
6. Personnel, medical, and similar files, the disclosure of which would clearly be an unwarranted invasion of personal privacy
7. Investigatory records compiled for law enforcement purposes
8. Material in reports of agencies responsible for regulating or supervising financial institutions (such as bank examiners' reports)
9. Geological or geophysical information and data (including maps) concerning wells

## FEDERAL PRIVACY ACT OF 1974

Congress passed the Federal Privacy Act (FPA) of 1974 to protect against violation of individual privacy resulting from misuse of federal agency information. The alleged misuse of information took many forms and involved both government and private sources. For example, Social Security cards were used for identification purposes, such as check cashing, even though the card states that it is not to be used for identification.

*Conflict.* Federal agency use and assembly of information involves an inherent conflict of values. Agencies need accurate, complete information to perform efficiently. However, the United States was established to promote individual freedom, which includes the right of privacy and to have a limited government. The FPA tries to strike a proper compromise between efficient government management and individual privacy.

*Main Provision.* The main provision of the FPA stops an agency from disclosing any record in a system of records by any means of communication to any person or agency without the prior written consent of the individual. This provision has several key points and many qualifications. The FPA is generally limited to federal agencies, although it also applies to federal contractors, including states or businesses receiving federal contracts, unless otherwise exempt. One other point about the FPA: An individual's name and address may not be sold or rented by a federal agency unless specifically authorized by another law.

Because many state governments and private company employers are federal contractors, they are covered by the Federal Privacy Act. Consequently, many employers are reluctant to give out information about employees or former employees (such as job references) to third parties such as other employers who might want to know how a worker performed for them. If former employers have information about former employees in a "system of records," the former employers may be reluctant to say anything without first getting prior written consent of the employees. Getting written permission in advance from former employees is cumbersome, so former employers might be unwilling to say anything to third persons about former employees. Much information employers have about former employees is contained in employee records and is based also on first-hand observation by supervisors. If the former employer discloses such information without first getting the former employee's written permission, one case has held that the former employer does not violate the Federal Privacy Act if the former employer consults personal memory but not any system of records in doing so.

Another Federal Privacy Act problem involves the disclosure of Social Security numbers through documents filed with Bankruptcy Courts. Persons whose Social Security numbers are available for anyone to see fear *identity theft.* The following case deals with an attempt by a paralegal who drafted bankruptcy petitions, from having his Social Security number publicly disclosed. The case includes discussion of two separate and distinct sources of privacy rights: the U.S. Constitution and the Privacy Act of 1974.

## In Re Crawford
### U.S. Court of Appeals (9th Cir.)
### 194 F.3d 954 (1999)

## Background and Facts

Ferm, who characterizes himself as an "independent paralegal," assists individuals in preparing bankruptcy petitions. He is a professional BPP (bankruptcy petition preparer). In mid-1965, he filed a motion with the Bankruptcy Court for the District of Nevada seeking leave to substitute an identification number other than his Social Security Number (SSN) on the bankruptcy petitions he prepares. The motion was motivated by Ferm's fear of credit card fraud. The bankruptcy court denied the motion in an order filed on August 21, 1995.

On September 5, 1995, Ibolya Rausch and Laorphus Crawford each filed pro se Chapter 7 petitions with the bankruptcy court. Each petition disclosed that Ferm had assisted in its preparation. Although Ferm completed required disclosure forms in connection with the petitions, he omitted his SSN. In response, appellee United States Trustee ("government") asked the bankruptcy court to fine Ferm $24,000, require him to disgorge the fees he earned from Rausch and Crawford, and hold him in contempt of the court's August 21, 1995, order. In a published opinion, the bankruptcy court fined Ferm a total of $800 for his failure to include his SSN on the documents relating to the Crawford and Rausch petitions. The district court in a published opinion affirmed the bankruptcy court. These appeals followed.

## Body of Opinion

**Judge Fletcher.** . . . Section 110 c [Ed.: of the Bankruptcy Code] requires that BPPs [Ed.: Bankruptcy Petition Preparers] include their SSNs on all documents filed with the bankruptcy court and authorities the imposition of a fine in the event of noncompliance. . . . Congress enacted this provision in 1994 as part of a larger effort to regulate nonattorney bankruptcy petition preparers:

"[Section 110] adds a new section to chapter 1 of title 11 United States Code to create standards and penalties pertaining to bankruptcy petition preparers. Bankruptcy petition preparers not employed or supervised by any attorney have proliferated across the country. While it is permissible for a petition preparer to provide services solely limited to typing, far too many of them also attempt to provide legal advice and legal services to debtors. These preparers often lack the necessary legal training and ethics regulation to provide such services in an adequate and appropriate manner. These services may take unfair advantage of persons who are ignorant of their rights both inside and outside the bankruptcy system." . . .

Ferm does not object to the bankruptcy court's *collection* of his SSN pursuant to § 110 c. He does, however, object to the subsequent *disclosure* of his SSN to the general public, an outcome that results from the fact that, by separate statutory provision, papers filed with the bankruptcy court become part of the public record. . . . Accordingly, we limit our inquiry today to the question of whether the disclosure of Ferm's SSN violated his constitutional or

statutory rights; we express no opinion regarding whether the mere collection of SSNs pursuant to [the bankruptcy code] invades any legally protected interest of BPPs. . . .

While the Supreme Court has expressed uncertainty regarding the precise bounds of the constitutional "zone of privacy," its existence is firmly established. . . . We have observed that the relevant Supreme Court precedents delineate at least two distinct kinds of constitutionally-protected privacy interests: "One is the individual interest in avoiding disclosure of personal matters, and another is the interest in independence in making certain kinds of important decisions.". . . . Ferm argues that the disclosure of his SSN implicates the first of the two threads, sometimes referred to as the right of "informational privacy." . . .

We agree with Ferm that the indiscriminate public disclosure of SSNs, especially when accompanied by names and addresses, may implicate the constitutional right to informational privacy. As the Fourth Circuit recognized in *Greidinger v. Davis*, "the harm that can be inflicted from the disclosure of a SSN to an unscrupulous individual is alarming and potentially financially ruinous." . . . In an era of rampant identity theft, concern regarding the dissemination of SSNs is no longer reserved for libertarians inveighing against the specter of national identity cards. . . . ("Armed with one's SSN, an unscrupulous individual could obtain a person's welfare benefits or Social Security benefits, order new checks at a new address on that person's checking account, obtain credit cards, or even obtain a person's paycheck.") Unlike a telephone number or even a name, an individual's SSN serves as a unique identifier that cannot be changed and is not generally disclosed by individuals to the public.

Judicial and legislative actions in other contexts also support the conclusion that the disclosure of SSNs can raise serious privacy concerns. . . . For example, courts have interpreted Exemption 6 of the Freedom of Information Act (FOIA) . . . to forbid the disclosure of SSNs. . . . Congress, for its part, has enacted measures to control the collection and dissemination of SSNs by government agencies, including the Privacy Act, discussed in more detail below, and the Driver Privacy Protection Act . . . (barring states from disclosing "personal information," including SSNs, contained in motor vehicle licensing records).

The right to informational privacy, however, "is not absolute; rather, it is a conditional right which may be infringed upon a showing of proper governmental interest." . . . . Our precedents demand that we "engage in the delicate task of weighing competing interests" to determine whether the government may properly disclose private information. . . . Relevant factors to be considered include:

. . . the type of record requested, the information it does or might contain, the potential for harm in any subsequent nonconsensual disclosure, the injury from disclosure to the relationship in which the record was generated, the adequacy of safeguards to prevent unauthorized disclosure, the degree of need for access, and whether there is an express statutory mandate, articulated public policy, or other recognizable public interest militating toward access . . .

This list is not exhaustive, and the relevant considerations will necessarily vary from case to case. In each case, however, the government has the burden of showing that "its use of the information would advance a legitimate state interest and that its actions are narrowly tailored to meet the legitimate interest. . . . In most cases, it will be the overall context, rather than the particular item of information that will dictate the tipping of the scales. . . . Compare *Roe v. Sherry*. . . . (Navy's interest in investigating a serious crime outweighed privacy interest in HIV test results) with *Doe v. City of New York* . . . (holding that HIV status generally falls within the constitutional right to informational privacy).

In filling his side of the scales, Ferm makes much of the ruinous consequences that can flow from identity theft. . . . He also notes that the bankruptcy court has not established any safeguards to prevent disclosure of his SSN to unscrupulous third parties—as part of the bankruptcy case, a BPP's SSN becomes part of the public record, available for inspection. . . .

Properly understood, Ferm's complaint is this: The disclosure of his SSN makes him vulnerable to being a victim of certain crimes. While this surely implicates Ferm's informational privacy interests, it does not appear to constitute a more serious invasion of those interests than many other requirements imposed by government. Enhanced risk, in fact, obtains anytime the government requires an individual to deposit identifying information in the public record. To weigh properly the privacy interest involved, the dire consequences of identity theft must be discounted by the probability of its occurrence. Surely government disclosure does enhance the risk of identity theft. However, the realization of the injury still requires two additional, nongovernmental elements: (1) an identity thief and (2) a vulnerable account. In that regard, Ferm's circumstance is different from the individual, for example, who is required to disclose her HIV status, sexual orientation, or genetic makeup. Unlike these personal facts, a SSN is not inherently sensitive or intimate information, and its disclosure does not directly lead to injury, embarrassment or stigma. . . .

The government fills its scales with arguments that, in the final analysis, are more weighty than those made by Ferm. First, the government points to the important legislative purposes behind . . . [Ed.: the bankruptcy code, which requires disclosure of the SSN] as did the courts below. . . . As noted above § 110 [Ed: of the bankruptcy code] was enacted to remedy what was perceived to be widespread fraud and unauthorized practice of law in the BPP industry. This certainly constitutes an important governmental interest. There is no doubt, moreover, that the gathering of BPP SSNs directly serves this interest by facilitating the governmental monitoring and policing of individual BPPs. . . .

After weighing the relevant considerations, we conclude that the speculative possibility of identify theft is not enough to trump the importance of the governmental interests behind [relevant sections of the Bankruptcy Code]. . . . In short, the balance tips in the government's favor. Accordingly we cannot say that Congress transgressed the bounds of the Constitution in enacting the statutes at issue here. . . .

## Section 7 of the Privacy Act

The Privacy Act of 1974 includes a provision meant to control the collection and disseminaiton of SSNs by government agencies. . . . Ferm contends that the relevant bankruptcy forms that he was required to complete did not include the disclosures required by Section 7(b) of the Privacy Act. The government responds by noting that Section 7(a)(2)(A) of the Privacy Act does not apply "to any disclosure which is required by Federal statute." . . . Because the disclosure of Ferm's SSN was expressly required by . . . [Ed.: the bankruptcy code], the government reasons that Section 7 is wholly inapplicable here. The government is mistaken. A close reading of Section 7 makes it clear that Section 7(a)(2)(A)'s exclusion for federal statutes only pertains to the limitation recited in Section 7(a)(1)—that no right, benefit, or privilege be denied to any individual for refusing to disclose her SSN.

Ferm's argument, nonetheless, is unavailing. Ferm has conceded that he has no objection to the *collection* of his SSN, and thus has waived any objection stemming from the method of collection employed by the government here. Section 7(b) has no bearing on the public *disclosure* of SSNs by the government, the only issue in dispute in these appeals. . . .

## Judgment and Result

Judgment of the district court is affirmed. Preparer failed to show reasonable cause excusing his failure to disclose his SSN.

## Questions

1. The case above dealt with an individual's privacy rights under federal constitutional law (*zone of privacy*) and privacy under Section 7 of the Privacy Act of 1974. What are some similarities and differences between the two?
2. Are Social Security Numbers (SSNs) of bankruptcy petition preparers (BPPs) found on public documents? Did the Bankruptcy Code, a federal law, require that SSNs be included on all documents filed with the bankruptcy court? Why?
3. Did the bankruptcy petition preparer object to the collection of his SSN, or something else?
4. Given the fact that more than 1.4 million bankruptcy petitions are filed annually, does this suggest that quite a number of persons are exposed to bankruptcy filings and conceivably could have access to bankruptcy petitions of others from which they could get ideas about items to include in their own petitions?
5. Have courts ever interpreted any federal statutes as forbidding the disclosure of SSNs?
6. Some county courthouses now post all court records—including divorce proceedings and bankruptcies—on a Web site. What privacy issues does that raise?

## Government in the Sunshine Act

The Government in the Sunshine Act became federal law in 1976. It is sometimes called an **open meeting law**. Its main objective is to open up the official decision-making process of the federal government. The Sunshine Act requires that an agency headed by a collegial body must not conduct or dispose of agency business unless every portion of the business meeting is open to the public. A collegial body is two or more individuals heading an agency, a majority of whom are presidential appointees confirmed by the U.S. Senate. Thus, the Sunshine Act would apply to the Federal Trade Commission because it is headed by five presidentially appointed, Senate-confirmed commissioners. The Sunshine Act would not apply to the U.S. Environmental Protection Agency, because only one person—the administrator—heads it.

## Protection for Federal Whistleblowers

*Whistleblowers* are people who expose waste, fraud, and abuse in an organization. Generally speaking, people praise whistleblowers, because who can be in favor of the wrongdoings that whistleblowers expose? Yet when people do blow the whistle, those in the organization who are engaged in the allegedly improper conduct frequently retaliate against the whistleblowers, often by demoting, reassigning, or firing them. This occurs because frequently the person on whom the whistle is blown is the whistleblower's own boss or agency. Bosses and coworkers do not like criticism, and they retaliate by finding some shortcoming in the whistleblower's job performance as a pretext for punishing him or her for the whistleblowing. In other words, the boss finds the whistleblower is "stealing paper clips" (which, of course, is wrong) and uses it as the basis for punishment, even though the real reason is to even the score.

Many statute-specific whistleblower protections have been in place for years. For example, the Clean Water Act and OSHA contain protections for employees who blow the whistle on violations. These protections apply to both private- and public-sector employees.

*The Civil Service Reform Act.* In 1978 Congress passed the Civil Service Reform Act (CSRA), which protects many, but not all, civilian federal employees. The CSRA established the Merit Systems Protection Board (MSPB) to hear whistleblower complaints of federal employees and also created the Office of Special Counsel (OSC) to investigate and champion federal employee whistleblowers. The CSRA's whistleblower protections failed miserably. (In fact, one occupant of the Special Counsel's office gave seminars to federal agencies on how to fire whistleblowers!)

President George H. W. Bush signed into law the Whistleblower Protection Act of 1989 to amend and strengthen the CSRA's whistleblower protections. It does several things to help federal employees who blow the whistle in federal agencies, including the following:

- It gives whistleblowers a cause of action to pursue their own case if the OSC does not do so after a certain time. (The CSRA allowed only the OSC to pursue whistleblower complaints.)
- It lessens the burden of proof the whistleblower must meet to prove a connection between the whistleblowing and the whistleblower's punishment.

- It restates the OSC's primary mission as being protection of federal employees who whistleblow rather than protecting the Civil Service System by punishing the supervisor who punishes whistleblowers.

*Problems in Dealing with Whistleblowers.* Significant problems remain with both the Whistleblower Protection Act of 1989 and whistleblowing generally. First, the 1989 Act exempts many federal agencies from its protections, including any federal corporation (e.g., TVA, the Federal Deposit Insurance Corporation, the Resolution Trust Corporation (charged with the savings and loan cleanup), the CIA, and the FBI.)

A major dilemma left unsolved after the 1989 Act is dual causation (also referred to as the *nexus* problem) whistleblowing, which happens when a whistleblower does something wrong at work that is either preceded or followed by an act of whistleblowing. Then, after both events have occurred, the supervisor disciplines the whistleblower in some way, such as not giving a salary increase. The question is, was the failure to give a salary increase the result of the whistleblowing or because the employee genuinely deserved no pay increase? If the employee complains that the boss was punishing him or her for whistleblowing, and the boss points out the whistleblower's faults, who prevails? This dual causation problem is present with all whistleblower protection statutes, not just the 1989 Act.

## CONTROLLING ADMINISTRATIVE AGENCIES

The growth of administrative agencies over the past sixty years has been tremendous. Consult Figure 6.1 earlier in this chapter to see the large number of federal employees. Some functions the agencies perform are essential and many more are desirable, but society has limited resources and wants limited intrusion into its members' lives. Thus, ways have been developed to legally and economically control administrative agencies at all levels of government. The following sections discuss such controls.

## THE COURTS

Administrative agency actions are reviewable by courts, the major legal control over administrative agencies. Generally, state courts review state administrative agency actions, and federal courts review federal agency actions. This rule has exceptions. Judicial review of agency action is established by the Administrative Procedure Act (APA) at the federal level and by state APAs and common law at the state level. Courts can overturn agency actions for the following reasons:

1. The agency violated the U.S. Constitution.
2. The agency acted *ultra vires* (beyond its statutory authority).
3. The agency action was arbitrary, capricious, or an abuse of discretion, or it broke some other law.
4. The agency did not follow legal procedures.
5. The agency adjudication was unsupported by substantial evidence.

*Evidence to Support Agency Action.* The concept of limited judicial review of administrative action permits courts to review questions of law and lets agencies decide the facts. Agency fact decisions must be supported by evidence. Courts use two separate tests to judge whether the evidence is sufficient to support administrative agency actions: (1) the substantial evidence test, and (2) the arbitrary, capricious, and unreasonable test. The **substantial evidence test** is used to review adjudications (agency orders resulting from hearings) and formal and hybrid rule making.[2]

The **arbitrary, capricious, and unreasonable test** is usually used to judge informal rule making unless a statute requires the stricter substantial evidence rule. This test comes from the federal Administrative Procedure Act and is not as strict as the substantial evidence test. In other words, the federal agency does not have to produce as much evidence to justify what it does under the arbitrary, capricious, and unreasonable rule as it does under the substantial evidence test.

## Sunset Laws

So-called **sunset laws** have been enacted at different levels of government. They terminate administrative agencies in one of several ways: cutting off the agency's budget, revoking the law that creates the agency, or requiring periodic renewal of the law creating the agency. For example, every time an agency's budget is up for renewal, the sun could set on all or part of that agency's operations. Other laws have the same objective but are called by other names. Budgets (via appropriations bills) could be sunset laws for an agency or its programs.

## Ombudspersons

Agency employees who check to see that the agency is operating properly are called ombudspersons. In other words, an agency polices itself when it uses **ombudspersons**. Universities, cities, states, and various federal departments have such employees who are sometimes known by other names, such as inspectors general. The jurisdiction of ombudspersons may be broad or narrow. For example, some university ombudspersons may investigate student complaints but not those of the faculty.

## Federal Civil Rights Suits

Federal civil rights suits refer to lawsuits based on Sections 1981, 1982, and 1983 of Title 42 of the U.S. Code. These sections allow people whose federal civil rights are denied by private individuals or by state or municipal officials to sue the wrongdoer in federal court. These laws can be used to hold state or municipal agency employees liable for abusing their power and violating people's civil rights. Possible remedies available for federal civil rights violations include injunctions, actual damages, and punitive damages.

Examples of federal civil rights violations that subject state or municipal officials to liability include the following:

---

[2]The term *hybrid rule making* refers to a process an agency uses to make regulations that add to the notice and comment (*Federal Register* notice of the rule and comments—often critical—filed by the public in response to agency proposals) procedures agencies follow in informal rule making. Added procedures could include public hearings.

1. A municipality refuses to license a public coffeehouse run by skateboarders, solely because the officials do not like skateboarders.
2. A radical (right- or left-wing) student group is denied access to a state-owned auditorium when such access is routinely granted to other public groups (assuming no other basis for the denial exists).
3. State welfare administrators refuse to conform to federal welfare standards that require a hearing before ending welfare payments.

*Gonzaga University v. Doe* provides a recent U.S. Supreme Court decision refusing to allow a s 1983 suit when a student was denied teacher certification because of alleged violations of the Family Educational Rights and Privacy Act (FERPA) by a professor.

## Gonzaga University v. Doe
### United States Supreme Court
### 122 S.Ct. 2268 (2002)

### Background and Facts

As a student at Gonzaga University, a private educational institution in Washington State, Doe planned to become a public elementary school teacher in that state after graduation. Washington at the time required all new teachers to obtain an affidavit of good moral character from their graduating colleges. Petitioner League, Gonzaga's teacher certification specialist, overheard one student tell another that Doe had engaged in sexual misconduct. League then launched an investigation, contacted the state agency responsible for teacher certification, identifying Doe by name and discussing the allegations. League finally told Doe he would not receive his certification affidavit.

Doe sued Gonzaga and League in state court under § 1983 alleging a violation of the Family Educational Rights and Privacy Act of 1974 (FERPA), which prohibits the federal funding of schools that have a policy or practice of permitting the release of students' educational records without their parents' written consent.

A jury awarded Doe compensatory and punitive damages on the FERPA claim of over $1 million. The Washington Court of Appeals reversed in relevant part, concluding that FERPA does not create individual rights and thus cannot be enforced under § 1983.

The Washington State Supreme Court reversed the Court of Appeals. In so doing the State Supreme Court acknowledged that FERPA does not give rise to a private cause of action. However, it reasoned that the nondisclosure provision creates a federal right enforceable under § 1983. Gonzaga appealed to the U.S. Supreme Court.

### Body of Opinion

**Chief Justice Rehnquist.** . . . Like the Washington Supreme Court and the state court of appeals below, other state and federal courts have divided on the question of FERPA's enforceability

under § 1983. The fact that these courts have relied on the same set of opinions from this Court suggests that our opinions in this area may not be models of clarity. . . .

Congress enacted FERPA under its spending power to condition the receipt of federal funds on certain requirements relating to the access and disclosure of student educational records. The Act directs the Secretary of Education to withhold federal funds from any public or private "educational agency or institution" that fails to comply with these conditions. . . .

Doe contends that this statutory regime confers upon any student enrolled at a covered school or institution a federal right, enforceable in suits for damages under § 1983, not to have "educational records" disclosed to unauthorized persons without the student's express written consent. But we have never before held, and decline to do so here, that spending legislation drafted in terms resembling those of FERPA can confer enforceable rights. . . .

Since *Pennhurst*, only twice have we found spending legislation to give rise to enforceable rights. In *Wright v. Roanoke Redevelopment and Housing Authority* . . . , we allowed a § 1983 suit by tenants to recover past overcharges under a rent-ceiling provision of the Public Housing Act, on the ground that the provision unambiguously conferred "a mandatory [benefit] focusing on the individual family and its income." The key to our inquiry was that Congress spoke in terms that "could not be clearer," and conferred entitlements "sufficiently specific and definite to qualify as enforceable rights under *Pennhurst*." . . .

Our more recent decisions, however, have rejected attempts to infer enforceable rights from Spending Clause statutes. . . .

Doe reads this line of cases to establish a relatively loose standard for finding rights enforceable by § 1983. He claims that a federal statute confers such rights so long as Congress intended that the statute "benefit" putative plaintiffs. . . . He further contends that a more "rigorous" inquiry would conflate the standard for inferring a private right of action under § 1983 with the standard for inferring a private right of action directly from the statute itself, which he admits would not exist under FERPA. . . .

. . . [T]here is no question that FERPA's nondisclosure provisions fail to confer enforceable rights. To begin with, the provisions entirely lack the sort of "rights-creating" language critical to showing the requisite congressional intent to create new rights. . . . Unlike the individually focused terminology of Titles VI and IX, . . . FERPA's provisions speak only to the Secretary of Education, directing that "[n]o funds shall be made available" to any "educational agency or institution" which has a prohibited "policy or practice." . . .

## Judgment and Result

Doe loses. FERPA's provisions create no personal rights to enforce under § 1983.

## Questions

1. Did FERPA itself specifically allow individuals to sue violators of FERPA's privacy rights? If not, what does § 1983 add to FERPA that FERPA lacked itself?

2. Did the Supreme Court admit that sometimes in the past its decisions had allowed federal rights to be inferred from general spending statutes, which is what the plaintiff, Doe, argued? How did the Supreme Court distinguish those cases? By saying the rights conferred "could not be clearer" in the other cases, whereas here it was not so clear that the statute intended to benefit individuals?

## LEGISLATIVE VETOES

A legislative veto is the U.S. House or Senate or both saying to a regulator, "We invalidate your regulation." Because Congress created most administrative agencies, some argue that it should have the power to veto particular agency regulations it does not like.

The **legislative veto** is controversial for several reasons. First, it interferes with the orderly rule-making process (described in Chapter 7). Second, Congress arguably takes an inconsistent position when it vetoes a regulation after it gave the agency the power to make the regulation by passing an enabling statute. Supporters of the legislative veto first point to it as a way to get government off the people's backs, thereby helping to increase productivity.

In 1983 the U.S. Supreme Court decided in *I.N.S. v. Chadha*, that federal legislative vetoes are unconstitutional unless they involve both houses of Congress and the president as well. In other words, if the Congress wants to legislatively veto an administrative regulation, it must do so by passing a statute. Therefore, the legislative veto will be less frequently used than if only one house of Congress, acting alone, could veto a regulation.

## FEDERAL TORT CLAIMS ACT

*Sovereign Immunity.* The federal government and its agencies are protected from lawsuits by the sovereign immunity doctrine. As a result, the Defense Department is not liable to soldiers injured when poor battle plans cause high casualties. Also, federal employees as individuals are protected from suit based on their official acts. For example, if a mail carrier puts a Social Security check in the wrong mailbox, causing a retiree to miss a car payment and resulting in the repossession of the retiree's car, neither the federal government nor the carrier is liable, with some exceptions.

*Waiver.* The federal government is liable for damages, injuries, property loss, or death if it has waived its sovereign immunity and the claimant otherwise establishes a theory of recovery. One important instance in which the federal government has waived its sovereign immunity is in the Federal Tort Claims Act. By virtue of this act, the federal government allows suit against itself, its agencies, and employees for torts they commit.[3] If, for example, an Internal Revenue Service (IRS) agent trespasses into a person's business to obtain evidence, the federal government and the employee as an individual would be liable, assuming no valid defense is available.

*Limits.* Six important limits have been placed on the liability of federal agencies and their employees.

1. The law of the state where the alleged wrong occurred defines whether the behavior causing the suit is a legal wrong. For example, if the alleged wrong were an invasion of privacy and had occurred in Alabama, but Alabama did not recognize invasion of privacy as a civil wrong, no basis would exist for suit under the Federal Tort Claims Act.
2. The alleged wrong must be within the scope of the federal employee's official duties.
3. Recoveries under this act include damages and injunctions; punitive damages are not available.
4. The Federal Tort Claims Act does not waive sovereign immunity for discretionary, policy conduct or for misrepresentations, whether negligent or intentional. Thus, when a federal regulator has the option to do or not do certain things and the outcome damages a member of the public, the federal agency is not liable. However, when the regulator undertakes mandatory functions affecting regulated parties, the regulator is liable for negligence under the Federal Tort Claims Act if those decisions cause damage.
5. The Federal Tort Claims Act does not waive sovereign immunity when the federal official negligently or intentionally misrepresents something. *Lemke* discusses this exception further.
6. There is a two-year statute of limitations for tort claims against the United States. Specifically, claims must be presented in writing to the appropriate federal agency within two years after such claim accrues.

Certain additional procedures apply to particular agencies. The following case deals with a claim against the U.S. Postal Service by a person injured when a mail truck struck her.

---

[3] The Federal Tort Claims Act (FTCA) does not waive sovereign immunity for certain intentional torts (assault, battery, false imprisonment, false arrest, malicious prosecution, abuse of process, libel, slander, misrepresentation, deceit, or interference with contract rights). However, the FTCA waives intentional tort immunity when the tort is committed by investigative or law enforcement officers.

## Kokotis v. U.S. Postal Service
U.S. Court of Appeals (4th Cir.)
223 F.3d 275 (2000)

### Background and Facts

On October 29, 1995, Evelyn Kokotis was injured in an automobile accident. The collision was allegedly due to the negligence of a Postal Service employee. Two days later, Kokotis was sent a Standard Form 95 (SF 95) to facilitate the filing of an administrative claim pursuant to the Federal Tort Claims Act (FTCA). A letter from the Postal Service accompanied the SF 95. The letter explained in multiple places, and in boldface and capitalized text, that Kokotis had two years to file a complete claim. The letter also stated, in boldface text, that for a claim to be considered complete an exact sum certain dollar amount must be included. Moreover, the SF 95 itself included numerous similar warnings. The form even indicated in italics above the entry for the total amount of the claim that *"failure to specify may cause forfeiture of your rights."* The box above the space for the claimant's signature on the SF 95 contained the following language in boldface capitals: *"I certify that the amount of claim covers only damages and injuries caused by the accident above and agree to accept said amount in full satisfaction and final settlement of this claim."*

In December 1995, approximately one month after the accident, Kokotis filed an SF 95 with the Postal Service without including a sum certain. Instead, the cover letter accompanying the form stated that Kokotis was still undergoing medical treatment and included an itemization of Kokotis's medical bills to date. Kokotis submitted supplemental letters to the Postal Service on February 27, 1996, March 25, 1996, December 12, 1996, August 21, 1997, and January 22, 1998. As of the August 21, 1997, letter (the last letter sent before the statute of limitations expired), the total damages claimed were $4,546.79. Kokotis finished the medical treatment for her accident on September 25, 1997, approximately one month before the statute of limitations expired.

On March 3, 1998, four months after the statute of limitations had expired but prior to final agency action, Kokotis submitted a revised SF 95 requesting a sum certain in the amount of $19,000. The Postal Service denied Kokotis's claim. The Postal Service explained that since the claim was not completed within the FTCA's two-year limitations period, it could not be considered. Kokotis's request for reconsideration of this decision was denied.

Kokotis filed suit for damages against the Postal Service on March 12, 1999. The Postal Service moved to dismiss the complaint for lack of subject matter jurisdiction. The district court granted the motion, holding that Kokotis's failure to identify a sum certain within the two-year statute of limitations deprived it of jurisdiction over her suit. The district court declined to toll the statute of limitations on the grounds that there was no misleading conduct on the part of the United States. Kokotis appealed.

### Body of Opinion

**Chief Judge Wilkinson.** Kokotis seeks to recover against the government under the limited waiver of sovereign immunity embodied in the FTCA. Sovereign immunity can be waived only by the sovereign; the circumstances of its waiver must be scrupulously observed and not expanded by the courts. . . . Precisely because the FTCA constitutes a waiver of sovereign immunity, plaintiffs like Kokotis must file an FTCA action in careful compliance with its terms. . . . A key jurisdictional prerequisite to filing suit under the FTCA involves the presentation of an administrative claim to the government within two years of the incident. . . . Moreover "the requirement of filing an administrative claim is jurisdictional and may not be waived." . . .

An administrative claim must be properly presented. The FTCA's implementing regulations consider a claim to be properly presented when the government receives a completed SF 95 (or other written notification of an incident), and "a claim for money damages in a sum certain.". . . Requesting a sum certain is a necessary element of any FTCA administrative claim. Failure to request a sum certain within the statute of limitations deprives a district court of jurisdiction over any subsequently filed FTCA suit. . . .

The sum certain requirement is not a trap for the unwary. Rather, this requirement allows an agency to assess a claim's settlement value. . . . Since the FTCA links both the authority to settle a claim and the source of settlement funds to the amount of the underlying claim, the Act's purpose is frustrated if the administrative claim does not indicate a specific amount of money. . . .

If the FTCA plaintiffs were allowed to pursue Kokotis's preferred route of not submitting a sum certain, the government's ability to determine a claim's value would be impaired. This, in turn, might push the government toward several unsatisfactory options: (1) channel all decisions to the highest levels in order to assure the decision to settle was made by someone authorized to do so; or (2) resist or postpone settlement so long as the amount of the claim could not be ascertained. Either way the burden on the government would increase and the FTCA's goal of efficiently handling claims against the government would be undermined.

Notwithstanding the government's general interest in the sum certain requirement, Kokotis asserts that the requirement should not strictly be applied against her. She first contends she provided enough information to the Postal Service, in the form of periodic supplemental letters, for the agency to estimate the value of her claim. We disagree. Kokotis provides no explanation for how the Postal Service could have predicted a 418 percent increase in the size of her claim. Kokotis's last pre-statute of limitations supplemental letter of August 21, 1997, indicated total damages of $4,546.79; her post-statute of limitations request sought $19,000. Moreover, even if Kokotis were correct that the Postal Service could somehow have estimated the value of her claim, she cannot escape the FTCA's unwavering requirement of submission of a sum certain within two years of the incident. . . . No exception exists for cases where the agency might have been able to estimate the value of a claim, and courts cannot insert into the FTCA administrative process special provisions that the statute does not contain. . . .

Kokotis next argues that she could not submit a sum certain before her treatment was complete and the extent of her injuries were known. While the record indicates Kokotis' last medical treatment occurred one month before the filing period expired, that fact is beside the point. Every limitations period embodies the possibility that a complaint must be filed before the claimant's knowledge is complete. That possibility, however, affords no basis for disregarding the interest of finality embodied in a statute of limitations that a legislative body has chosen to enact. . . .

Kokotis advances one further argument for why she should be excused from the sum certain requirement. She claims that she did not estimate her damages for fear that a low figure would be settled quickly and that a high figure would discourage settlement altogether. Such strategic calculations on the part of a claimant cannot be allowed to set aside the conditions attached to the sovereign immunity waiver. . . . Standardized requirements promote the efficient resolution of large volumes of claims. The assessment of individual claimants of their own settlement prospects cannot be permitted to supersede the regulatory requirements to which all other claimants are expected to adhere.

Kokotis next argues that because she presented a sum certain before final action on her claim, it is an amendment that relates back to her December 1995 filing. We disagree. An amendment of a claim can only occur if a complete claim, including a sum certain, is filed before the statute of limitations expires. . . . The regulation states that "a claim shall be deemed to have been presented when the U.S. Postal Service receives . . . a claim for money damages in a sum certain. . . . " . . . Since Kokotis's December 1995 filing did not include a sum certain, it was not "presented" within the meaning of [Ed: the regulation]. The regulation further states that only a "claim presented in compliance with [Ed: the regulation]" can be amended before final agency action. . . . Since Kokotis's original filing did not include a sum certain, it was not presented in compliance with [Ed.: the regulation] and therefore not subject to amendment. . . .

## Judgment and Result

District court's judgment in favor of Postal Service is affirmed. Plaintiff loses.

## Questions

1. How much time does someone have in which to file a claim after being injured by a Postal Service employee? Didn't Kokotis actually file a claim before the two-year statute of limitations was up? Why, then, didn't she recover?
2. Why did not Kokotis's amendment to her claim "relate back" in time to her original claim so that her completed claim could be considered "filed" prior to expiration of the statute of limitations?
3. What ethical arguments can be made in support of the statute of limitations? Against it? Refer back to Chapter 1 to answer this.

## CHAPTER SUMMARY

Administrative law deals with laws and regulations affecting administrative agencies. Administrative agencies are nonlegislative, nonjudicial governmental lawmakers. Such agencies exist at the federal, state, and local levels of government.

Administrative agencies exist to provide expertise, to oversee socialized harm, to protect the weak, to provide economy in government regulation, and to correct wrongs resulting from class struggle.

Legislatures give administrative agencies the legal authority to regulate by passing enabling acts.

Agencies have the authority to promulgate regulations. Regulations can be either interpretative or substantive. Substantive regulations are also known as legislative regulations.

The federal Administrative Procedure Act (APA) sets out the rules by which federal administrative agencies make regulations, adjudicate, and carry out their executive function.

The Federal Register Act created the Federal Register system.

In 1966 Congress enacted the Freedom of Information Act, which allows persons to obtain information from federal administrative agencies.

The Federal Privacy Act of 1974 restricts what information persons may obtain from a federal agency in a system of records under certain circumstances.

To open up federal agency management, Congress passed the Government in the Sunshine Act, also known as the *open meeting law*.

Federal agency employees—called *whistleblowers*—who expose waste, fraud, and abuse in government are protected by a number of federal statutes. One such law is the Whistleblower Protection Act of 1989.

Ways of controlling federal administrative agencies include the courts (that is, by suing the agency), sunset laws, ombudspersons, and the Federal Tort Claims Act.

## ■ MANAGER'S ETHICAL DILEMMA

Thomas Gaubert was the major shareholder and chairman of the board of IASA, the Independent American Savings Association, a Texas-chartered and federally insured savings and loan association (S&L). (FHLBB) sought an IASA merger with Investex Savings, a failing Texas S&L. Because FHLBB was concerned about Gaubert's other financial dealings, its officials requested that he sign a *neutralization agreement* that effectively removed him from IASA's management. They also asked him to post a $25 million interest in real property as security for his personal guarantee that IASA's net worth would exceed regulatory minimums. Gaubert agreed to both conditions. Federal officials then provided regulatory and financial advice to enable IASA to consummate the merger with Investex. Throughout this period, the regulators instituted no formal action against IASA. Instead, they relied on the likelihood that IASA and Gaubert would follow their suggestions and advice.

In 1986, the regulators threatened to close IASA unless its management and board of directors were replaced; all of the directors agreed to resign. The new officers and directors were recommended by the FHLBB (the regulators). After the new management took over, FHLBB officials became more involved in IASA's day-to-day business. The regulators recommended the hiring of a certain consultant to advise IASA on operational and financial matters. Regulators advised IASA concerning whether, when, and how its subsidiaries should be placed into bankruptcy. Regulators mediated salary disputes and urged IASA to convert from state to federal charter.

Although IASA was thought to be financially sound while Gaubert managed it, the new directors soon announced that IASA had a substantial negative net worth. You are Gaubert. You decided to sue the FHLBB for negligent regulation causing your stock in IASA to decline in value. What legal arguments is Gaubert likely to face under the Federal Tort Claims Act?

## DISCUSSION QUESTIONS

1. Is the often-heard allegation that "regulators are liberals" true? Would the extensive regulations in consumer matters, environmental affairs, equal employment opportunity, anti-trust, and handgun control lend credence to this idea? How about regulations restricting access to pornography, regulating the use of marijuana and other drugs, restricting abortions, limiting the use of bankruptcy, imposing tough vagrancy laws, and imposing dress codes (no public nudity)?

   Consider further regulations that impose food-labeling requirements, require driver's licenses, restrict entry into various occupations by imposing occupational licenses, regulate clothing labels, or disclose terms of auto leases. What part of the political spectrum favors these regulations?

2. This chapter tells us that the federal Sunshine Act requires open meetings by agencies headed by a collegial body composed of two or more individual members. Does the Sunshine Act apply to the U.S. Department of Justice? Who heads this department? [*Nichols v. Reno*, 931 F. Supp. 748 (D. Colo., 1996)].

3. Former U.S. government employees and political employees brought a common law right of privacy claim against the first lady and former White House staff, which alleged the first lady and the staff requested Federal Bureau of Investigation (FBI) files of plaintiffs for the improper purpose of obtaining embarrassing or damaging information for partisan political purposes. Does the federal privacy act preempt (that is, "knock out," or invalidate) the common law tort of invasion of the right of privacy, or merely add to common law privacy rights? [*Alexander v. F.B.I.*, 971 F. Supp. 608 (1997)].

4. What are some of the reasons for the growth of administrative agencies? Which reasons are the most persuasive today?

5. What are the controls on administrative agencies?

6. The Federal Tort Claims Act lets people sue and recover damages from the U.S. government for torts (noncontractual civil wrongs) that federal employees commit. The act does not, however, let a person recover punitive damages against the U.S. government. In one case, a government employee negligently drove a federal car and permanently brain damaged an innocent victim. The victim's relatives sued and recovered $1,300,000 for the victim, who was in a permanent coma. Was this jury award punitive and therefore not allowed by the Federal Tort Claims Act? [*Flannery v. U.S.*, 718 F.2d 108 (4th Cir. 1983)].

7. Is the Texas Parole Board an agency covered by the federal Administrative Procedure Act? [*Johnson v. Wells*, 566 F.2d 1016 (5th Cir. 1978)].

8. Congress and congressional committees have much valuable information about the Central Intelligence Agency. Can the public get this information by bringing a freedom of information suit against Congress? [*Paisley v. C.I.A.*, 724 F.2d 201 (D.C. Cir. 1984)].

9. The FBI was investigating Tom Miller. It went to the Fort Worth National Bank to get records on Miller's bank account and use of money orders. The bank turned such information over to the FBI without Miller's consent. Miller claimed this action violated the Federal Privacy Act. In doing so, he argued that a national bank is an agent of the federal government and is thus covered by the Federal Privacy Act. Is Miller correct? [*Ausherman v. Stump*, 643 F.2d 715 (10th Cir. 1981)].

**Use your InfoTrac password to look up articles on http://www.infotrac-college.com**

Keywords: *Administrative Procedure Act, Freedom of Information Act, Federal Privacy Act, Sunshine Act, whistleblowers.*

For suggested readings, please visit this book's Web site at **http://fisher.westbuslaw.com** (click on "Internet Applications").

# GOVERNMENT REGULATION: ANATOMY AND ENFORCEMENT OF A REGULATION

## POSITIVE LAW ETHICAL PROBLEMS

"Our company is being singled out for an affirmative action inspection even though we are not at the top of the computer-generated inspection list," argued Mr. Reilly, an executive at Beverly Enterprises.

"Well, it is true that Beverly was third on a list of three, but there were good reasons for selecting you," answered Mr. Busch, an official at the Office of Federal Contract Compliance Programs (OFCCP), which conducts affirmative action inspections.

"Well, we have 699 plants around the United States and we are 100 percent in compliance. Your administration of your computer-generated search violates the U.S. Constitution's Fourth Amendment's unreasonable search protections," responded Reilly.

Who was right?

"The no-lead regulation is arbitrary and capricious because studies indicate that the lead in gasoline is just one contributor to the lead in people's blood. Furthermore, no one knows exactly how much lead in the air will endanger people's health. Therefore, EPA's no-lead regulation for gasoline is invalid, and we should challenge it in court," concluded an executive at the Ethyl Corporation. Was he successful?

*"OF EVEN GREATER IMPORTANCE, THOUGH, IS THE PURPOSE BEHIND THE REQUIREMENT THAT THE PARTIES BE ABLE TO COMMENT ON THE RULE WHILE IT IS STILL IN THE FORMATIVE OR PROPOSED STAGE. THE PURPOSE IS BOTH (1) TO ALLOW THE AGENCY TO BENEFIT FROM THE EXPERTISE AND INPUT OF THE PARTIES WHO FILE COMMENTS WITH REGARD TO THE PROPOSED RULE, AND (2) TO SEE TO IT THAT THE AGENCY MAINTAINS A FLEXIBLE AND OPEN-MINDED ATTITUDE TOWARDS ITS OWN RULES."*

*—JUDGE WILKEY
IN NATIONAL
TOUR BROKERS
ASS'N. V. UNITED
STATES (1978)*

This chapter discusses the legislative, judicial, and executive functions of administrative agencies: making regulations, adjudicating (deciding cases), and enforcing agency statutes and regulations.

## THE FUNCTIONS OF ADMINISTRATIVE AGENCIES

Figure 7.1 sets out the major steps that could be involved in the life of a federal regulation and shows the adjudicatory, legislative, and executive jobs of the typical agency.

## EXECUTIVE

The *executive* functions involve law enforcement and administration. These functions consist of investigating and enforcing regulations and doing the scores of mundane tasks that make any organization run, such as hiring, firing, and issuing licenses.

**FIGURE 7.1 MAJOR STEPS IN THE LIFE OF A FEDERAL REGULATION (REG) INFORMAL RULE MAKING**

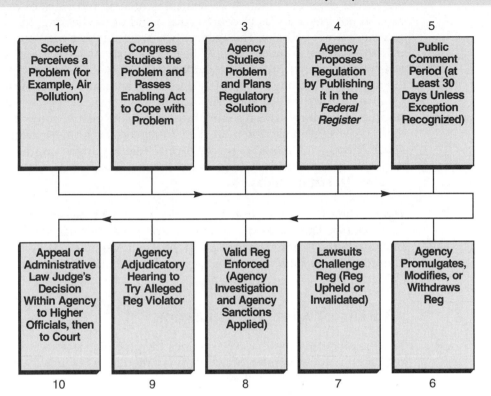

## ADJUDICATIVE

Agency *adjudication* refers to hearings before administrative law judges (ALJs), who are legally independent of agency prosecutors, investigators, and rule makers. ALJs make rulings on admissibility of evidence (the rules of evidence are usually more lenient here than in courts) and control the conduct of the hearing.

## LEGISLATIVE

The *legislative* function of an administrative agency refers to rule making. The three kinds of rule making are informal, formal, and hybrid.

*Informal Rule Making.* Informal rule making uses the notice and comment process discussed later in this chapter. Agencies usually make regulations in this way. Essentially, in the process, a federal agency places a notice of **proposed rule making** in the *Federal Register*, receives comments from interested people on the proposed regulation, makes any changes, and promulgates the regulation. No trials or hearings are held. No face-to-face contact is made between the regulator and the public. Regulation making done this way takes place on paper or over the Internet. If a court challenge is offered to an informal rule, the arbitrary, capricious, and unreasonable evidentiary standard is used to review it.

*Formal Rule Making.* Formal rule making occurs when a statute requires rule making on the record. A notice of the proposed rule making takes place, and a hearing follows: Witnesses give testimony under oath, transcripts of testimony are made, cross-examination of witnesses occurs, and rules of evidence apply, though not as strictly as in courts. At the end of the hearing, the agency makes written, formal findings. The agency then promulgates a regulation based on the evidence at the hearing. Courts use the substantial evidence test to decide whether the agency has enough evidence to justify the regulation's existence.

Formal rule making is extremely expensive and can be slow. A classic example occurred when the Food and Drug Administration spent approximately ten years to promulgate a regulation setting the appropriate peanut content of peanut butter.[1] The lengthy transcript (more than 7,700 pages) is formal rule making and free speech gone wild, and shows why formal rule making is impractical despite its desirable qualities such as cross-examination. Thus, formal rule making is rarely required by statutes today.

*Hybrid Rule Making.* Hybrid rule making is a cross between formal and informal rule making. The notice and comment aspects of informal rule making are combined with the requirement of a public hearing. Also, the substantial evidence test is used to judge sufficiency of agency evidence to support the regulation.

## THE LIFE OF A FEDERAL REGULATION

The remainder of this chapter examines the possible steps in the life of a federal regulation. Not every step occurs in every regulation's life, although some regulations follow each possible step.

### STEP 1. SOCIETY PERCEIVES A PROBLEM

Society often perceives problems before legislatures do. Individuals may bring problems to the attention of the legislature by writing letters, forming citizens' groups, hiring lobbyists, and making campaign contributions. Congress must then study the problem to understand its exact nature. Members of Congress do not personally study all problems brought to their attention; no one has that much time. Instead, each member of Congress has a sizable staff, often exceeding 100 people. In addition, the congressional committees (and often subcommittees) have large staffs who do the work of studying problems.

### STEP 2. CONGRESS PASSES AN ENABLING ACT

People sometimes blame administrative agencies for causing the oversupply of regulations. This action is analogous to a patient blaming an optometrist for the patient's bad eyesight when told to get glasses. The doctor is doing only what the patient asks. Similarly, the legislature tells agencies what to do when it passes an enabling act.

Statutes that empower administrative agencies to make regulations are enabling acts. Agency regulations are valid only if the legislature gives the agency the necessary power. Agencies have no inherent power to make legally binding regulations.

---

[1] The content was set at 90 percent peanuts. The case is *Corn Prod. Co. v. FDA*, 427 F.2d 511 (3d Cir., 1970), *cert. denied sub. nom. Derby Foods, Inc. v. FDS*, 400 U.S. 957 (1970).

They may do only what the legislature lets them do in enabling acts. (Under discussion here are legislative regulations only, not interpretative regulations.)

The following is an **enabling act**. It is a section of a federal statute called the Sarbanes-Oxley Act of 2002 that gives a federal agency (here the Securities and Exchange Commission) the power to make regulations. This enabling act (below) is the exact wording Congress used to tell the Securities and Exchange Commission to make a rule.

### SEC. 407 DISCLOSURE OF AUDIT COMMITTEE FINANCIAL EXPERT.

(a) RULES DEFINING 'FINANCIAL EXPERT'—The Commission shall issue rules, as necessary or appropriate in the public interest and consistent with the protection of investors, to require each issuer, together with periodic reports required pursuant to Sections 13(a) and 15(d) of the Securities Exchange Act of 1934, to disclose whether or not, and if not, the reasons therefor, the audit committee of that issuer is comprised of at least 1 member who is a financial expert, as such term is defined by the Commission.

(b) CONSIDERATIONS—In defining the term 'financial expert' for purposes of subsection (a), the Commission shall consider whether a person has, through education and experience as a public accountant or auditor or a principal financial officer, comptroller, or principal accounting officer of an issuer, or from a position involving the performance of similar functions—

(1) an understanding of generally accepted accounting principles and financial statements;

(2) experience in—
(A) the preparation or auditing of financial statements of generally comparable issuers; and
(B) the application of such principles in connection with the accounting for estimates, accruals, and reserves;

(3) experience with internal accounting controls; and

(4) an understanding of audit committee functions.

(c) DEADLINE FOR RULEMAKING—The Commission shall—

(1) propose rules to implement this section, not later than 90 days after the date of enactment of this Act; and

(2) issue final rules to implement this section, not later than 180 days after that date of enactment.

## STEP 3. AN AGENCY STUDIES THE PROBLEM

When the legislature passes an enabling statute, it has implicitly said that society has a problem. The enabling statute tells an agency to do something about the problem and gives it some guidelines to make regulations to solve the problem. Before an agency can propose or promulgate a regulation, it must conduct a study. The study can be done in-house or contracted out to a consulting firm or to university professors.

*For more information about the Federal Trade Commission, see* **http://www.sec.gov**

When the legislature passes an enabling statute, it has implicitly said that society has a problem. The enabling statute tells an agency to do something about the problem and gives it some guidelines to make regulations to solve the problem. Before an agency can propose or promulgate a regulation, it must conduct a study. The study can be done in-house or contracted out to a consulting firm or to university professors.

The study is the key to the regulation because it is the scientific or factual justification for the regulation. For example, if the SEC promulgates a regulation forcing companies to explain whether or not they have a "financial expert" on the company's audit committee and, if not, why not, companies may ask "why" they should be forced to do so. In response, the SEC may refer the companies to Section 407 of the Sarbanes-Oxley Act, the law that tells the SEC to make such regulations to protect the public investors by making sure someone on the audit committee knows how to read and understand financial statements. Company (called "issuers" by federal securities law) financial statements should tell potential investors the true state of the company's finances. Company financial statement "shenanigans" that cost investors millions because the statements portray a "sound" company when the company actually is not (Enron?), enticing investors to buy securities in those companies, should not be permitted to occur.

## STEP 4. THE AGENCY PROPOSES A REGULATION

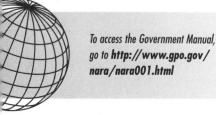

The Web site for the Federal Register can be found at http://www.gpo.gov/ su_doc/aces/aces140.html

After the agency concludes its study, it drafts a regulation based on the study's conclusions. Different agency offices or personnel examine the draft regulation, such as the Office of General Counsel, the agency's lawyers, economists, and scientists, to try to find problems with it.

Once the agency's draft regulation has been reviewed within the agency, the heads of the agency sign it and send it to the *Federal Register* Office in the National Archives and Records Service, where the draft regulation is published in a daily edition of the *Federal Register*. Additionally, with the advent of the Internet, many federal agencies also publish proposed regulations, public comments thereto, and promulgated regulations on it so the public can have greater access to agency actions. Consult the particular agency's Web site for recent rule making activity.

*The Law Governing Federal Agencies' Regulation Making.* The federal law governing regulation making comes from the Administrative Procedure Act (APA), which governs most federal agencies. The APA's regulation-making rules do not apply to U.S. military or foreign affairs functions, to matters relating to agency management and personnel, or to public property, loans, grants, benefits, or contracts. Also, state and municipal regulation making is not covered by the federal APA. Many states have state APAs that govern state administrative agencies. In addition to the APA, special statutes, such as the Occupational Safety and Health Act, sometimes put other requirements on agency rule making.

*The Notice in the Federal Register.* When an agency proposes a regulation, general notice of the proposed regulation must be published in the *Federal Register*, with two exceptions: when people subject to the regulation are named and either (1) are personally served or (2) otherwise have actual notice.

To access the Government Manual, go to http://www.gpo.gov/ nara/nara001.html

*Contents of Notice.* The following items must be in the notice of the proposed rule making published in the *Federal Register*:

1.  The time, place, and nature of public regulation making in general
2.  The laws the agency says give it the authority to make the proposed rule

3. The provisions of the proposed rule or a description of the subjects and issues involved (In other words, the rule itself does not have to be published when it is proposed.)

***Regulations That Need Not Be Published.*** Interpretative regulations, general policy statements, or rules of agency organization, procedure, or practice do not have to be published in the *Federal Register* because they are too general or trivial and because courts do not treat such items as law. One other instance excuses an agency from giving notice of a proposed substantive regulation. When an agency for good cause finds that notice and public procedure thereon are impracticable, unnecessary, or contrary to the public interest, *Federal Register* notice is not required of even a substantive regulation.

The Department of Transportation provides a variety of information at **http://www.dot.gov**

In the following case, *Truckers United For Safety v. Fed. Highway Administration*, which reason did the court give for excusing *Federal Register* notice?

## Truckers United For Safety v. Fed. Highway Administration
U.S. Court of Appeals (D.C. Cir.)
139 F.3d 934 (1998)

### Background and Facts

Truckers United For Safety (TUFS), a nonprofit trade association of motor carriers, petitioned the court for review of a portion of the regulatory guidance issued by the Federal Highway Administration for private parties seeking to comply with motor carrier safety regulations.

TUFS contends that the Administration should have afforded interested parties notice and an opportunity to comment under the Administrative Procedure Act (APA).

### Body of Opinion

**Judge Rogers.** Under the Motor Carrier Act of 1935 and the Motor Carrier Safety Act of 1984, the Federal Highway Administration has the authority to issue regulations pertaining to commercial motor vehicle safety and to enforce those regulations. . . . Pursuant to that authority, the Administration promulgated the Federal Motor Carrier Safety Regulations, including the following regulations:

§ 390.11 Motor carrier to require observance of driver regulations.

Whenever . . . a duty is prescribed for a driver or a prohibition is imposed upon the driver, it shall be the duty of the motor carrier to require observance of such duty or prohibition. If the motorcarrier is a driver, the driver shall likewise be bound.

§ 395.3 Maximum driving time.

(a) Except as provided (elsewhere) . . . no motor carrier shall permit or require any driver used by it to drive nor shall any such driver drive:

(1) More than 10 hours following 8 consecutive hours off duty; or

(2) For any period after having been on duty 15 hours following 8 consecutive hours off duty.

(b) No motor carrier shall permit or require a driver of a commercial motor vehicle to drive, nor shall any driver drive, regardless of the number of motor carriers using the driver's services, for any period after—

(1) Having been on duty 60 hours in any 7 consecutive days if the employing motor carrier does not operate commercial motor vehicles every day of the week; or

(2) Having been on duty 70 hours in any period of 8 consecutive days if the employing motor carrier operates commercial motor vehicles every day of the week.

§ 395.8 Driver's record of duty status.

(a) Except for a private motor carrier of passengers (nonbusiness), every motor carrier shall require every driver used by the motor carrier to record his/her duty status for each 24-hour period using the methods prescribed (herein). . . .

(b) Failure to complete the record of duty activities of this section or § 395.15, failure to preserve a record of such duty activities, or making of false reports in connection with such duty activities shall make the driver and/or the carrier liable to prosecution. . . .

The administration has developed and periodically updated regulatory guidance in question-and-answer format to assist parties bound by these regulations. . . . In the most recent edition of this regulatory guidance, published in the Federal Register on April 4, 1997, the Administration "consolidated previously issued interpretations and regulatory guidance materials and developed concise interpretative guidance in question-and-answer form." . . . Three particular questions and answers within the guidance are of concern here. First and second, in interpretation of 49 C.F.R. § 395.3:

Question 7: What is the liability of a motor carrier for hours of service violations?

Guidance: The carrier is liable for violations of the hours of service regulations if it had or should have had the means by which to detect the violations. Liability under the Federal Motor Vehicle Safety regulations does not depend upon actual knowledge of the violations.

Question 8: Are carriers liable for the actions of their employees even though the carrier contends that it did not require or permit the violations to occur?

Guidance: Yes. Carriers are liable for the actions of their employees. Neither intent to commit, nor actual knowledge of, a violation is a necessary element of the liability. Carriers "permit" violations of the hours of service if they fail to have in place management systems that effectively prevent such violations. . . .

Third, in interpretation of 49 C.F.R. § 395.8:

Question 21: What is the carrier's liability when its drivers falsify records of duty status?

Guidance: A carrier is liable both for the actions of its drivers in submitting false documents and for its own actions in accepting false documents. Motor carriers have a duty to require drivers to observe the Federal Motor Carrier Safety Regulations.

. . . TUFS' further contention, that the set of three questions and answers in the regulatory guidance is invalid because the Administration did not provide interested parties with notice and an opportunity to comment in accordance with the APA is similarly unpersuasive. . . . Under the APA, legislative rules are subject to notice-and-comment requirements, whereas interpretative rules are not. . . . To distinguish between the two, the court asks

> "whether the purported interpretative rule has 'legal effect,' which in turn is best ascertained by asking (1) whether in the absence of the rule there would not be an adequate legislative basis for enforcement action or other agency action to confer benefits or ensure the performance of duties, (2) whether the agency has published the rule in the Code of Federal Regulations, (3) whether the agency has explicitly invoked its general legislative authority, or (4) whether the rule effectively amends a prior legislative rule." . . .

Although this inquiry may be "fuzzy" in some cases . . . in the instant case, each of these criteria points toward the same conclusion: the three questions and answers represent interpretative rules not subject to the APA's notice and comment requirements.

First, as discussed, the three questions and answers do not appear to impose a new strict liability standard on motor carriers, and thus the Administration has no apparent need to rely upon them for authority to take any enforcement action. The regulations in force both before and after the Administration issued the regulatory guidance provided that motor carriers have a duty to require their drivers' compliance with the regulations . . . and in particular, with the maximum hours of duty and record keeping regulations with which the regulatory guidance in question is concerned. . . . The regulatory guidance appears only to elaborate upon that duty, and then only in a manner consistent with earlier applications of the regulations. . . . Even if the regulatory guidance did not exist, the Administration could rely upon earlier authority to apply the rules embodied in the three challenged questions and answers.

Second, the regulatory guidance is not published in the Code of Federal Regulations. It was published only in the *Federal Register*, and the Administration gave no indication there that it would publish the Regulatory Guidance again elsewhere. . . .

Third, the Administration did not invoke its legislative authority in publishing the regulatory guidance. To the contrary, the Administration explained that this was "interpretative guidance" meant to "provide the motor carrier industry with a clearer understanding of the applicability of many of the requirements contained in the Federal Motor Carrier Safety Regulations in particular situations." . . . Although the label an agency places on a rule is not dispositive, . . . the label, as indicative of intent, does carry some weight in our consideration whether the underlying rule is legislative or interpretative.

Finally the three questions and answers do not amend a prior legislative rule. As noted, they appear consistent with prior law. . . .

All four factors indicate that the Administration was not required to afford interested parties notice and an opportunity to comment before promulgating the three questions and answers. . . .

## Judgment and Result

The Federal Highway Administration won. The Court of Appeals held the FHA's rules were interpretative. Therefore the FHA did not have to provide the public with notice and an opportunity to comment on the rules under the Administrative Procedure Act.

## Questions

1. Did the Federal Highway Administration give the public 30 days to comment on the proposed regulation?
2. Does the APA give a clear definition of "interpretative regulation" excusing compliance with the 30-day comment period? Who makes the initial determination that the regulation is "interpretative" justifying no commenting period? If no one such as TUFS here, challenges the agency determination that a regulation is interpretative, is not the agency's determination always right?
3. What is the purpose of the 30-day comment period between the proposal and promulgation of a federal rule?
4. How could the Internet facilitate the commenting process? Take a look at the Internet cites throughout this chapter. A number of federal agencies now allows the public to comment on proposed regulations over the Internet. Does this type of access make it easier for members of the public located in remote communities to comment on proposed regulations?

*Problems in Finding the Notice.* In the majority of cases, publication in the *Federal Register* is the only official notice the public gets before a regulation takes effect. The average person has never seen the *Federal Register*, let alone read a proposed regulation. The advent of the Internet now helps people find proposed regulations by using their home or office computers. They simply go to the proposing agency's Web site and look up 'proposed regulations' there.

Figure 7.2 is a proposed SEC regulation that requires issuers (companies) to identify financial experts on audit committees or explain whether or not—and, if not, why not—the audit committee is composed of a least one member who is a "financial expert."

Several points should be noted:

1.  What factors does the proposed regulation use to identify if a person is a "financial expert?" Does it require that the person have a Ph.D. in auditing? Be a straight "A" accounting major at an accredited college or university? Or what?
2.  Remarks are often made to the proposed regulation. Such remarks usually explain in layperson's terms what the proposed regulation is about. Note that the proposed reg does not require that a "financial expert" be on the audit committee, but, rather, the issuer must explain why no expert is on the audit committee if there is none. Perhaps business experience could substitute for educational credentials.
3.  The proposed regulations do NOT go into the *Code of Federal Regulations*.
4.  When the regulations are later promulgated, the introductory remarks explain that the promulgated regulation will go into 17 *C.F.R.* § 229.309.

## FIGURE 7.2 A Proposed Regulation

**SECURITIES AND EXCHANGE COMMISSION**

**Financial Expert.** This proposed disclosure requirement would increase the disclosure burden by requiring a registrant to report the number and names of persons that the board of directors has determined to be financial experts on its audit committee as well as whether the expert is independent, and if not, an explanation of why they are not. It would not require a registrant to have a financial expert on its audit committee. Item 401 of Regulations S-K and S-B already requires registrants to ascertain and disclose the business experience of all of its directors. The inquiry that registrants should make to satisfy this disclosure requirement should assist the registrant in determining whether a particular director is a financial expert under the rules. If the registrant does not have a financial expert, the rule only requires that the registrant explain why it does not have such a person on its audit committee. Therefore, we believe the added burden of the proposed rule would be minimal. For purposes of the PRA, we estimate that the proposed disclosure requirements regarding financial experts will result in a minimal incremental increase of 0.5 burden hours per issuer in connection with preparing each annual report.

**11. Add §229.308 to read as follows:**

**§229.309 (Item 309) Audit committee financial experts.**

Disclose the number and names of the persons that the registrant's board of directors has determined to be the financial experts serving on the registrant's audit committee, as defined in Section 3(a)(58) of the Exchange Act (15 U.S.C. 78c(a)(58)). Also disclose whether the financial expert or experts are independent as that term is used in Section 10A (m)(3) of the Exchange Act (15 U.S.C. 78j-1(m)(3)), and if not, an explanation of why they are not. If the registrant's board of directors has not determined that a financial expert is serving on its audit committee, the registrant must disclose that fact and explain why it does not have such an expert.

Instructions to Item 309.

1.  For purposes of the determination by the board of directors under this Item 309, the term "financial expert" means a person who has, through education and experience as a public accountant or auditor, or a principal financial officer, controller, or principal accounting officer, of a company that, at the time the person held such position, was required to file reports pursuant to Section 13(a) or 15(d) of the Exchange Act (15 U.S.C. 78m(a) and 78o(d)), or experience in one or more positions that involve the performance of similar functions (or that results, in the judgment of the board of directors, in the person's having similar expertise and experience), the following attributes:
    a.  An understanding of generally accepted accounting principles and financial statements;
    b.  Experience applying such generally accepted accounting principles in connection with the accounting for estimates, accruals, and reserves that are generally comparable to the estimates, accruals, and reserves, if any, used in the registrant's financial statements;
    c.  Experience preparing or auditing financial statements that present accounting issues that are generally comparable to those raised by the registrant's financial statements;
    d.  Experience with internal controls and procedures for financial reporting; and
    e.  An understanding of audit committee functions.
2.  If the board of directors has determined that a person is a financial expert because, in the board's judgment, he or she has similar expertise and experience to those enumerated, the registrant must disclose the basis for that determination.

## FIGURE 7.2  A Proposed Regulation, continued

3. In evaluating the education and experience of a person, the board of directors should consider the following factors in the aggregate:

   a. The level of the person's accounting or financial education, including whether the person has earned an advanced degree in finance or accounting;

   b. Whether the person is a certified public accountant, or the equivalent, in good standing, and the length of time that the person actively has practiced as a certified public accountant, or the equivalent;

   c. Whether the person is certified or otherwise identified as having accounting or financial experience by a recognized private body that establishes and administers standards in respect of such expertise, whether that person is in good standing with the recognized private body, and the length of time that the person has been actively certified or identified as having this expertise:

   d. Whether the person has served as a principal financial officer, controller or principal accounting officer of a company that, at the time the person held such position, was required to file reports pursuant to Section 13(a) or 15(d) of the Exchange Act, and if so, for how long;

   e. The person's specific duties while serving as a public accountant, auditor, principal financial officer, controller, principal accounting officer or position involving the performance of similar functions;

   f. The person's level of familiarity and experience with all applicable laws and regulations regarding the preparation of financial statements that must be included in reports filed under Section 13(a) or 15(d) of the Exchange Act;

   g. The level and amount of the person's direct experience reviewing, preparing, auditing or analyzing financial statements that must be included in reports filed under Section 13(a) or 15(d) of the Exchange Act;

   h. The person's past or current membership on one or more audit committees of companies that, at the time the person held such membership, were required to file reports pursuant to Section 13(a) or 15(d) of the Exchange Act;

   i. The person's level of familiarity and experience with the use and analysis of financial statements of public companies;

   j. Whether the person has any other relevant qualifications or experience that would assist him or her in understanding and evaluating the registrant's financial statements and other financial information and to make knowledgeable and thorough inquiries whether:

      i. The financial statements fairly present the financial condition, results of operations and cash flows of the registrant in accordance with generally accepted accounting principles; and

      ii. The financial statements and other financial information, taken together, fairly present the financial condition, results of operations and cash flows of the registrant; and

   k. In the case of a foreign private issuer, the person's level of experience in respect of public companies in the foreign private issuer's home country, generally accepted accounting principles used by the issuer, and the reconciliation of financial statements with U.S. generally accepted accounting principles.

4. Although the board of directors should consider the factors listed in Instruction 3, those factors are not replacements for, and a financial expert must satisfy, all of the attributes listed in Instruction 1 to this Item.

5. In the case of foreign private issuers with two-tier boards of directors, for purposes of this Item 309, the term "board of directors" means the supervisory or non-management board.

6. A registrant that is an Asset-Backed Issuer (as defined in §240, 13a-14(g) and §240-15d-14(g) of this chapter) is not required to disclose the information required by this item.

**12. Add §229.446 to read as follows....**

http://www.sec.gov/rules/proposed/33-8138.htm

*Inadequate Notice.* Suppose that a federal agency publishes a notice in the *Federal Register* asking the public what changes it would like to see in a statute the agency enforces. Assume the agency plans to turn these suggestions over to Congress, hoping it will pass amendments to the act the agency enforces. However, after the agency starts receiving the public's suggestions, the agency instead promulgates a regulation dealing with the matter. This action saves the agency from having to go to Congress to get a statute passed.

A problem could arise with this procedure—the problem of *notice*. Remember the APA notice requirements for proposed regulations: A federal agency must first give notice of a proposed regulation by publishing either the regulation in draft form or information about it in the *Federal Register*. *National Tour Brokers Association v. United States* says that a regulation promulgated without a prior notice is invalid.

## National Tour Brokers Ass'n v. United States
U.S. Court of Appeals (D.C. Cir.)
591 F.2d 896 (1978)

### Background and Facts

The National Tour Brokers Association (NTBA) was a group of travel agents. The NTBA sued the U.S. Interstate Commerce Commission (ICC). The ICC had promulgated regulations putting new, expensive duties on travel agents. The NTBA argued that the ICC did not first propose its regulations in the *Federal Register*, a requirement of the Administrative Procedure Act. The ICC did publish a *Federal Register* notice, but the notice did not mention any proposed regulation applying to tour brokers. The ICC argued that its action of publishing a general notice, asking for the public's ideas on how to limit tour brokers, was sufficient.

### Body of Opinion

**Judge Wilkey.** A. *Constructive Notice*

The first clause of § 553(b) provides for constructive notice: 'General notice of proposed rulemaking shall be published in the *Federal Register*.' We are unable to find that the Commission satisfied this requirement. It is true that the Commission published a general notice in the *Federal Register*, but it was not a notice of proposed rulemaking. A fair reading of that item clearly indicates that it was one looking toward the formulation of possible legislative amendments which might be proposed to Congress, not administrative rulemaking. It seems that the Commission changed its mind halfway through this proceeding and is now attempting to correct its procedural deficiencies by characterizing the proceeding *ex post facto* as informal rulemaking.

Agencies could in the future publish vague, ambiguous notices in the *Federal Register*, adverting obliquely to certain issues or proceedings, and then, months or years later, promulgate final rules and claim that constructive notice had been given. This cannot be the objective of the APA notice requirement.

The purpose of this (notice) requirement is clear—to put interested parties on notice that *administrative rule making* in certain areas is about to take place. We hold that the Commission failed to meet this requirement in this case. . . .

The legislative change sought in this case was basically an expansion of the authority of the ICC, while the administrative rules later issued addressed much more specific subjects such as territorial restrictions and bond amounts. . . .

B. *Actual Notice*

Section 553(b) allows the alternative of actual notice: " . . . unless persons subject thereto are named and either personally served or otherwise have actual notice thereof in accordance with law."

The Commission claims that actual notice was given to the parties at the oral hearing held 9 August 1976. The Commission's Chairman opened that hearing by outlining some of the questions the Commission hoped to resolve, among which was, "[I]f the Commission does decide that entry controls are no longer necessary, should we seek legislation or is some other course of action available?" This is clearly not a statement that a rulemaking proceeding is taking place. Rather, it is an inquiry asking whether it would be advisable to undertake a rulemaking proceeding. The statement of NTBA's counsel later at that hearing, in response to the Chairman's introductory remarks, was in conformity with this meaning. Counsel stated: Now, our position is this. We urge [the Commission] not to submit to Congress legislative recommendation for change in Section 211. We also urge that you not attempt a change in Section 211 administratively.

Counsel was simply stating that it did not think that an administrative rulemaking proceeding should be initiated. It was not an implicit concession that a rulemaking proceeding was then underway. . . .

Of even greater importance, though, is the purpose behind the requirement that the parties be able to comment on the rule while it is still in the formative or "proposed" stage. The purpose is both (1) to allow the agency to benefit from the expertise and input of the parties who file comments with regard to the proposed rule, and (2) to see to it that the agency maintains a flexible and open-minded attitude towards its own rules, which might be lost if the agency had already put its credibility on the line in the form of "final" rules. People naturally tend to be more close-minded and defensive once they have made a 'final' determination. . . . The purpose of § 553 is to "enable the agency promulgating the rule to educate itself before establishing rules and procedures which have a substantial impact on those regulated." . . .

The deficiencies in an approach whereby the agency issues final rules before it receives (and benefits from) comments and input from the parties is graphically illustrated in the instant proceeding. In its initial decision promulgating the final rules here in issue, the Commission stated that [i]n all but a few cases, such bonds [*i.e.*, tour broker surety bonds] will be written on a full collateral basis only, *i.e.*, the broker must post with the surety company the coverage amount in cash or acceptable investment bonds. Surety companies, even before issuing bonds on a full collateral basis, thoroughly investigate a bond applicant as to reputation, integrity, business ability, and financial stability. The possibility of questionable fly-by-night brokers is thereby all but eliminated.

As pointed out by petitioner the Commission may be in serious error about how tour broker surety bonding actually works. . . .

## Judgment and Result

The court invalidated the ICC's promulgated rules because the APA notice requirement had not been satisfied. The public had been denied its right to comment, and the ICC had thereby deprived itself of help from the public in understanding the business it was trying to regulate.

## Questions

1. Did the agency (ICC) publish a notice of proposed rule making before it promulgated its rule? What effect did these actions have on the rule?

2. Because the ICC published a public notice in the *Federal Register* before promulgating the challenged regulation, how was the National Tour Brokers Association or any other member of the public harmed?

3. Did the court hold that the regulation in question was invalid because of what it did (a substantive flaw) or because of how the ICC promulgated it (a procedural defect)?

## Step 5. The Public Comments

Step 5 in Figure 7.1—the comment period—is crucial from the public's standpoint. During this time, anyone, whether a private business, a teenager, a state government official, or another federal official, may submit comments to the agency proposing the regulation.

*Time to Comment.* A federal agency must usually give the public at least thirty days to comment on a proposed regulation before its effective date. As a practical matter, federal agencies often give the public a much longer time, sometimes months, between proposal and the end of the comment period.

*Form for Comment.* Comments do not have to follow any particular form; a simple letter directed to the proposing agency is sufficient. A member of the public could say several things in a comment. Comments are usually critical of agency-proposed regulations. Consider the comment letters submitted by Mr. Dexter Peacock (Figure 7.3a) and Mr. Martin Winter (Figure 7.3b) in response to the SEC's proposed regulation in Figure 7.2. Note that Mr. Peacock is concerned that there might not be enough qualified people available to be "financial experts." Mr. Winter, on the other hand, lauds the SEC's efforts to require "financial literacy" on the audit committees. He does suggest an interesting modification to the SEC's proposal, however, namely that the SEC "financial expert" requirement be "phased in" over several years because, in his view, only about 10 percent of Fortune 250 companies (very large corporations) meet Sarbanes-Oxley's Section 407 "financial literacy" requirements. He goes on to observe that of the more than 10,000 companies filing periodic reports with the SEC, only about 10 percent probably satisfy Sarbanes-Oxley's "financial expert" test for an audit committee member.

*What Agencies Must Do with Comments.* After the comment period, the APA directs the agency to "consider" the relevant material presented. This consideration could lead the agency to promulgate the rules as they were proposed or to modify the proposed regulations to take the comments into account, or withdraw the regulations.

*Why Comment.* The principal importance of commenting lies in the public's ability to suggest changes in proposed regulations before they become law. In effect, the public is helping the agency write its regulations. As a practical matter, an

**FIGURE 7.3A  A COMMENT TO A PROPOSED REGULATION**

From: Peacock, Dexter [DexterPeacock@akllp.com]
Sent: Friday, November 15, 2002 2:33 PM
To: SEC (E-mail)
Subject: File No. S7-40-02

Gentlemen and Ladies: I have practiced securities law at a large law firm for 35 years. I have also served as a director of three NYSE companies and two banks, and am currently a director of a NYSE-listed company. I have served on the audit committees of two of the NYSE companies and chaired one of them.

I am concerned that the Commission greatly overestimates the number of people who can meet the requirements of Section 407 of Sarbanes-Oxley and who will be willing to serve in the capacity of a "financial expert" on an audit committee. I understand that the basic attributes of "financial expert" are set forth in federal law, and that the Commission cannot change them by rule. But the Commission does have considerable latitude in how to interpret this law, and it needs to do so as broadly as it can. I will not undertake an exhaustive discussion of the interpretative issues, but will call two to you attention.

1. Knowledgeable people who are considering whether to make themselves available as "financial experts" are worried about the first attribute—"understanding generally accepted accounting principles." A retired partner with 30 years of public company auditing experience at a Final Four accounting firm recently remarked to me that he was afraid he could not meet the "understanding of GAAP. . ." test, because he had been out of public accounting for two years and was "rusty" on some GAAP principles. Will this attribute be interpreted to require a current ability to pass the GAAP portion of the CPA exam? This question is not as absurd as it may sound; if the Commission is going to focus on substantive knowledge of GAAP, it is going to be propelled some distance down this very road. In my opinion, "knowledge of GAAP" ought to be interpreted the same way that we mean when we speak of a lawyer's "knowledge of the law"—which does not mean that the lawyer knows off the top of his head what the answer to a specific legal question is, but rather that he is familiar with the area, knows where to find the answer quickly, and knows how to interpret what he finds. I strongly urge the Commission to issue a reasonable interpretation of this attribute so that most retired auditors and virtually all CFO's are not disqualified out of hand.

2. What does experience in the preparation or auditing of financial statements of "generally comparable" issuer mean? I would suggest the Commission limit its elaboration of these words to its already-proposed requirement that such experience have been acquired in a public company, and specifically reject the interpretation that such experience must have been obtained in the same or a similar industry. Otherwise, we are going to find ourselves with not only a small pool of people but one further stratified by the industries in which they work or worked.

My principal concern, however, is that the stock exchanges appear to be headed for an incorporation of the SEC's definition of "financial expert" in the audit committee requirements contained in their listing agreements (see, e.g. NASDAQ's October 9, 2002 Rule 19b-4 filing). If this development proceeds in the direction it appears to be going, it will mean that every listed company will have to have a "financial expert" in its board. I simply do not think there are enough people who can meet these requirements to provide every listed company with a "financial expert." In fact, I think the Commission may be dismayed at how small the pool of "financial experts" turns out to be, even if it takes a liberal approach to the Section 407 rule.

In any case, there is an alternative. The market can decide for itself how important the presence of a financial expert is, on a company-by-company basis. If companies are unable, despite a continuing and good faith effort, to attract a financial expert to their board, then we should leave them to the discipline of the securities markets. I can find nothing in Sarbanes-Oxley that requires a different result. I think the Commission at least needs to contemplate the possibility (I think the probability) that hundreds of companies will face the theoretical requirement that they delist if all companies have to find a "financial expert", which could have a catastrophic result on their stockholders. I say "theoretical" because this will never be permitted to happen. But it will embarrass the exchanges and the Commission will set back corporate reform, and can be avoided with the application of a reality check.

**FIGURE 7.3B  A COMMENT TO A PROPOSED REGULATION**

**Martin E. Winter**
**101 East 52nd Street**
**6th Floor**
**New York, NY 10022**

Robert F. Burns, Esq.
Chief Counsel
Office of the Chief Accountant
U.S. Securities and Exchange Commission
450 Fifth Street N.W.
Washington, D.C.   20549

**Rulemaking Required by Section 407**
**of the Sarbanes-Oxley Act of 2002**

Dear Mr. Burns:

I understand that you are among those leading the effort on the part of the staff in advising the Commission with respect to the rulemaking on the definition of "financial expert" required by Section 407 of the Sarbanes-Oxley Act—an important matter that appears to have drawn relatively little commentary in the wake of the law's enactment. I write to offer a suggestion on this subject and share a few related views on corporate audit committees insofar as they may prove helpful to you and others at the agency in shaping the forthcoming rule proposal.

By way of background, I was once a principal with Arthur Young & Co. and continue to be a certified public accountant. I later served as the secretary and treasurer of a public company and as chief financial officer of a private investment firm. I currently serve as chief executive officer of independent Board Advisor Services LLC, a consulting firm that advises boards of directors on corporate governance, financial reporting, and accounting matters.

**Section 407 and Defining Financial Expertise**

*The Section 407 Mandate.* Over the last few years, many have called for and taken notable steps to strengthen the oversight and involvement of corporate audit committees in the financial reporting processes of their respective issuers. The national securities exchanges, for example, now require committee members to have some degree of financial "literacy"— a standard that, between the leading exchanges, leaves open the question of whether one must be able to read the music or simply be able to play by ear, as it were.

Section 407 of the Sarbanes-Oxley Act, however, now requires something substantially more: that issuers disclose whether or not the audit committee of that issuer is comprised of at least one member who is a "financial expert," as that term will be defined by the Commission in its forthcoming rulemaking. If no committee member is so qualified, the issuer will have to face the difficult task of stating the reason why not. Although styled as a disclosure rule, Section 407 and its ensuing rules should lead to new and welcome normative standards for the financial savvy of corporate audit committees.

*Financial Expertise.* The extent to which Section 407 and related provision of the Sarbanes-Oxley Act may bring about meaningful reforms in corporate governance and financial reporting will, to an important degree, turn on the manner in which the Commission delineates the financial expertise requirement. On this score, Congress has taken steps to ensure that certain critical qualifications be met. Specifically, Section 407 requires the Commission to consider whether the designated person has "through education and experience as a public accountant or auditor or a principal financial officer, comptroller, or principal accounting officer of an issuer, or from a position involving the performance of similar functions—

(1)   an understanding of generally accepted accounting principles and financial statements;

(2)   experience in—
     (A)  the preparation or auditing of financial statements of generally comparable issuers; and
     (B)  the application of such principles in connection with the accounting for estimates, accruals, and reserves;

---

**FIGURE 7.3B A COMMENT TO A PROPOSED REGULATION (CONTINUED)**

---

(3)  experience with internal accounting controls; and

(4)  an understanding of audit committee functions"

Some following this provision have expressed uncertainty about whether these considerations need only be reviewed by the Commission in formulating its definition of whether they must be part of any definition the agency adopts. In either case, these considerations represent a remarkable list. Among them, emphasis may need to be placed on the need for experience with "generally comparable issuers," particularly given that the Conference Committee saw fit to add this qualification to the already impressive set of criteria proposed by the Senate. In my view, seeking experience specific to the issuer's industry, size and financial complexity, for example, makes good sense.

**Near-Term Compliance Challenges**

For all the good embodied in the financial expert standard, meeting its terms by the end of this fiscal year and even perhaps the next may be difficult for a majority of our nation's public companies. My own review of the audit committee composition of the Fortune 250, a fairly seasoned and sophisticated sample group, suggested that less than ten percent would currently satisfy the considerations posed by Section 407. I expect that a review of the more than 10,000 public companies who file periodic reports with the Commission would reveal a similar gap and a much better sense of the absolute number of issuers who may struggle at the outset to meet the new audit committee standard, perhaps vying with each other in an early scramble to obtain the people and experience they need (particularly in view of recently imposed rules by the national securities exchanges, including a restriction on the total number of board memberships one person may hold). While I support the implementation of the new standards I fear that many issuers will feel pressured to fill the post with the first person they can find who meets the definition rather than searching for those best suited to advising them and comparable companies. Given the near-term compliance challenges the new standard will pose, some flexibility, consistent with Commission practice and other provisions of the Act, would likely improve the implementation and ultimate effectiveness of Section 406 and its related rules, Accordingly, I offer the following suggestion.

**A Possible Solution to this Near-Term Issue**

The Commission might, as it has in the past, allow for a phase-in period for compliance with the forthcoming financial expert standard during which audit committees could engage outside independent financial experts to satisfy the new rule. Among its provisions, the Sarbanes-Oxley Act cites the authority of public company audit committees to engage their own financial and other advisers, recognizing that many committees have engaged such advisers for some time as a matter of best practice. I believe that a phase-in period of this sort would be consistent with that provision and practice, and result in benefits to issuers and ultimately public investors as companies and boards could conduct more meaningful searches for the directors best suited to providing them with sound advice and judgment on financial matters borne of, among other things, experience with comparable issuers.

Given that possibility, I feel strongly that this option should be subjected to the rigors of the public notice and comment process through the forthcoming rule proposal. I believe that the ensuing commentary from those following Section 407 will bear out its merits. Finally, while others may disagree, I do not believe that an auditor could provide this service to a reporting company audit client given the primacy of its independence obligations and its public watchdog function.

I would be happy to discuss this suggestion and my other thoughts, or supplement them, should you think that would be helpful to you others at the Commission. You may reach me at the address above or by telephone at (212)759-4433. Many thanks for your consideration.

Sincerely,


Martin Winter

cc: Mr. Robert K. Herdman
    Giovanni P. Prezioso, Esq.
    Alan L. Beller, Esq.

agency need do nothing with public comments: The APA only tells agencies to consider comments. However, agencies do read, consider, and sometimes modify or even totally withdraw proposed regulations in response to comments. An example occurred when the Securities and Exchange Commission withdrew its proposed regulation that would have encouraged earnings projections in financial statements.[2] Public comments can significantly influence regulations.

## STEP 6. THE AGENCY PROMULGATES, MODIFIES, OR WITHDRAWS THE REGULATION

After the public comment period closes, the APA tells the federal agency proposing the regulation to consider the comments. The APA does not require that the agency write letters to all the commenters with the agency's reaction to the comments, nor does the APA require that the agency promulgate the regulation.

An agency can do three basic things after the public comment period ends: promulgate the regulation, modify the regulation and either promulgate it as modified or repropose it for another round of public comments with an eye toward eventual promulgation, or withdraw the regulation. Let us examine each of these alternatives.

*Promulgate Now.* If the agency is making a regulation on a topic that is noncontroversial, is knowledgeable about the matter to be regulated, and has no staffing, budgetary, or other problems, the regulation would probably be promulgated as proposed after the comment period ends. For an example of the promulgated reg on SEC financial experts on issuer audit committees, watch the SEC Web site (**http:/www.sec.gov**). When this text was written, there was no promulgated reg for the proposed reg in Figure 7.2.

*Modify and Repropose.* Suppose the agency does not have a full understanding of the problem or the subject matter is controversial. In such cases the public comments could educate agency personnel by pointing out flaws in the proposed regulations. This process is a great help to federal agencies and could prevent an ineffective or overly burdensome proposed regulation from ever being promulgated. It may be the greatest service a business or member of the public could provide in the entire regulatory process, and it does not cost much to make a comment. Furthermore, the number and nature of public comments indicate the extent of interest in a problem. Strongly adverse or favorable public comments signal likelihood of future success to an agency for a regulatory program.

*Withdraw.* Comments to an agency's proposed regulation sometimes indicate overwhelming criticism. In effect, the proposal is a dud, a trial balloon shot down for one reason or another. The proposing agency may withdraw the proposed regulation and throw it out.

## STEP 7. CHALLENGES IN COURT TO THE PROMULGATED REGULATION

After an agency promulgates a regulation, it has the practical effect of law; however, legal ways are available to challenging a regulation after promulgation. According to the APA, such challenges can occur if the regulation does any of the following:

---

[2]41 *Fed. Reg.* 19,982 (1976).

1. Violates the U.S. Constitution
2. Is arbitrary, capricious, an abuse of discretion, or otherwise not in accordance with law
3. Is beyond the authority (*ultra vires*) of the enabling act

***Violates the U.S. Constitution.*** A regulation that violates the U.S. Constitution is invalid. A regulation is presumed valid until a court decides otherwise. This standard applies whether it is a federal, state, or municipal regulation. Examples of an unconstitutional regulation are as follows:

1. At the federal level, the Internal Revenue Service's (IRS) promulgating a regulation that allows IRS agents to secretly enter private businesses without the owner's approval would violate the Fourth Amendment's unreasonable search and seizure prohibition.
2. At the state level, the state real estate licensing board's promulgating a regulation prohibiting people of Japanese ancestry from sitting for the state real estate licensing exam would violate the Fourteenth Amendment's equal protection clause.

***Is Arbitrary, Capricious, Etc.*** The terminology "arbitrary, capricious, an abuse of discretion, or otherwise not in accordance with law" refers to several reasons why agency regulations could be invalid. Evidence must exist to support agency regulations. Courts use two tests to determine whether the studies and data that agencies use to justify regulations are sufficient: (1) arbitrary, capricious, an abuse of discretion, and (2) substantial evidence.

The arbitrary, capricious, and abuse of discretion (A-C-A) standard controls informal rule making. This standard is more lenient than the substantial evidence test. It allows agencies to makes rules with fewer data, and studies and less evidence than the substantial evidence standard. The substantial evidence (SE) test is used for hybrid and formal rule making and any other rule making where a statute specifically requires it.

*Ethyl Corp. v. Environmental Protection Agency* illustrates that the arbitrary, capricious, and abuse test applies when agencies promulgate regulations.

## Ethyl Corp. v. Environmental Protection Agency
U.S. Court of Appeals (D.C. Cir.)
541 F.2d 1 (D.C. Cir.)

### Background and Facts

Lead "antiknock" compounds, when added to gasoline, dramatically increase the fuel's octane rating. Increased octane allows for higher compression engines, which operate with greater efficiency. Since 1923 antiknocks have been added to gasoline, and a large industry has developed to supply these compounds. Today, approximately 90 percent of motor gasoline manufactured in the United States contains lead additives, even though most 1975 and 1976 model automobiles are equipped with catalytic converters, which require lead-free gasoline. From the beginning, however, scientists have questioned whether the addition of lead to gasoline, and its consequent diffusion into the atmosphere

from the automobile emission, poses a threat to public health. . . . The reasons for concern are obvious (and essentially undisputed by Ethyl Corp. and the other petitioners who challenge the no-lead regulations): (1) lead in high concentrations in the body is toxic; (2) lead can be absorbed into the body from the ambient air; (3) lead particulate emissions from gasoline engines account for approximately 90 percent of the lead in our air. Despite these apparent reasons for concern, hard proof of any danger caused by lead auto emissions has been hard to come by because of the multiple sources of human exposure to lead.

Lead is found in the land, in the sea, in plants, in animals, and, ultimately, in humans. Traces of lead ranging from 10 to 40 micrograms per 100 grams of blood (10-40 mg/100g) are found in everyone, including those living in environments with almost no atmospheric lead. [National Academy of Sciences Report or NASR]

Human body lead comes from three major sources. In most people, the largest source is the diet. EPA estimates daily dietary lead intake for adults average 200–300 mg per day, with a range of 100–500 mg a day. . . . Absorption of dietary lead into the bloodstream is estimated at about 10 percent, although in children absorption may be as high as 50 percent. Thus, the average adult adds 20–30 mg of lead to his/her bloodstream from his/her diet alone. This daily intake, which may be highly variable depending on individual diets . . . is generally regarded as, for all practical purposes, uncontrollable.

A second major source, ingestion of lead paint by children with pica (the abnormal ingestion of nonfood substances, a relatively common trait in preschool children, particularly ages 1–3), is generally regarded as "the principal environmental source in cases of severe acute lead poisoning in young children." [NASR] . . . Limited control has been achieved in that lead paints are now rarely used, and are frequently banned by statute for interior surfaces.

The last remaining major source of lead exposure for humans is the ambient air. This source is easily the most controllable, since approximately 90 percent of lead in the air comes from automobile emissions, and can be simply eliminated by removing lead from gasoline. . . . Once lead is in the body, its source becomes irrelevant; all lead in the bloodstream is essentially fungible. Thus, so long as there are multiple sources of lead exposure it is virtually impossible to isolate one source and determine its particular effect on the body. The effect of any one source is meaningful only in cumulative terms. . . .

For years the lead antiknock industry has refused to accept the developing evidence that lead emissions contribute significantly to the total human lead body burden. In the Clean Air Amendments of 1970. . . Congress finally set up a legal mechanism by which that evidence could be weighed in a more objective tribunal. It gave the newly created EPA authority to control . . . any fuel additive whose emission "will endanger the public health or welfare." . . . It is beyond question that the fuel additive Congress had in mind was lead.

EPA published on January 31, 1971, advance notice of proposed rulemaking to regulate lead in gasoline. . . . Proposed regulations were issued one year later on February 23, 1972 supported by a document *Health Hazards of Lead*. Comments were invited for a 90-day period and were reopened for another 30 days. Public hearings were also held on these matters in Washington, D.C., Dallas, and Los Angeles. After a series of proposals and reproposals of no-lead regulations, the Natural Resources Defense Council [NRDC], a private environmental group, sued EPA to force it to promulgate the no-lead regulations pursuant to the Clean Air Act. Finally, on October 28, 1973, as a result of the NRDC lawsuit, EPA was ordered to publish a final decision as to whether lead additives should be regulated for health reasons. On November 28, 1973, EPA released its third health study on no-lead regulations and also promulgated its no-lead regulations. Lead additive manufacturers including Ethyl Corp. sued EPA on grounds that its no-lead regulations violated the Administrative Procedure Act's "arbitrary and capricious" standard.

## Body of Opinion

**Judge J. Skelly Wright.** In promulgating the low-lead regulations . . . EPA engaged in informal rule-making. . . . Our review of the evidence . . . requires us to strike "agency action, findings, and conclusions" that we find to be "arbitrary, capricious, and abuse of discretion, or otherwise not in accordance with law." . . . This standard of review is a highly deferential one. It presumes agency action to be valid. . . . Moreover, it forbids the court's substituting its judgment for that of the agency . . . and requires affirmance if a rational basis exists for the agency's decision. . . .

This is not to say, however, that we must rubber-stamp the agency decision as correct. To do so would render the appellate process a superfluous (although time-consuming) ritual. Rather, the reviewing court must assure itself that the agency decision was "based on a consideration of the relevant factors." . . . Moreover, it must engage in a "substantial inquiry" into the facts, one that is "searching and careful." . . . This is particularly true in highly technical cases such as this one. . . .

There is no inconsistency between the deferential standard of review and the requirement that the reviewing court involve itself in even the most complex evidentiary matters. . . . The immersion in the evidence is designed *solely* to enable the court to determine whether the agency decision was rational and based on consideration of the relevant factors. . . . It is settled that we must affirm decisions with which we disagree so long as this test is met. . . .

Thus, after our careful study of the record, we must take a step back from the agency decision. We must look at the decision not as the chemist, biologist or statistician that we are qualified neither by training nor experience to be, but as a reviewing court exercising our narrowly defined duty of holding agencies to certain minimal standards of rationality. . . . We must affirm unless the agency decision is arbitrary or capricious. . . .

Under Section 211(c)(1)(A) the Administrator may, on the basis of all the information available to him, promulgate regulations that

> control or prohibit the manufacture, introduction into commerce, offering for sale, or sale of any fuel or fuel additive for use in a motor vehicle or motor vehicle engine (A) if any emission products of such fuel additive will endanger the public health or welfare.

The Administrator cannot act under Section 211 . . . however, until after "consideration of all relevant medical and scientific evidence available to him, including consideration of other technologically or economically feasible means of achieving emission standards." . . .

In making his threshold determination that lead particulate emissions from motor vehicles "will endanger the public health or welfare," the Administrator provided his interpretation of the statutory language by couching his conclusion in these words: such emissions "present a significant risk of harm to the health of city children." . . .

Ethyl Corporation and other petitioners argue that the "will endanger" standard requires a high quantum of factual proof, proof of actual harm rather than of a "significant risk of harm." . . . Since, according to petitioners, regulations under Section 211 . . .

must be premised upon actual proof of actual harm, the Administrator has, in their view, no power to assess risks or make policy judgments in deciding to regulate lead additives. Moreover, petitioners argue, regulation must be based on the danger presented by lead additives "in and of themselves," so it is improper to consider, as the Administrator did, the cumulative impact of lead additives on all other sources of human exposure to lead. . . .

*The Precautionary Nature of "Will Endanger."* Simply as a matter of plain meaning, we have difficulty crediting petitioners' reading of the "will endanger" standard. The meaning of "endanger" is not disputed. Case law and dictionary definition agree that endanger means something less than actual harm. When one is endangered, harm is *threatened*; no actual injury need ever occur. Thus, for example, a town may be "endangered" by a threatening plague or hurricane and yet emerge from the danger completely unscathed. A statute allowing for regulation in the face of danger is, necessarily, a precautionary statute. Regulatory action may be taken before the threatened harm occurs; indeed, the very existence of such precautionary legislation would seem to *demand* that regulatory action precede, and, optimally, prevent the perceived threat. As should be apparent the "will endanger" language of Section 211 . . . makes it such a precautionary statute.

The Administrator read it as such, interpreting "will endanger" to mean "presents a significant risk of harm." . . . We agree with the Administrator's interpretation. This conclusion is reached not only by reference to the plain meaning of the statute, but by juxtaposition of Section 211 . . . with other sections of the Clean Air Act. . . .

*Summary of the Evidence* From a vast mass of evidence the Administrator has concluded that the emission products of lead additives will endanger the public health. He has handled an extraordinarily complicated problem with great care and candor. The evidence did not necessarily always point in one direction and frequently, until EPA authorized research, there was no evidence at all. The Administrator reached his conclusion only after hearings spread over several months, consideration of thousands of pages of documents, publication of three health documents, three formal comment periods, and receipt of hundreds of comments. Each study was considered independently; its worth was assessed only after it was measured against any critical comments. From the totality of the evidence the Administrator concluded that regulation under Section 211 . . . was warranted.

## Judgment and Result

The U.S. Court of Appeals held that the arbitrary and capricious standard justified its upholding EPA's no-lead regulations.

## Questions

1. What is the relation between the studies the regulator (EPA or the EPA Administrator here) uses to develop regulations and the arbitrary and capricious standard? Did EPA satisfy this standard when it regulated the lead in gasoline?

2. What would have to occur to the public's health if the Ethyl Corporation's interpretation of Section 211 of the Clean Air Act were followed? Would people have to actually experience illness before lead could be regulated? Who made the statutory decision to regulate lead in gasoline using the "will endanger standard"? Who made the regulatory decision? If someone wanted to blame EPA for regulating lead in gasoline hastily who should be assigned responsibility?

3. An environmental group (National Resources Defense Council) had to sue EPA to get it to perform its statutory duty to regulate lead under the Clean Air Act. What does this say about regulatory agencies? About the need for private environmental groups? Note in the Environmental Law chapter how many plaintiffs are private environmental groups.

4. Does lead have a helpful, harmful, or neutral effect on the human body? If the three major sources of lead in humans are diet, lead-based paint in the environment ingested by children, and airborne lead, as EPA concedes, why should the manufacturers of lead in gasoline be singled out for regulation? Is this not placing the burden for addressing a problem on one, albeit an important one, sector of society? How can this be justified?

5. How technically qualified are judges to assess the scientific studies that form the basis of regulations such as the no-lead regulations? Does the commenting process assist the judges in their job? How?

6. Of the several studies showing effects of lead on humans were these studies consistent in what they showed or was it simply a question of degree and not kind? Did EPA suppress these studies? How did it make them available to the public?

7. What was the nature of the rule making process that the EPA used to develop the no-lead regulations? The court at one point states that it was the informal rule making process and yet it notes that the EPA did hold public hearings during the rule making process. In so noting, what type of rule making actually was occurring?

8. What should happen to the evidentiary standard by which a regulation is judged if the regulation is, in fact, hybrid in nature? What evidentiary standard was used? Is there really any difference between the arbitrary and capricious standard as opposed to the substantial evidence test?

*Is Beyond the Authority* (**Ultra Vires**) *of the Enabling Act.* As discussed, an administrative agency may make a regulation only if the legislature gives it the power. Administrative agencies have no inherent power to make substantive regulations. A valid enabling act transferring regulation-making power from the legislature to the agency must exist.

An administrative agency acts *ultra vires* when it either makes regulations beyond the authority the enabling act grants or makes regulations where no enabling act exists at all. When an agency acts *ultra vires*, the courts discipline the agency by invalidating the regulation. *Ernst & Ernst v. Hochfelder* provides such an example. The enabling act in that case is the Securities Exchange Act of 1934. An important part of that act is Section 10b, which lets the Securities and Exchange Commission (SEC) make regulations covering fraud (which involves *scienter*, meaning "intent"). However, Section 10b of the act does not empower the SEC to make regulations covering *negligent* misrepresentations. In the *Hochfelder* case the U.S. Supreme Court was asked whether part of SEC Rule 10b-5 was *ultra vires* (outside the power granted by) Section 10b of the Securities Exchange Act of 1934.

---

## Ernst & Ernst v. Hochfelder
U.S. Supreme Court
425 U.S. 185 (1976)

---

### Background and Facts

Ernst & Ernst, an independent public accounting firm, audited a stockbroker. The stockbroker sold fraudulent securities to several investors, and the investors lost money on the securities. The investors sued the accounting firm under Section 10b of the Securities and Exchange Act and rule 10b-5 for negligently auditing the stockbroker. The investors claimed that if the accounting firm had audited the stockbroker properly, it would have uncovered the fraud. Rule 10b-5 made the accountants liable for negligent audits. The accountants argued that the enabling act (the SEC Act) prohibited fraud only, not negligence. Therefore, the accountants maintained that part of Rule 10b-5 was *ultra vires* the enabling act. As a result, they argued the rule was invalid when it tried to cover negligence.

### Body of Opinion

**Justice Powell.** We have addressed, to this point, primarily the language and history of § 10(b). The Commission contends, however, that subsections (b) and (c) of Rule 10b-5 are cast in language which—if standing alone—could encompass both intentional and negligent behavior. These subsections respectively provide that it is unlawful "[t]o make any untrue statement of a material fact or to omit to state a material fact necessary in order to make the statements made, in the light of the circumstances under which they were made, not misleading . . . " and "[t]o engage in any act, practice, or course of business which operates or would operate as a fraud or deceit upon any person. . . . "

Viewed in isolation the language of subsection (b), and arguably that of subsection (c), could be read as proscribing, respectively, any type of material misstatement or omission, and any course of conduct, that has the effect of defrauding investors, whether the wrongdoing was intentional or not.

We note first that such a reading cannot be harmonized with the administrative history of the Rule, a history making clear that when the Commission adopted the Rule it was intended to apply only to activities that involved scienter. More importantly, Rule 10b-5 was adopted pursuant to authority granted the Commission under § 10(b). The rulemaking power granted to an administrative agency charged with the administration of a federal statute is not the power to make law. Rather, it is "the power to adopt regulations to carry into effect the will of Congress as expressed by the statute." Thus, despite the broad view of the Rule advanced by the Commission in this case, its scope cannot exceed the power granted the Commission by Congress under § 10(b). For the reasons stated above, we think the Commission's original interpretation of Rule 10b-5 was compelled by the language and history of § 10(b) and related sections of the Acts. . . . When a statute speaks so specifically in terms of manipulation and deception, and of implementing devices and contrivances—the commonly understood terminology of intentional wrongdoing—and when its history reflects no more expansive intent, we are quite unwilling to extend the scope of the statute to negligent conduct. . . .

### Judgment and Result

Rule 10b-5 was partly invalid. Specifically, the part of the rule covering negligent acts was invalid because a rule must be within the authority of the enabling act. In this case, the enabling act was the Securities and Exchange Act of 1934. It let the SEC make rules covering fraud. It did not let the SEC make regulations covering negligence. Therefore, when Rule 10b-5 covered negligence, it went beyond the enabling act and was invalid to the extent it did so.

### Questions

1. Had the public accounting firm (Ernst & Ernst) committed fraud when it audited the brokerage firm's books? Had it committed negligence?
2. Did the SEC's Rule 10b-5 cover negligence? Did the enabling act (Section 10(b) of the 1934 Securities Exchange Act) cover negligence? What is wrong with a regulation that covers more than its enabling act?

## STEP 8. AN AGENCY ENFORCES VALID REG THROUGH INVESTIGATION, PROSECUTION, AND ADMINISTRATION

The executive function of an administrative agency includes such matters as issuing permits and licenses. These tasks often involve testing for practitioner competence as realtors, engineers, or accountants. It also includes the agency's prosecution for violations of its statutes and regulations.

*Permits and Licenses.* Not all agencies issue permits or licenses; however, the essence of administering many agency statutes and regulations often involves permits. For example, much of the almost 100-page Clean Water Act boils down to getting a permit to discharge anything into U.S. waters.

*Prosecuting.* If a person, business, or other entity violates a permit or an administrative statute or regulation, the agency enforcing the act or regulation must generally prove the violation. In other words, people are innocent of administrative violations until proven guilty. Prosecutorial discretion applies here: Namely, the agency may prosecute whomever it chooses, subject only to its judgment about the strength of each case, staff resources, and other factors known only to prosecutors.

*Searches and Investigations: Police and FBI.* Agencies must gather evidence to prove regulatory or statutory violations. Many times, alleged regulatory violations occur on private property such as in a factory, home, or store. The Fourth Amendment to the U.S. Constitution says that warrantless searches by government officials are illegal; however, in certain exceptional cases, warrantless searches by law enforcement officials are allowed.

*Administrative Searches Today.* Do administrative officials, not police or the FBI, need search warrants to do administrative searches? In two cases, *Camara*[3] and *See*,[4] the Supreme Court decided that administrative officials must have search warrants to do health and other administrative searches of homes (*Camara*) and businesses (*See*), unless the owner consents or an emergency exists. The Supreme Court modified its "administrators need a search warrant" rule in the later cases of *Colonnade*[5] and *Biswell*.[6] In those cases, the Court said that where a business is pervasively regulated (liquor in *Colonnade* and firearms in *Biswell*), the business expects no privacy. The Fourth Amendment's rule against warrantless searches does not apply; that is, warrantless searches of pervasively regulated businesses are legal. Then came the *Barlow's* case in 1978. In *Marshall v. Barlow's*, Bill Barlow demanded a search warrant before he would let the OSHA inspector onto his premises. The OSHA statute expressly allowed inspectors to enter private property without search warrants to see if OSHA regulations were being obeyed. The U.S. Supreme Court held in that case that OSHA's statutory right-of-entry provision for OSHA inspectors violated the U.S. Constitution's Fourth Amendment and therefore was invalid. In the year 2000 the U.S. Court of Appeals for the District of Columbia was asked to rule whether administrative plans to *randomly* search businesses to see of they were violating federal Affirmative Action were valid when the business was not otherwise

---

[3]*Camara v. Municipal Ct.*, 387 U.S. 523 (1967).
[4]*See v. City of Seattle*, 387 U.S. 541 (1967).
[5]*Colonnade Catering Corp. v. United States*, 397 U.S. 72 (1970).
[6]*United States v. Biswell*, 406 U.S. 311 (1972).

suspected of violating Affirmative Action. The *Beverly Enterprises v. Herman* case deals with this matter.

## Beverly Enterprises, Inc. v. Herman
U.S. District Court
130 F.Supp.2d 1 (D.D.C. 2000)

### Background and Facts

The plaintiff is an Arkansas corporation that operates nursing homes that provide skilled nursing care for veterans. In various contracts with the Veterans Administration, the plaintiff has agreed to be bound by the affirmative action provisions contained in Executive Order 11246. Executive Order 11246 requires that whenever the federal government purchases goods or services the government must insert a provision into the contract that prohibits the contractor from discriminating on the basis of race, sex, color, religion, or national origin. The executive order also requires that contractors establish and update a written affirmative action program and allows the Secretary of Labor to set guidelines for verifying compliance. If a contractor fails to comply with these guidelines, the Secretary of Labor is empowered to terminate all contracts with that contractor and order that the government not deal with that contractor until it complies with that executive order.

One method by which the Department of Labor secures compliance with affirmative action programs is through a corporate management review ("CMR"), an administrative search that formally includes a review of the company's affirmative action files, an on-site review of the company's headquarters and an off-site analysis. The process for selecting companies for review begins when federal contractors, such as the plaintiff, file an Equal Employment Opportunity Employer Information Report with the Equal Employment Opportunity Commission. The plaintiff's reports list the location of the plaintiff's headquarters, the number of employees, the number of facilities, and the plaintiff's industry. This information is entered into a computer and given to the Office of Federal Contract Compliance Programs (OFCCP) in the Department of Labor.

The OFCCP organizes the list of company headquarters into separate geographical lists corresponding to the jurisdictional territory of each OFCCP local office. The national office then sends each local office a list of the companies, placed in random order, which have headquarters in its jurisdiction ("CMR candidate list"). Defendant OFCCP claims the only criteria that affect the order and composition of the CMR candidate list are: (1) the geographical location of the company's headquarters, (2) the number of facilities the company owns, (3) the status of the company as a federal contractor and (4) the number of people the company employs. The plaintiff, however, argues that the computer program that generates the CMR candidate list considers other factors, including the company's industry.

The OFCCP local offices then are assigned to conduct a certain number of CMRs per year by their regional office. The area director for each local office starts at the top of the CMR candidate list and decides whether the office can review the candidate. A company may be rejected for review if it is out of business, its contract is completed, its contract is worth less than $50,000, it has fewer than 50 employees, there is no evidence of its contract with the government, it was reviewed within the past two years, it was reporting to the OFCCP under a Conciliation Agreement or it is a signatory to a consent decree. The director continues down the list until he or she has selected enough companies to review to fill the quota for that office. The national office director then confirms the accuracy of the area director's decisions. After this process is complete, the agency notifies the chosen companies of their selection and offers them an opportunity to request an explanation for their selection.

In 1998, the Little Rock, Arkansas, office of the OFCCP was assigned to choose one company in its jurisdiction for a CMR. According to the defendants, the plaintiff's name was placed third on a list of three candidates given to the area director Joel Maltbia by the national office. Mr. Maltbia claimed he rejected the first name on the list because the Federal Procurement Data System, the OFCCP's computer listing of federal contractors, did not list the company as having a current contract with the federal government. Mr. Maltbia eliminated the second name from the list because he believed that the company was already reporting to the OFCCP under a consent decree. By contrast, Mr. Maltbia found that the plaintiff did not meet any of the criteria for being rejected for review. Accordingly, Mr. Maltbia filled out rejection forms for the first two candidates on the list and recommended that the plaintiff be selected for review. Mr. Busch, the national office director, approved Mr. Maltbia's choice of the plaintiff for a CMR.

The plaintiff was informed of its selection in October 1998. Mr. Reilly, the plaintiff's deputy general counsel and vice president, met with OFCCP officials later that month to discuss the criteria by which the plaintiff was selected for a CMR review. Mr. Reilly expressed concerns that the plaintiff was being targeted for review because its other 699 facilities had been selected for other types of review on many occasions in the past few years. During this time, the plaintiff's companies were found to be in compliance 100 percent of the time. Mr. Reilly believed the meetings with OFCCP officials failed to address his concerns and he refused to let the defendant OFCCP conduct its review.

On May 17, 1999, defendant OFCCP filed an administrative complaint with the Department of Labor's Office of Administrative Law alleging that the plaintiff's refusal to submit to a CMR violated its obligations under Executive Order 11246. The plaintiff claimed it was not selected according to a neutral administrative plan as required by the Fourth Amendment. The OFCCP initiated an "expedited hearing." Under such a hearing discovery is limited to admissions, an exchange of witness lists, and oral depositions. The administrative law judge (ALJ) denied some of plaintiff's discovery requests because such requests are not allowed in expedited hearings. The ALJ found that the CMR review selection was valid. The Department of Labor Administrative Review Board affirmed the proposed administrative search. Plaintiff appealed to the federal district court.

## Body of Opinion

**District Judge Urbina.** . . . The plaintiff contends that the administrative decision should be set aside because the compliance review that the OFCCP seeks to conduct is "contrary to [the plaintiff's] Fourth Amendment rights protecting against an unreasonable administrative search." The defendant contends that the plaintiff has failed to present any evidence showing that its selection for a compliance review violated the plaintiff's Fourth Amendment rights. . . .

For an administrative search to be valid under the Fourth Amendment, an agency must first show probable cause. . . . The Supreme Court has held that probable cause is established when there is either "specific evidence of an existing violation" or the particular company was chosen according to "reasonable legislative or administrative standards." The Fifth Circuit has interpreted *Marshall* to require that the proposed search be: (1) authorized by statute; (2) properly limited in scope and (3) initiated in a proper manner. . . .

Here, the administrative search to enforce compliance with affirmative action programs was authorized pursuant to an executive order which has the force of law. . . .

Similarly, the plaintiff does not contest the defendants' assertion that administrative searches to confirm compliance with affirmative action programs are properly limited in scope. . . .

An administrative search violates the Fourth Amendment unless the agency shows the company's selection for the search is based on (1) specific evidence of an existing violation, (2) reasonable legislative or administrative standards that have been met with respect to that particular contractor, or (3) an administrative plan containing specific neutral criteria. . . . In this case, the defendants seek to prove that the plaintiff's selection for the search was made pursuant to an administrative plan containing specific neutral criteria. . . . Deciding whether the defendant OFCCP used neutral criteria is a factual determination. . . . Thus the court will overturn the agency's decision only if it is not supported by substantial evidence. . . .

General criteria used to create the CMR candidate list. . . . The defendant OFCCP claims that it uses four criteria in order to choose a contractor for a compliance review. . . . Specifically the agency claims that the local offices receive a randomized CMR candidate list of all companies that have: (1) identified themselves as a federal contractor; (2) maintained multiple establishments; (3) operated a corporate headquarters within that local office's jurisdiction and (4) employed 4,000 or more employees. . . . The area directors for each office then remove companies from the list if they are out of business, the contract between the government and the company has been completed, the contract was not for enough money to qualify for a review, there is no evidence of the contract, the headquarters was reviewed in the last two years, the company is already reporting under a conciliation agreement or the company is a signatory to a consent decree. . . . Based on the record, the court holds that substantial evidence supports the Board's ruling that the OFCCP uses neutral criteria to select a company for a compliance review.

The actual selection process. For a selection to be valid, an agency actually must apply the neutral criteria in making the specific contested selection. . . . The plaintiff charges that: (1) the defendants did not meet their burden of showing that the OFCCP considered only the four factors listed above in creating the CMR candidate list and (2) the area director failed to follow the procedures.

For the following reasons the court concludes that the agency's holding that the OFCCP followed its own neutral criteria is supported by substantial evidence.

The court rejects the plaintiff's first claim that the OFCCP used other factors in generating the list of candidates, because the Board's rejection of this theory was supported by substantial evidence. Specifically, the Board wrote:

> "The testimony of Lawrence and Busch is more than sufficient for the A.L.J. and for us to determine that OFCCP's administrative plan for preparing the CMR listing was neutral. . . .

This circuit has held that in order to prove that a company was properly selected for a compliance review from a computerized list, the employees of the agency need only attest that the target of the search was selected under the agency's normal procedures. . . . .

Plaintiff's second claim is that Mr. Maltbia improperly skipped to the third name on the CMR candidate list. . . . To prove its claim, the plaintiff believes it is entitled to the rejection reports and the CMR candidate list from which it was selected. . . . Although the Fifth Circuit has held this type of discovery was necessary in one case. . . this circuit has specifically rejected the holding in that case. . . . As discussed above, employees of the agency need only testify that they applied the proper neutral administrative standard. . . .

This holding also is supported by the testimony of Ms. Joyce and Mr. Busch, two current OFCCP officials, who testified that Mr. Maltbia acted properly according to OFCCP guidelines. . . . The plaintiff does not obtain the right to go through the OFCCP's files based on an unsubstantiated belief that the agency's employees are not telling the truth. . . .

## Judgment and Result

The federal district court held that OFCCP's proposed administrative search did not violate the Fourth Amendment.

## Questions

1. What was the legal basis on which the OFCCP proposed to search Beverly Enterprises?
2. What criteria went into the OFCCP's decision to conduct a CMR of Beverly Enterprises? Do you think that the court placed too much reliance on the "word" of the OFCCP officials that they used neutral criteria in generating the list without independent corroboration of that fact?
3. If plaintiff did not have the right to "go through the OFCCP's files based on unsubstantiated belief that the agency's employees were not telling the truth," why were OFCCP employees allowed to go through Beverly's files to find possible violations when Beverly employees said they were following the law? Should "trust" be a one-way street?

*The General Rule.* The *Barlow's* and *Beverly Enterprises* cases set out the general rule that search warrants are required before government inspectors can enter commercial facilities. But the *Colonnade* case (recognized in *Barlow's*) held that search warrants are not required in industries with a long history of pervasive regulation. Thus, in 1981 the U.S. Supreme Court held that federal mine safety inspectors needed no search warrant to inspect stone quarries. That case turned on whether the industry had a long history of government inspection. The U.S. Supreme Court said that it had. As a result, when government inspectors appear at a business, the manager must consider whether the particular business falls into the general rule of *Barlow's* (i.e., the business can demand a search warrant before admitting the inspectors) or whether the business falls within the *Colonnade* exception (government inspectors may enter without a warrant when the industry has a long history of pervasive government regulation).

*Practical Tip.* As a practical matter, many businesses and individuals admit government inspectors into their factories, farms, and homes without a warrant. Sometimes they do it on the belief that a cooperative attitude will cause the inspectors to be forgiving as well as reasonable. The action also suggests nothing either to hide or to arouse suspicion. Finally, some agencies, such as the Occupational Safety and Health Administration (OSHA), will do courtesy inspections of a business before the official inspection to point out areas in which the business needs to improve its safety and health performance to comply with OSHA regulations and not be fined.

*Administrative Sanctions.* A final part of agency enforcement is punishing those who violate its regulations or statutes. Agencies do not have the power to punish someone criminally, mainly because agency procedures do not give defendants (called *respondents*) all of the constitutional protections courts provide, such as the right to jury trial. However, many regulatory statutes have criminal sanctions. Agencies such as the FTC must therefore ask the U.S. Justice Department to bring criminal charges when such statutes are violated. In such situations the Justice Department has prosecutorial discretion—the power to bring or not bring criminal charges.

*Civil Penalties.* Many statutes also give administrative agencies the power to assess civil penalties. They enable agencies to use the stick of punishment while avoiding the delay caused by all of the procedural protections given to criminal defendants.

In the *United States v. Ward* decision on page 205, the U.S. Supreme Court upheld the idea that federal administrative agencies can assess a civil penalty.

## STEP 9. AGENCIES HOLD ADJUDICATORY HEARINGS

Adjudication is the third major function of administrative agencies. (The other two functions are legislative and executive.) *Adjudication* means that agencies hold hearings similar to courtroom trials. The federal Administrative Procedure Act provides the basic rules for agency hearings.

*The Hearing.* To visualize an agency hearing, think of an ordinary courtroom trial and eliminate the jury. The agency is the moving party, or prosecutor, where

## United States v. Ward
U.S. Supreme Court
448 U.S. 242 (1980)

### Background and Facts

The Clean Water Act prohibits the discharge of oil or hazardous substances into navigable U.S. waters. Violations can be punished with civil penalties of up to $5,000 per offense. The act also requires violators to report their violations to the U.S. Coast Guard, which sets the civil penalty for violators. Ward had an oil retention pit at a drilling site near Enid, Oklahoma. Oil escaped into Boggie Creek. Ward notified the Coast Guard of his violation. The Coast Guard (a federal agency in the Department of Transportation) imposed a civil penalty of $500 on Ward. Ward sued to stop collection of the penalty, claiming it violated his privilege against self-incrimination under the Fifth Amendment.

### Body of Opinion

**Justice Rehnquist.** At the time this case arose § 311(b)(3) of the act prohibited the discharge into navigable waters or onto adjoining shorelines of oil or hazardous substances in quantities determined by the President to be "harmful." Section 311(b)(5) of the Act imposed a duty upon "any person in charge of a vessel or of an onshore facility or an offshore facility" to report any discharge of oil or a hazardous substance into navigable waters to the "appropriate agency" of the United States Government. Should that person fail to supply such notification, he or she was liable to a fine of not more than $10,000 or imprisonment of not more than one year. Section 311(b)(5) also provided for a form of **use immunity**, specifying that "[n]otification received pursuant to this paragraph or information obtained by the exploitation of such notification shall not be used against any such person in any criminal case, except a prosecution for perjury or for giving a false statement." . . .

Section 311(b)(6) provided for the imposition of a "civil penalty" against "[a]ny owner or operator of any vessel, onshore facility, or offshore facility from which oil or any hazardous substance is discharged in violation" of the Act. In 1975, that subsection called for a penalty of up to $5,000 for each violation of the Act. In assessing penalties, the secretary of the appropriate agency was to take into account "the appropriateness of such penalty to the size of the business or of the owner or operator charged, the effect on the owner or operator's ability to continue in business, and the gravity of the violation." . . .

On or about March 23, 1975, oil escaped from an oil retention pit at a drilling facility located near Enid, Oklahoma, and eventually found its way into Boggie Creek, a tributary of the Arkansas River system. At the time of the discharge, the premises were being leased by respondent, L.O. Ward, who was doing business as L.O. Ward Oil & Gas Operations. On April 2, 1975, respondent Ward notified the regional office of the Environmental Protection Agency (EPA) that a discharge of oil had taken place. Ward later submitted a more complete written report of the discharge, which was, in turn, forwarded to the Coast Guard, the agency responsible for assessing civil penalties under § 311(b)(6).

After notice and opportunity for hearing, the Coast Guard assessed a civil penalty against respondent in the amount of $500. Respondent filed an administrative appeal from this ruling, contending inter alia, that the reporting requirements of § 311(b)(5) of the Act violated his privilege against compulsory self-incrimination. The administrative appeal was denied. On April 13, 1976, Ward filed suit in the United States District Court for the Western District of Oklahoma, seeking to enjoin the Secretary of Transportation, the Commandant of the Coast Guard, and the Administrator of EPA from enforcing §§ 311(b)(5) and (6) and from collecting the penalty of $500. On June 4, 1976, the United States filed a separate suit in the same court to collect the unpaid penalty. The District Court eventually ordered the two suits consolidated for trial.

Prior to trial, the District Court rejected Ward's contention that the reporting requirements of § 311(b)(5), as used to support a civil penalty under § 311(b)(6), violated his right against compulsory self-incrimination. The case was tried by a jury, which found that Ward's facility did, in fact, spill oil into Boggie Creek. The District Court, however, reduced Ward's penalty to $250 because of the amount of oil that had spilled and because of its belief that Ward had been diligent in his attempts to clean up the discharge after it had been discovered.

The United States Court of Appeals for the Tenth Circuit reversed. . . . Although admitting that Congress had labeled the penalty provided for in § 311(b)(6) as civil and that the use of funds collected under that section to finance the administration of the Act indicated a "remedial" purpose for the provision, the Court of Appeals tested the statutory scheme against the standards set forth in *Kennedy v. Mendoza-Martinez*, . . . and held that § 311(b)(6) was sufficiently punitive to intrude upon the Fifth Amendment's protections against compulsory self-incrimination. It therefore reversed and remanded for further proceedings in the collection suit.

The distinction between a civil penalty and a criminal penalty is of some constitutional import. The Self-Incrimination Clause of the Fifth Amendment, for example, is expressly limited to "any criminal case. . . . " Similarly, the protections provided by the Sixth Amendment are available only in "criminal prosecutions. . . . " Other constitutional protections, while not explicitly limited to one context or the other, have been so limited by decision of this Court. (Double Jeopardy Clause protects only against two criminal punishments); (proof beyond a reasonable doubt required only in criminal cases).

This court has often stated that the question of whether a particular statutorily defined penalty is civil or criminal is a matter of statutory construction. . . . Our inquiry in this regard has traditionally proceeded on two levels. First, we have set out to determine whether Congress, in establishing the penalizing mechanism, indicated either expressly or impliedly a preference for one label or the other. . . . Second, where Congress has indicated an intention to establish a civil penalty, we have inquired further whether the statutory scheme was so punitive either in purpose or effect as to negate that intention. In regard to this latter inquiry, we have noted that "only the clearest proof could suffice to establish the unconstitutionality of a statute on such a ground."

As for our first inquiry in the present case, we believe it quite clear that Congress intended to impose a civil penalty upon persons in Ward's position. Initially, and importantly, Congress labeled the sanction authorized in § 311(b)(6) a "civil penalty," a label that takes on added significance given its juxtaposition with the criminal penalties set forth in the immediately preceding subparagraph, § 311(b)(5). . . .

We turn then to consider whether Congress, despite its manifest intention to establish a civil, remedial mechanism, nevertheless provided for sanctions so punitive as to "transfor[m] what was clearly intended as a civil remedy into a criminal penalty." . . . In making this determination, both the District Court and the Court of Appeals found it useful to refer to the seven considerations listed in *Kennedy v. Mendoza-Martinez*. . . . This list of considerations, while certainly neither exhaustive nor dispositive, has proved helpful in our own consideration of similar questions, . . . and provides some guidance in the present case.

Without setting forth here our assessment of each of the seven Mendoza-Martinez factors, we think only one, the fifth, aids respondent. That is a consideration of whether "the behavior to which [the penalty] applies is already a crime." In this regard, respondent contends that § 13 of the Rivers and Harbors Appropriation Act of 1899, . . . makes criminal the precise conduct penalized in the present case. Moreover, respondent points out that at least one federal court has held that § 13 of the Rivers and Harbors Appropriation Act defines a "strict liability crime," for which the Government need prove no scienter. . . . According to respondent, this confirms the lower court's conclusion that this fifth factor "falls clearly in favor of a finding that § 311(b)(6) is criminal in nature.". . .

While we agree that this consideration seems to point toward a finding that § 311(b)(6) is criminal in nature, that indication is not as strong as it seems at first blush. We have noted on a number of occasions that "Congress may impose both a criminal and a civil sanction in respect to the same act or omission." . . . Moreover, in *Helvering*, where we held a 50 percent penalty for tax fraud to be civil, we found it quite significant that "the Revenue Act of 1928 contains two separate and distinct provisions imposing sanctions," and that "these appear in different parts of the statute. . . . " To the extent that we found significant the separations of civil and criminal penalties within the same statute, we believe that the placement of criminal penalties in one statute and the placement of civil penalties in another statute enacted seventy years later tends to dilute the force of the fifth *Mendoza-Martinez* criterion in this case.

In sum, we believe that the factors set forth in *Mendoza-Martinez*, while neither exhaustive nor conclusive on the issue, are in no way sufficient to render unconstitutional the congressional classification of the penalty established in § 311(b)(6) as civil. Nor are we persuaded by any of respondent's other arguments that he has offered the "clearest proof" that the penalty here in question is punitive in either purpose or effect. . . .

## Judgment and Result

The U.S. Supreme Court reversed the Court of Appeals decision. The Supreme Court decided the Clean Water Act's civil penalties provision was, in substance as well as in form, a *civil* not a *criminal* penalty. As such, the mandatory reporting of spills provision did not violate the Fifth Amendment's privilege against self-incrimination that applies to criminal acts.

## Questions

1. Were the punishments applied to the defendant civil or criminal? Which did the defendant argue they were?
2. Does the Fifth Amendment's privilege against self-incrimination apply in civil cases?

someone is accused of breaking agency regulations. A private person, often a business, is the defendant, also called the *respondent*. A private party can be the moving party under certain circumstances. Notice of agency adjudicatory hearings must include the time and place of the hearing and tell what the hearing will be about.

*Administrative Law Judge.* The presiding official at an adjudicatory hearing is an administrative law judge, formerly called the hearing examiner. Technically, this person is independent of the agency personnel prosecuting the case, which keeps the administrative law judge off the agency's prosecutorial team.

*Parties.* Parties to an agency adjudication may introduce evidence, witnesses, and arguments to support their position. Settlement offers are allowed. In fixing the time and place of the hearing, the convenience and necessity of the parties are taken into account.

## STEP 10. APPEAL OF ADMINISTRATIVE LAW JUDGE'S DECISION

Once an administrative law judge makes a decision, it can be appealed.

*Standing.* The standing doctrine says that only the person injured may sue (has standing) to correct a wrong. This doctrine also applies to actions by administrative agencies. Therefore, a farmer whose land is flooded by a new Tennessee Valley Authority dam has standing to sue TVA, since the farmer is injured.

*Exhaustion.* Generally, a person must go through an agency's decision-making structure before taking an agency action to court. This procedure is called the exhaustion doctrine. Its purpose is to give an agency a chance to do its job and correct its own mistakes by having an appeal process within the agency itself. The exhaustion doctrine also saves the time and expense of suing in court. Consider the case of Mildred Smith, who retires at age 65 and files for Social Security benefits. The Social Security office mistakenly confuses her with another Mildred Smith and declares her ineligible. Mildred appeals to a higher level *within* the Social Security administration, which corrects the mistake. Mildred's Social Security checks are on the way without her having to go to court.

*Exceptions to the Exhaustion Doctrine.* At times the exhaustion doctrine does not apply. If agency action would cause irreparable injury, exhaustion is excused. Exhaustion is also excused when an agency acts beyond its jurisdiction and when going through agency channels would be a futile effort.

*Appeals to the Courts.* A person suffering a legal wrong by agency action may take the matter to court. For example, suppose the state real estate commission suspends a realtor's license after an adjudicatory hearing. The realtor may appeal this action to a court.

*Appealable Agency Action.* Generally, only an agency's *final* action may be appealed to a court. This practice gives an agency the opportunity to correct itself before the courts do.

*Proper Court.* Once a federal agency takes final action, the action may be appealed to a federal district court unless a special statute provides for appeal to another court, such as a U.S. court of appeals. For example, Securities and Exchange Commission and Federal Trade Commission adjudications are appealed to a U.S. court of appeals.

Courts of appeals are not trial courts. They have no juries and hear no witnesses. They accept the evidence developed at the agency adjudicatory hearing. On the other hand, federal district courts are trial courts. Witnesses are heard, and evidence is presented. Thus, an agency case that comes to a federal district court is usually entirely retried (a *de novo* review). *De novo* court review insults an administrative agency because it implicitly says, "What you [the agency] have done has to be done all over again because what you did in some way is not good enough." When the facts developed at agency adjudications are accepted by U.S. courts of appeals, stature is given to agencies, saving everyone's time and resources by not having to retry cases.

*Ripeness.* The term *ripeness* refers to an administrative agency's action being developed enough to give the court a clear understanding of the problem. In other words, the agency must have acted officially and not just sent up trial balloons about what it might do. Courts will not review an agency's action unless it is ripe—that is, what the agency has done must be final or complete enough for a court to say it is legal or illegal. Ripeness is therefore an argument made by one who does not want the agency action challenged. Often, this is the agency itself.

The following is an example of ripeness in an administrative agency action. The Securities and Exchange Commission (SEC) proposes a regulation requiring that securities sales people have a college degree in finance. The National Association of Securities Dealers (NASD) immediately sues the SEC to invalidate the proposed regulation. The SEC would argue that the matter is not yet ripe, because the regulation is only proposed, not promulgated. The SEC would win based on the ripeness doctrine, because the SEC has not taken any definite, concrete final action but has merely proposed a regulation. On the other hand, the ripeness defense would be weaker if NASD were to sue after the SEC promulgates the regulation. Promulgation is a definite, concrete, final agency action that a court can sink its teeth into.

*Remedies a Court May Order for Agency Wrongdoings.* A reviewing court may declare agency action illegal and either force it to act or stop it from acting when any of the following occur:

1. An agency has been arbitrary, capricious, abused its discretion, or otherwise not acted in accordance with the law.
2. An agency has acted contrary to constitutional right, power, privilege, or immunity.
3. An agency acts beyond its statutory authority.
4. An agency acts without observing legal procedures.
5. An agency acts without substantial evidence to support it.

Agency hearings thus must satisfy different rules (constitutions, statutes, and even regulations). The set of rules that controls the hearing depends in part on the case's facts and the arguments the parties make.

## Some Added Help to Small Businesses When "Feds" Make Regulations

In 1980 Congress amended the APA to improve informal (notice and comment) rule making by passing the **Regulatory Flexibility Act** (RF Act), which strengthens the APA's notice requirements. As a practical matter, most small business people and the public generally do not know that a publication called the *Federal Register* exists. Furthermore, many do not read it even when they are aware of its existence. Congress knew this when it enacted the Regulatory Flexibility Act. One of the act's provisions encourages federal agencies to publish proposed rules having a substantial impact on small entities (small hospitals, municipal governments, and small businesses) in journals likely to be obtained by those entities—journals in addition to the *Federal Register*. Whether affected people will read the proposed regulations and take the initiative by sending critical comments to the proposing agency is uncertain. At least the RF Act is a step in the right direction.

## CONCLUDING POINTS ABOUT RULEMAKING

### NO RIGHT TO A HEARING

When a federal agency engages in informal rule making (notice and comment rule making), the U.S. Constitution's Fifth Amendment's due process clause does not require the agency to hold an evidentiary hearing. A practical effect for a business is that it never has a chance to hear the government's experts who gathered the evidence that was the basis for the agency's regulations. Therefore, the agency's experts are never cross-examined by business lawyers (helped by experts from outside the agency) who could point out weaknesses in the agency regulations. Any trial lawyer will point out that an important part of a trial is the right to cross-examine the opposition's witnesses.

### A WARNING

Although no Fifth Amendment right requires a hearing when an agency engages in informal rule making to make substantive regulations, specific agency statutes might require such a hearing. Even here, though, usually no provision to cross-examine opposing viewpoints is made. However, at least one U.S. court of appeals interprets the Administrative Procedure Act as allowing cross-examination on crucial administrative issues.

### REG-NEG: A POSSIBLE FUTURE DIRECTION FOR FEDERAL RULE MAKING

A statute enacted by the 101st U.S. Congress could have a significant impact on federal rulemaking. That law deals with what has come to be called **reg-neg**, regulations that are negotiated. Negotiated rule making differs from the "notice and comment" rule making discussed in this chapter. Basically, it involves the appointment of a committee by an official of the agency responsible for the rule. The committee is made up of the different constituencies likely to be affected by the regulation, who meet, share information relevant to drafting the proposed regulation, come up with a report (possibly containing a draft regulation), and then submit it to the agency with authority to promulgate it. This draft report would be a basis for the agency to propose and promulgate the rule in an environment in which all affected parties have agreed on the particulars of the rule, thus cutting down on the time to make the regulation. The act does not restrict challenges to the regulation that emerge from this process.

Whether in fact agreement could be reached on highly controversial rules (such as the EPA's 1,000-year containment rule for nuclear waste disposal) remains to be seen. Also, the reg-neg law could simply add another layer of bureaucracy to the rule making process. Finally, this process could bury or hide controversial rules from the public. After all, how many people now know how regulations are made? If the process is made even more complex and is hidden from sight in a committee, is the public interest served?

Congress renewed in 1996 legal authority for negotiated rule making but later repealed it.

## CHAPTER SUMMARY

Administrative agencies have three functions: executive, judicial, and legislative.

The three types of administrative rule makings are formal, informal, and hybrid.

The chronological steps in an informal federal rule making are society perceives a problem; Congress studies the problem and enacts an enabling act; the agency studies the problem and develops a regulatory solution; the agency proposes the regulation in the *Federal Register*; the public comments on the proposed regulation; the agency promulgates, reproposes, or withdraws the proposed regulation; lawsuits challenge the regulation, which is either upheld or wholly or partially invalidated; a valid regulation is enforced; an adjudicatory hearing is held at which the alleged violation of the regulation is tried; an appeal from the ALJ hearing to the court system is possible.

Several recent modifications to the process by which federal regulations are made have been introduced by the Regulatory Flexibility Act and negotiated regulation ("reg-neg") process, which is set to expire unless renewed by Congress.

The executive function of an administrative agency covers investigation, prosecution, and administration.

Administrative searches by government officials are illegal unless the inspector has a search warrant or some exception to the search warrant requirement exists, such as closely regulated businesses.

Administrative agencies do not have the power to punish someone criminally. Federal administrative agencies may assess a civil penalty.

Persons may challenge actions of administrative agencies in court. Requirements on those who seek to appeal agency actions to the courts include standing, primary jurisdiction, ripeness, and exhaustion.

Courts have a wide range of options in granting remedies for improper agency actions.

The Internet now offers businesses and persons generally more opportunity to participate in federal agency regulation making.

## ■ MANAGER'S ETHICAL DILEMMA

Tom Stebbins was the director of a conservatively run savings and loan (S&L) association in Grand Rapids, Michigan. Tom had always been careful to see that his S&L maintained ample capital, had a conservative loss ratio on total loans, and did not make high-risk loans. Now Tom learned the many failed S&Ls in other parts of the United States, particularly Texas, had not been managed as well. As a result, the nation's S&L crisis was forcing federal regulators to impose added fees on the properly managed S&Ls, such as Tom's, to pay part of the cost of those that were poorly run. Tom felt the federal government was punishing the "good managers" to pay for the shenanigans of the "fast-buck" artists who had taken over S&Ls during the deregulation and weak regulation era of the late 1970s and 1980s.

Had weak regulation contributed to the S&L crisis of the 1990s, which threatened to cost the entire nation $500 billion over a period of years? Tom wondered whether good businesspeople do not actually benefit from tough regulations, because they follow the law anyway while the "fly-by-night operators" take deposits away from legitimate S&Ls by offering interest rates that well-managed S&Ls cannot match? Then well-managed S&Ls pay a second time by having to contribute extra fees to pay off insured deposits when poorly managed S&Ls go under. Tom wondered, "Would not strong regulation really have been the friend of properly run S&Ls?"

## DISCUSSION QUESTIONS

1. Is there value in letting citizens know what their government is doing? One attempt to let the public know what an agency is doing can be found using the Internet. Describe the steps you would follow in finding regulations on cigarettes and smokeless tobacco. Would your answer be different if the regulations were merely proposed, but, as yet unpromulgated?

2. The secretary of transportation proposed an airport slot regulation. Northwest Airlines challenged that reg because the notice of *proposed* rule making did not say exactly what the *promulgated* reg would look like. Must the regulation itself be in the *Federal Register* notice when the agency proposes it? [*Northwest Airlines, Inc. v. Goldschmidt*, 645 F.2d 1309 (1981)].

3. What is informal rule making?

4. Give a disadvantage for small business people when a federal agency makes rules.

5. The proposed used car regulation in this chapter has had a lively existence. It was promulgated, then Congress, under authority of the enabling acts, legislatively vetoed it. A consumer group then sued Congress, claiming that Congress's legislative veto was unconstitutional. In 1983, the U.S. Supreme Court held that the two-house legislative veto was unconstitutional, making the used car regulation valid again. But this decision did not end the matter. The FTC, now headed by a Reagan-appointed committed to deregulation, then withdrew its promulgated used car regulation for further study. The used car reg was promulgated in 1984. The promulgated reg in Figure 7.5 is now in effect. A consumer group has again sued the FTC, claiming the reg is invalid for procedural reasons. That suit has now been decided in favor of the FTC (the rule is valid). Several enforcement actions have been brought by the FTC. The FTC also issued compliance guidelines in 1987 (52 *Fed Reg.* 18,552). Do you see why regulating is a *process* and not *static*?

6. The U.S. Environmental Protection Agency (EPA) proposed regulations setting air pollution standards for new or modified cement plants. The EPA did not make available test results and methodology used (in part) as the basis for these regulations until *after* promulgation. The Portland Cement Association sued the EPA claiming it had a right to see data that partially formed the basis for the regulations before Portland filed comments to the proposed regulations. Was it right? The case is *Portland Cement Association v. Ruckelshaus* (1974).

7. Should an agency have a duty to disclose its complete data base, including studies supporting its final regulation?

8. Should commentators have a duty to disclose their database to the agency proposing a regulation?

9. Joseph Burger owned and operated a junkyard in Brooklyn, New York. His business involved dismantling cars and selling their parts. At about noon on November 17, 1982, Officer Joseph Vega and four other plainclothes officers, all members of the Auto Crimes Division of the New York City Police Department, entered Burger's junkyard to conduct an inspection under the New York statutes regulating vehicle dismantlers. The Auto Crimes Division conducted about 10 routine inspections daily. They asked to see Burger's vehicle-dismantling license and "police book," which state law required that such businesses keep. Burger did not have such a book. The officers then asked to inspect Burger's lot and he agreed, though the officers lacked a search warrant. They copied vehicle inspection numbers (VINs) from several cars and, after checking the police department computer, learned that several vehicles in Burger's possession had been stolen. The police arrested Burger. Burger moved to suppress the evidence the police seized during their search on grounds that New York's statute authorizing administrative searches of junkyards was unconstitutional. The police argued that Burger's junkyard was a pervasively regulated business for which no search warrant was required, particularly in view of the New York statutes permitting such inspections. The New York Court of Appeals basically agreed with Burger, and New York appealed to the U.S. Supreme Court. What was the result? [*New York v. Burger*, 482 U.S. 691 (1987)].

10. What does the exhaustion doctrine mean?

11. Immigration and Naturalization Service (INS) officials conduct surprise raids on factories to look for illegal aliens. The officials entered a factory after getting search warrants. Some officials stood at the doors while others went through the factory, asking workers about their immigration status. Workers who could not answer the INS officials satisfactorily or produce immigration papers were arrested, often as many as half the workers in certain California factories. The U.S. Court of Appeals for the Ninth Circuit held that these searches were unconstitutional. That court reasoned the surprise raids were unconstitutional seizures of the entire factory's workforce. It also said that INS officials could not question workers individually unless officials had a reasonable suspicion the worker was an illegal alien. The INS appealed to the Supreme Court. Were the surprise raids unconstitutional? [*INS v. Delgado*, 466 U.S. 210 (1984)].

12. When a regulator issues a license, is it performing an executive or a judicial function?

13. When can a regulator search a business without a search warrant?

14. Can a regulator impose a civil penalty? A criminal penalty?

15. Describe an agency adjudicatory proceeding. What is a main difference between it and a jury trial in a court?

16. A bill before Congress would impose a civil penalty of $100,000 on prohibited insider trading in an issuer's securities. Why would the enforcer (U.S. government) prefer a *civil* rather than a *criminal* penalty?

17. A veteran brought before the Veterans Administration a constitutional challenge to a federal law limiting lawyers' fees to $10 for representing veterans. The law was passed in the 1860s to protect Civil War vets from exploitation. The lower federal court upheld the law. The veteran appealed to the U.S. Supreme Court. What was the result? *Walters v. National Association of Radiation Survivors*, 473 U.S. 305 (1985).

## INFOTRAC KEYWORDS

**Use your InfoTrac password to look up articles on http://www.infotrac-college.com**

Keywords: *Agency regulation enforcement, federal rule making.*

For suggested readings, please visit this book's Web site at **http://fisher.westbuslaw.com** (click on "Internet Applications").

# INTERNATIONAL BUSINESS: PUBLIC LAW

"Those fish may not enter the U.S.," said a U.S. Customs inspector to a Mexican fish processor.

"Why not?" asked a representative of the Mexican company. "These fish are just as good as those caught by U.S. fishermen."

"No, they are not," replied the U.S. inspector. "They were caught in violation of U.S. 'purse-seine' fishing requirements, and, because of this, the United States forbids their being imported."

May a GATT signatory nation forbid the importation of fish caught in international waters when the method of catch is illegal under that nation's laws?

"We have been sued in New York for over 2,000 deaths and 200,000 other injuries that occurred in Bhopal, India," shouted one Union Carbide Corporation (UCC) executive to another. Thousands of Indians and the Indian government sued UCC, the U.S. parent of Union Carbide of India Limited, in New York City for the damages done in India. UCC thought that India was the place to bring the lawsuit. Who was right?

*"THE WORLD IS YOUR OYSTER."*

— **SHAKESPEARE**

The one outstanding fact about international law is the absence of **positive law** in the international arena. That is, using John Austin's definition of law, no single sovereign or universal authority exists with the power to make rules binding on all persons, with sanctions imposed if the law is violated. Rather, in a crude sense, the law of the jungle—might makes right—prevails in international affairs. Of course, custom, fairness, private covenants, and treaties supplement the power ethic, but we should not forget that it is literally possible for nations to get away with what would be murder if committed by individuals—a sobering thought.

This chapter focuses on public institutional arrangements in international law under which business must operate. The following chapter examines business applications of international law.[1] This chapter will outline important treaties and institutions that influence commerce internationally, including the WTO, UNCITRAL, the EU, the NAFTA, and OPIC. It begins with an overview of basic definitions concerning international trade in the U.S. economy.

---

[1] The authors acknowledge use of *Import Practice: Customs and International Trade Law* by David Serko and *International Trade for the Nonspecialist* by various authors for ALI/ABA in preparing this chapter.

## DEFINITION AND SOURCES OF INTERNATIONAL LAW

For information on treaties holdings of the United Nations, go to http://www.un.org/law

When lawyers, international businesspersons, and diplomats refer to international law they are usually talking about treaties (also called conventions) between and among nations, customs, and recognized principles regulating independent nations in peace and war. Thus, Savigny's legal ethic of longstanding custom is important in the international area. We define international law, then, as the treaties, conventions, and customs nations observe in dealing with one another.

Treaties can be bilateral (between two nations) or multilateral (involving more than two nations). An example of a bilateral treaty is one between the United States and the People's Republic of China (PRC, or mainland China) authorizing certain trade between the two nations. An example of a multilateral treaty would be the World Trade Organization (WTO), successor to the General Agreement on Tariffs and Trade (GATT),[2] which now has more than 143 signatory nations, including the United States. The North American Free Trade Agreement (NAFTA) has, at this writing, three parties—Canada, the United States, and the United Mexican States (Mexico).

International law should be distinguished from municipal law, which refers to the domestic law of a particular country. For example, the law governing the speed limits on interstate highways in the United States is considered municipal law, even though, technically, cities generally do not set interstate speed limits. International law refers to treaties and customs that nations recognize in dealing with one another.

## NATURE AND EXTENT OF U.S. INTERNATIONAL TRADE

Economic isolationism results from passing laws that make it difficult or impossible for persons in the United States to buy and sell goods and services in foreign countries. High tariffs, quotas (limits on the number of goods that can be imported to the United States or exported from the United States), and trade barriers based on health, conservation, or other public policies are all examples of ways the legal system can stifle international trade. Isolationism is also referred to as protectionism.

The United States has learned the hard way that economic isolationism is a losing economic policy. The Tariff Act of 1930, known as the Smoot-Hawley Act, imposed extremely high tariffs on goods entering the United States. This act hurt foreign manufacturers, who in turn convinced their governments to retaliate by enacting high tariffs on U.S. goods. As a result of Smoot-Hawley and the resulting tariffs, international trade came to a standstill. Some say Smoot-Hawley even caused the Great Depression. Although its philosophy has been condemned, that act's structure is the basis for much of today's customs law, albeit in much amended form reflective of a less protectionist philosophy.

---

[2] GATT actually refers to two things: GATT, the agreement, and GATT, the organization. The agreement (covering only goods) supplemented by GATS (the General Agreement on Trade in Services) and TRIPS (the agreement on Trade-Related Aspects of Intellectual Property) (dealing with patents, copyrights, trademarks, trade secrets, and industrial designs) continues and is administered by the WTO. GATT, the organization, no longer exists because the WTO replaced it.

Other significant acts dealing with U.S. tariffs include the Reciprocal Trade Agreements Act of 1934, the Trade Act of 1974, and the Trade Agreements Act of 1979. The 1934 act gives the president the power to negotiate lower tariffs with other nations, which quite obviously, was a reaction to Smoot-Hawley. The 1974 act authorized the president to negotiate reduction of nontariff barriers. With the 1979 act, Congress continued to focus on nontariff matters such as countervailing duties, antidumping, and subsidies.

## CURRENT POLICY

Current U.S. policy generally favors international trade. The strongest evidence supporting this statement comes from the data in Figure 8.1. Despite the U.S. trade deficit for each of the past 10 years and its trend to increase, the United States generally has not raised tariffs on incoming goods; however, some significant exceptions should be noted. First an "off-the-books understanding" between Japanese and U.S. officials exists regarding the number of Japanese-made cars the United States will admit in any one year. In effect it is a voluntary quota, one of the most blatant forms of protectionism. Second, allegations persist that the U.S. dollar's decline against other currencies has been engineered by the U.S. government to create a trade barrier against foreign goods. The idea is that a cheap dollar makes foreign goods more expensive and hence less attractive for U.S. consumers. Third, even though the United States has approved the NAFTA, various concessions in the form of continued trade barriers against, among other things, Canadian peanut butter, were granted to gain U.S. congressional support for the NAFTA.

## THEORY OF COMPARATIVE ADVANTAGE

No discussion of international trade would be complete without mention of the theory of comparative advantage. David Ricardo, an Englishman who wrote in the nineteenth century, advanced the theory of **comparative advantage**. According to this idea, if there are two nations, both of which produce the same two products—say, wool and wine—and one nation is absolutely more efficient in producing both products, it would, nonetheless, be better for both nations if each specialized in making what it is *relatively* more efficient at making and then traded products with each other. The essence of comparative advantage is specialization.

*The Economist* magazine has called the theory of comparative advantage "the biggest idea in economics." It is the major—but not the only—reason behind international trade. In practical terms, this idea means that if nations trade with each other, they *all* become wealthier. This theory is the basis for GATT, NAFTA and other treaties promoting free or freer trade. Of course, promoting world peace is also a justification for free trade because people tend not to "bite the hand that feeds them."

The disadvantages of comparative advantage are several. First, it is a rational, but only partially empirical, theory. This means it has not been fully tested in the real world. In other words, some, but not overwhelming, evidence supports this theory. Second, major economic dislocations can occur when this theory is followed. One only need think of the many industrial plant closures in the United States and other major industrial nations and plant relocations to lower-cost nations to realize that the third- and fourth-quartile jobholders—"blue collar"—jobs are exiting the United States for foreign shores. The question then becomes, "Can the economically displaced workers be retrained for higher-skill jobs, or are these jobs beyond their capabilities?"

## Most Favored Nations ("Normal Trade") Clauses in Treaties

Note in Table 8.1 that the dollar amount of foreign goods imported into the United States is large. The United States imposes tariffs on many foreign goods. The United States also places different tariff rates on the same goods from different countries. Most favored nations (MFN) clauses, also called *normal trade*, in treaties give citizens or subjects of the contracting nations privileges accorded by either party to those of the most favored nations. For example, if the United States and China have a treaty with an MFN clause, then the United States must give China the lowest tariff rate on a particular good that it gives to any nation. MFN treatment includes, but is not limited to, tariff rates. A principal effect of MFN clauses is to reduce tariffs, which promotes free trade.

MFN treatment is one of the key features of the WTO, which administers international treaties to which more than 143 nations are signatories or observe (the U.S. Senate, as of this writing, has not ratified WTO, but the U.S. generally follows WTO provisions).

Some nations, such as Russia, do not have most favored nation status regarding shipping their goods into the United States. Other nations, such as the People's Republic of China, do have MFN status. Obviously, conferral of this status does not necessarily depend on whether the country involved is a communist or nondemocratic nation.

## INSTITUTIONS AFFECTING INTERNATIONAL BUSINESS

Business professionals should be familiar with several laws and institutions that affect international business. Included here are the WTO, UNCITRAL, the EU, OPIC, and NAFTA.

## World Trade Organization (and GATT, its predecessor)

*Information about GATT can be accessed at the Web site for the World Trade Organization at http://www.wto.org*

The General Agreement on Tariffs and Trade (GATT) took effect in 1947. It was replaced by the WTO in 1995. The WTO's main purpose is to reduce tariffs and trade restrictions. The WTO has had the practical effect of reducing today's tariffs by more than 25 percent from what they were a generation ago. Nations take actions under the WTO at meetings called *rounds*, which first began in the late 1940s. The first five rounds mainly concerned themselves with reducing tariffs, while later rounds, such as the seventh in 1979, called the Tokyo round, focused on simplifying the trade procedures that proved stumbling blocks to international trade. The most recent round occurred in Uruguay and has had several deadlines that have been missed. Three WTO (and GATT treaty) principles are among the most important:

## TABLE 8.1  U.S. EXPORTS, GENERAL IMPORTS, AND TRADE BALANCE IN GOODS: 1970 TO 2000

[In billions of dollars (43.8 represents $43,800,000,000). Domestic and foreign exports are f.a.s. value basis; general imports are on customs value basis.]

| Year | Total Goods[1] | | | Manufactured Goods [2][3] | | | Agricultural Products[4] | | | Mineral Fuels [3][5] | | |
|---|---|---|---|---|---|---|---|---|---|---|---|---|
| | Exports | Imports | Balance | Exports | Imports | Balance | Exports | Imports | Balance | Exports | Imports | Balance |
| 1970 | 43.8 | 40.4 | 3.4 | 31.7 | 27.3 | 4.4 | 7.3 | 5.8 | 1.6 | 1.6 | 3.1 | -1.5 |
| 1971 | 44.7 | 46.2 | -1.5 | 32.9 | 32.1 | 0.8 | 7.8 | 5.8 | 2.0 | 1.5 | 3.7 | -2.2 |
| 1972 | 50.5 | 56.4 | -5.9 | 36.5 | 39.7 | -3.2 | 9.5 | 6.5 | 3.0 | 1.6 | 4.8 | -3.2 |
| 1973 | 72.5 | 70.5 | 2.0 | 48.5 | 47.1 | 1.3 | 17.9 | 8.5 | 9.4 | 1.7 | 8.2 | -6.5 |
| 1974 | 100.0 | 102.6 | -2.6 | 68.5 | 57.8 | 10.7 | 22.3 | 10.4 | 11.9 | 3.4 | 25.5 | -22.0 |
| 1975 | 109.3 | 98.5 | 10.8 | 76.9 | 54.0 | 22.9 | 22.1 | 9.5 | 12.6 | 4.5 | 26.5 | -22.0 |
| 1976 | 117.0 | 123.5 | -6.5 | 83.1 | 67.6 | 15.5 | 23.3 | 11.2 | 12.1 | 4.2 | 34.0 | -29.8 |
| 1977 | 123.2 | 151.0 | -27.8 | 88.9 | 80.5 | 8.4 | 24.2 | 13.6 | 10.6 | 4.2 | 47.2 | -43.0 |
| 1978 | 145.9 | 174.8 | -28.9 | 103.6 | 104.3 | -0.7 | 29.8 | 15.0 | 14.8 | 3.9 | 42.0 | -38.1 |
| 1979 | 186.5 | 209.5 | -23.0 | 132.7 | 117.1 | 15.6 | 35.2 | 16.9 | 18.3 | 5.7 | 59.9 | -54.2 |
| 1980 | 225.7 | 245.3 | -19.6 | 160.7 | 133.0 | 27.7 | 41.8 | 17.4 | 24.3 | 8.2 | 78.9 | -70.7 |
| 1981 | 238.7 | 261.0 | -22.3 | 171.7 | 149.8 | 22.0 | 43.8 | 17.2 | 26.6 | 10.3 | 81.2 | -70.9 |
| 1982 | 216.4 | 244.0 | -27.6 | 155.3 | 151.7 | 3.6 | 37.0 | 15.7 | 21.3 | 12.8 | 65.3 | -52.5 |
| 1983 | 205.6 | 258.0 | -52.4 | 148.5 | 171.2 | -22.7 | 36.5 | 16.5 | 19.9 | 9.8 | 57.8 | -48.0 |
| 1984 | 224.0 | 330.7 | -106.7 | 164.1 | 230.9 | -66.8 | 37.9 | 19.3 | 18.6 | 9.7 | 60.8 | -51.1 |
| 1985 | 218.8 | 336.5 | -117.7 | 168.0 | 257.5 | -89.5 | 29.3 | 19.5 | 9.8 | 10.3 | 53.7 | -43.4 |
| 1986 | 227.2 | 365.4 | -138.2 | 179.8 | 296.7 | -116.8 | 26.3 | 20.9 | 5.4 | 8.4 | 37.2 | -28.8 |
| 1987 | 254.1 | 406.2 | -152.1 | 199.9 | 324.4 | -124.6 | 28.7 | 20.3 | 8.4 | 8.0 | 44.1 | -36.1 |
| 1988 | 322.4 | 441.0 | -118.6 | 255.6 | 361.4 | -105.7 | 37.1 | 20.7 | 16.4 | 8.5 | 41.0 | -32.5 |
| 1989 | 363.8 | 473.2 | -109.4 | 287.0 | 379.4 | -92.4 | 41.6 | 21.1 | 20.5 | 9.9 | 52.6 | -42.7 |
| 1990 | 393.6 | 495.3 | -101.7 | 315.4 | 388.8 | -73.5 | 39.6 | 22.3 | 17.2 | 12.4 | 64.7 | -52.3 |
| 1991 | 421.7 | 488.5 | -66.8 | 345.1 | 392.4 | -47.3 | 39.4 | 22.1 | 17.2 | 12.3 | 54.1 | -41.8 |
| 1992 | 448.2 | 532.7 | -84.5 | 368.5 | 434.3 | -65.9 | 43.1 | 23.4 | 19.8 | 11.3 | 55.3 | -43.9 |
| 1993 | 465.1 | 580.7 | -115.6 | 388.7 | 479.9 | -91.2 | 42.8 | 23.6 | 19.2 | 9.9 | 55.9 | -46.0 |
| 1994 | 512.6 | 663.3 | -150.7 | 431.1 | 557.3 | -126.3 | 45.9 | 26.0 | 20.0 | 9.0 | 56.4 | -47.4 |
| 1995 | 584.7 | 743.4 | -158.7 | 486.7 | 629.7 | -143.0 | 56.0 | 29.3 | 26.8 | 10.5 | 59.1 | -48.6 |
| 1996 | 625.1 | 795.3 | -170.2 | 524.7 | 658.8 | -134.1 | 60.6 | 32.6 | 28.1 | 12.4 | 78.1 | -65.7 |
| 1997 | 689.2 | 870.7 | -181.5 | 592.5 | 728.9 | -136.4 | 57.1 | 35.2 | 21.9 | 13.0 | 78.3 | -65.3 |
| 1998 | 682.1 | 911.9 | -229.8 | 596.6 | 790.8 | -194.2 | 52.0 | 35.7 | 16.3 | 10.4 | 57.3 | -47.0 |
| 1999 | 698.0 | 1,024.6 | -328.8 | 611.6 | 882.7 | -271.1 | 48.2 | 36.7 | 11.5 | 9.9 | 75.2 | -65.3 |
| 2000 | 781.9 | 1,218.0 | -436.1 | 691.5 | 1,012.7 | -321.3 | 53.0 | 39.2 | 13.8 | 13.4 | 135.4 | -122.0 |

[1]Includes nonmonetary gold, military grant aid, special category shipments, trade between the U.S. Virgin Islands and foreign countries and undocumented exports to Canada. Adjustments were also made for carryover. Import values are based on transaction prices whenever possible ("f.a.s." for 1974-79 and Customs value thereafter). Import data before 1974 do not exist on a transaction price valuation basis. [2]Manufactured goods include commodity Sections 5-9 under Schedules A and E for 1970-82 and SITC Rev. 3 for 1983-forward. Manufactures include undocumented exports to Canada, nonmonetary gold (excluding gold ore, scrap, and base bullion), and special category shipments. [3] Data for 1970-80 exclude trade between the U.S. Virgin Islands and foreign countries. Census data concordances link the 1980-92 trade figures into time series that are as consistent as possible. Data for 1970-79 are not linked and are from published sources. Import values are "f.a.s." for 1974-79 and Customs value thereafter; these values are based on transaction prices while maintaining a data series as consistent as possible over time. Import data before 1974 do not exist on a transaction price valuation basis. 1991 imports include revisions for passenger cars, trucks, petroleum and petroleum products not included elsewhere. [4]Agricultural products for 1983-forward utilize the latest census definition that excludes manufactured goods that were previously classified as manufactured agricultural products. [5]Mineral fuels include commodity Section 3 under SITC Rev. 1 for 1970-76, SITC Rev. 2 for 1977-82 and SITC Rev. 3 for 1983-forward.

*Source: Statistical Abstract of U.S., 2001.*

1. The WTO outlaws tariff discrimination for WTO members and requires MFN treatment for WTO members.
2. The WTO outlaws nontariff barriers; this provision plugs a loophole that could arise when member nations try to escape their obligations under item 1 by imposing quotas, health and safety standards, which actually are disguised trade barriers. The Dolphin case that follows, decided by a GATT panel, presented such a case. In that case, Mexico accused the United States of violating GATT's provision forbidding nontariff barriers when the United States required "dolphin-friendly" labels (under the Dolphin Protection Consumer Information Act) on tuna cans sold in the United States and prohibited entry into the United States of foreign tuna caught under circumstances violating a U.S. law (the Marine Mammal Protection Act), which protects animals such as dolphins.
3. WTO/GATT places caps on tariffs (called "Schedules of Concessions" under Article II of GATT); according to this idea, WTO members commit themselves to limits on tariffs on particular items from other WTO members. However, member nations need not have tariff rates identical with other WTO member nations on the same products. Thus Mexico prior to the NAFTA, had higher tariffs on certain goods entering Mexico from the United States than the United States imposed on identical goods entering the United States from Mexico (on certain items this continues to be true even under the NAFTA although Mexican tariffs against certain U.S. agricultural products are scheduled to be phased out under the NAFTA). However, under MFN principles, Mexico may not impose higher tariff rates on U.S.-made widgets entering Mexico than on identical Canadian widgets entering Mexico, because all three nations are WTO/GATT (and now NAFTA) signatories.

A nation may receive MFN treatment from the United States without being a member of the WTO. Also, membership in the WTO does not always entitle one to MFN treatment. Poland, a WTO member, for several years in the 1980s, was denied MFN treatment to induce domestic reforms designed to help the Polish people.

---

## GATT Dispute Settlement Panel Report:
## United States—Restrictions on Imports of Tuna

Reproduced with permission from *GATT Dispute Settlement Panel Report: United States—Restrictions on Imports of Tuna*, 1991 BDIEL AD LEXIS 67, © The American Society of International Law.

### Background and Facts

Purse-Seine Fishing of Tuna. The last three decades have seen the deployment of tuna fishing technology based on the "purse-seine" net in many areas of the world. A fishing vessel using this technique locates a school of fish and sends out a motorboat (a *seine skiff*) to hold one end of the purse-seine net. The vessel motors around the perimeter of the school of fish, unfurling the net and encircling the fish, and the seine skiff then attaches its end of the net to the fishing vessel. The fishing vessel then purses the net by winching in a cable at the bottom edge of the net, and draws in the top cables of the net to gather its entire contents.

Studies monitoring direct and indirect catch levels have shown that fish and dolphins are found together in a number of areas around the world and that this may lead to incidental taking of dolphins during fishing operations. In the Eastern Tropical Pacific Ocean (ETP), a particular association between dolphins and tuna has long been observed, such that fishermen locate schools of underwater tuna by finding and chasing dolphins on the ocean surface and intentionally encircling them with nets to catch tuna underneath. This type of association has not been observed in other areas of the world; consequently, intentional encirclement of dolphins with purse-seine nets is used as a tuna fishing technique only in the Eastern Tropical Pacific Ocean. When dolphins and tuna together have been surrounded by purse-seine nets, it is possible to reduce or eliminate the catch of dolphins through using certain procedures.

## Body of Opinion

### Marine Mammal Protection Act (MMPA).

. . . The Marine Mammal Protection Act (MMPA) regulates . . . the harvesting of tuna by United States fishermen and others who are operating within the jurisdiction of the United States. The MMPA requires that such fishermen use certain fishing techniques to reduce the taking of dolphin incidental to the harvesting of fish. The United States authorities have licensed fishing of yellowfin tuna by United States vessels in the ETP on the condition that the domestic fleet not exceed an incidental taking of 20,500 dolphins per year in the ETP.

The MMPA also requires that the United States Government ban the importation of commercial fish or products from fish caught with commercial fishing technology which results in the incidental killing or incidental serious injury of ocean animals in excess of United States standards. Under United States customs law, fish caught by a vessel registered in a country is deemed to originate in that country. As a condition of access to the United States market for the yellowfin tuna or yellowfin tuna products caught by its fleet, each country of registry of vessels fishing yellowfin tuna in the ETP must prove to the satisfaction of the United States authorities that its overall regulatory regime regarding the taking of marine mammals is compatible to that of the United States. To meet this requirement, the country in question must prove that the average rate of incidental taking of marine mammals by its tuna fleet operating in the ETP is not in excess of 1.25 times the average incidental taking rate of United States vessels operating in the ETP during the same period.

The Panel noted that Mexico had argued that the measures prohibiting imports of certain yellowfin tuna and yellowfin tuna products from Mexico imposed by the United States were quantitative restrictions on importation under Article XI, while the United States had argued that these measures were internal regulations enforced at the time or point of importation under Article III:4 and the Note Ad Article III, namely that the prohibition of imports of tuna and tuna products from Mexico constituted an enforcement of the regulations of the MMPA relating to the harvesting of domestic tuna.

The Panel concluded from the above considerations that the Note Ad Article III covers only those measures that are applied to the product as such. The Panel noted that the MMPA regulates the domestic harvesting of yellowfin tuna to reduce the incidental taking of dolphin, but that these regulations could not be regarded as being applied to tuna products as such because they would not directly regulate the sale of tuna and could not possibly affect tuna as a product. Therefore, the Panel found that the import prohibition on certain yellowfin tuna and certain yellowfin tuna products of Mexico and the provisions of the MMPA under which it is imposed did not constitute internal regulations covered by the Note Ad Article III.

The Panel further concluded that, even if the provisions of the MMPA enforcing the tuna harvesting regulations (in particular those providing for the seizure of cargo as a penalty for violation of the Act) were regarded as regulating the sale of tuna as a product, the United States import prohibition would not meet the requirements of

Article III. . . . Article III:4 calls for a comparison of the treatment of imported tuna as a product with that of domestic tuna as a product. Regulations governing the taking of dolphins incidental to the taking of tuna could not possibly affect tuna as a product. Article III:4 therefore obliges the United States to accord treatment to Mexican tuna no less favorable than that accorded to United States tuna, whether or not the incidental taking of dolphins by Mexican vessels corresponds to that of United States vessels.

### Dolphin Protection Consumer Information Act (DPCIA).

The Panel examined the distinction between quantitative restrictions on importation and internal measures applied at the time or point of importation, and noted the following. While restrictions on importation are prohibited by Article XI:1, contracting parties are permitted by Article III:4 and the Note Ad Article III to impose an internal regulation on products imported from other contracting parties provided that it: does not discriminate between products of other countries in violation of the most-favored-nation principle of Article I:1; is not applied so as to afford protection to domestic production, in violation of the national treatment principle of Article III:1; and accords to imported products treatment no less favorable than that accorded to like products of national origin, consistent with Article III:4. . . .

The Panel noted that Mexico considered the labeling provisions of the DPCIA to be marking requirements falling under Article IX:1, which reads:

> Each contracting party shall accord to the products of the territories of other contracting parties treatment with regard to marking requirements no less favorable than the treatment accorded to like products of any third country.

The United States considered that the labeling provisions were subject not to Article IX but to the most-favored-nation and national-treatment provisions of Articles I:1 and III:4. The Panel noted that the title of Article IX is "Marks of Origin" and its text refers to marking of origin of imported products. The Panel further noted that Article IX does not contain a national-treatment but only a most-favored-nation requirement, which indicates that this provision was intended to regulate marking of origin of imported products but not marking of products generally. The Panel therefore found that the labeling provisions of the DPCIA did not fall under Article IX:1.

The Panel proceeded to examine the subsidiary argument by Mexico that the labeling provisions of the DPCIA were inconsistent with Article I:1 because they discriminated against Mexico as a country fishing in the ETP. The Panel noted that the labeling provisions of the DPCIA do not restrict the sale of tuna products; tuna products can be sold freely both with and without the "Dolphin Safe" label. Nor do these provisions establish requirements that have to be met in order to obtain an advantage from the government. Any advantage which might possibly result from access to this label depends on the free choice by consumers to give preference to tuna carrying the "Dolphin Safe" label. The labeling provisions therefore did not make the right to sell tuna or tuna products, nor the access to a government-conferred advantage affecting the sale of tuna or tuna products, conditional upon the use of tuna harvesting methods. The only issue before the Panel was therefore whether the provisions of the DPCIA governing the right of access to the label met the requirements of Article I:1.

The Panel noted that the DPCIA is based . . . on a finding that dolphins are frequently killed in the course of tuna-fishing operations in the ETP through the use of purse-seine nets intentionally deployed to encircle dolphins. The DPCIA therefore accords the right to use the label "Dolphin Safe" for tuna harvested in the ETP only if such tuna is accompanied by documentary evidence showing that it was not harvested with purse-seine nets intentionally deployed to encircle dolphins. The Panel examined whether this requirement applied to tuna from the ETP was consistent with Article I:1. According to the information presented to the Panel, the harvesting of tuna by intentionally encircling dolphins with purse-seine nets was practiced only in the ETP because of the particular nature of the association between dolphins and tuna observed only in that area. By imposing the requirement to provide evidence that this fishing technique had not been used in respect of tuna caught in the ETP the United States therefore did not discriminate against countries fishing in this area. The Panel noted that, under United States customs law, the country of origin of fish was determined by the country of registry of the vessel that had caught the fish; the geographical area where the fish was caught was irrelevant for the determination of origin. The labeling regulations governing tuna caught in the ETP thus applied to all countries whose vessels fished in this geographical area and thus did not distinguish between products originating in Mexico and products originating in other countries.

The Panel found for these reasons that the tuna products labeling provisions of the DPCIA relating to tuna caught in the ETP were not inconsistent with the obligations of the United States under Article I:1 of the General Agreement.

The Panel wished to underline that its task was limited to the examination of this matter "in the light of the relevant GATT provisions," and therefore did not call for a finding on the appropriateness of the United States' and Mexico's conservation policies as such.

The Panel wished to note the fact, made evident during its consideration of this case, that the provisions of the General Agreement impose few constraints on a contracting party's implementation of domestic environmental policies. The Panel recalled its findings. . . that under these provisions, a contracting party is free to tax or regulate imported products and like domestic products as long as its taxes or regulations do not discriminate against imported products or afford protection to domestic producers, and a contracting party is also free to tax or regulate domestic production for environmental purposes. As a corollary to these rights, a contracting party may not restrict imports of a product merely because it originates in a country with environmental policies different from its own.

. . . The Panel noted that the United States considered the prohibition of imports of certain yellowfin tuna and certain yellowfin tuna products form Mexico, and the provisions of the MMPA on which this prohibition is based, to be justified by Article XX(b) because they served solely the purpose of protecting dolphin life and health and were "necessary" within the meaning of that provision because, in respect of the protection of dolphin life and health outside its jurisdiction, there was no alternative measure reasonably available to the United States to achieve this objective. Mexico considered that Article XX(b) was not applicable to a measure imposed to protect the life or health of animals outside the jurisdiction of the contracting party taking it and that the import prohibition imposed by the United States was not necessary because alternative means consistent with the General Agreement were available to it to protect dolphin lives or health, namely international co-operation between the countries concerned.

## Conclusions

The prohibition of imports of certain yellowfin tuna and certain yellowfin tuna products of Mexico and the provisions of the Marine Mammal Protection Act under which it is imposed are contrary to Article XI:1 and are not justified by Article XX(b) or Article XX(g).

The tuna labeling provisions of the Dolphin Protection Consumer Information Act relating to tuna caught in the Eastern Tropical Pacific Ocean are not inconsistent with the obligations of the United States under Article I:1 of the General Agreement on Tariffs and Trade.

## Questions

1. Were the dolphins that the two U.S. statutes were attempting to protect in U.S. or international waters? How can U.S. statutes have extra-jurisdictional effect? If Mexico wants to export tuna caught in its waters or in international waters into the United States, is Mexico not imposing its environmental ideas on the U.S. consumers, that is, that dolphins should not be afforded much protection?

2. Was the Marine Mammal Protection Act attempting to protect U.S. citizens' health? Welfare?

3. What arguments did the United States advance to justify its limits on the importation of tuna? Animal rights? Did this relate to some feature of tunas? If it did not, how could the United States justify restricting the tuna if the purpose in so doing was to protect some other mammal not being imported into the United States?

4. How realistic is it for the GATT Panel to suggest that the United States could pursue its concern for dolphins by pursuing international cooperation between the two countries concerned? Is GATT not a form of international cooperation? Does GATT forbid countries from trying to protect marine mammals? If another country uses GATT to stymie protection of marine mammals, how likely is it to pursue cooperative efforts with the United States to achieve the same ends?

5. If the United States suddenly decided that goods could not be imported into the United States unless made under U.S. labor conditions (Fair Labor Standards Act for wages, Occupational Safety and Health Act for employment conditions, Workers' Compensation, ERISA, etc. protections), could it restrict imports of Mexican or any country's goods if not made under a comparable legal regime, according to the interpretation of GATT? What might be the legal justification the United States could advance to impose such a restriction? What would be the Mexican or other foreign nation legal challenge to such restrictions?

6. Does GATT completely disallow a member nation from protecting its citizens from harmful products entering its territory?

7. Are GATT panel deliberations open to the public? What legal ethics mentioned in Chapter 1 are or are not in evidence here?

## UNCITRAL

The United Nations Commission on International Trade Law (UNCITRAL) had its first meeting in 1966. The commission is composed of representatives from only 36 countries from all regions of the world. This small number permits a group that is workable in size. The commission meets approximately one month per year. It aims to promote the unification and harmonization of international trade by drafting *model laws*, which it presents to different nations with an eye toward encouraging each nation to enact them. The idea is that if each nation passes UNCITRAL's model statutes, eventually the goal of uniform national laws would be achieved. Presumably, trade barriers would decrease since trade laws would be similar from country to country. An example of a model act that UNCITRAL has drafted and the United Nations has approved is the Draft Convention on Contracts for the International Sale of Goods. This is patterned after Article 2 of the Uniform Commercial Code.

*The Web site for United Nations Commission on International Trade Law, UNCITRAL is located at* **http://www.uncitral.org**

## EUROPEAN UNION[3]

The Treaty of Rome, which was signed in 1957 and took effect in 1958, created the European Economic Community (EEC), also known as the Common Market. The EEC's main purpose is to promote tariff-free trade among its members and to have common tariffs for outsiders. Some see the EEC as a first step toward a politically united Europe. The EEC has legislative, executive, and judicial arms which in some ways have control of individual member nations. For example, the EEC's supreme court, called the Court of Justice, issues decrees that bind all member nations internally. In effect, this means that member nations are giving up a bit of their sovereignty. The Treaty of Rome's Articles 85 and 86 are laws forbidding anticompetitive acts by businesses within (and to some extent outside) the EEC, much as the antitrust laws do in the United States.

The following European nations belong to the EEC: Belgium, Denmark, France, Germany, Greece, Ireland, Italy, Luxembourg, the Netherlands, Portugal, Spain, and the United Kingdom. As of this writing, ten additional nations, many of which are former Eastern European communist nations, have been proposed for European Union membership.

### THE MAASTRICHT TREATY: CREATING THE EUROPEAN UNION (EU)

The Maastricht Treaty establishes the European Union (EU), originally consisting of twelve member nations, but, as of this writing, consisting of the fifteen EC nations (with more seeking admission). The Maastricht Treaty is a significant development along the road to European unification. It amends the Treaty of Rome and, as such, carries forward that Treaty's efforts to unify Europe.

From this point forward the terms European Community and European Union will be used interchangeably. In a technical sense the EC became part of the EU when the Maastricht Treaty went into effect. The EU encompasses the European

---

[3] The authors acknowledge relying on Leonard's *Guide to the European Union* in preparing this and the Maastricht Treaty segments.

Commission (which has authority in matters such as education, health, culture, and consumer protection), the Council of Ministers, the European Parliament, and the Court of Justice.

When most people think of the Maastricht Treaty, they think of the unified currency (the Euro) for member states. However, that treaty has the far broader objective of European integration politically, socially (with the current Social Chapter), and economically (by establishing a European currency, the euro, which took effect on January 1, 2002 for the "person on the street.")

An "opt out" provision permits Great Britain to stay out of the monetary union (euro) and the Social Chapter. As of this writing, Great Britain has exercised its option to stay out of the European currency.

## NAFTA[4]

On August 12, 1992, then President Bush reported completion of negotiations for a North American Free Trade Agreement (NAFTA) among the nations of Canada, Mexico, and the United States. As of this writing NAFTA has not been ratified by all three countries, although the U.S. House of Representatives approved NAFTA on November 17, 1993. Canada is the United States' largest trading partner and Mexico is third. Much debate has surrounded the net economic effects of NAFTA, and readers are referred to other sources to assess the merits of the arguments pro and con. Here, attention is devoted to the some important NAFTA provisions.

*Tariffs.* All tariffs on products traded among the member nations are scheduled to be eliminated within 15 years of NAFTA's implementation. U.S./Canada trade became essentially duty-free in 1998. All Mexican tariffs on U.S. exports into Mexico are scheduled to disappear in ten years except for those on corn and beans, which will end in fifteen years.

*Rules of Origin.* NAFTA is designed to lower tariffs only on goods made in North America. Rules of origin determine whether a product is made in North America. The idea is to keep Mexico or Canada from being "export platforms" for shipment duty-free of, say, Japanese goods to the United States through, for example, Mexico.

Rules of origin are important under NAFTA because even after it takes effect, NAFTA members may still have different tariffs on goods coming into them from non-NAFTA countries such as Japan. Thus if the United States had a 10 percent tariff on Japanese cars and Mexico had a 1 percent tariff on Japanese cars, a clever importer could first import the Japanese cars into Mexico, "wash" them of their identity by superficially "finishing" them (such as installing cigarette lighters in Mexico), and exporting them as "Mexican" cars to the United States with no tariff, because tariffs among NAFTA members are to be phased out ultimately.

Goods entirely made in the United States, Mexico, or Canada of composed entirely of NAFTA components are given duty-free treatment within the NAFTA region (the area of the member nations). Goods having non-NAFTA region parts might be given duty-free treatment if they have undergone a specified change in tariff classification. Here the rules of product origin are crucial. Under the

---

[4] The authors acknowledge reliance on U.S. State Department documents in preparing this segment.

NAFTA, the U.S./Canada Free Trade Agreement's (a predecessor to the NAFTA) rules of origin will be used for U.S./Canadian trade.

*NAFTA's Safeguards.* NAFTA has at least two safeguards to prevent a member nation such as the United States being overrun with imports from another member such as Mexico. One bilateral safeguard is the snap-back provision, which allows pre-NAFTA tariff rates to be reimposed for up to three, and in some cases four, years if import surges from Mexico to the United States seriously injure U.S. firms or workers. A second global safeguard permits the United States to place quotas or tariffs on Canadian or Mexican products if multilateral action is taken in response to imports causing or threatening substantial injury.

*NAFTA's Environmental Protections.*[5] NAFTA provides that each member nation has the right to set what it thinks is the appropriate level of protection for people, animals, and plants life or health, technically called sanitary, which relates to humans and animals, and phytosanitary, which relates to plants. This right is qualified by disallowing arbitrary or unjustifiable life or health provisions that would result in arbitrary or unjustifiable discrimination against another party's goods or be, in effect, a disguised trade restriction. Also, when a nation deals with animal or plant life or health, cost effectiveness of alternative ways of limiting risks must be considered.

Two other qualifications significantly limit environmental measures in order for them to be valid under NAFTA: They must be "necessary" to protect human, animal, or plant life or health at the level the particular nation selects. For example, for a zero level of risk, it would be necessary to have a low level of pesticide residue on lettuce. Second, environmental measures to protect human, animal, or plant life or health must be "based on scientific principles." Commentators have noted that genetic engineering does not appear to be covered under this part of the NAFTA.

NAFTA is generally seen as more environmentally friendly than GATT for several reasons. First, NAFTA requires that a scientific study support a standard even though other studies might lead to an opposite conclusion. The Uruguay round of GATT apparently would upset standards if contrary to "available scientific evidence," meaning that if several studies do not support the standard, the fact that one does support it would probably lead to the standard's being struck down. Second, GATT's Uruguay round forces environmental standards to be the "least restrictive to trade, taking into account technical and economic feasibility." NAFTA does not force the environmental standards of nations to be so accommodating to trade. Third, GATT's Uruguay round forces standards for humans as well as plants and animals life and health to meet cost and effectiveness standards, while the NAFTA requires cost and effectiveness only for animals and plants—not standards protecting humans. Fourth, GATT's Uruguay round requires environmental standards to be consistent with "human health risks to which people voluntarily expose themselves." Thus, if the nation is one where everyone smokes and drinks alcohol heavily, it would appear inconsistent to have stringent environmental standards concerning pesticide residues in food, because people are voluntarily exposing themselves to greater risks by their lifestyle. NAFTA has no such consistency requirement between environmental standards and the population's lifestyle.

---

[5] The authors acknowledge reliance on Steve Charnovitz, "NAFTA: An Analysis of its Environmental Provisions," *Environmental Law Reporter* (1993).

## OVERSEAS PRIVATE INVESTOR CORPORATION (OPIC)

The Overseas Private Investor Corporation (OPIC) is a U.S. government agency. It provides insurance to citizens and businesses against certain risks associated with doing business abroad. Included are such risks as confiscation (a foreign government's taking a foreign business's property in violation of international law), insurrection, repatriation problems (the inability to take earnings "out" of a foreign country), war, and revolution. OPIC premiums are based on the risk involved.

## U.S. INTERNATIONAL TRADE COMMISSION[6]

View information about the International Trade Commission at http://www.usitc.gov

In 1916 Congress established by statute the U.S. Tariff Commission. The name was changed in 1974 to the U.S. International Trade Commission (ITC). It provides studies, reports, and recommendations to the president, Congress, and other governmental bodies regarding tariffs and other international trade issues.

The ITC is an independent federal agency. It consists of six presidentially appointed commissioners who must be confirmed by the U.S. Senate. The commissioners' full terms are for nine years, although some commissioners serve only part of a term. The president designates the ITC chairperson and vice chairperson for two-year terms. Succeeding chairpersons may not be from the same political party. No more than three commissioners may be members of the same political party.

### ITC FUNCTIONS

The ITC must provide the president, the House Ways and Means Committee, and Senate Finance Committee with all the information it has when requested. The ITC must also conduct investigations on matters of international trade requested by either the president or Congress.

### GENERALIZED SYSTEM OF PREFERENCES

The president has the authority to lower U.S. tariffs, called *preferences*, on goods imported into the United States from certain developing countries. The ITC advises the president on the likely effect of such preferences on U.S. business and consumers.

### INDUSTRY ADJUSTMENTS TO IMPORT COMPETITION

Suppose a particular business, a particular industry, a particular union, or other industrial representative believes that an imported good poses a serious threat to a U.S. business. This U.S. business may petition the ITC to investigate the matter. If the ITC finds the import does threaten serious injury to the U.S. industry, it can recommend that the president take corrective action. The president has discretion

---

[6] The authors acknowledge reliance on government documents in preparing material on the International Trade Commission.

to increase tariff duties, impose a quota on the foreign goods, work out a marketing agreement of some sort, or assist U.S. workers, businesses, or communities adversely affected by the import.

## IMPORT INTERFERENCE WITH AGRICULTURAL PROGRAMS

The president also has the authority to direct the ITC to investigate to determine whether articles being imported render Department of Agriculture programs for agricultural commodities or products ineffective or that would reduce the amount of any product processed in the United States from such commodities or products. The president can limit such imports by either fees or quotas.

## COMPARING UNIT LABOR COSTS AMONG NATIONS

A quiet but important war is occurring today: It is the fight for the consumer's money among businesses from all over the world. U.S. firms must sell goods that compete with goods from Japan, Germany, The Netherlands, Sweden, and many other nations. One basic cost in international competition is labor. Table 8.2 compares U.S. unit labor costs with those of other nations. While labor is but one production cost, it is significant in most manufacturing enterprises.

## PROTECTING U.S. PATENTS, COPYRIGHTS, AND TRADEMARKS ABROAD: SPECIAL 301

The U.S. International Trade Commission (ITC) estimates that theft abroad of U.S. intellectual property costs its owners at least $43 billion in 1986 alone. Thieves in foreign countries pirate or counterfeit items such as computers, computer software, books, tapes, CDs, movies, auto parts, pharmaceuticals, and semiconductors. The pirates then sell copies of these items as the real McCoy.

The 1988 Trade Act states that international protection of intellectual property rights is vital to the international competitiveness of individuals and businesses in the United States who rely on protection of intellectual property rights. That Act also recognizes that U.S. businesses must have access to foreign markets. Further, a section of the 1988 Act—**Special 301**—also states as its purpose the development of a strategy to protect intellectual property rights and to assume market access for U.S. business.

*Special 301: A Major Purpose.* Special 301, as stated by then President Reagan at the bill's signing, is to "strengthen the ability of U.S. firms to protect their patented, copyrighted, or trademarked goods and ideas from international thievery."

*What Special 301 Requires.* Special 301 tells the U.S. Trade Representative (USTR) to, within 30 days following publication of the *National Trade Estimate Report,* designate nations that deny "fair and equitable market access to U.S. persons who rely on intellectual property protection."

*Identification of 301 Countries.* The USTR must identify as "priority foreign countries" those whose acts, practices, or policies are the most onerous and have the most adverse economic effect on the United States and who are not trying to negotiate in good faith to correct deficient intellectual property protection. In

## TABLE 8.2 NATIONAL LABOR COSTS IN SELECTED COUNTRIES

**Hourly compensation costs in U.S. dollars for production workers in manufacturing, 29 countries or areas and selected economic groups, selected years, 1975-2000**

| Country or Area | 1975 | 1980 | 1985 | 1990 | 1995 | 1997 | 1998 | 1999 | 2000 |
|---|---|---|---|---|---|---|---|---|---|
| **North America** | | | | | | | | | |
| United States | $6.36 | $9.87 | $13.01 | $14.91 | $17.19 | $18.27 | $18.59 | $19.11 | $19.86 |
| Canada | 5.96 | 8.67 | 10.95 | 15.95 | 16.10 | 16.47 | 15.60 | 15.65 | 16.16 |
| Mexico | 1.47 | 2.21 | 1.59 | 1.58 | 1.51 | 1.78 | 1.84 | 2.09 | 2.46 |
| **Asia and Oceania** | | | | | | | | | |
| Australia | 5.62 | 8.47 | 8.20 | 13.07 | 15.27 | 16.58 | 14.92 | 15.66 | 14.15 |
| Hong Kong SAR[1] | .76 | 1.51 | 1.73 | 3.20 | 4.82 | 5.42 | 5.47 | 5.44 | 5.53 |
| Israel | 2.25 | 3.79 | 4.06 | 8.55 | 10.54 | 12.04 | 12.02 | 11.91 | 12.88 |
| Japan | 3.00 | 5.52 | 6.34 | 12.80 | 23.82 | 19.54 | 18.29 | 20.89 | 22.00 |
| Korea | .32 | .96 | 1.23 | 3.71 | 7.29 | 7.86 | 5.67 | 7.05 | 8.13 |
| New Zealand | 3.15 | 5.22 | 4.38 | 8.17 | 9.91 | 10.80 | 9.01 | 9.14 | 8.13 |
| Singapore | .84 | 1.49 | 2.47 | 3.78 | 7.33 | 8.24 | 7.77 | 7.13 | 7.42 |
| Sri Lanka | .28 | .22 | .28 | .35 | .48 | .46 | .47 | .46 | - |
| Taiwan | .40 | 1.00 | 1.50 | 3.93 | 5.94 | 5.91 | 5.27 | 5.62 | 5.98 |
| **Europe** | | | | | | | | | |
| Austria | 4.51 | 8.88 | 7.58 | 17.75 | 25.32 | 21.97 | 22.21 | 21.85 | 19.46 |
| Belgium | 6.41 | 13.11 | 8.97 | 19.17 | 27.62 | 23.98 | 24.31 | 23.92 | 21.11 |
| Denmark | 6.28 | 10.83 | 8.13 | 18.04 | 24.07 | 22.03 | 22.69 | 22.96 | 20.44 |
| Finland | 4.61 | 8.24 | 8.16 | 21.03 | 24.10 | 21.32 | 21.66 | 21.33 | 19.50 |
| France | 4.52 | 8.94 | 7.52 | 15.49 | 20.01 | 17.99 | 18.28 | 17.98 | 16.38 |
| Germany, former West | 6.29 | 12.21 | 9.50 | 21.81 | 31.58 | 27.54 | 27.43 | 26.76 | 24.01 |
| Germany[2] | - | - | - | - | 30.26 | 26.36 | 26.28 | 25.64 | 22.99 |
| Greece | 1.69 | 3.73 | 3.66 | 6.76 | 9.17 | 9.20 | 8.91 | - | - |
| Ireland | 3.05 | 6.03 | 5.99 | 11.81 | 13.78 | 13.83 | 13.58 | 13.61 | 12.50 |
| Italy | 4.67 | 8.15 | 7.63 | 17.45 | 16.22 | 17.57 | 17.11 | 16.60 | 14.66 |
| Luxembourg | 6.50 | 12.03 | 7.81 | 16.74 | 22.62 | 18.74 | 18.70 | 18.65 | 16.69 |
| Netherlands | 6.58 | 12.06 | 8.75 | 18.06 | 24.12 | 20.82 | 21.40 | 21.30 | 19.08 |
| Norway | 6.77 | 11.59 | 10.37 | 21.47 | 24.38 | 23.72 | 23.50 | 23.91 | 22.05 |
| Portugal | 1.58 | 2.06 | 1.53 | 3.77 | 5.37 | 5.38 | 5.48 | 5.35 | 4.75 |
| Spain | 2.53 | 5.89 | 4.66 | 11.38 | 12.88 | 12.24 | 12.14 | 12.11 | 10.85 |
| Sweden | 7.18 | 12.51 | 9.66 | 20.93 | 21.44 | 22.22 | 22.02 | 21.60 | 20.14 |
| Switzerland | 6.09 | 11.09 | 9.66 | 20.86 | 29.30 | 24.19 | 24.38 | 23.56 | 21.24 |
| United Kingdom | 3.37 | 7.56 | 6.27 | 12.70 | 13.67 | 15.42 | 16.39 | 16.48 | 15.88 |
| **Trade-weighted measures [3]** | | | | | | | | | |
| **All 28 foreign** | | | | | | | | | |
| economies | 3.83 | 6.59 | 6.74 | 12.35 | 16.38 | 15.30 | 14.75 | 15.27 | 15.16 |
| OECD | 4.25 | 7.30 | 7.39 | 13.48 | 17.74 | 16.46 | 15.88 | 16.48 | 16.31 |
| less Mexico, Korea | 4.82 | 8.30 | 8.48 | 15.54 | 20.39 | 18.80 | 18.23 | 18.83 | 18.52 |
| Europe | 5.09 | 9.90 | 7.96 | 17.30 | 22.03 | 20.45 | 20.67 | 20.36 | 18.50 |
| Asian NIEs | .52 | 1.17 | 1.65 | 3.72 | 6.41 | 6.83 | 5.91 | 6.29 | 6.79 |

Dash means data not available.
[1]Hong Kong Special Administrative Region of China.
[2]Referred to as unified Germany in prior news releases.
[3]Because data for Germany (referred to as unified Germany in prior news releases)

*Source:* U.S. Department of Labor, Bureau of Labor Statistics (January 13, 2002) **http://bls.gov/news.release/ichcc.t02.htm**.

this respect, Congress determined that practices such as expropriation, restrictive licensing procedures, and "cultural sovereignty" barriers were undesirable. Once the USTR identifies priority foreign countries, it must investigate that nation's undesirable practices. The USTR must complete the investigation within six months and must also seek a bilateral solution with individual problem nations.

*Sanctions.* Assuming the offending nation refuses to cooperate, the USTR may sanction the country by raising duties or otherwise restricting imports from the problem country.

*Other Aspects of Special 301.* The USTR may add to the list of "priority foreign countries" at any time. The USTR also has the power to revoke priority foreign country status anytime, provided detailed reasons are given for such revocation.

Special 301 should not be confused with Super 301, which is also designed to strengthen the hand of U.S. trade negotiators to liberalize trade with foreign countries. Super 301 was used to retaliate against countries hostile to U.S. trade. One difference between Super 301 and Special 301 is that Special 301 is permanent while Super 301 expired after 1990. Renewal of Super 301 is considered from time to time.

## RESTRAINTS ON INTERNATIONAL BUSINESS

## U.S. ANTITRUST LAWS

*Extraterritorial Effect.* Suppose a Japanese firm and a Korean firm agree to fix prices on radios sold in France. The U.S. antitrust laws do not apply to such conduct that has no effect or contact with the United States. To say otherwise would mean that the United States could set the speed limits or antitrust laws in Paris. However, U.S. antitrust laws (discussed in other chapters) can apply to international business; that is, they can have extraterritorial effect (outside the United States). The Sherman Act specifically states that it applies outside the United States.

*U.S. Antitrust Law Control of Business Outside the U.S.* U.S. antitrust laws apply if anticompetitive activities outside the United States have some substantial effect within the United States. Thus, if the Japanese and Korean radio firms agree to fix prices on radios shipped to the United States and this agreement has a substantial effect within the United States, the U.S. antitrust laws apply and make it illegal.

*Who Can Sue for Extraterritorial Antitrust Violations.* Another way of asking who can sue is to ask whom the antitrust laws protect. Foreign and U.S. governments, U.S. and foreign businesses, and any other person injured may sue for violations of U.S. antitrust laws outside the United States, which have a substantial effect within the United States.

*Who Can Be Sued.* Quite a number of categories of persons can be sued for breaking U.S. antitrust laws in international settings. Assuming the jurisdictional requirements are met, foreign governments, U.S. and foreign businesses, and any person who violates U.S. antitrust laws can be sued for alleged violations.

*Antitrust Exemption.* The Export Trading Company Act was passed in 1982 to encourage U.S. business to engage in international trade. The principal reason for encouraging U.S. trade, which was to help correct the trade deficit, can be understood by examining Figure 8.1 showing the U.S. merchandise trade balance from 1970 through 2000. Several figures stand out: the trend of the trade deficits over the past decade fluctuated up and down but have been worsening, particularly in the most recent years; the import value for petroleum fell sharply until 1986 (due at least in part to the decline in the world oil prices); the value of U.S. agricultural exports *fell* sharply between 1984 and 1987; and the United States consistently imports more in dollar terms of transportation equipment (autos, buses, and trucks) as it exports. All of these facts support efforts to encourage U.S. business to export more, while assuming that import restrictions will not frequently be imposed.

The Export Trading Company Act (ETCA) tries to encourage U.S. businesses to increase exports by letting competitors form Export Trading Companies (ETCs) without the threat of U.S. antitrust liability. The ETCA sets up a procedure for companies to get a certificate of antitrust compliance from the secretary of commerce and the Justice Department. To obtain such certification the applicant must show it will not (1) substantially lessen competition or restrain trade in the United States or substantially restrain export trade of a competitor; (2) cause unfair competition; (3) affect the prices of goods or services in the United States; or (4) sell for competition or resell the exported goods within the United States. Thus, the ETCA amended the Sherman and FTC Acts dealing with antitrust.

## Antitrust in the European Union

The European Union (EU) has several provisions (especially Articles 85 and 86 of the Treaty of Rome, which established the EEC) that forbid anticompetitive business practices. Article 85 is similar to Section 1 of the Sherman Act.

*The Helms–Burton Act.*    Certain segments of the U.S. Congress and business community continue to feel hostility toward Fidel Castro and his communist revolution. In part this animus is due to the Cuban government's nationalization of assets of U.S. firms doing business in Cuba when Castro came to power in 1959.

In 1996 the U.S. Congress, led by Senator Jesse Helms of North Carolina and Congressman Dan Burton of Indiana, passed the Helms–Burton Act. This act has as its primary objective the economically isolating, in effect punishing, of Cuba for these earlier acts of confiscation. Helms–Burton attempts to achieve its objective by making certain acts illegal if done by a foreign business regarding such confiscated U.S. property. In other words, if a foreign business uses confiscated U.S. assets, that business is punished.

The punishment Helms–Burton imposes on foreign businesses takes several forms. One is the prevention of such foreign firms' executives from entering the United States. Also, foreign executives' families may not enter the United States to study or visit here. Another provision of Helms–Burton would allow U.S. firms whose Cuban property was seized by Castro to sue the company now using this property from Cuba in U.S. courts.

Helms–Burton is controversial. Many foreign governments and businesses have criticized Helms–Burton for violating principles of free economic trade. In fact, U.S. policy in general has favored free trade internationally since the 1930s, so, arguably, passage of Helms–Burton is at odds with U.S. trade policy. Critics point to the fact that the United States has robust trade with other communist nations, for example, the People's Republic of China (PRC), the largest communist nation and one of the most repressive governments in the world. The United States runs a trade deficit with the PRC of more than $50 billion per year. Critics of Helms–Burton also note that such laws invite other nations' retaliation against unpopular U.S. policies, which could ignite a series of international boycotts.

## KYOTO TREATY

The Kyoto treaty is a major international environmental initiative. It aims to have all major industrial countries (there are more than 30) reduce greenhouse gases (e.g., carbon dioxide) in order to halt or slow global warming. Such "warming" is believed to contribute significantly to long-term, adverse world climate change. The goal is to reduce 1990 greenhouse gas emissions by 5.2 percent to 7 percent by 2012. The reduction would be 7 percent for the United States.

Only one nation—Romania—has ratified the Kyoto treaty. Fifty-five nations must ratify this treaty to make it law.

The stated reasons for not ratifying Kyoto, in the case of the United States, are that making such a commitment to pre–1990 levels would severely slow economic development, particularly in the case of the United States, which produces about 25 percent of the world's goods and services. Also, the United States argues that it is a market for many other nation's goods, so any cutback on the U.S. propensity to consume would hurt other nations—often developing nations. Further, the United States contends that Kyoto has double standards, having a high standard for industrial nations such as the United States and *no* standards for India and China, whose economies are booming and who are significant sources of greenhouse gases (China is second and India is third as a world source of greenhouse gases). Because the United States is a major market for both Chinese and Indian goods, the Bush administration argues that imposing a high standard on the United States and *no* standard on China or India is counterproductive for them because it would reduce their major market.

The Bush administration has advanced some interesting ideas to soften the Kyoto treaty's impact on industrial nations. One is *credits*. According to this idea, a developed nation that helped reduce emissions in a developing nation would have its (the developed nation's) pollution "credited" or reduced by the amount of the emission cuts in the developed nation. So far this idea has not found broad support among other nations. Another idea is for nations to create *carbon dioxide sinks* by such methods as planting new forests. The sinks would absorb carbon dioxide and create oxygen, countering the greenhouse effect. This idea has also failed to win broad support.

As of this writing there is broad—although not universal—acceptance in the scientific community that global warming is occurring. Many scientists point to harmful climactic and economic effects of permitting this matter to go unchecked.

## CHAPTER SUMMARY

International law refers to treaties, customs, and recognized principles nations use to regulate their relations in war and peace. In light of John Austin's positive law, international "law" cannot follow positive law because no sovereign entity rules over all nations.

International trade is extensive and has tended to grow. The important most-favored-nation status tends to reduce tariffs among nations.

A number of institutions affect international trade, including the WTO, UNCI-TRAL, the EU, and OPIC.

U.S. antitrust laws can, under certain circumstances, regulate trade in foreign nations. The EU also in theory forbids certain anticompetitive practices.

The Helms–Burton Act aims to isolate Cuba in retaliation for seizure of U.S. firms' property during the communist takeover there in 1959. This law punishes certain foreign businesses using U.S. assets confiscated by the Castro government.

## MANAGER'S ETHICAL DILEMMA

"I'm sorry, sir," said the U.S. immigration and passport official to a Canadian business executive. "I can't admit you to the United States."

"This is outlandish," replied Herbert Smith, the CEO of Mega-Industries. "Why not? I'm not a runaway crook or drug dealer."

"No, but your company, Mega-Industries, bought property in Cuba, which formerly belonged to U.S. companies prior to Fidel

Castro's takeover in 1959. The U.S. congress has enacted the Helms–Burton Act, which forbids entry into the United States of executives of companies that traffic in assets of U.S. firms confiscated by the Castro government."

Is the U.S. immigration official correct?

## DISCUSSION QUESTIONS

1. At least one candidate for the U.S. presidency in the past two presidential elections has pressed for a tightening of U.S. tariffs and quotas to protect "blue collar" jobs, which are being lost to labor in nations with much lower-priced labor. What would be the pluses and minuses of such a proposal? Has this ever been tried before in the United States and what were the results?

2. What section of U.S. law would businesses with patents, trademarks and copyrights resort to if they felt their rights were being infringed?

3. In what way is Super 301 more potent that Special 301? Why is Super 301 less powerful than Special 301?

4. What relationship does the Generalized System of Trade Preferences have to tariffs?

5. What are the functions of the International Trade Commission?

6. What is the difference between the WTO's basic philosophy and that of the European Union? Or do they share a basic one-world approach?

### INFOTRAC KEYWORDS

**Use your InfoTrac password to look up articles on http://www.infotrac-college.com**

Keywords: *International business law, normal trade relations, tariff discrimination, OPIC, ITC, international antitrust, Helms–Burton Act.*

For suggested readings, please visit this book's Web site at **http://fisher.westbuslaw.com** (click on "Internet Applications").

# PRIVATE BUSINESS DEALINGS IN INTERNATIONAL CONTEXTS

## POSITIVE LAW ETHICAL PROBLEM

"If I have the U.S. copyrighted labels on my perfumes," said Jessica Wilson, a marketing executive of L'anza, a U.S. cosmetics manufacturer, "I have the right to stop someone from importing those products back into the United States." Wilson had sold her perfumes and other cosmetics to a British distributor for resale in Europe at a price far below what they sold to U.S. distributors. The British distributor had resold the perfumes and cosmetics to a Maltese distributor, who, realizing how high the U.S. price was, resold to Quality King, a U.S. distributor unauthorized by L'anza to sell in the United States.

Wilson believed that because L'anza's U.S. copyrighted label was still affixed to the cosmetics when they were shipped back into the United States without L'anza's approval, L'anza had the right to stop Quality King's distribution in the United States. Was she correct?

Businesses are becoming international, even small businesses such as Art's Oriental Rug Shop. Because of this trend, the average person must possess some knowledge of laws affecting international business. This chapter is devoted to explaining how commercial transactions can occur in the international context. Because, as the prior chapter explained, no sovereign exists with the power to make uniform rules governing all nations, it is necessary for businesses to know how private individuals and businesses must and can operate in this environment of plural sovereigns.

This chapter starts with an anatomy of an international business deal. Included here is a discussion of letters of credit and bills of lading. Then the matter of gray market goods, a common phenomenon on the international scene, is noted. Business on the international scene is extremely competitive, and bribery of foreign governments to obtain business is, unfortunately, not unknown. The Foreign Corrupt Practice Act has a direct bearing on many international business transactions involving U.S. business, and its limits will be explored. Several avenues for dispute settlement are also addressed.

*"WHEN YOU ARE AT ROME LIVE IN THE ROMAN STYLE; WHEN YOU ARE ELSEWHERE LIVE AS THEY LIVE ELSEWHERE."*

—ST. AMBROSE
(C 340–397)

## INTERNATIONAL BUSINESS DEALS

Art is an Atlanta, Georgia, rug dealer. He made a contract to buy 500 8-by-10-foot red, handwoven Turkish rugs for $200,000 from Ali, a rugmaker in Ankara, Turkey. The Art–Ali contract presents many practical problems, including the following:

1. How can Ali be sure that he will be paid after shipping the rugs?

2. How can Art be certain that he will get the rugs after paying for them?
3. Can Art stop the deal if Ali sends rugs that are different from the ones that Art ordered?

*For valuable federal resources, as well as law firm and law school links, go to* **http://www. findlaw.com**

You might look at the previous facts and say, "What's the problem? Art should simply mail Ali a check for $200,000, and Ali can send Art the rugs when the check clears." This scenario is possible. But what if Art is unsure that Ali will send the rugs once the check clears? What if Ali does not know if Art will pay? Art wants to keep the money until he gets the rugs. Ali wants to keep the rugs until he gets paid. If this standoff happens, the deal will never occur. Art and Ali mistrust each other.

Art and Ali's mistrust problem is solved by a letter of credit and a bill of lading. Both the letter of credit and the bill of lading use third parties—banks for the letter of credit and transport companies for the bill of lading. Assume that Art and Ali trust banks and transport companies more than they trust each other.

## Letters of Credit

A letter of credit is a bank's commitment to pay a definite amount of money or extend a certain amount of credit to a third person, called a *beneficiary*. The bank extends credit to the beneficiary because a customer (called the *account party*) pays the bank to do so. The bank extends credit to (pays) the beneficiary (Ali) when he gives the bank certain pieces of paper (often, bills of lading).

*The Independence Principle.* The general rule is that letters of credit are independent of the underlying contract (to buy rugs in the Ali–Art example). Therefore, if Ali sends blue rugs instead of red, the issuing bank must honor the letter of credit. It assumes that the beneficiary (Ali) presents the documents that the letter of credit requires, often a bill of lading. It also assumes that Ali (the seller) substitutes nonconforming goods (blue rugs instead of red) in good faith. *GATX Leasing Corp. v. DBM Drilling Corp.* illustrates the independence principle.

---

### GATX Leasing Corp. v. DBM Drilling Corp.
Texas Court of Appeals
657 S.W. 2d 178 (Tex. App. 4th Dist. 1983)

**Background and Facts**

DBM Drilling Corporation was the account party of an irrevocable letter of credit. DBM arranged with Frost National Bank to issue an irrevocable letter of credit to GATX Leasing Corporation to pay for a drilling rig. GATX presented documents to Frost National Bank as the letter of credit required. DBM, however, claimed that the oil rig itself did not live up to the contract DBM had with GATX. DBM sued to enjoin the Frost Bank from honoring the letter of credit.

**Issue**

May the account party on a letter of credit stop the issuing bank from paying the letter of credit when the goods do not conform to the underlying contract but the documents conform to the letter of credit?

**Decision**

No. The account party may not stop the issuing bank from paying an irrevocable letter of credit in the case of a mere breach of the underlying contract. It was not a case involving fraud or forgery by the beneficiary. Instead, the beneficiary and account party merely disagreed about whether the oil rig was being sold or leased.

*Stopping Payment on Letters of Credit: Forgery.* Assume that a letter of credit requires the seller to submit a bill of lading to get paid. If the seller submits a forged bill of lading and knows it, the buyer can stop payment on the letter of credit.

*Stopping Payment on Irrevocable Letters of Credit: Fraud.* The buyer can stop the issuer from paying a letter of credit if the beneficiary commits fraud in the underlying contract. *Sztejn v. J. Henry Schroder Banking Corp.* illustrates the rule.

---

## Sztejn v. J. Henry Schroder Banking Corp.
Supreme Court Special Term, New York County
177 Misc. 719, 31 N.Y.S. 2d 631 (1941)

### Background and Facts

Sztejn, a U.S. businessman, contracted to buy bristles from Transea Traders Ltd., located in India. Sztejn arranged for a letter of credit to pay for the goods. Transea fraudulently sent 50 crates with cow hair and other rubbish instead of the bristles agreed upon. Transea presented documents conforming to those that the letter of credit required. The buyer tried to stop the issuing bank from paying Transea's drafts drawn on the letter of credit. Transea argued that the letter of credit was independent of the bristle contract. Therefore, Transea claimed that the buyer could not stop payment of the letter of credit. Instead, it should sue Transea for breach of contract (a costly, slow, uncertain process).

### Issue

Can a buyer stop payment under an irrevocable letter of credit when the seller fraudulently ships nonconforming goods but presents documents (bills of lading) conforming to the letter of credit?

### Decision

Yes. The letter of credit ordinarily is independent of the underlying contract. Therefore, if the seller presents documents that conform to what the letter of credit requires, a court will not enjoin payment on the letter of credit. Here, the seller's fraud was called to the issuing bank's attention before presentation of the drafts and documents for payment. In such a case, the idea that the letter of credit is independent of the underlying contract should not be extended to protect a fraudulent seller.

The court noted that the seller would have won if the buyer had notified the bank of the seller's fraud after the bank had paid the letter of credit.

---

## BILL OF LADING

A bill of lading is a piece of paper that a transport company gives to someone. It shows three things:

1. A receipt for goods
2. A contract to transport the goods
3. Title to or ownership of the goods

## EXAMPLE OF AN INTERNATIONAL BUSINESS DEAL: THE ART–ALI CONTRACT

First, Art and Ali entered a contract for the rugs. (Recall Art is an Atlanta buyer; Ali is an Ankara, Turkey, seller.) Second, Art arranged with his Atlanta bank to issue a letter of credit to Ali, through which Art pays Ali (see Figure 9.1).

**FIGURE 9.1  ANATOMY OF AN INTERNATIONAL BUSINESS DEAL USING A LETTER OF CREDIT AND A BILL OF LADING: THE ART–ALI CONTRACT**

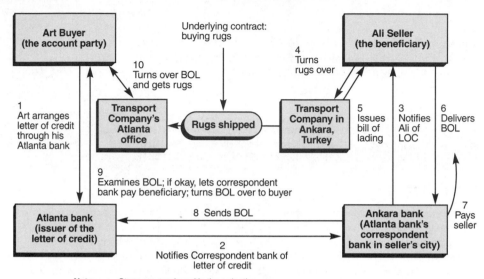

**Note:**
  a. Steps are numbered in the order they occur.
  b. The buyer (Art) is the account party of the letter of credit.
  c. The seller (Ali) is the beneficiary of the letter of credit.
  d. The buyer's bank is the issuer.
  e. The letter of credit and bill of lading are independent of the rug purchase contract.

Often the bank issuing the letter of credit arranges for another bank, called a *correspondent bank,* in the seller's city to physically issue the letter of credit to the seller. (Assume that the Atlanta bank has a correspondent bank in Ankara.) The letter of credit will set out certain conditions that the foreign seller (Ali) must meet before the seller can draw on the credit. Drawing on the credit is how the seller is paid. It happens when the seller writes a draft (a check) on the letter of credit. It can be understood by comparing the letter of credit with a checking account that someone else sets up for you. You can then write checks using someone else's money. The same thing is true for the letter of credit that the buyer of goods has set up for the foreign seller.

Next, Ali delivers the rugs to a transport company in Ankara, Turkey. The transport company gives Ali a bill of lading for the rugs. Recall that the bill of lading is three things: a receipt showing that Ali actually turned something over to the shipper, a contract where the shipper agrees to transport the rugs to Art, and a title showing that whoever has the bill of lading owns the goods. Ali turns over the bill of lading to either Art's Atlanta bank or, more likely, the Atlanta bank's correspondent bank in Ankara.

When Ali turns the bill of lading over to the Ankara bank, it pays Ali. The Ankara bank could also delay paying Ali until the Atlanta bank determines that the bill of lading conforms to the letter of credit's requirements, which would be the more cautious way for the Ankara bank to pay Ali. The Ankara bank then sends the bill of lading to Art's Atlanta bank. The Atlanta bank checks the bill of lading to see that it meets the letter of credit's terms.

Notice that Art's Atlanta bank will not check the rugs—just the bill of lading for the rugs. The contract for the rugs is independent from the letter of credit and bill of lading. If the bill of lading meets the letter of credit's requirements, Art's Atlanta bank credits the Ankara bank's account.

Art's Atlanta bank charges Art for the letter of credit. It then gives Art the bill of lading. Art takes the bill of lading to the transport company's local office and gets the rugs. The deal is complete. Ali has his money, and Art has his rugs.

## HARMONIZED TARIFF SCHEDULES

One crucial fact every business needs to know is whether the country where the good is to be imported imposes tariffs on such items, and, if they do, the amount. Tariffs can be very high—above 50 percent on some items or zero on other items such as original art works. It is interesting that a wool coat purchased for $600 in Britain incurs a higher duty than a $50 million Picasso painting.

One can find what, if any, tariffs exist on goods shipped into the United States by consulting the Harmonized Tariff Schedule of the United States. The International Trade Commission publishes this book in loose-leaf form. It has tariff rates for virtually all items. This book can usually be found in larger libraries.

## IMPORTING GRAY MARKET GOODS

*Gray market goods* refer to foreign-made goods bearing valid U.S. copyright, trademark, or other U.S. intellectual property protection that are imported into the United States without the consent of the U.S. trademark holder. At least three importing situations can give rise to gray market goods.

## CASE 1 GRAY MARKET GOODS

Here, a U.S. firm buys from an independent foreign firm both the rights to sell the foreign-made goods in the United States *and* the rights to register the foreign firm's trademark in the United States. Often the foreign manufacturer will have registered the foreign trademark in the United States. A U.S. firm would want to use the foreign firm's trademark because of the quality image associated with it. The gray market would arise if the foreign manufacturer exported its goods to the United States after having sold its trademark and the right to sell its goods in the United States to a particular U.S. firm. In such a case, the U.S. firm would be forced into intrabrand competition with the very trademark it had purchased. Intrabrand competition could also arise if the foreign manufacturer sold its products outside the United States and a third party bought them there and imported them into the United States to compete once again with a valid trademark holder of those foreign goods. U.S. Customs Service regulations outlawing case 1 gray market goods were upheld by the U.S. Supreme Court in *Kmart Corp. v. Cartier, Inc.*

## Case 2 Gray Market Goods

The second gray market situation occurs when a U.S. firm registers the U.S. trademark for goods made abroad by an affiliated manufacturer. In the most common case (called case 2a), a foreign parent firm controls U.S. distribution of its products by establishing a U.S. subsidiary. The subsidiary then registers a U.S. trademark under its own name, which is identical to the parent's foreign trademark. This type of gray market arises when a third party (such as Kmart) buys the foreign goods abroad either directly from the foreign parent or from another foreign source and imports them into the United States. U.S. discount stores such as Kmart buy from foreign parents because they can often get lower prices when the U.S. dollar is stronger than foreign currencies. Two variations on case 2 occur when a U.S. firm sets up a manufacturing subsidiary abroad (case 2b) or its own unincorporated manufacturing division (case 2c) to make its U.S. trademarked goods, and then imports them for U.S. distribution. Then the foreign subsidiary or unincorporated foreign division may sell goods to U.S. companies that are not distributors of the U.S. parent firm. Importing of this type of gray market good by affiliates of the U.S. trademark holder is allowed under U.S. Customs regulations. Estimates are that as much as 98 percent of gray market goods enter the United States in a case 2 scenario. In *Kmart Corp. v. Cartier, Inc.*, the U.S. Supreme Court upheld Customs Service regulations authorizing case 2 gray market goods by foreign affiliates of U.S. firms.

## Case 3 Gray Market Goods

The third type of gray market good occurs where a U.S. firm holding a U.S. trademark authorizes an independent foreign manufacturer the exclusive right to use the trademark in a particular foreign location, but it requires that the foreign manufacturer not import the trademarked goods into the United States. If the foreign manufacturer violates this agreement and ships the goods into the United States, or if a third party ships the goods into the United States, these foreign–made goods then compete in the United States with the U.S. manufacturer's domestic goods. This type of gray market good was declared illegal by the U.S. Supreme Court in *Kmart v. Cartier, Inc.*

## 1997 Supreme Court Case on Gray Market Goods

In 1997 the U.S. Supreme Court was again presented with situation akin to a gray market goods case, but this time the facts varied slightly: The gray market goods were manufactured in the United States and had labels bearing valid U.S. copyrights. What made the goods *gray* was the fact that the U.S. copyright holder had originally shipped the goods to foreign countries on the assumption that they would be sold there at much lower prices than in the United States, where marketing costs contributed to and justified a much higher price. The U.S. copyright holder did not want the goods shipped back to the United States, which made the goods *gray*, that is, improperly in the United States in the eyes of the U.S. manufacturer. Read the *Quality King Distributors v. L'anza Research International, Inc.* case to see whether the U.S. manufacturer was able to use the valid U.S. copyrighted labels as a basis for stopping the import of the goods. As you read the case, see whether you agree with Justice Stevens that this case is factually different enough from the *Kmart* case that it might not even involve *gray* market goods.

## Quality King Distributors, Inc. v. L'Anza Research International, Inc.
U.S. Supreme Court
523 U.S. 135 (1997)

### Background and Facts

Respondent L'anza, a California manufacturer, sells its hair care products in this country exclusively to distributors who have agreed to resell within limited geographic areas and only to authorized retailers. L'anza promotes its domestic sales with extensive advertising and special retail training. In foreign markets, however, it does not engage in comparable advertising or promotion. Its foreign prices are substantially lower than its domestic prices. It appears that after L'anza's United Kingdom distributor arranged for the sale of several tons of L'anza products, affixed with U.S. copyrighted labels, to a distributor in Malta, that distributor sold the goods to Quality King Distributors, Inc. Quality King then imported the goods back into the United States without L'anza's permission and resold them at discounted prices to U.S. dealers unauthorized by L'anza to sell its products.

L'anza filed suit alleging that Quality King's actions violated L'anza's exclusive rights under the Copyright Act of 1976, Sections 106, 501, and 602 to produce and distribute the copyrighted material in the United States. The federal district court rejected Quality King's "first sale" defense and entered judgment for L'anza. Concluding Section 602(a), which gives copyright owners the right to prohibit the unauthorized importation of copies, would be "meaningless" if Section 109(a) provided a defense, the Ninth Circuit Court of Appeals affirmed.

### Body of Opinion

**Justice Stevens.** Section 106(3) of the Copyright Act of 1976 . . . gives the owner of a copyright the exclusive right to distribute copies of a copyrighted work. That exclusive right is expressly limited, however, by the provisions of Sections 107 through 120. Section 602(a) gives the copyright owner the right to prohibit the unauthorized importation of copies. The question presented in this case is whether the right granted by Section 602(a) is also limited by Sections 107 through 120. More narrowly, the question is whether the "first sale" doctrine endorsed in Section 109(a) is applicable to imported copies. . . .

In *Bobbs-Merrill v. Straus* . . . this court held that the exclusive right to "vend" under the copyright statute then in force applied only to the first sale of a copyrighted work. Congress subsequently codified Bobbs-Merrill's first sale doctrine in the Act. Section 106(3) gives the copyright holder the exclusive right "to distribute copies . . . by sale or other transfer of ownership," but Section 109(a) provides: "Notwithstanding . . . Section 106(3), the owner of a particular copy . . . lawfully made under this title . . . is entitled, without the authority of the copyright owner, to sell or otherwise dispose of the possession of that copy." . . . Although the first sale doctrine prevents L'anza from treating unauthorized resales by its domestic distributors as an infringement of the exclusive right to distribute, L'anza claims that Section 602(a), properly construed, prohibits its foreign distributors from reselling its products to American vendors unable to buy from its domestic distributors.

The statutory language clearly demonstrates that the right granted by Section 602(a) is subject to Section 109(a). Significantly, Section 602(a) does not categorically prohibit the unauthorized importation of copyrighted materials, but provides that, with three exceptions, such "importation . . . is an infringement of the exclusive right to distribute . . . under Section 106. . . . " Section 106, in turn, expressly states that all of the exclusive rights therein granted—including the distribution right granted by Subsection (3)—are limited by Sections 107 through 120. One of those limitations is provided by Section 109(a), which expressly permits the owner of a lawfully made copy to sell that copy "notwithstanding the provisions of Section 106(3)." After the first sale of a copyrighted item "lawfully made under this title," any subsequent purchaser whether from a domestic or a foreign reseller, is obviously an "owner" of that item. Read literally, Section 109(a) unambiguously states that such an owner "is entitled, without the authority of the copyright owner, to sell" that item. Moreover, since Section 602(a) merely provides that unauthorized importation is an infringement of an exclusive right "under Section 106," and since that limited right does not encompass resales by lawful owners, Section 602(a)'s literal text is simply inapplicable to both domestic and foreign owners of L'anza's products who decide to import and resell them here. . . .

The court finds unpersuasive the Solicitor General's argument that "importation" describes an act that is not protected by Section 109(a)'s authorization to a subsequent owner "to sell or otherwise dispose of the possession of" a copy. An ordinary interpretation of that language includes the right to ship the copy to another person in another country. More important, the Solicitor General's cramped reading is at odds with Section 109(a)'s necessarily broad reach. The whole point of the first sale doctrine is that once the copyright owner places a copyrighted item in the stream of commerce by selling it, he has exhausted his exclusive statutory right to control its distribution. There is no reason to assume that Congress intended Section 109(a) to limit the doctrine's scope. . . .

### Judgment and Result

The first sale doctrine is applicable to imported copies. Thus, the U.S. copyright holder could not prevent the unauthorized import of the copyrighted goods here.

### Questions

1. What section of the Copyright Act of 1976 was L'anza relying on to stop the reshipment of the cosmetics back into the United States? What section was Quality King relying on to limit L'anza's rights under Section 602?

2. What is a gray market good? In a portion of the opinion omitted, Justice Stevens observes that ". . . we used those terms [gray market goods] to refer to the importation of foreign-manufactured goods bearing a valid U.S. trademark without the consent of the trademark holder. . . . We are not at all sure that those terms appropriately describe the consequences of an American manufacturer's decision to limit its promotional efforts to the domestic market and to sell its products abroad at discounted prices that are so low that its foreign distributors can compete in its domestic market." Is Justice Stevens saying that the *Quality King Distributors, Inc. v. L'Anza Research International, Inc.* case might not be a gray market case? Why?

3. Does the *Quality King* case exemplify a philosophy in favor of or against restraints on importation of goods? What about the copyright holder's right to limit distribution, including importation of copyrighted goods?

4. Had L'anza consigned (that is, kept title or ownership) the goods to foreign distributors and required that any foreign distributor not selling at retail in turn consign the goods to other distributors, do you think L'anza would have a stronger argument that it had the right to prevent shipment of the goods back into the United States? Why was it important to the Supreme Court that the title to the goods with the copyrighted labels had passed to the distributor? May a holder of a validly copyrighted label affixed to goods control who purchases the goods once they are sold? Why? What about consignments? What public policy is at work here?

5. What legal ethics are found in the *Quality King* decision?

6. Consider the following as a business ethics problem associated with gray market goods: Foreign manufacturers frequently sell their goods in different countries at different prices. Thus, for instance, a Japanese-made TV might be sold in Korea for $100 and in the United States for $200. In part, this market differentiation is based on the various standards of living among countries. One consequence of this differentiated pricing is that consumers in the "upscale" countries, such as the United States, are subsidizing the consumers in the lower-income countries in the sense that a U.S. consumer is contributing a higher amount to the Japanese manufacturer's development costs than is the Korean consumer. Consider this problem from the standpoint of the business ethics noted in Chapter 1.

## Other Rules Governing International Business

### The Foreign Corrupt Practices Act

In 1977 Congress passed the Foreign Corrupt Practices Act. It was amended in 1988. This act prohibits foreign corrupt practices by domestic concerns. Foreign corrupt practices are bribes. The act prohibits bribes to foreign officials (government employees) to influence official acts. For example, a U.S. company violates the act if it bribes an Iranian official to get oil drilling rights.

*Businesses Covered.* The Foreign Corrupt Practices Act (FCPA) covers businesses required to register their securities (called issuers) under the 1934 Securities Exchange Act. Covered businesses (issuers) can be corporations, partnerships, limited partnerships, business trusts, and unincorporated organizations. The FCPA also makes it illegal for any domestic concern to use the mails or interstate commerce to commit a foreign corrupt practice. Thus, the FCPA covers nonissuers of securities.

*People Covered, Penalties, and Loopholes.* People covered by the Foreign Corrupt Practices Act include an issuer's shareholders, officers, and directors who bribe to help the issuer. Violations of the Foreign Corrupt Practices Act are federal felonies. Punishments for certain individuals include five years in prison or a $100,000 fine, or both. Covered business issuers violating the act can be fined up to $2 million.

The act does not apply to the following:

1. Small bribes (called grease payments) to foreign officials
2. Bribes to private (nongovernmental) foreigners
3. Extortion payments (when the foreign official first asks for a bribe and the issuer pays it)
4. Payments that are legal under the written laws of the foreign official's country

## ACT OF STATE DOCTRINE

The Act of State Doctrine says that U.S. courts should accept foreign governments' official acts at face value. For example, if Japan gives two people a marriage license, the United States should not question its validity. This rule generally applies to a government's official acts within its territory.

*Reason for the Act of State Rule.* The act of state rule keeps U.S. courts out of foreign affairs. Under the U.S. Constitution, Congress and the president—not the courts—run foreign affairs.

*Business Example.* Suppose the government of South Africa owns all the country's diamond mines. Suppose, also, that no company can mine diamonds unless it has a government permit. If the South African government gives deBoors Company such a permit, the U.S. courts cannot say that the permit is illegal. This matter is South Africa's business, not that of the U.S. courts.

*State Securities Law Exception.* In the following case, Mr. Riedel, an Ohio resident, deposited $100,000 in a Mexican bank. He later transferred his certificate of deposit (CD) to another Mexican bank to get the certificate payable in U.S. dollars instead of Mexican pesos (which were declining in value). After he got his dollar-denominated CD, the government of Mexico issued currency regulations forcing Mexican banks to pay back depositors—both the interest and principal—only in pesos. Later, the Mexican government nationalized all that nation's banks. When the CD matured, the Mexican bank sent Riedel a check in pesos, which turned out to be worth only $53,276.63—much less than what he had deposited. He sued the Mexican bank in Ohio claiming, among other things, that the CD was a security under Ohio law; thus, the security had to be registered, which it was not. The U.S. Court of Appeals agreed with Riedel.

---

### Riedel v. Bancam, S.A.
U.S. Court of Appeals (6th Cir.)
792 F.2d 587 (1986)

**Background and Facts**

This appeal raises the question whether plaintiff-appellant, W. Christian Riedel, can maintain an action for alleged violations of Ohio securities law against defendant-appellee, Bancam, S.A. ("Bancam"), a Mexican bank that the Government of Mexico has nationalized. . . .

In January 1981, Riedel, a resident of the State of Ohio, asked Unibanco, S.A. ("Unibanco"), a Mexican bank, to transfer $100,000 to Banca Metropolitana, S.A. ("Bamesa"), another Mexican bank and a predecessor of Bancam, so that Riedel could purchase a dollar-denominated certificate of deposit from Bamesa. . . . On January 1, 1982, Bamesa and another Mexican bank merged, forming Bancam. On July 6, 1982, Riedel renewed the certificate for the last time and Bancam sent Riedel "Deposito de Dolares en Administracion a Plazo Fijo con Tasa Fija No. 077996" acknowledging an interest rate of 20.1737 percent per annum and a new maturity date of January 20, 1983. Neither Bamesa nor Bancam registered any of the certificates of deposit with either the Securities and Exchange Commission or the Ohio Division of Securities.

On August 13, 1982, the Government of Mexico issued rules governing the payment of bank deposits denominated in foreign currency which prohibited Mexican banks from using dollars to repay the holders of dollar-denominated certificates of deposit. The rules required Mexican banks to pay principal and interest on dollar-denominated deposits in pesos, at a rate of exchange substantially below the financial market exchange rate, rather than in dollars. On September 1, 1982, the Government of Mexico nationalized all privately owned Mexican banks. Consequently, Bancam, like every other banking institution in Mexico, became wholly owned by the Government of Mexico.

At maturity of the final renewal of the certificate of deposit, Bancam sent appellant a check in repayment of his certificate of deposit in the amount of 7,434,000 pesos in accordance with the exchange rate of 74.34 pesos to the dollar, the current legal exchange rate. Since the financial market exchange rate was approximately 149.5 pesos to the dollar, Riedel could only convert the 7,434,000 pesos to $53,276.63. Nevertheless, Riedel cashed the check.

On January 19, 1984, Riedel brought this action in the U.S. District Court for the Northern District of Ohio alleging violations of federal and Ohio securities laws. On June 7, 1984, Bancam filed a motion to dismiss the complaint. . . . Initially, Bancam argued that Section 4(a) of the Foreign Sovereign Immunities Act of 1976 ("FSIA"), precluded the District Court from asserting personal or subject matter jurisdiction over the action. Second, Bancam argued that the "act of state doctrine" and the Articles of Agreement of the International Monetary Fund ("Fund Agreement") required dismissal for failure to state a claim upon which the District Court could grant relief because Riedel based the action solely on the Government of Mexico's actions in issuing and enforcing currency exchange rules which required banks to repay dollar-denominated certificates of deposit in pesos. Third, Bancam contended that the complaint failed to state a cause of action because the certificates of deposit were not "securities." . . . The District Court concluded that it lacked jurisdiction over the Ohio securities law and breach of contract claims. The District Court stated that 28 U.S.C. § 1332 "does not permit a citizen of this state to sue a foreign government or agency thereof, in a federal district court."

This appeal raises several questions: (1) Whether the FSIA gives the District Court subject matter jurisdiction over Riedel's claims for breach of contract and violations of Ohio Revised Code ("ORC") Chapter 1707 ("Ohio securities law"); (2) Whether the act of state doctrine bars Riedel's claims against a Mexican bank that the Government of Mexico has nationalized.

## Body of Opinion

**Circuit Judge Cornelia G. Kennedy.** In this appeal, Riedel does not challenge the District Court's conclusion that the certificates of deposit that Bancam issued are not "securities" under federal securities law. Instead, Riedel argues that the "act of state doctrine" does not

bar his breach of contract and Ohio securities law claims. The District Court, however, did not refer to the "act of state doctrine" in denying Riedel's motion for a new trial. In addition to holding, as a matter of law, that the certificate of deposit involved in this case was not a "security" under federal securities law, the District Court ruled that it did not have jurisdiction over Riedel's breach of contract and Ohio securities law claims. The District Court concluded that: "Diversity jurisdiction pursuant to 28 U.S.C. Section 1332, does not permit a citizen of this state to sue a foreign government or agency thereof, in a federal district court." . . .

[W]e hold that the District Court properly concluded that it did not have jurisdiction under 28 U.S.C. § 1332 over the breach of contract and Ohio securities law claims.

We conclude, however, that the District Court may have had jurisdiction over the breach of contract and Ohio securities law claims under FSIA. Although the FSIA ordinarily entitles foreign states to immunity from federal jurisdiction, 28 U.S.C. § 1605(a)(2) creates a "commercial activity" exception to this immunity. Title 28 U.S.C. § 1605(a)(2) provides in pertinent part:

> A foreign state shall not be immune from the jurisdiction of courts of the United States or of the States in any case . . . in which the action is based upon commercial activity carried on in the United States by the foreign state; or upon an act performed in the United States in connection with a commercial activity of the foreign state elsewhere or upon an act outside the territory of the United States in connection with a commercial activity of the foreign state elsewhere and that act causes a direct effect in the United States.

We agree and hold that the sale of the certificates of deposit in this case was a "commercial activity." . . .

Under the "act of state doctrine," courts exercise jurisdiction but prudentially "decline to decide the merits of the case if in doing so we would need to judge the validity of the public acts of a sovereign state performed within its own territory."

In *Callejo v. Bancomer, S.A., supra,* the Fifth Circuit concluded that the "act of state doctrine" precluded the court from inquiring into the validity of Mexico's currency exchange regulations. . . . We agree with the Callejos that these securities claims are not barred by the act of state doctrine, since they are based on Bancomer's initial failure to register the certificates of deposit, not on Bancomer's later breach of the certificates by complying with Mexico's exchange control regulations. . . . We dismiss these claims, however, on the ground that the certificates of deposit sold by Bancomer were not "securities" within the meaning of the federal and Texas securities laws.

We adopt the reasoning of the *Fifth Circuit in Callejo v. Bancomer, S.A.,* regarding the "act of state doctrine." Consequently, we hold that the "act of state doctrine" precludes the District Court from addressing Riedel's breach of contract claim. Accordingly, we affirm the portion of the District Court's order denying Riedel's motion for a new trial on the breach of contract claim. The "act of state doctrine," however, does not bar the Ohio securities law claim. Riedel bases that claim on Bancam's failure to register the certificate of deposit with the Ohio Division of

Securities and not on Bancam's failure to repay dollars at the certificate's maturity.

We reject Bancam's contention that the certificates of deposit are not "securities" under ORC § 1707.01(B). Accordingly, we reverse the portion of the District Court's order denying Riedel's motion for a new trial on the Ohio securities law claim.

Since the District Court may have had subject matter jurisdiction, we remand the Ohio securities law claim for further proceedings consistent with this opinion.

## Judgment and Result

Accordingly, we affirm the portion of the District Court's order denying Riedel's motion for a new trial on the breach of contract claim, reverse the portion of the District Court's order denying Riedel's motion for a new trial on the Ohio securities law claim, and remand the Ohio securities law claim for further proceedings consistent with this opinion. (The U.S. Court of Appeals decided that despite the act of state doctrine, the plaintiff could question the legality of the Mexican government's rewriting the contracts under the Ohio securities law.)

## Questions

1. What rate of interest was Mr. Riedel earning on his certificate of deposit (CD) in the Mexican bank? Why do you suppose he was promised such a high rate of interest?
2. Is a CD a "security" under Ohio law?
3. A foreign nation that nationalizes all the banks in the country and rewrites the local banks' CD contracts to require payment of interest and principal in pesos instead of U.S. dollars, this is the act of a foreign state, giving rise to the "act of state" doctrine. Does the *Riedel* case create a state securities law exception to the act of state doctrine?
4. Did the court of appeals find that some of the acts involved in the *Riedel* case did give rise to the act of state defense?

## SETTLING INTERNATIONAL BUSINESS DISPUTES

Businesspersons who deal in the United States can often recite many problems that can ruin a business deal here. However, the difficulties increase dramatically when deals go international. Currency fluctuations, wars, confiscation, and economic boycotts all make dealing in foreign trade much riskier than conducting business domestically.

## WAYS OF SETTLING DISPUTES

Here we consider three ways of settling international disputes. Then our attention turns to two problems concerning international lawsuits by and against businesses. One deals with the Foreign Sovereign Immunities Act (FSIA) in the context of a currency devaluation, and the other deals with the *forum non conveniens* doctrine in the Bhopal Gas Plant Disaster.

*Private Settlement.* If trouble occurs with an international business deal, a person can do several things. First, the parties can work out their problems themselves, which is the less expensive, faster way to settle contract disputes. For this approach to work, the parties must be reasonable and flexible. The legal system should be avoided if possible because international litigation is filled with uncertainty and it is expensive. Most important, it can destroy a business's goodwill.

*Arbitration.* Second, the parties can put an arbitration provision in their contract. An arbitration provision names a neutral third person to settle contract disputes. Arbitration is slower and costs more than a private settlement but is faster and less expensive than suing in a court.

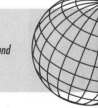

*Information about the American Arbitration Association can be found at http://www.adr.org*

*Lawsuit.* A third approach is for the parties to sue each other in court, but this process is expensive and slow. Also, finding a court that will handle international business disputes is difficult. For example, the International Court of Justice in The Hague, Netherlands, is not available for private lawsuits. Only governments can sue governments there.

One business can sue another business in a country's courts, but to do so, the business suing must locate the business sued in a country where jurisdiction exists. The parties can specify in their contracts which country's rules will apply in the settlement of contract disputes.

## SUING FOREIGN GOVERNMENTS

Foreign nations generally may not be sued. This is called the *sovereign immunity doctrine*. The U.S. Congress has enacted the Foreign Sovereign Immunities Act (FSIA), which makes foreign governments immune from suit in the United States. The FSIA has exceptions, however, which means that under certain circumstances, foreign governments *can* be sued in U.S. courts. These exceptions arise when (1) the foreign government waives (voluntarily gives up) the sovereign immunity defense, and (2) a foreign nation carries on a commercial activity in the United States.

*Riedel v. Bancam*, discussed earlier in this chapter, deals with the FSIA.

## FORUM NON CONVENIENS: WHERE TO SUE WHEN THINGS GO WRONG

*When faced with international business problems, a good resource would be the lawyer directory at http://www.martindale.com/locator/home.html*

The *forum non conveniens* doctrine is a rule of U.S. law that says that when a lawsuit may be brought in more than one court, the trial judge originally trying the case has the discretion to tell the litigants, "Go to another court; it is more convenient." The main factors the original judge should use in making that decision are matters of convenience, such as where the event giving rise to the suit occurred, where the witnesses are, and which court is more experienced in the type of litigation.

In the *Bhopal* case, victims of an industrial disaster in India sued Union Carbide Corporation (UCC) in New York City rather than in India, where the events occurred. The U.S. Court of Appeals sent the case back to India on grounds of *forum non conveniens*.

A related issue in the *Bhopal* case discusses whether the U.S. courts would have to honor an Indian court judgment against Union Carbide Corporation property *in the United States* if an attempt is made to collect that Indian judgment in the United States. The case answers yes to that question if Indian courts are impartial, their procedures are compatible with due process, and the Indian court has jurisdiction over the defendant.

Thus, U.S. courts often will enforce judgments from foreign countries' courts against U.S. businesses and individuals.

## EXPROPRIATION

*Expropriation* refers to a foreign government's seizing a business's assets in that country and giving less than fair value in return. This situation often happens following a foreign political revolution. The Iranian revolution in 1979 is an example. Millions, perhaps billions, of dollars of U.S. firms' assets were seized and inadequately paid for by the new Iranian government. Expropriation arises only if a U.S.

company has a plant or property in a foreign country. Therefore, companies in the United States do not have to worry about foreign expropriation.

## REPATRIATION

*Repatriation* means bringing back to the United States income and investments that U.S. businesses have earned or made in foreign countries. Many foreign countries lure U.S. businesses into them by telling of high profits that can be made there, sometimes forgetting to tell of limits on getting those profits back to the United States. U.S. businesses should make certain they ask whether a foreign country limits taking profits back to the United States.

---

### In Re Union Carbide Corp. Gas Plant Disaster
U.S. Court of Appeals (2nd Cir.)
809 F.2d 195 (1987)

---

### Background and Facts

This appeal raises the question of whether thousands of claims by citizens of India and the Government of India arising out of the most devastating industrial disaster in history— the deaths of over 2,000 persons and injuries of over 200,000 caused by lethal gas known as methyl isocyanate which was released from a chemical plant operated by Union Carbide India Limited (UCIL) in Bhopal, India—should be tried in the United States or in India. The Southern District of New York, John F. Keenan, *Judge*, granted the motion of Union Carbide Corporation (UCC), a defendant in some 145 actions commenced in federal courts in the United States, to dismiss these actions on grounds of *forum non conveniens* so that the claims may be tried in India, subject to certain conditions. The individual plaintiffs appeal from the order and the court's denial of their motion for a fairness hearing on a proposed settlement. UCC and the Union of India (UOI), a plaintiff, cross appeal. We eliminate two of the conditions imposed by the district court and in all other respects affirm that court's orders.

The accident occurred on the night of December 2–3, 1984, when winds blew the deadly gas from the plant operated by UCIL into densely occupied parts of the city of Bhopal. UCIL is incorporated under the laws of India. Fifty and nine-tenths percent of its stock is owned by UCC, 22 percent is owned or controlled by the government of India, and the balance is held by approximately 23,500 Indian citizens. The stock is publicly traded on the Bombay Stock Exchange. The company is engaged in the manufacture of a variety of products, including chemicals, plastics, fertilizers and insecticides, at 14 plants in India and employs over 9,000 Indian citizens. It is managed and operated entirely by Indians in India.

Four days after the Bhopal accident, on December 7, 1984, the first of some 145 purported class actions in federal district courts in the United States was commenced on behalf of victims of the disaster. On January 2, 1985, the Judicial Panel on Multidistrict Litigation assigned the actions to the Southern District of New York where they became the subject of a consolidated complaint filed on June 28, 1985.

In the meantime, on March 29, 1985, India enacted the Bhopal Gas Leak Disaster (Processing of Claims) Act, granting to its government, the UOI, the exclusive right to represent the victims in India or elsewhere. Thereupon, the UOI, purporting to act in the capacity of *parens patriae*, and with retainers executed by many of the victims, on April 8, 1985, filed a complaint in the Southern District of New York on behalf of all victims of the Bhopal disaster, similar to the purported class action complaints already filed by individuals in the United States. The UOI's decision to bring suit in the United States was attributed to the fact that, although numerous lawsuits (by now, some 6,500) had been instituted by victims in India against UCIL, the Indian courts did not have jurisdiction over UCC, the parent company, which is a defendant in the United States actions. The actions in India asserted claims not only against UCIL but also against the UOI, the State of Madhya Pradesh, and the Municipality of Bhopal, and were consolidated in the District Court of Bhopal.

By order dated April 25, 1985, Judge Keenan appointed a three-person Executive Committee to represent all plaintiffs in the pretrial proceedings. It consisted of two lawyers representing the individual plaintiffs and one representing the UOI. On July 31, 1985, UCC moved to dismiss the complaint on grounds of *forum non conveniens*, the plaintiffs' lack of standing to bring the actions in the United States, and their purported attorneys' lack of authority to represent them. After several months of discovery related to forum non conveniens, the individual plaintiffs and the UOI opposed UCC's motion. After hearing argument on January 3, 1986, the district court, on May 12, 1986, 634 F.Supp. 842, in a thoroughly reasoned 63-page opinion granted the motion, dismissing the lawsuits before it on condition that UCC:

(1) consent to the jurisdiction of the courts of India and continue to waive defenses based on the statute of limitations,

(2) agree to satisfy any judgment rendered by an Indian court against it and upheld on appeal, provided the judgment and affirmance "comport with the minimal requirements of due process," and

(3) be subject to discovery under the Federal Rules of Civil Procedure of the United States.

On June 12, 1986, UCC accepted these conditions subject to its right to appeal them; and on June 24, 1986, the district court entered its order of dismissal. In September 1986 the UOI, acting pursuant to its authority under the Bhopal Act, brought suit on behalf of all claimants against UCC and UCIL in the District Court of Bhopal, where many individual suits by victims of the disaster were then pending. . . .

India's interest is increased by the fact that it has for years treated UCIL as an Indian national, subjecting it to intensive regulations and governmental supervision of the construction, development and operation of the Bhopal plant, its emissions, water and air pollution, and safety precautions. Numerous Indian government officials have regularly conducted on-site inspections of the plant and approved its machinery and equipment, including its facilities for storage of the lethal methyl isocyanate gas that escaped and caused the disaster giving rise to the claims. Thus India has considered the plant to be an Indian one and the disaster to be an Indian problem. It therefore has a deep interest in ensuring compliance with its safety standards. Moreover, plaintiffs have conceded that in view of India's strong interest in its greater contacts with the plant, its operations, its employees, and the victims of the accident, the law of India, as the place where the tort occurred, will undoubtedly govern. In contrast, the American interests are relatively minor. Indeed, a long trial of the 145 cases here would unduly burden an already overburdened court, involving both jury hardship and heavy expense. It would face the court with numerous practical difficulties, including the almost impossible task of attempting to understand extensive relevant Indian regulations published in a foreign language and the slow process of receiving testimony of scores of witnesses through interpreters.

Having made the foregoing findings, Judge Keenan dismissed the actions against UCC on grounds of *forum non conveniens* upon the conditions indicated, after obtaining UCC's consent to those conditions subject to its right to appeal the order. After the plaintiffs filed their notice of appeal, UCC and the Union of India filed cross appeals.

Upon these appeals, the plaintiffs continue to oppose the dismissal. The Union of India, however, has changed its position and now supports the district court's order. UCC, as it did in the district court, opposes as unfair the condition that it submit to discovery pursuant to the Federal Rules of Civil Procedure without reciprocally obligating the plaintiffs and Union of India to be subject to discovery on the same basis so that both sides might be treated equally, giving each the same access to the facts in the others' possession.

Upon argument of the appeal, UCC also took the position that the district court's order requiring it to satisfy any Indian court judgment was unfair unless some method were provided, such as continued availability of the district court as a forum, to ensure that any denial of due process by the Indian courts could be remedied promptly by the federal court here rather than delay resolution of the issue until termination of the Indian court proceedings and appeal, which might take several years. UCC's argument in this respect was based on the sudden issuance by the Indian court in Bhopal of a temporary order freezing all of UCC's assets, which could have caused it irreparable injury if it had been continued indefinitely, and by the conflict of interest posed by the UOI's position in the Indian courts where, since the UOI would appear both as a plaintiff and a defendant, it might as a plaintiff voluntarily dismiss its claims against itself as a defendant or, as a co-defendant with UCC, be tempted to shed all blame upon UCC even though the UOI had in fact been responsible for supervision, regulation and safety of UCIL's Bhopal plant.

## Body of Opinion

### Circuit Judge Mansfield. 

The standard to be applied in reviewing the district court's forum non conveniens dismissal was clearly expressed by the Supreme Court in *Piper Aircraft Co. v. Reyno*, . . . as follows:

> The *forum non conveniens* determination is committed to the sound discretion of the trial court. It may be reversed only when there has been a clear abuse of discretion; where the court has considered all relevant public and private interest factors, and where its balancing of these factors is reasonable, its decision deserves substantial deference.

Having reviewed Judge Keenan's detailed decision, in which he thoroughly considered the comparative adequacy of the forums and the public and private interests involved, we are satisfied that there was no abuse of discretion in his granting dismissal of the action. On the contrary, it might reasonably be concluded that it would have been an abuse of discretion to deny a *forum non conveniens* dismissal. . . . Practically all relevant factors demonstrate that transfer of the cases to India for trial and adjudication is both fair and just to the parties.

Plaintiffs' principal contentions in favor of retention of the cases by the district court are that deference to the plaintiffs' choice of forum has been inadequate, that the Indian courts are insufficiently equipped for the task, that UCC has its principal place of business here, that the most probative evidence regarding negligence and causation is to be found here, that federal courts are much better equipped through experience and procedures to handle such complex actions efficiently than are Indian courts, and that a transfer of the cases to India will jeopardize a $350 million settlement being negotiated by plaintiffs' counsel. All of these arguments, however, must be rejected. . . .

Although the plaintiffs' American counsel may at one time have been close to reaching a $350 million settlement of the cases, no such settlement was ever finalized. No draft joint stipulation in writing or settlement agreement appears to have been prepared, much less approved by the parties. No petition for certification of a settlement class under Fed.R.Civ.P. 23 has ever been presented. . . . Most important, the UOI, which is itself a plaintiff and states that it now represents the Indian plaintiffs formerly represented by American counsel, is firmly opposed to the $350 million "settlement" as inadequate. Under these circumstances, to order a Rule 23 "fairness" hearing would be futile. The district court's denial of the American counsels' motion for such a hearing must accordingly be affirmed. . . .

As the district court found, the record shows that the private interests of the respective parties weigh heavily in favor of dismissal on grounds of *forum non conveniens*. The many witnesses and sources of proof are almost entirely located in India, where the accident occurred, and could not be compelled to appear for trial in the United States. The Bhopal plant at the time of the accident was operated by some 193 Indian nationals, including the managers of seven operating units employed by the Agricultural Products Division of UCIL, who reported to Indian Works Managers in Bhopal. The plant was maintained by seven functional departments employing over 200 more Indian nationals. UCIL kept at the plant daily, weekly and monthly records of plant operations and records of maintenance as well as records of the plant's Quality Control, Purchasing and Stores branches, all operated by Indian employees. The great majority of documents bearing on the design, safety, start-up and operation of the plant, as well as the safety training of the plant's employees, is located in India. Proof to be offered at trial would be derived from interviews of these witnesses in India and study of the records located there to determine whether the accident was caused by negligence on the part of the management or employees in the operation of the plant, by fault in its design, or by sabotage. In short, India has greater ease of access to the proof than does the United States.

The plaintiffs seek to prove that the accident was caused by negligence on the part of UCC in originally contributing to the design of the plant and its provision for storage of excessive amounts of the gas at the plant. As Judge Keenan found, however, UCC's participation was limited and its involvement in plant operations terminated long before the accident. Under 1973 agreements negotiated at arm's-length with UCIL, UCC did provide a summary "process design package" for construction of the plant and the services of some of its technicians to monitor the progress of UCIL in detailing the design and erecting the plant. However, the UOI controlled the terms of the agreements and precluded UCC from exercising any authority to "detail design, erect and commission the plant," which was done independently over the period from 1972 to 1980 by UCIL process design engineers who supervised, among many others, some 55 to 60 Indian engineers employed by the Bombay engineering firm of Humphreys and Glasgow. The preliminary process design information furnished by UCC could not have been used to construct the plant. Construction required the detailed process design and engineering data prepared by hundreds of Indian engineers, process designers and subcontractors. During the ten years spent constructing the plant, its design and configuration underwent many changes.

The vital parts of the Bhopal plant, including its storage tank, monitoring instrumentation, and vent gas scrubber, were manufactured by Indians in India. Although some 40 UCIL employees were given some safety training at UCC's plant in West Virginia, they represented a small fraction of the Bhopal plant's employees. The vast majority of plant employees were selected and trained by UCIL in Bhopal. The manual for start-up of the Bhopal plant was prepared by Indians employed by UCIL.

In short, the plant has been constructed and managed by Indians in India. No Americans were employed at the plant at the time of the accident. In the five years from 1980 to 1984, although more than 1,000 Indians were employed at the plant, only one American was employed there and he left in 1982. No Americans visited the plant for more than one year prior to the accident, and during the five-year period before the accident the communications between the plant and the United States were almost nonexistent.

The vast majority of material witnesses and documentary proof bearing on causation of and liability for the accident is located in India, not the United States, and would be more accessible to an Indian court than to a United States court. The records are almost entirely in Hindi or other Indian languages, understandable to an Indian court without translation. The witnesses for the most part do not speak English but Indian languages understood by an Indian court but not by an American court. These witnesses could be required to appear in an Indian court but not in a court of the United States. Although witnesses in the United States could not be subpoenaed to appear in India, they are comparatively few in number and most are employed by UCC which, as a party, would produce them in India, with lower overall transportation costs than if the parties were to attempt to bring hundreds of Indian witnesses to the United States. Lastly, Judge Keenan properly concluded that an Indian court would be in a better position to direct and supervise a viewing of the Bhopal plant, which was sealed after the accident. Such a viewing could be of help to a court in determining liability issues.

The first condition, that UCC consent to the Indian court's personal jurisdiction over it and waive the statute of limitations as a defense, are not unusual and have been imposed in numerous cases where the foreign court would not provide an adequate alternative in the absence of such a condition. . . . The remaining two conditions, however, pose problems.

In requiring that UCC consent to enforceability of an Indian judgment against it, the district court proceeded at least in part on the erroneous assumption that, absent such a requirement, the plaintiffs, if they should succeed in obtaining an Indian judgment against UCC, might not be able to enforce it against UCC in the United States. The law, however, is to the contrary. Under New York law, which governs actions brought in New York to enforce foreign judgments, . . . a foreign-country judgment that is final, conclusive and enforceable where rendered must be recognized and will be enforced as "conclusive between the parties to the extent that it grants or denies recovery of a sum of money" except that it is not deemed to be conclusive if:

(1) the judgment was rendered under a system which does not provide impartial tribunals or procedures compatible with the requirements of due process of law;

(2) the foreign court did not have personal jurisdiction over the defendant. . . .

UCC contends that Indian courts, while providing an adequate alternative forum, do not observe due process standards that would be required as a matter of course in this country. As evidence of this apprehension it points to the haste with which the Indian court in Bhopal issued a temporary order freezing its assets throughout the world and the possibility of serious prejudice to it if the UOI is permitted to have the double and conflicting staphhtus of both plaintiff and co-defendant in the Indian court proceedings. It argues that we should protect it against such denial of due process by authorizing Judge Keenan to retain the authority, after *forum non conveniens* dismissal of the cases here, to monitor the Indian court proceedings and be available on call to rectify in some undefined way any abuses of UCC's right to due process as they might occur in India.

UCC's proposed remedy is not only impractical but evidences an abysmal ignorance of basic jurisdictional principles, so much so that it borders on the frivolous. The district court's jurisdiction is limited to proceedings before it in this country. Once it dismisses those proceedings on grounds of *forum non conveniens* it ceases to have any further jurisdiction over the matter unless and until a proceeding may some day be brought to enforce here a final and conclusive Indian money judgment. Nor could we, even if we attempted to retain some sort of supervisory jurisdiction, impose our due process requirements upon Indian courts, which are governed by their laws, not ours. The concept of shared jurisdictions is both illusory and unrealistic. The parties cannot simultaneously submit to both jurisdictions the resolution of the pretrial and trial issues when there is only one consolidated case pending in one court. Any denial by the Indian courts of due process can be raised by UCC as a defense to the plaintiffs' later attempt to enforce a resulting judgment against UCC in this country.

## Judgment and Result

For these reasons we direct that the condition with respect to the discovery of UCC under the Federal Rules of Civil Procedure be deleted without prejudice to the right of the parties to have reciprocal discovery of each other on equal terms under the Federal Rules, subject to such approval as may be required of the Indian court in which the case will be pending. If, for instance, Indian authorities will permit mutual discovery pursuant to the Federal Rules, the district court's order, as modified in accordance with this opinion, should not be construed to bar such procedure. In the absence of such a court-sanctioned agreement, however, the parties will be limited by the applicable discovery rules of the Indian court in which the claims will be pending.

As so modified the district court's order is affirmed. (The U.S. Court of Appeals transferred this case to India.)

## Questions

1. Is it basically up to the discretion of the trial judge where the case is first brought to decide whether it should be sent to some other court because of *forum non conveniens*?

2. Where did the major event giving rise to the case occur? Where were the plant, the victims, and the witnesses?

3. What argument could be made for trying the Bhopal disaster case in New York City?

4. Would a New York or Bhopal jury be more likely to bring in a large damage verdict in the plaintiffs' favor?

5. What did the U.S. Court of Appeals do with the first condition, that Union Carbide Corporation (UCC) consent to the Indian court's personal jurisdiction over it and give up (waive) the statute of limitations as a defense? Do you think it is fair that a foreign nation such as India should be able to force a business to give up a defense it otherwise would have in the United States?

6. Why did the U.S. Court of Appeals knock out the trial court's second condition, that UCC must agree that an Indian court's judgment against UCC (should one be given) would bind UCC if the plaintiffs tried to enforce that judgment against UCC's property in the United States?

7. What reason did the U.S. Court of Appeals give for deleting the condition that UCC be subject to discovery in India according to United States—not Indian—rules of discovery? Can a U.S. court tell another nation's court system what procedural rules to use?

8. After this case the Indian government as representative of the victims filed a $3.3 billion lawsuit in an Indian court against UCC. That lower court rendered an interim decision against UCC in which UCC was told to pay immediately to the victims $270 million *before* final resolution of UCC's liability. UCC appealed this to an Indian appellate court, which on April 4, 1988, reduced to $195 million in immediate interim damages. In so doing the judge found UCC's liability adequately proven even though UCC argued that *no trial* had as yet determined that UCC was liable. Some see this decision as increasing the likelihood of a settlement. The $195 million award was to be divided as follows: $1,950 each for the minor injury victims, $3,900 each for the more seriously injured, and $7,800 each for survivors of the deceased or those suffering the most serious injuries. About 520,000 claims have been filed, but UCC claims that many are fraudulent. Even though the appellate court in India reduced the verdict by $75 million, it apparently went further in declaring that there was more than a prima facie case against UCC. UCC has argued that sabotage caused the disaster.

In 1989, the government of India and Union Carbide entered an agreement capping UC's damages to all Indian victims at $470 million. This settlement occurred after the Supreme Court of India decreed the award.

## CHAPTER SUMMARY

International business deals often use letters of credit and bills of lading to promote trust between the parties. Although letters of credit are independent of the underlying contract, under some circumstances courts will stop payment on *irrevocable* letters of credit.

Gray market goods refer to foreign-made goods bearing a valid U.S. trademark, which are shipped into the United States without the consent of the U.S. trademark holder. Most gray market goods are legally shipped into the United States. A Supreme Court decision tells us that U.S.-made goods with a copyrighted U.S. label may be shipped back into the United States without approval of the U.S. copyright owner if a legal "first sale" of the goods abroad has been transacted.

The Foreign Corrupt Practices Act makes it illegal for certain persons connected with U.S. corporations to use the mails or interstate commerce to bribe a foreign government official. This act exempts "grease" payments and certain other payments to foreigners.

## MANAGER'S ETHICAL DILEMMA

Bill Foster knew that his job was on the line. He had been the top salesperson for Airpower Company in Seattle, Washington, for several years, but this year was terrible. He sold international jumbo jets for passenger services, mainly concentrating his efforts in the Middle East and Far Eastern markets. International competitors, especially the European consortium, Flybus, was somehow winning orders that Bob had formerly obtained. He learned of the underlying reasons for his competitors' success during a conversation in a hotel bar in Bahrain, when a friend remarked, "Bob, you've got to start playing ball with some of these foreign buyers."

"What do you mean?" asked Bob.

"Payola, old boy. It works every time," said Pierre Goldfinger of France. "You simply make the foreign buyer a "consultant" and he pushes his client—usually a government-run airline—to buy your product, even if it is more expensive."

"But why would a foreign buyer's agent purchase a product that is more expensive than the European model?" quizzed Bill.

"Oh, that's an easy one. Simply point out that your company has higher-quality products. Foreign buyers don't want to have a plane crash on their hands with hundreds of angry relatives complaining that the government's procurement policies cost them their loved ones," rejoined Pierre.

"But Pierre, bribery of foreign government officials is illegal under U.S. law," Bill observed.

"Ah, you Americans are, how you say, 'hung up on legalities.' When in Rome, do as the Romans do, Bill. Everybody bribes a little, and it's for a good cause. Think of all of those American jobs you'd be saving in Seattle, to say nothing of your own." Pierre said, "Further, if other nations' laws do not forbid bribery of government officials, why should you be put at a disadvantage by your own country?"

Should Bill Foster "join the club" and bribe to get foreign government business as his foreign competitors appear to be doing?

## DISCUSSION QUESTIONS

1. This chapter quoted the *Kmart v. Cartier* case to define a gray market good as a foreign-made good bearing a valid U.S. trademark that is imported into the United States without the consent of the owner of that mark. What is it about the *Quality King Distributors, Inc. v. L'anza* case that might make one hesitant to conclude that the *Quality King* case is a gray market case? If the term *gray market* is not statutorily defined but, rather, is federal common law, might not the term be subject to interpretation and consequently given a broader definition by a later case such as *Quality King*? How much did the Supreme Court rely on the term *gray market good* in *Quality King* to make its decision?

2. This chapter showed the mechanics of an international contract between a U.S. buyer and a foreign seller. Describe how the deal would work if the foreign business had bought and the U.S. business had

sold. Who would arrange for the letter of credit? Who would draw on the letter of credit? Who would get the bill of lading? What would this person do with the bill of lading?

3. Suppose Art, the rug dealer in the scenario in this chapter, gets into a dispute with Ali, the Turkish rug seller. Why would Art not take the case to the International Court of Justice in The Hague, Netherlands?

4. What is a bill of lading?

5. Name the parties in a letter of credit and explain their function.

6. Why, as a practical matter, do people use letters of credit and bills of lading instead of dealing more directly with one another in international business?

7. If a beneficiary of a letter of credit presents fraudulent documents to the confirming bank to draw on the letter of credit, this act of fraud entitles an account party to get a court to enjoin payment under the letter of credit.

A letter of credit covered shipments of sugar. The letter provided that drafts were to be drawn under it only when invoices and warehouse receipts showed the sugar's "net landed weight." The invoices and receipts were presented to the bank, and credit was sought. The sugar was not actually weighed until four days after the request for credit. The buyer sued to enjoin (stop) the bank from issuing credit under the letter of credit. The seller of the sugar, attempting to get credit under the letter of credit, claimed that the bank *had* to honor the letter of credit because the seller presented the bank with documents that the letter of credit required. The buyer of the sugar, argued that there was fraud because the letter of credit required the seller to have the sugar weighed and to present a weight certificate to the bank before credit would be given. Because the seller presented the weight certificate to the bank four days *before* the sugar was officially weighed, the buyer claimed that this action was clearly fraudulent, justifying a court in enjoining the confirming bank from giving credit under the letter

of credit. Who was correct, buyer or seller? [*Old Colony Trust Co. v. Lawyers' Title and Trust Co.*, 297 F. 152 (2d Cir. 1924)].

8. Did Congress intend to do away with the act of state doctrine in private lawsuits where someone says that violations of the Foreign Corrupt Practices Act have occurred? In one case, Clayco Petroleum Corporation sued Occidental Petroleum Corporation (Oxy), claiming that Oxy's agents bribed a government official of the country of Umm Al Qaywayn unlawfully to obtain an offshore oil concession. Clayco claimed that in September 1969, Sheikh Ahmed (the ruler) told Clayco that it would get the oil concession. Clayco claimed that Oxy got the concession because Oxy bribed Ahmed. The Foreign Corrupt Practices Act prohibits corporations covered by the 1934 Securities Exchange Act or their agents from bribing foreign officials to get or keep business. Should Sheikh Ahmed's action in giving Oxy the oil concession be presumed legal as the act of state doctrine would require, or does the Foreign Corrupt Practices Act allow a U.S. court to examine the motives of a foreign government's giving the oil concession to Oxy? [*Clayco Petroleum Corp. v. Occidental Petroleum Corp.*, 712 F.2d 404 (9th Cir. 1983)].

## INFOTRAC KEYWORDS

**Use your InfoTrac password to look up articles on http://www.infotrac-college.com**

Keywords: *Gray market goods, Foreign Corrupt Practices Act, Act of State Doctrine, forum non conveniens, expropriation, repatriation.*

For suggested readings, please visit this book's Web site at **http://fisher.westbuslaw.com** (click on "Internet Applications").

# MODULE 3

# PRIVATE LAW AFFECTING ENTREPRENEURS

# TORTS: NEGLIGENCE, STRICT LIABILITY, AND INTENTIONAL TORTS

## POSITIVE LAW ETHICAL PROBLEMS

"It violates the University of Evansville's right of privacy for a former professor to use its name and abbreviation UE for his Web site and e-mail addresses," argued a UE official.

"No way," retorted William Felsher, a former UE professor. "I haven't violated UE's right of privacy by appropriating its name or likeness. UE is a corporation. Corporations have no right of privacy."

Do corporations have a common law right of privacy?

"My ex-husband tricked me. Before we signed the property settlement as part of our divorce, he represented that he had much less property than he actually had. As a result, I signed a property settlement agreement for about $500,000 less than I should have. But since I signed that agreement after my own attorney examined it, I guess that I am bound by it and can't get out of it," said Barbara Wilcox to her neighbor Beatrice Kayser. Is Ms. Wilcox correct?

"Texaco has just committed the largest wrong in the history of mankind," said a bystander to Mr. James Kinnear, president of Texaco. Mr. Kinnear was dumbfounded. A Texas jury had just returned a verdict of $10.53 billion, the largest verdict in the history of the law, against Texaco and in favor of Pennzoil. The jury had found that Texaco had wrongfully interfered with a contract Pennzoil had with Getty Oil. This history was not the kind Mr. Kinnear wanted to make. He told his lawyer to appeal the result because the trial had many questionable aspects, including the fact that the alleged Getty–Pennzoil contract was not even written and that the trial judge in the case had received a $10,000 campaign contribution from Pennzoil's attorney *after* the case had been assigned to the judge. Surely all of these facts would come out and would cause an appellate court to upset this outrageous miscarriage of justice, Mr. Kinnear thought. Was he right?

*"TORT LAW IS A LEGAL LABORATORY."*

—**PROSSER AND KEETON**
TORTS, 5TH ED.

Today, businesses face billion-dollar judgments based on tort law. Tort law is a major area of legal theories where liability results mainly from judges' opinions. This chapter surveys three major common law tort categories: negligence, strict liability, and intentional torts. (Refer to Figure 2.2 in Chapter 2 to visualize how torts "fit" into the legal system.)

## WHAT IS A TORT?

A tort is a breach of a noncontractual civil duty for which a court will provide a remedy. The word *tort* comes from the French word meaning to twist. In other words, torts are wrongs, or actions that are not straight but twisted. Torts are *civil wrongs*. Slander, libel, negligence, and fraud are examples of civil wrongs, which individuals do to other individuals (as opposed to society as a whole, which are criminal and not civil wrongs).

## PLACING TORTS IN GENERAL BUSINESS LAW

Figure 2.2 in Chapter 2 presents an overview of civil and criminal law. The negligence and strict liability areas show the placement of these torts. As you can see, such torts are civil, not criminal substantive law.

*This Web site provides abstracts to law review articles on various topics including torts:* **http://legalminds. lp.findlaw.com/**

Tort law is mainly state law; however, the Federal Tort Claims Act (FTCA) allows persons to sue the U.S. government for certain torts that its agents commit. It is possible for something to be a tort in one state but not another; and even if a particular tort (such as slander) exists in all states, each of the 50 states could define it differently. Although this inconsistency creates the opportunity for great diversity, not much variation exists from state to state in their torts and how they are defined. Some states, such as California and New York, however, often recognize new legal wrongs sooner than others.

The common law tradition is that judges make most tort law; that is, judges decide what is a "wrong," or a tort, and thereby determine community standards of right and wrong.

## TORTS COMPARED WITH CRIMES

Torts and crimes have differences and similarities, and they sometimes overlap. One similarity is that both try to stop wrongful conduct. An area of overlap is that some acts, such as striking another in anger, could be both a tort (battery) and a crime (criminal battery).

*For a Web site supported by Stanford and Cornell Law Schools, which has abstracts on legal topics including torts, go to* **http://www. lawreview.org**

However, torts differ from crimes in several ways. First, a person owes tort duties to another person. A person owes a duty to society not to commit crimes. This distinction, however, is not completely satisfactory because one owes tort duties to all individuals, which in a sense is society. Another difference between torts and crimes is who enforces them. It is society's representative, such as the district attorney, who enforces criminal law, whereas the injured victim enforces tort law. Of course, government as a representative of society can sue a person in tort for damages to government property.

Tort and criminal law also differ in their objectives. One of the objectives of criminal law is to punish. Tort law is usually compensatory, designed to restore the victim's position prior to the commission of the tort. Occasionally, tort remedies include punitive damages designed to punish the person committing the tort.

## TORT LAW IS A LEGAL LABORATORY

Tort law has been called a legal laboratory because courts' (judges') ideas change about what a tort is. For example, at one time invasion of privacy was not a tort but today it is. Also, certain torts apply to more situations now than they once did.

For instance, strict liability first applied to water leaking onto another's property and causing damage. Today it also arises regarding defective products, handling wild animals, flying airplanes, and other situations.

Tort law has been a growing trend, part of a tendency within the courts to recognize new kinds of wrongs.

## TORT CLASSIFICATIONS

Torts can be classified in several ways. One classification—property torts and torts against the person—focuses on the victim.

*Type of Victim: Property/Person.* Property torts include trespass and conversion, while torts against persons include assault and battery. In a way, all torts are against people because people own property and sue if it is damaged.

*Type of Wrong.* Another tort classification looks at the type of wrong. Torts can involve carelessness (negligence), ultrahazardous activities (strict liability), or be intentional in nature.

This chapter discusses negligence, strict liability, and intentional torts.

## NEGLIGENCE[1]

For a Web site that directs one to negligence cases, go to **http://www.yahoo.com/ government/law**

**Negligence** involves carelessness that injures others. It is a tort that can occur almost anywhere—while driving a car, doing an audit, or supervising one's children. Negligence has four parts: (1) duty, (2) breaking of the standard of care, (3) proximate cause, and (4) damages. All four parts must exist for negligence to occur.

## DUTY

The duty part of negligence usually arises by *operation of the law*, meaning that a court or legislature says a person owes a duty of care to others. People do not have to pay each other $2 per month to create these duties. The duty to drive carefully (as in most activities) arises automatically because a lawmaker says so.

Occasionally, however, the duty of care does arise by contract. For example, **malpractice** cases, which are, technically speaking, negligence suits, are brought against professionals such as physicians, lawyers, engineers, architects, veterinaries, and accountants who have not performed their contractual duties to their clients with requisite care. In other words, the duty to be careful *to the client* does generally arise by contract in the case of professionals, because the client *hired* the accountants, for example, to audit its financial statements. If, on the one hand, the accountants did it carelessly and made many errors, the accountants have broken their duty of care to the client, who could recover against the accountants for negligence.

On the other hand, what if the client had shown the poorly prepared financial statements to its bank to get a loan? The bank relies on the financial statements, makes the loan, the business goes bankrupt and does not repay the bank, and the

---

[1] Negligence is also discussed in Chapter 23 on product liability.

bank sues the accountants for negligently preparing the financial statements. Note that the bank never hired the accountants, so the accountants will defend by invoking the **privity rule**. The privity rule says that accountants only have a duty of care to people who hire them. In recent times, however, courts have created exceptions to the privity rule, making accountants liable for their negligence to more people than just their clients. Read the *First Florida Bank v. Max Mitchell & Co.* case to see what a major state's supreme court did when a third party (a bank) sued the accountants for negligently auditing its client's books, and the accountants raised the privity defense.

---

### First Fla. Bank v. Max Mitchell & Co.
Supreme Court of Florida
558 So.2d 9 (Fla. 1990)

### Background and Facts

Max Mitchell is a certified public accountant and president of Max Mitchell and Company, P.A. In April of 1985, Mitchell went to First Florida Bank for the purpose of negotiating a loan on behalf of his client, C. M. Systems, Inc. Mitchell advised Stephen Hickman, the bank vice-president, that he was a certified public accountant and delivered to Hickman audited financial statements of C. M. Systems for the fiscal years ending October 31, 1983, and October 31, 1984, which had been prepared by his firm. The October 1, 1984, audited statement indicated that C. M. Systems had total assets of $3,474,336 and total liabilities of $1,296,823. It did not indicate that C. M. Systems owed money to any bank, and in a later conference with Hickman, Mithcell stated that as of April 16, 1985, C. M. Systems was not indebted to any bank. At that time, Mitchell asked Hickman to consider a $500,000 line of credit for C. M. Systems.

Over the next several weeks, Mitchell had numerous discussions with Hickman concerning various line items in Hitchell's audit of C. M. Systems. Mitchell represented that he was thoroughly familiar with the financial condition of C. M. Systems. On May 23, 1985, Hickman asked Mitchell for interim financial statements for the period which ended on April 30, 1985. Mitchell advised that they would not be available for several more weeks. Hickman asked Mitchell if there had been any material change in the company's financial condition since October 31, 1984, and Mitchell said that he was not aware of any material changes. On June 6, 1985, the bank approved the request for a $500,000 unsecured line of credit to C. M. Systems. Thereafter, C. M. Systems borrowed the entire amount of the $500,000 credit line, which it has never repaid.

Subsequently, the bank discovered that the audit of C. M. Systems for the fiscal year ending October 31, 1984, had substantially overstated the assets, understated the liabilities, and overstated net income. Among other things, the audit failed to reflect that as of October 31, 1984, C. M. Systems owed at least $750,000 to several banks. In addition, several material changes had occurred in the company's balance sheet after the audit but prior to the approval of the line of credit.

The bank filed a three-count complaint against Mitchell and his firm. Because of the absence of privity between either Mitchell or his firm and the bank, the trial court granted Mitchell summary judgment on the negligence and gross negligence counts. The bank voluntarily dismissed the count based on fraud. Believing itself bound by prior decisional law of the state, the district court of appeal affirmed. Recognizing the public policy implications of the issue and the erosion of the privity doctrine in other areas of the law, the court posed the certified question for our consideration.

### Body of Opinion

**Judge Grimes.** The seminal case on this subject is *Ultramares Corp v. Touche*, . . . (1931), authored by Justice Cardozo. In that case the court held that a lender which had relied upon inaccurate financial statements to its detriment had no cause of action against the public accounting firm which had prepared them because of the lack of privity between the parties. In declining to relax the requirement of privity, the court observed:

> If liability for negligence exists, a thoughtless slip or blunder, the failure to detect a theft or forgery beneath the cover of deceptive entries, may expose accountants to a liability in an indeterminant [sic] amount for an indeterminant [sic] time to an indeterminant [sic] class. The hazards of a business conducted on these terms are so extreme as to enkindle doubt whether a flaw may not exist in the implication of a duty that exposes to these consequences.

. . . The court distinguished its earlier decision of *Glanzer v. Shephard*, . . . (1922), in which it had held that a public weigher was liable to the buyer of beans for the amount the buyer overpaid the seller in reliance on the weigher's erroneous certificate of weight. The court said that the use of the certificate was a consequence "which to the weigher's knowledge was the end and aim of the transaction,". . . and reasoned that, unlike the case before it, the bond between the weigher and the buyer "was so close as to approach that of privity, if not completely one with it." *Ultramares.* . . .

In purporting to reach a decision within the parameters of *Ultramares* and *Glanzer*, the New York Court of Appeals in *Credit Alliance Corp. v. Arthur Andersen & Co.*, . . . (1985), recently explained the circumstances under which recovery may be accomplished by persons in "near privity":

> Before accountants may be held liable in negligence to noncontractual parties who rely to their detriment on inaccurate financial reports, certain prerequisites must be satisfied: (1) the accountants must have been aware that the financial reports were to be used for a particular purpose or purposes; (2) in the furtherance of which a known party or parties was intended to rely; and (3) there must have been some conduct on the part of the accountants linking them to that party or parties, which envinces the accountants' understanding of that party or parties' reliance.

In the more than 50 which have elapsed since *Ultramares*, the question of an accountant's liability for negligence where no privity exists has been addressed by many courts. There are now essentially four lines of authority with respect to this issue.

(1) Except in cases of fraud, an accountant is only liable to one with whom he is in privity or near privity. . . .

(2) An accountant is liable to third parties in the absence of privity under the circumstances described in Section 552, *Restatement (Second) of Torts* (1976), which reads in pertinent part:

### § 552. Information Negligently Supplied for the Guidance of Others

(1) One who, in the course of his business, profession or employment, or in any other transaction in which he has a pecuniary interest, supplies false information for the guidance of others in their business transactions, is subject to liability for pecuniary loss caused to them by their justifiable reliance on the information, if he fails to exercise reasonable care or competence in obtaining or communicating the information.

(2) Except as stated in Subsection (3), the liability stated in Subsection (1) is limited to loss suffered:

 (a) by the person or one of a limited group of persons for whose benefit and guidance he intends to supply the information or knows that the recipient intends to supply it; and

 (b) through reliance upon it in a transaction that he intends the information to influence or knows that the recipient so intends or in a substantially similar transaction.

(3) An accountant is liable to all persons who might reasonably be foreseen as relying upon his work product. . . .

(4) An accountant's liability to third persons shall be determined by the balancing of various factors, among which are the extent to which the transaction was intended to affect the plaintiff, the foreseeability of harm to him, the degree of certainty that the plaintiff suffered injury, the closeness of the connection between the defendant's conduct and the injury suffered, the moral blame attached to the defendant's conduct, and the policy of preventing future harm. . . .

Some of the competing interests involved in selecting the proper standard for accountants' liability to third parties are set forth in Annotation, *Liability of Public Accountant to Third Parties*, 46 A.L.R.3d . . . (1972):

> It is contended by those favoring such liability that accountants, due to their professional status and the respect they command, invite reliance on their work by the business community, and that investors and creditors do, in fact, rely upon their accuracy and integrity; on the other hand, it is pointed out that unlike members of other professions, accountants have no control over the identity or number of those who rely on their work, and that imposition of liability, in negligence to third parties would place an enormous potential burden on the profession. Those in favor of expanding liability argue that the accounting profession no longer needs the protection of nonliability in this area, due to its wealth, and contend that the cost of insurance protection could be passed on to the client, stating that the innocent relier should not be damaged because of the error of the negligent accountant. In reply, it is observed that the cost of such insurance protection is prohibitive and, in many cases, that such coverage is not available at any price; furthermore, it is said, such higher costs would tend to lead to dominance of the profession by the large national accounting firms and to a curtailment of the availability of accountancy services to small businesses. Nor, it is contended, does the argument for extended liability take into consideration the ever more acute shortage of qualified public accountants in private practice. Those in favor of expanding liability argue that liability could easily be limited by the increased use of disclaimers and limited certifications, pointing to the success of the British experience in this area. Opponents, however, observe that the use of such devices is a commercial impossibility unless all accountants follow this practice, since it tends to dissatisfy the client, who will then turn to the use of other accountants not following this practice.

Upon consideration, we have decided to adopt the rationale of Section 552, *Restatement (Second) of Torts* (1976), as setting forth the circumstances under which accountants may be held liable in negligence to persons who are not in contractual privity. The rule shall also apply to allegations of gross negligence, but the absence of privity shall continue to be no bar to charges of fraud.

Because of the heavy reliance upon audited financial statements in the contemporary financial world, we believe permitting recovery only from those in privity or near privity is unduly restrictive. On the other hand, we are persuaded by the wisdom of the rule which limits liability to those persons or classes of persons whom an accountant "knows" will rely on his opinion rather than those he "should have known" would do so because it takes into account the fact that an accountant controls neither his client's accounting records nor the distribution of his reports. As noted by the North Carolina Supreme Court when it adopted a similar position in *Raritan River Steel Co. v. Cherry, Bekaert & Holland*, . . . (1988):

> We conclude that the standard set forth in the *Restatement (Second) of Torts* § 552 (1977) represents the soundest approach to accountants' liability for negligent misrepresentation. It constitutes a middle ground between the restrictive

*Ultramares* approach advocated by defendants and the expansive "reasonably foreseeable" approach advocated by plaintiffs. It recognizes that liability should extend not only to those with whom the accountant is in privity or near privity, but also to those persons, or classes of persons, whom he knows and intends will rely on his opinion, or whom he knows his client intends will so rely.

There remains the need to apply this rule to the facts at hand. At the time Mitchell prepared the audits for C. M. Systems, it was unknown that they would be used to induce the reliance of First Florida Bank to approve a line of credit for C. M. Systems. Therefore, except for the unusual facts of this case, Mitchell could not be held liable to the bank for any negligence in preparing the audit. However, Mitchell actually negotiated the loan on behalf of his client. He personally delivered the financial statements to the bank with the knowledge that it would rely upon them in considering whether or not to make the loan. Under this unique set of facts, we believe that Mitchell vouched for the integrity of the audits and that his conduct in dealing with the bank sufficed to meet the requirements of the rule which we have adopted in this opinion.

Accordingly, we answer the certified question in the affirmative. To the extent that they may conflict with this opinion, we disapprove the opinions in *Buchman, Investors Tax,* and *Gordon.* We quash the decision of the district court of appeal and remand the case for further proceedings.

## Judgment and Result

The Florida Supreme Court held that an accountant, who does not exercise reasonable and ordinary care in preparing the client's financial statements and who personally presents the client's statements to the third party to induce the third party to make a loan to the client, is liable to the third party (the bank) for negligence. In so doing the Florida Supreme Court did *not* follow the privity rule.

## Questions

1. If the privity rule says that accountants are not liable to people who do not hire them, why did the court in the *First Florida* case create an exception?
2. What is the rationale behind the privity rule? Does the privity rule make good sense in a fast-paced economy where third parties do not always have the time to examine financial statements in detail but who recognize the name of a prominent accounting firm known for its accuracy and integrity?
3. Should accountants be liable for their negligence to all third parties who might conceivably rely on the erroneous financial statements? What are the negatives of expanding the privity rule too much? What are the negatives in honoring the privity rule too much?
4. Would the following statement be an accurate rule to draw from the *First Florida* case? Accountants who audit a client's financial statements are liable to third persons for the client's business failure.

## STANDARD OF CARE

People have duties to be careful in all their activities. But how careful? The degree is indicated by the standard of care. The exact standard of care is what the ordinary, reasonable, prudent (ORP) person would do in the same situation. It is an objective and not a subjective standard. Therefore, *reasonable* is determined by an ORP person and not by the person accused of negligence. An ORP person is just like each of us except that s/he is always reasonable and prudent. When we occasionally are not, we have broken the standard of care that we owe others; breaking this standard is being *careless* in a legal sense.

The standard of care is objective, but it takes many factors into account. For example, if a driver has a car accident, the amount of traffic, visibility, weather conditions, and other factors determine the standard of care. The actual driver's conduct is compared with these conditions to see whether it meets the ORP person standard of care.

Many states recognize the **negligence per se** doctrine. It helps plaintiffs prove that defendants were careless. This doctrine says that a defendant breaks a duty of care by not obeying a statute (or regulation) setting a level of care (for example, speed limit laws) if the statute is intended to protect the plaintiff and prevent the type of loss the plaintiff suffers. *Munford, Inc. v. Peterson* illustrates negligence per se.

## Munford, Inc. v. Peterson
Supreme Court of Mississippi
368 So.2d 213 (1979)

### Background and Facts

**Justices Robertson, Walker, and Lee.** The parents and brothers of Scott Peterson instituted suit in the Circuit Court, First Judicial District of Harrison County, against Munford, Inc. and Tommy Blankenship for damages accruing by reason of the wrongful death of Scott Peterson. The jury returned a verdict in favor of the Petersons for $100,000, judgment was entered against Munford, Inc., and in favor of Blankenship, and Munford, Inc. appeals.

On the afternoon of May 28, 1975, Scott Peterson and four other boys planned to get together after baseball practice. Peterson and one of the boys were to spend the night at the home of Blankenship. Later that evening, one of them took the keys to the family car, found some vodka, and took it with him to the appointed meeting place (another boy's home). They all went to the Majic Market (owned and operated by the appellant), where they bought some orange juice and later drank it with the vodka. One of the boys was fifteen years of age, three of them were fourteen, and one was thirteen. After drinking the vodka, they went back to the Majic Market and one of the fourteen-year-olds entered the establishment and purchased a six-pack containing 14-oz cans of beer. The woman operator asked him if he was eighteen years of age. He replied in the affirmative, but she made no effort to have him prove his age or identify himself. The record indicates that he looked no older than a fourteen-year-old boy.

The boys went to David Black's house (one of the party) and drank the beer. They then decided to return to the Majic Market for more beer. The seventeen-year-old sister of Black refused to let him leave because she knew they were drinking beer. The other four drove to the Majic Market, where a different boy went in and bought a six-pack of beer (king-size). No inquiry was made concerning his age. They went out on a side road and drank the beer.

After consuming the second package of beer, the boys went back to the Majic Market, where one of them again entered the place and bought another six-pack without any questions being asked about his age. They drove out on the side road, drank the beer and began to ride around. About 4 A.M., Blankenship was driving the automobile and was traveling west on U.S. Highway 90. A hard rain had fallen, there was water on the road, he lost control of the vehicle, crossed the median and south lanes of the highway, hit the seawall, the automobile hurdled fifty-seven feet through the air, landed on the beach, and turned over five times, traveling 337½ feet. Scott Peterson was thrown out of the car and it rolled over him, fatally crushing his chest.

The declaration charged negligence against Munford, Inc. for selling beer to the boys in violation of the law, all of whom were under the age of 18 years, and who became intoxicated as a result of drinking the beer. Blankenship was charged with negligence in the operation of the vehicle. . . .

### Body of Opinion

**Justice Lee.** Under the common law, there is no action for damages in the selling or giving away of intoxicating liquors. The rule is stated in 45 AM.Jur.2d *Intoxicating Liquors* § 553, at 852 (1969), as follows:

At common law it is not a tort to either sell or give intoxicating liquor to ordinary able-bodied men, and it has been frequently held that in the absence of statute, there could be no cause of action against one furnishing liquor in favor of those injured by the intoxication of the person so furnished.

Where there is no statute pertaining to a subject, the common law prevails.

While the Wisconsin Supreme Court upheld the common-law principle stated above in *Garcia v. Hargrove*, 46 Wis.2d 724, (1970), (Wisconsin subscribes to the comparative negligence doctrine), the dissenting opinion of Chief Justice Hallows may have expressed a modern trend:

The time has arrived when this court should again exercise its inherent power as the guardian of the common law and hold upon general principles of common law negligence a person, who, when he knows or should have known a person is intoxicated, sells or gives intoxicating liquor to such a person, is guilty of a negligent act; and if such negligence is a substantial factor in causing harm to a third person, he should be liable with the drunken person under our comparative-negligence doctrine. Conceded, the common law in this state for almost 100 years has been to the contrary . . . but the basis upon which these cases were decided is sadly eroded by the shift from commingling alcohol and horses to commingling alcohol and horsepower.

However, in the discussion of the two questions presented here, we do not look to, or decide, the application of the common law in view of our statutes. Mississippi Code Annotated Section 67-3-53(b) (1972) provides the following:

In addition to any act declared to be unlawful by this chapter, or by Sections 27-71-301 through 27-71-347, and Sections 67-3-17, 67-3-27, 67-3-29 and 67-3-57, it shall be unlawful for the holder of a permit authorizing the sale of beer or wine at retail:

(b) To sell, give, or furnish any beer or wine to any person visibly or noticeably intoxicated, or to any insane person, or to any habitual drunkard, or to any person under the age of eighteen (18) years.

The declaration charged, among other things, that appellant sold beer to the minors in violation of Mississippi law and that such negligence contributed to the wreck and to the death of Scott Peterson. . . .

The principle that violation of a statute constitutes negligence per se is so elementary that it does not require citation of authority. When a statute is violated, the injured party is entitled to an instruction that the party violating the statute is guilty of negligence, and, if that negligence proximately caused or contributed to the injury, then the injured party is entitled to recover. The demurrer admitted that appellant violated the law and the evidence is undisputed that it did so. The demurrer was properly overruled and the peremptory instruction on negligence[2] was correctly given. The law is plain and unambiguous in prohibiting the sale, giving or furnishing beer or wine to any person under the age of eighteen years by the holder of such a permit. The method of determining a minor's age is for the proprietor to select. Suffice it to say, the responsibility is his to see that the law is not violated by him. . . .

The evidence is uncontradicted that appellant sold to the minors involved a quantity of beer in violation of the statute. . . . The facts in this case raise a jury issue as to whether or not there was causal connection between the incompetence of the driver as a result of drinking the beer, and the accident. It is required only that the intoxication be a contributing cause to the accident, not the sole proximate cause. The evidence was sufficient to withstand a motion for directed verdict and the verdict was not against the overwhelming weight of the evidence.

Appellant contends the trial court erred in refusing instructions on contributory negligence and assumption of risk and in granting an instruction that plaintiff was not negligent as a matter of law.

The appellant requested an instruction on assumption of risk, which was refused by the court. The court committed no error in refusing same.

The co-defendant Blankenship, who received a favorable verdict from the jury, requested an instruction on contributory negligence, which was refused. The appellant did not request such an instruction and cannot complain that the court erred in refusing that instruction to Blankenship.

The appellees requested and were granted the following instruction:

> The Court instructs the jury that as a matter of law in this case, the Plaintiffs' decedent was not negligent, nor at fault, nor to blame for his death; and cannot be charged with any negligence or fault.

Appellees seek the benefit of the statute to impose liability on appellant, yet argue that Scott Peterson was a member of a protected class and that he could not be guilty of negligence. We have stated hereinabove that the provision of the statute prohibiting sale of beer to persons under the age of eighteen years (and others named therein) is for the public safety.

The evidence is undisputed that Scott Peterson and the other boys pooled their money to buy the beer, that they were all together drinking it, that they all "felt no pain," that they were drinking the beer to make them feel good, and that Scott Peterson knew Blankenship had drunk a quantity of beer, in addition to drinking vodka. Appellant set up an affirmative defense of contributory negligence in its answer. The instruction directly contradicted the evidence and it precluded the jury from applying the law of comparative negligence, although the appellant did not request an instruction thereon, was highly prejudicial and constituted reversible error.

[The portion of the opinion upholding the admittedly "irregular" jury verdict is omitted. That verdict dismissed the case against defendant Blankenship, the driver of the car killing Peterson, while holding defendant/appellant Munford, Inc., liable. The Mississippi Supreme Court said this was not an error.]

## Judgment and Result

The Mississippi Supreme Court said that when a person violates a statute, that person breaks the negligence standard of care. The parents of the deceased person stated a cause of action based on negligence. Trial court errors against the defendant/appellant justified a new trial.

## Questions

1. How was the defendant business (Munford, Inc.) allegedly negligent? Did it drive the car that killed Peterson?
2. If a person violates a statute and injures a person the statute was intended to protect, is it negligence per se?
3. How do you explain the jury's refusal to hold liable the driver of the car while holding liable the business selling the beer?

---

[2] The Court instructs the jury in this case that the defendant, Munford, Inc., was negligent as a matter of law.

***Res ipsa loquitur*** is a Latin phrase meaning "the thing speaks for itself." It is another legal idea helping a negligence plaintiff prove the defendant broke the standard of care. Courts apply the idea where three facts occur:

1. Only the defendant controls what caused the harm.
2. The loss would not usually have happened except in the case of negligence.
3. The event must not have been due to any voluntary action or contribution by the plaintiff.

If these three facts occur, *res ipsa loquitur* allows an **inference of negligence**, meaning that a plaintiff has proven negligence unless a defendant has some defense.

## PROXIMATE CAUSE

A plaintiff must prove that a defendant proximately caused a plaintiff's injuries. Proximate cause means that a defendant's carelessness in fact caused a plaintiff's damage; that is, but for a defendant's carelessness, a plaintiff would not have been injured. A defendant's carelessness also must be close in time and space to justify holding a defendant liable. Courts use words such as *foreseeable* to decide the proximate cause issue. **Proximate cause**, in effect, says that a defendant is not liable for all injuries that he or she causes. For example, a defendant's negligence results in his factory's burning down, and the flames spread from building to building until the entire town burns. Proximate cause says that a defendant is liable for the first building's burning but not the whole town's destruction. Factors such as wind conditions and the efficiency of the fire department could counteract a defendant's carelessness. Also, public policy favors limiting people's negligence liability.

The following famous case, *Palsgraf v. Long Island Railroad Co.*, holds that the defendant was not liable for the plaintiff's injuries because the defendant's carelessness was not proximate to the plaintiff's loss.

## Palsgraf v. Long Island Railroad Co.
### New York Court of Appeals
### 162 N.E. 99 (1928)

### Background and Facts

Ms. Palsgraf stood on a railroad platform awaiting a train. A man on the same platform ran to catch another departing train. He jumped toward the moving train car and in so doing appeared unlikely to make, it so a railroad employee on the platform pushed him onto the car and another railroad employee on the car reached out to pull him aboard. In so doing, a package filled with explosives fell from the man's grasp onto the train tracks and blew up. The explosion in turn caused scales at the far end of the platform to fall onto Ms. Palsgraf. She sued the railroad for negligence and the railroad defended on grounds that it was not the proximate cause of her injuries.

### Body of Opinion

**Chief Judge Cardozo.** . . . The conduct of the defendant's guard, if a wrong in its relation to the holder of the package, was not a wrong in its relation to the plaintiff, standing far away. Relatively to her it was not negligence at all. Nothing in the situation gave notice that the falling package had in it the potency of peril to persons thus removed. Negligence is not actionable unless it involves the invasion of a legally protected interest, the violation of a right. "Proof of negligence in the air, so to speak, will not do." . . . If no hazard was apparent to the eye of ordinary vigilance, an act innocent and harmless, at least to outward seeming, with reference to her, did not take to itself the quality of a tort because it happened to be a wrong, though apparently not one involving the risk of bodily insecurity, with reference to someone else. "In every instance, before negligence can be predicated of a given act, back of the act must be sought and found a duty to the individual complaining, the observance of which would have averted or avoided the injury." . . .

One who jostles one's neighbor in a crowd does not invade the rights of others standing at the outer fringe when the unintended contact casts a bomb upon the ground. The wrongdoer as to them is the man who carries the bomb, not the one who explodes it without suspicion of danger. Life will have to be made over, and human nature transformed, before prevision so extravagant can be accepted as the norm of conduct, the customary standard to which behavior must conform. . . .

What the plaintiff must show is "a wrong" to herself; i.e., a violation of her own right, and not merely a wrong to someone else, not conduct "wrongful" because unsocial, but not "a wrong" to any one. . . . The risk reasonably to be perceived defines the duty to be obeyed. . . . Here, by concession, there was nothing in the situation to suggest to the most cautious mind that the parcel wrapped in newspaper would spread wreckage through the station. If the guard had thrown it down knowingly and wilfully, he would not have threatened the plaintiff's safety, so far as appearances could warn him. His conduct would not have involved, even then, an unreasonable probability of invasion of her bodily security. Liability can be no greater when the act is inadvertent. . . .

One who seeks redress at law does not make out a cause of action by showing without more that there has been damage to his person. If the harm was not wilful, he must show that the act as to him had possibilities of danger so many and apparent as to entitle him to be protected against the doing of it though the harm was unintended. . . .

## Judgment and Result

The New York Court of Appeals found for the defendant railroad.

## Questions

1. Clearly if the defendant railroad's employees had not bumped the package from the one passenger's arms, the explosion would not have occurred. Therefore the railroad caused plaintiff's injuries. Why then was defendant not liable to plaintiff?
2. Why was defendant's negligence not the proximate cause of plaintiff's injuries?
3. If the man carrying the package had sued the railroad for its employees' negligence, would the railroad have been liable to him?
4. Does proximate cause excuse a person from liability for failure to live up to the appropriate standard of care? Why?

## DAMAGES

If a defendant owes a duty of care to a plaintiff and breaks that duty, this act alone does not let the plaintiff recover. The breach of the duty must damage plaintiff, meaning that a defendant must have damaged plaintiff's person or property.

## DEFENSES TO NEGLIGENCE

Even if a plaintiff proves the four parts of negligence, a defendant can raise affirmative defenses. If defendant can prove any one affirmative defense, plaintiff's negligence claim is defeated. Two affirmative defenses are contributory negligence and assumption of risk.

*Contributory Negligence and Assumption of Risk.* **Contributory negligence** means that a plaintiff's own carelessness partly caused his or her loss. Contributory negligence generally prevents a plaintiff from recovering anything. This rule is harsh, because a plaintiff could be only 5 percent contributorily negligent and yet recover nothing. To reduce this harshness, some states have **comparative fault**. Comparative fault schemes vary among the states, but ordinarily a contributorily negligent plaintiff recovers damages reduced by the amount of his or her contributing fault. For example, if a plaintiff's damages are $10,000 and a plaintiff is 10 percent contributorily negligent, the plaintiff gets $9,000 if comparative fault applies.

**Assumption of risk** occurs when a plaintiff actually knows a risk exists and nonetheless engages in the activity. Spectators at baseball games probably assume the risk of being hit by a foul ball.

*Damage Apportionment.* Some states refine comparative fault by asking two questions. First, how much did the plaintiff's fault contribute to the accident? Courts reduce plaintiff's recovery by this percentage. Second, how much did the plaintiff's contributory negligence contribute to his or her damages? Courts reduce plaintiff's recovery again by this percentage. For example, a motorcyclist's failure to wear a protective helmet might contribute little to an auto collision; however, it might greatly increase his or her injuries.

## STRICT LIABILITY

**Strict liability** means that a person is liable for harm proximately caused, even though no fault is shown. The defendant merely did or failed to do something that is close enough to a plaintiff's damages to justifiably hold the defendant liable.

Strict liability can occur in many situations. Persons engaged in ultrahazardous activities are strictly liable to persons whom they proximately injure. Examples of ultrahazardous activities include dynamiting, fumigation, flying airplanes, and keeping wild animals. Courts also apply strict liability to defective consumer goods. Chapter 23 discusses this issue.

### WHY ALLOW ULTRAHAZARDOUS ACTIVITIES?

If ultrahazardous activities are so risky, why allow them? The reason is that their social value outweighs prohibiting them. However, individuals participating in ultrahazardous activities are liable for any harm that they proximately cause no matter how careful they are. Strict liability encourages people in ultrahazardous activities to be careful.

### DEFENSES TO STRICT LIABILITY

Assumption of risk can be a defense to strict liability. However, contributory negligence is generally not a defense in strict liability cases. *Indiana Harbor Belt Railroad v. American Cyanamid* presents a contemporary strict liability scenario—a toxic chemical spill.

## Indiana Harbor Belt Railroad Co. v. American Cyanamid Co.
U.S. District Court, Northern District of Illinois
517 F.Supp. 314 (1981)

### Background and Facts

American Cyanamid Company (Cyanamid) manufactured and shipped acrylonitrile, a hazardous, flammable, toxic substance. Cyanamid arranged for Missouri Pacific to transport acrylonitrile to Indiana Harbor Belt Railway's (Indiana Harbor) freight yard in Illinois. There the railroad car containing the substance was to be turned over to Conrail for delivery to Cyanamid in New Jersey. Upon arrival at Indiana Harbor's freight yard, substantial amounts of acrylonitrile leaked from the freight car. Indiana Harbor claims extensive damage to property, equipment, and the water supply over a two-mile area. The spill resulted in the evacuation of 3,000 people from their homes. It also caused extensive interference with railroad operations for a substantial time. Indiana Harbor spent much to fix its property. Indiana Harbor sued Cyanamid for its damages based on a strict liability theory. Cyanamid argued that even though acrylonitrile is a hazardous substance, strict liability only applies to ultrahazardous activities. Cyanamid claimed that common sense tells us that transporting a hazardous substance is not ultrahazardous or inherently dangerous.

### Body of Opinion

**District Judge Moran.** Cyanamid argues that dismissal of plaintiff's strict liability counts is required because no cause of action has been stated under Illinois law. They maintain that strict liability standards apply to activities that are inherently dangerous and that naturally and probably result in harm despite the exercise of the utmost care. They argue that Illinois law has limited the ultrahazardous activity concept to cases involving blasting or explosives and it has not been extended to the circumstances alleged in this case. They note that regardless of acrylonitrile's qualities as a hazardous substance, strict liability cannot be applied unless it is a hazardous activity. Defendant contends that their activity was not inherently dangerous as a matter of common knowledge or otherwise.

Plaintiff Sanders applies the same legal standards as Cyanamid but believes that Cyanamid's conduct fits within them. They acknowledge that these facts raise a question of first impression but argue that the allegations "fit comfortably within the contours of the Illinois absolute liability doctrine."

Indiana Harbor argues that Illinois courts apply strict liability principles when a peril with potentially grave consequences is introduced into the community. As they believe shipping acrylonitrile is intrinsically dangerous regardless of how careful the shipper may be, plaintiff urges that this court apply strict liability standards. . . .

Neither party has cited any Illinois authority discussing whether shipment of acrylonitrile is an inherently dangerous activity. The Illinois cases in this area have focused largely on blasting activities though they have not expressly limited the concept to this activity. . . .

There are two opinions that this court believes provide persuasive rationales for finding liability in analogous circumstances. In *Chavez v. Southern Pacific Transportation Co.* . . . (E.D.Calif. 1976), Southern Pacific transported eighteen boxcars loaded with bombs. The bombs exploded in a railroad yard causing personal injury and property damage. The court imposed strict liability because the defendant was engaged in an ultrahazardous activity. The court focused on the relative positions of the parties and the desirability of properly distributing the loss. The court emphasized that one who intentionally acts with knowledge that their activity may cause harm, despite the exercise of due care, should "in all fairness be required to compensate the other for the damage done."

The risk distribution justification for imposing strict liability is well suited to claims arising out of the conduct of ultrahazardous activity. The victims of such activity are defenseless. Due to the very nature of the activity, the losses suffered as a result of such activity are likely to be substantial—an "overwhelming misfortune to the person injured". . . . By indirectly imposing liability on those who benefit from the dangerous activity, risk distribution benefits the social-economic body in two ways: (1) the adverse impact of any particular misfortune is lessened by spreading its cost over a greater population and over a longer time period, and (2) social and economic resources can be more efficiently allocated when the actual costs of goods and services (including the losses they entail) are reflected in their price to the consumer. Both of these benefits may be achieved by subjecting Southern Pacific to strict liability.

## Judgment and Result

The U.S. District court decided that strict liability applied to the facts of this case.

## Questions

1. Does determining whether something is ultrahazardous depend on how much damage it causes? That is, is the ultrahazardous character known before or after a loss?
2. Might gas stations be ultrahazardous?

## INTENTIONAL TORTS

### INTENTIONAL TORTS COMPARED WITH CRIMES

**Intentional torts** are similar to and different from crimes. Both crimes and intentional torts are wrongs that usually involve some kind of intent; however, a few strict liability crimes do not involve intent. Both crimes and intentional torts are intentional wrongs, and indicate justification for punishing the wrongdoer. Also, the same act (assault and battery, for example) can be both an intentional tort and a crime.

The victims of intentional torts are individuals. Crimes, of course, have individual victims (for example, the person robbed). Because crimes are acts against general society, the punishment can be much greater, such as imprisonment or death. Society never sentences a person to prison or death for committing an intentional tort.

### INTENTIONAL TORTS COMPARED WITH NEGLIGENCE

Intentional torts are both different from and similar to the tort of negligence. The main difference is that the wrong in negligence is carelessness, but the wrong in intentional torts concerns some kind of intent. Also, punitive damages are possible for intentional torts but not for negligence.

Intentional torts and negligence have several similarities. First, both are torts, which are civil wrongs. The victims are individuals, not society in general. Second, victims can recover both nominal and compensatory damages for negligence and intentional torts.

## INTENTIONAL TORTS COMPARED WITH CONTRACTS

Contracts and intentional torts are both areas of civil law; neither is a crime. A person injured by either a breach of contract or an intentional tort can possibly recover both nominal and compensatory damages.

An agreement does not have to be broken to recover for an intentional tort, but a broken contract is required before a person can recover contract damages. Also, intentional tort victims can recover punitive damages, which is not possible for victims of broken contracts.

## REMEDIES FOR INTENTIONAL TORTS

Basically, the two types of remedies for tort victims are legal and equitable.

*Legal Remedies.* Legal remedies include various kinds of damages—nominal, compensatory, and punitive damages—all of which are monetary.

**Nominal damages** are a small amount of money that a victim receives when his or her right is broken but no substantial harm occurs. For example, Norman could throw a Coke on Bruce (a battery), but what real harm does Bruce suffer? Nominal damages are proper because no real harm was suffered.

**Compensatory damages** refer to money needed to "make a victim whole." In other words, the victim has a physical or financial loss of some sort. For example, if Arthur slanders Tom's accounting book (by saying it has too many errors when it really does not), sales of Tom's book could fall. Therefore, Tom can receive compensatory damage.

**Punitive damages** punish wrongdoers when their conduct is particularly outrageous. For example, when Norman throws a Coke on Bruce, it is proper to make Norman pay Bruce punitive damages.

*Equitable Remedies.* **Equitable remedies** include injunctions, specific performance, and accountings. Plaintiffs can recover these remedies only when their legal remedies are inadequate.

**Injunctions** are court orders to do or not do something. For example, a court might order a defendant not to trespass on a plaintiff's property.

**Specific performance** is basically a contract remedy, which orders a person breaking a contract to perform an obligation. This remedy is available only when legal remedies, such as money, are inadequate.

**Accountings** refer to court orders that direct someone, such as an agent, to present income and expense records to someone else. For example, if a former employee uses a former employer's trade secrets without authorization, the employee will have to account for (and turn over) any profits made.

## FRAUD[3]

**Fraud** is a misrepresentation of a material fact that the defrauding person knows about; the defrauding person intends to defraud, and the victim is damaged as a result of reasonably relying on the misrepresentations.

Fraud is one of the most frequently committed business torts and often occurs to persuade others to enter contracts. For example, if someone wants to sell a car,

---

[3] Fraud is also discussed in Chapter 22 under consumer protection.

what better way to sell it than by lying about, or understating, its true mileage? However, lying in this situation might involve fraud, and the victim can escape the contract and recover damages.

Because fraud is so common, a few other points should be noted.

First, the person misrepresenting must intend to defraud. If someone mistakenly misrepresents something, innocent misrepresentation—not fraud—occurs. The contract can be undone, but generally no damages can be recovered.

Second, either a buyer or seller (or both) can commit fraud in one contract.

Third, seller's talk, puffing, and opinions are different from misrepresentations of facts. Facts are objective, definite, or observable. For example, Jerry says his car will get 20 miles per gallon. This statement is a representation of fact because any person can determine its truth. If the statement is false, then it is a misrepresentation of fact. Puffing, opinions, or seller's talk are not misrepresentations of fact; they are subjective. For example, statements such as "This house is wonderful," "That car is the most stylish," or "That picture is beautiful" are subjective. Words such as *wonderful*, *most stylish*, and *beautiful* are opinion, not fact, and are unlike objective descriptions such as three feet or one carat. For fraud to exist, a misrepresentation of fact (not a misrepresentation of opinion) must be made.

Fourth, fraud can occur by **concealment**. That is, if a seller "keeps his or her mouth shut" instead of disclosing a material fact not easily discoverable by the other party, fraud can occur. In one case, a homeowner offered his house for sale. The other party bought the house but discovered later that the water was available only between 7 A.M. and 7 P.M. The seller had said that the buyer could have "all the water he wanted" and did not specify to the buyer that water would be available for only half of the day. The court said this case involved fraud by concealment. The seller had a duty to disclose material facts not readily ascertainable.

Unfortunately, much of the U.S. population will probably be a party to the type of agreement illustrated in the next case, because it involves a divorce property settlement. The case, *Hewlett v. Hewlett*, also shows that fraud can creep into such contracts.

## Hewlett v. Hewlett
### Missouri Court of Appeals
### 845 S.W.2d 717 (1993)

### Background and Facts

Robert T. and Patricia R. Hewlett were married on December 22, 1960, and they had three children during their 29-year marriage. Patricia worked as a full-time homemaker raising the couple's three children. Robert worked in the automobile sales industry for 30 years. He owned a partial interest in Bob Allen Ford Company and Bob Allen Investment Company, and also had certain other business and real estate interests. Robert handled all of the couple's financial matters. The Hewletts separated in January 1989. Robert filed for divorce on July 14, 1989. The parties signed a property settlement. The decree of dissolution was issued on January 2, 1990.

On December 21, 1990, Patricia filed a motion to set aside the judgment on the basis of her ex-husband's fraudulent representations incorporated in the property settlement. After an extensive hearing, the trial court made the following findings: That Robert incorrectly valued the marital assets and liabilities by at least $1,225,000; that Robert intended that Patricia rely upon his representations in negotiating the property settlement; that Patricia had a right to rely thereon; that Robert knew or should have known that these representations were false; and that Patricia was damaged by at least $500,000 as a result of her reliance upon Robert's representations. Based on these findings, the trial court set aside the decree of dissolution.

### Body of Opinion

**Judge Smart.** The trial court found the following assets of Robert were undervalued: His ownership interest in Bob Allen Investment Company, his ownership interest in MidAmerican Insurance Company, a Connecticut General Insurance policy, his

401(K) plan, and an account at United Missouri Bank. The trial court found that two debts were overstated. . . . Finally, the trial court found that Robert concealed the following assets: Stock in Kidder, Peabody; an interest in KCD Distributors; an interest in Transoceanic Casualty Company; a partnership interest in Hewlett-Wiegers Partnership; and facts related to the nature of the United Missouri Bank account and $24,000 spent from the account. . . .

In asserting a claim of fraud, a party must prove the following elements: (1) a representation; (2) its falsity; (3) its materiality; (4) the speaker's knowledge of the falsity (or the speaker's awareness that s/he lacks knowledge of its truth or falsity); (5) the speaker's intent that the statement be acted upon by the other party in the manner contemplated; (6) that party's ignorance of the falsity; (7) reliance on the truth; (8) right to rely thereon; and (9) injury. . . .

Mr. Hewlett owned a 50 percent interest in Bob Allen Investment Company. This company held as assets four parcels of real estate, an automobile dealership known as Metro Ford, and a leasing company known as Metro Leasing. The trial court found that Robert represented to Patricia and her counsel that his interest in the Bob Allen Investment Company had a value of $432,276, whereas, the court found, it was actually worth at least $1,400,000 even without inclusion of any factor for goodwill. Robert claims that he made no false representations regarding the value of the investment company. The record shows that he and his attorney provided Patricia and her attorney with many financial records. Robert stated that he relied on his accountant, Daniel Beattie, for the valuation of $432,276 and that the valuation was a statement of opinion, not one of fact. Robert states that Patricia and her attorney had the information, opportunity, and means to obtain an appraisal of the business, and since she chose not to obtain an appraisal, she is now barred from claiming fraud. Patricia's attorney in the divorce case, Mr. Williams, testified that he examined the financial information provided, and he decided that the estimates of value seemed appropriate to him.

Patricia claims that Robert knew the value of the investment company was much higher than the valuation he provided. . . . Patricia presented exhibits showing that prior to the dissolution hearing, Robert had valued the interest substantially higher in financial statements and corporate annual reports. Patricia presented the testimony of Mr. Beattie, who testified that he was never requested to formally appraise the investment company. Beattie stated that he was asked to prepare computations to enable Robert to find a formula for the purpose of valuing the dealership. Beattie testified that he did not know how the $432,276 value was determined by Robert, and that Robert's counsel told him the value was negotiated between the parties' counsel. Patricia presented as an expert Thomas Slack, who testified that Bob Allen Investment Company had a value of between $5,300,000 and $6,000,000. Slack valued the goodwill at $2,569,965.

Robert argues that the value he represented to Patricia ($432,276) was a statement of his opinion and not a statement of fact. A statement of value is ordinarily considered an opinion. The exception occurs when "the representing party has special knowledge and the other is ignorant in respect to the value which is known to the representing

party and the representations are made with intention that they be relied on." *Alexander v. Sagehorn* . . . (Mo. 1980). . . . Evidence was presented that Robert had special knowledge of the interest's value. Robert was actively involved in the auto dealerships as an executive as well as a major stockowner.

The second element, the representation's falsity, was shown by Slack's testimony as to the value of the interest and also by the tax returns and financial documentation presented at the hearing. . . . The materiality of the representation is clear since the interest in the company is a substantial marital asset. Element four, Robert's knowledge of the falseness of the representation (or his awareness that he did not know whether it was true or false), is shown by the testimony of his accountant that Hewlett and his attorney did not ask the accountant to appraise his interest in the company, but instead sought information as to computations which might be used to determine a formula for ascertaining value. The trial court could have inferred that Robert did not want the accountant to value his interest because he desired to come up with his own figure, in order to mislead.

Robert argues that Patricia had no right to rely on his representations because she had an attorney and had ample opportunity to make her own determinations. However, "[o]ne may act upon a positive representation of fact, notwithstanding that means of knowledge are open, particularly where the facts may be assumed to be within the knowledge of the person who declares it." *Alexander v. Sagehorn.* . . . If Robert had made no statement of value, Patricia may have taken some action to determine value, "but having been told by someone who purported to know, she relied on that figure." In this case, Patricia and her attorney had no obligation to determine value.

## Judgment and Result

For the plaintiff. The court of appeals decided that substantial evidence supported the trial court's setting aside the decree of dissolution based on fraud in the husband's financial statements shown to her.

## Questions

1. If a person misrepresents the value of something, is this act generally considered a representation of fact or opinion? Which would a defendant sued for fraud want it to be, fact or opinion? Why?

2. Was Patricia reasonable in her reliance on the figures Robert provided as to his net worth? Was her attorney reasonable in relying on the figures? Are attorneys supposed to be able to prepare financial statements? Did the accountant actually provide an appraisal of Robert's worth or just a formula for doing so? Does this excuse what the accountant did and put the blame for wrongdoing back on Robert's shoulders?

3. Would the scenario in the *Hewlett* case support or undercut the assertion made in Chapter 1, that positive law is the most one can expect of people in terms of ethical conduct?

## FALSE IMPRISONMENT

**False imprisonment** occurs when one person totally restrains another for an "appreciable period of time," such as even a few minutes. The person restrained need not be physically harmed because the confinement or restraint itself is the harm. Most cases say that the victim must be aware of the confinement when it happens before he or she can be falsely imprisoned. The confinement need not be in a room, although it often is.

*Remedies.* Persons falsely imprisoned can recover nominal damages (a very small amount of money). Actual or compensatory damages (money to cover real losses or injuries) are also available. The victim can recover punitive damages where the wrongdoer had a bad intent or recklessly disregarded a plaintiff's interests. However, a plaintiff receives no punitive damages when a defendant made a good-faith error.

*Defenses to False Imprisonment.* One of the main defenses to false imprisonment is the *shopkeeper's privilege*. Basically, this privilege allows a merchant with reasonable cause to detain a customer suspected of shoplifting for investigation, which must be conducted in a reasonable manner and time.

## INVASION OF PRIVACY

The intentional tort of **invasion of privacy** covers four loosely related but separate wrongs:

1. Intrusion upon a plaintiff's seclusion or into his or her private affairs
2. Public disclosure of private facts
3. Unauthorized appropriation of a person's name or likeness
4. Holding up a person in a false light

In other words, anyone who does any one of these four wrongs commits the tort of invasion of privacy.

*Intrusion upon Solitude or Seclusion.* **Intrusion upon solitude or seclusion** is one invasion of privacy. This invasion can occur if defendant sets up telescopes, listening devices, or snoops into a plaintiff's private life in a way that would be objectionable to a "reasonable person."

Unauthorized wiretapping of a plaintiff's private conversation has been held to be an intrusion upon a plaintiff's solitude and seclusion. An unauthorized photo of Herman using toilet paper for its intended purpose would usually invade his solitude or seclusion.

*Public Disclosure of Private Facts.* Public disclosure of private facts is a second type of invasion of privacy. The facts disclosed must be private. Courts have said that a person's personal finances and details about a personal part of the human body are private. Matters of public record, such as the amount of property taxes a homeowner pays, are not private facts.

*Unauthorized Appropriation.* The **unauthorized appropriation** of a plaintiff's name or likeness for a defendant's benefit frequently occurs in business cases. For example, Mace's Department Store advertises its dishes using Nancy Shurtz's name as a satisfied customer. The fact that Nancy uses Mace's dishes is no defense, because Nancy's privacy is the protected interest.

*False Light.* Holding up a person in a **false light** in the public eye can arise in many situations. For instance, Ralph's illegitimate use of Michael Jackson's name to suggest Michael's connection with Ralph's product, book, or company is a false light case.

One famous false light case involved a defendant's unauthorized use of plaintiff's name on a telegram to the governor. The telegram asked the governor to act in a certain way on a pending law. The plaintiff actually did not agree with the telegram. Therefore, the telegram held the plaintiff up in a false light.

*Defenses to Invasion of Privacy.* No right of privacy exists in the following situations:

1. When the matter published is of public or general interest
2. When the matter is privileged under libel and slander laws
3. When the individual claiming privacy consents to publication

*Felsher v. University of Evansville* is an invasion of privacy case, asking the question of whether a corporation has a right of privacy when its name or likeness has been appropriated without its permission.

## Felsher v. University of Evansville
### Supreme Court of Indiana
### 755 N.E.2d 589 (2001)

### Background and Facts

The University of Evansville is a not-for-profit corporation, originally founded at Moores Hill, Indiana, in 1854. Felsher was formerly a professor of French. The University terminated him in 1991.

In 1997 Felsher created Internet Web sites and electronic mail accounts containing portions of the names of Dr. James S. Vinson, president of the University; Dr. Stephen G. Greiner, vice president for Academic Affairs; and Dr. Larry W. Colter, Dean of the College of Arts and Sciences. Each of these addresses also contained the letters UE, which is a common abbreviation for the University of Evansville.

Felsher featured articles that he had written on the Web sites he created. The articles alleged wrongdoings by Vinson and other University employees. One article alleged that President Vinson violated the University Faculty Manual. In another article Felsher stated that one UE professor had publicly declared himself unqualified to teach one of his courses.

Using the e-mail accounts he created, Felsher sent mail to several universities nominating each of the University officials, in turn, for various academic positions. In his e-mail message, Felsher directed the reader to one of the Web pages he had created as a reference for the nominee's activities.

The University, Vinson, Greiner, and Colter filed this lawsuit alleging invasion of privacy, and Felsher then removed the e-mail addresses and the Web sites. Felsher later created another twelve Web sites containing roughly the same information as had appeared on the previously removed sites.

Pending resolution of the suit, the University sought and obtained a preliminary injunction prohibiting Felsher from engaging in certain Internet activities. The court denied Felsher's motion to remove the University as a plaintiff. The trial court found in favor of the University and its officials concluding that they have a protectable privacy interest in their rights to the exclusive use of their identities and that Felsher invaded this interest when he appropriated their names for use in e-mail correspondence and for his benefit in creating the Internet Web sites.

The trial court's order permanently enjoined Felsher from (1) appropriating the names and likenesses of the University, Vinson, Greiner, Colter or the name of any other person or individual associated with the University for any purpose; (2) using the e-mail addresses he created or any other e-mail addresses that incorporates the plaintiffs' names including "UE" or the name of any other person or individual associated with the University; (3) maintaining any web site with a URL or address containing any of the plaintiffs' names, including UE, or the names of any person or individual associated with the University; and (4) nominating Vinson, Greiner, Colter or any person or individual associated with the University for positions with any other schools, colleges, or universities.

The Court of Appeals affirmed and the Indiana Supreme Court granted certiorari on, among other things, whether UE as a corporation had a remedy based on the right of privacy.

## Body of Opinion

**Chief Justice Shepard.** . . . Felsher first argues that the trial court erred because the University is not entitled to an invasion of privacy claim.

Representatives of several news organizations, as amici curiae, support Felsher's petition . . . stating, "Well established privacy law . . . precludes corporations from bringing an action for invasion of privacy. Amici accurately assert that no other state has recognized a claim for invasion of privacy by a corporation.

The issue of whether a corporate entity is entitled to an invasion of privacy claim is one of first impression in Indiana. We begin our analysis by acknowledging the position taken in the Restatement (Second) of Torts § 652A (1)(1977): "One who invades the right of privacy of another is subject to liability for the resulting harm to the interests of the other."

This court has previously observed that the term "invasion of privacy" is a label used to describe "four distinct injuries: (1) intrusion upon seclusion, (2) appropriation of name or likeness, (3) public disclosure of private facts, and (4) false-light publicity. . . .

We explained that the four wrongs were separate and "united only in their common focus on some abstract notion of being left alone." . . . We indicated that "recognizing one branch of the privacy tort does not entail recognizing all four." . . .

The only injury at issue here is appropriation. The University argues that it may maintain an action for appropriation because the claim addresses a property interest rather than personal feelings. . . . The University also relies on Restatement § 652(I), which says, "Except for the appropriation of one's name or likeness, an action for invasion of privacy can be maintained only by a living individual whose privacy is invaded."

While we agree that an appropriation claim involves a privacy issue "in the nature of a property right," we think the University's reliance on the exception set forth in the Restatement is misplaced. Each of the comments to Restatement § 652(I) negates the inference that a corporation is entitled to an appropriation claim.

The first comment states that the privacy right is personal. This comment then states a rule: "The cause of action is not assignable, and it cannot be maintained by other persons." . . . The appropriation exception that follows addresses this rule, not the personal character of the right.

The second comment discusses the general requirement that "the action for the invasion of privacy cannot be maintained after the death of the individual whose privacy is invaded." This comment states an exception for appropriation actions due to its "similarity to an impairment of a property right . . . " The exception is clarified as a recognition of survival rights in an appropriation action.

Finally, the third comment declares, without exception, "A corporation, partnership or unincorporated association has no personal right of privacy." . . . The comment then states that a corporation has "no cause of action for any of the four forms of invasion covered by §§ 652B to 652E." . . . The following sentence in the comment indicates that although these Sections . . . do not entitle a corporation claim, a corporation has "a limited right to the exclusive use of its own name or identity in so far as they are of use or benefit, and it receives protection from the law of unfair competition. . . .

Therefore, we think these Restatement sections do not support the position that a corporation may bring an appropriation claim resting on notions of privacy. . . .

## Judgment and Result

The Indiana Supreme Court held that UE as a corporation did not have an appropriation of name or likeness claim based on invasion of privacy. The case was reversed in part and affirmed in part. [In an omitted part of the opinion, the Indiana Supreme Court said other grounds such as the state's unfair competition law and trademark statute as well as tortious interference with business relations did provide a basis for UE to prevail against defendant.]

## Questions

1. How did the defendant allegedly violate UE corporation's right of privacy?
2. Why shouldn't a corporation have a privacy right?
3. What ethics noted in the Chapter 1 are promoted by *not* allowing a corporation to have a right of privacy?

## CONVERSION

**Conversion** is the unauthorized and unjustified interference with the dominion and control of another's personal property. Personal property is anything movable; that is, things other than land and buildings can be converted.

Conversion is a wrong commonly called stealing. Conversion is not a crime, however, but an intentional tort.

Interfering with another's personal property must be intentional. The intent does not have to be to harm—just interfere.

*What Can Be Converted.* Any tangible personal property—such as a horse, car, or diamond ring, for example—can be converted. Modern courts say that intangible personal property can be converted. The conversion is particularly true when there is a tangible symbol of an intangible right (such as a stock certificate representing a share of stock, an insurance policy representing insurance, or a savings bank book representing a savings account).

Land and buildings cannot be converted. Neither can gravel, trees, or crops. But once severed from the land, gravel, trees, and crops can be converted.

*Examples of Conversion.* A person who steals personal property commits conversion, but subtler forms of conversion exist. A person buying or selling stolen goods is considered a converter, even if unaware that the goods are stolen. A person who rightfully gets possession of goods but who refuses to give them to the owner is also a converter.

## ABUSE OF PROCESS

The essential parts of **abuse of process** are an ulterior purpose and the willful act in the use of the process not proper in the regular conduct of the proceeding.

*Process* refers to civil or criminal legal procedures. Arrest warrants and service of a summons and complaint in civil cases are examples of process. When process is used properly, no tort occurs. However, the intentional tort of abuse of process occurs when a person misuses process—that is, when process justified for one purpose is used for an improper purpose.

Generally, malice is not required for abuse of process. The case or matter also does not have to end in a plaintiff's favor. The crux of abuse of process is improper use.

## WRONGFUL INTERFERENCE WITH CONTRACTUAL RELATIONS

The elements of **wrongful interference with contractual relations** are as follows:

1. A valid, enforceable contract exists between B and C
2. D, a third person, must know that the contract between B and C exists
3. D must intentionally induce B or C to break the contract between B and C

The intentional tort of wrongful interference with contractual relations makes contracts stable. This tort makes it wrong for a third person to upset an existing contract between two parties. Note that the defendant need not have either malice or bad faith.

Defenses to wrongful interference include lack of a part of the definition of this tort or justification. Justifications include moral, social, or economic pressures lawful in and of themselves. For example, if D's ads are so effective they cause B to break a contract with C, then it is considered economic justification.

In 1987 the Texas Court of Appeals decided *Texaco v. Pennzoil*. Pennzoil claimed that it had a contract to buy Getty Oil stock for a merger. After the alleged Getty-Pennzoil contract was formed, but before it was performed, Texas persuaded Getty to break its contract with Pennzoil and sell its stock to Texaco for a higher price. Pennzoil then sued Texaco on the theory that Texaco had wrongfully interfered with the Pennzoil-Getty contract. The result of this lawsuit in the Texas Court of Appeals follows.

## Texaco, Inc. v. Pennzoil Co.
Texas Court of Appeals (1st Dist.)
729 S.W.2d 768 (1987)

### Background and Facts

This appeal concerns a judgment awarding Pennzoil damages for Texaco's tortious interference with a contract between Pennzoil and the "Getty entities" (Getty Oil Company, the Sarah C. Getty Trust, and the J. Paul Getty Museum).

The jury found, among other things, that:

(1) At the end of a board meeting on January 3, 1984, the Getty entities intended to bind themselves to an agreement providing for the purchase of Getty Oil stock, whereby the Sarah C. Getty Trust would own 4/7th of the stock and Pennzoil the remaining 3/7th; and providing for a division of Getty Oil's assets, according to their respective ownership if the Trust and Pennzoil were unable to agree on a restructuring of Getty Oil by December 31, 1984;

(2) Texaco knowingly interfered with the agreement between Pennzoil and the Getty entities;

(3) As a result of Texaco's interference, Pennzoil suffered damages of $7.53 billion;

(4) Texaco's actions were intentional, willful, and in wanton disregard of Pennzoil's rights; and,

(5) Pennzoil was entitled to punitive damages of $3 billion.

The main questions for our determination are: (1) whether the evidence supports the jury's finding that there was a binding contract between the Getty entities and Pennzoil, and that Texaco knowingly induced a breach of such contract. . . .

Though many facts are disputed, the parties' main conflicts are over the inferences to be drawn from, and the legal significance of, these facts. There is evidence that for several months in late 1983, Pennzoil had followed with interest the well-publicized dissension between the board of directors of Getty Oil Company and Gordon Getty, who was a director of Getty Oil and also the owner, as trustee, of approximately 40.2 percent of the outstanding shares of Getty Oil. On December 28, 1983, Pennzoil announced an unsolicited, public tender offer for 16 million shares of Getty Oil at $100 each.

Soon afterward, Pennzoil contacted both Gordon Getty and a representative of the J. Paul Getty Museum, which held approximately 11.8 percent of the shares of Getty Oil, to discuss the tender offer and the possible purchase of Getty Oil. In the first two days of January 1984, a "Memorandum of Agreement" was drafted to reflect the terms that had been reached in conversations between representatives of Pennzoil, Gordon Getty, and the Museum.

Under the plan set out in the Memorandum of Agreement, Pennzoil and the Trust (with Gordon Getty as trustee) were to become partners on a 3/7ths to 4/7ths basis respectively, in owning and operating Getty Oil. Gordon Getty was to become chairman of the board, and Hugh Liedtke, the chief executive officer of Pennzoil, was to become chief executive officer of the new company.

The Memorandum of Agreement further provided that the Museum was to receive $110 per share for its 11.8 percent ownership, and that all other outstanding public shares were to be cashed in by the company at $110 per share. Pennzoil was given an option to buy an additional 8 million shares to achieve the desired ownership ratio. The plan also provided that Pennzoil and the Trust were to try in good faith to agree upon a plan to restructure Getty Oil within a year, but if they could not reach an agreement, the assets of Getty Oil were to be divided between them, 3/7ths to Pennzoil and 4/7ths to the Trust.

The Memorandum of Agreement stated that it was subject to approval of the board of Getty Oil, and it was to expire by its own terms if not approved at the board meeting that was to begin on January 2. Pennzoil's CEO, Liedtke, and Gordon Getty, for the Trust, signed the Memorandum of Agreement before the Getty Oil board meeting on January 2, and Harold Williams, the president of the Museum, signed it shortly after the board meeting began. Thus, before it was submitted to the Getty Oil board, the Memorandum of Agreement had been executed by parties who together controlled a majority of the outstanding shares of Getty Oil. The Memorandum of Agreement was then presented to the Getty Oil board, which had previously held discussions on how the company should respond to Pennzoil's public tender offer. A self-tender by the company to shareholders at $110 per share had been proposed to defeat Pennzoil's tender offer at $100 per share, but no consensus was reached.

The board voted to reject recommending Pennzoil's tender offer to Getty's shareholders, then later also rejected the Memorandum of Agreement price of $110 per share as too low. Before recessing at 3 A.M., the board decided to make a counterproposal to Pennzoil of $110 per share plus a $10 debenture. Pennzoil's investment banker reacted to this price negatively. In the morning of January 3, Getty Oil's investment banker, Geoffrey Boisi, began calling other companies, seeking a higher bid than Pennzoil's for the Getty Oil shares.

When the board reconvened at 3 P.M. on January 3, a revised Pennzoil proposal was presented, offering $110 per share plus a $3 "stub" that was to be paid after the sale of a Getty Oil subsidiary

("ERC"), from the excess proceeds over $1 billion. Each shareholder was to receive a pro rata share of these excess proceeds, but in any case, a minimum of $3 per share at the end of five years. During the meeting, Boisi briefly informed the board of the status of his inquiries of other companies that might be interested in bidding for the company. He reported some preliminary indications of interest, but no definite bid yet.

The Museum's lawyer told the board that, based on his discussions with Pennzoil, he believed that if the board went back "firm" with an offer of $110 plus a $5 stub, Pennzoil would accept it. After a recess, the Museum's president (also a director of Getty Oil) moved that the Getty board should accept Pennzoil's proposal provided that the stub be raised to $5, and the board voted 15 to 1 to approve this counterproposal to Pennzoil. The board then voted themselves and Getty's officers and advisors indemnity for any liability arising from the events of the past few months. Additionally, the board authorized its executive compensation committee to give "golden parachutes" (generous termination benefits) to the top executives whose positions "were likely to be affected" by the change in management. There was evidence that during another brief recess of the board meeting, the counteroffer of $110 plus a $5 stub was presented to and accepted by Pennzoil. After Pennzoil's acceptance was conveyed to the Getty board, the meeting was adjourned, and most board members left town for their respective homes.

That evening, the lawyers and public relations staff of Getty Oil and the Museum drafted a press release describing the transaction between Pennzoil and the Getty entities. The press release, announcing an agreement in principle on the terms of the Memorandum of Agreement but with a price of $110 plus a $5 stub, was issued on Getty Oil letterhead the next morning, January 4, and later that day, Pennzoil issued an identical press release.

On January 4, Boisi continued to contact other companies, looking for a higher price than Pennzoil had offered. After talking briefly with Boisi, Texaco management called several meetings with its in-house financial planning group, which over the course of the day studied and reported to management on the value of Getty Oil, the Pennzoil offer terms, and a feasible price range at which Getty might be acquired. Later in the day, Texaco hired an investment banker, First Boston, to represent it with respect to a possible acquisition of Getty Oil. Meanwhile, also on January 4, Pennzoil's lawyers were working on a draft of a formal "transaction agreement" that described the transaction in more detail than the outline of terms contained in the Memorandum of Agreement and press release.

On January 5, *The Wall Street Journal* reported on an agreement reached between Pennzoil and the Getty entities, describing essentially the terms contained in the Memorandum of Agreement. The Pennzoil board met to ratify the actions of its officers in negotiating an agreement with the Getty entities, and Pennzoil's attorneys periodically attempted to contact the other parties' advisors and attorneys to continue work on the transaction agreement.

The board of Texaco also met on January 5, authorizing its officers to make an offer for 100 percent of Getty Oil and to take any necessary action in connection therewith. Texaco first contacted the Museum's lawyer, Lipton, and arranged a meeting to discuss the sale of the Museum's shares of Getty Oil to Texaco. Lipton instructed his associate, on her way to the meeting in progress of the lawyers drafting merger documents for the Pennzoil-Getty transaction, to not attend that meeting, because he needed her at his meeting with Texaco. At the meeting with Texaco, the Museum outlined various issues it wanted resolved in any transaction with Texaco, and then agreed to sell its 11.8 percent ownership in Getty Oil.

That evening, Texaco met with Gordon Getty to discuss the sale of the Trust's shares. He was informed that the Museum had agreed to sell its shares to Texaco. Gordon Getty's advisors had previously warned him that the Trust shares might be "locked out" in a minority position if Texaco bought, in addition to the Museum's shares, enough of the public shares to achieve over 50 percent ownership of the company. Gordon Getty accepted Texaco's offer of $125 per share and signed a letter of his intent to sell his stock to Texaco, as soon as a California temporary restraining order against his actions as trustee was lifted.

At noon on January 6, Getty Oil held a telephone board meeting to discuss the Texaco offer. The board voted to withdraw its previous counterproposal to Pennzoil and unanimously voted to accept Texaco's offer. Texaco immediately issued a press release announcing that Getty Oil and Texaco would merge.

Soon after the Texaco press release appeared, Pennzoil telexed the Getty entities, demanding that they honor their agreement with Pennzoil. Later that day, prompted by the telex, Getty Oil filed a suit in Delaware for declaratory judgment that it was not bound to any contract with Pennzoil. The merger agreement between Texaco and Getty Oil was signed on January 6; the stock purchase agreement with the Museum was signed on January 6; and the stock exchange agreement with the Trust was signed on January 8, 1984. . . .

The parties agree that in our review, we are required to apply the substantive law of New York and the procedural law of Texas. . . .

## Body of Opinion

**Justice Warren.** Texaco argues first that there was no evidence or there was insufficient evidence to support the jury's answers to Special Issue No. 1. The jury found that the Trust, the Museum, and Getty Oil Company intended to bind themselves to an agreement with Pennzoil containing certain enumerated terms at the end of the Getty Oil Company board meeting on January 3, 1984. Texaco claims that not only is there insufficient evidence of any intent to be found but also that the "agreement" referred to in Special Issue No. 1 is too indefinite to be a legally enforceable contract.

Texaco contends that under controlling principles of New York law, there was insufficient evidence to support the jury's finding that at the end of the Getty Oil board meeting on January 3, the Getty entities intended to bind themselves to an agreement with Pennzoil.

Pennzoil responds that the question of the parties' intent is a fact question, and the jury was free to accept or reject Texaco's after-the-fact testimony of subjective intent. Pennzoil contends that the evidence showed that the parties intended to be bound to the terms in the Memorandum of Agreement plus a price term of $110 plus a $5 stub, even though the parties may have contemplated a later, more formal document to memorialize the agreement already reached. Pennzoil also argues that the binding effect of the Memorandum of Agreement was conditioned only upon approval of the board, not also upon execution of the agreement by a Getty signator. . . .

Thus, under New York law, the parties are given the power to obligate themselves informally or only by a formal signed writing, as they wish. The emphasis in deciding when a binding contract exists is on intent rather than on form. . . .

In its brief, Texaco asserts that, as a matter of black letter New York law, the "subject to" language in the press release established that the parties were not then bound and intended to be bound only after signing a definitive agreement, citing *Banking & Trading Corp. v. Reconstruction Finance Corp.* The court in that case stated that "if the agreement is expressly subject to the execution of a formal contract, this intent must be respected and no contract found until then." However, the court went on to say that where intent is less sharply expressed, the trier of fact must determine it as best he can. Although the intent to formalize an agreement is some evidence of an intent not to be bound before signing such a writing, it is not conclusive. The issue of when the parties intended to be bound is a fact question to be decided from the parties' acts and communications. . . .

Regardless of what interpretation we give to the conditional language in the press release, we conclude that it did not so clearly express the intent of the parties not to be bound to conclusively resolve that issue, as Texaco asserts. . . .

Texaco also contends that explicit language of reservation in drafts of Pennzoil's transaction agreement indicates the parties' expressed intent not to be bound without a signed writing. Texaco asserts that "Pennzoil's lawyers carefully stated that the parties' obligations would become binding only 'after the execution and delivery of this Agreement.'" . . .

A reasonable conclusion from reading the entire drafts is that the phrase "after the execution and delivery of this Agreement" was used chiefly to indicate the timing of various acts that were to occur, and not to impose an express precondition to the formation of a contract. Compare *Reprosystem* ("when executed and delivered," the agreement would become "a valid and binding agreement"). Again, the language upon which Texaco relies does not so clearly express an intent not to be bound to resolve that issue or to remove the question from the ambit of the trier of fact. . . .

Considering the type of action, the conduct involved, and the need for deterrence, we are of the opinion that the punitive damages are excessive and that the trial court abused its discretion in not suggesting a remittitur. Though our Texas guidelines are similar to those of New York, New York courts have adopted a more conservative stance on punitive damages. There is a point where punitive damages may overstate their purpose and serve to confiscate rather than to deter or punish. In this case, punitive damages of one billion dollars are sufficient to satisfy any reason for their being awarded, whether it be punishment, deterrence, or encouragement

of the victim to bring legal action. We conclude that the award of punitive damages is excessive by two billion dollars.

## Judgment and Result

If within thirty days from the date of this judgment, Pennzoil files in this Court a remittitur of two billion dollars, as suggested above, the judgment will be reformed and affirmed as to the award of $7.53 billion in compensatory damages and $1 billion in exemplary damages; otherwise the judgment will be reversed and remanded.

## Questions and Comments

1. After the Texas Court of Appeals case, Texaco appealed to the Texas Supreme Court, which, in a *two-sentence* decision made without hearing oral argument, refused to upset the Texas Court of Appeals decision. Texaco earlier had tried to get the federal courts to enjoin Texas's enforcement of its appeal bond law, which would have required that Texaco post $10.53 billion *before* it could appeal to the Texas Court of Appeals or the Texas Supreme Court. Texaco was successful in its attempt to get the U.S. District Court in New York to enjoin the full use of the Texas appeal bonding requirement. The federal district court reduced the appeal bond to $1 billion. The U.S. Court of Appeals for the Second Circuit in New York basically upheld the district court. During this time Texaco was able to appeal to the Texas Court of Appeals. However, Pennzoil appealed the federal injunction decree to the U.S. Supreme Court which *reversed* the lower federal court decision on the appeal bond issue. This forced Texaco into bankruptcy on Sunday, April 12, 1987, so that it could appeal the Texas Court of Appeals decision to the Texas Supreme Court. As already noted, the Texas Supreme Court wasted little ink in affirming the court of appeals decision, and left Texaco with a last appeal on issues of federal law only. Before that happened Texaco and Pennzoil settled their wrongful interference with contractual relations suit for $3 billion in cash. This settlement forced Texaco to reorganize.

2. Who was the contract between in the *Texaco–Pennzoil* case? Who interfered with this contract? Are punitive damages possible for this type of tort?

3. Was the contract in question written or oral? Is it not odd that a billion-dollar merger would be oral?

4. If it is uncertain whether Pennzoil and Getty intended to have a contract before there was a writing, who decides this matter?

5. The Texas Court of Appeals found no judicial misconduct when the trial judge in the case received a $10,000 campaign contribution from Pennzoil's lead attorney *after* the judge had been assigned the case. The Court of Appeals said that judges have to run election campaigns, that they need money to do so, and that it is logical that the lawyers would be contributors to these election campaigns.

## INTENTIONAL INFLICTION OF MENTAL DISTRESS

The tort **intentional infliction of mental distress** places liability on a person for intentionally causing severe emotional distress in situations where the actor's conduct goes beyond reasonable decency.

Intentional infliction of mental distress tries to protect people's peace of mind by allowing recovery if another person causes a plaintiff serious mental distress by an extremely outrageous act. An example would be wrapping a bloody dead rat in a loaf of bread and giving it to a sensitive person to open.

Intentional infliction of mental distress is a fairly new tort. Courts have for a long time given persons with physical injuries money for mental suffering "parasitic" (added on) to physical harm. The idea was that the victim was unlikely to be faking mental suffering if he or she had physical injuries.

Problems surround the whole notion of allowing recovery for mental injury without physical harm. First, mental suffering can be faked, allowing recovery for false claims. Second, this tort could flood the courts with lawsuits because of the large amount of mental stress in today's society. Third, this tort could encourage people to become crybabies, unable to stand the stress of modern life. Fourth, this tort could be a way for angry employees to get even with a boss who has properly disciplined them.

## DEFAMATION

*For help locating tort law, see*
*http://law2.house.gov*

**Defamation** has several key elements. First, a statement must be made by someone about another person. Second, the statement must hold up to ridicule, contempt, or scorn the person about whom the statement is made. Generally, favorable statements, such as "she is an intelligent person," are not defamatory because they fail to satisfy the holding up to ridicule, contempt, or scorn requirement. Third, the statement must be published. For defamation purposes, publication merely means that the statement is heard (if oral) or seen (if written) by at least one other person. Publication does not mean published in book form.

Defamation as an intentional tort is designed to discourage abuse of reputations and to protect a person's relations with other people. This tort tries to make liable a person who says or writes untrue statements about another that hold up the person spoken about to ridicule, contempt, or scorn in the minds of others.

Several defenses to defamation include the following:

1. Truth
2. Lack of an element of the definition
3. Privilege (absolute or qualified)

Truth can be used as a defense. If, for example, Sally says something true to Maggie that makes Irene look ridiculous, contemptible, or scorned, most states say that this type of statement is not defamation.

**Privilege** means that, even though a defendant has uttered or written statements that would otherwise be defamatory, a defendant is not liable because of some superior public policy of free expression. The two types of privileges are absolute and qualified. **Absolute privilege** means that a person may make the defamatory remark maliciously or without necessity. **Qualified privilege** is a right to make defamatory statements limited by motive and manner in which the remarks were made. Some examples of absolute privileged comments include remarks made on the floor of legislatures or at legislative hearings, executive communications, court or judicial hearings, husband–wife communications, and in publications consented to by the plaintiff.

The two types of defamation are libel and slander. Libel is written and slander is oral, although some difficult "in-between" areas exist. For example, are defamatory remarks spoken on television or radio slander or libel? Some courts have said that such remarks are libelous.

The *East v. Bullock's Inc.* case illustrates problems associated with alleged defamatory statements by an employer when evaluating an employee thought to have stolen from the employer. As you will see, the employer raised the qualified privilege defense.

---

## East v. Bullock's Inc.
Federal District Court (D. Arizona)
34 F.Supp.2d 1176 (1998)

---

### Background and Facts

Melinda Ann East was employed at the Bullock's department store in Scottsdale, Arizona, from July 10, 1991, until she was terminated on March 29, 1995. During the course of her employment, she worked in various positions. Initially, she was hired as a sales associate and paid on an hourly basis. In April of 1992, she was promoted to manager of the Young Men's department and reclassified as a salaried employee. From February of 1993 through May of 1993, she worked as a merchandise trainer and was again paid hourly. In May of 1993 she was named manager of the Children's department and paid on a salaried basis. In December of 1993, she became an assistant manager in the Designer Ladies Dresses department and was paid hourly. Thereafter, she assumed the position of selling manager in the Men's Polo department on a salaried basis. In November of 1994, Bullock's redefined the position of selling manager and, although East retained the title, she was reclassified as an hourly worker. She continued in this capacity until her March 1995 termination.

On October 30, 1994, Kerry McBay, the human resources manager at Bullock's Scottsdale store, met with East to discuss problems relating to East's timekeeping. East had neglected to "clock in" and "clock out" on a regular basis as required by Bullock's rules of conduct.

Sometime in early 1995, another manager at the Scottsdale store reported that East was making additions or corrections to her time records after the fact, rather than on a real time basis. Thereafter, Bullock's security department placed East under surveillance. Video cameras recorded her entrances and exits. On several occasions, between March 15, 1995, and March 25, 1995, East's time records failed to match the times when she was observed entering and exiting the store.

On March 28, 1995, Security Chief Dale Lindgren interviewed East. When queried about the time discrepancies. East denied intentionally misrepresenting her hours. She apologized if she had made any inadvertent errors. She stated that her failure to punch in and out could be attributed to her frequent reclassification from hourly to salaried. Salaried employees are not required to record their time.

After East's interview, she was suspended by Mr. McBay. Mr. McBay then sought direction from Denise Flynn, Bullock's vice-president of human resources. Ms. Flynn instructed Mr. McBay to terminate East. East was terminated on March 29, 1995.

At the time of East's termination, Ms. Flynn called Jill Lansdale, the Scottsdale store manager, and advised her of East's termination. Ms. Lansdale informed the senior managers in the store that East had been terminated for falsifying company documents.

Based on the foregoing events East filed a number of claims against Bullock's including the defamation.

### Body of Opinion

**District Judge Ezra.** . . . Count 3 of Plaintiff's Amended Complaint alleges defamation. Plaintiff argues that Ms. Lansdale, Bullock's vice-president of human relations, made statements to other managers that Plaintiff was terminated for falsifying company documents. Plaintiff attempts to characterize her termination as one for timekeeping theft and makes much of the fact that accusations of theft are per se defamatory. However, Plaintiff has not proffered any evidence that Ms. Lansdale said anything about theft.

Moreover, Plaintiff's defamation claim fails because Ms. Lansdale's statements were true, that is, Plaintiff was actually terminated for falsifying company documents, namely her time records. Although Ms. Lansdale did not independently investigate the grounds for Plaintiff's termination, she did not recklessly or negligently disregard the truth.

Finally, even if Ms. Lansdale's statements were not true, the statements were made in a meeting with other store managers. Bullock's argues that such statements fall within a qualified privilege under Arizona law. The Arizona Supreme Court recognized . . . a two-part test for determining whether a qualified privilege exists. First, the court must examine the circumstances to determine whether a privileged occasion arose. Second, once a conditional privilege applies, a plaintiff must prove the privilege was abused by proving actual malice or by demonstrating excessive publication. Abuse through "actual malice" occurs when the defendant makes a statement knowing its falsity or actually entertaining doubts about its truth. . . . Abuse through excessive publication results from publication to an unprivileged recipient not reasonably necessary to protect the interest upon which the privilege is grounded. . . . Although the second part of the test is usually a question of fact for the jury, the court may decide the issue if there is no evidence of malice or excessive publication.

In this case, Ms. Lansdale's publication of Plaintiff's termination to other managers is entitled to a qualified privilege based on "common interest." Occasions in which "one is entitled to learn from his associates what is done in a matter in which he has an interest in common with them," warrant a qualified privilege. . . . Co-managers in a company would have a common interest in learning of an employee's termination. Furthermore, because there is no evidence of actual malice or excessive publication, the court finds that the conditional privilege has not been abused.

## Judgment and Result

Statements by the store's vice-president of human relations that plaintiff was terminated for falsifying company documents were privileged from defamation action.

## Questions

1. Does the decision acknowledge that managers have a broad privilege that extends to even saying untrue statements about company employees if done at company meetings where such matters are appropriately discussed? What limits does the court place on statements made even during closed meetings? Can such discussions take place at a company picnic where many employees unrelated to personnel matters, such as custodians and stockholders, are present? What if family members who are not company employees are present at the picnic—what business do they have hearing about possible employee thefts of company property?

2. Does limited dissemination of allegedly defamatory remarks only within the affected organization tend to show the speaker's goodwill or is more required of supervisory personnel?

3. Are the arguments in favor of recognizing the qualified privilege doctrine especially strong today where employers are discovering that employee theft accounts for greater losses than those from shoplifters? If allegations that an employee is performing a given job unsatisfactorily prove to be untrue, does this error not stigmatize the employee? Does this type of incident not suggest that employers should be especially careful in appraising employee performance and corroborate allegations with *objective* evidence prior to making any allegations?

4. If East had shown that many other hourly employees of Bullock's routinely violated the time clock rule and were not disciplined at all, might this factor indicate that Bullock's was using East's violations as a pretext for dismissing her? Also, even if East and East alone were violating the time clock rule, might it not reveal prejudice against East if it could be shown that East's sales performance far exceeded that of her co-workers?

5. Most states do require that plaintiff prove damages before recovering in a slander case unless it is slander per se. The lack of malice, however, can mitigate A's damages.

6. The *East* case speaks of defamation (slander) per se in which statements injuring a person in her trade, business, or professional calling are made. In such cases damages or malice is presumed. Why?

## CHAPTER SUMMARY

Torts are breaches of noncontractual civil duties. Torts and crimes can overlap, but not all torts are crimes. Torts and contracts are both areas of civil law, but contract duties generally arise by agreements. Tort duties generally do not arise by agreement.

Remedies for torts include nominal, compensatory, and possibly punitive damages for intentional torts. Equitable remedies such as injunctions are also possible.

Torts can fall into the following categories: negligence, intentional torts, and strict liability torts.

Negligence involves duty, breach of the standard of care, proximately causing damages. Defenses to negligence include contributory negligence, assumption of risk, and lack of an element of the definition of negligence, for example, no duty.

Intentional torts include fraud, defamation, false imprisonment, conversion, wrongful interference with contractual relations, invasion of privacy, and abuse of process.

■ MANAGER'S ETHICAL DILEMMA ■

Oscar Fuller could not stand it anymore. He had been sued again because his business, which ran a skating rink, had put "see through" ceilings in the women's restrooms for surveillance purposes. A woman customer had learned of it and accused Oscar of peeping at her, which he denied doing. Not only that, she successfully sued his business for the intentional tort of invasion of the right of privacy and won both compensatory and punitive damages. What really irked Oscar was that he had installed the ceilings after another woman patron had been robbed and raped while in the restroom and had successfully sued him for negligence in not supervising his restrooms more carefully.

Now Oscar saw an opportunity to get legal liability under control. A tort reform bill had been introduced in the state legislature. The bill contained the following provisions: (1) a "cap" on pain and suffering awards of $300,000 per incident; (2) a $250,000 cap on punitive damages; (3) a requirement that negligence claims against businesses be arbitrated before being allowed to go to court and, if such claims went to court and the jury award was less than 30 percent above the arbitrator's award, the party moving the case to court would have to pay both parties' attorney fees; and (4) a no-fault legal regime for negligence claims against vehicle drivers.

What ethical considerations might enter Oscar's decision on whether to support this bill

## DISCUSSION QUESTIONS

1. Compelled self-defamation, sometimes called *compelled self-disclosure*, is a defamation doctrine that says the defamed person is forced by circumstances to reveal defamatory statements made about himself to third persons. For example, in applying for a job a person might be asked why they left a previous job. Suppose the former employer discharged the applicant for "theft of company property," but the employee disputes this claim. Nonetheless, rather than lying about it, the job applicant says, "My former employer dismissed me for allegedly stealing company property. I dispute his claim." The prospective employer decides not to hire the applicant, believing the former employer. The applicant then bring a defamation action against his former employer, arguing compelled self-disclosure ("I had to repeat my old employer's defamation to my new, prospective employer to be a truthful person.")

    Valencia made such a claim against Citibank International (Citibank) when she brought a defamation suit against Citibank. Specifically, Valencia alleged that Citibank's reasons for terminating her were false and that she was compelled to disclose the false reasons for her termination to prospective employers. Should the state of Florida (where this case arose) recognize the doctrine of compelled self-disclosure and permit the employee to sue the former employer for defamation when the former employer said nothing to anyone about why the former employee was terminated? [*Valencia v. Citibank International*, 728 So.2d 330 (Fla. Ct. App. 1999)].

2. Explain the difference between torts and crimes.

3. What does it mean to say that tort law is a legal laboratory?

4. List the four parts of the negligence definition.

5. How is the ORP person different from each of us?

6. Name two defenses to negligence.

7. What is the difference between intentional torts and crimes?

8. Is tort law generally state or federal law?

9. Define *fraud*.

10. A landlord had secretly installed a listening device in his tenants' bedroom. This device enabled him to monitor and record voices and sounds in the bedroom. The tenants did not claim that the landlord actually used the listening device. Did the tenants have a good claim for invasion of their right of privacy? [*Hamberger v. Eastman*, 206 A.2d 239 (N.H.1964)].

11. Hallmark Builders, Inc., sued a local television station for defamation. The local television newscast reported on problems encountered by new home buyers, including defects in construction. Did a close-up camera shot of hairline masonry cracks in the house accurately represent the cracks, or was this defamatory? [*Hallmark Builders Inc. v. Gaylord Broadcasting Co.*, 733 F.2d 1461 (11th Cir. 1984)].

12. A manufacturer's regional sales manager criticized a particular salesperson's job performance to the company president. The remarks related solely to the sales work for the company. Were these remarks privileged? [*Humphrey v. National Semiconductor Corp.*, 463 N.E. 2d 1197 (Mass. App. 1984)].

13. A motorcyclist was in an accident with a Postal Service jeep. The motorcyclist proved damages for injuries, medical expenses, pain and suffering, and disability and impairment amounted to $12,346.15. His negligence was 50 percent of the cause of the accident. The government showed that it sustained $589.67 in damages. The jurisdiction follows a comparative negligence scheme. What did each party recover? [*Wright v. United States*, 574 F.Supp. 160 (1983)].

14. Ernest Gortarez, age 16, and his cousin, Albert Hernandez, age 18, went to Smitty's store on January 2, 1979. About 8 P.M., Gortarez picked up a 59-cent vaporizer used to freshen the air in cars. He asked if he could pay for it in the front of the store when he finished shopping. The clerk said yes, but decided the request was suspicious and had a hunch that Gortarez would try to leave without paying. The two cousins finally left the store through an unattended checkout aisle. The clerk, Robert Sjulestad, had followed the two boys out of the store and had not seen them pay for or put down the vaporizer. Thus, the clerk thought they had shoplifted it. Sjulestad told the security guard and store manager, "Those two guys just ripped us off." The assistant manager and two other store employees followed the boys into the parking lot, where the guard flashed his police badge (he was an off-duty policeman moonlighting as a security guard). The guard said, "I believe you have something you did not pay for." The guard then seized Hernandez, put his arms on the car, and began searching him. Hernandez offered no resistance, even though Gibson did not ask for the vaporizer, nor did Gibson say what he was looking for. Gortarez saw Gibson grab his cousin and was outraged at this behavior. He used strong language to protest the detention and the search, yelling at Gibson to leave his cousin alone. Gortarez pushed Gibson away from his cousin. Gibson then put a choke hold on Gortarez for a period of time, even after Gortarez had advised the store employees that the vaporizer had been left in the store. When a carryout boy told the manager that he had found the vaporizer in a basket at the checkout lane, the two cousins were released. The cousins then sued Smitty's for false imprisonment. What was the result? [*Gortarez v. Smitty's Super Valu, Inc.*, 680 P.2d 807 (1984)].

## INFOTRAC KEYWORDS

**Use your InfoTrac password to look up articles on http://www.infotrac-college.com**

Keywords: *proximate cause, contributory negligence, strict liability, intentional torts, fraud, invasion of privacy, defamation.*

For suggested readings, please visit this book's Web site at **http://fisher.westbuslaw.com** (click on "Internet Applications").

# NATURE, DEFINITION, AND CLASSIFICATION OF CONTRACTS

*"FREE TO CHOOSE"*

—MILTON
FRIEDMAN

With this chapter we survey the law covering contracts. We shall define contracts, discuss how contracts fit into the U.S. legal system, and examine contract classifications as well as the basic rules of contract formation.

## HOW CONTRACTS FIT INTO THE MARKET ECONOMY

In introductory economics courses you learned about the market economy and the intersection of supply and demand curves, which set the price of goods and services. It is important to note that these supply and demand curves summarize not one but millions of **contracts**, which are agreements between buyers and sellers of all goods and services. In other words, contracts are the basis for the market economy. When people trade for money or exchange goods for goods (barter), they make contracts.

## TRENDS IN CONTRACT LAW

In the Middle Ages, people were born serfs or nobles. With a few exceptions, they kept their status of prince or serf for their entire lives. Serfs essentially were slaves with few rights; they had no freedom to enter contracts to work where they wanted in order to improve their economic and social status.

*A site dealing with business law and providing information about contracts in particular can be found at http://www.yahoo.com/government/law*

In the nineteenth and early twentieth centuries the market economy thrived, and individual freedom increased. People were free to work where they wanted and could own property in their own names. People could change their status by working and contracting. These freedoms continue today.

In the mid- and late twentieth century, two trends have emerged in contract law. The first trend has been toward long-term contracts. For example, a utility company may enter a 10- or 20-year contract to buy coal. Second, since the late 1970s, a definite trend toward monopolies has developed, which concentrates economic power. This second trend was intensified by the merger mania of the 1980s and 1990s. Because monopolies reduce the number of competitors, a few large businesses have great power to set contract terms. These terms include price, warranty, and quality standards.

## PHILOSOPHIES FOUND IN CONTRACT LAW

Several philosophies, or beliefs, are found in contracts. First is the *libertarian* idea that people have freedom of choice. For example, people can contract for a particular job, buy or rent a house, buy a Ford or a Cadillac, and spend or save all or part of their paychecks. Because individuals are free to choose and shape their lives, they answer these questions on an individual basis.

Another philosophy found in contracts is the *utilitarian* concept of the greatest good for the greatest number. Again, each individual determines the "greatest good" personally. For example, a person who contracts to go to school to learn to be an insurance broker believes spending money on education is more valuable than spending it on a car or a vacation. Another person might do the opposite.

Finally, contracts are not positive law using John Austin's definition of positive law (a command of government with sanctions if it is broken). Instead, private people (not government) make their own contracts. However, *contract law*, as distinct from contracts, is made by courts and legislatures and, thus, is positive law. Note also that court-ordered remedies for breach of contract are a type of sanction, and thereby satisfy part of Austin's positive law definition.

## LAW GOVERNING CONTRACTS

*For access to the Uniform Commercial Code, go to http://www.law.cornell.edu/topics/contracts.html*

The law governing contracts is generally state law, including state statutes or common law, or judge-made rules. Every state except Louisiana has passed the Uniform Commercial Code's (UCC) Article 2, which sets the rules for contracts dealing with goods. Real estate, services, and insurance contracts are controlled by common law and other state statutes.

## Contract Definitions[1]

Various legal scholars and authorities give us contract definitions. Members of the American Law Institute (ALI), a nongovernmental group of legal scholars including professors and practicing lawyers, read many cases and try to restate them in an easy-to-understand way. The ALI explains contracts in a set of books called the *Restatement, Second, Contracts.*

*Restatement's Contract Definition.* After reading thousands of cases, ALI scholars define a contract as follows: "A contract is a promise or a set of promises for the breach of which the law gives a remedy, or the performance of which the law in some way recognizes as a duty." Basically, this definition means that if a judge would make someone keep a promise, it is a contract. A problem with this definition is that a person has to sue to get a judge's decision.

*Common Definition of a Contract.* The common definition of a contract is "an agreement between competent parties enforceable in court." An agreement involves an offer and acceptance. The offer and acceptance must be bargained for. *Competent parties* refers to the idea that minority age, insanity, and drunkenness on the part of one or more persons will result in an agreement that is void or voidable.

*For additional information on contract law and business law in general, to to **http://www. lawreview.org***

The "enforceable in court" part of the contract definition refers to several points. First, not all agreements are legally enforceable contracts. Social agreements (or *dates*) are not contracts. For example, if Fred breaks a date with Marsha, Marsha *will not* get a judge to award her a remedy for breach of contract. Second, excited utterances (such as "I'll give a billion dollars to anyone who saves my drowning child," yelled by a mother to a crowd as she watches her child pulled under by an ocean current) do not give rise to contracts. Therefore, the hero who saves the woman's child is not entitled to a billion dollars given her excitement when she made the offer. Third, other problems (such as fraud, mistake, innocent misrepresentation, duress, unconscionability, or lack of a written contract where a writing is required) could make a contract unenforceable. Fourth, many contract definitions require that the parties give each other *consideration*. Consideration means that the contracting parties each have given up a right that was bargained for (asked for) by the other party. Consideration takes the form of a promise for a promise in a bilateral contract or a promise for an act in a unilateral contract.

## The Objective Theory of Contracts

The **objective theory of contracts** means that contracts are determined by what people appear to have done (which is "objective"), not what they think they have done (which is "subjective"). This theory of contracts forces judges to point to evidence people can see, such as a signed contract, to decide whether a contract exists.

For example, Jim thinks he is playing a joke on Sarah. He pretends to offer his $35,000 Cadillac to her for $15,000 and signs a contract saying so. He does not actually intend to follow through on such an offer. However, based on appearances,

---

[1] This chapter is a survey, not an in-depth treatment of contract law. Other contract topics such as consideration, illegality, and unconscionability are covered later under the topics of consumer protection and product liability.

any reasonable person would say Jim made an offer. Therefore, the objective theory of contracts says Jim and Sarah have a contract, assuming Sarah accepted, even if Jim does not want one.

## CONTRACT CLASSIFICATIONS

We shall now examine five different contract classifications:

1. Bilateral and unilateral
2. Express and implied
3. Valid, voidable, void, and unenforceable
4. Executed and executory
5. Quasi-contracts

### BILATERAL AND UNILATERAL CONTRACTS

The basis for the bilateral and unilateral contract classification is the number of promises.

When two people exchange promises—one promise for another—they make a **bilateral contract**. For example, Irving says to Herman, "Promise to paint my house, and I'll promise to pay you $500." If Herman promises to do so, he has made a bilateral contract with Irving.

A **unilateral contract** consists of a promise and an act. A person makes a promise and also asks for an act in return. One example is: "I'll pay you $500 (the promise) if you paint my house" (the requested act). The promise is the offer, and the offeree's performance of the requested act is the acceptance. Only when the requested act is complete is there a contract.

Note the difference between bilateral and unilateral contracts. In a situation involving a unilateral contract, the offeror asks for a return act ("paint my house"), not a promise. However, if an offeror asks for a return promise, he or she wants to enter a bilateral contract. Only a return promise (not an act) will form the contract in a bilateral case.

One other point: A person does not have to use the word *promise* to make a promise. Any words showing you promise (such as "okay," or "I agree") will do. *Davis v. Jacoby* examines the distinction between unilateral and bilateral contracts.

## Davis v. Jacoby
### Supreme Court of California
### 1 Cal. 2d 370, 34 P.2d 1026 (1934)

### Background and Facts

Caro Davis was the niece of Blanche and Rupert Whitehead, who were childless. The Whiteheads were very fond of Caro, who lived with them in California for a while. Then Caro married Frank Davis and moved to Canada.

When Mr. Whitehead became ill, he wrote to Caro and Frank. In the letter, he asked them to come to California and care for the Whiteheads until they died. In return for doing so, Mr. Whitehead

promised to give Caro everything in his will (estimated at $150,000 in 1931). Frank Davis sent a return letter saying he and Caro accepted Mr. Whitehead's offer. The Davises prepared to leave Canada but before leaving, they received word that Mr. Whitehead had committed suicide.

The Davises went to California to care for Mrs. Whitehead until she died. Soon after, they learned that Mr. Whitehead's will did not give them anything. The estate argued Mr. Whitehead's letter was an offer requesting an act (an offer for a unilateral contract).

Because the act (going to California and caring for the Whiteheads) was not done *before* Whitehead died, the estate executor argued there was no contract.

The Davises argued that Mr. Whitehead had asked for a *return promise* (not a return act). The Davises had made a return promise *before* Whitehead died.

## Body of Opinion

The theory of the trial court and of respondents of this appeal is that the letter of April 12 was an offer to contract, but that such offer could only be accepted by performance and could not be accepted by a promise to perform, and that said offer was revoked by the death of Mr. Whitehead before performance. In other words, it is contended that the offer was an offer to enter into a unilateral contract, and that the purported acceptance of April 14 was of no legal effect.

The distinction between unilateral and bilateral contracts is well settled in the law. It is well stated in Section 12 of the American Institute's *Restatement of the Law of Contracts* as follows: "A unilateral contract is one in which no promisor receives a promise as consideration for his promise. A bilateral contract is one in which there are mutual promises between two parties to the contract; each party being both the promisor and the promisee." This definition is in accord with the law of California.

In the case of unilateral contracts no notice of acceptance by performance is required. Section 1584 of the Civil Code provides: "Performance of the conditions of a proposal . . . is an acceptance of the proposal."

Although the legal distinction between unilateral and bilateral contracts is thus well settled, the difficulty in any particular case is to determine whether the particular offer is one to enter into a bilateral or unilateral contract. . . . By the provisions of the *Restatement of the Law of Contracts*, it is expressly provided that there is a presumption that the offer is to enter into a bilateral contract. Section 31 provides: "In case of doubt it is presumed that an offer invites the formation of a bilateral contract by an acceptance amounting in effect to a promise by the offeree to perform what the offer requests, rather than the formation of one or more unilateral contracts by actual performance on the part of the offeree." Professor Williston, in his *Treatise on Contracts*, volume 1 § 60, also takes the position that a presumption in favor of bilateral contracts exists.

In the comment following Section 31 of the *Restatement*, the reason for such presumption is stated as follows: "It is not always easy to determine whether an offeror requests an act or a promise to do the act. As a bilateral contract immediately and fully protects both parties, the interpretation is favored that a bilateral contract is proposed."

While the California cases have never expressly held that a presumption in favor of bilateral contracts exists, the cases clearly indicate a tendency to treat offers as offers of bilateral rather than of unilateral contracts.

Keeping these principles in mind, we are of the opinion that the offer of April 12 was an offer to enter into a bilateral as distinguished from a unilateral contract. Respondents argue that Mr. Whitehead had the right as offeror to designate his offer as either unilateral or bilateral. That is undoubtedly the law. It is then argued that from all the facts and circumstances it must be implied that what Whitehead wanted was performance and not a mere promise to perform. We think this is a non sequitur, in fact the surrounding circumstances lead to just the opposite conclusion. These parties were not dealing at arm's length. Not only were they related, but a very close and intimate friendship existed between them. The record indisputably demonstrates that Mr. Whitehead had confidence in Mr. and Mrs. Davis, in fact that he had lost all confidence in everyone else. The record indicates that Mr. Whitehead had become desperate, and that what he wanted was the promise of appellants that he could look to them for assistance. He knew from his past relationship with appellants that if they gave their promise to perform he could rely upon them. The correspondence between them indicates how desperately he desired this assurance. . . . "Will you let me hear from you as soon as possible—I know it will be a sacrifice but times are still bad and likely to be, so by settling down you can help me and Blanche and gain in the end." By thus specifically requesting an immediate reply Whitehead expressly indicated the nature of the acceptance desired by him, namely, appellants' promise that they would come to California and do the things requested by him. This promise was immediately sent by appellants upon receipt of the offer, and was received by Whitehead. It is elementary that when an offer has indicated the mode and means of acceptance, an acceptance in accordance with that mode or means is binding on the offeror.

Another factor which indicates that Whitehead must have contemplated a bilateral rather than a unilateral contract, is that the contract required Mr. and Mrs. Davis to perform services until the death of both Mr. and Mrs. Whitehead. It is obvious that if Mr. Whitehead died first some of these services were to be performed after his death, so that he would have to rely on the promise of the appellants to perform these services. It is also of some evidentiary force that Whitehead received the letter of acceptance and acquiesced in that means of acceptance. . . .

For the foregoing reasons we are of the opinion that the offer of April 12, 1931, was an offer to enter into a bilateral contract which was accepted by the letter of April 14, 1931. . . .

The judgment appealed from is reversed.

## Judgment and Result

The California Supreme Court held that Mr. Whitehead's letter to the Davises was an offer to enter a bilateral contract that Mr. Davis accepted by sending a letter of acceptance.

## Questions

1. If A says to B, "Come to California and I'll pay you $500," and B says, "I promise to come," is there a contract?
2. How does one distinguish between a unilateral and bilateral contract?
3. Was it clear whether the contract sued upon here was unilateral or bilateral? Is there a preferred construction if there is doubt? Why?

## EXPRESS AND IMPLIED CONTRACTS

**Express contracts** are those having the terms completely stated in words. Such contracts can be either oral or written. A contract between a homeowner and a home buyer covering many details in selling a house is an example of an express, written contract. Calling the local pizza shop and ordering a 14-inch pizza with mushrooms and sausage to be delivered to your dorm room is an example of an express oral contract, if the pizza shop accepts the order.

**Implied contracts** can also be inferred from the parties' conduct even though nothing is said. Such contracts are implied in fact, meaning the facts justify assuming that the parties intend a contract. Two kinds of implied contracts are contracts implied in law and contracts implied in fact.

The following example involves an implied-in-fact contract. A student is in a bookstore, picks out a book, takes it to the cashier, and puts down the necessary money. The clerk makes change and bags the book. Nothing is said, yet the parties' conduct shows they intended to make a contract.

## VALID, VOIDABLE, VOID, AND UNENFORCEABLE CONTRACTS

A contract is valid if it has no legal flaws. A **valid contract** is enforceable under virtually all circumstances.

Contracts are **voidable** when they have certain defects that could, but not necessarily will, make the contract unenforceable. At least one of the parties may escape voidable contracts by noting the defect. Defects making contracts voidable include fraud, innocent misrepresentation, and lack of contractual capacity (such as minority). For example, a 10-year-old who signs a contract to buy a Cadillac can avoid the contract because she or he is a minor.

Sometimes contracts have such serious flaws that they are called legally void. **Legally void** means no contract could have existed at all—ever. A contract can be void even though a piece of paper exists saying that it is a contract.

Factors that make an attempted contract void include illegality of the subject matter (such as contracts to commit murder), contracts against public policy, and attempts by persons adjudged legally insane to contract.

**Unenforceable contracts** are those failing to meet a procedural or formal requirement that makes them unenforceable. A *procedural flaw* would be not suing within the statute of limitations period. A *formal error* would involve making an oral contract when the statute of frauds requires a written one.

## EXECUTED AND EXECUTORY CONTRACTS

We can also classify contracts according to the degree to which they have been performed. Contracts partly performed or totally unperformed are **executory contracts**. Contracts fully performed by both parties are **executed contracts**.

It is possible for a contract to be fully performed (an executed contract) by one party and unperformed or partly performed (an executory contract) by the other party. For example, Claude Teagarden pays Bill Haymaker $10 to mow his lawn. Teagarden has fully executed his part of the contract, but Haymaker's part is executory until he finishes mowing.

## QUASI-CONTRACTS

A **quasi-contract** is not a contract but a legal idea that lets judges force a contract on parties even though they did not have one. The term *quasi-contract* means "like a contract." Quasi-contracts are also known as contracts implied in law, meaning a judge creates them.

*Purpose of the Quasi-Contract Theory.* The quasi-contract theory exists to prevent unjust enrichment. It applies in situations where one person confers benefits on another when it is reasonable to believe payment is expected, no gift is intended, and where no contract exists. A judge will tell the person receiving the benefits to pay the reasonable value, as set by the judge, of the benefits received.

*Example of a Quasi-Contract.* The following example involves a quasi-contract. Charles Walker calls Ace Painting Company (Ace) and tells the painters to paint his building. Ace mistakenly drives up in front of Bill Eshee's building and starts painting. Eshee sees the Ace truck and realizes they should be painting Walker's building next door. Eshee says nothing, hoping for a free paint job. When Ace finishes the job, Mr. Ace says to Eshee: "Well, Mr. Walker, how do you like the paint job?" Eshee replies, "It's great. But I'm Eshee. Walker's building is next door."

To allow Eshee to get a free paint job when he had reason to know that pay was expected would be unjust enrichment. Ace has no contract with Eshee. However, Ace can ask a judge to apply the quasi-contract idea to let Ace recover the reasonable value of the benefits Eshee got.

*Limits on Quasi-Contracts.* At times a judge will not allow a person to use the quasi-contract concept. If the person receiving benefits does not have a reasonable opportunity to reject the benefits before getting them, judges will not allow quasi-contract recovery. For example, suppose Ace Painting Company had painted Eshee's building, and Eshee had not known about the job until completion. Eshee would not have to pay on the basis of quasi-contract because he had no reasonable opportunity to reject the benefits.

A quasi-contract also does not apply when parties have a valid contract covering the matter. For example, suppose Ace Painting Company has a contract to paint Walker's building for $1,000. Ace's crew does the job, but Mr. Ace discovers that the job costs are $2,000. He cannot use the quasi-contract concept to recover $2,000 because his contract for $1,000 controls.

The *Matter of Estate of Milborn* case gives an example of a quasi-contract.

### Matter of Estate of Milborn
Illinois Appellate Court, Third District
122 Ill. App. 3d 688, 78 Ill Dec. 241, 461 N.E.2d 1075 (1984)

#### Background and Facts

The plaintiffs, Paul and LaVon Campbell, filed combined claims against the estate of Gertrude Milborn, deceased, seeking $5,000 for services performed for the decedent.

The only evidence at trial consisted of the unrebutted testimony of the plaintiffs. LaVon Campbell stated that except for the last few months of decedent's life, all meals during a five-year period from 1977 until the decedent's death in 1982, came from the Campbells' kitchen. Mrs. Campbell also did the housecleaning for the decedent and most of the laundry. Both of the plaintiffs made sure that the decedent took her medicine every day and in the proper dosages.

Paul Campbell testified that he mowed the decedent's lawn, cared for the yard, and patched the roof. While the decedent was hospitalized during the last few months of her life, Mr. Campbell was given a power of attorney authorizing him to handle the decedent's financial matters. Mr. Campbell also provided transportation for the decedent when she needed to see out-of-town doctors.

Both plaintiffs testified that they expected compensation for most of the services they performed. The court, sitting without a jury, found that the plaintiffs had established an implied contract with the decedent and allowed their claim in the amount of $5,000. The executor appeals.

## Body of Opinion

**Justice Heiple.**    There are two kinds of implied contracts: contracts implied in law (also called quasi-contracts) and contracts implied in fact. The trial court found that there was an implied contract between the decedent and the plaintiffs but did not specify which kind. The executor contends that the plaintiffs failed to prove either type of implied contract.

A contract implied in fact is one whereby a contractual duty is imposed by reason of a promissory expression which may be inferred from the facts and circumstances and the expressions on the part of the promissor which show an intention to be bound. The record in the present case reveals no specific acts, conduct or circumstances which permit us to infer a promissory expression or intent to be bound. There is no evidence of mutual understanding between the parties or the implied terms of the alleged agreement. Thus, there was no contract implied in fact.

A contract implied in law differs from a contract implied in fact in that it arises by implication of law wholly apart from the usual rules relating to contracts and does not depend on an agreement or consent of the parties. A contract implied in law is equitable in nature, predicated on the fundamental principle that no one should unjustly enrich himself at another's expense. Where services are rendered by one person for another which are knowingly and voluntarily accepted, the law presumes that such services were given and received in the expectation of being paid for and implies a promise to pay their reasonable worth. When set in the context of a claim against a decedent's estate, the facts giving rise to a quasi-contract must be proven by clear and convincing evidence.

The executor does not deny that the plaintiffs performed services which were knowingly and voluntarily accepted by the decedent. In fact, the executor presented no evidence at all on behalf of the estate. The executor's argument is that there was no quasi-contractual liability because the plaintiffs failed to prove by clear and convincing evidence that the decedent requested and expected to pay for the plaintiffs' services.

The plaintiffs were not required to prove that the decedent requested their services. As previously stated, where useful services are knowingly and voluntarily accepted, the law presumes that such services were given and received in the expectation of being paid for and implies a promise to pay. It is true that a person who officiously confers a benefit upon another is not entitled to be compensated therefor. However, it is not the absence of a request which bars recovery but the officiousness of the claimant's conduct.

Officiousness is synonymous with meddlesomeness and can be described as volunteering one's services where they are neither

asked for nor needed. *Webster's Third New International Dictionary* 1567 (1976). Despite the fact that the plaintiffs were not competent witnesses as to any request made by the decedent it would be unreasonable for us to assume, based on the nature of the work performed by the plaintiffs and the duration of their service, that the decedent made no request whatsoever. Furthermore, it cannot be said that the plaintiffs' services were unneeded.

According to Mrs. Campbell, the decedent lived alone and never cooked. She would only eat when food was brought to her. Doctors would prescribe medication for the decedent only if someone else would give it to her. Mr. Campbell performed all of the yard work and building maintenance. The decedent may not have required twenty-four hour nursing care, but it is obvious that she was unable to properly care for herself. In view of the fact that the plaintiffs were unable to obtain assistance from the decedent's family, their services were not only needed, they were essential and definitely not officious. Even without clear proof of a request by the decedent, her knowing and voluntary acceptance of the plaintiffs' necessary services over a five-year period raises a promise implied in law to pay the reasonable value of such services.

Next, the executor argues that the plaintiffs intended their services to be gratuitous. Gratuitous intent in cases of this type can be shown in one of two ways. The first is by the conduct of the claimant. With regard to the plaintiffs' intent and expectations, counsel for the executor made the following statement during closing argument: "I think that the testimony of the claimants show that one party expected to receive payment, that is the Campbells, certainly no contradiction at all on that." Based on the record, we agree with this conclusion. Having conceded that the plaintiffs' conduct did not demonstrate a gratuitous intent, the executor may not now argue to the contrary.

Gratuitous intent may also be presumed in certain cases. Where persons live together as members of one family, a promise to pay for services of one to another is not implied from the mere rendition and acceptance of such services. Absent a showing of an express or implied in fact contract for payment, the services are presumed to be gratuitous. Blood kinship is not necessary in order to raise the presumption. The rule rests upon the idea of mutual dependence between those who are members of one *immediate* family even though there may be no tie of blood or affinity.

The executor acknowledges that the plaintiffs are not related to the decedent by blood or marriage and did not share the same house as the decedent. Nonetheless, the executor asks us to extend the presumption of gratuitous intent because of the bond of friendship between the plaintiffs and decedent and because the plaintiffs loved the decedent and treated her as a member of the family.

A bond of friendship between parties who do not live as members of an immediate family is not regarded by the law as sufficient to raise a presumption of gratuitous intent. . . .

The final issue is whether the plaintiffs proved that their claim was worth $5,000. Mrs. Campbell testified that she arrived at a value of $5,000 based on the fact that her mother was paying $1,700 per month for nursing home care. Although the plaintiffs did not provide the decedent with twenty-four hour care as a nursing home, $5,000 is still a nominal figure which breaks down to approximately $60 per month for the plaintiffs' five years of service.

To recover under a quasi-contract, the plaintiffs are required to prove the reasonable value of their services. The executor certainly cannot argue that $60 per month is an excessive or unreasonable value to place on three meals per day, part-time nursing care, housecleaning, maintenance work and transportation. We find that $5,000 was a reasonable value to place on the plaintiffs' services and affirm the judgment of the circuit court of Hancock County.

## Judgment and Result

The Court of Appeals held that the Milborn estate was liable on a quasi-contract theory to the Campbells for services rendered to Mrs. Milborn before she died.

## Questions

1. Is a quasi-contract a contract that a court forces on a situation where the parties had no contract in fact? Why does the court impose a contract when none in fact existed?
2. If B, an unemployed painter, paints C's house during the night but C did not want the paint job, can B recover from C based on quasi-contract? How does this example differ from the *Milborn* case?

## THE MAKING OF A CONTRACT: THE OFFER

A contract is a legally enforceable agreement between competent parties. *Agreement* means mutual assent. Courts usually say that agreements are made up of offers and acceptances. Therefore, the first step in making a contract is for one person to make an **offer** to another. The person making the offer is called the **offeror**. The person to whom the offer is made is called the **offeree**.

What is an offer? An offer is made when the offeror in some way tells the offeree that the offeror wants to enter a contract with the offeree. The offer indicates what the offeror will do and what is wanted in return from the offeree, along with a definite willingness to commit. Offers can be made expressly or by implication. For example, an express offer occurs when a person signs a written contract to buy a house. An offer can also be made by implication. If Barbara Winslow enters Kmart, sees a blouse she likes, and takes it to the cashier, Winslow has made an offer by implication. The cashier then rings up the sale, puts the blouse in a bag, and hands it to Winslow. During this transaction, no words have been spoken, yet a contract has been made between Winslow and Kmart.

An easy way to think about making contracts is to remember the formula: offer + acceptance = contract.[2] The remainder of this chapter will examine offers and acceptances.

## INTENT NEEDED TO MAKE AN OFFER

An offer must be made with **objective intent**, which is how something looks to a reasonable person. If a person *appears* to be making an offer, then an offer has been made—even if the offeror does not intend to make an offer. What a person *thinks* has occurred is called **subjective intent**. It is objective, not subjective, intent that decides whether a person has made an offer.

---

[2] Keep in mind the *Restatement, Second's* definition of contract: "A contract is a promise or set of promises for the breach of which the law gives a remedy, or the performance of which the law in some way recognizes as a duty."

## UNENFORCEABLE OFFERS

*Jokes or Excited Utterances.* If an offer is clearly made as a joke or **excited utterance**, it is not a legally enforceable offer at all. So if an offeree accepts an offer that obviously is a joke, no contract exists. Similarly, if in an excited moment a person shouts that a huge, clearly unrealistic reward will be given, an offer has not been made. A person who accepts such an offer does not form a contract.

*Social Offers.* **Social offers** are not legally enforceable offers. For example, if Bill asks Mary to go to a party and then breaks the date, Mary cannot recover from Bill for breach of contract.

*Agreements to Agree.* **Agreements to agree** are not legally binding contracts. Rachael's statement to Bruce, "I agree that at some future time we shall make a contract to pay you a bonus for coming to work for my company," is not a legally binding contract because it provides no present commitment to an agreement.

*Statements Showing Intent.* Statements showing intent do not in and of themselves create contracts.

*Sham Transactions.* Sometimes people make what appear to be contracts to cheat creditors or the Internal Revenue Service. These transactions that are contracts in form but not in substance are referred to as **sham transactions**. For example, Harvey Slater, about to go bankrupt, contracts to sell his farm to his son Jim for $5, on the understanding that Jim would return the property to Harvey later; but Harvey's creditors can reclaim the farm from Jim because the contract was a sham or fraud on his creditors. No reasonable person viewing this arrangement would say objectively that intent to form a contract existed. Also, Harvey and Jim did not even subjectively intend to contract.

## INVITATIONS TO NEGOTIATE

When two people are negotiating, not all of their statements are offers, sometimes not even the first one. Instead, their first remarks are often **invitations to negotiate**. These invitations are not offers and, if accepted, do not become contracts. They are merely attempts to *feel out* the other party to strike the best deal if an offer and acceptance ever are made. They often take the form of questions, such as "Would you like to buy my Ford for $1,900?" Ads in newspapers and on television and radio are usually invitations to negotiate if they are general, incomplete, and not addressed to anyone in particular. Thus, it is usually the customer who comes into the store to make an offer, which the merchant may either accept or reject. If the rule were otherwise and merchants' ads were offers, merchants would have to carry huge inventories to avoid contract liability (if many customers accepted the offers in the ads).

Sometimes media ads are offers. If the ad is definite, complete, certain, and limited to certain specific items, it is more likely an offer than an invitation to negotiate.

## CERTAINTY

Generally, offers must be certain and definite. This rule helps courts decide the proper remedy if a contract is broken. An acceptance of an indefinite offer generally results in no contract. For example, an offer to lend money as a borrower's needs required was held to be too uncertain. Another offer stating that hay was to be measured according to government rule when several such rules existed was also held to be too indefinite.

The nine exceptions to the rule that offers (acceptances and the resulting contracts) must be definite are as follows:

1. *Trade custom.* Trade custom can clear up an offer's indefiniteness. For example, failure to state a price when it is understood in the trade that market price at the time of delivery was intended will be considered definite.
2. *Previous dealings.* When parties have dealt with one another before and have followed a practice that clears up a vague contract term, courts hold that the offer and contract are not void for lack of definiteness.
3. *Implicit terms.* Some terms in an offer are not expressly stated, but courts nonetheless find them to be implicit. Thus, if a contract fails to state a required performance time, it has been held that performance is to be within a reasonable time.
4. *Open terms in sale of goods contracts.* The UCC allows contract terms such as price or quantity to be valid if a commercially reasonable way of filling them later is available.
5. *Contracts of indefinite length.* Offers for contracts whose performance covers an indefinite period are valid. Courts find the necessary definiteness by allowing either to cancel any time. For example, Sarah is to be Beatrice's cook as long as Beatrice lives, or as long as Sarah performs satisfactorily.
6. *Cost-plus contracts.* In cost-plus contracts, one person agrees to purchase something and pay another's costs plus a fee calculated on some other basis, such as a percentage of the cost. Even though Mike does not know the total cost of building the Empire State Building, his offer to pay Tom his costs plus 10 percent for the project is definite enough.
7. *Requirements and output contracts.* A requirements contract exists when one person agrees to buy all of its requirements from another. Requirements contracts are valid even when a party does not know the exact requirements when the contract is made. Thus, offers to buy all of one's requirements are definite enough. Similarly, output contracts that are offers to sell another all that one produces are definite enough for courts. The indefiniteness arises because no one knows exactly what the production output will be.
8. *Retainer contracts.* The following is an example of a retainer contract. Bob Wilson wants an attorney's services for one year. He offers George Blackstone $10,000 to be his attorney. If Blackstone accepts, this contract is valid even though neither Blackstone nor Wilson knows exactly what services Blackstone will perform in the coming year. In fact, Blackstone may do nothing, but courts usually require Blackstone to exercise good faith in deciding what actions he should take for Wilson.
9. *Incorporation of another writing.* An offer and resulting contract that are too uncertain can be made certain if it refers to another writing. In one case, a building contract lacked crucial terms such as square footage but referred to the building plans and specifications, which cleared up the indefiniteness.

## COMMUNICATION REQUIREMENT OF OFFERS

Offers must be communicated before they are effective. For example, Marianne writes out an offer to Mike and puts it in her desk drawer. Mike secretly learns of the letter and calls Marianne to accept the offer. There is no contract in this case because the offer was not communicated to Mike by Marianne or her agent. Now assume Marianne has communicated her offer to Mike, the offeree. Mike then has the power to accept and thereby bind Marianne to a contract.

## HOW OFFERS END

Offers end in a number of ways other than by acceptance, including the following:

1. Time lapse
2. Revocation
3. Rejection
4. Counteroffer
5. Death or insanity of the offeror or offeree
6. Destruction of essential subject matter
7. Intervening or subsequent illegality

*Time Lapse.* Because offers do not last forever, the offeror may state how long the offer will be open. The offer will remain open as long as the offeror states unless it is revoked or ended before that time. When the stated time ends, so does the offer.

If the offer does not say how long it will remain open, the offer lasts for a reasonable time. *Reasonable* takes into account the nature of the subject matter, any trade custom, and similar factors.

*Revocation.* Offerors revoke offers. **Revocation** means recalling or calling back an offer. Offerors generally may revoke an offer any time before acceptance. Revocations need not be in any particular form and take effect when communicated to the offeree. This communication can be indirect. If the offeree accepts before the offer's revocation, a contract exists and the later revocation has no effect on the contract. Public offers are usually revocable if made in a manner similar to the original offer. Revocations need not be communicated to all persons who read the original public offer. Once an offeror revokes an offer, the offeree's later acceptance does not form a contract.

If the offeror promises that the offer will remain open for a stated period of time, may the offeror revoke before that time expires? Yes, assuming no option or firm offer exists. *Gibbs v. American Savings & Loan Association* illustrates the revocation of an offer.

*Exceptions to Revocation.* **Options** are offers that stop the offeror from revoking the offer during the stated option period or until a certain date. The option is irrevocable for the option period because the offeree gives the offeror consideration (something of value). Options are an exception to the general rule that offers are revocable.

For example, if Ken Zeigler offers his farm to Tim Danielson for $100,000 and Danielson is interested but wants to think about it, an option is the answer. Assume Danielson offers Zeigler $500 if Zeigler will hold open his offer to sell the farm for 30 days, and Zeigler agrees. This arrangement is an option because Danielson has not yet bought the farm but he still has time to think about it. If Danielson exercises the option within the 30 days, he must pay Zeigler $100,000 in addition to the option price. (Sometimes the option amount is applied to the purchase price, sometimes not.) If Danielson thinks over the offer during the 30 days and decides not to exercise it, Zeigler keeps the $500 and the farm, and the offer to sell the farm ends.

Two last points: First, just because people call an offer an *option* does not mean it is an irrevocable offer. The offeree must give the offeror consideration (something of value) to turn an ordinarily revocable offer into an irrevocable option contract. Second, options can be given on anything, not just real estate.

Firm offers are a second exception to the general rule that offers are revocable at any time. A **firm offer** is a written offer made by a merchant for the sale or purchase of goods, assuring that the offer will be irrevocable for the period of time stated in the offer (up to a three-month maximum, which is renewable). The UCC is the law creating firm offers. Every state but Louisiana recognizes UCC firm offers. Note that the firm offer does not exist for realty or services.

## Gibbs v. American Savings & Loan Association
California Court of Appeals, Second District
217 Cal. App. 3d 1372, 266 Cal.Rptr. 517 (Cal.App. 2 Dist. 1990)

### Background and Facts

In August 1984, James and Barbara Gibbs submitted an offer for $180,000 to American Savings to purchase a house in Woodland Hills, which American Savings had taken back through foreclosure. American Savings, through its employee, Dorothy Folkman, agreed that the Gibbs could move into the subject property and rent it until the close of escrow. No action was taken on this offer.

On March 27, 1985, pursuant to a request by Ms. Folkman, the Gibbs submitted a new offer because American Savings could not find their original offer. The purchase price was again $180,000. On the morning of June 6, 1985, the Gibbs received a counteroffer from American Savings containing several additional terms and conditions, but with no mention of purchase price. According to Barbara Gibbs, she immediately drove to her husband's job site where she and her husband signed this counteroffer. She drove to her office, typed an envelope with a certified mail tag, placed the counteroffer in the envelope, and before 10 o'clock that morning, she handed it to the mail clerk at her office, instructing him to mail it for her.

At approximately 11 A.M. that same morning, Barbara Gibbs had a telephone conversation with Dorothy Folkman in which Folkman said the counteroffer was in error, because American Savings had intended to increase the sales price to $198,000. Folkman also advised Gibbs that because of this error, the counteroffer was revoked.

American Savings took the position that no contract had been formed. The Gibbs insisted that they had accepted the counteroffer before it was revoked and that a contract thus existed. The Gibbs brought action for damages, specific performance, breach of contract, and declaratory relief. After trial, the court found that Barbara Gibbs did not place the acceptance of the counteroffer in the course of transmission when she gave it to the mail clerk in her office on June 6, 1985; thus there was no acceptance on that date. The postmark on the envelope was June 7, 1985. Dorothy Folkman's oral revocation of the counteroffer on June 6, 1985, preceded the Gibbs' acceptance of that counteroffer on June 7 and therefore no contract for sale of the property was ever formed. The Gibbs appeal judgment.

### Body of Opinion

In a case such as this, where there is no request for a statement of decision, "it must be presumed that every fact essential to the judgment was proved and found by the court." . . . In accordance with these well-established rules of appellate review, we find substantial evidence supports the trial court's judgment. Barbara Gibbs testified that she received the counteroffer from American Savings at about 8:45 or 9 A.M. on June 6, 1985. She and her husband signed the counteroffer at 9:39 A.M. that day. She then drove about one mile to her office, prepared an envelope and certified mail receipt, and gave the ready-to-mail, signed counteroffer to the mail clerk in her office for mailing. This purportedly occurred before 10 A.M. on June 6.

Barbara Gibbs further testified that the clerk brought the mail to the Woodland Hills Post Office and returned with her receipt by 10:15 A.M. on June 6. However, the certified mail receipt was not produced at trial, and the envelope in which the signed counteroffer was mailed to American Savings was postmarked June 7, 1985, not June 6. According to the Domestic Mail Manual of the United States Postal Service, Section 144.471, the date shown in the meter postmark of any type of mail must be the actual date of deposit. Section 144.534 of the manual provides that metered mail bearing the wrong date of mailing shall be run through a canceling machine or otherwise postmarked to show the proper date. The postmarked envelope constitutes substantial evidence that the acceptance was mailed on June 7, not June 6.

Civil Code Section 1583 provides: "Consent is deemed to be fully communicated between the parties as soon as the party accepting a proposal has put his acceptance in the course of transmission to the proposer," . . . This rule has long been interpreted to require that the acceptance be placed out of the control of the accepting party in order to be considered "in the course of transmission." . . . Typically, this is found when the acceptance is delivered to the post office.. . . California's 'effective upon posting' rule, as codified in Section 1583, thus holds that an acceptance of an offer is effective and deemed communicated upon its deposit in the mail. . . .

The postmark on the counteroffer in the case before us shows such deposit occurred on June 7, 1985, not on June 6. The counteroffer was not placed in the course of transmission beyond the control of the offeree when Barbara Gibbs gave it to the mail clerk in her office with instructions to deliver it to the post office. It was placed in the course of transmission within the meaning of Civil Code Section 1583 when it was deposited with the United States Postal Service on June 7, 1985.

It is basic contract law that any offer may be revoked any time prior to acceptance. . . . Both Barbara Gibbs and Dorothy Folkman from American Savings testified that they spoke together on the telephone on the morning of June 6, 1985. During that call, Folkman became aware of American Savings' error in failing to include the $198,000 purchase price in the counteroffer, advised Barbara Gibbs of the error and stated that American Savings was revoking the counteroffer. Inasmuch as the counteroffer was revoked on June 6, prior to the Gibbs' acceptance, no contract was formed.

A similar result was reached in the Florida case of *Kendel v. Pontious* (Fla.App. 1971). . . . In *Kendel*, the buyers delivered their signed acceptance to their attorney who was to mail it to the seller. Before the attorney mailed the signed acceptance to the seller, the seller revoked the offer. The court held delivery to the buyers' attorney did not constitute posting. No contract was formed because the seller's revocation preceded the mailing of the acceptance.

We find no reason to depart from this well-reasoned law.

## Judgment and Result

The court of appeals affirmed the trial court's finding that the seller had revoked its counteroffer before the buyer accepted it.

## Questions

1. Who had made the first offer in this case? Why was it not accepted by American Savings?
2. Why was American Savings' correspondence on the morning of June 6, 1985, deemed a counteroffer if it was for the same price as the Gibbs' original offer?
3. May a written counteroffer be revoked orally?
4. If an offer is revoked before acceptance, does a contract exist? Is that the scenario that occurred here?

*Revocation in Unilateral Contracts.* A unilateral contract is a promise requesting an act in return. If an offeror makes an offer requesting an act and the offeree starts performing the act, can the offeror revoke the offer before the offeree completes the act? Many courts say no, allowing the offeree reasonable time to complete the requested act. They suspend the offeror's power to revoke during this period.

*Rejection.* A **rejection** is the offeree's unequivocal refusal of an offer communicated to the offeror. The legal effect of a rejection is to end the offer. Thus, a rejection followed by an acceptance does not form a contract. The following are rejections in response to offers: "No," "Never," "I don't want that," and words or indications of similar import. The offeree's *questions* to the offeror concerning the offer are *not* rejections and do not end the offer. Also, conditional acceptances (such as "I accept if you paint the fences") are rejections. Thus, they end offers, and are offers from the original offeree to the original offeror.

*Counteroffer.* Counteroffers end offers. Counteroffers are statements by offerees to offerors changing the terms in the original offer. Implicitly, a counteroffer amounts to an offeree's saying to an offeror, "I do not want your original offer, but I am making you this offer instead."

A counteroffer could be made even if an offeree tried to accept an offer. Common law says that any addition or change—even a small, unintentional one—of the offeree's acceptance turns an acceptance into a counteroffer. The UCC changes this rule somewhat when goods are involved. (See the "Acceptance" section for further discussion.)

*Death or Insanity of the Offeror or Offeree.* If either the offeror or offeree dies or becomes insane after the offer is made but before acceptance, the offer ends automatically.

*Destruction of Essential Subject Matter.* Destruction of the subject matter of an offer before acceptance ends the offer. For example, if Charles offers to sell Melinda his Ford and while Melinda is thinking about the offer the car burns up, the offer to sell the car ends. In contrast, if the car's cigarette lighter is stolen before Melinda accepts the offer, this event would not end the offer because the cigarette lighter is not an essential subject matter of the offer.

*Intervening or Subsequent Illegality.* The following example involves intervening or subsequent illegality: Suppose John Sluck offers Ray Jordan 50 barrels of whiskey for $100 per barrel. If it becomes illegal to make and sell alcoholic beverages before Ray accepts, Sluck's offer would automatically end. If the contract becomes illegal after acceptance but *before* performance, the contract duties end due to illegality.

The next section discusses the second half of agreement—the acceptance.

## THE MAKING OF A CONTRACT: THE ACCEPTANCE

Once the offeree has an offer, she or he has the power to accept it. Acceptance merges the offer and acceptance into a contract binding both the offeror and offeree. An **acceptance** is an assent by the offeree to the offer's terms. The acceptance can occur by word or act. The offeree must simply communicate the intent to accept to the offeror; she or he does not even have to use the word "accept."

*Glover v. Jewish War Veterans* examines the issue of intent to accept.

### Glover v. Jewish War Veterans of the United States
Municipal Court of Appeals for the District of Columbia
68 A.2d 233 (1949)

#### Background and Facts

The issue determinative of this appeal is whether a person giving information leading to the arrest of a murderer without any knowledge that a reward has been offered for such information by a nongovernmental organization is entitled to collect the reward. The trial court decided the question in the negative and instructed the jury to return a verdict for defendant. Claimant appeals from the judgment on such instructed verdict.

The controversy grows out of the murder on June 5, 1946, of Maurice L. Bernstein, a local pharmacist. The following day, June 6, Post No. 58, Jewish War Veterans of the United States, communicated to the newspapers an offer of a reward of $500 "to the person or persons furnishing information resulting in the apprehension and conviction of the persons guilty of the murder of Maurice L. Bernstein."

Notice of the reward was published in the newspaper June 7. A day or so later Jesse James Patton, one of the men suspected of the crime, was arrested and the police received information that the other murderer was Reginald Wheeler and that Wheeler was the "boyfriend" of a daughter of Mary Glover, plaintiff and claimant in the present case. On the evening of June 11 the police visited Mary Glover, who in answer to questions informed them that her daughter and Wheeler had left the city on June 5. She told the officers she didn't know exactly where the couple had gone, whereupon the officers asked for names of relatives whom the daughter might be visiting. In response to such questions she gave the names and addresses of several relatives, including one at Ridge Spring, South Carolina, which was the first place visited by the officers and where Wheeler was arrested in company with plaintiff's daughter on June 13. Wheeler and Patton were subsequently convicted of the crime.

Claimant's most significant testimony, in the view that we take of the case, was that she first learned that a reward had been offered on June 12, the day after she had given the police officers the information which enabled them to find Wheeler. Claimant's husband, who was present during the interview with the police officers, also testified that at the time of the interview he didn't know that any reward had been offered for Wheeler's arrest, that nothing was said by the police officers about a reward, and that he didn't know about it "until we looked into the paper about two or three days after that."

## Body of Opinion

**Associate Judge Clagett.**  We have concluded that the trial court correctly instructed the jury to return a verdict for defendant. While there is some conflict in the decided cases on the subject of rewards, most of such conflict has to do with rewards offered by governmental officers and agencies. So far as rewards offered by private individuals and organizations are concerned, there is little conflict on the rule that questions regarding such rewards are to be based upon the law of contracts.

Since it is clear that the question is one of contract law, it follows that, at least so far as private rewards are concerned, there can be no contract unless the claimant when giving the desired information knew of the offer of the reward and acted with the intention of accepting such offer; otherwise the claimant gives the information not in the expectation of receiving a reward but rather out of a sense of public duty or other motive unconnected with the reward. "In the nature of the case," according to Professor Williston, "it is impossible for an offeree actually to assent to an offer unless he knows of its existence." After stating that courts in some jurisdictions have decided to the contrary, Williston adds, "It is impossible, however, to find in such a case [that is, in a case holding to the contrary] the elements generally held in England and America necessary for the formation of a contract. If it is clear the offeror intended to pay for the service, it is equally certain that the person rendering the service performed it voluntarily and not in return for a promise to pay. If one person expects to buy, and the other to give, there can hardly be found mutual assent. These views are supported by the great weight of authority, and in most jurisdictions a plaintiff in the sort of case under discussion is denied recovery."

The American Law Institute in its *Restatement of the Law of Contracts* follows the same rule, thus: "It is impossible that there should be an acceptance unless the offeree knows of the existence of the offer." The *Restatement* gives the following illustration of the rule just stated: "A offers a reward for information leading to the arrest and conviction of a criminal. B, in ignorance of the offer, gives information leading to his arrest and later, with knowledge of the offer and intent to accept it, gives other information necessary for conviction. There is no contract."

We have considered the reasoning in state decisions following the contrary rule. Mostly, as we have said, they involve rewards offered by governmental bodies and in general are based upon the theory that the government is benefited equally whether or not the claimant gives the information with knowledge of the reward and that therefore the government should pay in any event. We believe that the rule adopted by Professor Williston and the *Restatement* and in the majority of the cases is the better reasoned rule and therefore we adopt it. We believe furthermore that this rule is particularly applicable in the present case since the claimant did not herself contact the authorities and volunteer information but gave the information only upon questioning by the police officers and did not claim any knowledge of the guilt or innocence of the criminal but only knew where he probably could be located.

## Judgment and Result

The court of appeals agreed with the lower court's decision and found for the defendant. The plaintiff did not intend to accept the offer when she did the act the offer requested because she did not know the offer existed.

## Questions

1. Must an offeree intend to accept when doing an act requested in an offer for a unilateral contract?
2. Is the rule different if the offeror of a reward is the government? Why?
3. If a person is asked for information, what should he or she do before answering?

---

The offeree usually has a choice about accepting or rejecting an offer. In a few cases (such as public accommodations, including motels, hotels, or restaurants), the federal Civil Rights Act of 1964 requires that hotels and restaurants accept customers' offers to use their facilities. This act assumes that the customer is able to pay and no public health, safety, or other laws would be broken. Years ago, the Waldorf–Astoria Hotel legally refused to house Fidel Castro because he insisted on bringing live chickens into his room—a clear breach of public health laws.

Also, a merchant's power to accept or reject a customer's offer may be limited by the FTC's regulations forbidding bait-and-switch advertising.

## HOW TO ACCEPT

Acceptance must be done in the way the offeror requests. For example, if the offeror says, "Accept by mail," a telephoned acceptance is invalid and no contract results. If the offeror says, "Accept by return mail," the acceptance must be sent on the same day that the offer was received. If the offeror does not specify a way to accept and the offeror mailed or telegraphed the offer, the offeree may use either to accept.

Consider another example of the rule that acceptance must be done as the offeror requests. If the offeror says, "Paint my house and I'll pay you $500," a promise to paint the house is not acceptance; the offeror asked for painting, not a promise to paint.

The exactness rule regarding acceptance is common law, which applies to realty and services. In the case of goods, the UCC permits the parties or circumstances clearly to specify a way to accept. If neither the parties nor circumstances clearly indicates the medium (e.g., phone or mail) to use, the UCC permits any reasonable way in the situation. *Champagne Chrysler-Plymouth, Inc. v. Giles* examines the proper form of acceptance.

### Champagne Chrysler-Plymouth, Inc. v. Giles
Florida Court of Appeals
388 So.2d 1343 (1980)

### Background and Facts

For a number of weeks prior to mid-January 1978, Champage Chrysler-Plymouth Inc. advertised, in a thirty-second spot commercial on a Saturday television program called "Miami All Star Bowling," that it was giving away a new Plymouth Arrow to anyone who bowled a 300 game on the televised program that day. Giles unquestionably was aware of this advertising. Apparently believing that Champagne's offers could only be withdrawn by a revocation commensurate to the offer itself, Giles, in mid-February 1978, put up his pin money and entered the week-long tournament which culminated with the finals carried, as usual, on the "Miami All Star Bowling" television show of February 17, 1978. Giles qualified for the finals and, as the reader may have already surmised, threw twelve strikes in a row for a 300 game. Although otherwise rewarded with cash prizes, free Pepsi and the like, Giles called upon Champagne for his just desserts.

Not bowled over by this request, Champagne responded that it had made no offer of an automobile on February 17 and, for that matter, had not been offering such a prize for over a month of Saturdays. Its position, simply stated, was that Giles was aiming at the wrong pocket. Giles sued.

Champagne's defense was that its offer of a prize *on and for* a particular Saturday television show meant that it made an offer good for that show only. Since no such offer was made on February 17, the day Giles rolled a 300 game, Champagne had no liability. Giles responded that Champagne had place mimeographed flyers and printed posters containing its offers in nearly every bowling alley, and some of this advertising was still posted as of February 17. The trial court, viewing Champagne's earlier offer unrevoked and outstanding as of February 17, and there being no doubt that Giles rolled a 300

game, entered summary judgment as to liability in favor of Giles.

Its bubble thus burst, Champagne appealed. We agree with Champagne that the mimeographed flyer offering a car as a prize for any 300 game bowled on the televised program, even if it remained posted on February 17, 1978, expired by its own terms. In the case of a unilateral contract:

"As the obligation is, before acceptance, on one side only, the proposer being bound to comply with his proposal, while the other party is under no obligation, and under no peril until acceptance, the provision of the offer as to time of acceptance is viewed with strictness.". . .

The television commercials and printed posters present a different problem. The present state of the record does not reflect whether these were unilateral offers limiting the time of acceptance by their express terms or were offers requiring revocation. While the trial court was correct that there was no genuine issue of material fact that appropriate revocation did not occur, the issue as to whether revocation was required remained. If, in fact, the television commercials were unilateral contracts, it would not have been necessary for Champagne to take any steps to revoke the offers made by it on prior television programs, since these offers would have expired by their own terms on the dates made and would not have been outstanding as of February 17, 1978. Since the record contains no clear and undisputed evidence of the words used on the cardboard poster (purportedly still displayed on February 17) and thus does not eliminate the distinct possibility that these were unilateral contracts requiring no revocation, it was error for the trial court to enter summary judgment for Giles. In this respect, as well as in respect to the issue of whether Giles believed that Champagne's offer of a car was outstanding as of February 17, we find that there were genuine issues of material fact still extant at the time of the entry of summary judgment.

Accordingly, we reverse the summary judgment entered in favor of Giles and remand this cause for further proceedings consistent with this opinion.

which expired by their own terms with no revocation being required to end any offer.

## Judgement and Result

The Florida Court of Appeals decided that Giles did not accept the car dealer's mimeographed offer. As to the television and printed posters, the matter was sent back to the trial court to determine if the words on the printed posters were offers for unilateral contracts

## Questions

1. Must an offeree accept an offer exactly for the acceptance to be effective? Why?
2. Why is not substantial performance by the offeree close enough to be acceptance?

## WHO CAN ACCEPT

Only the offeree can accept an offer. The offer could be directed to one person, a small group of people, or the general public.

What is the effect of an acceptance by someone to whom the offer was not directed? The acceptance is ineffective, and no contract results. However, the original offeree could treat this "acceptance" as an offer and accept it, thereby forming a contract.

## SILENCE AS ACCEPTANCE

Silence is generally not acceptance, which prevents an offeror from forcing the offeree to reply to an offer to avoid contract liability. For example, suppose a television store with a large inventory of new televisions sends out postcards describing in detail a particular model, offering it for $500, and providing that if the store has not heard from the customer in the next five days, it will treat the customer's silence as acceptance. Must the customer send in a postcard rejecting the offer to avoid a contract? No. Silence generally is not acceptance.

Two exceptions to the general rule that silence is not acceptance are trade customs and previous dealings. If failure to respond to an offer is regarded as acceptance in a particular trade, then the offeree must reject the offer to avoid contract liability. Previous dealings regarding silence refer to prior contracts that require the offeree to respond to avoid contract liability. For example, in some book and record clubs, members agree in advance to take the monthly selection unless they send in a stop order or rejection notice.

*Unordered Goods in the Mail.* Section 3009 of the federal Postal Reorganization Act of 1970 permits people receiving unordered goods in the mail from businesses to keep, use, discard, or dispose of the goods in any manner without any obligation whatsoever to the sender. It is also possible that the senders of unordered merchandise through the mails could be violating laws forbidding use of the mails to defraud and unfair methods of competition under the Federal Trade Commission Act.

## ACCEPTANCES ADDING TO OR VARYING FROM THE OFFER: COMMON LAW EXACTNESS RULE

Is an acceptance effective if it adds to or changes a term in the offer? The answer depends on what was offered. If the offer was for realty, services, or insurance, acceptances must be exact, or the common law exactness or **mirror image** rule. The acceptance must exactly mirror what was offered to protect offerors from being forced into contracts they never intended, which would occur if offerees could add to or change the offer and have it bind the offeror.

The following is an example of the common law exactness rule. Tom Simon offers his house to Joe Blanc for $75,000. Blanc says, "I accept. Paint it white." Blanc accepted but added a new term, therefore, no contract is formed between Simon and Blanc for Simon's house because Blanc's acceptance was not exact. Putting it another way, Blanc's acceptance was *not* the mirror image of Simon's offer. To force Simon to sell a "white house" would force him into a contract his offer never suggested.

## Acceptance Adding to or Varying from the Offer: The UCC Rule

The common law exactness or mirror image rule for acceptances is not followed when goods—distinguished from realty, services, or insurance—are involved. Acceptances of offers to buy or sell goods may add to or change the offer and still be acceptances forming contracts. For example, Sellit says to Buyit, "I'll sell you my car for $500." Buyit responds, "I'll take it; put new seat covers on it." Sellit clearly intended to sell the car but nothing in the offer mentions new seat covers. Is there a contract? If so, what are the terms?

The UCC sets out the rules for contracts dealing with goods. Acceptances with added terms are acceptances of the original offer *and* an offer back to the original offeror regarding the added term. In other words, a contract is formed regarding what the original offeror offered, such as in the situation with the car. The buyer is bound to the original offer only. The buyer's *added term* (the seat covers) in the acceptance is essentially a new offer made to the original offeror. The original offeror in the preceding example has sold his or her car and does not have to put seat covers on the car.

## When Is an Acceptance Effective?

If an offeror says that an acceptance is effective only when received, it is effective only when the offeror receives it. If the offeror fails to say anything about an acceptance's effective date, a mailed acceptance is effective on the date it was sent with correct postage and address, also known as the **mailbox rule**; acceptance takes effect when the offeree drops the acceptance in the mailbox or other appropriate receptacle. This rule applies even if the letter of acceptance never reaches the offeror.

A telegraphed acceptance is effective when given to the telegraph office official. Again, if the offeror specifies that a telegraphed acceptance is effective only when received, this restriction must be observed.

The telephone can also be used to accept unless the parties involved say otherwise or state law requires a written contract.

## Acceptances at an Auction

Who accepts and who offers at an auction? The auctioneer makes invitations to negotiate, and the audience's bids are offers. The auctioneer accepts these offers when his or her hammer falls to the auction block. Because a bid is an offer, the bidder may withdraw it any time before acceptance. If a bid is accepted, a contract results that binds both the bidder and auctioneer. If the bids are not high enough to satisfy the auctioneer, must the highest bid be accepted? The answer to that question depends on whether the auction is "with or without reserve." If an auction is "with reserve," the auctioneer may withdraw an item if the bids are too low. If the auction is "without reserve," the highest bidder's offer must be accepted no matter how low it is.

## CONSIDERATION

We have already discussed the parts of a contract, which are the offer and the acceptance. This section of the chapter looks back at the agreement to determine whether it meets another test: Consideration. In a technical sense, consideration is a bargained for benefit to the promisor or a detriment to the promisee. Nontechnically, consideration means that both the offeror and offeree to the contract must bargain for and give up a right in order to make the other's promise or act enforceable.

*Benefit to the Promisor.* Consideration can be a benefit to the promisor. For example, B promises to pay A $500 if A promises to paint B's house. B's promise to pay A benefits A. B's promise is, therefore, consideration that makes A's promise to paint enforceable. The same is true about A's promise to paint: It makes B's promise to pay enforceable.

*Detriment to the Promisee.* A legal detriment means that someone gives up a right to do something. Referring to the painting example, B's promise to pay A $500 is a detriment to B, because B gives up the right to $500. Note that here B's giving A $500 is also a benefit to A in addition to being a detriment to B. A detriment to the promisee is consideration for the promise if the promisor bargained for it, which is true even if the promisor gets no benefit when the promisee does what the promisor bargained for. The *Hamer v. Sidway* case illustrates this type of consideration.

### Hamer v. Sidway
Court of Appeals of New York
27 N.E. 256 (1891)

### Background and Facts

William E. Story, Sr., was the uncle of William E. Story, Jr. At a family dinner, the uncle promised to pay the nephew $5,000 if he would not drink, use tobacco, swear, play cards or billiards for money until the nephew became 21 years old.

The nephew followed the uncle's request. Upon reaching the age of 21, the nephew asked his uncle for the $5,000. The uncle sent the nephew a letter telling how hard he had worked for the money and went on to say that he hoped the nephew would not waste it. The uncle also said he was pleased that the nephew had followed his request. The uncle added, "You shall have the $5,000, as I promised you. I had the money in the bank the day you were 21 years old. You shall have the money certain. You can consider this money on interest."

The nephew agreed the money should stay with the uncle "on interest" as the letter described. Two years later the uncle died without having paid the nephew anything. The nephew sued the uncle's estate for the money. The estate argued that the uncle's promise was not binding because the nephew had given the uncle no consideration.

## Body of Opinion

**Judge Parker.** . . . The defendant contends that the contract was without consideration to support it, and therefore invalid. He asserts that the promisee, by refraining from the use of liquor and tobacco, was not harmed, but benefited; that that which he did was best for him to do, independently of his uncle's promise—and insists that it follows that, unless the promisor was benefited, the contract was without consideration—a contention which, if well founded, would seem to leave open for controversy in many cases whether that which the promisee did or omitted to do was in fact of such benefit to him as to leave no consideration to support the enforcement of the promisor's agreement. Such a rule could not be tolerated, and is without foundation in the law. The Exchequer Chamber in 1875 defined "consideration" as follows: "A valuable consideration, in the sense of the law, may consist either in some right, interest, profit, or benefit accruing to the one party, or some forbearance, detriment, loss, or responsibility given, suffered, or undertaken by the other.". . . Anson. Cont. 63. "In general, a waiver of any legal right at the request of another party is a sufficient consideration for a promise.". . . Pollock in his work on Contracts (page 166), after citing the definition given by the Exchequer Chamber, already quoted, says: "The second branch of this judicial description is really the most important one. 'Consideration' means not so much that one party is profiting as that the other abandons some legal right in the present, or limits his legal freedom of action in the future, as an inducement for the promise of the first."

Now, applying this rule to the facts before us, the promisee used tobacco, occasionally drank liquor, and he had a legal right to do so. That right he abandoned for a period of years upon the strength of the promise of the testator that for such forbearance he would give him $5,000. We need not speculate on the effort which may have been required to give up the use of these stimulants. It is sufficient that he restricted his lawful freedom of action within certain prescribed limits upon the faith of his uncle's agreement, and now, having fully performed the conditions imposed, it is of no moment whether such performance actually proved a benefit to the promisor, and the court will not inquire into it; but, were it a proper subject of inquiry, we see nothing in this record that would permit a determination that the uncle was not benefited in a legal sense.. . .

## Judgment and Result

The nephew wins.

## Questions

1. Consideration is said to be either benefit to the promisor or detriment to the promisee. Who was the promisor, the uncle or the nephew? Who was the promisee?
2. Does *Hamer v. Sidway* find that the uncle had benefited from the nephew's failure to drink, smoke, and so on?
3. Did the nephew give up a legal right which, arguably, was not a benefit to the uncle? Is this situation what is meant by detriment to the promisee without there being benefit to the promisor?

## REASON FOR THE CONSIDERATION RULE

The reason for requiring consideration is to satisfy the basic natural law idea of fairness. Both sides of a contract should give something to the other to have a binding agreement.

## "BARGAINED FOR" PART OF THE CONSIDERATION DEFINITION

The "bargained for" part of the consideration definition means that the person receiving the benefit (or requesting the other party to suffer a detriment) must have requested or bargained for the benefit (or detriment). The idea is to stop the promisee from giving the promisor something she or he does not want to make the promisor's promise binding. For example, Bob says that he will pay Davy $500 if Davy promises to paint Bob's house. Instead of promising to paint, Davy promises Bob a fur cap. Davy's promising to give Bob the fur cap is a benefit to Bob but Bob did not bargain for (or want) the cap. Because Bob has "bargained for" the promise to paint and not the cap, only the promise to paint is consideration in this case.

## ADEQUACY OF CONSIDERATION

Adequacy of consideration means: Did you get "enough" under the terms of the contract, or did you pay too much? Courts (judges) do not usually examine the adequacy of the consideration because of freedom of contract.

*Freedom of contract* means the parties to the contract, not a judge, decide what and how much consideration each gives the other. Each individual protects his or her own best interest. For example, suppose Ray Jordan agrees to pay Virginia Mosley $10,000 for her clunker of a car. After making the contract, Jordan has second thoughts and refuses to pay. Mosley sues him for breach of contract. Jordan defends by claiming that Mosley's car is worth $2,000, not $10,000. Said another way, Jordan claims Mosley's consideration is inadequate. However, this claim is no defense for Jordan. Jordan must bargain for the best price possible before entering the contract. If he cannot get a fair price, he should not buy the car. In a free market economy, Jordan, not a judge, protects Jordan's interest.

At times the courts will rule consideration is inadequate. Generally, the exceptions involve uneven exchanges suggesting duress or undue influence. For example, an uneven exchange of the same currency ($50 U.S. for $100 U.S.) will cause a court to say the consideration is inadequate.

## WHEN CONTRACTS SHOULD BE IN WRITING: THE STATUTE OF FRAUDS RULE

As a general business policy, it is good advice to write down and have both parties sign all contracts. Virtually all states have a **Statute of Frauds**, which requires that certain contracts dealing with certain subjects be evidenced by a signed writing. If contracts falling into these subject matter areas are oral, but the Statute of Frauds says they should be evidenced by a signed writing, the contract is said to be unenforceable. Then, the party trying to enforce the contract cannot enforce it if the defendant (person against whom the contract is asserted) raises the Statute of Frauds defense.

Statutes of Frauds are state laws and thus the exact coverage varies somewhat from state to state. The Uniform Commercial Code (UCC) also has a Statute of Frauds requirement for certain types of subject matter.

*Reason for the Writing Requirement.* The reason for the Statute of Frauds is to prevent persons from introducing fraudulent or perjured testimony to "prove" the formation of contracts dealing with important (realty), costly (expensive goods), complex (contracts that cannot be completed within one year), or unusual contracts (guaranty contracts or contracts in consideration of marriage). The thinking is that unless a writing signed by the party to be charged exists, contracts dealing with these matters should not be enforceable.

*Categories of Contracts Required to Be Written.* Generally, the areas in which contracts must be evidenced by a signed writing include transfers of interests in real estate (generally including leases of over one year); contracts for the sale of expensive goods (the UCC sets the amount at $500 or more); guaranty contracts (contracts under which one person agrees to pay another's debts if the other does not pay); contracts that cannot by their terms be completed within one year; contracts in consideration of marriage.

*Special Statute of Frauds Rules.* Several refinements of the aforementioned Statute of Frauds rule should be noted. First, if a contract falls into any one of the aforementioned categories of contract, the contract must be evidenced by a signed writing. For example, a contract requiring an accounting firm to provide services for two years must be evidenced by a signed writing even though it is not for the sale of goods over $500. It is enough that one part of the Statute requires a writing to make the contract come within the Statute's terms.

A second point involves the signing. Ideally both parties should sign the contract, but the Statute of Frauds only requires that "the party to be charged"—the defendant—sign the contract. Signing can consist of a person's actual signature but can also be a stamped signature or even initials rather than one's full name. Note that if one party signs and the other does not, the contract would be enforceable against the signer but not against the nonsigner, unless some exception to the signer rule applies. At least three important exceptions to the "signer" rule may affect the sale of goods between merchants. If two merchants orally negotiate a contract for the sale of goods and one of the merchants sends the other a written confirmation of the sale and the receiving merchant does not object to the confirmation within 10 days of receipt, the nonsigning merchant is bound to the contract even though that merchant did not sign it. Note that this only applies in the case of the sale of goods under the UCC. A second exception to the writing requirement involves specially made goods. When a seller substantially starts to make specially ordered goods, no writing is required. A third exception involves part performance of a contract for goods costing $500 or more; an oral contract is enforceable for that part of the contract the buyer has paid for, but the remainder of the contract is unenforceable.

Another subtlety involves the sale of goods for $500 or more. What if a contract is for 500 widgets, each of which cost $2. Is this viewed as 500 contracts for $2, which obviously would not have to be written, or one contract for $1,000, which would have to be written? Courts often view it as one contract for 500 widgets, which, because it is over $500, requires a writing.

With respect to the provision requiring contracts that by their terms cannot be completed within one year to be written, the year starts to run from the date the contract is formed. Thus, a contract for exactly one year whose performance starts the day the contract is formed need not be written to be enforceable. However, a contract formed on July 1, 2003, whose performance is to start September 1, 2003, and is to last until August 1, 2004, would have to be in a signed writing to be enforceable because the time from formation to finish of performance is 13 months. Also, some contracts appearing to last for more than a year actually are not required to be written. For example, a contract for Tom to be Fred's cook for the rest of Tom's life does not have to be written because Tom could die tomorrow (even though we hope he does not). This contract is exempt from the writing requirement even if Tom lives for more than one year.

*Form of the Writing to Satisfy the Statute of Frauds.* The writing to satisfy the Statute of Frauds must identify the parties and subject matter, indicate that a contract exists, and state essential terms (price, quantity, time of performance, credit terms). The UCC is quite liberal with respect to specific terms generally allowing a contract for goods to be enforceable if the quantity and parties are named and some sort of signature exists (e.g., a stamped name anywhere on the document) even if the price is not, provided a mechanism, such as the market price, exists to "fill the gaps."

The following case indicates that not all courts will find the Statute of Frauds satisfied even where the contract is for a substantial amount.

## James v. Safari Enterprises, Inc.
### Court of Appeals of Georgia
### 537 S.E.2d 103 (2000)

### Background and Facts

On May 5, 1998, James was the high bidder at a foreclosure sale on two parcels of land. Safari Enterprises, Inc. was conducting the sale pursuant to a power of sale contained in a security deed. Michael Safari, an owner and officer of Safari Enterprises, had also bid on the properties, but James outbid him. The parties did not execute any memorandum of sale on the transaction, and James denies that the parties entered into a binding sales contract.

James testified that when she placed her bid she was unaware that the security deed reflected a second mortgage on the property and that the property was subject to a first mortgage. She first learned of this fact when Safari Enterprises' attorney told her after the fact. She told the attorney that if she had bid on a second mortgage, she was not interested in purchasing the properties. She then left to check the records. Once she confirmed that a large first mortgage existed, she immediately returned to the attorney and told him she did not wish to consummate the deal.

Safari Enterprises' lawyer acknowledged that following the sale, he did tell James that the deeds were not first mortgages, but he says that James did not voice any hesitation about the transaction. Instead, the lawyer said that she told him she had to leave for about 30 minutes to get the money for the purchase from her bank. He relayed this to Michael Safari, who then left, anticipating that the deal with James would close. According to the lawyer, it was only when James returned that she told him she did not wish to close on the transaction.

Safari Enterprises sued James for specific performance of the transaction. James sought summary judgment on several grounds including the statute of frauds. The trial court denied the motion stating that it found no authority for James' position that the statute of frauds applied to a foreclosure sale. And even assuming that the statute of frauds did apply, the trial court found that Safari Enterprises reasonably relied on James' high bid as evidence of her intention to purchase the property, thus removing the sale from the statute of frauds. James appealed the trial court's decision.

### Body of Opinion

**Presiding Judge Pope.** Under Georgia's statute of frauds, "(a)ny contract for sale of lands, or any interest in, or concerning lands" must be in writing and signed by the party to be charged. . . . And in an early opinion, our Supreme Court held that the statute of frauds applies to nonjudicial foreclosure sales made pursuant a power of sale in a security deed. . . . Accordingly, the statute of frauds applies to the sale in this case unless it falls into one of the recognized exceptions.

The trial court found that Safari Enterprises' reliance upon James' high bid removed the transaction from the statute of frauds. . . . That section provides that the statute of frauds does not extend to a situation "where there has been performance on one side, accepted by the other in accordance with the contract." We find, however, that this case is controlled by [a statute] which states:

> The specific performance of a parol contract as to land shall be decreed if the defendant admits the contract or if the contract has been so far executed by the party seeking relief and at the instance or by the inducements of the other party that if the contract were abandoned he could not be restored to his former position. . . .

Here, James denies the contract. But an award of specific performance may still be made under [state statute] where the contract is partially performed. . . . The statute defines what constitutes partial performance: (1) full payment, (2) partial payment and possession, or (3) possession and valuable improvements. . . .

Here, none of these factors are present. James simply made a bid for the property, which Safari Enterprises accepted. No partial performance of the contract occurred. The transaction, therefore, stays within the confines of the statute of frauds. And in the absence of a writing signed by James detailing the terms of the transaction, James is not bound.

### Judgment and Result

The Court of Appeals reversed the trial court's judgment. In so doing it held that James was not bound.

### Questions

1. Does the court of appeals admit that oral contract dealing with realty can sometimes be enforceable even though there is no writing? Under what circumstances?
2. Do statutes of frauds support or undercut the ethic of "keeping one's word"?

## CHAPTER SUMMARY

Contracts are the basis of the market economy.

A contract is an agreement between competent parties and is enforceable in court.

The *Restatement, Second, Contracts* definition of contracts is "a promise or set of promises for the breach of which the law gives a remedy, or the performance of which the law in some way recognizes as a duty."

Courts generally apply an objective test to decide whether a contract exists when the parties disagree as to whether they have formed a contract.

Classifications of contracts include bilateral and unilateral; express and implied; executed and executory; valid, void, voidable and unenforceable; and quasi-contracts.

The two major components of a contract are the offer and the acceptance. Offers are made by the offeror and can only be accepted by the person or persons to whom the offeror intended to make the offer.

Offers end in several ways, including death or insanity of the offeror or offeree before acceptance, destruction of an essential subject matter before acceptance, intervening illegality before or after acceptance but before performance, counteroffer before acceptance, and rejection of the offer before acceptance.

At common law, acceptances must mirror or exactly conform to the offer. The Uniform Commercial Code has liberalized the rules of acceptance. Sometimes courts will impose a contract on a situation in which one person has conferred benefits onto another under circumstances where the conferee knows or should know that compensation was expected and no gift was intended.

Consideration is generally required to make contracts enforceable. Consideration refers to the voluntary relinquishment of a known right that is bargained for in exchange for someone else's right.

The Statute of Frauds requires that contracts dealing with certain subject matter be evidenced by a signed writing to be enforceable.

■ **MANAGER'S ETHICAL DILEMMA**

Emil Tyden had a great idea. After many hours of experimenting in his laboratory, he developed a cure for baldness in men. He carefully tested his formula and, after repeated instances of success, he decided to approach the World Drug Company to see if it was interested in buying the formula. He met a Ms. Colgrove who asked Emil what he had discovered. He replied, "A cure for male baldness."

Ms. Colgrove expressed interest and asked to see his formula. Emil thought for a minute. He had worked hundreds of hours developing the formula. What assurances did he have that she would not write it down, tell him it was worthless, and then have World Drug Company start making it after claiming it had developed the product itself?

Discuss any of the material covered in the chapter that suggests a possible protection to assist Emil in deciding whether to reveal his information to Ms. Colgrove.

## Discussion Questions

1. The arrival of the Internet and Internet auctions presents challenges for the legal system. An example occurred recently where a computer-sophisticated eighth grader logged on to an Internet auction site and bid on a Van Gogh painting, a Viking ship replica, and several other items. Although unsuccessful on the Van Gogh painting, the youngster was the high bid on a 1971 Corvette, a wrestling belt, and a bed belonging to Canada's first prime minister, Sir John A. MacDonald. Bidding was at $12,000 on the bed when the boy entered a winning bid of $900,000. The parents of the boy were reportedly about to suspend their son's Internet privileges (and hopefully not give him credit card privileges). What defenses might be available to the boy and his parents for such purchases?

2. Must an offer be written in all cases?

3. Give an example of a written offer.

4. Does a contract exist if a person offers to sell her car for $400, but really does not intend to follow through on the offer, and the offeree accepts?

5. Give an example of an invitation to negotiate.

6. Name some characteristics of offers.

7. Who can accept an offer?

8. If B offers his house to C for $140,000, and C says, "I accept. Paint the house before I move in," has C accepted?

9. Is contract law positive law, or are contracts positive law?

10. Is contract law more consistent with a market or planned economy?

11. A landowner listed certain land with a realtor. When the brokerage listing agreement expired, the broker called the owner to see whether the property was still available for sale. The owner replied that the property was still available, but the tenant leasing it had the first option to buy. Shortly after this conversation, the broker secured an offer to buy from a third party. However, the tenant exercised the first option to buy, which prevented the third party from buying. The broker sued the owner for the brokerage commission, arguing that the realtor had satisfied the brokerage contract's terms by producing a ready, able, and willing buyer. Was the landowner's conditional acceptance of the broker's offer accepted by the broker, thereby forming a contract? [*Arthur Rubloff & Co. v. Drovers Nat. Bank of Chicago*, 80 Ill. App. 3d 867, 36 Ill. Dec. 194, 400 N.E.2d 614 (1980)].

12. Golestaneh offered to sell his Florida condominium to Mintzberg. The offeror's terms were: selling price $200,000 cash; closing date beginning of October; broker's commission to be split evenly between the parties; price includes light fixtures, carpeting, and major appliances. The prospective buyer, Mintzberg, sent the following letter to the seller: "This will confirm that the October 1, 1979, closing date is acceptable with the understanding that Mr. Mintzberg would prefer an earlier closing date. I would appreciate a more detailed explanation of your advice to my secretary regarding the maintenance charges." Was the buyer's letter an acceptance of the seller's offer? [*Mintzberg v. Golestaneh*, 390 So.2d 759 (Fla. App. 1980)].

## InfoTrac Keywords

**Use your InfoTrac password to look up articles on http://www.infotrac-college.com**

Keywords: *Theory of contracts, Statute of Frauds.*

For suggested readings, please visit this book's Web site at **http://fisher.westbuslaw.com** (click on "Internet Applications").

# PROPERTY

At one time, property law was the basis of the legal system. Today, as government has discovered ways to regulate and tax property, other rights, such as the right to one's job, are probably as important. This chapter surveys some basic property concepts such as title, property classifications, how property fits into the market economy, personalty, and realty. Also, given today's emphasis on entrepreneurship, ways to protect intellectual property are discussed.

> *". . . THE RIGHT OF THE OWNER TO USE HIS LAND IS NOT ABSOLUTE."*
>
> —MR. JUSTICE BRANDEIS, PENNSYLVANIA COAL CO. V. MAHON, 260 U.S. 393 (1992)

## DEFINITION OF PROPERTY

**Property** is the rights that one person has regarding other people with respect to something. This definition may sound a bit obscure, so let's discuss it further. It is common to hear someone describe a car as property. Technically, this definition is wrong. A car is something in which one or more persons have rights. For example, the *owner* has the right to use the car, but often the owner will have borrowed from a credit union or bank to buy the car. That lender will have a security interest (a type of mortgage) on the car, which gives the lender the right to seize the car if the owner/borrower defaults on the loan. Occasionally, the car owner will take the car to a repair shop to have it worked on. The mechanic will have the right to use the car to test it and a limited right to keep the car until the bill is paid. So you can see that many different persons have rights—that is, property—in the car.

*Property*, then, means the rights a person or people have to something. The property is *not* the object or thing (house, car, fishing pole, etc.) but the *rights* to that thing. Thus, the owner of the car has greater rights to the car than a thief, but the owner who misses a payment may have less right to the car than the credit union that repossesses the car.

## LEGAL PHILOSOPHIES REFLECTED IN PROPERTY LAW

Several legal ethics or philosophies are reflected in property law. Included here are positive law, historical jurisprudence, natural law, and Ehrlich's sociological philosophy of law. John Austin, who developed analytical positivism (discussed in Chapter 1), is credited with naming different property classifications. Such classifications are part of positive law even today. These classifications include personalty and realty.

The historic philosophy is evidenced by the idea that property rights are long-standing ideas that have been recognized since the ancient Greeks and Egyptians. Changing ideas of who can own property and what can be property reflect Ehrlich's sociological school of law, which emphasizes norms of conduct. For example, at one time slaves in the United States could not own property. Also, in the nineteenth century United States, African Americans could be property. Modern norms of conduct, however, reject the idea that only certain races can *own* property or that certain races can be property.

Natural law ideas of fairness found in the U.S. Constitution forbid government from taking property unless the government gives just compensation or fair market value to the owner.

## PROPERTY LAW IS STATE LAW

Property law is generally state, not federal, law. Thus, in the area of constitutional lawmaking, property law is generally left to the individual states. For example, the state of Michigan makes the rules about who owns cars, land, and other things in Michigan. With 50 states, 50 different rules could exist about a particular property question. For example, the state of Maryland might say that oral wills are valid, while Massachusetts might outlaw oral wills. Because of the federal system and the fact that each state makes its own property law rules, property law is quite complex.

Some federal laws do regulate property, however. The Fifth and Fourteenth Amendments say that property shall not be taken without due process of law. The U.S. Constitution also sets out the eminent domain rule, which means that private property may not be taken by the federal, state, or local governments or companies with eminent domain authority, without paying "just compensation"—fair market value. Several federal statutes also govern land sales contracts, including the Interstate Land Sales Full Disclosure Act (ILSFDA), which regulates the sale of undeveloped land by giving the buyer a three-day cooling-off period to escape the contract to buy.

## TITLE AND TITLE DOCUMENTS

Title refers to ownership. If someone owns land, a car, or sweater, that person has **title** to it. Title is different from **title documents**. Title is ownership, but a title document is a piece of paper saying who owns the object. Most items do not have title documents. For example, if someone were to ask you to prove that you own the shirt or blouse you are wearing, it would probably be difficult to do (unless you saved the sales receipt) because our clothing, furniture, and most household goods do not have title documents.

However, we do have title documents called **deeds** for land. Also, cars and trucks have title documents called *titles*.

The state government issues title documents to autos and trucks, but private parties write deeds to land. Also, deeds should be recorded, or noted in a record book on land titles at the Courthouse in the county where the land is located.

## PROPERTY CLASSIFICATIONS

Property can be classified in several ways. (Note that here we violate our earlier pure property definition that property is rights in some thing. Here we are treating property not as the rights but as the thing in which one has rights—the car, the land, the fishing pole.) One property classification includes realty, personalty, and fixtures. A second property classification refers to property as either tangibles or intangibles. A final classification is that of public and private property.

### PERSONAL PROPERTY

Personal property, also called **personalty**, refers to movables. (Things that cannot be moved are generally classified as realty.) Examples of personalty include clothing, automobiles, and furniture. This movable versus immovable distinction between realty and personalty is not perfect, because a shovelful of land can be moved and also the planet Earth moves through space, so arguably everything is always moving. Nonetheless the movable—immovable distinction is used here to distinguish personalty from realty.

### REAL PROPERTY

Real property, also called realty, refers to land and buildings. Realty is sometimes said to be immovable. A house is **realty**, as is a vacant lot. Realty also includes the air rights and subsurface rights to the land. A landowner who builds a skyscraper on her land would be using the air rights to her realty. Air rights are subject to the right of overflight by aircraft, which do not have to pay the realty owner for this right.

Realty owners have the rights to what is below their land, called *subsurface rights*. *Surface rights* can be sold separately from subsurface rights. A farmer does so by keeping the surface rights to raise crops and selling the subsurface rights to an oil company.

Trees, grass, and plants (called *fructus naturales*) that grow naturally on land without the help of humankind are part of the realty. Plants put on the land are also part of the realty. However, crops arising from vegetation helped partly by human effort (called *fructus industriales*) belong to whomever planted and grew them. Thus, the tenant who planted the strawberries—not the landlord—would be entitled to them.

## FIXTURES

An in-between category of property is called fixtures. A **fixture** is personalty attached to realty with the intent that it will become a permanent part of the realty. An oven sitting in an appliance dealer's showroom is personalty. When built into the wall of a home, the oven becomes a fixture.

Fixtures can regain their identity as personalty if severed from the realty. To decide whether personalty has become a fixture, four questions must be answered:

1. What does the person who owns the item (such as a microwave oven put in a wall cabinet) consider it to be—a fixture or personalty?
2. Who attached the item? If done by the realty owner, it is more likely a fixture.
3. How securely is the personalty attached to the realty? The more firmly attached the personalty is, the more likely it is a fixture. A sliding glass door, for example, would likely be a fixture, whereas a lamp nailed to the wall probably would remain personalty.
4. What function does the personalty have to the realty? A toilet is particularly and closely suited for use in a house. Thus, it would be part of the realty.

**Trade fixtures** are an exception to the idea that fixtures become part of the realty. Items such as signs and counters, which are firmly attached to the realty, remain the tenant's personal property.

## TANGIBLE AND INTANGIBLE PROPERTY

As already noted, all property is technically intangible because in a true sense, property refers only to rights in some thing. However, let us leave the world of pure property definitions. Instead, let us refer to property for the moment as the object (the car, land, or fishing pole) in which one has rights. Some property therefore is *tangible*, that is, can be seen, such as a car, land, or fishing pole. Other property—a patent, for instance—cannot be seen and is therefore *intangible*.

## PUBLIC AND PRIVATE PROPERTY

A third property classification is public and private property. This classification focuses on who owns the property. Your shirt or car would belong to one person. It therefore is private property. The Pentagon or the U.S. Supreme Court building would be public property because a government owns it.

## TYPES OF REAL PROPERTY ESTATES

Owners of realty have **estates** in the land and buildings on the land. The word *estate* makes a person think of a huge house and large lawn, but estate here means something different. It refers to an interest in the realty.

*Fee Simple Absolute.*  The highest estate in land (the maximum rights the law allows) a person can have is called a **fee simple absolute**. Phrases such as "to A and his heirs" or "to A" create a fee simple absolute.

The owner of a fee simple absolute may sell, give, or devise (give by a will) the realty.

Abstracts on various legal topics can be found at **http://www. lawreview.org**

*Life Estate.*  A **life estate** is an interest in realty for one's life but for no longer. When one dies, the realty belongs to someone else. Persons with life estates are called life tenants. Because the life tenant has the realty only for his or her life, this estate may not be transferred by will. It can, however, be sold or given away for the life tenant's life.

*Leaseholds.*  A person who leases another's realty has a **leasehold**, or leasehold interest. Persons with leaseholds are called *tenants*. Tenants do have only temporary rather than permanent rights to the realty. Leases may be for fixed periods or may run from period to period.

*Easements.*  An **easement** is a nonpossessory right to use someone else's realty for some purpose. For example, the telephone company might have an easement to string a phone line over your land, or a neighbor might have a right to use your driveway to get to her property.

The property subject to the easement is called the **servient estate**. The property enjoying the benefit of the easement is the **dominant estate**.

Several kinds of easements are easements appurtenant, easements in gross, affirmative, and negative easements. **Easements appurtenant** benefit another piece of land, which is usually adjacent to the servient estate. **Easements in gross** benefit a certain person or business. A powerline easement for a utility would be an easement in gross. An **affirmative easement** would exist when someone is given a right to use someone else's land. A **negative easement** prevents someone from doing something on one's land, such as stopping the building of a structure if it would block the sunlight to the dominant estate.

*Profits.*  **Profits** are a right to enter someone else's real estate to remove something, such as minerals, crops, or water.

*Licenses.*  A **license** is not a real property interest. Instead it is a right to use another's realty, such as the use of a seat in a football stadium for the game only or a seat in a movie theater during operating hours.

## WAYS TO HOLD TITLE TO REAL PROPERTY

Although it is certainly possible to own all the rights to real property, it is also possible to own rights with others. We shall now look at some types of joint realty ownership.

### TENANTS IN COMMON

**Tenants in common** occurs where two or more people have title to an interest in realty. Tenants in common can give, sell, or devise by will their individual interests in the realty. Each tenant in common has a

As the largest landowner in the United States, the Bureau of Land Management Web site provides a variety of information at **http://www.blm.gov**

right to the whole realty. The tenants in common can have equal or unequal rights to the whole. An example of tenancy in common occurs if Mr. Sims deeds his house to his son Ronald and his daughter Beverly as tenants in common. Both Ron and Beverly would have equal right to use the house.

## Joint Tenants

**Joint tenants** own realty together but with a **right of survivorship**. The right of survivorship refers to the idea that the joint tenants who die before other joint tenants lose all interest in the property. Thus, with three joint tenants, the last survivor takes all rights to the estate. When only one joint tenant is left, the survivorship feature is gone. Obviously, joint tenants may not convey their interest by will, which ends when they die, except for the last joint tenant. Joint tenancies are not favored because they involve a forfeiture, except for the surviving joint tenant.

However, joint tenants may convey their interest while they are alive. These transferees from a joint tenant become tenants in common regarding their share of the estate with the remaining joint tenants. To create a joint tenancy, however, the deed must specify that a joint tenancy exists.

## Tenancy by the Entirety

**Tenancy by the entirety** is a specialized form of joint tenancy: The joint tenants must be spouses. It involves a right of survivorship, so the surviving spouse takes the entire estate. Not all states recognize tenancy by the entirety, however.

## Tenancy in Partnership

The Uniform Partnership Act recognizes **tenancy in partnership**, which occurs when business partners own property—realty, personalty, or fixtures—together. This form of tenancy has the right of survivorship feature; that is, when a partner dies or departs from the business, the remaining partners take the departing partner's share.

## Real Estate Syndications

**Real estate syndications** arise when several persons own property. The vehicle for the joint ownership could be a limited partnership, partnership, trust, or corporation. In other words, the individual investor owns a limited partnership share but the limited partnership itself owns the real estate. Similarly, if the corporate form is used for the syndication, the corporation owns the realty and the individual investors are shareholders in the corporation. The form the syndication takes governs what law controls these organizations. For example, if the syndication takes the form of a trust, trust law will govern matters of management and transferability of syndication interests.

## Community Property

**Community property** exists in California, Arizona, Louisiana, Washington, Idaho, Nevada, Texas, and New Mexico. It applies only to the way married couples own property in those states. During the marriage, when one spouse acquires property, half of it belongs to the other spouse, even if the deed specifically is made out only in the name of one spouse. During the marriage, community property may not be sold or mortgaged without both spouses' approval.

## CONDOMINIUMS

A **condominium** is a way individuals can own the space between the walls of their unit. "Condo" owners have equal interests in the common areas of the entire complex: grounds, swimming pool, tennis court, driveway, elevator, sidewalks, and so on. Condo owners may sell or mortgage their interests subject to restrictions in the condo agreement, which sometimes can be very restrictive. Usually assessments or dues are charged monthly or annually to each unit to pay for maintenance and insurance on the common areas. In the case of high-rise condos, the owners actually own the bit of airspace their unit occupies.

## HOW PROPERTY IS ACQUIRED

Property may be acquired in several ways. This discussion analyzes the following ways of acquiring both realty and personalty:

1. Theft
2. Gift
3. Capture
4. Finding
5. Inheritance
6. Trust
7. Manufacture
8. Confusion
9. Purchase

## THEFT

Personal property may not legally be acquired by stealing it. The original owner of property can reclaim it if found in the hands of a thief or a good-faith purchaser from a thief. Thus, if a thief steals Mary's ring and sells it to Betty (a good-faith buyer who pays $500 believing that the thief really owns it), and Mary tracks it down, Mary can recover it from Betty. (Betty must find the thief and sue that thief for breach of warranty of title.) A thief may not pass good title to personalty. A taker (buyer or donee) from a thief gets no better title than the thief had: nothing.

The following case deals with an art dealer who buys an object for more than $1 million in the international art market under suspicious circumstances, hoping to resell it for $20 million to a rich museum. Did that art dealer obtain good title?

*Voidable Title.* A person who has voidable title to personalty may pass full title to a good faith purchaser for value. **Voidable title** means that someone got title to the goods by means that would permit O, the original owner, to recover the goods from T, the immediate transferee (the person with voidable title). Such means might include mistake, common nonphysical duress, fraud in the inducement, or

## Autocephalus Greek-Orthodox Church v. Goldberg
Federal District Court (S.D. Indiana)
717 F.Supp. 1374 (1989)

### Background and Facts

In this case the court is asked to decide the right of possession as between the plaintiffs, the Autocephalous Greek-Orthodox Church of Cyprus (Church) and the Republic of Cyprus and the defendants, Peg Goldberg (Goldberg) and Goldberg & Feldman Fine Arts, Inc., of four Byzantine mosaics created in the early sixth century. The mosaics, made of small chips of colored glass, were originally affixed to and for centuries remained in a church in Cyprus, a small island in the Mediterranean Sea. In 1974, Turkish military forces invaded Cyprus and seized control of northern Cyprus, including the region where the church is located. At some point in the latter 1970s, during the Turkish military occupation of Northern Cyprus, the mosaics were removed from their hallowed sanctuary. The plaintiffs, on one hand, claim that the Church has never intended to relinquish ownership of the mosaics, that the mosaics were improperly removed without the authorization of the Church or the Republic of Cyprus, and that the mosaics should be returned to the Church. The defendants, on the other hand, claim that export of the mosaics was authorized by Turkish Cypriot officials, and that in any event Goldberg should be awarded the mosaics because she purchased them in good faith and without information or reasonable notice that they were stolen.

Goldberg is president and majority shareholder of Goldberg & Feldman Fine Arts, Inc. . . . On July 1, 1988, Fitzgerald [another art dealer] informed Goldberg that he was aware of four early Christian mosaics that were for sale. Later that day, Fitzgerald introduced Goldberg to Michel van Rijn, a Dutch art dealer, and Ronald Faulk, an attorney from California. Goldberg knew very little about van Rijn or Faulk. She was told, however, that van Rijn was once convicted in France for forging Marc Chagall's signature to prints of that artist's work and that he also had been sued by an art gallery "for failure to pay money." . . . She also was aware that Faulk was in Europe to act as attorney for Fitzgerald and van Rijn.

At this July 1st meeting, van Rijn showed Goldberg photographs of the four Byzantine mosaics, and she immediately "fell in love" with them. . . . van Rijn told Goldberg that the seller of the mosaics was a Turkish antiquities dealer. In addition, he told her that the seller had "found" the mosaics in the rubble of an "extinct" church in northern Cyprus while serving as "an archaeologist from Turkey assigned to northern Cyprus." . . .

On July 3, 1988, while still in Amsterdam, Goldberg negotiated an agreement with van Rijn, Fitzgerald, and Faulk, whereby "the parties agreed to acquire the mosaics for their purchase price of $1,080,000 (U.S.)." . . . The agreement also provided that the parties would split the profits made on any future resale of the mosaics as follows: Goldberg & Feldman 50 percent; Fitzgerald 22.5 percent; van Rijn 22.5 percent; and Faulk 5 percent. This agreement was executed on July 4th in Amsterdam. . . .

Goldberg intended to sell the mosaics. Beginning in the fall of 1988, she contacted at least two people in an attempt to market and sell the mosaics. By October 1988, Goldberg had discussed the sale of the mosaics with Dr. Geza von Habsburg, an art dealer operating out of Geneva and New York. In October of 1988 von Habsburg contacted Dr. Marion True of the Getty Museum in California and discussed whether it would be interested in purchasing the mosaics for $20 million. Dr. True explained that the Getty does not collect Byzantine art and told von Habsburg that because of her close working relationship with Cyprus, it would be necessary for her to contact her friend Dr. Vassos Karageorghis about the mosaics. Dr. True had developed a working relationship with Dr. Karageorghis, and he had often spoken to her of Cyprus's attempts to recover the mosaics. Dr. True then called Dr. Karageorghis, who told her that export of the mosaics was not authorized by Cyprus and that the mosaics she described were the mosaics which Cyprus had been so interested in recovering. Dr. True gave Dr. Karageorghis the name of Geza von Habsburg and how to contact him.

In November 1988, Dr. Karageorghis and others in conjunction with Cyprus's Director General of the Ministry of Foreign Affairs, contacted the ambassador of Cyprus in Washington, D.C. They informed the ambassador of the mosaics' existence in the United States and suggested that immediate and discreet action be taken to recover the mosaics. The embassy then began working with its attorneys, the plaintiffs' Washington law firm in this case, to determine the location and possessor of the mosaics. . . .

The plaintiffs and their attorneys eventually learned that the mosaics were in Goldberg's possession in Indianapolis. The plaintiffs wrote to Goldberg requesting the return of the mosaics. Upon the defendants' refusal, the plaintiffs instructed their attorneys to file suit to recover the mosaics. . . .

### Body of Opinion

**District Judge Noland.** There are long-established rules of law in Indiana that a thief never obtains title to stolen items, and that one can pass no greater title than one has. . . . Therefore, one who obtains stolen items from a thief never obtains legal title to or right to possession of the item. . . .

In *Breckenridge v. McAfee* . . . (1876), one of the plaintiff's employees wrongfully and without the plaintiff's authorization took the plaintiff's wheat, sold it to defendants, and absconded with the money. The plaintiff sued for the return of the wheat, or if that was impossible, for money damages for the value thereof. At trial a jury returned a verdict for the plaintiff. The Indiana supreme court affirmed the judgment. . . .

Similarly, in *Torian v. McClure* . . . (1882) the thief rented a piano from the plaintiff. The thief then sold the piano to the defendant, a good faith purchaser for value. The plaintiff sued . . . for recovery of the piano. The trial court found for the plaintiff and ordered a return of the piano, or in the alternative money damages, and ordered money damages for the detention of the piano. The Indiana supreme court affirmed the judgment, including this conclusion of law:

> . . . that [the thief], at the time he sold the piano to the defendant, had no title thereto, and could confer none on the defendant, and that the plaintiff is the owner thereof.
>
> . . . This case as well stands for the proposition that a thief never acquires title to stolen property, and cannot pass any right to possession of stolen property to a subsequent transferee, including a *bona fide* purchaser for value.

Under Indiana law, as outlined, a thief obtains no title to or right to possession of stolen items and can pass no title or right to possession to a subsequent purchaser. The mosaics were stolen. For purposes of this analysis, it is of no significance whether Aydin Dikman originally stole the mosaics, or who originally stole them. Further, it matters not whether Goldberg purchased the mosaics from Dikman alone, or from only van Rijn and Fitzgerald. The evidence of theft and chain of possession under the facts of this case lead only to the conclusion that Goldberg came into possession of stolen property.

## Judgment and Result

The court concludes that the defendants were in wrongful possession of the mosaics and had to relinquish them to the plaintiff Church.

## Questions

1. If a person acquires goods from a thief but is unaware that the seller is a thief, can that person obtain valid title to the goods? Should the same rule apply to land (realty)? Why?
2. If a buyer acquires property from someone rightfully in possession but who wrongfully sells the property, does the buyer win over the property's original owner?
3. What business ethics noted in Chapter 1 are in evidence here? What legal ethics?

---

sale by someone lacking contractual capacity. T, the immediate transferee from the owner, may pass good title on to G, a good faith purchaser for value if G takes before O rescinds (tries to recover) title. For example, if Mary goes to a jeweler and buys a diamond ring and pays for it with a bad check, Mary gets voidable title to the ring. If Mary sells the ring for value (say $400) to Betty (a good faith purchaser who does not know of the fraud) Mary may pass full title to Betty. If the jeweler later learns that Betty has the ring, he cannot recover it. The idea behind voidable title is to encourage commerce by letting good faith purchasers for value keep personalty even though the seller's title was somewhat flawed.

In cases where T still retains the goods, O may recover them from T. Where O bails (loans) goods to T, and T unauthorizedly sells the goods to G (a good faith purchaser for value), O may recover the goods from G. The reasoning is as follows: As between two innocent persons (O and G), the law asks who has legal title and says that person (in this case, O) owns the goods. O did not give T any title, voidable or otherwise, when she loaned the goods to T. T in such a case merely had possession of the goods, but no voidable title, and thus T could merely transfer what she had—possession, but not title—to G.

*Buyer in the Ordinary Course of Business (BIOC).* Section 2-403(2) of the Uniform Commercial Code, enacted in 49 states (but not Louisiana) gives merchants a voidable title to goods entrusted to them. Specifically, any entrusting of possession of goods to a merchant who deals in goods of that kind gives the merchant the power to transfer all rights of the entruster to a **buyer in the ordinary course of business (BIOC).** Thus, if Mary takes her diamond ring to the jeweler to be cleaned and the jeweler sells it to another customer (a BIOC), the BIOC keeps the ring even though Mary can find the ring and the BIOC. (Mary could sue the jeweler for the tort of conversion, but she may not legally recover the ring from the BIOC.) The reason for letting the BIOC prevail is to encourage buying from merchants without the fear that what they buy can be reclaimed by someone else.

*Adverse Possession.* Realty, meaning land and buildings, may in a real sense be acquired by theft, although the technical name is adverse possession. **Adverse possession** occurs where someone openly, adversely, and continuously claims the land that is officially titled in someone else's name. In *Pieper v. Pontiff*, one state supreme court named the following six elements of an adverse possession claim to land (the case discusses the elements):

1. Under a claim of right
2. Actual
3. Open, notorious, and visible
4. Exclusive
5. Continuous
6. Peaceful

A statutory period (typically ranging from 10 to 20 years) in each state determines how long a person must continuously claim someone else's realty to acquire title by adverse possession. The time starts to run once someone occupies and exclusively controls the property. The occupation has to be continuous, but not necessarily constant. Regular use is sufficient. If one adverse possessor holds the property for less than the statutory period and sells it to another adverse possessor, the successive adverse possessors' occupation periods can be added together (called *tacking*) to satisfy the statutory period. The adverse element does not mean fighting mad, just against and not subservient to the owner on the deed. For example, a tenant is subservient and not adverse to the landlord simply because of being a tenant. A person can mistakenly hold another's land and still be adverse, as in the case of a mistaken boundary line matter.

## Pieper v. Pontiff
Supreme Court of Mississippi
513 So.2d 591 (1987)

### Background and Facts

On February 19, 1973, Mrs. Pontiff was conveyed a tract of land by her mother, Mrs. Hazel Reynolds, which was described in the warranty deed as having a northern boundary 289.7 feet along the south margin of a local road which intersects U.S. Highway 11. The land was also described as being located in the southeast quarter of the northwest quarter of Section 3, Township 2 North, Range 14 West, in Lamar County, Mississippi. On April 30, 1980, Mr. Pieper purchased property whose southern boundary was described as the south line of the northeast quarter of the northwest quarter of Section 3, Township 2 North, Range 14 West, in Lamar County, Mississippi. The above two described parcels of land overlap by 35 feet because the public road referred to in Mrs. Pontiff's deed is actually located in the northeast quarter of the northwest quarter and did not lie along the south line of the northeast quarter of the northwest quarter. The dispute as to ownership of this 35-foot strip of land arose when Mrs. Pontiff saw a "for sale" sign posted on the side of the road that she claimed as her property in December of 1982.

At trial, Mrs. Pontiff testified that her mother, Mrs. Hazel Reynolds, bought property in 1942, which contains the property deeded to Mrs. Pontiff. Mrs. Reynolds' deed was also in evidence. Mrs. Pontiff also testified that Highway 11 dissects this larger tract of land and that her mother conveyed her, in 1973, the property on the east side of Highway 11, which includes the 35-foot strip now in dispute. Mrs. Pontiff testified that in 1942, on this east side of Highway 11 (the property deeded to her), there were remnants of an old cabin and that her father used the property to pasture his cows. She also testified that this land, including the 35-foot strip, was under fence in order to keep the cows in. She also testified that there was timber on this property, including the 35-foot strip in dispute. Mrs. Pontiff further testified that when she bought the property in 1973, the fence, although in deterioration, was still standing. In 1982, the time the controversy over this 35-foot strip of land arose, the fence was practically all torn down except for some remnants and fence posts.

Mr. Jordan, a certified land surveyor for state-aid roads in the county, testified from the survey he made of this property in 1973 for Mrs. Pontiff. In his testimony he stated that Mrs. Pontiff's property and Mr. Pieper's property were separated by a fence line and that this fence line ran along the south margin of the county road. He also testified that he had lived in Purvis all of his life and that he had never known anyone else to make use of this disputed property other than the Reynolds since World War II. He testified that the property had always been bounded by a fence or a fence line along the side of the road. He further testified that no one else besides the Reynolds family had ever claimed that 35 feet of property. Finally, he testified that the iron stake which marks the section line was probably placed there by a surveyor hired by Mr. Pieper in 1982, and that, indeed, the north boundary described in Mr. Pieper's deed did not run along the south margin of this road, but was described as being the section line. He speculated that the old fence was originally put up just outside the section line (so that it ran along the road) simply because the road is a natural boundary.

Two other witnesses, long-time residents of the area, testified that the disputed land had always been known as belonging to the Reynolds family, and that the property had been under fence since the early 1940s.

On cross-examination of these witnesses, the testimony focused on what use had been made of the land since 1973, when Mrs. Pontiff bought it from her mother. Mrs. Pontiff testified that the land had not been put to any use other than for her and her husband to walk on when they came from Texas to visit her mother. She also testified that they had planted trees on the property and specifically had planted a pear tree, which eventually died, on this 35-foot strip. The other three witnesses testified that, to their knowledge, the land had not been used for gardening, farming, cutting timber, or grazing cattle in the past nine years.

Mr. Pieper did not put on any witnesses of his own, and only offered his deed into evidence to prove the boundary lines of his property. At the end of oral testimony, both sides offered into evidence records of the taxes paid on this property from 1973 to the present.

## Body of Opinion

We focus on the issue of adverse possession of the 35-foot strip of property in dispute.

Mr. Pieper incorrectly frames the issue in this case as to adverse possession. He correctly argues that there are six elements necessary to constitute an effective adverse possession claim: (1) under claim of right; (2) actual; (3) open, notorious and visible; (4) exclusive; (5) continuous and uninterrupted for 10 years, and (6) peaceful. However, he incorrectly applies these elements to Mrs. Pontiff rather than to Mrs. Hazel Reynolds, Mrs. Pontiff's mother and predecessor in title. There was testimony throughout the trial that Mrs. Reynolds acquired her property through warranty deed in 1942 and that she and her family used the property deeded to Mrs. Pontiff, including the 35 feet in dispute, to graze cows. The disputed property was under fence for that purpose from 1942 until the mid-1960s, and the fence remained in repair "well enough to keep cattle" until at least 1972 when Mr. Jordan surveyed it. In 1945, in a quiet title action, the chancery court decreed that Mrs. Reynolds'

property was bounded by the south margin of the public road. The decree assumed that the south margin of the road and the section line were one and the same. It was not until 1982, when Mr. Pieper hired a survey of the land pursuant to the boundaries set out in his deed, that the discrepancy came to light. Therefore, Mrs. Reynolds claimed the 35-strip from 1945 until she deeded it to Mrs. Pontiff in 1973.

The Reynolds family's use of this property was exclusive and peaceful, continuous for 41 years, actual, open and notorious and under claim of right, according to the evidence offered. In other words, there was much credible evidence that could lead the chancellor to conclude that title to the 35-foot strip of land had vested in Mrs. Hazel Reynolds by adverse possession before 1973, when it was deeded to Mrs. Pontiff.

It is upon the point of discrepancy in the 1945 decree of the chancery court that Mr. Pieper frames his second argument. He alleges that because Mrs. Pontiff's deed from her mother did not set out by legal quarter section that the disputed property was part of the deeded property, Mrs. Pontiff's claim to the property was ineffective. This Court held many years ago, and again more recently, that it does not matter whether land claimed under adverse possession be within or without the "call of the title deeds," *Evans v. Harrison*, (1922), or that it be in the same quarter section or section as the land lies which is described in the deed.

Finally, Mr. Pieper argues that the fence around the disputed property has been in disrepair since 1973, during Mrs. Pontiff's claim of right, and that, therefore, the fence was not enough to put anyone on notice that Mrs. Pontiff claimed the property. Again, Mr. Pieper applies the requirements of adverse possession to the wrong title claimant. Mrs. Pontiff's mother gave notice for more than forty years by a fence around the disputed property and by continued use of the property. Once title ripened by adverse possession in Mrs. Reynolds, it is not necessary that the fence be standing, or even in existence, when the suit is filed.

Once title to the disputed property ripened in Mrs. Reynolds by adverse possession, and once she conveyed the disputed property to her daughter, Mrs. Pontiff, Mr. Pieper could not divest Mrs. Pontiff of that title unless he adversely possessed against her, which he does not claim to have done. The chancellor did not err in quieting title to the disputed property in Mrs. Pontiff and dismissing Mr. Pieper's counterclaim.

## Judgment and Result

Finding no error, we affirm the chancellor's order confirming and quieting title in Myrna Reynolds Pontiff.

## Questions

1. Is it "fair," according to natural law principles, that one person should be able to "steal" another's land?
2. What are the six elements of adverse possession the Mississippi Supreme Court announces?
3. What legal ethics justify adverse possession?

## Gift

A **gift** refers to the voluntary transfer of title to property where the transferor receives nothing in exchange for the transfer. The giver of the gift is called the **donor** and the person receiving the gift is called the **donee**. Title to both realty and personalty can be acquired by an *inter vivos* gift. Inter vivos gifts refers to gifts between living persons, to be contrasted with gifts one makes by will at one's death. A deed is necessary to convey realty by gift. Generally a valid delivery of the deed must occur in the giving of a gift of realty. The types of gifts are inter vivos and gifts *causa mortis*.

The elements of a valid inter vivos gift are (1) donative intent, (2) delivery, and (3) acceptance. **Donative intent** refers to the idea that the gift giver must presently intend to make a gift, not just want to give at some unspecified future time.

**Delivery** involves the present handing over of control to something from the donor to the donee. Delivery can be either actual (the donor's handing over a ring to the donee) or constructive (the donor's handing over something *representing* the item being given, such as the keys to a car when one is giving a car).

**Acceptance** refers to the donee's agreeing to take control over the item given. Acceptance is generally presumed except when the gift would impose a hardship on the donee (for example, if someone gave a friend a piece of land with a toxic waste dump that cost more to clean up than the land was worth).

A **gift causa mortis** results when a donor thinks she or he is about to die, makes a gift because of this belief, and then actually dies because of the particular threat of death. The donor must die from that bout of that illness or operation that caused him or her to make the gift. For example, if the donor is about to undergo heart surgery, makes a gift in contemplation of this surgery, but survives, the gift is revoked. If the donor later undergoes heart surgery and dies, this event does not revive the gift causa mortis, unless of course the donor had again made such a gift.

## Capture

The *capture doctrine* is a way to acquire title to animals in the wild, but not animals in captivity, as in a zoo. Capture occurs when one takes physical possession of wild animals, but federal and state conservation laws place restrictions on capturing some types of wild animals.

## Finding

A person may acquire title to lost personalty by finding it. **Lost property** is personalty that has been unintentionally, involuntarily parted with by the owner. A **finder** is a person who locates lost property. The finder has a claim superior to all others except that of the owner who lost it.

*Statutes on Finding.* In some jurisdictions, statutes set out procedures to be followed in claiming lost property. Usually such statutes require advertising the object in specific enough terms to notify the loser that the property has been found and awaits his or her claiming it, while allowing enough detail to be held back to enable the finder to test the claimant's ability to identify it.

*Mislaid Property.* Mislaid property differs from lost property. Mislaid property is personalty one intentionally parts with but which one cannot recall parting with. Mislaid property remains the property of the one who intentionally parted with it but forgot it. Mislaid property does not become the property of the finder.

*Abandoned Property.* Abandoned property is personalty someone has intentionally and permanently parted with by leaving it in no one's custody. The first one to take possession of abandoned personalty becomes its owner.

## INHERITANCE

One way a person may acquire either realty or personalty is by inheriting it from the estate of a deceased person. Deceased persons' estates may transfer property to others either by the **statute of descent** or by **will**.

*Statute of Descent.* The statute of descent is a will made by the state legislature, which realizes that many people do not have wills (dying without a will is known as dying **intestate**) and so drafts a statute that distributes a decedent's property in accordance with the way the legislature thinks the decedent would want it distributed. The legislative determination of how most people would want their property distributed at their death might be entirely wrong. Nevertheless the statute of descent tells how a person's property is distributed unless that individual either dies without property or leaves a will.

*Wills.* A will is a piece of paper on which a **testator** (maker of the will) indicates the persons who will take his or her property when he or she dies. A will in the testator's (testatrix, if a woman) handwriting and signed by the testator is called a **holographic will**. It does not have to be witnessed to be valid in most states, but not all states recognize the validity of holographic wills. Wills that are not in the testator's handwriting generally have to be declared by the testator to be his or her will in the presence of two witnesses, who must sign in each other's presence. The testator must be the age specified by the legislature of the state in which she or he dies domiciled to be able to execute a valid will. The will requirements of witnesses, attestation, signing in the presence of witnesses, and being a certain age are referred to as **formal requirements**. If any one of them is lacking, the will is theoretically void. In practical terms, if a formal requirement is lacking but no one challenges it, the will probably transfers property to the persons named in it.

Wills are **ambulatory**, meaning that they may be changed any number of times before the testator dies unless the testator has made a binding contract to make a will. If the testator has made a binding contract to make a will, it is a debt of the estate. One reason wills are ambulatory is that they do not take effect until the testator dies. Before that time, a person named in the will merely has an expectancy, but no property rights in any of the testator's assets.

A testator's will may not be used to escape debts, even if the will does not mention the testator's wish to pay personal debts. The way the testator's creditors are assured of an opportunity to be paid is by the probate process. A **probate court** exists in virtually every county in the United States. The function of probate courts is to test the validity of deceased persons' wills. (Was it really her will?) Such courts also appoint administrators for estates of those dying without a will or without naming an executor. A person named in a will to manage and wind up the estate is called an **executor**. The executor's job is to collect all of the decedent's property, pay off his or her debts, and distribute any remaining property in accordance with the will or statute of descent. If the will names no one to be executor or if there is no will, the probate judge appoints someone—called an **administrator**—to wind up the estate as just described. After appointment of the executor or administrator, public notices are placed in newspapers of general circulation telling of the decedent's death and advising decedent's creditors where and when to present their bills for payment. Then a hearing is held, at which time creditors' claims can be presented, proven, and either allowed or disallowed by the probate court.

Allowed creditor claims are paid before bequests (personal property given by will) and **devises** (realty given by will) are made. It is possible that creditor claims could exhaust all of the decedent's property, in which case takers named in the will would get nothing.

## TRUSTS

One can acquire property as a trustee or as a trust beneficiary.

*Definition of Trust.* A **trust** is a way of owning property with two titles (that is, with two owners at the same time). The two titles are beneficial title, sometimes called **equitable title**, and legal title. Putting it another way, a trust is a legal relationship consisting of a settlor (the person who sets up the trust), a *res* (the property subject to the trust), a trustee (the person having legal title who manages the res), and a beneficiary (the person who receives the trust benefits and who holds beneficial title to the *res*). An indication of the settlor's intent is necessary to establish a trust for a legally recognized trust purpose. Also, some states require following certain formalities (writings, etc.) to establish a trust.

*Law Governing Trusts.* State law governs the setting up of trusts. State law and federal estate and gift tax law play an understandably vital role in the operation of trusts.

*Mechanics of Forming Trusts.* Trusts may have either realty or personalty as their *res*. State statutes determine whether trusts have to be written. Generally such statutes require trusts to be written when realty is the *res*. At common law oral trusts with any kind of *res* are possible and, in a few states, is still the law. As a practical matter, it is best to have a written trust.

*How Long Trusts Can Last.* A trust can be set up to last for as long as possible, provided that all interests the trust creates **vest** (take effect and become the property rights of someone) within any life (or lives) in being at the time the trust becomes effective, plus 21 years. This last statement is called the **rule against perpetuities**. It was announced in England hundreds of years ago to keep property from being tied up by any one person for an extended period of time. It is a populist idea, along the lines that every person should have a *shot* at becoming an owner of resources. This rule has also been followed in the United States—much to the dismay of lawyers because it is difficult to draft documents to satisfy it. However, this rule does not apply to some statutory trusts for employee retirements.

*Inter Vivos and Testamentary Trusts.* Trusts created and taking effect during the settlor's life are called *inter vivos* trusts. Trusts that take effect at the settlor's death are **testamentary** trusts. The degree of formality (witnesses, writing, etc.) needed to create a trust is greater for testamentary trusts, because requirements for executing a will must be observed.

*Reasons for Creating Trusts.* The trust arrangement allows one person (the settlor) to give property to another (the beneficiary) even though that person is unable to manage it. For example, a minor child, insane person, or a person inexperienced in managing property would represent appropriate reasons for setting up a trust. The settlor confers legal title on the trustee, who manages the *res* for the benefit of the beneficiary.

*Trustee's Duties.* Trustees hold the legal title to the trust *res*. As such, they have the duty to manage the *res* according to the terms set out in the instrument creating the trust. Trustees must not act negligently in managing the trust *res*. They must use the care and skill that ordinarily reasonable, prudent persons would use in managing their own affairs. Trustees are **fiduciaries**. As such, they have the highest duty of good faith in managing the trust. They must avoid conflicts of interest, such as selling trust assets to themselves. Trustees must account to the trust beneficiaries. The duty to account provides a way to guard against the trustee's abusing the trust's terms.

*Problems with the Trust.* Disputes can arise when the trust beneficiary (often a young person) thinks the trustee (often a bank) is mismanaging the trust. If the beneficiary sues the trustee for mismanagement or violation of one of the trustee's duties, the suit takes place in an equity court, not law court.

*Who Can Be a Trustee.* Virtually any legal person, natural (an individual) or artificial (a corporation), private or governmental, can be a trustee.

*How Trusts End.* Trusts end when the instrument creating them says they end. It is usually a definite date or when some purpose has been accomplished. Trusts may also be ended if all parties to it agree.

## MANUFACTURE

A person may acquire ownership of property by manufacturing it from materials she or he owns. However, others' patents may limit what one may make and how one may make it. Also, trademarks can limit how something is marketed.

## CONFUSION

Title to property may arise from a process known as **confusion** of fungible goods. **Fungible goods** are those that are uniform in size, shape, or nature, such as wheat or oil. If a grain elevator carelessly mixed a farmer's grain with others' grain, the farmer would have a claim on all of the grain needed to protect his or her interest.

## PURCHASE

**Purchase** is perhaps the most common means of acquiring property, both real and personal. Purchase occurs as the result of a contract, covered in Chapter 10. Recall that a contract is an agreement between competent parties enforceable in court.

A person can acquire either personalty or realty by contracting to buy it. It is also possible to exchange goods for goods or goods for services in a **barter** transaction. Most property, however, is acquired in exchange for money.

Generally, contracts can be oral unless realty or expensive goods valued at $500 or more are purchased, in which case *written* evidence of the contract, signed by the person against whom you are trying to enforce the contract, is necessary.

## USES OF PROPERTY

One basic right property owners have is to use whatever property rights they have in whatever way they see fit. For example, if someone owns a sailboat, that person can use the boat on a sunny Sunday afternoon in July.

### BAILMENT

Often, owners of personalty will want to lend their property to some friend. This type of relationship is called a bailment. A **bailment** is the separation of title and possession of personal, not real, property. The bailor is the owner of the property and the bailee is the borrower. The loaned property is called the bailed property.

*Types of Bailments.* The law recognizes three types of bailments: bailment for the sole benefit of the bailor; bailment for the sole benefit of the bailee; and mutual benefit bailment.

A **bailment for the sole benefit of the bailor** benefits only the owner of the bailed property. It would occur when the owner of a fur coat asks a friend to keep it for no charge but not use it while the owner goes on vacation.

**Bailments for the sole benefit of the bailee** arise if the borrower only is benefiting from using someone else's property. An example would be if a person asks her neighbor to borrow his lawnmower for no rental fee or other consideration and the neighbor agrees.

A **mutual benefit bailment** is created when Mary rents an auto from a car rental agency. Mary, the bailee, is getting use of the car. The car rental agency, the bailor, is getting money. Both bailee and bailor benefit, hence, the name mutual benefit bailment.

*Significance of the Different Types of Bailment.* The significance of the types of bailment is that the more a bailment benefits the bailee, the more care the bailee has to the bailed property. In a bailment for the sole benefit of the bailee, the bailee has a high standard of care. Under a mutual benefit bailment, the bailee has the duty of ordinary care. In bailments for the sole benefit of the bailor, the bailee has a slight duty of care.

In addition to the previously described duties of care, the bailee must also return the bailed property at the end of the bailment.

### LEASES, LICENSES, AND EASEMENTS

Owners of real estate could let others use their realty. Such use of another's realty could be a license, an easement, or a lease. A license is the right extended to a person to enter onto another's realty for a limited time and purpose. A patron's sitting in a movie theater is a license. An easement is also a nonpossessory interest in someone else's realty. An easement that exists to benefit a particular person is called an easement in gross, while an easement benefiting adjacent land is an easement appurtenant. A lease is a right to possess and use someone else's realty for a limited time, frequently referred to as landlord–tenant law.

*Kinds of Tenancies.* Tenancies, or landlord–tenant relationships, include tenancy for years, tenancy for period (or periodic tenancy), a tenancy at will, and a tenancy at sufferance.

A tenancy for years is misleading because it refers to a lease for a period of time expressly stated in the lease contract. For example, a lease for one month (even though not a year) is, in fact, a tenancy for years and gives the tenant the right to occupy the premises for one month. Note that the period can be for any definite length, but if the lease is for more than one year, it must be written to be enforceable. When the period stated in the lease expires, the lease ends even if no notice is given. Renewal provisions (if they exist and are exercised) allow tenants to remain in possession.

A periodic tenancy arises by a lease, but the lease does not state how long it lasts, although periodic rent is required. Periodic tenancies are automatically renewed unless properly ended. A lease creating a periodic tenancy might read: "The tenant must pay rent to the landlord on the first of the month." The period can be any length—a week, a month, a year. Holdover tenants from a tenancy for years can become periodic tenants when they pay weekly or monthly rent if no express term exists and no renewal clause under the first lease was exercised. Landlords in periodic tenancy situations must give tenants proper notice (usually notice must be a period's length in advance) to end a periodic tenancy.

A tenancy at will exists if the lease is "for how long we make it." Both tenant and landlord have little security in this arrangement because either may end it at any time without even giving notice. Holdover tenants can also fall into this category until such time as they become periodic tenants.

Tenants at sufferance is actually not a tenancy, but, rather, someone who legally occupies someone else's property as a tenant for years, for example, and the lease expires and the tenant stays on wrongfully. In such a case the tenant becomes a tenant at sufferance.

*Problem Areas in Landlord–Tenant Relations.* Problem areas in landlord–tenant relationships include the following:

- The amount of damage deposit the tenant is required to make when the lease is signed
- The procedures to be followed to determine the amount of damages caused by the former tenant and by the present tenant (Is there a walk-through inventory by landlord and tenant at both the start and end of the lease?)
- The date after the lease ends when the landlord has to refund the tenant's damage deposit
- The uses to which the tenant may and may not put the premises
- The degree to which the tenant must observe sanitation regulations in the apartment and in common areas
- The extent of security protection the landlord must provide

- The tenant's rights to deduct from rent amounts spent to make repairs the landlord must make
- The tenant's rights to withhold rent payments and stay in or leave the premises free of any obligation if the premises become uninhabitable due to causes beyond the tenant's control
- The extent to which class actions are allowable

*Some Traditional Common Law Rules with Respect to Leases.* These six common law rules have been changed in some jurisdictions by statute.

1. If the tenant leases both a building and the land on which the building sits, and the building is destroyed, the tenant is liable for rent on both the building and land unless a lease clause or statute excuses the rent.
2. The tenant has a duty to make minor repairs to keep the premises livable, such as repairing a broken screen.
3. The tenant has a duty to pay rent.
4. The tenant may **sublet** or assign his or her lease unless the lease prevents it.
5. If the tenant, tenant's family member, or guest is injured on the leased premises, the landlord is generally *not* liable, unless the injury resulted from some breach of a landlord's agreement to keep the premises in repair or the injury occurs in a common area (stairs, elevator, or deck) and is the result of the landlord's breaching a duty to maintain the premises.
6. The tenant has a duty not to commit waste on the premises.

## THE UNIFORM RESIDENTIAL LANDLORD TENANT ACT (URLTA)

Landlord-tenant law is state law. About one-third of the states have passed the Uniform Residential Landlord Tenant Act (URLTA). As the name suggests, this law only covers residential leases, not those where a business leases space for its offices. URLTA strikes a balance between landlord and tenant rights that is generally more favorable to tenants than were the generally landlord-biased common law rules on this topic. Check your state code to determine whether your state has adopted URLTA.

Among the topics URLTA addresses are deposits, subleasing, habitability, landlord right of access, landlord rules governing tenants, general landlord and tenant rights and duties, unconscionability, and exculpatory clauses.

*Deposits.* Deposits refer to amounts of money the tenant is required to leave with the landlord to protect some landlord interest. Cleaning deposits cover landlord costs of cleaning the premises after the tenant vacates the premises. URLTA permits landlords to include cleaning deposits in residential leases. However, **BOLD** print must identify nonrefundable cleaning deposits.

Security deposits cover damage to the premises, theft of items belonging to the landlord, or tenant departure prior to termination of the lease. In effect, security deposits are damages the tenant pays in advance to cover any violations committed. URLTA caps the size of security deposits. These caps or limits vary from state to state; state codes set the exact amount. Many states (including some without URLTA) require that landlords place security deposits in a separate account, and some states even require that tenants earn interest on security deposits. Common law, by contrast, allowed landlords to do what they wanted with security deposits.

Deposits for prepaid rent refers to amounts that landlords require tenants to pay up front (prior to entering the premises) to guarantee that rent will be paid. URLTA caps prepaid rent to one and one-half times the monthly rent.

*Subleasing.* A sublease occurs when a tenant transfers possession of the leased property to a third person for only part of the lease. The original tenant continues to pay rent to the original landlord in a sublease, and the sublessee becomes the tenant of the original tenant. The sublessee is not the tenant of the original landlord. The sublessee has no right to sue the original landlord if the original landlord fails to meet lease obligations. In such a case, if the landlord breaches any obligations, the sublessee must sue the original tenant, who, in turn, must sue the original landlord.

An assignment of a lease differs from a sublease in several respects. In a *lease assignment*, the original tenant turns over rights and duties to the assignee. The original tenant remains liable to the original landlord, but also the assignee is obligated to the tenant. Note also that the landlord remains liable to the original tenant and also becomes liable to the assignee. The assignee agrees to serve out the lease term and pay rent directly to the original landlord.

Common law rules allowed tenants to sublet or assign leases. The lease can, of course, take this right away from the tenant. A majority of states continue to allow tenants to sublet or assign the lease unless prohibited in the lease.

*Habitability.* Habitability requires that the leased property be *livable*, that is, it must have functioning plumbing and heat and be in good repair. Broken windows or leaky roofs would violate the habitability requirement. Amazingly, the common law did not impose a habitability requirement on the leased premises. Thus, the tenant could move into unlivable premises with no legal way of forcing the landlord to make repairs. Presumably, only people in desperate financial situations or unaware of the poor condition of the premises would lease such property.

Unlike the common law, URLTA imposes a warranty of habitability on the landlord of residential property. Tenants now have a legal basis to sue landlords who fail to provide livable premises. For example, if the plumbing does not work, the tenant can sue the landlord for breaching the warranty of habitability.

URLTA makes it unconscionable (illegal) for landlords to eliminate the warranty of habitability in residential leases.

*Landlord Right of Access.* Even though tenants have leased the premises, landlords may legally enter them under certain circumstances. First, the tenant may allow the landlord to enter. Second, URLTA and a majority of states allow the landlord to enter after giving advance notice. For example, the landlord might want to check the premises for radon or some other health hazard. URLTA requires that the landlord give the tenant two days notice except in the case of an emergency, such as a fire, in which case no advance notice is required. Tenants must be told the reason a landlord needs access. URLTA says that repairing, decorating, and cleaning are appropriate reasons for entering the tenant's premises. Third, governmental inspectors may enter if they have a warrant. Landlords must obey such warrants covering tenants' premises. Should the warrant prove defective, the tenant has recourse against the government inspectors, not the landlord.

*Landlord Rules.* It is common for landlords to impose rules on tenants covering matters such as who can park in the apartment parking lot; who can use the apartment swimming pool; who can use the apartment laundry; whether pets are allowed; and what are allowable noise levels. URLTA and all jurisdictions allow such rules if they apply to all tenants, they are definite, tenants are aware of the rules when they sign the lease, tenants are notified of rules changes, and the rules' purposes are for the tenants' general welfare, convenience, or safety. Extra charges for rules violations are upheld by courts if the rules are reasonable, even though the charge may amount to a large sum.

*Landlord's Rights and Duties.* The principal landlord right is to receive the tenant's rent on time. Tenants failing to pay their rent risk eviction, and landlords have the right to end the lease. URLTA requires that landlords give written notice that rent is overdue. If the tenant fails to pay rent within two weeks of receipt of an overdue notice, the lease is legally ended in thirty days. The *Lake County Trust Co. v. Wine* case illustrates a tenant's attempt to avoid paying a rent increase thought to be excessive.

## Lake County Trust v. Wine
### Court of Appeals of Indiana
### 704 N.E.2d 1035 (1998)

### Background and Facts

Williamsburg owns Williamsburg Manor, a residential community that provides mobile home lots for lease. The tenants of the park had executed written leases with Williamsburg that provided month-to-month tenancies. In November 1993, Williamsburg increased the rent for the lots from $221 to $236 per month, constituting a 7 percent increase. Many of the tenants vehemently protested the increase. Appellees, Terry and Sandra Wine, Ronald and Carol Niebauer, and other tenants of Williamsburg, paid their rent minus the increase; as a result, Williamsburg returned their checks with Notices to Quit. Several tenants were permitted to pay the required rent plus a late fee; however, the Niebauers and other ringleaders of the rent protest were not permitted to remain in Williamsburg under any circumstances. Williamsburg sued to evict the Niebauers, the Wines, and other tenants. The Wines' and Niebauers' eviction suits were consolidated. The Wines and the Niebauers counterclaimed on behalf of themselves and the other tenants of Williamsburg for breach of contract (and other grounds here omitted). The trial court certified the action as a class action. Williamsburg moved for summary judgment on the Niebauer class counterclaims; additionally, Williamsburg moved the court to decertify the class action. The trial court denied both motions and let the appeal proceed before it rendered a decision.

### Body of Opinion

**Judge Robb.** . . . Williamsburg argues that the trial court erred when it denied its motion for summary judgment on the Niebauers' class claim that a duty of good faith and fair dealing was expressly incorporated into the Williamsburg lease. Section 13 of the Williamsburg lease states that "the posted rules and regulations . . .

attached to this lease are part of this lease at the time of execution.". . . The preamble to the rules and regulations states:

> Williamsburg Manor is conceived as a community of neighbors living in harmony . . . not by rigid rules and regulations. . . . When these standards are fair, reasonable and logical . . . when they are applied and complied with on an impartial basis . . . each resident can be assured a maximum of freedom, privacy, safety and comfort. . . . [T]he spirit behind this statement is the Golden Rule: "Do unto others as you would have others do unto you."

. . . The Neibauer class argues that the language of the preamble to the rules and regulations imposes a duty of good faith which is expressly incorporated into the rental agreement. We disagree.

Rules of construction of contracts apply to leases. . . . In Indiana, the duty of good faith is applied in contract law only under limited circumstances such as those involving insurance contracts. . . . Finally, a contract may incorporate another unsigned writing when the contract expressly incorporates the terms of the writing. . . .

The duty of "fairness" outlined in the rules and regulations does not apply to the lease; rather, this duty is expressly limited to the statement it precedes: the rules and regulations. The preamble to the rules and regulations states: "the spirit behind *this statement* is in the Golden Rule" [emphasis added]. Thus, even assuming the language of the preamble implies a contractual duty of good faith, the preamble limits itself to the rules and regulations and therefore does not apply to the conditions of the lease. Although the language of the lease incorporates the terms and conditions of the rules and regulations, the terms of each document retain their original meaning and will only effectuate the intent clearly contemplated by the language of said instruments. Thus, a statement which limits the effect and scope of a clause will retain its meaning when incorporated into another document.

In the alternative, the Neibauer class claims that the duty of good faith and fair dealing should apply to leases in general. In particular, it argues that a sophisticated landlord has undue influence in the execution of a lease. Thus, they claim that without a duty of good faith Williamsburg can arbitrarily and unfairly raise the monthly rent. In general, however, contract law does not require such a duty:

> It is not the province of courts to require a party acting pursuant to such a contract to be "reasonable," "fair," or show "good faith" cooperation. Such an assessment would go beyond the bounds of judicial duty and responsibility. It would be impossible for parties to rely on the written expressions of their duties and responsibilities. . . .

The Neibauer class admits that Williamsburg had the right to raise rent; indeed, because the leases were month to month, Williamsburg and the tenants had the right to renegotiate the terms of the lease at the end of each successive tenancy. . . .

Williamsburg gave all of the tenants over one month's notice of the new monthly rent; therefore, the terms of the leases were clear and unambiguous. Under Indiana law, a person is presumed to understand and assent to the terms of the contracts they sign. . . . Aside from the fact that Williamsburg is a "corporate landlord," the Neibauer class cannot point to any undue influence or unequal bargaining power exercised by Williamsburg in the execution of their respective leases; therefore, as a matter of law, we are unwilling to extend a duty of good faith and fair dealing to corporate landlords. Like all tenants, the residents of Williamsburg were free to execute a lease with a different landlord if the terms of the lease were unacceptable.

By asking the court to apply a duty of good faith to an unambiguous lease, the Niebauer class is effectively requesting this court to rewrite the terms of an agreement where the intent of the parties is clear. Such an exercise of our discretion is without the boundaries of our authority and in clear contravention of contract law as outlined by our Supreme Court. . . .

## Judgment and Result

The Court of Appeals would not apply a duty of good faith and fair dealing to tenants' unambiguous lease with the mobile home park.

## Questions

1. Do rules of construction for contracts apply to leases?
2. Are persons who rent mobile home lots usually high or low income persons? Should the law protect such persons from exploitation? In Indiana is a duty of good faith "read into" residential lease contracts where tenants are low income persons?
3. Williamsburg Manor's rules and regulations spoke of a community governed by the spirit of the Golden Rule. Did the court say this spirit of the Golden Rule applied to the lease? Would Kant (mentioned in Chapter 1 in connection with the categorical imperative) have approved of what the court did here?
4. Was there any legally recognized reason why Williamsburg Manor could not increase the tenants' rent? If landlords could not raise rents, is it not possible that they might not cover their costs and eventually go out of business? Then where would the tenants go?
5. What check do tenants have on a landlord who apparently arbitrarily raises rents too much? Go elsewhere? What if there is no other trailer park in the vicinity?

As noted earlier, landlords have duties under URLTA including keeping the premises habitable, providing a place for garbage disposal, keeping utilities safe as well as operable (assuming the tenants pay their utility bills), obeying building and safety codes, and keeping common areas safe and clean.

*Tenants' Rights and Duties.* Tenants have a duty to pay their rent on time and follow rules governing the leased premises. Failure to pay the rent or follow the rules entitles the landlord to end the lease or impose added charges.

The tenant has a number of rights, including the right to habitable property and the right to repair and deduct the cost of repair from the rent payment. Under URLTA the landlord has 14 days to respond to tenants' demands to repair before the tenant can exercise self-help (repair them or hire someone to repair the problem). URLTA caps the amount of repairs tenants can engage in and deduct from the rent to the larger of $100 or half the month's rent. Amounts vary from state to state.

Occasionally, the leased premises are in such disrepair that the tenants can assert that they have been *constructively evicted*. If constructive eviction occurs, the tenant has the right to leave the premises with no further liability on the lease.

Exactly what amounts to constructive eviction will vary from case to case, but it could include, for example, lack of heat in a Boston apartment in January.

*Unconscionability.* Unconscionability means that a term in a contract such as a lease is unfair to the tenant to such an extent that a court will not enforce the provision. A provision could be unfair because the landlord had a much stronger bargaining position than the tenant, because the lease is offered on a "take it or leave it" basis, or because of some other factor. A lease that required that the tenant forfeit his car if he parked in the wrong parking spot would be unconscionable.

URLTA makes it unconscionable for landlords to deprive tenants of URLTA rights. Thus, it would be unconscionable for landlords to impose a lease provision taking away tenants' rights to have functioning plumbing.

*Exculpatory Clauses.* Perhaps you have heard of landlords who put terms in leases absolving the landlord from liability for tenant injuries or damages incurred during the lease. Generally, courts refuse to honor exculpatory clauses that totally exempt landlords from their own negligence. The validity of such clauses generally turns on the amount of the landlord's culpability (blameworthiness), as well as the source and nature of the tenant's injury. For example, if the tenant's spouse throws a rolling pin at the tenant and puts out the tenant's eye, the landlord will not be liable because landlords are not responsible for tenants' marital bliss. On the other hand, if the tenant slips and falls because the landlord has not repaired loose tile after having been informed and after having had sufficient time to remedy the matter, the landlord will probably be liable for the tenant's damages even though the lease has an exculpatory clause exonerating the landlord from such liability.

The *Steward ex rel. Stewart v. Aldrich* case shows that at least one state's supreme court has held that landlords will not be liable for injuries to third persons caused by tenants' animals.

## Steward ex rel Stewart v. Aldrich
Supreme Judicial Court of Maine
788 A.2d 603 (2002)

### Background and Facts

In December of 1997, Aldrich rented an apartment to Donald and Robin Bailey pursuant to a month-to-month agreement. The tenancy agreement was not in writing and, according to Aldrich, most of the terms were "implied," and the obligations of the parties were governed by "reasonableness." For example, Aldrich indicated that it was "understood" that he would perform traditional landlord functions like making repairs and plowing snow, and the tenants would be responsible if they caused excessive damage to the apartment. The Baileys took possession of the apartment at either the end of December 1997 or the beginning of January 1998.

Aldrich indicated that he had evicted tenants in the past. He had always given tenants whom he was evicting a 30-day notice of eviction. According to him, the tenants would either leave or, upon realizing that he was "serious," would correct the underlying problem that had led him to begin eviction proceedings. He did not recall ever giving a seven-day notice of eviction, but believed it was his right to do so.

Aldrich did not prohibit his tenants form having dogs. The rules regarding animals were also governed by an implied rule of reason. For example, Aldrich testified that it was understood that the tenants could not have an inordinate number of dogs (e.g., ten), and that the tenants were expected to keep the dogs on a leash when outside the apartment. The parties dispute whether Aldrich specifically told the Baileys that they could get a dog. He testified that he did not recall discussing the subject of dogs with the Baileys before he found out that they had one. The Baileys testified that they asked Aldrich whether they could get a dog and he told them that he would not have a problem if they did.

The Baileys acquired a dog, an Akita, sometime in the spring of 1998. On April 24, 1998, the dog attacked the Baileys' two year-old daughter and created a serious wound in her head.

On July 28, 1998, seven year-old Kristen Stewart, who was a friend of the Baileys' daughter, arrived unexpectedly at the Baileys' apartment. Robin Bailey was getting ready to go to the doctor's office, but told Kristen that she could stay while she got ready. Robin went into the bedroom to get ready, and Kristen stayed in the living room with the dog. A few minutes later Robin heard a scream and rushed to the living room to find that Kristen had been attacked by the dog and received injuries to her face from the attack.

Stewart alleges that Aldrich had a duty to ensure that the premises he rented to tenants did not possess any dangerous conditions and that he violated this duty by allowing the Baileys to remain in the apartment with a dog that he knew to be dangerous. The court granted Aldrich's motion for a summary judgment, and this appeal by Stewart followed.

## Body of Opinion

### Justice Clifford

. . . Although there is a dispute about whether Aldrich knew that the dog had previously bitten the daughter of his tenants, the Baileys presented sufficient evidence to support a finding that he did. Further, although the trial court did not explicitly draw the inference that knowledge of the previous attack meant that the landlord should have known that the dog was dangerous or had vicious propensities, a factfinder could reasonably draw such an inference from the evidence.

A landlord is generally not liable for a dangerous condition that comes into being after the lessee takes exclusive possession and control of the premises. (*Nichols v. Marsden* . . . ); see also *Restatement (Second) of Torts*, § 355 (1965) ("a lessor of land is not subject to liability to his lessee or others upon the land with the consent of the lessee or sub-lessee for physical harm caused by any dangerous condition which comes into existence after the lessee has taken possession"). A landlord is liable for defective or dangerous conditions on his property under the exclusive control of his tenants only when the landlord:

a) fails to disclose the existence of a latent defect which he knows or should have known existed but which is not known to the tenant[s] nor discoverable by [them] in the exercise of reasonable care;

b) gratuitously undertakes to make repairs and does so negligently; or

c) expressly agrees to maintain the premises in good repair.

*Nichols* (summarizing prior precedent)

Stewart does not contend that any of the *Nichols* exceptions apply in this case. Rather, she contends that Aldrich has not satisfied the predicate condition of *Nichols* that he had no control over the dangerous condition because Aldrich could have terminated the rental agreement after he learned that the Bailey's dog was vicious. Stewart argues that because Aldrich had the power to coerce the Baileys into getting rid of the dog by threatening to terminate the tenancy by eviction, he had "control" over the dog's presence on the premises, and consequently cannot avoid liability under the test articulated in *Nichols*. We are unpersuaded by her argument.

Stewart is correct that *Nichols* requires the landlord to establish the absence of "control" in order to avoid liability for a dangerous condition on the premises. . . . Accordingly, in order to avoid liability for harm caused by a dangerous condition on the premises, the landlord

must show that he did not have the requisite control and that none of the three enumerated *Nichols* exceptions apply. The dispositive issue here is whether Aldrich, because he could have evicted the Baileys, or not renewed their tenancy, retained "control" over the presence of the dog on the premises at the time of the attack within the meaning of *Nichols*. The mere power to coerce the conduct of tenants through the threat of eviction or by refusing to renew the tenancy, however, is not the "control" contemplated by *Nichols*.

Although we have not explicitly defined the word "control," the cases applying *Nichols* illustrate that "control" means a power over the premises that the landlord reserves pursuant to the terms of the lease or the tenancy, whether express or implied, and does not include the incidental control that comes from being able to threaten tenants with nonrenewal of a lease or with eviction. Landlords have been held liable for dangerous conditions because of the retention of "control," but those cases generally involve facts where some power is reserved by the landlord pursuant to the terms of the lease. . . . If landlords retain control over common areas in the rental property, they can consequently be held liable for dangerous conditions in those areas. Moreover, landlords may retain control over non-common areas when they reserve certain rights or responsibilities over the premises by the terms of the lease or tenancy. . . . We have never held, however, that the landlord retains control over the premises merely because he has the power to coerce tenants through the power of eviction or nonrenewal of a lease.

Understanding "control" in this way is also consistent with our concept of leaseholds. A bedrock principle of our jurisprudence has been that a lease or tenancy is equivalent to a conveyance for almost all purposes, and when a tenant assumes exclusive control and possession of the premises the tenant becomes like the owner of the property for most purposes. . . .

## Judgment and Result

The landlord won.

## Questions

1. Could persons coming onto leased premises who are injured by the tenant's dog possibly recover from the *tenant* who owned and had the right to control the dog?

2. The general, over-arching principle the court seems to focus on is control. For instance, what does the court say is the general rule about landlord liability for injuries caused by unsafe conditions arising after the property is leased where there is no agreement to repair? If the landlord retains control over the land, may the landlord be held liable? Do landlords have liability for unsafe conditions and defects in the common areas available to the public? Are landlords liable for any conditions existing before or at the time the property is leased?

3. Would holding a landlord liable for injuries caused by the tenant's dog be an extension or contraction of liability over the usual rule holding the tenant liable? Why would a person want to sue the landlord rather than the more obvious candidate for liability, the tenant?

## CHAPTER SUMMARY

Property is the bundle of rights one person has with respect to another person with respect to the thing. Property is not the thing, but the rights someone has in the thing.

Title refers to ownership of property. Title documents refer to pieces of paper that officially say who has property rights in something. Title documents exist for land, vehicles, and a few other things.

Property law is generally state law; thus, the rules of property law vary from state to state.

Property can be classified as realty, personalty, or fixtures.

Property can be acquired in a number of ways, including capture, manufacture, gift, purchase, theft (under some circumstances), as a trust beneficiary, finding, and confusion.

Property may be used in various ways, including bailing property, leasing realty, or conveying an easement.

URLTA sets rules governing residential leases in some states.

## ◼ MANAGER'S ETHICAL DILEMMA

Beatrice Kayser was the president of Smokey Mountain Realty of Knoxville, Tennessee. Beatrice prided herself on the fact that her firm had been in business for more than 25 years and had increased its sales volume each year. Customers trusted her firm and the salespeople worked hard. One day Beatrice received a report from the U.S. Environmental Protection Agency. The report noted a colorless, odorless gas called radon that seeps from underground uranium decays into radioactive particles which enter human lungs and cause cancer. EPA estimated that radon might be responsible for 5,000 to 20,000 lung cancer deaths per year (out of the total 140,000 annual deaths from lung cancer). Figure 12.1 was developed by EPA and shows the radon amounts and associated health risks.

According to the study, several states have much greater potential for harmful radon levels in the home. The states in which it is estimated that 25 percent or more of the homes have excessive radon levels in residences are Indiana, Pennsylvania, Wisconsin, Minnesota, North Dakota, Colorado, and Wyoming. States where 20 to 25 percent of the homes have radon levels

above safe levels include Kansas, Rhode Island, and Massachusetts, while in Connecticut, Missouri, Tennessee, and Kentucky about 15 to 20 percent of the homes have unhealthy levels. In Michigan, 10 to 15 percent of the homes have unsafe radon levels.

The study also indicated that radon risks increased up to 15 times for smokers than for nonsmokers. Thus, smoking in a house with elevated radon levels should not be allowed. The study recommended that homeowners test their homes for radon to see whether they exceed the level at which EPA recommends corrective action—4 picocuries per liter of air. This level is about equal to 200–300 chest X-rays per year, or to smoking half a pack of cigarettes per day. Radon detection tests cost about $15 for each room. If excess radon is found, correction costs (involving ventilation and sealing cracks in the house's foundation and from underground pipes) range from $500 to $2,000 in most cases.

Beatrice realized she was selling real estate in a high-risk state for radon. None of her fellow realtors knew about this risk, nor did many homeowners. What should she do now that she is aware of it?

## FIGURE 12.1 HEALTH RISKS ASSOCIATED WITH EXPOSURE TO RADON

| Radon Level pCl/l | Estimated Number of Lung Cancer Deaths Due to Radon Exposure (out of 1,000) | Comparable Exposure Levels | Comparable Risk |
|---|---|---|---|
| 200 | 400–700 | 1,000 times average outdoor level | More than 60 times nonsmoker risk |
| | | | 4 pack-a-day smoker |
| 100 | 270–630 | 100 times average indoor level | |
| | | 100 times average outdoor level | 20,000 chest x-rays per year |
| | | | 2 pack-a-day smoker |
| 20 | 60–210 | | 1 pack-a-day smoker |
| 10 | 30–120 | 10 times average indoor level | |
| | | | 5 times non-smoker |
| 4 | 13–50 | | 200 chest x-rays per year |
| 2 | 7–30 | 10 times average outdoor level | |
| | | | Non-smoker risk of dying from lung cancer |
| 1 | 3–13 | Average indoor level | |
| | | | 20 chest x-rays per year |
| 0.2 | 1–3 | Average outdoor level | |

*Source:* U.S. Environmental Protection Agency.

## DISCUSSION QUESTIONS

1. Great discussion today surrounds whether zoning of real property is necessary. At least one major U.S. city (Houston, Texas) has no zoning requirements. In effect, someone may legally put a chicken coop into an upscale residential neighborhood. On the other hand, zoning laws create, as well as destroy, property values by restricting what landowners can do with their land. Suppose you are a city council member of a medium-sized city that is considering revamping its zoning laws. Would you be in favor of more restrictive, less restrictive, or no zoning laws? Why?

2. If a person pays taxes on property that she claims by adverse possession and had occasionally mowed the land, is this enough to prove exclusive and adverse possession? [*Crowden v. Grantland*, 510 So.2d 238 (Ala. 1987)].

3. Is acceptance of a gift generally presumed? [*Smith v. Fleming*, 358 S.E.2d 900 (Ga.App. 1987)].

4. An owner of land bequeathed it to a Jesuit College. The college learned that a tenant operated an "adult" bookstore on the property and understandably wanted the tenant to leave. The tenant claimed that it had a 10-year oral lease. Could the college evict the tenant on grounds that no valid lease existed? [*William Henry Brophy College v. Tovar*, 619 P.2d 19 (1980)].

5. A lease agreement specified no animals, birds, pets, motorcycles, waterbeds, trucks, jeeps, or vans on the premises at any time. The lease also provided for a $50 fine for each violation. Berlinger had a motorcycle on his patio on October 10, 13, 24, and November 7, 1979. The landlord assessed a $200 fine for violating the lease's rule. Berlinger moved out without paying the fine, and the landlord tried to withhold $200 from his security deposit. Berlinger objected on grounds that the fine was excessive and the rule was arbitrary. Was it? [*Berlinger v. Suburban Apartment Management*, 454 N.E.2d 1367 (1982)].

6. Morton executed a will leaving most of his $55,000 property to a friend and to the First Presbyterian Church. He was 85 when he executed the will. Morton lived in a motel. He would go on walks and return with his pants soiled because he had voided in public. Morton forgot how to play checkers, and other evidence showed that he often forgot to pay

his rent or would forget and pay twice. He left only $1,000 each to two nephews. They challenged Morton's will on grounds that he lacked the requisite mental capacity when he wrote the will. Did the nephews win? [In *Re Estate of Morton*, 428 P.2d 725 (1967)].

7. Charrier, an archeologist, discovered artifacts in graves of Tunica Indians on land owned by the State of Louisiana. He sold the artifacts to a university for $175,000. Louisiana claimed that it owned the property. Charrier argued that the artifacts were abandoned property. Who won? [*Charrier v. Bell*, 389 So.2d 155 (1979)].

## INFOTRAC KEYWORDS

**Use your InfoTrac password to look up articles on http://www.infotrac-college.com**

Keywords: *Real property law, personal property, tenants in common, inheritance, testamentary trusts, lease law, landlord rights, tenants rights, easements.*

For suggested readings, please visit this book's Web site at **http://fisher.westbuslaw.com** (click on "Internet Applications").

# INTELLECTUAL PROPERTY
# AND TECHNOLOGY

---

## POSITIVE LAW ETHICAL PROBLEMS

"I was Playboy 'Playmate of the Year' in 1981, and I'm entitled to use that fact on my Web page," claimed Terri Wells.

"Oh, no, you're not," said a Playboy Enterprises Inc. representative. "You are using the trademarked terms 'Playmate' and 'Playboy' on your Web site without our permission, which is trademark infringement and trademark dilution."

Is unauthorized use of another's trademark on one's Web page trademark infringement and/or dilution?

"We were first to register the Internet domain name sportys.com, but someone else has the trademark to 'sporty's'," said the CEO of Sporty's Farm.

"So you are worried about the trademark owner to 'sporty's' taking the Internet domain name away from us because he had the trademark before we registered the Internet domain name?" asked Ken Curry his assistant.

"Right," replied the CEO. "But I think we can we sue the trademark owner first and get a declaratory judgment that we own the Internet domain name 'sportys.com' and if the trademark owner of 'sporty's' wants to buy the domain name from us it can."

"But aren't we prevented from doing this by the Anticybersquatting Consumer Protection Act?" asked Curry.

"Oh, no," answered the CEO, "because what we did occurred before that Act was passed. That Act only applies to cybersquatting occurring after the Act was passed."

Was the CEO correct?

"Napster is violating the federal copyright laws by allowing the downloading of our copyrighted music," alleged John Smith, an executive of A&M Records.

"No, Napster is only facilitating Internet users sharing music files. Napster itself copies nothing. Therefore Napster is not violating federal copyright law," answered Sam Brown, a Napster official.

"Yes, it is. Someone can violate federal copyright law by helping others who are unlawfully copying, which is exactly what Napster is doing by establishing a mechanism for the exchange of copyrighted material."

Who was right?

---

*"AMERICA IS A LAND OF WONDERS, IN WHICH EVERYTHING IS IN CONSTANT MOTION AND EVERY CHANGE SEEMS AN IMPROVEMENT. THE IDEA OF NOVELTY IS THERE INDISSOLUBLY CONNECTED WITH THE IDEA OF AMELIORATION."*

—DE
TOCQUEVILLE
*DEMOCRACY IN AMERICA* (1835)

---

Ideas are the fodder of the entrepreneur. Ideas can rise to the form of personal property that the legal system will protect. Several devices protect these ideas, including quasi-contracts, trade secrets, copyrights, trademarks, and patents. The following discussion examines each of these protections.

An *idea* of some kind is the basis of any business. The ability to conceive of an idea sufficiently novel, feasible from a cost standpoint, and offering market appeal is the basis for many fortunes. Consider, for example, Forbes' 1999 choice as the "richest person in the world": Bill Gates. Twenty years ago, this man was a college dropout. But he had ideas and he knew how to exploit them.

Federal and state codes and cases and links to law schools are available at **http://www. findlaw.com**

Once an idea is disclosed, however, competitors as well as customers learn of it and are not reluctant to "clone" it to profit themselves. The innovator of ideas has a need to protect the idea while at the same time disclosing it in order to enjoy the fruits of the innovation. Although the discussion here is geared to helping businesspersons exploit their inventions under the cover of some legal protection, we should not lose sight of the fact that some social justification must be present for legal protection in the first place. Hence, society is constantly balancing social costs of providing legal protection for ideas against the social benefits from developing legally protected ideas. The "law giveth and the law taketh away," and what protection society confers on an idea conceiver can be removed if the protection has been abused. What constitutes abuse of legal protection and what is creative use of the law is not always an easy matter to resolve as the cases in this chapter reveal.

A free e-mail service providing legal information may be accessed through **http://www. lawnewsnetwork.com**

This chapter covers the legal protections of quasi-contracts, trade secrets, trademarks, copyrights, and patents. After examining these legal protections in detail, we briefly note some aspects of law as applied to e-mail and the Internet. Lastly, international protections for intellectual property is covered.

## QUASI-CONTRACT

Quasi-contracts are not contracts at all. Rather, the judge says that something "like a contract," hence *quasi-contract*, will be regarded as existing in order to prevent unjust enrichment. The idea is that one person has received benefits for which she knows or should know that pay is expected and injustice would result by not holding her liable. If a judge decides in plaintiff's favor, the recovery is the reasonable value of the benefits conferred.

A simple example like one from Chapter 11 helps explain quasi-contract. Suppose an "Ace Painting Service" truck drives up in front of your house, and house painters say to you, "Hi, Mr. Smith, we'll have your house painted in no time." In fact, Smith lives next door. You say nothing because you are Mr. Jones, and the painter mistakenly starts to paint your house. You let him proceed, knowing that he is painting the wrong house. He finishes and asks for pay. You then refuse, pointing out that Smith lives next door.

The judge will not let you cheat the painter. The judge will impose a quasi-contract to allow the painter to recover the reasonable value of the paint job. The reason? You knew that professional painters expect to be paid for their work; you had an opportunity to reject the benefits but you craftily decided to be silent and collect the benefits. The law will not allow you to wrongfully profit at the painter's expense.

But then you might ask, "What if you were not standing in front of your house when the painter drove up? What if the painter mistakenly paints your house, and it looks great. Can the painter here assert quasi-contract as a way to shake money out of your pockets? Here, the answer is no because you were not in a position to reject the benefits. The benefits were being imposed without your knowledge. To hold otherwise would enable unemployed painters to sneak out to people's houses at night and foist all sorts of unwanted benefits on them in the hopes of using quasi-contract principles to recover. Here the circumstances do not justify paying the painter.

## QUASI-CONTRACT COMPARED TO CONTRACT IMPLIED-IN-FACT

Contracts implied by facts (or implied-in-fact) indicate that the parties actually intended for a contract to exist although their express language is not sufficient to create one. In the case of contracts implied in law (quasi-contracts), neither the facts nor the language indicate any intention of the parties to have a contract.

## APPLYING QUASI-CONTRACT TO BUSINESS IDEAS

As you might suspect, quasi-contracts can help inventors. Consider the following example: Edison, an inventor, has worked on a unique toy doll that teaches children to speak French in a programmed way. He writes to Mega Company and asks whether they might be interested in hearing about a toy he believes has incredible market potential. A Mega executive writes back to Edison and asks for details about the toy, explaining that he must know more about it prior to Mega's deciding whether to sign Edison up.

If Edison discloses everything about his doll (including the years of development work and drawings), Mega might reject the idea and then copy it and manufacture it without giving Edison a dime of royalties. On the other hand, Mega might, in fact, be working on just such a device that, coincidently, Edison was developing also.

Deciding who is exploiting whom and thus who is entitled to quasi-contract protection in such a case is not easy as the following case demonstrates. There, the court said that quasi-contract protection might be appropriate. Note, however, that other cases have held that where an express contract exists, courts do not generally impose a quasi-contract theory to allow recovery for a business idea. The reasoning is that if a judge imposes a quasi-contract in cases where a contract actually exists, it would amount to the court's substituting a new contract—in effect, changing the terms the parties themselves had agreed upon.

---

### Kaplan v. Michtom
Federal District Court, S.D. N.Y.
17 F.R.D. 228 (1955)

### Background and Facts

The defendant Gillette Company seeks to dismiss a complaint in an action to recover the reasonable value of an idea for a doll with hair that could be given a permanent wave. Plaintiff claims that defendants wrongfully appropriated his idea after plaintiff confidentially disclosed it to him.

Plaintiff made his confidential disclosure to various representatives of the defendants in an attempt to sell his idea. He wrote a letter advising defendant he had an idea in which defendant might be interested and asking defendant whether it would like to know the details. Plaintiff received a reply, enclosing a "detailed state-

ment of . . . policy on suggestions from outside sources," and advising him that if the terms were agreeable, he should complete and return the statement "and we will be happy to consider your suggestion." The letter expressed the hope that the writer would "hear from you again soon." It does not appear what the statement of policy provided or whether plaintiff signed it. Plaintiff then wrote a letter to the defendant in which he "communicated his idea" to it. The defendant did not answer his letter until about two months later, when it advised the plaintiff that a doll such as suggested had been planned for more than six months, to be manufactured by certain of the other defendants named in this suit.

This case is presently at the stage of the proceedings where a motion to dismiss the complaint has been made. The issue before the court is whether it appears to a certainty that the plaintiff would not be entitled to relief under any state or federal laws.

## Body of Opinion

**District Judge Edelstein.** The main contention of the defendant is that the complaint is defective against it because of the absence of any allegation of "anything to limit the rights" of that defendant, which I take to mean the absence of an express agreement. No express agreement is alleged. Nevertheless, the allegations of the complaint are sufficient to permit the plaintiff to adduce proof in support of his claim on the basis of which he would be entitled to recover. . . .

Defendant cites *Williamson v. N.Y. Central R.R.* . . . for the proposition that there can be no protection of an "abstract idea" not reduced to a "concrete form" at disclosure in the absence of an express contract; and *Grombach Production v. Waring* . . . for authority that in a business idea case there can be no contract implied in law. . . . In view of the court's own definition of a contract implied in law, I have difficulty in understanding its conclusion that the jury could not be permitted to find such a contract based on the usage in the particular trade. It would seem that there has been a "curious admixture of the principles of quasi and implied-in-fact contracts.". . . 31 *Cornell Law Quarterly* 382, 389. Nevertheless, the decision in negation of the existence of a contract implied in law in the absence of an express contract was based upon "prior gratuitous, unsolicited disclosure." Whether the plaintiff's disclosure in the case at bar was gratuitous and unsolicited is a matter of proof. It is to be noted, moreover, that the *Grombach* case apparently involved an "abstract idea," communicated in telephone conversations, a written

"presentation" having been rejected as evidence in the case. The decision of the Court of Appeals was not placed on the ground that the idea had not been reduced to "concrete form" at disclosure, nor is there any indication in the opinion that the issue ought to be treated as relevant. In any event, it is impossible to determine from the complaint precisely what the form of the disclosure was in this case.

It is certainly proper for courts to be "assiduous in defeating attempts to delve into the pockets of business firms through spurious claims for compensation for the use of ideas. Thus, to be rejected are attempts made by telephoning or writing vague ideas to business corporations and then seizing upon some later general similarity between their products and the motions propounded as a basis for damages.". . . But whether this is such a case cannot be determined from the complaint. It does not appear to a certainty that plaintiff will be unable to prove a state of facts giving rise to a right of recovery in quasi-contract. . . .

## Judgment and Result

The court refused to dismiss plaintiff's complaint. A trial could go forward, at which plaintiff might be able to prove grounds for a quasi-contract recovery.

## Questions

1. Did the judge in the *Kaplan* case allow the inventor to recover on a quasi-contract theory? What problems does the plaintiff face in proving his case?
2. Did the defendant solicit plaintiff's idea in *Kaplan*? If not, does the case suggest any reason why a court should be careful not to accept at face value plaintiff's quasi-contract claim?

## TRADE SECRETS

**Trade secrets** refer to information a person has that is used in a business and gives advantage over competitors who do not know or use it. Trade secrets can consist of formulas, patterns, devices, or compilation of information used in one's business. Two types of information that can be trade secrets are (1) product formulas, manufacturing processes, ingredient suppliers, and packaging suppliers that one uses in the manufacture of one's products; (2) customer lists and price information. The formula for Coca-Cola is a trade secret known by few persons.

Note that recording or registering a trade secret is not required in obtaining this protection. However, one must take reasonable steps to keep the secret. In deciding whether to accord business information trade secret status, courts examine whether a business took substantial steps to keep the information secret. For example, having employees sign confidentiality agreements with respect to the secret information would be a definite step in furtherance of establishing trade secret status.

Trade secret law is common law, not statutory. Further, it is state, not federal, law, so potential for variation exists among the states in terms of protection. Thus, one should look to large, commercial states such as New York, which have many opportunities for making trade secret pronouncements. The *Geritrex* case is a New York decision.

## Geritrex Corp. v. DermaRite Industries, LLC
U.S. District Court (S.D. N.Y.)
910 F.Supp. 955 (1996)

### Background and Facts

Geritrex was founded approximately 18 years ago by Madaio. Its manufacturing and sales operations are based at one site in Mount Vernon, New York. Geritrex currently has approximately 250 customers. Total sales for 1994 were $2.2 million, and Madaio projected that sales for 1995 would total $1.8 million.

In April 1994, defendant Braunstein began working at Geritrex as its vice-president of sales. He left Geritrex in late March 1995. It is undisputed that while he was employed by Geritrex, he had access to its customer list and information concerning which customers purchased which products or received discounted prices. Braunstein currently owns a minority equity position in DermaRite, serves as its president, and runs its sales operations.

In August 1994, John Zimmerman joined Geritrex, where he served as production manager. He left Geritrex in late May 1995. While Zimmerman was employed by Geritrex, he was involved in all facets of production and had access to product formulations and to information about prices and suppliers of ingredients and packaging. Zimmerman began working for DermaRite in early June 1995. In addition to setting up DermaRite's manufacturing facility, his duties include formulating products, managing production, and obtaining ingredients and packaging.

DermaRite was formed in May 1995 by Braunstein and Israel Minzer, a businessman with contacts in the nursing home industry. Zimmerman testified that he completed the development of at least one DermaRite product by the end of August 1995 and finished work on the remainder of the 20 products in DermaRite's product line by the end of September 1995. According to Braunstein, DermaRite currently has about 35 customers, 12 of which were formerly Geritrex customers. Total sales as of the date of the preliminary injunction hearing were approximately $100,000. Braunstein offered testimony, as yet uncontroverted, that approximately $30,000 in sales is attributable to former Geritrex customers.

Plaintiff requests a preliminary injunction prohibiting defendants from competing with plaintiff for six months on the ground that Zimmerman and Braunstein signed confidentiality and noncompetition agreements during their employment with Geritrex. Plaintiff also asks for preliminary injunctions forbidding defendants from continuing to use its product formulations, manufacturing processes, supplier information, customer list, and price information on the ground that defendants have misappropriated plaintiff's trade secrets.

### Body of Opinion

**Judge Conner.** Plaintiff . . . asserts that it is entitled to a preliminary injunction on the ground that DermaRite, Zimmerman, and Braunstein misappropriated information proprietary to Geritrex in order to develop and market DermaRite's products. To establish misappropriation of a trade secret, plaintiff must prove that: "(1) it possessed a trade secret, and (2) [defendants are] using that trade secret in breach of an agreement, confidence, or duty, or as a result of discovery by improper means.". . . "A trade secret may consist of any formula, pattern, device or compilation of information which is used in one's business, and which gives him an opportunity to obtain an advantage over competitors who do not know or use it.". . . Plaintiff has identified two types of information that it alleges constitute trade secrets. The first is the product formulas, manufacturing processes, ingredient suppliers, and packaging suppliers that it uses in the manufacture of its products. The second is its customer list and price information.

Although New York courts have identified a number of factors that courts may look to in determining whether information constitutes a trade secret, . . . the most important consideration is whether the information is kept secret. . . . Plaintiff must show that it took substantial measures to protect the secret nature of its information. . . .

With respect to the information about plaintiff's manufacturing processes and product formulas, it is clear from the evidence before us that plaintiff did not take substantial measures to keep that information secret. . . . It is clear that the file copies [of batch records] were accessible, as cartons of batch products (some unsealed) were stored in several unlocked areas of the Geritrex facility. . . . Furthermore, nothing prevented an employee from copying a batch record while he or she was working with it. The batch records were not stamped confidential. . . . Zimmerman's uncontroverted testimony established that he regularly and quite openly took work, including batch records, home. . . . Michael Bernstein, the operations director, frequently worked on batch records in the cafeteria where any employee or visitor to the Geritrex plant could have had access to the records. . . . This evidence persuades us that plaintiff did not make substantial efforts to limit access to this information to employees who needed to know the product formulations.

Plaintiff contends that the Geritrex facility had only two doors, both locked, and that access to the building is limited to employees and escorted visitors. While this fact is indicative of some attempts at secrecy . . . , it is not determinative in view of the overwhelming indications that plaintiff did not take substantial measures within the plant to protect the confidentiality of the product information from visitors or from employees who had no need to know it. Indeed, Madaio has admitted that he relied on the professional ethics of his production employees to keep Geritrex's product information secret, which simply does not constitute substantial efforts at secrecy.

We may make short shrift of plaintiff's argument that the source of the packaging for its products constitutes a trade secret. Anyone may easily determine the manufacturer of the containers for plaintiff's products by picking up the package and reading the manufacturer's name. Information that is readily ascertainable in this fashion does not constitute a trade secret. . . . Furthermore, plaintiff has presented no credible evidence at this time from which we could determine whether it has made substantial efforts to keep secret the sources of the ingredients used in its products.

Because Geritrex failed to take substantial measures to keep this alleged proprietary information secret, plaintiff has not demonstrated a likelihood of success on the merits, or even the existence of a serious question for litigation, on the issue of whether information regarding its product formulations, manufacturing processes, ingredient sources or packaging constitutes a trade secret.

Turning to plaintiff's contentions with respect to its customer argument is somewhat stronger, though ultimately unsuccessful. Although there is no evidence before us at this time that this information was marked confidential or that access to it was limited to sales personnel, the members of the sales force had, for the most part, signed confidentiality and noncompetition agreements. Braunstein, whether he signed the agreement or not, admits that Madaio presented it to him. Braunstein was therefore aware that plaintiff sought to keep its customer list and price information confidential. Hence, there is at least some indication that plaintiff made efforts to keep its customer list and price information secret, and plaintiff may well succeed in establishing that this information constitutes a trade secret.

Even if we assume that Geritrex's customer list and price information are trade secrets, however, plaintiff has not presented convincing evidence that demonstrates that DermaRite has been using that information to compete for Geritrex customers. As head of sales for Geritrex, Braunstein undoubtedly had access to its customer list and price information. He has also acknowledged that while he worked for Geritrex, he added some business cards to the file of business contacts that he has developed over the course of his 20-year career. Braunstein does not deny being aware of

Geritrex's relationships with "a handful" of the customers that he has contacted, but he maintains that he has gathered his information about potential customers from a number of sources, including publicly available directories of nursing homes and hospitals and Minzer's apparently extensive contacts in the nursing home business. Indeed, Braunstein has testified that only 12 of DermaRite's 35 customers are former Geritrex customers. Braunstein has also offered uncontroverted testimony that DermaRite's two largest customers, responsible for approximately $60,000 in sales, were never Geritrex customers. Based on this evidence, we cannot find, at this juncture, that plaintiff is likely to succeed in demonstrating that defendants have used Geritrex's customer list and price information to lure away its customers. Plaintiff has, however, demonstrated that a serious question for litigation exists on this issue.

## Judgment and Result

Plaintiff showed that a sufficiently serious question for further litigation existed (need for a trial) regarding whether one former employee had signed a noncompetition agreement. However, neither the product formulas and processes, the packaging suppliers, nor the ingredient sources were trade secrets. The plaintiff did show that a sufficiently serious question for litigation existed as to whether a competitor used a manufacturer's allegedly secret customer list and price information.

## Questions

1. What items did plaintiff claim were trade secrets?
2. Why was plaintiff successful on some but not all of the trade secret claims?
3. What risks does society face if "too many things" are found to be trade secrets? Does such a finding stifle competition?
4. If, as the court says, the plaintiff relied on the "professional ethics" of the production employees to keep Geritrex's product formulas secret, which "simply does not constitute substantial efforts at secrecy," what does this judgment say about the court's regard for "ethics outside of the positive law"? Do they exist? Does your answer support the claims that positive law has risen to the status of an ethic?
5. Does a business need to register anything to claim trade secret protection?

## COPYRIGHTS

**Copyright law** protects original works of authorship fixed in any tangible medium of expression. Ideas alone are not copyrightable because they are not tangible. If an idea is made tangible, such as when written into a book, it may be copyrighted. Something is *tangible* if the work of authorship can be perceived,

reproduced, or otherwise communicated either directly or indirectly or with the aid of a machine or device. Thus, Web pages, which can be perceived with the aid of a computer, are copyrightable (assuming they meet the originality requirement). In short, copyright protects ideas that are creative, original, and which are in some type of fixed form.

*For help with intellectual property matter or any legal matter in your community, access the attorney index at **http://www. martindale-hubbel.com**, choose Lawyer Locator*

## RIGHTS OF COPYRIGHT HOLDER

Copyright owners have several rights. First, there is the right to copy or reproduce the copyrighted material. Second, they have the right to produce derivative works based on the copyrighted material. Derivative works are works based on one or more preexisting works, such as translations, musical arrangements, condensations, or any other form in which a work can be recast. Third, copyright owners have the exclusive right to display or perform the copyrighted material. Fourth, they have the exclusive right to distribute (sell or lease) the copyrighted material.

Copyrights last for the lifetime of the owner plus 70 years, if the copyright arose *after* January 1, 1978. (The copyright term is 95 years for corporations if the copyright arose after January 1, 1978.) Copyrighted material used without permission is an infringement. Damages can be obtained from infringers.

## TYPES OF COPYRIGHT INFRINGEMENT

There are several ways one can violate another's copyright. First, one can commit **direct infringement**. This occurs when one, for example, directly copies another's copyrighted material without a defense. Second, one can commit **contributory copyright infringement**. This happens when one knows or has reason to know of a third person's copyright infringement and induces, causes, or materially contributes to that person's infringing conduct. Actual knowledge is not required, just reason to know of the other's infringing conduct. For example, if one operates an Internet bulletin board service (BBS) and knows or should know that a subscriber is placing others' copyrighted material on the bulletin board, then the bulletin board owner would be liable for contributory copyright infringement, absent a defense (the Digital Millennium Copyright Act, discussed next, does provide some defenses for OSPs and BBSs). **Vicarious copyright infringement** occurs when one has the right and ability to supervise the infringing activity and also has a direct financial interest in the infringing activity. The Napster case presents issues of contributory and vicarious copyright infringement, as well as several possible defenses.

### A&M Records v. Napster, Inc.
U.S. Court of Appeals (9th Cir.)
239 F.3d 1004 (2001)

**Background and Facts**

In 1987, the Moving Picture Experts Group set a standard file format for the storage of audio recordings in a digital format called MPEG-3, abbreviated as MP3. Digital MP3 files are created through a process colloquially called *ripping*.

Ripping software allows a computer owner to copy an audio compact disk (audio CD) directly onto a computer's hard drive by compressing the audio information on the CD into the MP3 format. The MP3's compressed format allows for rapid transmission of digital audio files from one computer to another by electronic mail or any other file transfer protocol.

Napster facilitates the transmission of MP3 files between and among its users. Through a process commonly called "peer-to-peer" file sharing, Napster allows its users to (1) make MP3 music files stored on individual computer hard drives available for copying by other Napster users; (2) search for MP3 music files stored on other users' computers; and (3) transfer exact copies of the contents of other users' MP3 files from one computer to another via the Internet. These functions are made possible by Napster's MusicShare software, available free of charge from Napster's Internet site, and Napster's network servers and server-side software. Napster provides technical support for the indexing and searching of MP3 files, as well as for its other functions, including a chat room, where users can meet to discuss music, and a directory where participating artists can provide information about their music.

Plaintiffs claimed Napster users are engaged in the wholesale reproduction and distribution of copyrighted works, all constituting direct infringement. The district court agreed. The court of appeals upheld the district court's determination that as much as 87 percent of the files available on Napster may be copyrighted and that more than 70 percent may be owned or administered by plaintiffs. The court of appeals also rejected Napster's "fair use" defense on grounds that Napster has a harmful effect on plaintiffs' current and future digital download market. The court of appeals then turned to the contributory and vicarious copyright infringement issues.

## Body of Opinion

**Circuit Judge Beezer.** . . . We first address plaintiffs' claim that Napster is liable for contributory copyright infringement. Traditionally, "one who, with knowledge of the infringing activity, induces, causes or materially contributes to the infringing conduct of another, may be held liable as a 'contributory' infringer." . . . Put differently, liability exists if the defendant engages in "personal conduct that encourages or assists the infringement." . . . The district court determined that plaintiffs in all likelihood would establish Napster's liability as a contributory infringer. The district court did not err; Napster, by its conduct, knowingly encourages and assists the infringement of plaintiffs' copyrights.

Contributory liability requires that the secondary infringer "know or have reason to know" of direct infringement. . . . The district court found that Napster had both actual and constructive knowledge that its users exchanged copyrighted music. The district court also concluded that the law does not require knowledge of "specific acts of infringement" and rejected Napster's contention that because the company cannot distinguish infringing from noninfringing files it does not 'know' of the direct infringement. . . .

It is apparent from the record that Napster has knowledge, both actual and constructive, of direct infringement. Napster claims that it is nevertheless protected from contributory liability by the teaching of *Sony Corp. v. Universal Studios, Inc.* . . . We disagree. We observe that Napster's actual, specific knowledge of direct infringement renders *Sony*'s holding of limited assistance to Napster. We are compelled to make a clear distinction between the architecture of the Napster system and Napster's conduct in relation to the operational capacity of the system.

The *Sony* court refused to hold the manufacturer and retailers of videotape recorders liable for contributory infringement despite evidence that such machines could be and were used to infringe plaintiffs' copyrighted television shows. *Sony* stated that if liability "is to be imposed on petitioners in this case, it must rest on the fact that *they have sold equipment with constructive knowledge of the fact that their customers may use that equipment to make unauthorized copies* of copyrighted material." . . . The *Sony* court declined to impute the requisite level of knowledge where the defendants made and sold equipment capable of both infringing and "substantial noninfringing uses." . . .

We are bound to follow *Sony*, and will not impute the requisite level of knowledge to Napster merely because peer-to-peer file sharing technology may be used to infringe plaintiffs' copyrights. . . . We depart from the reasoning of the district court that Napster failed to demonstrate that its system is capable of commercially significant noninfringing uses. . . . Consequently, the district court placed undue weight on the proportion of current infringing use as compared to current and future noninfringing use. . . . The instant appeal occurs at an early point in the proceedings and "the fully developed factual record may be materially different from that initially before the district court. . . . " Regardless of the number of Napster's infringing versus noninfringing uses, the evidentiary record here supported the district court's finding that plaintiffs would likely prevail in establishing that Napster knew or had reason to know of its users' infringement of plaintiffs' copyrights.

This analysis is similar to that of *Religious Technology Center v. Netcom Online Communication Services, Inc.*, which suggests that in an online context, evidence of actual knowledge of specific acts of infringement is required to hold a computer system operator liable for contributory copyright infringement. . . .

We agree that if a computer system operator learns of specific infringing material available on his system and fails to purge such material from the system, the operator knows of and contributes to direct infringement. . . . Conversely, absent any specific information which identifies infringing activity, a computer system operator cannot be liable for the exchange of copyrighted material. . . .

We nevertheless conclude that sufficient knowledge exists to impose contributory liability when linked to demonstrated infringing use of the Napster system. . . . The record supports the district court's finding that Napster has actual knowledge that specific infringing material is available using its system, that it could block access to the system by suppliers of the infringing material, and that it failed to remove the material. . . .

We turn to the question of whether Napster engages in vicarious copyright infringement. Vicarious copyright liability is an "outgrowth" of respondeat superior. . . . In the context of copyright law, vicarious liability extends beyond an employer/employee relationship to cases in which a defendant "has the right and ability to supervise the infringing activity and also has a direct financial interest in such activities." . . .

The district court determined that plaintiffs had demonstrated they would likely succeed in establishing that Napster has a direct financial interest in the infringing activity. . . .We agree. Financial benefit exists where the availability of infringing material "acts as a 'draw' for customers." . . .

The district court determined that Napster has the right and ability to supervise its users' conduct. . . . (finding that Napster's representations to the court regarding "its improved methods of blocking users about whom rights holders complain . . . is tantamount to an admission that defendant can, and sometimes does, police its service.") We agree.

The ability to block infringers' access to a particular environment for any reason whatsoever is evidence of the right and ability to supervise. . . . Here, plaintiffs have demonstrated that Napster retains the right to control access to its system. Napster has an express reservation of rights policy, stating on its Web site that it expressly reserves the "right to refuse service and terminate accounts in [its] discretion, including, but not limited to, if Napster believes that user conduct violates applicable law . . . or for any reason in Napster's sole discretion, with or without cause."

To escape imposition of vicarious liability, the reserved right to police must be exercised to its fullest extent. Turning a blind eye to detectable acts of infringement for the sake of profit gives rise to liability. . . .

Our review of the record requires us to accept the district court's conclusion that plaintiffs have demonstrated a likelihood of success on the merits of the vicarious copyright infringement claim. Napster's failure to police the system's "premises," combined with a showing that Napster financially benefits from the continuing availability of infringing files on its system, leads to the imposition of vicarious liability. . . .

## Judgment and Result

The court of appeals held that plaintiffs demonstrated likelihood of success on the contributory infringement and vicarious infringement claims. Also, the court of appeals rejected the "fair use" defense.

## Questions

1. Did Napster commit direct copyright infringement? How could it be said to violate the federal copyright laws?
2. Who committed contributory or vicarious copyright infringement? Must there be direct infringement prior to finding contributory or vicarious infringement? What is the difference between contributory and vicarious copyright infringement?
3. What defenses did Napster raise?

---

Copyright law is federal, so if a person copyrights something, that protection is effective for the entire United States. Such protection makes it illegal for someone else to *copy* another's copyrighted material. However, if someone else *independently* develops exactly the same thing—admittedly, a highly unlikely occurrence—that is made without copying, it, too, could theoretically be copyrighted.

Copyright protection has defenses or loopholes. For example, 70 years after an author dies, the copyrighted matter may be used without paying a royalty. Also, copying copyrighted material is allowed if done for fair use. *Fair use* includes instruction, research, and criticism. Factors that courts take into account in determining fair use include (1) the purpose and character of the use (is it educational, which is more likely to be fair use, or commercial, which is less likely to qualify as fair use?); (2) the nature of the copyrighted material (factual material is more likely to be subject to fair use than creative material); (3) the amount that is copied (the more copied, or the more crucial passages copied, the more likely that there is infringement); (4) the effect of the copying on the marketability of the copyright holder's copyrighted material.

Also, if one obtains a *release* or permission to reproduce the copyrighted material from the copyright holder (usually for a fee or royalty), one may copy or engage in one of the other rights reserved to the copyright holder.

There are other defenses to copyright infringement. The *first sale doctrine* holds that the owner of a copy of a copyrighted work may sell that copy without committing copyright infringement. For example, you may sell a CD you purchased at a music store. You may NOT, however, copy that CD and resell it. Another defense is *public domain*. The Congressional Record, court decisions, and matters on which the copyright has expired are all in the public domain and can be copied, displayed, distributed, or used for derivative works without violating the copyright.

## Digital Millennium Copyright Act (DMCA)

The Digital Millennium Copyright Act (DMCA) was passed on October 28, 1998, and directed to be effective October 28, 2000. Part of its principal functions are to apply federal copyright law to the Internet and to create four different safe harbors (areas of nonliability) for online service providers (OSPs) from primary federal copyright liability, contributory and vicarious copyright liability.

One of the major concerns leading to passage of the DMCA was potential copyright liability of OSPs, such as America Online, and Web pages offering interactive bulletin board services (BBSs). When situations arise where third parties transmit or post copyrighted materials without authorization and without the OSP or BBS's knowledge or consent, the OSP or BBS could be subjected to contributory or vicarious copyright infringement.

The DMCA recognizes four distinct Internet activities and provides *safe harbors* (areas of nonliability) for OSPs and BBSs regarding them: (1) storing matter; (2) linking matter; (3) providing conduit service (e-mail); and (4) caching (storing matter for a short time). Any one of these four activities by third-party users could involve an OSP or BBS in copyright infringement by transmitting infringing matter using the OSP or BBS. Hence, the DMCA provides four distinct safe harbors for OSPs and BBSs for each of the four functions.

Although each safe harbor is different, several steps are needed to qualify for any of them. First, defendants must implement a policy to terminate repeat offenders. Second, defendants must design their systems to accommodate copyright protection measures. After these initial steps, elaborate measures come into play to qualify for a particular safe harbor.

Generally speaking, OSPs are not liable under the DMCA for storing and linking copyright violations of their users if the OSP lacks actual knowledge of the infringement, if the OSP derives no financial benefit from the infringement, and the OSP has notice and "take down" procedures upon actually discovering infringement by a user. Other conditions exist for caching and conduit safe harbors.

## TRADEMARKS

**Trademarks** refer to any word, letter, number, design, picture, or combination to designate someone's goods. "Pepsi" and "Coke" are examples of trademarks. Trademarks can fall into one of several categories: federal statutory trademarks, common law trademarks, and state trademarks.

Federal trademarks are created when one registers the mark under the Lanham Act. This law protects the mark for 20 years for marks registered before November 16, 1989; registrations granted after November 16, 1989, have a 10-year, renewable term.

Anyone using the trademark without authorization **infringes** the mark and is liable for an accounting to the copyright holder for profits, destruction of the infringing copies and plates, and possibly an injunction. The Lanham Act permits services to be given **service marks**. The act permits the mark to be either *on* the goods or on the packaging, displays, tags, or product labels.

Common law trademarks are created by use long enough so that the public associates the producer with that particular mark. Common law marks last as long as they are properly used. Although there is *federal* trademark law, the federal government has not preempted state law in this area. States control trademarks regarding matters solely within each state (intrastate commerce). State trademark law varies from state to state.

*Public Service Co. of N.M. v. Nexus Energy Software, Inc.* illustrates an alleged federal trademark infringement where both firms compete on the Internet.

## Public Service Co. of N.M. v. Nexus Energy Software, Inc.

U.S. District Court (D. Mass.)

36 F.Supp.2d 436 (1999)

### Background and Facts

Plaintiff Public Service Co. of New Mexico (PNM) sued Nexus Energy Software, Inc., because of Nexus's use of the mark "eNERGYplace" and the domain name "energyplace.com." PNM claims that Nexus's use of these marks infringes its service mark "Energy Place," Federal Registration No. 2,181,294.

PNM is a publicly traded utility company operating in New Mexico. In 1996, PNM developed its Energy Place information service. This service is a consumer hotline that, among other things, directs customers to vendors who supply energy efficient products. PNM's registration of "Energy Place" states that the use of the mark is for:

> . . . providing information services regarding the most efficient and cost-effective use of energy resources; providing energy audits for industrial, commercial, and residential consumers; energy consulting services; managing energy consumption for industrial and commercial consumers; promoting public awareness for the need for more efficient and cost-effective use of energy resources. . . .

Energy Place operates on the Internet where it has received inquiries from throughout the United States. In addition to its Internet site, Energy Place advertises through television, radio, and the mail.

Nexus is a Massachusetts company founded in 1997. In April 1998, Nexus began operation of its Internet site, which offers consumers various services to analyze their energy needs. Nexus uses the mark "eNERGYplace" in connection with its site. Shortly thereafter, Nexus sought trademark protection for its "eNERGYplace" mark. In July 1998, PNM notified Nexus of its own mark "Energy Place"; one month after the Patent and Trademark Office (PTO) denied Nexus's trademark application citing the likelihood of confusion with PNM's mark. After settlement negotiations between the parties broke down, PNM filed this suit for a preliminary injunction against Nexus's use of the mark.

### Body of Opinion

**District Judge Harrington.** To determine whether the plaintiff is likely to prevail on its claim of trademark infringement,

the court must determine (1) whether the trademark is valid; and (2) whether Nexus has infringed the mark. The court finds that PNM is likely to succeed on both points.

First, the court finds that Nexus is unlikely to succeed on its claim that PNM's trademark is invalid because it is generic or descriptive and therefore rules that the trademark is valid. Terms eligible for trademark protection lie on a spectrum of distinctiveness: on one end of the spectrum are generic terms that are not eligible for trademark protection; in the middle of the spectrum are descriptive terms that can be protected only if they have acquired a secondary meaning; at the far end of the spectrum are suggestive, arbitrary, or fanciful terms that are eligible for trademark without proof of secondary meaning. . . . Nexus argues that the term "Energy Place" is generic or, at most, descriptive.

The court's analysis begins with the fact that PNM's mark is registered, and, thus, is entitled to a presumption of validity. . . . This presumption "entitles the plaintiff to a presumption that its registered trademark is not merely descriptive or generic, or, if merely descriptive, is accorded secondary meaning.". . . Nexus can rebut this presumption by showing that the term is a generic name for goods or services or that the term is descriptive and has not acquired secondary meaning.

Nexus has produced no evidence showing that "Energy Place" is a generic term for consumer service relating to energy information, products, and services. The question of whether a term is generic is one of fact: do consumers associate the term with the product rather than the brand of a product? . . . Nexus' numerous exhibits indicate that many power companies have mailing addresses that include the term "Energy Place" and that some corporations have used energy place in their name, but this does not demonstrate that "Energy Place" is the generic term used by consumers for sites where they can find information regarding energy information, products, and services.

Having found that the term "Energy Place" is not a generic name for sites where consumers can find information regarding energy information, products, and services, the court must still address whether the term is merely "descriptive" of the product—in which case the trademark would be invalid without a showing of secondary meaning—or whether the term is suggestive, in which case the trademark is valid without any showing of secondary meaning. The court finds that the term "Energy Place" is "suggestive," and, thus, that the trademark is valid.

"A term is suggestive if it requires imagination, thought, and perception to reach a conclusion as to the nature of goods. A term is descriptive if it forthwith conveys an immediate idea of the ingredients, qualities, or characteristics of the goods." . . . Trademark law limits the protection accorded merely descriptive terms because they are a poor means of distinguishing between competing services and because descriptive terms are often necessary for a company to describe its services to consumers. . . . Given the wealth of synonyms in the English language, such concerns are reduced when the term is merely suggestive. . . .

Although the term "Energy Place" suggests that it is a place related to energy, it does not convey an immediate idea of the ingredients, qualities, or characteristics of the services PNM offers. . . . Moreover, competitors are left with a variety of terms to describe their competing services, one example being energy information services. Consequently, the court finds that the term "Energy Place" is not "merely descriptive," and that the trademark is valid.

The court also finds that Nexus's use of the mark "eNERGYplace" and the domain name "energyplace.com" likely infringes PNM's trademark. The essential element of a trademark infringement claim is likelihood of confusion. In assessing likelihood of confusion, the following factors guide the court: the similarity of the marks; the similarity of the goods; the relationship between the parties' advertising; the classes of prospective customers; evidence of actual confusion; the defendant's intent in adopting its mark; and the strength of the plaintiff's mark. . . .

In analyzing these factors the court concludes that on balance they support a finding of likelihood of confusion:

1. *Similarity of Marks*: The two marks look virtually identical and sound identical.
2. *Similarity of Services*: Although there are some differences in the services offered, both parties offer consumers information relating to energy services.
3. *Channels of Trade*: Both parties compete on the Internet. Both parties are trying to lure the same customers, although there are some differences in the services offered and in the geographical regions served—PNM serves primarily New Mexico, while Nexus serves primarily customers in states that have deregulated their energy supplier (generally the Northeast).
4. *Nexus's Intent in Adopting Its Mark*: Nexus apparently adopted its mark with no knowledge of PNM's mark; it has, however, knowingly continued to use PNM's trademark since July of 1998.
5. *Evidence of Actual Confusion*: PNM demonstrated that consumers trying to reach PNM's "Energy Place" site on the Internet are likely to be directed to a page that initially displays the term

"eNERGYplace" that then fades to "eNERGYguide." Furthermore, information on this page tells consumers that the new name for "eNERGYplace" is "eNERGYguide."
6. *Strength of PNM's Mark*: PNM's mark is sufficiently distinct to warrant protection—it is registered, it has been used for over two years, and PNM has invested in various types of advertising of its mark, thus creating some goodwill.

In balance, the court finds that it is reasonably probable that PNM would succeed in proving a likelihood of confusion between its mark and Nexus's mark. . . .

## Judgment and Result

The term "Energy Place" was not "merely descriptive," and the utility's trademark in that term was valid. Nexus's use of the mark "eNERGYplace" and the domain name "energyplace.com" likely infringed PNM's "Energy Place" trademark, warranting issuance of a preliminary injunction stopping Nexus's use of its mark and all variants of the terms that differ only in capitalization or italics and the domain name "energyplace.com" within 30 days of this order.

## Questions

1. In determining whether PNM's trademark was valid, how important is its characterization as *generic*? Is it better for a trademark claimant that its mark is descriptive? Can descriptive marks be valid? Does being suggestive help a descriptive mark become legally valid?
2. What value was it to PNM that its mark was already registered by the Patent and Trademark Office?
3. Once it is determined that a mark is valid, the next problem is to decide whether the other mark infringes it—that is, are the two marks likely to be confused? What were the six elements that the court of appeals relied on to resolve the "likelihood of confusion" issue in a trademark case? Does the ruling suggest that the trademark claimant must have actually have used its mark in order to claim trademark infringement?
4. Does the fact that defendant is in Massachusetts while plaintiff was thousands of miles away in New Mexico enter into the "likelihood that the parties do not compete"?
5. How can Nexus claim that it had no knowledge of plaintiff's mark if plaintiff's mark was already registered and the register is public? Wouldn't a trademark search have disclosed plaintiff's prior mark, making defendant's claim that it did not know of plaintiff's prior mark at best negligent and at worst a lie?
6. Of the legal ethics noted in Chapter 1, which is/are most prominent here?

## TRADEMARK DILUTION

Trademark dilution refers to the lessening of the capacity of a famous trademark to identify and distinguish goods or services, regardless of competition between the owner of the famous mark and other parties. Trademark dilution also can occur even without a likelihood of confusion, mistake, or deception between the protected mark and the allegedly diluting mark.

Trademark dilution finds its origin in a 1927 *Harvard Law Review* article written by Professor Frank I. Schechter. Schechter claimed that trademarks do more than identify the source of goods. Instead, he claimed trademarks can create consumer desire to purchase more if the marked goods are satisfying. Thus, even noncompeting goods could infringe a trademark by what is called *dilution*, or a "whittling away" of the trademark by others.

In 1995 the Federal Trademark Dilution Act became law. It adopts Professor Schechter's ideas. The act only protects famous marks, based on their national recognition and the inadequate protection that the hodge-podge of state antidilution laws offer to trademark holders. To prove trademark dilution a plaintiff must establish that (1) it has a famous trademark, and (2) that defendant's use is commercial and in commerce and is likely to cause dilution.

Successful plaintiffs bringing antidilution actions may only get injunctive relief unless they can prove the defendant intended to trade on the owner's reputation or to cause dilution of the famous mark. States may also protect against dilution because the federal act does not preempt state antidilution laws. Noncommercial use of a mark is a defense to an antidilution suit.

The *Playboy Enterprises, Inc. v. Welles* case shows how trademark dilution can overlap with other trademark issues in the context of Internet advertising. The case also discusses several trademark defenses, such as fair use and nominative use.

## Playboy Enterprises, Inc. v. Welles
U.S. Court of Appeals (9th Cir.)
279 F.2d 796 (2002)

### Background and Facts

Terri Welles was on the cover of Playboy in 1981 and was chosen to be the Playboy Playmate of the Year for 1981. Her use of the title "Playboy Playmate of the Year 1981," and her use of other trademarked terms on her Web site are at issue in this suit. During the relevant time period, Welles's Web site offered information about and free photos of Welles, advertised photos for sale, and advertised membership in her photo club, and promoted her services as a spokesperson. A biographical section described her selection as Playmate of the Year in 1981 and her years modeling for Playboy Enterprises, Inc. (PEI). After the lawsuit began, Welles included discussions of the suit and criticisms of PEI on her Web site and included a note disclaiming any association with PEI.

PEI complains of four different uses of its trademarked terms on Welles's Web site: (1) the terms "Playboy" and "Playmate" in the metatags (hidden codes used by some search engines to determine the content of Web sites in order to direct searchers to relevant sites) of the Web site; (2) the phrase "Playmate of the Year 1981" on the masthead of the Web site; (3) the phrases "Playboy Playmate of the Year 1981"

and "Playmate of the Year 1981" on various banner ads, which may be transferred to other Web sites; and (4) the repeated use of the abbreviation "PMOY '81" as the watermark on the pages of the Web site. PEI claimed that these uses of its marks constituted trademark infringement, dilution, false designation of origin, and unfair competition. The district court granted defendants' motion for summary judgment. PEI appeals.

### Body of Opinion

#### Circuit Judge Nelson.

. . . Trademark Infringement.

Except for the use of PEI's protected terms in the wallpaper of Welles's Web site, we conclude that Welles's uses of PEI's trademarks are permissible, nominative uses. They imply no current sponsorship or endorsement by PEI. Instead, they serve to identify Welles as a past PEI "Playmate of the Year."

We articulated the test for a permissible, nominative use in *New Kids On The Block v. New America Publishing, Inc.* The band, New Kids On The Block, claimed trademark infringement arising from the use of their trademarked name by several newspapers. The newspapers had conducted polls asking which member of the band New Kids On The Block was the best and most popular. The papers' use of the trademarked term did not fall within the traditional fair use doctrine. Unlike a traditional fair use scenario, the defendant newspaper was using the trademarked term to describe not its own product, but the plaintiff's. Thus, the factors used to evaluate fair use were inapplicable. The use was nonetheless permissible, we concluded, based on the nominative nature.

We adopted the following test for nominative use:

First, the product or service in question must be one not readily identifiable without use of the trademark; second, only so much of the mark or marks may be used as is reasonably necessary to identify the product or service; and third, the user must do nothing that would, in conjunction with the mark, suggest sponsorship or endorsement by the trademark holder. . . .

To satisfy the first part of the test for nominative use, the "product or service in question must must be one not readily identifiable without use of the trademark." This situation arises "when a trademark also describes a person, a place, or an attribute of a product" and there is no descriptive substitute for the trademark. In such a circumstance, allowing the trademark holder exclusive rights would allow the language to "be depleted in much the same way as if generic words were protectable." In *New Kids*, we gave the example of the trademarked term, "Chicago Bulls." We explained that "one might refer to the 'two-time world champions' or 'the professional basketball team from Chicago,' but it's far simpler (and more likely to be understood) to refer to the Chicago Bulls." Moreover, such a use of the trademark would "not imply sponsorship or endorsement of the product because the mark is used only to identify its source." Thus, we concluded, such uses must be excepted from trademark infringement law.

The district court properly identified Welles's situation as one which must also be excepted. No descriptive substitute exists for PEI's trademarks in this context. . . .

The second part of the nominative use test requires that "only so much of the mark or marks may be used as is reasonably necessary to identify the product or service." *New Kids* provided the following examples to explain this element: "A soft drink competitor would be entitled to compare its product to Coca-Cola or Coke, but would not be entitled to use Coca-Cola's distinctive lettering." Similarly, in a past case, an auto shop was allowed to use the trademarked term "Volkswagen" on a sign describing the cars it repaired, in part because the shop "did not use Volkswagen's distinctive lettering style or color scheme, nor did it display the encircled 'VW' emblem." Welles's banner advertisements and headlines satisfy this element because they use only the trademarked words, not the font or symbols associated with the trademarks.

The third element requires that the user do "nothing that would, in conjunction with the mark, suggest sponsorship or endorsement by the trademark holder." . . . It would be unreasonable to assume that the Chicago Bulls sponsored a Web site of Michael Jordan simply because his name appeared with the appellation "former Chicago Bull." Similarly, in this case, it would be unreasonable to assume that PEI currently sponsors or endorses someone who describes herself as a "Playboy Playmate of the Year in 1981." The designation of the year, in our case, serves the same function as the "former" in our example. It shows that any sponsorship or endorsement occurred in the past.

In addition to doing nothing in conjunction with her use of the marks to suggest sponsorship or endorsement by PEI, Welles affirmatively disavows any sponsorship or endorsement. Her site contains a clear statement disclaiming any connection to PEI. Moreover, the text of the site describes her ongoing legal battles with the company.

For the foregoing reasons, we conclude that Welles's use of PEI's marks in her headlines and banner advertisements is a nominative use excepted from the law of trademark infringement.

Metatags.

Welles includes the terms "playboy" and "playmate" in her metatags. Metatags describe the contents of a Web site using keywords. Some search engines search metatags to identify Web sites relevant to a search. Thus, when an Internet searcher enters "playboy" or "playmate" into a search engine that uses metatags, the results will include Welles's site. Because Welles's metatags do not repeat the terms extensively, her site will not be at the top of the list of search results. Applying the three-factor test, for nominative use, we conclude that the use of the trademarked terms in Welles's metatags is nominative. . . .

Forcing Welles and others to use absurd turns of phrase in their metatags, such as those necessary to describe Welles, would be particularly damaging in the Internet search context. . . . We can hardly expect someone searching for Welles's site to imagine the same phrase proposed by the district court to describe Welles without referring to Playboy—"the nude model selected by Mr. Hefner's organization. . . ." Yet if someone could not remember her name, that is what they would have to do. . . .

There is simply no descriptive substitute for the trademarks used in Welles's metatags. Precluding their use would have the unwanted effect of hindering the free flow of information on the Internet, something which is certainly not a goal of trademark law. . . .

We conclude that the metatags satisfy the second and third elements of the test as well. . . .

Wallpaper/watermark.

The background, or wallpaper, of Welles's site consists of the repeated abbreviation "PMOY '81," which stands for "Playmate of the Year 1981." Welles's name or likeness does not appear before or after "PMOY 1981." . . . Accepting, for the purposes of this appeal, that the abbreviation "PMOY" is indeed entitled to protection, we conclude that the repeated, stylized use of this abbreviation fails the nominative use test.

The repeated depiction of "PMOY '81" is not necessary to describe Welles. . . .

Trademark Dilution.

The district court granted summary judgment to Welles as to PEI's claim of trademark dilution. We affirm on the ground that all of Welles's uses of PEI's marks, with the exception of the use in the wallpaper, which we address separately, are proper, nominative uses. We hold that nominative uses, by definition, do not dilute the trademarks.

Federal law provides protection against trademark dilution:

The owner of a famous mark shall be entitled, subject to the principles of equity and upon such terms as the court deems reasonable, to an injunction against another person's commercial use in commerce of a mark or trade name, if such use begins after the mark has become famous and causes dilution of the distinctive quality of the mark. . . .

Dilution, which was not defined by the statute, has been described by the courts as "the gradual 'whittling away' of a trademark's value." Traditionally, courts have recognized two forms of dilution: blurring and tarnishment. Blurring occurs when another's use of a mark creates "the possibility that the mark will lose its ability to serve as a unique identifier of the plaintiff's product." Tarnishment, on the other hand, occurs "when a famous mark is improperly associated with an inferior or offensive product or service." As we recognized in Panavision, dilution may occur through uses on the internet as well as elsewhere.

Dilution works its harm not by causing confusion in consumers' minds regarding the source of a good or service, but by creating an association in consumers' minds between a mark and a different good or service. As explained in a First Circuit case, in dilution (as compared to infringement) "an entirely different issue is at stake—not interference with the source signaling function but rather protection from an appropriation" of or free riding on the investment (the trademark holder) has made in its [trademark]." Thus, for example, if a cocoa maker began using the "Rolls Royce" mark to identify its hot chocolate, no consumer confusion would be likely to result. Few would assume that the car company had expanded into the cocoa making business. However, the cocoa maker would be capitalizing on the investment the car company had made in its mark. Consumers readily associate the mark with highly priced automobiles of a certain quality. By identifying the cocoa with the Rolls Royce mark, the producer would be capitalizing on consumers' association of the mark with high quality items. Moreover, by labeling a different product "Rolls Royce," the cocoa company would be reducing the ability of the mark to identify the mark holder's product. If someone said, "I'm going to get a Rolls Royce," others could no longer be sure the person was planning on buying an expensive automobile. The person might just be planning on buying a cup of cocoa. Thus, the use of the mark to identify the hot chocolate, although not causing consumer confusion, would cause harm by diluting the mark.

Uses that do not create an improper association between a mark and a new product but merely identify the trademark holder's products should be exempted from the reach of the anti-dilution statute. Such uses cause no harm. The anti-dilution statute recognizes this principle and specifically excepts users of a trademark who compare their product in "commercial advertising or promotion to identify the competing goods or services of the owner of the famous mark."

For the same reason uses in comparative advertising are excepted from anti-dilution law, we conclude that nominative uses are also excepted. A nominative use, by definition, refers to the trademark holder's product. It does not create an improper association in consumers' minds between a new product and the trademark holder's mark.

When Welles refers to her title, she is in effect referring to a product of PEI's. She does not dilute the title by truthfully identifying herself as its one-time recipient any more than Michael Jordan would dilute the name "Chicago Bulls" by referring to himself as a former member of that team, or the two-time winner of an Academy Award would dilute the award by referring to him or herself as a "two-time Academy Award winner." . . . Of course, the conferrer of such honors and awards is free to limit the honoree's use of the title or references to the award by contract. So long as its use is nominative, however, trademark law is unavailing.

The one exception to the above analysis in this case is Welles's use of the abbreviation "PMOY" on her wallpaper. Because we determined that this use is not nominative, it is not excepted from the anti-dilution provisions. . . .

## Judgment and Result

Defendant's use of plaintiff's trademarks in Web site's headlines and banner ads was nominative use. Defendant's use of "playboy" and "playmate" in metatags was nominal use. Defendant's repeated, stylized use of "PMOY 1981" on her Web site wallpaper (background) was not nominative use.

## Questions

1. Did Welles's Web site disclaim any association with PEI (the plaintiff)? Was Welles's unauthorized use of PEI's trademarks on her Web site without PEI's permission legal?
2. PEI sued Welles for both trademark infringement and trademark dilution. What is the difference between these two types of wrongs? Is the "nominative use" defense recognized for both types of wrongs? Why might Welles's use of "PMOY" on her Web site wallpaper not be nominative use?
3. What is the difference between the two types of trademark dilution—blurring versus tarnishment?
4. What is the difference between the fair use and nominative use defenses in trademark infringement?
5. Was Welles's use of PEI's trademarks in her Web site's metatags permitted? Is there any danger of a non-trademark owner's overuse of another's trademarks in their metatags?
6. Does the anti-dilution statute permit comparative advertising even though a famous trademarked product in commerce is mentioned without the mark holder's permission?

## CYBERSQUATTING AND THE ANTICYBERSQUATTING CONSUMER PROTECTION ACT

**Cybersquatting** occurs when one person registers as an Internet domain name another's trademarked name or similar name before the trademark owner registers it as an Internet domain name. It is common for brand names such as "coca-cola" to want to use their name as an Internet URL (address) because people trying to locate "coca-cola" on the Internet instinctively use a trademarked name in first attempts to find a company's Web page.

Unfortunately, traditional brick-and-mortar firms have been slow to adapt to the Internet and often find their trademarked names or close approximations are taken by cybersquatters. Cybersquatters are often willing to sell the Internet domain name (the trademark of someone else) back to the trademark owner for a pretty penny. It was this sort of exploitation that Congress sought to remedy when it passed the Anticybersquatting Consumer Protection Act (ACPA) in 1999.

*Information about a true brick-and-mortar company can be found at* **http://www.lowes.com.**

The ACPA allows trademark holders to sue civilly one who in bad faith registers, traffics in, or uses a domain name that falls into either of two categories: a distinctive mark or a famous mark. Not all uses of others' trademarks are necessarily illegal because they could be done in good faith. For example, Thunderbird owners who love their favorite car and are unassociated with Ford Motor Company could legally use 'thunderbirdclub.org' as a Web site even though it uses Ford's trademarked Thunderbird name. Also, trademark law allows comparative advertising where a competitor points out how her product is factually better than a competitor's trademarked product. For example, a competitor of Dodge motor cars could register a comparative domain name site "dodgesucks.com" in which a Dodge competitor's factually better features such as cargo space, gas mileage, and stopping distance are noted.

The act identifies nine factors to guide courts in deciding if cybersquatting is in bad faith:

1. The trademark or other intellectual property rights of the person, if any, in the domain name
2. The extent to which the domain name consists of the legal name of the person or a name that is otherwise commonly used to identify that person
3. The person's prior use, if any, of the domain name in connection with the bona fide offering of any goods or services
4. The person's bona fide noncommercial or fair use of the mark in a site accessible under the domain name
5. The person's intent to divert customers from the mark owner's online location to a site accessible under the domain name that could harm the goodwill represented by the mark, either for commercial gain or with the intent to tarnish or disparage the mark, by creating a likelihood of confusion as to the source, sponsorship, affiliation, or endorsement of the site
6. The person's offer to transfer, sell, or otherwise assign the domain name to the mark owner for financial gain without having used, or having an intent to use, the domain name in the bona fide offering of any goods or services, or the person's prior conduct indicating a pattern of such conduct
7. The person's provision of material and misleading false contact information when applying for the registration of the domain name, the person's intentional

failure to maintain accurate information, or the person's prior conduct indicating a pattern of such conduct

8. The person's registration or acquisition of multiple domain names that the person knows are identical or confusingly similar to marks of others that are distinctive at the time of registration of such domain names, or dilutive of famous marks of others that are famous at the time of registration of such domain names, without regard to the goods or services of the parties

9. The extent to which the mark incorporated in the person's domain name registration is or is not distinctive and famous within the meaning of the Trademark Act.

The ACPA allows courts to add even more factors to determine if a cybersquatter is acting in bad faith.

The ACPA prohibits holding someone liable as a cybersquatter if the defendant believed, with reasonable grounds, that the use of the domain name was fair or otherwise lawful. Courts may order forfeiture or cancellation of the domain name or its transfer to the mark owner in appropriate cases. The ACPA remedies include injunctions, recovery of defendant's profits, actual damages, attorneys' fees, and statutory damages in an amount of at least $1,000 and up to $100,000 per domain name, as the court considers just.

The *Sporty's Farm L.L.C. v. Sportsman's Market* case presents a recent decision under the act.

## Sporty's Farm LLC v. Sportsman's Market, Inc.
U.S. Court of Appeals (2nd Cir.)
202 F.3d 489 (2000)

### Background and Facts

Sportsman's is a mail-order catalog company that is quite well known among pilots and aviation enthusiasts for selling products tailored to their needs. Recently it has expanded to cover tools and home accessories. The company annually distributes 18 million catalogs nationwide, and has yearly revenues of about $50 million. Aviation sales account for about 60 percent of Sportsman's revenue, while non-aviation sales comprise the remaining 40 percent.

In the 1960s, Sportsman's began using the logo "sporty" to identify its catalogs and products. In 1985, Sportsman's registered the trademark "sporty's" with the U.S. Patent and Trademark Office. Since then, Sportsman's has complied with all statutory requirements to preserve its interest in the "sporty's" mark. "Sporty's" appears on the cover of all Sportsman's catalogs; Sportsman's international toll free number is 1-800-4sportys; and one of Sportsman's domestic toll free phone numbers is 1-800-Sportys. Sportsman's spends about $10 million per year advertising its "sporty's" logo.

Omega is a mail-order catalog company that sells mainly scientific process measurement and control instruments. In late 1994 or early 1995, the owners of Omega, Arthur and Betty Hollander, decided to enter the aviation catalog business and, for that purpose, formed a wholly owned subsidiary called Pilot's Depot, LLC. Shortly thereafter, Omega registered the domain name sportys.com with NSI. Arthur Hollander was a pilot who received Sportsman's catalogs and thus was aware of the "sporty's" trademark.

In January 1996, nine months after registering sportys.com, Omega formed another wholly owned subsidiary called Sporty's Farm and sold it the rights to sportys.com for $16,200. Sporty's Farm grows and sells Christmas trees, and soon began advertising its Christmas trees on a sportys.com Web page. When asked how the name Sporty's Farm was selected for Omega's Christmas tree subsidiary, Ralph S. Michael, the CEO of Omega and manager of Sporty's Farm, explained that "in his own mind and among his family, he always thought of and referred to the Pennsylvania land where Sporty's Farm now operates as Spotty's farm. The origin of the name derived from a childhood memory he had of his uncle's farm in upstate New York. As a youngster, Michael owned a dog named Spotty. Because the dog strayed, his uncle took him to his upstate farm. Michael thereafter referred to the farm as Spotty's Farm. The name Sporty's Farm was a subsequent derivation." There is no evidence in the record that Hollander was considering starting a Christmas tree business when he registered sportys.com or that Hollander was ever acquainted with Michael's dog Spotty.

In March 1996, Sportsman's discovered that Omega had registered sportys.com as a domain name. Thereafter, and before Sportsman's could take any action, Sporty's Farm brought this declaratory judgment action seeking the right to continue its use of sportys.com. Sportsman's counterclaimed and also sued Omega as a third party defendant for trademark infringement, trademark dilution under the Federal Trademark Dilution Act. While this litigation was going on, Sportsman's used "sportys-catalog.com" as its primary domain name.

The trial court rejected Sportsman's trademark infringement claim because confusion in the marketplace is unlikely, given that they are in wholly unrelated businesses. However, on the trademark dilution claim, where likelihood of confusion is unnecessary, the district court found for Sportsman's saying that "sporty's" was a famous mark and Sporty's Farm and Omega had diluted "sporty's" because registration of sportys.com as a domain name compromises Sportsman's Market's ability to identify and distinguish its goods by precluding Sportsman's Market from using its unique identifier. The district court issued an injunction forcing Sporty's Farm to relinquish all rights to sportys.com. Sportsman's later acquired the domain name.

The matter was appealed to the U.S. Court of Appeals. During the appeal the U.S. Congress enacted the Anticybersquatting Consumer Protection Act (ACPA) and the Court of Appeals used it to decide the case rather than sending the matter back to the district court.

## Body of Opinion

**Circuit Judge Calabresi.** . . . While this appeal was pending, Congress passed the ACPA. That law was passed "to protect consumers and American businesses, to promote the growth of online commerce, and to provide clarity in the law for trademark owners by prohibiting the bad-faith and abusive registration of distinctive marks as Internet domain names with the intent to profit from the goodwill associated with such marks—a practice commonly referred to as 'cybersquatting.' . . . Congress viewed the legal remedies available for victims of cybersquatting before passage of the ACPA as 'expensive and uncertain.' . . .

Under the new Act, we must first determine whether 'sporty's' is a distinctive or famous mark and thus entitled to the ACPA's protection. . . . The district court concluded that 'sporty's' is both distinctive and famous. We agree that 'sporty's' is a 'distinctive' mark. As a result, and without casting any doubt on the district court's holding in this respect, we need not, and, hence, do not, decide whether 'sporty's' is also a 'famous' mark. . . .

The next question is whether domain name sportys.com is "identical or confusingly similar to" the 'sporty's' mark. . . . As we noted above, apostrophes cannot be used in domain names. . . . As a result, the secondary domain name in this case (sportys) is indistinguishable from the Sportsman's trademark (sporty's). . . . We therefore conclude that, although the domain name sportys.com is not precisely identical to the 'sporty's' mark, it is certainly "confusingly similar" to the protected mark. . . .

We next turn to the issue of whether Sporty's Farm acted with a "bad faith intent to profit" from the mark 'sporty's' when it registered the domain name sportys.com. . . . The statute lists nine factors to assist courts in determining when a defendant has acted with a bad faith intent to profit from the use of a mark. But we are not limited to considering just the listed factors when making our determination of whether the statutory criterion has been met. . . .

We hold that there is more than enough evidence in the record below of 'bad faith intent to profit' on the part of Sporty's Farm . . .

so that "no reasonable factfinder could return a verdict against" Sportsman's. . . . First, it is clear that neither Sporty's Farm nor Omega had any intellectual property rights in sportys.com at the time Omega registered the domain name. . . . Sporty's Farm was not formed until nine months after the domain name was registered, and it did not begin operations or obtain the domain name from Omega until after this lawsuit was filed. Second, the domain name does not consist of the legal name of the party that registered it, Omega. . . . Moreover, although the domain name does include part of the name of Sporty's Farm, that entity did not exist at the time the domain name was registered.

The third factor, the prior use of the domain name in connection with the bona fide offering of any goods or services, also cuts against Sporty's Farm since it did not use the site until after this litigation began, undermining its claim that the offering of Christmas trees on the site was in good faith. . . . Further weighing in favor of a conclusion that Sporty's Farm had the requisite statutory bad faith intent, as a matter of law, are the following: (1) Sporty's Farm does not claim that its use of the domain name was 'noncommercial' or a 'fair use' of the mark; (2) Omega sold the mark to Sporty's Farm under suspicious circumstances . . . ; and (3) as we discussed above, the 'sporty's' mark is undoubtedly distinctive. . . .

The most important grounds for our holding that Sporty's Farm acted with a bad faith intent, however, are the unique circumstances of this case. . . . We know from the record and from the district court's findings that Omega planned to enter into direct competition with Sportsman's in the pilot and aviation consumer market. . . . It cannot be doubted that Omega registered sportys.com for the primary purpose of keeping Sportsman's from using that domain name. . . . Finally, the explanation given for Sporty's Farm's desire to use the domain name, based on the existence of the dog Spotty, is more amusing than credible. . . . There is ample evidence that Sporty's Farm acted with a 'bad faith intent to profit' from the domain name sportys.com as those terms are used in the ACPA. . . .

Under the ACPA, damages are unavailable to Sportsman's since sportys.com was registered and used by Sporty's Farm prior to passage of the new law. . . .

We conclude . . . that damages are not available to Sportsman's under the FTDA. The district court found that Sporty's Farm did not act willfully. . . . Thus, even assuming the 'sporty's' mark to be famous, we cannot say that the district court clearly erred when it found that Sporty's Farm's actions were not willful. . . .

## Judgment and Result

The injunction issued by the district court was proper under the new anticybersquatting law, but damages are not available to Sportsman's under the ACPA or the FTDA.

## Questions

1. Does the Anticybersquatting Consumer Protection Act forbid ALL cybersquatting?
2. Why didn't the plaintiff in the above case win damages?

# PATENTS[1]

Patent protection is conferred exclusively by federal rather than state law. A **patent** is a legal monopoly conferred by the government (the patentor) on the private party (the patentee). The patent entitles the patentee to exclude anyone else from making, using, or selling the patented item for a period of 20 years from the date of the application. After a patent expires, the patentee loses rights to the invention. There is a proposal to change patent protection to 17 years from time of patent conferral to bring the United States in line with other nations.

An inventor might not obtain a valid patent if the invention was in public use or on sale in the United States for more than one year prior to the filing of the patent application. An inventor's own use and sale of the invention for more than a year before the patent application is filed bars rights to a patent just as effectively as though this use and sale had been by someone else. Patent protection under U.S. law is limited to the United States and does not extend beyond its borders.

The importance of patents was recognized early in the Constitution's statement of policy directed toward "promotion of science and the useful arts." A patent is, in effect, a contract between the government and the inventor. In return for a legal monopoly, the inventor discloses his idea to the public. Further refinements of a patent can extend its life beyond the original patent's 20 years. Because the patent rights accrue to the patentee and any heirs and assigns, the patentee may assign those rights. Patents are also inheritable.

Items that can be patented under section 101 of the Patent Act include "any new and useful process, machine, manufacture, or composition of matter, or any new and useful improvement thereof." Thus, the Patent Act recognizes four categories of patentable inventions under section 101: (1) machines, (2) processes, (3) composition of matter, and (4) manufacture. Machines refer to any device, apparatus, or mechanism made up of coordinated parts that when placed in motion yield an intended result. *Machine* is broadly defined. *Process* covers chemical, mechanical, or mode of treatment of matter to produce a given result. A process might, for example, change something into a different state or matter. *Composition* includes mixtures and chemical unions that can take the form of gases, solids, and fluids. *Manufacture* is a catchall category that could cover items not specifically allowed by the other three categories.

Even if something is a machine, process, composition of matter, or manufacture, four other requirements must be met before something can be patented: novelty, utility, disclosure, and nonobviousness. First, in the *novelty* requirement for patents, *novel* means that something is not found in the store of common knowledge. Novel means new. The Patent Act lays out three conditions to decide whether something is new:

1.  The item must not be previously patented, described in U.S. or foreign publication, or known or used by someone else in the United States.
2.  The item should not have been described in anyone else's previous U.S. patent application.

---

[1] The authors acknowledge relying on Mark Holmes, "A Primer for Patents for the General Practitioner," *Texas Bar Journal* 50, 976 (1987).

3. The item must be made by someone else who has not tried to abandon or hide the item.

The second major requirement for obtaining a patent is that the item must be **useful** (have utility or beneficial use). Most commentators regard this stipulation as easily satisfied.

**Disclosure** refers to the third requirement that the inventor tell the public how the item is made, how to make it, and the best uses of it.

Finally, the **nonobviousness** requirement means that the item when made was not readily seen by someone possessing average skill in the area of endeavor. The idea of nonobviousness is to advance the field.

## VIOLATION OF SOMEONE'S PATENT: INFRINGEMENT

**Infringement** occurs when someone uses someone else's patent without permission. Infringement suits are brought only in federal court. One way for someone to avoid a patent infringement suit and still use the patented item is to obtain a **patent license** from the patent holder, which typically involves paying a royalty to the patentee.

The recovery that one can receive after proving patent infringement can be huge. However, the litigation costs to an individual inventor can wipe out most of any patent recovery. A large corporation can contest an inventor's patent for years, during which time the clock on the patent is ticking away. Professor Kearns, a Wayne State University engineering professor, was able to recover millions of dollars from automobile manufacturers for infringement of his invention: the intermittent windshield wiper for autos. But was Kearns able to convince a court to extend his patent for a period equal to that during which automakers challenged his patent? The *Kearns v. Chrysler Corp.* case provides an answer.

### Kearns v. Chrysler Corp.
U.S. Court of Appeals (Fed. Cir.)
32 F.3d 1541 (1994)

#### Background and Facts

In 1982, Kearns filed an action against Chrysler alleging infringement of U.S. patents 3,351,836, 3,564,374, 3,602,790, and 3,581,178, all relating to electronic intermittent windshield wipers (IWWs) for use in automobile vehicles. At the time the suit was filed, Kearns had three similar suits pending against other automobile manufacturers and distributors involving the same patents.

On October 22, 1982, proceedings in the Chrysler action were stayed pending resolution of the earlier filed suits. The stay was instituted pursuant to Chrysler's stipulation that it would be "bound by the judgment as to the validity of . . . U.S. patents Nos. . . . " in either Ford, Wood Motors, or SWF, whichever was the last to be adjudicated. The stipulation expressly provided, however, that Chrysler would "not be bound by any consent judgment."

In 1989, shortly before the Ford case went to trial, Chrysler renewed its stipulation regarding the issues of invalidity and

unenforceability. Subject to continuation of the court-ordered stay, Chrysler agreed to be "bound by the judgment (excluding a consent judgment) in the *Kearns v. Ford* case, . . . as to the validity and enforceability of the patents involved in that action that are also involved in this action.

. . .

The liability phase of the Ford case commenced on January 3, 1990. . . . On March 9, 1990, the district court entered partial judgment that the specified claims were valid, enforceable, and infringed by Ford. . . .

The damage phase of Ford was tried . . . in April 1990. The jury was unable to reach a unanimous verdict and a second trial on damages was held in July 1990. A second jury . . . returned a unanimous verdict in favor of Kearns awarding $5,163,842 for the period from April 3, 1978, through 1988. . . . Although damages for the period from 1972 to April 3, 1978, remained in dispute, Ford and Kearns eventually reached a settlement as to the total amount of liability. . . .

The Chrysler case returned to active status in early 1991. On February 20, 1991, the district court issued a pretrial order stating that the issues to be adjudicated at trial concerned "infringement, damages, and willfulness." On May 3, 1991, Chrysler filed a motion to have the pretrial order modified to add patent validity as an issue for trial. In support of its motion, Chrysler argued that the pretrial stipulations . . . did not bar Chrysler from challenging the patents. . . . Chrysler claimed that because the final judgment in *Ford* was entered pursuant to a settlement agreement between Ford and Kearns, it was a "consent judgment" within the meaning of the stipulations.

The district court rejected Chrysler's argument, noting that although a settlement had been reached in *Ford* on the issue of damages, the issue of validity was "hotly" contested by the parties at trial, resulting in a unanimous jury verdict and a final judgment in favor of Kearns. . . .

By court order, the Chrysler action was split into separate jury trials on the issues of liability and damages. On December 10, 1991, the jury returned verdicts that Chrysler's accused IWW circuits, designated the "1977 Circuit" and the "1980 Circuit," infringed Kearns patents. On June 11, 1992, the same jury returned a verdict that Chrysler's infringement was not willful and assessed a reasonable royalty of $.90 per unit for a total of 12,564,107 infringing units. Pursuant to the jury's verdicts, the district court entered final judgment in favor of Kearns in the amount of $18,740,465.43, including prejudgment interest and costs. . . . Both Chrysler and Kearns appealed.

## Body of Opinion

**Circuit Judge Lourie.** . . . Shortly before trial, Kearns expanded his claim for relief to include injunctive relief. Kearns believed that Chrysler's infringement deprived him of the "full value" of his patents during their respective terms by effectively extinguishing his exclusive right to sell his patented IWW systems to automobile manufacturers. Kearns urged that Chrysler should be enjoined from manufacturing infringing IWW systems for a period of sufficient duration "to put him in [a] position where the harm [caused by] past infringement during the terms of the patents in suit is rectified." The district court refused to grant such relief because the patents had already expired. The court concluded that "there is nothing in statute or common law giving Kearns the right to an injunction against practicing the disclosures in an expired patent."

In arguing that the district court erred in denying him post-expiration relief, Kearns claims that the $11 million damage award is not adequate to compensate him for the loss he sustained as a result of Chrysler's infringement. Kearns contends that Chrysler's infringement stripped him of "exclusive time" over his patents in violation of his rights under the U.S. Constitution and the patent laws, and that he is entitled to have that time restored to him. That contention, however, finds no basis in the statutory scheme governing patent infringement remedies.

Under the laws enacted by Congress, a patent grants the patent owner the right to exclude others from making, using, or selling the claimed invention in the United States for the term of

17 years. . . . When that exclusive right is infringed, the patent owner is authorized to obtain compensation in the form of damages, measured, e.g., by lost profits or a reasonable royalty. . . . Moreover, the statute expressly provides for the grant of injunctions "in accordance with the principles of equity." . . . In view of the fact that the principal right afforded by a patent is the "right to exclude," we have noted that "the nature of the patent grant . . . weighs against holding that monetary damages will always suffice to make the patentee whole." . . . Indeed, while monetary relief is often the sole remedy for past infringement, it does not follow that a monetary award is also the sole remedy against future infringement." . . . However, §283 relief is available only to "prevent the violations of any right secured by patent." Thus, when the rights secured by a patent are no longer protectable by virtue of expiration or unenforceability, entitlement to injunctive relief becomes moot because such relief is no longer available. . . .

An invention claimed in a patent passes into the public domain upon termination of the patent's 17-year statutory term. Because the rights flowing from a patent exist only for the term of the patent, there can be no infringement once the patent expires. Here, all the asserted patents expired before the commencement of trial. Therefore, Kearns "can no longer obtain injunctive relief with respect to [those patents]." . . . Granting the relief requested by Kearns would impermissibly extend the statutory term beyond that established by Congress. Congress has the power to provide for patent term extension in appropriate circumstances . . . but it has not done so here and we cannot legislate in its place. . . . The expiration of Kearns's patents precludes the grant of injunctive relief and the judgment for $11 million in damages thus amounts to adequate and full compensation under the law for Chrysler's past violation of his patent rights. . . .

We sympathize with Kearns's complaint that his patents have expired without his ever being able to exclude others from practice of his invention, especially since he is an individual inventor contending with a multitude of giant corporations. While it is of course the essence of a patent that it provides the right to exclude, the same statute that grants that right also permits other parties, including accused infringers, to challenge the validity of a patent and to contest a charge of infringement. . . . Moreover, entitlement to an injunction implementing the right to exclude, as compared with only assessing damages against an infringer, in not absolute even during the life of a patent, but is discretionary. . . . Here, because Kearns's patents have expired, the district court certainly did not abuse its discretion in denying injunctive relief.

It is unfortunate that Kearns feels that he never enjoyed an exclusive status under his patents, but that is simply a consequence of the right of others to challenge his patents and the fact that his patents have expired. The patent statute does provide for increased damages and attorney fees as additional relief for aggrieved patent owners . . . but Kearns did not persuade the district court that he was entitled to such relief.

We therefore conclude that the district court properly granted summary judgment in favor of Chrysler on Kearns' request for post-expiration injunctive relief.

Kearns argues that the district court erred in granting Chrysler's motion for summary judgment on Kearn's claim for damages based on lost profits, rather than a reasonable royalty. A patent owner bears the burden of proof on damages. . . . Kearns has not carried that burden with respect to lost profits.

A lost profits award is appropriate only if the patent owner can prove there was a reasonable probability that "but for" the infringement, it would have made the infringer's sales. . . . Where, as here, a patent owner fails to prove lost profits, the court is left with no alternative but to have damages determined on the basis of a reasonable royalty. . . .

## Judgment and Result

Kearns was given no court order that would, in effect, have extended the life of his patent beyond the statutory period of 17 years (recently extended to 20 years). Evidence supported the finding of infringement, and Kearns was entitled to a reasonable royalty, but not lost profits. Chrysler lost on the royalty issues. Kearns lost on the lost profit and post-patent injunctive relief issues.

## Questions

1. Did Kearns recover lost profits from Chrysler? A reasonable royalty?
2. What was Kearns's argument that he was entitled to injunctive relief beyond the statutory period from the time he was granted the patent, that is, beyond 17 years (now 20 years)? Why did he fail on this issue? Is that answer troubling in light of the "little, but brilliant, guy" tied up in litigation with "corporate giants" for the period of his patent who was never able to exploit it to the extent he otherwise would have?
3. How much did Kearns recover from Chrysler? A footnote [omitted] pointed out that Kearns "fired several of his attorneys and attempted to conduct massive multiple suits pro se." Recall pro se suits mean Kearns acted as his own attorney. A newspaper account reported that Kearns spent almost all of his recoveries on attorney fees and actually netted little if anything from this litigation. How might the patent laws be amended to rectify this apparent injustice to inventors? Or was it injustice?
4. Why was the claim against Ford relevant in Kearns's suit against Chrysler?

In the next patent case, *Diamond v. Diehr*, the U.S. Supreme Court decided that computer programs meeting certain criteria are patentable.

## Diamond v. Diehr
U.S. Supreme Court
450 U.S. 175 (1981)

## Background and Facts

Respondents filed a patent application claiming invention for a process for molding raw, uncured synthetic rubber into cured precision products. While it was possible, by using well-known time, temperature, and cure relationships, to calculate by means of an established mathematical equation when to open the molding press and remove the cured product, according to respondents the industry had not been able to measure precisely the temperature *inside* the press, thus making it difficult to make the necessary computations to determine the proper cure time. Respondents characterized their contribution to the art to reside in the process of constantly measuring the temperature inside the mold and feeding the temperature measurements into a computer that repeatedly recalculates the cure time by use of the mathematical equation and then signals a device to open the press at the proper time. The patent examiner rejected respondents' claims on the ground that they were drawn to nonstatutory subject matter under 35 U.S.C. § 101, which provides for the issuance of patents to "[w]hoever invents or discovers any new and useful *process,* machine, manufacture, or composition of matter, or any new and useful improvement thereof. . . . " The Patent and Trademark Office Board of Appeals agreed, but the Court of Customs and Patent Appeals reversed.

## Body of Opinion

**Justice Rehnquist.** We have before us today only the question of whether respondents' claims fall within the § 101 categories of possibly patentable subject matter. We view respondents' claims as nothing more than a process for molding rubber products and not as an attempt to patent a mathematical formula. We recognize, of course, that when a claim recites a mathematical formula (or scientific principle or phenomenon of nature), an inquiry must be made into whether the claim is seeking patent protection for that formula in the abstract. A mathematical formula as such is not accorded the protection of our patent laws, and this principle cannot be circumvented by attempting to limit the use of the formula to a particular technological environment. Similarly, insignificant postsolution activity will not transform an unpatentable principle into a patentable process. To hold otherwise would allow a competent draftsman to evade the recognized limitations on the type of subject matter eligible for patent protection. On the other hand, when a claim containing a mathematical formula implements or applies that formula in a structure or process which, when considered as a whole, is performing a function which the patent laws were designed to protect (e.g., transforming or reducing an article to a different state or thing), then the claim satisfies the requirements of § 101.

Because we do not view respondents' claims as an attempt to patent a mathematical formula, but rather to be drawn to an industrial process for the molding of rubber products, we affirm the judgment of the Court of Customs and Patent Appeals.

## Judgment and Result

Respondents' claims recited subject matter that was eligible for patent protection under § 101.

(a) For purposes of § 101, a "process" is "an act, or a series of acts, performed upon the subject-matter to be transformed and reduced to a different state or thing. If new and useful, it is just as patentable as is a piece of machinery. . . .

(b) While a mathematical formula, like a law of nature, cannot be the subject of a patent, respondents do not seek to patent a mathematical formula, but instead seek protection for a process of curing synthetic rubber. Although their process employs a well-known mathematical equation, they do not seek to pre-empt the use of that equation, except in conjunction with all of the other steps in their claimed process. . . . The questions of whether a particular invention meets the "novelty" requirements of 35 U.S.C. § 102 or the "nonobviousness" requirements of § 103 do not affect the determination of whether the invention falls into a category of subject matter that is eligible for patent protection under § 101.

(c) When a claim containing a mathematical formula implements or applies the formula in a structure or process which, when considered as a whole, is performing a function which the patent laws were designed to protect (e.g., transforming or reducing an article to a different state or thing), then the claim satisfies § 101's requirements.

## Questions

1. When Congress amended the Patent Act in 1952 by replacing the word *art* with *process*, did Congress intend to expand or reduce the number of patentable items? Does this interpretation reflect a current legal norm, that is, the promotion of entrepreneurship?
2. Could Einstein have obtained a patent on his famous theory of relativity, $E = MC^2$? Why?
3. Are math formulas patentable? Would a math formula that is part of a process for molding raw, uncured synthetic rubber into cured precision products be patentable?

## INTERNET, E-MAIL, AND SOME ASPECTS OF LAW AFFECTING THEM[2]

Few technologies have had the impact of the Internet (also known as the World Wide Web or WWW) and the related e-mail. Although the Internet was first developed in the 1960s in the United States so that defense contractors could communicate with each other, the Internet did not mature to the point where large numbers used it until the mid- to late 1980s. Today, the Internet and e-mail are available to anyone with access to a computer with a modem. The media through which the "net" and e-mail operate include telephone lines, coaxial cable, and radio waves using satellite transmission.

Congress and the courts have been active in making law regulating cyberspace. In 1997, the U.S. Supreme Court in *Reno v. A.C.L.U.* invalidated two parts of the Communications Decency Act (CDA) designed to protect minors from "obscene" and "indecent" material on the Internet. In so doing, the Supreme Court ruled that the First Amendment's free speech protections, with attendant possible restraints, apply to the Internet. Obscene speech and child pornography are not protected by the First Amendment.

---

[2] The authors acknowledge reliance on articles in the "Suggested Readings" section found on the publisher's Internet pages for this textbook.

## International Protection of Intellectual Property[3]

Protection for intellectual property rights has existed since at least the mid-1800s with passage of the Paris Convention for the Protection of Industrial Property Rights and the Berne Convention for the Protection of Literary and Artistic Works. More recent treaties such as GATT/WTO and NAFTA require that signatories provide legal protection for intellectual property such as patents, trademarks, and copyrights.

The Uruguay round of trade negotiations resulted in an agreement known as Trade-Related Aspects of Intellectual Property. One major feature of this agreement was to broaden former GATT coverage to require that members provide legal protections for intellectual property. WTO provisions coming out of the Uruguay round require that members must provide for trademark registration and renewal. WTO members must also provide for patent protection. WTO also creates a uniform term for protecting patents (20 years from the date of application). In late 1995, the United States amended its patent laws to conform to the WTO patent term.

Two other GATT/WTO features that will affect intellectual property are reciprocity and most-favored nation (MFN) status. Reciprocity refers to one nation's according nationals from other GATT/WTO signatories the same rights (such as intellectual property protections) that it gives its own nationals. Thus, a foreign manufacturer would appear to be entitled to the same rights as a domestic manufacturer. With respect to MFN, GATT/WTO members must generally give other nations the same advantages they give to a particular nation. This provision should drive down trade barriers to foreign trade enjoying intellectual property protection (such as patents for computer chips). Trade secret protections under GATT/WTO are recognized and are referred to as *undisclosed information*.

NAFTA also has provisions directed to intellectual property protection. It requires signatory nations to establish patent protection. NAFTA also recognizes trademarks and mandates an original term of at least 10 years, which is renewable. With respect to trade secrets, NAFTA precludes governmental disclosure of certain manufacturer data obtained under regulatory authority. For example, drug manufacturers' test data turned over to regulators would not be discoverable.

In addition to WTO/GATT and NAFTA protections, the United States unilaterally provides protection for intellectual property against foreign pirating under Special 301.

---

[3] The authors acknowledge reliance on articles in the "Suggested Readings" section found on the publisher's Internet pages for this textbook.

## CHAPTER SUMMARY

Quasi-contracts are not contracts, but, instead, are judicially imposed devices like (quasi-) contracts. They are designed to prevent unjust enrichment where benefits have been conferred under circumstances where the conferee knows or should know that pay is expected. They are usually not imposed if the parties have an express or implied-in-fact contract.

Trade secrets may consist of any formula, pattern, device, or compilation of information used in one's business, giving one an opportunity to obtain an advantage over competitors who do not know or use it. Examples of trade secrets include product formulas, manufacturing processes, customer lists, and price information.

Copyright protection affords protection for works expressed in a tangible medium, such as songs, books, plays, pictures, and movies. For works created after January 1, 1978, the length of protection is the life of the author plus 70 years. The criterion for obtaining copyright protection is originality. The Digital Millennium Copyright Act contains several safeharbors insulating OSPs from copyright liability when OSP subscribers commit copyright infringement. There are several types of copyright infringement including direct, contributory, and vicarious infringement. Many defenses to copyright infringement exist including fair use and the material is in the public domain.

Trademarks can arise from federal protection. Trademarks are designed to distinguish goods (or services) from competing products. Such protection is available if one complies with federal statutes. Trademark protection lasts 10 years for marks granted after November 16, 1989 and is renewable. The test for trademark infringement is likelihood of confusion, mistake, or deception. The Anticybersquatting Consumer Protection Act outlaws bad-faith cybersquatting.

Functional patent protection, which is distinguished from design patents, is available to protect machines, processes, composition of matter, or manufactured items. Patent protection lasts for 20 years from the date of the application. Criteria for patent protection are that the item must be new, nonobvious, utilitarian, and disclosed. If someone other than the patent holder makes, sells, or uses items having the patented invention, he or she may be subject to infringement suits.

Internet domain names can obtain federal intellectual property protection such as trademark protection. A number of federal statutes aim to protect children in various ways from Internet abuses. Privacy of Internet users is also protected in various ways.

### ■ MANAGER'S ETHICAL DILEMMA

Dennis Lilly had a device that would convert raw sewage into environmentally harmless and commercially viable fertilizer. He did not have the resources to develop and market his finding. He knows that patent, trademark, and copyright protection are available, but  he wonders if it is worth pursuing such protections. He has a friend, Mr. Wollin, a successful entrepreneur, who is interested in his invention. What would you advise Lilly to do prior to seeking financial assistance from Wollin?

## DISCUSSION QUESTIONS

1. A celebrity named O.J. Simpson tried to register at the federal registry his name and nickname, including "O.J. Simpson," "O.J.," and "The Juice" for use with a broad range of goods, including figurines, trading cards, sportswear, medallions, coins, and prepaid telephone cards. After the marks were approved for registration by an examiner in the U.S. Patent and Trademark Office, the marks were published in the *Official Gazette* in accordance with federal law.

   William B. Ritchie filed oppositions to registration of these marks, asserting they were not registerable on either of two statutory grounds: first, that the marks are immoral or scandalous matter and should be denied registration under § 2(a) of the Lanham Act; and second, that one of the marks is primarily merely a surname and thus not registerable under § 2(e)(4) of the Lanham Act.

   Should a U.S. Court of Appeals allow Ritchie to challenge the registration, and did he establish a reasonable belief that he would be damaged by the registration? [*Ritchie v. Simpson*, 170 F.3d 1092 (1999)].

2. Must a newspaper claiming copyright ownership in an ad it wrote for someone else give a specific and separate copyright notice in the ad? Would a copyright notice properly affixed to the newspaper as a whole cover individual ads in that newspaper? [*Eastern Pub. and Advertising, Inc. v. Chesapeake Pub. and Advertising, Inc.*, 831 F.2d 488 (4th Cir. 1987)].

3. Can a telephone directory be copyrighted? [*Southwestern Bell Media, Inc. v. Trans Western Pub., Inc.*, 670 F.Supp. 899 (D. Kan. 1987)].

4. May a court award attorney fees to the winning party in a patent infringement suit? [*Afros S.p.A. v. Krauss-Maffei Corp.*, 671 F. Supp. 1402, reargument denied 671 F. Supp. 1458 (D. Del. 1987)].

5. Was a U.S. patent on double-sided floppy disc drives that had a fixed lower head infringed by an imported device with movable lower heads, but that were more rigid than those of prior art? [*Tandon Corp. v. U.S. International Trade Com'n*, 831 F.2d 1017 (C.A. Fed. Cir. 1987)].

6. May someone prove that a competitor's patent is invalid? [*Afros S.p.A. v. Krauss-Maffei Corp.*, 671 F. Supp. 1402, reargument denied 671 F. Supp. 1458 (D. Del. 1987)].

7. If a word is generic it may not get trademark protection. Is the term *Gear* generic as applied to clothing? [*Gear, Inc. v. L.A. Gear California, Inc.*, 670 F. Supp. 508 (S.D. N.Y. 1987)].

8. A trademark acquires a secondary meaning when it is shown that the primary significance of the term in the minds of the consuming public is the producer not the product. Is the crux of the secondary meaning doctrine that the trademark comes to identify not only the goods but the source of the goods, even though the relevant consuming public might not know the producer's name? [*Centaur Communications Ltd. v. A/S/M Communications, Inc.*, 830 F.2d 1217 (2d Cir. 1987)].

9. Was a store owner's transmission of a radio broadcast, including music, in the workplace to benefit the employees a public performance subject to copyright control? [*Merrill v. County Stores, Inc.*, 669 F. Supp. 1164 (D. N.H. 1987)].

---

### INFOTRAC KEYWORDS

**Use your InfoTrac password to look up articles on http://www.infotrac-college.com**

Keywords: *Intellectual property, copyright infringement, DMCA, trademarks, trademark dilution, cybersquatting, patent infringement, e-mail privacy, Internet privacy, Special 301.*

---

For suggested readings, please visit this book's Web site at **http://fisher.westbuslaw.com** (click on "Internet Applications").

# MODULE 4

# LAW AFFECTING THE BUSINESS
# HUMAN RESOURCES DEPARTMENT

**CHAPTER 14**

Common Law Rules in
Employer–Employee Relations

**CHAPTER 15**

Important Statues in
Employer–Employee Relations

**CHAPTER 16**

Employment Discrimination

**CHAPTER 17**

Federal Labor Law:
Unionization and Collective Bargaining

## POSITIVE LAW ETHICAL PROBLEMS

"I apprehended a robber at our store and instead of being rewarded, I was fired!" exclaimed Antonio Feliciano.

"Well, you were fired because you violated the company policy of not resisting robbers," replied an executive of 7-Eleven Inc., Feliciano's employer.

Is it wrongful for an employer to fire a worker for defending himself during a robbery at the employer's business?

"But the alleged acts—even if true—certainly do not bind us, the Boy Scouts—because the scout masters receive no pay from us," said Mike Malloy, a Boy Scouts of America representative who was reviewing a complaint filed by a former Boy Scout alleging that a scout master had sexually molested him years earlier.

"Ah," replied the attorney for the alleged victim, "but principals are bound by the acts of agents, even if they work for nothing."

"I doubt that. But even if it is true," continued Malloy, "the Boy Scouts clearly got no benefit from such allegedly outrageous conduct. It was beyond the scope of the scout master's duties."

Should a principal be liable for a volunteer agent's sexual molestation of a person the agent was charged with supervising, or does the outrageousness of such acts remove them from the scope of the job?

*"QUI FACIT PER ALIUM FACIT PER SE." (A PERSON WHO ACTS THROUGH ANOTHER IS LEGALLY RESPONSIBLE JUST AS THOUGH HE OR SHE HAD ACTED PERSONALLY.)*

—AGENCY
PRINCIPLE

This chapter begins a series dealing with employer–employee relations. It examines common law rules governing employers' relations with individual employees. Chapters 15 and 16 look at statutes altering or adding to some of the common law rules. Chapter 17 examines federal labor law and dealing with employees on a collective basis.

## EMPLOYER–EMPLOYEE LEGAL CLASSIFICATIONS

The terms **employer** and **employee** are helpful descriptions of functional relationships, but they do not have much legal significance. Rather, the archaic-sounding labels *master–servant*, *principal–agent*, and *employer–independent contractor* are the legal categories for most employer–employee relations.

A **master–servant relationship** arises when a person (the "master") employs another person (the "servant") to perform physical tasks not involving the making of contracts with third persons. The task is often a menial sort, such as gardening or cleaning. The **principal–agent relationship** occurs when one person (the principal) employs another (the agent) to enter business relations (usually contracts) with third persons. It differs from the master–servant situation in that the objective of a principal–agent relationship is to establish legal relations with third persons. The master–servant relationship does not have this objective. Legal relations, however, may result through a servant's torts, which injure a third person. (Recall that torts are breaches of civil duties, such as slander or assault.)

*The congressional Web site at* **http://thomas.loc.gov** *provides links to state law and employment classifications*

The **employer–independent contractor relationship** results when one person (the employer) hires another (the independent contractor) to work for the employer. In this relationship, the employer does not have the right to control the means by which the independent contractor performs the work. The principal or master in the agent or servant case, however, has the right to control both the *means* by which the job is to be done and the *end* or *object* of the work. In the independent contractor relation, the employer does retain the right to control the end or object of the work. Otherwise, independent contractors could choose to do nothing if they wished—certainly not something that someone would pay another to do.

An employee could be an agent or servant with respect to one part of the job and an independent contractor with respect to another part. For example, an insurance salesperson could be an agent with respect to the representations made to prospective customers in selling insurance policies but an independent contractor when driving to see a customer. Calling an employee an agent, servant, or independent contractor does not per se establish that relationship. Rather, courts will examine the substance of the relationship to determine which relationship exists.

## WHO MAY BE PRINCIPALS

The general rule is that one who has the mental capability to act on one's own behalf may be a principal.[1] Minors may be principals if they are old enough to comprehend the nature and significance of the act undertaken on their behalf. Minors may also void a contract made on their behalf, as they could if they had acted for themselves. Because legally a corporation is considered a person, corporations may be principals. Partnerships and trusts may also be principals. However, legal incompetents, such as insane people, and unincorporated associations may not be principals.

## WHO MAY BE AGENTS, SERVANTS, AND INDEPENDENT CONTRACTORS

One may be an agent, servant, or independent contractor for another person as long as one has the mental and physical capability to perform and understand the significance of the acts undertaken. Minors may be agents unless they are too young to meet the physical or mental requirements of the task. Corporations, trusts, and partnerships may be agents. All of the aforementioned people may be agents, assuming that the principal has in some way authorized the agent to act.

---

[1] Throughout the chapter, principal is treated as synonymous with master or employer in the case of an independent contractor.

## EFFECT OF DIFFERENT EMPLOYER–EMPLOYEE CLASSIFICATIONS

The basic common law classifications of employees are important because, generally, legal liability is greater for the employer when the employee is classified as an agent or servant rather than as an independent contractor. The principal in a principal–agent situation and a master in a master–servant context have the right to control the agent or servant to a greater extent than does an employer in an employer–independent contractor situation.

Someone who commits a crime or a tort or breaks a contract is liable. Within the concept of vicarious liability, or **respondeat superior**, if one person does something, another is legally responsible. The respondeat superior concept applies across the board to agency or master–servant relations in private enterprise or governmental contexts. It does *not* usually apply to employer–independent contractor situations, except where the independent contractor performs **nondelegable duties** or engages in ultrahazardous activities for the employer. In the field of employer–employee relations, the exact category of that relationship—principal–agent or master–servant on the one hand or employer–independent contractor on the other—plays a large role in determining the employer's liability for the employee's acts.

Before illustrating the consequences of the various employer–employee classifications, let us look at the rule that agency relationships are consensual and usually contractual. **Consensual relations** are those that are entered by mutual consent but that do not necessarily possess all of the elements of a contract. As a practical matter, most agency arrangements are contractual, because agents want payment for their services. However, a neighbor or friend doing a good deed by running an errand for a sick friend would be a **gratuitous agent** if no pay were received for such help.

The respondeat superior rules establishing vicarious liability apply to both gratuitous as well as paid servant and agents. The *Lourim v. Swensen* case presents the respondeat superior concept in the context of a gratuitous servant/agent who supervised minor children as a Boy Scout leader. Given the fact that many families today have two wage earners who often must place their minor children in day care centers, the liability implications of the *Lourim* case are tremendous. One might further extrapolate beyond day care to primary schools, secondary schools, colleges, universities, and even churches. A segment of the opinion omitted dealt with Oregon's willingness to subject churches to vicarious liability for alleged sexual abuse by priests against children who attend church functions.

Note that in *Lourim* the question arose about whether the agent's allegedly outrageous acts were "outside the scope of employment," meaning they were not done "at work," resulting in no employer liability. The Supreme Court of Oregon decided, however, that the nature of the alleged acts—sexual molestation—did not render them beyond the scope of employment.

## TYPES OF AGENTS

To search for various aspects of state law, go to **http://www. alllaw.com/state_resources/ state_law_search**

In a discussion of agents only—not servants or independent contractors—several types of agents should be noted. The **general agent** is someone having authority to act on another's behalf in many different types of transactions or to handle all matters involved with a particular business. When professional athletes appoint business

# Lourim v. Swensen
Supreme Court of Oregon
977 P.2d 1157 (1999)

## Background and Facts

This case arises out of the allegations by the plaintiff that he was sexually abused by his Boy Scout leader, Swensen, approximately 30 years earlier, when plaintiff was a minor. In 1995, plaintiff brought the present action against Swensen, as well as the Cascade Pacific Council and Boy Scouts of America (collectively, the Boy Scouts) claiming that Swensen had sexually abused him from 1965 through 1967. The complaint alleges that between 1965 and 1967 Swensen was a volunteer Boy Scout leader, duly authorized by the Boy Scouts to act as such. As part of his volunteer duties, he was directed to fulfill the role of troop leader or assistant troop leader to plaintiff's troop.

Plaintiff and his family became close to Swensen, and Swensen was a frequent guest in their home. Swensen gained the trust and confidence of plaintiff's family as a suitable friend, guide, mentor, and role model to plaintiff, then an adolescent. By virtue of that relationship, Swensen gained the support and permission to spend substantial periods of time alone with plaintiff. Swensen also won the friendship of plaintiff himself. He was plaintiff's mentor and role model. Swensen gained the opportunity to socialize with plaintiff and to spend time alone with him and together with other boys in remote places. Swensen used his position of trust to gain opportunity to touch plaintiff physically. Eventually, Swensen committed a series of sexual assaults on plaintiff when plaintiff was a minor. Plaintiff alleges Swensen's assaults were manipulations committed in connection with his duties as troop leader.

As against the Boy Scouts, the complaint alleges that the Boy Scout organizations are vicariously liable for Swensen's tortious conduct under the doctrine of respondeat superior.

The Boy Scouts moved to dismiss the action on the grounds that both claims are time-barred and that the complaint fails to state ultimate facts sufficient to constitute a tort claim for vicarious liability based on the doctrine of respondeat superior. The trial court granted defendants' motion as to all claims. Plaintiff appealed.

On appeal the Court of Appeals affirmed the decision of the trial court. That court concluded that plaintiff's complaint states no facts from which it reasonably could be concluded that Swensen's sexual assaults on plaintiff were within the scope of employment.

The case was then appealed to the Oregon Supreme Court.

## Body of Opinion

**Justice Gillette.** A complaint is sufficient to state a cause of action for vicarious liability based on the doctrine of respondeat superior if the allegations that it contains, if true, would establish that the employee's acts were committed within the scope of his or her employment. . . . In *Chesterton v. Barmon* . . . this court set out three requirements that must be met to establish that an employee's conduct was within the scope of employment: (1) the conduct must have occurred substantially within the time and space limits authorized by the employment; (2) the employee must have been motivated, at least partially, by a purpose to serve the employer; (3) the act must have been of a kind that the employee was hired to perform. Applying that framework to this case, the court of appeals held that the complaint failed to state a claim because

". . . there simply are no allegations of fact that satisfy all three of the elements of vicarious liability. In particular, there are no facts from which it reasonably could be concluded that Swensen's sexual assaults were acts of a kind [an] employee was hired to perform."

. . . Accepting the allegations in the complaint as true and drawing all reasonable inferences in the plaintiff's favor, a jury reasonably could infer that the sexual assaults were merely the culmination of a progressive series of actions that involved the ordinary and authorized duties of a Boy Scout leader. . . . A jury also reasonably could infer that Swensen's performance of his duties as troop leader with respect to plaintiff and his family was a necessary precursor to the sexual abuse and that the assaults were a direct outgrowth of and were engendered by conduct that was within the scope of Swensen's employment. . . .

Notwithstanding that conclusion, the Boy Scouts argue that dismissal of the complaint is proper on a ground not considered by the court of appeals. . . . They assert that the doctrine of respondeat superior is premised on the existence of a master/servant relationship which, they argue, is not adequately alleged in the present complaint. For the following reasons, we disagree.

It is well established that one can be a servant even though the service is performed gratuitously. . . . The relevant inquiry in determining whether a master/servant relationship exists for respondeat superior purposes is whether the master has the right to control the actions of the servant. . . . We must determine whether plaintiff has adequately alleged that the Boy Scouts had the right to control Swensen's actions.

The complaint alleges that "at all relevant times, Swensen was a volunteer Boy Scout leader, duly authorized by the Boy Scouts and the Cascade Pacific Council to act in that capacity" and that "as part of the volunteer duties with the Boy Scouts and the Cascade Pacific Council, Swensen was directed to fulfill the role of troop leader or assistant troop leader to plaintiff's troop". . . .

A jury could reasonably infer from the allegation that "Swensen was directed to fulfill the role of troop leader or assistant troop leader to plaintiff's troop" that the Boy Scouts directed the activities and, thus, that the Boy Scouts had the right to control Swensen's activities. . . . In this regard, although the complaint does not contain a specific allegation setting forth the typical duties of a troop leader or what, specifically, Swensen was directed to do as a Boy Scout leader, such an allegation is unnecessary.

## Judgment and Result

The Supreme Court of Oregon held that the plaintiff stated a cause of action in his complaint and if he could later prove at trial the allegations in his complaint, he could recover against Cascade Pacific Council and the Boy Scouts of America for the alleged actions of the scout master on grounds of respondeat superior.

## Questions

1. How could the Boy Scouts of America be liable for actions of a scout master? Can a principal be liable for acts of an agent? What is the reason for the respondeat superior principle?
2. Must the person who injures the third party be a paid employee of the person sued under respondeat superior? Must the injured party work for the employer sued?

3. Given the inflammatory nature of the alleged actions of the agent/servant (scout master) here, how could it rationally be claimed that a scout master's sexually molesting a boy scout could ever be done for the benefit of the Boy Scouts of America?
4. In a part of the opinion omitted, the Supreme Court of Oregon stated that the child abuse claim was not time barred even though it was raised 30 years after the alleged abuse. The court stated that the statute of limitations extended to "three years from when the plaintiff discovered the causal connection between the child abuse and his injuries." Might not psychological development injuries be undiscovered until a person entered professional counseling years after the child abuse, thus justifying the extension of the statute of limitations?

managers to handle their endorsements, exhibitions, and media appearances, keep their books, and file their tax returns, the business managers are general agents. The manager of a neighborhood Kroger or Safeway supermarket is also a general agent.

A **del credere agent** is one who sells goods for another on credit and guarantees that, if the buyer does not pay, the agent will pay. This agent is similar to a guarantor, someone who agrees to pay the debt of another only if the primary obligor (debtor) does not pay. A guarantor can guarantee any type of obligation, but a *del credere* agent usually guarantees only a buyer's credit for goods purchased.

A **special agent** is one employed to accomplish a particular task. For example, if one desires to sell a particular oil painting, the agent employed to make such a sale is a special agent. The significance of terms such as *general agent* or *special agent* arises, for example, with respect to the ending notice that the principal must give third persons who have dealt with the principal through the agent. Actual notice of a general agent must be given by the principal to third persons who have dealt with a general agent in the past. No such actual notice would be required for third persons who have dealt with the principal through the special agent appointed to handle a particular transaction.

## WHY EMPLOY AN INDEPENDENT CONTRACTOR

An important basic principle in employer–employee relations is that the employer and employee can play a large part in determining their legal relationship to one another. They can put terms in their employment contract and conduct themselves in ways that have been legally recognized by courts in establishing the employer–employee relationship they desire. As long as the employer and employee put words in their agreement that accurately describe the legal relationship (principal–agent, master–servant, or employer–independent contractor) they want, *and* as long as they act as the words say, their relationship will most likely be recognized by the courts as what they claim it to be.

Many factors influence an employer's decision to employ a servant rather than an independent contractor. The employer's desire to exercise (or not exercise) control is a key factor. The more right to control that employers exercise over the means their employees use to do their work, the more likely a master–servant relationship exists. The advantage to the employer is that the work can be done exactly as the employer wishes. The disadvantages to the employer in hiring a servant instead of an independent contractor primarily involve cost.

The potentially higher cost of hiring an employee instead of an independent contractor comes from the employer's tort liability for the servant's acts while working. The employer is generally not liable for an independent contractor's torts committed while working on the employer's behalf unless the work is inherently dangerous. Many statutes impose taxes such as Social Security and workers' compensation on employers who hire employees *but* not on employers who hire independent contractors. Given the substantial (and increasing) Social Security liability for employers, the desire to minimize the impact of the Social Security tax is a significant consideration for an employer. The *Toyota Motor Sales v. Superior Court* case illustrates the employer's tort liability for servants as opposed to independent contractors. The tests for determining whether someone is a servant or independent contractor are the same in the tort and Social Security situations. The *Toyota* case lists these tests.

## Toyota Motor Sales v. Superior Court
California Court of Appeals, Second District
220 Cal. App. 3d 864, 269 Cal. Rptr. 647 (1990)

### Background and Facts

This case arises from a rear-end automobile accident that occurred on August 26, 1987, in the city of Torrance, California. The defendant, Christopher Heard, while delivering a pizza from Numero Uno No. 12, a pizza franchise owned by Mr. Lee, so operated his vehicle as to cause it to collide with the rear of the plaintiff's vehicle. As a result, plaintiff sustained damages that included $13,000 in medical expenses and $900 in property damage.

On July 8, 1988, plaintiff filed suit against Lee, Heard, and Toyota. She alleged that Heard was negligent in the operation of the vehicle and that Lee, as his employer, was vicariously liable under the doctrine of respondeat superior. The cause of action against Toyota alleged that it had defectively designed the seat belt installed in plaintiff's vehicle and that the belt's failure upon impact had contributed to her injuries.

Plaintiff made a demand upon the defendants for $500,000 to settle the entire case. Subsequently, Heard entered into a separate settlement with plaintiff for $100,000, which the court, on August 10, 1989, found to be in good faith within the meaning of Section 877.6. The evidence in support of that determination included the fact that Heard was a 21-year-old student with few, if any, assets other than coverage for his car under his father's liability policy. The amount paid in settlement represented the full policy limits. Toyota did not object to the trial court's good faith determination with respect to this settlement.

Plaintiff then entered into a separate settlement with Lee in consideration of the payment of the sum of $15,000 which represented the full amount provided by Lee's liability policy. Over Toyota's objection, the trial court found this settlement to be in good faith. Based thereon, Toyota's cross-complaint against Lee for comparative equitable indemnity was dismissed. Toyota then filed a timely petition for a writ of mandate.

### Body of Opinion

**Associate Justice Croskey.** It is clear from a review of the record, that the good faith determination made by the trial court was based on its conclusion that Heard was not an employee of Lee, but, rather, was an independent contractor. On that assumption Lee would have no liability to plaintiff, as the only theory against Lee asserted by plaintiff was based upon the doctrine of respondeat superior. There was no claim that Lee was independently negligent in hiring or using Heard's delivery services. In such circumstances, a settlement of $15,000 would clearly justify a finding that it was made in good faith. On the other hand, if Heard was an employee of Lee, acting in the course and scope of his employment at the time of the accident, then Lee might well be exposed to the potential of unlimited liability and the question of good faith would depend upon the trial court's evaluation of other factors (e.g., plaintiff's probable recovery and the extent of Lee's wealth) which were not reached or considered by the court. . . .

The evidence, relevant to the legal status of Heard, offered by Lee and apparently relied upon by the court was that he (1) provided his own car, expenses and insurance, (2) was paid on a commission (10 percent) basis for each delivery, (3) agreed to pay his own payroll (FICA) and income taxes, (4) agreed to provide his own worker's compensation coverage, and (5) had signed a written agreement with Lee which acknowledged his status as an "independent contractor." Lee, in accordance with the agreement, paid Heard for his services each day in cash an amount equal to 10 percent of the total charges for the pizzas delivered.

The evidence emphasized by Toyota demonstrated that Heard (1) was requested by Lee to work between 5:00 P.M. and 9:00 P.M. each day, (2) delivered pizzas at the times and to the customers and in the quantities as directed by Lee, (4) collected the money indicated on the customer's bill prepared by Lee and returned it (with any "shortages" to be deducted from the commission), and (5) could be terminated by Lee at any time "For Any Reason Whatsoever" upon 24 hours written notice to him.

The most significant factor in determining whether the status of a person performing services for another is an employee or an independent contractor is the right to control the manner and means of accomplishing the result, that is, the details of the work. "If the employer has the authority to exercise complete control, whether or not that right is exercised with respect to all details, an employer–employee relationship exists". . . . Other factors are also to be considered. They, including the issue of employer control, are set forth in *Restatement (Second) of Agency* Section 220, as follows:

1) A servant is a person employed to perform services in the affairs of another and who with respect to the physical conduct in the performance of the services is subject to the other's control or right to control.

2) In determining whether one acting for another is a servant or an independent contractor, the following matters of fact, among others, are considered:
   a) the extent of control which, by the agreement, the master may exercise over the details of the work;
   b) whether or not the one employed is engaged in a distinct occupation or business;
   c) the kind of occupation, with reference to whether, in the locality, the work is usually done under the direction of the employer or by a specialist without supervision;
   d) the skill required in the particular occupation;
   e) whether the employer or the workman supplies the instrumentalities, tools, and the place of work for the person doing the work;
   f) the length of time for which the person is employed;
   g) the method of payment, whether by the time or by the job;
   h) whether or not the work is a part of the regular business of the employer;
   i) whether or not the parties believe they are creating the relation of master and servant; and
   j) whether the principal is or is not in 'business' . . .

However, the cases which have recognized the Restatement's multiple factor enumeration have emphasized that employer control is clearly the most important and the others merely constitute 'secondary elements'. . . . Moreover, it is not the control actually exercised, but that which may be exercised which is determinative. . . .

"One of the means of ascertaining whether or not this right to control exists is the determination of whether or not, if instructions were given, they would have to be obeyed." . . . The real test has been said to be "whether the employee was subject to the employer's orders and control and was liable to be discharged for disobedience or misconduct; and the fact that a certain amount of freedom of action is inherent in the nature of the work does not change the character of the employment where the employer has general supervision and control over it." . . . "Perhaps no single circumstance is more conclusive to show the relationship of an employee than the right of the employer to end the service whenever he sees fit to do so.". . .

Indeed, the unlimited right to discharge at will and without cause has been stressed by a number of cases as a strong factor demonstrating employment. . . .

In light of such rules, it appears to us that the undisputed evidence in this case may be characterized very simply. Lee hired Heard to deliver pizzas to Lee's customers and directed and controlled: (1) the number, nature, and type of pizzas to be delivered; (2) the time when such deliveries would take place; (3) the persons and locations to whom they would be delivered, and (4) the price to be charged for each pizza and the total amount of money to be collected from each customer. In short, Lee determined what would be delivered, when and to whom, and what price would be charged. What portion of Heard's work was left to his discretion and not subject to Lee's control? Did it include anything more than the route Heard would take to a customer's home or how fast he would drive? Such factors generally have been considered to be simply a freedom inherent in the nature of the work and not determinative of the employment relation. . . . Moreover, it is at least arguable that Lee had the right to control this aspect of Heard's work as well. It would be Lee's obvious purpose and desire, and thus clearly part of Heard's responsibility, to get the fresh, warm pizza to the customer as soon as possible. Indeed, it will doubtless be argued at trial that Heard's preoccupation with the necessity of prompt delivery contributed in some manner to the accident which allegedly caused plaintiff's injuries.

Essentially, the only evidence offered in support of the claim that Heard was an independent contractor was that he provided his own car, expenses and insurance. . . . He was subject to Lee's total control as to all aspects of his job. . . . When Heard reported to work, how long he worked, when he made deliveries, and to whom and for what purpose were all dictated and controlled by Lee. Heard was at no risk whatever with respect to Lee's business or any of the pizza sales which were the subject of Heard's delivery services (except that his commission was subject to a charge for any "shortages"). His only responsibility was to deliver, collect the money, and return. Finally, Lee retained the express contractual right to terminate the relationship at any time and without cause.

The remaining factors relied upon by Lee are entirely self-serving or equivocal and are of little or no value on the issue. The fact that Heard was paid on a commission basis is equally consistent with employee status. The agreement characterizing the relationship as one of "client–independent contractor" will be ignored if the parties, by their actual conduct, act like "employer–employee". . . . Indeed, the attempts to conceal employment by formal documents purporting to create other relationships have led the courts to disregard such terms whenever the acts and declarations of the parties are inconsistent therewith. . . .

Finally, the requirements that Heard pay his own payroll and income taxes and provide his own worker's compensation insurance are of no help whatever to Lee. These are merely the legal consequences of an independent contractor status, not a means of proving it. An employer cannot change the status of an employee to one of independent contractor by legally requiring him to assume burdens which the law imposes directly on the employer. . . .

## Judgment and Result

The trial court judgment was modified. The Court of Appeals told the trial court to reexamine whether Lee's settlement with plaintiff was in good faith. This rehearing was necessary because the trial court had incorrectly decided that the pizza delivery boy (Heard) was an independent contractor and not a servant or agent. The Court of Appeals held the delivery boy was an agent or servant, not an independent contractor.

## Questions

1. Why would Lee want his pizza delivery people to be independent contractors instead of agents or servants?
2. Who pays both the employer's and employee's Social Security taxes if the employee is an independent contractor? Is this a reason employers want employees to be independent contractors?
3. Who is liable for an independent contractor's torts committed on the job?

The *Toyota* case shows us the general rule that employers are liable for acts of agents or servants within the scope of their employment. It also listed the tests courts follow to determine if a worker is an independent contractor. Even if a worker is found to be an independent contractor, there are times when courts will STILL hold the employer liable for the independent contractor's acts. This happens when the nondelegable duty doctrine applies. This occurs when the work is inherently dangerous or involves a duty imposed by statute, contract, franchise, charter, or common law. *Pusey v. Bator* provides an example.

## Pusey v. Bator
Supreme Court of Ohio
762 N.E.2d 968 (2002)

## Background and Facts

In April 1987, Wilson, on behalf of Greif Brothers, entered into a contract with Youngstown Security Patrol, Inc. (YSP) to supply a uniformed security guard to "deter theft and vandalism" on Greif Brothers' property during specified hours. Wilson told YSP's owner and president, Carl Testa, that he wanted the security guard to periodically check the parking lot and the inside of the building. Other than those instructions, Wilson did not instruct Testa in the manner that YSP was to protect Greif Brothers' property.

The written security agreement did not specify whether the guard was to be armed or unarmed, and Wilson and Testa both later testified that they never discussed the subject. At least some of the YSP security guards assigned to watch Greif Brothers carried firearms.

On June 30, 1991, Testa hired Eric Bator as a YSP guard. Notes on Bator's application indicate that Bator was hired as an unarmed guard but that he would take the necessary training by the state to become certified as an armed guard. Nevertheless, because he felt uneasy performing his security guard duties without a weapon, Bator took his gun, in a briefcase, to work with him. Bator testified that his supervisor knew Bator carried a gun and that he was unlicensed to work as an armed guard. The supervisor denied this.

Bator was the guard assigned to Greif Brothers' property from 11 P.M., August 11, to 7 A.M., August 12, 1991. At approximately 1 A.M., Bator looked out a window in the guard office and saw two persons, Derrell Pusey and Charles Thomas, walking through Greif Brothers' parking lot. Bator used the radio in the office to inform a YSP guard on duty at another location that two people were on Greif Brothers' property.

Bator, without his gun, walked out of the building but remained on the porch outside the office door. When Bator stepped out from the doorway, the men stopped walking and looked toward him. Both men had their hands behind their backs. Bator estimated that he was 20 feet from the men. Bator twice asked the men if he could help them; neither man responded but instead looked at the other and then back at Bator.

Bator testified that Charles then removed his hands from behind his back, and Bator saw that he was holding a bag. When the bag was in motion, it sounded like metal was hitting together inside it. Bator again asked the men what they wanted. Bator testified Derrell then asked, "Are you open for business?" Bator replied that the business was closed and that he was the night guard. According to Bator, Derrell then became angry and called Bator a "mother ———ker." Derrell's outburst frightened Bator, who quickly stepped into the guard office, retrieved his gun, and returned outside.

Bator testified he held the gun below his waist pointed toward the ground and again asked the men to tell him what they wanted. Derrell swore at Bator again, further frightening him, and Bator raised the gun to be sure they saw it. Bator then ordered them to lie down on the ground with their arms outstretched. Charles complied but Derrell got down on the ground but did not put his arms out as told. Bator told the men he felt safer with them on the ground. Derrell replied, "——ck you," and made a quick movement like he was reaching in his back pocket. Bator thought Derrell was reaching for a weapon, so he fired his gun, hitting Derrell in the back of the head. Bator went inside, radioed for an ambulance and backup support. During this time, Charles tried to leave but was stopped by a YSP supervisor who quickly arrived on the scene.

Derrell died from the wound and his estate filed a wrongful death action against Bator, YSP, and Greif Brothers. YSP and Bator settled with the estate (represented by Ms. Pusey, Derrell's mother) as the jury trial began, leaving only Greif Brothers as a defendant. The trial court found for Greif Brothers. The court of appeals affirmed. Pusey appealed to the Ohio Supreme Court.

## Body of Opinion

**Justice Douglas.** . . . In making its determination that Greif Brothers are not liable for damages resulting from Derrell's death, the trial court first determined that YSP was an independent contractor and not an employee of Greif Brothers. This was an important factor in the court's ultimate decision because, whereas an employer is liable for the negligent acts of its employees committed within the scope of employment, an employer of an independent contractor generally is not liable for the negligent acts of the independent contractor. . . .

"The chief test in determining whether one is an employee or an independent contractor is the right to control the manner or means of performing the work." . . . If such right is in the employer, the relationship is that of employer and employee; but if the manner or means of performing the work is left to one responsible to the employer for the result alone, an independent contractor relationship is created. . . .

We find that, even when viewed in the light most favorable to Pusey, the evidence clearly established YSP's status as an independent contractor. Greif Brothers specified the result . . . deter vandals . . . but the details . . . were left to YSP. . . .

As stated previously, an employer is generally not liable for the negligent acts of an independent contractor. There are, however, exceptions to this general rule, several of which stem from the nondelegable duty doctrine. Nondelegable duties arise in various situations that generally fall into two categories: (1) affirmative duties that are imposed on the employer by statute, contract, franchise, charter, or common law and (2) duties imposed on the employer that arise out of the work itself because its performance creates dangers to others, i.e., inherently dangerous work. . . . If the work to be performed fits into one of these two categories, the employer may delegate the *work* to an independent contractor, but he cannot delegate the *duty*. In other words, the employer is not insulated from liability if the independent contractor's negligence results in a breach of duty.

Pusey claims that hiring armed guards to protect property creates a nondelegable duty because the work is inherently dangerous. . . .

Work is inherently dangerous when it creates a peculiar risk of harm to others unless special precautions are taken. . . .

To fall within the inherently dangerous exception, it is not necessary that the work be such that it cannot be done without the risk of harm to others, or even that it be such that it involves a high risk of such harm. It is sufficient that the work involves a risk, recognizable in advance, of physical harm to others, which is inherent in the work itself. . . .

The exception does not apply, however, where the employer would reasonably have only a general anticipation of the possibility that the contractor may be negligent in some way and thereby cause harm to a third party. For example, one who hires a trucker to transport his goods should realize that if the truck is driven at an excessive speed, or with defective brakes, some harm to persons on the highway is likely to occur. An employer of an independent contractor may assume that a careful contractor will take routine precautions against all of the ordinary and customary dangers that may arise in the course of the contemplated work. . . .

We find that work such as YSP was hired to perform does create a peculiar risk of harm to others. . . .

## Judgment and Result

For plaintiff Pusey. The case was remanded to the trial court to see if, in fact, Derrell's death resulted from YSP's negligence.

## Questions

1. Was YSP, the security firm providing the guards, Greif's employee or an independent contractor?
2. Under what circumstances is it possible for an employer of an independent contractor to be liable for the independent contractor's on-the-job negligence?
3. Following 9/11, security takes on added significance. In that regard, does *Pusey v. Bator* indicate that employers of security firms will incur more or less liability for their security guards?

## HOW AGENCY AUTHORITY IS CREATED

Employees can obtain authority to do their work in at least four ways: express authority, implied authority, apparent authority, and ratification.[2] Each is discussed in detail in the following paragraphs. The points to watch for are the formalities necessary to create the authority, when the authority is created, and how and when the authority ends.

### EXPRESS AUTHORITY

**Express authority** is created when the employer (or principal or master) orally or in writing tells the employee (or agent, servant, independent contractor) to do something. Most agency situations have no formal requirements (writings or documents of appointment) for conferring express authority. An exception occurs in the case of real estate agents whose appointments as agents must be evidenced by a writing in many states. A rationale for the writing requirement in this case is that the transaction that a realtor enters on the principal's behalf (sale of realty) must be evidenced by a signed writing, as should the agency contract, because it is also of great legal significance. However, in many other situations in which the contract the agent enters with the third person on the principal's behalf is just as significant, the underlying agency contract does not have to be evidenced by a signed writing to satisfy most states' statute of frauds.[3] No writing is required to establish the principal–agent relationship.

As a matter of good business practice, the principal and agent (or master and servant, or employer and independent contractor) will want to have the terms of their employment relation spelled out in as much detail as possible to provide for contingencies. **Powers of attorney** refer to a particular kind of express authority that can be created only in writing. A person who is not a licensed attorney but who acts for another under a document called a power or letter of attorney is legally an **attorney in fact**, not an **attorney at law**. (The latter is the licensed professional attorney most people refer to as a lawyer.) Powers of attorney usually apply only with respect to future—not past—matters.

### IMPLIED AUTHORITY

An agent or servant receives **implied authority** by reasonable inference from the express authority, by conduct of the principal and agent, and by circumstances creating an emergency or necessity that the agent (servant) have such authority. What the principal and agent (or servant) do with respect to each other—not with respect to third persons—is a factor that, in many cases, decides whether the agent (or servant) has implied authority. Mere assumptions by a third person that an agent has implied authority to do something will not give implied authority to an agent (or servant). Without a special statute, mere relationships such as husband

---

[2] A few jurisdictions also recognize inherent authority, which is such power an agent or servant has by virtue of the agency itself. This authority exists to protect people harmed by a servant or agent claiming to have authority.

[3] Equal dignity statutes exist in most states, however, and do require the contract between the agent and the principal to be written if the statute of frauds requires the contract the agent enters on the principal's behalf be written.

and wife, father and son, mother and daughter do not create implied authority to act as an agent or servant for the other party.

An example of implied authority's arising from express authority would be a principal's telling an agent to hire a secretary for the office. The principal's direction to the agent to hire a secretary is express authority. Implied authority, reasonably flowing from such express authority, would probably include the authority to offer a reasonable salary to a promising applicant. Implied authority would not allow the agent to hire two secretaries or promise a car to an applicant to induce acceptance. Neither act is implied from the express authority because it goes beyond what a reasonable person would infer is necessary to accomplish the express authority.

Implied authority arising from emergency or necessity occurs where an unexpected contingency creates a situation in which the agent is unable to contact the principal, and the principal has given no express instructions to the agent on how to handle the matter. The unexpected contingency must be an emergency requiring immediate attention to protect property or person.

## Apparent Authority

**Apparent authority** is authority an agent may acquire by words or conduct of the principal that leads a third person to believe that the agent has authority. The entire agency may be created by apparent authority. Also, agents with express authority may have their agency powers increased by apparent authority. The appearance must come from some act—or omission where the principal had a duty to act—of the principal and not of the agent.

For example, assume an employee has no express or implied authority to sell. If the boss watches the employee make a sale in front of a customer, the boss's failure to stop the employee creates the appearance (to the customer) that the employee has authority to sell. The *Northington* case illustrates an alarming apparent authority problem.

---

### Northington v. Dairyland Ins. Co.
Supreme Court of Alabama
445 So.2d 283 (1984)

#### Background and Facts

Appellant, Eunice Northington, appeals from the trial court's summary judgment in favor of Dairyland Insurance Company, Inc. in an action alleging breach of contract and fraud. We affirm.

In September 1981, Ms. Northington went to Mr. Leonard Wills and discussed the possibility of obtaining insurance for her automobile. Mr. Wills, who owns and operates Wills Realty and Insurance Company, Inc., is an independent insurance agent for various companies, including Dairyland, and is an insurance broker for other companies. On November 30, 1981, Ms. Northington gave Mr. Wills a cash payment of $80, and Mr. Wills advised her that she had full automobile insurance coverage on her automobile as of that date. Ms. Northington did not fill out an application for insurance or sign any other form at that time or at any subsequent time in connection with her insurance coverage.

Ms. Northington attempted to contact Mr. Wills subsequently to discuss the fact that she had never received her insurance policy papers. On the few occasions when she reached Mr. Wills, he maintained to Ms. Northington that she had full insurance coverage, but did not inform her of the particular insurance company through which she was allegedly insured.

On December 16, 1981, Ms. Northington was involved in a one-vehicle automobile accident. She made a claim to Mr. Wills for coverage of the damages under her alleged insurance policy. Mr. Wills advised her to get two estimates on the damage and not to worry.

In January 1982, following the accident, Mr. Wills informed Ms. Northington that she had insurance with Dairyland Insurance Company, Inc., and that this insurance would cover the damage to her automobile. In February 1982, Mr. Wills accepted a further payment of $37.55 from Ms. Northington to be applied to the cost of her insurance.

In fact, Mr. Wills never made application to Dairyland for insurance on Ms. Northington's behalf. Nor did Mr. Wills forward the premium payments from Ms. Northington or any notice of loss from the accident to Dairyland.

On April 8, 1982, Ms. Northington filed a complaint against Leonard Wills, Wills Realty and Insurance Company, Inc., and Dairyland Insurance Company. She alleged breach of contract and fraud against the defendants.

On January 27, 1983, Dairyland filed a motion for summary judgment. As grounds for the motion, Dairyland asserted that there was no material dispute as to the facts and that at no time did Dairyland write a policy of insurance for Ms. Northington, that at no time was Ms. Northington, prior to her accident, informed that she had a policy of insurance with Dairyland, and that the actions of Dairyland's agent, Mr. Wills, exceeded the scope of his authority.

The trial court granted Dairyland's motion for summary judgment. Ms. Northington appeals, alleging that the trial court erred in finding that there was no genuine issue of material fact as to Dairyland's liability. Her basic argument is that Dairyland is bound by the representations that she was fully insured made by Mr. Wills acting under apparent authority as a general agent for Dairyland. We do not agree.

## Body of Opinion

**Justice Faulkner.** First, it is clear that Mr. Wills could not be considered an actual agent of Dairyland in his transactions with Ms. Northington, since he exceeded the scope of his actual authority as defined in the agency agreement existing between him and Dairyland. That agreement stated, in part:

(1) Pursuant to request that the underwriting facilities of the Company be made available to the Agent, the Company hereby grants authority to the Agent to solicit proposals for insurance for such classes or risks as the Company from time to time may authorize to be solicited, and to collect, receive and receipt for premiums of insurance tendered by the Agent to and accepted by the Company subject, however, to restrictions placed upon such Agent by the laws of the state or states in which such Agent is authorized to write insurance business and to the terms and conditions hereinafter stated; provided, however, that the acceptance by the Agent of any premiums or the giving of a receipt therefor shall in no wise obligate the Company other than in accordance with the written instructions of the Company.

Agents shall have authority to bind insurance for classifications of risks and types of vehicles that are normally written by the Company. When a signed application is submitted, with a premium deposit of at least two months' premium, coverage is bound as of the time and date the application is signed by both the applicant and agent. All bound business must be submitted with cash and must be promptly forwarded to a Dairyland office.

Since Mr. Wills willfully breached the agency agreement by failing to follow the above procedures in securing insurance for Ms. Northington, he cannot be considered an actual agent so as to bind Dairyland in this case. . . .

Ms. Northington, nevertheless, asserts that Dairyland is liable for Mr. Wills's representations under the doctrine of apparent authority and estoppel.

In *Roberts & Sons v. Williams*, . . . this court said:

Where the evidence shows that the actor has been held out by the alleged principal, as being his agent or as possessing the authority assumed by such agent within the scope of the principal's business, the doctrine of apparent authority can be invoked by one who has been misled to his detriment. . . .

The following was written in *Automotive Acceptance Corporation v. Powell*:

The doctrine of apparent authority does not rest upon what one thinks an agent's authority may be, or what the agent holds out his authority to be; rather, the doctrine of apparent authority is based on the principal's holding the agent out to a third person as having the authority under which he acts. The following statement on the doctrine of apparent authority is found in Am.Jur.2d, Agency, Sec. 74, p. 476:

'The apparent power of an agent is to be determined by the acts of the principal, and not by the acts of the agent; a principal is responsible for the acts of an agent within his apparent authority only where the principal by his acts or conduct has clothed the agent with the appearance of authority, and not where the agent's own conduct and statements have created the apparent authority.'

'Apparent authority' is such as a principal knowingly permits an agent to assume or holds him out as possessing. It seems to be generally held that an agent's authority must be based upon the conduct of the principal and not of the agent.

These statements indicate that in order for a principal to be held liable under the doctrine of apparent authority and estoppel, the principal must have engaged in some conduct which led a third party to believe that the agent had authority to act for the principal. Reviewing the record, we find no evidence whatsoever that Dairyland indicated to Ms. Northington or led her to believe that Mr. Wills had authority to act for the company in the manner in which he acted. No one, other than Mr. Wills, made any representations to Ms. Northington or engaged in any conduct on behalf of Dairyland in this case. Since an agent's apparent authority must be based on conduct of the principal and not of the agent, and Dairyland engaged in no conduct which gave the impression of Wills's authority, we hold that Dairyland is not liable for Wills's representations.

## Judgment and Result

As indicated above, Mr. Wills was not an agent for Dairyland in his transactions with Ms. Northington; he, therefore, had no authority to bind Dairyland by his representations. Accordingly, there was no genuine issue of material fact against Dairyland. Dairyland, therefore, was entitled to summary judgment. Affirmed.

## Questions

1. Does apparent authority come from acts or omissions of the principal, which lead third persons to believe the agent had authority?
2. Why was Dairyland Insurance Co., the putative principal, not liable for failing to tell Ms. Northington that Mr. Wills was not its agent?
3. Does this case help explain why insurers have insureds send premiums directly to the company (the insurer) instead of paying the agent directly?

## RATIFICATION

An employer (or principal or master) may confer authority retroactively on a person for an act already done. This practice is known as ratification. **Ratification** is the acceptance by one of all benefits and burdens of an act done on one's behalf by another person who, at the time the acts were performed, had no authority to act for the ratifier. A simple example of ratification occurs when X, a customer, walks into S's furniture store and, without S's authority, sells a chair to C, another customer, for $20 more than list price. If S soon learns of this sale and then approves of its terms (and, presumably, collects the purchase price from X), S is said to have ratified X's act of selling the chair.

The six requirements for ratification are as follows:

1. One person without any authority or exceeding his or her authority purports to act for another.
2. The person for whom the acts were done was legally able to do those acts, both at the time they were done and when they were ratified. In other words, the acts themselves were legal and not crimes, and the principal was not insane or drunk at the time of ratification.
3. The person for whom the acts were done has full knowledge of all material circumstances of the acts done on his or her behalf when ratification occurs.
4. The ratification occurs while the third person is a party to that contract; if the third person disclaims the contract before ratification, the principal will not be able to ratify.
5. Ratification is of the entire transaction done on the principal's behalf.
6. The person for whom the unauthorized act was done (the alleged principal), not the person who actually did the act, is the ratifying party.

## COMMON LAW DUTIES THAT MASTERS OWE SERVANTS

*Masters*—employers of those who are legally termed *servants*—owe their employees several duties that arise automatically between the master and servant, even without an express contract. One is the duty to provide a safe place to work, not necessarily a risk-free place to work but merely a relatively safe place. This duty attaches when employees are actually or constructively doing their jobs. Masters' common law duty to provide a relatively safe work place for employees applies, irrespective of how many or how few servants masters have working for them.

Remember this point when the discussion turns to state workers' compensation statutes for servants and agents, because many of these laws do not cover employers with fewer than a certain number of employees.

Masters generally have a duty to provide employees with tools with which to perform their work. The employers' common law duty extends to providing employees with safe tools as well. The master and servant might agree that the servant will provide the tools. If so, courts could rely on this factor in holding that the relationship is actually employer–independent contractor rather than master–servant. It could, in turn, mean that the independent contractor (the employee) is the only one liable for torts committed on the job—a favorable conclusion from the employer's standpoint and an unfavorable result from the employee's view.

The courts have generally imposed a duty on masters to pay their servants the reasonable value of their services, even if no specific mention is made of payment, providing the servant's services are of a type for which compensation is usually paid and inferring that compensation expected is reasonable under the circumstances.

## COMMON LAW DUTIES THAT PRINCIPALS OWE AGENTS

In a gratuitous agency the agent agrees to work for nothing. Most agencies, however, are designed to pay the agent. Usually an agency contract—either written or oral—exists that will either specifically state an amount of pay for the entire period of the agency, provide a rate of pay if the agency has no definite term, or note conditions (such as production of a ready, able, and willing buyer for realty at the seller's asking price) on the contract.

If by chance the principal and agent neglect to mention the matter of the agent's pay, courts will examine the circumstances of the agency—matters such as the reasonable expectations of the parties, whether agencies of the sort at hand generally involve pay—to decide whether to infer a duty to pay the agent, and in what amount.

The failure to mention the agent's pay does not necessarily mean that the agent is not entitled to pay. Put another way, if nothing is said about paying the agent, the agency is not necessarily gratuitous. Also, if a person acts on another's behalf without authorization and that person ratifies the purported agent's acts, the agent is entitled to be paid. The duty to pay the agent, when such a duty is present, usually rests on the principal.

If an agent has a right to compensation, a number of actions can deprive the agent of this right:

- The agent violates the fiduciary duty owed to the principal.
- The agent fails to fulfill the conditions required of him or her by the agency contract.
- The terms of an agency contract are known to be illegal (such as a violation of the federal antitrust laws).
- The agent waives—voluntarily gives up—the right to pay.
- The agent materially fails to follow instructions.
- The agent commits **fraud** or **conversion** against the principal.

If the agent is careless in performing agency duties, thereby injuring the principal, the agent does not totally lose the right to be paid. Rather, the agent's compensation is reduced by the damage to the principal.

An **advance** is money an agent may obtain before making a sale. Although agents have no automatic right to advances, the agency contract can provide for them. A surprising number of cases allow an agent to keep all advances, even though sales commissions equal to advances were not made. An agent who represents both parties to a transaction is not entitled to be paid by either unless both parties are aware of the **dual agency** and approve of it.

Other common law obligations that a principal owes an agent are a **duty to reimburse** the agent for ordinary and necessary expenses incurred while performing agency duties. If an agent receives a fine or penalty for violation of the law in performing agency duties, the principal would not have to reimburse the agent for the violation, because it would not be ordinary and necessary to perform the agency duties. Except under exceptional circumstances, such as an emergency, the principal has no duty to reimburse the agent for expenses incurred resulting from a violation of the principal's instructions.

The principal owes agents a **duty to indemnify** them for losses sustained and for liabilities they incur in performance of agency duties. This obligation applies only if the agent is not breaching a duty to the principal. For example, if the agent fails to use proper care and injures a third person, the principal has no duty to indemnify the agent for the liability to the injured person.

As with masters and servants, the principals owe agents a duty of care. That duty of care is based on common law negligence principles. The elements of negligence are duty, breach of the standard of care, proximate cause, and damages. Defenses to negligence include contributory negligence, assumption of risk, the statute of limitations, and lack of an element of the definition of negligence, such as no duty.

## COMMON LAW DUTIES THAT AGENTS OWE PRINCIPALS

Agents owe their principals a number of duties. Such obligations include the duty to use care and skill in performing for the principal, the duty to be faithful to the principal in performing agency functions and not self-deal (the fiduciary duty), and the duty to follow instructions. These duties arise automatically by establishment of the agency relation.

### DUTY TO ACCOUNT

The agent's duty to account arises either when the principal turns property over to the agent for use in performing agency duties or when a third person turns property over to the agent on the principal's behalf. The agent must not only account to the principal whenever the principal demands it, but the accounting must also be accurate. The agent has a duty to turn over property of the principal in the agent's possession when the principal demands it. If the agent refuses, the agent is liable to the principal for conversion. What satisfies the agent's duty to account? In one case, the agent's preparation of an income tax return covering the principal's business that the agent managed was said to satisfy the agent's duty to account.

## DUTY TO USE CARE AND SKILL

The duty to use care and skill in performing the principal's work is usually satisfied by using the standard of ordinary care in the occupation at hand. However, if the principal's project fails, the agent is not necessarily liable for failing to fulfill the duty and care or skill, because this duty does not make an agent an insurer. An agent can be an insurer of the principal's enterprise, although such an obligation will not be imposed under general agency law. The level of care and skill for gratuitous agents is often lower than that for compensated agents. Gratuitous agents are, however, liable for gross negligence and negligence in performing their agency duties.

Today's highly competitive business environment creates pressures on principals to keep agents' salaries low. Often, this pressure means that employers "churn" their employees so that they cannot develop seniority and make high incomes associated with seniority. In such environments, employees may be performing satisfactorily and yet be fired to keep costs down. How can this practice happen legally? If the level of skill and care that an employee must demonstrate is subjective, that is, dependent on what a particular employer says is appropriate, then the employee can, in effect, be fired anytime: the employer can simply make impossible demands on the employee, such as increase the employee's workload or assign ridiculous things, and when the employee makes an error, as is likely to happen when employee is overworked, or refuses the ridiculous request, the employer can, with a straight face, tell the employee that he or she is "not meeting standards." In answer to this problem, at least one court has applied an objective "reasonable person standard" to judge whether an agent is performing his or her job satisfactorily.

## DUTY TO FOLLOW INSTRUCTIONS

The agent has a duty to follow the principal's instructions. It has been said that this duty is not limited to reasonable instructions, but if the principal were to ask the agent to kiss every client who enters a contract with the agent on the principal's behalf, the agent would not have to perform. A kiss under such circumstances would probably amount to the tort of battery—a civil wrong. Agents have no duty to follow instructions if doing so constitutes a tort or crime. If an agent fails to follow the principal's legal instructions, the agent is liable for damages resulting from such breach of duty.

## FIDUCIARY DUTY

The most prominent of the agent's responsibilities to the principal is the fiduciary duty. A fiduciary is one who owes great faith, loyalty, and accountability to another. Some courts have included many of the agent's duties to the principal, such as the duty to account and the duty to follow instructions, under the umbrella term *fiduciary duty*. Here, **fiduciary duty** is given a more limited scope, covering the agent's duty to act for only one principal, the duty not to profit at the principal's expense, the duty to communicate to the principal information relevant to the agency, and the duty not to act adversely to the principal's interests. If the agent violates the fiduciary duty, the principal may recover damages or obtain appropriate equitable relief. The fiduciary duty exists even in the case of gratuitous agents.

Some aspects of an agent's fiduciary duty extend beyond the time the agent ends the agency. For example, the agent's duty not to disclose trade secrets continues after an agent ceases employment for the principal who owns those secrets. This duty does not last interminably, but reasonable time and geographic parameters are read into it.

Of the duties agents owe principals, probably the one most involving ethics is the fiduciary duty. *American Express Financial Advisors, Inc. v. Topel* illustrates problems that can arise in this area.

---

# American Express Financial Advisors, Inc. v. Topel
U.S. District Court (D. Colorado)
38 F.Supp.2d 1233 (1999)

## Background and Facts

For five years, Mr. Topel worked as a financial planner for American Express (AMEX) pursuant to a written contract with AMEX. Mr. Topel received copies of both his Planner Agreement and separate documents setting forth certain key terms of this contract prior to starting work as an agent for AMEX. Mr. Topel signed the Planner Agreement as a condition of his affiliation with AMEX. Pursuant to the Planner Agreement, Mr. Topel received training and what AMEX characterizes as confidential trade secret information, comprised of customer identities, addresses, financial holdings, investment objectives, and buying preferences.

The Planner Agreement, which Mr. Topel now seeks to avoid, prohibits him for a period of one year after resigning from AMEX, from soliciting or selling investments and financial services, directly or indirectly, to those AMEX customers in the territory he served or learned about through AMEX.

According to AMEX, after Mr. Topel tendered his resignation in late May 1997, it learned that he was violating the terms of his Planner Agreement and was actively soliciting and diverting the AMEX customers he serviced on its behalf. AMEX brought an action against Topel for, among other things, breach of his fiduciary duty to AMEX.

## Body of Opinion

**Judge Babcock.** Colorado law provides that "unless otherwise agreed, an agent is subject to a duty to his principal to act solely for the benefit of the principal in all matters connected with the agency." . . . While an agent is entitled to make some preparations to compete with his principal after the termination of their relationship, an agent violates his duty of loyalty if he engages in pre-termination solicitation of customers for a new competing business. (See *Koontz v. Rosener* . . . by working to set up a competing business while still engaged by plaintiff, defendants violated their duty of

loyalty); (see also *Community Counselling Serv., Inc. v. Reilly* . . . during period of employment, employee cannot solicit for himself future business which his employer requires him to solicit for his employer).

As the undisputed facts make clear, Mr. Topel solicited customers for his new venture while he was still affiliated with AMEX. . . . In some instances, there is evidence that Mr. Topel ignored his AMEX customers' requests to keep their investments with AMEX. . . . He also sent correspondence to his AMEX customers to solicit them for his new venture while he was still employed by AMEX and, in at least one instance, on an AMEX letterhead. . . . There is no genuine issue regarding whether Mr. Topel's activities violated his fiduciary duty of loyalty to AMEX. Therefore, AMEX is entitled to summary judgment on this claim.

## Judgment and Result

The financial planner breached his fiduciary duty toward the corporation, his former employer.

## Questions

1. How would you define *fiduciary duty*? What instances of violation of this duty were present in the *Topel* case?
2. Is the fiduciary duty owed by the agent to the principal? By the principal to the agent? Why or why not?
3. Is the fiduciary duty owed by servants to masters? By masters to servants? Why or why not?
4. What ethics mentioned in the first chapter are implicit in the fiduciary duty? Can you think of any way in which the fiduciary duty could be improved—that is, made more fair to both employees as well as employers?
5. Does the court acknowledge times when agents may do things that might not be entirely to the principal's benefit, even though the employee is drawing a paycheck from the principal?

## COMMON LAW DUTIES THAT SERVANTS OWE MASTERS

Generally, servants owe masters the same duties that agents owe principals. They owe masters a fiduciary duty, a duty to follow legal instructions, a duty to use ordinary care and skill in performance of servant duties, and a duty to communicate information to a master. The scope of the servant's duties is considerably narrower than an agent's because the servant, by definition, is one who may not enter contracts with third persons on the master's behalf. The last remark can easily mislead one into a false sense of certainty because determining who is a servant and who is an agent is often difficult, particularly when one realizes that courts have held that a person may be an agent with respect to one part of a job, a servant with respect to another part of a job, and an independent contractor with respect to yet another part of the same job.

## AGENT OR SERVANT LIABILITY THIRD PERSONS: TORTS

An agent or servant is liable for torts committed against anyone, regardless of whether the tort is committed within or beyond the scope of the agency. For example, if an agent commits fraud to induce a third person to enter a contract with the agent's principal, the agent would be liable for the fraud. This liability stands even if the principal ratified the contract by retaining the benefits of the agent's fraud. However, the tort victim may *not* obtain a double recovery (once from the agent and once from the principal). If the third person recovers once from the agent or servant, the third person is entitled to no further recovery against the principal.

The agent or servant would be entitled to be **indemnified** by the principal if the determination were made that the agent broke no duty owed to the principal at the time the agent was subjected to liability. The agent or servant would have no right of indemnity against the principal if the agent was not following instructions, was outside the scope of his or her authority during commission of the torts, or violated any of the duties owed the principal at the time the tort was committed.

The respondeat superior principle is the basis for subjecting one person to legal liability for the acts or omissions of another; that is, one person (principal or master) who does not personally commit a tort or enter a contract is held or sought to be held for a tort committed by another or a contract entered by another on that person's behalf. According to this doctrine, principals or masters are legally answerable for the acts or omissions of their servants or agents *within the scope of their employment*. The respondeat superior principle applies to both master–servant and principal–agent relationships. Recall, however, that the servant's express and implied authority is more limited than the agent's, because the servant has no authority to enter contracts on the master's behalf, while the agent does.

The **scope of employment** notion subjects a master or principal to liability for job-related acts or omissions of servants and agents. It is synonymous with authority concepts (express authority, implied authority, apparent authority, and ratification) introduced earlier, in that these authority bases set the employee's job parameters and, in so doing, establish the extent of the employer's liability for the employees.

The problem of determining where an agent's responsibilities end—the extent of the scope of employment—and where an agent's duty begins is difficult to ascertain in general terms. Consider the following. If a servant hired to deliver packages negligently drives too fast for road conditions and injures a third person, why should the master be liable? After all, the servant was hired to deliver packages, not to drive negligently into third persons. In other words, masters and principals could, and do, argue that the servant's or agent's committing a tort while performing duties in and of itself removes the act from within the scope of the agency. However, courts do not accept this categorical argument, because doing so would insulate masters and servants from liability in every tort situation. Yet, it must still be determined when a tort is within the scope of employment so as to subject the principal to vicarious liability. Generally, a case-by-case determination is necessary.

## AGENT LIABILITY TO THIRD PERSONS: CONTRACTS

Agents may be subjected to liability to third persons with respect to contracts in three ways: on the contract, for the tort of fraud, or for **breach of warranty of authority**. All three legal theories will not be available in any single suit, although they would all likely be pleaded. Then, as the evidence develops to support one but not the others, some would be dropped.

A number of contract situations exist in which an agent will be held contractually liable to a third person. An agent for a **nonexistent principal** is liable on the contract to third persons who deal with the agent. The two most common nonexistent principal situations are a corporate promoter making contracts for a corporate principal that has not yet been legally organized and an agent entering a contract for an organization that is formed but is not a legal entity (an unincorporated fraternity, for example).

If an agent enters a contract with a third person on the principal's behalf and the agent acts within his or her authority, discloses the fact of agency and the principal's identity to the third person, and properly executes the contract, the principal and not the agent will be bound to the contract. The principal, and not the agent, will have the right to sue to enforce the contract that the agent entered on the disclosed principal's behalf.

Several situations exist, however, in which an agent may be liable to the third person when the agent enters a contract on behalf of the existing principal. On the mechanical side, the agent may improperly execute the contract. This problem generally involves a written contract. In such a case, a properly signed contract—one that binds only the principal—will identify the principal by name with the agent's name and the fact of agency disclosed, usually immediately below the principal's name, as in the following example:

ABC Company
by John Johnson, Agent

A contract executed in this way would bind ABC Company and not John Johnson, even though Johnson signed the contract. The reason Johnson is not bound, assuming no special facts such as nonexistent principal, is that Johnson signed the contract in a representative capacity.

However, what if John Johnson merely signs his name and nothing else to the contract, even though he intends to bind only his principal? In this **undisclosed principal** situation, the fact of agency and the principal's identity are both undisclosed to the third party. The cases dealing with the matter are not in agreement on whether Johnson should be held personally and exclusively, or whether extrinsic evidence (evidence outside of the contract) should be allowed to show that another person (the principal) is supposed to be bound. Some courts do not allow such evidence and some do.

The third person must elect which party—agent or principal—to subject to liability. Many cases allow the third person to elect to sue an agent and the principal when the principal becomes disclosed. Only one recovery, however, is allowed. Given this fact, the safest course to follow from the agent's position is to sign the principal's name and then the agent's name with an indication of agency. A **partially disclosed principal** exists where agents sign their names and identify themselves as agents but omit the principal's name. Generally, a third person may hold either the agent or the undisclosed (or partially disclosed, if that is the case) principal to the contract.

## LIABILITY FOR CRIMES

### EMPLOYEE LIABILITY

A person who commits a crime is liable for it. It makes no difference whether that person is an agent, employee, servant, or independent contractor when the crime occurs. People are *personally* liable for their crimes.

What if a boss orders employees to commit crimes as part of their work, and the employees obey the boss and are criminally prosecuted? Obedience to a boss's command is not a criminal defense. What if the boss threatens to fire employees who refuse to commit crimes as part of their jobs? For example, a truck dispatcher may set timetables for truckers at levels that are impossible to meet if highway speed limits are obeyed. Threat of job loss is not a criminal defense. Employees sometimes mistakenly believe that their bosses are ordering them to commit crimes, because employees think committing a crime is the only way to do the job. A clever employee might be able to do the job legally. For example, in our truck dispatcher example, the truck driver might have been able to meet timetables by taking a shorter route or by making shorter meal stops.

### EMPLOYER LIABILITY

If an employer personally commits a crime, the employer is criminally liable. Thus, if Mr. H. L. Box, an accountant, cheats on a client's income tax return to reduce the client's taxes, Box is criminally liable, even though he committed the crime to help the client. Presumably, Box also intended to help his own business by committing the crime.

What if, instead of personally filling out a false tax return, Box tells his younger assistant, Jack Zeigler, to cheat on the client's return? Zeigler follows instructions, cheats, and is caught. Both Zeigler and Box are criminally liable. Zeigler, the employee, is liable because he personally committed the crime (following the boss's orders is no defense), and Box is liable based on criminal conspiracy rules.

A **criminal conspiracy** is an agreement with an intent to commit an unlawful act or a lawful act in an unlawful way. Exactly how the intent to commit the unlawful act (or lawful act in an unlawful way) must be shown is not always clear. Often, a substantial act to carry out the illegal act shows the needed intent. In our tax evasion example, Zeigler's falsifying and filing a client's tax return would show intent. Thus, both Box and Zeigler would be liable for a criminal conspiracy to violate the income tax law.

## CORPORATE EMPLOYERS

What about corporate employers' liability for employee crimes? Corporations present special problems, because they are artificial persons who can act only through their employees. Corporate employers are liable for employee crimes on the following occasions: if a court applies the respondeat superior principle or (in many situations) if strict liability criminal statutes exist.

## RESPONDEAT SUPERIOR

The respondeat superior principle also applies to many crimes. Hence, a corporation is criminally liable for its employees' crimes committed on the job to benefit the corporation. For example, a corporate engineer who breaks a law against submitting a false pollution compliance report commits a crime. (The engineer would be criminally liable because the engineer did the act.) The corporate employer would also be liable because the crime was within the scope of the employee's job and was done on the employer's behalf.

The respondeat superior principle makes the corporate employer liable for employee crimes committed *within the scope of the employee's job* and for the employer's benefit. (In other words, the corporate employer is not answerable for employee crimes committed off duty.) Corporate employers are liable under respondeat superior for employee on-duty crimes even if the corporate employer told the employee not to commit the crimes.

*U.S. v. Gibson Products* shows how a corporate employer was held criminally liable for an employee's crimes. The main reason for the respondeat superior in this case was that the employee performed the criminal acts within the scope of the agent's duties, which led the court to apply the respondeat superior doctrine to hold the corporation (but *not* the corporate president) criminally liable.

---

### United States v. Gibson Products Co., Inc.
U.S. District Court Southern District of Texas
426 F.Supp. 768 (1976)

### Background and Facts

Defendant corporation, Gibson Products Company, Inc., in this consolidated action stands charged in 19 counts with knowingly making false entries on ATF Form 4473 in connection with the sale of firearms to foreign citizens. In Cr. No. 76-B-262, the defendant Pedro G. Alvarado was charged in five of said counts as a co-defendant with Gibson Products. Alvarado pled guilty to one count, and the other four counts in the indictment were dismissed as to him, thus removing him from this prosecution. In Cr. No. 76-B-393, this defendant, Gibson Products, was alone charged in the remaining 14 counts. These two consolidated actions were called for trial on November 8, 1976, and, a jury being waived, said actions proceeded to trial before the Court.

### Body of Opinion

**District Judge Cox.** The Court, having heard all of the evidence, finds, beyond a reasonable doubt, that Gibson Products Company, Inc., has operated a department store located in McAllen, Texas, for many years. In January 1969, Gibson Products

Company applied for and was issued a license to be a dealer in firearms, other than destructive devices, or ammunition for other than destructive devices. The application for such license was made by Jack Hanshaw, who was identified as the corporation's president. Pedro G. Alvarado, a long-standing employee, had been placed in charge of the hardware and sporting goods department, and, on said application, was designated as "Sporting Goods Manager." While in such capacity and during the period of time from February 11, 1975, through November 14, 1975, the said Alvarado did manage the department, selling, among other items, guns (long guns and hand guns) and ammunition. There was no evidence to indicate that the designation originally given to Pedro G. Alvarado on the application had been changed and none to indicate that some other employee was in charge of the sporting goods department during the period in which the illegal gun sales were made.

The Court further finds, beyond a reasonable doubt, that Pedro G. Alvarado sold certain hand guns to foreign citizens and made false entries on ATF Forms 4473 in regard to each sale involved in this trial. Fictitious names and other fictitious information was entered on the forms. On a few occasions, Alvarado received a bribe or kick-back from the purchaser in connection with the illegal sales. However, such illegal activity and the receipt of kick-backs by Alvarado did not change his status as department head. Alvarado's actions in selling the aforementioned guns were in the course and scope of his employment, because that was his job. Alvarado deposited the full retail price of every gun sold in the store's cash register.

The Court also finds, beyond a reasonable doubt, that Hanshaw rarely went down on the sales floor. When he did audit the ATF 4473 Forms, he concerned himself only with inventory control of individual guns, not with proper completion of the statutorily required information.

In addition, the Court finds, beyond a reasonable doubt, that, in connection with several of the illegal sales, Alavardo received a benefit individually, either a small money kick-back or "ego satisfaction." However, since Alvarado was not himself knocking down, it goes without saying that all of the sales were also intended to benefit the corporation. It was the purpose of the store, and of Alvarado as manager of the department, to sell merchandise and encourage customers to return to the store. The major beneficiary of the sales was the corporation. Reference to gun sales as a "loss leader" does not change the situation. As the Court understands it, loss-leader merchandise is generally a part of the profit-making plan of a retail sales business. The Court concludes that Hanshaw was derelict in his supervision of the gun sales, especially in view

of the fact that gun sales are strictly regulated by the United States government, and considering the potential for abuse given an unsupervised department.

In determining if the factual situation which existed in this case, as found by the Court beyond a reasonable doubt, constitutes a violation of 18 U.S.C. § 922 (m), it is necessary to review the law applicable here.

Criminal liability for the commission of certain offenses may be imputed to a corporate defendant. . . . Because corporations act only through human agents, the requisite level of intent, here, a "knowing" act, must be imputed to the corporation. This theory, known in civil tort as *respondeat superior*, can be applied to corporate defendants in criminal cases. . . .

The Court must determine whether this corporate defendant, under the facts found by the Court, had the requisite intent, and whether the evidence shows beyond a reasonable doubt that the acts were done deliberately and with knowledge. . . . The circuit courts have required that a finding of intent to benefit the corporation is necessary to hold the corporation criminally liable for illegal acts. The acts must also have been performed in the scope of the agent's duties. . . .

Defendant argues that the corporate president gave specific instructions to Alvarado and to all gun sales personnel, prohibiting them from making false entries on the Form 4473. This argument is no legal persuasion to the Court. . . .

The Court concludes that the evidence, as the Court has found it, beyond a reasonable doubt, establishes that Alvarado acted within the scope of his employment, and with an intent to benefit the corporation, when he made the illegal entries on Form 4473. The Defendant Gibson's Products Company, Inc., is therefore guilty of Counts 1 through 5 in Criminal Action No. 76-B-262 and is guilty of Counts 1 through 14 in Criminal Action No. 76-B-393.

## Judgment and Result

The federal district court held *both* Pedro Alvarado, the employee who committed the crime, *and* Gibson Products Company, Inc., the corporate employer, liable for the crime of falsifying the government form regarding gun sales.

## Questions

1. What reasons did the court give for subjecting the corporate employer to criminal liability for the employee's crimes?
2. Is it possible to imprison a corporate employer held criminally responsible for an employee's on-the-job crimes?

## SOME LIMITS ON CORPORATE CRIMINAL LIABILITY

The **superior agent rule** says that corporations are liable only for crimes of high-level employees (superior agents). This rule limits corporate criminal liability to some extent. It is justified, in part, by the basic fairness of holding corporations liable for crimes committed by employees close enough to the corporate inner circle to say the corporation itself knew. Although this idea has some appeal, strictly speaking, corporations cannot know anything, because they are artificial persons. Also, problems exist in defining how high in the corporate structure employees must be before they can be called superior agents. These and other problems have led some jurisdictions to reject the superior agent rule.

A second limit on corporate criminal liability for employee crimes is the requirement that the crime be within the scope of the employee's job and done for the corporation's benefit. Consider an extreme example. A small, incorporated supermarket has a deliveryman. While delivering groceries to a customer, the deliveryman rapes the customer. Because this crime would be beyond the scope of the employee's job and not for the corporate employer's benefit, the deliveryman's corporate employer would not be criminally liable for the rape. The employee's crime must relate directly to the employee's duties and be intended as part of or incident to the employee's job before the corporate employer will be criminally liable.

## HOW AGENCIES END

An agency relationship may end in many ways. An initial distinction should be made between the power and the right to end an agency relation. An agency relationship is a voluntary, consensual relationship. In addition, courts refuse to enforce personal service contracts because, among other things, they violate the U.S. Constitution's Thirteenth Amendment slavery prohibition; therefore a principal or agent always has the power—not necessarily the right—to end agency arrangements. If an agent or principal ends an agency relationship without the right to do so, the principal or agent breaking the contract will be liable to the other for contract damages and whatever other remedies are appropriate in the situation. Thus, agencies may end at any time by either the principal's or agent's decision to end the arrangement.

Probably the usual way agencies end is by finishing the work the agent was hired to do or by arrival of the date at which the contract calls for the agency to end. The principal and agent may voluntarily agree between themselves to end the agency at any time, irrespective of what the agency agreement may say about the termination date.

The death of either the principal or agent ends the agency by **operation of law**, as does insanity of either principal or agent. Bankruptcy of the principal—and, in some cases, the agent—will end the agency. If the agent becomes physically or legally incapacitated (for example, loss of a professional license), the agency terminates. If it becomes impossible to perform due to loss or destruction of essential subject matter, the agency relation ends. Illegality of the agency's object or even sudden shifts in the economy (for example, economic depression) or in the political climate (for example, war) may result in an agency's ceasing.

Many of the prior observations made about an agency's ending apply with equal force to ending master–servant and employer–independent contractor arrangements.

For further information on agency law, go to the Web site for the Council on State Governments at http://www.statesnews.org

## ENDING THE EMPLOYMENT RELATIONSHIP: EMPLOYMENT AT-WILL

About 55 percent of the nonfarm workforce in the United States is not protected by union contracts or by civil service statutes. Many of these workers legally operate as at-will employees; that is, they have no written contract for a definite term. In at-will employment situations, the general rule has traditionally been that either the employer or the employee may end the working relationship any time for almost any (or no) reason. (Dismissals for protected union activities are prohibited, and are discussed in Chapter 17; dismissals prohibited by the civil rights laws are discussed in Chapter 16.)

On the surface, the employment at-will rule appears fair to both workers and employers. After all, both have the power to end the employment relationship. In practice, the rule generally favors employers, especially when jobs are scarce. Thus, the rule gives employers a strong disciplinary tool against employees. Used constructively, the employment at-will rule helps employers enforce their common law right to have workers follow instructions. Obedience can help production and harmony. If an employee at-will disobeys a direct order, the employer can fire that worker immediately.

Unfortunately, some employers lean on at-will employees to induce them to do questionable, unethical, or even illegal things. Also, some employers are not above terminating employees in questionable circumstances, such as just before an employee would be entitled to a large bonus. Such wrongful firings represent the negative or dark side of the at-will rule.

*Wrongful Dismissal Lawsuits in General.* Lawsuits based on wrongful dismissals have become common in most states. Two studies of California (generally a leader in legal developments) wrongful dismissal cases indicated that plaintiffs win 90 to 95 percent of the cases going to the jury. Damage awards averaged $450,000 and $548,000 in the two studies.

*Employee Actions Causing Wrongful Dismissals.* Employee actions prompting dismissals run the gamut, including major blunders. In the *Mau* case, an employee of 28 years who had worked his way up to be head mailroom clerk was fired for neglecting to send out 300 retirees' pension checks.[4] He lost his wrongful dismissal suit in the Nebraska Supreme Court. Employee actions are sometimes heroic. Recall the *Geary* case in Chapter 1, where Geary, a U.S. Steel salesman, went over his immediate boss's head to report a defect in a company product.[5] The company later withdrew the product from the market. U.S. Steel then fired Geary, who sued unsuccessfully in the Pennsylvania Supreme Court. *Geary* was a 1974 case, and *Mau* was decided in 1980. Both follow the traditional common law rule that an employer may fire an at-will employee any time for almost any reason.

*Legal Limits on Wrongful Dismissals.* The at-will rule remains, but it is being modified by statutes and judicial decisions. Several states have private-sector whistleblower statutes protecting against wrongful dismissal. Although no federal statute forbids wrongful dismissals in all situations, specialized federal laws

---

[4] *Mau v. Omaha Nat. Bank*, 207 Neb. 308, 299 N.W.2d 147 (1980)
[5] *Geary v. U.S. Steel Corp.*, 456 Pa. 171, 319 A.2d 174 (1974)

such as the National Labor Relations Act and Title VII of the Civil Rights Act of 1964 do give some protections in limited circumstances.

Courts in at least 30 states now provide some rights against wrongful dismissal. (In 1979, only about 15 states gave this protection.) Reasons for judicial relief can be grouped under contract and public policy headings.

If an employer and employee have an express contract covering the subject of grounds for dismissal, generally courts will honor its terms. For example, the contract could simply recite the general at-will rule allowing dismissal any time for almost any reason, or it could list the grounds for dismissal, such as insubordination or theft of company property.

Problems arise when no written contract exists or when the written contract either ignores, partially covers, or is ambiguous on the dismissal. Courts can then do one of several things. First, they can uphold the firing by citing the general rule. Second, more than 20 states allow recovery on an implied contract basis. Under this idea, courts interpret vague language in recruitment brochures, company manuals, and the like as meaning that the employer will dismiss employees only for "good cause." Third, courts can refuse to allow at-will employee terminations on the grounds that they violate a strong public policy. In one case, *Petermann v. International Brotherhood of Teamsters*, an employee was subpoenaed to testify before a state legislative committee.[6] The employer told him to give false testimony. The employee disobeyed, told the truth, and was fired. The employee won his claim for wrongful dismissal, even though the employment relationship was at-will. The Supreme Court of California reasoned that coercing perjury is "patently contrary to public policy." Fourth, some courts rely on promissory estoppel to hold an employer liable for promises made in company personnel manuals regarding dismissal procedures. Promissory estoppel holds a promisor liable for promises made when the promisee justifiably relies on the promise, the promisor knows or should know the promisee will act or forebear in reliance, and substantial injustice can be prevented only by holding the promisor liable.

The *Feliciano v. 7-Eleven, Inc.* case illustrates an attempt by an employer to escape liability when it dismissed an employee for violating company policy. Note that the West Virginia Supreme Court of Appeals was asked by a federal court whether West Virginia recognizes a public policy exception to wrongful dismissal when an employee is engaged in self-defense.

*Notice of the Agency's Ending.* Sometimes an agency ends with bad feelings between the principal and agent. This animosity may cause a disgruntled agent to enter unauthorized contracts on the principal's behalf merely to even the score against the former principal. It is also possible that the agent may forget or carelessly enter a transaction after the agency relationship has ended. Is the principal bound by an agent's contracts made on the principal's behalf after the agency has ended?

The answer depends on the type of agency, whether the third person who enters the contract after the agency ended ever had previous dealing with the principal through the agent, the manner in which the agency ends, and whether the principal gives the third person notice of the agency's termination.

---

[6] 174 Cal. App. 2d 184, 344 P.2d 25 (1959)

## Feliciano v. 7-Eleven, Inc.
Supreme Court of Appeals of West Virginia
559 S.E.2d 713 (2001)

### Background and Facts

The plaintiff, Antonio Feliciano, was employed as a retail sales clerk by the defendant, 7-Eleven, Inc., at its Baker Heights store, located in Berkeley County, West Virginia. At approximately 4:00 A.M. on July 14, 2000, a woman, wearing a mask and pointing a firearm, demanded that store employees, including Feliciano, give her the store's money. During this incident, certain employees emptied the cash register and, while the woman was focused upon another employee, Feliciano grabbed and disarmed her. Feliciano continued to restrain the would-be robber until local law enforcement authorities arrived on the scene and apprehended her.

Following this incident, 7-Eleven terminated Feliciano, who was an at-will employee, for failure to comply with its company policy which prohibits employees from subduing or otherwise interfering with a store robbery. Feliciano then filed a civil action against 7-Eleven in the Circuit Court of Berkeley County alleging that he had been wrongfully discharged, in contravention of West Virginia public policy, for exercising his right to self-defense. The defendant removed the suit to the United States District Court for the Northern District of West Virginia, Martinsburg Division, based upon diversity of citizenship and moved to dismiss Feliciano's claim, contending that he had failed to state a claim upon which relief could be granted.  In considering this motion, the district court encountered a legal conundrum which it has certified to the Supreme Court of Appeals of West Virginia. Applying West Virginia substantive law, the court ruled by order entered February 28, 2001, that "unless the West Virginia Supreme Court of Appeals holds otherwise, the Court concludes self-defense is not a substantial public policy in West Virginia," which ruling, if upheld, would result in the dismissal of Feliciano's complaint for failure to state a meritorious claim for wrongful discharge. Pursuant to this decision, the district court certified its question of law to the West Virginia Supreme Court of Appeals.

### Body of Opinion

**Justice Davis.** . . . The single issue presented for resolution by this Court is the certified question posed by the United States District Court for the Northern District of West Virginia: "Whether the right of self-defense is a 'substantial public policy' exception to the at-will employment doctrine, which provides the basis for a wrongful discharge action?" . . .

The jurisprudential history of this State, however, clearly demonstrates the existence of a public policy favoring an individual's right to defend him/herself. From the earliest reported cases to present day decisions, this Court has repeatedly recognized and safeguarded an individual's right to defend him/herself against an unprovoked assailant. In the course of these opinions, we have defined the nature of the right to self-defense, holding that [w]hen one without fault himself is attacked by another in such a manner or under such circumstances as to furnish reasonable grounds for apprehending a design to take away his life, or to do him some great bodily harm, and there is reasonable grounds for believing the danger imminent, that such design will be accomplished, and the person assaulted has reasonable ground to believe, and does believe, such danger is imminent, he may act upon such appearances and without retreating, kill his assailant, if he has reasonable grounds to believe, and does believe, that such killing is necessary in order to avoid the apparent danger; and the killing under such circumstances is excusable, although it may afterwards turn out, that the appearances were false, and that there was in fact neither design to do him some serious injury nor danger, that it would be done. But of all this the jury must judge from all the evidence and circumstances of the case. . . .

More recently, we have similarly observed that

[A] defendant who is not the aggressor and has reasonable grounds to believe, and actually does believe, that he is in imminent danger of death or serious bodily harm from which he could save himself only by using deadly force against his assailant has the right to employ deadly force in order to defend himself. . . .

In fact, the right to self-defense is so entrenched in the common law of this State that, some 80 years ago, this Court, while considering a defendant's plea of self-defense, obviated the need for meaningful discussion thereof by remarking that "[t]he law of self-defense is so well understood and has been so many times laid down by prior decisions as to need no additional affirmation in this case." . . . Furthermore, we previously have recognized that the right to self-defense extends to one's place of employment:

[I]n defending himself, his family or his property from the assault of an intruder, one is not limited to his immediate home or castle; his right to stand his ground in defense thereof without retreating extends to his place of business also and where it is necessary he may take the life of his assailant or intruder. . . .

Hence, it goes without saying that an individual's right to self-defense in West Virginia has been sufficiently established in and clarified by our State's common law so as to render it a substantial public policy.

While we recognize this substantial public policy of an employee's right to defend him/herself against bodily injury, we nevertheless must also be mindful of an employer's corresponding duty to safeguard its employees and patrons. . . . Thus, while a particular employee may assert his/her right to self-defense, an employer also has an interest in protecting its staff and customers from harm that may befall them as a result of the employee's actions in defending him/herself. For example, in the case *sub judice*, it is quite possible that someone, be it Feliciano, his coworker, or an innocent bystander, could have been injured in the course of Feliciano's attempts to defend himself. While it is indeed quite fortunate that no such injuries resulted, we must still account for this very real possibility. Accordingly, we find that while an employee has a right to self-defense, such right must necessarily be limited in its scope and available in only the most dangerous of circumstances. Therefore, we hold that when an at will employee has been discharged from his/her employment based upon his/her exercise of self-defense in response to lethal imminent danger, such right of self-defense constitutes a substantial public policy exception to the at-will employment doctrine and will sustain a cause of action for wrongful dismissal. Consistent with our prior precedent, we hold further that an employer may rebut an employee's *prima facie* case of wrongful discharge resulting from the employee's use of self-defense in response to lethal imminent danger by demonstrating that it had a plausible and legitimate business reason to justify the discharge.

As this case is presently before the Court upon certification of a question of law, we are not at liberty to decide whether the facts support Feliciano's cause of action for wrongful discharge. However, as guidance for future cases, we find the following elements of the tort of wrongful discharge . . . to be particularly instructive to a determination of whether an employee has successfully presented a claim of relief for wrongful discharge in contravention of substantial public policy:

1) [Whether a] clear public policy existed and was manifested in a state or federal constitution, statute or administrative regulation, or in the common law (the *clarity* element).
2) [Whether] dismissing employees under circumstances like those involved in the plaintiff's dismissal would jeopardize the public policy (the *jeopardy* element).
3) [Whether the] plaintiff's dismissal was motivated by conduct related to the public policy (the *causation* element).
4) [Whether the] employer lacked overriding legitimate business justification for the dismissal (the *overriding justification* element).

This succinct summary merely reiterates the procedures we previously have delineated in the foregoing discussion and decision of this case. . . .

### Judgment and Result

The Supreme Court of Appeals of West Virginia answered "yes, but with limitation" to the question submitted by the U.S. District Court as to whether West Virginia had a substantial public policy of an employee's right to defend him/herself against bodily injury.

### Questions

1. What is the "employment at will" doctrine? Does it have exceptions?
2. How convinced are you that Felciano will recover when his case returns to federal district court?

Considering the most significant of these factors—notice to the third person of the agency's termination—the principal must give actual notice to third persons who have dealt with the principal through the agent. **Actual notice** is a phone call, personal visit, or letter. Of these methods, a certified letter probably provides the best evidence that the third person has received actual notice, although large certified mailings can be costly. **Constructive notice** is to be contrasted with actual notice. Constructive notice of any agency's termination must be given to people other than those who have dealt through the agent. A paid advertisement in a newspaper or trade journal giving public notice of an agency's termination is an example of constructive notice.

No notice of any kind need be given to third persons upon termination of a special agent hired to accomplish a particular task. If the agency ends by the principal's death, in most cases, the agent's authority ends at that time. This situation can create hardship for an agent who, while in good faith not knowing that principal has died, enters a contract with a third person on the principal's behalf. Generally, the agent will be liable on the contract, even though it was understood that the agent was acting only in an agency capacity in entering the contract. One effective lobbying group—commercial banks—has succeeded in reversing this rule regarding their ability to pay checks written by a depositor before death but presented for payment after death. The bank is viewed as an agent of people with checking accounts, so the death ending the agent's authority rule does not apply here according to Section 4-405 of the Uniform Commercial Code (the law in the District of Columbia and 50 states).

## CHAPTER SUMMARY

Employers' relations with their employees generally fall into one of the following categories: master–servant, principal–agent, and employer–independent contractor. The terms *employer–employee* are generally not recognized by the courts as a separate legal category.

The respondeat superior principle establishes the idea that one person can be liable for another's actions if the nonactor has the right to control the means and ends of the actor's job. Respondeat superior applies in principal–agent situations to hold principals liable for their agent's actions within the scope of their jobs. Respondeat superior also holds masters liable for their servants' actions within the scope of their employment. Respondeat superior does not generally apply in the case of employers and independent contractors.

The rules permit almost anyone to be an agent, servant, or independent contractor who demonstrates the mental and physical capability to perform and understand the significance of the acts undertaken. Corporations, trusts, and partnerships can be agents.

The ways of creating authority in an agent or servant include conferring express authority, implied authority, apparent authority, and ratification.

Masters and principals owe their employees several duties, including the duty to provide safe working conditions, the duty to instruct, the duty to pay, and the duty to provide tools to perform their jobs. Principals also owe agents the duty to reimburse them for reasonable expenses incurred in carrying out the agency, as well as the duty to indemnify agents for losses sustained in the agency.

Agents owe principals the duty to account, the duty to use care and skill, the duty to follow instructions, and the fiduciary duty. The fiduciary duty is broad and covers such matters as being honest and avoiding conflicts of interest with one's principal.

Agents who are authorized to contract on their principal's behalf are generally not personally liable on such contracts if the agent signs in a representative capacity and the principal's identity is known to the other contracting party.

Employees who commit crimes on the job are personally liable for them. Employers can be liable for their employees' crimes if courts apply the respondeat superior doctrine or the criminal conspiracy doctrine. Generally, corporate executives are not criminally liable for their employees' crimes if the executives did not authorize or know of the crimes. Defenses to employers prosecuted for employee crimes include the superior agent rule and the scope of employment doctrine.

When agencies end, the principal should notify third parties. Actual notice of the agency's ending should be given to third persons with whom the principal has dealt through the agent, and constructive notice given to other third parties.

The employment at-will doctrine permits either the employer or employee to end an employment relationship at any time for almost any reason. Exceptions to the employment at-will rule tend to protect the employee. Such exceptions include the tort of wrongful dismissal, implied contract limits on employers' dismissal rights, public policy exceptions, and the promissory estoppel theory.

## ■ MANAGER'S ETHICAL DILEMMA ■

While on duty for the North Carolina Highway Patrol, Trooper Chris T. Phillips stopped to order food from the drive-through window of a Taco Bell restaurant in Black Mountain, North Carolina. Restaurant Management of Carolina, L.P. owned and operated the restaurant under a franchise agreement with Taco Bell Corp. Apparently recognizing that the trooper had ordered food, an employee of the restaurant, Jason Paul Jones, spat in the trooper's food before serving it to him. Shortly thereafter, while consuming the food, the trooper noticed a substance on the food that appeared to be human saliva. He returned immediately to the restaurant and spoke to the shift manager, who denied any knowledge of the incident. Nonetheless, the trooper reported the incident to the local police department and to his supervisor. A State Bureau of Investigation laboratory report later confirmed the presence of human saliva in the food. Two days later, Jones revealed to his shift supervisor that he spat in the trooper's food because he had been "harassed" by local police officers for skateboarding and thought the trooper-customer could have been one of the officers.

The trooper brought actions against Jones, restaurant management, and Taco Bell. Following pleadings and discovery, the trial court granted summary judgment in favor of restaurant management and Taco Bell. The trooper appealed. What was the result?

## DISCUSSION QUESTIONS

1. A real estate agent may not lie to would-be purchasers if asked whether the former occupant of a home had AIDS, because so doing would be fraud or misrepresentation. On the other hand, the agent has a fiduciary duty to the seller, whom the agent represents, to attempt to sell the property as well as not to disclose unauthorized information.

   In California, a Realtor representing a seller was sued by a buyer on grounds that the Realtor failed to disclose that, in the previous five years, five murders had taken place in the house the Realtor sold. The customer said the brokers should disclose matters related to the house that would have a psychological impact on the buyer. Do you agree? [*Reed v. King*, 145 Cal. App. 3d 261 (1983)].

2. Michael Auston, a shift supervisor at the A.B.P. Midwest, Inc., allegedly asked Sharon Paul, an employee at A.B.P., "What are you two lesbians doing tonight?" It was uncontested that the persons referred to as "two lesbians" were Sharon Paul and Norma Mae O'Brien. When Auston made this allegedly defamatory statement, was he acting within the scope of his employment? [*O'Brien v. A.B.P., Inc.*, 814 F.Supp. 766 (D. Minn. 1992)].

3. The common law rules controlling the employer–employee relationship were developed many years ago when employers and employees often knew each other personally and took a personal interest in each other. Is this true today? Why? Do you think this shift in some way explains why statutes have supplemented the common law rules?

4. What are some of the common law duties that employers owe employees? Do these rules tend to favor either the employer or the employee, or are they neutral in operation?

5. What are the advantages and disadvantages to employers in having agents or servants instead of independent contractors?

6. What legal ethics discussed in Chapter 1 are served by holding an employer criminally answerable for an employee's on-the-job crimes? What legal ethics support holding an employer civilly liable for damages resulting from an employee's work-related crimes?

7. When an employer wrongfully discharges an employee by breaking an unexpired employment contract, the employee may sue the employer and recover damages. However, the employee has a duty to mitigate damages. Therefore, the employee must actively seek other employment. When an Indiana school board wrongfully dismissed an untenured teacher for filing a grievance, she sued the school board for damages. The board claimed the teacher did not try hard enough to find other work and thereby failed to fulfill her duty to mitigate her damages, and her damages should therefore be reduced. The teacher had unsuccessfully applied for teaching jobs at several other school systems in the area in which she lived. She argued that this satisfied her duty to mitigate damages. The school board, however, argued that she had to either take a job of a substantially different character or grade, or move to another community to find comparable work to fulfill her duty to mitigate damages. Who was correct? [*Board of Sch. Trustees v. Indiana Ed. Employment Relations Bd.*, 412 N.E.2d 807 (Ind. App. 1980)].

8. The question of the employer's right to dismiss an employee in an employment at-will arrangement is hotly contested today. One key issue is whether the employer has an unconditional right to dismiss without having or stating a reason. In one case, a woman sued her employer for an alleged breach of

an oral employment contract. She was hired for factory work in 1968 at $1.84 per hour. She allegedly was told that if she worked well, she would get better jobs with better pay. She claimed that she was harassed by her foreman because she refused to go out with him. His hostility, condoned—if not shared—by the company personnel manager, resulted in her being fired. A jury trial produced a $2,500 verdict. The employer appealed to the New Hampshire Supreme Court. What was the result? [*Monge v. Beebe Rubber Co.*, 114 N.H. 130, 316 A.2d 549 (1974)].

9. An assistant manager authorized repair work on a restaurant's neon sign. The restaurant owner refused to pay the repair bill. He argued that the assistant manager had authority only to take bids on the job, not contract for it. Did the assistant manager bind the restaurant based on inherent authority? [*Zanac, Inc. v. Frazier Neon Signs, Inc.*, 134 Ga.App. 501, 215 S.E.2d 265 (Ga.App. 1975)].

## INFOTRAC KEYWORDS

**Use your InfoTrac password to look up articles on http://www.infotrac-college.com**

Keywords: *Principal–agent relationships, respondeat superior, independent contractors, fiduciary duty, employment at-will.*

For suggested readings, please visit this book's Web site at **http://fisher.westbuslaw.com** (click on "Internet Applications").

# IMPORTANT STATUTES IN EMPLOYER–EMPLOYEE RELATIONS

"I fell 70 feet onto a concrete factory floor, and yet my employer claims I shouldn't get any workers' compensation benefits," said Francisco Ruiz, formerly employed at Belk Masonry Co.

"You should get zero workers' compensation benefits," argued Mr. Belk, "because you lied on your employment application. You presented a false Social Security number and a fake I-9 immigration card. You are an illegal alien!"

Should illegal aliens employed in the United States be entitled to workers' compensation benefits?

"We have been paid less than the Fair Labor Standards Act requires for minimum hourly wages," claimed Marcia Fazekas, a registered nurse who worked for Health Care Ventures.

"No, Marcia, you are professionals, and, as such, the minimum wage and hours provisions of the FLSA do not apply to the in-home care you provide," replied John Jones, an executive at Health Care Ventures, Fazekas' employer.

Are registered nurses performing home health care services for different clients "professionals" under the FLSA?

*"During 2000 over 45 million persons—one in six—received over $407 billion in benefits out of a 2000 federal budget of $1.788 trillion."*

—STATISTICAL ABSTRACT OF THE UNITED STATES

In Chapter 14 we saw some common law (judge-made) rules affecting employer–employee relations. Federal and state statutes have reshaped the entire area of employer–employee relations over the past 50 years. Such statutes address two major employee concerns: on-the-job safety and financial security. This chapter divides the statutes into two major areas. The first, job safety and statutory recovery, discusses *preventive* law (the Occupational Safety and Health Act—OSHA), and a *compensatory* law—workers' compensation. The second area, workers' financial security, covers the Employee Retirement Income Security Act of 1974 (ERISA), the Social Security Act, the Fair Labor Standards Act, unemployment compensation, the Family and Medical Leave Act of 1993, and plant closing legislation. Figure 15.1 presents a historical overview of statutes in the employer–employee area.

## JOB SAFETY AND STATUTORY RECOVERY

### WORKERS' COMPENSATION

In the early part of the twentieth century, state legislatures started establishing workers' compensation systems. The objective of these systems is to pay workers

## FIGURE 15.1 SIGNIFICANT STATUTES AFFECTING EMPLOYER–EMPLOYEE RELATIONS

(or their dependents) for work-related injuries, diseases, or death. Employers are liable for all such employee harm, even though the employer was not to blame. Put another way, employers are insurers of job-related harm to employees.

Early laws tended to cover only hazardous work, and even then they were not always welcomed. For example, Maryland enacted a law in 1902 setting up a cooperative accident fund for miners. It was held unconstitutional. Montana had a similar experience with its 1909 miners' compensation act. Although New York's 1910 compulsory workers' compensation act covered only a few hazardous jobs, it was likewise declared unconstitutional.

Finally, in 1917 the U.S. Supreme Court held that workers' compensation laws were valid exercises of a state's police power in *New York Central Railroad v. White* (243 U.S. 188). The *White* decision broke state resistance to workers' compensation. By 1920, only eight states were without a workers' compensation law. Today all states have workers' compensation laws, covering hazardous and most non-hazardous jobs.

*Common Law Fault.* Before workers' compensation laws, workers injured on the job recovered if they showed that employer **fault** (negligence) had injured them. It was a common law basis of recovery. Furthermore, even if employer fault were shown, the employer could escape liability by proving any *one* of the following defenses: (1) the injured employee's **contributory negligence** (i.e., the employee's own fault contributed to the employee's loss); (2) the worker's **assumption of risk** (i.e., the worker voluntarily performed a job knowing of the risk involved and was injured by this risk); or (3) a fellow servant's carelessness injured the worker, called the **fellow servant rule**.

The common law negligence rules just described prevented many injured workers or deceased workers' dependents from recovering for job-related injuries or death. The employers' argument on behalf of common law rules was essentially cost: common law rules kept worker claims low. Common law rules placed a large part of the cost of industrial injuries on the victims and their families and, indirectly, on society. For example, if an employee broke her back at work due in part to her own carelessness (contributory negligence), she recovered nothing.

*Shift to Workers' Compensation.* Common law rules were often harsh on injured and deceased workers' families. Many believed that using common law's fault idea was too crude to allocate the burden of industrial injury, disease, and death in a complex economy. To such people, these costs were simply part of the good or service produced and should be borne irrespective of fault by the party in the best position to administer them—the business producing the good or service. The business in turn passed this cost on to the consumers of the product or service.

Workers' compensation insurance is the mechanism for imposing these human costs on employers. Workers' compensation abandons common law fault principles in deciding who bears the cost of work-related injuries, diseases, and deaths. It makes the employer the insurer of these risks.

*Key Features of Workers' Compensation Statutes.* Workers' compensation statutes are state laws. And although they vary from state to state concerning the accidents and diseases covered, beneficiaries, and procedures, these laws have many similarities.

*Work-Related Requirement.* A worker (or dependent) may recover only for injuries, diseases, and death occurring on the job. For example, if an employee carelessly places a ladder against a wall at work, falls and sustains injuries, workers' comp pays. If that same accident had happened at home, workers' comp would not pay since the injuries would not be job-related.

Courts tend to construe the work-related requirement liberally. If doubt exists whether an injury occurred on or off the job, courts tend to say that "gray area" cases are work-related, allowing the worker to recover from workers' comp. For example, an accountant working for a large public accounting firm attended a day-long firm outing at a country club. On the way home at midnight, he was killed in an auto accident. A court held that this death was work-related, enabling the accountant's family to recover under workers' comp. If heart attacks are work-related, the claimant may recover even if the worker had a preexisting heart condition. Also, others cases have held that heart attacks at work resulting from psychic upset are recoverable.

Generally, workers' comp statutes do not allow employees to recover for self-inflicted injuries. This rule attempts to stop malingering (pretending one has a covered injury to collect benefits). Suicides present exceptional cases because malingering is unlikely. In one Delaware Supreme Court case (*Delaware Tire Center v. Fox*), the court indicated that certain suicides were compensable. According to *Fox*, a suicide is not willful for workers' comp purposes if an industrial accident was the main factor triggering the worker's suicide. Suicides are, thankfully, rare in the workplace. Back injuries are not. The most common worker compensation claims arise from back injuries. The *Ruiz v. Belk Masonry Co.* case illustrates a current workers' comp problem, should illegal aliens be allowed to collect?

---

## Ruiz v. Belk Masonry Co., Inc.
### Court of Appeals of North Carolina
### 559 S.E.2d 249 (2002)

### Background and Facts

Plaintiff Francisco Ruiz sustained an injury while employed as a construction worker for defendant Belk Masonry Company, Inc. on October 7, 1997. Plaintiff fell approxi-

mately 70 feet from a forklift onto a concrete floor and sustained a traumatic brain injury, a kidney contusion, and several fractures. He was transported to Carolinas Medical Center and was hospitalized until November 7, 1997. Plaintiff was them transferred to the Charlotte Institute of

Rehabilitation, where he received physical, occupational, and speech therapy, along with psychological counseling. Plaintiff was placed in an outpatient program under the care of his brother, Jose Ruiz, on December 3, 1997, and continued to participate in follow-up treatment with his treating physician, Dr. James T. McDeavitt. Dr. McDeavitt testified plaintiff reached maximum medical improvement on February 9, 1998. Dr. McDeavitt also testified plaintiff did not require 24-hour attendant care, and that with a vocational rehabilitation plan, plaintiff might be able to return to work.

Plaintiff presented the testimony of a vocational rehabilitation expert and a certified life care planner. The life care planner testified that plaintiff needed 24-hour care. Patrick Clifford, a vocational rehabilitation expert, testified that plaintiff could not even perform sedentary work, had limited ability to walk or drive, and had limited cognitive abilities.

Plaintiff was an illegal or undocumented alien at the time of his hiring and at the time of the accident. Plaintiff presented a false Social Security card and I-9 form to defendant–employer when he was employed.

## Body of Opinion

**Judge McGee.** Defendants first argue the Commission erred in awarding workers' compensation benefits to plaintiff because plaintiff was an illegal alien. We disagree.

Defendants argue the statutory construction of [Ed.: state statutes] . . . does not allow for illegal aliens to be classified as "employees." Defendants further argue plaintiff does not have an earning capacity. However, [Ed.: a state statute] . . . defines "employee" as "every person engaged in an employment under any appointment or contract of hire or apprenticeship, express or implied, oral or written, including aliens, and also mirrors, whether lawfully or unlawfully employed." . . .

[Ed.: State law] does not preclude plaintiff from receiving workers' compensation benefits based solely on his status as an illegal alien. "The philosophy which supports the [Workers'] Compensation Act is that the wear and tear of the workman, as well as the machinery, shall be charged to the industry." . . . "The primary purpose of legislation of this kind is to compel industry to take care of its own wreckage." . . . These principles are still relevant today and in the particular situation before us. We agree with the deputy commissioner's finding in this case that we "must also be aware the defendant-employer received the benefits of plaintiff's labor up to the time of the injury, and it would be repugnant to now deny plaintiff a benefit of the same agreement." . . .

Defendants next argue the Commission erred in awarding plaintiff benefits for attendant care. Defendants contend no competent evidence exists to support the findings of fact that, in turn, would support the Commission's conclusion that plaintiff is entitled to attendant care services at a rate of eight dollars an hour for sixteen hours a day. We disagree.

Whether a plaintiff does or does not receive attendant care benefits is a conclusion of law which must be supported by finding of fact. On an appeal from an opinion and award from the Commission, the standard of review for this Court "is limited to a determination of (1) whether the Commission's findings of fact are supported by any competent evidence in the record; and (2) whether the Commissions's findings justify its conclusions of law." . . .

Defendants argue the Commissions' finding that "plaintiff is in need of attendant care and defendant have not provided it" is not supported by competent evidence. "The facts found by the Commission are conclusive upon appeal to this Court when they are supported by competent evidence, even when there is evidence to support contrary findings." . . . FUrthermore, the "finding of fact by the Industrial Commission are conclusive on appeal is supported by any competent evidence." . . .

The Commission found the following facts in its opinion and award:

9. Mr. Jose Ruiz indicated that plaintiff cannot take care of himself. Mr. Ruiz has to cook, clean, wash, shop, and pay bills, among other things, for plaintiff. He turns on plaintiff's shower and has to assist plaintiff into the shower. Plaintiff can bathe himself while he sits on a stool. Mr. Ruiz indicated that plaintiff cannot cook because he will leave the stove on or forget about the food on the stove. Plaintiff needs assistance walking because he is not stable on his feet and may fall at any time.

10. Mr. Jose Ruiz indicated that he is not able to hold a full-time job because it is unsafe to leave plaintiff at home for a long period and he therefore works four or five hours per day, five days a week, and otherwise he is always with plaintiff.

. . .

16. Paula Medina, a registered nurse with a Master's degree in health administration who also is a certified life planner, drafted a life care plan for plaintiff at the request of Patrick Clifford. As a part of this plan, she indicated that plaintiff would need attendant care for the remainder of his life. Jose Ruiz has been providing care to plaintiff but will be unable to continue if he is not paid.

Defendants argue the testimony of plaintiff's brother and Paula Medina in incompetent, and they offer conflicting evidence to rebut this testimony. Specifically, defendants offer the testimony of plaintiff's treating physician that plaintiff has improved steadily, plaintiff can remain at home unattended, and vocational rehabilitation would be appropriate for plaintiff. Defendants contend this testimony is the only credible testimony concerning plaintiff's health. However, the Commission "is the sole judge of the credibility of the witnesses and the weight to be given their testimony." Thus, the Commission may assign more weight and credibility to certain testimony than other. Moreover, if the evidence before the Commission is capable of supporting two contrary findings, the determination of the Commission is conclusive on appeal.

After a careful review of the record before us, we find there is competent evidence to support the findings of fact made by the

Commission, and these findings support the Commission's conclusions of law. . . .

## Judgment and Result

Plaintiff wins. The Court of Appeals affirmed the award of the Commission.

1. What had Ruiz done that in the eyes of the employer deprived him of the right to workers' compensation benefits?
2. Did all of the evidence at the Workers' Compensation Commission hearing support Ruiz's claim? Was there conflicting evidence? Who resolves the conflict?

*Certain But Limited Recovery.* One feature of workers' comp is the certain recovery given to all covered employees. If an employee has an injury, a schedule sets dollar values for many specific losses. For example, the schedule may allow $5,000 for a hand, $7,500 for an arm, and $10,000 for an eye. For unscheduled losses, a percentage of disability is determined. This partial (or total) disability recovery is related to an employee's earnings. In either case, employees are handed checks for the amount the workers' comp benefit schedule says they get—no more, no less. Thus, this recovery is certain. It does not depend on winning a jury verdict. The common law defenses of contributory negligence, the fellow servant rule, and assumption of risk are not available to employers under workers' comp because the employer is an insurer (presumed liable provided the worker loss relates to the job). Fault is not an issue as it is in negligence cases.

*Exclusivity of Remedy.* Workers' comp statutes eliminate employee common law and statutory claims against employers, making the workers' comp statute the *only* legal basis for an employee to recover from the employer, co-workers, and employer's executives for job-related injuries, diseases, or death. The employee is guaranteed a workers' comp recovery for these events.

What if the employee's actual expenses or losses from a work-related accident are more than what workers' comp allows? The injured employee recovers *only* the scheduled amount, because workers' comp statutes are bargains between employees and employers. Even if a harm is worth more to one person than to another, an employee cannot forgo the workers' comp recovery and sue on common law principles instead. Employees are limited to workers' comp recovery for work-related injuries, disease or death, even if a particular employee's real losses are far greater than what workers' comp allows. This limited exclusive remedy is a major benefit to employers. Such a benefit is greater in inflationary times because workers' comp benefits are usually not inflation indexed. Also, workers' comp benefits are often conservative, partly because they try to project mythical average employees' losses (in calculating, for example, the value of an arm).

Workers' comp's exclusive remedy rule applies only to employee lawsuits against their employers. In other words, workers' comp says its recoveries are the only ones available against an employer. However, it does *not stop* an employee from suing a *third party* on common law or other statutory principles for job-related injuries, disease, or death. For example, employees of insulation installers have sued the manufacturer of asbestos insulation for diseases caused by inhaling asbestos fibers. One such manufacturer, the Manville Corporation, entered bankruptcy due to such third-party claims.

*Nonapplication to Independent Contractors.* Most state workers' compensation statutes apply only to employees (agents and servants), not to independent contractors. This limitation has great financial consequences for business. Specifically, business would prefer to have independent contractors rather than employees (agents and servants) because it does not directly pay their workers' comp insurance costs. Workers' comp costs are high and rising because of increased medical and hospital costs and the pressures to expand job relatedness to include more employee injuries and disease under workers' comp coverage.

*Funding.* Virtually all state workers' comp systems force employers to pay for industrial injuries, accidents, and deaths in one of three ways: by purchasing insurance from industrial insurers, by **self-insuring** (large employers set up contingency funds to cover risks to workers), or by using a state fund to which covered employers contribute.

*Administration.* Workers' comp systems are run by state administrative agencies. Such names as "industrial commissions" are common for such bodies. These agencies **adjudicate** worker claims (for example, they decide whether a disease is job-related). No juries are involved, only an administrative law judge. Decisions of such industrial boards may be appealed to the courts. The agencies also enforce the law by making sure required employers have workers' comp coverage.

*Employees Covered.* State workers' compensation laws cover most employees. However, farm workers, workers in the home, and federal workers (covered by federal laws) are not covered by state workers' comp laws.

*Mandatory or Elective.* State workers' comp laws are either elective or mandatory. In the case of mandatory statutes, a state could require employers having a certain minimum number of employees (three is a common number) to have workers' comp coverage. Many states allow employers to elect workers' comp coverage or common law negligence. If an employer chooses the latter, the defenses of contributory negligence, assumption of risk, and the fellow servant rule are not available. One advantage to the employee if an employer elects not to have workers' comp coverage is that the workers' comp recovery limit does not apply. An injured employee may recover at common law all provable damages. Because of its limited benefit schedule, full recovery is often not true where workers' comp controls.

## OCCUPATIONAL SAFETY AND HEALTH ACT (OSHA)

The Occupational Safety and Health Act is a federal law passed in 1970. In the four years before OSHA was passed, more U.S. workers were killed at work than were killed in the Vietnam War. About 2 million were disabled each year by work-related accidents. The *President's Report on Occupational Safety and Health* (1972) estimated that 100,000 deaths per year were attributable to occupational diseases and illnesses from exposure to chemical and physical hazards. Congress tried to stop this carnage in the workplace when it passed OSHA. President Nixon signed it into law on December 29, 1970, and OSHA took effect on April 28, 1971.

For regulations, inspections, and processes of the Occupational Safety and Health Administration, go to *http://www.osha.gov*

*OSHA's Objectives.* OSHA tries to make the workplace safe and healthy for workers and to preserve the country's human resources. When OSHA became law, it covered about 57 million workers in about four million businesses, large and small, affecting interstate commerce.

*OSHA Administration and Records.* The Occupational Safety and Health Administration (also known as OSHA) administers and enforces the act.

OSHA puts a record-keeping burden on employers. Four types of records must be kept:

1. Enforcement records
2. Research records
3. Job-related injury and accident records
4. Records of job hazards

*OSHA Standards.* How does OSHA propose to accomplish its objective of making the workplace safer and healthier? The answer is familiar: by regulations. The three types of OSHA standards are interim, permanent, and temporary emergency. The *interim standards* were applicable for two years after the act's passage. The secretary of labor was allowed to use any national consensus standard of a nationally recognized standards setting organization (e.g., professional engineering groups' standards) for this purpose. The *permanent standards* are the basic OSHA regulations setting workplace safety and health requirements. Permanent standards may be set any time after consulting with the OSHA Advisory Committee. *Temporary emergency standards* last only six months and provide some protection while OSHA develops a permanent standard. For instance, OSHA has imposed an emergency standard for vinyl chloride (a carcinogen).

OSHA regulations vary from industry to industry. The regulations detail how to carry on work to avoid accidents and promote health. For example, hearing loss results from overexposure to job noise. An OSHA regulation (found in 29 CFR §1926.101) tells when and which earplugs must be used in construction work.

OSHA standards come from several places. OSHA got many of its standards from private organizations such as the American National Standards Institute and the National Fire Protection Association. Such privately developed standards were called national consensus standards. They were advisory occupational safety and health standards from federal standards already established under prior federal laws. (An example is the Walsh–Healey Act, which forbids the federal government from buying more than $10,000 of goods made under unsanitary or hazardous working conditions.)

*National Institute of Occupational Safety and Health (NIOSH).* The National Institute of Occupational Safety and Health (NIOSH) is a research institute that develops **criteria documents**, which are studies telling how much of a substance causes diseases, how much noise causes deafness, and so on. A few OSHA standards (specific numbers, amounts, levels, and the like) are based partly on criteria documents.

*State OSHAs (SOSHAs).* OSHA lets states develop standards and plans to regulate job safety and health. If a state assures it will regulate its plan as effectively as the federal plan, the state—not the OSHA—regulates workplace safety and health in that state. At least half of the states have assumed OSHA administration and enforcement.

*Steps in OSHA's Operation.* Figure 15.2 details how OSHA works. In step 1, Congress passed the Occupational Safety and Health Act. This delegated rule-making authority from Congress to the Occupational Safety and Health Administration (actually the secretary of labor). The act also sets out a general duty standard for employers based on common law principles. It provides: "Each employer shall furnish to each of his employees employment and a place of employment which are free from recognized hazards that are causing or are likely to cause death or serious physical harm to his [or her] employees."

The act itself (OSHA) creates only one workplace safety and health standard, the **general duty standard** just quoted. The OSH Act is an *enabling* act. It is a delegation of regulation-making authority from Congress to an administrative agency. OSH Administration worker safety and health standards are promulgated as regulations by the secretary of labor as part of the Department of Labor.

Reread Chapters 6 and 7 on the anatomy of a federal regulation if you do not recall how notice and comment regulation making takes place (Step 2 in Figure 15.2). In *Whirlpool Corp. v. Marshall*, the U.S. Supreme Court upheld an OSHA regulation that lets employees refuse to do their work if they reasonably believe death or serious injury will result *and* if they believe they have no less dangerous way of doing the job.

In step 3, OSH Administration inspectors conduct surprise inspections of factories and other workplaces that the OSH Act covers. These inspections are designed to see whether a business follows OSHA standards. Recall from Chapter 8 that a

## FIGURE 15.2 How OSHA Works

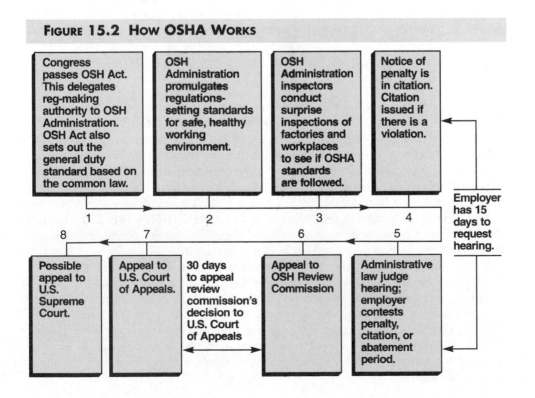

business person has a right of privacy. This protection lets a business demand a search warrant from the OSHA inspector before admitting that person. The act allows an employer and an employee representative to walk with the OSHA official during an inspection.

Step 4 in OSHA's operation is the possible issuance of an OSHA citation. An OSHA citation lists alleged employer violations of OSHA. It also contains a notice of penalties for the various alleged violations as well as an **abatement period**. The abatement period tells an employer how much time it has to correct an OSHA violation.

Employer penalties for OSHA infractions exist for nonserious violations or for serious, nonwillful violations. If a violation is willful and repeated, penalties up to $10,000 are possible. Additionally, a six-month period of imprisonment is possible if an employee death results from an OSHA violation.

In step 5 of OSHA's operation, an employer receiving an OSHA citation has 15 days to contest the citation, penalty, or abatement period. Such a challenge takes place before an administrative law judge, who is basically a federal judge. (Refer to Chapters 6 and 7 on enforcement of a federal regulation if you need to recall how an administrative hearing differs from a trial court.) The administrative law judge hears witnesses, other evidence, and legal arguments, decides factual and legal issues, and enters an order.

Step 6 in OSHA's operation involves a possible appeal of the administrative law judge's order to the Occupational Safety and Health Review Commission, which is an appellate administrative review. Once the Occupational Safety and Health Review Commission enters its order, an employer or the secretary of labor has 30 days to appeal to a U.S. Court of Appeals. Twelve of these courts are spread throughout the United States. Their decisions can possibly be taken to the U.S. Supreme Court (steps 7 and 8 in OSHA's operation). A leading OSHA practicing lawyer suggests that employers appeal Occupational Safety and Health Review Commission orders to U.S. courts of appeals. This lawyer reported that about half of the time the courts of appeals reverse Review Commission orders.

*Criticisms of OSHA.* OSHA is hated by many businesses for several reasons. First, OSHA has many vague regulations. For example, OSHA had a regulation requiring "all places of employment, passageways . . . be kept clean and orderly." What is "clean and orderly" to a businessperson may not be so to an OSHA inspector. In one case, a business was cited for violating this regulation.

Second, other OSHA regulations are quite detailed about trivial matters. One U.S. Secretary of Labor (Ray Marshall) has called OSHA regulations nit-picking. No detail is too small for OSHA regulations. For example, 29 CFR § 1910.25(b)(1)(ii) of the 1977 OSHA regulations contain detailed requirements for permissible irregularities in western hemlock used for ladder construction.

Third, business has to pay for OSHA's requirements. No matter how great OSHA may be, the one who pays has less enthusiasm. Fourth, some of OSHA's enforcers were allegedly arrogant and high-handed, with an adversarial rather than supportive attitude toward business. "We are out to get you" rather than "we are out to help you improve" was the perception some businesses had of OSHA. Whether this assessment was accurate or just an excuse attempting to divert attention from OSHA violations probably cannot be answered the same way in all cases.

Fifth, many have questioned OSHA's judgment in regulating trivial matters having little bearing on worker safety and health. For example, one early OSHA regulation (later amended) prohibited ice in drinking water. Because OSHA has always had a limited enforcement staff, its job of improving workplace safety and health has been allegedly shortchanged by its spending excessive time on trivia.

*OSHA Changes.* In the Appropriations Act of 1977, Congress told OSHA to get rid of "nuisance standards" (trivial regulations or those unrelated to OSHA's safety and health objectives). President Carter also told executive departments (such as Labor, which houses OSHA) to reduce and simplify regulations. OSHA got these messages on October 24, 1978, when OSHA published a final rule in the *Federal Register* (43 F.R. 49726) revoking about 900 OSHA regulations.

Other suggestions for OSHA improvement include more frequent inspection of high-risk industries (such as construction) and less frequent inspection of less hazardous workplaces (such as real estate offices), *de minimis* (little) notices (or warnings) for small or technical standards violations with no direct bearing on health and safety, simplified standards, further reduction of unneeded standards, and increasing help to businesses so they can comply with the standards.

One of the most persistent areas of controversy under OSHA concerns workplace inspections. Employers frequently complain that OSHA inspectors are officious and lack judgment resulting in employer fines for what are, essentially, trivial regulations infractions.

On the other hand, employees complain that employers have complained to the point that OSHA inspectors now "look the other way," often ignoring serious safety violations with resulting hazardous conditions for workers. The *Irving v. U.S.* case presents an interesting twist on this theme: while workers are not entitled to sue employers for injuries sustained by OSHA violations, could workers bring a Federal Tort Claims Act case against the OSHA when OSHA inspectors negligently inspect an employer's workplace proximately causing a worker's injury?

## Irving v. United States
U.S. Court of Appeals (1st Cir.)
162 F.3d 154 (1998)

### Background and Facts

In 1979, Somersworth Shoe Company operated a manufacturing plant in New Hampshire. On October 10 of that year, the plaintiff Gail Merchant Irving, a Somersworth employee, was stamping innersoles by means of a marker machine. At one point, she went behind her workbench to obtain materials from the die rack. In the process, she dropped a glove. When she stooped to retrieve it, her hair was drawn into the vacuum created by the high speed rotation of a drive shaft that delivered power to an adjacent "die-out" machine. She sustained horrific injuries.

Irving sued the United States under the Federal Tort Claims Act (FTCA) claiming that inspectors employed by the Occupational Safety and Health Administration (OSHA) negligently performed their duties and thereby proximately caused her injuries. The case traveled an inexcusably long and tortuous route to a decision on the merits—a route that included four detours to the U.S. Court of Appeals for the First Circuit. Ultimately, the district court, proceeding under a legal framework established by a panel of the First Circuit, concluded that the FTCA's discretionary function exception did not bar Irving's claim; that the OSHA inspector acted negligently; and that such negligence was actionable under applicable state law.

A divided panel of this court affirmed the judgment . . . but the full court, acting sua sponte [on its own motion] withdrew the opinion and ordered rehearing en banc, principally to review the important question of whether the FTCA's discretionary function exception foreclosed the plaintiff's negligent inspection claim.

## Body of Opinion

**Circuit Judge Selya.** . . . In this instance, the plaintiff claims that workplace inspections, negligently performed by OSHA compliance officers, proximately caused her injuries. In analyzing the nature of this conduct, we begin with the language of the OSH Act because "it will most often be true that the general aims and policies of the controlling statute will be evident from its text" . . . and, in turn, these aims and policies will offer valuable insights into the nature of the conduct.

In relevant part, the OSH Act authorizes the Secretary of Labor to "inspect and investigate during regular working hours and at other reasonable times, and within reasonable limits and in a reasonable manner, any such place of employment and all pertinent conditions, structures, machines, apparatus, devices, equipment, and materials therein." . . . Under this authority, OSHA conducts both programmed general administrative inspections—known in the bureaucratic argot that OSHA so readily attracts as "full-scope" or "wall-to-wall" inspections—and more focused efforts pinpointed to threats of imminent danger. Aside from a reasonableness limitation on the time and manner of inspections, the statute places virtually no constraint on the Secretary's discretion to conduct such inspections in any way that she deems fit. . . .

It [Congress] left the scope and detail of OSH Act inspections to the Secretary's discretion. Had Congress wished to impose upon OSHA an obligation to inspect every corner of every plant that it visited, we think it is highly likely that Congress would have expressed its intention by choosing language comparable to that which it used in crafting the [Federal Mine Safety Act].

We recognize that, by its plain terms, the OSH Act confers discretion only upon the Secretary, not upon compliance officers—and it is the latter's conduct that concerns us. Nevertheless, the legislative rules governing the authority of compliance officers mimic the statute and grant these officials broad discretion over the scope, manner, and detail of general administrative inspections. The regulations' stated goal is "to set forth general policies for enforcement of the inspection, citation, and proposed penalty provisions of the Act." . . . Echoing the language of . . . the Act], Section 1903.3 of the regulations confers upon compliance officers the unbridled power, subject only to limits of reasonableness, to enter workplaces, inspect any piece of equipment or other pertinent item, and interview any person in order to carry out the Secretary's statutory mission. . . .

To be sure, the regulations contain a sprinkling of mandatory directives. . . . (obligating compliance officers, inter alia, to present their credentials at the start of an inspection, to use "reasonable precautions" when taking photographs and samples, to wear appropriate protective clothing, to avoid "unreasonable disruption" of the workplace, and to "confer with the employer" in order to inform him of "any apparent safety or health violations disclosed by the inspection"). Save for these and, for our purposes, other similarly innocuous details, the regulations neither mandate a particular modus operandi for conducting inspections nor otherwise materially restrict compliance officers' flexibility. Of particular importance, the regulations do not prescribe any specific regimen governing the scope or detail of general administrative inspections performed by compliance officers. . . .

The function of an OSHA compliance officer is an integral part of OSHA's enforcement policies. When conducting inspections under the auspices of an administrative plan, OSHA compliance officers are expected to study the layout of the facility they are about to investigate, to review its health and safety records, and to interview employer and employee representatives during the inspection about working conditions. One might expect that as a result of such study, OSHA inspectors will make daily judgments about what risks and safety issues most urgently require their attention. At bottom, OSHA inspectors must visit numerous workplaces, all of which present different challenges and issues, and they simply cannot be expected to inspect every item in every plant. The day-to-day decisions made by compliance officers thus further OSHA's enforcement policy of ensuring adequate safety in workplaces with a view toward efficient and effective use of limited resources, and are thus grounded in policy. . . .

We are not persuaded by plaintiff's contention that all inspections ought to be painstakingly comprehensive because individual companies rely on OSHA inspections to improve their health and safety conditions. The OSH Act, in no uncertain terms, places primary responsibility for workplace safety on employers, not on the federal government. . . .

## Judgment and Result

Plaintiff loses. The Federal Tort Claims Act does not allow tort claims such as plaintiff's negligent OSHA inspection claim, which are based on discretionary functions. The manner of conducting OSHA inspections is discretionary.

## Questions

1. Is the OSH Act mandatory, meaning that it forces the government to do certain things and if it does not it can be sued for not doing them? Or is the OSH Act discretionary, meaning that the act essentially lets the OSHA do whatever it wants in carrying out the Congressional mandates and thus the OSHA is immune from suit if it does not observe the OSH Act? Note that this mandatory/discretionary characterization was essential to the success of plaintiff's suit.

   Did the court admit that the OSHA really is a hodge-podge of mandates and discretion?
2. When conducting OSHA inspections under an administrative plan, what are OSHA inspectors expected to do? Anything?
3. Under OSHA, who has the primary responsibility for workplace safety—employers or the Occupational Safety and Health Administration? Why? Is this reasonable in light of employers' desire to "cut costs to the bone" and thereby skimp on safety if at all possible?

## WORKERS' FINANCIAL SECURITY

### FAIR LABOR STANDARDS ACT

Congress enacted the Fair Labor Standards Act (FLSA) in 1938. The act's purpose was to eliminate labor conditions that did not allow employees to maintain minimum living standards. The belief was that substandard wages and working hours impaired employee health and welfare. Thus, Congress declared that poor labor conditions burdened commerce and led to unfair competition among the states.

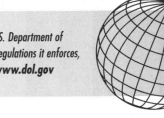

*To access the U.S. Department of Labor and the regulations it enforces, go to http://www.dol.gov*

Two of the FLSA's main provisions direct employees to pay their workers at least minimum wages and limit the hours employees can work unless they are paid overtime (higher) wages. The FLSA also establishes equal pay, record keeping, and child labor standards. These rules affect more than 50 million full-time and part-time workers.

The FLSA has recently been criticized as causing unemployment in certain labor sectors. Some maintain that such unemployment reflects that minimum wage rates are set above the value of the services these people have to offer.

*Covered Workers.* The FLSA covers workers in interstate commerce (such as interstate bus drivers) and workers producing goods for interstate commerce (such as the employees in Hastings, Michigan, who make piston rings for shipment throughout the United States). The following businesses are covered by the FLSA:

1. Laundries or dry cleaners
2. Construction firms
3. Hospitals
4. Schools (including higher education) whether public or private
5. Retail or service businesses with certain levels of annual gross incomes
6. Any other business having annual gross sales or business of certain levels

A business whose *only* regular employees are the owner or members of the owner's immediate family is not covered by the FLSA.

Federal employees are subject to the FLSA's minimum wage, overtime, child labor, and equal pay provisions. State and local government employees are covered by the FLSA's child labor and equal pay provisions only if they are in traditional governmental activities. (The U.S. Supreme Court indicates that schools, hospitals, parks, fire prevention, police protection, sanitation and public health, and recreation are considered traditional governmental activities.) Minimum wage and overtime provisions do not apply to state and local traditional governmental activities. Thus, for example, equal pay would have to be given to male and female state park employees doing the same work, but the state park does not have to pay the minimum federal wage or abide by the federal maximum working hours. (However, about three-fourths of the states have state wage and hour laws that could apply to state government employees.)

Some employees who do not work for businesses covered by the FLSA might still get the FLSA's minimum wage, maximum hours (overtime pay), equal pay, and child labor protections if they individually engage in interstate commerce. Such employees include those who regularly cross state lines in their work.

*FLSA Wage Standards.* Workers covered by the FLSA have a legal right to $5.15 per hour starting September 1, 1997. Covered workers also have a right to overtime pay at no less than one and one-half times the employees' regular rate after 40 hours of work in the work week.

Covered employers may sometimes pay less than the minimum wage. Learners, apprentices, and handicapped workers may, under certain circumstances, be paid less than the minimum wage. Full-time students in retail or service businesses, agriculture, or higher education institutions may be paid less than the minimum federal wage. (Keep in mind that most states have minimum wage laws that might cover students and others not federally protected.) Special certificates issued by the Department of Labor's wage and hour administrator must be obtained to pay these groups subminimum wages.

Industry wage orders may set minimum rates below the generally applicable FLSA minimum wage in Puerto Rico, the Virgin Islands, and American Samoa.

*FLSA Exemptions.* Despite being employed by a covered firm, some employees are not covered by the FLSA's minimum wage provisions. Others are not protected by the overtime sections. Still others get no wage or hour protection at all. The following jobs are exempt from both the FLSA's minimum wage and overtime provisions:

1. Executive, administrative, and professional employees, including teachers and academic administrative employees in elementary and secondary schools (outside salespeople are also included)
2. Employees of certain individually owned and operated small retail or service establishments not part of a covered enterprise
3. Employees of certain seasonal amusement or recreational establishments, employees of certain small newspapers, switchboard operators of small telephone companies, workers/sailors employed on foreign vessels, and employees engaged in fishing operations
4. Farm workers employed by anyone who used no more than 500 person-days of farm labor in any calendar quarter of the preceding calendar year
5. Casual babysitters and people employed as companions to the elderly

Certain workers are exempt from the FLSA's overtime provisions only (although many make beyond the minimum wage, and that protection is not worth much to them anyway).

As noted, professional employees are exempt from both the FLSA's minimum wage and overtime provisions. Is a home care nurse working for a private clinic a professional? Read *Fazekas v. Cleveland Clinic Found. Health Care* to find out.

*FLSA Child Labor Provisions.* The FLSA child labor provisions are partly designed to keep children in school and out of work that is harmful to their health or well-being. The U.S. Secretary of Labor publishes lists of hazardous farm and nonfarm occupations in which minors may not work. Department of Labor regulations controlling youth nonfarm jobs differ somewhat from those covering farm jobs.

*FLSA Record Keeping.* The FLSA requires employers to keep records on wages and hours. Most of the information is of the kind generally maintained by employers for other laws. These records do not have to be in any particular form. Time clocks need not be used.

## Fazekas v. Cleveland Clinic Foundation Health Care
U.S. Court of Appeals (6th Cir.)
204 F.3d 673 (2000)

### Background and Facts

Plaintiffs Marcia Fazekas, Carole Leland, Carole Pernell, Susan Shelko, and Rebecca Winfield, registered nurses formerly employed by the defendant, performed home health care visits for patients in the Cleveland metropolitan area during 1995 and 1996. These visits generally involved treating patients for diagnosed medical conditions, designing health care protocols for individual patients, and educating the patients and their families regarding participation in ongoing treatment. The plaintiffs also supervised home health care visits made by licensed practical nurses and kept administrative records for all visits to patients under their care.

The plaintiffs' individual employment relationships with the defendant were defined by signed employment agreements. As set forth in each standard agreement, the scheduling of a registered nurse's home health care visits was governed by the "25/15 Plan," which required each nurse to make at least 25 visits to patients and be on call at least 15 hours per week. Patients beginning a course of home health care treatments would be screened initially by a Health Care Ventures nursing supervisor, who would then assign each patient to one of the registered nurses performing home visits. Each nurse would then be responsible for developing an initial treatment plan for her new patient and scheduling all necessary home visits in accordance with that plan. Health Care Ventures provided guidelines for the patients' home visit schedules, but the nurses themselves devised each patient's individual treatment plan and were responsible for subsequent revisions in treatment protocols.

The nurses were compensated on a per-visit basis. Pursuant to an attachment to the employment agreement, the nurses received $30 for each home visit during periods when they were not on call, and $32 per visit when on call. The agreements were modified from time to time, so that eventually the nurses also received $37 for each visit involving infusion therapy, and $50 for each initial assessment of a new patient. These payments included compensation for all attendant transportation and administrative duties connected with the actual visits themselves.

The "25/15 Plan" was apparently designed to approximate a 40-hour work week. Nevertheless, the plaintiffs contended that they regularly made more than 25 total visits per week and generally documented 50 to 80 hours per week of work done in conjunction with these visits. Regardless of whether the plaintiffs worked more than 40 hours during any one week, they still received the standard per-visit fee for each home visit.

The plaintiffs were all separated from employment with Health Care Ventures on or about November 4, 1996. In 1997, they filed a complaint in federal district court alleging that Health Care Ventures violated the Fair Labor Standards Act by not paying them time-and-a-half for hours worked in excess of 40 hours per week.

In addressing the cross motions for summary judgment, the district court held that the defendant had satisfactorily shown that the plaintiffs were exempt from the overtime requirements of the act because they were "employed in a bona fide . . . professional capacity" as that term had been construed by the Department of Labor. The court thus granted the defendant's summary judgment motion, in an order that the plaintiffs now appeal.

### Body of Opinion

**Circuit Judge Daughtrey.** Under the Fair Labor Standards Act, employers must pay employees time-and-a-half for all hours worked over 40 hours per week. . . . Persons employed in a "bona fide . . . professional capacity," however, are exempted from the overtime pay requirements. . . . The act give the Secretary of Labor the power to determine which jobs qualify as bona fide professional employment. . . . In general, however, the professional exemption is to be narrowly construed to further Congress's goal of providing broad federal employment protection. . . .

Labor Department regulations construing and enforcing the act outline several requirements for employment purported to be professional in nature:

The term *employee employed in a bona fide . . . professional capacity* shall mean any employee:

a) Whose primary duty consists of the performance of . . . [w]ork requiring knowledge of an advanced type in a field of science or learning customarily acquired by a prolonged course of specialized intellectual instruction and study . . . and

b) Whose work requires the consistent exercise of discretion and judgment in its performance; and

c) Whose work is predominantly intellectual and varied in character (as opposed to routine mental, manual, mechanical, or physical work) and is of such character that the output produced or the result accomplished cannot be standardized in relation to a given period of time; and . . .

d) Who is compensated for services on a salary or fee basis at a rate of not less than $170 per week. . . .

In a dispute over whether overtime should have been paid, the employer bears the burden of showing that the professional exemption applies to the employees. . . . In this case, the plaintiffs concede that their work as registered nurses making home health care visits required knowledge of an advanced type and the consistent exercise of discretion and judgment and that it was predominantly intellectual and varied in character. They contest whether Health Care Ventures has shown that they were paid on a "fee basis."

According to the Department of Labor regulations, courts should encounter "[l]ittle or no difficulty" in determining whether a particular employment arrangement involves payment on a fee basis:

> Such arrangements are characterized by the payment of an agreed upon sum for a single job regardless of the time required for its completion. These payments in a sense resemble piece-work payments with the important distinction that, generally speaking, a fee payment is made for the kind of job which is unique rather than for a series of jobs which are repeated an indefinite number of times and for which payment on an identical basis is made over and over again.

In this case the plaintiffs were paid an agreed-upon sum for each visit regardless of the time spent on each visit. The parties dispute, however, whether home health care visits are "unique" and thus whether per-visit payment for these visits can be considered payment on a fee basis. Heeding the Supreme Court's command that the Secretary's interpretation of Department of Labor regulations is controlling unless "plainly erroneous or inconsistent with the regulations," . . . both parties present Department of Labor documents that purportedly articulate the Department's official position regarding the uniqueness of each home health care visit.

Health Care Ventures offers as evidence the June 1992 response of the Acting Administrator of the Wage and Hour Division of the Department to request for advise from counsel for an employer operating a home health care service. In its request for advice, the employer described a scenario in which it paid registered nurses on a per-visit basis to provide health care services to clients in their homes. According to the employer, "no employee will perform what is essentially a single repetitive task . . . over and over. Each patient's needs and situation [would be] different, and would be individually assessed and treated by the employee as the employee deems necessary during each visit. The employees must use independent, professional and largely unsupervised judgment on a case-by-case basis." In a written opinion letter, the Acting Administrator agree that these positions would meet the exemptions requirements of [Ed.: federal regulations] and, in particular, that the per-visit pay plan would qualify as compensation on a fee basis within the meaning of [federal regulations].

In response, the plaintiffs offer an internal memorandum dated October 1, 1994, from counsel for the Wage and Hour Division in response to a request from the National Association for Home Care for a formal opinion as to whether per-visit compensation of a registered nurse making home visits constitutes a fee basis of payment under the Department of Labor regulations. In its letter, the Association argues that each visit made by a registered nurse to a patient's home is necessarily unique. In the response, counsel for the Department's Wage and Hour Division disagreed, concluding:

> [W]e think that payment on a "per visit" basis is probably not the type of fee payment arrangement contemplated by the regulations. Section 541.313(d) refers to payment methods made

to singer, artists, and illustrator/writers to demonstrate the adequacy of a fee payment, i.e., whether the amount of payment meets the regulation's requirement that the rate of pay is "not less than $170 per week to a professional employee." The use of these professional occupations to demonstrate this point suggests to us that the character or nature of the job itself must be unique, and not simply that the performance of the job vary from day to day. While we recognize that the nurse will necessarily make professional judgments and assessments based on his or her skills in providing patient care on each visit, such work is not unique in character because unlike work performed by a singer, artist, or illustrator, the work performed by the nurse is generally repetitive and not original in character. . . .

However, as of the date of pendency of oral argument in this case, the Administrator of the Wage and Hour Division has not issued an opinion contrary to the position taken by the Administrator in 1992, to the effect that supervising nurses in a situation such as the one now before us are exempt employees.

In deciding which of the opinions, issued by the Division during different administrations, may help decide this case, we note that not all opinion letters of an administrative agency are worthy of deference by the courts. However, the Supreme Court has indicated that an opinion of the Administrator of the Wage and Hour Division of the Department of Labor has persuasive value if the position of the Administrator is well-considered and well-reasoned. . . .

The district held that the 1992 written opinion of the Acting Administrator, and not the 1994 internal memorandum, represented the Department's position on the question at issue in this case. We agree with the district court that the Acting Administrator's 1992 opinion letter is a controlling interpretation, that it is not inconsistent with the language of the regulation nor plainly erroneous. . . .

## Judgment and Result

The Court of Appeals affirmed the district court's holding that plaintiffs were engaged in a bona fide professional capacity, both because their duties required advanced knowledge and discretion and because they paid on a fee basis.

## Questions

1. Did the Court of Appeals hold that the work of nurses performing home health care would *always* qualify for the professional exemption and, hence, not be covered by the FLSA minimum hourly wage provision?

2. What impact does a decision such as that in the *Fazekas* case have on controlling national health care costs? Note that opinion letter the Court of Appeals followed was issued by the first Bush administration, while the more recent one relied upon by plaintiffs came from the Clinton administration. Does it seem odd to rely on an older document rather than a more recent document in interpreting a regulation?

*FLSA Enforcement.* The U.S. Department of Labor's Wage and Hour Division administers and enforces the FLSA against business. It also enforces the FLSA against state and local governments, federal employees of the Library of Congress, U.S. Postal Service, Postal Rate Commission, and the Tennessee Valley Authority. The U.S. Civil Service Commission enforces the FLSA for all other federal employees.

To see that the FLSA is followed, the Department of Labor's Wage and Hour Division has authority to investigate and gather data from an employer on wages, hours, and other employment conditions or practices. The division can tell an employer to change its way of operating so that it obeys the FLSA.

*FLSA Sanctions.* Willful violations of the FLSA are crimes carrying fines up to $10,000. Criminal convictions may result in imprisonment. Civil penalties are possible for violators of the FLSA's child labor provisions. It is an FLSA violation to fire or in any other manner discriminate against an employee who files a complaint or participates in an FLSA proceeding.

*Recovery of Back Wages.* One of the FLSA's remedies for workers is the possibility of recovering amounts they were underpaid. The statute of limitations is two years for recovery of back pay. If a willful violation occurs, the statute of limitations is three years. Workers can recover unpaid minimum or overtime wages in several ways:

1. The Department of Labor's Wage and Hour Division may supervise such payments.
2. The Secretary of Labor may sue for back wages *and* an equal amount as liquidated damages.
3. An employee may file a private suit for back pay *and* an equal amount as liquidated damages, plus attorney's fees and court costs.
4. The secretary of labor may get an injunction to stop anyone from violating the FLSA, including wrongful withholding of the proper minimum wages.

## EQUAL PAY ACT

The Equal Pay Act of 1963 amends the Fair Labor Standards Act (FLSA) and is part of the FLSA. The Equal Pay Act makes it illegal to pay different wages based on sex to men and women doing substantially the same work. If the jobs require equal skill, effort, and responsibility, and if working conditions are similar, pay to men and women must be equal. Because the act is federal law, it applies in all states to all businesses affecting interstate commerce, meaning that the Equal Pay Act applies to most businesses and labor unions as well. It also covers federal, state, and local government employees. The Equal Pay Act applies to most employees subject to the FLSA, including executive, administrative, professional, and outside sales personnel.

If a bank has two tellers—one a man, the other a woman—but each has slightly different tasks, the bank must pay them the same wages. Jobs do not have to be identical for the Equal Pay Act to apply. It is enough that they are substantially equal. Otherwise employers could easily defeat the Equal Pay Act's purpose to pay men and women the same amount for the same work by creating some small difference in their jobs and basing differences in pay on this inequality. If an employer violates the Equal Pay Act, it may not lower an employee's wages to eliminate the differential.

Suppose a wage difference is only partly based on sex. The difference is totally illegal. However, the Equal Pay Act does allow wage differences between men and women if based on factors other than sex. Such factors as bona fide seniority systems, merit systems, or systems rewarding productivity do not violate the act.

## Unemployment Compensation

The Social Security Act of 1935 established today's federal-state unemployment insurance system. The U.S. Supreme Court upheld its constitutionality in 1937. The system's basic idea is to pay workers something so that they can survive when they lose their jobs because of adverse business conditions.

*From Where Does the Money Come.* The money to pay unemployment compensation comes from federal payroll taxes imposed on employers. If states have unemployment insurance programs meeting federal requirements, employers pay state rather than federal unemployment taxes. (This state tax is credited against federal unemployment taxes.) By 1938, every state had enacted an unemployment compensation act.

*Which Employers Are Covered.* Any employer with one or more employees who worked some part of 20 or more weeks per year must pay federal (or state) unemployment taxes. Also covered are employers paying wages of $1,500 or more in any calendar quarter. The preceding are federal minimums that all state unemployment programs must meet. States may force more employers to pay unemployment taxes. A few do; for example, at least four states cover domestic employees who are not covered federally. Certain employers are exempt from unemployment taxes: employers of labor for educational, religious, and charitable institutions; employers of certain farm labor; employers of federal or state government labor; and employers of labor for the family.

*Which Employees Are Covered.* The unemployment system provides benefits only for employees working for covered employers (those paying unemployment taxes). In other words, if an employee works for an exempt employer and loses a job, no unemployment benefits are available.

Both federal and state law set unemployment eligibility requirements. Federal law sets certain coverage floors, or minimums. States may set how long a person must have worked to be eligible for unemployment benefits. For example, a person joining the labor force from high school who has never worked and is immediately unemployed is not entitled to unemployment benefits. States set earnings requirements before a person is entitled to unemployment benefits. Federal law does not set either earnings or minimum work requirements.

*Amount of Benefits.* The length and amount of unemployment benefits vary from state to state. All states give at least 26 weeks' coverage. Some go as high as 39 weeks. Additionally, various federal laws provide supplemental unemployment income when state unemployment income runs out. In some instances, this supplement (when added to state benefits) has lasted for as long as 65 weeks. Refer to Table 15.1 for data concerning the various states' unemployment benefits.

**TABLE 15.1 STATE UNEMPLOYMENT INSURANCE BY STATE AND OTHER AREA: 1999**
**(6,951 REPRESENTS 6,951,000.)**

| State or Other Area | Benefi-ciaries, First Pay-ments (1,000) | Benefits Paid (mil. dol.) | Avg. Weekly Unem-ploy-ment Benefits (dol.) | State or Other Area | Benefi-ciaries, First Pay-ments (1,000) | Benefits paid (mil. dol.) | Avg. Weekly Unem-ploy-ment Benefits (dol.) | State or Other Area | Benefi ciaries, First Pay-ments (1,000) | Benefits Paid (mil. dol.) | Avg. Weekly Unem-ploy-ment Benefits (dol.) |
|---|---|---|---|---|---|---|---|---|---|---|---|
| Total | 6,951 | 20,270 | 212 | KY | 104 | 240 | 201 | OH | 228 | 688 | 224 |
| AL | 128 | 192 | 156 | LA | 74 | 187 | 162 | OK | 45 | 121 | 209 |
| AK | 46 | 123 | 182 | ME | 33 | 81 | 192 | OR | 143 | 429 | 223 |
| AZ | 71 | 150 | 157 | MD | 97 | 271 | 205 | PA | 402 | 1,350 | 251 |
| AR | 77 | 162 | 197 | MA | 182 | 822 | 279 | RI | 44 | 141 | 246 |
| CA | 1,048 | 2,634 | 158 | MI | 323 | 880 | 238 | SC | 96 | 194 | 185 |
| CO | 55 | 159 | 241 | MN | 100 | 357 | 279 | SD | 8 | 16 | 170 |
| CT | 109 | 372 | 225 | MS | 55 | 110 | 153 | TN | 151 | 323 | 184 |
| DE | 23 | 56 | 204 | MO | 132 | 293 | 175 | TX | 359 | 1,189 | 225 |
| DC | 17 | 60 | 235 | MT | 25 | 56 | 181 | UT | 38 | 98 | 205 |
| FL | 223 | 670 | 212 | NE | 26 | 55 | 177 | VT | 18 | 45 | 203 |
| GA | 163 | 281 | 199 | NV | 65 | 192 | 216 | VA | 92 | 179 | 187 |
| HI | 31 | 130 | 278 | NH | 15 | 35 | 208 | WA | 190 | 906 | 276 |
| ID | 44 | 102 | 200 | NJ | 256 | 1,077 | 277 | WV | 52 | 129 | 198 |
| IL | 307 | 1,169 | 241 | NM | 30 | 86 | 178 | WI | 209 | 475 | 223 |
| IN | 112 | 271 | 210 | NY | 417 | 1,639 | 232 | WY | 11 | 27 | 201 |
| IA | 81 | 180 | 227 | NC | 216 | 428 | 219 | PR | 117 | 237 | 103 |
| KS | 53 | 158 | 237 | ND | 12 | 40 | 201 | VI | 2 | 4 | 173 |

*Source:* U.S. Employment and Training Administration, *Unemployment Insurance Financial Data Handbook.*

Generally, only certain causes entitle one to collect unemployment benefits. For example, economic recessions or depressions causing a person to be laid off generally entitle the person to benefits. If another job with someone else opens up, the unemployed person cannot turn it down and draw unemployment until his old job reappears. Every state unemployment compensation law requires that a person be available for, seeking, and able to work to collect benefits. If a person voluntarily quits a job without good cause, refuses suitable work, or is dismissed for improper conduct at work, he or she has no right to unemployment compensation.

Most state laws refuse to give unemployment benefits to workers on strike. The state of New York is an exception. The employer in the following case sued the state, claiming that this law violates the federal Constitution because it is **preempted** by the federal Social Security Act and the National Labor Relations Act. The U.S. Supreme Court said that the New York Unemployment Compensation Act is constitutional in *New York Telephone Company.*

Employers today, especially small employers, increasingly lease their workers from employment agencies. Who is responsible for FICA (Social Security) and FUTA (unemployment taxes) is such a case? The *U.S. v. Garami* case provides an answer.

# U.S. v. Garami
U.S. Dist. Ct., M.D. Fla.
184 B.R. 834 (2002)

## Background and Facts

Tidy Maid is a residential and commercial cleaning service run by the debtor, Imre Garami. An office manager assists Mr. Garami with the administrative functions of the business, and Tidy Maid uses from 12 to 18 cleaners. For economic reasons, the debtor Imre Garami, d/b/a (do business as) Tidy Maid began leasing his employees from Sunshine Staff Leasing, Inc. ("Sunshine") beginning in October of 1993. Under the lease agreement, Sunshine provides weekly payroll checks to the commissioned Tidy Maid cleaners in exchange for a fee totaling 3 percent of the gross payroll. Sunshine is responsible for paying withholding taxes and FICA. This arrangement also enables Tidy Maid cleaners and the debtor to obtain health insurance through Sunshine.

The debtor and Tidy Maid's office manager are responsible for the day-to-day supervision of the cleaners. Tidy Maid hires, fires, trains, assigns, and controls the cleaners and provides them with transportation to and from their work assignments, cleaning materials, and vacuum cleaners. Sunshine's role is limited. It pays the cleaners' commissions according to instructions given by Tidy Maid and arranges for an initial drug test.

Prior to the contract with Sunshine, Tidy Maid's taxes were done with the help of a firm of CPAs. The debtor has no knowledge of whether Sunshine has paid tax liabilities as required under its contract with Tidy Maid.

This controversy arises out of the United States' claim that the debtor owes unpaid FICA (Form 941) liabilities for the last quarter of 1993 which it alleges were generated with respect to the leased employees. The United States takes the position that Tidy Maid rather than Sunshine was the employer of the leased employees and that Tidy Maid rather than Sunshine is responsible for allegedly unpaid employment tax liabilities. The debtor takes the position that Sunshine is liable.

Although Tidy Maid contends that all appropriate moneys have been sent to Sunshine, the government maintains that it has no proof that the taxes have been paid. Sunshine, who is not a party to the action at this time, pays the taxes for the leased employees under its own employer identification number. The government's position appears to be that unless it receives information from Sunshine breaking down Sunshine's lump payment by individual tax identification numbers or proof that taxes have been paid for all of the employees Sunshine leases, the government will hold the debtor responsible for all of the taxes. The government contends that the federal obligation is that of the person who meets the qualifications of an employer, and that the debtor, not Sunshine, is such person. The bankruptcy court held for Tidy Maid, and the United States appealed to the federal district court which tried the matter *de novo* (reintroduced all evidence and witnesses).

## Body of Opinion

**Judge Fawsett.** . . . The Internal Revenue Code requires employers to deduct withholding taxes and pay FICA (Social Security) and FUTA (federal/state unemployment taxes) on employees' wages. . . . An "employer" is defined as "the person for whom an individual performs or performed any service, of whatever nature, as the employee of such person except that— (1) if the person for whom the individual performs or performed the services does not have control of the payment of the wages for such services the term "employer" . . . means the person having control of the payment of such wages. . . ." The determination of the employer–employee relationship involves an analysis of 20 common law factors which are as follows:

(1) whether the worker must comply with the other person's instructions about when, where, and how to work;
(2) whether the worker is trained by the person for whom the services are performed;
(3) whether the worker's services are integrated into the business operations;
(4) whether the services must be rendered personally by the worker;
(5) whether the person for whom the services are performed hires, supervises, and pays assistants;
(6) whether there is a continuing relationship between the worker and the person for whom the services are performed;
(7) whether the person for whom the services are performed establishes set hours of work;
(8) whether the worker must devote substantially full time to the business of the person or persons for whom the services are performed;
(9) whether the work is performed on the premises of the person for whom the services are performed;
(10) whether the person for whom services are performed retains the right to set the order or sequence of tasks;
(11) whether the worker is required to submit oral or written reports;
(12) whether payment is made by hour, week, or month rather than lump sum;
(13) whether the workers' business and/or traveling expenses are paid;
(14) whether the worker must supply tools, materials, and other equipment;
(15) whether the worker makes a significant investment in facilities used to perform services;
(16) whether a worker can realize a profit or suffer a loss as a result of services;
(17) whether a worker performs services for more than one firm at a time;

(18) whether a worker makes services available to the general public;

(19) whether the person for whom the services are performed has the right to discharge a worker; and

(20) whether a worker has the right to terminate the working relationship without incurring liability.

These criteria are ordinarily used to distinguish between an employee and an independent contractor but are equally applicable to determine by whom an individual is employed. . . . No one factor is controlling, but a critical question is whether the person for whom the work is performed has the right to control the activities of the individuals whose status is in issue, not only as to results but also as to the means and method to be used for accomplishing the result. . . . A contract which purports to create an employer–employee relationship is not controlling where an analysis of the common law factors as applied to the facts of the particular situation establish that such a relationship does not exist. . . .

Whether or not two parties stand in an employer–employee relationship is a factual question. . . . In factually similar situations involving leasing corporations, courts have declined to find that workers were employees of the corporations from which they were leased. . . . This court finds that Tidy Maid's employees are no exception and that the Bankruptcy Court erred in its ruling to the contrary. The administrative acts performed by Sunshine of arranging for the initial drug testing, providing the cleaners with information about the health insurance, and providing W-4 forms do not supersede the economic reality of the employer–employee relationship that the cleaners have with Tidy Maid. Sunshine generates payroll checks based on the information supplied to it by Tidy Maid. There is no evidence to suggest that Sunshine would pay the cleaners and file the employment taxes regardless of whether Tidy Maid submits payment. . . .

Although Sunshine contractually agrees to pay the employment taxes of Tidy Maid's cleaners, such an agreement does not relieve that actual employer, Tidy Maid, of the obligation to pay those taxes. . . . Because each taxpayer has a nondelegable duty to timely perform its federal income tax obligations, a contract with a third party does not relieve it of its duty to do so. THerefore, in the instant case, although the debtor may have paid the appropriate taxes to Sunshine for forwarding to the United States, until payment is actually made to the government, the responsibility for such payment rests on the shoulders of the debtor. . . .

It appears that the Bankruptcy Court's ruling was influenced by the seeming unfairness of the burden this result places on a debtor who is making a good-faith attempt to comply with the law. In the instant case, the debtor may be able to secure proof of payment from Sunshine that would satisfy the government's demands. As problems such as those presented become more widespread, it is up to Congress, not the court, to fairly and affirmatively accommodate the peculiarities of staff leasing into this country's internal revenue system.

## Judgment and Result

Tidy Maid loses. It must pay FICA and FUTA taxes for workers it leased from Sunshine.

## Questions

1. Leasing staff—that is, hiring "temps"—is increasingly common in the United States. Does this case provide comfort to an employer who leases its staff from such an employee leasing service on the assumption that the leasing service will make appropriate FICA and FUTA payments to the appropriate taxing authorities out of a lump sum the leasing employer gives to the lessor employer?

2. Shouldn't a leasing employer demand from the firm from whom it leases workers a breakdown of amounts paid to employees and amounts withheld for various tax payments?

*Experience Rating.* An employer may reduce its unemployment tax liability if its employees are unemployed less than the average. This reduction occurs because of the experience rating factor. **Experience rating** relates a particular employer's unemployment tax rates to employment rates. If an employer has steady levels of employment so that its workers are seldom out of work, it will have a low experience rating, which means lower unemployment taxes for that particular employer. Experience ratings are affected by all employers' employment levels. During high unemployment, all employers pay higher unemployment taxes, because more people are drawing from the unemployment fund.

*Exhaustion of Unemployment Benefits.* When unemployment benefits (both state and supplemental federal benefits) run out, a worker is left to public works employment (if it is available), welfare, charity, or the generosity of friends and relatives to survive.

## SOCIAL SECURITY[1]

To access the Social Security Administration's Web site, go to **http://www.ssa.gov**

Marv Wollin had been a tool and die worker with American Machine Company for 45 years. He started work at age 20 after serving three years in the U.S. Army. Marv had managed to put his two children through college at State University and had fully paid for his house. He was planning to retire the next year. Both he and his wife were in good health and they hoped to move to Florida. Marv started calculating his retirement, knowing he would receive a monthly retirement check from the company retirement fund. He also knew he would start getting a Social Security check but was uncertain whether his Social Security income would be taxed. He also wondered whether his Social Security income would be cut, because he had heard the Social Security system was going bankrupt. He was concerned that his working part-time might cause him to lose his monthly Social Security income.

Let us examine the answers to these uncertainties.

*Background.* The Social Security Act took effect in 1935. Its original purpose was to provide a minimal income for retired workers. The original act did not provide for survivors of a worker who died in the prime of life, leaving a family. In 1939, an amendment to the act increased coverage to pay dependents of a worker who died. The 1935 Act gave only the worker—no dependents—money to live on in retirement. The 1939 amendments gave a retirement income to certain of the worker's dependents.

The 1935 Act gave nothing to workers who were totally disabled. It was not until July 1957 that Social Security Act disability insurance benefits were first given to workers who lost income due to total disability.

In 1965, the Social Security program was amended to include Medicare, which assures hospital and medical insurance protection to people 65 and over. Since 1973, Medicare coverage has been available to people under age 65 entitled to disability checks for two or more consecutive years. The 1973 amendments also cover people with permanent kidney failure who need dialysis or kidney transplants. Additional medical problems are added to the coverage from time to time.

*Workers Covered.* In 1935 the Social Security program covered only workers in industry and commerce. The 1950s saw the program expand to cover household and farm employees, people in the U.S. armed forces, members of the clergy, most self-employed people, and most state and local employees. Today, most workers in the United States (nine out of ten, according to the U.S. Department of Health and Human Services) are covered by Social Security.

*Administration.* The Social Security program is run by the Social Security Administration in the U.S. Department of Health and Human Services. Employers and the self-employed send in periodic (monthly or more frequent) Social Security taxes to a Federal Reserve bank or designated commercial bank.

Employers must keep records for Social Security purposes. Employee names, earnings, Social Security numbers (no two are alike), and other information must be kept for four years after the taxes are due. Government officials may inspect employer Social Security records.

---

[1] The authors acknowledge the assistance of Social Security Administration brochures in preparing this section.

*Types of Social Security Benefits.* About one out of six persons in the United States gets some form of Social Security benefit. Retirement checks are what most people think of when the term *Social Security* is mentioned. People today can start receiving retirement benefits at age 62. People who wait until age 65 before retiring draw larger benefits than those retiring earlier. Even after early retirees reach age 65, they draw less than those who waited. After workers retire, what kind of benefits can they expect? Three factors influence the size of retirement benefits: (1) the average yearly earnings covered by Social Security, (2) the age at retirement, and (3) the number of dependents.

The Social Security Act provides, in addition to retirement benefits, disability and survivors' benefits. A worker becoming severely disabled before age 65 can receive disability checks under Social Security. Disability for Social Security purposes exists if a person has a severe physical or mental condition that prevents working and is expected to last (or has lasted) for at least 12 months or is expected to end in death. Blindness is an example. Disability checks start on the sixth full month of a worker's disability and continue as long as the disability lasts. Severely disabled workers (e.g., those totally blinded) can get benefits even if they manage to do *some* work. The size of the disability benefit is currently tied to one's age and work credit.

For adults, one of the most frequent disabilities is back injuries. The following case presents a common claim for Social Security disability payments and provides a flavor of the problems associated with such claims.

---

## Schmidt v. Apfel
### Federal District Court (D. Kansas)
### 39 F.Supp.2d 1291 (1999)

## Background and Facts

Vera Schmidt applied for disability benefits on July 11, 1994, stating that she had become disabled on February 16 of that year. The claim was denied initially and on reconsideration. An administrative law judge (ALJ) denied her claim on January 26, 1996. He determined that Schmidt was unable to return to her former employment, but that she could perform other work in the national economy. Schmidt's appeal from this decision was denied on February 12, 1997. She then instituted the present action.

At the time of the hearing before the ALJ, Schmidt was 53 years old. She had a high school education, and had worked as a print shop worker, a bookkeeper, and a gas station attendant. After the date of her alleged disability, she briefly returned to the print shop on a part-time basis. She was not engaged in any substantial gainful activity at any time since February 16, 1994.

On February 7, 1994, Schmidt saw a chiropractor, Stephen Dent, complaining of pain in the thoracic and lumbar areas. Dent reported a "decreased" range of motion in these areas, and wrote in his notes that Schmidt had "acute moderate thoracic strain." He prescribed ice packs and scheduled Schmidt for another visit in two days. Schmidt continued to see Dent on several occasions up to January 20, 1995. Schmidt contacted Dr. Ted R. Cook, her family physician, on March 8, 1994. Dr. Cook reported that "Vera is in

today wanting an evaluation of her back for Workman's Comp." He noted that Schmidt had been seeing Dent who was treating a rib between her scapula, "usually getting the rib popped back in place when she is in his office but as soon as she gets home she does something and it pops right back out."

She reported back pain, but stated that it "seems to be much better" since she began taking Flexeril, which she took at night because it made her drowsy. Dr. Cook examined Schmidt and found "very tender areas" near the spine. He found no neurological deficits and no paresthesia. He prescribed Lodine 300 mg. for Schmidt to take with the Flexeril.

Dr. Cook saw Schmidt on a number of occasions during 1994. On March 11, Dr. Cook reported that Schmidt stated she was continuing to see Dent for her lumbar strain and that she was "60 to 70% improved." Dr. Cook's examination indicated "moderate spasm" in the lumbar region, and that Schmidt has "good range of motion." He advised her to modify her work activities so that she didn't have to lift so much and to exercise. On May 2, he reported that Schmidt showed "significant spasm" in the thoracic region, but did not show any tenderness in the joints or lumbar region.

On May 4, 1994, Schmidt had seen orthopedist Dr. Jay Stanley Jones. Dr. Jones found Schmidt's x-rays showed some thoracic area spinal degeneration. He wrote that Schmidt had "a chronic overuse syndrome seeing that she gets better over the weekends and then when she returns to work she gets worse." He decided to keep Schmidt off work for a week and prescribed Feldene. "If this improves her symptomatology," he wrote, "I am going to recommend a job change."

In May, Schmidt reported to Dr. Jones that there was little change in her condition, although she was a "little bit better." On June 22, she saw Dr. Jones complaining of "increasing back pain" which was "localized over the scapula."

In August, Schmidt reported that her back condition hadn't changed, that she felt it was "as good as she is going to be" and that she wanted to schedule a functional capacity examination. On September 29, Dr. Jones wrote that Schmidt should sit at a desk or stand in one position for "brief periods" only. She should not use a keyboard or do bookkeeping or other repetitive work with her hands. However, Dr. Jones indicated that Schmidt's "impairment rating" for her back was only 8 percent.

The hearing before the ALJ was conducted on September 27, 1995. Subsequent to the hearing, on November 1, 1995, Dr. Jones summarized his findings regarding Schmidt in a letter to her attorney. He wrote that Schmidt was being seen for severe shoulder pain, as well as carpal tunnel syndrome. He concluded that he did not believe Schmidt could perform even sedentary work because of her pain, which limited her to sitting for 10 minutes, and then standing or walking for 10 minutes. She could lift 5 to 10 pounds frequently, and 20 pounds occasionally. She had an "impingement syndrome" which restricted her ability to perform grasping, gripping, and reaching motions with her hands."

Schmidt testified at the hearing, stating that her pain is a dull pain in the upper part of her back. Schmidt testified that the pain becomes a stabbing pain when she stands for 10 minutes, does dishes, sits in a work position for 10 to 15 minutes, or lifts too much. When this happens, she sits in her recliner for 45 minutes to an hour. She can then resume work for a shorter period of time than she would have been able to perform but for the onset of the stabbing pain.

She also gets headaches that begin in her neck and move up. She treats these headaches with over-the-counter medicines and sitting in her recliner. She spends approximately five hours a day in her recliner.

Her hands and fingers get tingly and numb on occasion. Her hands hurt when her back hurts or when she has been using them. She often drops things and can no longer crochet. She continues to needlepoint, which she can do for 45 minutes, after which she relaxes in her recliner for 15 to 20 minutes before resuming. She prepares supper three times a week, each of which requires an hour of preparation. She no longer goes boating or fishing, or plays ball. She can read in her recliner and goes to her son's basketball games. She can lift 30 pounds, although she has found it difficult because it causes a sharp pain in her back. She can lift 15 pounds comfortably but not reliably. She takes medications only on an as-needed basis.

On a scale of one to ten, she has described her pain as an eight, when it has been aggravated by an activity such as doing dishes. After steroidal treatment, she testified that her pain diminished to a level of four or five for two or three weeks. None of her physicians has recommended surgery on her back or hands nor have they prescribed electronic pain blockers or back braces.

A vocational expert, Cindy Younger, also testified at the hearing. Younger testified that a person with Schmidt's vocational characteristics and residual function capacity (RFC) could lift 10 pounds frequently and 15 to 30 pounds occasionally and perform the job of bookkeeper, one of Schmidt's previous jobs. The ALJ asked Younger about the effect of a hypothetical RFC that would limit Schmidt to the frequent lifting of only nominal weights, occasional lifting of 10 to 15 pounds, with a limitation on standing no more than two to four hours per eight-hour shift.

Younger testified that such an RFC would not preclude working as a bookkeeper. She stated that Schmidt had acquired the skills to work in such a job from her previous employment and could work in the position of reception clerk, of which there were 2,630 positions in Kansas and 900 in the Wichita area.

The ALJ determined that there was no evidence Schmidt met or exceeded a listed impairment, that she could not return to work due to her medical condition, but that she could perform other work in the national economy. However, the ALJ also determines that Schmidt's claim of total inability to work was not credible. He noted several factors in reaching this conclusion: (1) that the objective medical records established "only minimal degenerative changes of the thoracic spine; (2) that there was a contradiction between the level of incapacity claimed by Schmidt and her normal daily activities.

## Body of Opinion

Under . . . [the U.S. Code] "the finding of the Secretary as to any fact, if supported by substantial evidence, shall be conclusive." Substantial evidence is more than a scintilla and is that evidence which a reasonable mind might accept as adequate to support a conclusion. . . .

This deferential standard of review does not apply to the Secretary's application of the law. . . . In determining whether the decision of the Secretary is based on substantial evidence, the court is not to re-weigh the evidence or substitute its judgment for that of the Secretary. . . . However, the court will not simply "rubber stamp" the decision of the Secretary.

The qualifications for disability insurance benefits under the Social Security Act are that the claimant meets the insured status requirements, is less than 65 years of age, and is under a "disability." . . . An individual "shall be determined to be under a disability only if his physical or mental impairment or impairments are of such severity that he is not only unable to do his previous work but cannot, considering his age, education, and work experience, engage in any other kind of substantial gainful work which exists in the national economy." . . .

The burden is on the claimant to prove the existence of a disability that prevents him from engaging in his prior work or a continuous period of twelve months. . . . If the claimant makes such a showing, the Secretary must show the claimant is able to do other work in jobs present in the national economy. . . .

The Secretary employs a five-step process in determining the existence of a disability . . . a process that ends at any point if the Secretary determines the claimant is disabled or not. The steps, in order, require determinations of whether the claimant: (1) is currently engaged in substantial gainful activity; (2) has a medically severe impairment or combination of impairments; (3) has an impairment equivalent to one of a number of extremely severe impairments listed in 20 C.F.R. Part 404, Subpt. P, App. 1; (4) is unable, due to the impairment, to perform past work; and (5) has the residual functional capacity to perform other work available in the national economy, considering age, education, and past work experience. . . .

The ALJ's decision correctly states and applies the relevant standards. . . . While Schmidt points to other indicia of physical impairments, it remains true that none of the impairments is more than minimal in nature. . . . In her appeal, Schmidt repeatedly argues that a person need not be completely disabled to be entitled to benefits. This is certainly true, but it misses the point here, which is that Schmidt's credibility as to her assertions of nearly complete disability—for instance, that she cannot perform sedentary work because she cannot hold a pen or pencil—are directly undermined by evidence that, for example, she performs needlework for as much as 45 minutes at a time. She also shops, cooks, keeps house, and attends her son's basketball games. Schmidt argues that the ALJ erred in not explicitly considering facts that would buttress her credibility. Schmidt fails to show any error, however. The ALJ con-

cluded that Schmidt's claims were partially credible, finding that she did suffer some moderate, non-disabling degree of pain. The allegedly corroborative evidence does not alter the inconsistencies noted in Schmidt's claims, which were noted by the ALJ. . . .

## Judgment and Result

Schmidt loses. The ALJ's decision was affirmed.

## Questions

1. Does someone who has never been employed qualify for Social Security disability payments?
2. What is RFC, and how does it relate to qualifying for Social Security disability payments?
3. If a worker is able to engage in some other job for which he or she is qualified, but not his or her original work, does it mean that he or she cannot recover Social Security disability income?
4. How common are back injuries? If a more relaxed standard of qualification applied to Social Security disability payments, what would happen to the Social Security budget and Social Security taxes? Given the elusiveness of objectively measuring whether someone has a back injury, does this play into the decision to have a "tough" test for such disability payments, as exemplified by the *Schmidt* case? How important was Schmidt's credibility in proving her claim?

*Building Work Credits.* Work credit refers to a minimum amount of time a person must work (covered by Social Security) before becoming eligible for benefits. Social Security work credit is measured in quarters of coverage. A worker can earn no more than four quarters of coverage for a year. The amount of covered earnings needed for a quarter of coverage will increase automatically in the future to keep pace with average wages.

If a worker does not work enough quarters to qualify for Social Security benefits, the worker gets no benefits. Also, such workers do not get back the Social Security tax they or their employer paid while they worked. However, work credit that workers earn stays on their records. Thus, if a person without enough work credit to qualify for Social Security returns to work, that person can add to work credit already earned and eventually could qualify for benefits.

The amount of Social Security benefits one eventually gets depends on average earnings during one's working years and on one's personal situation (e.g., being married with two dependents versus being single). Once the minimum work credits to qualify for Social Security are earned, working has no effect on the size of one's Social Security benefits. One's personal situation (e.g., marital status and number of dependents) then affects benefit size.

*Financing Social Security.* The employer and the employee pay equal Social Security taxes for the employee. The tax rate schedule for employers and employees is shown in Table 15.2. Note that it was set at 7.51 percent each (or

### TABLE 15.2 TAX RATE SCHEDULE FOR EMPLOYEES AND EMPLOYERS

**Percent of Covered Earnings**

| Years | For Retirement, Survivors, and Disability Insurance | Hospital Insurance | Employee and Employer Rate | Total |
|-------|------|------|------|-------|
| 1988–89 | 6.06 | 1.45 | 7.51 | 15.02 |
| 1990 and later | 6.20 | 1.45 | 7.65 | 15.30 |

*Source*: Social Security Administration.

14.3 percent total) of the employee's gross wages or salary for 1988 and 1989 and rose to 7.65 percent each (or 15.3 percent total) of the employee's gross salary in 1990.

Self-employed people now pay the same rate for Social Security as do employers and employees combined, because the benefits are the same for the self-employed as for employees. Table 15.3 shows Social Security tax rates for self-employed people. The maximum salary taxable is the same for employees and the self-employed.

*Social Security Features.* Social Security has a number of significant points.

1. Social Security *benefits* are not subject to state or local income taxes. However, a worker earning $20,000 pays a Social Security tax on the entire $20,000, even though that worker takes home less than $20,000 because of federal income taxes and other deductions. Thus, the worker is taxed (by the Social Security tax) on tax (the amount of the federal income tax taken from the worker's paycheck).
2. Social Security payments may not be garnished by the beneficiary's creditors.
3. Social Security benefits (of all types) increase if the cost of living increases.
4. A person must survive to get Social Security retirement benefits. Those who die before retirement will reap no personal benefit from their years of contributions, although their survivors, if any, might draw benefits.

*Social Security Changes.* The following changes were made to the Social Security system in 1983:

1. The COLA (cost of living adjustment) was modified to make inflows and outflows to the system more nearly equal.
2. People who first became federal workers on January 1, 1984, or later are now part of the system.
3. Social Security beneficiaries in certain cases now pay federal income taxes on their benefits. (Single retirees making more than $25,000 and couples receiving $32,000 from other sources can have as much as 85 percent of their Social Security benefits taxed.)

*Current Issue: Social Security Equity.* A matter not corrected in 1983 was the serious intergenerational wealth transfer now occurring under Social Security. Specifically, current retirees withdraw all they have paid into Social Security

### TABLE 15.3 TAX RATE SCHEDULE FOR SELF-EMPLOYED PEOPLE

**Percent of Covered Earnings**

| Years | For Cash Benefits | For Hospital Insurance | Total |
|---|---|---|---|
| 1984 | 11.40 | 2.60 | 14.00 |
| 1985 | 11.40 | 2.70 | 14.10 |
| 1986–87 | 11.40 | 2.90 | 14.30 |
| 1988–89 | 12.12 | 2.90 | 15.02 |
| 1990 and later | 12.40 | 2.90 | 15.30 |

*Source:* Social Security Administration.

within 18 to 24 months after retiring. These retirees then continue to draw Social Security benefits even if they have no financial need. In fact, millionaires may draw Social Security retirement benefits even after receiving all they have paid in. Further, current retirees will on the average draw four dollars in benefits for every one dollar they paid into Social Security. Who pays the missing three dollars? The working people who currently pay Social Security taxes. Thus, the intergenerational wealth transfer is away from the younger generation (who generally have a greater financial need) to the retirees, who often are doing well financially.

## REGULATION OF EMPLOYEE PENSIONS

Sara Coleman had contributed 6 percent of her weekly take-home pay to her employer's retirement plan for the past five years. She wondered what was being done with the money. Was it in safe or risky investments? She also was thinking of changing jobs. If she went to work for a new employer, would she lose her pension contributions, or would they follow her to her new job (that is, were they "portable")? She also asked her employer for information about the retirement plan. The employer refused to give her any information. Was Sara entitled to anything?

Private retirement plans, which are separate from Social Security, involve billions of employee (and often employer) dollars. If an employer sets up a qualified employee retirement plan, employer contributions are tax deductible from the employer's standpoint. Income earned on pension contributions while it accumulates, before it is paid out, is not subject to federal income taxation, and usually not to state and local taxes, either. When a person retires, however, amounts received from a qualified pension plan are taxed by federal, state, and local income tax laws. The assumption is that a retired worker will then be in a lower tax bracket, and the taxes paid will thus be lower.

The U.S. Internal Revenue Code sets the rules for establishing qualified employee retirement plans. The **coverage requirement** means that a certain percentage of all employees must be part of the retirement program. This requirement forces top management to spread benefits to lower-level employees.

In addition to the terms just discussed, you should be aware of several other pension-related terms. First, pensions can be *noncontributory* (where only the employer pays into them for the employees' retirement) or *contributory* (where the employees each pay at least part of the contribution). Second, in **defined**

**contribution** plans, the periodic payment into the pension plan is fixed, whereas in **defined benefit** plans, the periodic payment into the plan varies so that the benefits ultimately received will be a definite—often indexed—dollar amount. Generally, defined contribution plans are more favorable to employers because the amounts employers must pay into such plans are fixed, while amounts paid into defined benefit plans tend to increase as inflation makes it necessary to maintain benefit levels. Of course, if the plan's investment experience is favorable, the employer's contributions can decrease in a defined benefit plan so it can benefit employers.

## EMPLOYEE RETIREMENT INCOME SECURITY ACT OF 1974 (ERISA)

Many employees, such as Sara Coleman in the previous story, pay money into an employer-established retirement plan. Many, like Sara, wonder what protections the law provides for employee retirement plans. Congress enacted ERISA to deal with just those concerns to see that employee retirement plans provide the retirement income they are supposed to when they are supposed to.

*Fiduciary Duties.* ERISA tries to protect employee retirement plans in several ways. Although ERISA imposes other restrictions on employee retirement plans, the main ones are as follows. First, it creates *fiduciary duties* for plan managers and advisors. Second, it requires plan records and reports. Third, it sets plan investment restrictions. Fourth, it creates a federal corporation to insure employee benefits should the plan fail. Fifth, ERISA requires vesting of both employee and employer contributions. Sixth, it places funding requirements on certain plans.

ERISA's fiduciary duties for plan managers and advisors place the law's highest duty of care and good faith on such people. Specifically, plan managers and advisors should use the care that prudent people would use in managing their own assets. This high level of duty exists because employee retirement plans must be protected to make sure retirement income is available. Furthermore, plan managers and advisors have millions, sometimes hundreds of millions or even billions, of employee dollars under their control. The temptation to abuse this control is great; therefore, the deterrent against such abuse must also be great. The ERISA fiduciary duty applies to both retirement plan managers (those exercising control over the plan) and plan advisors who charge for their services.

The following case addresses the matter of self-dealing or the conflict of interest provision of ERISA. Specifically, ERISA forbids employers' retirement committees from causing their plan to engage in transactions that directly or indirectly transfer plan assets to parties in interest. In other words, retirement plan managers should not sell plan assets to themselves (presumably at bargain prices) or force the plan to buy assets from the managers' personal assets (undoubtedly at inflated prices). The idea is that plan managers should avoid conflicts of interest. What if an employer promises employees increased retirement benefits if they forgo age discrimination and ERISA claims against the employer? Is this transaction benefitting a party in interest (here the employer) prohibited? The *Lockheed Corp. v. Spink* case examines this issue.

## Lockheed Corporation v. Spink
U.S. Supreme Court
116 S.Ct. 1783 (1996)

### Background and Facts

Paul Spink was employed by Lockheed Corporation from 1939 until 1950, when he left to work for one of Lockheed's competitors. In 1979, Lockheed persuaded Spink to return. Spink was 61 years old when he resumed employment with Lockheed. At that time, the terms of the Lockheed Retirement Plan for Certain Salaried Individuals (Plan), a defined benefit plan, excluded from participation employees who were over the age of 60 when hired. This exclusion was expressly permitted by ERISA.

Congress later passed the Omnibus Budget Reconciliation Act of 1986 (OBRA). Section 9203(a) of OBRA repealed the age-based exclusion provision of ERISA, and the statute now flatly mandates that "[n]o pension plan may exclude from participation (on the basis of age) employees who have attained a specified age." Sections 9201 and 9202 of OBRA amended ERISA and ADEA (the Age Discrimination in Employment Act) to prohibit age-based cessations of benefit accruals and age-based reductions in benefit accrual rates.

In an effort to comply with these new laws, Lockheed ceased its prior practice of age-based exclusion from the plan, effective December 25, 1988. As of that date, all employees, including Spink, who had previously been ineligible to participate in the plan due to their age at the time of hiring became members of the plan. Lockheed made clear, however, that it would not credit those employees for years of service rendered before they became members.

When later faced with the need to streamline its operations, Lockheed amended the plan to provide financial incentives for certain employees to retire early. Lockheed established two programs, both of which offered increased pension benefits to employees who would retire early, payable out of the plan's surplus assets. Both programs required as a condition of the receipt of benefits that participants release any employment-related claims they might have against Lockheed. Though Spink was eligible for one of the programs, he declined to participate because he did not wish to waive any ADEA or ERISA claims. He then retired, without earning any extra benefits for doing so.

Spink brought this suit, in his individual capacity and on behalf of others similarly situated, against Lockheed and several of its directors and officers. Among other things, the complaint alleged that Lockheed and the members of the board of directors violated ERISA's duty of care and prohibited transactions provisions by amending the plan to create the retirement programs. Relatedly, the complaint alleged that the members of Lockheed's Retirement Committee, who implemented the plan as amended by the board, violated those same parts of ERISA. For these alleged ERISA violations, Spink sought monetary, declaratory, and injunctive relief pursuant to ERISA's enforcement provisions. Lockheed moved to dismiss the complaint for failure to state a claim, and the District Court granted the motion.

The Court of Appeals for the Ninth Circuit reversed. That court held that the amendments to the plan were unlawful under ERISA § 406(a)(1)(D), which prohibits a fiduciary from causing a plan to engage in a transaction that transfers plan assets to a party in interest or involves the use of plan assets for the benefit of a party in interest. The court reasoned that because the amendments offered increased benefits in exchange for a release of employment claims, they constituted a use of plan assets to "purchase" a significant benefit for Lockheed. Though the court found a violation of § 406, it decided that there was no need to address Lockheed's status as a fiduciary. The Supreme Court issued a writ of certiorari (the way to appeal a case to the Supreme Court).

### Body of Opinion

**Justice Thomas.** Nothing in ERISA requires employers to establish benefits plans. Nor does ERISA mandate what kind of benefits employers must provide if they choose to have such a plan. . . . ERISA does, however, seek to ensure that employees will not be left empty-handed once employers have guaranteed them certain benefits. . . . Accordingly, ERISA tries to "make as certain as possible that pension fund assets [will] be adequate" to meet expected benefits payments. . . .

To increase the chances that employers will be able to honor their benefits commitments—that is, to guard against the possibility of bankrupt pension funds—Congress incorporated several key measures into the Act. Section 302 of ERISA sets minimum annual funding levels for all covered plans . . . and creates tax liens in favor of such plans when those funding levels are not met. . . . Sections 404 and 409 of ERISA impose respectively a duty of care with respect to the management of existing trust funds, along with liability for breach of that duty, upon plan fiduciaries. . . . Finally, § 406 of ERISA prohibits fiduciaries from involving the plan and its assets in certain kinds of business deals. . . . It is this last feature of ERISA that is at issue today.

Congress enacted § 406 "to bar categorically a transaction that [is] likely to injure the pension plan." . . . That section mandates, in relevant part, that "[a] fiduciary with respect to a plan shall not cause the plan to engage in a transaction, if he knows or should know that such transaction constitutes a direct or indirect . . . transfer to, or use by or for the benefit of a party in interest, of any assets of the plan." . . . The question here is whether this provision of ERISA prevents an employer from conditioning the receipt of early retirement benefits upon the participants' waiver of employment claims. For the following reasons, we hold that it does not.

Spink . . . alleged that the members of Lockheed's Retirement Committee who implemented the amended Plan violated § 406(a)(1)(D) . . . . [T]he court of appeals erred in holding that the Retirement Committee members violated the prohibited transaction section of ERISA without making the requisite finding of fiduciary status. It is not necessary for us to decide the question whether the Retirement Committee members acted as fiduciaries when they paid out benefits according to the terms of the amended Plan, however, because we do not think that they engaged in any conduct prohibited by § 406(a)(1)(D).

The "transaction" in which fiduciaries may not cause a plan to engage is one that "constitutes a direct or indirect . . . transfer to, or use by or for the benefit of a party in interest, of any assets of the plan." . . . Spink reads § 406(a)(1)(D) to apply in cases where the benefit received by the party in interest—in this case, the employer—is not merely a "natural incident of the administration of pension plans." . . . Lockheed, on the other hand, maintains that a plan administrator's payment of benefits to plan participants and beneficiaries pursuant to the terms of an otherwise lawful plan is wholly outside the scope of § 406(a)(1)(D). . . . We agree with Lockheed.

Section 406 (a)(1)(D) does not in direct terms include the payment of benefits by a plan administrator. And the surrounding provisions suggest that the payment of benefits is in fact not a "transaction" in the sense that Congress used the term in § 406 (a). Section 406 (a) forbids fiduciaries from engaging the plan in the "sale," "exchange," or "leasing" of property . . . ; the "lending of money" or "extension of credit," . . . the "furnishing of goods, services, or facilities," . . . ; and the "acquisition . . . of any employer security or employer real property," . . . with a party in interest. . . . These are commercial bargains that present a special risk of plan underfunding because they are struck with plan insiders, presumably not at arms-length. . . . What the "transactions" identified in § 406 (a) thus have in common is that they generally involve uses of plan assets that are potentially harmful to the plan. . . . The payment of benefits conditioned on performance by plan participants cannot reasonably be said to share that characteristic.

According to Spink and the Court of Appeals, however, Lockheed's early retirement programs were prohibited transactions within the meaning of § 406 (a)(1)(D) because the required release of employment-related claims by participants created a "significant benefit" for Lockheed. . . . Spink concedes, however, that among the "incidental" and thus legitimate benefits that a plan sponsor may receive from the operation of a pension plan are attracting and retaining employees, paying deferred compensation, setting or avoiding strikes, providing increased compensation without increasing wages, increasing employee turnover, and reducing the likelihood of lawsuits by encouraging employees who would otherwise have been laid off to depart voluntarily. . . .

We do not see how obtaining waivers of employment-related claims can meaningfully be distinguished from these admittedly permissible objectives. Each involves, at bottom, a quid pro quo between the plan sponsor and the participant: that is, the employer promises to pay increased benefits in exchange for the performance of some condition by the employee. . . . By Spink's admission,

the employer can ask the employee to continue to work for the employer, to cross a picket line, or to retire early. The execution of a release of claims against the employer is functionally no different; like these other conditions, it is an act that the employee performs for the employer in return for benefits. Certainly, there is no basis in § 406 (a)(1)(D) for distinguishing a valid from an invalid quid pro quo. Section 406 (a)(1)(D) simply does not address what an employer can and cannot ask an employee to do in return for benefits. . . . Furthermore, if an employer can avoid litigation that might result from laying off an employee by enticing him to retire early, as Spink concedes, it stands to reason that the employer can also protect itself from suits arising out of that retirement by asking the employee to release any employment-related claims he may have.

In short, whatever the precise boundaries of the prohibition in § 406 (a)(1)(D), there is one use of plan assets that it cannot logically encompass: a quid pro quo between the employer and plan participants in which the plan pays out benefits to the participants pursuant to its terms. When § 406 (a)(1)(D) is read in the context of the other prohibited transactions, it becomes clear that the payment of benefits in exchange for the performance of some condition by the employee is not a "transaction" within the meaning of § 406 (a)(1)(D); it also would provide little guidance to lower courts and those who must comply with ERISA.

## Judgment and Result

The payment of benefits under an amended retirement plan, regardless of what the plan requires of the employees in return for those benefits, does not constitute a prohibited transaction under ERISA.

## Questions

1. ERISA makes it illegal for retirement plan fiduciaries to self-deal, that is, engage in transactions that are "direct or indirect . . . transfers to, or use by or for the benefit of a party in interest, of any assets of the plan." Why is the employer's conditioning an employee's right to retirement benefits on the employee's giving up an age discrimination or ERISA claim the employee would otherwise have against the employer not considered self-dealing? After all, is the employer not using plan assets to benefit the employer by "buying off" litigation claims?

2. Is perhaps the key to the *Lockheed* case that the employer was not taking away employee retirement benefits that had already vested but, rather, was *increasing* retirement benefits for those who relinquished their otherwise valid employment claims against Lockheed?

3. The Lockheed Plan was a defined benefit plan. What does such a plan entail?

*Records and Reports.* ERISA imposes records and reports requirements. The plan manager must record each individual plan participant's length of employment and the amount of **vested benefits**. An explanation of the retirement plan must be given to each employee. This explanatory brochure of the retirement plan must be simple enough for the average person to understand. It might include such things as circumstances causing loss of plan benefits, claims procedures, and eligibility requirements. Each employee retirement plan must prepare an annual report with opinions from both an independent actuary and an independent certified public accountant. Employees and the public have a right to see the retirement plan's annual report. Although ERISA imposes disclosure requirements, some suggest they are not as tough as those under the 1933 and 1934 federal securities acts.

*Investment Restrictions.* ERISA investment restrictions limit what the retirement plan manager can do with the millions or billions of dollars in the plan. Transactions between the plan manager and the plan are illegal. For example, the plan manager cannot sell his or her hula hoop factory to the plan because it would be a conflict of interest. Loans by the plan to the employer are also illegal. The plan can, however, own the employer's securities. For example, Sears' employee retirement plan is the largest stockholder in that company.

*Pension Benefit Guaranty Corporation.* ERISA created the Pension Benefit Guaranty Corporation (PBGC), designed to make sure employees get vested retirement benefits if the plan fails. Both the plan and the employer are required to repay amounts the PBGC has to pay employees, but limits exist on an employer's liability to repay the PBGC.

*Vesting.* An important ERISA reform is its *vesting requirements*. Vesting refers to rights that cannot legally be taken away. For example, workers who have vested pension rights cannot lose them by changing jobs. Often, both employees and employers pay toward an employee retirement plan. Before ERISA, employer contributions often did not vest until just before a worker retired. If a worker changed jobs, was fired, or for some other reason stopped working before vesting, the worker lost the entire employer retirement contribution (which might be 40 years' accumulation, in extreme cases). Before ERISA, if a large number of employees were fired just before vesting at retirement, the employer would get back all employer contributions for all such employees. The amounts would be used to pay benefits for other employees who remained until retirement, thus reducing the employer's retirement costs. Most scholars viewed this practice as inequitable, assuming employer contributions are a type of deferred pay (instead of a gift or tip from the employer). Employers argued that late vesting of their contributions reduced employee retirement costs.

ERISA requires 100 percent immediate vesting of employee pension contributions. After December 31, 1988, ERISA requires that employers' contributions must vest at least as rapidly as either one of the following vesting schedules:

1. Five-year "cliff" (all at once) vesting; that is, employees who have worked five years or more must be 100 percent vested regarding the employer's contribution to their retirement plan; or
2. Three- to seven-year graduated vesting; this approach requires that employees have the right to the employer's contribution to the employee's retirement plan according to the following schedule:

| Years of Service | Percentage Vested |
|:---:|:---:|
| 3 | 20 |
| 4 | 40 |
| 5 | 60 |
| 6 | 80 |
| 7 | 100 |

Does ERISA prevent a private employer's retirement plan from reducing retirement benefits by amounts received from other benefit plans? The *Alessi v. Raybestos-Manhattan Inc.* case says no.

## Alessi v. Raybestos-Manhattan, Inc.
U.S. Supreme Court
451 U.S. 504 (1981)

### Background and Facts

In two suits initiated in New Jersey state court, retired employees who had received workers' compensation awards subsequent to retirement challenged the validity of provisions in their employers' pension plans reducing a retiree's pension benefits by an amount equal to a workers' compensation award for which the retiree is eligible. Those private pension plans are subject to federal regulation under the Employee Retirement Income Security Act of 1974 (ERISA). The employers independently removed the suits to Federal District Court, where the judges in each suit held that the pension offset provisions were invalid under a provision of the New Jersey Workers' Compensation Act prohibiting such offsets; that Congress had not intended ERISA to preempt such state laws; that the offsets were prohibited by ERISA's provision, prohibiting forfeitures of pension rights except under specified conditions inapplicable to these cases; and that a Treasury Regulation authorizing offsets based on workers' compensation awards were invalid. The Court of Appeals consolidated appeals from the two decisions and reversed.

### Body of Opinion

**Justice Marshall.** 1. Congress contemplated and approved the kind of pension provisions challenged here.

Pension plan provisions for offsets based on workers' compensation awards do not contravene ERISA's nonforfeiture provisions. While (ERISA) prohibits forfeitures of vested rights, with specified exceptions that do not include workers' compensation offsets, nevertheless other provisions make it clear that ERISA leaves to the private parties creating the pension plan the determination of the content or amount of benefits that, once vested, cannot be forfeited. The statutory definition of "nonforfeitable" pension benefits . . . assures that an employee's claim to the protected benefit is legally enforceable, but it does not guarantee a particular amount or a method for calculating the benefit. . . . It is particularly pertinent that Congress did not prohibit "integration," a calculation practice under which benefit levels are determined by combining pension funds with other public income streams available to the retired employee. Rather, Congress accepted the practice by expressly preserving the option of pension fund integration with benefits available under both the Social Security Act and the Railroad Retirement Act. Offsets against pension benefits for workers' compensation awards work much like the integration of pension benefits with Social Security or Railroad Retirement payments, and thus the nonforfeiture provision has no more applicability to the former kind of integration than it does to the latter.

Although neither ERISA nor its legislative history mentions integration with workers' compensation, ERISA does not forbid the Treasury Regulation permitting reductions of pension benefits based on awards under state workers' compensation laws, or Internal Revenue Service rulings to the same effect. There is no merit in the argument that integration of pension funds with workers' compensation awards, which are based on work-related injuries, lacks the rationale behind ERISA's permission of integration of pension funds with Social Security and Railroad Retirement payments, which supply payments for wages lost due to retirement. Both the Social Security and Railroad Retirement Acts also provide payments for disability, and ERISA permits pension integration with such benefits as well as with benefits for wages lost due to retirement. Moreover, when it enacted ERISA, Congress knew of the IRS rulings permitting integration with workers' compensation benefits and left them in effect.

The New Jersey statute in question is preempted by federal law insofar as it eliminates a method for calculating pension benefits under plans governed by ERISA. The provision of ERISA, stating that the Act's provisions shall supersede any state laws that "relate to any [covered] employee benefit plan," demonstrates that Congress meant to establish pension plan regulation as exclusively a federal concern. Regardless of whether the purpose of the New

Jersey statute might have been to protect the employee's right to workers' compensation disability benefits rather than to regulate pension plans, the statute "relate[s] to pension plans" governed by ERISA because it eliminates one method for calculating pension benefits—integration—that is permitted by federal law, and the state provision thus is an impermissible intrusion on the federal regulatory scheme. It is of no moment that New Jersey intrudes indirectly, through a workers' compensation law, rather than directly, through a statute called "pension regulation," since ERISA makes clear that even indirect state action bearing on private pensions may encroach upon the area of exclusive federal concern. Moreover, where, as here, pension plans emerge from collective bargaining, the additional federal interest in precluding state interference in labor–management negotiations calls for preemption of state efforts to regulate pension terms.

## Judgment and Result

The U.S. Supreme Court held that ERISA does not stop a private pension plan from reducing retirement benefits by the amount of money obtained from workers' compensation awards received after retirement.

## Questions

1. Does ERISA have a provision that stops retirement plans from forfeiting pension benefits?
2. What is meant by *integration* with respect to retirement plans? Does integration reduce a person's retirement benefits or merely calculate those payments by taking into account benefits from other sources?
3. If state law prohibits pension offsets and ERISA allows them, which prevails? Why?
4. Explain what a pension offset provision is.

*ERISA Preemption.* Recall from Chapter 5 that federal preemption refers to a federal statute's (or regulation's) preventing state or local laws from dealing with a particular matter. For example, does ERISA preempt states from passing laws that affect employee benefit plans?

ERISA does have a specific preemption provision designed to promote national uniformity in employee pensions and other benefits. (ERISA covers employee benefits other than pensions.) However, states argue that ERISA's preemption provision is only partial, which would mean that states could regulate *some* areas of employee benefit programs.

In 1985 the U.S. Supreme Court decided *Metropolitan Life v. Massachusetts.* Massachusetts and 11 other states require private insurers to include mental health coverage in group insurance policies. Two private insurers, Metropolitan Life and Travelers Insurance Company, argued that ERISA preempted the states on this matter; that is, if each state could tell insurers what to put into their group policies, ERISA's national goal of uniformity would be lost. The Supreme Court decided that ERISA does *not* preempt state law on this matter. In other words, state law can force group insurers to cover certain risks such as alcoholism, drug treatment, and infant care.

*Reversion of Excess Plan Assets.* Employers sometimes go out of business. If they fully fund present and future liabilities under the employee benefit plan, the plan sometimes has excess assets (money left over after all obligations are paid. In one case, an employer amended its pension plan (before going out of business) to allow any excess plan assets to go to the employer. ERISA has an exclusive benefit rule that says that plans are only supposed to benefit participants and their beneficiaries plus pay reasonable plan administration costs.

In *Washington-Baltimore Newspaper Guide Local 35 v. The Washington Star Co.,* a federal court of appeals held that an employer's plan amendment allowing excess assets to revert to the employer did not violate ERISA's exclusive benefit rule.

## FAMILY AND MEDICAL LEAVE ACT OF 1993[2]

*The Family and Medical Leave Act of 1993 can be found on the Library of Congress Web site at http://thomas.loc.gov*

The first major piece of legislation President Clinton signed into law was the Family and Medical Leave Act of 1993. This law was passed in recognition of two demographic shifts in the workforce over the past three or four decades: first, the influx of women into the workforce, and second, the increase in single-parent families. This act aims to accommodate such new members of the workforce by mandating that employers provide leaves of absence to employees when leave is requested for certain family purposes, including birth of a child, placing a child for adoption or in foster care, the employee's ill health, or the ill health of an employee's family member.

The law has two important requirements. First, employers must give up to 12 weeks of leave in a calendar year to employees covered by the act's family or medical purposes. Employers do not have to pay employees during the leave, but employers must continue to provide health insurance during the leave. However, if the employee usually has to pay part or all of the health coverage while at work, then this requirement continues during the leave. Second, the employees are entitled to get their jobs back (or an equivalent job) at the end of the leaves.

Employees must provide employers with a 30-day advance notice of the request for a leave when need for such a leave is foreseeable. Obviously, a pregnancy is foreseeable, although predicting the exact time is problematic, and the required notice must be "practicable" in such cases.

Employers have a legal obligation to provide employees with written guidance as to the rights and obligations the FMLA requires.

Certain limitations affect coverage of the FMLA. It does not apply to employers who have just opened their business, because employees have no rights under the act until they have worked at least one year. Also, employers must have 50 or more employees before the FMLA applies.

Enforcement of the FMLA is similar to the federal Fair Labor Standards Act. Remedies for violating the FMLA include employment, reinstatement, and promotion. The secretary of labor may bring actions seeking injunctions against employers. Class actions under the act are allowed.

## COBRA

COBRA refers to the Consolidated Omnibus Budget Reconciliation Act of 1985. This Act was designed to provide temporary health insurance for workers who are terminated from their jobs. Coverage applies whether termination is voluntary (the worker quits) or involuntary (the worker is fired or laid off). There is no coverage if the worker is dismissed for gross misconduct. The period of coverage following termination is 18 months (up to 29 for disabled).

COBRA does not require employers to provide health insurance for workers or former workers. Rather, COBRA says that if an employer provides health insurance to workers, the *former* workers are covered for 18 (or 29, if disabled) months after termination. When the employment relationship ends, the former employee has an option: "opt out" of the former employer's health insurance (which ends the former employer's health insurance liability to that worker) or

---

[2] The authors acknowledge reliance on readings at the end of this chapter in preparing this segment.

continue under the former employer's policy for 18 (or 29, is disabled) months. Workers might opt out if they find a new job with health insurance. For those opting to continue under the former employer's insurance, coverage is the same as it was pretermination. Family members, for example, might be covered. The only catch is that the terminated employee must pay the full premium, plus a 2 percent administrative charge. Nonetheless, the former employee gets the advantage of the employer's group rate, which is usually lower than insurance as individual could purchase.

There are several ways a former employer may be relieved of COBRA's requirements to former employees:

1. COBRA does not apply (with some exceptions) to employers with fewer than 20 employees.
2. The employer may totally drop all health insurance for all past and present employees.
3. The terminated employee may take another job with health insurance coverage.
4. The worker can become eligible for coverage under a spouse's health plan.
5. The worker could become eligible for Medicare.
6. The 18-month (29 for disabled) period could expire.
7. The worker could stop paying premiums before the 18- (or 29-) month period expires.

Penalties exist for employers who disobey COBRA.

## PLANT CLOSING LEGISLATION

As plants across the United States close, particularly in the "rust belt" states of the Midwest and also in the Northeast, thousands of workers lose their jobs. Additionally, communities with unemployed workers suffer because the community's tax base can decline, along with schools and other public services. To soften the shock of sudden plant shutdowns, several states (including Maine, Wisconsin, Massachusetts, Maryland, Michigan, and Connecticut) and cities (Philadelphia and Vacaville, California) have passed laws at one time or another that require some type of preclosing notice to workers. Features of the notice can vary:

- The size of the business it applies to (often it only covers employers with 100 or more employees)
- How much advance notice of closing must be given (60 days is common, although the longer the notice, the more protection there is)
- The sanction for noncompliance (Wisconsin's sanction was at one time only $50 per worker—hardly a deterrent)
- Whether the notice is mandatory or voluntary (in some states such as Michigan, the notice has been voluntary with little if any compliance)

*Federal Plant Closing Statute.*[3] On August 4, 1988, federal plant closing legislation requiring advanced notice of certain layoffs and closings became law without President Reagan's signature. This law requires employers with more than 100 employees to give 60 days advanced notice if 50 or more employees at one

---

[3] The authors acknowledge Deloitte, Haskins, & Sells *DH&S Review* in preparing this segment.

site will lose their jobs because of a plant closing. A layoff notice must be given if 50 workers at one site will lose jobs and they are 33 percent or more of the workforce. Notice is also required if 500 or more employees are to be laid off, no matter what the circumstances.

In the *Fort Halifax Packing Company v. Coyne* case, the U.S. Supreme Court upheld the Maine plant closing legislation when challenged on grounds that ERISA and the National Labor Relations Act preempted it.

## CHAPTER SUMMARY

A number of statutes passed in the twentieth century affect employees' job safety and financial security.

Workers' compensation statutes provide money to workers who suffer on-the-job injuries, diseases, or death. These statutes impose no-fault liability on employers. Defenses to workers' comp claims include the fact that the employee intentionally caused the injury or was not at work at the time of the loss.

The federal OSHA statute tries to prevent injury and loss to employees while at work.

The Fair Labor Standards Act is the federal law that sets maximum hours and hourly wage minimums employers must pay their employees who affect interstate commerce. Some employees are exempt from either or both the maximum hours and minimum wage requirements.

The Equal Pay Act amends the Fair Labor Standards Act. The Equal Pay Act prohibits employers from paying different wages based on sex to men and women who do substantially equal work.

Unemployment compensation is a federal and state program designed to provide unemployed individuals with some support while they are unemployed. The money for this program comes from a federal payroll tax placed on employers. State unemployment taxes can be credited against the employer's federal unemployment tax liability if the state law meets federal requirements. Not all employees are covered by unemployment compensation.

Social Security taxes are imposed on employers and employees. Independent contractors pay both the employer's and employees' share of this tax. Social Security taxes are paid on an employee's gross income before income taxes are deducted.

ERISA is a federal statute designed to regulate private pension plans. ERISA imposes vesting requirements, imposes duties on retirement plan managers, and establishes the Pension Benefit Guaranty Corporation to insure plan benefits. ERISA does not require that employers have retirement plans.

The Family and Medical Leave Act of 1993 requires certain employers to provide leaves of absence when requested to certain employees for up to 12 weeks during each calendar year to take care of certain family and medical problems. Covered employees taking such leaves are entitled to get their jobs (or equivalent) back and to keep health insurance during the leave.

COBRA entitles terminated employees to obtain health insurance under certain circumstances.

Plant closing statutes in a number of states require that employers give employees advance notice if plants are about to close. In 1988, a federal plant-closing statute became law.

## ■ MANAGER'S ETHICAL DILEMMA

Dee Leacoca, the CEO (chief executive officer) of the Leacoca Motor Company of Detroit, Michigan, discovered that 16 percent of the cost of the cars his firm built was made up of employee health care costs. Dee wanted to reduce this cost and thereby make his cars more competitive with foreign manufacturers. Most foreign manufacturers operated in countries having national health insurance systems. Their workers' health costs were paid for by society (the country's government) rather than directly by the foreign manufacturer. Although foreign manufacturers had to pay taxes to support their governments' programs (including national health insurance), this cost was spread over the entire society rather than being concentrated on the employers. This system, in turn, made it relatively cheaper for foreign manufacturers to produce cars.

A bill that several car manufacturers wanted to be introduced in Congress was placed on Dee's desk for his reaction. The bill proposed establishing a national health care agency in the United States. Under the bill, physicians would be made federal employees and would receive subsidized medical school education (as they do now), and would receive starting salaries of $50,000 per year, which would rise to as high as $150,000 per year, depending on the physician's expertise, medical specialty, and years of experience, and scarcity of medical practitioners in the geographic region (SMSA, standard metropolitan statistical area). The federal health care agency would provide offices, nurses, hospitals, and staff. Also, liability limits of $500,000 per operation would be imposed for physician malpractice under this scheme, with arbitration rather than jury trials of malpractice claims in order to control medical costs.

Dee wondered whether he should throw his support behind this bill. What legal and business ethics mentioned in Chapter 1 are involved here? What would you do if you were in Dee's position?

## DISCUSSION QUESTIONS

1. "In 1992, petitioners, a group of probation officers, filed suit against their employer, the State of Maine, in the United States District Court for the District of Maine. The officers alleged the State had violated the overtime provisions of the Fair Labor Standards Act of 1938 (FLSA), . . . and sought compensation and liquidated damages." Should state employees be able to recover against a state that violates the federal Fair Labor Standards Act or does the Eleventh Amendment, which explicitly refers to states' immunity from suits by "Citizens of another State, or by Citizens or Subjects of any Foreign State," immunize states from suits brought by their own citizens? Note that the Eleventh Amendment literally does not immunize states from suits brought against them by their own citizens. [*Alden v. Maine*, 119 S.Ct. 2240 (1999)].

2. What are the principal benefits of the Fair Labor Standards Act? How could it be argued that the Fair Labor Standards Act causes unemployment among young workers who tend to have low skill levels? Does this argument suggest a possible modification in the FLSA? What are some arguments against exempting young workers from the FLSA's protections?

3. Who benefits from the Equal Pay Act? How can it be argued that men benefit from this law? What employers does it cover? Why should the Equal Pay Act cover governmental units?

4. What objectives does OSHA have? In what ways does OSHA achieve them? How does it not achieve its goals? In this regard, how can the reduction of OSHA regulations increase the likelihood of OSHA's success?

5. Does the "integration principle" announced in the *Alessi* case suggest a way to reduce the cost of employer retirement programs? Should the *Alessi* principle be extended to allow any (private or public) pension plan to reduce benefits by taking into account amounts received from other retirement plans? If all pension plans could be reduced, what would they be reduced to—some absolute dollar level?

6. Workers' compensation generally covers only injuries, disease, or death at work. Did the following death occur at work? An electric utility company's line foreman supervised correction of a power outage. He corrected the problem at 9:00 A.M. but remained subject to call. He headed home in a company car, did some personal shopping, and stopped at several bars. At 4:00 P.M., while drunk, he got into the company car, continued on his way home, and was killed in a two-car accident. Evidence showed the collision occurred when he turned to avoid hitting a pedestrian. His widow and children sued to recover workers' compensation. Was he at work when killed? [*Oakes v. W.C.A.B.*, 79 Pa. Cmwlth. 454, 469 A.2d 723 (1984)].

7. HPL Ohio, Inc., was cited for a serious violation of OSHA regulations requiring handrails on platforms higher than four feet. HPL's platform was seven feet high and did not have handrails. It was used for storage. Employees climbed on it about every three months. HPL argued that the violation was nonserious. Was it? [*HPL Ohio, Inc.*, 7 OSHC 21512 (1974)].

8. Employers Temporary Service, Inc. (E.T.S.) was an employment service. A 15-year-old applied for employment but misrepresented his age as 19 on the employment application. E.T.S. told the boy he would have to prove his age at his next visit to the hiring hall. No such proof was ever requested or offered. E.T.S. found the boy work at R.A. Young Industries, Inc. While running a power press there, the boy suffered amputation of two fingers and part of his hand. The boy sued the employers Young and E.T.S. for negligence. They defended by arguing the boy's exclusive remedy was under workers' compensation. The boy argued that people illegally employed (here, child labor) were not "employees" covered by workers' comp. (The workers' comp remedy would probably have been smaller than a judgment in a negligence suit, which would benefit the employers.) Who was right? [*Allossery v. Employers Temporary Serv., Inc.*, 88 Mich. App. 496, 277 N.W.2d 340 (1979)].

9. Employees are generally unable to collect unemployment insurance benefits if they voluntarily quit work. Brousseau was convicted of drunken driving, and a judge suspended Brousseau's driver's license. As a result, his employer fired Brousseau from his job as a truck driver and warehouse worker. Did Brousseau involuntarily lose his job so as to be eligible for unemployment compensation, or did his voluntary act of drunkenness disqualify him from unemployment benefits? [*Brousseau v. Maine Employment Security Com'n*, 470 A.2d 327 (Me. 1984)].

10. Social Security benefits are available for disabled workers under age 65. In one case, a 47-year-old drywall finisher suffered from heart disease, hypoglycemia, vertebrovascular insufficiency, mental depression, and possible emphysema. Was this condition a "slight neurosis, slight impairment of hearing and sight" not entitling him to Social Security disability benefits? [*Brady v. Heckler*, 724 F.2d 914 (11th Cir. 1974)].

## INFOTRAC KEYWORDS

**Use your InfoTrac password to look up articles on http://www.infotrac-college.com**

Keywords: *Worker's compensation, OSHA regulations, FLSA, unemployment compensation, social security, social security benefits, ERISA, FMLA.*

For suggested readings, please visit this book's Web site at **http://fisher.westbuslaw.com** (click on "Internet Applications").

# EMPLOYMENT DISCRIMINATION

## POSITIVE LAW ETHICAL PROBLEM

New Jersey's Casino Control Act made every state-licensed casino take affirmative action to ensure equal employment opportunity for women, racial minorities, and the disabled. To this end, the act required that casinos improve minority and female job representation in certain job categories if their minority and female representation within those categories fell below certain percentage goals set by New Jersey's Casino Control Commission. The aim of these quota-like requirements was not to remedy past or present discrimination against minorities or women. Instead, their main reason for existence, apparently, was to ensure that the large minority populations of certain New Jersey cities got a certain share of the jobs that would result from casino development.

In July of 1994, the Commission's minority goal for casino technician positions was 25 percent. Around that time, a white male named Karl Schurr applied for a position as a light and sound technician at a Resorts International Hotel casino in Jersey City. His main competitor for the position was Ronald Boykin, a black male whom Resorts' management regarded as equally qualified. For that reason, and because the casino's percentage of minorities in the light and sound technician category was 22.25 percent, the casino hired Boykin rather than Schurr.

Schurr then sued Resorts under Title VII of the 1964 Civil Rights Act, which forbids racial discrimination in employment no matter what the race of the victim. Was Schurr's suit successful? Regardless of what the law says, was it *right* that Boykin be favored over Schurr? What might justify such favoritism? Would Boykin's hiring be justified if it was intended to remedy past or present discrimination against racial minorities? Would it be justified if, as apparently was the case here, the aim was to give minorities some share of the jobs generated by casino development? What if the aim was simply to promote racial diversity for its own sake?

*"A PRACTITIONER IN THE [EMPLOYMENT DISCRIMINATION] AREA, BE IT STUDENT, ATTORNEY, BUSINESSPERSON, EMPLOYEE, GOVERNMENT OFFICIAL, OR UNION LEADER, CANNOT CONCENTRATE ALL ENERGIES ON ONE SOURCE OF RIGHTS OR REMEDIES. A POTENTIAL PLAINTIFF HAS A QUIVER OF REMEDIAL ARROWS; A POTENTIAL DEFENDANT MANY FLANKS TO COVER."*

— **M. PLAYER**
FEDERAL LAW OF
EMPLOYMENT
DISCRIMINATION,
2D ED. (1981)

This chapter discusses the most important federal laws forbidding discrimination in employment. Before the 1960s, there was little or no federal regulation of employment discrimination. During the 1960s and 1970s, however, that pattern changed dramatically. As a result, businesses now confront a maze of employment discrimination regulations. Today, federal law prohibits discrimination on the bases of age, gender, race, color, national origin, religion, and disability. Figure 16.1 summarizes the types of discrimination forbidden by the most important federal employment discrimination laws.

## Figure 16.1 Major Federal Employment Discrimination Laws

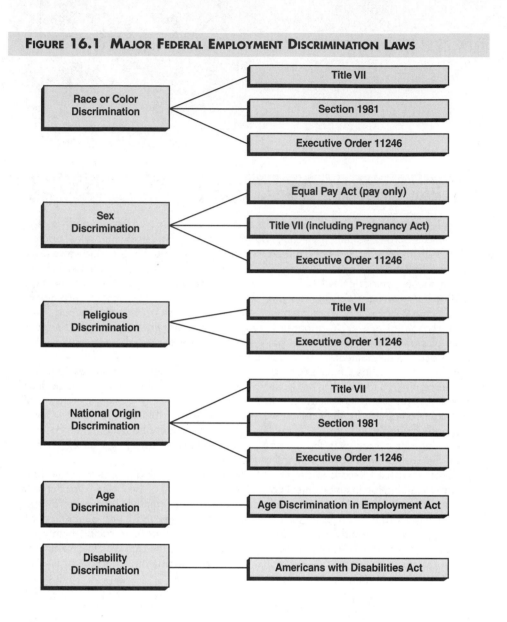

## The Equal Pay Act

The Equal Pay Act of 1963 (EPA) is an employment discrimination provision of limited scope. The EPA only forbids *gender* discrimination regarding *pay*. It commands that men and women performing equal work receive equal pay. The EPA was passed as an amendment to the Fair Labor Standards Act (FLSA),[1] and its coverage is similar to the FLSA's coverage. Unlike the FLSA, however, the EPA protects executive, administrative, and professional employees.

---

[1] The FLSA is discussed in Chapter 15.

## THE ELEMENTS OF AN EQUAL PAY ACT CASE

Although the Equal Pay Act forbids pay discrimination against both men and women, the usual EPA case involves an aggrieved woman. To recover, a woman must show that she has received lower pay than a male employee who performed substantially equal work for the same employer. Two jobs are substantially equal when they involve each of the following: (1) equal effort, (2) equal skill, (3) equal responsibility, and (4) similar working conditions. As the following *Fowler* case suggests, however, courts often do not consider these factors one by one.

---

### Fowler v. Land Management Groupe, Inc.
U.S. Court of Appeals for the Fourth Circuit
978 F.2d 158 (1992)

### Background and Facts

In 1987, the Land Management Groupe, Inc. (LMG) hired Barbara Fowler as a Project Manager at a starting salary of $32,000 per year. Fowler worked for LMG for approximately three years, until she was laid off in February 1990. During her three years with LMG, Fowler attained the title of vice-president of building development. Her salary at the time of her termination was $60,000.

After her departure from LMG, Fowler sued the firm in federal district court under the Equal Pay Act. After a jury trial, the jury entered a verdict in her favor. The court, however, granted LMG's motion for judgment notwithstanding the verdict (JNOV). Fowler appealed this ruling.

### Body of Opinion

**Chief Judge Ervin.** Under [the Equal Pay Act], a female plaintiff bears the burden of proof of establishing . . . that (1) her employer pays her a lower wage than a male counterpart (2) for equal work on jobs the performance of which requires equal skill, effort and responsibility. . . . The burden [then] shifts to the defendant to show, by a preponderance of the evidence, that the wage differential resulted from one of the allowable causes enumerated by the statute.

In reviewing a JNOV, we must view the evidence in the light most favorable to the non-moving party [Fowler]. JNOV is appropriate only when there is no legally sufficient evidentiary basis for a reasonable jury to have found for the non-moving party. . . .

The evidence shows that another vice-president of the company, Bruce Reese, was hired six months after Fowler. Reese's starting salary was $62,000 (compared to Fowler's $32,000). At the time LMG terminated Fowler's employment, Reese's annual salary was $73,500 (compared to Fowler's $60,000). . . .

LMG points to various aspects of the trial testimony which established that (1) Reese had certain professional qualifications that Fowler did not possess (he possessed an engineer's license and a surveyor's license); (2) Reese had greater practical experience; (3) Reese's expertise in site preparation and zoning were more useful to the company than Fowler's expertise in building construction because the majority of LMG's properties were not yet undergoing construction; (4) Reese's activities generated a greater share of the company's profits than did Fowler's activities; and (5) Reese was considered a more important employee of LMG.

While these justifications are persuasive, we do not believe they rise to such an overwhelming level that no reasonable jury could find that the pay differential was unjustified. Contradicting LMG's position, several LMG employees testified that they discerned no difference in the respective tasks performed by Reese and Fowler or in the degree of authority that they appeared to exercise on behalf of the company. . . . Furthermore, there is no evidence that Reese was ever called upon to use his engineering or surveying licenses while in the employ of LMG. Viewed in the light most favorable to Fowler, we believe the evidence adequately supports the jury's verdict.

### Judgment and Result

District court's grant of judgment notwithstanding the verdict to LMG reversed; jury verdict for Fowler stands.

### Questions

1. Notice that the jury decided in Fowler's favor, but that the trial judge decided for the employer anyway. Is this right? See Chapter 4.
2. Did the court of appeals say that it would have reached the same result the jury did had the case been tried before it? Check out the court's statement of the way in which it is supposed to handle appeals from a district court's JNOV decision.
3. How did the court dispose of the assertion that Reese's engineering and surveying licenses made his job and Fowler's job unequal? Was it right to do so?

The effort associated with a job is the amount of physical or mental exertion it requires. Skill involves the experience, training, education, and ability required by a job—not the skills the male and female employees actually possess. Responsibility (or accountability) refers to such things as the importance of the decisions made in a particular job or the degree of supervision the job requires. For example, bank employees whose loan decisions must be reviewed by a superior when the loan exceeds $10,000 probably are not equal to bank employees who can approve loans of up to $50,000 at their own discretion. Finally, working conditions refers to the quality of the employee's physical surroundings; the hazards the job creates; and factors such as heat, cold, inside or outside work, and exposure to fumes or toxic substances. Note that the working conditions for the positions being compared need only be similar, not equal.

## EPA Defenses

Once a plaintiff establishes the elements of an EPA claim, the defendant loses the case unless it proves that the pay disparity is justified by one of the act's four defenses: (1) seniority, (2) merit, (3) quality or quantity of production (e.g., a piecework system), and (4) any factor other than sex. To successfully use the first three defenses, employers ordinarily cannot rely on discretionary, subjective employee evaluation systems that might permit sex-based criteria to influence their decisions. Instead, employers usually must demonstrate that they used an organized system with fairly precise criteria that apply equally to employees of each sex and are communicated to all employees. The catchall any-factor-other-than-sex defense may include practices such as shift differentials or bonuses paid because a position is part of a training program.

## EPA Remedies

The EEOC's Web site is at http://www.eeoc.gov

Because the Equal Pay Act is part of the FLSA, its remedies resemble the FLSA remedies discussed in Chapter 15. In an EPA case, therefore, successful plaintiffs generally recover the amount of back pay lost because of the employer's discrimination. In addition, such plaintiffs may receive an equal amount as liquidated damages. Unlike the FLSA, however, the EPA is enforced by the Equal Employment Opportunity Commission (EEOC) rather than the Labor Department.[2] The EPA differs from many of the employment discrimination measures discussed later by not requiring private plaintiffs to submit their claims to the EEOC or a suitable state agency before a lawsuit may take place.

## Title VII of the 1964 Civil Rights Act

Due mainly to its scope, Title VII of the 1964 Civil Rights Act is the most important federal employment discrimination statute. Title VII prohibits employment discrimination based on race, color, religion, sex, and national origin. It forbids such discrimination in a wide range of employment contexts, and thus covers most significant terms, conditions, and benefits of employment.

---

[2] The EEOC is an independent federal agency with a sizable staff and many regional offices. It enforces most of the employment discrimination laws discussed in this chapter. It also interprets those laws by issuing regulations and guidelines.

## COVERAGE

*Covered Entities.* Title VII basically covers employers employing fifteen or more employees and engaging in an industry affecting interstate commerce. The term *employer* includes individuals, partnerships, corporations, labor unions (regarding their own employees), employment agencies (regarding their own employees), and state and local governments. Title VII also prevents unions and employment agencies from discriminating against their members and clients, respectively. For Title VII to apply in these two cases, the union usually must have fifteen or more members, and the employment agency must service an employer with fifteen or more employees. Note that the latter test differs from the test applied where an employment agency discriminates against its own employees. For example, a three-person employment agency is covered by Title VII if it discriminates against African-Americans when making job referrals to IBM, but Title VII would not cover the agency's refusal to hire a secretary because of his or her race. Similarly, a union with only ten employees but a hundred members is liable for discrimination against the members it represents, but not for discrimination against its own employees.

*Exclusions from Coverage.* Certain employers, employees, and employment relationships are specifically excluded from Title VII's coverage. First, Title VII does not apply to employer discrimination against independent contractors.[3] Second, Title VII's definition of the term *employer* specifically excludes Indian tribes and certain bona fide tax-exempt private clubs. Third, Title VII allows religious educational institutions to employ individuals of that religion to carry on their activities.

*Covered Decisions.* Recall that the Equal Pay Act only forbids sex discrimination regarding pay. The range of decisions covered by Title VII is much broader. Its sweeping provisions against employer, employment agency, and union discrimination cover almost all of the ways that these parties might disadvantage employees, clients, or members because their race, color, sex, religion, or national origin. Title VII also has a broad antiretaliation provision that forbids discrimination against any employee who has opposed an employment practice made illegal by Title VII; has exercised his Title VII rights; or has participated in any investigation, proceeding, or hearing under Title VII. Finally, Title VII forbids discrimination on the bases of race, color, sex, religion, or national origin in notices or advertisements.

## PROCEDURES

Private parties alleging a violation of Title VII cannot simply sue their employer at any time they desire. Instead, they must comply with certain procedures before doing so. The general aim of these procedures is to give the EEOC or state employment discrimination agencies the opportunity to settle the dispute or to sue in their own right in lieu of the private party's suit. The many details of these complex procedures are beyond the scope of this text, but two points should be kept in

*For directions on how to file a charge with the EEOC, see **http://www.eeoc.gov***

---

[3] The employee–independent contractor distinction is discussed in Chapter 14.

mind. First, the complaining party (complainant) must file a *charge* with a suitable state fair employment agency or (if no suitable state agency is available) with the EEOC within a specified time period after the alleged violation. This requirement gives the state agency or the EEOC the opportunity to take such action as it deems appropriate. Second, the EEOC's or the state agency's failure to take action satisfactory to the complainant ordinarily does not prevent the complainant from suing on his or her own behalf. In most such cases, the EEOC eventually issues a right-to-sue letter, which gives the claimant the power to sue.

## PROVING A TITLE VII VIOLATION

For there to be a violation of Title VII, a private plaintiff or the government must prove that the employer acted for discriminatory reasons when making the challenged employment decision. Proof of discrimination is easy where the employer has an express policy that discriminates on one of the bases forbidden by Title VII. The *Johnson Controls* case later in the chapter is an example. Proving discrimination also poses few problems where direct evidence of discrimination, such as testimony or documents, establishes a discriminatory motive.

However, if Title VII were limited to cases of this sort, it would be a paper tiger in the struggle against employment discrimination. Often, employers can discriminate without leaving such obvious evidence in their wake. Thus, various other methods of proving a Title VII violation are available. The most important of these are Title VII's disparate treatment and disparate impact theories. The details of these theories are critical in determining Title VII's impact, and those details have changed from time to time in response to political pressures. For this reason, and because of their complexity, we describe the disparate treatment and disparate impact theories in fairly general terms.

*Disparate Treatment.* Title VII's **disparate treatment theory** is most often used where a single plaintiff or a small number of plaintiffs allege some isolated instance or instances of discrimination that cannot be proven by direct evidence. The disparate treatment theory involves a three-stage order of proof.

1. First, the plaintiff must first establish a **prima facie case**: a case strong enough to require some rebuttal by the defendant. The evidence needed to establish a prima facie case varies from situation to situation, but usually that evidence is easy to produce. In a discriminatory hiring case, for example, the plaintiff might have to show that (1) he is within one of Title VII's five protected classes; (2) he applied for, and was qualified to perform, a job for which the employer was seeking applicants; (3) he was denied the job; and (4) the employer continued to seek applicants for the position after his rejection.
2. Once the plaintiff has established a prima facie case, the defendant must produce evidence that the challenged employment decision was made for legitimate, nondiscriminatory reasons or it will lose the case. In a hiring case, for example, the employer might claim that the reason for its refusal to hire the plaintiff was her lack of qualifications for the job.
3. If the defendant produces legitimate, nondiscriminatory reasons, the burden is on the plaintiff to show that the challenged employment decision was actually the result of discrimination. In most cases, a plaintiff who can show that

the employer's allegedly legitimate, nondiscriminatory reasons were only a pretext for a decision actually made with a discriminatory motive is usually in good shape. For instance, a black plaintiff might show that the employer's job qualifications were applied only to African-American jobseekers and not to their white counterparts.

*Disparate Impact.* Unlike the disparate treatment theory, Title VII's **disparate impact** (or adverse impact) **theory** is most often used in cases involving a large number of plaintiffs. This theory proceeds in three steps.

1. First, the plaintiffs must show that the employment practice they are challenging has an adverse impact (or disparate impact) on the basis of race, color, religion, sex, or national origin. The most common examples are employer rules such as testing, high school diploma, height, weight, and strength requirements that are neutral on their face, but that obviously can have a disproportionate adverse effect on certain groups protected by Title VII. Height and weight requirements for a particular job, for example, might well have this effect on women or on people of certain national origins. In addition, the disparate impact theory includes subjective employer practices such as hiring and promotion systems that permit discretionary, qualitative judgments.
2. Once the plaintiffs demonstrate adverse impact, the employer must show that the challenged practice is job-related for the position in question and consistent with business necessity. For example, an employer might argue that physical size is important for the proper performance of the job in question. If the employer fails to make the necessary showing, it loses the case.
3. If the employer makes the previous showing, the plaintiffs ordinarily will lose. But they have an alternate route to victory: showing that the employer's legitimate business needs can be advanced by an alternative employment practice that is less discriminatory than the challenged practice, and that the employer has failed to adopt such a practice. Women or national origin groups disadvantaged by a height or weight requirement, for instance, might argue that the employer's needs would be better met by a strength test and that such a test also would be less disadvantageous to them.

## DEFENSES TO TITLE VII CLAIMS

Even if a violation of Title VII is proven, an employer still emerges victorious if it can establish one of Title VII's various defenses. Title VII's most important defenses break down into three groups.

*Bona Fide Occupational Qualification.* Sometimes, one's gender, religion, or national origin is a genuine qualification for a particular job. In such cases, the **bona fide occupational qualification (BFOQ)** defense protects defendants from Title VII liability. As the following *Johnson Controls* case makes clear, however, the BFOQ defense is a narrow one. For one thing, the defense has no application to race or color discrimination. More importantly, for a BFOQ defense to exist, sex, religion, or national origin must be necessary for effective job performance. Thus, female gender is not a BFOQ for the job of airline flight cabin attendant. However, a firm that requires men to work as attendants in men's washrooms, or employs only women as fitters for women's undergarments, should not violate Title VII.

## Auto Workers v. Johnson Controls, Inc.
U.S. Supreme Court
499 U.S. 187 (1991)

### Background and Facts

Johnson Controls, Inc. manufactures batteries. Lead is a primary ingredient in its manufacturing process. Exposing female employees to lead creates a risk of harm to any fetus they may carry. For this reason, Johnson Controls excluded pregnant women or women who are capable of bearing children from jobs that involve exposure to lead.

A number of female plaintiffs began a federal district court class action alleging that Johnson Controls' policy was illegal sex discrimination under Title VII. After the district court entered a summary judgment for Johnson Controls and the court of appeals affirmed, the plaintiffs appealed to the U.S. Supreme Court.

### Body of Opinion

**Justice Blackmun.** The bias in Johnson Controls' policy is obvious. Fertile men, but not fertile women, are given a choice as to whether they wish to risk their reproductive health for a particular job. [The] policy explicitly discriminates against women on the basis of their sex. . . .

[But] an employer may discriminate on the basis of "religion, sex, or national origin in those certain instances where religion, sex, or national origin is a bona fide occupational qualification reasonably necessary to the normal operation of that particular business or enterprise." The BFOQ defense is written narrowly, and this Court has read it narrowly. . . .

Johnson Controls argues that its fetal-protection policy falls within the so-called safety exception [of] the BFOQ. Our cases have stressed that discrimination on the basis of sex because of safety concerns is allowed only in narrow circumstances. In *Dothard v. Rawlinson* (1977), . . . we allowed the employer to hire only male guards in contact areas of maximum-security male penitentiaries only because more was at stake than the individual woman's decision to weigh and accept the risks of employment. We found sex to be a BFOQ inasmuch as the employment of a female guard would create real risks of safety to others if [rape-related] violence broke out because the guard was a woman. Sex discrimination was tolerated because sex was related to the guard's ability to do the job—maintaining prison security. We also required in *Dothard* a high correlation between sex and ability to perform job functions, and refused to allow employers to use sex as a proxy for strength although it might be a fairly accurate one.

Similarly, some courts have approved airlines' layoffs of pregnant flight attendants . . . on the ground that the employer's policy was necessary to ensure the safety of passengers. In two of these cases, the courts pointedly indicated that fetal, as opposed to passenger, safety was best left to the mother.

Our case law, therefore, makes clear that the safety exception is limited to instances in which sex or pregnancy actually interferes with the employee's ability to perform the job. . . . [Thus,] we have no difficulty concluding that Johnson Controls cannot establish a BFOQ. Fertile women, as far as appears in the record, manufacture batteries as efficiently as anyone else. Johnson Controls' professed moral and ethical concerns about the next generation do not suffice to establish a BFOQ of female sterility. Decisions about the welfare of future children must be left to the parents who conceive, bear, support, and raise them rather than to the employers who hire those parents.

### Judgment and Result

Judgment in favor of Johnson Controls reversed; case returned to the lower courts for further proceedings consistent with the Supreme Court's opinion.

### Questions

1. Why did the plaintiffs have an easy time proving a Title VII case here?
2. How did the Court distinguish its decision in *Dothard v. Rawlinson*?
3. Do you think that concern for fetal life was Johnson Controls' real reason for excluding pregnant women from jobs that involve exposure to lead? Think of a more practical motive for the firm's policy. *Hint:* the Supreme Court's decision may have left *Johnson Controls* in a difficult legal position.

*Seniority.* An employer is not liable under Title VII if its alleged discrimination resulted from the operation of a bona fide seniority system. To be bona fide, a seniority system must at least treat all employees equally on its face, have been created for nondiscriminatory reasons, and operate in a nondiscriminatory fashion.

*Various Merit Defenses.* Title VII gives employers a defense if their alleged discrimination resulted from the operation of a bona fide merit system or a system that measures earnings by quality or quantity of production (e.g., a piecework system). Like their Equal Pay Act counterparts, these systems must be organized, communicated, and neutrally applied in order to protect employers. Title VII also protects employment decisions made as the result of a professionally developed ability test. Of course, such tests must be job-related. The EEOC has promulgated detailed guidelines on employee selection procedures for determining the validity of ability tests.

## REMEDIES FOR TITLE VII VIOLATIONS

Courts can order a wide range of remedies once the government or a private plaintiff wins a Title VII suit. If intentional discrimination results in lost wages, a private plaintiff can obtain back pay accruing from a date two years prior to the filing of the charge. Successful private plaintiffs may also recover attorney's fees at the court's discretion. Victims of intentional discrimination who suffer harms such as emotional distress, sickness, loss of reputation, and denial of credit also can obtain compensatory damages. Victims of intentional discrimination also can recover punitive damages in cases where the defendant was malicious or recklessly indifferent to the victim's rights. However, the sum of the plaintiff's compensatory and punitive damages cannot exceed certain amounts stated in the statute. These amounts vary with the size of the employer.

Title VII also gives courts much discretion to formulate equitable remedies appropriate to the violation. For example, a court might order that a private plaintiff be hired, reinstated, or given retroactive seniority. In addition, courts sometimes impose various affirmative action orders: for example, injunctions compelling active steps to recruit minorities. These include the ordering of quota-like preferences for minorities—and occasionally for women—in the employer's future hiring and promotion. For example, a court might order an employer with a long history of systematic discrimination to hire minorities at a certain rate until the minority percentage of the employer's work force equals the minority percentage in some relevant local population. In general, such remedies are permissible where they are needed to eliminate the effects of pervasive, persistent, and/or severe discrimination; they do not excessively or unnecessarily restrict the employment prospects of white people; and they do not require that unqualified people be hired or promoted. This is true even if the favored minority people were not themselves victims of illegal employment discrimination.

Quota-like remedial minority preferences favoring nonvictims also may appear in consent decrees that courts issue following the settlement of a Title VII suit. In fact, the Supreme Court has stated that the preferential relief agreed to in a consent decree sometimes can be broader than the relief a court could order on its own after a violation of Title VII.

As discussed in Chapter 5, however, reverse racial discrimination by the federal government now gets the same full strict scrutiny as racial discrimination against minorities. This may create an obstacle to remedial orders and consent decrees containing minority preferences.

## RACE AND COLOR DISCRIMINATION

Thus far, we have been discussing certain basic rules that apply to any Title VII suit. Now we examine in more detail Title VII's prohibited bases of discrimination—race and color, sex, national origin, and religion. Title VII's ban on race and color discrimination includes discrimination against blacks, other racial minorities, Eskimos, and Native Americans.

Title VII also forbids racial discrimination against whites. Does this mean that voluntary employer preferences favoring racial minorities cannot stand under Title VII? These voluntary racial preferences differ from the racial preferences discussed previously. Here, the question is whether a *private employer* violates Title VII when it institutes such a preference. Earlier, the question was whether a *court* could order such a preference as a remedy after it was shown that an employer had violated Title VII by discriminating against racial minorities, or could approve a racially preferential consent decree following Title VII litigation. In *Steelworkers v. Weber* (1979), the Supreme Court said that voluntary employer preferences survive a Title VII attack if they (1) are intended to open opportunities for minorities by admitting them to "traditionally segregated" job categories in which they have been underrepresented due to past discrimination; (2) do not unnecessarily trammel upon the interests of white employees, (3) are not an absolute bar to the advancement of white employees, and (4) are only temporary. As the following case makes clear, the *Weber* decision is very much alive today.

## Resorts International Hotel, Inc. v. Schurr
U.S. Court of Appeals (Third Circuit)
196 F.3d 486 (1999)

### Background and Facts

New Jersey's Casino Control Act requires that every state-licensed casino undertake affirmative measures to ensure equal employment opportunity for women, racial minorities, and the disabled. Among these measures is a requirement that casinos improve minority and female job representation in certain job categories, if their minority and female representation within those categories falls below certain percentage goals established by New Jersey's Casino Control Commission. In July of 1994, Karl Schurr, a white male, applied for a position as a light and sound technician at a Resorts International Hotel casino in Jersey City. Eventually, the casino narrowed the pool of people considered for the job to Schurr and Ronald Boykin, a black male. Resorts' management regarded Schurr and Boykin as equally qualified for the job. At that time, the minority goal for technician positions was 25 percent. Because the casino's percentage of minorities in that category was 22.25 percent, and because Schurr and Boykin were thought to be equally qualified, the casino's managers felt that they were obligated to hire Boykin. As a result, Boykin got the job.

After filing a charge of discrimination with the EEOC and the New Jersey Division of Civil Rights in January of 1995 and getting a right-to-sue letter over a year later, Schurr sued Resorts for racial discrimination under Title VII. After the federal district court granted Resorts' motion for summary judgment, Schurr appealed to the Third Circuit Court of Appeals.

### Body of Opinion

**Circuit Judge Mannsman.** The terms of Title VII are violated when an employer takes action "to discriminate against any individual with respect to his compensation, terms, conditions, or privileges of employment" or "to limit, segregate, or classify his employees . . . in any way which would deprive or tend to deprive any individual of employment opportunities or otherwise affect his status as an employee" on the basis of "race, color, religion, sex, or national origin." Although this language was initially construed as absolute—prohibiting all discrimination in employment—it is clear now that in certain circumstances, race-based employment decisions made pursuant to an affirmative action plan do not run afoul of the statute. . . . The parties in this matter agree that Schurr has established a prima facie case of race-based employment discrimination and that Resorts rested its decision not to hire Schurr on the terms of its affirmative action policy. Here, then, . . . the dispositive liability issue is the validity of Resorts' policy under Title VII.

We . . . are convinced that the affirmative action plan offered to rebut Schurr's prima facie case lacks the remedial purpose required by controlling precedent. In order to be characterized accurately as remedial, an affirmative action plan must be designed to correct a "manifest imbalance in traditionally segregated job categories" [quoting *Weber*]. The requirement that "manifest imbalance" relate to a traditionally segregated job category provides assurance that race will be taken into account in a manner consistent with Title VII's purpose of eliminating the *effects* of employment discrimination.

Under our reasonable interpretation of this standard, Resorts' affirmative action plan is deficient. The plan itself and the regulations which mandate the plan were not based on any finding of historical or then-current discrimination in the casino industry or in the technician job category; the plan was not put in place as a result of any manifest imbalance or in response to a finding that any relevant job category was or ever had been affected by segregation. Indeed, the case now before us is an unusual one in that there is no disagreement as to whether Resorts' plan or the . . . regulations [were] intended to remedy past or present discrimination. They were not. . . . The Casino Control Commission does not pretend otherwise. On appeal, the Commission makes the following statement relevant to the purpose underlying the act and the regulations:

> The Legislature recognized that a once-renowned tourist area had become blighted and had been largely abandoned by tourists. The Legislature was also aware [that] Atlantic City had and has a large minority population, and sought to ensure that the job creation which would accompany casino development would benefit all segments of the population.

The absence of any reference to or showing of past or present discrimination in the casino industry is fatal. The affirmative action plan relied on by Resorts in this Title VII action is invalid under the first prong of *Weber* and cannot form the basis for deviating from the antidiscrimination mandate of Title VII. Schurr, therefore, is entitled to summary judgment on the Title VII claim.

## Judgment and Result

The court of appeals reversed the district court's grant of summary judgment to Resorts on Schurr's Title VII claim, and ordered that Schurr be awarded summary judgment on that claim. The case was remanded to the district court for determination of the remedies to which Schurr was entitled.

## Questions

1. Notice that the court's decision in this case seems to leave Resorts and other casino owners between a rock and a hard place. Had Resorts not hired Boykin, it might have violated state law. But by hiring Boykin rather than Schurr, Resorts exposed itself to Title VII liability. Is there any way out of this trap?
2. Schurr also challenged the Casino Control Commission's minority employment goals on constitutional grounds, but his claim failed for reasons that have nothing to do with their constitutionality. What kind of a constitutional claim would Schurr have been making? What is the test of constitutionality the court would apply to such a claim? See Chapter 5.
3. Try to figure out how the Casino Control Commission's minority employment goals might fare under the second, third, and fourth elements of the *Weber* test. There probably is no clear answer to this question, but try anyway.

## SEX DISCRIMINATION

Although Title VII's ban on sex discrimination protects men as well as women, most Title VII sex discrimination cases involve female claimants. Because this provision was added to Title VII in a late amendment, there is little legislative history to assist courts in its interpretation. Clearly, however, Title VII's prohibition of sex discrimination applies only to gender-based discrimination. Thus, Title VII does not forbid discrimination on the bases of sexual orientation or transsexuality (although some states forbid the former).

Title VII's ban on sex discrimination involves a number of more or less distinct topics. They include:

1. *Sexual stereotyping.* Sexual stereotyping is employer behavior that discriminates against women by either assuming that women can only behave in a stereotypically "female" fashion, or requiring that they behave in such a fashion. For example, an employer might violate Title VII if it denies a female employee a job opportunity because it assumes that she is unaggressive, or instead penalizes her for acting aggressively.
2. *Preferences favoring women.* In 1987, the Supreme Court held that a voluntary county-wide affirmative action plan covering public employees did not violate Title VII even though the plan favored female employees over male employees in promotion decisions. In doing so, it applied the *Weber* tests for

voluntary racial preferences described earlier. Of course, the Court reformulated those tests to reflect gender rather than race.

3. *Pregnancy discrimination.* The Pregnancy Discrimination Act, which became effective in 1978, amended Title VII to make discrimination based on pregnancy, childbirth, or related medical conditions illegal. Thus, women are protected from such practices as being fired or refused a job merely because of pregnancy, childbirth, or related conditions. The Act also says that pregnancy and related conditions must be treated like other ailments similarly affecting an employee's ability to work. For example, an employer's sick leave, disability insurance, and health insurance policies must treat pregnancy like other ailments similarly affecting the ability to work.

4. *Sexual harassment.* Since the 1970s, two general theories of Title VII recovery for sexual harassment have emerged.[4] Both cover many kinds of unwelcome sex-related behavior—including sexual advances, requests for sexual favors, and other verbal or physical conduct of a sexual nature.

   The first sexual harassment theory is called **quid pro quo sexual harassment**. As its name suggests, this form of sexual harassment involves some kind of linkage, connection, or trade between the employee's submission to sex-related behavior and tangible job consequences. This linkage can be either express or implied. Thus, a male supervisor who fires a female subordinate because she refused to have sexual relations with him (or refused to submit to other kinds of sex-related conduct) violates Title VII. This would be true regardless of whether he expressly told the subordinate that she would be fired for refusing to submit. The same result would occur where submission is expressly or implicitly linked to other tangible job consequences such as promotions, raises, and performance evaluations. Many courts, however, require that the plaintiff show some tangible job detriment, usually one with financial consequences, in order to recover for quid pro quo sexual harassment.

   However, neither a quid pro quo nor a tangible job consequence is necessary when an employee sues for **work environment sexual harassment**. This is sexually related behavior that is so severe or pervasive that it creates an intimidating, hostile, or offensive working environment. Work environment sexual harassment may be individual or group behavior. For example, a supervisor might deluge a female subordinate with sexual propositions, touchings, and so forth; or co-workers might subject a female employee to a barrage of sex-related touchings, inquiries, jokes, comments, and general abuse. Here, there could be liability for work environment sexual harassment even if the employee is treated fairly regarding compensation, promotion, fringe benefits, and so forth. Because such behavior must be unwelcome, however, a female employee may not recover if she instigated the alleged harassment or willingly participated in it. More importantly, the harassment must be severe or pervasive for liability to exist.

   Although most sexual harassment cases involve male perpetrators, men clearly can sue for sexual harassment by women. The courts are split on the question of whether Title VII allows *sexual favoritism* suits. In these cases, an employee sues his or her employer because another employee has obtained an unfair employment advantage by submitting to sexual harassment or freely

---

[4] Similar principles apply to race, color, religion, or national origin harassment.

giving sexual favors. In *Oncale v. Sundowner Offshore Services, Inc.* (1998), the Supreme Court held that Title VII applies to same-sex sexual harassment. The following case seems to read *Oncale* narrowly.

## Bibby v. Philadelphia Coca-Cola Bottling Co.
U.S. Court of Appeals (Third Circuit)
260 F.3d 257 (2001)

### Background and Facts

John Bibby, who is gay, had worked for the Philadelphia Coca-Cola Bottling Company since 1978. When he returned to work late in 1993 after being treated for depression and anxiety, the company tried to fire him, but after Bibby filed a grievance and went through arbitration, he was reinstated and awarded back pay. About a year later, a male co-worker assaulted Bibby in a locker room. About a month after this, the same co-worker used his forklift truck to block Bibby's exit from a platform on which Bibby was working. The co-worker then yelled the following at Bibby: "Everybody knows you're as gay as a three dollar bill," "Everybody knows you're a faggot," and "Everybody knows you [engage in receptive anal intercourse]." Later that day, the co-worker called Bibby a "sissy." According to Bibby, supervisors harassed him by yelling at him, ignoring his reports of problems with machinery, and arbitrarily enforcing work rules against him where infractions by other employees would have been ignored. Bibby also claimed that graffiti of a sexual nature, some of them bearing his name, were written in the firm's bathrooms and allowed to remain on the walls longer than some other graffiti.

Late in 1998, Bibby sued the bottling company in federal district court for same-sex sexual harassment under Title VII. After the court granted the company's motion for summary judgment, Bibby appealed.

### Body of Opinion

**Circuit Judge Barry.** Title VII of the 1964 Civil Rights Act provides that "[i]t shall be an unlawful employment practice . . . to discriminate against any individual . . . because of . . . sex." It is clear, however, that Title VII does not prohibit discrimination based on sexual orientation. Congress has repeatedly rejected legislation that would have extended Title VII to cover sexual orientation. Thus, Bibby can seek relief under Title VII only for discrimination because of sex.

Until 1998, it was unclear whether and under what circumstances Title VII would apply in a case of sexual harassment where both the harasser and the victim were of the same sex. . . . In *Oncale v. Sundowner Offshore Services, Inc.* (1998), the Supreme Court unanimously held that Title VII does provide a cause of action for same-sex sexual harassment. . . . The Court reasoned that it is not the sex of the harasser or the victim that is important to a sexual harassment claim, but, rather, what is important is that the victim prove that the conduct at issue was not merely tinged with offensive

sexual connotations, but actually constituted discrimination because of sex. . . .

There are several situations in which same-sex harassment can be seen as discrimination because of sex. The first is where there is evidence that the harasser sexually desires the victim. . . . Same-sex harassment might also be found where there is no sexual attraction, but where the harasser displays hostility to the presence of a particular sex in the workplace. For example, a woman chief executive officer of an airline might believe that women should not be pilots, and might treat women pilots with hostility amounting to harassment. . . . In [such] situations, it would be easy to conclude that the harassment was caused by a general hostility to the presence of one sex in the workplace or in a particular work function, and therefore amounted to discrimination because of sex. Further, although it is less clear, a plaintiff may be able to prove that same-sex harassment was discrimination because of sex by presenting evidence that the harasser's conduct was motivated by a belief that the victim did not conform to the stereotypes of his or her gender. The gender-stereotypes method for proving same-sex sexual harassment is based on *Price-Waterhouse v. Hopkins* (1989), a case in which the Supreme Court [granted] the sex discrimination claim of a woman who had been denied partnership in an accounting firm at least in part on the basis that she was "macho," "overcompensated for being a woman," needed "a course in charm school," was "masculine," and was "a lady using foul language. . . ." Relying on *Price-Waterhouse,* . . . the Seventh Circuit held that where the evidence indicated that the harassment of a sixteen-year-old young man was motivated by his co-workers' belief that because he wore an earring he was not sufficiently masculine, there was sufficient evidence to support a finding that the harassment amounted to discrimination because of sex.

Thus, there are at least three ways by which a plaintiff alleging same-sex sexual harassment might demonstrate that the harassment amounted to discrimination because of sex. . . . Based on the facts of a particular case and the creativity of the parties, other ways in which to prove that harassment occurred because of sex may be available. That having been said, however, it is clear that whatever evidentiary route the plaintiff chooses to follow, he or she must always prove that the conduct at issue was not merely tinged with offensive sexual connotations, but actually constituted discrimination because of sex. Bibby simply failed in this respect; indeed, he did not even argue that he was being harassed because he was a man and offered nothing that would support such a conclusion. There was no allegation that his alleged harassers were motivated by sexual desire, or that they possessed any hostility to the presence of men in the workplace or in Bibby's particular job. Moreover, he did not claim that he was harassed because he failed to comply with societal stereotypes of how men ought to appear or behave, or that as a man he was treated differently than female co-workers. His claim was, pure and simple, that he was discriminated against because of his sexual orientation. No reasonable finder of fact could reach the conclusion that he was discriminated against because he was a man.[5]

Bibby argues that in reaching this conclusion, we will be placing an extra burden on gay and lesbian plaintiffs bringing an action for same-sex sexual harassment by requiring that such plaintiffs prove that their harassers were not motivated by anti-gay animus. Bibby is wrong. Whatever the sexual orientation of a plaintiff bringing a same-sex sexual harassment claim, that plaintiff is required to demonstrate that the harassment was directed at him or her because of his or her sex. Once such a showing has been made, the sexual orientation of the plaintiff is irrelevant. In addition, once it has been shown that the harassment was motivated by the victim's sex, it is no defense that the harassment may have also been partially motivated by anti-gay or anti-lesbian animus. For example, had the plaintiff in *Price-Waterhouse* been a lesbian, that fact would have provided the employer with no excuse for its decision to discriminate against her because she failed to conform to traditional feminine stereotypes.

## Judgment and Result

The court of appeals affirmed the district court's decision granting a summary judgment to the bottling company; Bibby loses.

## Questions

1. Assuming that Bibby actually had a good claim for same-sex sexual harassment, do you think that the harassment he suffered was severe or pervasive?
2. Is the court correct in concluding that the harassment Bibby suffered had nothing to do with his gender? For example, would co-workers have treated a woman (even a gay woman) the same way that they treated Bibby?
3. Did Bibby suffer the "gender-stereotyping" form of same-sex sexual harassment after all? What about the co-employee's statement that he was a sissy?
4. Notice that the court treats one form of sexual stereotyping as same-sex sexual harassment. Which form of sexual stereotyping is this?

---

[5] Given this conclusion, we need not reach the additional requirement that the alleged conduct was severe or pervasive enough to create an objectively hostile or abusive work environment [court's footnote].

---

## NATIONAL ORIGIN DISCRIMINATION

*The EEOC's guidelines on national origin discrimination are found under "Laws, Regulations, and Policy" at* **http://www.eeoc. gov**

Title VII's ban on national origin discrimination includes discrimination based on (1) a person's country of origin; (2) a person's ancestors' country of origin; or (3) a person's possession of physical, cultural, or linguistic characteristics shared by people of a certain national origin. For example, an employee has a Title VII case if he suffers discrimination because he was born in Germany. He would also have a Title VII case if he suffers discrimination because his parents were born there. Where discrimination is based on the employee's possession of physical, cultural, or linguistic traits, moreover, neither the employee nor his ancestors need have been born in a particular country for a Title VII claim to exist. Thus, a person of pure Brazilian ancestry might recover if she suffers discrimination because her employer thinks that she looks like, behaves like, or speaks like a German.

The EEOC has promulgated various guidelines on national origin discrimination. An employer's citizenship requirement, for example, violates Title VII if it has the purpose or effect of discriminating against an individual on the basis of national origin. Thus, if a northwest Montana logging company imposes a U.S. citizenship requirement for hiring lumberjacks, this could be a Title VII violation against Canadian lumberjacks.

Because formally neutral employer selection procedures such as tests, educational requirements, and interviews can disproportionately affect certain national origin groups, these procedures may violate Title VII. The EEOC's detailed guidelines on employee selection procedures set the standards such selection criteria must meet. However, a special rule applies to employer height and weight requirements. Because such requirements tend to exclude individuals on the basis of national origin, an employer must evaluate them for adverse impact, even if the employer's total selection process has no adverse impact on national origin groups. The EEOC also has stated that it will carefully evaluate national origin discrimination charges involving requirements that employees be fluent in English.

Finally, because job safety and efficiency often require that employees be competent in English and communicate in that language, the EEOC does not flatly ban speak-English-only rules in the workplace. Where such a rule is applied at all times in the workplace, the Commission presumes that it violates Title VII and closely scrutinizes it. Where such a rule is applied only at certain times, it is permissible if the employer can justify it by business necessity.

## DISCRIMINATION BASED ON RELIGION

Title VII prohibits most employment discrimination based on a person's religion. As you saw earlier in the chapter, however, religious educational institutions usually are immune from Title VII when they discriminate on the basis of religion. Also, religion occasionally may be a BFOQ.

Title VII's definition of religious discrimination is broad. Although not all courts might agree, the EEOC has suggested that the term *religion* includes almost all moral or metaphysical beliefs that are sincerely held with the strength of traditional religious views. Indeed, Title VII forbids employment discrimination against atheists because of their atheism. Besides forbidding discrimination based on religion as such, Title VII also prohibits discrimination based on religious observances or practices. Examples include grooming, apparel, and the refusal to work on the Sabbath. Some observances or practices, however, may interfere with an employer's business operations. Thus, discrimination based on such practices is justified if the employer demonstrates that it cannot reasonably accommodate the religious practice without undue hardship. An accommodation creates undue hardship if it imposes more than a minimal burden on an employer.

## SECTION 1981

The Civil Rights Act of 1866 was a post–Civil War statute designed to protect the civil rights of the newly freed slaves. A portion of the act called "Section 1981" has frequently been used to attack employment discrimination. Section 1981 mainly covers racial discrimination, but it also applies to discrimination against people of racially defined national origin such as Germans or Mexicans, and ethnic groups such as gypsies and Jews.

Section 1981 obviously protects fewer groups than does Title VII. But it does cover almost all the ways in which an employer might discriminate against the groups it does protect. Where it applies, moreover, Section 1981 has proven useful to plaintiffs. Title VII's methods of proving discrimination generally apply in Section 1981 suits. More importantly, plaintiffs in Section 1981 suits need not comply with Title VII's complex procedural requirements and may have more time in which to sue. In addition, Title VII's limits on compensatory and punitive damages do not apply in Section 1981 cases. For these reasons, Section 1981 has proven a useful supplement or alternative to Title VII, and plaintiffs sometimes include a Section 1981 count alongside a Title VII claim.

## Executive Order 11246

Originally issued in 1965, Executive Order 11246 forbids race, color, national origin, religion, and sex discrimination by certain federal contractors. The order is enforced and administered by the Office of Federal Contract Compliance Programs (OFCCP) of the Department of Labor, which has issued regulations to implement it. On occasion, Executive Order 11246 has been the basis for affirmative action plans preferring racial minorities.

## The Age Discrimination in Employment Act

The aim of the Age Discrimination in Employment Act of 1967 (ADEA) is to prohibit arbitrary age discrimination against employees and to ensure that employees are evaluated on the basis of ability rather than age. The act protects those who are at least 40 years of age, with no upper age limit. As the following *O'Connor* case makes clear, someone within that 40-and-over age group can recover for age discrimination regardless of whether the favored employee was inside or outside the group. In addition, a person age 40 or over probably can recover for age discrimination that favors either a younger or an older individual. Finally, those who are less than 40 years old receive no protection against age discrimination under the ADEA.

## O'Connor v. Consolidated Coin Caterers Corporation
U.S. Supreme Court
517 U.S. 308 (1996)

### Background and Facts

At the age of 56, James O'Connor was fired from his job with the Consolidated Coin Caterers Corporation. O'Connor's replacement was 40 years old. Alleging that he was fired because of his age, O'Connor sued Consolidated under the ADEA. After the federal district court granted Consolidated's motion for summary judgment and O'Connor appealed, the court of appeals affirmed. It did so because O'Connor's replacement was inside, rather than outside, the ADEA's protected 40-and-over age group. O'Connor appealed to the U.S. Supreme Court.

### Body of Opinion

**Justice Scalia.** [T]here must be at least a logical connection between each element of the [plaintiff's] prima facie case and the illegal discrimination for which it establishes a legally mandatory, rebuttable presumption. The element of replacement by someone under 40 fails this requirement. The discrimination prohibited by the ADEA is discrimination because of an individual's age, though the prohibition is limited to individuals who are at least 40 years of age. This language does not ban discrimination against employees because they are aged 40 or older; it bans discrimination against employees because of their age, but limits the protected class to those who are 40 or older. The fact that one person in the protected class has lost out to another person in the protected class is thus irrelevant, so long as he has lost out *because of his age*. Or to put the point more concretely, there can be no greater inference of *age* discrimination . . . when a 40-year-old is replaced by a 39-year-old than when a 56-year-old is replaced by a 40-year-old. Because it lacks probative value, the fact that an ADEA plaintiff was replaced by someone outside the protected class is not a proper element of the . . . prima facie case.

### Judgment and Result

Court of appeals decision in Consolidated's favor reversed; O'Connor's age discrimination case allowed to proceed.

### Questions

1. Does the Supreme Court's decision mean that O'Connor wins his suit against Consolidated?
2. Do you think that O'Connor should win in a case where his replacement is 65?
3. What would be the result if O'Connor had been 36 years old?

Like Title VII, the ADEA prohibits employer discrimination regarding almost all terms, conditions, and benefits of employment. The ADEA also resembles Title VII in forbidding employer retaliation against those who object to illegal age discrimination, file charges, or otherwise assist or participate in proceedings under the Act.

## ENTITIES COVERED

The ADEA covers employer discrimination by individuals, partnerships, employment agencies (regarding their own employees), labor organizations (regarding their own employees), and corporations that (1) are engaged in an industry affecting interstate commerce and (2) employ twenty or more persons. However, the Supreme Court has held that the ADEA does not eliminate the states' sovereign immunity against suits by private individuals, which may mean that most age discrimination suits against state and local governments must proceed under state law. The ADEA also covers referral activities by employment agencies of any size if they make referrals to a covered employer. Finally, the ADEA applies to labor unions in their role as employee representative. Here, the labor union usually must have twenty-five or more members.

## PROCEDURES

Like Title VII, the ADEA sets up a complex procedural path that private parties with age discrimination claims must follow. These procedural requirements, whose details are beyond the scope of this text, resemble Title VII's requirements but differ in a few particulars. The EEOC also can sue to enforce the act, and an EEOC suit blocks private suits involving the same alleged violation. For all ADEA actions, suit must be filed within two years of an alleged nonwillful violation, and within three years of an alleged willful violation.

## PROVING AN ADEA VIOLATION

The methods of proving an ADEA violation resemble the Title VII methods discussed earlier. Proving age discrimination is easy where the defendant has an express policy treating people differently because of their age. Other direct evidence of age bias such as testimony or documents obviously can be useful to plaintiffs as well. The ADEA also permits disparate treatment suits that resemble Title VII disparate treatment suits. Finally, some courts have used Title VII's disparate impact theory in ADEA suits.

## DEFENSES

Even if the plaintiff manages to prove unlawful age discrimination, the defendant triumphs if it can establish one of the ADEA's defenses. The Act has a seniority defense that resembles the corresponding defense under Title VII. The ADEA also allows the employer to use age criteria in bona fide employee benefit plans such as retirement, pension, and insurance plans. In addition, the ADEA allows an employer to discharge or otherwise penalize an employee for good cause. It also allows employers to use reasonable factors other than age in their employment decisions. Finally, the ADEA has a bona fide occupational qualification (BFOQ) defense that applies when age is reasonably necessary to effective job performance. Possible examples include age limits on school bus drivers, airplane and helicopter pilots, police, and firefighters.[6]

## REMEDIES

A successful ADEA plaintiff can recover unpaid back wages resulting from the discrimination. If the discrimination was willful, the plaintiff obtains an additional equal amount as liquidated damages. Generally, courts do not permit punitive damage recoveries, or recoveries for consequential damages such as pain, suffering, and emotional distress. Equitable remedies are also possible under the ADEA; they include court orders requiring hiring, reinstatement, and promotion.

## THE AMERICANS WITH DISABILITIES ACT

For years, the major federal law dealing with employment discrimination against disabled people was the Vocational Rehabilitation Act of 1973, which mainly applies to federal contractors and to programs receiving federal financial assistance. But this pattern of limited federal protection changed dramatically in 1990, when Congress enacted Title I of the Americans with Disabilities Act (ADA). Title I's procedures and remedies are the same as those for Title VII, and it is enforced by the EEOC.

### ENTITIES COVERED

Title I of the ADA covers employers that are engaged in an industry affecting interstate commerce and that have fifteen or more employees. The ADA's employers are basically the same as for Title VII; they include individuals, partnerships, corporations, colleges and universities, labor unions (with respect to their own employees), employment agencies (with respect to their own employees), and state and local governments. Not covered, however, are the U. S. government and corporations it wholly owns, Native American tribes, and certain tax-exempt private clubs. Like Title VII, the ADA also covers discrimination by unions against their members, and by employment agencies against their clients.

### PROHIBITED DISCRIMINATION

Under Title I, the covered entities just described may not discriminate against qualified individuals with a disability because of that disability. The act forbids such discrimination in a wide range of employment contexts, including hiring, firing, pay, promotions, job training, and many others. It also has an antiretaliation provision that resembles Title VII's antiretaliation provision.

The ADA's protected disabilities are (1) physical or mental impairments that substantially limit one or more of a person's major life activities, (2) any record of such an impairment, and (3) a person's being regarded as having such an impairment. The last two categories include people who have earlier been misdiagnosed as having some impairment, have recovered from an earlier impairment, or are regarded by others as having an impairment even though they might not. However, those who suffer discrimination due to their current use of illegal drugs are not considered "qualified individuals with a disability." Also, homosexuality, bisexuality, transvestism, transsexualism, pedophilia, exhibitionism, voyeurism, compulsive

---

[6] Also, a 1996 amendment to the ADEA says that employers do not violate the act when they discharge or refuse to hire certain firefighters and law enforcement officers.

gambling, kleptomania, pyromania, and certain other conditions or disorders are not disabilities. Furthermore, entities covered by the act may prohibit workplace drug or alcohol use, may require that employees not be under the influence of drugs or alcohol at the workplace, and may hold drug users or alcoholics to the same standards as other employees.

To be a *qualified* individual with a disability, a disabled job applicant or employee must be able to perform the essential functions of the job she desires or holds, either *with or without reasonable accommodation*. Thus, the ADA forbids handicap discrimination against impaired people who can perform the essential functions of the relevant job without any extra assistance from their employers. But it also requires that employers make reasonable accommodation to those who could perform the job's essential functions with such accommodation.

What is a reasonable accommodation? The ADA's definition of the term includes acts such as making facilities accessible and usable by people with disabilities; job restructuring; part-time or modified work schedules; reassignments; adjustments to equipment, examinations, and training materials; and others. But even if a reasonable accommodation is available, the employer need not provide it if such accommodation would impose an *undue hardship*. Undue hardship is defined as an act requiring significant difficulty or expense. Among the factors for determining whether an accommodation involves such difficulty or expense are its cost, the covered entity's financial resources, and the accommodation's effect on its business operations.

What is the relationship between the ADA's "reasonable accommodation" and "undue hardship" requirements? At first glance, it appears that these two standards overlap. For example, a proposed accommodation that causes an employer undue hardship is unlikely to be reasonable. Most courts avoid this problem by first asking whether the requested accommodation seems reasonable on its face— that is, whether it ordinarily would be reasonable or would be reasonable in the usual run of cases. If the plaintiff survives this hurdle, then the employer must prove specific circumstances that show undue hardship.

Figure 16.2 on page 442 recapitulates the preceding ADA requirements.

## DEFENSES

Certain factors already mentioned—for example, undue hardship, the plaintiff's use of illegal drugs, and others—effectively operate as defenses to an ADA suit. In addition, the act lists certain specific defenses. For example, it says that covered entities may use standards, tests, or selection criteria that disadvantage people with protected disabilities, if those standards, tests, or criteria are job-related and consistent with business necessity, and if no reasonable accommodation is possible. The ADA also lets employers require that an employee not pose a direct threat to the health and safety of other employees. In 2002, the Supreme Court upheld an EEOC regulation extending this defense to situations where the employee's disability threatens *his own* health or safety.

In recent years, the Supreme Court has been reading the ADA's definition of a disability narrowly. The most likely reasons are the amount of litigation the ADA would generate if more broadly construed, and the effect this might have on employer prerogatives and business productivity. In *Sutton v. United Airlines* (1999), the Court held that the ADA does not protect people whose medical conditions or other alleged disabilities are correctable. This case involved two sisters who were denied employment as commercial airline pilots because their uncorrected vision was in the 20/200 to 20/400 range, even though corrective lenses gave both women vision of 20/20 or better. The following unanimous *Williams* decision also seems to make it more difficult to mount an ADA suit.

## FIGURE 16.2 FINDING YOUR WAY THROUGH THE ADA

## Toyota Motor Manufacturing, Kentucky v. Williams
U.S. Supreme Court
122 S. Ct. 681 (2002)

### Background and Facts

Ella Williams began working at Toyota's Georgetown, Kentucky auto manufacturing plant in 1990. In 1993, Toyota assigned Williams to a team in its Quality Control Inspection Operations (QCIO). For a few years thereafter, Williams performed only two of the tasks undertaken by this unit: visually inspecting painted cars, and wiping painted cars with a glove. She performed each of these jobs satisfactorily. In 1996, Toyota required that all QCIO employees rotate through all four of the processes performed by that unit. This meant that Williams had to hold her hands and arms up around shoulder height for several hours at a time to use a sponge attached to a piece of wood to apply "highlight oil" to painted cars. As a result, Williams began experiencing pain in her

neck and shoulders. Later, she was diagnosed with a variety of physical ailments, among them carpel tunnel syndrome. After Williams asked to be reassigned to her pre-1996 jobs and Toyota denied the request, she was fired for excessive absences from work.

Then, after filing a charge with the EEOC and getting a right-to-sue letter, Williams sued Toyota under the Americans with Disabilities Act in a Kentucky federal district court. The district court held for Toyota, but the Sixth Circuit Court of Appeals reversed this decision. Toyota then appealed to the U.S. Supreme Court. The Court's review of the case was limited to the following issue: the proper standard for determining whether a person is substantially limited in performing manual tasks under the ADA's definition of a disability.

## Body of Opinion

**Justice O'Connor.** The ADA requires covered entities, including private employers, to provide "reasonable accommodation to the known physical or mental limitations of an otherwise qualified individual with a disability who is an applicant or employee, unless such covered entity can demonstrate that the accommodation would impose an undue hardship." The act defines a "qualified individual with a disability" as "an individual with a disability who, with or without reasonable accommodation, can perform the essential functions of the employment position that such individual holds or desires." In turn, a "disability" is: "(A) a physical or mental impairment that substantially limits one or more of the major life activities of such individual; (B) a record of such an impairment; or (C) being regarded as having such an impairment."

. . . The question presented by this case is whether the Sixth Circuit properly determined that Williams was disabled under subsection (A) of the ADA's disability definition at the time she sought an accommodation from Toyota. The parties do not dispute that Williams's medical conditions . . . amount to physical impairments. The relevant question, therefore, is whether the Sixth Circuit correctly analyzed whether these impairments substantially limited Williams in the major life activity of performing manual tasks. . . .

Our consideration of this issue is guided first and foremost by the words of the disability definition itself. "[S]ubstantially" in the phrase "substantially limits" suggests "considerable" or "to a large degree" [citing a Webster's dictionary]. The word "substantial" thus clearly precludes impairments that interfere in only a minor way with the performance of manual tasks from qualifying as disabilities. "Major" in the phrase "major life activities" means important [again citing the Webster's dictionary]. In order for performing manual tasks to fit into this category—a category that includes such basic abilities as walking, seeing, and hearing—the manual tasks in question must be central to daily life. If each of the tasks included in the major life activity of performing manual tasks does not independently qualify as a major life activity, then together they must do so.

That these terms need to be interpreted strictly to create a demanding standard for qualifying as disabled is confirmed by the first section of the ADA, which lays out the legislative findings and purposes that motivate the act. When it enacted the ADA in 1990, Congress found that "some 43,000,000 Americans have one or more physical or mental disabilities." If Congress intended everyone with a physical impairment that precluded the performance of some isolated, unimportant or particularly difficult manual task to qualify as disabled, the number of disabled Americans would surely have been much higher.

We therefore hold that to be substantially limited in performing manual tasks, an individual must have an impairment that prevents or severely restricts the individual from doing activities that are of central importance to most people's daily lives. The impairment's impact must also be permanent or long-term. . . .

While the court of appeals in this case addressed the major life activity of performing manual tasks, its analysis [focused on] Williams's inability to perform manual tasks associated only with her job. This was error. When addressing the major life activity of performing manual tasks, the central inquiry must be whether the claimant is unable to perform the variety of tasks central to most people's daily lives, not whether the claimant is unable to perform the tasks associated with her specific job. . . . There is no support in the act, our previous opinions, or the regulations for the court of appeals' idea that the question of whether an impairment constitutes a disability is to be answered only by analyzing the effect of the impairment in the workplace. . . . [T]he manual tasks unique to any particular job are not necessarily important parts of most people's lives. . . . In this case, repetitive work with hands and arms extended at or above shoulder levels for extended periods of time, the manual task on which the court of appeals relied, is not an important part of most people's daily lives. The court, therefore, should not have considered Williams's inability to do such manual work in her specialized assembly line job as sufficient proof that she was substantially limited in performing manual tasks. . . .

At the same time, the court of appeals appears to have disregarded the very type of evidence that it should have focused upon. It treated as irrelevant the fact that Williams can tend to her personal hygiene and carry out personal and household chores. Yet household chores, bathing, and brushing one's teeth are among the types of manual tasks of central importance to people's daily lives, and should have been part of the assessment of whether Williams was substantially limited in performing manual tasks.

The district court noted that at the time Williams sought an accommodation from Toyota, she admitted that she was able to do the manual tasks required by her original two jobs in QCIO. In addition, according to Williams's deposition testimony, even after her condition worsened, she could still brush her teeth, wash her face, tend her flower garden, fix breakfast, do laundry, and pick up around the house. The record also indicates that her medical conditions caused her to avoid sweeping, to quit dancing, to occasionally seek help dressing, and to reduce how often she plays with her children, gardens, and drives long distances. But these changes in her life did not amount to such severe restrictions in the activities that are of central importance to most people's daily lives that they establish a manual-task disability as a matter of law. On this record, it was therefore inappropriate for the court of appeals to grant partial summary judgment to Williams on the issue whether she was substantially limited in performing manual tasks, and its decision to do so must be reversed.

## Judgment and Result

The court of appeals' decision for Williams on the standard for assessing whether a person is substantially limited in performing manual tasks was reversed. The case was returned to the lower courts for proceedings consistent with the Supreme Court's opinion.

## Questions

1. Did Williams have an "impairment"? Why or why not?
2. Did Williams have an impairment that substantially limited one or more of her major life activities? Why or why not?
3. Why did the Supreme Court not discuss whether Williams could perform her job with a reasonable accommodation and whether Toyota could accommodate her without undue hardship?

Unlike most of the employment discrimination laws discussed in this chapter, the ADA does not contain a seniority defense. So what happens when a disabled employee's request for a reasonable accommodation collides with the defendant firm's seniority system? The following case deals with this problem.

## US Airways, Inc. v. Barnett
U.S. Supreme Court
70 U.S.L.W. 4285 (2002)

### Background and Facts

In 1990, Robert Barnett injured his back while working in a cargo-handling position at US Airways, Inc. Afterwards, Barnett was transferred to a less physically demanding position in the firm's mail room. Under US Airways' seniority system, other employees periodically could bid for this and other jobs within the company. In 1992, Barnett learned that at least two employees senior to him intended to bid for the mail room position. After Barnett asked US Airways to accommodate his disability by making an exception to its seniority system that would allow him to remain in the mail room, the firm refused and he lost his job.

Then, Barnett sued US Airways in federal district court under the ADA. His basic argument was that US Airways discriminated against him on the basis of his disability because it refused him the reasonable accommodation he had requested. After the district court held for US Airways and the court of appeals reversed that decision, US Airways appealed to the U.S. Supreme Court. It asked the Court to decide whether the ADA requires an employer to reassign a disabled employee to a position as a reasonable accommodation, even though another employee is entitled to the position under the employer's established and bona fide seniority system.

### Body of Opinion

**Justice Breyer.** The question in the present case focuses on the relationship between seniority systems and the plaintiff's need to show that an accommodation seems reasonable on its face, i.e., ordinarily or in the run of cases. We must assume that the plaintiff, an employee, is an individual with a disability. He has requested assignment to a mail room position as a reasonable accommodation. We also assume that normally such a request would be reasonable within the meaning of the statute, were it not for one circumstance, namely, that the assignment would violate the rules of a seniority system. Does this circumstance mean that the proposed accommodation is not a reasonable one?

In our view, the answer to this question ordinarily is "yes." The statute does not require proof on a case-by-case basis that a seniority system should prevail. That is because it would not be reasonable in the run of cases that the assignment in question trump the rules of a seniority system. To the contrary, it will ordinarily be unreasonable for the assignment to prevail.

Several factors support our conclusion that a proposed accommodation will not be reasonable in the run of cases. Analogous case law supports this conclusion, for it has recognized the importance of seniority to employee–management relations. This Court has held that,

in the context of a Title VII religious discrimination case, an employer need not adapt to an employee's special worship schedule as a reasonable accommodation where doing so would conflict with the seniority rights of other employees. The lower courts have unanimously found that collectively bargained seniority trumps the need for a reasonable accommodation in the context of the linguistically similar Rehabilitation Act. And several Circuits, though differing in their reasoning, have reached a similar conclusion in the context of seniority and the ADA. . . .

[T]he typical seniority system provides important employee benefits by creating, and fulfilling, employee expectations of fair, uniform treatment. These benefits include job security and an opportunity for steady and predictable advancement based on objective standards. They include an element of due process, limiting unfairness in personnel decisions. And they consequently encourage employees to invest in the employing company, accepting less than their value to the firm early in their careers in return for greater benefits in later years. . . . [T]o require the typical employer to show more than the existence of a seniority system [to defeat a "reasonable accommodation" claim] might well undermine the employees' expectations of consistent, uniform treatment. . . . That is because such a rule would substitute a complex case-specific "accommodation" decision made by management for the more uniform, impersonal operation of seniority rules. Such management decision-making, with its inevitable discretionary elements, would involve a matter of the greatest importance to employees, namely, layoffs. . . . We can find nothing in the statute that suggests Congress intended to undermine seniority systems in this way. And we consequently conclude that the employer's showing of violation of the rules of a seniority system is by itself ordinarily sufficient.

The plaintiff (here the employee) nonetheless remains free to show that special circumstances warrant a finding that, despite the presence of a seniority system . . . , the requested accommodation is reasonable on the particular facts. That is because special circumstances might alter the important expectations described above. The plaintiff might show, for example, that the employer, having retained the right to change the seniority system unilaterally, exercises that right fairly frequently, reducing employee expectations that the system will be followed. . . . The plaintiff might show that the system already contains exceptions such that, in the circumstances, one further exception is unlikely to matter. . . .

In its question presented, US Airways asked us whether the ADA requires an employer to assign a disabled employee to a particular position even though another employee is entitled to that position under the employer's established seniority system. We answer that *ordinarily* the ADA does not require that assignment. Hence, a showing that the assignment would violate the rules of a seniority system warrants summary judgment for the employer—unless there is more. The plaintiff must present evidence of that "more," namely, special circumstances surrounding the particular case that demonstrate the assignment is nonetheless reasonable.

## Judgment and Result

The Supreme Court vacated the court of appeals' decision and returned the case to the lower federal courts for proceedings consistent with its opinion.

## Questions

1. Did the Supreme Court hold that, where a request for reasonable accommodation collides with a seniority system, the request *always* fails? What did it hold?
2. Justice Breyer gave two examples of situations in which an employer might be required to grant a reasonable accommodation, even though its seniority system says otherwise. What are they? What justifies them?
3. Early in his opinion, Justice Breyer noted that, under the Vocational Rehabilitation Act, all courts considering the question held that seniority system provisions trump claims for reasonable accommodation. The Rehabilitation Act and the ADA are different statutes. So why should those decisions be persuasive here?

## STATE EMPLOYMENT DISCRIMINATION LAWS

A great many states have laws resembling Title VII and the ADEA, and many have statutes protecting the handicapped. Some of these measures impose tougher standards on employers than their federal counterparts. Also, some states go beyond federal law regarding the types of discrimination they forbid. Some, for example, prohibit unfavorable employment decisions based on a person's marital status, physical appearance, sexual orientation, political affiliation, off-the-job smoking, and AIDS infection.

In addition, some states and localities have enacted "pay equity" laws that could be regarded as **comparable worth** provisions. Most such laws apply only to public employment. Often they say that the relevant government unit(s) should not discriminate in pay between female-dominated jobs and male-dominated jobs, if those jobs have comparable overall worth to the employer. This is true even though the "male" and "female" jobs might be quite dissimilar. To determine the worth of dissimilar jobs, proponents of comparable worth sometimes give the different jobs point ratings under variables resembling the Equal Pay Act's equal work components (skill, responsibility, effort, and working conditions), total the point ratings, and then compare the totals. Once there were signs that Title VII would become a vehicle for comparable worth claims, but that possibility has receded over the years.

## CHAPTER SUMMARY

This chapter examines the major federal laws forbidding employment discrimination. It opens by discussing the Equal Pay Act (EPA), which forbids sex discrimination regarding pay. To recover under the EPA, claimants must show that they have received lower pay than an employee of the opposite sex who performed substantially equal work.

Then the chapter examines America's most important employment discrimination provision: Title VII of the 1964 Civil Rights Act. Title VII forbids all sorts of employment discrimination on the bases of race, color, religion, sex, and national origin. It mainly covers employers who employ more than fifteen employees.

Executive Order 11246 forbids certain federal contractors from discriminating on the same bases as Title VII. A post–Civil War antidiscrimination statute called Section 1981 also has been enlisted in the fight against employment discrimination.

## ■ MANAGER'S ETHICAL DILEMMA

You are the president of Planetary Highway, Inc., a medium-sized firm in a highly competitive segment of the telecommunications industry. Right now, Planetary is the leading firm in this segment, and its profitability is outstanding. The firm's success is due in large measure to Jim Sloan, Planetary's director of research. Jim's abilities have made him essential to the firm's continuing success.

In at least one respect, however, Jim is something less than a model manager. In recent years, Jim has had sexual relations with many of the company's female employees. It is difficult to say whether Jim's behavior really constitutes sexual harassment of either the quid pro quo or the work environment variety. For one thing, he is a very attractive and personable individual. For another, he is discreet. Also, Jim's "victims" seem to get more than their share of good raises, promotions, choice assignments, and so forth. Thus, these women are unlikely to complain about Jim's actions, or even to admit that they had sex with him.

By now, though, some of Planetary's other male and female employees have begun to get wind of what's going on. As a result, employee morale is beginning to suffer. Even if they have a claim under Title VII or state law, however, none of these suspicious employees could prove anything. Nonetheless, some of them are beginning to voice their suspicions both inside and outside the firm.

It is probably within your formal power to get Jim fired. Doing so, however, would hardly do Planetary or its shareholders any good. Worse yet, Jim has sufficient clout within the firm and on its board of directors that taking action against him could put your neck on the line. Even if Jim were canned, moreover, any one of Planetary's competitors would snap him up in an instant. This would probably be true even if they discovered the reason for his firing. Needless to say, Jim would vastly improve the competitive position of any firm acquiring his services.

Despite all the disadvantages of taking action against him, Jim's behavior still bothers you. What should you do?

---

Section 1981 covers some kinds of racial, ethnic, and racial/national origin discrimination.

The Age Discrimination in Employment Act forbids age discrimination against those age 40 and up. Its coverage, procedures, methods of proof, and defenses resemble those established by Title VII.

Finally, the Americans with Disabilities Act (ADA) forbids employment discrimination against qualified individuals with disabilities. Like the Age Discrimination in Employment Act, the ADA's coverage, procedures, methods of proof, and defenses resemble those set out by Title VII.

## DISCUSSION QUESTIONS

1. Opponents of certain 1991 amendments to Title VII charged that planned changes to the disparate impact method of proof would make Title VII a "quota bill." What they meant was that the changes would force employers to hire the "right numbers" of African Americans and other racial minorities to head off possible Title VII liability. Although this criticism might not apply to the legislation that actually emerged, how could the disparate impact method lead employers to "hire by the numbers"? *Hint*: Check out the second part of the disparate impact test and consider what might happen if it imposed a genuinely tough burden of proof on employers. On the other hand, what is likely to happen if the second portion of the disparate impact test is easy on employers?

   Finally, assuming solely for the sake of argument that the 1991 amendments force employers to prefer minorities in hiring and elsewhere, what would happen if they are sued by white people who suffer racial discrimination because employers have felt compelled to favor minorities?

2. What are the arguments for and against the quota-like minority preferences (or reverse discrimination) discussed in this chapter? First, consider some of the common criticisms of such practices. Are they consistent with the idea that individuals should be treated solely on the basis of their ability to perform the job in question? Are such practices fair to white employees or job applicants? What other objections to these preferences can you think of?

   After this, consider what might be said in favor of such practices. Do minorities deserve "reparations" for the generations of discrimination they have suffered? (Here, note that some beneficiaries of minority preferences may not themselves be victims of discrimination.) Would a system in which all employment decisions are made on a perfectly neutral color-blind basis really treat minorities fairly and equally? In answering this question, consider America's long history of prior discrimination against racial minorities, and the effect this may have had on their ability to compete equally in the employment market. Could minority employment preferences help give future generations of minorities the ability to compete on an equal basis, so that such preferences eventually become unnecessary? Would abandoning the current system of minority preferences endanger social harmony in future years? Are these preferences valuable because they promote workforce diversity? (But is diversity valuable *in itself*? Or is it supposed to be valuable because it furthers some of the policies just discussed? Does it promote any other important values?) What other arguments might support the preferential treatment of minorities in employment?

3. How do the various arguments and counterarguments made in the previous question apply to employment preferences in favor of *women*?

4. In the previous Manager's Ethical Dilemma, what kind of Title VII suit might the disgruntled employees conceivably be able to mount? What are their chances of success? Is it a good idea to allow such suits under Title VII? *Hint*: Check out the concluding portions of this chapter's discussion of sexual harassment.

5. Employment discrimination law recognizes the employer's need to run the business in an efficient and effective manner. In particular, it recognizes the employer's interest in ensuring that its employees be competent in performing their jobs. What rules discussed in the chapter specifically recognize these interests?

6. Look at the brief description of the *Sutton* case that precedes the *Williams* case in the chapter's discussion of the ADA. Did the Court say that employers can irrationally discriminate against people whose problems are correctable, but that employers must be careful with people who really do have problems and thus may really be unable to perform? Does this make any sense at all? What might motivate the Court's seemingly irrational position? Check out the next discussion question.

7. Arguably, the Supreme Court has been reading the Americans with Disabilities Act narrowly in order to prevent employers from being deluged with ADA claims. What might justify such a position?

8. Should Title VII be amended to forbid discrimination on the basis of sexual orientation? On the basis of transsexuality?

9. Notice that sex discrimination suits involving unequal pay can proceed under both the Equal Pay Act and Title VII. Do such suits involve the same legal requirements under each act? Some years ago, the Supreme Court held that when such suits proceed under Title VII, (1) the Equal Pay Act's defenses apply, but (2) the EPA's equal work requirement does not apply. At one time, this decision was thought to open the door for comparable worth suits under Title VII. (See the discussion of comparable worth in the section on state employment discrimination laws.) Why is this so? Why are comparable worth suits impossible under the Equal Pay Act?

10. For more than fifteen years, the Supreme Court has been grappling with the question of when employers are liable for sexual harassment committed by supervisors and other employees. Due to the confusions that have prevailed in the area, the chapter's discussion of sexual harassment does not include this subject. The main source of the Court's difficulties, one of your authors believes, is the Court's mistaken idea that Congress wanted the common law of agency to resolve the employer liability question.

Suppose that it is up to you to determine when employers should be liable for employee sexual harassment, and that you are starting with a clean slate. What about the view that, because the employer is a distinct entity from its supervisors and other employees, employers should *never* be liable for employee sexual harassment? What about the opposite view that employers should *always* be strictly liable for employee sexual harassment? If you would prefer some compromise between these extremes, consider the following questions. What kind of fault standard should apply to the employer? For example, is a negligence standard a good idea? Should it make a difference *what kind* of employee committed the harassment? For example, should it matter that the harasser was a supervisor or even a high-level executive? This ties in with another question: Would you want different rules for quid pro quo harassment and work environment harassment? Note that quid pro quo harassment usually is committed by supervisors, while work environment harassment may be committed by supervisors or by co-employees.

11. Most courts still seem to require that an employee suffer some kind of tangible job detriment, usually a detriment of a financial nature, in order to recover for quid pro quo sexual harassment. This appears to mean that employers will escape liability when a supervisor announces the quid pro quo to a subordinate, the subordinate calls the bluff, and then nothing happens. Should employers escape liability in cases of this kind? Assume that the supervisor's behavior did not rise to the level of work environment harassment.

## INFOTRAC KEYWORDS

**Use your InfoTrac password to look up articles on**
**http://www.infotrac-college.com**

Keywords: *Civil rights, Title VII, Title VII claims, race discrimination, sex discrimination, religious discrimination, age discrimination.*

For suggested readings, please visit this book's Web site at **http://fisher.westbuslaw.com** (click on "Internet Applications").

# FEDERAL LABOR LAW: UNIONIZATION AND COLLECTIVE BARGAINING

## POSITIVE LAW ETHICAL PROBLEM

"She's anti-union and committing an unfair labor practice because she is intentionally hiring fewer than 50 percent of the workers for her new firm from the old firm," argued Jim Fisher, a former employee of Piggly Wiggly Supermarket.

"Oh, she can hire whomever she wants, because she and her husband bought the supermarket and they are dropping some departments and adding others, so it's not a 'successor' firm," replied an onlooker.

When successor employers are deciding whom to hire from the former unionized employer's workforce, can they pick and choose employees based on employees' hostility to unions?

*"EMPLOYEES HAVE AS CLEAR A RIGHT TO ORGANIZE AND SELECT THEIR REPRESENTATIVES FOR LAWFUL PURPOSES AS THE RESPONDENT HAS TO ORGANIZE ITS BUSINESS AND SELECT ITS OWN OFFICERS AND AGENTS."*

— CHIEF JUSTICE CHARLES EVANS HUGHES
IN *NLRB V. JONES & LAUGHLIN STEEL CORP.*, 301 U.S. 1 (1937))

This chapter deals with the federal law of union organization and collective bargaining and focuses on three federal statutes: the National Labor Relations Act of 1935 (also called the Wagner Act), the Taft–Hartley Act (also known as the Labor–Management Relations Act of 1947), and the Landrum–Griffin Act (or Labor–Management Reporting and Disclosure Act of 1959).

## DEVELOPMENT OF LABOR LAW

In the 1800s the labor organization was treated by state law as a criminal conspiracy, a combination of employees withholding services from their employers. This rule gradually changed by the late 1800s when the legality of union efforts was judged by the ends it sought to achieve and the means used to reach these ends. Throughout the century, the court injunction was used to control unions.

The year 1890 witnessed the passage of the Sherman Act, which declared combinations in restraint of trade illegal. The effect of the Sherman Act on unions was soon felt when the *Danbury Hatters* case applied that act to union boycotting activities. Injunctive relief was used to stop picketing and strike activity and to kill the strike entirely. During this period and for a considerable time thereafter, the judiciary identified with ownership interests and consequently showed its hostile attitude toward unions by interpreting statutes to curb unions.

After an unsuccessful attempt in the Clayton Act of 1914 to exempt union activity from the antitrust laws, the Norris–LaGuardia Act was passed in 1932. Rather than outlawing the injunction against lawful union activity, the Norris–LaGuardia Act removed jurisdiction to enjoin peaceful labor disputes from the federal courts. The effect of this was to keep federal courts out of the process of regulating unions. (Note that state courts may issue injunctions in labor disputes.)

In 1926, prior to enactment of the Norris–LaGuardia Act, the Railway Labor Act was passed. As the name suggests, the function of the act was to regulate labor in the railroad industry.

The National Labor Relations Act became law in 1935. At that time it had two functions: (1) to provide a way for employees to say if they wanted a union, and (2) to set forth a code of unfair labor practices binding on employers only, with no prohibitions on unions. From the management viewpoint, this last feature of the NLRA was a shortcoming, and in 1947, with the conservative trend in the country, the Taft–Hartley Act (the Labor–Management Relations Act) was passed. It rewrote the original NLRA and provided a new code of unfair labor practices applicable to unions. It also outlawed **secondary boycotts**,[1] enforced collective bargaining agreements, and provided for a resolution of disputes affecting national health and welfare. It backed up these provisions with an 80-day injunction before a strike could be called, to encourage collective bargaining for the period.

Further reduction of union power came in 1959 in the Landrum–Griffin amendment to the Labor Management Relations Act. For the first time, Congress provided for federal regulation of the internal affairs of labor unions. In addition, further restrictions were placed on secondary boycotts and picketing during organizational campaigns.

In the 1980s the largest single factor affecting labor was the presidency of Ronald Reagan. Although once a union member and even a union president, President Reagan pursued labor policies generally opposed by union leaders. Some evidence, however, indicates that union *members* supported him.

Presidents have the power to appoint individuals who shared their union views to the federal judiciary and the National Labor Relations Board (NLRB), and these appointees may affect labor law years after the president leaves office. President Reagan's appointees generally went to bat for labor law cases that diluted the power of unions. Thus, labor law cases today reflect an increasingly hostile attitude toward unions. For example, in 1984 the U.S. Supreme Court decided *NLRB v. Bildisco & Bildisco*, holding that an employer may legally file a Chapter 11 bankruptcy petition and immediately dishonor an existing collective bargaining agreement without first talking to the union. Congress then modified the *Bildisco* decision by amending the bankruptcy code. The code now sets up a consultation process that employers must follow with the union and the bankruptcy court before seeking bankruptcy relief from collective bargaining agreements.

A second example of an increasingly hostile attitude of the law toward unions concerns the NLRB's reversal of its earlier ruling on a multiplant employer's shifting work from a high- to a low-labor-cost plant, often in another state. The NLRB had declared this action illegal in the 1982 case of *Milwaukee Spring Division of Illinois Coil Spring Company*. In 1984, after two Reagan appointees had joined the NLRB, the board reversed its 1982 decision. An employer may now legally switch work from a union plant covered by a collective bargaining agreement to a nonunion plant, solely because of lower labor costs. The employer in the *Milwaukee Spring* case did bargain with the union to an impasse

---

[1] *Secondary boycotts* refer to a bargaining technique and generally refer to requiring or forcing someone to stop handling another's products or doing business with another person. Put another way, a secondary boycott is any combination whose purpose and effect are to force customers or suppliers of an employer with which the union has a dispute to stop doing business with that employer. The union is one of the parties to the combination, and the other party is a customer or supplier of the employer.

before shifting work to the other plant. Thus, the employer must apparently consult with the union before shifting work.

Finally, although unions have faced hard times legally and economically in recent years, society still benefits from well-paid workers. After all, they are consumers and taxpayers. Who buys the products that businesses make? Who pays the taxes that support public schools and other public services? Working men and women—not robots. Labor must be competitively employed to maximize social welfare. Nonetheless, as U.S. business becomes increasingly internationalized, labor must recognize that pay levels are being set on a worldwide basis. Wage demands that are out of step with the world labor market run the risk of driving employers to lower-cost domestic or foreign markets.

## NATIONAL LABOR RELATIONS BOARD (NLRB)[2]

*For more information about the National Labor Relations Board, go to* **http://www.nlrb.gov**

The National Labor Relations Board was established by the National Labor Relations Act. The NLRB is a federal administrative agency whose function is to administer rights and duties arising under the NLRA and its subsequent amendments. More specifically, its two main jobs are to prevent unfair labor practices and to settle representation questions.

The NLRB has jurisdiction to the maximum extent allowable under the U.S. Constitution's commerce clause. The NLRB does not initiate its own proceedings; anyone except the NLRB may initiate proceedings pursuant to its powers.

Two types of proceedings can be initiated with the NLRB. One is the **complaint case** (C case), which alleges that an unfair labor practice has been committed. Unfair labor practices (ULPs) can be committed by the company or by the union. The second is the **representation case** (R case) in which a union seeks NLRB recognition as the employees' bargaining representative. Anyone but the NLRB can initiate R proceedings. In the C case, a charge can be filed by anyone except the NLRB. The complaint issues from the NLRB general counsel's employee. No power to review the general counsel's decision not to issue an order is currently available.

### NLRB JURISDICTION

The National Labor Relations Board, not a state or federal court, is the forum for trying unfair labor practices created under the National Labor Relations Act. In other words, when it holds a hearing before an administrative law judge, the NLRB is similar to a court. The NLRB is an administrative agency and thus performs other functions. This new forum was created to escape what many labor leaders perceived to be an employer-biased judiciary. Because the unions were dissatisfied with the businesspersons' forums (courts), they created their own forum—the NLRB—which was generally sympathetic to unions until the 1980s.

The NLRB has exclusive jurisdiction over unfair labor practices in and affecting interstate commerce. However, staff shortages and budgetary constraints have forced the NLRB to limit its jurisdiction over unfair labor practices in interstate commerce to those involving larger businesses.

---

[2] The authors acknowledge reliance on government publications in preparing this segment.

Certain employers are exempt by the NLRA, including federal, state, and municipal governments. Certain employees are also exempt by the NLRA, including supervisors, managers, agricultural workers, independent contractors, domestic workers (such as maids and housekeepers), people who work for parents or spouses, and workers covered by the Railway Labor Act.

The *Holly Farms Corp. v. NLRB* case shows how the U.S. Supreme Court has upheld an NLRB interpretation of the NLRA by covering "chicken catchers" and other workers closely allied to the agriculture industry. Recall that the NLRA specifically exempts farm workers from its protections.

## Holly Farms Corp. v. NLRB
U.S. Supreme Court
517 U.S. 392 (1996)

### Background and Facts

Holly Farms Corporation is a wholly owned subsidiary of Tyson Foods, Inc. Holly Farms is a vertically integrated poultry producer headquartered in Wilkesboro, North Carolina. Holly Farms' activities include hatcheries, a feed mill, an equipment maintenance center, and a processing plant.

"Broiler" chickens are birds destined for human food markets. Holly Farms hatches broiler chicks at its own hatcheries and immediately delivers the chicks to the farms of independent contractors. The contractors then raise the birds into full-grown broiler chickens. Holly Farms pays the contract growers for their services, but retains title to the broilers and supplies the food and medicine necessary to their growth.

When the broilers are seven weeks old, Holly Farms sends its live-haul crews to reclaim the birds and ferry them to the processing plant for slaughter. The live-haul crews—which typically comprise nine chicken catchers, one forklift operator, and one live-haul driver—travel in a flat-bed truck from Holly Farms' processing plant to the farms of the independent growers. At the farms, the chicken catchers enter the coops, manually capture the broilers, and load them onto the bed of the truck, and the live-haul driver returns the truck, with the loaded cases and crew, to Holly Farms' processing plant. There, the birds are slaughtered and prepared for shipment to retail stores.

In 1989, the Chauffeurs, Teamsters and Helpers, Local 391, filed a representation petition with the National Labor Relations Board, seeking an election in a proposed unit that included live-haul employees working out of Holly Farms' Wilkesboro processing plant. Over Holly Farms' objection, the Board approved the bargaining unit, ruling that the live-haul workers were "employees" protected by the NLRA rather than "agricultural laborers" excluded from the Act's coverage. The U.S. Court of Appeals for the Fourth Circuit enforced the Board's order. Other Federal Courts of Appeals have held that live-haul workers employed by vertically integrated poultry producers are engaged in "agriculture." The Supreme Court agreed to hear the case.

### Body of Opinion

The NLRA's protections extend only to workers who qualify as "employee[s]" under . . . the Act. The term "employee," NLRA . . . states, [does] not include any individual employed as an agricultural laborer. No definition of "agricultural laborer" appears in the NLRA. But annually since 1946, Congress has instructed, in riders to Appropriations Acts for the Board: "Agricultural laborer" for NLRA purposes, shall derive its meaning from the definition of "agriculture" supplied by the Fair Labor Standards Act. . . .

This definition includes farming in both a primary sense, which encompasses practices "performed by a farmer or on a farm as an incident to or in conjunction with such farming operations." When a statutory prescription is not free from ambiguity, the Board must choose between conflicting reasonable interpretations. Courts, in turn, must respect the judgment of the agency empowered to apply the law to varying fact patterns.

The Court confronts no contention that the live-haul crews are engaged in primary agriculture. Thus, the sole question the Court addresses and decides is whether the chicken catchers, forklift operators, and truck drivers are engaged in *secondary* agriculture. The live-haul activities are not "performed by a farmer." When an integrated poultry producer contracts with independent growers for the care and feeding of chicks hatched in the producer's hatcheries, the producer's status as a farmer ends with respect to those chicks. The producer does not resume farmer status when its live-haul employees arrive on the independent farms to collect broilers for carriage to slaughter and processing. This conclusion entirely disposes of the contention that the truck drivers are employed in secondary agriculture, for Holly Farms acknowledges that these crew members do not work "on a farm."

The more substantial question is whether the catching and loading of broilers qualifies as work performed "on a farm as an incident to or in conjunction with" the independent growers' farming operations. Holly Farms' position that this work is incident to the raising of poultry is a plausible, but not an inevitable, construction of the Fair Labor Standards Act. Hence, a reviewing court must examine the Board's position only for its reasonableness as an interpretation of the governing language.

The Board concluded that the collection of broilers for slaughter, although performed "on a farm," is not incidental to farming operations. Rather, the Board determined, the live-haul crews' work is tied to Holly Farms' processing operations. This is a reasonable interpretation of the statute. Once the broilers have grown on the farm for seven weeks, the growers' contractual obligation to raise the birds ends, and the work of the live-haul crew begins. The growers do not assist the crews in catching or loading the chickens, and the crews play no role in the growers' performance of their contractual undertakings. Furthermore, the live-haul employees all work out of the Wilkesboro processing plant, begin and end each shift by punching a timeclock at the plant, and are functionally integrated with other processing-plant employees. It was also sensible for the Board to home in on the status of the crews' *employer*.

The Board's decision adheres to longstanding NLRB precedent . . . and is supported by the construction of the Fair Labor Standards Act by the Department of Labor, the agency responsible for administering the FLSA. The Labor Department's regulations accord with the Board's conclusion that the live-haul crews do not engage in secondary farming and further demonstrate that the FLSA's meaning is not so plain [as to "agricultural laborer"] as to bear only one permissible construction. . . .

## Judgment and Result

The Supreme Court upheld the NLRB's interpretation of "employees" in the NLRA to cover live-haul workers as a bargaining unit. Such workers were not exempt as agricultural workers.

## Questions

1. The NLRA exempts from its coverage agricultural workers but does cover employees of employers in interstate commerce. Is it obvious or ambiguous that chicken catchers, forklift operators, and live-haul drivers fall into one category instead of the other type of worker?
2. Who has the primary responsibility for interpreting and administering the NLRA—the courts or the NLRB? Did the Supreme Court here seem to support the NLRB's interpretation of the National Labor Relations Act? Did this decision benefit unions or employers?
3. As an economic matter, will the Court's opinion in Holly Farms likely increase or decrease the cost of chickens for consumers?

*Union ULPs.* The Taft–Hartley amendments to the NLRA in 1947 added the following union ULPs:

1. Restraining or coercing employees in the exercise of their rights to form, join, or assist unions [§ 8(b)(1)]
2. Causing or attempting to cause an employer to discriminate against an employee in violation of § 8(a)(3) or causing or attempting to cause an employer to discriminate against an employee denied union membership for a reason other than nonpayment of union dues or fees [§ 8(b)(2)]
3. Refusing to bargain with an employer [§ 8(b)(3)]
4. Engaging in a secondary strike or picketing activity [§ 8(b)(4)]
5. Requiring as a condition to union membership a discriminatory or excessive fee [§ 8(b)(5)]
6. Causing or attempting to cause an employer to pay anything of value for service not performed (also known as the anti-featherbedding provision) [§ 8(b)(6)]

The 1959 Landrum-Griffin Act added two more union ULPs:

1. Picketing against any employer where an object thereof is forcing an employer to recognize or bargain with an uncertified union [§ 8(b)(7)]
2. Entering an agreement with an employer to engage in a secondary boycott [§ 8(e)]

Generally, state courts handle labor disputes that otherwise would be unfair labor practices but that do not qualify under the NLRB's jurisdictional tests. They do so by applying state common law (to the extent it exists) to resolve the matter. Because the concept of an unfair labor practice as developed under the National Labor Relations Act is unknown in most states, the law that courts hand out in this complex area of union–management relations is unsatisfactory. Also, the state court judges, many of whom hold antiunion biases, administer their own form of justice in labor disputes.

*Steps in ULP Cases.* An unfair labor practice (ULP) case (see Figure 17.1) begins when someone contacts the National Labor Relations Board and makes a charge against an employer or a union or both. A six-month statute of limitations exists on unfair labor practice charges, which means that filing of the complaint and service on the defendant must occur within six months after the alleged unfair labor practice has occurred. The NLRB gives priority to certain cases, including the secondary boycott, **hot cargo contract**,[3] organizational and recognition picketing, and discrimination against individual employees.

ULP charges filed by an individual can be disposed of short of issuance of a complaint by (1) **adjustment**, which is settlement informally or formally, (2) **dismissal**, which may be appealed to the NLRB general counsel, whose decision is final, or (3) **withdrawal** of the complaint.

If one of the aforementioned events does not occur, a complaint will issue from the NLRB. In certain rare instances the NLRB may get a temporary injunction or restraining order in a U.S. district court against an unfair labor practice. If the NLRB has reason to believe the charge is true, a mandatory injunction may issue. After the party accused of committing an unfair labor practice

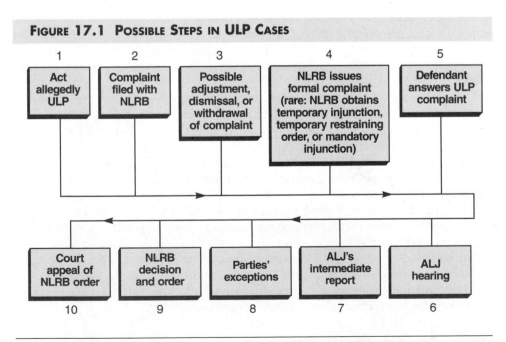

**FIGURE 17.1 POSSIBLE STEPS IN ULP CASES**

---

[3] Hot cargo contracts are made when a neutral employer (someone not involved in the labor dispute) agrees with the union to exert pressure on the employer with which the union has the dispute to help the union. Hot cargo refers to goods made or handled by an employer with whom the union has a dispute.

answers the complaint, the administrative law judge (ALJ) holds a hearing at which the charging party, as well as the respondent (defendant) and the general counsel of the NLRB, may participate. The judge at these hearings is the ALJ. Presentation of argument is similar to that followed in federal trial courts.

The ALJ makes an intermediate report with recommendations to which the parties may file exception. If none is filed, the NLRB adopts the intermediate report as its decision. If exceptions are filed, the NLRB considers the written records, usually without oral argument.

The level of proof by which one must establish one's case before the NLRB or one of the ALJs is the same as in most civil cases—preponderance of the evidence. If the NLRB determines that an unfair labor practice has been committed, it makes fact findings and issues a cease-and-desist or affirmative action order.

NLRB orders are reviewable by any one of three federal courts of appeals—the one where the firm does business, the District of Columbia court of appeals, or the court of appeals where the ULP occurred. If the NLRB's order is not enforced by the court of appeals, the NLRB may still issue a similar order and resist the court of appeals decision until the U.S. Supreme Court speaks or until enough courts of appeals prove antagonistic to the NLRB order.

## UNION–EMPLOYER CONFLICTS AND COMMON GROUNDS

*The home page for the International Brotherhood of Electrical Workers can be found at **http://www.IBEW.org/***

Chapter 1 discussed the legal ethic of power. Nowhere is the power ethic more apparent than in labor law. Employees unite to make one contract (collective bargaining agreement) with their employer to cover all of them. Previously, each made a separate contract with the employer but had no bargaining power as individuals. If one worker quit in disgust over low wages or poor working conditions, the employer was not affected. Thus, workers combined to get the strength of numbers. Few employers can afford to lose their entire workforce at once, which is possible if a union strikes.

The basic conflict between workers and their employer is that the employer wants the most work done under the cheapest working conditions at the lowest possible pay. Workers want the highest possible wages, the best working conditions, and the shortest hours.

The employer's job is to keep the cost of labor as low as possible because the employer has competitors (possibly both domestic *and* foreign) who are also fighting to keep their costs low. All of this cost control benefits consumers, who can buy products at the lowest possible price and in the quantities they want. (Compare this system with planned economics, where prices do not reflect market reality and shortages are common.)

Workers and employers do, however, share a common goal—preservation of the company, which represents jobs, incomes, and dividends. To the extent that workers and the employer consume the company product or service, they also share a desire to produce quality goods or services.

## UNION ORGANIZATIONAL EFFORTS

Consider the following example. Jack Driver, a former professional golfer who won the Masters and U.S. Open golf tournaments, made $3 million while on the pro golf tour. When Jack realized his playing days were numbered, he bought a Cincinnati, Ohio, company that manufactured golf clubs. The company had five clerical employees (two accountants and three secretaries), two full-time sales representatives, one club designer, and twenty-five production and maintenance employees.

Jack had ideas about how golf clubs should be designed. He thought there should be one style of club for pros and another for average players. Jack then built clubs incorporating these ideas. The sales of Jack's company tripled the year after the new clubs came on the market. Company profits tripled. Jack doubled his and the designer's salaries. He gave the sales reps $50,000 bonuses, and the clerical, production, and maintenance employees got merit increases of 20 percent that year. At a Christmas party at his house, Jack gave each employee a set of golf clubs and a Christmas card with a $100 bill, while everyone watched videotapes of Jack's U.S. Open victory.

Jack subsequently expanded his plant and doubled the number of production employees. He hired an MBA from State University to handle personnel problems, which had formerly been taken care of by Jack. The next year, Jack had too many employees to entertain at his house. Instead of a party, he put an extra $25 in everyone's Christmas cards. Some employees grumbled about the company's getting too big.

One day several of Jack Driver's employees discussed forming a union. Jack regarded this as ingratitude and became angry. He learned who the pro-union employees were and fired them for their beliefs. This action is an employer ULP [specifically, a Section 8(a)(1) violation]. The fired employees are entitled to reinstatement with back pay and seniority rights.

If Jack were to decide to preempt the union issue by setting up a union financed by the company, he would commit an employer ULP [specifically, a Section 8(a)(2) violation]. Employers may not give financial or other support to labor unions. **Checkoff** of union dues by an employer is an exception. An employer may petition the NLRB for a representation election if at least one union claims to represent its employees.

*Three Ways to Unionize.* Jack's employees can unionize in at least three ways:

1. By voting in a union at a representation election
2. By signing authorization cards
3. By the NLRB's ordering the employer to bargain with a union

The usual way to unionize is by voting at a representation election (R election) run by the NLRB. The employees vote by secret ballot. A majority vote is needed for union certification. What prompts the NLRB to hold an R election for a particular employer's workers is a request, or petition, from the employees, an outside union who wants to represent such employees, or the employer. Employers cannot make a request for an R election unless at least one outside union has sought to represent the employees.

Employees or outside unions may not request an election without a **showing of employee interest** in a union in which at least 30 percent of the employees support a vote. Usually the employees' showing of interest comes by their signing authorization cards saying they want an R election or that they want a particular union as their collective bargaining representative. Employers often complain that unions tell employees that the authorization cards merely request an election, when actually the cards authorize a particular union to represent the workers. Workers, employers claim, do not read what they sign. Workers may by authorization card designate a union as collective bargaining agent subject to an NLRB check for accuracy and authenticity.

When the NLRB receives an R petition accompanied by the required showing of employee interest, its regional director decides whether it has jurisdiction over the employer. Recall from the discussion earlier that the NLRB might or might not  refuse to take jurisdiction over many smaller businesses or certain other employers.

If the regional NLRB director concludes that it has jurisdiction over a particular employer, an attempt is made to hold a consent representation election. Sometimes employers claim, for example, union misrepresentation in obtaining employee authorization cards. If this claim is raised, the NLRB regional director will order a hearing on these objections. At the end of the hearing, the regional director will either order or not order a representation election.

One of the areas where the National Labor Relations Board has considerable discretion lies in deciding what is the appropriate bargaining unit for a particular employer. For example, a Kmart superstore might have several departments, and employees in some departments might desire one union's representation for the entire store while employees in another department—such as the meat cutters— might want a separate union because they are more skilled and could command higher wages. Is the bargaining unit the entire Kmart store or the meat department? The *Kmart Corp. v. NLRB* case tells us that the NLRB decides what the appropriate bargaining unit is.

## Kmart Corp. v. NLRB
U.S. Court of Appeals (7th Cir.)
174 F.3d 834 (1999)

### Background and Facts

Kmart owns and operates Super Kmart Centers throughout the United States. Much larger than a traditional Kmart store, Super Kmart Centers are vast, one-stop shopping centers open 24 hours per day, seven days per week. Each Super Kmart Center is organized into four divisions: (1) customer service, which includes cashiers, cash and general offices, and invoicing; (2) hardlines, which include items such as electrical appliances, toys, camera equipment, garden equipment, and sporting and automobile equipment; (3) softlines, which include items such as clothing, accessories, and jewelry; and (4) food, which includes items such as grocery, dairy, meat, produce, bakery, deli, health and beauty, as well as pet products and a food court. The food sections comprise approximately one-third of the total selling space in the store.

Kmart owns and operates two such stores in Bradley and Broadview, Illinois. Both of these stores include food divisions that consist of meat, deli, produce, and bakery departments. The Bradley meat department unit consists of some twenty-three people, including six meat cutters and a total of thirteen meat wrappers and perishable

service associates (PSAs), while the meat department at the Broadview store employs fourteen individuals, including four meat cutters and a total of eight meat wrappers and PSAs. The meat departments in both stores handle three varieties of meat products, including prepackaged products requiring no processing whatsoever, boxed fresh meat, and ground beef.

Meat cutters' responsibilities include preparing premixed ground beef for sale by running it through a patty machine that forms the beef into patties as well as preparing boxed meat by partitioning large pieces of meat enclosed in shipping boxes, known as *primals*, into either subprimal cuts, steaks, or roasts through repetitive slicing and trimming tasks. According to the record, the meat cutters use specialized meat-cutting skills.

The employees classified as meat cutters receive wages of approximately $17.50 per hour, more than three times as high as other employees in the Bradley and Broadview stores.

Meat wrappers operate wrapping machines and package and price the meat after it has been cut by the meat cutters. The meat wrappers earn wages slightly higher than the $5.50 per hour starting wages paid to meat department PSAs. The PSAs are responsible for continually stocking fresh and frozen meat counters, staffing gourmet and seafood counters, and preparing products such as meatloaf and shish kabobs, and their wages are equal to that of other employees in the store.

On October 10, 1996, Local 546 of the United Food and Commercial Workers Union (Local 546) filed a petition with the NLRB's regional office, seeking certification as the exclusive bargaining representative of the meat department's employees at the Broadview store, while on December 16, 1996, Local 1540 of the United Food and Commercial Workers Union (Local 1540) filed a petition with the NLRB's regional office seeking certification as the exclusive bargaining representative of all of the meat department employees at the Bradley store. The regional director for the two geographic regions ruled that the employee units petitioned for were appropriate. The director ruled specifically that those employees assigned to the two respective meat departments shared a "community of interests" separate from other employees at the two super Kmart Centers. Furthermore, the director found that the meat department employees utilized special skills, had separate daily supervision, and worked in physically separate areas. The director ordered that the representation elections be conducted among and limited to the meat department employees for both stores to determine whether they wished to be represented by the locals.

Following successful votes for unionization in the respective meat departments, the NLRB certified Local 1540 as representative of the meat department of the Bradley store and Local 546 as representative of the meat department employees at the Broadview store. After Kmart refused to recognize Local 1540 and Local 546 as representatives in the respective stores, each filed charges with the NLRB alleging that the refusals constituted unfair labor practices. The general counsel of the NLRB issued an unfair labor practice complaint against Kmart Later the NLRB issued decisions granting the unions' motions for summary judgment finding unfair labor practices by Kmart by refusing to bargain with the respective locals. Kmart appealed to the U.S. Court of Appeals.

## Body of Opinion

**Circuit Judge Coffey.** On appeal, we consider whether the NLRB reasonably determined that units consisting of meat department employees in two Kmart stores constituted appropriate bargaining units and therefore properly found that Kmart violated the National Labor Relations Act by refusing to bargain with the duly certified collective bargaining representative of the employees.

In reviewing the matter under consideration, we will sustain the Board's factual findings if the record as a whole provides substantial evidence to support them, even if we might justifiably have reached a different conclusion as a matter of first impression. . . .

This court recognizes that "the selection of an appropriate bargaining unit lies largely within the discretion of the Board, whose decision, 'if not final, is rarely to be disturbed. . . .'" . . . Accordingly, this court recognizes that the Board's unit determinations should not be reversed unless they are arbitrary or unreasonable. . . . To disqualify

a unit, the employer must establish "not that another unit is more appropriate, but that the unit selected is utterly inappropriate.". . . Furthermore, the court may not substitute its judgment for a rationally supported position adopted by the NLRB . . . and underlying factual findings must be upheld if they are supported by substantial evidence. . . .

. . . We defer "to reasonable NLRB conclusions in analyzing its application of the law to particular facts, in recognition of the Board's special function of applying the general provisions of the act to the complexities of industrial life.". . . Therefore we are of the opinion that the NLRB, in applying the traditional community of interest factors, including skills, experience, integration, supervisory structure, employee interchange, and wage rates, reasonably determined that a separate meat department bargaining unit was appropriate. . . .

Kmart contends that the Board's decision in this case amounts to improper "gerrymandering" of collective bargaining units because the Board should have accorded greater weight to evidence that store-wide, or "wall-to-wall" units are appropriate. The Board properly rejected this evidence because it was simply not relevant to the issue of whether the meat department units in the instant case are appropriate. The Board is not charged with determining the most appropriate unit, or required to engage in comparative analysis of the relative appropriateness of various potentially bargaining units. On the contrary, the employer must establish "not that the other unit is more appropriate, but that the unit selected is utterly inappropriate,". . . and Kmart has failed to do this in this case. . . .

## Judgment and Result

The U.S. Court of Appeals upheld the NLRB's decision to recognize the meat department as a bargaining unit separate from the rest of the Kmart Superstore.

## Questions

1. What legal body makes the initial decision as to what is an appropriate bargaining unit? If evidence supports another decision as to the appropriate bargaining unit, will the court of appeals reverse the decision of the NLRB? In effect, does this tendency make the NLRB the determiner of what an appropriate bargaining unit is?

2. What factors did the NLRB examine to determine whether the meat department was an appropriate bargaining unit?

3. The *gerrymandering* referred to in the opinion is a practice of arbitrarily drawing lines for congressional and other electoral offices in public elections to achieve political advantage for the one drawing the lines. By analogy, if the NLRB decides that a superstore can be divided into many different bargaining units, some wanting unions and others not, when, arguably, the majority of all workers storewide do not want a union, is not Kmart correct that this division is gerrymandering? After all, if you were a Kmart store manager, would you rather deal with the unionization issue on a storewide basis or a department-by-department basis?

## Preelection Campaign Statements

For more information about the United Auto Workers, go to http://www.uaw.org

Assuming the NLRB orders a representation election (R election), what may an employer say to its employees to influence the election? The NLRA recognizes that the employer has a free speech right created by the First Amendment of the U.S. Constitution and implemented by Section 8(c) of the NLRA. This right allows the employer to state its legal position and its views, arguments, or opinions on what unionization will mean, provided that no threats of reprisal or force or promises of benefits are made violating the NLRA's Section 8(a)(1) discussed previously. The idea is that R elections should be conducted in **laboratory conditions**—that is, they should take place in a clinical, dispassionate atmosphere for employees to judge whether to unionize.

The following *NLRB v. Vemco, Inc.* case illustrates employer remarks to employees prior to a representation election. It shows that the employer may legally predict that it might have to cut workers or suffer a layoff.

## NLRB v. Vemco, Inc.
U.S. Court of Appeals, Sixth Cir.
989 F.2d 1468 (1993)

### Background and Facts

In 1989 the United Auto Workers (UAW) filed charges with the NLRB alleging that Vemco, Inc., was engaging in certain unfair labor practices in violation of the NLRA during the course of the UAW's campaign to organize Vemco's employees. After hearings, an administrative law judge (ALJ) found that Vemco had engaged in numerous unfair labor practices related to the UAW's organizing efforts. He therefore ordered Vemco . . . to reinstate with back pay employees laid off allegedly because of union activity and to bargain on request with the UAW. On review, the NLRB affirmed the ALJ's decision with only slight modification.

Vemco, Inc., located in Grand Blanc, Michigan, supplies the automotive industry with large plastic exterior car parts requiring injection molding and sophisticated paint application. Vemco's executive management consists of Larry Winget, principal owner and president, Michael Torakis, vice president of finance and administration and secretary/treasurer, and James Schutz, vice president of manufacturing. . . .

Vemco's three operations are molding, paint, and assembly. The paint plant is considered state of the art. For the 1989 model year, the paint plant itself was subdivided into cladding and fascia lines, with the fascia line further split into a masking area and a paint area.

At the time it opened its doors and throughout the 1989 automotive year, Vemco had only one customer, Buick-Oldsmobile-Cadillac Division of General Motors (BOC). BOC contracted with Vemco for fascias and claddings for several of its car models. The contract called for delivery to commence in August 1988, with projected quantity requirements to increase weekly over the fall of the year as BOC increased its own manufacturing. The contractual penalty for a failure to deliver according to the industry practice of just-in-time (JIT) shipping causing downtime on a BOC assembly line ran as high as $25,000 per minute of downtime.

Vemco's high-tech paint system did not function as planned when Vemco began operations because of major technical problems in many of the components of the system. The company that designed and built the paint system eventually walked off the project, leaving Vemco to identify and correct these problems with its own personnel and other outside contractors. Ultimately, the system had to be redesigned and rebuilt at the same time BOC's increasing delivery requirements had to be met.

As a result of its technical problems, Vemco was unable to produce a product that consistently met quality standards the first time through and had to rework enormous numbers of unacceptable parts. Because of the severe economic consequences of a failure to timely deliver to BOC, Vemco ended up with many more employees working longer hours than originally forecast. By mid-December, Vemco was running a second shift on both the fascia and cladding lines, partially to relieve the sixty- to eighty-four-hour weeks its employees had been working and partially in anticipation of orders from Ford Motor Company, which, if obtained, would have required a fully trained second shift to produce.

By early 1989, Vemco succeeded in "debugging" in part its paint operation. As a result, work hours decreased and productivity increased. These productivity gains resulted in a shortage of workhours for Vemco's employees. By mid-January, both shifts on the fascia lines were reduced to a four-day workweek, and Vemco considered going to a three-day workweek. At this point, employees expressed unhappiness with the sharp decline in hours and apprehension over further hourly reductions and possible layoffs.

Vemco has a non-union philosophy that is clearly expressed in its Personnel Policies Handbook that all employees receive and sign for at the time of their orientation. Some Vemco employees, however, became interested in unionizing soon after the company opened and by late September employees made telephone inquiries of the UAW. An initial union meeting was held in early October 1988, attracting 50 employees. Periodic meetings were held thereafter, including more or less weekly gatherings between January and March of 1989. Both Schultz and Torakis were aware of general union activity by October 1988. Line supervisors, who were also aware of this general union activity, committed unfair labor practices during the period between Vemco's start-up and the March 1989 mass layoff.

## Body of Opinion

**Senior Circuit Judge Rosen.** . . . We examine the violations that may rely on protected speech before reviewing the evidence as a whole to determine whether a bargaining order is appropriate.

The violations that Vemco claims rely on protected speech related to predictions made to employees and the media, both verbal and written, that if the company were required to reinstate employees laid off on March 17, it might have to cut work hours or suffer another layoff because of lack of work. In discussing protected speech, the Supreme Court set forth its views on employer conduct in the course of an organizing campaign:

> An employer is free to communicate to his employees any of his general views about unionism or any of his specific views about a particular union, so long as the communications do not contain a "threat of reprisal or force or promise of benefit." He may even make a prediction as to the precise effects he believes unionization will have on his company. In such a case, however, the prediction must be carefully phrased on the basis of objective fact to convey an employer's belief as to demonstrably probable consequences beyond his control. . . .
> If there is any implication that an employer may or may not take action solely on his own initiative for reasons unrelated to economic necessities and known only to him, the statement is no longer a reasonable prediction based on available facts but a threat of retaliation based on misrepresentation and coercion, and as such is without the protection of the First Amendment [as implemented by Section 8 (c) of the NLRA]. *Gissel*, 395 U.S. at 617-19.

First, we note that it is not at all clear whether the Vemco prediction at issue is a prediction of the consequences of company unionization or, instead, a prediction of the consequences of an impending NLRB decision that might mandate reinstatement of the laid-off employees, regardless of the outcome of the organizing campaign. If the latter, it is not a violation of the Act; if the former, we believe it satisfies the *Gissel* prediction standard for the reasons discussed below. Thus, it is protected speech which must be excluded in a review of the record to determine the propriety of a rerun election. . . .

There was nothing to suggest that the predicted shortage of work was within Vemco's control and there was no implication that Vemco would implement a cutback in hours or a layoff solely on its own initiative for reasons unrelated to the economic necessity of adjusting to a shortage of work. Given the severe consequences of a failure to deliver according to JIT, it hardly seems likely Vemco would cut back if it had the work. Vemco therefore made a reasonable prediction based on available facts, and not a threat of retaliation based on misrepresentation and coercion. This prediction is protected employer speech under Section 8(c) and will not be used to determine whether a rerun election should be ordered.

The remaining violations are summed up as follows:

(1) Threat to close plant for noneconomic reasons in the face of an organizing campaign and to later reopening with new employees;

(2) Threat of harsher personnel decisions;

(3) Promise of benefits relating to the institution of recall rights and advance notice of weekend overtime;

(4) Confiscation of union literature;

(5) Solicitation of grievances; and

(6) Overly broad no-solicitation rule and threats of discriminatory discharge involving employee Hall.

These undisputed violations are sufficient to support the traditional remedy of a rerun election. They do not, however, warrant a bargaining order under either category set forth in *Gissel*.

## Judgment and Result

The court here decided that the employer committed ULPs while the employees were considering whether to unionize, and this justified a rerun representation election. However, the employer's statements that it might have to cut workers if required to reinstate laid-off employees was protected employer speech and not a threat.

## Questions

1. What test did the court follow to distinguish threats from employer's predictions of things to come?

2. What, if any, free speech rights does an employer have in telling its side of the story when confronting employee unionization efforts?

3. If an employer commits unfair labor practices during unionization efforts, what remedies are available?

If an employer commits ULPs in pre-R election campaign statements, several outcomes are possible. If the union wins the election, probably little other than tougher union bargaining on behalf of employees will happen after union certification as the employees' collective bargaining agent. If the union loses the election, the election could be rerun. Thus, an employer who has a good chance of winning an R election should either make no preelection statements to employees or be cautious about what is said. (If the union loses a close election, it will often claim that the employer statements were ULPs destroying the election laboratory conditions.) Another possibility if the employer commits preelection ULPs is that the NLRB will simply order the employer to bargain with the union. In effect, the NLRB administratively declares the union a winner even though it has not won an R election. The reason is that the employer has so tainted the election atmosphere that laboratory conditions are impossible to achieve. This remedy is ordered where a majority of the employees signed cards authorizing the union to be their bargaining agent.

In 1969, the Supreme Court decided the *Gissel* case, which is the leading case on NLRB remedies if employer preelection ULPs taint the R election. In *Gissel*, the U.S. Supreme Court had to decide whether a union could become the employees' NLRB certified representative solely by producing union authorization cards signed by a majority of employees. The Court said it was possible. The Supreme Court also had to decide whether the union could gain certification as the collective bargaining representative solely by NLRB certification where employer preelection ULPs made holding an R election in laboratory conditions impossible. The Supreme Court also said that this remedy was an NLRB option.

## Court Review of NLRB Union Certification

Suppose a representation election is held and the NLRB certifies a union as the employee bargaining representative. The employer may not go directly to court for a review of the certification. The employer may, however, refuse to bargain with the union. This refusal would probably be challenged as a ULP, would first go to the NLRB, and could later be appealed. At the court of appeals, the employer could raise the union certification issue as a defense to its refusal to bargain. As a result, the employer can indirectly get court review of NLRB certification of unions. Unions, by contrast, may not get court review of the NLRB refusal to certify the union as the employees' collective bargaining agent.

### Frequency of Representation Election

*Election Bar Rule.* Suppose an NLRB-run representation election is held and the union loses. What, if anything, stops the union from getting the required 30 percent showing of interest (by having employees sign authorization cards) the next week and petitioning the NLRB to hold another representation election? The answer is the **election bar rule**. The NLRA prevents an R election if one was held within the previous twelve months and the union was defeated. The NLRB has held that the twelve-month bar also applies if the union wins.

Several reasons support the election bar rule. First, it forces the employees to reflect soberly before initially voting for a union. Second, it reduces the disruption of the employer's business that R elections cause. Third, it reduces the drain on NLRB administrative resources that occurs whenever R elections are held.

*Contract Bar Rule.* Once a certified union and employer agree on a collective bargaining agreement, the NLRB will dismiss any attempt (such as another union's) to have a representation election while the contract is in effect. It is the **contract bar rule**. The reason for the rule is to preserve stable relations between labor and management. In effect, the contract bar rule stops workers from getting rid of or changing unions while a contract exists between an employer and the union certified by the NLRB as the employees' collective bargaining agent.

The contract bar rule has three exceptions.

1.  The collective bargaining contract is longer than three years.
2.  A union schism exists, or the union is defunct.
3.  The employer has greatly expanded its operations.

The three-year exception is easily understood. A union in a shaky position as the employees' bargaining representative might try for long-term employer–union contracts to protect its position as bargaining agent. The NLRB thus limits the contract bar period to three years.

**Schism**—the second exception to the contract bar rule—means that top union officials have a conflict or a split over fundamental union policy. A schism could occur if union leaders allegedly embezzle union assets. Related to schism is union **defunctness**, which refers to situations in which the union no longer operates. For instance, a union's not holding meetings or presenting employee grievances to management is evidence of defunctness. If a schism or defunctness occurs during the life of a collective bargaining agreement, a representation election can be held.

A great expansion or change in an employer's operations is a third exception to the contract bar rule and includes several things. First, if fewer than 30 percent of the current employees were at work when the present contract was entered, the contract bar rule does not apply. Second, the contract bar does not apply if either a merger of two or more operations creates an entirely new operation with major personnel changes *or* operations are resumed with new employees after the firm has been closed down for an indefinite period.

## RUNAWAY SHOP

Shortly after the union wins an R election, Jack decides to shut down his Cincinnati, Ohio, plant and open a newer factory in Sarasota, Florida. This action might or might not be legal under the NLRA. If Jack moves his plant solely to get economic advantages of lower taxes and a lower area wage scale in Sarasota, Florida, he does not commit a ULP. However, if he moves his plant to escape or discourage unions, he does commit a ULP [specifically, a Section 8(a)(3) violation]. These distinctions create the problem (or opportunity, depending on one's viewpoint) to avoid illegality by simply stating reasons for plant relocation solely on economic grounds.

What sanction is applied if Jack relocates solely to escape a union? The NLRB will not order Jack to move his plant back to Cincinnati (his original location from which he fled). However, Cincinnati unionized employees will be offered first opportunity on jobs at the new location in Sarasota and will be awarded relocation expenses if they take the new jobs.

Employers often have several plants—some union, some nonunion. Shifting work from high-cost unionized plants to lower-cost nonunion plants is tempting.

Unions argue that such shifts made while a collective bargaining agreement is in effect amounts to the employer's breaking the agreement. The *Milwaukee Spring II* case gives the NLRB's present view on such moves.

## BANKRUPTCY TO ESCAPE COLLECTIVE BARGAINING AGREEMENTS

Bankruptcy is sometimes available to escape union contracts. See the section, "Development of Labor Law," earlier in the chapter for discussion of this topic.

## GOING OUT OF BUSINESS

The U.S. Supreme Court has held that employers may shut down a plant completely (forever) without committing a ULP, provided the employer does not have the intent to discourage unionization elsewhere (at plants in other locations, for instance). Thus, if Jack Driver's Cincinnati, Ohio, plant unionizes, Jack may legally close the plant permanently if he does not want to deal with the union.

## DUTY TO BARGAIN

U union is NLRB certified as the collective bargaining representative of Jack Driver's production employees. The U representative approaches Jack to talk about entering a collective bargaining agreement. Jack says, "I don't believe in unions. I refuse to talk with you. My employees each have individual employment contracts. This suits me just fine. Get out." Jack has committed a ULP because employers have a duty to bargain, as do unions.

What does *duty to bargain* mean? May Jack meet once with the union representative, listen to the representative, and leave without saying anything? He may not. The NLRB and courts have added *good faith* to the duty to bargain, meaning that Jack must meet and discuss wages, hours, and working conditions with an open mind. The parties do not have to agree on anything, however.

In *NLRB v. American National Insurance* (1952), the U.S. Supreme Court said that an employer's presenting a comprehensive "management functions" clause to a union did *not* amount to a refusal to bargain in good faith. The clause in question kept standards for work schedules flexible at management's option. Nor was management's refusal to budge from its position a refusal to bargain in good faith. However, the employer did bargain over some terms in the union proposals in *American National*. If the employer had come to the bargaining table and claimed the right to control every aspect of the employees' jobs and adamantly refused to bargain or yield, this action would be a ULP [Section 8(a)(5) violation].

The Supreme Court has also held that employers and unions can bring economic pressures (e.g., strikes and lockouts) against each other before, during, and after meeting to bargain and still be bargaining in good faith, and hence not committing ULPs.

Often during bargaining, an employer will claim that it cannot afford a union demand. If the union asks the employer to prove this claim, the employer must document the claim or it violates the duty to bargain in good faith. However, the union demand for proof of employer inability to pay must be narrow and must not impose unreasonable demands on the employer.

An employer may not increase employee wages or employment terms without first bargaining with the union. To do so violates the duty to bargain in good faith, because it undercuts the negotiating process. However, employers may change wages or benefits after bargaining with the union over them, even if no agreement is reached.

**Boulwareism** is a violation of the duty to bargain in good faith. Boulwareism is an employer's careful study of all bargaining issues before meeting the union, and presenting its best offer to the union immediately on a take-it-or-leave-it basis. This process was developed by a General Electric Company executive. Although it eliminates the low-offer posturing that characterizes negotiations, it suggests a closed mind at the start of negotiations, which is apparently a fatal flaw.

## BARGAINING TOPICS

The NLRA requires that an employer bargain about wages, hours, and working conditions. If an employer refuses, it commits a ULP, but some items are not mandatory subjects of bargaining. In *NLRB v. Borg-Warner* (1958), the employer's insistence on a clause excluding the international union as a party was held not to be a mandatory subject of bargaining. Therefore, the employer's continued insistence about this point was a refusal to bargain in good faith.

The *Fibreboard v. NLRB* case holds that an employer's decision to end part of its operation and contract it out is a mandatory subject of bargaining. Therefore, employer's contracting out maintenance work (formerly done by unionized company employees) without first discussing it with the union was a ULP—a refusal to bargain about a mandatory subject of bargaining. Justice Stewart pointed out in a concurring opinion in *Fibreboard* that *any* management decision, such as how to market the company's product, could affect the employees' wages, hours, and working conditions. Does this decision mean the union must be consulted about all such managerial decisions? Stewart thought not, but he raised an interesting question about the limits of mandatory subjects of bargaining.

The *Radisson Plaza Minneapolis v. NLRB* case shows an employer's refusal to bargain in good faith.

### Radisson Plaza Minneapolis v. NLRB
U.S. Court of Appeals, Eighth Circuit
987 F.2d 1376 (1993)

#### Background and Facts

This case arose following allegations by unions representing Radisson's employees that the employer had failed to bargain with the union in good faith. The opinion contains specific examples that formed the basis for the charges filed with the NLRB. The NLRB essentially agreed with the union charges. Radisson appealed to the U.S. Court of Appeals.

#### Body of Opinion

Section 8(a)(5) of the Act makes it an unfair labor practice for an employer "to refuse to bargain collectively with the representatives of his employees." . . . Section 8(d) of the Act defines the duty to bargain

collectively as the mutual obligation of the employer and union "to meet at reasonable times and confer in good faith with respect to wages, hours, and other terms and conditions of employment, or the negotiation of an agreement. . . . "

Although the duty of bargaining in good faith does not require that the parties make particular concessions, it envisions "a sincere, serious effort to adjust differences and to reach an acceptable ground". . . Thus, an employer engages in bad faith or surface bargaining by conducting negotiations "as a kind of charade or sham, all the while intending to avoid reaching an agreement.". . .

In determining the existence of bad faith bargaining, we examine "the employer's conduct in the totality of the circumstances in which the bargaining took place.". . . Moreover, we have noted that "the Board not only looks to the employer's behavior at the bargaining table but also to its conduct away from the table that may affect the negotiations."... We have recognized that "the question of good faith bargaining is for the Board's expertise more than ours."... Consequently, we will affirm a finding by the Board of an employer's bad faith bargaining if it is supported by substantial evidence on the record as a whole."...

The Board based its finding that Raddison failed to bargain in good faith upon Radisson's engaging in unfair labor practices "away from the table," and surface bargaining during the sessions. We examine these contentions in turn.

The Board found that Radisson unlawfully refused to bargain with the unions concerning changes in employee working conditions. In September 1988, Radisson changed job assignments and schedules of some unit employees. In March 1989, Radisson unilaterally increased the base wage rate for 65 percent of unit employees. Radisson does not dispute that it rebuffed the unions' request for bargaining after the changes were made. Under the Act, wages, hours, and other terms and conditions of employment are mandatory subjects of bargaining, and any unilateral change in these items by a company, when accompanied by a refusal to deal with the incumbent union, constitutes a violation of the Act....

Radisson responds that it bargained over the changes before it made them. Further, it argues that the wage increase was exempt from the duty to bargain because it was a continuation of an established company practice.

Radisson's first argument is without merit. Radisson cites evidence that the parties had generally discussed company policies on wages and working conditions during the negotiations. Mere evidence of company policies concerning employment conditions, without more, however, is not the equivalent of notice to the union of specific changes or of bargaining to impasse over a specific proposal. Accordingly, Radisson may not claim that it bargained over the changes.

Second, Radisson's argument that the wage increase was exempt from the duty to bargain is misplaced. The Board applies this exemption only in cases where the wage increase is automatic and does not involve the exercise of a company's discretion. ... Here the Board found that Radisson exercised substantial discretion in determining both the timing and amount of the increases. Radisson granted the increases at irregular intervals, and only after a preliminary determination that its budget and competitive requirements would sustain the increase. Consequently, the Board correctly found that the wage and schedule changes were mandatory subjects of bargaining and that Radisson committed an unlawful labor practice by unilaterally altering them without notification to the unions.

Moreover, Radisson does not contest two of the Board's findings: (1) that Radisson violated 8(a)(5) and (1) of the Act by refusing the unions' March 14 request for information for an updated list of the unit employees' names, addresses, wages, and social security numbers and (2) that Radisson and its parent corporation violated Section 8(a)(1) of the Act by maintaining a rule in its employee handbook prohibiting employees from discussing their wages with anyone other than management. Consequently, we accord these findings summary enforcement.... Moreover, these findings remain relevant in determining whether Radisson bargained in bad faith. ...

Thus, the Board properly found that Radisson's conduct away from the bargaining table supported an inference that Radisson failed to bargain in good faith. Radisson treated the unions as irrelevant with respect to issues of vital significance, including wage and schedule changes, and then refused to provide the unions with basic information concerning unit employees.

Likewise, Radisson's conduct during the bargaining sessions supported the Board's finding that Radisson engaged in surface bargaining. First, the Board found that Radisson's chief negotiator, attorney Stokes, engaged in a pattern of dilatory conduct. Stokes cancelled three bargaining sessions, terminated five of eleven meetings significantly earlier than planned, and refused the unions' requests for more frequent sessions without explaining why he was unavailable. ... As a result, the parties had only seven meetings over eight months.

Additionally, the Board found that Stokes had engaged in obstreperous conduct during the meetings calculated to deter consensus. First, Stokes engaged in frequent filibusters in collateral matters, such as Secretary Califano's book on health care, the nature of unions in Sweden, and the character of a hotel in Williamsburg, Virginia. Second, Stokes continually reminded unions of their slim margin of victory, questioned whether they enjoyed majority support, and cited allegations of the unions' international affiliate's linkage to organized crime without any reference to how this purported affiliation was related to the negotiations.

Last, Stokes insisted on extreme gambits during bargaining sessions that the Board found supported the charges of surface bargaining. During the March 27 meeting, Stokes requested that the contract contain a clause relieving Radisson of its obligation to bargain should either of the unions be found to be "dominated by organized crime." Second, Stokes insisted at more than one meeting that the handbook form the basis of the agreement. The handbook contains a clause, however, permitting Radisson "to amend, modify, or discontinue any of the information or benefits contained herein." In the light of this provision, the unions' acceptance of Stokes's proposal would have permitted Radisson to unilaterally change working conditions whenever it pleased or to require the union to renegotiate working conditions at its whim.

The use of such tactics by Radisson provide substantial evidence to support the Board's finding that Radisson engaged in surface bargaining during the negotiation sessions. Thus the Board reasonably found that the totality of Radisson's conduct, both at and away from the bargaining table violated Sections 8(a)(1) and (5) of the Act.

## Judgment and Result

The court found that Radisson failed to bargain in good faith.

## Questions

1. What specific single act constituted failure of the employer to bargain in good faith? Or was it a series of acts?

2. How can a situation in which an employer unilaterally raises employees' wages without first discussing it with the union be considered a failure to bargain in good faith?

3. If an employer has a duty to bargain in good faith, is a failure to reach an agreement with the union considered a breach of the duty to bargain in good faith?

4. Do unions also have a duty to bargain in good faith?

## COLLECTIVE BARGAINING AGREEMENT

A collective bargaining agreement (CBA) is what a union negotiates with an employer on behalf of the employees. It is a contract that can have any number of terms in it, such as management function clauses, union recognition clauses, arbitration clauses, and no-strike clauses.

The U.S. Supreme Court decided in 1962 the case of *Sinclair Refining v. Atkinson*. This case held that a no-strike clause in a union–employer contract could not be enforced by injunctive relief in a federal district court. The main reason for the *Sinclair* decision was the **Norris–LaGuardia Act**, which prohibits federal courts from issuing injunctions in labor disputes. It was unsuccessfully argued in *Sinclair* that the situation was not a labor dispute about strikes because the union had signed the agreement containing the no-strike clause.

As noted earlier in this chapter, the injunction had been an effective employer weapon against unions before the 1930s. Since passage of the Norris–LaGuardia Act in 1932, the federal courts have been understandably reluctant to issue injunctions against union activity. However, the Norris–LaGuardia Act as amended does not preclude federal courts from issuing injunctions against labor unions in all situations. For example, the Taft–Hartley Act allows a federal district court to issue a back-to-work order for eighty days when a union strike has been called that threatens the national health or safety.

In the *Boys Markets* case (1970), the U.S. Supreme Court again looked at the enforceability of a no-strike clause contained in a union–employer collective bargaining agreement. The agreement there called for *binding arbitration* of the dispute causing the strike. The Supreme Court overruled the *Sinclair* case by saying that the federal district court could issue an injunction to enforce a no-strike clause where the collective bargaining agreement (CBA) had a binding arbitration clause covering the dispute. The idea behind the *Boys Market* decision was to promote arbitration. The importance of the arbitration clause became apparent in 1976 when the Supreme Court was again called upon in the *Buffalo Forge* case to enforce a no-strike clause where the arbitration clause in the CBA did not cover the dispute. The Supreme Court refused to enforce the no-strike clause because arbitration would not be furthered by doing so. Thus, if an employer negotiates a no-strike clause in the CBA, it should also seek an arbitration clause so the no-strike clause can be enforced in federal court.

## EMPLOYER ATTEMPT TO DISAVOW COLLECTIVE BARGAINING AGREEMENTS

One of the main objectives of the National Labor Relations Act is maintaining industrial peace and stability. Collective bargaining agreements support this NLRA objective because they encourage continuity of labor–management relations.

Recently, however, employers have sought to play "hardball" with unions. One technique is by attempting to disavow collective bargaining agreements shortly after they have been entered. Employers use this technique when they sense that union members are unhappy with collective bargaining agreement terms—for example, wage increases might be small, or employers might reduce fringe benefits. In such cases, union members feel their unions are charging them dues for which members are getting nothing. Read the following *Auciello* case to see an instance of employer attempts to disavow a day-old collective bargaining agreement.

For more information and history of the AFL/CIO, go to http://www. aflcio.org/home.htm

## Auciello Iron Works, Inc. v. NLRB
U.S. Supreme Court
517 U.S. 781 (1996)

### Background and Facts

Auciello Iron Works of Hudson, Massachusetts, had twenty-three production and maintenance employees during the period in question. After a union election in 1977, the NLRB certified Shopmen's Local 501, AFL-CIO, as the collective bargaining representative of Auciello's employees. Over the following years, the company and the Union were able to negotiate a series of collective bargaining agreements, one of which expired on September 25, 1988. Negotiations for a new one were unsuccessful throughout September and October 1988, however, and when Auciello and the Union had not made a new contract by October 14, 1988, the employees went on strike. Negotiations continued, nonetheless, and on November 17, 1988, Auciello presented the Union with a complete contract proposal. On November 18, 1988, the picketing stopped, and nine days later, on a Sunday evening, the Union telegraphed its acceptance of the offer. The very next day, however, Auciello told the Union that it doubted that a majority of the bargaining unit's employees supported the Union, and for that reason disavowed the collective bargaining agreement and denied it had any duty to continue negotiating. Auciello traced its doubt to knowledge acquired before the Union accepted the contract offer, including the facts that nine employees had crossed the picket line, that thirteen employees had given it signed forms indicating their resignation from the Union, and that sixteen had expressed dissatisfaction with the Union.

### Judgment and Result

The Supreme Court found for the National Labor Relations Board. Auciello's attempted disavowal of the day-old collective bargaining agreement was an unfair labor practice.

### Questions

1. How does the *Auciello* case holding further the objectives of the National Labor Relations Act?
2. Suppose an employer negotiates a collective bargaining agreement that is generous to its unionized workforce and shortly thereafter realizes its mistake. Does *Auciello* encourage such employers to carefully consider making collective bargaining agreements they will not be able to escape on "good faith belief" that the union suddenly has lost majority status?

## COLLECTIVE BARGAINING AGREEMENTS: ARBITRATION PROVISIONS

Arbitration provisions are put into collective bargaining agreements by employers and unions to settle labor disputes by using a neutral third party (the arbitrator) to resolve differences without going to court. Courts and Congress both favor arbitration of labor disputes (rather than having lawsuits in court) because this method enables private settlement of disputes. Because the arbitrator is selected by the parties and draws his or her authority from the collective bargaining agreement, courts give great weight to what the arbitrator decides. Thus, arbitration awards may be appealed to courts, but courts will not upset them if there is no arbitrator fraud or other misconduct.

The *Misco case* is a U.S. Supreme Court decision upholding an arbitrator's award when an employer challenged it in court.

## United Paperworkers International Union v. Misco, Inc.
U.S. Supreme Court
484 U.S. 29 (1987

## Background and Facts

Misco's (the employer) collective bargaining agreement with United Paperworkers union authorizes the submission to binding arbitration of any grievance that arises from the interpretation or application of the agreement's terms, and reserves to management the right to establish, amend, and enforce rules regulating employee discharge and discipline and setting forth disciplinary procedures. One of respondent's rules listed as causes for discharge the possession or use of controlled substances on company property. Isiah Cooper, an employee covered by the agreement who operated a hazardous machine, was apprehended by police in the back seat of someone else's car in respondent's parking lot with marijuana smoke in the air and a lighted marijuana cigarette in the front-seat ashtray. A police search of Cooper's own car on the lot revealed marijuana gleanings.

Upon learning of the cigarette incident, respondent discharged Cooper for violation of the disciplinary rule. Cooper then filed a grievance which proceeded to arbitration on the stipulated issue whether respondent had just cause for the discharge under the rule and, if not, the appropriate remedy. The arbitrator upheld the grievance and ordered Cooper's reinstatement, finding that the cigarette incident was insufficient proof that Cooper was using or possessed marijuana on company property. Because, at the time of the discharge, respondent was not aware of, and thus did not rely upon, the fact that marijuana had been found in Cooper's own car, the arbitrator refused to accept this fact into evidence. However, the District Court vacated the arbitration award and the Court of Appeals affirmed, ruling that reinstatement would violate the public policy "against the operation of dangerous machinery by persons under the influence of drugs." The court held that the cigarette incident and the finding of marijuana in Cooper's car established a violation of the disciplinary rule that gave respondent just cause for discharge.

## Judgment and Result

1. The Court of Appeals exceeded the limited authority possessed by a court reviewing an arbitrator's award entered pursuant to a collective-bargaining agreement.

(a) Absent fraud by the parties or the arbitrator's dishonesty, reviewing courts in such cases are not authorized to reconsider the merits of the award since this would undermine the federal policy of privately settling labor disputes by arbitration without governmental intervention. The parties having agreed to submit all questions of contract interpretation to the arbitrator, the reviewing court is confined to ascertaining whether the award draws its essence from the contract and does not simply reflect the arbitrator's own notions of industrial justice. As long as the arbitrator is even arguably construing or applying the contract and acting within the scope of his authority, the court cannot overturn his decision simply because it

disagrees with his factual findings, contract interpretations, or choice of remedies.

(b) The Court of Appeals was not free to refuse enforcement of the award simply because it considered the cigarette incident ample proof that the disciplinary rule had been violated, since no dishonesty is alleged here, and since improvident fact finding is hardly a sufficient basis for disregarding what the arbitrator appointed by the parties determined to be the historical facts. Nor is the arbitrator's refusal to consider the evidence of marijuana in Cooper's car a sufficient basis for nonenforcement, since the collective-bargaining agreement largely left evidentiary matters to the arbitrator, whose decision on this point was consistent with the practice followed by other arbitrators of refusing to admit evidence which a discharging party did not rely upon. Assuming that the arbitrator did err on this point, his error was not in bad faith or so gross as to amount to affirmative misconduct. Moreover, his decision not to consider the disputed evidence did not forever foreclose respondent's use of that evidence as a basis for discharge. Even if it were open to the court to find a disciplinary rule violation on the basis of that evidence, the court could not properly set aside the award because in its view discharge was the correct remedy, since arbitrators normally have wide discretion in formulating remedies. Although the agreement here may have limited the arbitrator's remedial discretion by giving respondent the unreviewable right to discharge violators of the disciplinary rule, the proper course would have been to remand to the arbitrator for a definitive construction of the contract in this respect.

2. The Court of Appeals erred in setting aside the arbitral award on public policy grounds. A court's refusal to enforce an arbitrator's *interpretation* of a collective-bargaining agreement is limited to situations where the contract as interpreted would violate "some explicit public policy" that is "well defined and dominant, and is to be ascertained by reference to the laws and legal precedents and not from general considerations of supposed public interests." *W. R. Grace & Co. v. Rubber Workers*, 461 U.S. 757, 766. An alleged public policy must be properly framed under the approach set out in *W. R. Grace*, and the violation of such policy must be clearly shown. Here, the court made no attempt to review existing laws and legal precedents, but simply formulated a policy against the operation of dangerous machinery under the influence of drugs based on "general considerations of supposed public interests." Even if that formulation could be accepted, no violation of the policy was clearly shown, since the assumed connection between the marijuana gleanings in Cooper's car and his actual use of drugs in the workplace is tenuous at best. It was inappropriate for the court itself to draw that inference, since such fact finding is the task of the arbitrator chosen by the parties, not the reviewing court. Furthermore, the award ordered Cooper's reinstatement in his old job or an equivalent one for which he was qualified, and it is not clear that he would pose a threat to the asserted public policy in every such alternative job.

## Questions

1. Whose idea was it to have an arbitrator resolve disputes between the employer and the workers?
2. Was the arbitrator dishonest, or did the arbitrator commit fraud in deciding the case?
3. Does *Misco* support or undercut arbitrators' decisions?
4. Which legal ethics support the *Misco* result?
5. Do any business ethics suggest *Misco* is the correct result?

Employers frequently try to escape collective bargaining agreements. For example, suppose Company X negotiates a collective bargaining agreement generous to the union and extravagant from X's standpoint. X soon realizes that it made a mistake in signing the agreement because its labor costs put it at a competitive disadvantage. Suppose X sells out to Y. Does Y, called a successor employer, have to honor X's CBA? The following case provides some answers.

## Bloedorn v. Francisco Foods, Inc.
U.S. Court of Appeals (7th Cir.)
276 F.3d 270 (2001)

### Background and Facts

Until 1999, the employees of the Piggly Wiggly grocery store in Ripon, Wisconsin were represented by the United Food and Commercial Workers Union, Local No. 73A, AFL-CIO-CLC (the "Union"). When the owner of the store announced his intent to sell the franchise to Francisco Foods, Inc. (FFI), FFI invited store employees to submit applications to work for the new owner. Fewer than half of the employees that joined the FFI workforce had previously worked for the prior owner, however, so that when the store reopened under FFI's ownership, a majority of the store's employees were not Union members, and consequently, FFI was not obliged to recognize and bargain with the Union.

The Regional Director (the "Director") of the National Labor Relations Board (the "NLRB" or the "Board") filed an administrative complaint charging that FFI had deliberately refused to hire a number of people who had worked for the store's previous owner in order to avoid having to bargain with the Union, in violation of Section 8(a)(1) and (3) of the National Labor Relations Act (the "Act"). The Director also asserted that FFI's refusal to recognize and bargain with the Union, and its failure to adopt and enforce the terms of the collective bargaining agreement that the Union had entered into with FFI's predecessor, constituted unfair labor practices that were contrary to Section 8(a)(1) and (5) of the Act. While the complaint was pending before an administrative law judge, the Director filed this action seeking interim injunctive relief pursuant to the Act. Specifically, the Director asked the district court to enter an order requiring FFI to offer employment to the employees of the prior owner that FFI had refused to hire, to recognize and bargain with the Union, and to restore employee working conditions (including wages and hours) to their state prior to FFI's takeover of the store, until such time as the Director's complaint was resolved by the Board. The district court denied the Director's request and the Director appeals to the Court of Appeals.

### Body of Opinion

**Circuit Judge Rovner.** . . . Pam Francisco had worked at the Ripon Piggly Wiggly for twenty-five years and had served as the store manager for the last six and one-half years prior to 1999. When the Bayers decided to sell the store, Francisco and her husband Tom formed FFI for the purpose of buying the store. . . . FFI and RSI (the predecessor owner/employer) entered into a purchase and sale agreement on March 10, 1999. . . . Because the final collective bargaining agreement between RSI and the Union contained no successor clause, FFI would not be required to recognize the Union if a majority of its employees were not already members of the bargaining unit—i.e., if they had not worked for RSI. . . .

In the weeks following the announcement of the forthcoming sale, Francisco had a number of conversations with store personnel regarding her intent vis à vis the Union. According to these individuals, although Francisco allowed for the possibility that the new employees might opt for Union representation, she did not plan to recognize the bargaining unit at the outset of her tenure as store owner.

1. As we noted above, Francisco on March 15 had purportedly told Ritchay—who was offered but did not accept a job with FFI—that "It wouldn't be a union. . ." . . . According to Ritchay, a couple of days later, Francisco qualified that remark by saying that "there wouldn't be a union, but if the employees wanted a union—the new employees wanted a union they could vote on it." . . . Ritchay testified that he subsequently told Francisco "if [fellow RSI employee] Bob Schumacher is going to be out there picketing that I wouldn't be able to cross the line.". . . His conversation with Francisco "kind of went back and forth," Ritchay testified, and then, "I kind of mentioned that you know Bob really wants the Union in here. She says that's not going to happen.". . .

2. According to RSI utility employee Adam Simonis—whom FFI hired—Francisco said to him between one and two weeks after the sale was announced that "she was going to let the employees decide whether or not they wanted" a union rather than recognizing the Union right away." . . .

Although Francisco denied making most of the remarks attributed to her by store employees . . . she concedes that she told staff that she "would not recognize the union automatically and [she] felt that it should be an employee decision."

As April gave way to May, however, a number of positions with FFI remained unfilled, and a number of RSI employees who had applied for jobs with FFI had not yet been told whether or not FFI planned to hire them. On May 11, 1999, just five days before FFI took over the store, the following language began to appear in FFI's hiring advertisements in the local papers:

No Experience Necessary We Will Train You! . . .

Meanwhile, in the weeks immediately preceeding FFI's takeover of the store, Francisco allegedly had a number of additional conversations with RSI employees that again touched upon the prospective status of the Union with FFI. The testimony of these employees suggests that Francisco was making hiring decisions with an eye to avoiding an obligation to recognize the Union. . . .

The Supreme Court has recognized that when "[a] new employer makes a conscious decision to maintain generally the same business and to hire a majority of its employees from [its] predecessor," it must bargain with the union that represented the predecessor's employees. . . . When FFI opened for business, only a minority of its non-supervisory employees (sixteen of thirty-nine) formerly had worked for RSI. Nominally, then, it had no obligation to bargain with the Union. It is the Director's theory, however, that FFI made its hiring decisions in a calculated manner aimed at ensuring that the former employees of RSI did not constitute a majority of the FFI workforce. Of course, FFI bore no obligation to hire any of RSI's employees. . . . Yet FFI was not free to make discriminatory hiring decisions with the purpose of avoiding a duty to bargain with the representative of RSI's workforce. . . .

"Of course, it is an unfair labor practice for an employer to discriminate in hiring or retention of employees on the basis of union membership or activity under § 8(a)(3) of the National Labor Relations Act. . . . Thus a new owner could not refuse to hire the employees of his predecessor solely because they were union members or to avoid having to recognize the union." . . .

This is precisely what the Director believes that FFI did in this case; and in so doing, he asserts FFI violated not only Section 8(a)(3) but also Section 8(a)(5) of the Act. Section 8(a)(3) bars an employer from making discriminatory employment decisions in order "to encourage or discourage membership in any labor organization. . . ." Section 8(a)(5) provides that an employer commits an unfair labor practice when he "refuse[s] to bargain collectively with the representative of the employees. . . ."

FFI contends for a variety of reasons that there is no substantial continuity of enterprise between RSI and FFI. First, FFI's organizational structure differs from RSI's in a number of respects: department heads have been given more supervisory authority, including the right to hire, discipline, and terminate employees. . . . ; positions have been created for a customer service manager, a maintenance manager, and a bookkeeper, none of which existed under RSI's ownership; . . . new job descriptions have been written . . . and employees have been cross-trained so that they can handle a variety of assignments. Second, FFI has stopped using some of RSI's vendors and has begun using others that RSI had not used. . . . Third, and finally, FFI has purchased new equipment (including checkout equipment and thermal printers) and changed its way of doing business to the extent that it no longer maintains handwritten customer accounts. . . . The record also reveals certain other changes: the store's floral department has been eliminated . . . ; its offering of bakery goods has been expanded . . . ; and, in general, Francisco is attempting to update the store. . . .

These changes notwithstanding, we think it likely that the Board will find there to be a substantial continuity between RSI and FFI. The continuity assessment takes into account several factors, including "whether the business of both employers is substantially the same; whether the employees of the new company are doing the same jobs in the same working conditions under the same supervisors; and whether the new entity has the same body of customers." . . . These factors tilt rather strongly in favor of a finding of substantial continuity. FFI operates the same Piggly Wiggly grocery store that RSI did. There was virtually no hiatus between RSI's departure as the owner and FFI's assumption of control. . . . With the exception of the new positions that FFI has created, FFI employees appear to be performing largely the same tasks, under comparable conditions, and under a number of the same supervisors, as RSI employees did; they are simply doing it under new ownership. Obvioiusly the nature of the products that the store sells has not changed—notwithstanding the changes in FFI's vendors—nor has the store's customer base. . . .

## Judgment and Result

The Court of Appeals held that there was ample evidence that FFI's hiring decisions were animated by an intent to avoid a duty to recognize and bargain with the Union. The Court of Appeals granted an interim injunction requiring the employer to offer employment to employees whom it had refused to hire.

## Questions

1. Must a buyer of a unionized business automatically bargain with the prior employer's union?
2. What does *continuity of enterprise* have on the successor employer's duty to bargain with the prior employer's union?
3. What if the successor employer hires one employee less than a majority of its unionized predecessor. Must it bargain with the prior employer's union?

## DEVICES AFFECTING UNION SECURITY

Four devices affecting union security are state right-to-work laws, closed shops, union shops, and agency shops.

*Right-to-Work Laws.* Right-to-work laws are state laws that let individuals working for unionized employers refuse to join the union and also not pay union dues or fees. Unions must represent all employees in the bargaining unit, even non-dues-paying, nonunion employees, called *free riders*. The **state right-to-work laws** are permitted by Section 14(b) of the NLRA. About half of the states have such laws.

State right-to-work laws are not union security devices. Right-to-work laws undercut unions and, depending on one's point of view, can be either condemned or supported. Familiarity with right-to-work laws helps one understand the union security devices of closed shops, union shops, and agency shops.

*Closed Shops.* The closed shop protects unions by requiring that employers hire only union member job applicants. In other words, before an employer can consider hiring a job applicant, the employer must first determine whether that applicant is a union member. If the applicant is not a union member, the person may not be hired.

Closed shops arise from closed-shop clauses put in union-employer collective bargaining agreements. The NLRA [in Sections 8(a)(3) and 8(b)(2)] now makes the closed shop illegal.

*Union Shops.* Union shops require an employee to join a union after a specified time frame (often 30 days) after going to work for a unionized employer. Collective bargaining agreements with union shop clauses create union shops. Union shops are legal under the NLRA.

*Agency Shops.* Agency shops originate from clauses put in union-employer collective bargaining agreements. Agency shops require that a person pay to the union an amount equal to union dues and fees after going to work for a unionized employer. This arrangement is legal. Agency shops do not require that an employee join the union—only that the employee pay to the union the dollar value of union dues and fees. In states with right-to-work laws so providing, employees do not even have to pay the equivalent of dues and fees (they can be free riders), and the union still has a duty to represent them.

If employees pay the equivalent of union dues and fees, why should they not join the union? The answer lies in the enforceability of union rules. If an employee is a union member, the employee must follow union rules. If union members violate these rules, they can be fined. These fines are enforceable in court (civilly, not criminally). However, employees who do not join the union but merely pay the equivalent of dues and fees are not subject to union fines. This fact is not well known, and it can affect union discipline.

## STRIKES AND LOCKOUTS

Strikes and lockouts are devices that unions and employers use to pressure one another to enter collective bargaining agreements with terms favorable to them. **Strikes** are used by unions. In a **lockout**, the employer temporarily refuses to let employees work. Thus, a lockout is an employer device to pressure employees. With some limits, strikes and lockouts are legal under the NLRA.

**Whipsaw strikes** refer to union strikes against one or a few, but not all, employers in a multiemployer bargaining group while union labor continues to work for one or a few employers. The union attempts to pressure the struck employers to agree to bargaining demands by putting them at a competitive disadvantage. Whipsaw strikes are legal. Employers in a multiemployer bargaining group often respond to whipsaw strikes with lockouts. Lockouts neutralize what would otherwise be the competitive disadvantage of whipsaw strikes. Lockouts in response to whipsaw strikes are also legal.

Employers may hire temporary or permanent replacements for employees on **economic strikes**. Economic strikers are entitled to full reinstatement when their permanent replacements leave unless strikers get equivalent work elsewhere. However, if employees strike in response to an employer ULP, the employer may only temporarily replace them. If the ULP strikers unconditionally offer to return to work, the employer must reinstate them fully.

## SECONDARY BOYCOTTS

Secondary boycotts generally refer to requiring or forcing someone to stop handling another's products or doing business with another person. Either unions or employers can commit them. Usually the NLRA makes secondary boycotts unfair labor practices and hence illegal. The NLRA condemns secondary boycotts essentially because it wants to confine labor disputes to the immediate parties (the employer and union directly involved). Thus, the NLRA legalizes direct economic weapons, called **primary activities**, by the union against the employer, such as primary strikes, and by the employer against the union, such as the lockout. However, the NLRA has a general policy forbidding unions or employers from involving third parties in their disputes. Again, the reason is to confine the dispute and minimize economic disruptions accompanying union–employer strife.

A secondary boycott could occur in the following manner. U union has a labor dispute with Jack Driver's golf company. Jack is the primary employer. If U union forces Kmart to stop buying golf clubs from Jack's company, it is engaging in a secondary boycott. Kmart is the secondary employer. U union's conduct violates the NLRA's prohibition on secondary boycotts. Jack, the primary employer, can sue and recover damages from U union. Jack may not get injunctive relief to stop this illegal boycott, although the NLRB could.

Another example of a secondary boycott prohibited by the NLRA Section 8(e) occurs if U union induces Jack to sign a collective bargaining agreement not to deal with any employer with whom U union has a dispute. The two exceptions to such agreements are on-site construction and the garment industry. These exceptions let employers agree with unions not to handle certain products of people with whom the union has a dispute.

In the *Woodwork Manufacturers Association v. NLRB* case, a question at issue was whether the carpenter's union committed a secondary boycott by refusing to handle prefitted doors (those not finished at the job site). The basis for the alleged secondary boycott was a "will not handle" clause in the union–building contractor collective bargaining agreement. [Recall that Section 8(e) of the NLRA makes it illegal for employers and unions to agree to boycott others' products.] The U.S. Supreme Court in the *National Woodwork Manufacturers* case refused to hold that the union's actions were a prohibited secondary boycott, because the clause was designed to preserve carpenters' on-site work, not to expand carpenters' work.

The union's intent in including the "will not handle" clause was not aimed at a secondary party (door manufacturers) but rather was to preserve work with the primary employer (the building contractors).

## VOTING OUT THE UNION: DECERTIFICATION ELECTIONS

Suppose Jack Driver's employees have had a union for three years. After assessing their costs (union dues, having to attend union meetings and pay attention to how the union is run, and lost work time from strikes) and benefits (higher wages and better working conditions), they decide that having a union is not worth the costs. Can they get rid of the union? Yes.

One way employees can eliminate an existing union is through a **decertification election**. One or several employees or another person or union acting for the employees may file a decertification petition with the NLRB. Along with the decertification petition, at least 30 percent of the employees must indication that they want decertification. The NLRB then conducts a decertification election by secret ballot. If a majority of employees vote to decertify the union, it no longer is the collective bargaining agent.

Employers may not file decertification petitions. If Jack Driver learns that some of his employees are unhappy with their union and encourages or helps them to file a decertification petition, he commits a ULP [Section 8(a)(1) violation].

## UNIONS FOR GOVERNMENT EMPLOYEES

The National Labor Relations Act does not cover employees in the public sector (government employees). The sovereignty doctrine, which says that the federal government is the supreme lawgiver (although in a democracy, the people are the ultimate source of lawmaking power), explains why federal workers are treated differently from private-sector employees regarding unions. State and municipal governments (in addition to the national or federal government) also give their workers fewer collective bargaining rights than business workers have.

### LABOR LAWS COVERING FEDERAL EMPLOYEES

When Congress passed the Civil Service Reform Act of 1978, it set up the Federal Labor Relations Authority. This body hears unfair labor practice complaints from federal workers. It also can hear requests that bargaining be allowed for certain issues. The catch is that, unlike employees who work for private businesses, federal workers may not bargain about wages, hours, and fringe benefits. Federal agencies (the employers) may, however, bargain about some aspects of their employees' jobs, such as work equipment, the number and grades of "job slots," and certain work rules. Federal employees (including postal workers) have no right to strike.

### LABOR LAWS COVERING STATE AND MUNICIPAL GOVERNMENT EMPLOYEES

Most states allow public employees to form unions. However, even though these states allow state workers to unionize, they do not let such workers strike, thus weakening state employee unions. A few states allow certain government workers to strike in limited circumstances. However, public workers, such as teachers, do occasionally have illegal strikes. As with businesses whose employees illegally strike, state and municipal governments sue for injunctions to order the employees back to work.

## CHAPTER SUMMARY

Labor unions in the United States were at one time treated as criminal conspiracies designed to restrain trade in the labor market. Over time, courts and the legislatures have recognized labor unions' legal right to exist. In recent years, however, labor union membership in the United States has declined both in absolute numbers and as a percentage of the nonfarm workforce.

The Supreme Court ruled in the *Danbury Hatters* case that labor unions were subject to the Sherman Act.

The Clayton Act in 1914 unsuccessfully tried to exempt labor unions from the federal antitrust laws.

In 1932 the Norris–LaGuardia Act removed federal court jurisdiction to issue injunctions in peaceful labor disputes.

The National Labor Relations Act, passed in 1935, established the National Labor Relations Board (NLRB). It specified unfair labor practices that employers, but not unions, can commit.

Employer unfair labor practices include restraining or coercing employees in their right to form, join, and assist unions; employer dominance of labor organizations; employer discrimination regarding hire or tenure to encourage or discourage union membership; employer discrimination against an employee who has filed charges or testified under the NLRA; employer refusal to bargain with employees; and an employer commission of secondary boycott.

In 1947 Congress enacted the Labor–Management Relations Act, also known as the Taft–Hartley Act. This act outlined for the first time unfair labor practices that labor unions could commit.

Two types of cases can come before the National Labor Relations Board: R (representation) cases and C (complaint) cases.

Three ways an employer's workers can unionize are by (1) voting in the union at a representation election; (2) employees signing cards authorizing that the union represent them; and (3) the NLRB ordering the employer to bargain with the union.

The election bar and contract bar rules limit the frequency of representation elections. Employers may move their operations if their reasons for doing so are solely economic and not motivated by anti-union animus. Employers who do move their plants to encourage or discourage unions commit an unfair labor practice.

Under certain circumstances an employer may enter bankruptcy to escape collective bargaining agreements.

A successor employer has an obligation to bargain in good faith with the union representing employees of the predecessor employer, assuming substantial continuity is demonstrated between the predecessor and successor employers.

Devices affecting union security include right-to-work laws, closed shops, union shops, and agency shops.

Lockouts refer to employer actions to temporarily refuse to let employees work. Strikes occur when workers withhold their services from employers.

■ **Manager's Ethical Dilemma**

Dan Williams owned a company in Wisconsin that made auto seat covers. Dan became alarmed at his labor costs, particularly because his foreign competitors paid their employees only one-third to one-half of what Dan paid its employees. Labor was a sizable component of his costs of production.

One day Dan decided to call the governors of Tennessee, Georgia, Mississippi, and Alabama to see whether they would be interested in having a 300–person factory relocated there.

The response was instantaneous and uniform: Each governor leaped at the opportunity! The different governors put forth packages offering Dan tax incentives (low or forgiven real property taxes, low unemployment taxes, low workers' compensation costs) and free buildings for several years. What ethical considerations (refer to Chapter 1) should Dan consider in deciding whether to remain in Wisconsin or relocate in another state?

## Discussion Questions

1. Why do you think labor union membership has dropped so significantly in the past 20 years? Notice a further trend in the United States: Medical doctors and psychologists, feeling the pinch of government constraints on permissible fee reimbursements, have recently taken steps to unionize. Thus, while the blue-collar workforce is becoming less unionized, the white-collar workforce is in the process of becoming more unionized. What ethics discussed in Chapter 1 might account for this trend?

2. Why do you suppose a separate "court" system has been established for the trial of unfair labor practices? The name of that court system is the National Labor Relations Board with its network of administrative law judges. How does the NLRB law judge (ALJ) hearing differ from the usual trial court? Is a jury ever part of an administrative hearing? Who benefits most in this setting? Who loses?

3. What evidence indicates that federal labor law has not always treated union and employer alike? When did employer unfair labor practices come into being? When were union unfair labor practices created?

4. Currently, intense employer pressure is present to decertify unions as collective bargaining agents. What factors in the business environment could account for their motivation? Are company-sponsored unions legal? What realities have unions run into in their incessant efforts for improved wages, hours, and working conditions?

5. How true do you think the following statement is? "The union movement in the United States prevented the country from becoming communistic."

6. In *Dal-Tex*, which follows, what was so threatening about the employer's remarks? Explain what we mean when we say that the atmosphere surrounding representation elections is supposed to be one of laboratory conditions.

In *Dal-Tex Optical* [132 NLRB 1782 (1962)], the NLRB held that the following employer statements were threats and hence exceeded the free speech right:

Two years ago the I.U.E. Union tried to organize this plant. It went to every length to cause trouble. It misrepresented all of the facts. It conducted a vicious campaign. It did not then, nor does it now, represent any optical laboratory in Texas. Our employees were not fooled and voted against the Union by a large majority. The Union lost the election. This election was conducted by a secret ballot and was a fair election, but the Union could not stand being beaten and attempted to set aside the election. It introduced evidence before the Board, which I considered then, and do now consider, to be false and perjured.

A year and a half after the election, the National Labor Relations Board, based upon such evidence, decided that the election should be set aside and a new one held. After another six months the Board then decided to hold another election next week. The Company does not agree with the Board, and has maintained and is going to maintain that the election held two years ago was a valid election. And the courts are going to have to decide whether this first election was valid. In the meantime, the company is permitting the holding of this new election on company property on September 22nd, because it feels that your rights can be better protected.

If the Union should win this election, which I don't think it can, the courts are still going to have to determine whether the Board was right or wrong. If the Board was wrong, which I firmly believe, the election to be held on September 22nd will not mean a thing if the Union wins it. My guess is that it will be another couple of years before this matter is settled. In the meantime, we will go on just as we are without any union. I am explaining all of this to you so you will understand that wild promises by this Union of what is going to happen here if the union wins don't mean a thing. I believe in law and order. When the courts decide the matter I will abide by the decision of the courts.

[After detailing some of the benefits employees were receiving:]

So, why should you want a union to represent you? Is it because you believe it can get you more than you now have, or have you been told the Union will run this plant? I have made it a practice of giving back in increased wages all efficiency gains during the year. During the year 1959, there were 270 individual raises given. During the year 1960, there were 298 raises given, and during this year already there have been 349 raises given. These are merit raises. These are raises that you get in addition to your profit sharing and pension plans. I not only provide for your old age and your family in case of your death, but as the efficiency improves you get the benefit of it in increased wages. Do you want to gamble all of these things? If I am required by the court to bargain with this union, whenever that may be, I will bargain in good faith, but I will have to bargain on a cold-blooded business basis. You may come out with a lot less than you have now. Why gamble because agitators make wild promises to you? If I am required to bargain and I cannot agree, there is no power on earth that can make me sign a contract with this union, so what will probably happen is the union will call a strike. I will go right along running this business and will replace the strikers. There has been a lot of talk about your being skilled workers. You only do one operation, and in a short period I can train anybody to do any of these operations, as we trained most of you. I am not afraid of a strike. It won't hurt the Company. I will replace the strikers. They will lose all of their benefits. Strikers will draw no wages, no unemployment compensation and be out of a job. The union won't pay you wages. The union has nothing to lose. You do all of the losing. No employee is so important that he or she cannot be replaced. I am not afraid of threats. Before the last election this union tried everything. Before this election is over, you will see how dirty the Union will get. It has no responsibility. It is not reasonable to believe that you would give up your individual rights to outside agitators and not be able to come to me as you have in the past with your problems. I cannot believe you want to change to the cold-blooded bargaining basis that must follow.

[In the September 19 speech he stated, among other things:]

Will the union get you more wages? No, who pays the wages? I do. I built this plant. I invest the capital. I see to it that it runs 52 weeks a year. I see that the orders come in. I have consistently turned back to you in increased wages all efficiency gains made by the Company. I give hundreds of increase[s] in wages that are merited. In 1960 I gave 349 raises. This year I have already given 442 raises. This is the right way to handle wages. The result is that you have the highest wages in the industry. This I can assure you, it is my position now, and it will be my position at all times, that you will get merit raises just as I have been giving them over the years. If you don't merit them, you will not get them. This is nothing new. It is the system I have operated on from the beginning. I do not have to, nor will I change it. If you believe promises the union makes you, you will find out the union doesn't pay wages. I do. The union doesn't give raises. I do. Now, please remember you have to compare your wages with those of other optical laboratories in Dallas, Texas. We are at the top. It does not make any difference what Collins Electric pays or any other industry. It is what is paid in our industry. No union and no company in our industry in Texas can match our wages and benefits.

7. Suppose a union does an ineffective job of representing its members during collective bargaining talks. To what standard does the U.S. Supreme Court hold unions in representing their members? The *Air Line Pilots Association v. O'Neill* case [111 S.Ct. 1127 (1991)] provides an answer.

**INFOTRAC KEYWORDS**

**Use your InfoTrac password to look up articles on http://www.infotrac-college.com**

Keywords: *Boycotts, unionization, ULP, collective bargaining, union decertification.*

For suggested readings, please visit this book's Web site at **http://fisher.westbuslaw.com** (click on "Internet Applications").

# MODULE 5

# LAW AFFECTING BUSINESS FINANCING

### CHAPTER 18
## Business Organizations

### CHAPTER 19
## Securities Regulation

# BUSINESS ORGANIZATIONS

*"TIS THE ONLY COMFORT OF THE MISERABLE TO HAVE PARTNERS IN THEIR WOES."*

*—CERVANTES,*
*DON QUIXOTE*

*"IF THERE WERE A READING PUBLIC NUMEROUS, DISCERNING, AND IMPARTIAL, THE SCIENCE OF ETHICS, AND ALL THE VARIOUS SCIENCES WHICH ARE NEARLY RELATED TO ETHICS, WOULD ADVANCE WITH UNEXAMPLED RAPIDITY."*

*—JOHN AUSTIN*

This chapter's objective is to survey the legal forms a business can take and to point out some advantages of each. A business can select from a wide variety of legal forms, including the sole proprietorship, business trust, partnership, limited partnership, limited liability partnership (LLP), limited liability company, (LLC) and corporation.

## SOLE PROPRIETORSHIPS

A sole proprietorship is simply any person in business to make a profit for himself or herself alone. According to the *Statistical Abstract of the United States* (2001 edition), for the year 1998 an estimated 17,409,000 nonfarm sole proprietorships filed federal tax returns in the United States. The same source estimated total business receipts from sole proprietorships for 1998 as $918 billion, with total net income of $226 billion.

### LEGAL FORM

A **sole proprietor** owns the business and its property in her or his individual name but may have employees to help in the business. The sole proprietor may operate under an assumed or fictitious name. For example, Jane Keeling may own a drugstore called "Arrow Pharmacy." States have fictitious name statutes, which require registry of assumed names; generally, the penalties for noncompliance with fictitious name statutes are not severe.

## REASONS FOR SOLE PROPRIETORSHIPS

Reasons for having sole proprietorships include simplicity, control, convenience, and privacy. Few legal formalities must be observed to form a sole proprietorship, although some rules apply. For example, a retailer must obtain a sales tax license and secure an occupational license before doing certain types of work. The state of Illinois, for example, requires licenses for more than 180 occupations ranging from florist to insurance broker.[1] The lack of such a license can mean that contracts entered by persons in such professions are unenforceable or void.

The Brady v. Fulghum case shows what can occur when a building contractor does not have an occupational license.

### Brady v. Fulgham
Supreme Court of North Carolina
308 S.E.2d 327 (1983)

### Background and Facts

Plaintiff brought this action for monies allegedly due under a contract for construction of a private dwelling. In affirming summary judgment for defendants, the Court of Appeals concluded that plaintiff, a general contractor, had not complied "substantially" with the statutory licensing requirements.

In February 1980, plaintiff agreed with defendants by written contract to construct their house for a price of approximately $106,850. Plaintiff began construction on or about March 13, 1980. Neither during the negotiation of this contract nor when he began performance was plaintiff licensed as a general contractor as required by North Carolina law.

Plaintiff was awarded his builder's license on October 22, 1980, having passed the examination on his second attempt. At that time, he had completed two-thirds of the work on defendants' house. Defendants paid plaintiff $104,000. Plaintiff by this legal action seeks an additional $2,850 on the original contract and $28,926.41 for "additions and changes" requested by defendants during construction.

### Body of Opinion

**Justice Exum.** The legislature has provided a mechanism for certification of general construction contractors. . . . This process . . . protects the public by insuring confidence and integrity within the construction industry. . . . Although the statute does not expressly preclude an unlicensed contractor's suit against an owner for breach of contract, *Builders Supply v. Midyette* . . . held the contractor may not recover on the contract or *in quantum meruit* when he has ignored the protective statute.

After *Midyette*, the Court of Appeals decided several cases including the one at bar, in terms of whether the contractor had "substantially" complied with the licensing statutes. . . .

Generally, contracts entered into by unlicensed construction contractors, in violation of a statute passed for the protection of the public, are unenforceable by the contractor. . . . A majority of jurisdictions adhere to this interpretation. . . . Reading these statutes as being designed to protect the public from irresponsible contractors, . . . most state courts find "no legal remedy for that which is illegal itself." . . . General contractors have been precluded from maintaining actions if they must rely on their illegal act to justify their recovery. . . . The unenforceability of such contracts by the contractor stems directly from their conception in the contractor's illegal act.

The express language of the North Carolina licensing statute indicates that it is designed to insure competence within the construction industry. . . . The legislature seeks to guarantee "skill, training and ability to accomplish such construction in a safe and workmanlike fashion." . . . In tandem, these requirements "protect members of the general public without regard to the impact upon individual contractors." . . .

In examining the licensing statute in question, we recognize the distinction between legislation designed to produce revenue and to protect the public. In the former situation, the legislature exercises its taxing authority. In the latter, it exercises its police power. Accordingly, when a legislature invokes its police power to provide statutory protection to the public from fraud, incompetence, and irresponsibility, as ours has done with the contractor licensing statutes, courts impose greater penalties on violators. . . . Making contracts unenforceable by the violating contractor produces "a salutary effect

---

[1] A complete list is published in *Conard, Knauss, and Siegel, Enterprise Organization* (Mineola, NY: Foundation Press, 1972), pp. 10–11.

in causing obedience to the licensing statute." . . . These public policy considerations militate against permitting unlicensed general construction contractors to enforce their contracts. . . .

In recognition of the essential illegality of an unlicensed contractor's entering into a construction contract for which a license is required and in order to give full effect to the legislative intent to furnish protection to the public by strict licensing requirements, we reject the doctrine of substantial compliance, cognizant that harsh consequences may sometimes fall on those who do contracting work without a license. . . .

We do recognize the minority rule, adhered to by our Court of Appeals, is not without some support. California applies the doctrine of substantial compliance in certain cases to avoid unnecessarily harsh results on unlicensed contractors who perform well. . . .

We agree that the existence of a license at the time the contract is signed is determinative and attach "great weight to the significant moment of the entrance of the parties into the relationship." . . . Accordingly, we adopt the rule that a contract illegally entered into by an unlicensed general construction contractor is unenforceable by the contractor. It cannot be validated by the contractor's subsequent procurement of a license. . . .

In this circumstance there can be no substantial compliance with the licensing statutes. Neither may the contractor recover for extras, additions, or changes made during construction commenced pursuant to the contract. Such a contract is not, however, void. Others not regulated by the licensing statutes passed for their protection do not act illegally in becoming parties to such a contract. The policy underlying the licensing statutes would not be served by preventing enforcement by those for whose protection the statutes were passed. These parties may enforce the contract against the unlicensed contractor. . . . Further, if a licensed contractor's license expires, for whatever reason, during construction, he may recover for only the work performed while he was duly licensed. If, in that situation, the contractor renews his license during construction, he may recover for work performed before expiration and after renewal. If, by virtue of

these rules, harsh results fall upon unlicensed contractors who violate our statutes, the contractors themselves bear both the responsibility and the blame.

Plaintiff was unlicensed at the time he negotiated and contracted with the defendants to construct their house. He illegally entered into the contract; it is, therefore, unenforceable by him. His subsequent procurement of a valid license cannot validate or make legal that which was illegal in its inception.

## Judgment and Result

Plaintiff loses. Failure to have the occupational license was fatal to the sole proprietor's recovery on the contract to build the house. His subsequent obtaining of the license did not make legal what was illegal at its inception.

## Questions

1. Did the contractor have an occupational license to build houses at the time he signed the contract to build the house? Did he obtain such a license after the house in question was built?
2. What is the purpose of occupational licenses? Note that the case mentions two types of occupational licenses—revenue raising and policing (governing practitioner ethical and technical qualifications). Which type of license was the contractor's license in the preceding case?
3. The plaintiff builder in the preceding case was a sole proprietor. Can it be said that sole proprietors have no restrictions on them with respect to entering certain businesses and making contracts?
4. Does the *substantial compliance* doctrine—which states that if one meets most, but not all, of a statute's requirements that the individual may recover under the statute—help one not in full compliance with the positive law? Did the court in the preceding case adopt or reject the substantial compliance doctrine?
5. Was anything structurally wrong with the house that plaintiff built? Could one argue that natural law (justice) lost to positive law (the licensing law) in this case?

## PARTNERSHIPS

At the Web site for Library of Congress are links to **http://thomas.loc.gov**

The 2001 edition of the *Statistical Abstract of the United States* reports an estimated 1,855,000 partnership tax returns were filed in the United States for 1998. Partnership gross receipts for 1998 (the most recent year for statistics) were estimated at $1,603 billion, operating at a total net income of $187 billion. The strengths of using the partnership as one's legal form of business arise from combining the broader talents and material resources of two or more people. The partnership form also has other advantages.

## PARTNERSHIP ADVANTAGES

A partnership is easy to form and does not require state approval. Property (real and personal) may be held and transferred by the partnership itself. The partnership may be ignored for federal income tax purposes. In such a case, the partnership income is divided among the partners according to the partnership agreement and taxed as part of their personal incomes. This procedure eliminates *double taxation*.

## PARTNERSHIP DISADVANTAGES

A major disadvantage of partnerships is liability exposure, meaning that if a partner or partnership employee (while at work) harms a third person, the victim can seize all the partnership's property as well as each individual partner's assets to pay the damages. For example, if two doctors are partners and one commits malpractice against a patient, the victim can take all the partnership's assets (as well as each partner's individual assets) to pay the loss.

Second, partners must keep minutes of meetings and business records. This requirement is imposed by the Uniform Partnership Act (UPA). Also, partnerships selling partnership interests interstate may have to register such interests as securities under the Federal Securities Act.

## PARTNERSHIP DEFINITION

The UPA's definition of a **partnership** is an "association of two or more persons to carry on, as co-owners, a business for profit." The UPA is the law in all but one state.

If two or more persons do not intend to carry on the business on a long-term basis, it probably is not a partnership. If two or more persons do charitable work, the association is not a partnership because it does not intend to make a profit. The fact that two or more people try but fail to make a profit in a business is irrelevant with respect to the partnership's existence. What is crucial is whether they *intend* to operate a business for profit. If they do, and they intend to do so over a period of time, they are partners.

## PARTNERSHIP EXISTENCE

No express agreement is needed between two or more people for a partnership to exist. In other words, the law may hold that two or more people are in a partnership even when they do not intend there to be one. Also, the fact that the parties have said their relationship is not a partnership is not conclusive. The courts use an objective, rather than subjective, test to determine the parties' intent to form a partnership.

*Example of the Objective Test.* One example in which two parties are partners (even though they did not intend to be partners) occurs when a corporation is defectively organized. Its "shareholders" are treated as partners even though the clear subjective intent that they desired shareholders' limited liability rather than general partners' unlimited liability.

*Proving a Partnership's Existence.* The burden of proving that a partnership exists is on the party claiming that it exists. Courts look at a number of factors to determine whether a partnership exists. Two of the most important factors are joint right to manage the business and sharing profits and losses.

*Profit Sharing.* Section 7 of the UPA declares that a person sharing the profits of a business with another is prima facie evidence that she or he is a partner in the business. **Prima facie** evidence means that the evidence is strong enough to allow a judge in a jury trial to let the partnership issue go to the jury, and it can justify (but does not require) a jury's finding that a partnership exists. However, the UPA goes on to say that no prima facie inference that a person is a partner shall be drawn if business profits are received in any of the following ways:

1. As a debt repayment by installments or otherwise
2. As wages of an employee or rent to a landlord
3. As an annuity to a widow or representative of a deceased partner
4. As interest on a loan, although the amount of payment varies with the business's profits
5. As consideration for the sale of a business's goodwill or other property by installments or otherwise

The sharing of gross returns (gross income before expenses are deducted to arrive at a profit figure) does not create a prima facie presumption of partnership. Sharing gross returns also does not establish a partnership's existence, regardless of whether the persons sharing them have a joint interest in property from which the returns are obtained. As these points suggest, the fact that two or more persons jointly own property does not necessarily mean they are partners. However, joint property ownership does not necessarily preclude the joint owners from being partners. Joint ownership is a neutral fact in determining partnership existence.

*Right to Manage.* The right to share in business management is one of the basic partnership attributes. However, a partnership agreement may confer the management power on one partner only, without destroying the business's legal nature as a partnership. On the other hand, proof that a person has a right to share in partnership management does not establish that he or she is a partner; however, when this fact is coupled with the additional fact of profit sharing, the presumption is that a person is a partner.

*Partnership as an Entity.* The law treats partnerships as legal entities for some purposes but not others. Partnerships are entities for bankruptcy, suing and being sued (in many states), and owning property. On the other hand, partnerships are not entities for liability purposes. Thus, if someone sues the partnership and gets a judgment that uses up and exceeds all the partnership's assets, individual partners' assets must go toward payment of the debt.

## FORMING PARTNERSHIPS

A partnership may be formed between two persons or among three or more persons. Good business practice suggests that the partnership contract be written. If a partnership agreement cannot by its terms be completed within one year, most states' statutes of frauds would require that the partnership agreement be written to be enforceable. For example, if two accountants agree to form a partnership for three years, this partnership agreement cannot be performed within one year and thus would have to be evidenced by a writing signed by the partners to be enforceable. If a partner does not want to honor a partnership agreement, courts will not force him or her into a partnership. In other words, specific performance will not be awarded for breach of a partnership agreement. Damages, however, are given when appropriate.

The *Dalton v. Austin* case shows some problems in determining if a partnership exists.

## Dalton v. Austin
Supreme Judicial Court of Maine
432 A2d. 774 (1981)

### Background and Facts

**Justice Nichols.** The Plaintiff, Emily Dalton (formerly Emily Ruebsamen), appeals from a judgment for the Defendant, Whitney W. Austin, Sr., entered by the Superior Court in Penobscot County after a jury-waived trial on her complaint for conversion of certain financial contributions she had made to a business in Bangor known as The Small Change Restaurant, of which Austin was originally the sole proprietor.

In March of 1974, the Plaintiff and Defendant reached an oral agreement concerning the business, the exact terms of which were the subject of conflicting testimony at trial. The Plaintiff, who had had prior experience in the restaurant business, testified that she and the Defendant agreed to be equal partners in the restaurant and that, in consideration of certain financial contributions she was to make to the business, the Defendant agreed to incorporate the business, turn those business assets to which he had title over to the corporation, and distribute stock to the Plaintiff and himself. It appears, however, that the Plaintiff did not expect the business to be incorporated until after she became involved in its operation.

The Defendant testified that he and the Plaintiff agreed to become partners and that in consideration for being made a partner, the Plaintiff initially contributed her automobile to the business. The Defendant's understanding of the agreement differed from the Plaintiff's, however, in that he did not recall promising to turn assets over to the corporation, or to have stock issued and distributed. Rather, his testimony suggests that the agreement contemplated that the Plaintiff would ultimately purchase the restaurant, thus leaving him "free and clear" of the business, a circumstance the Defendant desired for reasons of health and overwork. In response to questions posed by opposing counsel as to whether the Defendant agreed to transfer assets in his name to the corporation and distribute stock to the Plaintiff, the Defendant testified that he did not remember or understand the agreement but thought the heart of the agreement to be the Plaintiff's ultimate purchase of the entire business.

After the agreement was made, the Defendant no longer took an active part in management of the restaurant; the Plaintiff, on the other hand, operated the business on a day-to-day basis for several months. In the months that she managed the restaurant, the Plaintiff made major financial contributions to the business totalling $18,214.89. She made these contributions by directly paying the debts and operating expenses of the business. The Defendant testified that he had no knowledge of the nature or extent of her payments on behalf of the business and that he never personally received them.

Under Plaintiff's management, business income declined dramatically. After operating the business for several months, the Plaintiff finally asked the Defendant to distribute the stock and transfer the assets. The record does not disclose whether the business was ever incorporated. Stock, however, was never distributed, and the Defendant's testimony suggests that ownership of business-related assets was never transferred to a corporation. Instead, a closing date for sale of the restaurant to the Plaintiff was set. On the advice of her attorneys, however, she ultimately refused to purchase the business from the Defendant and he eventually closed the business when its management totally failed. Thereafter, he made several attempts to lease profitably the business and finally sold it to a lessee. The proceeds from the sale, according to the Defendant's testimony, were used to pay mortgagees and creditors whose claims apparently exceeded the gain from the sale. The Defendant claims to have paid the balance out of personal funds.

At trial, after testimony by the two parties was heard, the presiding justice found for the Defendant. The justice specifically found that the parties were partners and that their original agreement created a partnership. From that finding, he concluded that neither party had a cause of action for restitution or conversion. In response to the request of the Plaintiff's counsel for a specific finding on whether an agreement existed between the parties in which the Defendant was obliged to transfer assets to the corporation and distribute stock, the court declined to rule on the specifics of any such agreement. Rather, the court limited its ruling to finding generally that a partnership agreement existed and that any controversy over the business arising out of the partnership was properly the subject of an action for an accounting between partners.

On appeal here, the Plaintiff contends the Superior Court erred in finding a partnership and in concluding that an action for conversion or money had and received was inappropriate. . . .

The Plaintiff argues that the Superior Court erred in concluding a partnership existed because no evidence of co-ownership or sharing of profits appears on the record.

Under the Uniform Partnership Act . . . which Maine adopted in 1973, as under the common law, the existence of a partnership is an inference of law based on established facts. . . . Under the Act, a partnership is defined as "an association of 2 or more persons . . . to carry on as co-owners a business for profit."

Evidence relevant to the existence of a partnership includes evidence of a voluntary contract between two persons to place their money, effects, labor, and skill, or some or all of them, in lawful commerce or business with the understanding that a community of profits will be shared. . . . No one factor is alone determinative of the existence of a partnership, but the record before us supports the finding of the Superior Court.

While the specifics of the agreement were in dispute, evidence of an agreement between the parties existed. That agreement clearly related to operation of a business. Assets used in the business and capital contributions to the business were made by both parties. They consistently testified that both regarded themselves as partners. Finally, the Plaintiff actively managed the business for several months.

The Plaintiff contends, nevertheless, that there is no evidence of co-ownership or a sharing of profits. Under the Uniform Act, the concept of co-ownership does not necessarily mean joint title to all business assets. Rather, as the commentary to the Uniform Act suggests, the right to participate in control of the business is the essence of co-ownership. . . . Contrary to this Plaintiff's contention, then, the record sufficiently supports the existence of co-ownership inasmuch as it reveals that she actively managed the business for several months without the supervision of the Defendant. While the record is devoid of evidence that the parties shared profits, sharing is not required if, as the evidence shows in this case, the agreement itself implies that the parties contemplated the sharing of profits. In the case before us evidence of actual sharing of profits was naturally absent, given the financial straits of the business.

We conclude that the Superior Court did not err in concluding that Austin and Dalton were engaged in a partnership.

The Plaintiff also argues that the Defendant is liable to her for conversion under theories of unjust enrichment or quasi-contract. The Superior Court clearly rejected this argument on grounds that the controversy between the parties over monies spent by Dalton for the business arose out of the partnership itself, and thus the only appropriate remedy under Maine law was an action for accounting.

Under the Uniform Partnership Act, partners have a fiduciary responsibility toward the partnership which obliges them to account for disposition of partnership property. Section 302 of the Act, in pertinent part, gives any partner the right to an account in a wide variety of circumstances, many of which closely resemble the circumstances of the instant case. In particular, Section 302(1) gives a partner who has been "wrongfully excluded from the partnership business or possession of its property by his copartners" a right to a formal account. Similarly, Section 302(3) gives any partner the right to an account pursuant to the fiduciary duties of every partner set forth in § 301. Section 301 provides in part as follows:

> Every partner must account to the partnership for any benefit and hold as trustee for it any profits derived by him without the consent of the other partners from any transaction connected with the formation, conduct or liquidation of the partnership or from any use by him of its property.

These provisions reflect a strong legislative preference, borrowed from the common law, for efficient settlement of partnership disputes involving complex and multifarious aspects in a single proceeding. . . .

Thus, other courts have consistently held that an action derived from the common law brought by one partner against another is inappropriate when the subject matter of the action is directly related to partnership business or property. . . . In particular, this rule has been applied to actions for conversion of partnership property, actions necessarily involving breaches of fiduciary duty. . . .

In the case before us, the appropriateness of resolving the dispute between the parties through an action for an accounting is clear. The Superior Court concluded that a partnership agreement existed between the parties and that the restaurant business was conducted in the form of a partnership. Once an agreement to form the partnership was struck and business proceeded accordingly, it is apparent that the money the Plaintiff sought to recover in this action was funds spent by her in the course of conducting the partnership business. The circumstance that the parties may have agreed to do business in the corporate form at some later date does not alter the essential character of the form of the business association. . . .

The Plaintiff attempts to distinguish her action from the general rule precluding independent actions on grounds that it rests on a separate legal obligation arising out of the Defendant's alleged promise to incorporate the business, turn assets over to the corporation and distribute stock. In so arguing, she is suggesting that her claim falls within a select group of exceptions to the rule limiting a partner's remedies to an accounting.

Actions by one partner against another in tort or for restitution on a theory of implied contract or unjust enrichment have been allowed by courts in other jurisdictions when the wrong which a plaintiff alleged constituted an injury to an individual in contrast to a partnership interest. Similarly, independent actions have been allowed when the affairs of a partnership are really wound up and the issues before the court can be resolved without extensive study of the partnership accounts. . . . The record before us indicates that the basis of this Plaintiff's claim is intimately related to partnership affairs. Moreover, the record is replete with confusion and ambiguity concerning the winding up of the partnership as well as the manner in which the partnership property was ultimately liqui-dated. These circumstances both suggest the prudence of settling the dispute between these two litigants in one comprehensive proceed-ing for an accounting and provide adequate support for the finding below that an independent action was inappropriate.

## Judgment and Result

We conclude that there was no error when the Superior Court entered judgment for the Defendant. The Supreme Judicial Court of Maine agreed with the lower court that Dalton and Austin had a partnership even though no written partnership agreement existed, there was no sharing of profits, and business assets were not jointly owned.

### Questions

1. What factors were relied on by the Supreme Judicial Court of Maine to hold that a partnership existed between Dalton and Austin?
2. How did the court answer Dalton's specific arguments that no partnership existed?
3. Assuming Dalton and Austin agreed to organize the business in corporate form at a future date, did their agreement necessarily mean they did not have a partnership before that time?
4. Why are partners not allowed to sue each other for torts or breaches of contract in connection with the partnership? Are such wrongs one partner commits against another corrected in one lawsuit for an accounting?

## ASPECTS OF THE PARTNERS' RELATIONSHIP

The Uniform Partnership Act sets out a number of rights and duties that partners have with respect to one another. These rights and duties include the following:

1. The right to be repaid the partner's contribution and to share equally in the partnership profits after partnership debts are paid
2. The duty to contribute toward partnership losses (capital or other) according to the partner's share in the profits
3. The right to be indemnified respecting personal liabilities reasonably incurred by a partner in the ordinary and proper conduct or preservation of the part-nership business or property
4. The right to be repaid with interest any payment or advance beyond the amount of capital contribution
5. The right to manage the partnership along with the other partners
6. The duty to keep partnership books and the right to inspect and copy such books
7. The duty to render information to copartners regarding all things affecting the partnership
8. A fiduciary duty to copartners much the same as that owed by an agent to a principal
9. The right to a formal account as to partnership affairs if a partner is wrong-fully excluded from the partnership business or possession of its property by the copartners or if the right to account is provided in the partnership agree-ment or any other circumstances rendering an accounting just and reasonable

If the partnership is for a fixed term—say, two years—and the partnership con-tinues beyond the term without any express agreement, the UPA declares that the rights and duties of the partners remain the same as before expiration of the term.

*Partners' Agreements.* The Uniform Partnership Act allows partners' rights and duties to be varied by their partnership agreement. For example, partners could agree that only one of them has the right to manage the partnership business.

Another variation frequently encountered adjusts the profits to which each partner is entitled on the basis of capital contribution or time devoted to managing the partnership affairs.

Suppose, for example, a three-person partnership is composed of A, B, and C, with A and B each contributing 25 percent of the partnership capital and C contributing 50 percent. Even if A, B, and C all devote equal amounts of time to managing the partnership, C might be justified in insisting on a provision in the partnership agreement that gives him 50 percent of the profits. If no such provision is included, the partners will divide the profits equally, even though C paid in twice as much as A and B.

Partners are understandably optimistic about their business prospects. They therefore tend to speak only of dividing profits, neglecting to mention losses. If no mention is made of dividing losses but only of profit division, losses are divided in the same way as profits. C, therefore, should try to insert an additional sentence dividing losses equally (or even more favorably from his standpoint). Profits and losses, in other words, do not have to be divided equally among partners, nor do losses have to be divided in the same way as profits. However, if no partnership agreement on the point is specified profits and losses are divided equally.

*Partners' Salaries.* The UPA general rule is that partners are not entitled to salaries. This rule also exists where the UPA is not the law. The rule, however, may be changed to allow partners to receive salaries for partnership work if the partnership agreement so provides. A reason for the usual no-salary rule is that each partner is entitled to share partnership profits, presumably a salary substitute.

*Partners' Suits against One Another.* Partners may not sue one another on partnership matters except to end the partnership. This prohibition includes violations of the partnership rights and duties listed previously. The logic of this rule is similar to that of rules generally precluding a husband and wife from suing one another for certain torts: If they cannot get along, they should end their relationship permanently and not expect courts to resolve their differences. Thus, the partners should talk out their disagreements or sue to dissolve the partnership. They can then have one another's violation of partnership rights and duties taken into account in settling partnership accounts when the partnership is brought formally to an end.

*Partners' Liability for Copartners' Contracts and Torts.* Every partner is an agent of the partnership for the purpose of its business, which sounds as though the partnership is the party from whom recovery is ultimately sought and that the partnership is an entity. However, the UPA drafters generally rejected the idea that a partnership is an entity. The partners—both the one who injured another or entered the contract on the partnership's behalf and the other partners who were not involved—will be sought to be held by the third party. The question will often be, "Did the acting partner have authority to commit a tort or to contract on the other partners'—not the partnership's—behalf?" If the partner committing the tort had the authority to act, the nonacting partner will also be liable.

*Partners' Authority.* Partners can obtain authority from copartners through express, implied, and apparent authority, or through ratification. Partners may empower each other to act by expressly saying so orally or in a document. Written **express authority** is easier to prove than oral express authority. **Implied authority** arises from express authority and amounts to those acts that are reasonably necessary to accomplish the express authority but that cannot, as a practical matter, be elaborately described. For example, partners selling autos will authorize a copartner to sell the cars, but they will not in detail say, "Open the hood and show the prospect the engine. Describe the engine size. Open and shut the car door to show how solid the car is. Turn on the lights, windshield wipers, and radio to demonstrate how well they work." The assumption is that a thorough salesperson will do all of these things, but seldom will instructions be so elaborate as to mention all of these matters.

**Apparent authority** arises from some act or omission of a copartner, not the acting partner, that reasonably leads a third person to conclude that the partner has authority to act on a particular matter. The UPA notes that the "act of a partner which is not apparently for the carrying on of the business of the partnership in the usual way does not bind the partnership unless authorized by the other partners." The UPA also notes certain acts by a partner that would not bind the other partners unless the business has been abandoned or all other partners agree. Such acts include assigning partnership property in trust for creditors or on the assignee's promise to pay the debts of the partnership, disposing of the partnership's goodwill, confessing a judgment, submitting a partnership claim or liability to arbitration or reference, or doing any other act that would make it impossible to carry on the ordinary business of the partnership.

**Ratification** occurs when a partner commits an act unauthorized by the other partners, and the other partners later learn of the act and approve it. The legal effect of this after-the-fact authority is to bind the person ratifying.

The matter of a partner's liability for a copartner's tort is also addressed by the UPA. It states that any wrongful act or omission of any partner acting in the ordinary course of the business of the partnership or with the authority of the copartners and causing loss or injury to any third person subjects the acting partner and all other partners to joint and several liability. Under **joint and several liability**, a partner could be forced to pay the entire tort judgment obtained against a copartner who injured others within the scope of the partnership. All partnership property and all of each individual partner's property may be seized to pay the tort judgment against the individual partner who commits the tort if it is within the scope of the partnership.

A partner's liability for partnership torts is joint and several. In jurisdictions that have abolished contributory negligence in favor of a comparative fault system in tort law, this system could modify partners' tort liability to one of comparative negligence. A partner's liability for partnership contracts is joint.

## PARTNERSHIP PROPERTY

Land and buildings (realty) and personalty,[2] such as typewriters, automobiles, and calculators, are used by partnerships to generate income. Partnerships may own property in the partnership name, although partnership property may be held in a partner's name. It is one way partnerships are regarded by the Uniform Partnership Act as entities, because only entities may own property. Not all

---

[2] Personalty is a property classification and generally refers to movables. It is to be contrasted with realty (land and buildings, typically) and fixtures (things permanently attached to realty).

property has a title document (a piece of paper officially recognized as evidence of ownership). Realty and automobiles do have title documents (called *deeds* in the case of realty), and statutes require recording of titles before their validity is recognized in many circumstances. However, most other less substantial property (e.g., desks, chairs, computers, office equipment) do not have title documents. One way to establish who owns non-title-bearing property is by retaining the invoice issued by the seller when the item is purchased. Often the invoice contains the purchaser's name. The partnership's name on the purchase invoice would be evidence that the property belonged to the partnership.

The Uniform Partnership Act defines partnership property as all property originally brought into the partnership or later acquired on the partnership's account. The last clause suggests that keeping the purchase invoice for property without a title document is vital in establishing its identity as partnership property. If property is purchased with partnership funds, it is presumed to belong to the partnership unless a contrary intention appears.

Realty may be acquired in the partnership name. At the same time, realty titled in a partner's individual name is presumed to be partnership property if purchased with partnership funds. This presumption is rebuttable. If the partnership realty is in the partnership's name, it can be transferred only in the partnership name. Where title to partnership realty resides in a partner or partners and not in the partnership, the partner in whose name the realty is titled may convey it to a third person, and this act will bind the partnership if the third person is a good-faith purchaser for value without knowledge of any limit on the conveying partner's authority to transfer it. If the third person knows of the conveying partner's lack of authority to convey the realty or does not give fair value, the other partners may recover the property for the partnership.

*Individual Partner's Property Rights.* Assuming for a moment that property used by the partnership is partnership property, what rights does an individual partner have in it? The UPA identifies a partner's property rights as being three: rights in specific partnership property, an interest in the partnership, and the partner's right to take part in partnership management. The UPA further says that a partner is a co-owner with his or her partners of specific partnership property as a **tenant in partnership**.

Tenants in partnership have equal rights with other partners to possess specific partnership property for partnership purposes. This right may be modified or eliminated by the partnership agreement. However, a partner has no right to possess partnership property for any nonpartnership purpose unless the other partners agree. Thus, a partner in an insurance firm may not drive the partnership Buick up to Cape Cod for an extended weekend unless the other partners agree.

A partner's **interest in the partnership** is his or her share of the profits and surplus. It is personal property. A partner may sell or convey this interest in the partnership. Doing so does not of itself dissolve the partnership, nor does it make the buyer of the partnership interest a partner. Thus, the buyer of a partner's partnership interest is entitled to the assigning partner's share in the partnership profits, not to share or to manage the business, inspect partnership books, or require any information on account of partnership transactions.

The partnership's continuity and viability as a business is to some extent protected from creditors of individual partners by the UPA's rule that a partner's right in specific partnership property is not subject to attachment or execution.

Partnership creditors may attach and execute against partnership property to receive payment for partnership debts, however. Interestingly, homestead and other **exemptions** are not available to the partnership when its creditors seek **execution** against partnership property for partnership debts. Also, the UPA provides that a partner's right in specific partnership property may not be subjected to **dower** (claims by a wife against her husband's realty simply because she married him), **curtesy** (a husband's claim to his wife's realty simply because he married her and they had a child), or other claims of widows, heirs, or next of kin.

## PARTNERSHIP BY ESTOPPEL

**Partnership by estoppel** is a legal theory that a plaintiff will raise against a defendant to attempt to hold him or her for obligations of a partnership of which she or he actually is not a member. Partnership by estoppel applies when the defendant has by words or actions led the plaintiff to believe that the defendant is a partnership member, the plaintiff changes his position in reliance, and the plaintiff sustains damages as a result of relying on such partnership membership. In short, partnership by estoppel has three elements: reasonable reliance that another is a partnership member, change of position in reliance, and damages. The person asserted to be a partner by estoppel is not, in fact, a partner. Yet, if these three elements of partnership by estoppel can be established, the defendant is estopped (stopped) to say that he or she is not a partner, making the defendant liable to the plaintiff for the partnership obligation in question.

## LIMITED PARTNERSHIPS

Sometimes a person wishes to join another in a business but does not want to take an active role in managing the business or be subject to unlimited liability for partnership claims greater than the original capital contribution. Short of incorporating (with attendant double taxation, increased red tape in filing annual state reports, and the problems of qualifying to do intrastate business in other states), what, if anything, can be done to satisfy such a person?

The limited partnership is a possible answer to the problem just posed. The limited partnership is made possible because of the Uniform Limited Partnership Act (or the Revised Uniform Limited Partnership Act), which is the law in all states except Louisiana, plus the District of Columbia and the Virgin Islands. The Uniform Limited Partnership Act (ULPA) lists certain requirements for forming a limited partnership. A filing of the articles of limited partnership (partnership agreement) or a specified information document with a public office is required by each state's ULPA. Documentation requirements vary among the states' ULPAs, particularly with respect to the forms to be filed and the place of filing.

## PARTNERS IN LIMITED PARTNERSHIPS

Any limited partnership must have at least one **general partner**. This person's (or persons') liability for all the obligations of the limited partnership is unlimited. The **limited partner** (or partners) is liable, however, only for the amount of capital contribution he or she agreed to make.

## LIMITED PARTNER REGISTRY

Ordinary partnerships do not and may not have limited partners; only limited partnerships may do so. The reason for allowing the limited partnership to exist is to help the partnership attract investors. The limited partnership creditors are protected (from being misled into believing they are extending credit to a partner who has unlimited liability) by the registration of the limited partnership articles in a public office. Potential creditors of the limited partnership should go to such a registry to see whether the partnership is listed as limited. In the case of a limited partnership, note should be taken of which partners are limited.

## LIMITED PARTNERS ARE PASSIVE

The limited partner is supposed to be passive with respect to management of the limited partnership business. The more active a limited partner is in managing the firm's business, the greater the risk that the limited partner will become a general partner. If this situation occurs, the partner has unlimited liability.

The Revised Uniform Limited Partnership Act (RULPA) permits limited partners to engage in certain management functions while retaining their limited partner status. Among such actions are serving as an agent, contractor, or consultant for the limited partnership; serving as a surety for the limited partnership; approving or disapproving amendments to the limited partnership agreement; voting on dissolution, winding up, or transferring all or most of the limited partnership assets to others; changing the business in which the partnership is engaged; or removing a general partner.

The *Obert v. Environmental Research & Development* case raises several issues concerning limited partnerships including the following: May a corporation be a general partner in limited partnership? May the limited partners carry on the partnership following the discharge of the general partner for cause? Do a majority of the limited partners have a fiduciary duty to the general and remaining limited partners not notified of proposed action of removing the general partner? May the limited partners act without holding a meeting?

---

### Obert v. Environmental Research & Development
Supreme Court of Washington
112 Wash. 2d 323, 771 P.2d 340 (1989)

#### Background and Facts

Plaintiffs are approximately fifty entities and individuals, all of whom are limited partners of the Campus Park Associates Limited Partnership, a Washington limited partnership. The defendant, ERADCO, is a Washington corporation whose stock is owned entirely by Patrick and Rosemary Easter.

The primary asset of the Campus Park LP is an 83-acre parcel of rural land located in Federal Way, Washington, which was purchased for $2,472,333 in December 1978. In 1978, ERADCO sold limited partnership units of the Campus Park LP to the plaintiffs through the use of a private placement memorandum. At the time of the purchase of the partnership units, each of the Campus Park LP limited partners and ERADCO entered into a limited partnership agreement.

ERADCO acted as the general partner of Campus Park LP from its inception in 1978 until May 5, 1984. In May 1984, 74.4 percent of the ownership of Campus Park LP amended the limited partnership agreement and voted by proxy to remove ERADCO as general partner, electing the Pace Corporation (Pace), a Washington corporation, as successor general partner. On or about May 5, 1984, an amended certificate of limited partnership was filed with the State of Washington amending the limited partnership agreement and replacing ERADCO with Pace as the new general partner. A King County Superior Court Judge confirmed the replacement of ERADCO by Pace on November 27, 1984. A later amendment to the certificate of limited partnership was made, naming Robert Gerend as an additional cogeneral partner of the Campus Park LP.

At the bench trial, the court found that prior to its removal, ERADCO had breached several fiduciary duties owed to the Campus Park LP limited partners, specifically:

(a) ERADCO failed to provide audited financial statements as required by the Limited Partnership Agreement. Some financial statements were eventually produced, but they were not timely. . . .

(b) ERADCO failed to pay real estate taxes on the Campus Park property for the years 1979, 1980, 1981 and 1982 until late 1982. This was contrary to the terms of the Deed of Trust, placing the limited partnership in default of its deed to its seller.

(c) Defendants failed to keep a reserve account as set forth in the Limited Partnership Agreement for the payment of taxes and assessments.

(d) Defendants failed to keep adequate land management time records for the "actual time" it alleges it spent in managing the limited partnership property. This timekeeping requirement was provided for in the Limited Partnership Agreement and represented in the Private Placement Memorandum. . . . Finally, some of the entries were fictitious, leaving an overall lack of confidence in ERADCO's attention to this fiduciary duty.

(e) Defendants borrowed monies from the limited partnership's bank, Westside Federal Savings and Loan, for its own purposes and pledged as collateral the separate limited partnership savings accounts of Campus Park. Also used as collateral to secure their borrowings were the Limited Partnership accounts of other limited partnerships. Also as part of the collateral agreement with the bank, ERADCO and Easter agreed to restrict the use of those limited partner accounts for the duration of its loans. The monies were kept in a five and one-half percent (5-1/2%) interest bearing account rather than being placed in an account earning interest at the current market rate of at least twelve percent (12%) or more. This practice started in May 1981 with the Campus Park account and terminated May 1982 at the request of the Campus Park limited partners. ERADCO continues to use other limited partnership savings accounts as collateral for its separate borrowings. The State Securities Division asked ERADCO and Easter to stop this practice but it has continued the loans against the limited partnership savings accounts. [The trial court found that the amount of damage to the limited partners in lost interest as a result of these actions was $2,100.]

(f) In December 1983, ERADCO commingled the separate monies of the Campus Park limited partnership with its own monies in its corporate account at the First Interstate Bank. One Hundred Fifty-five Thousand Dollars ($155,000) of limited partnership funds were transferred from the Campus Park savings account at Westside Federal Savings and Loan into an ERADCO corporate checking and savings account, which account had approximately One Hundred Fifty Dollars ($150) of other funds in it. ERADCO commingled Campus Park limited partnership funds with its own with the clear purpose of inflating ERADCO's own financial statement for its own borrowings. This commingling was not disclosed to the limited partners at the time and was not reflected in any audited or unaudited financial statements of either ERADCO or Campus Park. It also subjected those funds to unlimited risk as ERADCO had not paid its withholding taxes to the IRS, which had begun action to collect the overdue taxes.

In addition, the trial court found that ERADCO was unable to substantiate approximately 75 percent of its land management fees that the limited partners had already paid ERADCO, an amount totalling $127,181.32.

Despite these breaches, ERADCO did make capital contributions to the Campus Park LP in the amount of $24,076.83, a portion of the amount required under the limited partnership agreement. Accordingly, the trial court found that ERADCO was entitled to recover its capital contribution, plus interest in the amount of $4,700.50. In further compliance with the limited partnership agreement, ERADCO performed "program management activities" and "land management activities," and also attempted to market the Campus Park LP real property. The trial court found that in performing its management duties, ERADCO advanced $169,790 in expenses on behalf of the Campus Park LP that are recoverable from the Campus Park limited partners under paragraph 9 of the limited partnership agreement. Finally, the trial court confirmed a total of $1,800 in terms against ERADCO awarded throughout the litigation.

The trial court concluded as a matter of law that the Campus Park general partner could be removed for cause upon a 66 percent vote, and thus confirmed the previous court order confirming ERADCO's removal and Pace's replacement as general partner. Further, the trial court held that as a result of ERADCO's fiduciary breaches it was not entitled to specific performance of the limited partnership agreement. Specifically, the trial court refused to enforce paragraphs 8 and 14 of the limited partnership agreement, denying defendant its 25 percent share of the profit.

The trial court ordered that the sums due each party should be offset against the other, with a net judgment entered in favor of ERADCO in the amount of $67,486.01, that was to be a lien against the property of the Campus Park LP, and paid in five equal annual payments commencing September 18, 1986. The trial court found that ERADCO did not violate the Washington State Securities Act or the Consumer Protection Act.

The Court of Appeals reversed in part when it held that pursuant to RCW 25.10.440 upon the removal of ERADCO as general partner, the failure of the limited partners *unanimously* to elect a successor general partner resulted in the dissolution of the partnership. Further, the court reversed the $169,790 award to ERADCO for reimbursement of advanced expenses as not supported by the findings of the trial court. The court also held that ERADCO had violated the Securities Act, and thus remanded for an award of attorney fees attributable to proving those violations. Finally, the court remanded for a determination of whether ERADCO had violated the Consumer Protection Act. . . .

As to the present status of the limited partnership, plaintiffs represent in their petition for review:

Since May, 1984 to the present, the Pace Corporation has managed the [Campus Park LP] property and acted in all respects as the [General Partner]. *No Motion for Stay of this authority has ever been proposed by ERADCO.* Indeed, Pace by its President,

Robert Gerend, personally guaranteed a $260,000 loan from Puget Sound Bank to the partnership in reliance on the court's ruling and the vote of the limited partners that he was the legal [General Partner]. . . . The partnership is presently solvent and well managed.

## Body of Opinion

**Justice Pearson.** . . . ERADCO contends the trial court abused its discretion when it denied ERADCO's prayer for specific performance of the profits clause in the Agreement, even though ERADCO breached its fiduciary duty to the limited partners.

Paragraph 8.5 of the Agreement provided for ERADCO to receive a subordinated 25 percent interest in the net profits of the Campus Park LP:

The General Partner shall receive a subordinated interest of 25% of the net cash proceeds from sale or refinancing of the property, provided, that said fee shall be postponed until all the partners have received cash distributions equal to 100% of their original investment.

This provision was to hold true even in an instance where the general partner was removed for cause:

In the event of, and upon the removal of the General Partner as provided in subparagraph 14.2.1 of this paragraph [Removal of the General Partner for cause], the General Partner shall receive in cash prior to said removal full payment of the subordinated interest as defined in paragraph 8.5 hereof . . . The subordinated interest shall be calculated as set forth in paragraph 8.5 above, with the exception that the sales price shall be determined by an independent M.A.I. appraisal, or a bona fide offer to purchase, whichever figure may be the greater, and shall further be treated as if the sale were a cash sale, and the General Partner shall receive his fee forthwith. . . .

Essentially, this provision converts ERADCO's subordinated profit, as provided for in paragraph 8.5, into a preferential profit on the occasion of a breach by ERADCO, and then, subsequently rewards ERADCO upon its removal for cause. While this is not immediately at issue, we note that the propriety of this paragraph is highly questionable, given the nature of the fiduciary relationship. See *Note, Partnership—Disclosure, Fairness and Substantive Administrative Regulation of a General Partner's Fiduciary Duty in a Real Estate Limited Partnership,* 50 Wash.L.Rev. 977 (1975). According to ERADCO's own calculations, this 25 percent subordinated interest is valued at approximately $634,000. This figure is based upon the trial court's finding that the value of the property was $7,000,000 on the date ERADCO was removed as the general partner.

Upon finding that ERADCO had breached its fiduciary duty to the limited partners, the trial court refused to invoke its equitable power to order specific performance of the Agreement and denied ERADCO its contractual 25 percent interest in the profits:

Paragraph 14 and paragraph 8 of the Limited Partnership Agreement, specifically as they relate to payment of twenty-five percent (25%) of the subordinated profits on sale of the property to the General Partner even when the General Partner is removed for cause, are against public policy as they operate as a disincentive to the limited partners to pursue an action for breach of fiduciary duty against the General Partner. A court acting in equity cannot reward a general partner who breaches its fiduciary duty and breaches the contract by awarding it a profit it has not earned.

We affirm the ruling of the trial court, and hold that it did not abuse its discretion in denying ERADCO's prayer for specific performance of the subordinated profit contractual provision.

Not unexpectedly, ERADCO argues to the contrary. First, ERADCO attempts to minimize the severity of the fiduciary breaches it committed by focusing on the lack of actual damage done to the limited partners. Second, ERADCO contends that since the nature of the fiduciary breaches it committed are unrelated to its contractual right to the 25 percent compensation under the Agreement, the trial court should have no discretion to deny ERADCO its profit. Nevertheless, we find ERADCO's analysis unpersuasive. In point of fact, such arguments attempt to equate a breach of a fiduciary duty to a mere breach of contract. Such is not the law, and a disservice to the law would be done were we to ignore the very real distinctions between the two:

Not honesty alone, but the punctilio of an honor the most sensitive, is then the standard of behavior. As to this there has developed a tradition that is unbending and inveterate. Uncompromising rigidity has been the attitude of courts of equity when petitioned to undermine the rule of undivided loyalty by the "disintegrating erosion" of particular exceptions. . . . Only thus has the level of conduct for fiduciaries been kept at a level higher than that trodden by the crowd. . . .

ERADCO incorrectly argues that *Cogan* stands for the proposition that a breaching fiduciary forfeits only those profits related to the breach. On its face, this argument boldly ignores the above quoted language from *Cogan*. It further ignores the trial court's power of discretion regarding the employ of specific performance. Finally, it fails to recognize that all of the profits arising out of the fiduciary relationship with the plaintiff in *Cogan* were denied. In that case, a real estate broker earned a secret commission by representing two parties in a transaction. The court disallowed all of the profit the fiduciary gained from the plaintiff, the party to whom the fiduciary breached its obligation. Nonetheless, the broker was allowed to retain the other principal's commission, an individual not a party to the action. In the case at hand, ERADCO's claim to 25 percent of the profits arises out of the agreement with the parties to whom it owed, and against whom it breached, a fiduciary duty.

This court has held that a denial of specific performance, in an instance of a fiduciary's breach, is in the sound discretion of the court:

The Restatement (Second) of Agency § 469 (1958) provides: "An agent is entitled to no compensation for conduct which is disobedient or which is a breach of his duty of loyalty." . . .

Therefore, once it determined a fiduciary breach had occurred, it is apparent the trial court did not err when it refused to consider the extent of the breaches, or the extent of the damage suffered by the plaintiffs as a result of those breaches. As reflected, *supra*, the court credited ERADCO the amount of its capital contribution plus interest.

Granting it breached its fiduciary obligation, ERADCO argues that the 74.4 percent of the limited partners who voted for ERADCO's removal and Pace's replacement as general partner breached their fiduciary duty by failing to hold a meeting and failing to notify ERADCO and the remaining limited partners of the proposed action. ERADCO's sole basis for this claim is a sentence in paragraph 14.6 of the agreement that provides: "The laws of the State of Washington pertaining to corporate proxies shall govern all Partnership proxies." ERADCO then cites a section of the Washington Business Corporation Act to support its position.

> Any action required by this title to be taken at a meeting of the shareholders of a corporation, or any action which may be taken at a meeting of the shareholders, may be taken without a meeting if a consent in writing, setting forth the action so taken, is signed by all of the shareholders entitled to vote with respect to the subject matter thereof. . . .

The Court of Appeals correctly held that the language of the Agreement, and the inapplicability of this statute, defeated ERADCO's claim.

As previously quoted, the Agreement provides:

> 14.2 Limited Partners shall only have the right to vote upon the following matters affecting the basic structure of the Partnership:
> 14.2.1 Removal of the General Partner for cause;
> 14.2.2 Election of a successor General Partner . . .

Additionally, the Agreement provides that a majority vote, defined as 66 percent shall effect passage of the action. Paragraph 14.6 provides: "Each unit holder entitled to vote may do so either in person or by *written proxy*."

There is absolutely nothing in the Agreement, however, that requires a meeting be held when a vote is taken by the limited partners. In fact, the language of paragraph 14.6 suggests otherwise when it allows a *written* proxy. Absent a required meeting, RCW 23A.08.265 is inapplicable. Accordingly, we affirm the Court of Appeals on this issue. . . .

## Judgment and Result

Accordingly, we reverse the Court of Appeals holding that the Campus Park LP was dissolved. We affirm the trial court's denial of specific performance of the subordinated profits clause. We affirm the Court of Appeals holding that the limited partners did not breach their fiduciary duties when they removed and replaced ERADCO. Finally, we remand to the trial court for consideration of those issues ruled upon by the Court of Appeals, but not raised in the petitions for review.

## Questions

1. What evidence indicated that the general partners were managing the partnership poorly? How serious is it if someone fails to pay real property taxes for three straight years?
2. May a corporation be a general partner? Does allowing a corporation to be a general partner defeat the purpose of requiring someone to be unlimitedly liable?
3. What danger is present in having a unanimity requirement for removal of the general partner by the limited partners? Explain.

## BUSINESS TRUSTS

It is possible to understand the business trust by first examining the trust device. A trust involves a settlor, a trustee, a beneficiary, and a res. The **settlor** has property that is to be the **res** (the subject matter of the trust). The **beneficiaries** are the person or persons who are to receive the benefits from the trust. The **trustee** is the person or institution that manages the trust property. A peculiar feature of a trust is that it has two titles (owners)—a legal title and a beneficial title. The trustee holds the legal title, and the beneficiary has the beneficial title (also called the *equitable title*). The beneficiary is usually unable or unwilling to manage property. A trust arrangement lets someone else (the trustee) manage the trust property, while another (the beneficiary) receives its benefits. With this background, we now turn to business uses and variations of the trust, including the business trust, the Massachusetts trust, and the real estate investment trust (REIT).

In a **business trust**, the managers are trustees and the shareholders are beneficial owners. The basic feature of the business trust is that property is placed in the hands of trustees who manage and deal with it for the use and benefit of the shareholders (who are the beneficiaries). The similarities to the trust are apparent. It is a specialized application of the conventional trust applicable to a business's organizational form.

The **Massachusetts trust** is a business organization where property is legally owned by trustees who manage the trust property for the benefit of holders of trust certificates, which are similar to stock certificates. The Massachusetts business trust is an unincorporated association organized under Massachusetts law for investing in real estate in much the same way as a mutual fund invests in corporate securities.

A **real estate investment trust (REIT)** is a financial device in which investors buy shares in a trust and the trust res is invested in real estate. The REIT (pronounced "reet") has been both in and out of favor as an investment device in the past decade.

## LIMITED LIABILITY PARTNERSHIPS (LLPs)

The proliferation of lawsuits directed at professionals, such as physicians, has led to the creation of a new legal form, **the limited liability partnership (LLP)**. These entities are creatures of state law, so individual state statutes must be consulted. Generally, however, LLP statutes are patterned after the Uniform Partnership Act with the exception that liability is limited for professional malpractice only. Thus, if five physicians are organized as an LLP and one physician removes a client's liver instead of appendix, only the physician who commits the malpractice will be liable to the injured patient or survivors. On the other hand, if the partnership fails to pay its phone bill, this contract liability is joint among all physician partners.

LLP statutes generally require annual reports to state officials.

## LIMITED LIABILITY COMPANIES (LLCs)

A recent development in business organizations is the **limited liability company (LLC)**. A number of states have passed laws creating variations of the LLC. Such laws are designed to attract business into a state authorizing the LLC, but given the fact that most states now allow such organizations, this objective is likely to be unrealized.

The LLC is a hybrid form of legal organization, taking some of the most advantageous attributes of partnerships *and* corporations and combining them to form the LLC. Specifically, the LLC is an entity similar to a corporation and has shareholders (called *members*) as does a corporation. LLC members have limited liability, as do corporate shareholders. Usually at least two members are required, but this format permits an unlimited number of LLC members (unlike subchapter S corporations). Also, few restrictions are placed on the type of members, and therefore even a corporation could be a "member."

The federal income tax treatment of LLCs is flexible. In 1996, the U.S. Treasury Department and the Internal Revenue Service (IRS) decided to adopt a check-the-box policy for federal income tax treatment of LLCs. Simply put, this regulation would allow LLCs (as well as unincorporated businesses) to decide whether they want to be treated as a corporation or a partnership for such taxes. Formerly, elaborate tests were used to decide whether a business fell into the "partnership" or "corporation" pigeonhole for federal income tax purposes. This new treatment cuts red tape.

However, some state income tax schemes tax LLC income. This problem is an entirely separate legal issue because states are separate sovereigns under federalism principles.

LLCs, however, do have disadvantages. LLC memberships are not freely transferable. This major limitation explains why LLCs have little future for large enterprises where investors often want to exit their investments quickly. Also, as already noted, some states treat LLCs as corporations and impose state income taxes on LLC income—clearly an unfavorable development. Finally, LLCs organized in states allowing such organizations may not have their legal status as LLCs recognized in other states not allowing such organizations.

## CORPORATIONS

Corporations play a major role in our economic and political life. The 2001 edition of the *Statistical Abstract of the United States* estimates that in 1998 (the latest year for which figures are available) 4,849,000 federal tax returns were filed from U.S. corporations. Total receipts for such corporations for the same year were $17.324 trillion, and with income of $1.091 trillion.

### DEFINITION OF A CORPORATION

The word *corporation* derives from the Latin word *corpus*, which means "body." A **corporation** is a legal person, body, or entity. It is intangible. True, many of the assets owned by the corporation, such as the corporate office building, are visible and tangible, as are the corporate officers, directors, and shareholders. They are not, however, the legal corporation.

What, then, is this legal person, body, or entity called a corporation? It is a **legal fiction**. It is made up, a notion created by the law to satisfy certain social and economic needs. The corporate form allows the small investor to participate in capitalism by dividing up corporate ownership into many small pieces, or **shares**. These shares are then sold to the members of the general public. People who purchase corporate shares are known as **shareholders** or **stockholders**. Although the corporate assets and the total stockholder interest in them can be huge, the shares are often sold at comparatively small prices, having no relation to the size of the corporation.

### LIMITED LIABILITY AND TRANSFERABLE SHARES

Another feature of corporations that encourages public purchasing of shares and enables the small investor to participate in corporations is the **limited liability** concept. This idea is an outgrowth of the concept that the corporation is an artificial, legal person. Because a corporation is an entity or a legal person, it can enter contracts. It may be a principal, and as such is liable for its agents' or servants' torts committed and for contracts entered on its behalf within the scope of their employment. However, the shareholders as shareholders generally are not liable for corporate obligations. This rule has some exceptions, but the important point is that one can purchase corporate stock and not be liable for any greater amount to the corporation or corporate creditors. In other words, the financial risk involved in purchasing corporate stock consists only in the amount one agrees to pay for the stock. If the corporation later goes insolvent, the corporate creditors may not seize the shareholders' individual assets to pay the corporate debt.

One other feature promoting popular participation in stock investment is **transferability of shares**. Although restricting share ownership is possible, most large corporations do not. By allowing transfer of its shares, a corporation enables the investor to sell the stock to another, thereby protecting the investor from being locked in to the corporation.

## PROFESSIONAL CORPORATIONS

At one time, professionals such as physicians, attorneys, CPAs, architects, and engineers could not organize in the corporate form. However, today many states allow professionals to create a different type of corporation called a **professional corporation** because all of the shareholders are required to be members of the same profession. Such corporations are often identified with the letters P.A. (professional association), P.C. (professional corporation), or S.C. (service corporation) as part of their name.

One of the major objectives behind professional corporations was to confer limited liability to the professionals/shareholders for the acts of other corporate employees (but not the actor herself or himself) while providing some flexibility in operating the profession or business.

Professionals such as CPAs who are shareholders in a P.C. have limited liability for the P.C.'s debts, with some exceptions. One area presenting an exception involves professional malpractice—negligence related to practicing as a professional. The tort liability of professionals, who are shareholders in a professional corporation, depends on the approach taken by the state's P.C. statute.

For purposes of this discussion, CPAs will be used to represent professionals in general. First, under a conventional corporate approach, one CPA shareholder is not liable for the professional torts of another CPA shareholder. However, some state P.C. statutes make CPA shareholders liable for both their own professional torts and those professional torts of those they supervise. Also, the Model Professional Corporation Act Supplement offers three alternatives, any one of which a state may adopt: (1) treat CPA shareholders as partners for purposes of professional torts (which would make the CPA shareholders vicariously liable for the professional torts of all coworkers); or (2) treat CPA shareholders as they would be treated under conventional corporation statutes (that is, the CPA shareholder would not be liable for other CPA shareholders' professional torts or those of other P.C. employees); or (3) "cap" the CPA shareholders' personal professional liability to an amount by which the P.C. shows financial responsibility (by insurance or surety bond).

Suppose a receptionist negligently spills hot coffee on a client. If this act by a P.C. employee is regarded as a professional tort (as incident to the professional service), the CPA shareholder would not be liable if alternative 2 were followed. However, the CPA shareholder would be liable under alternative 1. If alternative 3 were in effect in the state, the CPA shareholder would be liable up to the statutory cap on damages.

A second exception to limited liability concerns a CPA shareholder's vicarious liability for corporate employees' torts; liability will depend on when and where the tort occurred. Of course a CPA shareholder is personally liable for his or her own torts. Generally, CPA shareholders are liable for coworkers' on-the-job torts but not their off-the-job torts. Thus, if after work, an assistant accountant negligently runs down a little girl while driving to the Kroger store, the assistant accountant, but not the CPA shareholder, would be liable because the tort did not happen on the job.

## SUBCHAPTER S CORPORATIONS

Subchapter S corporations are a creation of the Internal Revenue Code Section 1371 and subsequent sections. This part of the IRC allows small corporations (as defined by the IRC) that meet certain conditions to elect to have undistributed taxable income taxed to its shareholders. The big tax advantage of such corporations is that Subchapter S status usually permits the corporation to avoid *corporate* income taxes, and corporate losses can be attributed to corporate shareholders. Of course corporate shareholders of Subchapter S corporations pay taxes on taxable distributions from the corporation to them.

## CORPORATIONS' CONSTITUTIONAL RIGHTS

A corporation, being a legal person or entity, is a "person" for purposes of both the U.S. and state constitutions. As discussed in Chapter 5, a corporation is a "person" entitled to due process and equal protection of the laws, which extend to people only. Also, corporations are protected by the Fourth Amendment to the U.S. Constitution, which includes the "right of the *people* to be secure in their persons, houses, papers, and effects, against unreasonable searches and seizures" (emphasis added).

However, corporations are not given all the protections possible under the federal Constitution. Corporations have no privilege against self-incrimination under the Fifth Amendment to the U.S. Constitution. Thus, the SEC or IRS could subpoena corporate books or records and the corporation would be unable to block such subpoena. However, corporate officers do have a privilege against self-incrimination regarding their oral testimony on official corporate duties. Thus, they could not be forced to testify orally against themselves, although corporate documents could be used against them.

Also, corporations are not "citizens" within the language of the Constitution conferring on citizens "all privileges and immunities of citizens of the several states." The significance of this distinction lies in the fact that a corporation does not legally exist outside of the state that creates it if *intrastate* (local) business is transacted in a second state. Corporations do exist outside the creating state regarding *interstate* business.

A corporation organized under the laws of California does not exist legally in Nebraska for purposes of doing intrastate business in Nebraska. The people trying to so operate would legally be a partnership unless they *qualified* to do intrastate business as a corporation in Nebraska. Although it is not exactly the same as reincorporating in Nebraska, certain documents must be filed with Nebraska state officials to enable the California corporation to transact intrastate business in Nebraska.

## LAW GOVERNING CORPORATIONS

The previous discussion points out a significant fact: Almost all business corporations are creations of state, not federal, law. Some are corporations federally chartered, such as the Tennessee Valley Authority. Some interest in passing a federal corporation statute pursuant to the national government's power to regulate interstate commerce continues to be mentioned. As of now, such a proposal is merely talk, but from a business standpoint, the advantage of uniformity and being a corporation in all states with one federal incorporation is apparent.

Currently, even though a corporation is created pursuant to one state's corporation law, other states and the national government may have the power to regulate that state's corporation. For example, if the corporation sells its securities in interstate commerce, the federal securities laws require the registration of securities to be sold. Also, as just discussed, if a corporation is organized in one state and does business in another, it will have to qualify to do intrastate business in the other state.

## BASIC CORPORATE DEFINITIONS

*For an example of a large corporation, visit the Web site for General Motors at* **http://www.gm.com**

A **domestic corporation** is organized under the state corporation law of the state in which it is located. For example, a corporation organized under the laws of the state of Michigan is a domestic corporation to the state of Michigan. It is contrasted with a **foreign corporation**, which is a corporation organized under the laws of a state other than the state it is in. For example, a corporation organized under Indiana law would be a foreign corporation in Michigan. The foreign-domestic distinction is unrelated to the physical location of a corporation's assets. Many corporations are Delaware corporations, even though they have little in the way of physical plants or equipment there.

**Governmental corporations** refer to organizations, such as the Federal Deposit Insurance Corporation, that have no profit motive but exist for a social goal. **Municipal corporations** refer to cities and towns that have been given charters by the state to govern a geographic area. **Corporations for profit** are to be contrasted with **corporations not for profit**. Profit corporations are those that may divide profits among shareholders; they do not necessarily have to earn a profit to be so classified. Nonprofit corporations are those that may not turn over earnings to their members. (Nonprofit corporations have no shareholders, merely members.) **Professional corporations** refer to corporations organized by members of certain professions (e.g., physicians, accountants, dentists, and attorneys). The professional corporation is relatively new and offers certain tax advantages and fringe benefits to professionals.

## MODEL BUSINESS CORPORATION ACT

The committee on Corporate Laws of the Section of Corporation, Banking, and Business Law of the American Bar Association is responsible for drafting the **Model Business Corporation Act** (hereinafter called the Model Act or MBCA). The Model Act is, as its name suggests, an attempt to give state legislatures ideas for desirable features that their state corporation statutes should include. It is up to the legislatures of the individual states whether to adopt the Model Act in whole or in part. Thus far, about half of the states have adopted, at least partially, the MBCA.

Why are states adopting the Model Act? In part, to do what the states of Delaware and New Jersey have long engaged in—attracting firms from other states to incorporate under their tax laws so the state can generate revenue from corporate franchise taxes. The Model Act is a liberal act from management's viewpoint. It gives management considerable power, arguably at the expense of corporate shareholders and creditors. For example, shareholders are given the right to examine corporate books and records but are discouraged from exercising this right by requiring that the shareholder either have been a shareholder for at least six months before requesting to see the books or own 5 percent of all outstanding corporate stock. Further, the shareholder must submit a request to see the book in writing and state the reason for the request. The corporation may then grant the shareholder's request at a reasonable time, if the shareholder's request is proper (determined in the first instance by corporate officials). Still, not all provisions of the Model Act are designed to place the shareholders and corporate creditors at the mercy of the corporate directors who are the legal managers of the corporation.

*The Wall Street Journal provides access to present and past business news at http://www.wsj.com*

An example of a provision in the Model Act that better provides a means for corporate creditors to sue the corporation is the **registered agent**. The Model Act requires the continuous maintenance of a registered agent for each corporation formed in a state having that act. In practical terms, this provision benefits the creditor of small, elusive corporations, of which there are many. Trying to find these corporations when one wants to sue them is difficult and frustrating because the corporation may have moved its principal place of business from the address given on the charter filed with the secretary of state. The Model Act says each corporation must maintain a registered agent. One might ask, "Why can't the corporate officials simply fail to designate a registered agent?" In the first instance, they must designate a registered agent as a condition to getting the secretary of state to file their charter so they may legally act as a corporation. Then one might ask, "Why can't the corporate officials let the registered agent resign or retire, or just fire the registered agent?" The Model Act provides that if for any reason the person indicated on the publicly filed document as being the registered agent cannot be located, the secretary of state will be the registered agent and may be served with process to sue the evasive corporation. The practical problem turns to collecting a default judgment against the corporation, but at least the Model Act provides some help to previously distressed litigants who sued corporations.

## HOW CORPORATIONS ARE FORMED

Unlike sole proprietorships and partnerships, corporations may be formed only with official government, usually state, authorization. The state authorization takes the form of granting a **charter** or officially filing articles of incorporation.

Before the 1900s, corporations were formed when a state legislature passed a special statute that granted certain people a corporate charter. As one might suspect, the inducements that led legislators to introduce charter bills in state legislatures for particular people were not always honorable. Bribes to legislators for this purpose were not unusual. However, starting in 1811 in the state of New York, and by the start of the twentieth century in most other states, the general **corporate enabling act** became common.

A general corporate enabling act is a state statute that establishes a procedure by which anyone who complies may become incorporated. The democratization of the ability to incorporate removed much corruption associated with corporate formation, although correspondingly reducing some state legislators' unofficial source of income. Today, virtually all states have general business, corporate enabling statutes that permit anyone to form a business corporation for any lawful purpose. (Sometimes, though, states require three natural persons to incorporate.) Some special requirements, often established by other state corporation statutes, impose stricter formation requirements than do general corporation acts. Businesses supposedly having a strong public interest, such as banks and insurance companies, must usually meet these more stringent formation and operational requirements.

The job of generating the idea and enthusiasm for forming a new corporation belongs to the **corporate promoter**. This person usually sells corporate **share subscriptions** to the corporation to be organized, purchases property, hires employees, and makes necessary leases so that when the corporate existence begins, it will be relatively ready to do business.

## PROMOTERS' PREINCORPORATION LEGAL DUTIES

Promoters of corporations about to be organized face a number of legal problems. If a promoter misrepresents facts about the corporation she or he is forming, the promoter may be liable on either a fraud or breach of fiduciary duty basis to people subscribing for shares in corporations in the organization stage. The promoter who enters preincorporation contracts on behalf of the corporation may face legal problems. The problem is that the contract is between the promoter and the third party (a building lessor, for example); the corporation must be substituted for the promoter on that preincorporation contract after the corporation comes into existence. Four legal theories have been used to effect this substitution: novation, continuing offer, adoption, and ratification.

*Novation.* The novation theory assumes that a new contract is formed between the corporation and the third party once the corporation comes into existence. The promoter drops out of the scene and does not become a party to the new contract. Also, the old contract between the promoter and third party is ended by mutual agreement. If the corporation never comes into existence, or if the corporation comes into existence and does not enter a new agreement with the third person, the promoter is liable for such contracts.

*Continuing Offer.* The continuing offer is another way to hold a corporation liable on a promoter's preincorporation contract. The promoter induces the third person to make an offer to the planned corporation, which can be accepted or rejected when the corporation comes into existence.

*Adoption.* The adoption theory holds a corporation liable on a preincorporation contract made on the yet-to-be-formed corporation's behalf if the corporation's directors, after the corporation comes into existence, approve of the contract and adopt it as their own. Adoption legally takes effect when the corporation approves the preincorporation agreement. Adoption does not relieve the promoter of liability to the third party, however, because basic contract law holds that two persons (in this case, the promoter and the corporation after it comes into existence) may not extinguish a third person's contract rights without his or her consent (in this case, the third party with whom the promoter made the preincorporation contract). What third person will give up a claim against a promoter when he or she does not have to? Thus, adoption is not entirely satisfactory from the promoter's standpoint, although later performance by the corporation on the contract relieves the promoter of liability.

*Ratification.* Ratification is an agency theory. It holds that if a person without authority acts as another's agent in a transaction, and the person for whom the act was done later learns fully of the act and approves it, this person will be bound. In ratification, the purported agent is given retroactive authority to act and is relieved of personal responsibility to the third person for his or her previously unauthorized act. Because ratification relates back in time, the act of the agent is the principal's act when the agent did it, and not later, when the principal ratifies it. The principal's ratification relieves the agent of liability and subjects only the principal to liability to the third person. Thus, in the promoter's reincorporation contract situation, he or she would prefer a jurisdiction that follows the ratification theory rather than the adoption theory of holding corporations for preincorporation contracts made on their behalf. Unfortunately for the promoters, most jurisdictions follow the adoption notion, partly because of the rule that, to have ratification, the principal must exist when the act was done on its behalf. By definition, a preincorporation contract occurs when the corporation does not exist. In such a case, ratification is not possible.

## CORPORATE EXISTENCE

Knowing when corporate existence begins can prevent many problems. The Model Business Corporation Act states that corporate life starts when the responsible public official (often the secretary of state of incorporation) issues the certificate of incorporation. In *Robertson v. Levy* a note was signed in the corporation's name before the corporation came into being. The incorporator was held personally liable on the note in that case.

*Another extensive corporate Web site is General Electric's at* **http://www.ge.com**

## DISREGARD OF CORPORATENESS

Occasionally, someone will follow all of the rules for forming a corporation and a court will nonetheless say that a corporation does not exist. Several legal names indicate this situation, including *alter ego*, *piercing the corporate veil*, and *disregarding corporateness*.

Why would a court say no corporation exists if the rules for forming a corporation have been followed? There are several possibilities.

- The corporation may be used to commit a fraud.
- The corporation may be used contrary to public policy.
- The people running the corporation may be mingling their business with the corporation's so the corporation actually is not a separate entity.

The *Agway, Inc. v. Brooks* case illustrates an attempt to pierce the corporate veil to hold corporate shareholders liable for their corporation's debts.

## Agway, Inc. v. Brooks
Supreme Court of Vermont
790 A. 2d 438 (2001)

### Background and Facts

Agway, Inc. is a farm feed, fertilizer and tool supplier with retail locations in Vermont. In 1981, Agway, the plaintiff, began supplying feed to John and Mary Brooks, for their dairy farm in St. Albans Bay. Plaintiff provided credit to John and Mary Brooks, using a commercial credit agreement that listed the Brooks as owners of a 225-acre farm (with an annual equity value of $300,000), farm equipment, a truck, and a car. This agreement was signed in 1982 and annually thereafter with the last agreement in 1987, and the last billing on this account in May of 1998.

In 1998, John Brooks and his brother, Mark Brooks, formed the "Brooks Brothers Farm" partnership, and appointed John Brooks as the managing partner. At approximately the same time, John Brooks formed a corporation called "Brooks Farm, Inc." owned by the "Brooks Brothers Farm" partnership. John Brooks served as the president and managing director of Brooks Farm, Inc., which issued fifty shares of stock to each of the brothers.

In 1994, plaintiff began supplying feed under a separate account to Brooks Farm, Inc. The account had originally been opened by Brooks Farm in 1984 with no separate credit agreement. In 1994, a credit manager for plaintiff reviewed this account. The credit manager was unable to find a credit application, and he therefore had "Inc." deleted from the account. From 1994 until April of 1998, plaintiff supplied and delivered approximately $45,000 worth of feed and beet pulp per month, under the Brooks Farm account, to John and Mary Brooks's farm.

In October of 1998, plaintiff filed suit against John and Mary Brooks, and later Mark Brooks, as individuals, seeking the balance on the Brooks Farm account as of June of 1998—approximately $154,000—plus interest. Defendants answered the complaint claiming that the debt belonged to the corporation and the suit against them as individuals should be dismissed. The court held a bench trial on January 24, 2000. The court dismissed Mary Brooks as a party but found John and Mark Brooks individually and jointly liable for the $154,000 debt. . . .

In concluding that defendants had failed to respect the corporate form, the court noted that John, Mary, and Mark Brooks owned the major business assets, including the land, livestock, farm buildings, and equipment; and that the corporation owned no assets or leases of any real value. Further, the court determined that John Brooks had moved money between his business and personal account without corporate resolutions or documentation, loaned money from the corporation without notes and repaid them with receipts. The court did not find fraudulent intent but rather determined that John Brooks had failed to "make a distinction between John Brooks the person, and John Brooks as president and managing director of Brooks Farm, Inc." The court concluded that John Brooks had "purposely set up the corporation without assets and ran it without a profit"; had created an undercapitalized corporation with the intention of isolating any business debt from his personal assets; and consequently had given plaintiff the reasonable belief that John and Mark Brooks were acting on their personal behalf rather than on behalf of a corporation. . . .

### Body of Opinion

**Chief Justice Amestoy.** . . . A corporation is a legal construct, limited to the powers given it by the sovereignty that creates it. . . . and generally independent of the individuals who own its stock even when it is owned by a sole shareholder. . . . Although shareholders are not generally liable for the debts of the corporation, shareholders can be held liable where the corporate form has been used to perpetuate a fraud or to shield the shareholders' assets against legitimate claims of a creditor. . . .

The court will look beyond the corporation to its shareholders for liability, that is, pierce the corporate veil, where the corporate form has been used to perpetuate a fraud. . . . and also where the needs of justice dictate. . . . Although an individual will not be held liable merely because he owns all the stock of the corporation, "in an appropriate case, and in furtherance of the ends of justice, a debtor corporation and the individual owning all its stock and assets will be treated as identical, independent of any question of fraud. . . . In cases not involving fraudulent activity, the court will look to the facts and circumstances of each case to determine whether the corporate veil should be pierced in the interests of fairness, equity, and the public need. . . .

In this case, although the trial court did not infer that defendants acted with fraudulent intent, the court found that the distinct corporate identity of Brooks Farm, Inc. was never respected. Our review of the record upon which the trial court based its findings supports its most critical determinations, including that Brooks Farm, Inc. had nothing of value, that there was no credible evidence of arm's length negotiations or lease arrangements for business assets of the corporation notwithstanding corporate resolutions to that effect; that the corporation "acted as a checkbook" to run milk payments through to creditors, that corporate account deliveries were often paid with John Brooks's personal credit cards, and that loans were made to and from the corporate account without notes and paid with receipts. In sum, the evidence viewed in the light most favorable to the prevailing party is a sufficient basis for the trial court's finding that defendant John Brooks purposely undercapitalized Brooks Farm, Inc. with the intention of isolating his debt from business and personal assets.

While it is doubtful that the court would have equitable cause to pierce the corporate veil merely because a closely held corporation did not follow corporate formalities, "equity . . . will not blindly accept mere corporate form over the actual substance of the transactions involved." . . . In this case there was substantial evidence of not only a lack of corporate formality, but more significantly, of the fact that Brooks Farm, Inc. was a mere corporate strawman for the Brooks Brothers Farm partnership and John and Mark Brooks's personal businesses—without assets, capital, or purpose beyond evading contract liability. We will uphold a trial court decision to pierce the corporate veil where it has done so, as in this case, to correct the use of the corporate form to evade legitimate claims of judgment creditors. . . .

## Judgment and Result

The individual shareholders were held personally liable for the corporation's debts.

## Questions

1. In general, in a close corporation (where the stock is owned by only one or a very few people) are the shareholders personally liable for the corporation's debts?
2. Under what circumstances can a corporate shareholder be held personally liable for the corporation's debts? How many of the assets the corporation used in its business were actually owned by the corporation instead of the corporate shareholders?
3. Would an individual shareholder ever be held personally liable for a corporation's debts simply because she owned ALL of the shares in the corporation?

## CORPORATE DIRECTORS

The Model Business Corporation Act declares that the directors are the corporate managers. However, the Model Act permits the charter to vary this requirement by naming another person or persons as corporate managers.

The directors do not have to be residents of the state of incorporation, nor do they have to be shareholders unless the charter so requires. The charter or bylaws may prescribe other director qualifications. The directors have authority to fix their compensation unless the charter provides otherwise.

*Number.* The number of directors may be as few as one or it may be (and usually is) more. The number of directors is fixed in the manner provided by the charter or bylaws, except that the first board of directors is fixed by the charter. The number of directors may be increased or decreased by periodically amending the charter or bylaws. A decrease in the number of directors may not shorten the term of an incumbent director.

*First Board.* The names and addresses of the first board of directors are stated in the charter. The first board of directors holds office until shareholders at the first annual shareholders' meeting elect directors. After that point, directors are normally elected at each annual meeting of the shareholders. A shareholder, unless stipulated otherwise in a special charter or bylaw provision, has as many votes as he or she has shares.

*Term.* A director, after the first board, has a term of office as provided for in the charter or bylaws (often one to three years). A director holds office until the successor has been elected and qualified.

*Vacancies.* Vacancies on the board of directors may be filled by an affirmative vote of a majority of the remaining directors even if it is less than a quorum. A director so elected to fill a vacancy occupies this position only for the unexpired term of the predecessor.

A director ceases being a director through expiration of the term of office, death, corporate dissolution, or removal by shareholders. In the case of director removal by shareholders, any director or all directors may be removed with or without cause by a majority vote of shares (not shareholders) entitled to vote in an election of directors. If the corporation has **cumulative voting**, a director or directors may not be removed if the vote cast against removal would be sufficient to elect such director if cumulatively voted at an election of the entire board.

*Quorum.* A majority of the number of directors established by the charter or bylaws is a quorum to transact business unless the charter or bylaws require more. Once a quorum is established at a directors' meeting, a majority of the quorum is the act of the board unless the charter or bylaws require more.

*Bylaws.* One of the directors' important tasks is the adoption of the first set of corporate bylaws, a set of rules governing internal operation of the corporation. Bylaws regulate who writes salary checks, who signs corporate contracts, how long officers hold office, what sort of notice is appropriate for directors' meetings, and many more equally mundane matters. The bylaws may contain any provision for the regulation and management of corporate affairs not inconsistent with the charter, applicable state and federal statutes, and state and federal constitutions.

*Meetings.* Directors usually hold meetings to decide matters relating to corporate management. Directors' meetings may be held anywhere. Time and place of regular board meetings are usually prescribed in the corporate bylaws. Notice need not be given to directors for regular board meetings. Notice is required, per the bylaws, for special directors' meetings. If a director attends a directors' meeting, notice of such meeting is waived unless the director attends for the sole purpose of objecting to the notice's inadequacy. The business to be discussed or transacted at a regular or special directors' meeting does not have to be mentioned in the meeting notice unless the bylaws require it.

The Model Act, in a sensible departure from tradition, makes it possible for directors to act without holding a meeting if they act unanimously and in writing. The logic of holding meetings is to fully discuss the issues. However, if all agree on a matter, considerations of speed and economy seem to suggest the wisdom of dispensing with meetings.

A question arises as to the validity of director meetings where notice and other procedural rights are not observed. Generally, the answer turns on where the notice requirements are found and against whom nonobservance of them (and, hence, invalidity of the corporate action) is asserted.

*Dividends.* From the shareholders' standpoint, few actions that directors take are as important as declaring dividends. The general rule is that the matter of dividend declaration is solely within the directors' discretion. In some cases a court has passed on the question of whether directors can ever abuse their authority to declare dividends. Dividends may be declared and paid in cash or other property. A distillery once paid its dividends in whiskey.

One limit on dividend declarations by directors is the requirement that **unrestricted, unreserved earned surplus** be available. Dividends may be declared and paid using **treasury shares**. After a dividend has been declared, but before its payment, the shareholders are creditors to the extent of the dividend declared. A stock dividend is merely a movement from the **capital surplus account** to the **paid in capital account** and the corporation's issuance of new pieces of paper (shares) to show that the equity remains the same after declaration and payment of a **stock dividend**, as does each shareholders' pro rata portion of corporate equity. A **stock split** (which entails no movement in the corporate capital accounts but rather a further division of the corporate equity) is not regarded legally as the same thing as issuance of a stock dividend.

*Conflicts of Interest.* A problem associated with corporate directors is that of conflicts of interest. Unlike corporate officers, directors are not agents of the corporation. Thus, directors have no fiduciary duties arising from an agency relationship. They do, however, owe the corporation a duty to avoid conflicts of interest. The Model Business Corporation Act takes a fairly liberal view in favor of upholding transactions in which an interested director transacts business with his or her corporation. The Model Act does not invalidate such transactions provided disclosure of the directors' interest has been made to the other board members (or the shareholders, if they are the approving authority in the matter) and the interested director's vote is not needed to approve the transaction *or* if the contract or transaction is, in fact, fair and reasonable to the corporation. An interested director (or directors) may be counted in calculating the presence of a director's quorum when action is taken on the transaction in question.

The board of directors may delegate its managerial authority to an executive committee if the charter or bylaws allow and a resolution by a majority of the corporate directors allows. If this delegation of authority is done, such action does not relieve the directors of their legal responsibility for corporate management.

*Duty of Care.* Corporate directors have a legal duty to the corporation and its shareholders to exercise independent judgment in making decisions charting the corporation's course in the seas of commerce. Thus, agreements with a shareholder or shareholder group in which directors try to precommit themselves to a particular course of action are invalid. The directors also owe a duty of care in exercising their independent judgment. One case stated this duty of care in the following way: "Corporate directors are not liable for honest mistakes made in the exercise of their authority if they exercise reasonable care and business judgment."

This standard of director care does not obligate directors to ensure the success of their decisions; if it did, directors would become too conservative and not venturesome. The encouragement of risk taking with other people's (corporate) property is called the **business judgment rule**. It protects both corporate directors and officers from damage liability to the corporation and shareholders for good-faith business mistakes. For example, the decision to develop the Edsel automobile was reputedly a $250 million error for the Ford Motor Company, yet no executive was held liable by shareholders or the Ford Motor Company for that blunder.

Another case, *Levine v. Smith*, presented in Discussion Questions at the end of this chapter, showed how the business judgment rule protected the General Motors board of directors when GM shareholders challenged the buyout of GM's largest shareholder, H. Ross Perot.

Another situation giving rise to allegations of director misconduct involves director failure to become sufficiently involved in the details of running the company. Just how involved should a director be in following the details of a business's operations?" The following case, *Barnes v. Andrews*, provides some answers.

## Barnes v. Andrews
U.S. Court of Appeals (2nd Cir.)
298 F. 614 (1924)

### Background and Facts

This is a final hearing on a bill in equity under the General Corporation Law of New York to hold liable the defendant as director for misprision of office. The corporation was organized under the laws of that state to manufacture starters for Ford motors and aeroplanes. On October 9, 1919, about a year after its organization, the defendant took office as a director, and served until he resigned on June 21, 1920. During the period over $500,000 was raised by sales of stock of the company, made through an agent working on commission. A force of officers and employees was hired at substantial salaries, and the factory, already erected when the defendant took office, was equipped with machinery. Starter parts were made in quantity, but delays were experienced in the production of starters as a whole, and the funds of the company were steadily depleted by the running charges.

After the defendant resigned, the company continued business until the spring of 1923, when the plaintiff was appointed receiver, found the company without funds, and realized only a small amount on the sale of its assets. During the incumbency of the defendant there had been only two meetings of directors, one of which (i.e., that of October 9, 1919) he attended; the other happening at a day when he was forced to be absent because of his mother's death. He was a friend of the president, who induced him, as the largest shareholder, to become a director, and his only attention to the affairs of the company consisted of talks with the president as they met from time to time.

The theory of the bill was that the defendant had failed to give adequate attention to the affairs of the company, which had been conducted incompetently and without regard to the waste in salaries during the period before production was possible. This period was unduly prolonged by the incompetence of the factory manager, and disagreements between him and the engineer, upon whose patents the company depended. The officers were unable to induce these men to compromise their differences, and the work languished from incompetence and extravagance. More money was paid the engineer than his royalty contract justified, and money was spent upon fraudulent circulars to induce the purchase of stock.

### Body of Opinion

**Judge Learned Hand.** This cause, may be divided into three parts: First the defendant's general liability for the collapse of the enterprise; second, his specific liability for overpayment made to Delano; third, his specific liability for the expenses of printing pamphlets and circulars used in selling the corporate shares.

The first liability must rest upon the defendant's general inattention to his duties as director. He cannot be charged with neglect in attending directors' meetings, because there were only two during his incumbency and of these he was present at one and had an adequate excuse for his absence from the other. His liability must therefore depend upon his failure in general to keep advised on the conduct of the corporate affairs. The measure of a director's duties in this regard is uncertain; the courts contenting themselves with vague declarations, such as that a director must give reasonable attention to the corporate business. While directors are collectively the managers of the company, they are not expected to interfere individually in the actual conduct of its affairs. To do so would disturb the authority of the officers and destroy their individual responsibility, without which no proper discipline is possible. To them must be left the initiative and the immediate direction of the business; the directors can act individually only by counsel and advice to them. Yet they have an individual duty to keep themselves informed in some detail, and it is this duty which the defendant, in my judgment, failed adequately to perform.

All he did was talk with Maynard as they met, while commuting from Flushing, or at their homes. That, indeed, might be enough because Andrews had no reason to suspect Maynard's candor, nor has any reason to question it been yet disclosed. But it is plain that he did not press him for details, as he should. It is not enough to content oneself with general answers that the business looks promising and that all seems prosperous. Andrews was bound, certainly as the months wore on, to inform himself of what was going on with some particularity, and, if he had done so, he would have learned that there were delays in getting into production which were putting the enterprise in most serious peril. It is entirely clear from his letters of April 14, 1920, and June 21, 1920, that he had made no effort to keep advised of the actual conduct of the corporate affairs, but had allowed himself to be carried along as a figurehead, in complete reliance upon Maynard. In spite of his own substantial investment in the company, which I must assume was as dear to him as it would be to other men, his position required of him more than this. Having accepted a post of confidence, he was charged with an active duty to learn whether the company was moving to production, and why it was not, and to consider, as best he might, what could be done to avoid the conflicts among the personnel, or their incompetence, which was slowly bleeding it to death.

Therefore, I cannot acquit Andrews of misprison in his office, though his integrity is unquestioned. The plaintiff must, however, go further than to show that he should have been more active in his duties. This cause of action rests upon tort, as much though it be a tort of omission as though it had rested upon a positive act. The plaintiff must accept the burden of showing that the performance of the defendant's duties would have avoided loss, and what loss it would have avoided. I pressed Mr. Alger to show me a case in which the courts have held that a director could be charged generally with the collapse of a business in respect of which he had been inattentive, and I am not aware that he has found one. . . .

But when a business fails from general mismanagement, business incapacity, or bad judgment, how is it possible to say that a single director could have made the company successful, or how much in dollars he could have saved? Before this case can go to a master, the plaintiff must show that, had Andrews done his duty, he could have made the company prosper, or at least could have broken its fall. He must show what sum he could have saved the company. Neither of these he has made any effort to do. . . .

It is, indeed, hard to determine just what went wrong in the management of this company. Any conclusion is little better than a guess. Still, some discussion of the facts is necessary, and I shall discuss them. The claim that there were too many general employees turned out to be true, but so far as I can see, only because of the delay in turning out the finished product. Had the factory gone into production in the spring of 1920, I cannot say, and plaintiff cannot prove, that the selling department would have been prematurely or extravagantly organized. The expense of the stock sales was apparently not undue, and, in any event, Andrews was helpless to prevent it, because he found the contract was an existing obligation of the company. So far as I can judge, the company had a fair chance of life, if the factory could have begun to turn out starters at the time expected. . . .

Suppose I charge Andrews with a complete knowledge of all that we have now learned. What action should he have taken, and how can I say that it would have stopped the losses? The plaintiff gives no definite answer to that question. Certainly he has no right to interject himself personally into the tangle; that was for Maynard to unravel. He would scarcely have helped to a solution by adding another cook to the broth. . . .

True, he was not very well-suited by experience for the job he had undertaken, but I cannot hold him on that account. After all, it is the same corporation that chose him which now seeks to charge him. I cannot agree with the language of *Hun v. Cary* that in effect he gave an implied warranty of any special fitness. Directors are not specialists, like lawyers or doctors. They must have good sense, perhaps they must have acquaintance with affairs; but they need not—indeed, perhaps they should not–have any technical talent. They are the general advisers of the business, and if they faithfully give such ability as they have to their charge, it would not be lawful to hold them liable. Must a director guarantee that his judgment is good? Can shareholders call him to account for deficiencies which their votes assured him did not disqualify him for his office? While he may not have been the Cromwell for that Civil War, Andrews did not engage to pay any such role.

I conclude, therefore, as to this first claim that there is no evidence that the defendant's neglect caused any losses to the company, and that, if there were, that loss cannot be ascertained.

The second question is of the defendant's responsibility for overpayments to Delano. . . . I shall, for the sake of argument, assume that he would be chargeable with any sums shown to have been paid to Delano in excess of his right under the contracts made with him. The facts are as follows:

On August 20, 1918, Delano contracted with Stickels, who later assigned his contract to the company, to give him an exclusive license on Delano's patent for a Ford starter over the United States and Canada, for which Stickels was to pay him certain royalties, with a yearly minimum of $15,000, payable quarterly in advance. In the same contract Delano also gave Stickels an exclusive license

on his patent for an aeroplane starter at a unit royalty, with an initial payment of $15,000, should the government give "satisfactory assurance" that a contract with it was "to be had." In addition, Delano was to have a yearly salary of $2,500 as a consulting engineer of the company and $25 a day while acting as such. By a supplemental contract, executed the same day, it was agreed that Delano might cancel the aeroplane license, if in any year the company did not make 1,000 starters. On September 26, 1918, Stickels announced that he was satisfied that he got proper government contracts and the second license went into effect.

The company's yearly engagements were, therefore, $15,000 "dead rent" on the Ford license, and an obligation to manufacture 1,000 aeroplane starters per annum. As the company never made any, Delano was free to cancel that license at any time after January 1, 1920, though not before. It is not clear from the evidence just what was done at that date, nor does it appear whether Delano had earlier received the initial aeroplane payment of $15,000. From the correspondence between him and Stickels . . . I gather that they had paid him $25,000 during January, thus treating the payment of royalties on 1,000 starters as an equivalent of their actual manufacture. That payment they agreed was to cover the year 1920 as well.

The books show payments of $36,500 to Delano for royalties between October 1, 1919, and June 21, 1920, and it is with these that the plaintiff would charge the defendant. . . . Thus, the record shows no excess payments with which on any theory the defendant could be charged, except on the theory that the company should have allowed Delano to cancel the aeroplane license. That however, was in the first place a matter of judgment, in which had he known it, the defendant might without liability have concurred with his fellows, and, in the second, was a question on which I should have no right to assume that his persuasion would have been effective. In judging the decision to hold the license, I should remember that under the modification of January 1920, it covered another year. Who shall say that that was beyond the limits of reasonable decision? As to this branch of the claim the bill must on this record be dismissed; but if, after what I have said, the plaintiff still wished to amend and raise the claim regularly, I will leave the question of amendment open for discussion.

The last question is of the amounts paid out for printing the circulars used to sell stock. There are three answers to this claim: First, that it resulted in no loss to the company; second, that Andrews was not responsible for the supposedly false statements in the circulars; and, third, that the charge is not within the pleadings.

First, it is by virtue of the circular that the company got all its money. However unlawful the means, they succeeded, and the treasury was better off than it would have been without the disbursement. How, then, can a corporation charge a director, while it holds or has enjoyed the fruits of the wrong? The supposedly defrauded stockholders might have rescinded their contract and recovered their payments. In that case the disbursement would be a loss, and all directors who participated in it, or should have stopped it would be liable; but since any such recovery is now impossible, it cannot be said that the plaintiff has suffered. The question becomes at once clear, if we substitute for a corporation an individual principal, who should have innocently used the money fraudulently obtained by his agent. He has suffered no pecuniary loss till he repays the victim or at least till he is sued. The disbursement may have been a wrong to the company, but no damage followed it, and without damage there can be no recovery.

Second, I do not think Andrews should be charged with such detail of supervision as was involved in going over the circulars personally. True, I have held him accountable for not acquainting himself with the conduct of the business more intimately than he did; but there is a limit. It seems to me too much to say that he must read the circulars sent out to prospective purchasers and test them against the facts. That was a matter he might properly leave to the officers charged with that duty. He might assume that those who prepared them would not make them fraudulent. To hold otherwise is practically to charge him with detailed supervision of the business, which, consistently carried out, would have taken most of his time. If a director must go so far as that, there would be no directors. . . .

## Judgment and Result

Plaintiff's claims were dismissed.

## Questions

1. Are directors held to any level of care in supervising corporate functions?
2. Of the plaintiff's three claims—general business failure of the company, overpayment of Delano, and putting out a fraudulent prospectus to sell company stock—which do you think is the strongest to hold a director liable?
3. What is the danger in holding directors to too high a level of care in performance of their duties?
4. Would you say that the *Barnes v Andrews* case supports or undercuts the "business judgment rule," which insulates directors for good-faith errors in corporate decision making?

---

*Director Loans.* A corporation may not loan money or use its credit to assist its directors unless shareholders authorize such acts in the particular matter at hand. However, corporate loans (or credit assistance) are permitted to help any corporate employee (including a director) if a board decides the loan or credit assistance may benefit the corporation. Thus, a corporation-supported credit union for its employees would, no doubt, pass legal muster, but a loan to a director for the purchase of a new sports car would probably not.

*Illegal Acts.* A number of particular problems involve director liability. The first concerns director declarations and authorizations of dividend payments that are contrary to the corporate statutes, charter, or bylaws. If directors engage in such conduct, they are liable to the corporation for such dividends to the extent they exceed what legally could have been declared and paid.

A director is not liable for an illegal dividend if he or she relies and acts in good faith upon the corporate financial statements represented to him or her by the corporate president or officer in charge of the accounting books or presented in a written report by an independent public or certified public accountant fairly to reflect the corporation's financial condition. This reliance assumes the director in good faith determined that the amount was available for any dividends.

Another question of director liability arises where it is unclear how a director voted on a particular matter whose legality is in question. If a director is present at a meeting, he or she is presumed to have agreed with the action taken unless his or her objection is entered in the minutes of the meeting or a written objection is filed at or immediately after the meeting. A director who voted openly for an action at the meeting may not later disclaim liability by filing a dissent to the action taken.

## CORPORATE STOCKHOLDERS

A person who owns a share of corporate stock is called a *stockholder*. A share of stock is illustrated in Figure 18.1. When a corporation first issues stock to stockholders,

## FIGURE 18.1 CORPORATE SHARE CERTIFICATE

they must pay the corporation the full amount for which the shares were issued. Persons who buy, are given, or to whom stock is transferred in good faith and without knowledge the corporation never got full consideration, are not personally liable to the corporation or its creditors for the unpaid part of the consideration.

Each outstanding share of stock has one vote on each matter voted at a shareholder meeting. However, the corporate charter (articles of incorporation) may give more or less than one vote for any share on any matter. Stockholders may vote their shares either in person or by stock proxy. A **stock proxy** is a shareholder's written authorization to someone else to vote the shares. Proxies last for a maximum of eleven months unless the proxy says otherwise. Figure 18.2 provides an example of a proxy.

*A great deal of information investors and stockholders can use can be found at the Web site for CNBC, cable TV's business channel at* **http://www.cnbc.com**

## CORPORATE OFFICERS

Corporate officers consist of a president, one or more vice-presidents as may be prescribed by the bylaws, a secretary, and a treasurer. Any person may hold more than one office at a time, but the offices of president and secretary must be held by different people. The board of directors selects the president, vice-president, secretary, and treasurer. The time and manner of officer selection is usually found in the corporate bylaws. Any other officers, assistant officers, or agents who are necessary may be elected or appointed by the board or chosen as the bylaws prescribe.

## FIGURE 18.2 CORPORATE STOCK PROXY

**E. I. DU PONT DE NEMOURS AND COMPANY**
**THIS PROXY IS SOLICITED BY ORDER OF THE BOARD OF DIRECTORS**

**P R O X Y**

The undersigned hereby appoints W. S. Carpenter, Jr., L. du P. Copeland, C. H. Greenewalt, and C. B. McCoy, or any of them, each with power of substitution, as proxies for the undersigned to attend the annual meeting of stockholders of said Company to be held in the Ballroom of the Hotel du Pont, Wilmington, Delaware, at 12 o'clock noon, on April 12, 1971, and thereat, or at any adjournment thereof, to vote and act with respect to all shares of the Common Stock of said Company which the undersigned is entitled to vote upon the election of directors, and upon the proposals set forth in the proxy statement for said meeting, and, in their discretion, upon any matters not known to the management at the time of the solicitation of this proxy which may properly come before the meeting; hereby ratifies and confirms all that said proxies or any of them or any substitute may lawfully do or cause to be done by virtue thereof, and hereby revokes all proxies heretofore given.

The undersigned instructs such proxies to vote FOR ☐ or NOT VOTE ☐ for the election of directors. The undersigned also instructs such proxies to vote as directed on the reverse side with respect to the nine proposals. If no direction is given, the shares represented by this proxy will be voted "For" the election of directors and "For" Proposal 1 and "Against" Proposals 2 through 9 as set forth in the Proxy Statement on the pages indicated.

The Board of Directors favors a vote "For" Management Proposal No. 1:           NO.066568
No. 1 (Page 10 of Proxy Statement)  For ☐ Against ☐

The Board of Directors favors a vote "Against" Stockholder Proposals Nos. 2 through 9:
No. 2 (Page 10 of Proxy Statement)  For ☐ Against ☐ | No. 6 (Page 14 of Proxy Statement) For ☐ Against ☐
No. 3 (Page 12 of Proxy Statement)  For ☐ Against ☐ | No. 7 (Page 15 of Proxy Statement) For ☐ Against ☐
No. 4 (Page 13 of Proxy Statement)  For ☐ Against ☐ | No. 8 (Page 15 of Proxy Statement) For ☐ Against ☐
No. 5 (Page 13 of Proxy Statement)  For ☐ Against ☐ | No. 9 (Page 16 of Proxy Statement) For ☐ Against ☐

PLEASE SIGN, DATE AND RETURN THIS PROXY, USING THE ENCLOSED POSTAGE PREPAID ENVELOPE

JOHN SMITH                                                30 SHARES
768 YOSEMITE DRIVE
MILFORD OH 45015                          066568

⑈066568⑈
Number used for machine counting of the vote

Dated_____1971. SIGN HERE_____
When signing as attorney, executor, administrator, trustee or guardian, please give full title as such. If the signer is a corporation, sign in the full corporate name by duly authorized officer

Agency law determines the relationship between a corporation and its officers. The corporation is the principal, and the officer is the agent. The types of agent's authority discussed in Chapter 14—express, implied, and apparent authority and ratification—apply to corporate officers. The express authority (and duties) of corporate officers and agents comes at least in part from the corporate bylaws. Also, board resolutions, which are formal acts of corporations and other official bodies, may spell out in greater detail the powers given to specific officers. For example, the bylaws may empower the corporate treasurer to handle the corporation's financial affairs.

A board resolution might further say that the treasurer may sign payroll checks if countersigned by the president. Implied authority for officers is that which is usual and necessary to carry out the express authority. Reference would have to be made to the express authority to determine the nature and extent of implied authority. Apparent authority comes from corporate officials' acting in an official capacity, which reasonably leads a third person to believe the officers have authority to engage in a task. Ratification occurs if the corporate principals (most likely, the directors) retroactively approve an act by an officer for which the officer had no authority to perform.

The length of time that a corporate officer holds office is determined by the corporate bylaws or the officer's employment contract. A principal always has the power, but not necessarily the right, to end an agent's employment. Thus, a corporation could always fire an officer, but it would be liable to the officer for breach of contract. The board of directors is the "person" having the authority to remove corporate officers.

## COMPARING BUSINESS FORMS

Corporations are inevitably compared with sole proprietorships, partnerships, and limited partnerships as organizational forms for carrying on business. Which is the best legal form for a business? The answer depends on the business and the businesspeople's objectives. Each has advantages and disadvantages based on its ease of formation, ease of operation (for example, absence of government red tape), attractiveness of the form as an investment vehicle, tax considerations, privacy, and control.

### CORPORATIONS

The corporate form scores well on attractiveness as an investment vehicle. Its limited liability feature for shareholders and its divisible share ownership whereby investors are not obligated to manage the corporation are attractive to the financially well-heeled and lazy investor. At best, the corporate form earns mediocre grades for ease of formation and ease of operation. Corporate formation has been eased by the Model Business Corporation Act, which requires only one incorporator, shareholder, and director for a one-person corporation. However, state approval is required, minimum capitalization is mandatory ($1,000, according to many state corporation laws), and reports to state government are necessary. All these factors hinder operation as a corporation. Corporate tax considerations likewise do not all cut unfavorably or favorably. Corporations are subject to federal, state, and municipal taxes. Corporations must also pay annual franchise taxes to the creating state government. (Workers' compensation tax, Social Security tax, and unemployment taxes must be paid by an employer regardless of the employer's legal form.)

Two taxing events arise when a corporation earns net income and distributes part or all of that income to its shareholders. The corporation itself pays a tax on that income, and the shareholder recipients of dividends pay a tax on the dividend income. Critics of the tax system refer to this as double taxation. However, practically speaking, this double taxation can be and frequently is eliminated in **close corporations** (corporations with few shareholders) where the shareholders and officers are the same people. In such situations, generous expense accounts and inflated salaries are given to corporate officers so that the profit or net taxable corporate income is low. Then little taxable income for the corporation and few taxable dividends for the shareholders remain.

Based on the hypothesis that the corporate officers and shareholders are the same people, giving officers the inflated salaries and expense accounts is a way to give them their dividends so that they are tax deductible to the corporation.

A warning is in order: The Internal Revenue Service is aware of this gimmick and limits corporate salaries to reasonable levels. Considerable manipulation and straining are done to establish a salary as reasonable. Also, certain small corporations may qualify for federal income taxation as Subchapter S corporations, which also eliminates double taxation. In larger corporations that are not close corporations, the ability to inflate corporate officers' salaries and expense accounts is also present, but its effect is negligible due to the comparatively small portion that officers' salaries and expense accounts take from total corporate profits.

Privacy and control are generally negative factors with respect to the corporate form. If a corporation's securities are registered for purposes of the Securities Act of 1933 or the Securities Exchange Act of 1934, the firm's financial statements are available to any member of the public. Also, corporate annual and quarterly reports are available to any shareholder in the company, no matter how small the holding. Thus, to learn what any corporation's net income is and other aspects of its operations, all a person has to do is buy one share of its stock. All annual reports with summaries of the firm's financial operations would be forthcoming. A limit on such availability of corporate information is the availability of its shares. If shares in a corporation are not for sale, they then are not a source of information. Stocks unlisted on a securities exchange are often unavailable for public purchase.

Control is a controversial area of corporate law. Legally, shareholders (the corporation's owners) are separated from management (the board of directors), which is not to say that shareholders may not be directors. Rather, directors are not required under corporate law to be shareholders. Directors thus do not have to own enough stock to elect themselves to the board. They merely have to win the votes of enough shares of owners to elect them to the board.

A number of commentators have discussed this phenomenon of separation of corporate ownership from control. Some commentators see a danger in this phenomenon in that accountability and efficiency are possibly lost when property owners do not control or decide matters concerning their property. The separation of ownership and control in corporations is not inevitable, however. Certainly, in close corporations the shareholders and directors are the same people. This separation is present in the largest corporations that produce the bulk of the nation's goods.

## SOLE PROPRIETORSHIPS

Sole proprietorships get favorable marks on ease of formation (no government approval or forms are required to organize them), ease of operation (books are not legally required, except for income tax purposes, and no annual reports need be sent to owners or government agencies except tax officials), and privacy (no reports are filed with regulatory agencies and therefore are not available to those who want to know how much money one makes). Sole proprietors also have, by definition, sole control of operation of their business. This control is a plus for this legal form.

Sole proprietorships get fair marks on taxation, particularly federal income taxation, because net income is taxable once to the sole proprietor, eliminating the double taxation present with corporation income. Also, various tax shelters such as annuities and Keogh plans are available to sole proprietors to diminish their federal income tax liability. Sole proprietors pay Social Security tax on net income over a certain minimum dollar amount at a certain percentage rate (15.30 percent in 1990 and beyond). It can actually be an advantage for a sole proprietor to pay some Social-Security tax, because to qualify for some of the preretirement disability benefits that are part of Social Security, a person must have paid Social Security taxes for a certain minimum number of quarters.

The factor on which sole proprietorships receive their least favorable mark is probably attractiveness to investors, because sole proprietorships are not designed to be joint or group undertakings. Any investment in the equity or capital of the business would likely turn the sole proprietorship into a partnership. Also, sole proprietors are vulnerable to unlimited personal liability to business creditors.

## PARTNERSHIPS

Partnership pros and cons are mentioned here briefly in relation to the six criteria used to compare partnerships to other business forms. Partnerships are easy to form. No written partnership agreement is necessarily required for most partnerships. No government permission is needed to organize them, nor is any legal minimum capital necessary. Also, only two persons are required to form a partnership, although it may include more. Ease of operation is high for partnerships, owing to the general absence of government supervision. However, partnerships are unattractive to potential investors (as partners, at least) due to the unlimited personal liability each partner has for all partnership debts.

Tax considerations are usually favorable for partnerships. The double taxation present for many corporations is lacking in partnerships. A partnership generally is not an entity for federal income tax purposes. Such federal taxes fall only once on partners, not on the partnership, as a general rule. Also, tax shelters such as Keogh plans and tax-sheltered annuities are available to partnerships. Privacy is generally great in a partnership, owing to the unavailability of public reports on partners' activities. Control, likewise, does not have to be shared with shareholders, although other partners have a right to manage, unless this right is given up as part of the partnership agreement.

## LIMITED PARTNERSHIPS

From the limited partner's standpoint, many of the attributes of limited partnership bear close resemblance to the corporation's. Thus, a limited partnership is an attractive investment vehicle in terms of potential liability to the limited partner, because his or her liability is limited to the amount contributed to the business. On the other hand, a limited partnership requires a state statute allowing such organizations to be formed. State approval must be obtained before forming these organizations, which means filling out forms and dealing with red tape.

The number of reports limited partnerships must file is not as great as with corporations. Tax ramifications for limited partnerships are generally about the same as for partnerships. Limited partnerships offer less privacy than partnerships, owing to the public filing of information pursuant to forming the limited partnership.

The control that a limited partner has in a limited partnership could be less than that of a shareholder, because the shareholder has a right to be a corporate director if she or he is able to muster sufficient votes to win a directorship. In a small corporation, being voted a director is a distinct possibility. This opportunity fades as corporate size increases. Thus, a shareholder could exercise some control over corporate management. In contrast, limited partners have no right to manage a limited partnership's assets, and if they do, their character as limited partners is lost, and with it they become personally liable for all the partnership's obligations. Table 18.1 compares sole proprietorships, partnerships, and corporations as legal forms for business.

## TABLE 18.1 COMPARING LEGAL FORMS OF BUSINESS

| Business Organiz-ational Form | Ease of Formation | Ease of Operation | Liability Exposure | Tax Consid-erations | Privacy | Control |
|---|---|---|---|---|---|---|
| 1. **Sole propri-etorship** | Easy to form; no agreement required. | Simplest form, except for govern-mental reports. | Unfavorable; unlimited personal liability. | No double taxation, but sole proprietor's income is subject to federal income taxation. | Yes; some reports. | Sole proprietor controls except for governmental regulation. |
| 2. **Partnership** | Easy to form; no written agreement required, but one is advisable; two or more carrying on as co-owners a business for profit; could have a partnership and not be aware of it; possible partnership share subject to registration as a security. | Easy to operate, except for governmental reports. | Unfavorable; unlimited personal liability for each partner for all partnership debts; any change in partnership membership dissolves partnership. | No double taxation; partnership income not taxed at partnership level but passes to individual partners, where it is taxed at individual tax rates. | Yes, except possible reports filed with governmental agencies may be public records. | Each partner has equal right to manage regardless of capital contribution unless contrary agreement. |
| 3. **Corporation** | Need state authorization (charter); possible need to register corporate securities before offering to public. | Neutral to poor; many governmental reports possible. | Favorable; shareholder liability limited to share subscription or share amount; shareholder not personally liable for corporate debts unless guarantor of them. | Favorable to poor depending on number of shareholders; double taxation (two taxing events) possible when corporate income taxed and shareholder dividend income taxed; Subchapter S corporation avoids double taxation. | Least private business form; corporate charter (articles of incorporation) is public record; various reports filed with federal agencies may be public records. | Management control of proxy system results in shareholder loss of control of board of directors in corporations with large number of shareholders. |

## CHAPTER SUMMARY

The U.S. legal system offers businesses a variety of legal forms in which to organize, including the sole proprietorship, the partnership, the limited partnership, the business trust, and the corporation.

In recent years, sole proprietorships in the United States numbered more than 16 million. Few legal formalities are involved in setting up sole proprietorships. Obtaining occupational and sales tax licenses are two requirements. However, sole proprietorships must obey the OSHA, Social Security, environmental, and many other laws that regulate businesses organized in other forms.

Partnerships in the United States number more than 1.58 million. Partnerships are associations of two or more persons to carry on as co-owners a business for a profit. The Uniform Partnership Act, which is the law in virtually all fifty states, governs the formation, operation, and termination of partnerships. Several persons can have a business partnership but be unaware that they are in one. An objective test is used to decide whether a partnership exists. Partners are personally liable for copartners' and partnership employees' torts committed within the scope of the partnership. Agency rules apply in determining whether partners have authority to act for the partnership. Partnerships can own property in the partnership name. Property used in a partnership can also be owned by individual partners.

Limited partnerships can be formed if states have statutes permitting their organization. Virtually all states have such statutes. Limited partnerships must have at least one general partner (who has unlimited liability for partnership obligations) and may have any number of limited partners (who have limited personal liability for the partnership's debts).

Corporations are legal, artificial persons. Most business corporations are created under state corporation statutes. Corporate shareholders generally have limited personal liability for corporate debts. The corporate charter (also known as the articles of incorporation) must be filed with and approved by the state of incorporation. A business corporation generally may incorporate in any state. Corporations can have perpetual life. The business judgment rule provides some protection for corporate management from damage liability to corporate shareholders and the corporation when management decisions prove financially unsuccessful.

When comparing the different forms of business organization, an entrepreneur should consider factors such as ease of formation, ease of operation, liability exposure, tax considerations, privacy, and control.

---

### ■ MANAGER'S ETHICAL DILEMMA ■

"I think it's wrong," said Harmon Wilcox. Harmon had loaned $1 million to his friend, Eddie Dow, or rather, Eddie's corporation, Dow Oldsmobile, Inc. Auto sales had fallen after gasoline prices had shot up following the most recent Mideast crisis. Consequently, Dow Olds, Inc. was unable to repay the loan. Now Harmon went to Eddie Dow and said, "Look, Eddie, we've been friends for years. You repay the loan your corporation obtained from me."

Eddie replied, "Harmon, look, I didn't borrow anything from you. My corporation did. It owes you the money—not me."

Harmon would hear none of that legal mumbo jumbo. "You borrowed the money. The law looks at substance, not form. No corporation walked into my office and asked for the loan. You did. Now you pay up."

What ethics are involved here?

## DISCUSSION QUESTIONS

1. H. Ross Perot was a General Motors (GM) director because he was GM's largest shareholder and thus could elect himself to the board of directors. He was publicly critical of GM's management. GM decided to remove Perot from its board by offering to buy his GM shares for almost $750 million—a "giant premium." Mr. Grobow and certain other GM shareholders thought GM's board was paying Perot "hush mail" in making the offer. They sued the GM board and Perot for wasting corporate assets in making such an offer. The GM board claimed that the "business judgment rule" made its offer to Perot legal. Who was correct? [*Levine v. Smith*, 591 A.2d 194 (1991)].

2. Which factors should a businessperson consider in selecting a legal form? Which factor is the most important? Is it advisable to answer the preceding question without knowing the nature and particulars of a person's business?

3. Jim Wheeler believed he had a great idea—turn used newspaper into cattle feed. He bought the necessary equipment, leased a building, and hired several employees. He signed contracts for these items as an agent for Delta Corporation. Delta had not yet been legally organized. Later, it came into existence as a Texas corporation. What is Jim's personal liability for Delta's preincorporation contracts?

4. A creditor sued a person he claimed was a partner, for partnership debts. The person the creditor claimed was a partner said he had no voice in partnership management even though he had cosigned a partnership note. Was the cosigner of a partnership note a partner? [*J.M. Schultz Seed Co. v. Roberts*, 451 N.E.2d 62 (Ind. App. 1983)].

5. Defendants loaned money to the KNK partnership. They put a number of terms in the loan agreement designed to ensure that KNK would be able to repay the loan.

   a. A statement was included in the agreement to the effect that defendants as creditors specifically said that they were creditors and not the borrowers' partners.

   b. Debtors were to receive their loan repayment from sharing their debtors' profits.

   c. Defendants had the option to become the borrowers' partners at a future date.

   d. Defendants called themselves trustees rather than partners.

   e. Defendants loaned securities instead of money.

   f. The securities that defendants loaned were not to be commingled with the borrowers' property.

   g. Defendants were at all times to be kept informed regarding transactions affecting the defendants' loan.

   h. Defendants were to receive all dividends and income accruing from the loaned securities.

   i. Defendants' borrowers could, with defendants' consent, substitute securities of equal value for any of the securities loaned.

   j. Borrowers could, with defendants' consent, sell any of the securities loaned to them if the proceeds went to the defendants. Another creditor of the KNK partnership claimed this loan agreement contained enough partnership elements to make the creditors partners in the KNK partnership. Was this creditor correct? [*Martin v. Peyton*, 246 N.Y. 213, 158 N.E. 77 (1927)].

6. A limited partnership agreement was signed by all the "partners." However, no one filed a limited partnership certificate with the appropriate public office. Did a limited partnership exist? [*Blow v. Shaughnessy*, 68 N.C. App. 1, 313 S.E.2d 868 (1984)].

7. Is use of a person's name in a business with that person's knowledge enough to justify finding the person was "held out" as a partner to establish liability under the doctrine of partnership estoppel? [*Brown v. Gerstein*, 460 N.E.2d 1043, 17 Mass. App.Ct. 558 (1984)].

### INFOTRAC KEYWORDS

**Use your InfoTrac password to look up articles on http://www.infotrac-college.com**

Keywords: *Partnerships, sole proprietorships, limited partnerships, business trusts, LLPs, LLCs, Subchapter S Corporations, Model Business Corporation Act.*

For suggested readings, please visit this book's Web site at **http://fisher.westbuslaw.com** (click on "Internet Applications").

# SECURITIES REGULATION

## POSITIVE LAW ETHICAL PROBLEMS

"You defrauded me! I trusted you. You were my broker. You sold the securities in my account and converted the proceeds for your own purposes without my approval," shouted Mr. William Wood, an elderly man in poor health, to his broker, Charles Zandford.

"So what are you going to do about it?" asked Mr. Zandford, Wood's former broker.

"I'm going to ask the SEC to sue you for fraud under section 10-b of the Securities Exchange Act of 1934," replied Wood.

"Well, they will lose because that law requires that the fraud be 'in connection with the sale or purchase of a security.' I didn't commit fraud when I sold your securities. I committed the fraud later, when I stole the money from your account, so the 1934 Act is inapplicable," answered Zandford.

Does the 1934 Securities and Exchange Act cover frauds occurring after a security is sold and in a broker's account where the securities are sold by the broker who "runs off with the client's money"? Are such frauds "in connection with the purchase or sale of a security"?

"How large must an error be in a corporation's SEC registration statement before it is 'material'?" asked Mary Barker. Mary had just lost money on BarChris Corp's bonds. She had invested after having read BarChris's financial statements included in the registration statement.

Ralph Foster, Mary's lawyer, replied, "Well, if the error would deter you, a reasonable investor, from putting your money in this company at the time you invested, it is 'material.' What sort of 'errors' were in BarChris's financials?"

"The registration statement said that the earnings per share were 75 cents, when they were actually 65 cents. Annual earnings of BarChris were said to be $9.1 million when, in fact, they were $8.5 million—an overstatement of more than $600,000. Contingent liabilities were said to be $750,000, when they actually were $1.1 million—about a 50 percent error."

Were these errors significant enough to be considered "material" entitling investors to recover their losses from BarChris directors?

*"TICKER TAPE AIN'T SPAGHETTI."*

— Fiorello LaGuardia

Federal securities laws are controversial. Investors' feelings vary. Some say, "These laws are great because they give me information to invest and protection if something goes wrong." Other investors are ignorant about the protections that such laws provide.

Businesses subject to federal securities laws also have mixed feelings about them. Some firms see such laws as evidence of the heavy hand of government regulation. They claim such rules add compliance costs and slow securities marketing.

They also say that such laws give the average investor more information than needed to make an investment decision. Other businesses accept securities regulation as a fact of life. They see it as necessary to keep out scoundrels and to maintain public confidence in the many reputable securities businesses.

## FEDERAL SECURITIES LAWS

When we speak of the federal securities laws, we are referring to twelve federal laws—six passed between 1933 and 1940, one enacted in 1968, two enacted in the 1970s, one enacted in 1984, one enacted in 1995, and one enacted in 2002:

1. The Securities Act of 1933
2. The Securities Exchange Act of 1934
3. The Public Utility Holding Company Act of 1935
4. The Trust Indenture Act of 1939
5. The Investment Company Act of 1940
6. The Investment Advisers Act of 1940
7. The Williams Act of 1968
8. The Securities Investor Protection Act of 1970
9. The Foreign Corrupt Practices Act of 1977
10. The Insider Trading Sanctions Act of 1984
11. The Private Securities Litigation Reform Act of 1995
12. The Sarbanes–Oxley Act of 2002

We look at each of these laws briefly and then examine in depth the Securities Act of 1933, the Securities Exchange Act of 1934, and the Foreign Corrupt Practices Act of 1977 (an amendment to the 1934 act).

### SECURITIES ACT OF 1933

The Wall Street Journal *Web site is a good place to keep up-to-date on federal securities laws and SEC rulings:* **http://www.wsj.com**

The Securities Act of 1933 (SA) sets out the rules for selling securities to the investing public. It basically deals with the **primary market** (the sale of new or just issued securities). Its main requirement is that securities be registered with the federal Securities and Exchange Commission before they are offered or sold.

### SECURITIES EXCHANGE ACT OF 1934

The Securities Act deals with the primary markets (*new* securities). Regulating all of the old securities bought and sold daily (the **secondary markets**) is a job of the Securities Exchange Act of 1934 (SEA). The SEA also created the Securities and Exchange Commission (SEC) to administer and enforce the federal securities laws.

### PUBLIC UTILITY HOLDING COMPANY ACT OF 1935

The Public Utility Holding Company Act of 1935 (PUHCA), administered by the SEC, aims to stop abuses in the financing and operations of gas and electric public utility holding companies.

## TRUST INDENTURE ACT OF 1939

The Trust Indenture Act of 1939 (TIA) regulates sale of debt securities (such as bonds) to the public. The law requires debt securities registered under the SA to satisfy TIA requirements as well. The TIA requires that the debt contract (trust indenture) contain certain provisions (which the SA does not require) to protect investors.

Some debt arrangements have a trustee who is supposed to look out for the lenders' (creditors') interest. The TIA requires that the trustee be independent of obligations other than those of the investors that the trustee is supposed to represent.

## INVESTMENT COMPANY ACT OF 1940

The Investment Company Act of 1940 (ICA) lets the SEC regulate publicly owned companies that invest and trade in securities. The ICA controls who can be managers, how much management can be paid, and how large sales charges can be. The authority of the ICA also extends to regulating the investment strategies of publicly owned companies and other such matters.

## INVESTMENT ADVISORS ACT OF 1940

The Investment Advisors Act of 1940 (IAA) gives the SEC the authority to regulate investment advisors. These are people who tell others where to invest their money.

## WILLIAMS ACT OF 1968

The Williams Act attempts to regulate tender offers (corporate takeovers brought about by the purchase by one corporation of another corporation's stock). Congress passed the Williams Act in 1968 in response to the increasing number of **hostile tender offers** in which the corporation targeted to be taken over does not want to be taken over.

The Williams Act sets requirements in two basic areas. First, it requires the offeror (person trying to take over a corporation) to file a statement disclosing information about the offer. Second, the Williams Act sets out procedural rules on tender offers (for instance, whether stockholders who tender their shares to the offeror may later withdraw their offer).

Individual states have also passed statutes that attempt to limit takeovers. These laws have been challenged on the grounds that, among other things, the Williams Act preempts them. In 1987 the U.S. Supreme Court held in *CTS Corporation v. Dynamics Corporation* that state statutes regulating tender offers are valid if they do not frustrate the Williams Act's purposes. In other words, it is possible that both state and federal statutes could regulate corporate takeovers.

## SECURITIES INVESTOR PROTECTION ACT OF 1970

The Securities Investor Protection Act of 1970 (SIPA) set up a federal corporation (Securities Investor Protection Corporation, or SIPC) to administer the liquidation of brokerage firms having financial problems. For example, investors whose stockbrokers are forced out of business by financial problems would present their claims to the SIPC for payment.

## FOREIGN CORRUPT PRACTICES ACT OF 1977

The Foreign Corrupt Practices Act of 1977 (FCPA) grew out of revelations in the 1970s that U.S. businesses would sometimes have to bribe foreign government officials, political parties, or political candidates to get business. The FCPA prohibits certain bribes to foreign officials and requires that certain businesses set up systems of internal control to enable responsible managers to know if such activity is going on. Greater discussion of this important law comes later in the chapter. The FCPA was amended in 1988.

## INSIDER TRADING SANCTIONS ACT OF 1984

In recent years, scandals have occurred involving corporate insider trading. Such trading undermines public confidence in the securities markets. To increase the risk to those engaging in insider trading, Congress enacted the Insider Trading Sanctions Act of 1984. This law significantly increases the possible punishment for those caught trading on inside information.

## PRIVATE SECURITIES LITIGATION REFORM ACT OF 1995

Current financial news and analysis can be found at **http://www.foxnews.com/cavuto**

Prior to passage of the Private Securities Litigation Reform Act of 1995 Congress found considerable evidence that abusive and meritless lawsuits were threatening the U.S. capital markets. These lawsuits were being generated by aggressive plaintiffs' attorneys, who would find investors who had lost money in high-risk companies such as computer technology firms or bio-tech companies and convince them that they could sue such companies alleging errors in documents filed with the SEC (such as registration statements). If such errors were found (or even alleged), often the companies found it cheaper to settle rather than fight the matter out in court where litigation costs can be astronomical.

In response to such perceived exploitative litigation, Congress passed the Private Securities Litigation Reform Act over President Clinton's veto. Some of the more significant features follow.

1. *This act replaces joint and several liability with proportionate liability in certain cases under the Securities Act of 1933 and Securities Exchange Act of 1934.* Specifically, under section 11 of the 1933 Act (which covers *primary offerings*), the joint and several liability rule no longer covers "outside directors." Under the 1934 SE Act (covering secondary offerings), joint and several liability no longer applies with respect to almost any defendant. Therefore, defendants' liability in such cases is limited to only the harm they caused the defendants. Prior to this change, a public accounting firm, for example, could be held liable for the entire loss plaintiff suffered even if the accounting firm were only 5 percent at fault. Exceptions to the elimination of "joint and several" liability include defendants who "knowingly" violate the securities laws.
2. *The act limits private class actions.* The biggest protection here is a requirement that the "lead plaintiff" be the "most adequate plaintiff" for all shareholders. A judge determines who the lead plaintiff is, usually the largest shareholder in the class. Before this act, a "professional plaintiff" could buy a share of stock in the company to be sued, join with an "entrepreneurial attorney," and if they

were the first to file the class action, they effectively controlled the entire class of stock. Now, professional plaintiffs are limited to major shareholders certified by a court.

3. *The act establishes penalties for abusive litigation.* Courts have the authority to shift defendants' attorney fees to plaintiffs for defenders against litigation held by a court to be without merit.

4. *The act limits damages.* Under the 1934 SE Act, the damages are limited to the difference between the purchase or sales price paid and the mean trading price of the security over a 90-day period, starting when the alleged misstatements about the security were given to the market.

5. *The act imposes whistle-blowing duties on independent public auditors who examine firms subject to federal securities acts.* Public auditors must bypass the issuer's management and whistle-blow directly to the board of directors if management has not taken appropriate action to remedy an illegal act reasonably likely to materially affect the issuer's financial statements. Also, the board must notify the SEC one business day after receiving the auditors' report and send a copy of the notice to the auditors. If they do not get this directors' notice to the SEC within one business day, the auditors must resign or themselves notify the SEC.

6. *Securities fraud is not a Racketeer Influenced Corrupt Organization Act (RICO) offense.* This provision has favorable damage implications for securities act defendants who have committed certain other offenses within a 10-year period.

7. *The act creates a "safe harbor" for certain forward-looking statements that issuers might wish to make concerning future earnings.* A problem with such statements in the past has been that potential investors rely too heavily on issuers' rosy earnings projections only to be disappointed when future profits do not appear and share prices drop. Disappointed investors are inclined to sue under the securities laws alleging they were misled by material statements or omissions in registration statements.

Forward-looking statements (such as earnings projections) by the issuer are legal if identified by the issuer as "forward-looking" and accompanied by cautionary statements that identify important factors that could cause actual results to differ materially from the forward-looking statement. Forward-looking statements can be oral or written. No duty requires that forward-looking statements later be updated.

The 1995 Act exempts forward-looking statements made by the issuer, a person acting on the issuer's behalf, an outside reviewer retained by the issuer to "tout" the issue, or an underwriter with respect to information provided by the issuer or derived from such information. This safe harbor rule does not apply if the issuer was convicted of certain felonies or has been subject to judicial decrees relating to securities law violations. Also, the safe harbor for forward-looking statements is unavailable for such statements regarding blank-check companies, issues of penny stocks, and going private transactions. Additionally, not covered by the safe harbor for forward-looking statements are such statements in financial statements conforming with generally accepted accounting principles (GAAP), representations in registration statement made in connection with tender offers or initial public offerings, and certain other situations.

## Sarbanes–Oxley Act of 2002

The Sarbanes–Oxley Act of 2002 is an outgrowth of the Enron, Tyco, Waste Management, and other management and accounting scandals in the late twentieth and early twenty-first centuries. The act is more than seventy pages long and deals with several topics:

1. *It establishes a Public Company Accounting Oversight Board.* The board can regulate, investigate, and oversee the accounting industry. It can also discipline accountants. The SEC has authority over this board.
2. *The act prohibits accountants from offering several types of consulting services to their audit clients who are publicly traded companies.*
3. *The act requires rotation of the "lead" auditor for a client every 5 years.*
4. *Certain document destruction is forbidden under federal obstruction of justice laws.* Penalties for such acts are increased to up to twenty years.
5. *There are now criminal penalties for "schemes or artifices" to defraud shareholders.* Penalties for defrauding pension funds are increased to ten years.
6. *The act requires the CEOs and chief financial officers (CFOs) of publicly traded companies to "certify" the financial statements of their companies.* Penalties for "knowingly or willfully" violating this with materially misleading information carry up to twenty-year prison terms. Seventh, the Act requires "real time" or very fast disclosure of possible material changes in publicly traded companies' financial condition.
8. *Publicly traded companies may not make loans to executives that are unavailable to persons outside the company.*
9. *The act limits executives' use of bankruptcy to avoid liability for securities law violations.*
10. *The act prohibits investment banks from punishing their own securities analysts who issue negative reports on their own clients.*
11. *Whistleblowers inside publicly traded companies are given increased protection from punishment by their own companies.*
12. *The statute of limitations for fraud suits under the Securities Exchange Act of 1934 is lengthened to two years/five years.* That is, a suit may be brought if within two years from discovery of the fraud provided that it is no more than five years from commission of the fraud. The prior statute of limitations was one year/three years under the SEA.

The Sarbanes–Oxley Act of 2002 makes most of its adjustments to the Securities Exchange Act of 1934, not the 1933 Securities Act.

## Definition of a Security

*The Web site for CNBC, NBC's business channel, provides a wealth of securities information and analysis at http://www.cnbc.com*

What is a security? The term *security* might mean different things in different statutes. To be safe, one should see if and how *security* is defined in the statute with which one is dealing.

***Securities Act of 1933 Definition.*** The Securities Act of 1933 provides a broad definition of *security*, similar to that found in other federal laws and in a number of state laws:

Any note, stock, treasury stock, bond debenture, evidence of indebtedness, certificate of interest or participation in any profit-sharing agreement, collateral-trust certificate, pre-organization certificate or subscription, transferable share, investment contract, voting trust certificate, certificate of deposit for a security, fractional undivided interest in oil, gas, or other mineral rights, or, in general, any interest or instrument commonly known as a "security," or any certificate of interest or participation in, temporary or interim certificate for, receipt for, guarantee of, or warrant of right to subscribe or purchase, any of the foregoing.

*Substance, Not Form.* The definition of *security* usually includes shares of stock. In one case, however, the U.S. Supreme Court held that shares of stock in a cooperative housing corporation were not securities. It reasoned that the incentive for buying was solely to get low-cost housing; it was not to invest for a profit. The Supreme Court emphasized that form should be disregarded for substance and that economic reality should be stressed. Thus, something being called "stock" does not conclusively mean that it is a security for purposes of a particular federal securities statute. The word *security* is not limited to equity or ownership interest.

*Howey Case Definition.* One problem area in defining the word *security* is in defining investment contracts. Often, a piece of paper called a security or stock is not involved, yet courts have often said that investment contracts are securities. In *SEC v. W. J. Howey Co.* [328 U.S. 293 (1946)], the U.S. Supreme Court said that the test for whether an investment contract is a security is whether "the person invests his money in a common enterprise and is led to expect profits solely from the efforts of the promoter or a third party." That case held that separate rows of orange trees accompanied by contracts to cultivate, pick, and sell the oranges were securities under the Securities Act of 1933. Other investment contracts that have been declared securities in given situations include whiskey warehouse receipts, merchandise-marketing programs, oil-drilling investment programs, farmlands and animals, and condominiums.

*Changing Philosophy Regarding Securities Protection.* In prior years, the changed composition of the U.S. Supreme Court prompted a narrower definition of *security*. The *Daniel* case was evidence of this trend. There, the U.S. Supreme Court decided a noncontributory, compulsory pension plan was not a security for purposes of either the Securities Act of 1933 or the Securities Exchange Act of 1934. As the *SEC v. Zandford* case decided in 2002 and presented later in this chapter illustrates, the Supreme Court may be modifying its "regulatory light" approach given the corporate abuses—Enron and WorldCom come to mind—of the early twenty-first century. Although *Zandford* involved neither of those companies, its 9–0 decision may signal a "second look" on the need for regulatory oversight of the financial markets in general and brokers in particular.

## RECENT SUPREME COURT CASE APPLICATIONS OF SECURITY DEFINITION

Generally speaking, when one thinks of a security, the first thing that comes to mind is a share of stock. However, when Congress passed the Securities Act of 1933 and the Securities Exchange Act of 1934, it was primarily concerned with transactions in securities traded in public markets. Thus, Congress did not intend the federal securities laws to apply to "the private sale of a substantial ownership interest" in a business simply because the transaction was structured as a sale of stock instead of assets. Thus arose the "sale of a business" exception to federal securities registration requirements. The *Landreth* case indicates that it is not always easy to determine whether something is a sale of a business involving a stock transfer or an investment in stock.

## Landreth Timber Co. v. Landreth
U.S. Supreme Court
471 U.S. 681 (1985)

### Background and Facts

Respondents father and sons, who owned all of the common stock of a lumber business that they operated, offered their stock for sale through brokers. The company's sawmill was subsequently damaged by fire, but potential purchasers were told that the mill would be rebuilt and modernized. Thereafter, a stock purchase agreement for all of the stock was executed, and ultimately petitioner company was formed by the purchasers. Respondent father agreed to stay on as a consultant for some time to help with the daily operation of the mill. After the acquisition was completed, the mill did not live up to the purchasers' expectations. Eventually, petitioner sold the mill at a loss and went into receivership. Petitioner then filed suit in Federal District Court for rescission of the sale of stock and damages, alleging that respondents had violated the registration provisions of the Securities Act of 1933 and the antifraud provisions of the Securities Exchange Act of 1934. The court granted summary judgment for respondents, holding that under the "sale of business" doctrine, the stock could not be considered a "security" for purposes of the Acts because managerial control of the business had passed into the hands of the purchasers, who bought 100 percent of the stock. The court concluded that the transaction thus was a commercial venture rather than a typical investment. The Court of Appeals affirmed.

### Judgment and Result

**Held:** The stock at issue here is a "security" within the definition of the Acts, and the "sale of business" doctrine does not apply.

(a) Section 2(1) of the 1933 Act defines a "security" as including "stock" and other listed types of instruments. Although the fact that instruments bear the label "stock" is not of itself sufficient to invoke the Acts' coverage, when an instrument is both called "stock" and bears stock's usual characteristics as identified in *Forman*, a purchaser justifiably may assume that the federal securities laws apply. The stock involved here possesses all of the characteristics traditionally associated with common stock. Moreover, reading the securities laws to apply to the sale of stock at issue here comports with Congress' remedial purpose in enacting the legislation to protect investors.

(b) When an instrument is labeled "stock" and possesses all of the traditional characteristics of stock, a court is not required to look to the economic substance of the transaction to determine whether the stock is a "security" within the meaning of the Acts. A contrary rule is not supported by this Court's prior decisions involving unusual instruments not easily characterized as "securities." Nor were the Acts intended, as asserted by respondents, to cover only "passive investors" and not privately negotiated transactions involving the transfer of control to "entrepreneurs."

(c) An instrument bearing both the name and all of the usual characteristics of stock presents the clearest case for coverage by the plain language of the definition. "Stock" is distinguishable from most if not all of the other listed categories, and may be viewed as being in a category by itself for purposes of interpreting the Acts' definition of "security."

(d) Application of the "sale of business" doctrine depends on whether control has passed to the purchaser. Even though the transfer of 100 percent of a corporation's stock normally transfers control, the purchasers here had no intention of running the sawmill themselves. Moreover, if the doctrine were applied here, it would also have to be applied to cases in which less than 100 percent of a company's stock was sold, thus inevitably leading to difficult questions of line-drawing. As explained in *Gould v. Ruefenacht*, coverage by the Acts would in most cases be unknown and unknowable to the parties at the time the stock was sold. Such uncertainties attending the applicability of the Acts would be intolerable.

### Questions

1. What was sold in *Landreth* was clearly "stock." How could any questions arise concerning its status as "security" requiring registration under the 1933 Securities Act?

2. When someone sells the assets of a business—rather than the stock that represents those assets—is it a "sale of a business" (and not a "sale of a security"), which is exempt from registration under the securities laws?

3. Why did the court refuse to apply the "sale of business" exception to the securities laws here? Is it because the buyer did not in fact manage ("hands on") the business and hence treated the business as an investment?

4. Does treating something as covered by the securities laws when it arguably might not be covered promote any business ethics noted in Chapter 1?

5. Of the legal ethics noted in Chapter 1, which one or two are most in evidence in the *Landreth* case?

## SECURITIES ACT OF 1933

Figure 19.1 provides an overview and summary of the Securities Act of 1933. The main objective of the Securities Act of 1933 (SA) is to provide the public with full and fair disclosure about new securities offered for sale.

## MAIN PROVISIONS

Issuers of new securities must register them with the SEC before offering them to the public. Registration takes place when a person files a registration statement with the SEC and the SEC approves the **registration statement** as a full and fair disclosure. Offering or selling securities in interstate commerce or by use of the mails is illegal unless one first registers them.

A registration statement consists of two parts: a **prospectus** and **Part II**. A copy of the prospectus must be given to the security buyer before or when the purchase occurs. It contains detailed information about the issuer, its officers, directors, assets, liabilities, and the business. As a practical matter, many buyers never ask for or read the prospectus before placing an order with their broker. By not reading a prospectus, the investor throws away a large part of the SA's protection. Undoubtedly, many investors do not want to wade through the detail that a

## FIGURE 19.1  OVERVIEW OF SECURITIES ACT OF 1933

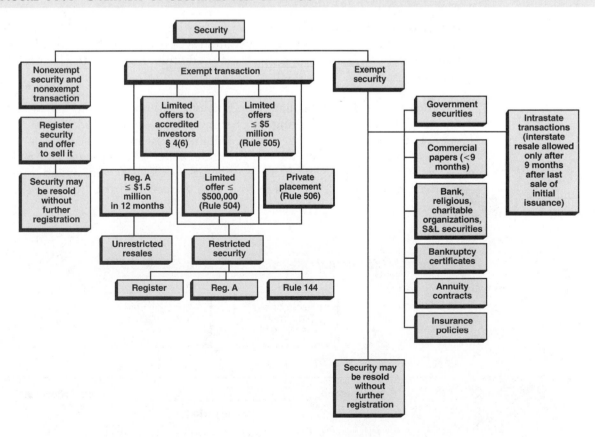

prospectus contains. Instead, they rely on their broker's judgments and the implied threat of withholding future business if the broker makes a mistake. Part II of the registration statement (containing various exhibits) need not ever be given to the investor. It is available for public inspection at the SEC.

*Registering Securities under the SA.* An issuer files information with the SEC in a proposed registration statement. Many professionals (accountants, lawyers, underwriters, geologists, and engineers, among others) might contribute to a particular registration statement. An issuer might not offer a security for sale until the registration statement becomes effective, which automatically occurs 20 days after the issuer files the proposed registration statement with the SEC. (This 20-day period is called the **waiting period**.) However, the SEC may accelerate or delay the registration statement's effective date. Delays occur when the SEC believes the registration statement is misleading or omits or falsely states information that investors need to evaluate the security.

*The Meaning of Registration.* The SEC does not judge a security's merits as an investment—that is, the SEC does not stamp a security as "a good buy" or "fools' gold." Instead, the SEC merely determines whether the registration statement gives prospective investors full and fair disclosure of facts pertinent to making an investment decision. If it does, a registration statement for garbage could be offered for sale. It cannot be stressed too strongly that a security registered with the SEC does not signify that the SEC thinks it is a good investment.

*Steps in Registration.* The registration process involves several steps. Who is involved in each step, and when can a security be offered and sold to the public? Figure 19.2 briefly describes the registration process under the SA of 1933. Keep in mind that a different registration is required under the Securities Exchange Act of 1934.

*Prefiling Period.* In the prefiling period, no offers to buy, offers to sell, or sales to the public may be made. During the prefiling period, the issuer may state preliminary negotiations or reach agreements with underwriters, because offers to underwriters are not covered by the act. An **underwriter** is a large, usually national, securities firm that buys the entire securities issue. Often, several underwriters are involved in a syndicate for a large issue. The underwriter distributes the security

**FIGURE 19.2 SECURITY REGISTRATION UNDER SA OF 1933**

through a network of securities dealers throughout the country. These dealers sell to the investing public. During the prefiling period, underwriters may not offer to sell securities to dealers, and dealers may not offer to buy securities.

*Waiting Period.* The waiting period is the period between the filing and the registration statement's effective date. The period is twenty days unless accelerated or delayed. Registration statements may be amended during this time. If the SEC does not ask for the amendment and an issuer files an amendment, the waiting period starts anew.

During the waiting period, contracts to sell the security are illegal; however, offers to sell or buy are allowed. Such offers may be written or oral, and oral offers are unrestricted. A written offer is technically a prospectus, which must contain certain information that is unavailable between filing and the effective date.

Two devices evade the limits on written offers during the waiting period: the **tombstone ad** and the **red herring prospectus**. A tombstone ad, so named because of its black borders, is a written ad for a security about to be issued that does not have enough information to make it a legal offer. The SEC requires that the tombstone ads contain certain language designed to tell the public that they are not legal offers. Various financial publications such as *Fortune* magazine or the financial sections of newspapers often carry tombstone ads.

A red herring prospectus is a prospectus with red printing that does not contain the price and certain other information. A red herring prospectus allows distribution of written information to investors during the waiting period without meeting all the technical requirements of a prospectus. Neither a tombstone ad nor the red herring prospectus is an offer. Either may be made in the waiting period. Neither is required to be made.

*Posteffective Period.* No limits are placed on offers or sales of securities after a security's registration statement takes effect. Generally, when investors buy a newly issued security, they must be given a prospectus (not the red herring prospectus, but the final, completed prospectus).

*Shelf Registration.* Two major problems that issuers face in selling new securities are timing and red tape. Timing refers to a time lag of several days usually occurring between an issuer's presenting a registration statement to the SEC and the SEC's approving it, which permits a public offering. The registration process reduces an issuer's flexibility in responding to rapidly changing securities markets. Red tape occurs when a securities issuer must prepare a registration statement (a lengthy, detailed report) before offering securities to the public.

The SEC has recently developed **shelf registration** to deal with these timing and red-tape problems. Shelf registration permits an issuer to prepare one registration statement covering any securities offering by the issuer for two years. Thus, an issuer can prepare a registration statement, receive SEC authorization for it, put securities "on the shelf" until the market is receptive, and sell them immediately.

## EXEMPTIONS FROM THE SECURITIES ACT OF 1933

Not all new securities or securities transactions have to go through the full registration process with the SEC. Certain securities and transactions in securities are exempt from all or part of the registration requirement. Exemptions are valuable because they save the issuer the time, money, and red tape of registration. Exemptions are strictly construed, and the person claiming an exemption has the burden of proving all facts to establish it. The Securities Act of 1933 (SA) has two types of exemptions: exempt transactions and exempt securities.

*The Meaning of Exemptions.* As a general rule, before newly issued securities can be offered or sold, they must be registered with the SEC as required by the Securities Act of 1933. Each time a sale of (or offers to sell) a new security is made, a registration statement has to be filed with the SEC unless exemptions apply. Exemptions excuse an issuer from filing a registration statement with the SEC, which is desirable for the issuer.

*Two Kinds of Exemptions.* The two general kinds of exemptions under the Securities Act of 1933 are exempt securities and exempt transactions. **Exempt securities** never have to be registered with the SEC before being offered for sale or before being sold.

An **exempt transaction** means that, when a particular sale (a transaction) of a security occurs, the seller does not have to register the security. However, before buyers of the first round of sales resell, they must file registration statements for later sales unless another exemption applies. In other words, a transaction exemption lasts for only one sale or round of sales. Therefore, a transaction exemption does not last as long as an exemption of a security.

*Exemption Trade-offs.* An important point about exemptions is that they are costly for business because they slow up selling securities and raising capital. On the other hand, exemptions generally lower investor protection, because information about the issuer and the security is generally not available in a government report.

## Exempt Transactions under the Securities Act of 1933

*Secondary Trading.* Sales by people other than the issuer or underwriter are exempt. The issuer is the source of the security, such as the corporation that issues its own stock. The underwriter is someone who buys from the issuer or the person who controls the issuer, such as the issuer's chief executive officer, a major stockholder, or several directors, with a view to distributing the security, usually by sale to the public. In other words, this exemption covers sales by securities dealers (stockbrokers) to the public and situations in which members of the public sell to their brokers.

Generally, this exemption is for secondary trading. The SA deals almost entirely with newly issued securities—the so-called primary market. Most securities sold daily on stock exchanges and over the counter involve secondary trading, that is, sales of already issued securities. New issues, although not unusual in a strong securities market, make up only a small fraction of daily trading. This loophole in the SA was plugged by the Securities Exchange Act of 1934, discussed later in this chapter.

*Private Placements.* Private placements occur when an issuer sells directly to a buyer without a public offering. Billions of dollars worth of securities are sold this way each year. An example is Chrysler Corporation's sale of bonds to an insurance company.

*Intrastate Offerings.* The intrastate offering exemption is for securities offered and sold within one state. The mails, telephone, or other interstate means of communication may be used if the issuer and all offerees and buyers are residents of one state. If a single offeree lives in another state, the entire exemption is lost.

*Regulation A.* The SEC promulgated Regulation A by authority of Section 3(b) of the Securities Act of 1933. This regulation relieves small security issues from the usual lengthy registration statement requirements by permitting short-form registration. It consists of a notice and offering circular filed with the SEC at least ten days before the public offering. The SEC currently defines a small issue as $1,500,000 or less in any twelve month period.

Integration rules treat several small securities issues of the same kind within a twelve month period as being one issue (integrated, or one). Thus, three $700,000 issues sold three months apart do not qualify as a small issue. The integration rules treat this as one $2,100,000 issue not qualifying for the small issue exemption, because it exceeds $1,500,000.

*Regulation D.* Regulation D exempts limited offerings from the Securities Act of 1933. Even though they are exempt, sellers of limited offerings must still give some notice to the SEC. Regulation D contains Rules 501 through 506.

*Rule 501.* The term *accredited investor* is used in limited offering exemptions. It includes the following:

1.  Any bank, insurance company, investment company, or employee benefit plan
2.  Any business development company
3.  Any charitable or educational institution with assets of more than $5 million
4.  Any director, executive officer, or general partner of the issuer
5.  Any person buying at least $150,000 of the securities if the purchase is 20 percent or less of the person's net worth
6.  Any person with a net worth of more than $1 million
7.  Any person with an annual income of more than $200,000

The idea is that accredited investors are sophisticated and rich and do not need securities law protection as much as do smaller investors.

*Rule 502.* Rule 502 deals with three Regulation D matters: (1) integration, (2) information, and (3) manner of offering and limits on resale. **Integration** in securities law means that securities sold at different times are treated as one offering. Integration can destroy a small issue or limited offering exemption. In other words, if the maximum amount that can be sold and still keep the exemption is $500,000, two separate $270,000 securities sales might be treated as one (integrated) $540,000 sale. Because this value exceeds the exemption amount, the securities have to be registered unless some other exemption applies. Securities offerings separated by more than six months are not part of one offering. Therefore, a sale of $400,000 in securities on January 5, 2000, and $400,000 in securities on July 10, 2000, are not integrated. Each would come within the $500,000 exemption.

No special information requirements must be satisfied when an issuer offers or sells securities under Rule 504 or only to accredited investors. If sales are made to unaccredited investors under Rule 505 or 506, all buyers must get certain information (a short-form prospectus) about the issuer.

Limits are placed on offering and resale of securities that are exempt under Regulation D. It is illegal to make a general offer or general solicitation of such exempt securities. Securities bought under Regulation D cannot be resold without registration unless another exemption is available.

*Rule 503.* Sellers must give notice to the SEC of any sales under Regulation D. Therefore, Regulation D does not totally eliminate red tape.

*Rule 504.* Rule 504 creates another exemption from the 1933 Securities Act's registration requirement. To qualify, the issuer must not sell more than $1 million of securities in any 12-month period. These sales may be to any number of purchasers, accredited or unaccredited. Rule 504 does not require giving any information to investors. Figure 19.3 illustrates rules 504, 505, and 506.

*Rule 505.* Under Rule 505 an issuer may sell up to $5 million of securities in any 12-month period to an unlimited number of accredited investors and up to 35 unaccredited investors. If any investors are unaccredited, all buyers must get certain information (a short-form prospectus) about the issuer.

*Rule 506.* An issuer can sell an unlimited amount of securities to accredited investors and up to 35 unaccredited investors. This rule assumes the seller reasonably believes the unaccredited investors can assess the risks before investing. If any investors are unaccredited, all buyers must get certain information (a short-form prospectus) about the issuer.

*Section 4(6).* Another exemption under the Securities Act of 1933 is Section 4(6). It exempts securities offerings up to $5 million when made only to accredited investors.

## Exempt Securities under the Securities Act of 1933

The previous discussion covers exempt transactions. Even if a particular transaction is not exempt, the securities themselves might be exempt from the SA's registration and disclosure requirements. Note that exempt securities are not exempt from the SA's antifraud and civil liability provisions—only from the disclosure and registration parts. In other words, anyone who commits fraud to sell an exempt security violates the SA. Also, keep in mind that a security exempt under the SA may not be exempt under the Securities Exchange Act of 1934.

### FIGURE 19.3  Regulation D Exemptions

| | Rule 504 | Rule 505 | Rule 506 |
|---|---|---|---|
| Number of buyers | Unlimited | Unlimlited for accredited; 35 for unaccredited | Unlimited for accredited; 35 for unaccredited |
| Amount | $1 million | <$5 million | Unlimited |
| Disclosure required | None | Disclosure to all, if any, unaccredited investors | Disclosure to all, if any, unaccredited investors |

The following securities are exempt from the SA's disclosure and registration requirements:

1. Securities issued or guaranteed by federal, state, or municipal governments, such as U.S. bonds and state securities
2. Commercial paper (promissory notes with a maturity of under nine months)
3. Bank, religious and charitable organizations, and savings and loans securities
4. Securities of common carriers subject to the Interstate Commerce Commission
5. Bankruptcy certificates
6. Annuity contracts
7. Insurance policies

## CIVIL LIABILITY UNDER THE SECURITIES ACT OF 1933

People can be held civilly liable under the Securities Act of 1933 (SA) if they offer to sell unregistered securities (a violation of Section 5 of the SA) or if the registration statement has material omissions or misstatements (violations of Section 11 of the SA). Section 11 violations deal only with securities registered under the SA. Section 12 of the SA puts civil liability on those committing fraud in the sale or offer of any security even if not registered under the SA. The remainder of this section deals with Section 11 violations—material omissions or misstatements in the registration statements.

*Section 11 Claims.* Section 11 of the SA allows those acquiring a security covered by a registration statement to recover damages if they show the following:

1. They acquired the security.
2. A registration statement covers the security.
3. The registration statement has a material misstatement or omission.
4. They lost money on the security.

Note that the investors need not show that they relied on the registration statement.

*Section 11 Defendants.* The following individuals can be sued in a Section 11 claim:

1. Signers of the security's registration statement (The issuer, the issuer's chief executive, financial and accounting officers, and a majority of the board all must sign the registration statement; therefore, they all may be sued.)
2. All directors
3. All people who agree to be directors
4. Experts agreeing to be named as having prepared all or part of the registration statement (which might include, among others, geologists, lawyers, accountants, and engineers)
5. All underwriters

*Extent of Liability and Recent Changes.* Not only may all the previously mentioned individuals be sued on a Section 11 claim, but some may also be jointly and severally liable for the claim. Thus, if an investor lost $100,000 and a director signed the registration statement, the individual director could be forced to pay the entire $100,000. Assuming the director paid the entire claim, the director would have a right of contribution from others liable for their proportionate share of the loss. Experts are liable only for the material omissions or misstatements in the part of the registration statement with which they were involved.

As noted earlier in this chapter, the 1995 Private Securities Litigation Reform Act exempts outside directors from joint and several liability. They are only pro-**portionately liable** for the harm they caused unless they knowingly violate the securities laws. For example, the dean of State University's business school who sits on the board of a local company that issues securities covered by a registration statement under the 1933 Act would not be jointly and severally liable for investors' losses but only proportionately liable for his negligence that may have contributed to the investors' loss. Obviously, such a provision encourages prominent citizens who are not employees of the issuer ("outsiders") to become directors. This practice is good public policy because it encourages a fresh look at the company's affairs by someone not closely associated with it on a day-to-day basis.

*Defenses to Section 11.* Given the great liabilities facing a wide variety of people under Section 11, the following defenses are available.

*Due Diligence.* Most defendants can raise the due diligence defense; however, the issuer may not, because it is liable in virtually all cases for material omissions or misstatements. **Due diligence** means that the individuals sued met a standard of care regarding information in their part of the registration statement. If the individuals are experts, such as lawyers, they have to meet the due diligence of their professions.

*Immateriality.* An omission or misstatement in the registration statement that is **immaterial** (a matter that the average prudent investor ought not to know before buying the security) is a defense. Part of the plaintiff security buyer's case is to show that the omission or misstatement was material. The defendant can, however, rebut this claim.

*Purchaser Knowledge.* The defendant's ability to show that the purchaser knew of the omission or misstatement when the security was bought is a defense.

*Other Causes of Damages.* A defendant can escape liability under Section 11 by showing that the plaintiff's loss was from causes other than the material omission or misstatement. For example, a general economic recession could account for a decline of the stock of all firms in an industry, aside from omissions or misstatements in the registration statement.

*No Reliance.* A Section 11 plaintiff need not prove reliance on the material error or omission. The defendant may, however, escape liability by proving that the plaintiff did not rely on the error or omission—an almost impossible task. However, if the plaintiff bought the security after the issuer released an income statement covering a period of a year or more after the registration statement took effect, the plaintiff must show reliance on the omission or misstatement.

*Statute of Limitations.* A peculiar one- to three-year statute of limitations exists for SA civil violations. Suits must be started one year after discovering the violation but in no case later than three years after the violation.

*Escott v. BarChris Construction Corporation* is the leading case interpretation of Section 11 of the Securities Act of 1933.

## Escott v. BarChris Construction Corporation
U.S. District Court (S.D. N.Y.)
283 F.Supp. 643 (1968)

### Background and Facts

Some investors bought bonds that BarChris Construction Corporation issued. BarChris's executives, attorneys, accountants, and underwriters prepared and filed a registration statement for the bonds. On May 16, 1961, the registration statement took effect. BarChris sold the bonds in May 1961 and used the money in its business, which was building bowling alleys. However, by 1962 it was obvious that there were too many bowling alleys. In October 1962, BarChris filed for bankruptcy. It defaulted on the bonds it had sold just a year earlier. Bond investors lost their money and pointed out the following errors in the bond registration statement.

### Summary

For convenience, the various falsities and omissions discussed in the preceding pages are recapitulated here.

1. 1960 Earnings
   (a) Sales

   | | |
   |---|---:|
   | Per prospectus | $ 9,165,320 |
   | Correct figures | 8,511,420 |
   | Overstatement | $   653,900 |

   (b) Net Operating Income

   | | |
   |---|---:|
   | Per prospectus | $ 1,742,801 |
   | Correct figure | 1,496,196 |
   | Overstatement | $   246,605 |

   (c) Earnings per Share

   | | |
   |---|---:|
   | Per prospectus | $ .75 |
   | Correct figure | .65 |
   | Overstatement | $ .10 |

2. 1960 Balance Sheet Current Assets

   | | |
   |---|---:|
   | Per prospectus | $ 4,524,021 |
   | Correct figure | 3,914,332 |
   | Overstatement | $   609,689 |

3. Contingent Liabilities as of December 31, 1960, on Alternative Method of Financing

   | | |
   |---|---:|
   | Per prospectus | $   750,000 |
   | Correct figure | 1,125,795 |
   | Understatement | $   375,795 |
   | Capitol Lanes should have been shown as a direct liability | $   325,000 |

4. Contingent Liabilities as of April 30, 1961

   | | |
   |---|---:|
   | Per prospectus | $   825,000 |
   | Correct figure | 1,443,853 |
   | Understatement | $   618,853 |
   | Capitol Lanes should have been shown as a direct liability | $   314,166 |

5. Earnings Figures for Quarter Ending March 31, 1961
   (a) Sales

   | | |
   |---|---:|
   | Per prospectus | $ 2,138,455 |
   | Correct figure | 1,618,645 |
   | Overstatement | $   519,810 |

   (b) Gross profit

   | | |
   |---|---:|
   | Per prospectus | $483,121 |
   | Correct figure | 252,366 |
   | Overstatement | $230,755 |

6. Backlog as of March 31, 1961

   | | |
   |---|---:|
   | Per prospectus | $ 6,905,000 |
   | Correct figure | 2,415,000 |
   | Overstatement | $ 4,490,000 |

7. Failure to Disclose Officers' Loans Outstanding and Unpaid on May 16, 1961 $   386,615

8. Failure to Disclose Use of Proceeds in Manner Not Revealed in Prospectus
   *Approximately* $ 1,160,000

9. Failure to Disclose Customers' Delinquencies in May 1961 and BarChris's Potential Liability with Respect hereto
   *Over* $ 1,350,000

10. Failure to Disclose the Fact that BarChris Was Already Engaged and Was About to be More Heavily Engaged in the Operation of Bowling Alleys

The investors who bought BarChris bonds and lost money sued the following:

1. BarChris's directors
2. BarChris's executive officers
3. BarChris's controller
4. BarChris's attorney
5. People who signed BarChris's registration statement for the bonds
6. The bond underwriters
7. Independent auditors who prepared financial statements that became part of the registration statement

Investors based their claim on Section 11 of the Securities Act of 1933. Section 11 allows buyers of securities covered by a registration statement to recover damages if they show the following:

1. They bought the security.
2. A registration statement covers the security.
3. The registration statement has a material misstatement or omission.
4. They lost money on the security.

## Key Points

[What follows are a number of the rulings the court made in the *BarChris* case.]

1. The provision of the Securities Act of 1933 imposing civil liability for material false statements and omissions in securities registration statement on directors of issuing corporation and others imposes liability upon director regardless of how new he is; presumption is that director knows his responsibility when he becomes a director, and he can escape liability only by using that reasonable care to investigate the facts which a prudent man would employ in management of his own property.

2. The evidence in this representative action by debenture buyers against the issuing corporation's nonofficer director who became a director on eve of the debenture financing, for damages resulting from false statements and material omissions in prospectus contained in registration statement for debentures was not sufficient to establish his due diligence defense.

3. The evidence in this representative action by debenture buyer against issuing corporation's "outside" director, who was a civil engineer, for damages resulting from false statements and material omissions in prospectus contained in registration statement for debentures failed to sustain his burden of proving his due diligence defense as to portions of statement other than audited 1960 figures.

4. The purpose of provision of Securities Act of 1933 imposing civil liability for false securities registration statement is to protect investors, and the "reasonable investigation" required of underwriters as one of prerequisites to avoid liability required more than mere accurate reporting in prospectus of data presented to them by corporate issuer; underwriters had to make some reasonable attempt to verify data submitted to them.

5. The extent to which underwriters must go in verifying data submitted to them by issuing corporation to avoid civil liability for false securities registration statement is one of degree and a matter of judgment in each case.

6. The evidence in this representative action by debenture buyers against the underwriters of debentures for damages resulting from false statements and material omissions in prospectus contained in registration statement for debentures established that the underwriters' counsel did not make a reasonable investigation of truth of prospectus which had not been made on authority of auditor as an expert.

7. The debenture underwriters whose counsel did not make a reasonable investigation of truth of portions of prospectus, contained in registration statement for debentures, not made on authority of auditor as an expert were bound by counsel's failure.

8. The evidence in this representative action by debenture buyers against the underwriters of debentures for damages resulting from false statements and material omissions in prospectus contained in registration statement for debentures failed to establish the underwriters' due diligence defense.

9. Under the Securities Act of 1933 the provision that no one shall be liable for false statements or omissions in securities registration statement as to part "not purporting to be made on the authority of an expert" if he had reason to believe that statements were true and that material facts were not omitted, only portions of debenture registration statement purporting to be made by issuing corporation's auditors constituted the expertised portions.

10. For purposes of "due diligence" defenses in this representative action by debenture buyers against the issuing corporation and others for false statements and omissions in the prospectus contained in registration statement for debentures, only consolidated balance sheet of corporation and its subsidiaries as of December 31, 1960, and statement of earnings and retained earnings for the five years then ended constituted the expertised portion, where corporation's auditors purported to certify only that portion.

11. The issuing corporation's executive vice president who was, in effect, the corporation's chief executive officer had no due diligence defenses . . . where vice president knew all relevant facts and could not have believed that there were no untrue statement or material omissions in prospectus.

12. The liability of an issuing corporation's director who signed securities registration statement for damages sustained as a result of false statements or material omissions in statement for the securities does not depend upon whether director read statement or, if he did, whether he understood what he was reading.

13. For purposes of the prospectus contained in the registration statement for bowling alley construction corporation's debentures, inclusion of bowling alley contract price as part of "scheduled," "unfilled orders" on corporation's books on designated date was erroneous and misleading, where contract was not signed until subsequent date, contract was canceled, and alley was never built.

14. The statement in the prospectus, contained in registration statement for bowling alley construction corporation's debentures, that $1,745,000 of proceeds of sale of debentures was to be utilized as "additional" working capital in "expansion" of bowling alley construction was false and misleading, where over 60 percent of the sum was immediately expended in other ways, primarily to pay prior debts incurred as result of bowling alley construction already undertaken.

15. The statement in the prospectus, contained in the registration statement for this bowling alley construction corporation's debentures, that, since the designated date, this corporation had been required to repurchase less than one-half of one percent of its customers' notes discounted by unaffiliated financial institutions was literally true but impliedly false and misleading, where outstanding notes of defaulting customers substantially exceeded the percentage, but immediate repurchase had not been demanded.

16. The omission of any reference to operation of bowling alleys in statement, in prospectus contained in registration statement for corporation's debentures, that corporation was engaged

in design, manufacture, construction, installation, modernizing, and repair of bowling alleys and manufacture and sale of related equipment rendered the description of this corporation's business incomplete and, therefore, misleading, even though this corporation actually operated only one alley prior to the date of this prospectus, in view of other bowling operations then intended or anticipated.

17. A materiality of false statement in, or omission from, a registration statement for a security is a prerequisite to liability in damages for such false statement or omission.

18. Under the Securities and Exchange Commission, regulation defining the word "material" as meaning "matters as to which an average prudent investor ought reasonably to be informed," refers to matters which an investor needs to know before he can make an intelligent, informed decision as to whether to buy the security involved.

19. As a prerequisite to civil liability for false statements in or omissions from security registration statements, a "material fact" is one which, if it had been correctly stated or disclosed, would have deterred or tended to deter average prudent investor from purchasing the securities in question.

20. For purposes of the prospectus contained in the registration statement for debentures issued by bowling alley construction corporation, sales, the net operating income, and earnings per share were overstated for year 1960. This was because profit had been claimed on alleys completed but not sold, money loaned had been improperly included in contract price and carried into profits, and alleys not completed had been treated as completed in applying the percentage of completion method in allocating sales to year 1960.

21. $50,000 of $125,000 due corporation as down payment on bowling alley constructed and sold by corporation constituted an overstatement of the corporation's current assets in the balance sheet included in the prospectus contained in the registration statement for the corporation's debentures, despite security given corporation. This was because that payment was overdue on both the down payment and on the notes given in payment of balance of purchase price.

22. The current assets of this bowling alley construction corporation were not grossly overstated in balance sheet included in prospectus contained in registration statement for corporation's debentures. This was because at most the net current assets should have been reduced by $609,689, which would have made them total $3,914,332 instead of $4,524,021.

23. As to prospectus contained in the registration statement for the corporation's debentures, the inclusion in the amount of this corporation's net sales for the three-month period of a figure constituting contract prices for bowling alleys constructed by the corporation and operated without sale by corporation's subsidiary during the period was improper.

24. The treatment of the bowling alley construction contract as a scheduled, unfilled order on the bowling alley construction corporation's books for purposes of the prospectus contained in the

registration statement for the corporation's debentures was inaccurate and misleading. This was because as of the date mentioned in the prospectus, the construction contract had not been signed, and no firm commitment existed.

25. In this representative action by debenture buyers against the issuing corporation's auditor for damages resulting from false statements and material omissions in prospectus contained in registration statement for debentures, the auditor had the burden of proving the due diligence defense.

26. Accountants should not be held to a standard higher than that recognized in their profession.

27. In regard to civil liability for a false securities registration statement, the accountant's S-1 review made, with reference to debenture registration statement, to ascertain whether material changes had occurred in the issuing corporation's financial position subsequent to the date of the certified balance sheet was not sufficient where accountant failed to take the steps prescribed by his employer or to spend adequate time on the task and was too easily satisfied with glib answers to his inquiries.

28. The evidence of this representative action by debenture buyers against the issuing corporation's auditor for damage resulting from false statements and material omissions in the prospectus contained in the registration statement for debentures failed to establish the auditor's due diligence defense.

29. The evidence in this representative action by debenture buyers against issuing corporation and others . . . failed to establish that the entire damage suffered by every plaintiff had been caused by decline in bowling industry in which corporation was involved, rather than errors and omissions in registration statement for which defendants were responsible.

## Judgment and Result

The court decided evidence indicated material misrepresentations and omissions in the registration statement. Its finding meant the bond buyers could recover from the accountants, directors, signers, and certain others if they did not establish a defense.

## Questions

1. Had the plaintiffs in the *BarChris* case bought BarChris bonds? How had they been damaged? Whom did the plaintiffs sue?
2. What does the fact that the plaintiffs were not repaid interest and principal on their bonds have to do with the registration statement?
3. Do the plaintiffs suing under the 1933 Securities Act for a material mistake or omission in the registration statement have to prove they relied on the registration statement's error to prove their case? What if the defendant shows that the plaintiff did not rely on the error?
4. What is the connection between a registration statement and the security?
5. What defenses were raised in *BarChris*?

## CRIMINAL PUNISHMENT UNDER THE SECURITIES ACT OF 1933

The Securities Act of 1933 (SA) has criminal sanctions. Committing fraud in the sale of securities (whether exempt or nonexempt) or willfully violating the SA is a crime. Possible punishment is up to five years in prison, a maximum fine of $10,000 or both.

## SECURITIES EXCHANGE ACT OF 1934

Figure 19.4 summarizes the Securities Exchange Act of 1934 (SEA). The SEA covers many different securities areas, unlike the Securities Act of 1933, which requires registration of new issues. The SEA concentrates on the secondary (used) securities and their markets. Among matters covered in the SEA are establishing the Securities and Exchange Commission and regulating the securities exchanges, dealers, and brokers, as well as publicly held companies.

As noted earlier in this chapter, the Private Securities Litigation Reform Act of 1995 substantially amended the 1934 SE Act. Refer to that discussion for particulars. One of the most significant amendments was changing the "joint and several" liability rule to "proportionate liability." Unlike the 1933 Act (where proportionate liability only applies to outside directors) the proportionate liability rule applied to all 1934 Act cases in which liability can be based on nonknowing (basically, negligent) conduct.

**FIGURE 19.4 OVERVIEW OF SECURITIES EXCHANGE ACT OF 1934 (SEA)**

The purposes of the Securities Exchange Act of 1934 include the following:

- Regulating securities markets
- Regulating securities traded in securities markets
- Registering and regulating broker-dealers, municipal securities dealers, securities, information processors, clearing agencies, and transfer agents
- Regulating publicly held companies
- Requiring public disclosure

## MAIN PROVISIONS

There are eight main provisions of the SEA:

1. Creation of the Securities and Exchange Commission
2. Registration requirements
3. Reporting requirements
4. Proxy solicitation rules
5. Regulation of credit in securities markets
6. Antifraud provisions
7. Insider trading information
8. Tender offer limits

In 2002 the Sarbanes–Oxley Act of 2002 took effect. This law was described in detail earlier in the chapter. It greatly enlarges oversight of the accounting industry.

## THE SECURITIES AND EXCHANGE COMMISSION

The Securities and Exchange Commission (SEC) is the leading enforcer of the federal securities laws. It enforces the Securities Act of 1933, the Securities Exchange Act of 1934, the Public Utility Holding Company Act of 1935, the Investment Company Act of 1940, the Investment Advisers Act of 1940, and the Trust Indenture Act of 1939. Interestingly, the SEC was established in 1934 by the Securities Exchange Act of 1934, one year after the first major federal act regulating securities—the Securities Act of 1933—became law. The Federal Trade Commission enforced the 1933 Act during its first year. This responsibility was transferred from the FTC to the SEC upon the SEC's establishment.

For more on the regulations and operations of the Security and Exchange Commission, go to **http://www.sec.gov**

The SEC promulgates rules and regulations, enforces them, and adjudicates cases where rules and regulations are allegedly violated. If this description sounds familiar, it should. The SEC is a federal administrative agency and performs most of the agency functions described in Chapters 6 and 7.

The Sarbanes–Oxley Act of 2002 established a new oversight board with responsibilities to investigate and oversee the accounting industry as well as discipline auditors violating standards. The SEC has direct authority over this board.

## SEA REGISTRATION REQUIREMENTS

To achieve the SEA's purposes of regulating securities and the securities markets, the SEA imposes registration requirements. Securities exchanges, security broker-dealers, municipal securities dealers, and certain securities must be registered with the Securities and Exchange Commission.

*Securities Registration.* The SEA requires that certain securities be registered with the SEC. Any security (bonds or equity security) traded on any national securities exchange must be registered unless it is exempt. Also, any company with 500 or more shareholders and more than $10 million in assets must register its equity (not debt) securities if they are traded in interstate commerce. Thus, securities traded over the counter (not on an exchange) must be registered if the issuer has more than $5 million in assets and 500 or more shareholders. It cannot be emphasized too strongly that SEA registration is in *addition* to registration under the Securities Act of 1933, discussed earlier.

*Reporting Requirements.* The Securities Exchange Act of 1934 requires that certain reports be filed with the SEC by issuers of securities registered under the SEA. (Recall that these securities are not necessarily the same as those registered under the SA.) Three of the more important reports a securities issuer must file with the SEC are as follows:

1. The 10-K report is an annual report on the issuer's operations. It is similar in some ways to the annual report that the issuer's management submits to shareholders. The 10-K must be audited by independent auditors.
2. The 10-Q report is an unaudited quarterly report of operations.
3. The 8-K report, known as the current report, is filed during the first ten days of the month following the happening of certain material events, such as a change in directors or an increase in authorized shares.

## SEA PROXY RESTRICTIONS

A proxy is a person who acts for another. In a corporation, a common practice for shareholders is to give the right to vote their shares to incumbent management or to a challenging group. When someone solicits proxies of shares registered under the SEA, the SEA and its rules and regulations impose certain requirements.

*Proxy Statement Requirements.* A proxy statement must accompany any proxy solicitation sent by the mails or in interstate commerce. The proxy statement contains facts about the person seeking the proxy. For example, if management asks for proxies when it wants to reelect itself (incumbent directors), the proxy statement will contain information about director shareholdings, salaries, and occupations. Each separate management proposal (such as approval of the independent accountants) and any shareholder proposals must be listed separately so that each can be voted on by the person whose proxy is sought. Management solicitation of proxies must include shareholder proposals if the shareholder owns 1 percent of the voting shares or $1,000 in market value of a voting security for at least one year. Limits are imposed on what shareholders can put in proxies. Proxies must have a space for the date and signature of the person giving them. The proxy, proxy statement, and accompanying material must be submitted to the SEC if the shares are registered under the SEA.

## SEA CREDIT RESTRICTIONS

Securities buyers are sometimes greedy. They want to give themselves leverage by putting a small amount down on a securities purchase and borrowing the rest, hoping the security swings wildly in value—in their favor. Such buying on margin contributed to the stock market crash of 1929. To control speculation the Federal Reserve Board sets margin requirements for securities dealers and brokers. These requirements determine how much credit a broker can extend to a securities buyer. For example, a 70 percent margin requirement means that the securities buyer must pay 70 percent of the security's price and can finance only 30 percent.

Other credit restrictions include prohibitions on brokers' hypothecating (using as collateral) a customer's securities unless the customer owes the broker for the securities. A customer who buys securities and wishes to take physical delivery of them (instead of holding them in a "street name") sometimes does not receive the securities for weeks. Understandably, the customer wonders whether the broker is using the securities as collateral for personal dealings.

## SHORT-SWING PROFITS

*Insiders.* An officer, director, or large shareholder (holder or beneficial owner of more than 10 percent of an equity class) is an insider for Section 16(b). Insiders often know a great deal more about the issuer than the market does. They could profit from this knowledge by trading in the issuer's securities. At one time, trading on such knowledge was thought to be a fringe benefit of being an insider. Then Congress enacted Section 16(b) of the Securities Exchange Act of 1934, its short-swing profits rule.

*Section 16(b).* Section 16(b) says that an insider must return to the issuer any profit from any sale and purchase or purchase and sale of the issuer's equity securities occurring within a six-month period. The intent of the insider is irrelevant. In other words, if the prohibited acts occurred within the six-month period, the insider is presumed to have used inside information to make the gain even if the insider actually had no information not known by the market. The idea behind the rule is to put all investors on the same footing by eliminating special advantages for insiders.

*Insider Reports.* Insiders must file reports of their holdings of the issuer's equity securities with the SEC and the securities exchange involved. Any change must be reported to the SEC within twenty days. Note that this requirement does not stop insiders from trading in the issuer's stock and keeping the profits. Also, this rule does not stop an insider from trading in another company's stock and making a profit within a six-month period, because the investor, by definition, is not an insider in the other issuer.

*Exceptions.* The short-swing profit rule has exceptions for odd-lot transactions (fewer than one hundred shares) and transactions involving low dollar amounts.

*Straw People.* Insiders may not act through *straw people* (friends or relatives); nor may insiders pass on information to friends or relatives so they can act for themselves. Such gains are recoverable by the issuer.

## SECTION 10(B) AND RULE 10B-5

Section 10(b) of the Securities Exchange Act of 1934 is the anti-fraud section of the statute. Rule 10b-5 promulgated under it is aimed at preventing fraud in buying and selling securities. The rule's language clearly says that it applies to "any person," meaning corporate insiders and outsiders. In this way, Rule 10b-5 is broader than Section 16(b). On the other hand, it is similar to Section 16(b) because it can stop profit taking in the firm's securities by corporate insiders who have inside information that is unavailable to the general public.

*Rule 10b-5 Application.* Rule 10b-5 applies to all securities. Virtually any fraud in connection with the sale or purchase of any security where the mails or an instrumentality of interstate commerce is involved is covered by Rule 10b-5. Rule 10b-5 applies even to securities otherwise exempt, such as government bonds. The rule applies even if the securities do not have to be registered under the SEA (because, for instance, the issuer has fewer than 500 stockholders). Unlike Section 16(b), only a sale or purchase (not both) of securities is required to violate Rule 10b-5.

Rule 10b-5 makes illegal any device, scheme, or artifice to defraud; any untrue statement, or any act, practice, or course of business that operates as a fraud in connection with the sale or purchase of a security. In the *Texas Gulf Sulphur* case, a mineral company drilled core samples in Canada that suggested a lucrative strike. The company was unsure whether the samples gave a true or misleading indication of the extent of minerals in the area. It issued an ambiguous press announcement about the matter. Later, it made a press announcement telling of a profitable strike. Between these announcements, corporate officers and their relatives bought or placed orders to buy company stock, which zoomed up in price after the news of the strike was publicly announced.

Was the first ambiguous press announcement followed by the insider buying a device, scheme, or course of business operating as a fraud in connection with the sale or purchase of securities in violation of Rule 10b-5? Read the next case to find out.

---

## SEC v. Zandford
U.S. Supreme Court
535 U.S. 813 (2002)

### Background and Facts

Between 1987 and 1991, Zandford was employed as a securities broker in the Maryland branch of a New York brokerage firm. In 1987 he persuaded William Wood, an elderly man in poor health, to open a joint investment account for himself and his mentally retarded daughter. According to the SEC's complaint, the "stated investment objectives for the account were 'safety of principal and income.'" The Woods granted respondent Zandford discretion to manage their account and a general power of attorney to engage in securities transactions for their benefit without prior approval. Relying on Zandford's promise to "conservatively invest" their money, the Woods entrusted him with $419,255. Before Mr. Wood's death in 1991, all of that money was gone.

In 1991, the National Association of Securities Dealers (NASD) conducted a routine examination of respondent's firm and discovered that on over twenty-five occasions, money had been transferred from the Woods' account to accounts controlled by respondent. In due course, respondent Zandford was indicted in the United States

District Court for the District of Maryland on 13 counts of wire fraud in violation of 18 U.S.C. § 1343. The first count alleged that Zandford sold securities in the Woods' account and then made personal use of the proceeds. Each of the other counts alleged that he made wire transfers between Maryland and New York that enabled him to withdraw specified sums from the Woods' accounts. Some of those transfers involved Zandford writing checks to himself from a mutual fund account held by the Woods, which required liquidating securities in order to redeem the checks. Zandford was convicted on all counts, sentenced to prison for 52 months, and ordered to pay $10,800 in restitution.

After Zandford was indicted, the SEC filed a civil complaint in the same District Court alleging that Zandford violated § 10(b) and Rule 10b-5 by engaging in a scheme to defraud the Woods and by misappropriating approximately $343,000 of the Woods' securities without their knowledge or consent. The SEC moved for partial summary judgment after Zandford's criminal conviction, arguing that the judgment in the criminal case estopped Zandford from contesting facts that established a violation of § 10(b). Zandford filed a motion seeking discovery on the question whether his fraud had the requisite "connection with" the purchase or sale of a security. The District Court refused to allow discovery and entered summary judgment against Zandford. It enjoined him from engaging in future violations of the securities laws and ordered him to disgorge $343,000 in ill-gotten gains.

The Court of Appeals for the Fourth Circuit reversed the summary judgment and remanded with directions for the District Court to dismiss the complaint. It first held that the wire fraud conviction, which only required two findings—(1) that Zandford engaged in a scheme to defraud and (2) that he used interstate wire communications in executing the scheme—did not establish all the elements of a § 10(b) violation. Specifically, the conviction did not necessarily establish that his fraud was "in connection with" the sale of a security. The court then held that the civil complaint did not sufficiently allege the necessary connection because the sales of the Woods' securities were merely incidental to a fraud that "lay in absconding with the proceeds" of sales that were conducted in "a routine and customary fashion." Zandford's "scheme was simply to steal the Woods' assets" rather than to engage "in a manipulation of a particular security." Ultimately the court refused "to stretch the language of the securities fraud provisions to encompass every conversion or theft that happens to involve securities." Adopting what amounts to a "fraud on the market" theory of the statute's coverage, the court held that without some "relationship to market integrity or investor understanding, there is no violation of § 10(b)."

The Supreme Court granted the SEC's petition for a writ of certiorari to review the Court of Appeals' construction of the phrase "in connection with the purchase or sale of any security." Because the Court of Appeals ordered the complaint dismissed rather than remanding for reconsideration, the Supreme Court assumes the allegations contained therein are true and affirm that disposition only if no set of facts would entitle the SEC to relief. The Supreme Court did not reach the question of whether the record supports the District Court's grant of summary judgment in the SEC's favor—a question that requires all potential factual disputes to be resolved in Zander's favor.

## Body of Opinion

**Justice John Paul Stevens.** . . . Section 10(b) of the Securities Exchange Act makes it "unlawful for any person . . . to use or employ, in connection with the purchase or sale of any security . . . , any manipulative or deceptive device or contrivance in contravention of such rules and regulations as the [SEC] may prescribe." . . . Rule 10(b)-5, which implements this provision, forbids the use, "in connection with the purchase or sale of any security," of "any device, scheme, or artifice to defraud" or any other "act, practice, or course of business" that "operates . . . as a fraud or deceit." . . . Among Congress' objectives in passing the Act was "to insure honest securities markets and thereby promote investor confidence" after the market crash of 1929. . . . More generally, Congress sought "'to substitute a philosophy of full disclosure for the

philosophy of *caveat emptor* and thus to achieve a high standard of business ethics in the securities industry.'" . . .

Consequently, we have explained that the statute should be "construed 'not technically and restrictively, but flexibly to effectuate its remedial purposes,'" . . . In its role enforcing the Act, the SEC has consistently adopted a broad reading of the phrase "in connection with the purchase or sale of any security." It has maintained that a broker who accepts payment for securities that he never intends to deliver, or who sells customer securities with intent to misappropriate the proceeds, violates § 10(b) and Rule 10(b)-5. . . .

The SEC claims respondent [Zandford] engaged in a fraudulent scheme in which he made sales of his customer's securities for his own benefit. Respondent [Zandford] submits that the sales themselves were perfectly lawful and that the subsequent misappropriation of the proceeds, though fraudulent, is not properly viewed as having the requisite connection with the sales; in his view, the alleged scheme is not materially different from a simple theft of cash or securities in an investment account. We disagree.

According to the complaint, respondent [Zandford] "engaged in a scheme to defraud" the Woods beginning in 1988, shortly after they opened their account, and that scheme continued throughout the two-year period during which respondent made a series of transactions that enabled him to convert the proceeds of the sales of the Woods' securities to his own use. . . .

Taking the allegations in the complaint as true, each sale was made to further respondent's fraudulent scheme; each was deceptive because it was neither authorized by, nor disclosed to, the Woods. . . . Indeed, each time respondent "exercised his power of disposition for his own benefit," that conduct, "without more," was a fraud. . . . In the aggregate, the sales are properly viewed as a "course of business" that operated as a fraud or deceit on a stockbroker's customer. . . .

## Judgment and Result

Reversed. SEC wins. The sale of the client's securities where the broker used the proceeds to buy cars and pay personal bills was a sale covered by § 10(b) and Rule 10(b)-5.

## Questions

1. Did Zandford have a fiduciary duty to Woods? Did he breach it in a fraudulent scheme in connection with securities sales?
2. Did the Supreme Court adopt a broad or narrow reading of § 10(b) and Rule 10(b)-5? Does such a reading increase or decrease investor confidence in brokers?
3. Does what Zandford did undercut the "integrity of the stock market" or was what he did (essentially running off with the money in the client's account) really only peripherally related to the stock market?
4. Is the philosophy of § 10(b) and Rule 10(b)-5 one of "caveat emptor" or "full and fair disclosure"?

*Examples of Rule 10b-5 Violations.* Some specific fraudulent acts include knowingly spreading false rumors about securities issuers to affect the issuer's securities prices, matching buy and sell orders from different people (such as two brokers from the same firm), a broker's *churning* a customer's account, or one person's simultaneously buying and selling the same security (wash sales) to give the appearance of market activity in the stock. The list is unlimited. *SEC v. Zandford* is a recent U.S. Supreme Court ruling indicating how broadly that court reads the "fraud in connection with the purchase or sale" requirement of section 10(b) and Rule 10(b)-5.

## SEC v. Texas Gulf Sulphur Co.
U.S. Court of Appeal (2d. Cir.)
401 F.2d 833 (1968)

### Background and Facts

Texas Gulf Sulphur Company (TGS) explored for minerals in Canada. Preliminary drilling on November 12, 1963, suggested that TGS had found a rich mineral deposit. Between November 12, 1963, and April 16, 1964, before the extent of the discovery was confirmed, various TGS officers, directors, and employees used this material inside information to buy TGS stock in the open market. They did not disclose the Canadian find to the public before their purchases. Word of the TGS Canadian find spread on Wall Street. On April 12, 1964, TGS issued a press release designed to lower public expectations about the nature and extent of the Canadian discovery. During this time, various TGS directors, officers, and employees continued to buy TGS stock. On April 16, 1964, TGS held a press conference where it announced a discovery of at least 25 tons of ore (very good news). Twenty minutes later, Coates, a TGS director, bought 2,000 shares for family trusts through his broker son-in-law, who also bought 1,500 shares for himself and his customers. TGS stock rose from 17-3/8 on November 8, 1963, to 37 on April 16, 1964, the day of the public announcement of the Canadian mineral find. The SEC sued TGS officers, directors, and employees under Section 10(b) of the Securities Exchange Act of 1934 (SEA) and Rule 10b-5. The SEC accused the insiders of trading in TGS stock based on material inside information undisclosed to the general investing public or the particular sellers.

### Body of Opinion

**Circuit Judge Waterman.** This action was commenced in the United States District Court for the Southern District of New York by the Securities and Exchange Commission (the SEC) pursuant to Sec. 21(e) of the Securities Exchange Act of 1934 (the Act), against Texas Gulf Sulphur Company (TGS) and several of its officers, directors and employees, to enjoin certain conduct by TGS and the individual defendants said to violate Section 10(b) of the Act, and Rule 10b-5 (the Rule), promulgated thereunder, and to compel the rescission by the individual defendants of securities transactions assertedly conducted contrary to law. The complaint alleged (1) that defendants Fogarty,

Mollison, Darke, Murray, Huntington, O'Neill, Clayton, Crawford, and Coates had either personally or through agents purchased TGS stock or thereon from November 12, 1963, through April 16, 1964, on the basis of material inside information concerning the results of TGS drilling in Timmins, Ontario, while such information remained undisclosed to the investing public generally or to the particular sellers; (2) that defendants Darke and Coates had divulged such information to others for use in purchasing TGS stock or calls or recommended its purchase while the information was undisclosed to the public or to the sellers; that defendants Stephens, Fogarty, Mollison, Holyk, and Kline had accepted options to purchase TGS stock on Feb. 20, 1964, without disclosing the material information as to the drilling progress to either the Stock Option Committee or the TGS Board of Directors; and (3) that TGS issued a deceptive press release on April 12, 1964. The case was tried at length before Judge Bonsal of the Southern District of New York, sitting without a jury. Judge Bonsal in a detailed opinion decided, *inter alia*, that the insider activity prior to April 9, 1964, was not illegal because the drilling results were not "material" until then; that Clayton and Crawford had traded after that date; that Coates had committed no violation as he did not trade before disclosure was made; and that the issuance of the press release was not unlawful because it was not issued for the purpose of benefiting the corporation, there was no evidence that any insider used the release to his personal advantage and it was not "misleading, or deceptive on the basis of the facts then known." . . . Defendants Clayton and Crawford appeal from that part of the decision below which held that they had violated Sec. 10(b) and Rule 10b-5 and the SEC appeals from the remainder of the decision which dismissed the complaint against defendants TGS, Fogarty, Mollison, Holyk, Darke, Stephens, Kline, Murray, and Coates.

[What follows are a number of the rulings the court made in the *Texas Gulf Sulphur* case. The case is the leading interpretation of Rule 10b-5.]

1. The essence of the rule of the Securities and Exchange Commission providing that it is unlawful for any person, directly or indirectly, by use of any means or instrumentality of interstate commerce, or of mails, or of any facility of any national securities

exchange, to engage in any act which operates as fraud or deceit is that anyone who, trading for his own account in securities of his corporate employer, has access, directly or indirectly, to information intended to be available only for corporate purpose and not for personal benefit of anyone may not take advantage of such information knowing it is unavailable to the investing public.

2. Not only are directors or management officers of corporation "insiders" within rule of Securities and Exchange Commission, so as to be precluded from dealing in stock of corporation, but any one in possession of material inside information is an "insider" and must either disclose it to investing public, or, if he is disabled from disclosing it in order to protect corporate confidence, or he chooses not to do so, must abstain from trading in or recommending securities concerned while such inside information remains undisclosed.

3. Individuals, who were insiders within meaning of rule of Securities and Exchange Commission precluding insiders from dealing in stock of corporation without disclosing material inside information, were not justified in engaging in insider activity because disclosure of material inside information was forbidden by legitimate corporate activity of acquisition by the corporation of options to purchase land surrounding mineral exploration site, and if information was material, individuals should have kept out of the stock market until disclosure of inside information was accomplished.

4. An insider, within meaning of the rule of the Securities and Exchange Commission, is not always foreclosed from investing in his own corporation merely because he may be more familiar with corporation's operations than are outside investors, and the duty of the insider to disclose information or duty to abstain from dealing in corporation's securities arises only in those situations which are essentially extraordinary in nature and which are reasonably certain to have substantial effect on the market price of the security if extraordinary situation is disclosed.

5. An insider is not obligated by the rule of the Securities and Exchange Commission to confer on outside investors the benefit of his superior financial or other expert analysis of the value of securities of a corporation by disclosing his educated guesses or predictions, and the only regulatory objective is that access to material information be enjoyed equally, and such objective requires nothing more than disclosure of basic facts so that outsiders may draw on their own evaluative expertise in reaching their own investment decisions with knowledge equal to that of insiders.

6. The basic test in determining whether information of insider is "material inside information," so that insider must disclose information or refrain from dealing with stock or securities of corporation, is whether a reasonable man would attach importance to information in determining his choice of action in transaction in question, and that encompasses any fact which in reasonable and objective contemplation might affect value of corporation's stock or securities.

7. "Material inside information" which insider is required by rule of Securities and Exchange Commission to disclose before dealing in stock and securities of corporation includes not only information disclosing earnings but also those facts which affect the probable future of the corporation and those which may affect desire of investors to buy, sell, or hold corporation's securities.

8. Whether facts in possession of insider are material inside information within rule of Securities and Exchange Commission, so that insider cannot deal in stock without disclosing information, when facts known to insider relate to particular event and are undisclosed will depend at any given time on balancing of both, indicated probability that event will occur and anticipated magnitude of event in light of totality of corporation's activity.

9. Knowledge by corporation and certain of its officers and employees of remarkably rich ore drill core was "material inside information" within meaning of rule of Securities and Exchange Commission so that they were required to divulge such information before purchasing stock of corporation.

10. The core of rule of Securities and Exchange Commission providing that it shall be unlawful to use any means or instrumentality of interstate commerce, or of mails, or of any facility of any national securities exchange to make untrue statement of material fact or to omit such statement is implementation of congressional purpose that all investors should have equal access to rewards of participation in securities transactions, and that all members of investing public should be subject to identical market risks, including risk that one's evaluative capacity or one's capital available to put at risk may exceed another's capacity or capital.

11. Even if insiders were in fact ignorant of broad scope of Securities and Exchange Commission and purchased stock as to which they had material inside information under mistaken belief as to applicable law, such ignorance did not insulate them from consequences of their acts in purchasing the stock without first disclosing the material inside information.

12. Insider violated rule of Securities and Exchange Commission and Securities Exchange Act by "tipping" outsider individuals or "tippees" concerning the material inside information about remarkably rich ore drill core made by corporation.

13. Insider, who knew that corporation drilled a core to determine whether ore was present, though he did not know that drilling disclosed remarkably rich ore, but who thereafter participated in program of corporation for acquisition of land surrounding site of drilling, and who then purchased for the first time a call on 100 shares of stock of corporation, possessed material "inside information" so as to make his purchase violative of rule of Securities and Exchange Commission and Securities Exchange Act.

14. Effective protection of the public from insider exploitation of advance notice of material information in violation of rule of Securities and Exchange Commission and Securities Exchange Act in purchase of stock by insider requires that time that insider places an order for stock, rather than time of its ultimate execution, be determinative, otherwise insiders would be able to beat the news of the material inside information to the public.

15. Insider, who had knowledge of remarkably rich ore discovery by corporation, and who telephoned his orders for stock in corporation to broker with instructions to buy at opening of midwest stock exchange the morning that material inside information was disclosed to the public, beat the news and violated rule of Securities and Exchange Commission and Securities Exchange Act.

16. Before insiders may act on material inside information about corporation by purchasing stock in corporation, such information

must have been effectively disclosed to the public in a manner sufficient to insure availability of information to investing public, or there is a violation of rule of Securities and Exchange Commission and Securities Exchange Act.

17. Where formal announcement to entire financial news media has been promised by corporation in prior official release known to news media, all insider activity with respect to stock of corporation must await dissemination of promised official announcement or there is violation of rule of Securities and Exchange Commission and Securities Exchange Act.

18. Insider, who knew of remarkably rich ore discovery by corporation, and who placed his telephone order for stock of corporation about twenty minutes after official news release by corporation of the material inside information violated rule of Securities and Exchange Commission and Securities and Exchange Act, since public did not have equal opportunity to make informed investment judgments by time insider ordered stock.

19. Beliefs of certain insiders, who purchased stock of corporation after learning inside material information that corporation had made a rich ore discovery, that news of ore strike was sufficiently public at time they ordered stock were of no avail to them and did not prevent their purchases of stock from violating rule of Securities and Exchange Commission and Securities Exchange Act, if those beliefs of insiders were not reasonable under circumstances.

20. A member of the top management of a corporation was under duty, before accepting stock option, to disclose any material inside information he may have possessed concerning rich ore discovery by corporation, and rescission of stock option would be directed, where he did not disclose such information to option committee.

21. Dominant congressional purposes underlying Securities Exchange Act of 1934 were to promote free and open public securities markets and to protect investing public from suffering inequities in trading, including specifically, inequities that follow from trading that has been stimulated by publication of false or misleading corporate information releases.

22. Phrase "in connection with purchase or sale of any security" by deceptive device within meaning of rule of Securities and Exchange Commission and Securities Exchange Act making such purchase or sale unlawful means that device employed whatever it might be, be of a sort that would cause reasonable investors to rely thereon, and, in connection therewith, so relying cause them to purchase or sell corporation's securities. . . .

23. Congress by Securities Exchange Act intended to protect investing public in connection with purchases or sales on exchanges from being misled by misleading statements promulgated for or on behalf of corporations irrespective of whether insiders contemporaneously traded in securities of corporation and irrespective of whether corporation or its management had an ulterior purpose or purposes in making official public release. . . .

24. When materially misleading corporate statements or deceptive insider activities have been uncovered, courts should broadly construe phrase "in connection with purchase or sale of any security" by deceptive device as used in rule of Securities and Exchange Commission and Securities Exchange Act.

25. The rule of Securities and Exchange Commission forbidding misleading corporate statements is violated whenever assertions are made by corporation in manner reasonably calculated to influence investing public, by means of financial news media, if such assertions are false or misleading or are so incomplete as to mislead irrespective of whether issuance of release was motivated by corporate officials for ulterior purposes.

26. If corporate management demonstrates that it was diligent in ascertaining information issued by means of financial media was the whole truth and that such diligently obtained information was disseminated in good faith there is no violation of rule of Securities and Exchange Commission forbidding deceptive statements by corporations. . . .

27. Choice by corporation of ambiguous general statement concerning ore discovery rather than summary of specific facts could not reasonably be justified by corporation by any claimed urgency due to rumors, in order to defend charge that corporation violated rule of Securities and Exchange Commission and Securities Exchange Act.

28. Choice by corporation of ambiguous general statement concerning ore discovery rather than summary of specific facts could not be justified on ground that corporation desired to avoid liability under rule of Securities and Exchange Commission and Securities Exchange Act for misrepresentation in event that mining project failed.

29. Choice by corporation of ambiguous general statement of ore discovery rather than summary of specific facts could not be justified on ground that explicit disclosure of facts might have encouraged rumor mill which corporation was seeking to allay, in order to avoid violation of rule of Securities and Exchange Commission and Securities Exchange Act.

## Judgment and Result

[The court held that certain insiders violated Section 10(b) and Rule 10b-5.] For reasons which appear below, we decide the various issues presented as follows:

1. As to Clayton and Crawford, as purchasers of stock on April 15 and 16, 1964, we affirm the finding that they violated 15 U.S.C. § 78j(b) and Rule 10b-5 and remand, for a determination of the appropriate remedy.

2. As to Murray, we affirm the dismissal of the complaint.

3. As to Mollison and Holyk, as recipients of certain stock options, we affirm the dismissal of the complaint.

4. As to Stephens and Fogarty, as recipients of stock options, we reverse the dismissal of the complaint and remand for a further determination as to whether an injunction should issue.

5. As to Kline, as a recipient of a stock option, we reverse the dismissal of the complaint and remand with directions to issue an order rescinding the option and for a determination of any other appropriate remedy in connection therewith.

6. As to Fogarty, Mollison, Holyk, Darke, and Huntington, as purchasers of stock or calls thereon between November 12, 1963, and April 9, 1964, we reverse the dismissal of the complaint and find that they violated 15 U.S.C. § 78j(b) and Rule 10b-5, and remand, for a determination of the appropriate remedy.

7. As to Clayton, although the district judge did not specify that the complaint be dismissed with respect to his purchase of TGS stock before April 9, 1964, such a dismissal is implicit in his treatment of the individual appellees who acted similarly. Consequently, although Clayton is named only as an appellant, our decision with respect to the materiality of K-55-1 (a core drilling sample) renders it necessary to treat him also as an appellee. Thus, as to him, as one who purchased stock between November 12, 1963, and April 9, 1964, we reverse the implicit dismissal of the complaint, find that he violated § 78j(b) and Rule 10b-5, and remand, for a determination of the appropriate remedy.

8. As to Darke, as one who passed on information to tippees, we reverse the dismissal of the complaint and remand, for a determination of the appropriate remedy.

9. As to Coates, as one who on April 16th purchased stock and gave information on which his son-in-law broker and the broker's customers purchased shares, we reverse the dismissal of the complaint, find that he violated [the 1934 Securities Exchange Act] and Rule 10b-5, and remand, for a determination of the appropriate remedy.

10. As to Texas Gulf Sulphur, we reverse the dismissal of the complaint and remand for a further determination by the district judge in the light of the approach taken in this opinion. . . .

## Questions

1. Who are insiders for purposes of Section 10(b) of the Securities Exchange Act and Rule 10b-5?
2. If a person is an insider, how does that status affect that person's ability to deal in the issuer's securities?
3. What does the insider trading rule apply to? Stocks? Bonds? Puts? Calls? Anything else?
4. Does the insider trading rule apply only to corporate issuers?
5. How long after inside information becomes public must an insider wait before dealing in the firm's security?

Almost 30 years after the *Texas Gulf Sulphur* case, the U.S. Supreme Court was presented with the question of whether an "outsider" could be liable to the source for misappropriating inside information under section 10b and Rule 10b-5. *United States v. O'Hagan* deals with this issue.

## United States v. O'Hagan
U.S. Supreme Court
521 U.S. 642 (1997)

### Background and Facts

After Grand Metropolitan PLC (Grand Met) retained the law firm of Dorsey & Whitney to represent it regarding a potential tender offer for the Pillsbury Company's common stock, respondent O'Hagan, a Dorsey & Whitney partner who did no work on the representation, began purchasing call options for Pillsbury stock, as well as shares of the stock. Following Dorsey & Whitney's withdrawal from the representation, Grand Met publicly announced its tender offer, the price of Pillsbury stock rose dramatically, and O'Hagan sold his call options and stock at a profit of more than $4.3 million. A Securities and Exchange Commission (SEC) investigation culminated in a 57 count indictment alleging, among other things, that O'Hagan defrauded his law firm and its client, Grand Met, by misappropriating for his own trading purposes material, nonpublic information regarding the tender offer. The indictment charged O'Hagan with securities fraud in violation of § 10(b) of the Securities Exchange Act of 1934 and SEC Rule 10b-5. . . . A jury convicted O'Hagan on all counts, and he was sentenced to prison. The Eighth Circuit reversed all of the convictions, holding that § 10(b) and Rule 10b-5 liability may not be grounded on the "misappropriation theory" of securities fraud on which the prosecution relied. . . .

### Body of Opinion

**Justice Ruth Bader Ginsburg.** This case concerns the interpretation and enforcement of § 10(b) . . . and rules made by the Securities and Exchange Commission pursuant to these provisions, Rule 10b-5. . . . Two prime questions are presented. The first relates to the misappropriation of material, nonpublic information for securities trading; [the second is omitted here]. In particular, we address and resolve these issues: (1) Is a person who trades in securities for personal profit, using confidential information misappropriated in breach of a fiduciary duty to the source of the information, guilty of violating § 10(b) and Rule 10b-5? . . . [The second, not involving § 10(b) is omitted.] Our answer to the first question is yes. . . .

The Eighth Circuit rejected the misappropriation theory as a basis for § 10(b) liability. We hold, in accord with several other Courts of Appeals, that criminal liability under § 10(b) may be predicated on the misappropriation theory. . . .

Under the "traditional" or "classic theory" of insider trading liability, § 10(b) and Rule 10b-5 are violated when a corporate insider trades in securities of his corporation on the basis of material, nonpublic information. Trading on such information qualifies as a "deceptive device" under § 10(b), we have affirmed, because "a relationship of trust and confidence [exists] between the shareholders of a corporation and those insiders who have obtained confidential information by reason of their position with that corporation." . . . That relationship, we recognized, "gives rise to a duty to disclose [or to abstain from trading] because of the necessity of preventing a corporate insider from . . . taking unfair advantage of . . . uninformed . . . stockholders." . . . The classic theory applies not only to officers, directors, an other permanent insiders of a corporation, but also to attorneys, accountants, consultants, and others who temporarily become fiduciaries of a corporation. . . .

The "misappropriation theory" holds that a person commits fraud "in connection with" a securities transaction, and thereby violates § 10(b) and Rule 10b-5, when he appropriates confidential information for securities trading purposes, in breach of duty owed to the source of the information. . . . Under this theory, a fiduciary's undisclosed, self-serving use of a principal's information to purchase or sell securities, in breach of a duty of loyalty and confidentiality, defrauds the principal of the exclusive use of that information. In lieu of premising liability on a fiduciary relationship between company insider and purchaser or seller of the company's stock, the misappropriation theory premises liability on a fiduciary turned trader's deception of those who entrusted him with access to confidential information.

The two theories are complementary, each addressing efforts to capitalize on nonpublic information through the purchase or sale of securities. The classic theory targets a corporate insider's breach of duty to shareholders with whom the insider transacts; the misappropriation theory outlaws trading on the basis of nonpublic information by a corporate "outsider" in breach of a duty owed not to the trading party, but to the source of the information. The misappropriation theory is thus designed to "protect the integrity if the securities markets against abuses by 'outsiders' to a corporation who have access to confidential information that will affect the corporation's security price when revealed, but who owe no fiduciary or other duty to that corporation's shareholders."

In this case, the indictment alleged that O'Hagan, in breach of a duty of trust and confidence he owed to his law firm, Dorsey & Whitney, and to its client, Grand Met, traded on the basis of nonpublic information regarding Grand Met's planned tender offer for Pillsbury common stock. This conduct, the Government charged, constituted a fraudulent device in connection with the purchase and sale of securities.

We agree with the Government that misappropriation as just defined, satisfies § 10(b)'s requirement that chargeable conduct involve a "deceptive device or contrivance" used "in connection with" the purchase or sale of securities. We observe, first, that misappropriators, as the Government describes them, deal in deception. A fiduciary who "pretends loyalty to the principal while secretly converting the principal's information for personal gain," . . . "dupes" or defrauds the principal. . . .

We turn next to the § 10(b) requirement that the misappropriator's deceptive use of information be "in connection with the purchase or sale of a security." This element is satisfied because the fiduciary's fraud is consummated, not when the fiduciary gains the confidential information, but when, without disclosure to the principal, he uses the information to purchase or sell securities. The securities transaction and the breach of duty thus coincide. This is so even though the person or entity defrauded is not the other party to the trade, but is, instead, the source of the nonpublic information. . . . A misappropriator who trades on the basis of material, nonpublic information, in short, gains his advantageous market position through deception, he deceives the source of the information and simultaneously harms members of the investing public. . . .

The misappropriation theory targets information of a sort that misappropriators ordinarily capitalize upon to gain no risk profits through the purchase or sale of securities. Should a misappropriator put such information to other use, the statute's prohibition would not be implicated. The theory does not catch all conceivable forms of fraud involving confidential information; rather, it catches fraudulent means of capitalizing on such information through securities transactions.

The Government notes another limitation on the forms of fraud § 10(b) reaches: "The misappropriation theory would not . . . apply to a case in which a person defrauded a bank into giving him a loan or embezzled cash from another, and then used the proceeds of the misdeed to purchase securities." . . . In such a case, the Government states, "the proceeds would have value to the malefactor apart from their use in a securities transaction, and the fraud would be complete as soon as the money was obtained." . . . In other words, money can buy, if not anything, then at least many things; its misappropriation may thus be viewed as sufficiently detached from a subsequent securities transaction that § 10(b)'s "in connection with" requirement would not be met. . . .

The misappropriation theory comports with § 10(b)'s language, which requires deception "in connection with the purchase or sale of any security," not deception of an identifiable purchaser or seller. The theory is also well tuned to an animating purpose of the Exchange Act: to insure honest securities markets and thereby promote investor confidence. . . .

## Judgment and Result

O'Hagan violated the Securities and Exchange Act's Section 10(b).

## Questions

1. Was O'Hagan an insider trading on insider information? If not, how could he be liable under Section 10(b)?

2. If O'Hagan's conduct violated Section 10(b), a misrepresentation must have occurred. Where was the misrepresentation by O'Hagan here? His failure to disclose his personal trading to the persons from whom he bought Pillsbury shares? Or his failure to disclose to Grand Met and his law firm—the source of the information? Was his misrepresentation an affirmative misrepresentation or misrepresentation by concealment?

*Tippees.* A tippee is someone getting material nonpublic information about an issuer from an insider. Is tippee trading in the company's security illegal? Not always. If the insider breaks a fiduciary duty to the issuer by disclosing the information to the tippee, it is illegal for the tippee to trade in the issuer's securities unless the tippee discloses the tip before trading. On the other hand, if the insider is not breaking a fiduciary duty by disclosing information to the tippee, the tippee may trade or act on the information. The *Dirks v. SEC* case so held.

## INSIDER TRADING SANCTIONS ACT

In 1984 Congress enacted the Insider Trading Sanctions Act to regulate insider trading. That act has the following provisions:

1. *Civil penalties.* The SEC is authorized to seek civil penalties in federal court against anyone buying or selling securities while possessing material nonpublic information.
2. *Triple damages.* Damages of up to three times the profit made (or loss avoided) by using nonpublic information are possible. (Before this statute, recovery was limited to giving up any profits.)
3. *Criminal penalties.* Criminal penalties for insider trading are increased from $10,000 to $100,000.
4. *Stock options.* Insider trading in stock options is explicitly stated as being illegal.
5. *Aiders and abettors.* The SEC can sue anyone aiding and abetting someone else who communicates material nonpublic information. No triple damages are available against aiders and abettors.
6. *Statute of limitations.* This statute contains a five-year statute of limitations.
7. *No definition.* The act does not define insider trading or material nonpublic information.

## TAKEOVER BIDS (TENDER OFFERS)

*Definitions.* A takeover bid, or tender offer, occurs when someone publicly offers to buy stock from a corporation's shareholders at a set price. Shareholders can then tender their stock to the offeror. Shareholders do not have to tender their stock. The offeror must give all who tender the same price. Acceptance of tendered stock is sometimes conditioned on a certain percentage—often a controlling percentage—of the stock being tendered. Shareholders may withdraw tendered stock for the first seven days of a tender offer. They may also withdraw their tendered shares if they are not purchased after sixty days following the start of the offer.

Tender offers are one way a person (including a corporation) or group can take control of a corporation. The corporation whose stock is sought is called the **target corporation**. The one offering to buy the securities is the **tender offeror**.

*Federal Regulation.* The Securities Exchange Act of 1934 (SEA) and the Williams Act of 1968 (amending the SEA) regulate tender offers. If a tender offer would result in the offeror's owning more than five percent of a class of securities registered under the SEA, the offeror must file with the SEC and furnish each offeree certain data. That data must have five items:

1. The offeror's background
2. Where the offeror gets the money to make the offer
3. Why the tender offer is made
4. How many shares are owned
5. Any relevant contracts, arrangements, and understandings

Also, any person who acquires more than 5 percent of any security registered under the SEA must file the prior five-point report with the SEC and the target corporation ten days after getting more than 5 percent ownership.

*Purpose of Regulating Tender Offers.* Tender offers can be friendly to the target corporation's management. Often, however, the target's management sees tender offers as threats to their jobs. This perception has led to **golden parachutes**—contracts with high severance pay that existing managers give themselves if a takeover is successful and the new owners fire them.

In an unfriendly takeover bid, the tender offeror often tells the target's shareholders that existing management is stupid and lazy. The tender offeror then may offer the target's shareholders much more than market value for their stock. Existing managers, in turn, caution shareholders not to sell because they think that the tender offerors would ruin the company and its communities by closing plants and firing hard-working employees. Federal law (the SEA) helps target shareholders get the facts from both sides in such a takeover fight by letting existing management know that its corporation is a target.

*Misstatements.* Misstating or omitting a material fact, or engaging in any fraudulent, deceptive, or manipulative acts in connection with a tender offer, is unlawful. In the following case, a shareholder of a target company claimed that a series of tender offers resulted in her not benefiting as much as she would have had the first tender offer been the only one, which violated the Williams Act's prohibition against fraudulent, deceptive, or manipulative acts or practices. Read the *Schreiber* case to see whether the Supreme Court agreed with her.

## Schreiber v. Burlington Northern, Inc.
U.S. Supreme Court
472 U.S. 1 (1985)

### Background and Facts

On December 21, 1982, Burlington Northern, Inc., made a hostile tender offer for El Paso Gas Co. Through a wholly owned subsidiary, Burlington proposed to purchase 25.1 million El Paso shares at $24 per share. Burlington reserved the right to terminate the offer if any of several specified events occurred. El Paso management initially opposed the takeover, but its shareholders responded favorably, fully subscribing to the offer by the December 30, 1982, deadline.

Burlington did not accept those tendered shares; instead, after negotiations with El Paso management, Burlington announced on January 10, 1983, the terms of a new and friendly takeover agreement. Pursuant to the new agreement, Burlington undertook, *inter alia*, to (1) rescind the December tender offer, (2) purchase 4,166,667 shares from El Paso at $24 per share, (3) substitute a new tender offer for only 21 million shares at $24 per share, (4) provide procedural protections against a squeeze-out merger[1] of the remaining El Paso shareholders, and (5) recognize "golden parachute" contracts between El Paso and four of its senior officers. By February 8, more than 40 million shares were tendered in response to Burlington's January offer, and the takeover was completed.

The rescission of the first tender offer caused a diminished payment to those shareholders who had tendered during the first offer. The January offer was greatly oversubscribed and consequently those shareholders who retendered were subject to substantial proration. Petitioner Barbara Schreiber filed suit on behalf of herself and similarly situated shareholders, alleging that Burlington, El Paso, and members of El Paso's board of directors violated § 14(e)'s prohibition of "fraudulent, deceptive or manipulative acts or practices . . . in connection with any tender offer." She claimed that Burlington's withdrawal of the December tender offer was a "manipulative" distortion of the market for El Paso stock. Schreiber also alleged that Burlington violated § 14(e) by failing in the January offer to disclose the "golden parachutes" offered to four of El Paso's managers. She claims that this January nondisclosure was a deceptive act forbidden by § 14(e).

The District Court dismissed the suit for failure to state a claim. The District Court reasoned that the alleged manipulation did not involve a misrepresentation, and so did not violate § 14(e). District Court relied on the fact that in cases involving alleged violations of §10(b) of the Securities Exchange Act, this Court has required misrepresentation for there to be a "manipulative" violation of the section.

The Court of Appeals for the Third Circuit affirmed.

## Body of Opinion

**Chief Justice Burger.** We are asked in this case to interpret § 14(e) of the Securities Exchange Act. The starting point is the language of the statute. Section 14(e) provides:

> It shall be unlawful for any person to make any untrue statement of a material fact or omit to state any material fact necessary in order to make the statements made, in the light of the circumstances under which they are made, not misleading, or to engage in any fraudulent, deceptive, or manipulative acts or practices, in connection with any tender offer or request or invitation for tenders, or any solicitation of security holders in opposition to or in favor of any such offer, request, or invitation. The Commission shall, for the purposes of this subsection, by rules and regulations define, and prescribe means reasonably designed to prevent, such acts and practices as are fraudulent, deceptive, or manipulative.

Petitioner relies on a construction of the phrase, "fraudulent, deceptive, or manipulative acts or practices." Petitioner reads the phrase "fraudulent, deceptive or manipulative acts or practices" to include acts which, although fully disclosed, "artificially" affect the price of the takeover target's stock. Petitioner's interpretation relies on the belief that § 14(e) is directed at purposes broader than providing full and true information to investors. . . .

She argues, however, that the term *manipulative* takes on a meaning in § 14(e) that is different from the meaning it has in § 10(b). Petitioner claims that the use of the disjunctive or in § 14(e) implies that acts need not be deceptive or fraudulent to be manipulative. But Congress used the phrase "manipulative or deceptive" in § 10(b) as well, and we have interpreted manipulative in that context to require misrepresentation. Moreover, it is a "familiar principle of statutory construction that words grouped in a list should be given related meaning." *Securities Industry Assn. v. Board of Governors, FRS* (1984). All three species of misconduct, i.e., "fraudulent, deceptive, or manipulative," listed by Congress are directed at failures to disclose. The use of the term *manipulative* provides emphasis and guidance to those who must determine which types of acts are reached by the statute; it does not suggest a deviation from the section's facial and primary concern with disclosure or congressional concern with disclosure which is the core of the Act.

Our conclusion that *manipulative* acts under § 14(e) require misrepresentation or nondisclosure is buttressed by the purpose and legislative history of the provision.

The expressed legislative intent was to preserve a neutral setting in which the contenders could fully present their arguments. The Senate sponsor went on to say:

> We have taken extreme care to avoid tipping the scales either in favor of management or in favor of the person making the takeover bids. § 510 is designed solely to require full and fair disclosure for the benefit of investors. The bill will at the same time provide the offeror and management equal opportunity to present their case.

To implement this objective, the Williams Act added §§ 13(d), 13(e), 14(d), 14(e), and 14(f) to the Securities Exchange Act. Some relate to disclosure; §§ 13(d), 14(d), and 14(f) all add specific registration and disclosure provisions. Others—§§ 13(e) and 14(d)—require or prohibit certain acts so that investors will possess additional time within which to take advantage of the disclosed information.

Section 14(e) adds a "broad antifraud prohibition," *Piper v. Chris Craft Industries, Inc.*, modeled on the antifraud provisions of § 10(b) of the Act and Rule 10b-5. It supplements the more precise

---

[1] A "squeeze-out" merger occurs when Corporation A, which holds a controlling interest in Corporation B, uses its control to merge B into itself or into a wholly owned subsidiary. The minority shareholders in Corporation B are, in effect, forced to sell their stock. The procedural protection provided in the agreement between El Paso and Burlington required the approval of non-Burlington members of El Paso's board of directors before a squeeze-out merger could proceed. Burlington eventually purchased all the remaining shares of El Paso for $12 cash and one-quarter share of Burlington preferred stock per share. The parties dispute whether this consideration was equal to that paid to those tendering during the January tender offer.

disclosure provisions found elsewhere in the Williams Act, while requiring disclosure more explicitly addressed to the tender offer context than that required by § 10(b). . . .

Nowhere in the legislative history is there the slightest suggestion that §14(e) serves any purpose other than disclosure, or that the term *manipulative* should be read as an invitation to the courts to oversee the substantive fairness of tender offers; the quality of any offer is a matter for the marketplace.

To adopt the reading of the term *manipulative* urged by petitioner would not only be unwarranted in light of the legislative purpose but would be at odds with it. Inviting judges to read the term *manipulative* with their own sense of what constitutes "unfair" or "artificial" conduct would inject uncertainty into the tender offer process. An essential piece of information—whether the court would deem the fully disclosed actions of one side or the other to be *manipulative*—would not be available until after the tender offer had closed. This uncertainty would directly contradict the expressed congressional desire to give investors full information.

## Judgment and Result

1. *Manipulative* acts under § 14(e) require misrepresentation or nondisclosure. To read the term *manipulative* in § 14(e) to include acts that, although fully disclosed, "artificially" affect the price of the takeover target's stock, conflicts with the normal meaning of the term as connoting conduct designed to deceive or defraud investors by controlling or artificially affecting the price of securities.

2. This interpretation of the term *manipulative* as used in § 14(e) is supported by the provision's purpose and legislative history. The purpose of the Williams Act, which added §14(e) to the Securities Exchange Act, was to ensure that public shareholders who are confronted with a tender offer will not be required to respond without adequate information. Nowhere in the legislative history is there any suggestion that § 14(e) serves any purpose other than disclosure, or that the term *manipulative* should be read as an invitation to the courts to oversee the substantive fairness of tender offers; the quality of any offer is a matter for the marketplace.

3. Applying the above interpretation of the term *manipulative* to this case, respondents' actions were not manipulative. (Plaintiff lost.)

## Questions

1. What are the objectives of the Williams Act, which governs tender offers?
2. Do Sections 14(e) and 10(b) of the 1934 SEA have similar purposes?
3. Describe how plaintiff was wronged by the tender offer process.
4. Was it possible for the Supreme Court to find *for* plaintiff? Why did it refuse to do so?
5. To whom does the tender offeror owe a duty not to be manipulative—to its own shareholders or to the target's shareholders?
6. What is the natural law philosophy in the Williams Act?

## CRIMINAL VIOLATIONS OF SEA

Violations of the SEA or its rules and regulations must be willful to be crimes. Section 32 of the SEA makes criminal the willful and knowing making of a statement in a required report, application, or document that is false or misleading in any material respect. An example of a Section 32 violation is an accountant's signing a corporation's financial statements as being fair representations of the firm's financial status when the accountant knows they are not. Accountants have been convicted for committing this federal felony.

Punishment can be up to five years in prison, up to a $100,000 fine, or both for SEA criminal violations. Conviction for a criminal violation prevents certain benefits under the securities laws (for example, use of the small issue exemption under the Securities Act of 1933 or association with a registered investment company).

## FOREIGN CORRUPT PRACTICES ACT

*Internal Reports.* The Foreign Corrupt Practices Act (FCPA) has three principal sections: 102, 103, and 104. Section 102 establishes internal reporting requirements for companies subject to the FCPA. These requirements are designed to put management in a position to know whether bribes are being paid directly or indirectly to foreign officials or political parties or candidates.

*Foreign Corrupt Practices.* Section 103 prohibits foreign corrupt practices—bribes—by issuers. An issuer is any firm required to register its securities under the 1934 Securities Exchange Act. The FCPA also makes it illegal for any U.S. citizen or domestic concern to use the U.S. mail or interstate commerce to commit a foreign corrupt practice. As such, the FCPA covers nonissuers of securities.

*Penalties.* Violations of the FCPA are federal felonies. An issuer committing prohibited foreign corrupt practices is subject to a fine of not more than $2,000,000. The fine could be a substantial deterrent to small firms. For large concerns, the stigma of a conviction would be more adverse than the size of the fine. Any officer or director of an issuer or stockholder acting on the issuer's behalf who willfully violates the corrupt practices applicable to issuers can be fined not more than $100,000, imprisoned for not more than five years, or both. The same penalties apply to domestic concerns, officers, directors, and shareholders acting on behalf of domestic concerns who bribe foreign officials or political party officials, or any person with reason to know his or her bribe will end up in the hands of a foreign official, foreign political candidate, or party official. (For more about the FCPA, see Chapter 9.)

## STATE SECURITIES REGULATION

Each individual state has the power to regulate securities within its borders. The federal constitutional basis for such state authority is found in the Tenth Amendment to the U.S. Constitution, which reserves power to the states that is not expressly given to the national government or retained by the people. The specific reserved power that the states invoke to regulate securities is the police power—the power to regulate to promote the health, safety, morals, and general welfare of the state.

*To check out individual state securities laws go to **http://www. prairienet.org/~scruffy/f.htm***

Some states were in the securities regulation business long before the federal government was. In 1911, Kansas was the first state to attempt to regulate securities. Other states have adopted securities laws, called **blue-sky laws**, designed to prevent sale by unscrupulous people of securities that represent nothing more than an interest in the blue sky. About half the states have passed the Uniform Securities Act as their blue-sky law.

Other states have their own blue-sky laws, which are usually of three types: licensing, disclosure, and fraud. The licensing type requires sellers of securities to obtain state licenses before engaging in the securities business. Such laws impose a duty on licensed sellers to disclose to prospective purchasers information germane to the security. The disclosure type of blue-sky law is akin to the philosophy of the Federal Securities Act of 1933, which is also one of full and fair disclosure. The idea is that the investor should be provided with all relevant facts about the issues before deciding whether to invest. People who provide facts are liable for falsity or omission of material facts. A registration statement similar to that filed under the Securities Act of 1933 furnishes investors with facts relevant to their decision to invest. The fraud type of blue-sky law forbids misrepresentation in the sale of securities. A violation of such statutes usually results in civil (damages and injunctions) and criminal sanctions.

State regulation of securities has been uneven. In some states, saying that such regulation exists is a joke, even though statutes are on the books. In other states—and they constitute a minority—regulation does exist. In fairness to the states, the same securities being regulated once by the feds and once by the states no doubt has caused a number of states not to regulate securities, even though they have the constitutional authority to do so.

The 1995 Private Securities Litigation Reform Act has amended the 1933 Securities Act as well as the 1934 Securities Exchange Act. A major change this act affects is the introduction of proportional liability (rather than joint and several liability) in certain situations.

The Sarbanes–Oxley Act of 2002 creates a new accounting standards and oversight panel, limits consulting services by audit firms of publicly traded clients, mandates rotation of lead auditor partners, and increases criminal penalties for obstruction of justice and schemes or artifices to defraud. It also imposes new rules on corporate governance. Finally, it protects research analysts from being punished by their firms for criticizing firm clients, and increases the time that investors have to sue for securities fraud.

## CHAPTER SUMMARY

A number of federal laws attempt to regulate the sale of securities. Two of the most important such laws are the Securities Act of 1933 and the Securities Exchange Act of 1934.

The Supreme Court defines *security* by using the *Howey* case definition. According to this definition, an investment in a common enterprise for profit expectation from third-party efforts qualifies something as a security. Courts examine the substance, not form, of an investment to determine whether it is a security.

The main objective of the Securities Act of 1933 is to provide full and fair disclosure of new securities offered for sale. This act does not require the government to tell the public whether an investment is good or bad. The 1933 Securities Act requires that nonexempt securities be registered with the SEC.

The Securities Exchange Act of 1934 created the Securities and Exchange Commission (SEC). The SEC is charged with administering many laws that regulate the securities markets.

The Securities Exchange Act of 1934 regulates the secondary market, made up of "used" or already issued securities. The 1934 Act requires that certain securities be registered unless exempt. The 1934 Act also imposes proxy statement requirements, credit restrictions, short-swing profit prohibitions, and antifraud provisions. Civil and criminal sanctions may be brought for violations of the 1934 Securities Exchange Act.

State laws also regulate the sale of securities.

---

### ■ MANAGER'S ETHICAL DILEMMA

"I got information from a company whistleblower, who said the company had nonexistent assets, so I advised clients to short the stock [sell stock they did not own and buy such stock to cover later when the stock price hopefully is lower] and when the company collapsed, my clients made money," said Ray Dirks, a securities analyst.

"But Ray," said a friend, "that's illegal. You were a tippee, and tippees who receive any information from insiders are strictly prohibited from trading in the stock."

"Oh, no," replied Dirks. "I was neither an 'insider' nor a 'tippee' from an insider who was violating any duty owed to the issuer. Therefore, I could trade in the issuer's stock using insider information."

"That's hogwash," said the friend. "There is an absolute prohibition on tippees' trading in an issuer's stock."

What do you think? Should a tippee trade in an issuer's stock?

## DISCUSSION QUESTIONS

1. Discussion is currently ongiong about the creation of a new body to regulate both commodities exchanges, currently regulated by the Commodities Futures Trading Commission (CFTC), and the securities exchanges, now regulated by the Securities and Exchange Commission (SEC). What do you see as the pros and cons of such a proposal?

2. In 1986 and 1988, the Colorado Springs–Stetson Hills Public Building Authority issued a total of $26 million in bonds to finance public improvements at Stetson Hills, a planned residential and commercial development in Colorado Springs. Central Bank served as the bond trustee for the bond issues.

   The bonds were secured by landowner assessment liens, which covered about 250 acres for the 1986 bond issue and about 272 acres for the 1988 bond issue. The bond covenants required that the land subject to the liens be worth at least 160 percent of the bonds' outstanding principal and interest. The covenants required AmWest Development, the developer of Stetson Hills, to give Central Bank an annual report containing evidence that the 160 percent test was met.

   In January 1988, AmWest provided Central Bank an updated appraisal of the land securing the 1986 bonds and of the proposed liens to to secure the 1988 bonds. The 1988 appraisal showed land values almost unchanged from the 1986 appraisal. Soon afterward, Central Bank received a letter from the senior underwriter for the 1986 bonds. Noting that property values were declining in Colorado Springs and that Central Bank was operating on an appraisal over more than sixteen months old, the underwriter expressed concern that the 160 percent test was not being met.

   Central Bank asked its in-house appraiser to review the updated 1988 appraisal. The in-house appraiser decided that the values listed in the appraisal appeared optimistic, considering the local real estate market. He suggested that Central Bank retain an outside appraiser to conduct an independent review of the 1988 appraisal. After an exchange of letters between Central Bank and AmWest in early 1988, Central Bank agreed to delay independent review of the appraisal until the end of the year, six months after the June 1988 closing on the bond issue. Before the independent review was complete, however, the Authority defaulted on the 1988 bonds.

   First Interstate and Jack Naber had purchased $2.1 million of the 1988 bonds. After the default, First Interstate and Naber sued the Authority, the 1988 underwriter, a junior underwriter, an AmWest director, and Central Bank for violations of Section 10(b) of the Securities Exchange Act of 1934. The complaint alleged that the Authority, the underwriter defendants, and the AmWest director had violated Section 10(b) for its conduct in aiding and abetting the fraud. A federal district court found for defendant Central Bank (the bond trustee). The U.S. Court of Appeals for the Tenth Circuit reversed, holding that there is a Section 10(b) aiding and abetting civil claim when: (1) there is a primary violation of 10(b); (2) there is recklessness by an aider and abettor (here, Central Bank, the bond trustee for failure to update the appraisal in a timely fashion); and (3) substantial assistance is given to the primary violator by the aider and abettor (i.e., would the 1988 bond issue have been marketable had the trustee reappraised the land that secured the bond issue?).

   The bond trustee (Central Bank) appealed to the U.S. Supreme Court arguing that Section 10(b) of the 1934 Act, coupled with a federal aiding and abetting statute, does not create a private aider and abettor cause of action. Who won? [*Central Bank v. First Interstate Bank*, 114 S.Ct. 1439 (1994)].

3. Winans was coauthor of a *Wall Street Journal* investment advice column that, because of its perceived quality and integrity, had an impact on the market prices of the stocks it discussed. Although he was familiar with the *Journal*'s rule that the column's contents were the *Journal*'s confidential information prior to publication, Winans entered into a scheme with Felis and another stockbroker who, in exchange for advance information from Winans as to the timing and contents of the column, bought and sold stocks based on the column's probable impact on the market. They then shared their profits with Winans. On the basis of this scheme, Winans and Felis were convicted of criminal violations of Section 10(b) of the Securities Exchange Act of 1934. The Court of Appeals affirmed. Winans appealed to the U.S. Supreme Court, arguing that the alleged fraud victim, the *Journal*, was not a buyer or seller of the stocks traded and thus the fraud was not covered by Section 10(b) of the Securities Exchange Act, because it requires fraud "in connection with the purchase or sale of any security." What was the result? [*Carpenter v. United States*, 108 S.Ct. 316 (1987)].

4. Securities brokers get commissions whenever a customer buys or sells a security (even if the customer loses money). Commissions may tempt brokers to urge customers to buy and sell securities frequently, even if such sales or purchases are not in the customer's best interests. Such frequent broker-encouraged trades are called *churning*. Is churning a

violation of the Securities Exchange Act of 1934; that is, is it considered a fraud in connection with the purchase and sale of securities? [*Costello v. Oppenheimer & Co., Inc.*, 711 F.2d 1361 (7th Cir. 1983)].

5. Are punitive damages recoverable under a Rule 10b-5 claim? [*Meyers v. Moody*, 693 F.2d 1196, rehearing denied 701 F.2d 173 (5th Cir. 1983)].

6. A newspaper financial columnist bought stock in a company. He then wrote a column advising people to buy that stock. He did not mention in his column that he owned stock in the recommended company. The column appeared, the stock rose, and the columnist sold his stock, making a profit. Does this conduct (known as *scalping*) violate Section 10(b) of the Securities Exchange Act of 1934 and Rule 10b-5? [*Zweig v. Hearst Corp.*, 594 F.2d 1261 (9th Cir. 1979)].

7. Michael Moss owned 5,000 shares of Deseret Pharmaceutical Company. Warner-Lambert Company wanted to buy Deseret stock to take over the company. Warner hired Morgan Stanley, Inc. to recommend an appropriate price to offer Deseret's shareholders. Courtois, a Morgan Stanley employee, learned of the possible Warner purchase of Deseret. On November 30, 1976, Courtois and two friends, Newman and Antoniu, bought 11,700 shares of Deseret (including Moss's stock) at $28 per share. The next day, December 1, 1976, the New York Stock Exchange stopped trading in Deseret for six days when Warner announced it would buy Deseret stock for $38 per share. Newman, Courtois, and Antoniu sold their 11,700 shares and made a big profit. Did they violate Section 10(b) of the 1934 Securities Exchange Act and Rule 10b-5 by buying Deseret stock, knowing of Warner-Lambert's upcoming offer and without telling existing Deseret stockholders about it when they bought their stock? [*Moss v. Morgan Stanley, Inc.*, 719 F.2d 5 (2d Cir. 1983)].

8. A securities broker was making a sales pitch to Edna Brown. Edna was not sure whether buying stock in the recommended company was a good investment. The broker pulled out a prospectus that the company had filed with the SEC and said, "Edna, the SEC has registered this stock. Therefore, you can bet your last dollar that it's a good investment." Do you agree? When the SEC registers a new security under the 1933 Securities Act, what is the SEC saying?

9. Sometimes one corporation will try to buy another corporation's stock from existing shareholders to take control of the corporation. This offer is called a *tender offer*. The tender offer price per share is usually above the share's existing market price. The company to be taken over is called the *target company*. The target company's management gets nervous when another firm tries to take it over. Why?

Because one of the first things the buyer does is fire the target firm's existing management. Can the target company's management get a court to stop a takeover by showing that the group making the tender offer did not disclose material financial information about two members of the takeover group? [*Pabst Brewing Co. v. Kalmanovitz*, 551 F. Supp. 882 (D.C. Del. 1982)].

10. Must people making a tender offer disclose their general business philosophy to the target corporation's shareholders? Existing management of Pabst Brewing Company argued that Kalmanovitz, who owned a competing brewery, planned to shut down several Pabst plants if his takeover bid succeeded. Pabst management thought Pabst shareholders should know of Kalmanovitz's plan before they sold their stock to Kalmanovitz. [*Pabst Brewing Co. v. Kalmanovitz*, 551 F. Supp. 882 (D.C. Del. 1982)].

11. Suppose Sally Morgan is an insider under Rule 16(b). She buys and sells 100 shares of her company's stock within a five-month period, making $1,000 on the deal. Assume that she did not actually use any inside information when she made her purchase and sale. Has she violated Rule 16(b), and can the company recover the $1,000? [*Smolowe v. Delendo Corp.*, 136 F. 2d 231 (2d Cir. 1943)].

12. Why should management know if one of its employees is violating the Foreign Corrupt Practices Act? (See Section 102 of the Foreign Corrupt Practices Act.)

13. Mr. Chiarella worked as a markup man in Pandick Press's New York composing room. Chiarella handled announcements of corporate takeover bids. When a corporation delivered these documents to Pandick Press, the names of the acquiring and target corporation were hidden by either fake names or blank spaces. The corporations sent the true names on the night of the final printing. Mr. Chiarella figured out the target companies' names (the companies being bought) before the final printing from other information in the documents. Without telling anyone what he knew, Chiarella bought stock in the target companies. He then sold it soon after the takeover attempts became publicly known. He made more than $30,000 through this method over fourteen months. The SEC investigated him, and he agreed to return the profits to the people from whom he had bought the stock. His employer fired him, and he was later indicted for violating Section 10(b) of the Securities Exchange Act of 1934 and Rule 10b-5. Chiarella was convicted. He appealed first to the court of appeals, which affirmed his conviction. He then appealed to the U.S. Supreme Court, arguing that his failure to inform sellers of the stock in target companies he had bought was not a fraud under

Rule 10b-5 of the Securities Exchange Act of 1934. Does a duty to disclose under Section 10(b) arise just because Chiarella had nonpublic information? [*Chiarella v. United States*, 445 U.S. 222 (1980)].

14. The SEC charged that Texas International Company's (TI) president, George Platt, while in the stands at a track meet, told his son and Barry Switzer, University of Oklahoma football coach, that TI was going to sell a company (Phoenix Resources) it controlled. Platt and Switzer allegedly bought stock in Phoenix Resources and sold it at a profit. Did Platt intentionally tip Switzer in violation of his (Platt's) fiduciary duty to Phoenix Resources shareholders, making Switzer's action illegal tippee trading? [*SEC v. Platt*, 565 F. Supp. 1244 (W.D. Okl. 1983)].

## INFOTRAC KEYWORDS

**Use your InfoTrac password to look up articles on http://www.infotrac-college.com**

Keywords: *Securities regulation, Private Securities Litigation Reform Act, Sarbanes–Oxley Act, Regulation D, Rule 10b-5, blue-sky laws.*

For suggested readings, please visit this book's Web site at **http://fisher.westbuslaw.com** (click on "Internet Applications").

# MODULE 6

# LAW AFFECTING THE MARKETING DEPARTMENT

**CHAPTER 20**
## Antitrust Law

**CHAPTER 21**
## Federal Trade Commission Act, Franchising, and Unfair Competition

**CHAPTER 22**
## Consumer Protection

# ANTITRUST LAW

## POSITIVE LAW ETHICAL PROBLEM

Barkat U. Khan had long wanted to run a gas station, but when he got his chance, things didn't work out. Khan contracted with State Oil Company to lease and operate a gas station and convenience store owned by State Oil. The contract said that Khan would get his gasoline supply from State Oil at a price equal to a suggested retail price set by State Oil, minus a margin of 3.25 cents per gallon. Khan could charge his station's customers any gasoline price he wanted, but if the price charged was higher than State Oil's suggested retail price, the excess was to be rebated to State Oil. Khan also could sell gasoline for less than State Oil's suggested retail price, but any such decrease obviously would reduce his margin.

About a year after Khan began operating the gas station, he fell behind in his lease payments. State Oil then gave notice of its intent to terminate the agreement and began a state court proceeding to evict Khan. But Khan had a plan to avoid this fate. Khan sued State Oil in federal court, alleging that, by its contract with him, State Oil had fixed prices violation of Sherman Act Section 1. Had the agreement with State Oil not existed, Khan claimed, he could have charged different prices based on the different grades of gasoline he offered, thereby achieving increased sales and profits.

Assuming that State Oil really had fixed his resale prices, Khan's antitrust argument seemed solid. The courts had long held that *vertical price-fixing* (price-fixing down the chain of distribution, usually between a supplier and a retailer) automatically violates Sherman Act Section 1. The main reason is that such price-fixing stifles *intrabrand* competition—competition among sellers of the same brand—which hurts consumers of that brand. But at least in part, the contract about which Khan was complaining fixed *maximum* prices. How does this hurt consumers? Does it make sense to read Section 1 as automatically barring the fixing of maximum prices?

*"People of the same trade seldom meet together, even for merriment and diversion, but the conversation ends in a conspiracy against the public, or in some contrivance to raise prices."*

—ADAM SMITH,
THE WEALTH OF
NATIONS (1776)

Free-market economies tend to be more efficient and productive than other kinds of economies. This is primarily due to the economic competition they foster. Yet the very freedom that helps promote competition also can frustrate it. Business firms sometimes use their freedom to restrain competition and thereby increase their profits. For example, competitors might agree to fix artificially high prices or to suppress competition by dividing territories among themselves. Also, one competitor may come to dominate its market, and then use the resulting economic power to hurt consumers, its remaining competitors, or other firms. For example, a business that monopolizes its industry may be able to maximize its profits by raising prices and restricting output.

Businesses have used these and other *restraints of trade* for centuries. Over those same centuries, the law sometimes has tried to prevent such anticompetitive behavior. The common law, for instance, has long prohibited certain trade restraints and other anticompetitive practices. In late-nineteenth century America, however, the common law was increasingly perceived as an inadequate tool for containing anticompetitive behavior. The main reason was the array of problems created by the unprecedented growth in the size and power of business organizations. In response, Congress enacted the **antitrust laws**.[1] This chapter examines the body of law courts have created as they fleshed out these statutes.

## THE EMERGENCE OF ANTITRUST LAW IN THE UNITED STATES

The arrival of large corporations and industrial combines during the latter part of the nineteenth century was accompanied by economic abuses. For example, railroads often charged high rates to customers with little economic power and low rates to powerful shippers (sometimes by secret rebates). Such abuses led to passage of the Interstate Commerce Act of 1887, which established the Interstate Commerce Commission to regulate railroads in general and their rates in particular.

Regulated industries like railroads may be *natural monopolies*: industries in which a particular market is most economically served by one firm. (Electrical power generation is another likely example.) In such cases, the antitrust regulation is thought to be inappropriate because it seeks to promote competition, and competition is not socially beneficial where a genuine natural monopoly exists. By the late nineteenth century, however, industries other than natural monopolies also exhibited abuses. At that time, lines of business such as fuel oil, cotton, and sugar were dominated by combinations of several firms called *trusts*.[2] The tactics that trusts used to gain and hold power in their industries—for example, below-cost pricing and business espionage—provoked widespread criticism. Also, many felt that the economic concentration the trusts created and the private power they exerted were inconsistent with freedom and democracy. At a minimum, trusts that subdued their competitors gained some ability to raise prices above competitive levels. At worst, some believed, they would control the political processes and create a social environment in which large groups dominate and the individual counts for nothing.

The public outcry against the trusts and their abuses eventually led to enactment of the federal antitrust laws. The first of these laws, the **Sherman Act**, was passed by Congress in 1890. Section 1 of the Sherman Act forbids "[e]very contract, combination in the form of trust or otherwise, or conspiracy, in restraint of trade or commerce among the several States, or with foreign nations." Section 1 covers many different anticompetitive practices involving *joint action*: collaboration by two or more parties. Section 2 of the Sherman Act says that "[e]very person who shall monopolize, or attempt to monopolize, or combine or conspire

---

[1] Many of the states also have antitrust laws. Because the federal antitrust laws are more important, and because the state laws vary, the latter are not discussed here.

[2] A trust might be defined as a property right held by one party for the benefit of another. Typically, the person holding the right, called the *trustee*, manages the property for the benefit of someone else, the *beneficiary*. For the trusts in question here, stockholders in several different companies transferred their shares to a set of trustees, in exchange for certificates entitling them to a percentage of the combined earnings of the jointly managed companies.

with any other person or persons, to monopolize any part of the trade or commerce among the several States, or with foreign nations, shall be deemed guilty of a felony." Basically, Section 2 forbids monopolization and attempts to monopolize. Notice that unlike Section 1, Section 2 has no joint action requirement; action by one party can violate Section 2.

Responding to perceived inadequacies in the Sherman Act, Congress supplemented it by enacting the **Clayton Act** in 1914. Section 3 of the Clayton Act makes it unlawful to sell or lease commodities (goods), where the sale or lease is made on the condition that the buyer or lessee not use or deal commodities sold or leased by a competitor of the seller or lessor, and where the effect of the sale or lease may be to substantially lessen competition or tend to create a monopoly. Section 3 mainly applies to three kinds of potentially anticompetitive behavior: tying contracts, exclusive dealing contracts, and requirements contracts. Section 7 of the Clayton Act governs mergers. Under Section 7, the test for liability is the same as under Section 3: whether the merger substantially lessens competition or tends to create a monopoly. Section 8 of the Clayton Act forbids interlocking corporate directorates: situations in which one person serves on competing corporations' boards of directors.

Clayton Act Section 2 prohibited price discrimination—charging similarly situated buyers different prices for a product. In 1936, Section 2 was amended by the **Robinson-Patman Act**, which prohibits price discrimination and related offenses. Finally, the year 1914 also witnessed Congress's passage of the **Federal Trade Commission Act**. Chapter 21 discusses this act in detail.

## THE DEBATE OVER ANTITRUST POLICY

Many antitrust provisions are vague, and the legislative history behind them does not clearly fix their meaning either. Thus, the formulation of antitrust law is largely up to the courts. What general views about the purposes of antitrust law should guide courts in this endeavor? Over the past several decades, two general approaches have dominated the antitrust policy debate. Although they go by various names, we will call them the "Chicago School" view and the "traditional" view.

According to the Chicago School view, the primary, if not the sole, purpose of the antitrust laws is to promote economic efficiency. This, Chicago School theorists assume, maximizes the economic welfare of consumers. The traditional view, by contrast, says that the antitrust laws should promote other values in addition to efficiency. Some traditionalists remain attached to the ideal of an economy dominated by small entrepreneurs. Some say that concentrated economic power is inconsistent with democracy and liberty in the long run, and that for this reason the antitrust laws should be used to break up such concentrated power. These values should prevail, some traditionalists maintain, even if they involve losses in economic efficiency. To the Chicago School theorists, on the other hand, size and economic concentration are not necessarily bad, as long as competition exists and efficiency is maximized. In their view, the traditionalists' position often boils down to protecting competitors rather than promoting competition.

How does the clash between Chicago School and traditionalist views affect antitrust law? Three practical differences stand out. First, the traditionalists favor more antitrust enforcement than does the Chicago School. Specifically, the traditionalists regard more kinds of business behavior as violations of the antitrust laws. Second, the traditional view is very concerned about economic concentration, while the Chicago School is less bothered by it. To the Chicago School, a firm's large size often is its reward for being a superior competitor, and to punish size is to discourage competitive activity. The traditionalists, however, worry about the economic and political power possessed by large firms and the uses to which it will be put. Finally, the Chicago School is less concerned about so-called vertical restraints (restraints down a firm's chain of distribution) than is the traditionalist camp. This reflects the Chicago School view that, for example, price-fixing between manufacturers and retailers or agreements whereby manufacturers assign territories to particular retailers are not necessarily anti-competitive on balance.

## THE SHERMAN ACT: PRELIMINARIES

### THE ACT'S REACH

Congress got power to enact the Sherman Act from the U.S. Constitution's commerce clause, which enables it to regulate commerce among the states. As discussed in Chapter 5, Congress's commerce clause regulatory power includes intrastate matters that have a substantial impact on interstate commerce. Thus, the Sherman Act extends to (1) activities that interfere with the flow of commerce among the states, and (2) activities inside a particular state that substantially affect commerce among the states. As a practical matter, the Sherman Act probably reaches most anticompetitive activities that occur solely within a particular state.

In addition to regulating anticompetitive conduct that involves or affects interstate commerce, the Sherman Act also regulates conduct that restrains trade or commerce with foreign nations. Like the former assertion of regulatory power, the latter has its basis in the commerce clause, which also allows Congress to regulate foreign commerce. To oversimplify a complex subject, the Sherman Act's regulation of foreign commerce basically covers anticompetitive activities that affect the U.S. economy. These activities may be undertaken by (1) foreign firms within the United States, (2) foreign firms outside the United States, or (3) American firms outside the United States. In all such cases, the U.S. government or a private plaintiff must get jurisdiction over the defendant.

### CRIMINAL PROSECUTIONS

Liability for violations of the Sherman Act may be both criminal and civil. Criminal prosecutions are initiated by the Antitrust Division of the Justice Department.[3] The maximum fine for a corporation found guilty of a Sherman Act criminal violation is $10 million. Individuals are punishable by fines of up to $350,000 and jail sentences of up to three years.

*On antitrust enforcement by the FTC, see* **http://www.ftc.gov**

A Sherman Act criminal defendant can enter one of three pleas—guilty, not guilty, or *nolo contendere*. A defendant who pleads *nolo contendere* can be criminally punished to the same degree as a defendant who pleaded guilty or who was

---

[3] The Federal Trade Commission also enforces the antitrust laws. See Chapter 21.

proven guilty following a not-guilty plea. But unlike a defendant who pleads guilty, a defendant who pleads *nolo contendere* neither admits nor denies the criminal charges. This means that the plea cannot be used to prove liability in a private plaintiff's subsequent civil suit against the defendant. When the defendant pleads guilty or is found guilty after a not-guilty plea, by contrast, a private plaintiff can use the previous criminal conviction to help make its civil case. This feature of the *nolo contendere* plea naturally makes it attractive to alleged antitrust violators, and settlements of criminal antitrust cases often involve such pleas.

## CIVIL SUITS

Both the Justice Department and private parties may sue antitrust violators civilly. The courts have broad injunctive powers in cases of this kind. For example, they may order the defendant to cease business and sell its assets (called *dissolution*), to sell its own stock or assets or those of an acquired firm (called *divestiture*), or to separate itself from some functional level of its operations such as retailing (called *divorcement*). An antitrust violator might also be enjoined to refrain from certain conduct in the future. If the parties settle the case, the court or the Justice Department completes a legally enforceable consent decree approving the terms of the settlement. Typically, a consent decree obligates the defendant to do something to remedy the effects of its anticompetitive behavior, or to refrain from such behavior in the future. Like a plea of *nolo contendere*, a consent decree does not constitute an admission of guilt or liability, and does not prove liability in subsequent civil litigation.

In addition, private parties who win a civil Sherman Act case recover **treble damages** plus attorney's fees from the defendant. This means that a successful private plaintiff gets three times its actual damages (plus attorney's fees). One reason for awarding treble damages is to supplement government enforcement of the antitrust laws by giving private parties an incentive to sue. Because such suits can be abused, however, courts have limited the availability of private treble damage claims. To get damages, a private plaintiff must show that the defendant's conduct harmed its business or property. In addition, that harm must constitute *antitrust injury*. This means that the defendant's allegedly unlawful conduct must cause injury of the type the antitrust laws were intended to prevent. For example, a private plaintiff cannot recover damages when the defendant's allegedly unlawful conduct increases the competition the plaintiff must face. Here, there may be harm to business or property, but that harm is not an antitrust injury because the antitrust laws aim to promote competition, not to prevent it.

The antitrust laws' **standing** requirements are another important obstacle to private suits. Standing rules appear in many different legal contexts; the general idea uniting them is that there must be a fairly direct and tangible connection between the alleged violation and the injury the plaintiff suffered. In other words, standing is a question of the plaintiff's proximity to the violation.

In *Illinois Brick Co. v. Illinois* (1977), the state of Illinois sued Illinois Brick and other concrete block manufacturers for price-fixing. Because Illinois Brick had not sold directly to the state but instead to masonry subcontractors who then sold to the state, the Supreme Court held that the state lacked standing to sue. This was true even though the subcontractors had passed on the costs created by the defendants' price-fixing—costs that probably constituted harm to business or property and antitrust injury. *Illinois Brick* at least means that only direct purchasers from members of an illegal price-fixing conspiracy have standing to sue. One justification for this rule is the possibility of multiple recoveries where several indirect purchasers buy from a direct purchaser; another is the difficulty of apportioning damages among the various parties affected by the price-fixing. Nonetheless, later cases suggest that an indirect purchaser has standing where (1) it buys from the direct purchaser under a fixed-quantity, cost-plus contract enabling the direct purchaser to pass on any price increases and obligating the indirect purchaser to buy a fixed quantity despite the price increase, or (2) the indirect purchaser owns or controls the direct purchaser.

## SHERMAN ACT SECTION 1

Section 1 of the Sherman Act forbids every contract, combination, or conspiracy in restraint of trade. This language presents two initial problems. First, what is a "contract, combination, or conspiracy," and how is its existence proven? Second, does the word *every* mean that *all* contracts, combinations, and conspiracies in restraint of trade are illegal?

### JOINT OR CONCERTED ACTION

Sherman Act Section 1's "contract, combination, or conspiracy" language requires *joint action* or *concerted action*. Purely unilateral action is insufficient for a Section 1 violation. In other words, Section 1 requires collaboration between two or more parties. Who or what counts as a separate party for this purpose? Under Section 1, a corporation cannot engage in joint action with itself or its employees. Also, a firm's employees cannot jointly act among themselves unless they collaborate with some independent party. In a 1984 case, furthermore, the Supreme Court held that a corporation cannot engage in concerted action with a wholly owned subsidiary. However, this rule may not cover all partially owned subsidiaries. One justification for all these rules is that in each case, the participants in the joint action are not completely distinct from one another. Also, collaboration among these participants probably creates less threat to competition than collaboration among parties who are genuinely distinct from one another, and who may be competitors.

Assuming that the participants in illegal concerted action are distinct from one another, how does a private plaintiff or the government prove the necessary contract, combination, or conspiracy? This question is important because sophisticated business managers do not make express agreements to restrain trade, or leave few tracks if they do. This means that courts sometimes must infer or imply concerted action from the parties' behavior and other relevant facts and circumstances. Most of the cases considering such inferences have involved alleged *horizontal* collaboration: joint action among competitors.

Where it exists, of course, direct evidence of an agreement such as documents or testimony often makes it easy to prove concerted action. In other cases, the question is what circumstantial evidence will do the job. Courts generally agree that without anything more, mere *conscious parallelism*—identical or similar conduct by competitors—does not prove an agreement to engage in that conduct. In a competitive market, for example, one might expect two competitors to charge identical or nearly identical prices at any particular point in time. But joint action may be found when conscious parallelism is accompanied by certain "plus factors." Plus factors include whether the defendants have a rational economic interest in conspiring, whether the defendants' parallel behavior is improbable unless there was an agreement, whether the defendants committed past antitrust violations, and whether they took action to further the alleged conspiracy after directly communicating with each other. Related to this last factor is another consideration that sometimes has led to Section 1 liability: exchanges of information between competitors, especially price information.

## RULE OF REASON AND PER SE VIOLATIONS

Section 1 expressly states that *every* contract, combination, or conspiracy in restraint of trade is illegal. Finding this standard impractical, in 1911 the Supreme Court held that Section 1 only forbids *unreasonable* restraints on trade. This **rule of reason** approach means that courts consider the economic impact of particular restraints on a case-by-case basis. Naturally, they look for evidence that the defendants' joint action had anticompetitive effects. But they also consider whether that behavior had a procompetitive impact or produced some social benefit such as increased efficiency. Of course, it is unclear just what balance of competitive over anticompetitive effects suffices to make a trade restraint unreasonable.

The rule of reason approach enables courts to make sensitive, case-by-case determinations about the anticompetitive effects of particular business behavior. But it is questionable whether courts can do this difficult job well. Even if the rule of reason standard does not strain judges' abilities, it certainly consumes their time. In addition, that standard obviously gives little guidance to business. For these reasons, the Supreme Court has fashioned **per se rules** under Sherman Act Section 1. Under the per se approach, certain kinds of anticompetitive conduct are *conclusively presumed* to violate Section 1. Issues such as standing and antitrust injury aside, in a per se case the only thing necessary for Section 1 liability is that the plaintiff or the government prove the relevant concerted action. The idea behind per se violations is that some kinds of business conduct are so often anticompetitive and without redeeming social value that it is useless and wasteful to consider their effects on a case-by-case basis. The virtues of per se rules mirror the disadvantages of the rule of reason approach: (1) per se rules are relatively easy, quick, and inexpensive for courts to apply; and (2) they give businesses more definite guidance about what they can and cannot do. Because per se rules are relatively clear, they also may deter antitrust violations. The main disadvantage of per se rules is their inflexibility.

Therefore, Section 1 of the Sherman Act recognizes two kinds of antitrust violations: (1) rule of reason violations, and (2) per se violations. In a rule of reason case, a private plaintiff or the government must (1) prove the concerted action in question; and (2) convince the court that its anticompetitive effects are sufficiently great, and its countervailing virtues sufficiently few, to justify liability. In a per se case, the plaintiff or the government need only prove the relevant joint action.

## PER SE VIOLATIONS

The rule of reason is the "default rule" under Sherman Act Section 1. Unless the challenged economic behavior fits within one of the "per se" categories described next, it is handled under the rule of reason. Now we consider the types of conduct that are said to be illegal per se under Sherman Act Section 1. Their number has been dwindling over the past 20 to 30 years. As you will see, moreover, some of these per se rules resemble the rule of reason.

*Vertical Price-Fixing.* Since 1911, **vertical price-fixing** or **resale price mainte-nance (RPM)** has been a per se violation. The main reason is that such agreements inhibit *intrabrand* competition. Suppose that the Wonder Widget Company requires all its Philadelphia-area dealers to sell at or above a certain price. How much price competition will there be for Wonder Widgets in the Philadelphia area?

Traditionally, the per se rule for vertical price-fixing has not covered two kinds of behavior that resemble vertical price-fixing. First, the per se rule generally has not applied to price-fixing in **consignment** arrangements. In a consignment, the seller (the consignor) retains another party (the consignee) to act as its agent in selling its goods, while retaining title to those goods. Because the seller/con-signor keeps title, and because owners should have the right to sell their own goods at their own price, a price-fixing agreement between consignor and con-signee should not violate Section 1. Over the years, courts have nibbled away at this rule, but for the most part it still stands.

Second, due to the need to prove joint action, certain kinds of *suggested retail prices* and *refusals to deal* do not violate Section 1. A manufacturer who merely sug-gests a retail price to its distributors does not engage in vertical price-fixing—even if the distributors follow the suggestion. The same is true of a manufacturer that announces that it will terminate any distributor who fails to follow its sug-gested prices, and then backs up the threat. In each case, the courts say, there is insufficient evidence of concerted action. A refusal to deal, moreover, represents the kind of free choice our system usually seeks to protect. However, joint action may be found if, in addition to the threatened refusal to deal, the manufacturer engages in some collaborative behavior to get its distributors to comply. For example, illegal vertical price-fixing may exist where a manufacturer enlists com-plying dealers to help police the price-fixing scheme. However, a manufacturer's termination of a price-cutting retailer after complaints from other retailers, with-out more, probably does not violate Section 1.

Supreme Court cases of the past twenty-odd years cast some doubt on the con-tinued per se illegality of vertical price-fixing. In 1977, the Supreme Court moved vertical *territorial* restraints—i.e., manufacturers' assigning their retailers to terri-tories—from the per se category to the rule of reason category. In doing so, the Court showed the influence of the Chicago School economic ideas discussed at the beginning of the chapter. It conceded that vertical territorial restraints inhibit intrabrand competition. But, the Court added, they may also promote interbrand competition. For example, vertical territorial restraints may enable manufacturers to attract competent and aggressive retailers, and may give such retailers an incentive to heavily promote the product and to offer good service. All these things may stimulate competition among brands and thereby benefit consumers. Without the territorial restraint, though, another retailer (called a *free-rider*) might benefit from a "good" retailer's promotional and service activities while stealing its business because, by not doing those things itself, it can offer lower prices. Without the territorial restriction, therefore, no one may have a sufficient incentive to engage in such valuable activities as promotion and service. The bottom line, said the Court, is that vertical territorial restrictions involve a complex mix of effects: They may inhibit intrabrand competition while sometimes promoting interbrand competition. Because the latter effect may sometimes predominate, they should be examined under the flexible rule of reason standard rather than a rigid per se rule.

Why does the law on vertical territorial restraints matter here? It matters because the arguments just made probably apply to vertical price-fixing as well as to vertical territorial restraints. That is, a vertical price-fixing scheme may help manufacturers attract superior retailers and give those retailers the incentive and the means to give good service and aggressively promote the product. Like vertical territorial restrictions, therefore, vertical price-fixing may present a complex mix of effects and be better treated under the rule of reason.

With all this in mind, perhaps it is not surprising to see the following *Khan* case make vertical maximum price-fixing a rule of reason violation rather than a per se violation. Vertical minimum price-fixing, however, remains a per se violation.

## State Oil Co. v. Khan
United States Supreme Court
522 U.S. 3 (1997)

### Background and Facts

Barkat U. Khan and his corporation contracted with State Oil Company to lease and operate a gas station and convenience store owned by State Oil. The agreement provided that Khan would obtain the station's gasoline supply from State Oil at a price equal to a suggested retail price set by State Oil, less a margin of 3.25 cents per gallon. Under the agreement, Khan could charge any amount for gasoline sold to the station's customers, but if the price charged was higher than State Oil's suggested retail price, the excess was to be rebated to State Oil. Khan could sell gasoline for less than State Oil's suggested retail price, but any such decrease would reduce his 3.25 cents-per-gallon margin. About a year after Khan began operating the gas station, he fell behind in his lease payments. State Oil then gave notice of its intent to terminate the agreement and began a state court proceeding to evict Khan.

Khan then sued State Oil in federal court, alleging that State Oil had fixed prices violation of Sherman Act Section 1 by preventing Khan from raising or lowering retail gas prices. But for the agreement with State Oil, Khan claimed, he could have charged different prices based on the different grades of gasoline he sold, thereby achieving increased sales and profits. The district court granted State Oil's motion for summary judgment, but the court of appeals reversed. State Oil appealed to the U.S. Supreme Court.

### Body of Opinion

**Justice O'Connor.** Although the Sherman Act, by its terms, prohibits every agreement in restraint of trade, this Court has long recognized that Congress intended to outlaw only unreasonable restraints. As a consequence, most antitrust claims are analyzed under a "rule of reason," according to which the finder of fact must decide whether the questioned practice imposes an unreasonable restraint on competition, taking into account a variety of factors, including specific information about the relevant business, its condition before and after the restraint was imposed, and the restraint's history, nature, and effect. Some types of restraints, however, have such predictable and pernicious anticompetitive effect, and such limited potential for procompetitive benefit, that they are deemed unlawful per se. Per se treatment is appropriate once experience with a particular kind of restraint enables the Court to predict with confidence that the rule of reason will condemn it. Thus, we have expressed reluctance to adopt per se rules with regard to restraints imposed in the context of business relationships where the economic impact of certain practices is not immediately obvious. . . .

*Albrecht v. Herald Co.* (1968) . . . involved a newspaper publisher who had granted exclusive territories to independent carriers subject to their adherence to a maximum price on resale of the newspapers to the public. . . . The Court concluded that it was per se unlawful for the publisher to fix the maximum resale price of its newspapers. The Court acknowledged that maximum and minimum price fixing may have different consequences in many situations, but nonetheless condemned maximum price fixing for substituting the perhaps erroneous judgment of a seller for the forces of the competitive market. . . . In a vigorous dissent, Justice Harlan asserted that the majority had erred in equating the effects of maximum and minimum price fixing. Justice Harlan pointed out that, because the majority was establishing a per se rule, the proper inquiry was "not whether dictation of maximum prices is ever illegal, but whether it is *always* illegal."

. . . [O]ur reconsideration of *Albrecht's* continuing validity is informed by several of our decisions, as well as a considerable body of scholarship discussing the effects of vertical restraints. Our analysis is also guided by our general view that the primary purpose of the antitrust laws is to protect interbrand competition. Low prices, we have explained, benefit consumers regardless of how those prices are set, and so long as they are above predatory levels, they do not threaten competition. Our interpretation of the Sherman Act also incorporates the notion that condemnation of practices resulting in lower prices to consumers is especially costly because cutting prices in order to increase business often is the very essence of competition. So informed, we find it difficult to maintain that vertically imposed maximum prices could harm consumers or competition to the extent necessary to justify their per se invalidation.

We recognize that the *Albrecht* decision presented a number of theoretical justifications for a per se rule against vertical maximum price fixing. But criticism of those premises abounds. The *Albrecht* decision was grounded in the fear that maximum price fixing by suppliers could interfere with dealer freedom. In response, as one commentator has pointed out, the ban on maximum resale price limitations declared in *Albrecht* in the name of "dealer freedom" has actually prompted many suppliers to integrate forward into distribution, thus eliminating the very independent trader for whom *Albrecht* professed solicitude. . . . The *Albrecht* Court also expressed the concern that maximum prices may be set too low for dealers to offer consumers essential or desired services. But such conduct, by driving away customers, would seem likely to harm manufacturers as well as dealers and consumers, making it unlikely that a supplier would set such a price as a matter of business judgment. In addition, *Albrecht* noted that vertical maximum price fixing could effectively channel distribution through large or specially advantaged dealers. It is unclear, however, that a supplier would profit from limiting its market by excluding potential dealers. Further, although vertical maximum price fixing might limit the viability of inefficient dealers, that consequence is not necessarily harmful to competition and consumers. Finally, *Albrecht* reflected the Court's

fear that maximum price fixing could be used to disguise arrangements to fix minimum prices, which remain illegal per se. Although we have acknowledged the possibility that maximum pricing might mask minimum pricing, we believe that such conduct—as with the other concerns articulated in *Albrecht*—can be appropriately recognized and punished under the rule of reason. . . .

After reconsidering *Albrecht*'s rationale and the substantial criticism the decision has received, we conclude that there is insufficient economic justification for per se invalidation of vertical maximum price fixing. . . . [T]he court of appeals noted that the district judge was right to conclude that if the rule of reason is applicable, Khan loses. . . . [Nonetheless], the matter should be reviewed by the court of appeals in the first instance. We therefore vacate the judgment of the court of appeals and remand the case for further proceedings consistent with this opinion.

### Judgment and Result

The Supreme Court vacated the court of appeals decision reversing the district court's decision granting State Oil's motion for summary judgment, and returned the case to the lower courts for further proceedings consistent with its opinion.

### Questions

1. Does *Khan* mean that vertical maximum price-fixing is always legal under Section 1?
2. Do you see anything in the Court's opinion which would suggest that the fixing of *minimum* prices should no longer be per se illegal?
3. What did the Court mean when it said that low prices do not threaten competition so long as they are above predatory levels?"

*Horizontal Price-Fixing.* Horizontal price-fixing is concerted action to fix prices by competitors at the same level. Its effect is to defeat interbrand competition: competition among brands of the same product. For this reason, and because its procompetitive effects seem few, horizontal price-fixing is the classic Sherman Act Section 1 per se violation. Horizontal price-fixing also includes agreements among competitors on matters that affect price—for example, agreements on the amount of goods the competitors will make, sell, or buy. Despite the *Khan* case, Section 1's per se ban on horizontal price-fixing most likely still includes the setting of maximum prices as well as the setting of minimum prices.

Horizontal price-fixing cases often involve a problem discussed earlier: proving concerted action. The courts generally agree that simple "price parallelism"—a situation where competitors are following the same price—does not violate Section 1 unless there is other evidence of joint action to fix prices. (In a competitive market, after all, one would expect competitors to be charging roughly the same price at any point in time.) The courts also have agreed that simply following an industry "price leader," without more, does not violate Section 1. (In the automobile and steel industries, for example, competitors traditionally would follow price increases announced by those industries' price leaders at the time, General Motors and U.S. Steel.) Although it is difficult to generalize about this subject, exchanges of price information also probably do not violate Section 1 by themselves. As discussed earlier, the additional considerations—the "something more"—that might render any of the above a Section 1 violation include the defendants' possession of a rational economic interest in conspiring, parallel behavior that is unlikely without an agreement, any past antitrust violations by the defendants, and the defendants' taking action to further the alleged conspiracy after directly communicating with each other.

*Horizontal Division of Markets.* Agreements by competitors to divide markets can take many forms. Perhaps the most common example is concerted action dividing territories among competitors—for example, an agreement that each competitor will sell only in its own particular region. But competitors might also agree to divide customers—for example, competitors A and B might agree that A will sell only to retailers, while B will sell only to wholesalers. In addition, competitors might divide product types—for example, competitors X, Y, and Z might agree that each will sell different sizes of ball bearings. In such cases, of course, the plaintiff or the government will have the now-familiar problem of proving joint or concerted action.

The division of territories, customers, or products reduces interbrand competition. (Sometimes, in fact, such an agreement may give one firm an effective monopoly within a particular territory or for a particular product.) For this reason, such agreements are per se violations of Sherman Act Section 1. However, some lower federal courts and some commentators have held or suggested that the rule of reason should apply in cases where the conspiring competitors lack market power and/or their agreement has positive procompetitive benefits. For example, suppose that three widget firms agreeing to allocate territories form 10 percent of the national market, and that each faces powerful competitors within its territory. Or suppose that, as part of their agreement to develop a new jet aircraft, two co-venturers agree that each will sell the plane to different customers. If the plane is valuable and it would not be developed without the division of customers, should the agreement be per se illegal?

*Group Boycotts.* A group boycott might be defined as joint action involving a refusal to deal with a particular firm or firms. (As we saw earlier, however, a purely unilateral refusal to deal does not violate Section 1.) Group boycotts can assume various forms. Perhaps the most common and most harmful example is an agreement by firms within an industry not to deal with suppliers or customers who deal with a competitor. For example, Firms A, B, and C in the widget industry might agree not to sell to retailers who market widgets manufactured by a competitor, Firm D. If the boycott works, D might be weakened or forced out of business, which would mean less competition in the widget industry. Alternatively, the boycott might make D cooperate with A, B, and C in some other anticompetitive conduct. Suppose for example that A, B, and C had initiated their boycott because D refused to join their price-fixing scheme.

Boycotts like those just described are per se illegal. But this might not be true where the conspiring firms lack market power (what if A, B, and C together had

10 percent of the widget market?), or where the boycott might promote efficiency or some other important value. In such cases, the rule of reason applies.

*Tying Contracts.* A **tying contract** (or tie-in) is a contract in which a seller conditions the buyer's purchase of one product (the **tying product**) on the buyer's purchase of another product sold by the seller (the **tied product**). For example, a firm might condition the sale of its copiers (the tying product) on the purchase of its copier paper (the tied product). Under Section 1 of the Sherman Act, the tied or tying "product" might be a service as well.[4] The main argument for suppressing tying contracts is that they distort competition in the tied product market. In the previous example, competition in the copier paper market might be distorted if consumers want the seller's copiers badly enough.

Courts apply a modified rule of per se illegality to tying contracts. This means that a tying contract is per se illegal if certain tests are met:

1. The tying and tied products are distinct items.
2. The seller has required the buyer to buy the tied product in order to obtain the tying product (the tie-in).
3. The seller has market power in the tying product market.
4. The tie-in affects a substantial amount of commerce in the tied product market.

The following *Eastman Kodak* case states and applies this test. The test's most important element, the market power requirement, might be satisfied by showing that the seller has a large share of the tying product market, or a patent in the product.

---

## Eastman Kodak Co. v. Image Technical Services, Inc.
### U.S. Supreme Court
### 504 U.S. 451 (1992)

### Background and Facts

The Eastman Kodak Company manufactured and sold high-volume photocopier equipment and micrographic equipment (e.g., scanners, microfilm viewers, and other such items). Kodak's equipment and the parts for that equipment were not compatible with competitors' machines and parts. Kodak provided its customers with service and parts for its machines. It made some of the parts itself; the rest were made to order for Kodak by independent original-equipment manufacturers. Beginning in the 1980s, eighteen independent service organizations (ISOs) began servicing Kodak equipment. In response, Kodak instituted a policy of selling replacement parts only to buyers of its equipment who used Kodak service or repaired their own machines. It also got the original equipment manufacturers to sell parts only to Kodak. Due to these and other steps taken by Kodak, the ISOs could

not obtain Kodak parts and some went out of business. Also, customers were forced to switch to Kodak service even though they preferred the ISOs' service.

The ISOs then sued Kodak in federal district court. Among other things, they alleged that Kodak violated Sherman Act Section 1 by tying the sale of Kodak service to the sale of Kodak parts. The district court granted Kodak's motion for summary judgment, but the court of appeals reversed this decision. Kodak appealed to the U.S. Supreme Court.

### Body of Opinion

**Justice Blackmun.** Because this case comes to us on petitioner Kodak's motion for summary judgment, the evidence of the ISOs is to be believed, and all justifiable inferences are to be drawn in their favor. . . . A tying arrangement is an agreement by a party

---

[4] As you will see later in the chapter, however, under Clayton Act Section 3, both the tied and the tying products must be commodities (i.e., goods).

to sell one product but only on the condition that the buyer also purchases a different (or tied) product, or at least agrees that he will not purchase that product from any other supplier. Such an arrangement violates Section 1 of the Sherman Act if the seller has appreciable economic power in the tying product market and if the arrangement affects a substantial volume of commerce in the tied market. Kodak did not dispute that its arrangement affects a substantial volume of interstate commerce. . . .

For the ISOs to defeat a motion for summary judgment on their claim of a tying arrangement, a reasonable trier of fact must be able to find, first, that service and parts are two distinct products, and, second, that Kodak has tied the sale of the two products. For service and parts to be considered two distinct products, there must be sufficient consumer demand so that it is efficient for a firm to provide service separately from parts. Evidence in the record indicates that service and parts have been sold separately in the past and still are sold separately to self-service equipment owners. Indeed, the development of the entire high-technology service industry is evidence of the efficiency of a separate market for service. . . . [Also,] the ISOs have presented sufficient evidence of a tie between service and parts. . . .

Market power is the power to force a purchaser to do something that he would not do in a competitive market. It has been defined as the ability of a single seller to raise price and restrict output. The existence of such power normally is inferred from the seller's possession of a predominant share of the market.

The ISOs contend that Kodak has more than sufficient power in the parts market to force unwanted purchases of the tied market, service. The ISOs provide evidence that certain parts are available exclusively through Kodak. The ISOs also assert that Kodak has control over the availability of parts it does not manufacture. . . . The ISOs also allege that Kodak's control over the parts market has excluded service competition, boosted service prices, and forced unwilling consumption of Kodak service. . . . [T]his evidence [is] sufficient to entitle the ISOs to a trial on their claim of market power. . . . We therefore affirm the denial of summary judgment [to Kodak] on the ISOs' Section 1 claim.

## Judgment and Result

The court of appeals decision denying Kodak's motion for summary judgment is affirmed. The case continues in the district court.

## Questions

1. What was the tying product here? What was the tied product?
2. In which market or markets was Kodak said to have market power?
3. Why did the Court conclude that Kodak might have sufficient market power in the tying product market?

## SHERMAN ACT SECTION 2

Sherman Act Section 2 forbids monopolization and attempts to monopolize.[5] We now consider each of these subjects in turn.

## MONOPOLIZATION

Monopolies reduce consumer welfare because monopolists can raise prices above free-market levels, usually restricting output in the process. Who qualifies as a monopolist under Section 2 of the Sherman Act? First, note that Section 2 does not require—and seldom involves—concerted action. Normally, that is, a single firm violates Section 2. Traditionally, this has occurred when (1) the firm has monopoly power; in (2) the relevant product and territorial market; and (3) the firm acquired or maintained that monopoly power with intent to monopolize. As you will see, the following *Microsoft* case downplays intent in its statement of this test's third element.

In economic terms, **monopoly power** might be defined as the ability to raise prices above the competitive level for a sustained time period, and to profit by doing so. Courts interpreting Section 2, however, normally define it as a percentage.

---

[5] Section 2 also forbids conspiracy to monopolize. Because this offense requires concerted action, and because most conspiracies to monopolize probably violate Sherman Act Section 1 in some way or another, this book does not discuss the subject.

Perhaps the most commonly stated number is 70 percent of sales in the product-territorial market. In other words, if the ratio of the defendant's sales in the product-territorial market to total sales in that market equals or exceeds 70 percent, the monopoly power test probably is met.

But what is the product-territorial market? The **product market** depends heavily on the question of *substitutability*: whether there are reasonable substitutes for the specific product the defendant sells. For example, suppose that the XYZ Corporation, with 100 percent of the widget market, tries to charge a monopoly price for its widgets. This strategy obviously will fail if gidgets are perfect substitutes for widgets, and if buyers can readily obtain all the gidgets they need. If so, why define the product market as merely involving widgets rather than widgets plus gidgets? And why worry just because XYZ has monopoly power in the widget market?

In determining which substitutes to include in the product market, courts examine several factors. To illustrate them, consider the Supreme Court's 1956 decision in *United States v. E.I. du Pont de Nemours & Co.* (the "cellophane case"), where the Court concluded that other flexible wrapping materials such as aluminum foil, wax paper, and saran wrap were reasonable substitutes for cellophane. DuPont's 20 percent share of this broader product market meant that it was not liable under Section 2 even though it had almost 75 percent of the cellophane market. The Court concluded that many of the substitutes had qualities—for example, flexibility, transparency, and permeability—similar to those consumers sought in cellophane. The Court also found that, because one or more of the substitutes competed with cellophane in each of its uses, the substitutes were functionally interchangeable with it. Finally, the Court judged that there was "cross-elasticity of demand" between cellophane and its substitutes; for example, an increase in the price of cellophane would cause increased demand for the substitutes.

In addition to determining the product market, courts in Section 2 cases also must determine the **territorial market** (or geographic market). The territorial market is that region in which a firm can increase its price without attracting new competitors and without losing sales to competitors outside the region. Suppose that the relevant product market is widgets and that the ABC Corporation has 10 percent of widget sales nationally, but 85 percent of sales in the Rocky Mountain region. But is the Rocky Mountain region the correct territorial market? To make such a determination, courts look at several factors. For example, if transportation costs are high, maybe widgets will not flow from other parts of the country to the Rockies once XYZ raises prices, which suggests that the Rocky Mountain area is the correct territorial market. Also, if price movements within the Rocky Mountain area do not correlate with price movements elsewhere, maybe we have another reason to think that this area is a self-contained territorial market. On the other hand, maybe consideration of such factors (and others) would force a court to conclude that the geographical market is the whole United States, or some segment of the country besides the Rocky Mountain region.

By itself, monopoly power in an appropriate product-territorial market is not enough for liability under Section 2. Traditionally, the defendant also must have had an intent to monopolize. In theory, this intent is absent, and Section 2 liability does not exist, when a firm acquires its monopoly innocently. For example, a company might get a monopoly simply by offering better products and services, or by historical accident (e.g., the last survivor in a dying industry).

Find the full text of the Microsoft case at **http://www.findlaw. com**, under "Laws: Cases and Codes." Remember that this is a June 2001 decision of the D.C. Circuit.

Intent to monopolize means an intent either to *acquire* or to *maintain* monopoly power. Each kind of intent normally is inferred from the defendant's behavior. (This is why the following *Microsoft* case puts so much emphasis on Microsoft's conduct and does not use the word "intent.") Intent to acquire monopoly power is easy to prove where the defendant has acquired its monopoly though practices such as below-cost pricing. A monopoly obtained through the acquisition of competitors probably meets the test as well. Intent to maintain monopoly power almost certainly exists where a monopolist engages in monopolistic pricing. The *Microsoft* decision describes some other ways in which a firm might maintain monopoly power and thus violate Section 2.

---

## United States v. Microsoft Corporation
U.S. Court of Appeals (D.C. Circuit)
253 F.3d 34 (2001)

---

### Background and Facts

In May of 1998, the Justice Department sued the Microsoft Corporation in federal district court for various antitrust violations, among them the unlawful maintenance of a monopoly in the personal computer operating system market under Sherman Act Section 2. After long and complex proceedings, the district court entered its final judgment in mid-2000. Among other things, it found Microsoft liable for monopolization of the PC operating system market under Section 2. Microsoft appealed this ruling and others to the D.C. Circuit Court of Appeals.

### Body of Opinion

**Per Curiam.** Section 2 of the Sherman Act makes it unlawful for a firm to "monopolize." The offense of monopolization has two elements: (1) the possession of monopoly power in the relevant market, and (2) the willful acquisition or maintenance of that power as distinguished from growth or development as a consequence of a superior product, business, acumen, or historic accident. The district court applied this test and found that Microsoft possesses monopoly power in the market for Intel-compatible PC operating systems. Focusing primarily on Microsoft's efforts to suppress Netscape Navigator's threat to its operating system monopoly, the court also found that Microsoft maintained its power not through competition on the merits, but through unlawful means. . . . We begin by considering whether Microsoft possesses monopoly power, and, finding that it does, we turn to the question of whether it maintained this power through anticompetitive means. . . .

**Monopoly Power.** While merely possessing monopoly power is not itself an antitrust violation, it is a necessary element of a monopolization charge. The Supreme Court defines monopoly power as the power to control prices or exclude competition. More precisely, a firm is a monopolist if it can profitably raise prices substantially above the competitive level. Where evidence indicates that a firm has in fact profitably done so, the existence of monopoly power is clear. Because such proof is only rarely available, courts more typically examine market structure in search of circumstantial evidence of monopoly power. Under this structural approach, monopoly power may be inferred from a firm's possession of a dominant share of a relevant market that is protected by entry barriers. . . . The district court considered these structural factors and concluded that Microsoft possesses monopoly power in a relevant market. Defining the market as Intel-compatible PC operating systems, the district court found that Microsoft has a greater than 95 percent share. . . . Microsoft argued that the district court incorrectly defined the relevant market. . . .

Because the ability of consumers to turn to other suppliers restrains a firm from raising prices above the competitive level, the relevant market must include all products reasonably interchangeable by consumers for the same purpose. In this case, the district court defined the market as the licensing of all Intel-compatible PC operating systems worldwide. . . . Calling this market definition far too narrow, Microsoft argues that the district court improperly excluded three types of products: nonIntel-compatible operating systems (primarily Apple's Macintosh operating system, Mac OS), operating systems for non-PC devices (such as handlheld computers and portal Web sites), and "middleware" products, which are not operating systems at all. . . .

The district court found that consumers would not switch from Windows to Mac OS in response to a substantial price increase because of the costs of acquiring the new hardware needed to run Mac OS (an Apple computer and peripherals) and compatible software applications, as well as because of the effort involved in learning the new system and transferring files to its format. The court also found the Apple system less appealing to consumers because it costs considerably more and supports fewer applications. . . . [W]e have no basis for upsetting the court's decision to exclude Mac OS from the relevant market.

[Regarding] Microsoft's challenge to the district court's exclusion of nonPC-based competitors, such as information appliances (hand-held devices, etc.) and portal Web sites that host server-based software applications, . . . the district court found that because information appliances fall far short of performing all of the functions of a PC, most consumers will buy them only as a supplement to their PCs. The district court also found that portal Web sites do not presently host enough applications to induce consumers to switch, nor are they likely to do so in the near future. . . . [W]e adhere to [both conclusions].

This brings us to Microsoft's main challenge to the district court's market definition: the exclusion of middleware. . . . Operating systems perform many functions, including allocating computer memory and controlling peripherals such as printers and keyboards. Operating systems also serve as platforms for software applications. They do this by "exposing"—i.e., making available to software developers—routines or protocols that perform certain widely used functions. These are known as Application Programming Interfaces or APIs. . . . Every operating system has different APIs. Accordingly, a developer who writes an application for one operating system and wishes to sell the application to users of another must modify, or "port," the application to the second operating system. This process is both time-consuming and expensive. "Middleware" refers to software products that expose their own APIs. Because of this, a middleware product written for Windows could take over some or all of Windows's valuable platform functions—that is, developers might begin to rely upon APIs exposed by the middleware for basic routines rather than relying upon the API set included in Windows. . . . The more developers could rely upon APIs exposed by such middleware, the less expensive porting to different operating systems would be. Ultimately, if developers could write applications relying exclusively upon APIs exposed by middleware, their applications would run on any operating system on which the middleware was also present. Netscape Navigator and Java—both at issue in this case—are middleware products written for multiple operating systems.

Microsoft argues that, because middleware could usurp the operating system's platform function and might eventually take over other operating system functions (for instance, by controlling peripherals), the district court erred in excluding Navigator and Java from the relevant market. The district court found, however, that neither Navigator, Java, nor any other middleware product could now, or would soon, expose enough APIs to serve as a platform for popular applications, much less take over all operating system functions. . . . Microsoft fails to challenge these findings, instead simply asserting middleware's potential as a competitor. These test of reasonable interchangeability, however, required the district court to consider only substitutes that constrain pricing in the reasonably foreseeable future, and only products that can enter the market in a relatively short time can perform this function. Whatever middleware's ultimate potential, the district court found that consumers could not now abandon their operating systems and switch to middleware in response to a sustained price for Windows above the competitive level. . . .

Having thus properly defined the relevant market, the district court found the Windows accounts for a greater than 95 percent share. The court also found that even if Mac OS were included, Microsoft's share would exceed 80 percent. Microsoft challenges neither finding, nor does it argue that such a market share is not predominant. . . .

**Anticompetitive Conduct.** [H]aving a monopoly does not by itself violate Section 2. A firm violates Section 2 only when it acquires or maintains, or attempts to acquire or maintain, a monopoly by engaging in exclusionary conduct, as distinguished from growth or development as a consequence of a superior product, business acumen, or historic accident. In this case, after concluding that Microsoft had monopoly power, the district court held that Microsoft had violated Section 2 by engaging in a variety of exclusionary acts (not including predatory pricing), to maintain its monopoly by preventing the effective distribution and use of products that might threaten that monopoly. Specifically, the district court held Microsoft liable for [among other things]: (1) the way in which it integrated Internet Explorer (IE) into Windows; [and] (2) its various dealings with original equipment manufacturers (OEMs). . . .

*Licenses Issued to Original Equipment Manufacturers.* The district court condemned a number of provisions in Microsoft's agreements licensing Windows to OEMs because it found that Microsoft's imposition of these provisions . . . serves to reduce usage share of Netscape's browser and, hence, protect Microsoft's operating system monopoly. . . . In particular, the district court condemned the license provisions prohibiting the OEMs from: (1) removing any desktop icons, folders, or "Start" menu entries; [and] (2) altering the boot sequence. . . .

[T]he first license restriction . . . thwarts the distribution of a rival browser by preventing OEMs from removing visible means of user access to IE. The OEMs cannot practically install a second browser in addition to IE . . . in part because pre-installing more than one product in a given category can significantly increase an OEM's support costs, for the redundancy can lead to confusion among novice users. That is, a certain number of novice computer users, seeing two browser icons, will wonder which to use when and will call the OEM's support line. Support calls are extremely expensive and, in the highly competitive original equipment market, firms have a strong incentive to minimize costs. . . . Therefore, we conclude that the [first] license restriction is anticompetitive. . . .

The second license provision at issue prohibits OEMs from modifying the initial boot sequence—the process that occurs the first time a consumer turns on the computer. Prior to the imposition of that restriction, among the programs that many OEMs inserted into the boot sequence were Internet sign-up procedures that encouraged users to choose from a list of IAPs, many of which . . . used Navigator rather than IE in their internet access software. . . . Because this prohibition has a substantial effect in protecting Microsoft's market power, and does so through a means other than competition on the merits, it is anticompetitive. . . .

*Integration of IE and Windows.* Technologically binding IE to Windows, the district court found, both prevented OEMs from pre-installing other browsers and deterred consumers from using them. In particular, having the IE software code as an irremovable part of Windows meant that pre-installing a second browser would increase an OEM's product testing costs, because an OEM must test and train its support staff to answer calls related to every software product preinstalled on the machine; moreover, pre-installing a browser in addition to IE would to many OEMs be a questionable use of the scarce and valuable space on a PC's hard drive. . . . [The district court's] findings of fact center upon three specific actions Microsoft took to weld IE to Windows: excluding IE from the "Add/Remove Programs" utility; designing Windows so as in certain circumstances to override the user's choice of a default browser other than IE; and commingling code related to browsing and other code in the same files, so that any attempt to delete the files containing IE would, at the same time, cripple the operating system. . . .

Microsoft had included IE in the Add/Remove Programs utility in Windows 95, but when it modified Windows 95 to produce Windows 98, it took IE out of the Add/Remove Programs utility. This change reduces the usage share of rival browsers not by making Microsoft's own browser more attractive to consumers, but rather by discouraging OEMs from distributing rival products. Because Microsoft's conduct, through something other than competition on the merits, has the effect of significantly reducing usage of rivals' products and hence promoting its own operating system monopoly, it is anticompetitive . . .

Microsoft designed Windows 98 so that using Navigator on Windows 98 would have unpleasant consequences for users by, in some circumstances, overriding the user's choice of a browser other than IE as his or her default browser. . . . Because the override reduces rivals' usage share and protects Microsoft's monopoly, it too is anticompetitive. . . .

Putting code supplying browsing functionality into a file with code supplying operating system functionality ensures that the deletion of any file containing browsing-specific routines would also delete vital operating system routines and thus cripple Windows. As noted above, preventing an OEM from removing IE deters it from installing a second browser because doing so increases the OEM's product testing and support costs; by contrast, had OEMs been able to remove IE, they might have chosen to pre-install Navigator alone. . . .

## Judgment and Result

The court of appeals affirmed the district court's decision that Microsoft violated Section 2 of the Sherman Act. On that issue, it returned the case to the district court and gave the district court broad discretion to fashion an appropriate remedy. In late 2001, the Justice Department and Microsoft agreed to settle the case.

## Questions

1. According to the district court (and, apparently, the court of appeals), what was the *territorial* market in this case?
2. Why was Microsoft so anxious to include Mac OS, handheld devices, portal Web sites, and middleware within the product market?
3. In the portion of the court's opinion regarding anticompetitive conduct (intent to acquire or maintain monopoly power), we omitted much of the court's very lengthy and detailed discussion, which included topics such as Microsoft's relations with America Online. So far as the disposition of the case is concerned, why did these omissions not matter?

## ATTEMPTS TO MONOPOLIZE

The paradox of Sherman Act Section 2—that preventing anticompetitive market structures might mean deterring good competitors—also arises when we consider attempts to monopolize. In a 1993 case, the Supreme Court held that liability for an attempt to monopolize requires (1) predatory or anticompetitive conduct by the defendant, (2) with a specific intent to monopolize, and (3) a dangerous probability of achieving monopoly power. A dangerous probability of achieving monopoly power is unlikely to exist if the defendant's market share is less than 50 percent. In some cases, the defendant's predatory or anticompetitive conduct might prove a specific intent to monopolize. One possible example of such conduct is below-cost pricing.

## CLAYTON ACT SECTION 3

Clayton Act Section 3 forbids the selling or leasing of commodities (goods) on the condition that the buyer or lessee not use or deal commodities sold or leased by a competitor of the seller or lessor—where the effect of this sale or lease may be to substantially lessen competition or tend to create a monopoly in any line of commerce. Section 3 mainly applies to tying contracts, exclusive dealing contracts, and requirements contracts. (Because Section 3 requires a sale or a lease, it does not govern consignment arrangements.) We consider requirements and exclusive dealing contracts together.

## TYING CONTRACTS

Section 3 of the Clayton Act governs tying contracts only when both the tied and the tying products are commodities. That difference aside, today most courts impose the same requirements for tying contract liability under both Sherman Act Section 1 and Clayton Act Section 3. This means that when considering tying contracts under Clayton Act Section 3, the four-part test discussed earlier applies.

## EXCLUSIVE DEALING AND REQUIREMENTS CONTRACTS

An **exclusive dealing contract** is a sales contract in which the buyer agrees to deal only in the seller's goods and/or not to deal in the goods of the seller's competitors. For example, a gas station might agree to sell only gasoline produced by a certain oil company, and not to sell gasoline produced by other oil companies.

In a **requirements contract**, the buyer agrees to purchase all its requirements of a particular commodity from the seller. For example, an electrical utility might agree to buy all the coal required for one of its generating stations from a particular coal company, thus preventing other coal companies from competing for its business.

Both exclusive dealing contracts and requirements contracts inhibit interbrand competition by preventing the seller's competitors from vying for the buyer's business. In our previous examples, the effect of the exclusive dealing or requirements contract is to prevent other oil companies or coal companies from competing for the gas station's or the utility's business. However, because firms have rational motives for entering into requirements contracts, which ensure them a source of supply, maybe their business would never have been the competitors' to obtain. Furthermore, because they may reduce a manufacturer's sales and distribution costs, attract good retailers, and give them an incentive to push the product, exclusive dealing and requirements contracts may sometimes enhance competition and efficiency. But on other occasions they simply are imposed by a powerful seller that wants to foreclose competition.

In addition to creating possible Section 3 liability, exclusive dealing and requirements contracts may also be rule of reason violations under Sherman Act Section 1. The standards for liability are basically the same under each act. Today, the most important factor courts consider is the degree to which the contract forecloses competition in the relevant market. This basically involves the percentage market share taken up by the challenged contract (*qualitative substantiality*), not the absolute dollar value of the contract (*quantitative substantiality*). If the foreclosure is less than 20 to 30 percent, liability probably will not exist. (Of course, this determination may require difficult product and territorial market questions.) Another factor is the duration of the agreement. Exclusive dealing or requirements contracts with shorter time periods and/or easy-to-use termination provisions are more likely to escape liability than contracts of longer duration that cannot easily be terminated. A third factor is the presence or absence of entry barriers to the affected market; the easier that market is to enter, the less likely that the exclusive dealing or requirements contract will violate Section 3.

## CLAYTON ACT SECTION 7

Section 7 of the Clayton Act forbids the acquisition of a firm's stock or assets, where the effect of this acquisition is to substantially lessen competition or tend to create a monopoly. In effect, Section 7 forbids certain mergers.[6] A merger might be said to occur where one firm buys enough of another firm's stock or assets to give the buying firm control over the firm that is bought. Defined narrowly, a merger occurs when two or more firms combine, with one of these firms continuing to exist while the other becomes part of (merges into) the survivor. Defined more broadly, the term merger also includes situations where one corporation buys a controlling interest in another corporation's stock but both corporations continue to exist; here, the buyer (the parent firm) controls the seller (the subsidiary) because the parent elects the subsidiary's board of directors. Finally, the term merger can include a consolidation, in which two or more corporations combine to form a new business entity. In this chapter, all these various combinations will be treated as mergers and as potentially subject to Clayton Act Section 7.

### GENERAL POLICY CONSIDERATIONS

*The Justice Department's merger guidelines can be found at* **http://www.usdoj.gov**, *under "Legal Documents."*

One reason for Sherman Act Section 1's concern with joint action is that joint action usually poses a greater threat to competition than purely unilateral behavior. At first glance, this threat to competition seems to compound when two businesses not only act jointly, but merge. Contracts, combinations, and conspiracies may eventually end as each of the once-collaborating firms goes its own way, but mergers create a more permanent union between businesses. For this reason, one might expect the courts to announce per se rules against mergers. As we will see, however, some mergers pose little threat to competition. Others may have social benefits that offset their potential to harm competition. For example, mergers can enhance efficiency by creating economies of scale, and by enabling the acquiring firm to make better use of the acquired firm's assets. Also, the threat of a takeover can force managers to behave efficiently. If the takeover in question is per se illegal, this threat—and its benefits—would disappear.

For the reasons just suggested, courts must exercise some discretion in merger cases. This means that the "law" under Section 7 is less a matter of definite rules to be followed than of factors to be considered on a case-by-case basis. For several reasons, merger law probably is more uncertain today than it has been in the past. For one thing, the Supreme Court has not issued a major Section 7 decision for some time. In the meantime, Chicago School ideas have gained influence. Were the Court to decide an important merger case today, therefore, it might well give more weight to economic efficiency concerns than in the past, and less to political

---

[6] Under the Hart–Scott–Rodino Antitrust Improvements Act of 1976, moreover, certain mergers require premerger notification to the FTC and the Justice Department. The act also creates a waiting period during which these agencies decide whether to challenge the merger.

values such as the desire to limit corporate size. Further increasing the uncertainty faced by firms that contemplate a merger are the inevitable changes in FTC and Justice Department enforcement policy that accompany the arrival of a new administration in Washington.

## TYPES OF MERGERS

Mergers come in three basic varieties. A **horizontal merger** is a merger between two (or more) competitors. In a **vertical merger**, a firm acquires either a customer (called forward integration) or a supplier (called backward integration). The term **conglomerate merger** covers all other kinds of mergers. Perhaps the most common kind of conglomerate merger, one sometimes called a pure conglomerate merger, occurs when the merging firms do not compete and have no evident economic relationship. Another type of conglomerate merger, the product extension merger, involves firms that make different products which nonetheless involve similar manufacturing or marketing techniques. In a geographic extension merger, finally, the two firms make the same product, but in different geographical markets. As the preceding definitions should suggest, merger cases often require that courts determine product and territorial markets. The considerations relevant to such determinations are much the same as in Sherman Act Section 2 cases.

*For some information on premerger notification see **http://www.ftc. gov**/under "Antitrust/Competition."*

*Horizontal Mergers.* Horizontal mergers threaten competition for at least three reasons. First, they obviously eliminate competition between the merging firms. Second, the firm resulting from the merger may have enough market power to distort competition. Third, the merger may increase concentration in the industry, making it easier for industry members to collude.

In determining whether a horizontal merger violates Section 7, courts typically sift and weigh a number of factors. Heading the list is the market share of the firm resulting from the merger. Another important factor is the market structure of the industry. For example, a merger creating a firm with a 20 percent market share is more worrisome in a highly concentrated market than in an unconcentrated one, because the opportunities for anticompetitive collaboration are greater in the first case. For similar reasons, courts also look for a trend toward greater (or lesser) concentration in the industry. In particular, they are concerned about the increase in concentration resulting from the merger itself. In weighing some of the factors just discussed, courts may employ the Herfindahl–Hirschmann Index (HHI) found in the Horizontal Merger Guidelines produced by the Justice Department and the FTC in 1992 and revised in 1997. The following *Heinz* case provides one example of the HHI's application. But the Guidelines and the HHI are not binding on the courts.

As the *Heinz* case illustrates, courts in horizontal merger cases examine other factors besides the market-structure issues just discussed. One such factor is the extent to which the merging firms actually compete; if they do not, how much will the merger diminish competition? Another factor is the nature of the acquired firm. That firm may have special competitive advantages; on the other hand, it may be a failing company whose market share overstates its strength. Yet another factor is the nature of the firm resulting from the merger. For example, that firm may be able to challenge a hitherto-dominant industry leader due to its size and resources, its efficiency, or its ability to innovate. A final factor concerns the possibility of new entrants into the industry—whether barriers to entry are low or high. If the barriers are low, for example, there may be little reason to worry about anticompetitive collaboration among existing firms in the industry, because the opportunity to reap excessive profits may attract new competitors. In fact, the likelihood of potential competition may keep existing competitors from cooperating to thwart competition in the first place.

When reading *Heinz*, keep in mind that the court is deciding whether a lower court should have issued a preliminary injunction against a horizontal merger, and not whether there is liability under Section 7. But the factors the court discusses are the same factors any court would consider in determining the ultimate legality of the merger.

---

## Federal Trade Commission v. H.J. Heinz Co.
U.S. Court of Appeals (D.C. Circuit)
246 F.3d 708 (2001)

### Background and Facts

In the year 2000, the U.S. baby food market was dominated by three firms: Gerber Products Company (65 percent market share); H.J. Heinz Company (17.4 percent); and Milnot Holding Corporation, the owner of Beech-Nut (15.4 percent). (However, Heinz was the largest baby food producer worldwide.) More than 90 percent of American supermarkets carried Gerber's products, while some 40 percent carried Heinz's baby food and about 45 percent Beech-Nut's. Heinz's sales tended to come from northern New England, the Southeast, the deep South, and the Midwest; Beech-Nut's sales were concentrated in New York, New Jersey, California, and Florida. Heinz marketed itself as a value brand with a shelf price several cents below Gerber's price, while Beech-Nut touted its product as a premium brand with prices only slightly below Gerber's prices.

Early in 2000, Heinz and Beech-Nut entered into a merger agreement. A few months later, the FTC sued for a preliminary injunction against the merger in federal district court. After the district court denied preliminary injunctive relief, the Commission appealed to the D.C. Circuit Court of Appeals.

### Body of Opinion

**Circuit Judge Henderson.** Section 7 of the Clayton Act prohibits acquisitions, including mergers, "where in any line of commerce or in any activity affecting commerce in any section of the country, the effect of such acquisition may be substantially to lessen competition, or to tend to create a monopoly." The Congress used the words "may be substantially to lessen competition" to indicate that its concern was with probabilities, not certainties. Merger enforcement, like other areas of antitrust, is directed at market power. It shares with the law of monopolization a degree of schizophrenia: an aversion to potent power that heightens risk of abuse, and tolerance of that degree of power required to attain economic benefits. . . .

In Section 13(b) of the FTC Act, the Congress provided a mechanism whereby the FTC may seek preliminary injunctive relief preventing the merging parties from consummating the merger until the Commission has had an opportunity to investigate and, if necessary, adjudicate the matter. . . . Section 13(b) provides for a grant of a preliminary injunction where such action would be in the public interest—as determined by a weighing of the equities and a consideration of the Commission's likelihood of success on the merits. . . .

**Likelihood of Success.** To determine likelihood of success on the merits, we measure the probability that, after an administrative hearing on the merits, the Commission will succeed in proving that the effect of the Heinz/Beech-Nut merger "may be to substantially lessen competition, or tend to create a monopoly" in violation of Section 7 of the Clayton Act. This court and others have suggested that the standard for likelihood of success on the merits is met if the FTC has raised questions going to the merits so serious, substantial, difficult, and doubtful as to make them fair grounds for thorough investigation, study, deliberation, and determination by the FTC in the first instance and ultimately by the court of appeals. . . . In *United States v. Baker-Hughes, Inc.* (D.C. Cir. 1990), we explained the analytical approach by which the government establishes a Section 7 violation. First, the government must show that the merger would produce a firm controlling an undue percentage share of the relevant market and would result in a significant increase in the concentration of firms in that market. Such a showing establishes a presumption that the merger will substantially lessen competition. To rebut the presumption, the defendants must produce evidence that shows that the market-share statistics give an inaccurate account of the merger's probable effects on competition in the relevant market. If the defendant successfully rebuts the presumption of illegality, the burden of producing additional evidence of anticompetitive effect shifts to the government, and merges with the ultimate burden of persuasion, which remains with the government at all times. . . .

*Prima Facie Case [presumption].* Merger law rests on the theory that, where rivals are few, firms will be able to coordinate their behavior, either by overt collusion or implicit understanding, in order to restrict output and achieve profits above competitive levels. Increases in concentration above certain levels are thought to raise a likelihood of interdependent anticompetitive conduct. Market concentration, or the lack thereof, is often measured by the Herfindahl–Hirschmann Index (HHI).[7] Sufficiently large HHI figures establish the FTC's prima facie case that a merger is anticompetitive. The district court found that the pre-merger HHI score for the baby food industry is 4,775, indicative of a very highly concentrated industry. The merger of Heinz and Beech-Nut will increase the HHI by 510 points. This creates, by a wide margin, a presumption that the merger will lessen competition in the domestic jarred baby food market. Here, the FTC's market concentration statistics are bolstered by the indisputable fact that the merger will eliminate competition between the two merging parties at the wholesale level, where they are currently the only competitors for what the district court described as the second position on the supermarket shelves. . . . Finally, the anticompetitive effect of the merger is further enhanced by high barriers to market entry. The district court found that there had been no significant entries in the baby food market in decades and that new entry was difficult and improbable. This finding largely eliminates the possibility that the reduced competition caused by the merger will be ameliorated by new competition by outsiders. . . .

*Rebuttal Arguments.* The appellees [mainly Heinz] first contend, and the district court agreed, that Heinz and Beech-Nut do not really compete against each other at the retail level. Consumers do not regard the products of the two companies as substitutes, the appellees claim, and generally only one of the two brands is available on any given store's shelves. Hence, they argue, there is little competitive loss from the merger. This argument has a number of flaws which render clearly erroneous the court's finding that Heinz and Beech-Nut have not engaged in significant pre-merger competition. First, . . . the district court failed to address the record evidence that the two do in fact price against each other, and that, where both are present in the same areas, they depress each other's prices as well as those of Gerber, even though they are virtually never all found in the same store. . . . [Second,] the court's conclusion concerning pre-merger competition does not take into account the indisputable fact that the merger will eliminate competition at the wholesale level between the only two competitors for the "second shelf" position. Competition between Heinz and Beech-Nut to gain accounts at the wholesale level is fierce. . . .

The appellees' second attempt to rebut the FTC's prima facie showing is their contention that the anticompetitive effects of the merger will be offset by efficiencies resulting from the union of the two companies, efficiencies which they assert will be used to compete more effectively against Gerber. . . . Nevertheless, the high market concentration levels present in this case require, in rebuttal, proof of extraordinary efficiencies, which the appellees failed to supply. . . .

The appellees claim next that the merger is required to enable Heinz to innovate, and thus to improve its competitive position against Gerber. Heinz and Beech-Nut asserted, and the district court found, that without the merger the two firms are unable to launch new products to compete with Gerber because they lack a sufficient shelf presence. This kind of defense is often a speculative proposition. In this case, given the old-economy nature of the industry as well as Heinz's position as the world's largest baby food manufacturer, it is a particularly difficult defense to prove. . . .

[T]he district court dismissed the likelihood of collusion derived from the FTC's market concentration data. . . . The combination of a concentrated market and barriers to entry is a recipe for price coordination. Where rivals are few, firms will be able to coordinate their behavior, either by overt collusion or implicit understanding, in order to restrict output and achieve profits above competitive levels. The creation of a durable duopoly affords both the opportunity and the incentive for both firms to coordinate to increase prices. . . . Because the district court failed to specify any structural market barriers to collusion that are unique to the baby food industry, its conclusion that the ordinary presumption of collusion in a merger to duopoly was rebutted is clearly erroneous. . . .

**Weighing of the Equities.** Although the FTC's showing of likelihood of success creates a presumption in favor of preliminary injunctive relief, we must still weigh the equities in order to decide whether enjoining the merger would be in the public interest. The principal public equity weighing in favor of issuance of preliminary injunctive relief is the public interest in effective enforcement of the antitrust laws. . . . The district court found, and there is no dispute, that if the merger were allowed to proceed, subsequent administrative and judicial proceedings on the merits will not matter because Beech-Nut's manufacturing facility will be closed, the Beech-Nut distribution channels will be closed, the new labels and recipe will be in place, and it will be impossible as a practical matter to undo the transaction. Hence, if the merger were ultimately found to violate the Clayton Act, it would be impossible to recreate premerger competition. . . . On the other side of the ledger,

---

[7] The department of Justice and the FTC rely on the HHI in evaluating proposed horizontal mergers. The HHI is calculated by totaling the square of the market shares of every firm in the relevant market. For example, a market with ten firms having market shares of 20 percent, 17 percent, 13 percent, 12 percent, 10 percent, 10 percent, 8 percent, 5 percent, 3 percent, and 2 percent has an HHI of 1,304. If the firms with 13 percent and 5 percent market shares were to merge, the HHI would increase by 130 points. . . . Under the Merger Guidelines a market with a postmerger HHI above 1,800 is considered highly concentrated, and mergers that increase the HHI in such a market by over 50 points potentially raise significant competitive concerns. Mergers producing an increase in the HHI of more than 100 points in such markets are presumed likely to create or enhance market power or facilitate its exercise. Although the Merger Guidelines are not binding on the courts they provide a useful illustration of the application of the HHI [court's footnote].

appellees claim that the injunction would deny consumers the pro-competitive advantages of the merger. The district court found that if the merger were preliminarily enjoined, the injury to competition would be irreversible: that is, the merger would be abandoned and could not be consummated if ultimately found lawful. . . . [But] the appellees acknowledge that there is no alternative buyer for Beech-Nut, and the court found that it is not a failing company but rather a profitable and ongoing enterprise. If the merger makes economic sense now, the appellees have offered no reason why it would not do so later. . . .

**Conclusion.** It is important to emphasize the posture of this case. We do not decide whether the FTC will ultimately prove its case or whether the defendants' claimed efficiencies will carry the day. Our task is to review the district court's order to determine whether, under Section 13(b), preliminary injunctive relief would be in the public interest. . . . We conclude that the FTC has raised serious and substantial questions [about the legality of the merger]. We also conclude that the public equities weigh in favor of preliminary injunctive relief. Accordingly, we reverse the district court's denial of preliminary injunctive relief and remand the case for entry of a preliminary injunction pursuant to Section 13(b) of the Federal Trade Commission Act.

## Judgment and Result

The court of appeals reversed the district court decision denying the FTC's motion to preliminarily enjoin the Heinz-Beech Nut merger, and ordered the district court to grant the injunction. *Note*: As of late 2001, it appeared that Heinz had abandoned the merger.

## Questions

1. Did the court of appeals hold that the merger could never proceed? That is, did its decision leave Heinz with no option except an appeal to the U.S. Supreme Court?
2. Look at the portion of the court's opinion where, after citing the *Baker-Hughes* case, it discusses its approach. Toward the end of that discussion, the court talks about the government's need to produce additional evidence of an anticompetitive effect. Yet nothing like that appears in the remainder of the opinion. Why not?
3. In footnote 7, check the HHI calculations presented there. Then, use the HHI formula to check the district court's HHI calculations that are presented in the court of appeals' decision. Your results on this inquiry should be similar, but not exactly on target. What might account for the discrepancy? *Hint*: Add the market shares for Gerber, Heinz, and Beech-Nut.

*Vertical Mergers.* Vertical mergers have at least four possible anticompetitive effects. First, they may block competitors' access to a share of some market. For example, if a retailer acquires a supplier, competitors of the supplier will not be able to compete for the retailer's business. Similarly, if a supplier acquires a retailer, the supplier's competitors cannot compete for the retailer's business. Second, vertical mergers can eliminate a potential competitor from the acquired firm's market. This potential competitor is the acquiring firm itself, which might have entered the acquired firm's market on its own if the merger had not occurred. A third, and related, effect of vertical mergers is to eliminate the benefits of threatened competition in the acquired firm's market. In our previous example, the threat that the acquiring firm will enter the acquired firm's market might prevent the acquired firm and its competitors from making the industry look more attractive to potential entrants by colluding to raise prices. Finally, vertical mergers can affect competition by discouraging new competitors from entering some market. If supplier S acquires retailer R, R's resulting disappearance as a source of business may deter potential competing suppliers from entering S's industry. The same may be true if R acquires S.

The main factor courts consider in vertical merger cases is the share of the relevant market in which, due to the merger, competition no longer occurs. In a merger between supplier S and retailer R, for example, courts may condemn the merger if R's share of the relevant retail market is sufficiently large. Of course, courts also examine the other considerations just discussed, where they are important. They may also consider historical trends in the industry (e.g., is it becoming more or less concentrated?), as well as the acquiring firm's history (e.g., has it made similar acquisitions in the past?). Over the past 25 years or so, courts have come under some criticism for not considering the possible efficiency gains resulting from vertical mergers. If nothing else, such mergers usually reduce transaction costs.

*Conglomerate Mergers.* Two important factors that courts consider in conglomerate merger cases have already been discussed. First, such a merger obviously eliminates the possibility that the acquiring firm might have entered the acquired firm's market on its own, thereby increasing competition in that market. Second, such a merger makes it impossible for the acquiring firm's potential entry to keep the acquired firm and its competitors from colluding to raise prices. Conglomerate mergers might also give the acquired or acquiring firm too great an edge over their competitors. For example, accessing the acquired firm's resources and/or expertise may enable the acquiring firm to dominate its market and to deter new entrants to that market. The first two factors have usually been the most important considerations in conglomerate merger litigation. Other considerations include such now-familiar issues as the acquired firm's market share, the degree of concentration in its market, and barriers to entering that market.

## THE ROBINSON–PATMAN ACT

The Robinson–Patman Act is primarily concerned with price discrimination: a seller's charging different prices to different buyers of the same product. Why is this a problem? One cause for concern is that large buyers might overcome their smaller competitors by using their market power to extract price concessions from suppliers. For example, concessions from food processors might enable a supermarket chain to undersell local "Mom and Pop" grocery stores. Because they represent less business to food suppliers than the chain does, the smaller groceries typically could not get a similar deal. This scenario is one example of **secondary line price discrimination**, which involves economic injury to competitors of the favored *buyer*. A similar phenomenon, called **tertiary line price discrimination**, involves economic injury to competitors of the *favored buyer's buyers*. For example, suppose that a large food wholesaler gets price concessions from a food processor, passes those savings on to its customers, and these grocery stores thereby get an edge over their competitors.

Another form of price discrimination, called **primary line price discrimination**, involves economic injury to competitors of the *discriminating seller*. For example, a large manufacturer might finance its low prices in areas where it faces strong competition by charging higher prices in areas where competition is weak. As a result, it may obtain a significant advantage over its competitors. For most of its history, the Clayton Act's original Section 2 was primarily concerned with primary line price discrimination. In 1936, however, Section 2 was amended by the Robinson–Patman Act. As its legislative history makes abundantly clear, the Robinson–Patman Act's main aim was to protect small retailers against their bigger and more powerful competitors by forbidding price discrimination in those competitors' favor. Thus, the act forbade secondary and tertiary line price discrimination as well as primary line discrimination. As we will see, the Robinson–Patman Act also prohibits discrimination regarding matters other than price.

The Robinson–Patman Act has been controversial ever since the time of its consideration and passage. To see why, first observe that the price discrimination forbidden by the act often benefits consumers. A major reason that chain stores have prospered, for example, is that they often offer consumers lower prices. Indeed, the standard criticism of the Robinson–Patman Act is that it protects competitors rather than protecting competition. To this, a defender of the act might reply that competitors who overcome their rivals by offering lower prices may then become oligopolists or even monopolists, or at least may get the market power to engage in anticompetitive practices. But in theory, at least, the other provisions of the antitrust laws can deal with such behavior. Due in part to such misgivings, government enforcement of the Robinson–Patman Act has been minimal for some time. Thus, private suits are now the main vehicle for enforcing the act's provisions.

## JURISDICTIONAL REACH

The Robinson–Patman Act applies only to price discrimination and other acts that occur "in commerce." This normally means that one of the sales involved in the price discrimination or other discrimination must cross state lines. Thus, an Indiana manufacturer probably would not violate the act if it sold at different prices to two or more Indiana customers.

## PRICE DISCRIMINATION

Price discrimination is forbidden by Section 2(a) of the Robinson–Patman Act. In addition to the in-commerce requirement, Section 2(a) liability requires the following:

1. *A sale*—Not included are offers to sell, leases, consignment arrangements, and refusals to deal.
2. *Of commodities (or goods)*—Thus, sales of services, real estate, and intangibles are not covered.
3. *Of like grade and quality*—A difference in grade or quality, of course, can justify a difference in price. Such a difference must be based on a physical difference that affects the commodity's acceptability to buyers. By themselves, differences in a product's brand name or label are not sufficient.
4. *To different competing customers at a different price or prices*—Normally, it is permissible to charge different prices to wholesalers than to retailers, or to buyers who do not compete in the same geographic market.
5. *Probable injury to competition*—This element varies with the type of price discrimination at issue. Primary line discrimination requires the greatest probability of injury to competition. If the following *Brooke Group* case is any guide, injury to a competitor—for example, lost sales—is insufficient for liability. In all likelihood, the motives of the price-discriminating firm are not the critical thing either. Rather, liability requires some fairly significant actual or potential detriment to competition.

   Secondary- and tertiary-line discrimination, however, require less likelihood of injury to competition. Here, it is generally sufficient for liability if the prices a seller charges competing buyers display sustained and substantial differences. Minor or short-term differences, however, may not be sufficient for liability.

## Brooke Group Ltd. v. Brown & Williamson Tobacco Corp.
### U. S. Supreme Court
### 509 U.S. 209 (1993)

### Background and Facts

In 1980, the Liggett Corporation (later renamed the Brooke Group Limited) introduced a line of economy generic cigarettes called "black and white" cigarettes. As the market for these economy cigarettes expanded, other cigarette manufacturers began their own offerings in this segment. Among them was the Brown & Williamson Tobacco Corporation (BW), which competed with Liggett by offering discriminatory volume discounts to wholesalers. This triggered a rebate war in the economy segment, a war BW apparently was winning. By the end of the war, Liggett claimed, BW was selling its black and whites at a loss.

Eventually, Liggett sued BW, alleging that BW's rebates constituted illegal price discrimination under Section 2(a) of the Robinson–Patman Act. Liggett claimed that BW's below-cost sales amounted to predatory pricing, and that the ultimate aim of such pricing was to force Liggett to raise its prices on generic cigarettes. This, Liggett further contended, would narrow the difference between generic and branded cigarette prices, thus restraining the growth of the economy segment and preserving BW's excessive profits on its branded cigarettes. Liggett also claimed that, to avoid prolonged losses on the generics that had become its main line of business, it had to go along with BW's scheme.

After a 115-day trial, the jury returned a $49.6 million treble damages verdict in Liggett's favor. The district court, however, decided that BW was entitled to judgment as a matter of law and therefore set aside the jury's verdict. After the court of appeals affirmed this decision, Liggett appealed to the U.S. Supreme Court.

### Body of Opinion

**Justice Kennedy.** By its terms, the Robinson–Patman Act condemns price discrimination only to the extent that it threatens to injure competition. . . . Liggett contends that BW's discriminatory volume rebates to wholesalers threatened substantial competitive injury by furthering a predatory pricing scheme designed to purge competition from the economy segment of the cigarette market. This type of injury, which harms direct competitors of the discriminating seller, is known as primary-line injury. We last addressed primary-line injury over twenty-five years ago, in *Utah Pie Co. v. Continental Baking Co.* (1967). . . . *Utah Pie* has often been interpreted to permit liability for primary-line price discrimination on a mere showing that the defendant intended to harm competition or produced a declining price structure. The case has been criticized on the grounds that such low standards of competitive injury are at odds with the antitrust laws' traditional concern for consumer welfare and price competition. . . . As the law has been explored since *Utah Pie*, it has become evident that primary-line competitive injury under the Robinson–Patman Act is of the same general character as the injury inflicted by predatory pricing schemes actionable under Section 2 of

the Sherman Act. . . . Accordingly, whether the claim alleges predatory pricing under Section 2 of the Sherman Act or primary-line price discrimination under the Robinson–Patman Act, two prerequisites to recovery remain the same. First, a plaintiff seeking to establish competitive injury resulting from a rival's low prices must prove that the prices complained of are below an appropriate measure of its rival's costs. . . . The second prerequisite to holding a competitor liable . . . is a demonstration that the competitor had a reasonable prospect . . . of recouping its investment in below-cost prices. For the investment to be rational, the predator must have a reasonable expectation of recovering, in the form of later monopoly profits, more than the losses suffered. . . . That below-cost pricing may impose painful losses on its target is of no moment to the antitrust laws if competition is not injured: it is axiomatic that the antitrust laws were passed for the protection of *competition*, not *competitors*. . . .

These prerequisites to recovery are not easy to establish, but they are not artificial obstacles to recovery; rather, they are essential components of real market injury. As we have said in the Sherman Act context, predatory pricing schemes are rarely tried, and even more rarely successful. . . . It would be ironic indeed if the standards for predatory pricing liability were so low that antitrust suits themselves became a tool for keeping prices high. . . .

There is . . . sufficient evidence in the record from which a reasonable jury could conclude that for a period of approximately eighteen months, BW's prices on its generic cigarettes were below its costs, and that this below-cost pricing imposed losses on Liggett that Liggett was unwilling to sustain. . . . Liggett has failed to demonstrate competitive injury as a matter of law, however, because its proof is flawed in a critical respect: the evidence is inadequate to show that in pursuing [its] scheme, BW had a reasonable prospect of recovering its losses from below-cost pricing through slowing the growth of generics. . . .

Based on Liggett's theory of the case and the record it created, there are two means by which one might infer that BW had a reasonable prospect of producing sustained supracompetitive pricing in the generic segment adequate to recoup its predatory losses: first, if generic output or price information indicates that oligopolistic price coordination in fact produced supracompetitive prices in the generic segment; or second, if evidence about the market and BW's conduct indicate that the alleged scheme was likely to have brought about tacit coordination and oligopoly pricing in the generic segment, even if it did not actually do so.

In this case, the price and output data do not support a reasonable inference that BW and the other cigarette companies elevated prices above a competitive level for generic cigarettes. . . . Not only does the evidence fail to show actual supracompetitive pricing in the generic segment, it also does not demonstrate its likelihood. At the time BW entered the generic segment, the cigarette industry as a whole faced declining demand and possessed substantial excess capacity. These circumstances tend to break down patterns of oligopoly pricing and produce price competition. . . . Tacit coordination is facilitated by a stable market environment, fungible products, and a small number of variables upon which the firms seeking to coordinate their pricing may focus. Uncertainty is an oligopoly's greatest enemy. By 1984, however, the cigarette market was in an obvious state of flux. The introduction of generic cigarettes in 1980 represented the first serious price competition in the cigarette market since the 1930s. This development was bound to unsettle previous expectations and patterns of market conduct and to reduce the cigarette firms' ability to predict each others' behavior. The larger number of product types and pricing variables also decreased the probability of effective parallel pricing. In order to coordinate in an effective manner and eliminate price competition, the cigarette companies would have been required, without communicating, to establish parallel practices with respect to each of these variables, many of which, like consumer stickers or coupons, were difficult to monitor. . . .

Even if all the cigarette companies were willing to participate in a scheme to restrain the growth of the generic segment, they would not have been able to coordinate their actions and raise prices above a competitive level unless they understood that BW's entry into the segment was not a genuine effort to compete with Liggett. If even one other firm misinterpreted BW's entry as an effort to expand share, a chain reaction of competitive responses would almost certainly have resulted, and oligopoly discipline would have broken down, perhaps irretrievably. . . . Liggett argues that the means by which BW signaled its anticompetitive intent to its rivals was through its pricing structure. According to Liggett, maintaining existing list prices while offering substantial rebates to wholesalers was a signal to the other cigarette firms that BW did not intend to attract additional smokers to the generic segment by its entry. But . . . [t]he likelihood that BW's rivals would have regarded its pricing structure as an important signal is low, given that Liggett itself, the purported target of the predation, was already using similar rebates. . . .

### Judgment and Result

Court of appeals decision in BW's favor affirmed. Liggett's Robinson–Patman claim fails and BW wins.

### Questions

1. What were the two requirements Liggett had to meet in order to demonstrate the necessary probability of injury to competition? Which one did it fail to satisfy? Why?
2. Why does below-cost pricing suggest predatory intent?
3. Make an argument that Liggett's motives for suing BW were anticompetitive.

---

*Two Defenses to Price Discrimination.* There are two accepted defenses to price discrimination:

1. *Cost justification.* Section 2(a) permits otherwise-illegal price discrimination where the price differential is due to differences in the commodity's cost of manufacture, sale, or delivery that result from the different methods or quantities in which the commodity is sold. To prove this defense, the defendant must group its customers into different categories according to their buying characteristics, and show that this grouping justifies its price differentials. Despite the difficulties such proof creates, the defense still can allow sellers to escape Robinson–Patman liability in cases where the price differential reflects genuine differences in the costs of servicing particular customers. Quantity discounts are one possibility.

2. *Meeting competition.* Section 2(b) of the Robinson–Patman Act insulates a seller from liability where its price discrimination took place "in good faith to meet an equally low price of a competitor." The aim of this defense is to prevent normal price competition from violating the Robinson–Patman Act. The standard for granting the defense is whether a reasonable person would believe that by charging the lower price, he would meet the equally low price of a competitor. Although this test requires that the seller have some more or less reliable information about the competitor's price, it does not demand absolute certainty. Note, however, that a seller normally cannot undersell a competitor, but only meet its price.

## BUYER INDUCEMENT OF DISCRIMINATION

Robinson–Patman Act Section 2(f) makes it illegal for a buyer to knowingly induce or receive a discriminatory price that violates Section 2(a). The aim of Section 2(f) is to penalize not only sellers who charge discriminatory prices, but the buyers who demand them. However, such buyers are not liable under Section 2(f) if the seller has a valid defense to price discrimination liability.

## OTHER FORMS OF SELLER DISCRIMINATION

Sellers can discriminate among customers in other ways than by the prices they charge. Thus, the Robinson–Patman Act penalizes three other methods by which sellers might discriminate among buyers. Unlike Section 2(a) liability, in all three cases no harm to competition is necessary for liability.

Section 2(c) of the act forbids sellers from paying, and buyers from accepting, commission or brokerage payments that are not in compensation for services rendered in connection with the sale or purchase of goods. Section 2(c)'s aim is to prevent indirect price discrimination in the form of fake commissions or brokerage payments to the buyer or its agents. Robinson–Patman Act Section 2(d) makes it illegal for a seller to pay a customer "for any services or facilities furnished by or through such customer" in connection with the sale of the product, unless the payment is available on proportionately equal terms to all competing customers. For example, a manufacturer cannot pay one of its retailers to advertise the product unless it offers essentially the same deal to its other retailers. Section 2(e) imposes a similar restriction on sellers who themselves furnish such services or facilities to their buyers. Note that unlike Section 2(c)'s ban on discriminatory commission or brokerage payments, the buyer is not liable under Sections 2(d) and 2(e). Also, there is a "meeting competition" defense under Sections 2(d) and 2(e).

## INTERLOCKING DIRECTORATES AND OFFICERS

"Competitors" that share officers and directors may be competitors in name only. Clayton Act Section 8 says that no person shall serve as a director, or as an officer chosen by the directors, of two corporations that: (1) each have capital, surplus, and undivided profits aggregating more than $10 million; and (2) are so situated that an anticompetitive agreement between them would violate the antitrust laws. However, Section 8 does not govern banks, banking associations, and trust companies. Also, the $10 million figure is adjusted yearly by an amount equaling the percentage increase or decrease in the gross national product (GNP).

In addition, Section 8 does not prohibit simultaneous service by an officer or director if: (1) the "competitive sales" of either corporation are less than $1 million, (2) the "competitive sales" of either corporation are less than 2 percent of that corporation's total sales, or (3) the "competitive sales" of *each* corporation are less than 4 percent of that corporation's total sales. "Competitive sales" are the gross revenues for all products and services sold by one corporation in competition with the other. Like the $10 million figure, the $1 million figure is adjusted yearly according to the percentage change in the GNP. This provision's apparent aim is to allow people to serve as officers or directors of two firms that are very small or that do not compete to any significant extent, even though they meet the basic tests for Section 8 liability.

## ANTITRUST EXEMPTIONS

Many activities are exempt from the antitrust laws. Most of these exemptions are explicitly stated in a statute, while some result from judicial decisions. Speaking generally, these exemptions reflect the notion that in some cases, the procompetitive policies underlying the antitrust laws should be superseded by other values. (Of course, self-interested political forces may also explain some exemptions.) The following list of antitrust exemptions is not exhaustive.

### THE STATE ACTION EXEMPTION

In *Parker v. Brown* (1943), the Supreme Court held anticompetitive activities by private raisin growers and packers exempt from the antitrust laws because those activities were authorized by state regulation. Federalism was the basis for this state-action exemption. However, the state regulation protected by *Parker v. Brown* may sometimes reflect the political influence of private firms that desire to avoid competition. To minimize this possibility, the Court has formulated two criteria for the state-action doctrine's application. First, the restraint on competition must be clearly articulated and affirmatively expressed as state policy. Second, that policy must be actively supervised by the state.

The point of the first test is to assure that the state actually has intended to displace competition in a particular area. It includes situations in which a state has clearly permitted, but not commanded, some anticompetitive practice. The "active supervision" test requires that the state exercise sufficient independent judgment and control over the allegedly anticompetitive practices that their details are the product of deliberate state intervention, rather than the result of private agreements. In the case where it enunciated this test, the Court found that price-fixing by state-regulated title insurance companies violated the Sherman Act, in part because the states essentially ratified the companies' rates, instead of setting them or at least scrutinizing them more carefully.

So far, we have been considering regulation by the state itself. What about anticompetitive behavior sanctioned by such local units of government as cities, counties, and townships? Here, state action immunity exists only if the subdivision acts under a state mandate and the challenged anticompetitive practice was a clearly foreseeable consequence of that mandate. However, it is not necessary that the state actively supervise the local unit's implementation of the mandate. Under these tests, the anticompetitive consequences of local zoning regulation probably would be shielded from the antitrust laws, while the anticompetitive consequences of a city's home-rule powers might not.[8]

### PETITIONING THE GOVERNMENT

In 1961, the Supreme Court held that the antitrust laws do not prohibit two or more people from associating together to persuade the government to enact a law

---

[8] Due to fear that application of the antitrust laws to local governments might result in crippling treble damage liability, Congress passed the Local Government Antitrust Act of 1984. The act bars federal antitrust damage suits against local governments, their officials and employees (when acting in their official capacity), and private persons (for actions directed by a local government). However, injunctive relief remains available.

with an anticompetitive impact. The reason was that the antitrust laws should not regulate political activity—even political activity with anticompetitive aims—because such activity implicates First Amendment values. However, this exemption does not cover "sham" political action that really is an attempt to suppress competition. In one such case, for example, the Supreme Court refused to exempt a group of large trucking firms that routinely opposed all applications by smaller truckers before state and federal agencies.

## UNION ACTIVITY

Trade unions may seek to monopolize the labor supply within a particular market, and strikes arguably resemble group boycotts. For this reason, organized labor's well-being might be endangered were the antitrust laws applicable to unions and their activities. Thus, labor unions, most union activities, and collective bargaining agreements generally are exempt from the antitrust laws. However, the exemption does not apply if a union engages in anticompetitive activity with a nonlabor group.

## OTHER EXEMPTIONS

Many regulated industries such as insurance; banking; airline and rail transportation; electric, gas, and water utilities; financial services; and others are exempt from the antitrust laws to a greater or lesser extent. Often, the administrative bodies regulating such industries deal with matters that otherwise would be antitrust issues. Federal law also exempts certain agricultural cooperatives from antitrust regulation. Federal law also exempts certain joint export activities by American companies, so long as they do not affect prices within the United States The aim of these combinations is to help American firms better compete against foreign cartels.

## CHAPTER SUMMARY

Sherman Act Section 1 forbids various contracts, combinations, or conspiracies in restraint of trade. Some of these are called per se violations. Here, the behavior in question is deemed so inherently anticompetitive that Section 1 liability is automatic once it is proven. Section 1 per se violations include horizontal and vertical price-fixing, the horizontal division of markets, group boycotts, and tying contracts. All other potentially anticompetitive contracts or combinations are called rule of reason violations. Here, in addition to proof of the offending behavior, an individualized inquiry into the economic effects of that behavior is necessary before Section 1 liability will exist.

Section 2 of the Sherman Act forbids monopolization and attempts to monopolize. Monopolization requires (1) a firm with monopoly power (determined primarily by market share), in (2) the relevant product and territorial market, and (3) the firm's acquisition or maintenance of that monopoly power with intent to monopolize. Section 2 liability for an attempt to monopolize requires (1) that the defendant has engaged in predatory or anticompetitive conduct, (2) with a specific intent to monopolize, and (3) with a dangerous probability of achieving monopoly power.

■ Manager's Ethical Dilemma

"Those chiropractors are stealing our patients," said Dr. Smith to Dr. Jones. "And they're not doing them much good, either." Both Smith and Jones are medical doctors. Due to their concerns, they sent letters to their lobbying groups and to the American Medical Association. Their letters urged that these groups pressure Congress and the state legislatures to enact tougher education requirements for chiropractors, tougher chiropractor licensing standards, and fee caps for chiropractic services. Drs. Smith and Jones also joined a large group of medical doctors who agreed not to refer patients to chiropractors even in situations where they felt that chiropractic treatment might do those patients some good. Instead, they agreed to send their patients to fellow MDs specializing in orthopedics.

Is all of this ethical behavior on the two doctors' part? What factual question will definitely affect your answer? *Note:* This scenario is loosely based on *Wilk v. American Medical Association* [895 F.2d 352 (7th Cir. 1990)].

Section 3 of the Sherman Act forbids the sale or lease of commodities on the condition that the buyer or lessee not use or deal commodities sold or leased by a competitor of the seller or lessor, where this would substantially lessen competition or tend to create a monopoly. Section 3 applies mainly to tying contracts, exclusive dealing contracts, and requirements contracts.

Clayton Act Section 7 forbids mergers that substantially lessen competition or tend to create a monopoly. Section 7's discretionary standards vary depending on whether a horizontal merger, a vertical merger, or a conglomerate merger is present.

Section 8 of the Clayton Act forbids certain interlocking directorates and officers between business firms.

The Robinson–Patman Act mainly concerns price discrimination, which may be of the primary line, secondary line, or tertiary line variety. It also forbids buyer inducement of price discrimination, discriminatory commission or brokerage payments, discriminatory payments to a customer, and the discriminatory furnishing of services or facilities to customers.

Many kinds of behavior are exempt from the antitrust laws. The most important antitrust exemptions are (1) the state action exemption, (2) a "political action" exemption, and (3) an exemption for union activity.

## DISCUSSION QUESTIONS

1. In the famous *Alcoa* case, where Alcoa had 90 percent of the U.S. market for virgin aluminum ingot, the court held that Alcoa intended to maintain monopoly power because it maintained excess production capacity, grabbed every new opportunity to make or sell aluminum, and thus kept new competitors from entering the industry. *Alcoa* may have come close to holding that the mere possession of monopoly power proves intent to monopolize. If so, is this a good or a bad result? What bad things are monopolists—even innocent monopolists—likely to do with monopoly power once they get it? On the other hand, might they not face new entrants to the industry if they try these bad things? Or will barriers to entry always or nearly always prevent new competitors from entering the industry? Finally, will firms' competitive juices flow more weakly if they know

that the ultimate reward of competitive effort—domination of an industry—will only get them in legal trouble under Section 2?

2. The chapter states the arguments made by the Supreme Court in its 1977 *Sylvania* case, where it held that vertical territorial restrictions should be treated as rule-of-reason violations rather than per se violations. Do you find these arguments persuasive? If so, should they be extended to justify rule-of-reason status for the vertical fixing of minimum prices?

3. As the chapter should make clear, Chicago School thinking is coming to dominate the antitrust laws. Go through the chapter and identify as many examples as you can. In each case, say *why* the development in question exemplifies Chicago School thinking.

4. All things considered, do you believe that the Chicago School approach is preferable to the traditional approach? Or is it the other way around?

5. Does the Robinson–Patman Act protect competitors more than it protects competition? How much does it protect competition? Should it be repealed? Why is it unlikely to be repealed any time soon?

6. Is the state action exemption a good idea? Whose interests do the "state policies" protected by the exemption tend to serve? Is federalism just a fig leaf covering anticompetitive behavior in this case?

7. One Chicago School argument against the per se rule for tying contracts says that if the seller has market power in the tying product, it can distort competition in other ways than by using a tying contract. For example, such a seller might simply use its market power to charge a higher price for the tying product, rather than by linking it to something else. In other words, there is only so much "monopoly profit" that the seller can derive from its market power in the tying product, and it matters little how the seller chooses to exercise that power. The apparent implication of the argument is that cracking down on tie-ins only treats a symptom, and does not address the source of the problem: the seller's market power in the tying product market.

    What do you think about this argument? What provision of the antitrust laws addresses what this argument regards as the real problem: market power in the tying product market?

8. During the 1960s and early 1970s, the Supreme Court apparently thought that horizontal mergers are a serious threat to competition. At that time, the Court sometimes struck down mergers that did not greatly increase industry concentration. Perhaps the best example is the Court's 1966 decision in *United States v. Von's Grocery Co.*, where the third largest retail grocery chain in the Los Angeles market (with 4.7 percent of all sales) acquired the sixth largest firm in that market, and the resulting firm accounted for only 7.5 percent of sales in the market. Does this result make any sense?

9. Is the Herfindahl–Hirschmann Index (HHI) for horizontal mergers a good idea? Is it just a misleading attempt to quantify the unquantifiable? On the other hand, doesn't the HHI at least give businesses some idea when they might run afoul of Clayton Act Section 7? And might it not force some consistency into government enforcement and judicial decisions under Section 7?

10. It has been argued that the rules for *proving* horizontal price-fixing and other kinds of horizontal collaboration under Sherman Act Section 1 allow a good deal of horizontal collaboration to escape Section 1 liability. This is especially true of the rule that merely following a price leader, by itself, does not violate Section 1. Is this a valid argument? What might be said in defense of the proof rules for horizontal collaboration?

## INFOTRAC KEYWORDS

**Use your InfoTrac password to look up articles on http://www.infotrac-college.com**

Keywords: *Sherman Act, vertical price fixing, price fixing, monopolization, Clayton Act, horizontal merger, conglomerate merger, Robinson–Patman Act, price discrimination, interlocking directorates, antitrust exemptions.*

For suggested readings, please visit this book's Web site at **http://fisher.westbuslaw.com** (click on "Internet Applications").

# FEDERAL TRADE COMMISSION ACT, FRANCHISING, AND UNFAIR COMPETITION

## POSITIVE LAW ETHICAL PROBLEM

The price inflation that afflicted the United States during the 1970s had definite consequences for the Orkin Exterminating Company. From 1966 until 1975, Orkin had
offered its customers contracts for "lifetime" termite protection and control. The contracts said that this guarantee would remain in effect for the lifetime of the covered
structure, so long as the customer continued to pay the annual renewal fee. After
increasing costs made the contracts too expensive, Orkin decided that it had to get
out of them. In 1980, therefore, the firm began notifying its 1966–1975 "lifetime"
customers that it was going to increase its annual renewal fees by about 40 percent.
Despite many complaints, most customers accepted the increase. One reason they
caved in was that signing on with Orkin's competitors often left them no better off
than under Orkin's revised plan. Also, Orkin instituted an "accommodation program" in which it explained its changed position to complaining customers and
thereby mollified some of them. Although a few persistent customers did escape the
rate increase through the program, most complaining customers were not made
aware of this possibility.

Was Orkin's behavior ethical? In any event, was it legal? The Federal Trade
Commission (FTC) thought not. In 1984, the FTC issued an administrative complaint
charging that Orkin had committed an unfair act or practice in violation of FTC Act
Section 5. Did the Commission wins its case?

In the previous chapter, you saw that the Sherman, Clayton, and Robinson–
Patman Acts forbid various anticompetitive practices. Section 5 of the Federal
Trade Commission Act of 1914, which prohibits unfair methods of competition,
does much the same. By forbidding unfair or deceptive acts or practices, moreover, Section 5 also protects consumers. Both of these missions—promoting competition and protecting consumers—are entrusted to the Federal Trade
Commission (FTC), which the FTC Act created in 1914.

This chapter opens by examining the FTC, its enforcement devices, and its role
in attacking anticompetitive behavior. The chapter's main concern, however, is
the Commission's regulation of unfair and deceptive business conduct, especially
deceptive advertising. The chapter then outlines some of the remedies the FTC
employs in advertising cases, as well as its regulation of franchising. The chapter
concludes by considering a federal statute—Section 43(a) of the Lanham Act—
that provides a civil remedy for false or deceptive advertising and certain other
kinds of unfair competition.

## THE FEDERAL TRADE COMMISSION

The Federal Trade Commission (FTC) is an independent federal administrative agency. It is not part of the executive branch of government and is not so subject to political control as agencies located within the executive branch. The FTC is headed by five commissioners, appointed by the president and confirmed by the Senate for staggered seven-year terms. The president also designates one of the commissioners as chairman of the FTC.

The FTC has several regional offices. These offices are the usual starting point for businesses or consumers wishing to contact the FTC about possible violations of the laws it enforces. The addresses and territorial coverage of the FTC's regional offices can be found at its Web site, http://www.ftc.gov.

### FUNCTIONS

Today, the FTC's main functions can be grouped under two headings: (1) maintaining economic competition, and (2) consumer protection. In other words, the FTC tries to encourage business competition that is both free and fair. The Commission promotes free competition by enforcing both the antitrust statutes discussed in Chapter 20 and FTC Act Section 5's ban on unfair methods of competition. The FTC's consumer protection mission has three main components. First, Section 5 enables the Commission to regulate *unfair* acts or practices by businesses. Second, Section 5 also gives the Commission the power to regulate *deceptive* acts or practices. The most important example is deceptive advertising. Third, the FTC enforces a number of specific federal consumer protection measures, some of which are discussed in the next chapter. The Commission also enforces various other miscellaneous federal statutes.

*For a list of the federal statutes the FTC enforces, see* ***http:// www.ftc.gov/ogc/stats.htm***

### FTC REGULATION UNDER SECTION 5

FTC Act Section 5 is worded in a broad and general fashion. One reason for its vagueness is that there are too many kinds of unfairness and deception for Congress ever to specify in a single statute. Another is that the ingenuity of unscrupulous businesspeople continually produces novel forms of unfairness, deception, and anticompetitive activity. Thus, Congress probably had little choice but to announce general standards, and to delegate the power to enforce those standards to an agency such as the FTC.

This necessary flexibility, however, comes at a price. Due to Section 5's generality, businesses sometimes have difficulty determining whether their activities will run afoul of the FTC. As you will see shortly, however, the FTC has taken a number of steps to address this problem.

Another implication of Section 5's generality is that the FTC has considerable freedom to determine how aggressively it regulates business misbehavior. In fact, the FTC's conception of its role—and thus its effect on business activity—has varied over the years. This is because the economic philosophies of the commissioners and the political allegiances of the administrations appointing them go some way toward determining the FTC's course. In the 1970s, for example, the Commission was an activist agency that constantly attempted to define and enforce stricter rules against alleged business misconduct. During the 1980s, on the other hand, the FTC tended to be more skeptical about the virtues of government regulation and to stress the economic costs of such regulation.

## FTC Rules, Guides, and Other Standards

Due to the generality of FTC Act Section 5 and some other laws the Commission enforces, businesses need authoritative guidance about what is legal and illegal under these provisions. To supply such guidance, the FTC uses various devices, including advisory opinions, industry guides and other policy statements, and trade regulation rules. These devices are cooperative procedures that try to promote voluntary compliance by business.

Although it is not obligated to do so, the FTC may respond to business queries about the legality of proposed conduct by issuing an **advisory opinion**. For example, a firm contemplating a particular marketing technique may be able to get an advisory opinion giving it some idea of whether the FTC will act to block the use of that technique. **Industry guides** and other FTC policy statements basically are FTC interpretations of the statutes it enforces. Although they generally lack the force of law, industry guides and other policy statements may violate some other, more authoritative, standard such as a **trade regulation rule**. Like industry guides and policy statements, FTC trade regulation rules interpret the statutes the Commission enforces. For example, they may specify particular practices that the FTC deems deceptive or unfair. To enact a trade regulation rule, the Commission must undertake a formal rule-making proceeding. Trade regulation rules have the force of law, and their violation can trigger FTC enforcement efforts.

## FTC Enforcement Devices

The main way that the FTC enforces its statutes and rules is through formal administrative action. After considering FTC administrative enforcement in some detail, we briefly consider some other enforcement devices at the Commission's disposal.

### Formal FTC Action

*Initiation of Proceedings.* Sometimes the initiative for FTC administrative action comes from the FTC's own investigations of possible illegal activity. On other occasions, the action is initiated by an informal complaint. Informal complaints may come from government bodies, from businesses, or from consumers. Once it receives an informal complaint, the FTC must decide whether to investigate the matter. If the Commission does investigate, it may ultimately decide that the case should be closed or settled. But the investigation also may result in a formal complaint against the alleged violator (the respondent).

*FTC Administrative Hearings.* Even after a formal complaint is issued, the FTC and the respondent still may settle the case. If this does not happen, the case goes to an FTC administrative hearing (also called an adjudicative proceeding). The hearing resembles a court trial. It is presided over by an administrative law judge, without a jury. After hearing evidence and the legal arguments made by counsel for the respondent and the FTC, the administrative law judge issues an initial decision.

*Commission Orders.* An initial decision against the respondent in an FTC administrative proceeding typically is accompanied by an order. The most common such order is called a **cease-and-desist order**, or C & D order. As its name suggests, a C & D order is a command ordering the respondent to cease certain behavior. However, Commission orders sometimes go beyond a simple command to cease and desist. The FTC may, for example, compel a respondent to make affirmative disclosures, to divest itself of certain assets or stock, or to make restitution to injured parties. In cases involving deceptive or unfair advertising, the Commission may also issue the affirmative disclosure, corrective advertising, and all-products orders described later in the chapter. Parties who violate the terms of a Commission order are subject to civil penalties.

As noted earlier, the FTC may settle a case with the alleged violator either before or after the issuance of a formal complaint. Such settlements involve a **consent order**. Where a consent order is worked out, the FTC agrees not to pursue the case further, in return for the respondent's promise to refrain from engaging in certain behavior. The respondent need not admit any violation of the law. The penalties for failure to obey a consent order are the same as for the failure to observe a normal Commission order.

*Further Review.* Where no settlement occurs, the administrative law judge typically decides for or against the respondent. This initial decision usually becomes the decision of the full Commission unless the Commission decides to review it, or either party appeals to the full Commission. The full Commission's decision may be appealed to the U.S. Courts of Appeals and then to the U.S. Supreme Court.

## OTHER ENFORCEMENT DEVICES

In various situations, the FTC may sue for **injunctive relief** in federal district court. Also, the Commission may obtain federal district court **civil penalties** in certain cases involving unfair or deceptive acts or practices. This can happen where (1) a private party knowingly violates a trade regulation rule defining such acts or practices; or (2) a private party knowingly violates a C & D order involving such acts or practices, even if the order involved some other party. To illustrate the second situation, suppose that the FTC orders a manufacturer to cease making certain untrue advertising claims. If a competitor of the manufacturer makes the same untrue claims with knowledge of the order, the FTC may sue to impose a civil penalty.

In two other situations involving unfairness or deception, the FTC may sue in state or federal court for **redress** to consumers or other injured parties. A business may be required to make such redress where it (1) violates any trade regulation rule defining such acts or practices; or (2) violates a C & D order imposed on *it* because of such acts or practices. The redress available to injured parties may include the rescission or reformation of contracts, the refund of money, the return of property, payment of damages, or public notice of the unfair or deceptive practice.

## The FTC and Anticompetitive Behavior

As we have stressed, one of the FTC's missions is to promote free economic competition. The main kinds of anticompetitive behavior with which the FTC is concerned are the orthodox antitrust violations described in Chapter 20. The FTC has authority to enforce the Clayton Act and the Robinson–Patman Act.[1] In the *Heinz* case in Chapter 20, for example, the Commission sued to enjoin a merger under Section 7 of the Clayton Act. Also, FTC Act Section 5's broad "unfair methods of competition" language covers all behavior made illegal by the Sherman Act.

Section 5 also lets the FTC attack anticompetitive conduct outside the letter or spirit of the other antitrust statutes. In one such case, the Supreme Court held that the Sperry and Hutchinson Company's attempt to suppress trading stamp exchanges that dealt in its S & H Green Stamps violated Section 5, even though the attempt did not violate either the letter or the spirit of the antitrust laws. Finally, Section 5 gives the FTC the power to proceed against potential or incipient violations of the antitrust laws.

## Unfair and Deceptive Acts or Practices

Section 5's prohibition of unfair and deceptive acts or practices gives the FTC power to regulate a wide range of activities harmful to consumers, especially deceptive advertising. When the Commission attacks business behavior under this portion of Section 5, it may do so on either of two bases. It may argue that the act or practice violates Section 5 because it is *unfair*, or because it is *deceptive*. This section considers each of these standards in turn, and then examines some matters that specifically pertain to advertising.

### Unfairness

Many unfairness cases proceed under standards promulgated by the FTC in 1980. These standards require that the offending practice cause injury to consumers and that this injury be: (1) substantial, (2) not outweighed by any offsetting consumer or competitive benefits the practice produces, and (3) not reasonably avoidable by consumers. Substantial harm includes monetary losses and unwarranted health and safety risks to consumers, but it is unlikely that emotional distress or the perceived offensiveness of an advertisement qualify.

The second element of the test—that the harm the challenged practice causes not be outweighed by its benefits to consumers or to competition—requires the FTC to balance the practice's costs against its benefits. Only when the practice is injurious in its net effects does it satisfy this second test. For example, a seller's failure to disclose complex technical data about its products might not be unfair if the data is of marginal usefulness to consumers and disclosure would significantly raise the product's price.

Finally, the FTC considers an injury not reasonably avoidable when the challenged act or practice significantly interferes with consumers' ability to make

---

[1] Also, companies planning certain kinds of mergers are required to give premerger notification to the FTC and the Justice Department, and supply certain information to these agencies as well.

informed decisions that would have prevented the injury. Such interference can occur where a seller fails to disclose important performance data regarding its product, and the buyer lacks sufficient information to meaningfully compare the product with other products. The Commission has also suggested that this test is met when sellers exercise undue influence over highly susceptible consumers—as, for example, when questionable cures are marketed to seriously ill cancer victims.

## Orkin Exterminating Co. v. Federal Trade Commission
U.S. Court of Appeals (11th Circuit)
849 F.2d 1354 (1988)

### Background and Facts

From 1966 until 1975, the Orkin Exterminating Company had offered its customers contracts for "lifetime" termite protection and control. The contracts said that the guarantee would remain in effect for the lifetime of the covered structure, so long as the customer paid the annual renewal fee. After inflation and increasing costs made the contracts too expensive, Orkin decided that it had to get out of them. In 1980, therefore, the firm began telling its 1966–75 "lifetime" customers that it would increase its annual renewal fees by about 40 percent. Despite many complaints, most customers accepted the increase. One reason they did so was that signing on with Orkin's competitors often left them no better off than under Orkin's revised plan. Also, Orkin instituted an "accommodation program" in which it explained its new position to complaining customers and thereby mollified some of them. Although a few persistent customers escaped the rate increase through the program, most complaining customers were not made aware of this possibility.

In 1984, the FTC issued an administrative complaint charging that Orkin had committed an unfair act or practice in violation of FTC Act Section 5. The administrative law judge found against Orkin, issuing an order requiring it to roll back the fees in its pre-1975 contracts to the levels originally stated in those contracts. The full Commission affirmed this decision, and Orkin appealed to the Eleventh Circuit Court of Appeals.

### Body of Opinion

**Clark, Circuit Judge.** Section 5 declares that "unfair or deceptive acts or practices in or affecting commerce" are unlawful; it also empowers the Commission to prevent certain entities from engaging in behavior that constitutes "unfair or deceptive acts or practices". . . . In 1980, the Commission promulgated a policy statement containing an abstract definition of "unfairness" which focuses upon unjustified consumer injury. Under the standard enunciated in this policy statement:

> To justify a finding of unfairness the injury must satisfy three tests. It must be substantial. It must not be outweighed by any countervailing benefits to consumers or competition that the practice produces; and it must be an injury that consumers themselves could not reasonably have avoided.

. . . The first prong of the unfairness standard requires a finding of substantial injury to consumers. In finding that Orkin's conduct had caused the requisite harm, the Commission said: "The harm resulting from Orkin's conduct consists of increased costs for services previously bargained for and includes the intangible loss of the certainty of the fixed price in the contract." The Commission's finding of substantial injury is supported by the undisputed fact that Orkin's breach of its pre-1975 contracts generated, during a four-year period, more than $7,000,000 in revenues from renewal fees to which the company was not entitled. As the Commission noted, although the actual injury to individual customers may be small on an annual basis, this does not mean that such injury is not substantial.

As for the second prong of the unfairness standard, the Commission noted that "conduct can create a mixture of both beneficial and adverse consequences." But because the increase in the fee was not accompanied by an increase in the level of service provided or an enhancement of its quality, the Commission concluded that no consumer benefit had resulted from Orkin's conduct. . . .

With regard to the third prong of the unfairness standard, the Commission concluded that consumers could not have reasonably avoided the harm caused by Orkin's conduct. . . . The Commission determined that "neither anticipatory avoidance nor subsequent mitigation was reasonably possible for Orkin's pre-1975 customers." Anticipatory avoidance through consumer choice was impossible because these contracts give no indication that the company would raise the renewal fees as a result of inflation, or for any other reason.

As for mitigation of consumer injury, the Commission concluded that the company's "accommodation program" could not constitute an avenue for avoiding injury because relief from Orkin's conduct was available only to those customers who complained about the increases in the renewal fees. . . . The Commission also rejected the claim that customers could have avoided their injuries by electing to transfer their business to one of Orkin's competitors. . . . [S]ome of Orkin's competitors did testify that they would assume the company's pre-1975 contracts at the renewal fees stated therein. Yet there is no evidence that Orkin's pre-1975 customers could have contracted with competitors for a renewal fee that would be subject to increase only upon structural modifications of the subject property. Because Orkin failed to present such evidence, it was not error for the Commission to rule summarily that this purported avenue of relief did not create a real choice to consumers who might seek to avoid their injuries.

## Judgment and Result

The Circuit Court of Appeals affirmed the Commission's decision and its order against Orkin.

## Questions

1. By charging higher renewal fees, Orkin broke the contracts it had made with its "lifetime" customers. This meant that the promises contained in those contracts were worthless. Why did the FTC not treat this as deception (rather than unfairness) under Section 5?

2. How did the Commission and the court deal with the argument that because the harm to each individual consumer was relatively low, no "substantial injury" occurred?

3. The court discussed two ways in which Orkin's customers might reasonably have avoided injury under the third part of the FTC's unfairness test. What were they?

## DECEPTION

Many deception cases apply standards found in the Commission's 1983 policy statement on that subject. The standards say that, to violate Section 5 on grounds of deceptiveness, advertising and other allegedly deceptive behavior must involve (1) a material; (2) representation, omission, or practice that is likely to mislead; (3) a consumer acting reasonably under the circumstances. The *Novartis* case applies much the same test.

*Representation, Omission, or Practice Likely to Mislead Consumers.* Many kinds of business behavior can violate Section 5's ban on deceptive acts or practices. Often, a seller's advertisements or other statements involve express claims that can be proven false. In addition, false claims can sometimes be implied from the circumstances. Implied representations can arise from the product's physical appearance, the circumstances of the transaction, the seller's express representations, and ordinary consumer expectations. For example, a product that looks new but actually is used may create an implied representation that it really is new. In one case, moreover, the FTC found an implied assertion that Listerine mouthwash can prevent and cure colds and sore throats because the following two representations appeared close together in Listerine's advertising: "Kills Germs by Millions on Contact" and "For General Oral Hygiene, Bad Breath, Colds, and Resultant Sore Throats." Sellers also can deceive by omitting significant facts. For example, claims that a product cures baldness may violate Section 5 if they are not accompanied by a statement that most forms of baldness cannot effectively be treated.

In all of these situations, the express statement, implied statement, omission, or practice must be likely to mislead consumers. (Actual deception, however, is not necessary.) Often, this test requires the FTC to determine the truth or falsity of the respondent's express and implied claims. In addition, the Commission may require sellers to substantiate objective claims about their products by showing that they have a reasonable basis.

*The "Reasonable Consumer" Test.* To violate Section 5, deceptive behavior also must be likely to mislead consumers who have acted reasonably under the circumstances. The reason for this requirement is to protect sellers from all the ignorant, foolish, or outlandish misconceptions to which some consumers are subject. As the FTC put it nearly forty years ago:

Some people, because of ignorance or incomprehension, may be misled by even a scrupulously honest claim. Perhaps a few misguided souls believe, for example, that all 'Danish Pastry' is made in Denmark. Is it therefore an actionable deception to advertise 'Danish Pastry' when it is made in this country? Of course not.[2]

Due to the "reasonable consumer" test, many familiar kinds of advertising statements usually do not violate Section 5. Statements of opinion are one example. Subjective claims such as taste, feel, appearance, and smell are another. The same is true for obviously exaggerated statements that amount to sales talk or "puffing." The Commission also may be reluctant to proceed against deceptive advertising where the consumer easily can evaluate the product or service, it is inexpensive, and it is frequently purchased. In such situations, sellers have little incentive to misrepresent because they want to encourage repeat purchases.

Critics of the Commission's approach toward deception have argued that the reasonableness standard may protect some unscrupulous advertising schemes aimed at the unsophisticated, naive, and gullible. Although this could be true, the Commission has indicated that when advertising is targeted toward a specific audience, it will examine the ad's effect on a reasonable member of that audience. Ads claiming miracle cancer cures, for example, are not judged from the perspective of a healthy person. On the other hand, a similar advertisement aimed at the medical profession would be judged in light of the knowledge and sophistication possessed by a reasonable member of that group.

*Materiality.* Insignificant forms of deception, one would think, should be of little concern to the FTC. Thus, the Commission has declared that only *material* misrepresentations, omissions, or practices violate Section 5's ban on deceptive acts or practices. Material information is information that is important to reasonable consumers and therefore should affect their conduct regarding a product or service, especially their decision to purchase it. Examples include statements or omissions regarding a product's cost, safety, purpose, effectiveness, performance, quality, durability, or warranties. In addition, the Commission has said that express claims and intentional implied claims are material.

## REMEDIES IN ADVERTISING CASES

Several types of orders are possible after successful Commission administrative action against unfair or deceptive advertising;

- The FTC may simply order the respondent to cease and desist from certain advertising claims.
- The Commission may condition the respondent's resumption of such claims upon its obtaining proper scientific evidence to support them.
- The Commission may order the inclusion of certain statements in subsequent advertising through either affirmative disclosure of information or corrective advertising. A corrective advertising requirement demands disclosure in future ads regardless of their content; an affirmative disclosure requirement demands disclosure only when the ad makes certain specific claims.

---

[2] *Heinz v. W. Kirchner* 63 F.T.C. 1282, 1290 (1963).

- The FTC may issue an all-products order extending to products or services other than the products or services covered by the original offending advertisement.
- In certain cases, the FTC may also seek the civil penalties or consumer redress discussed earlier in the chapter.

## FIRST AMENDMENT CONSIDERATIONS

As discussed in Chapter 5, commercial advertising receives an intermediate degree of constitutional protection that is less strong than the protection afforded political speech. Because Commission orders under FTC Act Section 5 restrict commercial speech, constitutional challenges to the Commission's regulation of advertising are possible. As the *Novartis* case suggests, however, such challenges have not seriously affected the FTC's regulation of advertising. The main reason for giving constitutional protection to commercial speech is to remove government-created obstacles to the flow of commercial information, and thus to promote informed consumer choice. This is consistent with the FTC's mission of eliminating deceptive and unfair advertising. In fact, the Constitution does not protect false or misleading advertising. This insulates much of the FTC's regulation of advertising from constitutional attack. Occasionally, however, courts may modify or narrow the scope of a Commission order on constitutional grounds.

---

## Novartis Corporation v. Federal Trade Commission
### U.S. Court of Appeals (D.C. Circuit)
### 223 F.3d 783 (2000)

### Background and Facts

Novartis Corporation manufactures and markets Doan's back pain remedies. Novartis was formed by a 1996 merger between Ciba-Geigy AG and Sandoz AG. From 1988 through 1996, Ciba-Geigy ran a series of advertisements claiming that the pills were a remedy specifically for back pain, and that they contained a special ingredient not found in other over-the-counter analgesics.

In 1998, the FTC undertook an administrative action against Novartis, alleging that the Ciba-Geigy advertisements violated Section 5 of the FTC Act. According to the Commission, the ads did so by making unsubstantiated implied claims that, because of their special ingredients, Doan's pills were better at relieving back pain than other over-the-counter pain medicines. The administrative law judge (ALJ) found that the ads were deceptive in violation of Section 5, and issued an order prohibiting Novartis from making unsubstantiated claims of superior efficacy for Doan's pills. However, the judge denied the FTC's request for a corrective advertising order. Later, the full Commission affirmed both the administrative law judge's finding that there was deception under Section 5 and its remedial order, but it reversed the ALJ on the corrective advertising question. The Commission ordered Novartis to include the following disclaimer in future advertisements: "Although Doan's is an effective pain reliever, there is no evidence that Doan's is more effective than other pain relievers for back pain." This statement was to continue for one year and until Doan's advertising had cost

Novartis a sum equal to the average annual amount spent for Doan's ads over the eight years of the challenged advertising campaign. Novartis appealed to the District of Columbia Circuit Court of Appeals.

### Body of Opinion

**Circuit Judge Henderson.** Novartis first challenges the Commission's finding that the advertisements were deceptive in violation of Section 5 of the act. The FTC applies a three-pronged test to determine deceptive advertising, asking whether (1) a claim was made, (2) the claim was likely to mislead a reasonable consumer, and (3) the claim was material. Novartis does not dispute that the Doan's advertisements made the implied claim charged or that it is likely to deceive, but does contest the Commission's finding that the claim was material. . . .

Under the Commission's test, a material claim is one that involves information that is important to consumers and, hence, likely to affect their choice of, or conduct regarding, a product. The Commission has historically *presumed* materiality for certain categories of claims: (1) all express claims; (2) intentional implied claims; and (3) claims that significantly involve health, safety, or other areas with which the reasonable consumer would be concerned, including a claim that concerns the purpose, safety, efficacy, or cost of the product or service, its durability, performance, warranties, or quality, or a finding by another agency regarding the product. The Commission applied the presumption here because it found the implied claim was intentional and involved both a health matter and the product's purpose and efficacy. . . . The Commission's finding of materiality is substantially supported by the evidence it cited, including the opinions of both sides' experts. Accordingly, we reject Novartis's challenge and uphold the Commission's finding of an implied deception claim in violation of the act.

Next, Novartis asserts that the corrective advertising remedy is without sufficient record support. In *Warner-Lambert Co. v. FTC* (D.C. Cir. 1977), we affirmed the Commission's statutory authority to impose corrective advertising and approved the standard it adopted for doing so:

> If a deceptive advertisement has played a substantial role in creating or reinforcing in the public's mind a false and material belief which lives on after the false advertising ceases, there is clear and continuing injury to competition and to the consuming public as consumers continue to make purchasing decisions based on the false belief. Since this injury cannot be averted by merely requiring respondent to cease disseminating the advertisement, we may appropriately order respondent to take affirmative action designed to terminate the otherwise continuing ill effects of the advertisement.

This language dictates two factual inquiries: (1) Did respondent's advertisements play a substantial role in creating or reinforcing in the public's mind a false belief about the product? and (2) Would the belief linger on after the advertising ceases? While the evidence is thin and somewhat fragmentary, we have weighed the expert testimony and, taken as a whole, we find that the record supports the Commission's conclusion.

On the standard's first prong, the Commission . . . based [itself] almost exclusively on the opinion of the FTC counsel's expert witness Michael B. Mazis that the Doan's advertising campaign created a continuing belief in the product's superiority. Mazis, in turn, based his opinion primarily on two studies. . . . We conclude that Mazis's opinion testimony constitutes substantial evidence in support of the Commission's holding that the Doan's advertisements created or reinforced false beliefs in the product's efficacy. We also believe that the record sufficiently supports the Commission's finding that the advertisements' effects are likely to linger. The Commission rested its finding primarily on the conclusion of [one of

the studies just mentioned]. . . . We cannot say this was an irrational inference. . . .

Finally, Novartis challenges the corrective remedy on the ground that it impermissibly restricts Novartis's free speech in violation of the First Amendment. . . . In *Central Hudson Gas & Electric Corp. v. Public Service Commission* (1980), the United States Supreme Court set out the standards applicable to governmental restrictions on commercial speech:

> . . . The state must assert a substantial interest to be achieved by restrictions on commercial speech. . . . [T]he restriction must directly advance the state interest involved; the regulation may not be sustained if it provides only ineffective or remote support for the government's purpose. Second, if the governmental interest could be served as well by a more limited restriction on commercial speech, the excessive restrictions cannot survive.

The remedy here advances precisely the "interest involved," namely the avoidance of misleading and deceptive advertising. Further, . . . whether a corrective remedy imposes a restriction greater than necessary to serve the interest involved goes to the appropriateness of the order under the Commission's two-pronged standard addressed above. Because the standard has been satisfied here, . . . we conclude that the Commission's remedy is not overly broad.

### Judgment and Result

Novartis's appeal was denied; Novartis is liable under Section 5 and the corrective advertising remedy stands.

### Questions

1. Novartis never expressly claimed that Doan's pills are more effective than other pain remedies in alleviating back pain. How, then, was it liable for deception under Section 5?
2. The court found Novartis's advertising claims to be material for two reasons. What were they?
3. Check Chapter 5's discussion of First Amendment attacks on commercial speech. Is the description of the *Central Hudson* test there essentially the same as the quotation from *Central Hudson* found in the opinion here?

## FTC REGULATION OF FRANCHISING

The term **franchise** is not consistently defined. It might be described as a relationship in which one party (the **franchisee**) gets the right to sell another party's (the **franchisor's**) goods or services under a marketing plan substantially dictated by the franchisor. Often, the franchisor gives the franchisee assistance in setting up the business, and allows the franchisee to operate under its trademark or trade name. Typically, the franchisee pays a purchase price for these benefits, and may also have to pay the franchisor a percentage of its income, sales, or supply expenses. Common examples of franchised businesses include fast-food restaurants, hotel and motels, hair-styling salons, gas stations, employment agencies, motor vehicle dealerships, and farm equipment distributors.

Franchising has enjoyed tremendous growth in recent decades. It has been estimated that more than 500,000 franchises operated in the United States during the mid-1990s, and that they accounted for over one-third of the nation's total retail sales. It also has been claimed that the number of people working for franchised outlets rose from 3.5 million in 1975 to about 7 million in the early 1990s, and the number probably has risen since then. The reasons for franchising's growth seem obvious. The relationship gives franchisors a relatively easy method for expanding into new markets, while at the same time receiving payments from franchisees. For franchisees, the relationship provides a chance to run "their own" business, while benefitting from the franchisor's resources, expertise, and brand name.

Franchise agreements usually are standard-form contracts drafted by the franchisor and offered to the franchisee on a take-it-or-leave-it basis. They typically cover subjects such as the royalties the franchisee must pay, any financing the franchisor might provide, whether or when the franchisor can terminate the franchisee, the franchisee's duty not to compete after the relationship ends, and many others. Many people believe that, on average, franchisors have greater bargaining power than do franchisees. It seems safe to say that the typical franchisor's understanding of the agreement's terms exceeds that of the typical franchisee. Also, franchisors may often have a greater choice of potential franchisees than would-be franchisees have of franchisors. However, franchisors have little rational incentive to mistreat capable, efficient, and productive franchisees.

## STATE REGULATION OF FRANCHISING

The perceived imbalance in power between franchisor and franchisee had led to increasing regulation of the relationship. The starting point for determining these two parties' legal relationship, of course, is the contract between them. To protect franchisees, some courts have supplemented or modified such contracts in various ways. A few have allowed franchisees to recover for the breach of fiduciary duties owed them by the franchisor (e.g., a duty to terminate the relationship only for good cause). A few courts have found that the franchise contract contains an implied covenant of good faith and fair dealing running from the franchisor to the franchisee (and perhaps vice versa). This covenant might be breached when, for example, the franchisor opens a new franchised outlet too near an existing outlet.

In general, state statutory regulation of franchising is more significant than the common law doctrines just described.[3] Many states require the disclosure of certain information to potential franchisees. Many such disclosures may be required; our following discussion of FTC regulation provides numerous examples. Many states also require that franchisors register with state authorities. As part of the registration process, franchisors usually must file various documents with the state. Examples include filings regarding the franchisor's business,

---

[3] Some states have "business opportunity" statutes that may or may not cover franchising. A business opportunity typically involves a sale of goods or services enabling the buyer to start a business. Examples include vending machine routes and businesses involving the assembly of parts in one's home.

officers and directors, litigation and bankruptcy history, intellectual property, and finances—as well as documents explaining many aspects of the franchisor's relationship with its franchisee. Finally, many states regulate the ongoing franchise relationship after it has been formed. The most common examples are the numerous state statutes that block franchisors from terminating or refusing to renew franchisees unless the termination or nonrenewal was for good cause. Other subjects that may be regulated include the notice required before termination, the duration of the franchise term, franchisor discrimination against particular franchisees, franchisee covenants not to compete after the relationship ends, and exclusive franchisee territories.

## THE FTC'S FRANCHISING RULE

The FTC's response to the problems posed by franchising came in the form of a 1979 trade regulation rule. The FTC rule preempts inconsistent state regulation of franchising. For the most part, however, it is only a disclosure regulation.

*You can find the full FTC franchising rule at **http://www.ftc.gov** under "Legal Framework." The rule's citation is 16 C.F.R. part 436.*

The rule defines the term *franchise* as any continuing commercial relationship in which a franchisee offers or sells goods or services, where the relationship meets either of the two following descriptions. In each case, the franchisee must be required to pay the franchisor a fee of $500 or more within the first six months of the business's operation or the rule does not apply.

1. A franchisee offers or sells goods or services that are (a) identified by the franchisor's trademark, trade name, or other commercial symbol; or (b) required to meet the franchisor's quality standards (where the franchisee operates under the franchisor's trademark, trade name, or other commercial symbol). For the FTC rule to apply in either case, the franchisor also must either (a) exert significant control over the franchisee's method of operation, or (b) give the franchisee significant assistance in its method of operation. Thus, the Benson Bicycle Company is covered by the FTC's rule if it exerts significant control over its franchisees or gives them significant assistance, and if (a) the franchisees sell its "Voyageur" bikes, or (b) the franchisees bear the "Benson" name and sell bikes that are not identified with Benson but that do have to meet Benson's quality standards.

2. A franchisee offers or sells goods or services supplied by the franchisor, or by someone dictated by the franchisor. Here, the FTC rule applies only if the franchisor secures retail outlets, accounts, vending machine sites, rack displays, or other sales displays for the franchisee. Note that in this case the franchisee is not selling products or services identified with the franchisor or subject to the franchisor's quality standards.

The FTC rule says that a franchisor can commit an unfair act or practice under FTC Act Section 5 in any of the following ways, among others. The usual Section 5 remedies and enforcement devices apply in such cases.

1. *Failing to furnish any prospective franchisee with certain written information.* The voluminous information required by the Commission includes the following: the franchisor's name, address, and principal place of business; the trademarks, trade names, and other commercial symbols identifying the goods

or services offered to the franchisee; the business experience of the franchisor's directors and officers; certain crimes of which these people may have been convicted; certain civil judgments that may have been obtained against them; any bankruptcies they have suffered; a factual description of the franchise being offered; the total and recurring charges the prospective franchisee will have to pay; the people with whom the franchisee will have to deal; property or other things the franchisee will have to lease or rent; a description of any financing arrangement offered by the franchisor; any limitations on the products or services the franchisee may sell, the customers to whom he or she may sell, or the territory within which he or she may sell; the duration of the agreement and the conditions under which its renewal, termination, or modification may occur; the franchisee's post-termination rights and obligations; details concerning any training program offered by the franchisor; and the franchisor's balance sheet statement for the most recent fiscal year. This list is incomplete; the relevant disclosures fill several pages in the *Code of Federal Regulations*.

All the disclosures required by the rule must be contained in a single disclosure statement or prospectus. The cover of this prospectus must bear the following statement:

**Information for Prospective Franchisees Required by Federal Trade Commission**

\* \* \*

To protect you, we've required your franchisor to give you this information. *We haven't checked it, and don't know if it's correct.* It should help you make up your mind. Study it carefully. While it includes some information about your contract, don't rely on it alone to understand your contract. Read all of your contract carefully. Buying a franchise is a complicated investment. Take your time to decide. If possible, show your contract and this information to an advisor, like a lawyer or an accountant. If you find anything you think may be wrong or anything important that's been left out, you should let us know about it. It may be against the law.

There may also be laws on franchising in your state. Ask your state agencies about them.

FEDERAL TRADE COMMISSION
Washington, D.C.

2. *Making any representations that state a specific level of potential sales, income, or profit for the prospective franchisee,* UNLESS: (a) there is a reasonable basis for the representations, the franchisor has material demonstrating their reasonableness, and it makes that material available to prospective franchisees or to the FTC upon demand; and (b) the representations and the assumptions underlying them are set forth in a single written document that is furnished to each prospective franchisee to whom the representations are made. In addition to stating certain specific information detailed in the regulations, this document must include the following statement.

**CAUTION**

These figures are only estimates of what we think you may earn. There is no assurance you'll do as well. If you rely upon our figures, you must accept the risk of not doing as well.

3. *Making any representations to a prospective franchisee that state a specific level of sales, income, or profit for existing outlets of the franchise business being offered.* However, such representations are permissible if conditions like those stated above are met. Here, though, the FTC requires the following statement:

**CAUTION**

Some outlets have [sold] [earned] this amount. There is no assurance you'll do as well. If you rely upon our figures, you must accept the risk of not doing as well.

4. *Failing to include the following statement on the cover sheet of the written documents required by requirements 2 and 3 above:*

**INFORMATION FOR PROSPECTIVE FRANCHISEES ABOUT FRANCHISE [SALES] [INCOME] [PROFIT] REQUIRED BY THE FEDERAL TRADE COMMISSION**

To protect you, we've required the franchisor to give you this information. *We haven't checked it and don't know if it's correct.* Study these facts and figures carefully. If possible, show them to someone who can advise you, like a lawyer or an accountant. Then take your time and think it over.

If you find anything you think may be wrong or anything important that's been left out, let us know about it. It may be against the law.

There may also be laws on franchising in your State. Ask your State agencies about them.

FEDERAL TRADE COMMISSION
Washington, D.C.

## LANHAM ACT SECTION 43(A)

Deceptive or unfair advertising cases under FTC Act Section 5 often are begun by the respondent's competitors. The best this tactic can achieve, however, is a C & D order against the respondent. How might the injured party obtain damages for the offending advertisement as well? Perhaps the best option is to sue under Section 43(a) of the Lanham Act.

The language of Section 43(a) is too complicated for easy restatement. Its most important provision basically allows civil recoveries for advertising statements that misrepresent the nature, attributes, or geographic origin of goods or services. The goods or services in question can be either the advertiser's goods and services or a competitor's goods and services. For instance, the Wisdom Widget Company might use Section 43(a) to sue Wonder Widgets both for false advertising claims Wonder makes about its own widgets, and for Wonder's false advertising claims about Wisdom's widgets. In addition to false statements, Section 43(a) creates liability for ads that are likely to deceive purchasers. The section probably covers deceptive omissions as well. However, there is no Section 43(a) liability for statements of opinion.

In addition to false or misleading advertising, Section 43(a) also covers several other kinds of commercial misbehavior. Indeed, the section might be said to create a federal law of unfair competition. Thus, Section 43(a) permits civil claims for the following:

- *Trademark infringement*. This includes both registered and unregistered trademarks.
- The form of common law invasion of privacy that involves appropriating another's name or likeness for commercial purposes. For example, suppose that a manufacturer of golf clubs uses Tiger Woods's name or likeness to promote its clubs without Woods's permission.
- *Trade dress infringement*. A product's trade dress might be defined as its overall appearance and sales image. As the following *Wal-Mart* case states, trade dress may once have been limited to the product's packaging or "dressing," but now it includes the product's design as well. Section 43(a) allows product manufacturers to recover against those who use a substantially similar trade dress to identify or promote their products, where this is likely to cause confusion about the products' origin. In *Wal-Mart*, the Court held that Section 43(a) trade dress suits can succeed only where the plaintiff's product has developed a secondary meaning. In trademark law, this occurs when a substantial number of buyers have firmly identified the mark with a particular source of goods or services. To take one of the Court's examples, suppose that the XYZ Corporation makes "Tasty" bread. Suppose further that due to XYZ's long use of this term, its extensive advertising, and its many sales of "Tasty" bread, a substantial number of consumers identify the "Tasty" mark with XYZ. Once this happens, that mark will have acquired secondary meaning.
- *Palming off* or *passing off*. These terms include all sorts of falsehoods designed to make consumers believe that one's own goods are those of a competitor. For example, a firm might imitate a popular competitor's packages, labels, containers, trademarks, trade names, and so forth.

## Wal-Mart Stores, Inc. v. Samara Brothers, Inc.
U.S. Supreme Court
529 U.S. 205 (2000)

### Background and Facts

Samara Brothers, Inc. manufactured a line of children's clothing with a distinctive design that featured hearts, flowers, fruits, and the like. In 1995, Wal-Mart Stores, Inc. contracted with Judy-Philippine, Inc. to manufacture a line of children's clothing for sale in Wal-Mart stores. This line of clothing closely resembled the Samara Brothers design; in fact, Wal-Mart sent Judy-Philippine photographs of Samara's garments and instructed Judy-Philippine to base its design upon them. After Judy-Philippine copied sixteen of Samara's designs for Wal-Mart, Wal-Mart made more than $1.15 million in gross profits from the sale of these "knockoffs."

Samara sued Wal-Mart for, among other things, infringement of unregistered trade dress under Lanham Act Section 43(a). After

federal district court and circuit court decisions for Samara Brothers, Wal-Mart appealed to the United States Supreme Court.

### Body of Opinion

**Justice Scalia.** In addition to protecting registered [trade]marks, the Lanham Act, in Section 43(a), gives a producer a cause of action for the use by any person of "any word, term, name, symbol, or device, or any combination thereof . . . which . . . is likely to cause confusion . . . as to the origin, sponsorship, or approval of his or her goods . . . " The breadth of the definition of marks registerable under [trademark law] . . . has been held to embrace not just word marks, such as "Nike," and symbol marks, such as Nike's "swoosh" symbol, but also "trade dress"—a category that originally included only the packaging, or "dressing," of a product, but in recent years has been expanded by many courts of appeals to encompass the design of a product. These courts have assumed . . . that trade dress constitutes a "symbol" or "device" for purposes of the relevant sections, and we do likewise. . . . This reading . . . is buttressed by a recently added subsection of Section 43(a), Section 43(a)(3), which refers specifically to "civil action[s] for trade dress infringement under this chapter for trade dress not registered on the principal register."

The text of Section 43(a) provides little guidance as to the circumstances under which unregistered trade dress may be protected. It does require that a producer show that the allegedly interfering feature is not "functional," and is likely to cause confusion with the product for which protection is sought. Nothing in Section 43(a) explicitly requires a producer to show that its trade dress is distinctive, but courts have universally imposed that requirement, since without distinctiveness the trade dress would not cause confusion as to the origin, sponsorship, or approval of the goods, as the section requires. . . . [C]ourts have held that a mark can be distinctive in one of two ways. First, a mark is inherently distinctive if its intrinsic nature serves to identify a particular source. In the context of word marks, courts have applied the now-classic test originally formulated by Judge Friendly in which word marks that are arbitrary ("Camel" cigarettes), fanciful ("Kodak" film), or suggestive ("Tide" laundry detergent) are held to be inherently distinctive. Second, a mark has acquired distinctiveness, even if it is not inherently distinctive, if it has developed secondary meaning, which occurs when, in the minds of the public, the primary significance of a mark is to identify the source of the product rather than the product itself. . . .

[W]ith respect to at least one category of mark—colors—we have held that no mark can ever be inherently distinctive. . . . We held that a color could be protected as a trademark, but only upon a showing of secondary meaning. . . . It seems to us that design, like color, is not inherently distinctive. The attribution of inherent distinctiveness to certain categories of word marks and product packaging derives from the fact that the very purpose of attaching a particular word to a product, or encasing it in a distinctive packaging, is most often to identify the source of the product. . . . Consumers are predisposed to regard those symbols as indication of the producer, which is why such symbols almost automatically tell a customer that they refer to a brand and immediately signal a brand or a product source. And where it is not reasonable to assume consumer predisposition to take an affixed word or packaging as indication of source—where for example the affixed words [are] descriptive of the product ("Tasty" bread) or of a geographic origin ("Georgia"

peaches)—inherent distinctiveness will not be found. . . . In the case of product design, as in the case of color, we think consumer predisposition to equate the feature with the source does not exist. Consumers are aware of the reality that, almost invariably, even the most unusual of product designs—such as a cocktail shaker shaped like a penguin—is intended not to identify the source, but to render the product itself more useful or more appealing. . . .

Consumers should not be deprived of the benefits of competition with regard to the utilitarian and aesthetic purposes that product design ordinarily serves by a rule of law that facilitates plausible threats of suit against new entrants based upon alleged inherent distinctiveness. . . . Competition is deterred, not merely by successful suit, but by the plausible threat of successful suit. . . . [T]he producer can ordinarily obtain protection for a design that *is* inherently source-identifying (if any such exists), but that does not yet have secondary meaning, by securing a design patent or a copyright for the design. . . . The availability of these other protections greatly reduces any harm to the producer that might ensue from our conclusion that a product design cannot be protected under Section 43(a) without a showing of secondary meaning. . . .

We hold that, in an action for infringement of unregistered trade dress under Section 43(a) of the Lanham Act, a product's design is distinctive, and therefore protectible, only upon a showing of secondary meaning.

## Judgment and Result

The Supreme Court held that in a trade dress suit under Section 43(a), a product design is distinctive, and therefore protectible, only upon a showing of secondary meaning. The circuit court decision for Samara was reversed, and the case was returned to the lower federal courts for proceedings consistent with the Supreme Court's opinion.

## Questions

1. So far as Section 43(a) is concerned, the apparent effect of the Court's decision is to let Wal-Mart appropriate Samara's design and to make money by doing so. At first glance, this might look like an awful result. What would Justice Scalia say in reply to such a claim?
2. Why did the Court conclude that a product's design is not inherently distinctive?
3. Assuming that there is such a thing, suppose that your firm manufactures a product with a genuinely distinctive design that has not acquired secondary meaning. What can your firm do to legally protect that design?

■ MANAGER'S ETHICAL DILEMMA

Nelson Eiland, a college professor, and Tom Neilson, an executive at a major advertising agency, are brothers-in-law. Over Christmas dinner one year, Nelson initiated a familiar exchange between himself and Tom.

NELSON: "Well, Tom, tell me: How many poor fools have you hoodwinked this year?"

TOM: "Nelson, we've been through this before. Firms that `hoodwink' people with their advertisements can get in trouble with the FTC."

NELSON: "And you know that's not what I'm talking about. The problem isn't illegal behavior; the problem is what's perfectly *legal*. You guys spend all your time dreaming up ways to manipulate people into buying things they don't need, and the law does nothing about it."

TOM: "Hey, people can always turn off the set if they don't like what's in our ads. No one's forcing them to do anything. Don't you know that water consumption from flushing toilets goes up dramatically when the commercials come on?"

NELSON: "Come off it. The whole point of a lot of modern advertising is to overcome people's will and reason through `hidden persuaders' of all kinds. And it works."

TOM: "If only it were that easy!"

NELSON: "False humility will get you nowhere. If that kind of advertising is so useless, why have so many corporations spent so much money on it for so long?"

TOM: "Because they don't know whether it works or not, and they don't want to take a chance. You know that old business lament: 'Half our advertising budget is wasted, but we don't know which half.'"

NELSON: "But you admit that some of it works. That means that in some cases people buy Product A when Product B would better suit them, or buy things that they don't really want or need at all. And that means that people don't get the most utility for their hard-earned dollars. Worse yet, it means that, for society as a whole, money is diverted from pressing public needs like better schools and a decent environment, and instead funneled toward stupid consumer baubles."

TOM: "Aha! Just like I always suspected! You think *you* know better. You think *you* know what people *really* want and need. You *know* they'd really be happier driving a Honda Civic than a five-series BMW. Or using public transportation rather than driving cars at all."

NELSON: "What I'm trying to do is to distinguish between ads that appeal to the intrinsic merits of the product and ads that appeal to irrational drives. Like hidden and half-hidden sexual pitches, for instance. By associating a product with sexual titillation, you make people more likely to buy it. And you also steer social resources toward consumption and away from better things. So people wind up with a product that meets their needs less well than some alternative expenditure of the money, and we wind up with misallocated societal resources. And the guy who buys the BMW doesn't get the girl, either."

TOM: "Like it or not, sometimes they do. And even if they don't, maybe that guy who buys the BMW *thinks* he can attract good-looking women, so he's a little happier."

NELSON: "Oh, my gosh! And you accused *me* of paternalism! Happiness and the good life—courtesy of Madison Avenue! Why not just wire the electrodes to the pleasure centers in our brains and have done with it?"

TOM: "Hey, why not?"

NELSON: "*Human dignity* is why not. Immanuel Kant said that we should treat people as *ends* and not just as *means* to our own ends. By that he meant that we shouldn't use people, and that we should appeal to their reason when we're trying to persuade them to do something—not employ manipulative techniques on them. So you shouldn't use manipulative techniques on people to get them to buy things, even if that somehow would make them happier."

TOM: "You can't eat `reason' and `dignity.'"

Who do think has gotten the better of this exchange? Why?

## CHAPTER SUMMARY

The Federal Trade Commission enforces many federal statutes involving competition and consumer protection. The most important of these laws is Section 5 of the FTC Act, which empowers the Commission to regulate unfair methods of competition and unfair and deceptive acts or practices. In enforcing all these various measures, the FTC may issue advisory opinions, industry guides and other policy statements, and trade regulation rules. (An example of the latter is the Commission's rule on franchising.) It also may enforce these measures through its own administrative proceedings. The most common remedy issued after a successful FTC proceeding is a cease-and-desist order. The FTC and the alleged violator also may settle the case through a consent order.

Although FTC Act Section 5 reaches beyond the antitrust laws, the FTC mainly attacks the orthodox antitrust violations described in Chapter 20 when it employs Section 5's "unfair methods of competition" language. Section 5's "unfair acts or practices" jurisdiction covers all kinds of actions that harm consumers. For liability to exist under this part of Section 5, the act or practice must produce consumer injury that is (1) substantial, (2) not outweighed by any consumer or competitive benefits the practice produces, and (3) reasonably avoidable by consumers. Section 5 "deceptive acts or practices" liability exists when there is (1) a material representation, omission, or practice; (2) that is likely to mislead a consumer; (3) acting reasonably under the circumstances. This part of Section 5 applies mainly to deceptive advertising.

The FTC also regulates franchising. It does so primarily by controlling the disclosures that the franchisor makes to the franchisee before the franchise relationship is formed. Many states regulate franchising as well.

Section 43(a) of the Lanham Act provides a federal civil remedy for deceptive advertising. The section also covers unfair competitive tactics such as palming off one's goods as another's, imitating a competing product's trade dress, infringing another's trademarks, and appropriating another's name or likeness for commercial purposes. By now, Section 43(a) has evolved into a general federal law of unfair competition.

## DISCUSSION QUESTIONS

1. Suppose that the manipulative advertising described in the preceding dialogue really works, and that it has all the bad effects Nelson describes. What does FTC regulation of advertising, as currently constituted, do about it?

2. Philosophers sometimes distinguish between *deontological* ethical theories and *consequentialist* ethical theories. Extreme (or strict) deontological theories say that certain actions are right or wrong, irrespective of their consequences. Extreme consequentialist theories say that in evaluating the goodness or badness of an action, its consequences are all that matter. The main example is a moral theory called *utilitarianism*, which says that the criterion for evaluating actions is the amount of net pleasure, happiness, or satisfaction they produce. In the preceding dialogue, which paragraph expresses strict deontological views? Where are utilitarian views expressed?

3. Manipulative advertising often is said to have two bad effects (assuming that it works). First, it makes people buy the wrong products for their needs (e.g., a sports car rather than a minivan, or vice-versa), and thus to leave them with less utility per dollar spent. Second, it makes people too obsessed with material things and thereby stimulates lots of needless consumption of those things. Pick out the places in the dialogue where Nelson makes each of these arguments. Pick out the place where Tom seems to concede the first argument while maintaining that

people get extra utility even when they are manipulated. Can one of these two effects of manipulative advertising exist alone without the other? Finally, do you think that manipulative advertising works as well as both Tom and Nelson think it works?

4. Is the FTC's "reasonable consumer" test for deception cases a good idea? Will it block FTC action in cases where unscrupulous parties prey upon human weaknesses such as greed, gullibility, and lack of business sophistication? Examples include hard-sell pitches for get-rich-quick schemes such as the purchase of oil and gas leases, jewels, or real estate that are claimed to be valuable but in fact are nearly worthless. Can the purchasers in such cases generally be said to have acted reasonably? If not, should the FTC try to protect fools from their folly, or should it take the attitude that in such cases people simply have to take care of themselves?

5. Is the First Amendment protection of commercial speech (discussed in Chapter 5) a good idea? If the doctrine were ever seriously applied to FTC regulation of deceptive and unfair advertising, might it not block such regulation? In that event, wouldn't advertisers have more freedom to deceive and manipulate consumers? Thus, isn't the doctrine potentially an unjustified boon to business?

On the other hand, the First Amendment protection of commercial speech has never been a big impediment to FTC regulation of advertising. And, as we asked earlier, how well does advertising deceive and manipulate consumers in any event?

As Chapter 5 makes clear, furthermore, the doctrine tends to *promote* competition in many cases. It does so mainly by knocking down advertising bans in professions such as law and accounting.

Which view strikes you as more correct?

6. All things considered, do you think that the FTC's regulation of franchising does much to protect franchisees? Should the Commission regulate franchising in the more comprehensive fashion adopted by many states?

7. As means of counteracting previous deceptive advertising, how effective are corrective advertising and affirmative disclosure orders likely to be?

8. Notice that some FTC adjudications begin with complaints from a competitor. Notice also that competitors often sue competitors under Section 43(a). Of course, such complaints or suits often are responses to genuine abuses. But is it possible that on some occasions competitors might use the law as an offensive weapon, and thereby gain an advantage that they could not gain through competition? Is this just an inevitable cost of regulation?

9. Why does the FTC impose a materiality requirement in deception cases under Section 5?

10. State and federal regulation of franchising assumes that, due to the franchisors' superior bargaining power, franchisees need legal protection against their franchisors. Is this assumption really valid?

## INFOTRAC KEYWORDS

**Use your InfoTrac password to look up articles on http://www.infotrac-college.com**

Keywords: *FTC act, unfair business practices, deceptive practices, cease-and-desist order, anticompetitive behavior, regulation of franchising, Lanham Act.*

For suggested readings, please visit this book's Web site at **http://fisher.westbuslaw.com** (click on "Internet Applications").

# CONSUMER PROTECTION

*"THERE'S A SUCKER BORN EVERY MINUTE."*

— P.T. BARNUM

Total retail trade in the United States amounted to $3.082 trillion in 2000, according to the 2001 *Statistical Abstract of the United States*. Although most purchases result in satisfied customers, some purchases produce consumer agony.

Tension exists between consumers and business. On one hand, business would like to produce goods with a short life (so the market is constantly rejuvenated), to sell goods at the highest price, and to forget the consumer once the purchase is made. The consumer, on the other hand, wants the highest-quality, lowest-priced goods and services, trouble free—but if anything goes wrong, everyone in the production and distribution cycle should be eternally responsible.

## DEFINING A CONSUMER

A consumer is any person who buys goods or services for personal consumption. A widow who buys aluminum siding for her house is a consumer, as are a five-year-old who buys an ice cream cone and Bill Gates (reputedly the richest American) when he buys a new suit. We are all consumers in our personal capacities.

## ARGUMENTS FAVORING CONSUMER PROTECTION

Why protect consumers? First, natural law with its basic notions of fairness suggests an equalization of economic power. The law has traditionally said it at least protects the weak from the strong. In this view, consumers are small, defenseless people pitted against industrial giants like Exxon and General Motors. According to this argument, they therefore deserve protection.

A second reason for protecting consumers is to protect businesses. This rationale seems strange when consumers and businesses are often seen as adversaries. However, the key word *honest* must be added before *businesses*. If a consumer buys inferior goods or is cheated by *one* business, sales could be diverted from a more ethical merchant. By establishing standards, consumer protection protects honest merchants who offer value to consumers. It does so in two ways. First, it makes life difficult for scoundrels. Second, it encourages people to buy more and with less hesitation, because they know that if their purchases are unsatisfactory, they are protected.

## ARGUMENTS AGAINST CONSUMER PROTECTION

Many reasons exist for *not* protecting consumers. The first reason is the cost. Consumer protection can raise the price of goods and services if merchants pass the price increase along to their buyers. How would consumer protection raise prices? One way is by requiring producers to test products more thoroughly before selling them. Increased testing means increased cost, which often means that consumer goods would increase in price.

A second reason for not protecting consumers is suggested by the *caveat emptor* doctrine. Are people helpless babies? No. They vote, have sex, smoke, and drink at increasingly younger ages. The theory is that turnabout is fair play. If people are mature and self-reliant in those areas, they can watch out for their own pocketbook interests.

## SOURCES OF CONSUMER PROTECTION LAW

Consumer protection rules are made by courts, legislators, and administrative agencies. Furthermore, consumer protection occurs at federal, state, and municipal levels.

The many sources of consumer law yield complexity. For example, fifty different state statutes can govern a consumer's right to revoke acceptance of a contract with a door-to-door salesperson. Such a situation obviously could complicate life for the sales manager of a national magazine publisher selling door-to-door.

## FEDERAL TRADE COMMISSION (FTC)

To access the major federal agency responsible for protecting consumers, go to **http://www. ftc.gov**

No federal consumer protection agency is officially called a "consumer protection agency." However, because one of the Federal Trade Commission's (FTC's) main jobs is consumer protection, practically speaking it is, in part, a federal consumer protection agency. The FTC, discussed in Chapter 21, was established in 1914 to regulate trade to keep markets competitive. The focus of FTC activity was not directly on consumers but rather on preserving competition. To the extent that the market is competitive, consumers benefit through lower prices, better service, and higher-quality products.

## CONSUMERISM

In the 1930s, Congress amended the FTC Act to allow the FTC to inform and protect consumers directly. Since that time, the FTC has conducted studies of many industries—life insurance, funeral homes, and auto repair, among others—with an eye toward pointing out how consumers are not getting the "biggest bang for their buck." For example, the life insurance industry study pointed out that term insurance provides the most life insurance protection per dollar of premium cost. In effect, it is a better buy than whole life insurance. Yet, life insurance companies market whole life insurance as more desirable than term insurance. The FTC believed consumers were being misled by the life insurance industry. Factors such as building up savings, rather than the amount of low-cost insurance protection per dollar, support buying whole life insurance.

Putting aside the relative merits of term versus whole life insurance, the FTC's studies of the insurance industry and certain other industries have produced hostility toward the FTC from certain businesses. No business likes to have its practices questioned, particularly those who are pulling their own weight through productive activities in a free competitive market economy. Competition is the regulator that keeps prices low, service good, and quality high. If competition cannot force businesses to produce a cheaper, higher quality, and better serviced product, the theory maintains, it cannot be done. If government tries to do it, what happens? Costs can get out of control, and the product or service does not reflect what consumers are willing to pay, given the market discipline of keeping costs within market price.

Thus, the FTC's cracking the whip on businesses is seen by some as misplaced. They ask, "Why not crack the whip on welfare recipients and other nonproductive beneficiaries of government benefits?" An answer to this question is that the FTC tries to protect honest, efficient businesses (as well as consumers) by informing consumers about who are the honest, efficient producers and what are the best buys. Remember that the FTC costs society money. The question becomes, "Does the FTC save consumers more than it costs taxpayers?" If it does, it is cost-justified.

## FTC CONSUMER PROTECTION REGULATIONS

Since the FTC consumer protection laws are discussed extensively in Chapter 21, here we discuss only five FTC consumer protection regulations. The FTC has authority under the Federal Trade Commission Act to promulgate regulations preventing unfair competition and unfair or deceptive acts and practices. The FTC has promulgated many consumer protection regulations. Four important regulations discussed here are the bait-and-switch regs, the reg modifying the holder-in-due-course rule, the mail-order merchandise reg, the three-day cooling off reg for door-to-door sales, and the telemarketing rule.

*http://www.consumer.gov* *provides a gateway to many sites of interest to consumers.*

*Bait and Switch.* Robert Berry sat dejectedly in his appliance store. He had fifty expensive color console TVs in his inventory that he had to sell because it was costing him a bundle to floor plan them (finance them at the local bank). Richard May, one of Robert's hotshot salespeople, suggested that Robert aggressively advertise new black-and-white portable TVs for $10 each. Richard told Robert to do one of three things when a customer came in. Robert was to say that he had just sold the last $10 set, or he was to say he could not find the $10 sets, or he was to bad-mouth the $10 sets and direct the customer to the expensive color consoles, which the store would sell at a rock-bottom price. Should Robert approve Richard's idea?

Richard's idea as stated violates the FTC regs, "Guides on Bait Advertising." **Bait advertising** occurs when a business advertises goods or services at a low price to attract buyers into the seller's business. The seller then switches the buyer to more expensive products or services. Among practices prohibited by the FTC regs are having salespeople refuse to show the low-priced, bait item; indicating that the bait item will not be available for a long time; having an inadequate supply of the bait item; or telling employees to sell items other than the bait item when a customer seeks the bait item.

*Modification of the Holder-in-Due-Course Rule.* Bill Vanderpuddle was excited. He had just bought a new digital camera from E-Z Electronics Company. Bill did not have the full $500 purchase price, but E-Z had him sign a **negotiable note** for $400 plus interest and pay $100 down. Bill took the camera home, used it a couple of times, but discovered that prints created using the digital camera were of much poorer quality than they should have been. Bill returned the camera to E-Z but got the runaround. ("It will take a month to get the parts and another two weeks to get it repaired.") Bill told the E-Z manager he would stop making his installment payments on the camera unless he got better service. The E-Z manager told Bill the negotiable note he had signed had been sold to City Bank, and, since the bank was a **holder in due course**, it was not subject to Bill's claim against E-Z. (A holder in due course is a good-faith purchaser for value without notice of any personal defenses such as the breach of warranty Bill might have against E-Z.) The E-Z manager told Bill that his claims (such as Bill's warranty claim that the camera did not work) were personal (between Bill and E-Z only) and could not be asserted by Bill when the bank tried to collect monthly payments on the installment note. Bill was angry. He bought a defective digital camera and had lost his bargaining power with the seller (the ability to stop monthly payments) because the seller had sold to a holder in due course the negotiable note Bill used to buy the camera. It did not seem fair.

What happened in this fictional story occurred daily before the FTC promulgated its reg changing the holder-in-due-course (HIDC) rule. The **HIDC rule** is of common law origin. It was later codified (made part of a lengthy commercial law statute) in the Uniform Commercial Code (UCC). The purpose of the HIDC rule is to encourage people to buy negotiable instruments (**commercial promissory notes** and other **commercial paper** having a certain form). The HIDC rule encourages buying commercial paper because it is a "courier without luggage"—someone or something that is not weighed down by personal defenses between the person who issued the commercial paper and the only one originally accepting it as payment. The idea is to make commercial paper the same thing as money.

The HIDC rule made commercial paper a money equivalent, but it did so at the expense of consumers like Bill Vanderpuddle. The same problem occurs when consumers enter installment contracts with a **waiver-of-defenses clause** in which third parties, such as banks, who buy an installment contract, even though not involving a negotiable instrument, are free of the consumer-buyer's defenses against the sellers. This waiver-of-defenses clause has the same effect on finance companies and banks who buy seller's installment contracts as does the HIDC rule: It frees them from defenses the consumer has against the seller.

To correct the perceived injustice to consumers caused by the HIDC rule and defense waiver clauses, the FTC promulgated a reg in 1976 that, to a limited extent, changed the HIDC rule and defense waiver clauses. Banks and consumer finance companies who buy commercial paper on consumer installment contracts with defense waiver clauses and who would otherwise have been holders in due course are now subject to consumer claims and defenses against the seller. Bill Vanderpuddle now has a claim (probably breach of warranty) against the bank that justifies his stopping payments until the camera is fixed.

Several points need to be made about the FTC reg modifying the HIDC rule and defense waiver clauses. First, the reg applies only to individual consumers, not to businesses that purchase goods or services. Second, it applies to consumer purchases or leases of either goods or services. Third, it does not apply to credit card issuers. Therefore, if Bill buys a camera at Kmart with a Visa card and the camera doesn't work, he must still pay Visa for the camera. He has lost his bargaining power with Kmart because the camera has been paid for by Visa.

*Mail-Order Merchandise.* Carl Johnson had always wanted to win the Lake St. Helen annual fishing contest. He received his spring copy of the famous L.L. Toadstool Sporting Goods catalog, advertising a set of dry flies for $15.95, a fly rod for $60, and fishing tackle for $20. He sent in his order on April 1. It was received by L.L. Toadstool on April 5. L.L. Toadstool knew on April 10 that it would be unable to fill Carl's order until June 1, due to a run on fishing equipment, but L.L. Toadstool did not tell Carl of this delay. On May 15, Carl still had not received his fishing gear. The Lake St. Helen's contest was almost over. What rights (if any) does Carl have against L.L. Toadstool?

The Federal Trade Commission Act outlaws unfair methods of competition and unfair or deceptive acts and practices. This act gives the FTC power to promulgate regulations declaring certain specific acts unfair methods of competition and unfair or deceptive acts and practices. Thus, the FTC has made a **thirty-day regulation governing mail-order merchandise**. The rule makes it an unfair method of competition and an unfair or deceptive act and practice for a seller to solicit orders for merchandise from the buyer through the mails unless the seller reasonably expects to be able to ship the goods within 30 days (or less if the seller promises a shorter time) after getting a properly completed order. In other words, mail-order companies cannot entice buyers to order and send their money and then sit on the orders. Sellers must ship promptly (within 30 days).

If sellers cannot ship mail-ordered merchandise within a 30-day period, they must tell buyers that they may either cancel their orders and receive a prompt refund or get delayed shipment. The sellers must tell buyers about such delays within a reasonable time after the seller realizes a delay is likely.

What happens if sellers break this FTC 30-day rule? The FTC can issue a formal or informal complaint against the alleged reg breaker. An FTC administrative hearing possibly followed by an appeal to a federal court of appeals is then possible. Only the courts have the power to punish violators of FTC regs. The FTC can issue a cease-and-desist (C&D) order against reg breakers. Court-ordered civil penalties up to $10,000 per violation of FTC C&D orders are possible. The FTC 30-day mail-order rule exempts the following transactions:

1. Subscriptions (such as magazines sales) ordered for serial delivery after the first shipment complies with this reg
2. Orders of seeds and growing plants
3. COD (cash on delivery) orders (delay is tolerated here because the consumer has not sent in any money)

The FTC's 30-day mail-order rule does not preempt state or municipal laws that are not inconsistent with it or that put equal or greater burdens on mail-order sellers. The FTC rule does replace state or municipal rules that put lesser duties on mail-order sellers.

***Cooling-Off Period for Door-to-Door Sales.*** The doorbell rings. The homeowner goes to the door. There stands a smiling aluminum siding salesperson. Such people hypnotize consumers with talk. Before the homeowner knows it, he has signed a contract to have aluminum siding installed for $5,000. He has agreed to pay five days later when the siding is installed. As the consumer lies in bed the night of the purchase, he realizes he could have the same job done at half the cost by a carpenter friend. What can consumers do in situations such as this one?

First, they should ask the seller to release them from the contract. Unperformed contracts can be ended by the parties' agreement anytime before both finish performing. This scenario is possible but unlikely to happen. Second, many state statutes provide three-day cooling-off periods in such cases. They usually apply only to door-to-door salespeople who call on consumers. (In other words, consumers do not have three days to escape contracts they make in stores.) These state laws are discussed later in the chapter under the heading "State Statutes Protecting Consumers." A third suggestion involves a Federal Trade Commission regulation that makes it an unfair and deceptive act or practice for any door-to-door seller not to furnish a buyer with a fully completed receipt or contract copy with substantially the following notice:

> You, the buyer, may cancel this transaction at any time prior to midnight of the third business day after the date of this transaction. See the attached notice-of-cancellation form for an explanation of this right.

The completed receipt or contract copy must also contain a completed notice-of-cancellation form. This form helps the buyer cancel any contract made with a door-to-door salesperson. The cancellation right must be exercised within three business days after making the contract. The contract, receipt, and notice-of-cancellation form must all be in the same language (all in Spanish, for example, for Spanish-speaking people).

This FTC rule applies to the sale, lease, or rental of consumer goods or services with a purchase price of $25 or more.

The following sales are *not* covered by the FTC rule:

1. Sales made by prior negotiations when the buyer visited the seller's permanent showroom
2. Sales wherein the buyer has the right to rescind the transaction under the Consumer Credit Protection Act or its regs

3. Sales wherein the buyer first contacted the seller, and the goods or services are needed for the buyer's personal emergency, and the buyer gives the seller a separate, signed statement in the buyer's handwriting describing the situation and waiving the right to cancel within three business days

4. Sales made and completed entirely by phone or mail and without any other contact between the buyer and seller's agent before the delivery or performance

5. Sales of realty (houses, buildings, and land), insurance, or securities or commodities from a broker registered with the Securities and Exchange Commission

6. Sales wherein the *buyer* first contacted the *seller* and asked the seller to visit the buyer's home for repair or maintenance purposes

Door-to-door sellers who do not give the receipt or contract and notice-of-cancellation form as required break FTC regs, resulting in a possible court-imposed $10,000 civil penalty.

*Telemarketing Rule.* The Federal Trade Commission regulates telemarketing. Telemarketing refers to a plan, program, or campaign conducted to induce the purchase of goods or services by one or more telephones and involves more than one interstate telephone call. The FTC has promulgated a telemarketing rule setting out the requirements for telemarketers.

The FTC rule covers both goods and services sold over the telephone, but not Internet sales. The FTC rule covers only marketing initiated by the telemarketer/seller but not when the buyer first contacts the seller. The FTC rule does not cover marketing that consists only of intrastate telephone calls.

When the FTC telemarketing rule applies, the seller must disclose to the customer in a clear, conspicuous manner before the customer pays the following information:

- Total costs
- Material conditions/limits/restrictions to buy/lease the goods/services
- Any policy of not refunding, exchanging, cancelling, repurchasing, and stating all material terms regarding that policy
- Disclosure of prize promotion scheme odds of receiving the prize and whether the odds are not calculable in advance, factors used in calculating the odds; that no purchase or payment is necessary to win a prize or participate in the prize promotion, with instructions on how to participate or an address or local or toll-free telephone number to which customers may write or call for information on how to participate

If the FTC telemarketing rule applies to the marketing plan, telemarketers may not make any calls before 8 A.M. or after 9 P.M. local time.

Several things are not considered telemarketing under the FTC rule. One of these is solicitation of sales through the mailing of a catalog that describes or illustrates the goods or services offered for sale. Thus, a mail-order catalog company that merely conducts a mailing encouraging consumers to call the company in response to the catalog would not be subject to the FTC's telemarketing rule, even if the mail-order company provides the caller with further information about products or attempts to sell callers other products.

## Consumer Privacy Regarding Finances: Gramm–Leach–Bliley Act

Increasingly, consumers are concerned about their privacy. A key area of privacy concern involves one's personal finances. If Mr. Crooked has Mary Jones's Social Security number and her mother's maiden name, Crooked could have the ability to access Mary's bank accounts, stock brokerage accounts, credit union accounts, pension assets, and credit cards. Clearly, financial institutions such as banks and credit card issuers have much important information about each of us. It is very tempting for financial institutions, which have databases disclosing consumer preferences and payment patterns, to sell or exchange this information with other businesses.

Concerns about such disclosures led Congress to enact the Gramm–Leach–Bliley Act (GLB) in 1999 to create privacy rights for consumers and duties for "financial institutions." Title V of GLB declares that "it is the policy of Congress that each financial institution has an affirmative and continuing obligation to respect the privacy of its customers and to protect the security and confidentiality of those customers' nonpubllic personal information."

GLB protects consumers by imposing initial and annual privacy notification and disclosure requirements on financial institutions. GLB regs require that consumers be given the opportunity to "opt out" of information sharing with third parties and nonaffiliated parties. Thus, a credit card company must let Mary Jones know about her right to "opt out" of the credit card company's program, which would otherwise permit it to sell Mary's financial information to Big Credit Company, an unrelated company that Mary does not deal with directly.

The GLB notice from financial institutions to consumers must be CONSPICUOUS. The GLB privacy notice must be delivered such that the consumer is reasonably assured of receiving it in writing (the U.S. mail is a reasonable way). Posting on a bulletin board at a branch credit union office would NOT be reasonable notice, nor would e-mailing when the consumer does not use e-mail.

A consumer may "opt out" in several ways including mailing the "opt out" notice back to the financial institution within thirty days of receipt or calling a toll-free number.

Nine areas must be addressed in an FTC (the lead agency) privacy notice: (1) nonpublic information collected; (2) nonpublic information shared; (3) affiliates/nonaffiliates with whom the information is shared; (4) the aforementioned information regarding prior customers; (5) the aforementioned information regarding third party independent contractors with whom the information is shared; (6) the right to and how to opt out of information sharing with third parties; (7) how "opt out" applies to the Fair Credit Reporting Act; (8) how security and confidentiality are protected; and (9) legal exceptions.

GLB imposes a prohibition on a financial institution's sharing account information for telemarketing purposes. GLB authorizes several federal agencies to develop privacy regulations. Included among these agencies are the Federal Trade Commission, the Federal Reserve Board, the Office of Thrift Supervision, the Office of the Comptroller of the Currency, the Federal Deposit Insurance Corporation, the National Credit Union Association, and the Securities and Exchange Commission. The privacy regulations are standardized for the federal agencies to facilitate understanding.

## TRUTH-IN-LENDING ACT

The Truth-in-Lending Act is actually a major part of the Consumer Credit Protection Act. It became federal law on May 29, 1968. The purpose of the Truth-in-Lending Act is to better inform consumers about credit terms. The act enables consumers to learn the cost of credit and helps them compare credit costs from different sources.

Truth-in-Lending does not set maximum or minimum credit charges. (However, state usury laws, which vary from state to state, do limit what creditors may charge.) Truth-in-Lending ensures that the customer is advised of all costs and conditions of credit.

## REGULATION

Truth-in-Lending is not fully self-executing. In other words, a federal agency (the Board of Governors of the Federal Reserve Board) has authority under the act to promulgate regulations spelling out the act's requirements in detail. The basic Truth-in-Lending regulations make up **Regulation Z**. The Truth-in-Lending Act went into effect July 1, 1969. From that date forward, all covered creditors have had to comply with the act and Regulation Z.

## TYPES OF CREDIT COVERED

Only certain types of credit are covered by Truth-in-Lending's requirements. Basically, it covers only credit not exceeding $25,000 that is extended to individuals for personal, family, household, or agricultural purposes. However, all real estate credit extended to individuals for personal, family, household, or agricultural purposes is covered, no matter what the amount.

Some forms of credit are exempt from Truth-in-Lending. Loans to businesses are exempt, as are loans to federal, state, and local governments. However, if a governmental unit—federal, state, or local—extends credit to an individual for personal, family, household, or agricultural purposes, it must comply with Truth-in-Lending. Another Truth-in-Lending exemption exists for transactions in securities or commodity accounts with a broker-dealer registered with the Securities and Exchange Commission. A third exemption exists for some types of transactions under regulated public utility tariffs. Finally, consumer loans exceeding $25,000 are also exempt (except for real estate).

The *In Re Hill* case illustrates the sanctions that can be applied to lenders who fail to disclose fully to borrowers in real estate transactions.

## TYPES OF CREDITORS COVERED

Any person or business regularly extending or arranging for credit to individuals for personal, family, household, or agricultural purposes must comply with Truth-In-Lending. Banks, savings and loan associations, department and other retail stores, credit card companies, automobile dealers, credit unions, consumer finance companies, and mortgage bankers are covered. Some less obvious individuals or businesses covered by Truth-in-Lending are hospitals, doctors, physicians, dentists, plumbers, and electricians who regularly extend or arrange for credit.

## In Re Hill
U.S. Bankruptcy Court (D. Maryland)
213 B.R. 934 (1996)

### Background and Facts

Ms. Veda T. Hill is a Chapter 13 bankruptcy debtor who seeks to rescind and avoid the mortgage of Allright Mortgage Co. on her home, to reduce Allright's claim by offset, to be awarded statutory damages, and to obtain other related relief. The complaint asserts three alleged violations of the Federal Truth-In-Lending Act (TILA). Based on these alleged violations, plaintiff seeks a determination that she has properly rescinded Allright's security interest on her home and that Allright's mortgage is avoided. Plaintiff granted the mortgage to secure a loan for home improvements and bill consolidation. Plaintiff has also objected to Allright's secured claim on the same grounds. The two matters have been consolidated.

Three three alleged violations of TILA are as follows: (1) Allright improperly disclosed (and it charged plaintiff twice for) a $236.11 advance interest payment; (2) Allright improperly failed to disclose to plaintiff a $15 courier fee as a Finance Charge, and it should not have calculated the fee as part of the Amount Financed, resulting in an understatement of the Annual Percentage Rate (APR) disclosed to plaintiff; and (3) Allright improperly failed to disclose to plaintiff that a $2,000 broker's fee was a Finance Charge, and it should not have included the fee as part of the Amount Financed, causing a further understandment of the APR disclosed to plaintiff.

Allright loaned the borrowers $25,000. Material disclosures on Ms. Hill's Federal Loan Disclosure Statement were: APR—20.7320%; Amount Financed—$24,250.00; Finance Charge—$55,018.71; and Total Payments—$79,268.71. The term of the loan was 180 months with monthly payment of $439.07, and a call provision after five years. Settlement on the mortgage loan occurred on April 9, 1992. From the gross amount of $25,000, defendant deducted . . . "Brokers' fees" of $2,000 and a fee of $15 for a "Courier to record documents." Interim interest of $236.11 was not deducted. Allright escrowed $10,500 for the home repairs, and $9,956.87 was left and described as "Cash to Borrower."

### Body of Opinion

. . . The first alleged violation of TILA upon which plaintiff seeks judgment involves an interim interest charge of $236.11 that was paid by plaintiff prior to its due date and deducted from the amount distributed to Ms. Hill. Plaintiff alleges that Allright collected the $236.11 as a prepaid Finance Charge, as part of the Amount Financed, and again by deducting it from the proceeds that were distributed to plaintiff.

The parties do not dispute that Allright was entitled to charge plaintiff the $236.11 in interest that was due on May 1. The expense was properly allocated as a Finance Charge. . . . However, by deducting the charge from the proceeds but not from the Amount Financed, Allright was collecting the $236.11 twice—first as a

Finance Charge and second, in part, as interest. In other words, Allright collected interest on prepaid interest, and this increased collection extends over the life of the loan. A prepaid Finance Charge should be subtracted from, and not included in, the Amount Financed. . . . The fact that borrowers made a voluntary choice makes no different. . . . Therefore the interim interest charge was improperly disclosed under TILA.

The second violation of TILA that plaintiff was alleged is that the fee for courier service charged by the attorney handling the settlement was a Finance Charge. It is undisputed that plaintiff was charged a $15 fee for having a courier record the mortgage documents. Further, this was not reimbursement for an actual cost, but was an approximation based on a standard charge. This expense was deducted from the Amount Financed rather than disclosed as a Finance Charge, and plaintiff has alleged that this allocation was improper and violated TILA. . . .

The court concludes that Allright did not act improperly in deducting the courier fees from the Amount Financed as such charges are not a Finance Charge. Mr. Rubenstein as settlement attorney, made the courier charge to cover, on the average, his costs. Allright did not require or retain his charge for itself.

[W]hether a particular expense constitutes a Finance Charge under TILA . . . must be examined. Certain charges may be excluded as Finance Charges if they are bona fide, reasonable in amount, and relate to one of the following:

1) fees for title examination, abstract of title, title insurance, property survey, and similar purposes.
2) fees for preparing deeds, mortgages, and reconveyance, settlement, and similar documents.
3) notary, appraisal, and credit report fees.
4) amounts required to be paid into escrow or trustee accounts if the amounts would not otherwise be included in the finance charge. . . .

However, fees are Finance Charges if the creditor either requires the fee or retains a portion of the fee for itself. . . .

Where a broker is required, as in the instant case, the broker's fee must be included as a Finance Charge. . . . It does not matter that the lender does not retain part of the broker's fee for itself, especially when the lender benefits from the broker's services. . . .

While it is true that plaintiff contacted Mr. Hyleigh of her own volition and not through Allright, it was acknowledged that Allright only made loans through brokers, except for two or three refinancings over fifteen years, and that this arrangement benefitted Allright in many ways. . . . The fact that Allright did not expressly require plaintiff to use a particular broker . . . does not alter the court's conclusion. United Mortgage brokered about 20 percent of Allright's loans. . . .

Because Allright required plaintiff to use the services of a broker, the broker's fee charged to plaintiff was required by TILA to be included as a Finance Charge. . . . Moreover, a recent amendment to TILA supports the court's conclusion by expressly including as an example of finance charges "borrower-paid mortgage broker fees, including fees paid directly to the broker or the lender (for delivery to the broker) whether such fees are paid in cash or financed.". . . These amendments are not, however, applicable to this case because this action was commenced before June 1, 1995. . . . They are referred to here merely as not expressing an intent contrary to the court's conclusions.

For these reasons, the court finds that Allright violated TILA by not disclosing the $2,000 broker's fee as a Finance Charge, and by including the broker's fee in the Amount Financed. . . .

A potential problem for plaintiff is that her right to rescind the transaction was limited by a three-year statute of limitations period after Allright failed to disclose material information properly to plaintiff. . . . The limitations period commenced running on the date the transaction was consummated. . . .

In the instant case, the loan transaction was consummated on April 9, 1992. . . . Plaintiff did not give Allright notice of her intent to rescind based on the improper broker's fee until October 10, 1995, more than three years after the loan had settled. . . .

Plaintiff's first attempt to rescind the transaction, however, via letter to Allright, occurred within three years, on March 6, 1995, although it did not mention the broker's fee. Similarly, plaintiff filed the complaint initiating this action on April 7, 1995, also within three years, but it also did not raise the broker's fees issue. Nevertheless, on February 5, 1996, the court granted plaintiff's motion to amend her complaint and her objection to Allright's claim that she filed on April 24, 1995, without objection from Allright. Plaintiff's amended complaint related back to the date of the timely original pleading because the added material concerning the broker's fee arose out of the same conduct, transaction, or occurrence. . . .

In the alternative, plaintiff may raise her TILA violation claims at any time as a matter of defense by way of recoupment or setoff. . . .

In the TILA context, courts have held that a defense based upon TILA can be raised in a foreclosure or other proceeding at any time. . . . Allright chose to file a foreclosure against Ms. Hill in state court. Ms. Hill then instituted this bankruptcy action. Following that, Allright sought to collect on the alleged debt by filing a proof of secured claim. Ms. Hill filed an objection to the proof of claim raising her TILA claims defensively.

Specifically, in the bankruptcy context, courts have held that when the creditor files a proof of claim, the debtor may defend against that claim by raising TILA as a defense at any time. . . . Thus, Ms. Hill's defense to the proof of claim based on TILA is not time-barred.

Contrary to Allright's contention, Ms. Hill did prove actual damages at trial. The method of measuring the actual damages under TILA is the amount by which the Finance Charge is understated. . . . Ms. Hill presented proof from Mr. Rubenstein that he did not disclose the broker fee in the Finance Charge. Thus, the Finance Charge was understated by $2,000. In addition, two statutory penalties of $1,000 each are invoked for the disclosure violations and for the failure to honor the rescission. . . .

Allright is entitled to judgment in its favor regarding the $15 courier fee; because of Allright's failure to disclose the $2,000 broker's fee as a Finance Charge was a violation of TILA, plaintiff is entitled to rescind the loan transaction, avoid the deed of trust, and cancel interest and settlement cost charges; and for the TILA violations plaintiff should recover actual damages of $2,000 for the broker's fee and $2,000 statutory damages. These remedies should be implemented by way of recoupment or set off. . . .

## Judgment and Result

The court finds that (1) the $236.11 interim interest charge was incorrectly classified and double charged; (2) Allright did not violate TILA with respect to the $15 courier fee; and (3) plaintiff is entitled to judgment for a violation of TILA involving the $2,000 broker's fee.

## Questions

1. How did plaintiff/borrower get around the three-year statute of limitations for raising TILA violations?
2. What rate of interest did plaintiff pay on her home improvement and cash advance loan? Does the federal TILA set a federal maximum rate of permissible interest on consumer loans? How, then, can a loan be rescinded if the consumer/debtor agreed up front to the loan? What if the loan terms were not clearly disclosed up front as "Finance Charges"?
3. What were the most egregious nondisclosures of the loans here: the "double interest," the courier charges, or the broker's fee?
4. What charges may be excluded as Finance Charges: title examination fees; title abstract fees; title insurance; property survey; deed preparation fees; mortgage preparation fees; reconveyance fees; settlement fees; notary fees; credit report fees; amounts required to be paid into escrow or trustee accounts if the amounts would not otherwise be included in the finance charge?
5. Putting aside the legalities of plaintiff's loan, what do you think about the financial wisdom of the terms of this loan? Does the fact that plaintiff ended up in bankruptcy suggest an answer to this question?

## DISCLOSING CREDIT TERMS

As mentioned, one of Truth-in-Lending's main aims is to increase consumer credit information. Regulation Z requires consumer credit information to be clear, conspicuous, and written. Truth-in-Lending and Regulation Z require disclosure of charges consumers must pay to get credit—including, in most cases, the finance charge and the annual percentage rate.

## Finance Charge and Annual Percentage Rate

Disclosure of the **finance charge** and disclosure of the **annual percentage rate (APR)** are the two most important ideas coming from Truth-in-Lending. These requirements tell consumers at a glance how much they are paying for credit in two ways—in dollar terms (the finance charge) and as a percentage of the loan (the annual percentage rate, or APR). The APR and finance charge must appear on the face of the periodic statement that creditors send to consumers.

The words *finance charge* and *annual percentage rate* must stand out clearly. In some transactions involving the sale of dwellings, that total dollar finance charge need not be stated, but the annual percentage rate must be disclosed.

Neither Truth-in-Lending nor Regulation Z sets maximum, minimum, or any charges for credit (state usury laws control this). Both require creditors to show consumers any finance charges and whatever annual percentage rate is charged. The annual percentage rate must be accurate to the nearest one-quarter of one percent.

## Credit Cards

The Truth-in-Lending Act and Regulation Z also cover the **credit card**—a single credit device used to get money, property, labor, or services on credit.

Credit cards may not be issued except in response to a request or application or as a renewal of, or substitute for, an accepted credit card. An **accepted credit card** is a credit card that the cardholder has requested or applied for and received, has signed or used, or has authorized another person to use. Any credit card issued in renewal of, or in substitution for, an accepted credit card becomes an accepted credit card when received by the cardholder.

The "accepted credit card" concept means only that the person who accepts a card is liable for its use. However, Truth-in-Lending limits a cardholder's liability for unauthorized use to $50 or to the amount of money, property, labor, or services obtained by unauthorized use before the card issuer is notified, whichever is lower. As a matter of goodwill, some credit card companies do not subject cardholders to even the $50 amount for unauthorized card use.

Unauthorized credit card use occurs, for example, when someone loses his wallet containing his credit cards, and someone finds it and makes charges on the cards. The cardholder would be liable up to only $50. What if spouses separated? Might one become liable for the other's use of credit cards obtained while they were happily married? The case on the following page gives an answer.

## Credit Advertising

Advertising of credit is covered by Truth-in-Lending. No ad for credit may tell consumers that a specific down payment, installment plan, or amount of credit can be arranged unless the creditor usually arranges terms of that type.

Creditors cannot tell consumers of a specific credit term unless all other terms are clearly and conspicuously stated. This rule applies to newspaper, TV, and radio advertising. It also covers all other ads, such as those in magazines, leaflets, flyers, catalogs, public address system announcements, direct mail literature, window displays, and billboards.

## Oclander v. First National Bank of Louisville
Kentucky Court of Appeals
700 S.W.2d 804 (1985)

### Background and Facts

Appellant, Monica Oclander, appeals from the summary judgment of the Jefferson Circuit Court against her in the sum of $11,319.43 with 12 percent interest from March 23, 1983, and costs on the appellee bank's suit on credit card charges made on appellant Monica's Mastercard open-end credit plan with the bank. We affirm.

We need not burden this opinion with a detailed factual presentation of this case inasmuch as its facts are of record and the parties and their counsel are familiar with them. We recite only those necessary to this appeal.

The credit card charges in question were made by Bonifacio Aparicio, appellant's estranged husband and co-defendant. The account was opened October 20, 1981, with cards issued to both. The credit limit was $400. In July 1982, Monica notified the bank that she was separated from Bonifacio. It "blocked" the account from additional charges and by letter forwarded to her advised her how to apply for and use its standard divorce and separation affirmation form to be completed and returned to the bank to restore her credit. She completed and returned them on August 9, 1982, indicating she had destroyed one of the two credit cards issued to her and Bonifacio and retained the other. Relying on this representation, the bank "unblocked" the account under the impression it was for her credit alone. Apparently she had not destroyed the one because various charges were made on the account ostensibly by Bonifacio in Spain between October 29, 1982, and November 30, 1982, the card's expiration date.

Congress recognized some time ago that the area of credit card liability needed to be dealt with in a uniform manner. Accordingly, 15 U.S.C.A. § 1643 provides protection for a card holder against "unauthorized" charges made on an account. Obviously, this was to protect the card holder in cases where the card had been stolen or lost and was being used to make "unauthorized" charges. § 1643 limits the liability of a card holder where there has been "unauthorized use." Title 15 U.S.C.A. § 1602(o) defines the term "unauthorized use" to mean "a use of a credit card by a person other than the card holder who does not have actual, implied, or apparent authority for such use and from which the card holder receives no benefit." If the person using the card has either actual, implied, or apparent authority then the charges are authorized and the limitations imposed by § 1643 do not apply and Ms. Oclander would be liable for all charges made on the account as set out under the "Terms of Agreement." Thus, the issue of liability turns on whether the charges made by Bonifacio Aparicio were authorized.

Apparent authority exists where a person has created such an appearance of things that it causes a third person to reasonably and prudently believe that a second party has the power to act on behalf of the first person.

In the present case, the Bank had sent a "Divorce and Separation Affirmation" along with a letter setting out what needed to be done to release Ms. Oclander from liability. The letter was specific and stated as follows:

Be advised that signing this in no way releases either party at this time, that the individual to be responsible must complete the application in full, both to update our file and to determine whether or not they qualify for an account in their name alone. If they do qualify for credit in this manner, the other party's name will be dropped. Otherwise, no charges are to be made on this account and both parties are responsible until the balance is reduced to zero.

The Bank then stated that it had "blocked" the account and that no further charges were to be made until the conditions in the above letter were met. Obviously, the intention of the Bank was to protect both itself and its customer from the abuses that have occurred in this case. Ms. Oclander stated that she was in possession of both the cards and destroyed one and retained the other for her use. Relying on these statements, the Bank removed the "block" from the account and Ms. Oclander was allowed to continue making charges on the account. What the Bank requested of Ms. Oclander was not unreasonable and would have protected all concerned if Ms. Oclander's statements had been accurate. . . . Bonifacio Aparicio did in fact have a card in his possession with his name on it as a joint card holder and presented the card to merchants who had no reason to question his authority to use it. Mr. Aparicio was in possession of a card which was a representation to merchants (third parties) to whom they were presented that he (second parties/card bearers) was authorized to make the charges. This is not a case where charges were made on an expired card, or the card was obtained through fraud or other wrongdoing. Mr. Aparicio was actually in possession of one of the cards and at all times was ostensibly authorized to make charges on the account. If Ms. Oclander had accurately explained the situation to the Bank and told them that Mr. Aparicio was in possession of one of the cards, or at the very least, that she did not have possession of both cards, then the Bank would have maintained the "block" it had originally placed on the account in July, and none of the charges made during Mr. Aparicio's buying spree would have been chargeable to the Bank.

The Bank did not even require that the cards be surrendered but only that they be accounted for by Ms. Oclander. Ms. Oclander failed to do so, and as a result the Bank has suffered damages for which she should be held accountable.

We find no merit to Monica's argument that there is a material dispute of fact over the bank's delay in placing an "overseas block" on the account. We find none. It placed the "block" as soon as it could after it became apparent something was amiss.

## Judgment and Result

The lower court's judgment is affirmed. The bank wins.

## Questions

1. Do people who obtain credit cards have potentially unlimited liability for unauthorized use of their credit cards? Why or why not?

2. Did the court in the *Oclander* case interpret the charges there as authorized?
3. Would any business ethics support the *Oclander* result?
4. Of the legal ethics noted in Chapter 1, which supports the result in *Oclander*?

### PENALTIES

Criminal and civil penalties can be imposed for violating the Truth-in-Lending Act. Fines up to $5,000, prison terms up to one year, or both are possible for willful violators of Truth-in-Lending or its regulations. The injured consumer may also sue civilly and recover twice the amount of the finance charge (but not less than $100 or more than $1,000) plus court costs and reasonable attorney fees.

### CREDITOR RECORDS

Creditors must save their papers for at least two years from the transaction date to prove compliance with Truth-in-Lending and its regulations. Government enforcement agencies have the right to inspect creditors' records to see that they are complying with the act and its regs.

### ENFORCERS

The two enforcement groups for Truth-in-Lending and its regs are private and public. Private enforcers are consumers whose rights under the act are violated.

Which agency enforces the act depends on what type of creditor allegedly violated it. In other words, no single federal agency enforces the act, making it confusing for consumers to know to which agency to complain.

### FAIR CREDIT REPORTING ACT

The Fair Credit Reporting Act (FCRA) is a federal law passed in 1970. Its main purpose is to provide accurate current information about consumers, but not about businesses. Consumer credit information used to get a job, insurance, or credit is covered by the act. The FCRA also makes illegal the disclosure of consumer credit information to third parties with no legitimate need to know the information.

### HOW THE FCRA WORKS

Suppose Mike Harrison tries to charge a purchase at Mace's department store but is turned down. Mike asks why and is told an unfavorable credit report has been filed on him. Mike cannot think of any reason for having a bad credit report; he has always paid his bills on time. He asks Mace's department store who supplied the credit report, but the store refuses to tell him unless he pays $10. What are Mike's rights?

Under the Fair Credit Reporting Act, consumers have the right to know the credit reporting agency that turns in reports that are the basis for the denial of credit. Furthermore, the consumer has a right to the information in any credit report the business relies on in this matter. Because the information must be given free of charge to the consumer, Mace's must give Mike the information in the credit report it used to evaluate his creditworthiness and may not charge him $10. Mike does not, however, have a right to the report itself.

Suppose that after Mace's gives Mike the free credit report, Mike finds the credit reporting agency has confused him with a Mike Harrimon. He can then force the credit reporting agency to correct the credit report and notify any credit or insurance recipient of the report for the six months before the error. If the erroneous credit concerned employment, Mike is entitled to have the correction sent to any potential employer receiving the incorrect report within the past two years.

The Fair Credit Reporting Act also entitles consumers to stop credit reporting agencies from disclosing accurate credit information if the requester wants it for noncommercial reasons.

## SANCTIONS

The Fair Credit Reporting Act lets consumers sue anyone violating it. Damages, attorney fees, and court costs are recoverable. Also, the Federal Trade Commission has authority to enforce the Fair Credit Reporting Act. The *Houghton* case illustrates the FCRA in operation.

---

### Houghton v. Insurance Crime Prevention Institute
U.S. Court of Appeals (3d Cir.)
795 F.2d 322 (1986)

#### Background and Facts

On November 29, 1984, Joseph M. Houghton filed a complaint alleging that defendants, the Insurance Crime Prevention Institute (ICPI), an organization funded by property and casualty insurance companies, and John Andrew Hoda, an employee of ICPI, violated the FCRA by obtaining under false pretenses information on a consumer from a consumer reporting agency. The complaint alleged that on or about July 6, 1982, Hoda, on behalf of ICPI, an agency which seeks to investigate suspected fraudulent claims, submitted to the Mid-East Index Bureau, a division of Central Index Bureau (CIB), card files stating that Houghton was involved in an accident on October 15, 1980, and that he had made a claim with Kemper Insurance Company regarding the accident. Houghton contends this information was false and fraudulent, because he was not involved in an accident on that date, had made no claim with Kemper as of that time, and had no bodily injury claim pending with Kemper at that time. The complaint alleges that defendants knew or should have known that this information was false and fraudulent and that defendants submitted the information to CIB so that, in return, defendants could obtain from CIB its accumulated confidential medical records, documents and information from other insurance carriers about Houghton.[1]

The complaint alleges that defendants had no permissible purpose under FCRA to obtain the information from CIB, a consumer reporting agency within the meaning of the Act, and that defendants disseminated to others the information received with the specific intent to discredit and harass plaintiff and to interfere in his personal affairs. Houghton sought compensatory and punitive damages, attorneys' fees and costs.

Defendants filed an answer on January 14, 1985, denying the material allegations in the complaint and asserting an affirmative defense that the complaint was barred by the two-year applicable statute of limitations set forth in FCRA. Since the action complained of took place on July 6, 1982, it is apparent that the complaint filed November 29, 1984, was not filed within the two-year period.

Houghton then amended the complaint to include the following paragraph:

Plaintiff did not become aware of the existence of said [index] card . . . prior to October 24, 1983, when a copy of said card was forwarded to plaintiff's counsel by the Secretary and Counsel of the American Insurance Association. . . . Moreover, plaintiff exercised all due diligence in obtaining said card and could not have obtained said card sooner, as plaintiff on numerous occasions

---

[1] The parties explained at oral argument that CIB works under a cooperative arrangement permitting access to its information only to those who provide it with information.

prior to October 24, 1983, demanded of CIB all cards and reports in their possession regarding plaintiff, but said card was either inadvertently or intentionally withheld until October 24, 1983.

By this amendment, Houghton sought to invoke the discovery rule to toll application of the two-year statute of limitations until his discovery of the relevant facts.

The district court then granted the motion to dismiss, holding:

> Plaintiff's amended complaint is barred by the two-year statute of limitations in the Fair Credit Reporting Act, and does not come within the "discovery" exception therein since the disclosure was not one required to be disclosed by defendants to plaintiff and the Central Index Bureau, which made the disclosure to its subscribers, is not a defendant.

## Body of Opinion

**Circuit Judge Sloviter.** The Fair Credit Reporting Act was passed in 1970 to insure that consumer reporting agencies exercise their "grave responsibilities" regarding the "assembling and evaluating [of] consumer credit and other information on consumers" with "fairness, impartiality, and a respect for the consumer's right to privacy."

Congress found that the "banking system is dependent upon fair and accurate credit reporting" and that an "elaborate mechanism [had] developed" concerning the credit and general reputation of the consumer.

The act provides that a consumer reporting agency may furnish a consumer report in certain enumerated circumstances and no other. The act provides for both criminal penalties and civil liability, which may include compensatory and punitive damages, costs and attorneys' fees. The United States district courts have jurisdiction over suits brought under the statute.

The act contains a statute of limitations, limiting suit to two years from the date the liability arises, with one exception. The applicable section provides:

> An action may be brought within two years from the date on which the liability arises, except that where a defendant has materially and willfully misrepresented any information required under this subchapter to be disclosed to an individual and the information so misrepresented is material to the establishment of the defendant's liability to that individual under this subchapter, the action may be brought at any time within two years after discovery by the individual of the misrepresentation.

Since the complaint was admittedly filed more than two years after the alleged violation of the Act, the only basis appellant argues to overturn the dismissal is by application of the discovery rule to the statute of limitations. Appellant cites to various state cases which, in the consumer context, have tolled the limitations statute until discovery by plaintiff of the wrongful act.

Appellant contends that these cases are applicable to the facts at bar since, despite due diligence, he did not become aware, nor would he have become aware, of the fraudulent submission of a false report until CIB finally released the report to him, which was

October 24, 1983. His suit was filed within two years of that date. He argues that as a matter of policy, and in the interest of justice, the time in which an injured party should have the right to sue for the wrongful submission of false information to a consumer reporting agency should be counted from the date of discovery.

If Houghton prevails on his legal position that a plaintiff has two years from the discovery of the violation, it would be irrelevant that in this case he would have had sufficient time to have filed his action in the period between October 1983 when the information was released to him and July 1984 when the statute of limitations barred the action. If a discovery rule is not applied, other plaintiffs would be barred from suit even if they were unaware of the relevant facts throughout the entire statutory period. Nonetheless, we cannot accept the extension of the discovery rule to this statute. . . .

In examining the statute of limitations set forth in the FCRA, the plain language of the act shows Congress' intent to permit tolling of an FCRA action only in a precisely defined situation. By its terms, it only permits tolling in the case of a material and willful misrepresentation by a defendant of information required to be disclosed under the act which is material to defendant's liability. Plaintiff does not challenge the district court's holding that the statutory tolling provision does not apply to these defendants because none of the disclosure provisions of the act imposed an obligation on these defendants to disclose to plaintiff the information pertinent here. CIB, the one entity which arguably had such an obligation, an issue we do not decide here, was not made a defendant in this lawsuit.

If we construe the statute as permitting us to imply a discovery exception to circumstances other than the one which Congress explicitly set forth, we would be rendering superfluous the discovery exception which Congress did set forth. This we may not do. The Supreme Court has stated that where Congress has enunciated an exception to a general prohibition, "additional exceptions are not to be implied in the absence of evidence of a contrary legislative intent." In this case, the statutory language clearly evidences the legislative intent. If the discovery rule is to be made generally applicable to FCRA cases, it must be done by congressional action.

## Judgment and Result

District Court judgment dismissing plaintiff's complaint is upheld. Houghton loses.

## Questions

1. How long did Mr. Houghton wait after discovering the allegedly improper submission of the information here before starting his suit?
2. Was Mr. Houghton wronged by an apparent violation of the Fair Credit Reporting Act here?
3. Does the *Houghton* case represent a triumph of procedural law over substantive law?
4. What do you think of the business ethics of Mr. Hoda of the Insurance Crime Prevention Institute?
5. What legal ethic(s) support what Mr. Hoda allegedly did?

## EQUAL CREDIT OPPORTUNITY ACT

The Equal Credit Opportunity Act (ECOA) was passed in 1974 and took effect in 1975. As a federal law, it applies in all fifty states.

Five revelations were made during consideration of the ECOA bill:

1. Getting credit is harder for single women than it is for single men.
2. When women marry, creditors make them reapply for credit in their husband's name; men do not have to do the same thing.
3. Creditors will not loan money to a married woman in her own name.
4. Creditors will usually not consider a married working woman's income when a married couple applies for a loan.
5. Divorced or widowed women find it difficult to reestablish credit.

The ECOA responded to these concerns by placing requirements on financial institutions and other firms extending credit on a regular basis. Covered lenders must make credit available to all creditworthy customers without regard to sex or marital status. A 1976 amendment to the ECOA prohibits credit discrimination by commercial lenders based on an applicant's national origin, race, religion, color, or age. The ECOA also makes it unlawful for any creditor to discriminate against any applicant with respect to any aspect of a credit transaction, because all or part of the applicant's income derives from any public assistance program.

## ECOA APPLICATIONS

Firms in the business of extending credit may not ask credit applicants about their marital status. This rule has exceptions. A lender may ask credit applicants about their marital status to determine its rights and remedies regarding a particular loan. For example, the lender could ask a woman if anyone else is going to be a co-obligor on the debt, or it could inquire about a woman's income sources. If she says she has no source of income except for her husband's income, questions about her marriage would then seem appropriate. Also, creditors may consider state property laws (such as community property in the southwestern states) directly or indirectly affecting creditworthiness.

Lenders may not deny credit to married women who apply for it individually (without their husbands). Lenders may ask a married woman only about the sources of income she intends to rely on in applying for credit (including income from a part-time job that is income producing on a regular basis, welfare, alimony, separate maintenance payments, or child support). Just because the creditor must take these sources of income into account does not mean a loan must be made. If credit applicants fail to meet creditworthiness requirements, the ECOA does not require that the creditor extend them credit.

The ECOA prohibits discrimination in credit extension based on age. A creditor may ask a credit applicant's age if it is to be used to determine the amount and probable continuance of income levels or credit history. Similarly, a creditor does not violate the ECOA by asking or considering the age of an elderly applicant when the age of such an applicant is to be used by the creditor in extending credit in favor of such an applicant. Using an empirically derived credit system that considers age is permissible if the system complies with Federal Reserve regs. However, an elderly applicant's age may not be given a negative value in such system.

Asking credit applicants whether their income comes from any public assistance program does not violate the ECOA if it is done to determine the amount and probable continuance of income levels or to determine credit history. Welfare payments and government benefits must be taken into account by creditors in determining a credit applicant's income, which does not mean a creditor must loan money to applicants who are otherwise not creditworthy.

The ECOA prohibits discrimination in extending credit based on race. For example, suppose Harvey Slater, an African American mail carrier, is turned down by a savings and loan association for a home loan. The stated reason is the "instability of real estate in that part of town." This categorical refusal to finance real estate purchases in declining neighborhoods (called **redlining**) violates the ECOA's prohibition if race is the real reason for the credit rejection.

Note four aspects about the ECOA.

1. It restricts only commercial lenders (not friends, family, or those making loans who are not in the credit business).
2. It preserves lenders' rights to reject loan applicants because they are not creditworthy. For example, "slow-pay, no-pay" debtors can still be turned down for loans.
3. It does not require lenders to make loans.
4. It limits the basis for which creditors can turn down loan applicants.

## OTHER ECOA PROVISIONS

*Creditor Deadline.* The ECOA requires a creditor to notify an applicant of its action on a credit application within thirty days of receiving a completed application.

*Specificity Requirement.* The ECOA requires creditors to be specific in telling credit applicants why they are denied credit. Creditors may not deny credit simply because the applicant "is not creditworthy" or because the applicant did not meet a minimum score on the lender's application test. Credit rejections may be oral if the creditor did not act on more than 150 credit applications in the prior year.

*ECOA Enforcement.* Private parties and administrative agencies make up the two general categories of ECOA enforcement.

*ECOA Remedies.* Damages, punitive damages designed to punish intentional violators, and injunctions are possible remedies when a private party sues an alleged violator. Court costs and attorney fees can be assessed against violators of the ECOA. Lawsuits by private parties must be started within two years of an ECOA violation (or within one year after an enforcement agency sues).

The *Bowen v. First Financial Services, Inc.* alleges an ECOA violation.

## FAIR CREDIT BILLING ACT

Suppose your name is John W. Smith—a common name. Suppose further that you have Visa and MasterCard credit cards. Given your name, being billed for someone else's purchases would not be impossible. If your monthly MasterCard statement (or billing from any business using credit cards) contains errors, what can you do?

## Bowen v. First Family Financial Services, Inc.
U.S. Court of Appeals (11th Cir.)
233 F.3d 1331 (2000))

## Background and Facts

In 1996 Bowen and Ford, the plaintiffs, separately obtained small loans from First Family Financial, and as part of their transactions, each of them was required to sign a two page document entitled in bold lettering: "ARBITRATION AGREEMENT." The agreement provides that First Family and the consumer "agree to arbitrate, under the following terms, all claims and disputes between you and us, except as provided otherwise in this agreement." In a more specific provision, the agreement states that it applies to "all claims and disputes arising out of, in connection with, or relating to: . . . any claim or dispute based on a federal or state statute."

In August of 1997, Bowen and Ford filed this putative class action. They contend that the Truth in Lending Act (TILA) grants consumers a non-waivable right to obtain judicial, as distinguished from arbitral, redress of statutory violations, including the right to do so through a class action. That is the basis of their claim that First Family's requirement that they sign the arbitration agreement violated the ECOA because it forced them to waive their right to litigate TILA claims in order to obtain credit. The complaint sought actual and statutory damages as well as declaratory and injunctive relief. Other than their challenge to the arbitration agreement requirement, the plaintiffs did not claim that First Family had violated a substantive provision of the ECOA, the TILA, or any of the provisions of the Consumer Credit Protection Act (of which the ECOA and TILA are a part).

The federal district court concluded that the plaintiffs had failed to plead how they exercised a right under the Consumer Credit Protection Act or how First Family had discriminated against them in response to their exercising such a right. Thus the court granted First Family's motion for judgment on the pleadings and dismissed the case with prejudice. The plaintiffs appealed to the Court of Appeals.

## Body of Opinion

**Circuit Judge Carnes.** Enacted as part of the Consumer Credit Protection Act, the ECOA proscribes discrimination in the extension of credit by making it:

Unlawful for any creditor to discriminate against any applicant, with respect to any aspect of a credit transaction—

1) on the basis of race, color, religion, national origin, sex or marital status, or age (provided the applicant has the capacity to contract);

2) because all or part of the applicant's income derives from any public assistance program; or

3) because the applicant has in good faith exercised any right under the Consumer Credit Protection Act. . . .

If a creditor violates [the Act], the ECOA provides that the aggrieved applicant, either through an individual suit or a class action, shall recover any actual damages sustained by the applicant, punitive damages, reasonable attorney's fees and costs, and any necessary equitable relief.

The TILA is part of the Consumer Credit Protection Act, and it imposes disclosure obligations upon creditors and authorizes consumers to recover both actual and statutory damages when a creditor makes inaccurate or inadequate disclosures. . . . The "right under the Consumer Credit Protection Act " upon which the plaintiffs base their . . . ECOA claim is the purported right under the TILA to litigate, both individually and as a class action, statutory claims for disclosure violations. They contend that First Family discriminated against them "with respect to any aspect of a credit transaction" by requiring them, as a condition of obtaining credit, to agree in advance to arbitrate any claims under the Consumer Credit Protection Act, including any claims under the TILA.

In order to establish a violation of the [relevant section of the Consumer Credit Protection Act] a plaintiff must show that: (1) he exercised in good faith (2) a right under the Consumer Credit Protection Act, and (3) as a result, the creditor discriminated against him with respect to the credit transaction. . . . As an initial premise of the plaintiffs' argument in this case is that the TILA grants consumers a non-waivable right to litigate, individually and through a class action, any claims arising under the statute. This right to litigate TILA claims, the plaintiffs maintain, is prospectively waived by the arbitration agreements that First Family requires credit applicants to sign. Because a credit applicant would be denied credit if he declined to sign the arbitration agreement in order to preserve his right to litigate under the TILA, the plaintiffs argue that First Family discriminates against applicants based on a good faith exercise of their rights under the Consumer Credit Protection Act, in violation of [relevant sections of] the ECOA and its implementing regulation. . . . But how were these plaintiffs discriminated against? . . .

The plaintiffs here have not alleged that First Family threatened to refuse their loan application, unless they signed the arbitration agreement, and they have not alleged that there were any pre-existing rights that had arisen in connection with a prior loan to the plaintiffs.

The plaintiffs attempt to overcome the difficulties surrounding the "good faith" exercise of rights and discrimination elements of [the relevant section of the statute] by contending that one of the ECOA's implementing regulations . . . prohibits a creditor from presenting an unlawful term as a mandatory condition of the loan agreement. We doubt that the existence of that regulation dispenses with the statutory requirements that there be an exercise of rights and discrimination resulting therefrom. But even if it does, a more basic problem for the plaintiffs, and one that we rely upon to dispose of their claim, is their position's fundamental premise that the TILA confers upon consumers a nonwaivable right to litigate—as distinguished from arbitrate—claims brought under that statute.

The fact that Congress has enacted a statute which creates substantive rights and provides judicial remedies to vindicate those substantive rights does not mean it has created a nonwaivable, substantive "right" to judicial redress. . . . As the Supreme Court has explained repeatedly, "by agreeing to arbitrate a statutory claim, a party does not forgo the substantive rights afforded by the statute; it only submits to their resolution in an arbitral, rather than judicial forum.". . .

While the legislative history of [the relevant statutory section] shows that Congress thought class actions were a significant means of achieving compliance with the TILA . . . , it does not indicate that Congress intended to confer upon individuals a non-waivable right to pursue a class action nor does it even address the issue of arbitration. . . .

We hold that for purposes of the ECOA . . . Congress did not create a nonwaivable right to pursue TILA claims in a judicial forum, either individually or through a class action. . . .

## Judgment and Result

The court of appeals decided that plaintiffs did not state a cause of action under the ECOA by requiring consumers to submit TILA claims to arbitration as a condition to obtaining a loan.

## Questions

1. Does the ECOA forbid creditors from forcing debtors to sign agreements to arbitrate Truth-in-Lending Act claims as a condition to obtaining a loan?
2. What difference does it make to a debtor that she has to submit a TILA claim to arbitration rather than suing on it in court?
3. Do creditors generally favor arbitration over court settlement of TILA claims? Why?
4. What philosophies of law mentioned in Chapter 1 are evidenced in the *Bowen* decision? Power? Fairness?

## BILLING ERRORS

The Fair Credit Billing Act of 1975 establishes a way for consumers to do something about credit card billing errors. It applies only to credit cards, not to other billing arrangements. Because it is a federal law, it applies in all states. If a consumer sends a written billing complaint to a creditor within sixty days of receiving the allegedly erroneous bill, that creditor must acknowledge the consumer's complaint within thirty days. The consumer's complaint to the credit card issuer must be written. The credit card issuer must either explain the alleged error in writing or correct the error within two billing cycles, but in no case more than ninety days after receiving the cardholder's complaint.

## DISCOUNTS

The Fair Credit Billing Act deals with credit card purchases. It allows a retailer who accepts credit cards to offer discounts to cash customers (those not using credit cards). This option recognizes the service fee that merchants pay to credit card companies. However, the act forbids merchants who honor credit cards to raise retail prices for cardholders over what cash customers pay without the discount. Note that the act does not require discounts for cash customers.

## CREDIT REPORTING

The Fair Credit Billing Act restricts a card issuer's reporting past due payments to third parties (for example, credit bureaus). Federal law requires a credit card issuer to inform the cardholder if and to whom it discloses a credit cardholder's past due amounts.

## FAIR DEBT COLLECTION PRACTICES ACT

The Fair Debt Collection Practices Act, which took effect on March 15, 1978, is a federal law and therefore applies in all states, the District of Columbia, and U.S. territories. The general purpose of the Fair Debt Collection Practices Act is to end abusive, deceptive, and unfair debt collection practices by debt collectors. It tries to see that people are treated fairly by debt collectors. The law does not permit debt collectors to use unjust means to collect debts. However, this act does not cancel consumer debts.

### WHAT DEBTS ARE COVERED

Only personal, family, and household debts are covered by the Fair Debt Collection Practices Act. For example, if Juan Rodriguez buys a stereo on credit for home use, his debt is a consumer debt covered by the act. However, if Juan Rodriguez buys a stereo on credit to play music in the waiting room of his advertising firm, the debt is not a consumer debt because the stereo is used for business and not personal consumption purposes. The Fair Debt Collection Practices Act does not protect business debtors. Presumably, business debtors can protect themselves.

### DEBT COLLECTORS

A debt collector (for purposes of this act only) is anyone other than the creditor who regularly collects debts for others. In other words, the Fair Debt Collection Practices Act does not apply to creditors who collect their own debts. Today it covers the creditor's attorney's collection efforts, although formerly it did not. The exception for creditors is a loophole in the Fair Debt Collection Practices Act, which is justified because of the belief that the creditor fears losing the debtor's goodwill and future business and will therefore civilize the creditor's debt collecting. Because debt collectors who collect others' debts and sell nothing themselves have no goodwill to protect, the act applies to them.

*Contacting a Debtor.* A debt collector may contact a debtor in person or by mail, telephone, or telegram. The contact may not occur at inconvenient or unusual hours, such as before 8:00 A.M. or after 9:00 P.M., or at inconvenient or unusual places unless the debtor agrees. A debt collector may not contact a debtor at work if the debtor's employer disapproves.

Within five days after the debt collector first contacts the debtor, the debt collector must send the debtor written notice telling the amount the debtor owes, who the creditor is, and what the debtor should do if the debtor believes the money is not owed.

A debt collector may not contact a debtor if the debtor sends a letter within thirty days after first being contacted, saying that no money is owed. However, a debt collector may start to collect again if the debtor is sent proof of the debt—for example, a copy of the bill.

A debt collector must stop contacting a debtor if the debtor says to do so in writing. Once a debt collector is told not to contact a person, the debt collector may no longer do so, except to confirm no further contact. Also, the debt collector may notify a debtor that some specific action may be taken, such as suing the debtor to collect, but only if the debt collector or creditor usually takes such action, that is, actually sues.

*Contacting Others about a Debtor's Bills.* Debt collectors may contact any person to locate a debtor. Debt collectors may tell people they contact only that they want to locate the debtor, not why they want to locate the debtor. The debt collector must not tell anyone that the debtor owes money. Also, the debt collector must not use a postcard or an envelope identifying the writer as a debt collector when contacting anyone while trying to locate the debtor.

*Prohibited Collection Practices.* A debtor may not harass, oppress, or abuse any person. Examples of prohibited practices include the following:

1. Using threats of violence to anyone or anyone's property or reputation
2. Publishing lists of consumers' names, saying that the consumers refuse to pay their debts (except to a credit bureau)
3. Using obscene or profane language
4. Repeatedly using the telephone to annoy anyone
5. Telephoning any person without identifying the caller
6. Advertising the debtor's debt
7. Using false statements to collect a debt, such as falsely implying that the debt collector is a U.S. or state government official or an attorney; falsely implying that the debtor committed a crime or that the creditor will seize, garnish, attach, or sell the debtor's property unless the debt collector or creditor intends to do so and it is legal to do so; saying that an action will be taken against the debtor if it can't legally be taken
8. Giving false credit information about the debtor to anyone else
9. Sending the debtor anything that looks like an official document, such as a summons and complaint, that might be sent by any court or U.S. agency, such as the Federal Trade Commission, or any state or municipal court or agency
10. Using any false name
11. Being unfair in debt collection, including the following examples:
    a. Collecting any amount greater than what the debtor owes
    b. Depositing any postdated check before the date on that check
    c. Making the debtor accept collect calls or pay for telegrams
    d. Contacting the debtor by postcard
    e. Taking or threatening to take the debtor's property unless allowed by statute
    f. Putting anything on an envelope other than the debt collector's name and address, even the debt collector's name may not be used if it shows it is about collection of a debt

Again, the prohibited practices listed apply only to **debt collectors** as defined by the act. A creditor is not a debt collector and thus is not prohibited by the act from doing any of the listed practices. However, other laws do prohibit some of these acts by creditors.

## DEBTOR CONTROL OVER SPECIFIC DEBTS

Aside from paying legal debts, the debtor has some control under the Fair Debt Collection Practices Act. If the debtor owes several debts to a single creditor, any payment made must be applied as the debtor directs. For example, the debtor may owe money for one purchase having a higher carrying charge than do other purchases. The debtor may have the creditor apply the payment to the debt with the higher carrying charge. A creditor may not apply a debtor's payment to a debt that the debtor believes is not owed.

## DEBTOR REMEDIES

If the creditor breaks the Fair Debt Collection Practices Act by doing one or more of the prohibited acts listed, the debtor may sue the creditor in state or federal court. The statute of limitations is one year. The debtor can recover damages, attorney fees, and court costs. If the creditor violates the act and injures several debtors, the act allows class actions with damage recovery up to $500,000.

## DEBTOR COMPLAINTS

The debtor can complain instead of suing. If a debt collector breaks the Fair Debt Collection Practices Act or a debtor has questions about it, the debtor may write to the FTC. The following case illustrates the Fair Debt Collection Practices Act.

---

### Venes v. Professional Service Bureau, Inc.
Court of Appeals of Minn.
353 N.W.2d 671 (1984)

### Background and Facts

Robert and Jane Venes are farmers living in Waukon, Iowa. Their farm suffered heavy financial losses. From 1975–1976, [the] Venes were forced to assign all of their income except $300 a month to the mortgage holder of the farm to prevent foreclosure. The farm operation started improving in 1977.

The Venes had major medical expenses not covered by insurance, including the birth of children in 1976 and 1978. In addition they paid bills for extended cancer treatment for both Robert Venes's father and brother. The brother died in 1978 and the father in 1980. By 1978 Venes were unable to keep up with payments owed to the Mayo Clinic for family medical bills.

The Mayo Clinic assigned a balance of $552.40 to PSB for collection. The clinic has a long-standing policy of not charging patients interest and did not authorize PSB to collect interest on the Venes account. PSB employees made a series of collection calls to Venes, starting in September 1979 and following at approximately two-week intervals.

Jane Venes testified that she received at least four calls although she told the first caller that her family did not deal with collection agencies. She hung up on one caller when his questions became detailed and prying. He immediately called back. She said the calls disrupted her work schedule and left her with the impression that PSB's object was to keep her on the telephone as long as possible to interrupt her day as much as possible.

Robert Venes received six calls. He told callers that he had not received notice of the assignment and would deal only with Mayo

Clinic. During one call a PSB employee who identified himself as "Mr. West" became abusive. He called Venes a "deadbeat" and threatened, "If you know what's good for you and your family, you'll stay out of the state of Minnesota." West refused to reveal his real name in that or subsequent calls, although Robert Venes repeatedly requested it.

In April 1980, PSB brought an action against Venes in Minnesota. The complaint sought interest on the account balance from December 14, 1977. Due to a communication problem between Venes and their Minnesota attorney, they failed to answer the complaint. A default judgment for $690, including $107 interest, was obtained and filed in Venes's home county in Iowa.

Robert Venes paid the principal amount to the Mayo Clinic and traveled to Rochester to hire another attorney to reopen the interest issue. Venes incurred attorney fees of $3,827.40 in vacating the judgment and bringing a motion for summary judgment to prevent collection of the interest. The trial court dismissed PSB's interest claim on the grounds that the Mayo Clinic does not charge patients interest as a matter of policy and that PSB has no greater rights than its assignor.

Venes subsequently brought action against PSB for violation of the Fair Debt Collection Practices Act based on the calls and PSB's suit to collect interest.

At trial Robert Venes testified that PSB's conduct had been irritating, insulting, and threatening and had angered him. He said he always had been a nervous person. He claimed the stress of the calls and the litigation aggravated his preexisting medical problems, such as migraines, ulcers, and his spastic bowel syndrome. Jane Venes confirmed that calls irritated her husband's nervous condition.

The jury awarded Venes $1,000 for out-of-pocket expenses, $3,900 for attorney fees for the prior action, and $6,000 for emotional distress. In addition, the trial court awarded $2,000 statutory damages and $1,500 attorney fees for the instant action. PSB appealed the damage awards for emotional distress, for out-of-pocket expenses, and for attorney fees incurred in the prior action.

## Body of Opinion

First, PSB challenges the award of damages for emotional distress. A consumer injured by a debt collector's failure to comply with the provisions of the Fair Debt Collection Practices Act is entitled to recover actual damages, including damages for intentional infliction of emotional distress.

The jury, by special verdict, found that PSB violated 15 U.S.C. § 1692f by attempting to collect interest not due the underlying creditor. It also found that PSB harassed Venes in violation of one or more subdivisions of 15 U.S.C. § 1692d:

(1) The use or threat of use of violence or other criminal means to harm the physical person, reputation, or property or any person.

* * *

(5) Causing a telephone to ring or engaging any person in telephone conversation repeatedly or continuously with intent to annoy, abuse, or harass any person at the called number.

* * *

(6) . . . [T]he placement of telephone calls without meaningful disclosure of the caller's identity.

The jury awarded $6,000 damages for emotional distress suffered as a result of these violations.

PSB argues that even if it violated the act, its actions were inadequate as a matter of law to justify an award of damages for emotional distress. Although the question may be a close one, we find that the evidence considered in the light most favorable to the Venes was sufficient to sustain the award. . . .

In this case PSB made a series of calls to Venes. In one a PSB employee became abusive, called Robert a "deadbeat" and threatened him to "stay out of Minnesota if you know what's good for you and your family." PSB argues that the caller's conduct was at worst in bad taste. We disagree. It was a fact question for the jury whether PSB's conduct was simple bad taste or extreme and outrageous. The jury reasonably could have found it was extreme and outrageous, particularly in light of Robert's medical problems.

In addition, PSB sought to collect interest from Venes even though the Mayo Clinic, the assigning creditor, did not charge patients interest and did not authorize PSB to do so. PSB attempted to collect interest on Venes' account even after it received notice that the principal amount was paid in full.

There was evidence at trial that each year the Mayo Clinic assigned approximately 1,500 accounts averaging $1,000 each to PSB for collection. The clinic has a published policy of not charging patients interest. It did not authorize PSB to charge interest on accounts assigned for collection. PSB was aware of the Mayo Clinic policy on interest. PSB did not inform the clinic that it was charging interest. It did not pay the clinic any of the interest it collected. PSB has continued to charge interest on some clinic accounts despite a court ruling that it is entitled to no more than its assignor.

A creditor has a right to urge payment of a just debt and to resort to proper legal procedures to enforce such payment. In this case, the jury could find that PSB exceeded its legal rights and recklessly or intentionally inflicted severe emotional distress upon Robert Venes.

Second, PSB contends that the trial court erred in submitting attorney fees for the first action to the jury as an element of actual damages in this case. The company admits that the legal fees incurred in the first action were the result of its violation of the Fair Debt Collection Practices Act, but argues: (1) Venes waived the right to collect attorney fees by not seeking them in the prior action, and (2) there is no statutory authority for treating attorney fees as actual damages. . . .

The purpose of the act, as reflected in 15 U.S.C. § 1692, is to eliminate abusive debt collection practices, to protect consumers and redress their injuries. Civil suits will deter abusive practices only if it is economically feasible for consumers to bring them. Unless consumers can recover attorney fees it may not be possible for them to pursue small claims. As Venes' attorney argued forcefully to the jury, unscrupulous collection agencies have little to fear from such suits if consumers must pay thousands of dollars in attorney fees to protect hundreds. Congress recognized this problem and specifically provided for the award of attorney fees to successful plaintiffs. 15 U.S.C. § 1692k(a)(3). It would be unfair to deny Venes attorney fees simply because they were incurred in a prior action which established the violation rather than in the instant proceeding.

## Judgment and Result

We affirm the verdict that PSB violated two provisions of the Fair Debt Collection Practices Act and affirm the award of damages for emotional distress, out-of-pocket expenses, and attorney fees for the prior action establishing one of the violations.

## Questions

1. What specific acts allegedly violated the Fair Debt Collection Practices Act?
2. What business ethics are reflected in the FDCPA?
3. How is the legal ethic of realism shown in the case?
4. Who benefits and who loses as a result of the FDCPA?

## ELECTRONIC FUND TRANSFER ACT

The U.S. Treasury Department makes millions of Social Security payments using electronic fund transfers (EFTs). Thousands of automated tellers process on average 2,000 transactions per month. A number of financial institutions have pay-by-phone services. All of these devices to transmit money are referred to as electronic fund transfers.

EFTs include several banking and payment systems that use computers and electronic technology. Such systems eliminate checks and reduce paper steps in transmitting funds, which greatly reduces transaction costs.

In 1978 Congress passed the Electronic Fund Transfer Act (EFTA), which went into effect in 1979. The EFTA, along with the regulations the Federal Reserve system promulgates under it, set out the liability rules governing EFTs. The EFTA itself defines such transfers as

[A]ny transfer of funds, other than a transaction originated by check, draft, or similar paper instrument, which is initiated through an electronic terminal, telephonic instrument, or computer or magnetic tape so as to order, instruct, or authorize a financial institution to debit or credit an account. Such term includes, but is not limited to, point-of-sale transfers, automated teller machine transactions, direct deposits or withdrawals of funds, and transfers initiated by telephone.

The definition does not include check guarantee and authorization services, or check systems involving electronic processing.

### GENERAL CONSUMER PROTECTIONS

If a consumer receives EFT services, the financial institution must disclose all of the terms, including the following:

1. The customer's liability for unauthorized transfers caused by loss or theft of the card, code, or other access device
2. Whom to call and the phone number in case of theft or loss
3. The charges for using the EFT system
4. What systems are available, including limits on frequency and dollar amounts
5. The consumer's rights to see transactions in writing
6. Ways to correct errors
7. The consumer's rights to stop payments
8. The financial institution's liability to the consumer
9. Rules concerning disclosure of account information to third parties

*Records.* The EFTA sharply reduces, but does not eliminate, the amount of paper in fund transfers. Financial institutions must give customers periodic statements describing types, amounts, dates, transferees, and locations of transfers. Timing of the periodic statements depends on the account activity and nature of the account.

Financial institutions must also notify consumers if an automatic deposit is not made as scheduled. This provision helps consumers avoid overdrawing their accounts.

*Unauthorized Use.* If the access device to the EFT system is lost, stolen, or misplaced, the EFTA limits the consumer's liability to $50 if the consumer notifies the financial institution within two business days of learning of such loss or theft. Liability limits climb to $500 if notification happens after the second business day. Finally, the consumer can have unlimited liability if notification does not occur within sixty days after receiving a periodic statement reflecting the unauthorized transfer.

*Mistakes.* Consumers discovering errors in their periodic statements must notify the financial institution within sixty days after receiving the statement. The notice can be oral or written. It must contain the following information:

- The consumer's account number and name
- The statement that an error has been made, along with an indication of the amount of the alleged error
- The reasons the consumer believes an error has been made

The financial institution has ten days to investigate the alleged error and report to the consumer, or the financial institution may credit the consumer's account and take forty-five days to investigate. If an error is discovered, the financial institution has one day to adjust the consumer's account. If no mistake has been made, however, the financial institution has to give the consumer a full, written report with conclusions.

Financial institutions failing to make transfers according to account terms are liable for all damages that the errors proximately caused. This provision assumes the account had sufficient funds to otherwise make the transfer.

*Sanctions and Damages.* If a financial institution violates the EFTA, a consumer may recover actual damages plus punitive damages of not more than $1,000 in a single action nor less than $100; in class actions the limit is the lesser of $500,000 or 1 percent of the financial institution's net worth. The EFTA has criminal sanctions. It is a federal misdemeanor for a financial institution to violate the EFTA. A $5,000 fine and up to one year's imprisonment are possible. It is a federal felony for people to fraudulently use EFT devices. Sanctions in such cases include a $10,000 fine and ten years' imprisonment.

## Criticism of the EFTA

The banking community has criticized the EFTA. The criticism centers on the absence of a fault standard in the EFTA's liability provisions. That is, even if the consumer negligently loses the EFT access device, the consumer's maximum loss is $50, assuming timely notice is given. Banks argue that consumers' incentive to be careful would increase if they had to bear the full loss for their own negligence. As it is, the financial institution incurs this loss unless it passes it on to all EFT users, in which case careful users pay for mistakes of the careless.

In the *Ognibene* case the bank transferred money from a customer's account to a con man to whom the customer had loaned his card for purposes of seeing whether the automated teller machine worked. In fact the con man worked a scam, withdrawing money from the customer's account unbeknownst to the customer. Was this transfer authorized, where the customer bore the loss, or an unauthorized transfer where the bank sustained the loss? (The con man had disappeared.) Read the *Ognibene* case to see the result.

## Ognibene v. Citibank, N.A.
Civil Court of the City of New York, Small Claims Part.
446 N.Y.S.2d 845 (1981)

### Background and Facts

Plaintiff seeks to recover $400 withdrawn from his account at the defendant bank by an unauthorized person using an automated teller machine. The court has concluded that plaintiff was the victim of a scam which defendant has been aware of for some time.

Defendant's witness, an assistant manager of one of its branches, described how the scam works: A customer enters the automated teller machine (ATM) area for the purpose of using a machine for the transaction of business with the bank. At the time that he enters, a person is using the customer service telephone located between the two automated teller machines and appears to be telling customer service that one of the machines is malfunctioning. This person is the perpetrator of the scam and his conversation with customer service is only simulated. He observes the customer press his personal identification code into one of the two machines. Having learned the code, the perpetrator then tells the customer that customer service has advised him to ask the customer to insert his Citicard into the allegedly malfunctioning machine to check whether it will work with a card other than the perpetrator's. When a good samaritan customer accedes to the request, the other machine is activated. The perpetrator then presses a code into the machine, which the customer does not realize is his own code which the perpetrator has just observed. After continuing the simulated conversation on the telephone, the perpetrator advises the customer that customer service has asked if he would try his Citicard in the allegedly malfunctioning machine once more. A second insertion of the cards permits cash to be released by the machine, and if the customer does as requested, the thief has effectuated a cash withdrawal from the unwary customer's account.

Plaintiff testified that on August 16, 1981, he went to the ATM area at one of defendant's branches and activated one of the machines with his Citibank card, pressed in his personal identification code and withdrew $20. While he did this a person who was using the telephone between plaintiff's machine and the adjoining machine said into the telephone, "I'll see if his card works in my machine." Thereupon he asked plaintiff if he could use his card to see if the other machine was working. Plaintiff handed it to him and saw him insert it into the adjoining machine at least two times while stating into the telephone, "Yes, it seems to be working."

Defendant's computer records in evidence show that two withdrawals of $200 each from plaintiff's account were made on August 16, 1981, on the machine adjoining the one plaintiff used for his $20 withdrawal. The two $200 withdrawals were made at 5:42 P.M. and 5:43 P.M. respectively; plaintiff's own $20 withdrawal was made at 5:41 P.M. At the time, plaintiff was unaware that any withdrawals from his account were being made on the adjoining machine.

The only fair and reasonable inferences to be drawn from all of the evidence are that the person who appeared to be conversing on the telephone observed the plaintiff enter his personal identification code into the machine from which he withdrew $20 and that he entered it into the adjoining machine while simulating a conversation with customer service about that machine's malfunctioning. It is conceded in the testimony of defendant's assistant branch manager that it would have been possible for a person who was positioned so as to appear to be speaking on the telephone physically to observe the code being entered into the machine by plaintiff. Although plaintiff is not certain that his card was inserted in the adjoining machine more than twice, the circumstances indicate that it was inserted four times. No issue of fraud by plaintiff or anyone acting in concert with him has been raised by defendant. Having observed plaintiff's demeanor, the court found him to be a credible witness and is of the opinion that no such issues exist in this case.

### Body of Opinion

**Judge Mara T. Thorpe.** The basic rights, liabilities, and responsibilities of the banks which offer electronic money transfer services and the consumers who use them have been established by the federal legislation contained in 15 U.S.C.A. 1693 et seq., commonly called the Electronic Fund Transfers Act (EFT). Although the EFT Act preempts state law only to the extent of any inconsistency . . . to date New York State has not enacted legislation which governs the resolution of the issues herein. Therefore, the EFT Act is applicable.

The EFT Act places various limits on a consumer's liability for electronic fund transfers from his account if they are "unauthorized." Insofar as is relevant here, a transfer is "unauthorized" if (1) it is initiated by a person other than the consumer and without actual authority to initiate such transfer, (2) the consumer receives no benefit from it, and (3) the consumer did not furnish such person "with the card, code or other means of access" to his account. . . .

In an action involving a consumer's liability for an electronic fund transfer, such as the one at bar, the burden of going forward to show an "unauthorized" transfer from his account is on the consumer. The EFT Act places upon the bank, however, the burden of proof of any consumer liability for the transfer. . . . To establish full liability on the part of the consumer, the bank must prove that the transfer was authorized. To be entitled to even the limited liability imposed by the statute on the consumer, the bank must prove that certain conditions of consumer liability, . . . have been met and that certain disclosures mandated . . . have been made.

Plaintiff herein met his burden of going forward. He did not initiate the withdrawals in question, did not authorize the person in the ATM area to make them, and did not benefit from them.

However, defendant's position is, in essence, that although plaintiff was duped, the bank's burden of proof on the issue of authorization has been met by plaintiff's testimony that he permitted his card to be used in the adjoining machine by the other person. The court does not agree.

The EFT Act requires that the consumer have furnished to a person initiating the transfer the "card, code, or other means of access" to his account to be ineligible for the limitations on liability afforded by the Act when transfers are "unauthorized." The evidence establishes that in order to obtain access to an account via an automated teller machine, both the card and the personal identification code must be used. Thus, by merely giving his card to the person initiating the transfer, a consumer does not furnish the "means of access" to his account. To do so, he would have to furnish the personal identification code as well. See 12 C.F.R. 205.2(a)(1), the regulation promulgated under the EFT Act which defines "access device" as "a card, code or other means of access to [an] . . . account or *any combination thereof*" [emphasis added].

The court finds that plaintiff did not furnish his personal identification code to the person initiating the $400 transfer within the meaning of the EFT Act. There is no evidence that he deliberately or even negligently did so. On the contrary, the unauthorized person was able to obtain the code because of defendant's own negligence. Since the bank had knowledge of the scam and its operational details (including the central role of the customer service telephone), it was negligent in failing to provide plaintiff-customer with information sufficient to alert him to the danger when he found himself in the position of a potential victim. Although in June 1981, after the scam came to defendant's attention, it posted signs in its ATM areas containing a red circle approximately 2-1/2 inches in diameter in which is written "Do Not Let Your Citicard Be Used For Any Transaction But Your Own," the court finds that this printed admonition is not a sufficient security measure since it fails to state the reason why one should not do so. Since a customer of defendant's electronic fund transfer service must employ both the card and the personal identification code in order to withdraw money from his account, the danger of loaning his card briefly for the purpose of checking the functioning of an adjoining automated teller machine would not be immediately apparent to one who has not divulged his personal identification number and who is unaware that it has been revealed merely by virtue of his own transaction with the machine.

Since the bank established the electronic fund transfer service and has the ability to tighten its security characteristics, the responsibility for the fact that plaintiff's code, one of the two necessary components of the "access device" or "means of access" to his account, was observed and utilized as it was must rest with the bank.

For the forgoing reasons and in view of the fact that the primary purpose of the EFT Act and the regulation promulgated thereunder is the protection of individual consumers . . . , the court concludes that plaintiff did not furnish his code to anyone within the meaning of the Act. Accordingly, since the person who obtained it did not have actual authority to initiate the transfer, the transfer qualities as an "unauthorized" one under 15 U.S.C.A. 1693a(11) and the bank cannot hold plaintiff fully liable for the $400 withdrawal.

To avail itself of the limited liability imposed by the act upon a consumer in the event of an "unauthorized" transfer, the bank must demonstrate (1) that the means of access utilized for the transfer was "accepted" and (2) that the bank has provided a way which the user of the means of access can be identified as the person authorized to use it. . . . One definition of "accepted" under the act is that the consumer has used the means of access. . . . Both of the foregoing conditions of liability have been met here since plaintiff used the means of access to his account to withdraw the $20 and had been given a personal identification code.

Additionally, the bank must prove that it disclosed to the consumer his liability for unauthorized electronic fund transfers and certain information pertaining to notification of the bank in the event the consumer believes that an unauthorized transfer has been or may be effected. . . . Defendant did not establish that it made such disclosures to plaintiff. Accordingly, it is not entitled to avail itself of the benefit of the limited liability for unauthorized transfers imposed upon consumers by the Act.

For the foregoing reasons, judgment shall be for plaintiff in the sum of $400.

## Judgment and Result

Plaintiff wins $400 from Citibank because Citibank transferred money from plaintiff's account without authorization.

## Questions

1. Was state or federal law the basis for regulating electronic fund transfers?
2. Must a consumer prove that an unauthorized transfer from his account has occurred? Must the bank or consumer prove the consumer authorized the transfer?
3. When the consumer turned his card over to the crook, who used it to withdraw from the consumer's account, hadn't the customer authorized the withdrawal?

## BANKRUPTCY

In our consumption-oriented society, advertising, credit availability, and peer pressure encourage us to buy in excess. Consumers overindulge. How do consumers spell relief? B-A-N-K-R-U-P-T-C-Y. Bankruptcy provides a type of consumer protection by offering a fresh start to people in debt.

The Bankruptcy Reform Act of 1978 (Bankruptcy Code) took effect on October 1, 1979. It is the first complete revision of federal bankruptcy law since 1938. (States have no bankruptcy laws.) The Bankruptcy Code provides two general types of relief for consumer debtors: (1) straight bankruptcy, which can be voluntary or involuntary, and (2) adjustment of debts of individuals with a regular income.

## STRAIGHT BANKRUPTCY

Straight bankruptcy (filed as Chapter 7 bankruptcy) refers to the process by which people turn over their property to the trustee in bankruptcy, and in return the bankruptcy court cancels their debts. This relieves people of their debts and allows them to get a fresh start. A **straight bankruptcy** lets consumer-debtors avoid their debts. These bankruptcies provide a safety valve; a relief from bad luck, bad economic conditions, bad management, or a combination of these.

Straight bankruptcy can be voluntary or involuntary. Debtors may voluntarily enter bankruptcy by filing a petition for relief. Creditors may put a debtor into involuntary bankruptcy if the debtor owes at least $5,000 in unsecured debt. Specifically, three creditors with unsecured claims of at least $5,000 can put someone into involuntary bankruptcy if twelve or more creditors have made claims, and one creditor with at least $5,000 in unsecured claims can do so. If the debtor is unable to pay debts as they mature, a court will order relief in an involuntary bankruptcy.

In straight bankruptcies, debtors turn all of their **nonexempt property** over to the bankruptcy trustee (an official of the bankruptcy court). The Bankruptcy Code lets debtors keep their **exempt property**. People can determine whether their property is exempt in bankruptcy through the federal Bankruptcy Code (law), which lists what property is exempt for bankruptcy or permits alternative state exemptions. Thus, the code lets states replace the **federal exemptions** with **state exemptions**; more than thirty states have done so thus far. State exemptions are usually less favorable to the debtor than the federal exemptions.

The debtor's nonexempt property is divided among the creditors. Not all creditors have equal rights to share the debtor's remaining property. A pecking order exists that requires all claims at a particular level to be fully paid before anything is paid to the next lower level of creditors. That order is as follows:

1. Secured creditors (those with secured claims on particular property of the debtor have first claim on that property)
2. Bankruptcy administration costs
3. Debts that the debtor's business incurs in the ordinary course of the debtor's business after an involuntary case starts but before an order for relief or trustee's appointment
4. Employee wage, salary, and commission claims (with a maximum of $2,000 multiplied by the number of employees) earned within 90 days before filing for bankruptcy
5. Claims for contributions to employee benefit plans arising from employee services within 180 days of filing for bankruptcy (maximum of $2,000 per employee)
6. Unsecured claims of grain farmers against grain elevators for grain or grain proceeds. Also, unsecured claims of $2,000 or less per individual of U.S. fishers against fish storage or fish processing plants

7. Consumer prepayments or deposits (maximum of $900 per consumer)
8. Taxes
9. General creditors (for example, those selling to the debtor on open account)

After all the creditors' claims are examined, the trustee distributes the debtor's property in accordance with these priorities. General creditors usually fare poorly, receiving about a nickel for every dollar the debtor owes them. At the end of the process, the bankruptcy judge enters an order discharging all dischargeable debts. The debtor (consumer) now has a fresh start.

## BANKRUPTCY CONSUMER PROTECTIONS

The new Bankruptcy Code provides certain protections for consumers but also places some limits on consumer bankruptcy.

*Discharge.* The **discharge** in effect cancels the debtor's debts. Technically, it bars the creditor from enforcing the debt unless the debtor reaffirms the debt. As the main reason for going bankrupt, it was a key provision under prior bankruptcy laws and is part of the new Bankruptcy Code.

*Limits on Who Can Go Bankrupt.* A consumer may voluntarily enter bankruptcy. Farmers may now file for voluntary bankruptcy.

*Difficulty in Reaffirmation of Debts.* Debtors do not want to reaffirm debts discharged in bankruptcy. When a person goes bankrupt and gets a debt discharged, a creditor often will not sell to that debtor again without a promise to pay the debts discharged in bankruptcy. This demand kills the main reason for going bankrupt. Although this tactic once was allowed and still is permitted under the new Bankruptcy Code, more procedural protections are given to the debtor. The purpose of these protections is to discourage reaffirmation.

Under the recent bankruptcy changes, the reaffirmation can take place only after the debtor's rights and the effects of reaffirmation have been fully explained to the debtor by the judge in a bankruptcy court hearing after the judge finds that reaffirmation does not impose an undue hardship on the debtor or a dependent of the debtor. Reaffirmation itself must occur before a debtor receives a bankruptcy discharge. Furthermore, the debtor may rescind the reaffirmation within sixty days after making it.

*Bankruptcy for Less-Than-Honest Debtors.* Under prior law, if a debtor lied in a loan application, got the loan, and later tried to go bankrupt to discharge the loan, bankruptcy was denied. The old rule required a debtor to be completely honest to go bankrupt. The new Bankruptcy Code limits this rule by letting the debtor go bankrupt but denying discharge for the debts about which the debtor lied to obtain, while allowing discharge for other debts.

*Limited Utility Service Cutoff.* When a debtor does not pay utility bills, the utilities cut off power or telephone service. The new Bankruptcy Code requires the bankruptcy trustee to deposit money with the utility within twenty days after entry of an order for relief. If the trustee does not provide a deposit, the utility may stop service.

*Nullification of Bankruptcy Clauses.* Bankruptcy clauses are put into contracts such as leases and provide that if a debtor files for bankruptcy, the debtor's property interest, lease, or contract ends automatically. These clauses are now invalid under the new Bankruptcy Code—another debtor protection.

*Waiver of Exemptions Not Allowed for Nonpurchase Money Security Interests.* Recall that certain of the debtor's property (exempt property) may not be taken by creditors to pay the debtor's bills. If a debtor borrows money and uses as collateral property the debtor already owns, a nonpurchase money loan is made. In other words, the debtor is not using the borrowed money to buy the collateral. If the collateral is exempt property (such as a car), creditors often require debtors to waive their exemption in the collateral as a condition to getting the loan. This is called an *exemption waiver*. It hurts debtors and helps creditors to protect consumer debtors. The Bankruptcy Code invalidates exemption waivers when exempt property is used as collateral for nonpurchase money loans.

*The Perez Doctrine.* The Perez doctrine says that state law is invalid if it penalizes or punishes people for exercising their federal bankruptcy rights. This doctrine arose from a 1965 case in which Adolpho Perez, an uninsured motorist, had an auto accident in Tucson, Arizona, that injured Miss Pinkerton. She sued him and won a $2,425.98 judgment. Perez immediately went bankrupt to escape his debts, including the accident judgment. Arizona had a statute suspending the driver's license of anyone going bankrupt to escape debts arising from auto accidents. Perez claimed that this statute violated the federal supremacy clause. The U.S. Supreme Court agreed with Perez, saying in effect that state law may not penalize a person for exercising the federal right to go bankrupt. This doctrine obviously benefits consumers.

## BANKRUPTCY LIMITS

The new Bankruptcy Code is not entirely debtor oriented. It places some limits on bankruptcy as a consumer protection. First, a consumer may obtain a straight bankruptcy only once every six years. Second, certain debts are nondischargeable—that is, they cannot be gotten rid of by going bankrupt. Such debts include taxes (state, federal, and municipal) under certain circumstances, educational loans coming due within five years of filing for bankruptcy, intentional tort judgments (e.g., assault, battery, libel, slander, or fraud), child support or alimony obligations, liability for breach of a trust or fiduciary duty, fines owed to governments, and unscheduled debts (i.e., the debtor does not list them as being owed).

*"Loading Up" with Luxury Purchases Immediately Before Filing for Bankruptcy.* Typically, before individuals file for bankruptcy they are emotionally depressed. What better way to fight "the blues" than by going on a spending spree? Buy that Cadillac, that new suit, that Caribbean cruise, and expensive meals with the idea that one is going bankrupt anyway, so these debts will be cancelled, too. The Bankruptcy Code, as amended in 1984, stops this practice by prohibiting discharge of a debtor from any debt for money, property, services if this debt was obtained by false pretenses, false representation, or actual fraud other than a statement respecting the debtor's financial condition. Consumer debts owed to a single creditor (such as a credit card company) and aggregating more than $500

for "luxury goods or services" incurred by an individual debtor on or within forty days before filing an order for relief are presumed nondischargeable. Luxury goods or services do not include goods or services reasonably acquired for the support or maintenance of the debtor or a dependent of the debtor.

The following case presents the "loading up" problem by an individual debtor who made thirty-eight separate purchases totaling $1,017.17 on her MasterCard within the forty-day period before the bankruptcy court entered the order for relief. Read the case to see which, if any, of these debts were discharged.

## In Re Tondreau

U.S. Bankruptcy Court (N.D. Indiana)
117 B.R. 397 (1989)

### Background and Facts

On April 27, 1985, Marie Madeleine Tondreau (the debtor) completed an Application for MasterCard and Cardholders Agreement requesting a MasterCard with a credit limit of $500. The Credit Union approved Marie's application on May 17, 1985, and thereafter issued a MasterCard to her. Between May 1985 and July 1986, the Credit Union raised the limit on the debtor's MasterCard account from $500 to $1,000. On July 8, 1986, the Credit Union issued a letter to her informing her that her MasterCard account exceeded the assigned limit of $1,000 by $166.83. The Credit Union further notified her that it would revoke her MasterCard privileges if she failed to bring the account within the assigned spending limit by July 18, 1986. On July 21, 1986, after the date set for revoking the debtor's credit card privileges, the Credit Union issued notice to Marie informing her that it had decided to terminate her credit card and asked her to return the MasterCard to the Credit Union. The notice listed the reasons for its action as "MasterCard Overlimit and Loan Delinquent." Marie testified at trial that she received both the July 8, 1986, letter and the termination notice from the Credit Union. She testified that upon receiving the notice from the Credit Union she understood that her MasterCard privileges were revoked.

Following the termination of her credit card privileges, the statements concerning Marie's MasterCard account reflect the following activity:

#### August 25, 1986 Statement

| | |
|---|---|
| Payments | -0- |
| New Activity | 61.77 |
| Finance Charge | 16.71 |
| New Balance | $1,165.47 |

#### September 23, 1986 Statement

| | |
|---|---|
| Payments | 270.00 |
| New Activity | -0- |
| Finance charge | 14.86 |
| New Balance | 910.33 |

#### October 23, 1986 Statement

| | |
|---|---|
| Payments | -0- |
| New Activity | 404.07 |
| Finance charge | 14.82 |
| New Balance | 1,329.22 |

#### November 24, 1986 Statement

| | |
|---|---|
| Payments | -0- |
| Credits | 375.54 |
| Adjustments | 10.00 |
| New Activity | 988.64 |
| New Balance | 1,952.32 |

At trial the debtor testified that the transactions recorded on the October 23, 1986, and November 24, 1986, statements were charge purchases for ordinary living expenses for herself, such as groceries, gasoline, cigarettes, household toiletries, car parts/service, shoes, prescriptions, eye glasses, and lumber for repairing the porch on her home. Marie had no dependents at the time she made the credit card purchases, although her boyfriend lived with her off and on during 1986 and therefore may have used some of the items purchased. Marie stated that her boyfriend made some of the purchases himself using her credit card but indicated that he did so with her permission. She explained that throughout 1986 she worked at St. Paul's Retirement Community and earned a salary of approximately $15,000 annually. She further testified that her income was sufficient to cover her living expenses until September of 1986, when she contacted an attorney about the possibility of filing a bankruptcy petition. She testified that her attorney informed her that once she filed for bankruptcy, she should no longer use any of her credit cards. Marie filed her bankruptcy petition on October 28, 1986.

### Body of Opinion

#### Robert K. Rodibaugh, Senior Bankruptcy Judge.

The issue before the court is whether any portion of the debtor's obligation to the Credit Union on her MasterCard account may be excepted from the debtor's discharge under Section 523(a)(2). This section provides in relevant part:

(a) A discharge . . . does not discharge an individual debtor from any debt—

(2) for money, property, services, or an extension, renewal, or refinancing of credit, to the extent obtained by—

(A) false pretenses, a false representation, or actual fraud, other than a statement respecting the debtor's or an insider's financial condition; . . .

(C) for purposes of subparagraph A) of this paragraph, consumer debts owed to a single creditor and aggregating more than $500 for "luxury goods or services" incurred forty days before the order for relief . . . are presumed to be nondischargeable; "luxury goods or services" do not include goods or services reasonably acquired for the support or maintenance of the debtor or a dependent of the debtor. . . .

The exception to discharge provided by Section 523 (a)(2)(A) is construed liberally in favor of the debtor and strictly against the party asserting the exception. . . . To have a debt declared nondischargeable in bankruptcy under Section 523 (a)(2)(A), the burden is on the plaintiff to prove each of five elements including:

(1) that the debtor made the representations;
(2) that at the time the representations were made he knew them to be false;
(3) that the representations were made with the intention and purpose of deceiving the creditor;
(4) that the creditor reasonably relied on the representations;
(5) that the creditor sustained the alleged injury as a proximate result of the representations having been made. . . .

The standard of review is that of clear and convincing evidence. . . . If plaintiff, however, is able to show that the debtor's obligation falls within Section 523 (a)(2)(C), the debt is presumed to be nondischargeable.

Reviewing the debtor's testimony and the other evidence presented herein, the court finds that the Credit Union has met its burden of showing that the obligations incurred on her MasterCard from September 20, 1986, to October 27, 1986, should be excepted from the debtor's discharge. The court notes that the debtor made four small purchases on her MasterCard in July of 1986. Thereafter on August 27, 1986, and September 19, 1986, the debtor made two payments on her MasterCard account in the amounts of $170 and $100, which apparently brought the account current and within the designated credit line of $1,000. Then, beginning on September 20, 1986, the debtor made thirty-eight separate purchases totalling $1,017.17 on her MasterCard within the 40-day period before the court entered the order for relief in her case. . . . The debtor made the purchases at a variety of businesses including Osco's, Baker's Shoes, Saveway Shoes, Super America, 9 West, South Bend Clinic, Joseph's Shoes, The Ridge Company, Auto Works, Seven Eleven, Hub Cap Annie, Rainbow Muffler, Williams Home Center and C&B Optical. These transactions, although individually quite small in amount (all under $50.00 but one) doubled the outstanding balance on the debtor's

MasterCard account, bringing it $952.32 over her $1,000 line of credit.

Considering the nature of the items purchased, the court concludes that most of them would not qualify as "luxury goods or services" under Section 523 (a)(2)(C). Hence, the presumption of nondischargeability set forth in Section 523 (a)(2)(C) does not apply to most of the items purchased. This conclusion, though, does not end the court's inquiry in this case. The Credit Union still has the opportunity to prove that the debtor knowingly made false representations in order to obtain an extension of credit on her MasterCard account. The court believes that the Credit Union has met its burden with respect to this issue.

Courts have considered various factors in determining whether a debtor's use of a credit card amounts to a false representation which should be excepted from the discharge under Section 523 (a)(2)(A). These factors include:

(1) The length of time between the credit card charges and the filing of the petition in bankruptcy.
(2) Whether the debtor consulted an attorney about bankruptcy before making the charges.
(3) The number of charges made.
(4) The amount of the charges.
(5) Whether the debtor made several charges on the same day or at the same store below the amount at which the seller would seek approval of the charges.
(6) Whether the charges represent an abrupt change in the debtor's use of the credit card.
(7) Whether the charges exceeded the credit limit of the account.
(8) The debtor's financial circumstances when the charges were made.
(9) Whether the debtor was employed at the time.
(10) Whether the debtor had reasonable prospects for employment or a reasonable expectation of additional income.
(11) The debtor's financial sophistication.
(12) Whether the items charged were superfluous.

. . . Another important factor to consider is whether the debtor used the credit card after receiving notice that it had been revoked.

In this case the court finds that each time the debtor used her MasterCard after she had notice that the Credit Union had revoked her account privileges, she falsely represented that she was entitled to use the MasterCard. In order to facilitate her use of the MasterCard after the Credit Union suspended her credit card privileges and her balance was well above her line of credit, the debtor made purchases under $50 which were unlikely to be detected immediately by the Credit Union since most businesses are not required to get authorization for purchases under $50. Using this system the debtor generated a total new debt to the Credit Union of $1,017.17 in just over one month's time often making several charges on the same day at the same store in amounts below $50. In doing so, the court finds the debtor knowingly violated the terms of her MasterCard account. . . .

The court believes the Credit Union has come forward with sufficient evidence to show that the debtor falsely represented the status of her MasterCard account to the various businesses where she made purchases on her MasterCard after her account had been closed.

## Judgment and Result

The bankruptcy court refused to allow the credit card purchases made within the forty-day period prior to the court's entering the order for relief to be discharged in bankruptcy. Such purchases were deemed to be made by a debtor who falsely represented that she was entitled to use her credit card, with intent to deceive the creditor, and the businesses that sold items to the debtor reasonably relied on such false representations.

## Questions

1. Were the purchases of shoes under $50 "luxury goods"? How then could the court say that such purchases were nondischargeable?
2. Was it really the "false pretense" aspect of using a credit card whose privileges had been terminated that rendered these rather small purchases nondischargeable?
3. Why should purchases made after consulting an attorney become suspect and possibly less likely to be dischargeable?
4. Does this case and bankruptcy law in general support the authors' assertion that "positive law has become the ethical ceiling in our society"?

## DEBT ADJUSTMENT (CHAPTER 13 BANKRUPTCY)

In addition to allowing straight bankruptcy, the Bankruptcy Code allows individuals to adjust their debts in which the amount owed all creditors is reduced, maturities are extended, or some combination of the two is followed. Courts sometimes let debtors adjust their debts by paying only 15 percent (or occasionally less) of their debts as payment in full. Unlike straight bankruptcy, no express limit is placed on the frequency of debt adjustment. However, bankruptcy judges have discretion to deny this type of relief.

Any individual with a regular income (even welfare or alimony income), with less than $269,250 (the amount is now indexed so it creeps up annually) in *unsecured* debt (no mortgage or security interest) and less than $807,750 (again, the amount is indexed so it changes annually in *secured* debt (a mortgage or security interest), qualifies for a debt adjustment under the Bankruptcy Code. Thus, a small, sole proprietorship (as well as a consumer) could adjust its debts.

The preceding discussion covers only some aspects of the federal Bankruptcy Code as it applies to consumers. The Bankruptcy Code's treatment of business and municipalities will not be discussed.

## 1984 AMENDMENTS AFFECTING CONSUMERS

In 1984 Congress amended the Bankruptcy Code. The amendments affect consumers going bankrupt in several ways. First, consumer-debtors owing mainly consumer debts and entering Chapter 7 (straight bankruptcy) must be advised of the availability of Chapter 13 as an alternative.

Second, the bankruptcy court has the power to dismiss Chapter 7 petitions if a debtor has demonstrated a prior or substantial abuse of the bankruptcy process.

Third, motor vehicle drivers becoming liable while legally intoxicated (drunken drivers) can no longer have such judgments discharged in bankruptcy.

Fourth, as already mentioned, consumer debtors who "load up" (buy luxury goods and services or obtain $1,000 or more in credit card cash advances right before filing for bankruptcy to maximize use of the exemptions) will find it harder to get debts for such purchases discharged. Specifically, if a debtor incurs consumer debts owed to a single creditor and aggregating more than $500 for luxury goods or services within forty days before filing for bankruptcy, such debts are presumed nondischargeable. Also presumed nondischargeable are cash advances aggregating more than $1,000 under an open-end credit plan obtained by an individual debtor on or within twenty days before filing for bankruptcy.

Fifth, in Chapter 13 cases unsecured creditors now have a veto over the plan in certain circumstances.

In early 2000, Congress considered amending the Bankruptcy Code to make it tougher in certain situations for consumers earning a substantial income to go bankrupt and escape certain debts. President Clinton promised to veto such amendments, arguing that low-income persons need the escape valve that bankruptcy provides.

## CHAPTER SUMMARY

A number of situation-specific consumer protection laws have been developed by Congress, the Federal Trade Commission, the courts, and the states.

The Federal Trade Commission has promulgated several regulations designed to protect consumers, including the bait-and-switch reg, the modification of the holder-in-due-course rule, the mail-order merchandise rule, the regulation establishing a cooling-off period for door-to-door sales, and the telemarketing rule.

Congress passed a number of statutes that protect consumers. The Consumer Product Safety Act, the Truth-in-Lending Act, the Fair Credit Reporting Act, the Equal Credit Opportunity Act, the Fair Debt Collection Practices Act, the Electronic Fund Transfer Act, and the federal Bankruptcy Code.

State laws such as the Uniform Commercial Code (UCC), Uniform Consumer Credit Code, usury laws, occupational licensing laws, and state consumer protection agencies all protect consumers.

### ▌ MANAGER'S ETHICAL DILEMMA ▌

Sanford Frederickson worked for E.F. Hutton, a company that sold investment securities in many states. Frederickson would draft a prospectus describing the investment and would then send it out to prospective investors in all twenty states. In order to make one investment opportunity more attractive, Frederickson negligently misrepresented the risk involved in certain tax shelter investments offered to Henry Blankenheim and Philip Kaefer. Frederickson stated the investments were "good"; that he had placed other clients in an earlier investment with the same people, and it was doing well; that he had his own money in this venture; that the forms Blankenheim and Kaefer were to sign to buy this stock were just administrative formalities and meant nothing; and that the reason the buyers needed to sign the purchase forms was because neither Frederickson nor E.F. Hutton was receiving commissions on this sale. The purchase forms the buyers signed contained hold-harmless provisions according to which the buyers agreed to exonerate the sellers from any loss buyers incurred on the investments and also agreed that the sellers made no representations to the buyers about the securities. The buyers bought about $230,000 in these securities from E.F. Hutton.

The investments proved unsuccessful, and Blankenheim and Kaefer lost all they had put into the tax shelters. They sued E.F. Hutton and Frederickson on a misrepresentation theory because the investments did not live up to Frederickson's representations. Frederickson and Hutton pointed out to Blankenheim and Kaefer that they were sophisticated businesspeople who knew they had signed a hold-harmless agreement. Should hold-harmless agreements exonerate businesses that negligently misrepresent what they sell to the buyers? [Blankenheim v. E.F. Hutton & Co., Inc., 266 Cal. Rptr. 563 (Cal. App. 6 Dist. 1990)]

## DISCUSSION QUESTIONS

1. You are Sally Cotter, a vice-president at First National Bank, a multistate bank that is considering expanding its offerings to small consumers. George Miracle, a new MBA, has come forward with the following proposal: First National Bank has a large consumer credit card operation. He proposes offering an insurance policy to each of these credit cardholders for $19.95 per year, which if all accepted, would generate almost $20 million in revenue for the bank. Specifically, Miracle's plan would offer to protect existing and new credit cardholders from losses if their credit cards were stolen or used without the authorization of the person whose name is on the card. His proposal would hold harmless from liability cardholders for losses above $50 if they notified the bank within three days of discovering unauthorized use of the credit card. As Miracle's superior, what do you say in response to his proposal?

2. What legal institutions have been most active in the consumer protection movement? Would a business prefer that a court, a legislature, or an administrative agency develop consumer rights? Which legal institution is generally more capable of producing sweeping, immediate social and economic changes?

3. What are the costs of consumer protection? What are the possible costs of consumer protection that consumers must bear? For example, does business have compliance costs with credit disclosure and more restrained debt collection? Who pays these costs? What would be the costs (and who would bear them) of not having consumer protection laws? Are consumer protection costs a factor no matter what is done or not done?

4. Which consumer protection laws are enforced by consumers? Which by courts? Which by administrative agencies? Of these enforcers, which is likely to be most effective? Why?

5. Consumer protection has been criticized by some as paternalistic, that is, someone or some agency is looking out for consumer interests. Should consumers look out for their own interests? Realistically, can consumers protect themselves when dealing with large businesses? Which does consumer protection help or hurt more—the ethical, fair-dealing businesses, or the unethical?

6. The Federal Bankruptcy Code protects consumers by allowing them to turn over their property to a bankruptcy trustee and in exchange receive a discharge of their bad debts. Not all debts are dischargeable through bankruptcy. For example, educational loans are not dischargeable unless they cause an undue hardship on the debtor. In one straight bankruptcy case, the debtors, Mr. and Mrs. Rice, owed $3,025 in student loans. Their monthly payment on these loans was $36. Mrs. Rice attended college for one-half semester. Mr. Rice attended college for one and one-half semesters. The Rices quit college because they lacked money and had family responsibilities. They made no effort to repay their loans. The Rices were married with four children ages 17, 15, 14, and 12, who lived at home. The children did not work. Mr. Rice was a maintenance man. Mrs. Rice was a psychiatric aide. Their combined monthly take-home pay was $1,268. Their budget showed $1,237 in expenses, leaving them $31 per month surplus if the $36 per month educational loan payment were not made. If the student loan payments were made, their monthly budget showed a $5 deficit. Should the educational loan be discharged as creating an undue hardship on the debtor? [*In re Rice*, Bankr. S.D. 13 B.R. 614 (1981)].

7. The Fair Credit Reporting Act is a federal law designed to stop the reporting of obsolete credit information used in obtaining jobs, insurance, or consumer credit. In one case brought under this act, Mr. Fite, a youth, had been convicted in 1972 in federal court of stealing government property. He was sentenced under the Youth Corrections Act, a federal law. The sentence was suspended, and he was put on one year's probation. Before the year was up Mr. Fite was unconditionally discharged and his conviction was automatically set aside. In August 1973, Mr. Fite was hired as an insurance salesman. His employer obtained a credit report from the Retail Credit Company that fairly and accurately reported Mr. Fite's arrest, conviction, and the setting aside of the conviction. He lost his job. He then tried to obtain a court order under the Fair Credit Reporting Act stopping the Retail Credit Company from reporting his arrest, conviction, and its setting aside to its customers and from maintaining any record of such facts. What was the result? [*Fite v. Retail Credit Company*, 386 F.Supp. 1045 (D. Mont. 1975)].

8. Sharpstown Dodge, Inc. sold Thornhill a van. Thornhill financed the van through Chrysler Credit Corporation. The amount financed was $4,292.38. The finance charge was $1,403.26. The total was to be repaid in 42 monthly installments. Thornhill claimed (correctly) that Sharpstown and Chrysler charged him 42 cents too much interest (that is, one penny per month too much interest). Thornhill claimed he was entitled to recover a statutory forfeiture under Texas law because of the interest overcharge. What result? [*Thornhill v. Sharpstown Dodge Sales, Inc.*, 546 S.W.2d 151 (1976)].

9. On May 27, 1980, a salesman for City Home Service, a siding and home repair company, called on

Arelenar and William James at their home in Canton, Mississippi. After giving his sales pitch for vinyl siding, the salesman completed some, but not all, blanks in an installment sales contract. The Jameses signed the contract despite its omissions and the fact that some handwritten parts could not be read. Two days later, the salesman returned with another contract. In it all blanks were filled in and readable. The Jameses signed this substitute contract covering the same siding purchase as the previous contract. After making two payments on the siding, the Jameses sued for penalties and to cut off the contract. They argued that the defects in the first contract violated the Truth-in-Lending Act. Specifically, the Jameses said the act requires contract terms to be disclosed when the contract is signed. City Home Service defended by saying the second contract signed two days later was part of one continuous deal (covering three days). City Home claimed the second contract cured any disclosure defects in the first contract. The district court agreed with City Home. The Jameses appealed. What result? [*James v. City Home Service, Inc.*, 712 F.2d 193 (5th Cir. 1983)].

10. Should a manufacturer be liable for the violation of a consumer protection regulation on the ground that the manufacturer failed to monitor the retailer's marketing practices? The parents of a two-year-old boy sued the manufacturer of a "lawn dart" made and distributed by Regent Sports Corporation under the name "Slider Jarts." The plaintiff, a little boy, was injured when the point of a lawn dart penetrated his skull and entered his brain when he walked away from his parents (unsupervised) and into the path of a lawn dart thrown by an eight-year-old girl. The dart was sold two days before this event by a Walgreen Drug store. Plaintiffs charged Regent Sports Corporation with liability under the Consumer Product Safety Act for manufacturing and distributing a product labeled "hazardous" under federal regulations. What result? [Aimone by *Aimone v. Walgreen's Co.*, 601 F.Supp. 507 (E.D. Ill. 1985)].

## INFOTRAC KEYWORDS

**Use your InfoTrac password to look up articles on http://www.infotrac-college.com**

Keywords: *consumer protection, bait and switch, telemarketing rule, Gramm–Leach–Bliley Act, Truth-in-Lending Act, Regulation Z, Fair Credit Reporting Act, Equal Credit Opportunity Act, Fair Credit Billing Act, Fair Debt Collection Practices Act, Electronic Fund Transfer Act, straight bankruptcy.*

For suggested readings, please visit this book's Web site at **http://fisher.westbuslaw.com** (click on "Internet Applications").

# MODULE 7

# Law Affecting the Manufacturing Department

# PRODUCT LIABILITY

## POSITIVE LAW ETHICAL PROBLEM

Roberto Martinez knew perfectly well that it is dangerous to try to put a 16-inch tire on a 16.5-inch rim. And even if he had not known, the prominent warning on the 16-inch Uniroyal Goodrich tire he was installing would have told him about the danger. Due to what may have been an understandable mistake, however, Martinez tried to install the 16-inch Uniroyal Goodrich tire on a 16.5-inch rim. As the warning predicted, the tire exploded when Martinez made the attempt, and he was injured.

Martinez then sued Uniroyal Goodrich for his injuries. His theory was that Goodrich could have designed the tire so as to avoid the risk he faced, and that its failure to do so made it liable. Goodrich responded by claiming, among other things, that its very conspicuous warning was sufficient to protect installers like Martinez, and should therefore protect it from liability. Who is right? That is, should the presence of an adequate warning be allowed to compensate for a less-than-safe design? Assume that a safer design was possible, and do not worry about any contributory fault on Martinez's part.

*"THE NINETEENTH-CENTURY LAW OF PRODUCT LIABILITY, SUCH AS IT WAS, EMBODIED THE PRINCIPLE OF CAVEAT EMPTOR: 'LET THE BUYER BEWARE.' TODAY THIS PRINCIPLE STRIKES MANY AS INHUMANE. PERHAPS FOR THIS REASON, TWENTIETH-CENTURY PRODUCT LIABILITY LAW EMBODIES THE OPPOSITE PRINCIPLE—CAVEAT VENDITOR, OR 'LET THE SELLER BEWARE.' AS WE ARE INCREASINGLY LEARNING, HOWEVER, THIS ISN'T TOO WONDERFUL, EITHER."*

— ANONYMOUS

Product liability law determines when manufacturers and sellers of defective goods are civilly liable to purchasers of those goods or other parties harmed by the defect.[1] Although product liability often is regarded as a consumer matter, many product liability suits are brought by businesses against other businesses that sold them defective products. This chapter first examines the most important **theories of product liability recovery**. These theories of recovery are legal rules stating the things a plaintiff must prove in order to recover damages from a seller of defective goods; sometimes plaintiffs employ several of these theories simultaneously. The chapter then discusses several legal problems that are common to the most important theories of recovery, but that often are resolved differently from theory to theory. We begin with theories of product liability recovery based on contract reasoning.

## CONTRACT THEORIES OF PRODUCT LIABILITY RECOVERY

Nineteenth-century contract law was highly individualistic. One example was freedom *of* contract—the parties' ability to set their own terms. Another was freedom *from* contract—a tendency to bind parties contractually only when they

---

[1] Chapter 22 discusses some state and federal regulations that police various aspects of consumer transactions but do not involve the recovery of damages for defective goods.

clearly expressed their willingness to be bound. For instance, sellers usually were bound only on those terms to which they had expressly assented. Indeed, some states made sellers contractually liable for defective goods only if they used words like "warrant" or "guarantee" while describing those goods.

Today, things are quite different. Now sellers can be bound on the basis of implied promises about their goods—promises created not by words, but by operation of law. When this happens, government denies traditional freedom of contract by dictating contract terms. In addition, now it is much easier for sellers to be bound on express statements that they make. In fact, the range of things considered "express statements" has expanded considerably. For all these reasons, modern sellers are less "free from" contractual liability, too.

Today, there are three important contract-based theories of product liability recovery. Each involves a product **warranty**: a promise regarding the nature of the product sold. In a breach-of-warranty suit, the plaintiff claims that the product failed to conform to the seller's promise. Today this promise may be *express* (made in words or in some behavior from which a verbal promise can be inferred) or *implied* (created by operation of law). Thus, we have an **express warranty** theory of recovery and two implied warranty theories—the **implied warranty of merchantability** and the **implied warranty of fitness for a particular purpose**.

Each of these three warranty theories is created by Article 2 of the **Uniform Commercial Code** (the UCC or Code). The UCC is a uniform act drafted by legal scholars and practitioners and eventually enacted in much the same form by the states. Article 2 of the Code governs the **sale of goods**; other transactions usually are controlled by the common law of contracts. Goods basically are movable things. Services and real estate do not qualify, although most kinds of farm products and other foodstuffs are regarded as goods. In determining whether a contract is for the sale of goods, various borderline situations arise. One problem concerns services in which goods play a role—for example, hair or beauty treatments, or the installation of an automobile battery. In such cases, the test for applying Article 2 is whether the good is the dominant part of the transaction. The installation of a car battery, for instance, probably is a sale of goods, but for a hair or beauty treatment the service element probably predominates.

## EXPRESS WARRANTY

The term *express warranty* usually means a warranty that the seller states in actual words, whether written or oral. The Code's express warranty provision, however, also includes certain conduct from which a verbal promise can be inferred. UCC Section 2-313(1) says that a seller can create an express warranty by (1) making any affirmation of fact or promise regarding the goods sold, (2) making any description of such goods, or (3) providing a sample or model of such goods. A seller is liable for breach of express warranty when its products fail to conform to an affirmation, description, sample, or model it has made or given.

*Affirmations and Descriptions.* Any affirmation of fact or promise involving the goods can create an express warranty. For example, a seller who states or promises that a truck can or will handle a 5,000-pound load normally creates an express warranty to that effect. Closely related to this first means of creating an express warranty is the second: making a description of goods sold. A description includes statements that goods are of a certain brand, type, or model (e.g., that a vehicle is a "Nissan Pathfinder LE"); descriptive adjectives characterizing the product (e.g., "radial" tires); and drawings, blueprints, or technical specifications. Also, the statement in the following *Daughtrey* case probably is best classed as a description. Neither an express warranty by fact or promise nor an express warranty by description requires that the seller use such formal words as *warrant* or *guarantee*. Also, each warranty can be either written or oral.

Although the line between the two groups is hazy, it is important to distinguish (1) affirmations of fact or promise and descriptions from (2) statements of value or opinion and statements that amount to sales talk or puffing. Statements of the second kind are not express warranties. For example, a seller who represents a boat's value by telling the buyer that "You could resell this boat next year for $5,000" or who says, "In my opinion, this boat will hold up for five years," normally is not liable if the statement turns out to be false. Sellers also may make statements of value or opinion when they make a more or less definite assertion about a subject that is inherently a matter of judgment; the seller's statement about the grade of a diamond in *Daughtrey* might be an example. But *Daughtrey* also asserts that in such cases and others, courts are more likely to conclude that an express warranty exists if the seller is knowledgeable about the goods sold and the buyer is not.

Sellers also do not make express warranties when they engage in sales talk or puffing. For example, sellers ordinarily are not liable for statements such as, "I know you'll be happy with this boat," or, "Boats like this one have traditionally been known for quality."

*Samples and Models.* The third way for a seller to create an express warranty is by giving a sample or model of the goods to be sold. A sample is an object taken from the actual collection of goods that the seller intends to sell, while a model is a replica offered for inspection when the actual goods are not available. Where either a sample or a model is given, there is an express warranty that the remaining goods conform to the sample or the model.

*The Basis-of-the-Bargain Requirement.* All three express warranties identified by Section 2-313(1) must be "part of the basis of the bargain." The meaning of this phrase is unclear. Before enactment of the UCC, the buyer had to actually—and strongly—rely on the warranty in order to recover. Some courts still interpret the UCC's basis-of-the-bargain test as requiring some significant degree of reliance by the buyer. Others only require that the warranty be a factor in the buyer's decision to purchase. Presumably, this means some lesser degree of reliance than required by pre-Code law. The *Daughtrey* case does not require any reliance on the buyer's part; it seems to bind the seller to all statements that otherwise qualify as express warranties.

*Advertisements and the Like.* Statements in advertisements, catalogs, brochures and so forth can be express warranties. But they may not be part of the basis of the bargain where it is unclear whether or how much the buyer relied on the statement in making the purchase—for example, where an ad appeared well before the sale. Also, advertisements often are filled with sales talk.

## Daughtrey v. Ashe
Supreme Court of Virginia
413 S.E.2d 336 (1992)

### Background and Facts

W. Hayes Daughtrey contacted Sidney Ashe, a jeweler, about the purchase of a diamond bracelet for his wife. Ashe showed Daughtrey a diamond bracelet that he offered to sell for $15,000. His only description of the bracelet when talking to Daughtrey was to call it "nice." When Daughtrey later phoned Ashe to say that he would buy the bracelet, Ashe completed an appraisal form containing the following language:

| DESCRIPTION | APPRAISED VALUE |
|---|---|
| platinum diamond bracelet, set with 28 brilliant full ct diamonds weighing a total of 10 carats. H color and v.v.s. quality. | $25,000.00 |

The term v.v.s. is one of the highest quality ratings for diamonds.

Daughtrey eventually bought the bracelet. However, he never saw the appraisal form before the sale, because Ashe placed it inside the box containing the bracelet. Later, Daughtrey discovered that the diamonds in the bracelet were not of v.v.s. quality. He demanded that Ashe replace the bracelet with a bracelet containing diamonds of that quality, but Ashe only offered to refund the purchase price upon Daughtrey's return of the bracelet. Because diamonds had increased in value since the sale, Daughtrey refused. Then he sued Ashe for breach of an alleged express warranty that the bracelet contained v.v.s. diamonds. The trial court denied Daughtrey's claim and Daughtrey appealed.

### Body of Opinion

**Justice Whiting.** Ashe contends that his statement of the grade of the diamond is a mere opinion and thus cannot qualify as an express warranty. . . . However, here, Ashe did more than give a mere opinion of the value of the goods; he specifically described them as diamonds of "H color and v.v.s. quality." Ashe did not qualify his statement as a mere opinion. And if one who has superior knowledge makes a statement about the goods sold and does not qualify the statement as his opinion, the statement will be treated as a statement of fact. Nor does it matter that the opinions of other jewelers varied in minor respects. All of them said, and the trial judge found, that the diamonds were of a grade substantially less

than v.v.s. . . . Given these considerations, we conclude that Ashe's description of the goods was more than his opinion; rather [it was] a statement of fact.

Next, Ashe maintains that because the description of the diamonds as v.v.s. quality was not discussed, Daughtrey could not have relied upon Ashe's warranty, and thus it cannot be treated as "part of the basis of the bargain." In our opinion, the "part of the basis of the bargain" language of UCC Section 2-313 does not establish a buyer reliance requirement. Instead, this language makes a seller's description of the goods that is not his mere opinion a representation that defines the obligation. . . . We conclude from the language used in Section 2-313 and the Official Comment thereto that the drafters of the Uniform Commercial Code intended to modify the traditional requirement of buyer reliance on express warranties. . . . We note that "induce" and "reliance" appear nowhere in Section 2-313, as contrasted with the reference to buyer reliance in the subsequent Section, UCC Section 2-315, dealing with an implied warranty of fitness for a particular purpose. . . .

Ashe introduced no evidence of any factor that would take his affirmation of quality out of the agreement. Therefore, his affirmation was a part of the basis of the bargain. Accordingly, we hold that Daughtrey is entitled to recover for his loss of bargain.

### Judgment and Result

Trial court judgment in Ashe's favor reversed. Case returned to the trial court for a determination of Daughtrey's damages.

### Questions

1. Why was Ashe not liable for his statement that the bracelet was "nice?"
2. In the text, we suggested that statements of opinion may include more or less definite assertions about matters that are inherently subject to judgment, and that a statement about the grade of a diamond may qualify. Why did the court conclude that Ashe's statement about the grade of the diamond was not a statement of opinion?
3. According to the Virginia Supreme Court, what does the basis-of-the-bargain requirement mean?

## IMPLIED WARRANTY OF MERCHANTABILITY

An implied warranty is a contractual promise arising by operation of law. Implied warranties represent government intervention to dictate the terms of a contract; they exist because the law says they exist. Implied warranties regarding the sale of goods have been created because legislatures and courts believe that consumers need additional legal protection against sellers with whom they cannot deal on equal terms. One important implied warranty in Article 2 of the UCC is the implied warranty of merchantability created by Section 2-314. That section states: "a warranty that the goods shall be merchantable is implied in a contract for their sale if the seller is a merchant with respect to goods of that kind."

*The Merchant Requirement.* Note from the language just quoted that for the implied warranty of merchantability to exist, the seller must be a **merchant** rather than a casual, one-time seller. For our purposes, the term *merchant* includes two kinds of sellers. The first involves those who regularly deal in products of the kind at issue in the case. Drug stores, hardware stores, and car dealers are examples. Thus, the implied warranty of merchantability does not accompany a business law professor's sale of a used car. The second kind of merchant includes people who regularly perform services involving the provision or installation of goods. Electricians, plumbers, carpenters, and heating supply contractors are examples.[2] In both cases, finally, the seller must be a merchant with respect to goods of the *kind sold*. For instance, Section 2-314 does not cover the sale of a used car by a sporting goods store.

*What Is Merchantability?* If the seller is a merchant with respect to the goods sold, those goods carry an implied warranty that they are merchantable. What qualities must the goods possess in order to meet this test? UCC Section 2-314(2) states that such goods must at least (1) pass without objection in the trade under the contract description; (2) in the case of fungible goods, be of fair average quality; (3) be fit for the ordinary purposes for which such goods are used; (4) be of even kind, quality and quantity within each unit (e.g., case, package, or carton) and among all such units; (5) be adequately contained, packaged, and labeled as the agreement may require; and (6) conform to any promises or affirmations of fact made on the container or label. The following *Keaton* case involves the third and fifth of these requirements.

The most important merchantability requirement is Section 2-314's command that the goods be fit for the ordinary purposes for which such goods are used. This requirement often is interpreted to mean that the goods must meet the reasonable expectations of the average consumer. This type of broad, discretionary test is almost inevitable, given the wide range of products sold today and the even wider range of defects they can present. As a result, implied warranty of merchantability cases often are decided on the basis of their particular facts.

Sometimes it is easy to determine whether goods satisfy the reasonable-consumer-expectation test. This is most true where they fail to perform properly or have harmful side effects in their ordinary uses. For example, an adhesive that fails to bind or that corrodes the things it touches is not merchantable. On the other hand, goods do not have to be perfect to be merchantable. In some cases, courts rely on prevailing industry practices or government health and

---

[2] However, note that the problem of Article 2's application to mingled goods/services situations may arise here.

safety regulations in formulating the merchantability standard. Finally, some courts, like the *Keaton* court, say that there is no implied warranty of merchantability recovery for obvious or reasonably discoverable defects.

Other situations present more difficult problems. One such problem arises where the harm caused by the defect is improbable. In cases involving an allergic reaction to the product, for example, courts often find that there was a breach of the implied warranty of merchantability where it was reasonably foreseeable that an appreciable number of people would suffer the reaction. Another problem involves sales of contaminated food or drink. Here, different courts have applied different merchantability standards. Under the foreign-natural test, the plaintiff recovers when the thing causing the injury is foreign to the food product in question (e.g., an open safety pin in a serving of fish), but not when it is natural to the food product (e.g., a fishbone in a serving of fish). Today, however, most courts use the standard reasonable consumer expectations test in this situation.

## Keaton v. A.B.C. Drug Co.
Georgia Supreme Court
467 S.E.2d 558 (1996)

### Background and Facts

Marilyn Keaton entered an A.B.C. Drug Company (ABC) store to buy laundry detergent and liquid bleach. After picking up some detergent, she proceeded to the bleach aisle, where bottles of bleach were stacked to a height above her eye level. Keaton reached up, grasped the handle of a half-gallon bottle of bleach, and began pulling it down from the shelf. As she did so, bleach splashed onto her face, causing injury to one of her eyes. The cause of the injury was a loose cap on the bottle. Keaton did not see that the cap was loose.

Keaton sued ABC under the implied warranty of merchantability in a Georgia trial court. After the jury found in her favor, the trial court denied ABC's motion for judgment notwithstanding the verdict. However, a Georgia intermediate court of appeals reversed the trial court's decision. Keaton then appealed to the Georgia Supreme Court.

### Body of Opinion

**Chief Justice Benham.** Keaton alleged a claim of breach of implied warranty under [UCC Section 2-314(2)(c)], asserting that the bleach container was not fit for the ordinary purposes for which it was intended. There was evidence presented at trial regarding the elements required to prove a claim under subsection (c), but also regarding the elements required to prove a claim under subsection (e), which provides a claim for breach of implied warranty if a product is defective via its container or packaging. We conclude that the jury was authorized to find that ABC, as a merchant of bleach, was required to adequately contain and package the bleach that it sold. Because bleach which spills via a loose cap is

not adequately contained or packaged, a claim under subsection (e) is supported. Because we hold that the evidence presented at trial supported a claim under subsection (e), under the right-for-any-reason theory, it is unnecessary for us to review the claim under subsection (c). . . .

Keaton's claim . . . is not defeated by an alleged failure to exercise care for her own safety. . . . The [Georgia] Court of Appeals has held that the law of implied warranty will not avail against patent defects, nor against latent defects which are either disclosed or are discoverable by the exercise of caution on the part of the purchaser. The bleach in this case was located at a height above Keaton's eye level, and it is undisputed that the top was not off [and that there was nothing] noticeably wrong with the bottle. Therefore, there was no patent or obvious defect. It was a jury question whether Keaton failed to exercise caution for her own safety.

### Judgment and Result

Intermediate appellate court decision reversed; Keaton wins.

### Questions

1. What would the result have been if Keaton had seen the loose bottle cap? What result if she should have seen it?
2. Which two merchantability definitions did the court consider here? On which did it base its decision? Did the court say that Keaton could not recover under the version it rejected?
3. What do you think that the court meant when it invoked the "right-for-any-reason theory?"

## IMPLIED WARRANTY OF FITNESS

UCC Section 2-315 provides that: "[w]here the seller at the time of contracting has reason to know any particular purpose for which the goods are required and that the buyer is relying on the seller's skill or judgment to select or furnish suitable goods, there is . . . an implied warranty that the goods shall be fit for such purpose." Section 2-315 first requires that the seller have reason to know the particular purpose for which the buyer desires the goods. In many 2-315 cases, the buyer clearly makes his or her needs known. But since the test is the seller's reason to know, the seller may be liable where the buyer's purpose is evident from the surrounding facts and circumstances even though it is not openly disclosed. Second, the seller must have reason to know that the buyer is relying on the seller's skill or judgment to select suitable goods. Third, a Code drafters' comment to Section 2-315 states that the buyer must actually rely on the seller's skill or judgment. Once these tests are met, the goods then carry an implied warranty that the goods are fit for the buyer's particular purposes.

The last two requirements pose few problems where the buyer asks for a product that will perform in certain ways and declares that it is up to the seller to select such a product. However, they are difficult to satisfy where the buyer is more knowledgeable than the seller, insists upon a certain brand, submits specifications for the goods to be purchased, or actually selects them. Recovery also is unlikely where the buyer conducts its own test of the product and bases its purchase decision on those tests.

How does the implied warranty of fitness differ from the implied warranty of merchantability? For one thing, the seller must be a merchant for the implied warranty of merchantability to exist, but there is no merchant requirement under the implied warranty of fitness. Secondly, the implied warranty of merchantability requires only that the goods be fit for their *ordinary* purposes, while the fitness warranty says that the goods must be fit for the buyer's *particular* purposes. For example, if a novice camper goes to a sporting goods store, requests a sleeping bag suitable for temperatures as low as minus 20 degrees Fahrenheit, and is sold a bag perfectly suitable for normal use but not for the requested temperature, an implied warranty of fitness claim can be made, but not a claim based on the implied warranty of merchantability. However, if the sleeping bag is totally defective and thus worthless for any purpose, the plaintiff can use both implied warranties. Finally, the implied warranty of fitness arises in a less common situation than the implied warranty of merchantability: basically, the case where the buyer has put himself in the seller's hands by making his needs known and requesting that the seller select suitable goods.

The *Sportmart* case on page 655 elaborates upon the distinction between the ordinary and the particular purposes for which goods are sold. It holds that, for an implied warranty of fitness claim to exist, there must actually be a "particular purpose" for which the goods were sold.

## TORT THEORIES OF PRODUCT LIABILITY RECOVERY

Besides freedom of contract and limited liability, nineteenth-century economic individualism also had implications for tort law. The most important such implication was the principle of "no liability without fault." Like the contract

## Sportmart, Inc. v. Spirit Manufacturing Co.
Northern District of Illinois
1999 U.S. Dist. LEXIS 7556 (1999)

### Background and Facts

Sportmart, Inc., a sporting goods retailer, contracted with the Spirit Manufacturing Company, a manufacturer of exercise equipment, for Spirit to build treadmills to be sold under a private Sportmart label. The electric motors for the treadmills were manufactured by the Baldor Electric Company. Due to defects in many of the motors, Sportmart experienced a large number of customer complaints about, and returns of, the treadmills built by Spirit. Eventually, Sportmart sued Spirit under, among other things, the implied warranties of merchantability and fitness for a particular purpose. Then Sportmart moved for summary judgment on these two claims.

### Body of Opinion

**District Judge Leinenweber.** Under the implied warranty of merchantability, goods must be "fit for the ordinary purposes for which such goods are used". . . . The court finds, for the reasons discussed [in the Background and Facts] above, that a significant percentage of the treadmills were not fit for the ordinary purposes for which treadmills are used, and therefore Spirit breached the implied warranty of merchantability.

Sportmart's [other] count is for breach of the implied warranty of fitness for a particular purpose. This implied warranty applies where the "seller at the time of contracting has reason to know any particular purpose for which the goods are required and that the buyer is relying on the seller's skill or judgment to select or furnish suitable goods." Sportmart argues that the treadmills were sold for residential use only, therefore satisfying the "particular purpose" requirement. Further, Sportmart alleges [that] its purpose in buying the treadmills differed from the ordinary retail situation because Spirit knew that Sportmart intended to place its reputation on the line by marketing the treadmills under its own private label. Spirit responds that Sportmart's purpose in buying the treadmills was the ordinary purpose of buying treadmills for resale to retail customers. As Sportmart cannot show that it had a "particular purpose" for the goods, Spirit argues, the warranty of fitness for a particular purpose does not apply.

The court finds that the implied warranty of fitness does not apply to this situation. The comments to the Uniform Commercial Code explain the difference between "particular purpose" and "ordinary purpose" using shoes as an example. "Shoes are generally used for the purpose of walking upon ordinary ground, but a seller may know that a particular pair was selected to be used for climbing mountains." The court finds that Spirit's sale of the treadmills to Sportmart is analogous to selling shoes for walking on ordinary ground. Sportmart acknowledges that it purchased the treadmills for the purpose of reselling them to its retail customers, who in turn planned to use them for exercising at home. The court finds that both Sportmart's intended use and the retail customers' intended use are the ordinary uses one would expect from a sporting goods store and a retail purchaser of treadmills. Further, the court fails to see how Spirit's knowledge that the treadmills would bear Sportmart's label changes their intended use. Whether the treadmills were marketed under [Sportmart's] label or a different name, Sportmart purchased the treadmills for the same purpose, namely resale to retail customers for their use as exercise equipment. The court finds that summary judgment for Sportmart is not appropriate for [this count]. Further, the court finds that Spirit is entitled to judgment in its favor on this count as a matter of law.

### Judgment and Result

The court granted Sportmart's motion for summary judgment on the implied warranty of merchantability count, but denied it on the implied warranty of fitness count. It went on to hold for Spirit on the latter count.

### Questions

1. Why did the court spend little time discussing Sportmart's implied warranty of merchantability claim?
2. It looks as if Baldor Electric is the party truly at fault here. Even so, Baldor's fault is irrelevant to Sportmart's implied warranty claims against Spirit. Why is this so?
3. From the facts given, do you think that Spirit could recover against Baldor under the implied warranty of merchantability?
4. Suppose that Sportmart were to sue Baldor under the implied warranty of merchantability. (In fact, it did just that in an Arkansas state court.) What legal problem would such a suit create? Check out the remainder of the chapter.

---

tendencies discussed earlier, this meant limited liability for sellers of defective goods. Another reason for this limited liability, some say, was the perceived need to promote industrialization by protecting infant manufacturing industries. If such industries had been required to pay their way by compensating everyone injured by their products, the argument runs, their profitability would have been endangered, their survival imperiled, and the country's industrialization retarded.

By now, however, the industrial system's survival is not an issue and the old no-liability-without-fault mentality has bitten the dust. The most important example of this new mentality is the emergence of **strict liability**—liability without fault—in the product liability sphere. But there are other reasons for strict liability's emergence—reasons represented by the terms *risk spreading* and *socialization of risk*. Imposing strict product liability on sellers and manufacturers helps protect consumers, but it imposes additional costs on those businesses. Because they are subject to increased liability, they must self-insure or purchase liability insurance. But if most competitors are in roughly the same boat, they can pass on these costs to consumers in the form of higher prices. Thus, the economic losses caused by defective goods are spread out or "socialized" by imposing those costs on the people who benefit from strict liability.

Negligence law has long been available to parties who sue for injuries and other losses caused by defective goods. Beginning mainly in the 1960s, however, negligence was supplemented by the emergence of strict product liability.[3] The most important version of strict product liability was the rule stated by Section 402A of the *Restatement (Second) of Torts*.[4] Section 402A was promulgated by the American Law Institute in 1965, and adopted by many states thereafter. In 1998, the American Law Institute published a *Restatement (Third) of Torts—Products Liability*. The authors of the new *Restatement* apparently wished to avoid traditional labels like *negligence* and *strict liability*. Because most states still adhere to negligence and Section 402A, however, we discuss these traditional theories first. Then we examine the *Restatement (Third)*, which may represent the future evolution of product liability law.

## Negligence

In product liability cases based on a seller's or manufacturer's alleged negligence, plaintiffs must prove a **breach of duty** on the defendant's part. This normally means that the defendant failed to act as a reasonable person would have acted under the circumstances. In product liability cases, this most often happens where the defendant failed to (1) properly manufacture, package, or handle the goods; (2) make an adequate inspection of the goods; (3) provide an adequate warning of hazards associated with the goods; or (4) properly design the goods.

*Improper Manufacture, Packaging, Handling, or Inspection.* Negligence suits alleging a manufacturer's careless construction, handling, or inspection of the goods often pose problems for plaintiffs, because evidence of the breach usually is under the defendant's control. However, the doctrine of **res ipsa loquitur** discussed in Chapter 10 sometimes helps plaintiffs establish a breach of duty.

---

[3] Negligence and strict liability are discussed in Chapter 10.

[4] The *Restatements* are statements of common law (and occasionally statutory) rules authored by the American Law Institute, a body of distinguished legal scholars and practitioners. The *Restatements* are not legally binding by themselves, but they often influence courts. It is not uncommon for state courts to adopt *Restatement* rules within their states.

Cases alleging a wholesaler's or retailer's negligent failure to inspect involve different considerations. Most states hold that such intermediaries have no duty to inspect goods sold them by another party, unless they knew or had reason to know of defects in those goods. In addition, there generally is no duty to inspect where this would be unduly difficult, burdensome, or time-consuming. Unless a defect is obvious or virtually certain to occur, therefore, there is no duty to inspect a product that is packaged in a sealed container which is not to be opened before the sale.

However, where an intermediary is not merely a conduit for the goods but is actively involved in their preparation or installation, it is liable for a failure to spot defects that are reasonably discoverable from the preparation or installation work done. A car dealer, for example, may be liable for the failure to discover defects that are reasonably apparent from its normal handling of a car that it offers for sale.

Finally, where either manufacturers or intermediaries have a duty to inspect and a reasonably discoverable defect exists, other duties may arise. Depending on the circumstances, such defendants may be required to warn purchasers of the defect, to repair the product, or simply not to sell it.

*Duty to Warn.* Courts consider many factors when determining whether a seller or manufacturer has a duty to give buyers and users of its products a suitable warning of risks associated with those products. The first and most important is whether harm is foreseeable. Another is the severity or magnitude of this foreseeable harm. Yet another is whether a warning is likely to be effective in reducing the risk of harm. A further factor is the burden that providing a warning imposes on the seller or manufacturer. Finally, courts often consider whether the buyer or user is likely to realize the danger. For this reason, there ordinarily is no duty to warn about obvious product dangers. A sporting goods store, for example, need not warn buyers that hunting knives are dangerously sharp.

A warning's suitability is decided on a case-by-case basis. This same is true for a related question: Which parties is the seller required to warn? For example, is a drug manufacturer required to warn physicians, patients, or both? Finally, in two situations even a perfectly suitable and thoroughly communicated warning may not protect a seller from negligence liability. First, the warning may be of no avail to the seller if it could feasibly make the product safe for its foreseeable uses. Second, a warning may not protect a seller who markets a product that is extremely unsafe even with the warning.

*Design Defects.* Even if a product is manufactured according to specifications, it may pose an unacceptable risk of harm because of its faulty design. Thus, manufacturers generally have a duty to design their products so that they are safe for any reasonably foreseeable use. However, other factors besides the reasonable foreseeability of harm and the severity of that harm help determine the manufacturer's design duty. One factor working in the defendant's favor in design defect cases is the product's compliance with government product safety standards. Another is the design's similarity to the design of similar products in the industry at the time of the sale. Yet another is that the product embodies the contemporary state of the art (the state of existing scientific and technical knowledge). A further consideration benefiting manufacturers is the product's social utility. Defendants sometimes escape liability in situations where making the product safer would cause a significant reduction in its social value. In some cases of this kind, courts may consider the safety and effectiveness of alternative designs and the cost of safer designs.

## STRICT LIABILITY

Strict liability is liability irrespective of fault. By now, some form of strict product liability has been adopted by most states. These states usually employ Section 402A of the *Restatement (Second) of Torts*. Section 402A exemplifies the demise of the nineteenth-century principle of no liability without fault. Where sellers and manufacturers are able to pass on the costs that Section 402A imposes, it also facilitates risk-spreading or socialization of risk.

*The Requirements of Section 402A.* Section 402A states: "One who sells any product in a defective condition unreasonably dangerous to the user or consumer or to his property is subject to liability . . . if (a) the seller is engaged in the business of selling such a product, and (b) it is expected to and does reach the user or consumer without substantial change in the condition in which it is sold." This rule applies even though "the seller has exercised all possible care in the preparation and sale of his product." Thus, Section 402A imposes strict liability on certain product sellers. If the section's tests are met, those sellers are liable no matter how careful their behavior, and plaintiffs need not prove a breach of duty.

However, Section 402A applies only in certain circumstances. First, the seller must be engaged in the business of selling the product that harmed the plaintiff. This test resembles UCC Section 2-314's merchant requirement. Thus, Section 402A does not cover occasional sales by those not regularly selling the product as a business. A housewife's twice-a-year sales of home-grown vegetables or a used car dealer's sale of camping equipment, for instance, are not within Section 402A. Second, the product must be one that is expected to reach the consumer without substantial change in its condition, and in fact does reach the consumer without undergoing any such change. This requirement protects sellers from liability where their products were substantially modified before reaching the plaintiff and the modification helped cause the plaintiff's injury.

The key problem under Section 402A is determining whether the product was in a defective condition that made it unreasonably dangerous to the user or consumer or to that person's property. The defective condition requirement, which resembles UCC Section 2-314's test of fitness for the goods' ordinary purposes, often is defined by the reasonable expectations of the average consumer. But for Section 402A to apply the product also must be unreasonably dangerous. This means that it must have some significant and unexpected capacity to cause personal injury or property damage. For instance, butter is not unreasonably dangerous because it contains cholesterol, but it would be so regarded if it is contaminated with lead. Due to the unreasonably dangerous requirement, Section 402A covers a narrower range of product defects than the implied warranty of merchantability. A coffee maker that simply fails to operate should not create 402A liability, but a coffee maker that short-circuits and causes a fire probably would. However, some courts have dispensed with the unreasonably dangerous requirement, or blurred it together with the defective condition requirement in various ways.

*Design Defects and Failure to Warn.* Courts routinely allow failure-to-warn and design defect cases to be brought under Section 402A. As the following *Port Authority* case illustrates, the factors considered in such cases resemble those considered in negligence cases involving an alleged failure to warn or defective design. This is true even though Section 402A is supposed to be a strict liability provision for which the defendant's fault is irrelevant.

*Unavoidably Unsafe Products.* Should strict liability apply where the defendant markets a product that is likely to harm a certain number of people, but that also does considerable good and that cannot be made safer without sacrificing that utility? Examples might include some of the drugs used to treat cancer or AIDS. In such cases, defendants may be able to use the "unavoidably unsafe product" defense set out in comment k to Section 402A. Comment k says that such "unavoidably unsafe products," if properly prepared and accompanied by proper directions and a proper warning, are not defective or unreasonably dangerous. Under the "learned intermediary" doctrine, drug manufacturers normally may rely on the prescribing physician to warn the ultimate consumer about the risks of a prescription drug.

*Wholesalers and Retailers.* Section 402A covers wholesalers, retailers, and other parties down the chain of distribution when they sell products that are unreasonably dangerous because of manufacturing defects. This is true even if such parties were in no way at fault. However, some states protect such intermediaries by statute. Typically, such laws immunize these intermediaries from liability if (1) the plaintiff can get state court jurisdiction over the responsible manufacturer, and (2) the manufacturer is neither insolvent nor likely to become so.

## Port Authority of New York and New Jersey v. Arcadian Corporation
U.S. Court of Appeals (Third Circuit)
189 F.3d 305 (1999)

### Background and Facts

On February 26, 1993, terrorists detonated an explosive device under the World Trade Center, causing six deaths, many injuries, and massive property damage. Among the ingredients contained in this bomb were ammonium nitrate and urea designed, manufactured, and marketed by the Arcadian Corporation and two other firms. These substances were sold to be used as fertilizer and were not explosive in themselves, but the terrorists made them explosive through the addition of various easily obtainable substances. Indeed, ammonium nitrate and urea had displayed their explosive potential on a few occasions in the past. The two most important examples were an accidental ammonium nitrate explosion during the 1940s in Texas City, Texas, and the bombing of a University of Wisconsin building by anti-Vietnam War protesters during the 1960s. Although it was possible to reduce, if not eliminate, the explosive properties

of such fertilizer products through certain chemical means, the defendants did not do so.

The owner of the World Trade Center, the Port Authority of New York and New Jersey, sued Arcadian and the other two firms in a New Jersey trial court. The Port Authority made three claims: (1) that the defendants negligently failed to design and manufacture their fertilizer products in such a way as to reduce or eliminate their explosive potential; (2) that the defendants were strictly liable because the products were defective and unreasonably dangerous when sold; and (3) that the defendants failed to warn the distributors who bought those products that they could be modified to become explosive, and failed to instruct the distributors to ensure that subsequent purchasers had legitimate reasons for buying the products. After the case was removed to federal district court, the court dismissed the plaintiffs' complaint for failure to state a claim upon which relief could be granted. The plaintiffs appealed to the Third Circuit Court of Appeals.

## Body of Opinion

**Circuit Judge Roth.** The district court found it was not necessary to make a determination whether New York or New Jersey law applies to the complaint. Instead, the district court determined that the complaint failed to state a claim under the law of either state. . . . Because we agree that dismissal is required under both New Jersey and New York law, we similarly need not decide the choice-of-law issue. . . .

Under New Jersey law negligence is no longer viable as a separate claim for harm caused by a defective product. Even though plaintiff alleges a negligence claim in Count I, this count . . . falls within the New Jersey Product Liability Act (NJPLA), which is the sole basis of relief under New Jersey law available to consumers injured by a defective product. Similarly, under New York law theories of negligence and strict liability for design and warning defects are functionally equivalent.

We find that defendants owed no duty to plaintiff under either New Jersey or New York law. First, the manufacturer of a raw material that is not in itself dangerous has no legal duty to prevent a buyer from incorporating the material into another device that may be dangerous. . . . Second, manufacturers have no duty to prevent a criminal misuse of their products which is entirely foreign to the purpose for which the product was intended. . . .

In the instant case, there is no allegation that the fertilizer products were dangerous in and of themselves. Under plaintiff's own allegations, the raw ammonium nitrate and urea sold by defendants were not explosive until the terrorists purposefully manipulated and adulterated them by mixing them together with additional chemicals such that they were transformed into energized materials that could be incorporated into an explosive charge. The danger to plaintiff was presented not by the raw materials, but by a bomb that incorporated the raw materials after they had been substantially altered. In addition, defendants had no control over the fertilizer once it was sold and no control over the final assembly of the bomb.

Moreover, under the NJPLA a plaintiff must prove that the product causing the harm was not reasonably fit, suitable, or safe for its *intended* purpose. The unforeseeable misuse of a product may not give rise to strict liability. "A product is not in a defective condition when it is safe for normal consumption and handling" [quoting a comment to Section 402A].

[Finally,] the alteration and misuse of defendants' fertilizer products were not objectively foreseeable. . . . We agree with the district court's conclusion that no jury could reasonably conclude that one accidental explosion fifty years ago, one terrorist act in this country almost thirty years ago, and scattered terrorist incidents throughout the world over the course of the last thirty years would make an incident like the World Trade Center bombing more than a remote or theoretical possibility. . . . The district court's conclusion is consistent with the refusal of the New Jersey Supreme Court to impose a duty in cases involving outrageous misuses of a product wholly unrelated to its intended purpose, where such a duty would expose manufacturers to endless liability. . . .

The district court dismissed plaintiff's failure-to-warn claims on two independent grounds: first, that defendants owed no duty to warn the middlemen; second, that plaintiff is unable to allege facts showing that such a warning would have prevented the harm. We agree with the district court on both theories.

Plaintiff alleges that defendants owed a duty to warn the distributor, wholesalers, retailers, and other suppliers not to sell the fertilizers to customers without confirming that buyers in the general and unrestricted public market have legitimate and lawful purposes for use of defendants' products. . . . [P]laintiff can cite no authority (and we can find none) under either New Jersey or New York law which supports the existence of a duty to warn middlemen that consumers, after purchasing their products, may alter the products and harm third parties. The district court properly dismissed the failure-to-warn claim on this ground. . . .

In addition, we agree with the district court that plaintiff is unable to allege facts showing that an adequate warning would have prevented the harm. The district court observed correctly that under both New Jersey and New York law, a plaintiff must show [causation] in a failure-to-warn claim. . . . Applying this law, we must agree with the district court's reasoned elaboration of why the failure-to-warn claim must fail.

> In light of the elaborate efforts the terrorists went through to commit their heinous crime, it would defy all logic, common sense, and fairness, . . . to presume that the World Trade Center bombing would have been prevented had defendants warned their middlemen not to sell to terrorists because terrorists might use the fertilizer to create a bomb. Given the terrorists' obvious determination, the court cannot presume that even if the middlemen heeded this warning, the terrorists' plan would have been thwarted.

## Judgment and Result

The court of appeals affirmed the district court's dismissal of the Port Authority's complaint.

## Questions

1. The New Jersey product liability statute seems to have been modeled on Section 402A. Go through the elements of Section 402A and try to determine whether they have been satisfied here.
2. Might the defendants have an abnormal-use defense here? Check the section on product liability defenses toward the end of the chapter.
3. The court did not consider the ease or cost of altering the fertilizer products to render them less easily modifiable into explosives. Suppose that it was very cheap and easy to accomplish this modification and that any such modification would be 100 percent effective. Should this change the result on the Port Authority's design defect claim?
4. The court did not discuss the amount of the Port Authority's claimed damages or the assets possessed by the defendants. Even so, make a guess about the financial impact on the defendants if the Port Authority had won here.

## THE *RESTATEMENT (THIRD)*

Section 1 of the *Restatement (Third): Product Liability* states its basic rule: "One engaged in the business of selling or otherwise distributing products who sells or distributes a defective product is subject to liability for harm to persons or property caused by the defect." Notice that, unlike Section 402A, the *Restatement (Third)* does not require that the product be unreasonably dangerous. However, it resembles 402A by only covering manufacturers and commercial sellers who are engaged in the business of selling the kind of product that injured the plaintiff. Also like 402A, Section 1 covers not only manufacturers but other sellers down the product's chain of distribution.

The *Restatement (Third)* has special rules governing sales of product components, prescription drugs, medical devices, food products, and used goods. But its most important specific rules come in its Section 2, which elaborates on Section 1 by defining the term *product defect*. Section 2 identifies three such defects:

1. *Manufacturing defects.* A product contains a manufacturing defect when it departs from its intended design. Examples include products that fail to meet specifications because they are incorrectly assembled, physically flawed, or damaged. For liability to exist, the product must have been in such a condition when it left the defendant's hands.
2. *Inadequate instructions or warnings.* Liability for manufacturing defects is strict; it applies even though all possible care was exercised in the preparation of the product. Under the *Restatement (Third)*, however, liability for the other two kinds of product defects involves something more like negligence. *Restatement* Section 2 says that a product is defective due to inadequate instructions or warnings when reasonable instructions or warnings could have reduced the product's foreseeable risks of harm, the seller failed to provide such instructions or warnings, and this made the product not reasonably safe. Here, manufacturers and sellers are only liable for reasonably foreseeable harms; they are not required to protect against every conceivable risk that their products might present. Most likely the other failure-to-warn factors discussed earlier apply under the *Restatement (Third)* as well. As also was true under negligence and 402A, there is no duty to warn about obvious and generally known risks. As before, finally, courts have to consider various factors and circumstances in determining both the reasonableness of the instructions or warnings, and the parties other than the immediate buyer who are entitled to such instructions or warnings.
3. *Design defects.* According to the *Restatement (Third)*, a product is defective in design when the foreseeable risks of harm it poses could have been reduced or avoided by a reasonable alternative design, and the omission of the alternative design makes the product not reasonably safe. The plaintiff must prove that such a reasonable alternative was, or reasonably could have been, available at the time of sale. How do courts determine whether an alternative design is reasonable and whether the product is unsafe without it? They consider and weigh a broad range of factors, most of which are stated in the following *Martinez* case. These factors resemble those used in design-defect cases under Section 402A. As *Martinez* also makes clear, the *Restatement (Third)* takes the position that a warning does not substitute for the provision of a reasonably safe design.

## Uniroyal Goodrich Tire Co. v. Martinez
Texas Supreme Court
977 S.W. 2d 328 (1998)

### Background and Facts

Roberto Martinez was injured while installing a Uniroyal Goodrich tire on a motor vehicle. The injury occurred when the 16-inch tire exploded while Martinez was attempting to mount it on a 16.5-inch rim. He made the attempt despite the presence of a prominent warning label on the tire. The warning specifically stated that one should never mount a 16-inch tire on a 16.5-inch rim, and that doing so could cause severe injury or death because the tire would explode.

Martinez sued Goodrich under strict liability in a Texas trial court. His theory was not that the warning was inadequate, but rather that the exploding tire was defective because Goodrich had failed to use a safer alternative bead design that would have kept it from exploding. The jury found for Martinez, awarding him $5.5 million in actual damages and $11.5 million in punitive damages. After reducing the punitive damages award pursuant to a settlement agreement between the parties, the trial judge awarded Martinez about $10.3 million. A Texas appeals court upheld the trial court's award of actual damages, but reversed its punitive damages award. Goodrich appealed to the Texas Supreme Court.

### Body of Opinion

**Chief Justice Phillips.** We must decide whether a manufacturer who knew of a safer alternative product design is liable in strict products liability for injuries caused by the use of its product that the user could have avoided by following the product's warnings. . . .

This court has adopted the products liability standard set forth in Section 402A of the *Restatement (Second) of Torts*. . . . To prove a design defect, a claimant must establish, among other things, that the defendant could have provided a safer alternative design. Implicit in this holding is that the safer alternative design must be reasonable, i.e., that it can be implemented without destroying the utility of the product. The newly released *Restatement (Third) of Torts: Product Liability* carries forward this focus on reasonable alternative design. . . . To determine whether a reasonable alternative design exists, and if so whether its omission renders the product unreasonably dangerous (or, in the words of the new *Restatement*, not reasonably safe), the finder of fact may weigh various factors bearing on the risk and utility of the product. One of these factors is whether the product contains suitable warnings and instructions. The new *Restatement* likewise carries forward this approach:

A broad range of factors may be considered in determining whether an alternative design is reasonable and whether its omission renders a product not reasonably safe. The factors include, among others, the magnitude and probability of the foreseeable risks of harm, the instructions and warnings accompanying the product, and the nature and strength of consumer expectations regarding the product, including expectations arising from product portrayal and marketing. . . . The relative advantages and disadvantages of the product as designed and as it alternatively could have been designed may also be considered. Thus, the likely effects of the alternative design on production costs; the effects of the alternative design on product longevity, maintenance, repair, and aesthetics; and the range of consumer choice among products are factors that may be taken into account. . . .

Goodrich urges this court to depart from this standard by following certain language from comment j of the *Restatement (Second) of Torts*. Comment j provides in part: "Where warning is given, the seller may reasonably assume that it will be read and heeded; and a product bearing such a warning, which is safe for use if it is followed, is not in defective condition, not is it unreasonably dangerous." The new *Restatement*, however, expressly rejects the Comment j approach. . . . "[I]nstructions and warnings may be ineffective because users of the product may not be adequately reached, may be likely to be inattentive, or may be insufficiently motivated to follow the instructions or heed the warnings. However, when an alternative design to avoid risks cannot reasonably be implemented, adequate instructions and warnings will normally be sufficient to render the product reasonably safe. Warnings are not, however, a substitute for the provision of a reasonably safe design."

Goodrich argues that . . . it is still entitled to judgment as a matter of law because no safer alternative was available. In response, Martinez points to the evidence that Goodrich's competitors, and eventually Goodrich itself, adopted [a safer tire bead design]. Goodrich counters that this alternative design is not in fact safer because if the tire is matched to the wrong rim size, the bead will never seat on the rim and it will inevitably explode during use. . . . Martinez, however, offered some evidence that his alternative design not only would have prevented the injury, but also that it would not have introduced other dangers of equal or greater magnitude. . . . [The] evidence does not conclusively prove that the [new design] would have introduced into the product other dangers of equal or greater magnitude. There was thus an issue of fact regarding whether a reasonable alternative design existed, which the jury resolved in favor of Martinez.

### Judgment and Result

The Texas Supreme Court affirmed the decision of the intermediate appellate court. Martinez wins.

### Questions

1. Why did the court hold that a suitable warning cannot insulate the defendant from liability where a better alternative design is available?

2. Did the court hold that the presence or absence of a suitable warning is *irrelevant* to determining liability in design-defect cases?

3. Should this case be taken as holding that manufacturers must adopt the safest possible design, no matter what the cost?

4. Due in part to extenuating circumstances not presented above, the Texas Supreme Court also rejected Goodrich's contention that Martinez was guilty of contributory negligence. But suppose that Martinez actually was contributorily negligent. Would this necessarily have defeated his claim? See the section on defenses toward the end of this chapter.

Table 23.1 provides a summary of the major product liability theories and their characteristics.

## TABLE 23.1 THE MAJOR PRODUCT LIABILITY THEORIES COMPARED

| Theory | Tort or Contract? | Type of Defendant | Nature of Product |
|---|---|---|---|
| Express warranty | Contract | Seller of goods | Not as expressly warranted |
| Implied warranty of merchantability | Contract | Merchant for goods sold | Most often, not fit for ordinary purposes for which such goods used |
| Implied warranty of fitness | Contract | Seller of goods | Not fit for buyer's particular purposes |
| Negligence | Tort | Seller of goods | Defective due to seller's failure to behave like reasonable person in manufacturing, inspecting, designing, and giving warnings about the product |
| Section 402A | Tort | Seller engaged in business of selling product sold | Defective and unreasonably dangerous |
| *Restatement (Third)* | Tort | One engaged in the business of selling product | Defective |

## OTHER THEORIES OF PRODUCT LIABILITY RECOVERY

### THE MAGNUSON–MOSS ACT

The federal Magnuson–Moss Warranty Act of 1975 contains many consumer protection provisions. Here, we focus on the act's provisions concerning warranty liability for sellers. Other portions of the act impose requirements regarding the full, fair, timely, and conspicuous disclosure of warranty terms to consumers.

*Look for the FTC regulations accompanying the Magnuson–Moss Act at* **http://www.ftc.gov**

The Magnuson–Moss Act says that where sellers of a consumer product costing more than $10 per item give a written warranty covering that product, they must designate the warranty as either full or limited. A consumer product is tangible personal property normally used for personal, family, or household purposes. Sellers who give a full warranty must (1) obligate themselves to remedy or repair the product in case of a defect, and (2) enable the consumer to obtain either a replacement product or a refund of the purchase price after a reasonable number of unsuccessful attempts to remedy the defect. Any other written warranty given by a seller of consumer products costing more than $10 per item should be designated as a limited warranty. In this case, sellers are only bound to whatever they promise in the warranty. Note that nothing in the act requires that sellers give a written warranty, and that sellers can avoid the previous requirements simply by not giving such a warranty.

## MISREPRESENTATION

Product liability law has long allowed consumers and other parties to recover for misrepresentations made by sellers of products they buy. Section 9 of the *Restatement (Third)* continues this tradition. Its rule applies only to merchant-like sellers engaged in the business of selling or otherwise distributing the product in question. The section includes fraudulent, negligent, or innocent misrepresentations made by such sellers. The misrepresentation must involve a material fact concerning the product—a fact that would matter to a reasonable buyer. Thus, inconsequential misstatements, sales talk, and statements of opinion do not create liability. However, Section 9 does not require that the product be defective. Unlike past law, moreover, Section 9 does not require that the misrepresentation be made to the public, or that the plaintiff have justifiably relied upon it. However, the misrepresentation must have caused the plaintiff to suffer personal injury or property damage.

## INDUSTRYWIDE LIABILITY

All the product liability theories just discussed require that the product defect cause the injury or other loss the plaintiff has suffered. However, some courts have dispensed with this requirement in certain cases. In doing so, they have held defendants liable where it is unclear whether they manufactured the specific product that caused the plaintiff's injury. This has occurred where the plaintiff was injured by a standardized product manufactured by many firms and is unable to prove which of several possible defendants actually was responsible for the injury. Several cases of this sort have involved DES, an anti-miscarriage drug causing various delayed diseases in the daughters of women to whom it was administered. A similar approach has been used in some decisions involving claims based on long-term exposure to asbestos.

In such cases, the courts in question apportion liability among the firms in the industry that might have produced the product that harmed the plaintiff, usually on the basis of market share. These courts often differ on the legal rationales for their decisions, and on many other more specific points. However, some courts considering the question have followed traditional causation rules and have rejected this whole approach to the problem. In such states, a plaintiff generally must prove that a particular defendant's product caused the harm of which she complains.

## DAMAGES

At this point in the chapter, we shift our focus from the theories of product liability recovery to some important problems that cut across the theories, and that may be resolved differently from theory to theory. These problems often are important factors in determining whether a plaintiff will recover. In the discussion that follows, we only consider how these problems affect the six most important theories of recovery discussed above.

One of the most important considerations affecting a plaintiff's choice of a product liability theory is the type(s) of damages that can be recovered under that theory. In addressing this question, we first consider the kinds of damages that might be recoverable in the normal product liability case. Then we consider which damages can be obtained under each of our six major theories of recovery. After that, the text briefly examines some statutory measures reducing the damages plaintiffs can recover.

### TYPES OF DAMAGES

The damages a plaintiff might recover in a product liability case break down into three general categories, one of which has several subcategories. It is possible for a single product liability suit to involve all these types of damages.

1. **Basis-of-the-bargain damages** (also called direct economic loss or harm to the product itself). These damages compensate buyers for the "lost" or "missing" value of defective goods. They are measured by the value of the goods as contracted for (generally the value as warranted, the sale price, or some reasonably anticipated value), minus the value of the goods as received.
2. **Consequential damages.** These damages comprise various harms that result from a product defect, but that are more remote from the defect than basis-of-the-bargain damages. Consequential damages include **personal injury**, **property damage**, and **indirect economic loss**. Personal injury most often means bodily harm of some kind. Usually included under the personal injury heading are losses attributable to pain and suffering, mental distress, inconvenience, loss of companionship and consortium, injury to reputation, lost earnings, and so forth. Property damage is damage to property of the plaintiff other than the defective product that she purchased. As its name suggests, indirect economic loss covers a wide range of economic harms resulting from the product defect. Examples include lost profits and loss of business goodwill.
3. **Punitive damages.** Punitive damages are not awarded to compensate plaintiffs for harm they have suffered. Instead, they are imposed as an extra penalty for especially bad behavior by the defendant, and as a deterrent to such behavior by the defendant and by others. The behavior justifying a punitive damages award usually involves an intentional or reckless disregard for the

safety of those likely to be affected by the goods. Examples include concealing known product dangers, consciously violating government or industry product safety standards, and maintaining grossly inadequate testing or quality control procedures.

## Damages under the UCC

Because they traditionally have been unavailable in contract cases, punitive damages usually cannot be obtained in express and implied warranty suits. Determining the other damages to which successful warranty plaintiffs are entitled can be a complex matter. An important factor affecting this question is whether there was **privity of contract**—a direct contractual relationship—between the plaintiff and the defendant.

Plaintiffs who dealt directly with—who are "in privity" with—the defendant collect basis-of-the-bargain damages. In addition, such plaintiffs can recover the various types of consequential damages if certain tests are met. UCC Section 2-715(2)(b) allows a buyer to recover for personal injury and property damage proximately resulting from his seller's breach of warranty. Although the Code does not define the term *proximately*, it probably refers to personal injury or property damage that is a reasonably foreseeable consequence of the breach. Section 2-715(2)(a)'s test for recovery of indirect economic loss is the seller's reason to know about the buyer's needs and requirements for the goods. For example, if a seller is familiar with his buyer's business and thus has reason to know how goods sold to the buyer will be used, the seller should be liable for indirect economic loss caused by defects in those goods.

What happens when there is no privity of contract between plaintiff and defendant? As you will see in the next section, plaintiffs who did not deal directly with the defendant sometimes cannot recover anything at all under the UCC. Even where such plaintiffs can recover, moreover, the types of damages available to them are limited. In general, such plaintiffs are (1) quite likely to recover for personal injury, (2) fairly likely to recover for property damage, (3) unlikely to recover basis-of-the-bargain damages, and (4) quite unlikely to recover indirect economic loss.

## Tort Damages

As the following *Alloway* case suggests, tort theories are best suited for obtaining personal injury, property damage, and (where appropriate) punitive damages. These theories are fairly poor vehicles for recovering indirect economic loss and basis-of-the-bargain damages. Despite a few differences, negligence law, Section 402A, and the *Restatement (Third)* generally speak with the same voice on these questions.

## Tort Reform Measures

The policies of risk-spreading and socialization of risk discussed earlier have not been trouble-free. Over the past few decades, some observers have argued that there is a crisis in the tort system generally, and in product liability law particularly. Attention has centered on the greater ease with which plaintiffs have been able to recover, and the increasing recoveries they have received. The resulting economic burden on sellers and manufacturers, it is claimed, makes it more difficult and more expensive for them to obtain liability insurance. Firms that cannot obtain insurance and that cannot self-insure might be wiped out by a single huge product liability judgment. For those who can get insurance, its greater costs have become increasingly difficult to pass on. Where these costs can be passed on, consumers have less money to spend. Consumers may also suffer as manufacturers fearful of massive product liability suits are deterred from worthwhile product innovations.

The preceding scenario has not persuaded everyone. For example, some people have blamed the increase in insurance premiums on the industry itself. Still, perceptions like those just described have created a *tort reform movement*. Its aim has been to reduce the economic pressure on firms and their insurers. Most tort reform measures have tried to scale back damage recoveries. For example, some states have limited recoveries for noneconomic loss, most often by putting a definite dollar cap (e.g., $250,000 or $500,000) on such recoveries. Also, many states restrict punitive damage recoveries in various ways. They may do so by capping punitive damages at some definite dollar figure (e.g., $250,000), or at some multiple of the plaintiff's compensatory damages (e.g., three times compensatory damages). Some states also bifurcate, or separate, the procedure for determining whether to award punitive damages and the procedure for determining their amount.

## Alloway v. General Marine Industries
Supreme Court of New Jersey
695 A.2d 264 (1997)

### Background and Facts

In July of 1990, Samuel Alloway purchased a new thirty-three foot Century Grande XL boat from the Mullica River Boat Basin, which in turn had purchased it from General Marine Industries (GMI). The cost was $61,070. Due to a defective seam in the boat's swimming platform, it sank three months later while docked at a marina. After Alloway paid $2,490 of the $2,500 deductible under his insurance policy, the insurer spent an additional $40,106.63 to repair the boat.

Then, Alloway sued Mullica and GMI under various theories. He eventually assigned most of those claims to his insurer. But he retained tort claims against GMI for the $2,490 and for the difference between the boat's purchase price and the boat's market value in its defective condition. A New Jersey trial court granted GMI's motion to dismiss for failure to state a claim, but an intermediate appellate court reversed. Alloway appealed to the New Jersey Supreme Court.

### Body of Opinion

**Justice Pollock.** The issue is whether the plaintiff may rely on theories of strict liability and negligence to recover damages for economic loss resulting from a defect that caused injury only to the boat itself. . . . The question reduces to whether plaintiff may use tort theories to recover the lost benefit of [his] bargain from [GMI]. . . .

Allocation of economic loss between a manufacturer and a consumer involves assessment of tort and contract principles in the determination of claims arising out of the manufacture, distribution, and sale of defective products. Generally speaking, tort principles are better suited to resolve claims for personal injuries or damage to other property. Contract principles more readily respond to claims for economic loss caused by damage to the product itself. Various considerations support the distinction. Tort principles more adequately address the creation of an unreasonable risk of harm when a person or other property sustains accidental or unexpected injury. When, however, a product fails to fulfill a purchaser's economic expectations, contract principles, particularly as implemented by the UCC, provide a more appropriate analytical framework. Implicit in the distinction is the doctrine that a tort duty of care protects against the risk of accidental harm and a contractual duty preserves the satisfaction of consensual obligations. . . .

By enacting the UCC, the legislature adopted a comprehensive system for compensating consumers for economic loss arising from the purchase of defective products. The UCC represents the legislature's attempt to strike the proper balance in the allocation of the risk of loss between manufacturers and purchasers for economic loss arising from injury to a defective product. Consequently, the UCC provides for express warranties regarding the quality of goods, as well as an implied warranty of merchantability and an implied warranty of fitness for a particular purpose. When a seller delivers goods that are not as warranted, the buyer may recover the difference between the value of the defective goods and their value if they had been as warranted. . . .

The vast majority of courts across the country have concluded that purchasers of personal property, whether commercial entities or consumers, should be limited to [economic loss] recovery under contract principles. . . . Scholars likewise have criticized the extension of strict liability to include claims for purely economic loss. . . . Following the majority rule, the American Law Institute's proposed *Restatement (Third) of Torts: Products Liability* defines economic loss to exclude recovery under tort theories for damage to a product itself. . . .

In addition to the right to recover under the UCC, victims of fraud or unconscionable conduct possess substantial rights to recover for common-law fraud or for violations of various state and federal statutes. The UCC expressly provides that "unless displaced by the particular provisions of this Act, the principles of law and equity, including the law merchant and the law relative to capacity to contract, principal and agent, estoppel, fraud, misrepresentation, duress, coercion, mistake, bankruptcy or other validating or invalidating cause shall supplement its provisions.". . . Additionally, the legislature has adopted the Consumer Fraud Act, which provides generous protection to defrauded consumers. . . . Another [New Jersey] statute, the Truth-In-Consumer Contract, Warranty and Notice Act, protects consumers by requiring that consumer contracts be clearly written and understandable. . . . Congress has provided further protection for consumers. For example, the Magnuson–Moss Warranty Act . . . offers consumers a basis in federal law for recovering damages. . . . In sum, judicial decisions and statutory enactments, including the UCC, protect consumers from overreaching. Against this background, a tort cause of action for economic loss duplicating the one provided by the UCC is superfluous and counterproductive. . . .

Over thirty years ago, before the adoption of the UCC, this court, concerned about the ability of consumers to reach remote parties in a chain of distribution, perceived the need to provide those consumers with a tort action. In the interim, the UCC has taken effect. . . . Under the UCC, as construed by this court, moreover, the absence of privity no longer bars a buyer from reaching through the chain of distribution to the manufacturer.

## Judgment and Result

Intermediate appellate court decision reversed; trial court decision dismissing Alloway's claims reinstated. Alloway cannot recover in tort for economic loss.

## Questions

1. Of the types of damages discussed in the text, which one is Alloway pursuing in this case?
2. Suppose that when the boat sank, damaged along with it was a new $3,000 computer that Alloway planned to use in his home. Does the New Jersey Supreme Court's opinion rule on this particular loss?
3. What is the significance of the court's reference to privity in the last paragraph of the decision? (*Hint:* Is it easier to recover outside privity under the UCC or under tort theories?) Check the next section of this chapter.

## WHO CAN RECOVER AGAINST WHOM? THE NO-PRIVITY DEFENSE

Yet another manifestation of the individualism that underlay much nineteenth-century law was the traditional rule that there is no liability outside privity of contract. **Privity of contract** is the existence of a direct contractual relationship between two parties. The attitude underlying the rule was that manufacturers and sellers only had duties toward the parties with whom they directly dealt, and not remote parties down the product's chain of distribution. The traditional rule may also have reflected the perceived need to protect infant manufacturing industries. Manufacturers obtained such protection because under the no-privity rule, plaintiffs injured by defective goods had to sue their immediate seller, with suits proceeding up the chain of distribution until they reached guilty manufacturer. In part because the various intermediaries may have been relatively blameless, manufacturers sometimes could escape liability for the consequences of their defective products.

Over the past century, the old no-privity defense has lost most of its former importance in the product liability area. Despite its diminished importance,

## FIGURE 23.1 A HYPOTHETICAL CHAIN OF DISTRIBUTION

however, the no-privity rule still retains some influence—especially in cases arising under the UCC. Our discussion of the rule's contemporary impact uses the illustrative chain of distribution in Figure 23.1. Suits between parties in the normal contractual chain of distribution (e.g., consumer-wholesaler) often are described as involving vertical privity. Suits between a party who is not part of this contractual chain (e.g., a family member or bystander) and one who has sold the goods (e.g., a retailer) often are said to involve horizontal privity.

## PRIVITY UNDER THE UCC

The effect of the no-liability-outside-privity defense in cases brought under the Uniform Commercial Code is a confused subject. Here, we first discuss the three versions of the provision (UCC Section 2-318) that is supposed to govern this question. Then, we describe the factors that often influence courts when they decide whether the plaintiff can recover against a remote defendant under the UCC.

UCC Section 2-318 comes in three alternative versions from which the states can choose. Alternative A extends the seller's express or implied warranty to any natural person who is in the family or household of his (the seller's) buyer or who is a guest in the buyer's home, if it is reasonable to expect that such a person would use, consume, or be affected by the goods and if that person suffers personal injury from a breach of the warranty. Alternative A does not significantly extend the seller's liability to parties outside privity of contract. In Figure 23.2, for example, its only real impact is to raise the possibility that a family or household member or a guest may be able to sue the retailer for personal injury.[5]

*Most states' versions of Section 2-318 can be found at http://www.law.cornell.edu, under "Constitutions & Codes," "State Constitutions & Codes."*

---

[5] Of course, the consumer also would be able to sue the retailer. Under a literal reading of Alternative A, however, the consumer would not be able to sue other parties up the vertical chain of distribution.

Alternatives B and C go much further. Alternative B extends the seller's express or implied warranty to any natural person who may be reasonably expected to use, consume, or be affected by the goods and who suffers personal injury from a breach of the warranty. Alternative C is much the same, but it allows recovery by any person (not just natural persons) who is "injured" (not just injured in person) by the breach. In an appropriate case, liability under Alternatives B and C might extend from the component parts manufacturer to the bystander in Figure 23.2.

The literal language of Section 2-318's three alternatives is not a good guide to the courts' behavior in UCC cases where privity is absent. Alternatives B and C obviously are very flexible on their face. And while Alternative A is fairly precise, a Code drafters' comment to Section 2-318 suggests that the courts are free to extend the seller's liability beyond Alternative A's explicit limits. To add to the confusion, some states have departed from Section 2-318 by adopting their own privity provisions.

Among the states as a whole, therefore, considerable uncertainty exists regarding the UCC plaintiff's ability to recover outside privity. Here, we only can list some of the factors making such recovery more or less likely.[6] The first such factor, one suggested by the "reasonable to expect" language of Section 2-318, is the reasonable foreseeability that a party like the plaintiff would suffer harm from the product defect in question. The second factor is suggested by the "natural person" language of Alternatives A and B. This factor is the nature of the plaintiff. On the whole, ordinary consumers stand a better chance of recovering outside privity than do business concerns. The third factor is the type of damages the plaintiff has suffered. This factor was discussed in the preceding section. To review, a UCC plaintiff who lacks privity of contract with her defendant is most likely to recover for personal injury and property damage, in that order. However, recoveries for basis-of-the-bargain damages are infrequent and recoveries for indirect economic loss rare.

## PRIVITY IN TORT CASES

Today the no-privity defense usually is ineffective when the plaintiff sues in tort. In negligence cases, the general test for recovery outside privity is whether it was reasonably foreseeable that the product defect would cause harm of the sort suffered to a plaintiff of the sort injured. Although the results of this test vary with the facts of the case, it allows suits against very remote parties in an appropriate situation. Only rarely does Section 402A pose privity problems of either a horizontal or a vertical nature. Indeed, many courts have allowed bystanders to recover under Section 402A. *The Restatement (Third)* does not have a privity provision. But it does say that whether a product defect caused harm should be determined by the prevailing rules on causation in tort. This might mean that a test of reasonable foreseeability will usually govern privity questions under the *Restatement (Third)*.

The following case grapples with privity problems under UCC Section 2-318.

---

[6] Another such factor is the type of warranty at issue. In general, plaintiffs outside privity who have relied on an express warranty made to them by advertising, brochures, and so forth have a better chance of recovery than implied warranty plaintiffs.

## Minnesota Mining & Manufacturing Co. v. Nishika, Ltd.
Supreme Court of Minnesota
565 N.W. 2d 16 (1997)

### Background and Facts

James Bainbridge and Daniel Fingarette [the claimants] established a plan for a three-dimensional photography business through four independent companies. In January of 1988, Bainbridge met with officials of the Minnesota Mining & Manufacturing Company (3M) to seek assistance with the three-dimensional film development process. Bainbridge testified that he told 3M all about his planned business, including his need for quality emulsion and backcoat sauce to process the film. In mid-1989, 3M formulated a new emulsion that it claimed would work well with the film development process. 3M apparently understood that this emulsion would be used in combination with a backcoat sauce that 3M had also developed.

In December 1989, 3M began selling the new emulsion and backcoat sauce components to two of the claimants' four companies, but not to the two others. After Bainbridge and Fingarette began using 3M's new emulsion in December 1989, a problem emerged with the film development process. Specifically, the photographs faded, losing their three-dimensional effect. By early 1990, the claimants experienced a significant decline in camera sales. 3M eventually solved the problem, but the claimants' business ultimately failed.

The claimants' four companies sued 3M in a Texas trial court alleging, in part, breach of express and implied warranties. They argued that the photographic fading was caused by the incompatibility of 3M's new emulsion and its old backcoat sauce, which, in turn, undermined confidence in their business. The jury concluded that 3M breached an express warranty for the emulsion and implied warranties for the emulsion and the backcoat sauce. Applying Minnesota law, the trial court awarded the four firms $29,873,599 in lost profits. An intermediate appellate court upheld this award. The Texas Supreme Court withheld final judgment and certified the following question to the Minnesota Supreme Court: "For breach of warranty under [Minnesota's version of UCC Section 2-318], is a seller liable to a person who never acquired any goods from the seller, directly or indirectly, for pure economic damages (e.g., lost profits), unaccompanied by any injury to the person or the person's property?" This question was relevant to the two plaintiff companies that had not dealt directly with 3M, but had suffered lost profits due to its various breaches of warranty. In the following opinion, the Minnesota Supreme Court answers the question.

### Body of Opinion

**Chief Justice Keith.** The certified question asks this court to consider whether a seller may be held liable for breach of warranty to a plaintiff who never used, purchased, or otherwise acquired goods from the seller, for lost profits unaccompanied by personal injury or property damage. Unlike the other two plaintiffs, [two of them] did not deal directly with 3M nor did they use, purchase, or

otherwise acquire the 3M goods at issue. . . . Hence, [they] premise their recovery of lost profits on the statutory extension of warranty protection to certain noncontracting parties ("third-party beneficiaries"). The third-party beneficiaries provision of Minnesota's Uniform Commercial Code addresses the reach of express and implied warranties to "injured" parties lacking privity of contract with the seller. Essentially, the provision broadens the reach of warranties by narrowing the lack-of-privity defense: "A seller's warranty whether express or implied extends to any person who may reasonably be expected to use, consume or be affected by the goods and who is injured by breach of the warranty. A seller may not exclude or limit the operation of this section." The term "person" includes corporations and other business organizations. . . . Minnesota's current version [of Section 2-318] is somewhat broader than the broadest of three options recommended by the drafters of the model UCC in 1966. . . . Alternative C is identical to current Minnesota law, but allows a seller to exclude or limit the operation of the provision if injury to the person is not involved. We agree with 3M that the statute is not so clear and free from ambiguity that we may disregard legislative intent . . . or the consequences of a particular construction. The unadorned term "injured" is not defined in the UCC, nor is it used elsewhere in the text of Article 2. As applied to [two of the plaintiffs], the reach of [the] section is unclear. . . .

Under [this] section, this court has sanctioned the recovery of lost profits (one form of economic loss) by a third-party beneficiary whose damages arose from a remote seller's breach of warranty. We have also indicated that plaintiffs who never used, purchased, or otherwise acquired defective goods may qualify as third-party beneficiaries when they suffer property damage. But this court has never gone so far as to hold that [the] section reaches a plaintiff who is seeking lost profits unaccompanied by physical injury or property damage and who never used, purchased, or otherwise acquired the goods in question. To do so, we believe, would expand warranty liability well beyond the limits contemplated by the legislature. . . .

Our understanding of the background and aims of [Minnesota's privity provision] leads us to conclude that the scope of a seller's liability for breach of warranty should recede as the relationship between a "beneficiary" of the warranty and the seller's goods becomes more remote. . . . [T]hose who purchase, use, or otherwise acquire warranted goods have standing to sue for purely economic losses. Those who lack any such connection to the warranted goods must demonstrate physical injury or property damage before economic losses are recoverable. . . . Any other result implies almost unlimited liability for sellers of warranted goods. If [the] section were interpreted as the plaintiffs advocate, it seems that [their] individual employees, or perhaps even their families, would have standing to sue 3M for causing the loss of their jobs or even a decline in their wages. . . . The plaintiffs appear to advocate warranty recovery as a catch-all alternative for plaintiffs with no viable legal basis for suit. The risk, however, is that the fortuitous existence of a warranty—between some seller and some buyer, somewhere—would allow remote yet foreseeable parties to recover for their hampered expectations, while others in similar circumstances—but who could not identify a warranty—would not. Confronted with liability of this magnitude, sellers would be encouraged to attempt to disclaim warranties or exclude consequential damages remedies—affecting both the immediate buyer and third-party beneficiaries alike. We therefore reject the plaintiffs' reading of the statute—an interpretation that would likely lead to a variety of unreasonable, unjust, and absurd results that we cannot imagine were intended by the legislature. In light of the statute's language and purpose, and consistent with the legislature's apparent intent, the best reading of [the] section is that noncontracting parties who never used, purchased, or otherwise acquired the seller's warranted goods may not seek lost profits, unaccompanied by physical injury or property damage, for breach of warranty under the statute.

## Judgment and Result

The Minnesota Supreme Court answered the Texas Supreme Court's certified question in the negative. This meant that two of the four plaintiff corporations could not recover lost profits. In *Minnesota Mining & Manufacturing Co. v. Nishika, Ltd.*, 953 S.W.2d 733 (Tex. 1997), the Texas Supreme Court applied the present case to deny these two firms recovery.

## Questions

1. Look at the text's three factors for determining privity questions under the UCC and apply them to the facts in this case. In which direction does each of the factors pull?
2. How is this case different from the other cases in which the Minnesota Supreme Court had let the plaintiff recover outside privity of contract under the UCC?
3. What would be the result if one of the plaintiff companies had suffered property damage due to the defect in the product? Could the company recover for the property damage? For its lost profits?

## LIABILITY DISCLAIMERS

A product liability **disclaimer** is a sales contract provision attempting to eliminate or modify the seller's liability for product defects under one or more theories of recovery.[7] Where a disclaimer is enforceable, it erases or reduces the seller's liability under a particular theory or theories of recovery. The main policy argument for enforcing disclaimers is freedom of contract. Also, because goods accompanied by an effective disclaimer are likely to be cheaper than other goods, enforcing disclaimers can increase the choices available to buyers. By enforcing disclaimers, courts effectively give buyers a choice between paying a higher price and getting an "insurance policy" against defects (the seller liability that is likely without a disclaimer), or paying a lower price while accepting a greater risk of an uncompensated defect (because the disclaimer would block recovery).

Today, these freedom-of-contract-based arguments pack less weight than they did a century ago. As a result, disclaimers often are not enforced. The main reason why these arguments tend to be unpersuasive is that disclaimers sometimes are imposed rather than freely bargained and accepted. Often, a disclaimer is offered on a standardized, take-it-or-leave-it basis by a seller of superior business sophistication, and is accepted without dissent by a consumer who has not read or understood the disclaimer prior to making the purchase. However, where the buyer is a knowledgeable business entity that has understood and freely bargained a disclaimer, these observations are much less valid and courts are more likely to enforce disclaimers.

---

[7] As used here, the term *disclaimer* includes limitations on the duration of a warranty. For example, a seller might include contract language attempting to limit the implied warranty of merchantability's coverage to one year from the sale or to the duration of an express warranty.

The legal rules on the enforceability of disclaimers are complicated. One reason for this complexity is that the law often tries to make case-specific decisions regarding disclaimers, enforcing them when it appears that they resulted from a free, equal, and knowing bargaining process, and invalidating them in other cases. Another reason for this complexity is that some theories of recovery—mainly the UCC's two implied warranties—are more hospitable to disclaimers than other theories. We begin our discussion of this subject by considering some relatively easy cases. Then we turn to the complex rules governing implied warranty disclaimers.

## THE EASY CASES

*Express Warranty Disclaimers.* It is difficult to disclaim an express warranty. UCC Section 2-316(1) says that an express warranty and language negating or limiting it should be read consistently if possible, but that the negation or limitation is "inoperative to the extent that such construction is unreasonable." Because an express warranty is a freely made contractual promise, disclaiming it usually is unreasonable. By successfully disclaiming, the seller would effectively be taking away with one hand what it freely and openly gave with the other.

*Disclaimers and Tort Liability.* Disclaimers of negligence liability can be regarded as contractually created forms of the negligence defense known as **assumption of risk**. As you will see later in the chapter, assumption of risk protects defendants from liability if the plaintiff's acceptance of the risk (here, the disclaimer) is knowing and voluntary. Today, it is difficult for a negligence disclaimer to meet these tests, and such disclaimers often are ineffective. If there is a disparity in bargaining power between plaintiff and defendant, courts often say that the voluntariness test has not been met. Inconspicuous disclaimers and disclaimers failing to state that *negligence* liability is being disclaimed often fail to satisfy the knowledge standard. Thus, disclaimers of negligence liability rarely succeed in consumer cases, and may fail in many other situations as well. However, such disclaimers often are enforced in commercial deals between business parties of relatively equal bargaining power, if the disclaimer clearly refers to negligence liability and it is evident that the parties actually negotiated it.

Disclaimers usually are ineffective in 402A cases, especially where the plaintiff is an ordinary consumer. However, some courts have upheld disclaimers of 402A liability in situations like those where negligence disclaimers are enforced.

The *Restatement (Third)* says that disclaimers are ineffective in cases involving personal injury, but declines to state a rule for property damage and indirect economic loss cases. Although the new *Restatement* does not specifically address the subject, it is difficult to believe that it would block disclaimers negotiated in commercial deals between business parties of relatively equal sophistication and bargaining power.

## IMPLIED WARRANTY DISCLAIMERS

Figure 23.2 outlines the inquiries that courts may be required to make in cases where the enforceability of implied warranty disclaimers is at issue. Our presentation basically follows Figure 23.2.

*The Basic Tests.* UCC Section 2-316(2)'s basic tests for the enforceability of implied warranty disclaimers seem to make it easy for sellers to disclaim implied warranties. To disclaim the implied warranty of merchantability, the seller must

**FIGURE 23.2 THE ENFORCEABILITY OF IMPLIED WARRANTY DISCLAIMERS**

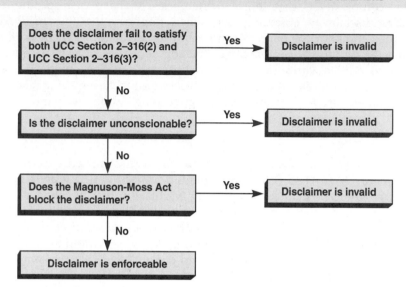

use the word *merchantability*, and the disclaimer must be conspicuous if it is in writing. To disclaim the implied warranty of fitness for a particular purpose, the disclaimer must be in writing and must be conspicuous. The general test for conspicuousness is whether a reasonable person ought to have noticed the disclaimer. Usually, disclaimers written in capital letters, bold face, larger type, or type of a contrasting color meet this test. Note that—unlike a fitness warranty disclaimer—a disclaimer of the implied warranty of merchantability may be oral. Note also that while all disclaimers of the latter warranty must use the word *merchantability*, no special form is needed to disclaim the implied warranty of fitness. A statement such as "THERE ARE NO WARRANTIES WHICH EXTEND BEYOND THE DESCRIPTION ON THE FACE HEREOF" suffices to disclaim that warranty.

***Additional Ways to Disclaim Implied Warranties.*** UCC Section 2-316(3) states some additional ways in which an implied warranty can be disclaimed. The first is by using phrases like "as is," "with all faults," and "as they stand." Although the Code does not expressly say so, many courts have held that such terms must be conspicuous to be effective as disclaimers.

Section 2-316(3) also provides that if the buyer inspects the goods and fails to discover a reasonably apparent defect, he will not have an implied warranty suit for the defect. Also, if the seller requests that the buyer inspect, the buyer refuses, and there is a reasonably apparent defect that the inspection would have revealed, the buyer will not have an implied warranty suit for that defect. Finally, an implied warranty can be disclaimed by course of dealing (previous conduct between the parties), course of performance (the parties' previous conduct under the contract in question), and usage of trade (a commercial practice having wide acceptance in the relevant locality or business).

***Unconscionability.*** From the discussion thus far, you might think that disclaiming implied warranty liability is easy for any seller (or seller's attorney) who takes the time and trouble to use the proper legal boilerplate. The following *Myers* case might reinforce this conclusion. Even if a disclaimer meets Section 2-316's lenient tests for enforceability, however, it can still be invalid if it is found to be unconscionable. UCC Section 2-302 gives a court broad powers to invalidate or modify contract provisions it concludes are unconscionable. The Code does not define the term *unconscionable*; in practice, it means little more than "grossly unfair." Courts using Section 2-302 have considerable discretion to determine whether a particular contract or contract term is unconscionable.

In exercising this discretion, courts consider a wide range of factors. They usually examine the substantive terms of the contract—those contract provisions creating the parties' rights and duties—and their tangible impact on the buyer. Disclaimers, which clearly are substantive contract terms, often leave the buyer without a legal remedy for defective goods. Sometimes this is an important factor influencing courts to find them unconscionable. Courts also consider procedural factors such as differences in bargaining power; one party's lack of education, intelligence, or experience; the seller's use of high-pressure sales tactics or "sales hype"; and technical, confusing, well-hidden, or inconspicuous contract language. Such factors obviously can assume importance in cases involving implied warranty disclaimers. However, disclaimers that meet Section 2-316(2)'s tests should at least be conspicuous.

Courts frequently find implied warranty disclaimers unconscionable in consumer cases. This is especially true where a consumer has suffered personal injury. In cases where the plaintiff is a business or commercial entity, however, many courts still refuse to apply Section 2-302, or find disclaimers conscionable even if they do apply the section. Even in this situation, though, a few courts have held disclaimers unconscionable.

*The Impact of Magnuson–Moss.* Like the Code's unconscionability doctrine, the Magnuson–Moss Act also blocks the enforceability of certain otherwise-valid implied warranty disclaimers. The act does so by restricting a seller's ability to disclaim implied warranties or limit their duration where it gives a written warranty to a consumer for the sale of a consumer product costing more than $10 per item. If the seller gives a full warranty, it cannot disclaim, modify, or limit any implied warranty. If the seller gives a limited warranty, it cannot disclaim or modify any implied warranty. But it can limit the implied warranty's duration to the duration of the written warranty if this is done conspicuously, the limitation is for a reasonable time period, and the limitation is not unconscionable. These rules are a significant restriction on sellers' ability to disclaim implied warranties in consumer cases. However, sellers can avoid the Magnuson–Moss Act's restrictions by refusing to give a written warranty. In such situations, the disclaimer could be placed on some other writing.

---

## Myers v. A.O. Smith Harvestore Products, Inc.
Court of Appeals of Idaho
757 P.2d 695 (1998)

### Background and Facts

Dale and Ila Myers operated a dairy farm near New Plymouth, Idaho. They purchased a "feed storage and delivery system" manufactured by A.O. Smith Harvestore Products, Inc. (AOS). The system consisted of a silo and a power-operated unloading unit. The Myerses' silo allowed the hay it contained to deteriorate. The result was decreased milk production and lost profits.

The Myerses sued AOS in an Idaho trial court under various theories of recovery, among them the implied warranties of merchantability and fitness. The trial court granted AOS's motion for summary judgment on these claims, and the Myerses appealed.

## Body of Opinion

**Chief Judge Walters** [AOS] asserts that as a matter of law [the implied] warranties were disclaimed. . . . Ordinarily, to be effective an implied warranty disclaimer must comply with UCC Section 2-316(2), which provides:

> (2) Subject to subsection (3) [not applicable here], to exclude or modify the implied warranty of merchantability or any part of it the language must mention merchantability and in the case of a writing must be conspicuous, and to exclude or modify any implied warranty of fitness the exclusion must be by a writing and conspicuous. Language to exclude all implied warranties of fitness is sufficient if it states, for example, that "There are no warranties which extend beyond the description on the face hereof."

"A term or clause is conspicuous when it is so written that a reasonable person against whom it is to operate ought to have noticed it. A printed heading in capitals is conspicuous. . . . Language in the body of a form is 'conspicuous' if it is in larger or other contrasting type or color." UCC Section 1-201(10).

Here, [the Myerses'] order form or purchase contract directed and required the buyer's signature not on the front of the form but on its reverse side. The side of the form upon which the signatures appear included the following bold heading and paragraph:

> SECOND DISCLAIMER
>
> NO OTHER WARRANTY, EITHER EXPRESS OR IMPLIED AND INCLUDING A WARRANTY OF MERCHANTABILITY AND FITNESS FOR A PARTICULAR PURPOSE HAS BEEN OR WILL BE MADE BY OR IN BEHALF OF THE MANUFACTURER OR THE SELLER OR BY OPERATION OF LAW WITH RESPECT TO THE EQUIPMENT AND ACCESSORIES OR THEIR INSTALLATION, USE, OPERATION, REPLACEMENT OR REPAIR.

Dale and Ila Myers signed this form and initialed an "ACKNOWLEDGMENT AND RELIANCE" to [this] effect:

> I HAVE READ AND UNDERSTOOD THE TERMS AND CONDITIONS OF THIS PURCHASE ORDER INCLUDING THE WARRANTIES, DISCLAIMERS AND TERMS AND CONDITIONS HEREIN GIVEN TO ME, EITHER BY THE MANUFACTURER OR THE SELLER. I RELY ON NO OTHER PROMISES OR CONDITIONS AND REGARD THAT AS REASONABLE BECAUSE THESE ARE FULLY ACCEPTABLE TO ME.

[T]he question whether the disclaimer statement and acknowledgment was sufficiently conspicuous to effect a waiver is a question of law for the court. The language quoted above is *labeled* as a disclaimer in large, bold, capital letters, and also is *written* in bold,

capital letters. We hold that the disclaimer was conspicuous and that the language effectively excluded implied warranties of merchantability and fitness for a particular purpose. Our holding is in accord with the conclusions reached by other courts which have examined nearly identical documents.

Even if [it is] conspicuous, the Myerses suggest [that] the disclaimer clause should not be effective because a [sales] representative told Dale Myers that the side of the form containing the parties' signatures did not relate to his purchase. However, upon examining the referenced testimony we find a slightly different account of the execution of the document. On direct examination, Dale Myers testified:

> Q: [T]here was [sic] some statements made by Mr. Collette concerning the back of this contract. What were those statements?
>
> A: To the best of my recollection, Mr. Collette said that "That part of this contract has nothing to do with the equipment you're purchasing, the price of that equipment or anything of that nature. The back of this contract is the fine print, and you can read it." He handed me a pencil.
>
> I started to read it, and to me, it's small print, I did not read the whole thing. And he says, "When you get through, you can initial it here and sign it here."
>
> That's what I done [sic].

Here, the disclaimer was *not* part of the small print also appearing on the signature page. We find little in this testimony to suggest that Dale Myers was directed to ignore the disclaimer. On the contrary, he apparently was allowed to read it. Finding no reason to refuse to enforce the clause, we hold that the implied warranty claims were barred by the disclaimer.

## Judgment and Result

Trial court decision on the implied warranty claims affirmed; the Myerses lose on those claims.

## Questions

1. Compare AOS's disclaimer to the language of Section 2-316(2). Why did the disclaimer successfully insulate AOS from implied warranty liability?
2. What legal doctrine might the Myerses' attorney have used to attack AOS's disclaimer? Under that doctrine, what arguments could he or she have made? On the facts of this case, however, what objection to the use of this doctrine would many courts still make?
3. Why did the court not have to consider the Magnuson–Moss Act here?

## Remedy Limitations

Immediately following the implied warranty disclaimer in the *Myers* case, the following language appeared: "NEITHER THE MANUFACTURER NOR THE SELLER SHALL BE LIABLE BY VIRTUE OF THIS WARRANTY, OR OTHERWISE, FOR ANY SPECIAL OR CONSEQUENTIAL LOSS OR DAMAGE... RESULTING FROM THE USE OR LOSS OF THE USE OF EQUIPMENT AND ACCESSORIES." This statement is a **remedy limitation**. Unlike disclaimers, which attack the plaintiff's theory of recovery, an enforceable remedy limitation prevents plaintiffs from recovering certain damages while leaving the theory of recovery intact. Thus damages that have not been excluded by a remedy limitation still can be recovered by the plaintiff as long as all liability under that theory has not been disclaimed. For example, suppose that a seller fails to properly disclaim the implied warranty of merchantability but does manage to exclude liability for consequential damages. Here, a buyer with a good implied warranty of merchantability claim still could recover basis-of-the-bargain damages. Because they can involve large dollar claims, the usual remedy limitation attempts to exclude consequential damages. Often, such exclusions are coupled with contract language limiting recovery to the repair or replacement of defective products or parts.

In tort cases, the tests for enforcing remedy limitations resemble those previously discussed for disclaimers. Under the UCC, remedy limitations are handled under different provisions than those governing disclaimers. UCC Sections 2-719(1) and 2-719(3) allow the seller to limit the buyer's remedies in express and implied warranty cases. Section 2-719(3), however, raises the possibility that a limitation of consequential damages will be unconscionable. It suggests that such a limitation may be unconscionable where the plaintiff's loss is "commercial." It is unclear what Code means by this term, but it might include all kinds of damages except personal injury and punitive damages. Where the loss is deemed commercial, courts presumably must make case-by-case determinations under the criteria described in the previous section. Section 2-719(3) also states that a limitation of consequential damages is prima facie unconscionable where the plaintiff has suffered personal injury resulting from the sale of consumer goods (goods used for personal, family, or household purposes). The "prima facie" language probably means that the limitation of consequential damages is presumed to be unconscionable unless the seller can demonstrate otherwise.

The *Moorer v. Hartz Seed Co.* case on page 678 involves a situation where the plaintiff's loss was "commercial." It illustrates the courts' tendency to find remedy limitations (and disclaimers) conscionable where the plaintiff is a party of at least some business sophistication who does not suffer personal injury.

## Timing Provisions

Product liability law puts various limitations on the time period within which suit must be brought. Here, we divide these restrictions into statutes of limitations and statutes of repose.

# Moorer v. Hartz Seed Co.
Middle District of Alabama
120 F. Supp.2d 1283 (2000)

## Background and Facts

Moorer Seed Company (MSC) was primarily engaged in the business of cleaning seeds; but it also purchased seeds to plant, harvest, and sell. MSC purchased some soybean seeds from the Hartz Seed Company. Each invoice accompanying seed delivered to MSC had the language **"ADDITIONAL TERMS, CONDITIONS AND LIMITED WARRANTY ON BACK"** placed immediately above the customer's signature line. One paragraph of these terms and conditions went as follows:

> **LIMITATION OF LIABILITY.** BUYER'S EXCLUSIVE REMEDY SHALL BE FOR DAMAGES, AND SELLER'S TOTAL LIABILITY FOR ANY AND ALL LOSSES AND DAMAGES ARISING OUT OF ANY CAUSE WHATSOEVER (WHETHER SUCH CAUSE BE BASED IN CONTRACT, NEGLIGENCE, STRICT LIABILITY, OTHER TORT, OR OTHERWISE) SHALL IN NO EVENT EXCEED THE PURCHASE PRICE OF THE GOODS IN RESPECT TO WHICH SUCH CAUSE ARISES OR, AT SELLER'S OPTION, THE REPLACEMENT OF SUCH GOODS, AND IN NO EVENT SHALL SELLER BE LIABLE FOR INCIDENTAL, CONSEQUENTIAL, OR PUNITIVE DAMAGES RESULTING FROM ANY SUCH CAUSE . . .

After taking delivery, MSC transferred the seeds to five farmers with whom it had contracted to grow soybeans. Some of the seeds did not germinate properly and MSC claimed that it suffered consequential damages on the deal. Later, MSC sued Hartz under various theories, including express warranty. Hartz moved for summary judgment. Among Hartz's arguments was a claim that the contract language just quoted blocked MSC from recovering any consequential damages.

## Body of Opinion

**Chief Judge Albritton.** Defendants do not seek summary judgment as to . . . MSC's claim for breach of express warranty. However, defendants contend that their potential liability on [this claim] is limited to the purchase price paid by MSC. . . .

Alabama law specifically allows parties, by agreement, to fashion their own remedies [quoting UCC Section 2-719]. . . . In the present case, there is a very specific provision limiting any recovery by MSC to the purchase price of the soybean seeds. Such stipulated remedies and limitations of consequential damages are frequently enforced where the injured party is a business person suffering commercial loss. MSC responds [by arguing] that the limitation-of-liability clause is unconscionable. . . . Section 2-719(3) of the UCC states: "Consequential damages may be limited or excluded unless the limitation or exclusion is unconscionable. Limitations of consequential damages for injury to the person in the case of consumer goods is prima facie unconscionable but limitation of damages where the loss is commercial is not."

Under Alabama law, the court decides as a matter of law whether a contract clause is unconscionable. In support of its argument, MSC relies primarily on another case from this district, *Majors v. Kalo Laboratories, Inc.* (1975), where the court refused to enforce a limitation-of-damages clause, finding it to be unconscionable. In *Majors*, the defendant-retailer sold soybean inoculant to the plaintiff-farmer. The plaintiff brought suit against the retailer, claiming substantial damages due to crop failure resulting from an alleged defect in the inoculant. The retailer defended on the grounds that the plaintiff was limited to the price of the product as stated on the product's package and advertising brochures. . . . Evidence was submitted to the court which showed that, prior to shipment to the plaintiff, the defendant-retailer was aware that its product was experimental and of uncertain quality. This information was not made known to the plaintiff. The court, in finding that the limitations clause was unconscionable, focused on the fact that the inoculant's defect was latent and that it caused large and unforeseeable consequential damages to the plaintiff-farmer. . . . The court also found it significant that the retailer had not informed the plaintiff of the experimental nature of the product.

In contrast to the *Majors* decision, there is the more recent response of the Supreme Court of Alabama . . . in *Southland Farms, Inc. v. Ciba-Geigy Corp.* (1991), which [considered] whether a particular limitation-of-remedies clause was unconscionable under Alabama law. The *Southland Farms* case involved the sale of agricultural chemical products by the defendant to a plaintiff farming corporation. After having used the chemicals on its potato fields, the plaintiff suffered damage to its crop caused by nut grass and potato rot. The chemicals had been intended to prevent such damage. The chemical containers were labeled with a limitation-of-remedy provision and an exclusion of consequential damages. The Supreme Court, in concluding that the limitation-of-remedy provision was enforceable, stated that the clear public policy in Alabama is to allow a seller to limit the remedies available to a buyer. . . . [T]he Supreme Court noted several reasons why these limitations-of-remedies clauses have become accepted in the agricultural chemical industry: (1) the vagaries of nature and the nature of such products; (2) the fact that the numerous factors affecting crop yield are beyond the manufacturer's control; (3) the fact that if the potential for consequential losses were shifted to the seller, the cost of the product would be prohibitive; and (4) the fact that crop insurance is available to the farmer to mitigate any burdensome effect that such an exclusion would have.

This court concludes, in light of the plain language of the UCC and the *Southland Farms* decision, that the limitation-of-remedies clause in the present case is not unconscionable. The *Majors* opinion . . . involved a different factual scenario. There, the court was presented with abundant evidence that the defendant, while attempting to completely limit its liability, was knowingly misrepresenting the experimental qualities of its product to the plaintiff. . . . It was the express intent of the drafters of Alabama's Commercial Code to allow sophisticated business people to work out their own affairs. In the present case, there is an agreement between sophisticated businesses to allocate certain risks to the buyer, MSC. This allocation is explicitly allowed for under Code Section 2-719(3). . . . There is much more to the growth of a successful soybean crop than germination rates. If the defendants are potentially liable for all consequential damages arising from crop failure, the cost of their products would be prohibitively expensive. Finally means are available for buyers to mitigate any burdensome effects a limitation-of-remedies provision might have. Here, MSC has largely avoided any potential difficulties by having a limitation-of-remedies provision of its own with its contract farmers.

## Judgment and Result

The court held that Hartz's limitation of consequential damages was valid under the UCC and was not unconscionable. For other reasons, however, it denied Hartz's motion for summary judgment on its

argument that the limitation-of-remedies clause prevented recovery on MSC's express warranty claim.

## Questions

1. In this case, Hartz's "additional terms and conditions" included a disclaimer that satisfied UCC Section 2-316(2), but Hartz did not argue that this clause knocked out MSC's express warranty claim. Instead, it tried to limit MSC's damages on the express warranty claim. Why do you think that Hartz followed this strategy?
2. Suppose that the facts in a subsequent Alabama case resemble the facts in this case, except that the plaintiff in the later case is a farmer like the plaintiff in the preceding *Myers* case. Suppose further that you are an attorney representing this farmer. What language in the preceding opinion would be helpful to you in trying to distinguish your case from *Moorer v. Hartz Seed Company*?
3. What policy arguments did the court use to justify its decision?

## STATUTES OF LIMITATIONS

Product liability suits under the UCC are governed by Section 2-725(1), which states: "An action for breach of any contract for sale must be commenced within four years after the cause of action has accrued."[8] Section 2-725(2) says that the normal time of a cause of action's accrual is the time the breach occurs, and makes this the time the seller offers to deliver the defective goods to the buyer. However, Section 2-725(2) changes the time of accrual to the time when the breach was or should have been discovered where "a warranty explicitly extends to future performance of the goods and discovery of the breach must await the time of such performance." Determining when this exception applies can be difficult. For example, the later date of accrual may apply if the goods are sold with a "Lifetime Guarantee" or are warranted for "25,000 miles or five years."

In tort suits, the applicable statutes of limitations typically are shorter than the UCC statute of limitations. However, this shorter period normally begins to run only at the time of the injury, or the time the plaintiff discovered or should have discovered the defect. For this reason, the tort standard often is more favorable to the plaintiff.

Some states also have special statutes of limitations that override their regular UCC and tort statutes of limitations where they apply. Examples include special limitations for delayed manifestation injuries such as those caused by long-term exposure to asbestos; and for cases involving death, personal injury, and property damage.

[8] The Code also requires that the plaintiff notify the seller of any breach of warranty within a reasonable time after the buyer discovered or should have discovered that breach. There usually is no notice requirement in tort cases involving defective goods.

## STATUTES OF REPOSE

Statutes of repose try to limit seller and manufacturer liability for products that have been used for extended time periods. A statute of repose normally begins to run at the time the product is sold to the first purchaser in the chain of distribution who is not buying for resale (thus excluding middlemen), and usually continues for ten to twelve years thereafter. In a state with a ten-year statute of repose, a buyer who buys the product for purposes other than resale and never resells it cannot recover for losses occurring more than ten years after the purchase. This is true even if the suit was commenced quickly enough to satisfy the applicable statute of limitations.

Closely resembling statutes of repose are the useful safe life statutes created by some states. These laws prevent recovery for losses occurring after the product's "useful safe life" has passed. This is the period during which the product is normally likely to perform in a safe manner. In some states, there is a presumption that the useful safe life ceases ten or twelve years after the product is delivered to the first buyer who does not purchase for resale. In such states, the useful safe life defense resembles a statute of repose.

## DEFENSES INVOLVING THE PLAINTIFF'S BEHAVIOR

In a broad sense, the term *defense* refers to any legal argument a defendant uses to defeat a plaintiff's claim. In a product liability suit, for example, a defendant might allege the plaintiff's failure to comply with a statute of limitations, the absence of privity, or the existence of an enforceable disclaimer. Here, however, we discuss defenses that involve the plaintiff's behavior. Traditionally, product liability law has recognized three such defenses: product misuse (or abnormal use), contributory negligence, and assumption of risk. Today, however, product liability law increasingly tends to apportion damages between the plaintiff and the seller under doctrines such as **comparative negligence** and **comparative fault**. Before considering these doctrines, we must first examine the traditional defenses.

### THE TRADITIONAL DEFENSES

*Product Misuse.* Product misuse or abnormal use occurs when a product is used in some unusual, unforeseeable way, and this causes the injury or loss for which the plaintiff sues. Examples of product misuse include mishandling the product, materially altering it, and failing to follow the manufacturer's instructions. Abnormal use has been a complete defense for the defendant in warranty, negligence, and 402A cases. However, the defense is not available where the defendant has reason to foresee the misuse and fails to take reasonable precautions to protect against it.

*Contributory Negligence.* Contributory negligence is the plaintiff's failure to exercise reasonable care for his or her own safety. If the plaintiff fails to exercise such care and this failure causes the injury or loss for which she sues in negligence, the defendant has a defense to that suit. In product liability cases, many kinds of behavior can qualify as contributory negligence. Perhaps the most common example is the simple failure to notice a dangerous but plainly apparent product defect. Many forms of product misuse also amount to contributory negligence.

Traditionally, contributory negligence has been a complete defense even where the plaintiff's carelessness was relatively slight. This rule has long worked to the advantage of defendants in negligence suits. It has also created an all-or-nothing situation in which slightly careless plaintiffs recovered nothing, while plaintiffs who were only somewhat more careful obtained a large damage award. In response to these perceived injustices, most states have enacted some form of **comparative negligence** for negligence suits. All systems of comparative negligence require that the factfinder determine the degree to which each party's negligence caused the injury, and state this in percentage terms. Then, the court allocates damages on this basis by reducing the plaintiff's recovery in proportion to his percentage share of the negligence causing the injury. In a *pure* system of comparative negligence, this allocation of damages occurs no matter what the plaintiff's and the defendant's relative shares of the negligence causing the injury. Thus, a plaintiff suffering losses of $10,000 would recover $4,000 if the factfinder determines that the defendant's share of the negligence causing the injury was 40 percent and the plaintiff's share was 60 percent. In states with a *mixed* system of comparative negligence, however, this percentage allocation of losses operates only where the defendant's share of the negligence causing the injury is greater than (or greater than or equal to) 50 percent. Under this comparative negligence system, the plaintiff in the preceding example would recover nothing.

In states that have not adopted comparative negligence, contributory negligence remains a defense to product liability suits based on a negligence theory. Some states have allowed contributory negligence to be a defense in warranty suits, and some have not. Contributory negligence usually has not been a defense in 402A cases. Where it exists, comparative negligence obviously is available in a negligence suit. But it is difficult to generalize about comparative negligence's application to other theories. Here, much may depend on how the state's comparative negligence statute is written—whether, for example, it only applies to negligence suits.

*Assumption of Risk.* Assumption of risk is the voluntary acceptance of a known risk of harm. It differs from contributory negligence because it involves a subjective test: actual knowledge of the risk. Suppose that the plaintiff consumes a soft drink containing a plainly visible decomposed mouse. If the plaintiff simply failed to notice the condition of the drink, only contributory negligence could be raised as a defense. But if the plaintiff was aware of the defect and consumed the drink anyway, assumption of risk would be available to the defendant. Like product misuse, assumption of risk traditionally has been a defense in negligence, warranty, and 402A cases.

## The Movement Toward Comparative Fault

Although not all states have joined the bandwagon, recent years have witnessed a general movement toward a system of comparative fault in product liability cases. Where comparative fault applies, the traditional rules just discussed no longer control. Although comparative negligence and comparative fault are often used interchangeably, they probably should be distinguished. Technically, comparative negligence compares only the plaintiff's and the defendant's *negligence*, while comparative fault compares all kinds of fault, such as negligence, contributory negligence, assumption of risk, product misuse, and others. Comparative fault operates much like comparative negligence, except that it considers all these kinds of fault, and not just the parties' negligence. Like comparative negligence, comparative fault may operate in either a pure or a mixed fashion. However, it is not always clear which theories of recovery permit a comparative fault defense.[9]

## CHAPTER SUMMARY

Today, the five most important theories of product liability recovery are (1) express warranty (made by affirmation of fact or promise, description, sample, or model); (2) implied warranty of fitness for a particular purpose (made when the seller has reason to know the buyer's needs and that the buyer was relying on the seller's skill or judgment); (3) implied warranty of merchantability (made by merchants who sell goods); (4) negligence (which assumes many forms); and (5) strict liability (mainly under Section 402A of the *Restatement (Second) of Torts*, which applies when merchant-like sellers sell products that are defective and unreasonably dangerous). A few minor theories of recovery exist as well. To all this, we add the new scheme of recovery created by the *Restatement (Third) of Torts: Product Liability*.

Several problems cut across the theories of recovery just described; they are resolved differently from theory to theory. These include (1) the damages obtainable; (2) the effect of the old no-liability-outside-privity-of-contract defense; and (3) the effect of disclaimers and remedy limitations. The states' various limitations on the time within which suit can be brought also vary somewhat from theory to theory. Finally, the traditional defenses of assumption of risk, contributory negligence, and product misuse vary somewhat in their effect from theory to theory. Currently, however, there is a broad movement toward comparative fault in this area. As a result, the traditional defenses are less important than they were formerly.

---

[9] The *Restatement (Third)* has a broadly worded "comparative responsibility" provision that apportions liability among the plaintiff, the seller, and distributors.

---

■ **MANAGER'S ETHICAL DILEMMA** ■

Fred Smith, an in-house attorney for one of the firms in the farm equipment market, apparently is having a mid-life crisis. He is discussing his feelings with Norma Thomas, a hotshot young MBA with the company.

FRED: "Year after year, we take these poor farmers to the cleaners with our standard-form implied warranty disclaimers, and it's beginning to get me down."

NORMA: "Why? It's legal, isn't it?"

FRED: "What's legal isn't always what's right. Sometimes businesses have to recognize moral obligations that go beyond just obeying the law."

NORMA: "Well, I don't know about that. But even assuming you're right, what's so awful about implied warranty disclaimers? They're in the contract, aren't they? And don't they have to be conspicuous, too? So why can't people just take a walk if they don't like our terms?"

Continued

## ■ MANAGER'S ETHICAL DILEMMA

FRED: "Every firm in our industry uses the same standard-form implied warranty disclaimers."

NORMA: "So that must mean that they're acceptable. Don't you think some competitor would offer different terms if it thought it could get an edge that way?"

FRED: "Good God, Norma! Who ever reads those things? *I* don't, and I'm a lawyer! Do *you* read them? Besides, some of those clauses are so filled with legalese that they're not so easy to read and understand. And to tell you the truth, some of our customers probably can't read very well. Even if they could and even if they made the effort, would they understand what an implied warranty is and what it means to disclaim it?"

NORMA: "So you seem to be saying that courts should never enforce implied warranty disclaimers. But doesn't that deprive consumers of an important option? An implied warranty is a lot like an insurance policy, because it says that if the goods are defective, you can recover against the seller. But why shouldn't consumers have the option to buy a product without this insurance policy and pay a lower price? Shouldn't a `moral' company give people that choice?"

FRED: "But you've missed my whole point! Usually, our buyers don't have the foggiest idea what they're getting! But maybe you have an argument—if we try harder to make our customers aware. For example, we might have our sales people explain the disclaimer in everyday language and thus give our customers a clear choice."

NORMA: "I wonder how many firms would or could operate that way. For example, your system probably would make it tougher to predict our liability exposure, so we might need more insurance coverage. Also, we'd need better internal record-keeping. Stuff like this probably would increase our internal costs, cut our profits, and generally make us less competitive."

FRED: "In that case, the law should require enhanced disclosure of warranty terms, so that all competitors would be in the same boat."

NORMA: "Oh my God! *More* regulation!"

FRED: "So what? Business has to be made to do what's right."

NORMA: "But what *is* right here? All the things you're suggesting cost money. If everyone has to do these things, the cost of products almost certainly will be higher. That's true even where people reject my "insurance policy.""

FRED: "Who cares? Free, informed, rational choice is central to human dignity and human autonomy."

NORMA: "But the consequence of your `human dignity' and `human autonomy' is that consumers have less money than they otherwise would."

FRED: "Consequences don't matter where a *principle* is at stake."

NORMA: "Oh really? Me, I'll take the money."

Who do you think has gotten the best of this exchange? Why?

## DISCUSSION QUESTIONS

1. One general trend within twentieth century product liability law has been the blurring of the line between tort and contract. From the materials in this chapter, identify some instances where the requirements established by particular tort and contract theories are very similar.

2. Is the implied warranty of merchantability a good idea? If it did not exist, would buyers probably be paying less for the products they buy, or more? In the former case, why shouldn't they have the choice of getting less legal protection in exchange for a lower price, or paying more to get an express warranty of some kind? But will sellers offer an express warranty in such situations? Or will competition require them to do so?

   On the other hand, are there simply certain minimum obligations of commercial responsibility that should apply to sellers regardless of what deal they might make with their buyers? If so, is an implied warranty of merchantability one of those obligations?

3. The applicable product liability rules often vary considerably depending on whether the plaintiff is an ordinary consumer, on the one hand, or a business entity, on the other. Review this chapter and identify as many examples of this divergence as you can. Why does the law make this distinction? Should this distinction be made in all cases involving "business" plaintiffs? For example, should a gas station that is operated as a sole proprietorship be treated the same as the IBM Corporation?

4. In strict liability cases, sellers and manufacturers are liable regardless of whether they were at fault. Is this morally right? In other words, is it fair to penalize innocent people? On the other hand, is it right to allow a seriously injured plaintiff to receive no compensation for injuries caused by a defective product? How does the risk-spreading strategy balance these competing moral concerns?

5. What do you think about the *Martinez* case earlier in the chapter? Leaving aside the question of Martinez's contributory fault, why shouldn't a seller who gives an adequate warning of risks associated with the product be allowed to escape liability? On

the other hand, consider the likely real-world effects if other courts follow the rule in the *Martinez* case. What will manufacturers have to do?

6. What do you think about the tort reform movement? Is it a praiseworthy effort to scale back the ridiculous excesses of the product liability explosion? Or is it a cynical ploy to allow businesses to evade their moral responsibilities and increase their profits? Does the truth lie somewhere between these extremes?

7. Do you agree with the court's definition of the basis-of-the-bargain requirement in the *Daughtrey* case? Should Daughtrey be able to recover for breach of a promise on which he did not rely? On the other hand, didn't Ashe make a *promise* that he broke? Should Daughtrey recover for that reason alone?

8. Some *deontological* moral theories say that the test for the morality of an action is its own nature: In this view, some things are inherently right or wrong, and that's it. On the other hand, *consequentialist* moral theories say that the morality of actions should be judged by their consequences. In the Manager's Ethical Dilemma, who is the deontologist and who the consequentialist?

9. What do you think about the result in the *Myers* case? If you don't like that result, make a legal argument for the result you prefer.

10. Why are uniform acts often so unclear? Article 2 of the UCC is a notorious example. How could a body of illustrious experts come up with such confused provisions as, for example, the three versions of UCC Section 2-318? *Hints*: By what process does a uniform act actually become law? Do all the interested parties agree about what commercial law should be like? Don't the drafters of a uniform act have to think about these things? In fact, who says that the drafters agree about what rules are best?

## INFOTRAC KEYWORDS

**Use your InfoTrac password to look up articles on http://www.infotrac-college.com**

Keywords: *warranty of merchantability, product liability, product liability recovery, strict liability, MagnusonMoss Act, tort damages, tort reform, privity, unconscionability, limitation of liability.*

For suggested readings, please visit this book's Web site at **http://fisher.westbuslaw.com** (click on "Internet Applications").

# ENVIRONMENTAL LAW

## POSITIVE LAW ETHICAL PROBLEMS

"You are just putting the chemical plant in our backyards because we are black. It's environmental racism," claimed Ms. Florence Robinson.

"It is unfortunate that the original zoning placed this industrial complex next to the community of Alsen. This does not appear to be intentionally racist," responded a Louisiana official.

Does the location of industrial plants in historically black neighborhoods amount to environmental racism?

"They want to find me guilty of a crime just because a few bits of dirt were pushed into a lake," said John Smith, a real estate developer.

"It is a crime," answered a California official, "if you don't have an NPDES permit!"

Is it a crime to bulldoze dirt into a lake without a permit?

> *"A RIVER IS MORE THAN AN AMENITY, IT IS A TREASURE."*
>
> **— JUSTICE OLIVER WENDELL HOLMES, JR.,** IN *NEW JERSEY V. NEW YORK*, 283 U.S. 336 (1931)

> *ELEVEN PERCENT OF ALL U.S. WOMEN WILL CONTRACT BREAST CANCER DURING THEIR LIVES.*
>
> **— ADVERTISEMENT BY GENERAL ELECTRIC**

> *APPROXIMATELY ELEVEN PERCENT OF ALL MEN IN THE U.S. WILL CONTRACT PROSTATE CANCER DURING THEIR LIVES.*
>
> **— STATISTICAL ABSTRACT OF THE UNITED STATES**

It is difficult to speak about environmental law without falling victim to the high-sounding platitudes used by commencement speakers. For example, "The problems we face in this area will be with us for thousands of years." "Our solutions to these problems could determine the future of humanity." Unfortunately, in the case of environmental law, many of these observations are true.

This chapter surveys several federal statutes addressing various environmental problems: water and air pollution, waste disposal, and extinction of life forms. The chapter ends with a glimpse at environmental trends.

## THE ENVIRONMENTAL ETHIC

While recognizing the flaws in the words *conservative* and *liberal*, we might say that environmental law shares both aspects. It is conservative because it aims to maintain and improve the quality of the air, water, and life generally and to strike an appropriate balance between present consumption and maintenance for future generations of the earth. However, liberals also have seized upon environmental and resource scarcity as areas that demand social control.

Environmental law has been criticized by both the politically conservative and liberal sectors. Conservatives point out that the estimated $1 trillion cost of toxic waste cleanup in the United States has bankrupted many "names" in Lloyds of London, which has insured toxic cleanups in the United States. As the sector that will immediately be called on to spend this amount, business conservatives rightfully ask, "Is environmental control worth it?" Thus, such persons often demand a cost–benefit analysis. If benefits outweigh costs, then the argument is settled. One problem, though, is that cleanup costs are definite, while benefits are not. How much is it worth to reduce the incidence of breast cancer in women, which studies have linked to environmental causes? How much is it worth to reduce emphysema, bronchitis, and heart disease, all of which have been linked to environmental causes? What is the value of a blue sky? We rightfully ask these questions when we are called upon to spend billions to cope with environmental problems. Ultimately, society pays in poorer health, property damage, and possible long-term habitat destruction, on the one hand, or in high environmental cleanup and maintenance costs, on the other. Table 24.1 presents the cost–benefit trade-off associated with a variety of health and safety regulations.

Some political liberals (in particular, certain poverty and minority groups) criticize the environmental movement as elitist. They see environmentalism as an attempt to prevent lower socioeconomic classes from enjoying the good life already enjoyed by many environmentalists. The good life, as they see it, necessitates some environmental degradation and resource exhaustion. They say it is is not fair to prevent them from enjoying the material things that economically privileged middle and upper classes have had for years.

## An Improvement in Calculating GDP

Gross domestic product (GDP) is the prime measure of national economic welfare. Until 1994, GDP did not measure all positive environmental benefits such as cleaner air and water, fewer health problems, and less property damage. Following 1994, efforts to take pollution control into account were made.

## Overview of Environmental Law

Before examining specific environmental statutes, consider the following observations about environmental law. First, if the number of environmental laws on the books is any indication of environmental concern, then the United States is environmentally concerned. The following list includes some important environmental laws:

- National Environmental Policy Act of 1969
- Clean Water Act (formerly known as the Federal Water Pollution Control Act, or simply the FWPCA)
- Clean Air Act
- Federal Noise Control Act of 1972
- Resource Conservation and Recovery Act of 1976 (RCRA)
- Federal Insecticide, Fungicide, and Rodenticide Act (FIFRA)
- Toxic Substances Control Act (TOSCA)
- Marine Protection, Research, and Sanctuaries Act of 1972
- Energy Supply and Environmental Coordination Act of 1974
- Endangered Species Act
- Safe Drinking Water Act of 1974
- Nuclear Waste Policy Act
- Comprehensive Environmental Response Compensation and Liability Act (CERCLA)

## TABLE 24.1 RISKS AND COST-EFFECTIVENESS OF SELECTED REGULATIONS, BY COST PER PREMATURE DEATH AVERTED

| Regulation* | Year Issued | Health or Safety | Agency | Baseline Mortality Risk per Million Exposed | Cost per Premature Death Averted |
|---|---|---|---|---|---|
| | | | | | million $ |
| Unvented Space Heater Ban | 1980 | S | CPSC | 1,890 | 0.1 |
| Aircraft Cabin FireProtection Std. | 1985 | S | FAA | 5 | 0.1 |
| Auto Passive Restraint/SeatBelt Std. | 1984 | S | NHTSA | 6,370 | 0.1 |
| Steering Column Protection Std.** | 1967 | S | NHTSA | 385 | 0.1 |
| Underground Construction Stds.*** | 1989 | S | OSHA-S | 38,700 | 0.1 |
| Trihalomethane Drinking Water Stds. | 1979 | H | EPA | 420 | 0.2 |
| Aircraft Seat Cushion Flammability Std. | 1984 | S | FM | 11 | 0.4 |
| Alcohol and Drug Control Stds.*** | 1985 | H | FRA | 81 | 0.4 |
| Auto Fuel-System Integrity Std. | 1975 | S | NHTSA | 343 | 0.4 |
| Stds. for Servicing Auto Wheel Rims*** | 1984 | S | OSHA-S | 630 | 0.4 |
| Aircraft Floor Emergency Lighting Std. | 1984 | S | FAA | 2 | 0.6 |
| Concrete & Masonry Construct. Std.*** | 1988 | S | OSHA-S | 630 | 0.6 |
| Crane Suspended Pers. Platf'm Std.*** | 1988 | S | OSHA-S | 81,000 | 0.7 |
| Passive Restraints—Truck & Bus (P) | 1989 | S | NHTSA | 6,370 | 0.7 |
| Side-Impact Stds. for Autos (Dynamic) | 1990 | S | NHTSA | na | 0.8 |
| Children's Sleepwear Flam'lity Ban**** | 1973 | S | CPSC | 29 | 0.8 |
| Auto Side Door Support Stds. | 1970 | S | NHTSA | 2,520 | 0.8 |
| Low-Alt. Windsh'r Equip. & Train. Std. | 1988 | S | FAA | na | 1.3 |
| Electrical Equip't Stds. (Metal Mines) | 1970 | S | MSHA | na | 1.4 |
| Trenching & Excavation Stds.*** | 1989 | S | OSHA-S | 14,310 | 1.5 |
| Traffic Alert & Collision Avoidance Sys. | 1988 | S | FAA | na | 1.5 |
| Hazard Communication Std.*** | 1983 | S | OSHA-S | 1,800 | 1.6 |
| Side-ImpactTruck, Bus, & MPV (P) | 1989 | S | NHTSA | na | 2.2 |
| Grain Dust Explosion Prev'n Stds.*** | 1987 | S | OSHA-S | 9,450 | 2.8 |
| Rear Lap/Shoulder Belts for Autos | 1989 | S | NHTSA | na | 3.2 |
| Radionuclides—Uran. Mines Stds.*** | 1984 | H | EPA | 6,300 | 3.4 |
| Benzene NESHAP (Fugitive Emis'n) | 1984 | H | EPA | 1,470 | 3.4 |
| Ethylene Dibromide Drinking Water Std. | 1991 | H | EPA | na | 5.7 |
| Benzene NESHAP(Coke By-Prod.)*** | 1988 | H | EPA | na | 6.1 |
| Asbestos Occup'l Exposure Limit*** | 1972 | H | OSHA-H | 3,015 | 8.3 |
| Benzene Occup'l Exposure Limit*** | 1987 | H | OSHA-H | 39,600 | 8.9 |
| Electrical Equip. Stds. (Coal Mines)*** | 1970 | S | MSHA | na | 9.2 |
| Arsenic Emis'n Stds.—Glass Plants | 1986 | H | EPA | 2,660 | 13.5 |
| Ethylene Oxide Occup'l Expos. Limit*** | 1984 | H | OSHA-H | 198 | 20.5 |
| Arsenic/Copper NESHAP | 1986 | H | EPA | 63,000 | 23.0 |
| Haz Waste List—Petrol. Refin. Sludge | 1990 | H | EPA | 210 | 27.6 |
| Cover/Move Uran. Tail'gs (Inact. Sites) | 1983 | H | EPA | 30,100 | 32.0 |
| Benzene NESHAP (Trans. Oper'ns) | 1990 | H | EPA | na | 33.0 |
| Cover/Move Uran. Tailings (Act. Sites) | 1983 | H | EPA | 30,100 | 45.0 |
| Acrylonitrile Occup'l Expos. Limit*** | 1978 | H | OSHA-H | 42,300 | 52.0 |
| Coke Ovens Occup'l Expos. Limit*** | 1976 | H | OSHA-H | 7,200 | 64.0 |
| Lockout/Tagout*** | 1989 | S | OSHA-S | 4 | 71.0 |
| Asbestos Occup'l Expos. Limit*** | 1986 | H | OSHA-H | 3,015 | 74.0 |
| Arsenic Occup'l Expos. Limit*** | 1978 | H | OSHA-H | 14,800 | 107.0 |
| Asbestos Ban | 1989 | H | EPA | na | 111.0 |
| Diethylstilbestrol (DES) Cattlefeed Ban | 1979 | H | FDA | 22 | 125.0 |
| Benzene NESHAP (Waste Oper'ns) | 1990 | H | EPA | na | 168.0 |
| 1,2-Dichloropropane Drink. Water Std. | 1991 | H | EPA | na | 653.0 |
| Haz Waste Land Disposal Ban (1st 3rd) | 1988 | H | EPA | 2 | 4,190.0 |
| Municipal Solid Waste Landfill Std. (P) | 1988 | H | EPA | <1 | 19,107.0 |
| Formaldehyde Occup'l Expos. Limit*** | 1987 | H | OSHA-H | 31 | 86,202.0 |
| Atrazine/Alachlor Drinking Water Std. | 1991 | H | EPA | na | 92,070.0 |
| Haz Waste List—Wood Preser. Chems. | 1990 | H | EPA | <1 | 5,700,000.0 |

*Source:* J.F. Morall, III, "A review of the record." Regulation, vol. 10, no. 2, p. 30. Updated by the authors and published in Executive Office of the President, *The Budget for Fiscal Year 1992.* CEQ, *Environmental Quality.*

Continued

## TABLE 24.1 CONTINUED

*Notes:* \*=70-year lifetime exposure assumed unless otherwise specified; \*\*=50-year lifetime exposure; \*\*\*=45-year lifetime exposure; \*\*\*\*=12-year lifetime exposure; na=not available. Abbreviations—CPSC: Consumer Product Safety Commission; MSHA: Mine Safety and Health Administration; EPA: Environmental Protection Agency; NHTSA: National Highway Traffic Safety Administration; FAA: Federal Aviation Administration; FRA: Federal Railroad Administration; FDA: Food and Drug Administration; OSHA-H: Occupational Safety and Health Administration, Health Standards; OSHA-S: Occupational Safety and Health Administration, Safety Standards. Potential benefits other than avoiding premature death are not included. Other benefits could include avoiding risks that are not life threatening and benefits that are not related to health.

*The Web site to one of the oldest environmental groups, the Sierra Club, can be found at* **http://www.sierraclub.org**

The list is long but not complete. International environmental law includes treaties (such as the Antarctic Treaty), international conventions (such as the International Convention for the Regulation of Whaling), and international agreements (such as the Agreement on the Conservation of Polar Bears). On the state level, environmental protection statutes and municipal ordinances are designed to maintain environmental quality (such as "green belt" ordinances around municipalities designed to limit growth and be buffer zones against unsightly urban sprawl).

Although space limits prevent comments on every environmental law, this chapter will survey some of the more important or popular acts: the National Environmental Policy Act of 1969 (NEPA), the Clean Water Act, the Clean Air Act, RCRA, TOSCA, CERCLA, the Nuclear Waste Policy Act, and the Endangered Species Act. Suggested readings at the chapter's end provide good sources if readers want more information on other acts or greater detail on the acts covered here.

## PRINCIPAL ACTORS OR INSTITUTIONS

*The Web site for the U.S. Environmental Protection Agency is found at* **http://www.epa.gov** *The Environmental Defense Fund, a private environmental organization, has a Web site at* **http://www.edf.org**

No single institution exists in the development of environmental law. Instead, a number of sectors in society have shaped such law, including private environmental groups, the U.S. Environmental Protection Agency (EPA), other federal administrative agencies (including the Department of Interior), the president, Congress, state administrative agencies, and the courts (mainly federal but increasingly state).

The Council on Environmental Quality (CEQ) formerly oversaw federal agency compliance with the environmental impact statement requirement. Additionally, CEQ used to issue an annual report on the state of the environment. The Clinton administration essentially eliminated the CEQ by cutting its staff to almost zero. Thus, other organizations, such as citizen groups, must now monitor federal agency compliance with the EIS requirement as well as issue annual reports documenting environmental welfare.

## NATIONAL ENVIRONMENTAL POLICY ACT

The National Environmental Policy Act of 1969 (NEPA) was signed into law on January 1, 1970, by President Nixon. The act's name is misleading because it sounds like a law to correct all sorts of environmental harm. However, it does no such thing, directly. NEPA does three things:

1. It establishes the Council on Environmental Quality (CEQ). (The CEQ was to be eliminated, but the Bush Administration has continued its existence, though as a severely truncated agency.)
2. It requires federal agencies to take environmental concerns into account when they take certain actions.
3. It requires federal agencies to prepare detailed environmental statements (popularly called environmental impact statements, or EISs) in certain situations.

Before NEPA was passed, one federal agency (the old Atomic Energy Commission, or AEC) tried to take environmental factors into account in licensing a nuclear power plant. The AEC was successfully sued for doing so, the argument being that taking environmental concerns into account was *ultra vivres* (beyond the power of) the AEC. Soon thereafter, NEPA was passed to correct this issue by requiring federal agencies to consider environmental harms from the project *before* it is started and to reduce the harshness of environmental impacts wherever possible.

NEPA declares the following to be a *continuing* national environmental policy:

> [The Federal Government is] to use all practicable means and measures, including financial and technical assistance, in a manner calculated to foster and promote the general welfare, to create and maintain conditions under which man and nature can exist in productive harmony, and fulfill the social, economic, and other requirements of present and future generations of Americans.

To put this national environmental policy into operation, NEPA recognizes some specific federal responsibilities:

1. To fulfill the responsibilities of each generation as trustee of the environment for succeeding generations
2. To assure for all Americans safe, healthful, productive, and esthetically and culturally pleasing surroundings
3. To attain the widest range of beneficial uses of the environment without degradation or risk to health or safety
4. To preserve important historic, cultural, and natural aspects of our national heritage
5. To achieve a balance between population and resources permitting a high standard of living
6. To enhance the quality of renewable resources and to help enable the recycling of depletable resources

Note that these federal responsibilities are not required. NEPA qualifies the federal agency duty to achieve with "all practicable means" language. In other words, federal agencies must use all means to promote recycling, resource-balancing, population preservation, historic preservation, and the other responsibilities, if they are practicable.

## ENVIRONMENTAL RIGHTS

NEPA does not give people any national right to a healthy environment. If polluted air causes lung cancer or carcinogenic water causes bladder cancer, NEPA is not violated. NEPA merely says that each person *should* enjoy (not *will* enjoy or has a right to enjoy) a healthful environment. NEPA is not a potent statute in many ways.

## ENVIRONMENTAL IMPACT STATEMENTS

NEPA requires all federal agencies to prepare environmental impact statements (EISs) in two cases: (1) when the agency sends a proposed law to Congress, and (2) whenever the agency proposes major federal action significantly affecting the quality of the human environment. NEPA requires that five items be contained in an EIS:

1. The environmental impact of the proposed action
2. Any adverse environmental effects of the proposed action
3. Alternatives to the proposed action
4. The relation between short-term uses of the environment and the maintenance and enhancement of long-term productivity
5. Any irreversible and irretrievable resource commitments involved in an agency action about to be implemented

Most lawsuits dealing with NEPA have concerned EISs. As the core of NEPA, the EIS requirement is called the action-forcing part of NEPA because it requires federal agencies to prepare an EIS.

*Failure to Prepare an EIS.* Nothing happens if a federal agency fails to prepare an EIS unless someone sues the agency. If someone takes the agency to court and the court decides the agency should have prepared an EIS, the court enjoins (stops) the project until an EIS is prepared. Generally, if an EIS is adequate, with all five items that all EISs must contain, a federal project can go ahead.

*Length of EIS.* Under new Council on Environmental Quality (CEQ) regulations, EISs are supposed to be no longer than 150 pages in ordinary circumstances. Extraordinary circumstances justifying longer EISs would be "super-colossal" projects, such as the Alaskan pipeline (that EIS was 12,000 pages).

*Inadequate EIS.* A federal agency can be sued if its EIS is inadequate, and the project can be stopped. For example, if the EIS fails to consider alternatives to the proposed project or if the EIS lacks any of the other five items an EIS should contain, a court will stop the project until the agency makes the EIS adequate.

*The Public and an EIS.* A member of the public can obtain an EIS. Recall that a federal agency prepares a separate EIS for each of its major federal actions significantly affecting the quality of the human environment. Thus, anyone may ask the particular federal agency for a copy of an EIS for a particular federal project.

The public also has a right to participate in writing an EIS. The CEQ regulations set out steps a federal agency must follow in writing an EIS. The agency writes a draft EIS and submits copies to CEQ and any other federal agencies with expertise on the project. For example, the Army Corps of Engineers would have expertise in a TVA dam proposal. How the public would learn about a draft EIS is uncertain, because CEQ's EIS regulations do not require *Federal Register* notice of a particular project's EIS availability.

After receiving agency and public comments, the agency writing the EIS considers the comments, might modify the EIS to take account of the comments, and then publishes the final EIS. If significant changes are made in the final EIS after comments are received, the changes are submitted for public and agency comment again before the final EIS is published. This entire EIS public and agency commenting process is similar to the proposal-comment-promulgation process for federal regulations discussed in Chapter 7. The public helps to write EISs by making comments in response to proposed EISs.

*Substantive Requirements.* NEPA's action-forcing EIS requirement originally was procedural. That is, as long as a major agency action affecting the environment was accompanied by an EIS document containing the five basic EIS requirements, courts tended to say that NEPA's EIS requirements were met. However, the courts now generally look at the substance of the EIS and what it actually says to see whether NEPA's requirements have been met.

*Interest of Business in EIS.* Federal agency actions could require an EIS, such as EPA's issuing NPDES permits[1] to sources, the Interior Department's issuance of grazing permits on western land, and the Interior Department's leasing federal land (one-third of U.S. land belongs to the U.S. government) to oil and other companies for mineral exploration. Unless an agency prepares an EIS, the agency's conferrals of a permit to a business could be invalid. Thus, business has a dollar-and-cents interest in EISs. The *Public Citizen v. U.S. Trade Representative* case shows how the entire U.S. business community can be affected by an EIS issue. Even though NAFTA's passage was undoubtedly a major federal action significantly affecting the quality of the human environment, a federal court of appeals held that no EIS was required for NAFTA. The court reasoned that the president was not a federal "agency" for NEPA purposes and that there was no "final" agency action when the president submitted NAFTA to Congress for approval. Therefore, no EIS was required for NAFTA. Do you think the court caved in to political pressures to have NAFTA take effect?

On a smaller level, NEPA issues affect businesspeople such as land developers and timber harvesters. Often a federal agency such as the National Park Service (part of the Department of the Interior) is called upon to determine whether "cutting 200 ancient trees to build a parking lot in a national park will have "major" environmental effects. The *Coalition for Canyon Preservation v. Slater* case illustrates the problem and shows how agencies go about deciding such matters.

---

[1]NPDES stands for National Pollutant Discharge Elimination System, the permit scheme set up to implement EPA regulations limiting what people may dump into the nation's waters.

## Coalition for Canyon Preservation v. Slater
U.S. District Court (D. Montana)
33 F.Supp.2d 1276 (1999)

### Background and Facts

This case involves a challenge to a decision by the National Park Service (NPS) to construct a parking lot on the east side of the Going to the Sun Road (GTSR) at the Avalanche Creek area of Glacier National Park. The NPS issued an Environmental Assessment (EA) in April of 1996 for the project. A little over one year later, the service issued a Finding of No Significant Impact (FONSI) in July of 1997. The Coalition seek a declaratory judgment that defendants have violated the National Environmental Policy Act (NEPA). . . . The Coalition also wants an injunction barring defendants from construction of the proposed parking lot and access road unless and until they have complied with the National Environmental Policy Act. . . . The Avalanche Creek Area is located at the confluence of Avalanche and McDonald Creeks several miles upstream of McDonald Lake adjacent to the Going to the Sun Road (GTSR). Currently, the east side of the GTSR in the the area contains a campground. It has an asphalt and handicapped accessible boardwalk through the Trail of the Cedars. It is the trailhead for the two-mile hike to Avalanche Lake. The Trail of the Cedars and Avalanche Lake are both popular with Glacier visitors.

The west side of the GTSR in the Avalanche area has a twelve-table picnic area, restrooms, and twenty parking spaces that abut the southbound lane of traffic of the GTSR. Because the Trail of the Cedars and the trailhead to Avalanche Lake are on the east side of the road, and the parking to the west, there is considerable pedestrian traffic across the GTSR. Additionally, automobiles create roadside parking along both shoulders of the GTSR in order to visit the popular area. Some of this parked traffic is illegal.

Responding to the increased visitor use and the perceived need to find a long-term solution, the National Park Service conducted and completed an Environmental Assessment (EA) for a parking lot on the east side of GTSR in 1984. . . . The lack of funding meant no action was taken on the 1984 plan.

Finding a solution for the congestion in the Avalanche Creek area was revisited by the National Park Service in 1995–1996. That consideration culminated in the Environmental Assessment and FONSI which are the subject of this case. . . . The Environmental Assessment resulted in the designation of a preferred alternative by the National Park Service which calls for a parking lot on the east side of GTSR in the Avalanche Creek area. The Coalition charges that too much is at stake to go forward without benefit of a full-blown Environmental Impact Statement.

### Body of Opinion

**District Judge Molloy.** The heart of the controversy is the impact the parking lot might have on the vegetation at the site where the proposed alternative is to be constructed. It is a forest classified as cedar-devil's club habitat with trees dating to 1517. It is an area with vegetation that the Environmental Assessment admits is rare and vulnerable to extinction. The cedar-devil's club habitat in the Avalanche Creek area is the largest in Montana. It is significant in other ways because it marks the eastern-most location of cedar-devil's club habitat in the North American continent. . . .

The Draft Environmental Assessment supporting the current proposal characterized the effects of development of the parking facility as follows: Further permanent loss of this rare and unique habitat, whether it be mature or successional forest constitutes a long-term significant impact." . . . Curiously, the Final Environmental Assessment omitted this language, but did note that the habitat "is an extremely significant resource due to its age, rarity (and) biogeograhic uniqueness." . . . The language of the draft implies the need for an Environmental Impact Statement while the final language is somewhat less demanding but it too implies the need for an EIS to consider the project's impact on an extremely significant resource.

. . . Public comment on the Environmental Assessment also focused on the anticipated removal of trees from the old-growth forest to accommodate the parking lot. The public comment was nearly universally against the proposed parking lot. . . .

The National Environmental Policy Act (NEPA) requires agencies to prepare an Environmental Impact Statement (EIS) for each "major Federal action significantly affecting the quality of the human environment. . . . The policy behind NEPA is "to ensure that an agency has at its disposal all relevant information about environmental impacts before the agency embarks on the project." . . .

An Environmental Assessment (EA) is a first step under NEPA to determine whether or not projected impacts of a project may be "significant." . . . Based on the significance determination made in the EA, the agency must then prepare an EIS or FONSI. . . . Here, the National Park Service made a determination of no "significant impact" and issued a FONSI. A Finding of No Significant Impact is reviewed under the arbitrary and capricious standard. . . . This standard requires that the "court must ensure that the agency has taken a 'hard look' at the environmental consequences of its proposed action." . . .

A court may reverse an agency decision when it offers an explanation for its decision that runs counter to the evidence before the agency. . . .

In reviewing agency decisions not to prepare an Environmental Impact Statement, the inquiry by the district court centers on the reasonableness of the Finding of No Significant Impact. "If substantial questions are raised regarding whether the proposed action may have a significant effect on the human environment, a decision not to prepare an Environmental Impact Statement is unreasonable." . . .

Agencies may reach a FONSI if mitigation measures are proposed that directly address the impacts identified in the Environmental Assessment. . . . Here, the National Park Service proposes to remove the picnic area on the west side of GTSR to allow for restoration of the habitat there. It then argues that this undertaking mitigates the impacts that will result from constructing the parking lot on the east side of the road. However, the Environmental Assessment is deficient in yet another way. There is insufficient scientific analysis that the area to the west will regenerate, or that its regeneration is sufficient mitigation to the loss of the habitat to the east. The National Park Service conclusion that it will regenerate is speculative. Finally, there is no dispute that regeneration, if successful, would take centuries. The measure of mitigation would be nearly half of the next millennium. . . .

The mitigation resolution here proposed does not meet the test.

## Judgment and Result

The District Court granted the injunctive relief sought by the Canyon Coalition. The agency had to prepare an EIS.

## Questions

1. What did the court in this case say were NEPA's purposes? Had the National Park Service (and other agencies) prepared an EIS or merely an EA? Who initially decides whether a federal action is "significant" from an environmental standpoint?
2. How does an EA relate to an EIS and a FONSI?
3. Who decides to make an EA and FONSI? Do "development-oriented" agencies tend to ignore EIS requirements as "just another form to fill out" before getting on with the important activity of development?
4. Did the court determine that the National Park Service had taken a "hard look" at the plaintiffs' environmental concerns? Notice who the plaintiffs were in the case. Does their involvement support the notion that private environmental groups—not CEQ— are the main enforcers of NEPA?

## CLEAN WATER ACT

The Environmental Protection Agency tries to control water pollution by keeping unwanted matter out of the rivers, lakes, and streams of the United States. The Clean Water Act (formerly the Federal Water Pollution Control Act, or FWPCA) first set goals in stages: swimmable, fishable waters by 1983 zero discharge of pollutants by 1985. The act tries to stop water pollution by making it illegal to discharge pollutants from point sources into waters of the United States without an NPDES permit.

Let us look more closely at the elements of this definition. A pollutant could be anything foreign to water in its natural state (such as heat, sewage, or any chemical). "Waters of the United States" is so broad a phrase that, technically speaking, a person pouring Scotch into water needs an NPDES permit. It is called a commerce clause definition of water. Recall from Chapter 5 that the federal government may regulate almost anything *affecting* interstate commerce. Because all water in some way affects interstate commerce, anytime anyone puts a pollutant into water, an NPDES permit may be needed.

An NPDES permit is a piece of paper every discharger from a **point source** (a discrete point such as a pipe or outlet as opposed to general runoff) needs before it is legal to put any pollutant into any lake, river, or stream in the United States (even a lake, river, or stream on one's own land). Such a permit must be obtained from the EPA before one can legally discharge anything into U.S. waters. In the permit, the EPA sets limits on what the permit holder can put into the water.

How does the EPA decide what amounts of which pollutants can be put into the water? Recall the steps in how a regulation is made, discussed in Chapter 7. The Clean Water Act is an enabling act. It directs the EPA to conduct studies that tell which pollutants are harmful and how harmful they are. From these studies EPA proposes and promulgates regulations limiting harmful amounts of pollutants.

The Clean Water Act set out phases of pollution control for point source dischargers to meet. Municipalities were to meet secondary treatment levels by 1977, which involved letting the large items settle out and chlorinating the rest. **Best**

**practicable treatment control** (BPT) levels were to be met by 1983. Industrial dischargers were held to stricter discharge limits—BPT by 1977 and **best available treatment** (BAT) control levels by 1983. These industrial limits apply only to businesses that dump pollutants directly into U.S. waters (as opposed to those discharging into sewers).

Understanding the EPA's water pollution regulations requires knowledge of two other aspects: **effluent guidelines** and **effluent limitations**. The Clean Water Act puts all direct industrial dischargers into U.S. waters into a number of categories. The EPA then set ranges of discharge for each of the industrial groups. Within an industrial group (textile mills, for example) a particular plant dumping waste directly into a stream would have an effluent limitation set for it. (The word *effluent* refers to waste dumped into the water.) This effluent limit for a particular textile mill would be taken from the range of limits in the effluent guidelines for all textile mills. The effluent limit for the particular mill would be put into an NPDES permit.

Every direct point source discharger into U.S. waters, including municipalities, businesses, farms, and all other point source dischargers, must have an NPDES permit. Many industries discharge into municipal sewers, but municipal treatment plants were not equipped to filter out heavy metals and other toxic substances common in industrial discharge.

Some things are not point sources and do not need NPDES permits. For instance, general runoff from a farmer's field at no particular point needs no NPDES permit. Pollutants from general land runoff are treated by **area-wide waste treatment programs** under the Clean Water Act. An example of such a program might be a buffer zone of grass or vegetation next to a stream to filter the runoff before it goes into the water. Starting on October 1, 1993, storm water runoff on land will require a permit under the SWPPP (Storm Water Pollution Prevention Plan), and such runoff must be treated to remove pollutants before being discharged from one's land.

## MIDCOURSE CORRECTIONS

Between 1972 (when the present Clean Water Act's structure and goals were set) and 1985 (by which time the act's goals were to be attained), the act called for midcourse corrections (adjustments in the act) through the 1977 amendments to the Clean Water Act. They moved some compliance dates from July 1, 1983, to July 1, 1984.

The midcourse corrections tried to toughen treatment of extremely dangerous water pollutants (toxins) and loosen up on less harmful pollutants by establishing three broad groups of pollutants: conventional, nonconventional, and toxic. A discharger has to treat pollutants in a discharge according to the group into which it falls. **Best conventional treatment** (BCT) control is required for conventional pollutants. Best available treatment (BAT) control (the strictest standard) is required for both toxins and nonconventional pollutants (a catchall category).

The moving back of the dates, the loosening of pollution control requirements on some pollutants, and the tightening up on toxins were in recognition of the huge costs of water pollution control, the large number of noncompliers with the July 1, 1977, phase one deadline, and the need to control deadly pollutants.

The new midcourse correction standards provided in the 1977 amendments to the Clean Water Act are applied to individual business and municipal dischargers through NPDES permits issued to each discharger by the EPA. The 1972 act required the same thing. As of February 12, 1980, individual point source dischargers in the United States had been issued 58,907 NPDES permits (43,512 to nonmunicipal entities such as businesses and 15,395 to municipalities).

The 1977 amendments also expanded the regulatory framework by authorizing EPA to issue **best management practices** regulations to control certain parts of the plant operations to restrict toxic runoff and hazardous materials. An example of the best management practice might be a tarp put over a coal pile to limit rain from washing off untreated impurities into the streams or sewers. EPA has discretion about whether to require best management practices and how stringent to make them. Table 24.2 provides information on water pollution levels.

## CRITICISMS

A primary criticism of the Clean Water Act is its cost to public and private sectors. The 1997 Statistical Abstract sets the public sector cost at $26.9 billion and the private sector cost at $78.3 billion for the year 1993 alone. The inevitable question is, what would the quality of water be if we did not spend this money to clean it?

Another criticism of water pollution control is the inflexibility of the regulators. For example, why should all discharge pipes in a factory have to meet the same effluent limits if it is cheaper to eliminate pollutants entirely from some pipes and to let others discharge more? As long as the total amount of pollutants discharged from all the plant's outlets is the same as if each individual outlet discharged exactly the same amount, society is not hurt. This idea is reflected in the bubble policy. Think of an entire factory as having a bubble over it. The factory is viewed as having an allowable discharge limit, but individual factory pipes discharging pollutants may dump different levels of pollutants as long as the total plant's discharge does not exceed the plant limit. The bubble concept has been tried for air pollution, but its application to water pollution is in the developmental stages.

One evidence of flexibility in the Clean Water Act was the extension of phase two deadlines (the July 1, 1983, dates of BAT for industry and BPT for municipalities) to July 1, 1984, and in some cases mid-1987. Another bit of flexibility was the 1977 amendments' new pollutant classifications (conventional, nonconventional, and toxic), which set different pollution control levels based on the harm each causes—that is, more treatment for more harmful pollutants such as toxins, less treatment for less harmful conventional pollutants. Table 24.2 provides some information on the various levels of water quality conditions in the United States.

## ENFORCEMENT

The Clean Water Act has both civil and criminal sanctions. Either private parties or the governmental bodies (the EPA, the U.S. Justice Department, or state government if it has assumed administration of the NPDES permit program) can enforce the act. The governmental units may bring either civil suits (for example, to enjoin or stop dumping of pollutants into streams) or criminal suits.

Violators of the Clean Water Act are liable for damages, civil penalties, cleanup costs, fines, and prison terms. *Colvin v. United States* illustrates that businesses must have NPDES permits to dump even small amounts into United States waters.

## TABLE 24.2 U.S. WATER QUALITY CONDITIONS BY TYPE OF WATERBODY: 1998

[Section 305(b) of the Clean Water Act requires states and other jurisdictions to assess the health of their waters and the extent to which their waters support water quality standards. Section 305(b) requires that states submit reports describing water quality conditions to the Environmental Protection Agency every 2 years. Water quality standards have three elements (designed uses, criteria developed to protect each use, and an antidegradation policy. For information on survey methodology and assessment criteria, see report.]

| Item | Rivers and Streams (miles) | Lakes, Reservoirs, and Ponds (acres) | Estuaries (sq. miles) | Great Lakes Shoreline (miles) | Ocean Shoreline (miles) |
|---|---|---|---|---|---|
| Total size | 3,662,255 | 41,593,748 | 90,465 | 5,521 | 66,645 |
| Amount accessed[1] | 842,426 | 17,390,370 | 28,687 | 4,950 | 3,130 |
| Percent of total size | 23 | 42 | 32 | 90 | 5 |
| Amount accessed as— | | | | | |
| Good[2] | 463,441 | 7,927,486 | 13,439 | 85 | 2,496 |
| Good but threatened[3] | 85,544 | 1,565,175 | 2,766 | 103 | 257 |
| Polluted[4] | 291,264 | 7,897,110 | 12,482 | 4,762 | 377 |
| Percent of accessed as— | | | | | |
| Good[2] | 55 | 46 | 47 | 2 | 80 |
| Good but threatened[3] | 10 | 9 | 10 | 2 | 8 |
| Polluted[4] | 35 | 45 | 44 | 96 | 12 |
| Amount impaired by leading sources of pollution:[5] | | | | | |
| Agriculture | 170,750 | 2,417,801 | 1,827 | 133 | 48 |
| Atmospheric deposition | (NA) | 616,701 | 2,922 | 1,017 | (NA) |
| Forestry | 20,020 | (NA) | (NA) | (NA) | (NA) |
| Habitat Modification | 18,451 | 417,662 | (NA) | (NA) | (NA) |
| Hydromodification | 57,763 | 1,179,344 | 531 | (NA) | (NA) |
| Industrial discharges/point sources | 13,795 | 502,760 | 1,926 | 140 | 52 |
| Irrigated crop production | 31,156 | 410,204 | (NA) | (NA) | (NA) |
| Land disposal of wastes | 19,928 | 381,073 | 1,508 | (NA) | 117 |
| Municipal point sources | 29,087 | 866,116 | 3,528 | 120 | 96 |
| Natural sources | 33,004 | 654,812 | 5,223 | (NA) | (NA) |
| Nonirrigated crop production | 46,484 | 553,064 | (NA) | (NA) | (NA) |
| Resource extraction | 25,231 | (NA) | (NA) | (NA) | (NA) |
| Urban runoff and storm sewers | 32,310 | 931,567 | 3,482 | 134 | 236 |

NA Not available. [1] Includes waterbodies accessed as not attainable for one or more uses. Most states do not assess all their waterbodies during the 2-year reporting cycle, but use a "rotating basin approach" whereby all waters are monitored over a set period of time. [2] Based on accessment of available data, water quality supports all designated uses. Water quality meets narrative and/or numeric criteria adopted to protect and support a designated use. [3] Although all assessed uses are currently met, data show a declining trend in water quality. Projections based on this trend indicate water quality will be impaired in the future, unless action is taken to prevent further degradation. [4] Impaired or not attainable. The reporting state or jurisdiction has performed a "use-attainability analysis" and demonstrated that support of one or more designated beneficial uses is not attainable due to specific biological, chemical, physical, or economic/social conditions. [5] Excluded unknown and natural sources.
*Source:* U.S. Environmental Protection Agency, *National Water Quality Inventory: 1998 Report to Congress*, June 2000

## Colvin v. United States
U.S. District Court, Central District of California
181 F.Supp.2d 1050 (2001)

## Background and Facts

Between approximately July 1996 and February 1997 Colvin arranged for 5.4 million pounds of screw press rejects ("waste") to be dumped on the Lady Lu Ranch ("Lady Lu"). Lady Lu is located on the northern shoreline of the Salton Sea. Once deposited on Lady Lu, the waste was spread by Colvin, using a bulldozer, throughout Lady Lu. Some of the waste ended up in the Salton Sea. [It is irrelevant whether Colvin dumped the waste into the middle of the Sea or placed the waste in contact with the Sea at the shoreline, knowing that the tides would transport the waste out to sea.]

On September 9, 1997, Colvin was charged in a one-count indictment with discharging pollutants into navigable waters of the United States without a permit, in violation of the Clean Water Act. At the end of a five-day jury trial, the court read the following jury instructions, in pertinent part:

In order for the defendant to be found guilty . . . the government must prove each of the following beyond a reasonable doubt:

- First, the defendant knowingly discharged a pollutant;
- Second, the pollutant was discharged from a point source;
- Third, the pollutant entered waters of the United States; and
- Fourth, the discharge was unpermitted.

    The term *point source* is defined in the Clean Water Act to mean "any discernable, confined, and discreet conveyance, including but not limited to any . . . container . . . or vessel . . . from which pollutants are or may be discharged."

Trucks and bulldozers that discharge pollutants are point sources.

In order for the Salton Sea to constitute a water of the United States, as defined by the Clean Water Act, you must find beyond a reasonable doubt any one of the following:

1)    that the Salton Sea is used by interstate or foreign travelers for recreational or other purposes; or

2)    that the Salton Sea may provide a habitat for migratory birds or endangered species.

The jury convicted Colvin on May 21, 1999. The conviction was affirmed by the United States Court of Appeals for the Ninth Circuit on March 12, 2001.

## Body of Opinion

**District Judge Timlin.** The evidence not presented at trial that Colvin submits in support of his motion is a Supreme Court decision, *Solid Waste Agency of Northern Cook County v. Army Corps of Eng'r.* . . . (2001) ("SWANCC"), that was decided after he was convicted. According to Colvin, SWANCC invalidates the basis for his conviction.

A brief review of CWA jurisprudence is necessary in order to understand the import of SWANCC and its effect on Colvin's underlying conviction. The CWA, also known as the Federal Water Pollution Control Act, . . . prohibits the unpermitted discharge of a pollutant from a point source into a water of the United States.

The United States Army Corps of Engineers ("Corps"), to which Congress has delegated the responsibility of "protecting the quality of our Nation's waters" by, inter alia [Ed.: among other things] promulgating regulations under the CWA, . . . has accorded various interpretations to "water of the United States," or "navigable waters." . . . "Navigable waters" has included, inter alia, "waters such as intrastate lakes, rivers, streams. . . . Mudflats, sandflats. . . playa lakes, or natural ponds, the use and degradation or destruction of which could affect interstate or foreign commerce. . . ." . . . In 1986, the Corps enacted the "Migratory Bird Rule.". . . Attempting to "clarify the reach of its

jurisdiction, the Corps stated that Section 404 of the CWA extends to intrastate waters which are or would be used as habitat by birds protected by Migratory Bird Treaties; or which are or would be used as habitat by other migratory birds which cross state lines; or which are or would be used as habitat for endangered species. . . . "

The SWANCC Court reviewed the authority of the Corps to promulgate the Migratory Bird Rule. . . . It held that the Corps' construing the term "navigable intrastate waters" to include isolated, non-navigable intrastate waters used as a habitat by migratory birds as an independent basis to assert jurisdiction under the CWA exceeded the authority granted to it under the CWA. . . . However, the SWANCC court did not invalidate other Corps interpretations . . . of navigable waters, including all traditional navigable waters, all interstate waters, all tributaries to navigable or interstate waters, all wetlands adjacent to any and all such waters, and all waters that are subject to the ebb and flow of the tide. . . . See, e.g., . . . *Idaho Rural Council v. Bosma,* . . . "The Ninth Circuit defines waters of the United States broadly" and that, even after SWANCC, "waters of the United States include at least some waters that are not navigable in the classical sense, such as non-navigable tributaries and streams" . . .

**Salton Sea.** The trial court record reflects that the Salton Sea is a popular destination for out-of-state and foreign tourists, who fish and recreate in and on its waters and shoreline. Some tourists visit the Salton Sea for medicinal purposes, believing its water is good for their skin. Other international and domestic visitors frequent the Salton Sea to water ski, fish, hunt ducks and race boats and jet skis on the Sea. Many Canadian tourists frequent the Sea in winter, while many others use it in the summer. The record further shows that the Sea ebbs and flows with the tide. Under most any meaning of the term, the Salton Sea is a body of "navigable water" and "water of the United States."

Thus, even after SWANCC, the CWA authorizes federal jurisdiction over illegal discharges into the Salton Sea. . . . Therefore, as Colvin illegally discharged waste into the Salton Sea, SWANCC does not establish that Colvin is "actually innocent" of a the crime for which he was convicted.

**Point Source.** Colvin has proffered no new evidence regarding his contention that the bulldozer with which he spread waste into the Salton Sea was not a "point source" under the CWA. As such, he is barred from bringing such a claim. . . . Regardless, it is well established that bulldozers and similar vehicles may be "point sources" under the CWA when they are, as here, utilized to spread waste. See, e.g., *Borden Ranch P'ship v. United States Army Corps of Eng'r.,* . . . holding that bulldozers and tractors used to pull waste through soil were "point sources" and commenting that the definition of "point source" is "extremely broad." . . . .

## Judgment and Result

The federal district court held that the lake in which defendant discharged pollutants was "navigable water" under the Clean Water Act. It also held that the bulldozer was a "point source" under the CWA.

## Questions

1. Is it a crime to discharge pollutants into navigable waters of the U.S. without an NPDES permit?
2. How could it be argued that a bulldozer is a "point source," given the fact that a bulldozer is not permanently on the shore of the lake?
3. Doesn't the idea that a body of water is "navigable" mean that it has some sort of "interstate" aspect? Recall from Chapter 5 that the federal government may regulate only matters that are interstate or which "affect" interstate commerce.

## 1987 AMENDMENTS

In the space of approximately eighty-three pages, Congress comprehensively amended the Clean Water Act (CWA) with the passage of the Water Quality Act of 1987. Essentially these amendments fine-tune the CWA and do not make major structural changes to it.

*Aspects of the CWA Left Unchanged.* The principal part of the Clean Water Act for controlling direct discharges from point sources into the nation's waters is the NPDES permit system. This system remains after the 1987 Act subject only to "fine-tuning." Similarly, the Act retains the concepts of point source discharges, nonpoint source discharges, and publicly owned treatment works (POTW).

*Specific Features of the CWA the 1987 Act "Fine-Tunes."* First, the 1987 Act alters criminal penalties. For negligent violations of NPDES permits or negligently introducing any pollutant or hazardous substance into a sewer system a person knows or reasonably should have known could cause personal injury or property damage, fines are at least $2,500 to a maximum of $25,000 per day or one year in prison, or both. For repeat offenders, punishment for negligent violations can be double the maximum for first violations.

Second, **knowing violations** of an NPDES permit or a pretreatment program result in fines of no less than $5,000 per day and not more than $50,000 per day or imprisonment of three years, or both.

Third, a fine of up to $250,000 or imprisonment up to fifteen years or both is possible for the offense of **knowing endangerment**. This violation involves an entity with an NPDES permit knowingly placing another person in imminent danger of death or serious bodily injury. Organizations can be fined not more than $1 million under this provision. Sanctions for repeat offenders are doubled for both fines and imprisonment.

Fourth, any person who knowingly makes any material false statement in a report, record, or document filed under the act can be fined not more than $10,000 or imprisoned up to two years, or both.

Fifth, civil penalties for certain violations are increased from a maximum of $10,000 per day to $25,000 per day. Good-faith efforts to comply may be considered in setting the amount of these penalties.

Sixth, administrative penalties can be assessed by the administrator of EPA for NPDES violations.

Seventh, a new provision referred to as **anti-backsliding** prevents reissuance of an NPDES permit with less stringent limits than the permit it replaces. The intent of anti-backsliding provisions is to maintain pollution control; unfortunately, some exceptions are permitted.

## CLEAN AIR ACT[2]

### PRE-FEDERAL AIR POLLUTION CONTROL

The first statutory attempts to control air pollution were made by the states. Uneven standards and enforcement were common. Various common law doctrines, such as nuisance, were also available to private party plaintiffs, but these were inadequate for broad pollution control efforts.

### FEDERAL AIR POLLUTION CONTROL

In 1955, for the first time, a federal statute dealt with air pollution. It merely authorized research and federal technical and financial assistance. In 1963, Congress passed the Clean Air Act, the first federal attempt to regulate by controls applicable directly to polluters. The statute had two main flaws: it did not define air pollution, merely saying that it was designed to prevent and control air pollution; and enforcement was hampered by a requirement that courts were to give consideration to the practicability and physical and economic feasibility of stopping pollution.

### 1965 AMENDMENTS

The 1965 amendments to the Clean Air Act attacked the problem of air pollution caused by automobiles and trucks by authorizing emission standards for mobile sources. The U.S. Public Health Service was to set the number. Again, however, economic and technical feasibility conditions affecting the development of such standards curbed development of meaningful emission controls.

### 1967 AMENDMENTS

The Clean Air Act was again amended in 1967. The theory behind these amendments was that air cleanup requires a national effort but that states should keep the primary authority for doing so. The 1967 amendments required that states establish **ambient air quality standards** for air quality control regions that are state and federally determined. After the air quality standards were determined, states were required to establish **state implementation plans** to achieve ambient air quality standards.

From the environmental viewpoint, weaknesses of the Clean Air Act after the 1967 amendments included the continued failure to define air pollution, the economic and technical feasibility conditions to the standards, the absence of private suit provisions, the lack of citizen surveillance, and excessive discretion in the act's administration.

### 1970 AMENDMENTS

The 1970 amendments to the Clean Air Act provided a definition of air pollution and eliminated the economic and technical feasibility loophole that previously existed. However, this law was still not strong. It had two functional elements—

---

[2] The authors acknowledge reliance on government documents in preparing this segment.

programs to furnish technical and financial help, and regulatory authority. A puzzling feature of the 1970 amendments was their continued declaration that the prevention and control of air pollution was the primary responsibility of the states, clearly a holdover from the 1955 act. Even though technical research is the heart of good air pollution regulations, the pattern has been to underfund air pollution research by about one third of its statutory authorization. Short-funding a regulatory program with criminal penalties has serious adverse implications, because judicial challenge is often directed to the scientific evidence behind the regulations.

Three objectives of the 1970 amendments were to establish the nondeterioration principle, primary air quality standards, and secondary air quality standards. **Primary air quality standards** are ambient or general environmental standards that outdoor air must meet to protect the public health. The time set for achievement of primary air quality standards was 1975. The **secondary standards** are designed to protect public welfare, including the avoidance of any adverse effects on any human-made or aesthetic aspects of the environment. They were to be achieved within a "reasonable" time after 1975. Some ambient standards were set by the 1967 amendments and others by the 1970 amendments. Since its establishment in 1970, the EPA's administrator is the party legally authorized to determine ambient air quality standards through promulgating regulations that set forth numbers indicating the amount of a particular air pollutant that will be legally tolerated.

## POLLUTANTS COVERED

Only about six pollutants are covered by the ambient air quality standards: hydrocarbons, carbon monoxide, sulfur dioxide, nitrogen oxides, particulates, and photochemical oxidants. Actually, more than six substances are now covered because hydrocarbons, particulates, and photochemical oxidants are generic, embracing more than one element. The Clean Air Act allows expansion of the list of air pollutants. Additionally, the 1970 amendments further authorize the EPA administrator to establish **direct emission standards** for any stationary source emitting substances designated by the administrator as hazardous, which may cause or contribute to mortality or irreversible or incapacitating illness). Vinyl chloride, asbestos, beryllium, mercury, and benzene have thus far been designated hazardous pollutants. Finally, the 1970 amendments give the EPA administrator authority to set **standards of performance** for new sources that contribute significantly to air pollution or endanger the public health or welfare.

## BASIC CONCEPTS

At this point, noting some basic air pollution concepts under the Clean Air Act may be helpful. The first is the **air quality control region** (AQCR). The entire area of the United States is divided into 247 air quality control regions, as designated by the EPA administrator, often consisting of several states having common topography, climactic, and air pollution characteristics. The AQCR has not proven successful as an air pollution cleanup technique mainly due to political reasons. For example, governors of some western and midwestern states see other governors, particularly those of eastern states, as wanting to clean up the air in eastern states at a cost of western and midwestern jobs. The second air pollution concept is that of criteria documents—scientific studies that set forth parameters for primary and secondary ambient air quality standards. They provide the support for the administrator's decision to set ambient air quality standards at a particular level and prevent accusations that the administrator pulled numbers out of thin air.

The heart of the federal air pollution control program—and the third important term in air pollution control under the Clean Air Act—is the state implementation plan (SIP). Each state submits a plan (SIP) to the EPA administrator to achieve the federally set primary and secondary air quality standards. **Nondeterioration standards** were made a mandatory part of the SIP after the Sierra Club successfully sued the EPA administrator to force such an inclusion. States were given until January 31, 1972, to submit proposed SIPs to EPA for approval. The EPA could either approve or disapprove all or part of the SIP. If EPA approved a SIP, it became part of federal law. The EPA may amend a SIP to conform to federal ambient air criteria.

The SIPs contain a compilation of state air pollution statutes, regulations plus municipal ordinances, emission limits, schedules and timetables for compliance, land use controls, and transportation control plans.

## ENFORCEMENT

Enforcement under the Clean Air Act has several aspects. Elaborate information-gathering provisions authorize the EPA administrator to require any emission source to install, use, and maintain monitoring equipment and to establish and maintain air pollution records. EPA officials are given a right of entry onto the premises of pollution sources. All information the administrator requires of pollution sources is publicly available, except for trade secrets. However, in the case of emission data, no trade secret protection is available.

Violations of the Clean Air Act can lead to civil penalties or criminal sanctions. The act also includes authority for citizen suits against any person (including the U.S. government) allegedly in violation of the Clean Air Act. This provision is the basis for a number of environmental group suits against the EPA to force promulgation of regulations. On a number of occasions the EPA has failed to meet statutory deadlines for promulgation of regulations or has promulgated weak regulations.

The EPA has emergency power to go to court to shut down any source or combination of sources that presents imminent, substantial danger to health. This power was used in 1971 in Birmingham, Alabama, to close steel mills, among other things.

**Mobile sources** account for slightly more than 50 percent of the air pollution in the United States. The EPA has emission standard authority for two general moving sources: all new vehicles, and engines in vehicles used on streets, as well as aircraft engines. Additionally, the EPA has the authority to regulate vehicular fuel, since this affects vehicular emissions.

In the following case, Virginia sued the federal government claiming that the Clean Air Act's enforcement mechanisms against the states violate federalism. See what a U.S. Court of Appeals did with this claim.

## Commonwealth of Virginia v. United States
U.S. Court of Appeals
74 F.3d 517 (4th Cir. 1996)

### Background and Facts

Virginia says that this dispute arises out of two major ongoing disputes with EPA regarding the Commonwealth's compliance with the federal Clean Air Act (CAA). One dispute, according to the complaint, involves Virginia's alleged failure to develop and submit to EPA an approvable vehicle inspection and maintenance (I and M) program and a volatile organic compound (VOC) reduction plan for Northern Virginia and Richmond. The other dispute involves Virginia's alleged failure to submit to EPA an approvable Title V stationary source operating permit program.

The chief mischief-maker here is ozone, the pollutant that most often causes a particular region's air to violate federal standards. Ozone is one of the primary components of smog. In sufficiently high concentrations, ozone causes chest pains, coughing, nausea, irritation of the throat and increased susceptibility to respiratory infection. Excessive ozone can also damage forests and crops.

Ozone is formed when volatile organic compounds (VOCs) react with nitrogen oxides in the presence of sunlight and heat. . . . "VOC is the collective name given to pollutants that [contain carbon and] are gases at room temperature." Automobile exhaust is a VOC source. Although most nitrogen oxides are made naturally, automobile exhaust increases atmospheric nitrogen oxide levels. Thus, auto exhaust, as a source of both VOCs and nitrogen oxides, is a major cause of increased ozone levels. Because by 2010 the number of miles driven in the United States will increase by an estimated 60 percent, the nation faces a real potential for ever-increasing amounts of pollution from automobile exhaust.

The CAA authorizes the EPA Administrator to promulgate national ambient air quality standards (NAAQS). An area that does not meet the minimum level of air quality mandated by the NAAQS is considered to be a "non-attainment area." With respect to the pollutant ozone, an area's degree of nonattainment may be classified as marginal, moderate, serious, severe, or extreme.

By 1989 more than 90 of the nation's urban areas were in nonattainment of the NAAQS for ozone, raising a health concern for as many as 95 million Americans. As a result, Congress in 1990 extensively amended the CAA in an effort to cope with the increasingly severe problem of unhealthy ozone levels throughout the country.

The CAA's complex statutory and regulatory scheme calls upon the states to shoulder a large portion of the difficult task of cleaning up the nation's air. The 1990 amendments extended deadlines (that had existed under earlier versions of the CAA) for states to reach full attainment with respect to ozone levels and set new deadlines for states to achieve lesser (but still maintaining) reductions of ozone. The 1990 amendments also encourage states to design and implement an operating permit program intended to regulate stationary sources of air pollution, such as factories and power plants.

### Body of Opinion

**Court of Appeals Judge Michael.** Under Title I of the CAA, if a state has an area within it that EPA has classified as being in moderate, serious or severe nonattainment with respect to ozone, the state must devise and implement a "state implementation plan" (SIP) that reduces VOC emissions within the area by 15 percent ("a 15% Plan"). . . . The SIP must include a program of vehicle inspection and maintenance that will reduce automobile exhaust's contribution to air pollution (an "I & M Program").

Title I imposes sanctions on states that fail to comply with its provisions. States may, for example, be prevented from spending federal highway money in nonattainment areas. . . . This loss of highway money is automatic and mandatory if the state fails to implement an adequate SIP within 24 months of EPA's finding that a proposed SIP is deficient. . . . Even before this two-year period expires, EPA may (after first going through a notice-and-comment rulemaking proceeding) block the state from spending federal highway funds in nonattainment areas. . . . However, highway money may not be blocked—under either the mandatory or the discretionary sanction provisions—for projects that "likely will result in a significant reduction in, or avoidance of, accidents." . . .

Nor may money be blocked if it is to be spent on transportation projects that would encourage conservation and that would tend to result in less pollution from automobiles, i.e., public transit programs, development of park-and-ride facilities, construction of high-occupancy vehicle lanes and the like. . . .

The state's failure to submit a valid SIP also causes the EPA to subject private industry to more stringent permitting requirements. . . . This sanction is mandatory after 18 months and (as with the highway sanction) is discretionary at any time after EPA has found a proposed SIP to be inadequate. . . .

Finally, if two years pass after a SIP is first found to be deficient or the state's submission of a proposed SIP to EPA is found to be administratively incomplete, EPA must impose a "federal implementation program" (FIP) on those areas of a state that are in nonattainment. . . . "The FIP provides an additional incentive for state compliance because it rescinds state authority to make the many sensitive technical and political choices that a pollution control regime demands." . . .

Title V of the CAA requires states to administer permitting programs intended to regulate stationary sources of air pollution. . . .

Once EPA rejects a proposed Title V permitting program, the state has 18 months to correct any problems EPA has with the proposed plan. If the state does not correct the problems within 18 months, EPA must impose either the highway sanction or the permitting sanction described above. . . . Six months later, if the problems remain uncorrected, EPA must impose the remaining sanction. . . . In addition, EPA may impose these sanctions earlier, but (as in the

Title I context) it first must go through a notice-and-comment rule-making proceeding. . . . Finally, if EPA has not approved a state's Title V Program by November 15, 1995 (five years after enactment of the 1990 Amendments), EPA must promulgate and administer a federal Title V permitting program (a FIP) within the state.

## Judgment and Result

Virginia lost. The Court of Appeals held that the CAA's provision denying states the right to appeal EPA decisions to federal district courts, requiring instead appeals directly to the Court of Appeals, was valid. The Court of Appeals only decided this jurisdictional issue, not whether Congress, through the EPA, could impose environmental mandates on states.

Because the Northern Virginia area has been in "serious" nonattainment with respect to ozone levels, and because the Richmond area has been in "moderate" nonattainment, Virginia is subject to Title I. Virginia is also subject to Title V.

EPA took final action by letter on January 20, 1994, finding that Virginia's Title I (I & M and 15% Plan) submissions were incomplete, in part because Virginia only submitted draft regulations to EPA instead of final, permanent regulations. On December 5, 1994, EPA took final action disapproving on substantive grounds Virginia's Title V Program, . . . in part because Virginia limited judicial review of permitting decisions to those litigants who could prove that they had a "pecuniary and substantial interest" in the outcome of the litigation. . . .

EPA's actions prompted Virginia to file on January 9, 1995, under . . . [the U.S. Code] a three-count complaint against EPA in the United States District Court for the Eastern District of Virginia, asking that certain CAA provisions be declared unconstitutional on their face. . . .

A reading of the complaint thus leaves no doubt that Virginia seeks to reverse final EPA action. Because jurisdiction under [the CAA] turns on whether final agency action is the target of the challenger's claim, it is of no consequence that Virginia has armed itself with the Constitution. . . .

It is settled that "when Congress has chosen to provide the circuit courts with exclusive jurisdiction over appeals from agency [actions], the district courts are without jurisdiction over the legal issues pertaining to final [actions]—whether or not those issues arise from the statutes that authorized the agency action in the first place." . . . CAA . . . channels review of final EPA action exclusively to the courts of appeals, regardless of how the grounds for review are framed. . . .

Virginia makes several points in contending that [the CAA]. . . does not, or at least should not be allowed to, restrict final action review to the circuit courts.

Because Congress wanted prompt and conclusive review in air quality controversies, it channeled (to the courts of appeals) all challenges, regardless of their basis, of EPA rules and final actions. See *Palumbo* . . . "exclusive jurisdiction in the court of appeals avoids duplicative review."

## Questions

1. Did the Court of Appeals actually make a decision on the politically sensitive issue of whether Congress can command (under the Clean Air Act) states to set up I & M (inspection and maintenance) programs? Or did the Court duck the issue?
2. One of the judges in the *Virginia v. U.S.* case was former U.S. Supreme Court Justice Lewis Powell of Virginia. He sat on the case during oral argument but did not participate in the decision of the case. Why would a Virginian sit on such a case?
3. Was the gist of Virginia's constitutional and jurisdictional argument this: That if the CAA is unconstitutional and the CAA says that challengers to it must go to the Court of Appeals and not the District Courts, then the District Courts really do have jurisdiction because the entire CAA (including the jurisdictional route bypassing the District Court) is invalid? Or that constitutional claims should be handled in the district courts and review of agency actions should be dealt with as the CAA prescribed, in the Courts of Appeal? Did either of these arguments prevail?
4. Despite the court's unwillingness to answer many questions the *Virginia* case raises, the opinion does contain a good discussion of SIPs, FIPs, nonattainment areas, and NAAQSs. How does each of these Clean Air Act concepts try to clean up the nation's air? How far were Northern Virginia and Richmond out of compliance with the 1990 amendments that were passed five years before this suit? What does this indicate about the air quality in these areas?
5. What development does the Court cite as likely to occur by the year 2010 with respect to air pollution caused by vehicle emissions in the United States? That the number of miles driven is likely to increase by 60 percent? What does this mean regarding air pollution? That even if we produce vehicles emitting less ozone and other pollutants, that gains will be offset by increased driving? Table 24.3 provides air pollution concentration levels.

## CONTROVERSIAL ISSUES

Before the 1977 amendments to the Clean Air Act, several controversial legal issues had to be settled: whether automobile emission standards should be extended or postponed; whether air quality in regions already cleaner than ambient air quality

TABLE 24.3 NATIONAL AMBIENT AIR POLLUTANT CONCENTRATIONS: 1990 TO 1999

[Data represent annual composite averages of pollutant based on daily 24-hour averages of monitoring stations, except carbon monoxide is based on the second-highest, nonoverlapping, 8-hour average; ozone, average of the second-highest daily maximum 1-hour value; and lead, quarterly average of ambient lead levels. Based on data from the Aerometric Information Retrieval System. mg/m³ = micrograms of pollutant per cubic meter of air; ppm = parts per million]

| Pollutant | Unit | Monitoring Stations, Number | Air Quality Standard[1] | 1990 | 1994 | 1995 | 1996 | 1997 | 1998 | 1999 |
|---|---|---|---|---|---|---|---|---|---|---|
| Carbon monoxide | ppm | 388 | [2]9 | 5.8 | 5.1 | 4.6 | 4.3 | 3.9 | 3.8 | 3.7 |
| Ozone | ppm | 703 | [3].12 | 0.112 | 0.107 | 0.112 | 0.105 | 0.105 | 0.110 | 0.107 |
| Ozone | ppm | 705 | [4]0.08 | 0.085 | 0.084 | 0.087 | 0.083 | 0.082 | 0.086 | 0.085 |
| Sulfur dioxide | ppm | 480 | .03 | 0.081 | 0.0069 | 0.0056 | 0.0056 | 0.0054 | 0.0053 | 0.0052 |
| Particulates (PM-10) | µg/m³ | 954 | [5]50 | 29.2 | 26.0 | 24.8 | 23.9 | 23.8 | 23.6 | 23.9 |
| Nitrogen dioxide | ppm | 230 | .053 | 0.020 | 0.020 | 0.019 | 0.018 | 0.018 | 0.018 | 0.018 |
| Lead | µg/m³ | 175 | [6]1.5 | 0.1 | 0.05 | 0.05 | 0.04 | 0.04 | 0.04 | 0.04 |

[1] Refers to the primary National Ambient Air Quality Standard that protects the public health. [2] Based on 8-hour standard of 9 ppm. [3] Based on 1-hour standard of 0.12 ppm. [4] Based on 8-hour standard of 0.08 ppm. [5] The particulates (PM-10) standard replaced the previous standard for total suspended particulates in 1987. [6] Based on 3-month standard of 1.5 µg/m³.
*Source*: U.S. Environmental Protection Agency, *National Air Quality and Emissions Trends Report*, annual.

standards should be allowed to deteriorate so that economic development could occur; whether new construction and hence increased population sources and expansion of old sources would be allowed in areas that had not yet attained ambient air quality standards; and whether faster and more effective enforcement of the act could be achieved.

## 1977 AMENDMENTS

In August 1977 President Carter signed the Clean Air Act amendments into law. The amendments further extended the auto emissions reduction deadline (originally set for 1975 and later postponed to 1978) for unburned hydrocarbons to 1980 and for carbon monoxide to 1981. The nitrogen oxide standard was relaxed from 0.4 to 1.0 gram per mile.

The 1977 amendments require studies of excess sulfates from catalyst-equipped cars that had shown some early problems in this area. EPA measurements of sulfate concentrations along the Los Angeles freeway system during a two-year study indicate the problem is less serious than at first feared. The 1977 amendments also extended National Academy of Sciences health studies of auto pollutants.

The 1977 Clean Air Act amendments deal with the second major problem—**prevention of significant deterioration** of air cleaner than ambient standards—by saying, in general, that some deterioration may take place but in different amounts in different areas. The 1977 amendments divide areas having cleaner than national standards into three classes. Class I areas are those in which little deterioration may take place. Mandatory Class I areas are international parks, national wilderness areas exceeding 5,000 acres, national memorial parks exceeding 5,000 acres, and national parks exceeding 6,000 acres. In Class II areas, only moderate air quality deterioration will be allowed. In Class III areas, significant deterioration will be allowed but may not exceed national ambient standards.

The principal practical issue involved in nondeterioration is whether western states' pristine air will give way to development of the region's coal resources. An answer to this question will be provided by the states' governors, because, according to the 1977 amendments, all clean air areas are Class II (except parks and wilderness areas designated by Congress as Class I in the amendments) unless the governor designates them as Class I or Class III. Thus, the 1977 amendments confer considerable power on a western state governor to promote air quality or economic development.

The third major air pollution problem addressed by the 1977 amendments involves nonattainment areas—areas that do not meet ambient air quality requirements. Because many areas presently do not meet national ambient air quality standards (NAAQS), and because each state SIP contains a **preconstruction review mechanism** to ensure that new source construction will not interfere with attainment or maintenance of NAAQS, it is questionable whether any new construction or expansion of existing facilities should be allowed in "dirty air" areas. EPA has proposed an **emission offset policy** that would allow new air pollution in present dirty air areas, provided that the net effect of the new emissions, together with reductions from existing sources below SIP requirements, does not worsen PAQSs (primary air quality standards) but contribute to reasonable progress in attaining such standards.

The 1977 amendments adopted the proposed EPA emission offset policy in modified form by allowing new sources in dirty air areas "only if they attain the lowest achievable emission rates" and if other sources in the state under the same ownership or control are in compliance with relevant emission control provisions. The state must reduce emissions in the dirty air area each year and make progress toward meeting the 1982 or 1987 deadline for attainment of NAAQS.

Improving Clean Air Act compliance and enforcement is the fourth major area tackled by the 1977 amendments. In an unusual attempt to gain industry's compliance with air pollution control regulations, the amendments establish a scheme that sets an economic penalty equal to the economic benefit of being out of compliance. Among the other new enforcement provisions is a requirement of **economic impact statements** (EIS) for new regulations under the Clean Air Act, including an evaluation of employment losses resulting from new regulations and studies of potential employee dislocation that the act will cause. Energy-related or economic emergencies will provide temporary relief from the act's regulations.

## AIR POLLUTION COSTS AND BENEFITS[3]

In its 1980 annual report, the Council on Environmental Quality (CEQ) estimates that $299.1 billion will be spent on air pollution control alone between 1979 and 1988. Given the magnitude of past and projected expenditures on air pollution, what are the resulting benefits? Probably the major benefit—improved public health—will never be known, because we can only speculate about what might have been had no pollution abatement occurred.

According to a recent CEQ annual report, scrubbers designed to control sulfur dioxide and particulate control systems have reduced violations of standards for those pollutants. However, increased emphasis on coal as an energy source could cause other noncriteria pollutants such as nitrates, trace metals, and organic carcinogens to increase. The Bush Administration's policy is one of

[3] Table 24.5 lists pollutant standard values for the six major criteria pollutants.

"voluntary control" regarding limiting CO2 and other air pollutants. The Bush position is based largely on the premise that increased studies are needed to assess environmental harms from air (and other) pollutants.

Carbon monoxide and photochemical oxidants are the principal air pollution problems in U.S. cities. The areas having ozone standard violations are large cities. Ozone has several known adverse health effects.

Global air pollution problems include the carbon dioxide greenhouse effect, the turbidity effect, and potential depletion of the ozone layer. The **greenhouse effect** refers to the increased temperatures at lower atmospheric levels caused by increased carbon dioxide, which tends to retain solar energy in the lower atmosphere. The projection is that if we use up fossil fuels at an accelerated rate, the $CO_2$ level will double by 2025 and will be seven to eight times the present level by 2100. A doubling of the $CO_2$ level would raise global temperature 2° to 3° C, a major environmental threat. **Turbidity**—the presence of microscopic particulates in the air—tends to counteract the $CO_2$ greenhouse effect somewhat. Analyses since 1970, however, show no clear global cooling or heating trend. Depletion of the ozone layer is caused at least in part by use of flourocarbons (propellants for certain aerosols such as hair sprays). The depletion of the ozone layer continues. One result is increased susceptibility to skin cancer.

*Northern Baton Rouge Environmental Assoc. v. LA DEQ* deals with a stationary air pollution source being placed in a minority neighborhood. It raises questions of *environmental racism*.

## North Baton Rouge Environmental Assoc. v. LA. DEQ
Court of Appeals of Louisiana (First Circuit)
805 So.2d 255 (2001)

### Background and Facts

On December 23, 1997, Paxon Polymer Company (later acquired by Exxon) submitted to the Louisiana Department of Environmental Quality (DEQ) an application for a Part 70 Operating Permit for the construction and operation of a new polypropylene production unit adjacent to its existing Baton Rouge Polyolefins Plant (BPRO). Polypropylene is a nonhazardous food-grade plastic material used in the manufacture of many commonly used household products. The plant is located in East Baton Rouge Parish, which, for the past several years, has been designated part of a five parish nonattainment area for ozone pollution.

Nonattainment status signifies that an area has failed to meet the National Ambient Air Quality Standard for specific pollutants. For this reason, facilities in the area have undertaken mandatory and voluntary changes aimed at reducing the proportion of ozone that is related to industrial activities. In return, the participating facilities receive economic benefits and security for future business operations.

To accommodate industrial growth in nonattainment areas, state and federal agencies responsible for controlling ozone have developed incentive-based regulations aimed at reducing the proportion of ozone emissions related to industrial activities. These regulations allow new permits to be issued where new emissions are "offset" by past emission reductions and the Lowest Achievable Emissions Rate (LAER) is achieved by the new or modified emissions source. These offsets or emissions reduction credits (ERCs) encourage voluntary overcompliance and are set at a higher figure than the emissions that the offsets cover: e.g., in this instance, a ratio of 1.2 to 1. Over time, air emissions will decrease, and a net air quality benefit will occur in the nonattainment area.

These ERCs are calculated in tons per year (TPY) and are evidenced by, and registered in, the ERC bank established by DEQ pursuant to Louisiana's statutes. The ERC bank allows deposits of ERCs only when the applicant voluntarily reduces volatile organic compounds (VOC) emissions by more than is required by law (i.e., they are surplus) and only when said applicant agrees to permanently reduce such emissions through accepting enforceable permits or orders. Reductions cannot be creditable as offsets if they are required by law; they must be voluntary and in excess of legal requirements. Once created, banked ERCs are protected and can be used by the certificate owner or the owner by transfer. If a company desires to make improvements or additions to its facility that would result in an emissions increase, it must acquire credits from the bank (either its own, or by contract from someone else) and "cash" them out at a ratio of 1.2 banked TPY of new emissions. These ERCs can, within ten years, be utilized by the same facility, between different facilities of the same company, or transferred between companies for the construction projects of new projects. This emissions trading market allows companies seeking to build new plants or to expand existing plants to purchase pollution reductions. Pursuant to DEQ regulations, a Nonattainment New Source Review (NNSR) is required for any modification to an existing stationary source that will cause an increase of 25 tons per year or more of VOCs.

The net increase in VOC emissions associated with the Exxon BRPO polypropylene project is 32.54 TPR. Therefore, offsets were required at a ratio of 1.2 to 1, totaling 39.05 TPY. Accordingly, on January 20, 1998, BRPO received a transfer of 40 tons of VOC emissions credits from the account of Exxon's Baton Rouge Chemical Plant. DEQ notified Exxon on January 23, 1998, that its permit application was administratively complete. An ERC bank certificate was issued by DEQ on February 18, 1998, reflecting that 40 tons were transferred and applied to offset emissions for the BRPO Title V permit.

Copies of a draft permit were forwarded to Exxon, the East Baton Rouge Parish Library and the EPA on June 25, 1998. On July 7, 1998, DEQ published a public notice in the Baton Rouge daily newspaper, *The Advocate*, asking for public comments on the proposed facility. On July 23, 1998, the EPA sent a letter to DEQ expressing concerns over the draft permit for Exxon's polypropylene plant, particularly regarding Exxon's proposed offsetting, alternative site analysis, and compliance with other new source requirements under state and federal law. DEQ responded to and addressed each question posed by EPA and provided back-up documentation where necessary. On August 7, 1998, DEQ received a letter from the North Baton Rouge Environmental Association (NBREA) requesting a public hearing in the nearby Alsen community and a ninety-day extension of the public comment period.

After addressing the concerns raised by the EPA, DEQ received oral approval from EPA for a proposed air permit. Notice of the public hearing was published in *The Advocate* in an enlarged format on September 15, 1998; however, prior to the announcement in the newspaper, Exxon notified NBREA of the date and location of the public hearing. A copy of the public notice was also hand-delivered to NBREA's president, Ms. Juanita Stewart. Pursuant to a request from Ms. Florence Robinson of NBREA, DEQ forwarded a copy of the draft permit and application to the Southern University Library.

On October 12, 1998, Ms. Mary Lee Orr, executive director of LEAN, also sent a public letter to DEQ requesting a 30-day extension of the public comment period. DEQ held a public hearing at the Alsen Community Center on October 14, 1998, at which time the public comment period was extended until 4:30 p.m. on October 30, 1998. Air permit no. 2581–VO was ultimately issued by DEQ on November 24, 1998. Since that date, the BRPO plant has been constructed, and, it commenced operation in May 2000.

## Body of Opinion

**Judge Pettigrew.** Following DEQ's decision to grant a permit to Exxon for construction of the polypropylene facility, NBREA and LEAN filed the instant action seeking judicial review. . . . The district court ruled in favor of DEQ . . . and held DEQ did not abuse its discretion in granting the permit to Exxon. . . . This appeal followed. . . .

In their initial assignment of error, NBREA and LEAN contend that the district court erred in upholding the issuance of the permit in light of evidence that DEQ and Exxon failed to comply with Nonattainment New Source Review requirements. Specifically,

NBREA and LEAN argue that despite the fact that the record did not demonstrate compliance with federal law and state air regulations, DEQ granted a permit to Exxon, and the district court affirmed this decision. . . .

NBREA and LEAN argue that it was Exxon's burden, as the permit applicant, to demonstrate its compliance with [Ed: state law] and the federal Clean Air Act.

In its brief to this court, Exxon notes that NBREA and LEAN never raised the issue of compliance prior to their appeal to the Nineteenth Judicial District Court. Despite Exxon's objection, the district court, in its oral reasons for judgment issued on March 15, 2000, ruled that this was a legal issue and that NBREA and LEAN were not necessarily required to raise same during the public comment period. The district court also stated:

> One of the legal issues is applicants shall be in compliance at all existing stationary sources owned or operated by the applicant. . . . I did not see in the record that Exxon showed that it was in compliance at all existing stationary sources owned or operated by applicant. Exxon's brief at page 20 says Exxon BRPO has a compliance history of no violations in over eleven years, . . . but I don't believe it specifically states that all existing or stationary sources owned or operated by applicant are in compliance. . . . Pursuant to the district court's ruling. . . Exxon supplemented the record...with a Certificate of Compliance. . . . Said Certificate of Compliance stated in pertinent part that:
>
> . . . All existing stationary sources owned or operated by *Exxon Chemical Americas* (applicant), or by any person controlling, controlled by, or under common control with the applicant, in the state were in compliance with (or in compliance with a schedule of compliance to meet) all applicable state and federal emission limitations and standards, the Federal Clean Air Act, and all conditions in a state or federally enforceable permit as of November 24, 1998.

Accordingly, we find this assignment of error to be without merit. . . .

In their third assignment of error, NBREA and LEAN contend that the district court failed to rule on DEQ's noncompliance with this court's ruling . . . which requires DEQ to respond to their charge that the permitting of this facility is tantamount to environmental racism.

At the public hearing held regarding the permitting of the Exxon facility on October 14, 1998, Ms. Florence Robinson, a member of NBREA, charged:

> Alsen is probably one of the best examples of environmental racism in the nation. The problem here goes far beyond mere environmental justice concerns. It is a case of outright discrimination. Many do not like to hear the term racism today, claiming that that is all in the past. Unfortunately, Alsen has been forced to continue to endure the racist actions of the past. The decision to industrialize Alsen was not made by the people of Alsen. In fact, because of their race, the people of Alsen were deliberately and systematically denied the right to participate in government and shape their own destinies. Now, Alsen is told it must live with these racist decisions. This is clearly an injustice, and is un-American.

In a letter addressed to DEQ and dated October 30, 1998, Exxon responded to the environmental justice concerns expressed by Ms. Robinson. Exxon cited a history of voluntary emissions reductions and stated that it did not feel that the allegations of environmental discrimination were valid. Additionally, DEQ, in its Public Comment Response Summary, responded to Ms. Robinson's comments and stated:

> The property owned by Exxon Chemical Americas upon which the polypropylene unit will be constructed is within the industrial areas designated by The Plan of Government of the Parish of East Baton Rouge and the City of Baton Rouge for industrial development. . . . The property was confirmed to be zoned M-2 Heavy Industrial.

The district court, in its reasons for judgment, stated:

> It is unfortunate that the original zoning placed this industrial complex next to the community Alsen. The fact that it was done a long time ago, doesn't make any difference in considering environmental justice, because a lot of things were done a long time ago that were not right. . . . Placing this industrial area in the neighborhood of the Alsen community does not appear to be intentionally racist. It's between a railroad and a river in a

relatively rural area. Exxon has used a plant facility already in existence. They're actually putting out less pollution than the plant that was there previously. . . . Should they locate it in another industrial area? Well, that only moves the problems to somebody else's city. . . .

## Judgment and Result

For defendant Exxon. There was no environmental racism, nor was there a violation of new source permitting in nonattainment areas.

## Questions

1. Were NBREA and LEAN governmental or private citizen groups? Was there some support for their position from the U.S. EPA?
2. How convincing do you find the DEQ response to allegations of environmental racism? How about that of the district court on the same issue?
3. Does the case indicate that there can be industrial development in areas where there is noncompliance with the Clean Air Act? Is this good or bad?

---

Much air pollution is the result of motor vehicles. The *Haney* case illustrates the temptation to tamper with cars' pollution control equipment.

## United States v. Haney Chevrolet, Inc.
U.S. District Court (M.D. Fla.)
371 F.Supp. 381 (1974)

## Background and Facts

The United States alleges that on or about July 26, 1972, Haney Chevrolet, Inc., an automobile dealer in Orlando, Florida, sold a new 1972 Chevrolet Corvette, Model LT-1, to William L. Ellis of Orlando, Florida. The United States further alleges that on or about August 23, 1972, Haney Chevrolet, Inc., violated [the Clean Air Act] by knowingly removing the original carburetor and its accompanying idle speed solenoid from that Corvette and replacing the carburetor without replacing the idle speed solenoid and knowingly rendering inoperative the transmission-controlled spark system on the Corvette. (The United States consolidated for trial these two devices or systems into one count.) Each of these devices or systems is alleged to be an emission control device or element of design which was installed on the Corvette by the manufacturer in compliance with the regulations promulgated by the Administrator of the Environmental Protection Agency pursuant to Title II of the Clean Air Act.

Prior to trial the parties stipulated . . . the following facts. . . .

1. The defendant, Haney Chevrolet, Inc., is a corporation organized under the laws of the State of Delaware . . . and is engaged in the sale and distribution of new Chevrolet motor vehicles within the Middle District of Florida.

2. On . . . July 26, 1972, Haney Chevrolet, Inc. sold the 1972 Chevrolet Corvette . . . to William L. Ellis for personal use and not for resale, and . . . William L. Ellis [took] delivery of [the] 1972 Chevrolet Corvette. . . .

3. On . . . August 23, 1972, Donald McDowell, on instructions given him by Douglas Irvine, the then Haney Chevrolet Service Manager, removed the original carburetor and accompanying idle speed solenoid from said Chevrolet Corvette, and installed a new carburetor without said idle speed solenoid, thereby rendering the idle speed solenoid inoperative.

4. On . . . August 23, 1972, Donald McDowell, on instructions given him by Douglas Irvine, rendered inoperative the transmission control spark system on said Chevrolet Corvette.

5. The transmission control spark system and the idle speed solenoid are emission control devices or elements of design within the meaning of [the Clean Air Act] and the regulations promulgated thereunder.

There remained for trial by the jury two genuine issues of fact raised by defendant's affirmative defenses:

1. Whether or not Donald McDowell, a mechanic of the defendant, and/or Douglas Irvine, defendant's service manager, were acting within the scope of their employment or agency with Haney

Chevrolet, Inc., on or about August 23, 1972, when the idle speed solenoid was removed from said Chevrolet Corvette and when the transmission control spark system on said Chevrolet Corvette was rendered inoperative; and

2. Whether or not Donald McDowell and/or Douglas Irvine knowingly removed or rendered inoperative said devices or systems with the intent that they remain permanently removed or inoperative. . . .

## Body of Opinion

**Judge Young.** For reasons set forth it is ordered that a directed verdict be entered on the Government's civil penalty claim in favor of the plaintiff. There remains at the conclusion of all the evidence no genuine issue of fact for determination by the jury on either of the questions specified to be tried before the jury. Without weighing the credibility of the witnesses, there can be but one reasonable conclusion as to the verdict in this case; therefore, a directed verdict in favor of the plaintiff is required. . . .

On the agency question which was specified before trial for determination by the jury, the evidence presented dictated but one conclusion: that defendant's service manager and mechanic were acting within the scope of their employment with the defendant on or about August 23, 1972, when they removed the idle speed solenoid and rendered inoperative the transmission controlled spark system on Mr. Ellis' Chevrolet Corvette. It is uncontroverted that the defendant's service manager and mechanic removed or rendered inoperative these emission control devices in the regular course of the duties in the defendant's service garage during their normal day-to-day activities and in the general furtherance of defendant's business interests. Clearly, neither Mr. Irvine nor Mr. McDowell performed any of this work on the Corvette toward any personal ends; rather, the work was done to serve the defendant's business interests. Under Florida law, an employer is liable for the improper acts of its employees or agents committed in the scope of their employment, even though they may have deviated from the employer's instructions. . . . Therefore, a directed verdict in favor of the United States is required on this issue.

The other question which was specified prior to trial for determination by the jury involves the issue of whether or not the defendant's service manager and mechanic knowingly removed or rendered inoperative these emission control devices or systems with the intent that they remain permanently removed or inoperative. Defendant has contended that its employees removed or rendered inoperative said devices or systems with the intent that they remain so only temporarily until a solution to the Corvette's engine problems could be found. Defendant further contended that to leave the devices engaged on the Corvette until a solution was found would present a fire hazard to the occupants of the vehicle. . . .

The statute states that it is unlawful for a dealer "knowingly to remove or render inoperative" certain emission control devices or elements of design from a vehicle. It is well-settled that an act is done knowingly when it is done voluntarily and intentionally, and not by mistake or accident. The Court interprets that the prohibited act of "removal or rendering inoperative a device or element of design" is complete within the meaning of this statute when the dealer knowingly removes or renders inoperative the emission control devices or elements of design on a particular vehicle and voluntarily relinquishes custody and control of the vehicle, (or custody and control by an agent or employee of the dealer) with the emission control devices or elements of design removed or rendered inoperative.

While common sense dictates that the dealer or an agent or employee of the dealer may remove or render inoperative any such emission control devices or elements of designs on a vehicle for purposes of testing that vehicle while in his custody and control, the statute must be interpreted to prohibit the dealer or his agent or employee from removing or rendering inoperative any such emission control devices or elements of design and thereafter releasing such vehicle from his custody and control without first reengaging and making operative all devices or elements of design previously removed or rendered inoperative by him.

In this case it is uncontroverted that Mr. Irvine, defendant's service manager, voluntarily permitted Mr. Ellis to take his Corvette from defendant's service garage after the idle speed solenoid had been removed and the transmission controlled spark system had been rendered inoperative. Thereafter, Ellis traded in the Corvette at a dealer in St. Petersburg who in turn sold the vehicle with the solenoid still removed and the TCS system still inoperative to another private party.

There is therefore no possible construction of the evidence which could be other than that the defendant, through its employees, permitted the Corvette to leave the custody and control of the defendant with the solenoid removed and the TCS system inoperative. On the second remaining issue then this Court concludes that the plaintiff is entitled to prevail as a matter of law and there is nothing to submit to a jury. . . .

## Judgment and Result

A civil penalty of $500 was imposed on Haney Chevrolet, Inc. No injunction (court order against repeat offenses, violation of which would be a crime) was imposed on Haney Chevrolet because the court thought repeat offenses were unlikely.

## Questions

1. If a corporation cannot do anything for itself but must act through its agents, why was the suit brought against Haney Chevrolet, Inc., instead of the service manager, Doug Irvine, or the mechanic who actually removed the solenoid at Irvine's direction?

2. How does it reflect on the ability of U.S. car manufacturers to build effective air pollution devices in 1972 if the Chevy dealer had to remove an air pollution control device to keep the Corvette from starting on fire? (Fortunately, since that time air pollution control technology has improved.)

3. Why should Haney Chevrolet, Inc., be liable here at all if illegal acts are beyond the scope of the agent/servant's duties?

4. Was the $500 civil penalty excessive, too lenient, or about right? How much harm can removing the air pollution control device on one car do?

## 1990 Amendments[4]

In November 1990 President Bush signed into law the Clean Air Act of 1990, which contained the first major amendments to the Clean Air Act since 1977. Before discussing changes the 1990 Amendments make, it is important to emphasize that much of the Clean Air Act's structure—such as SIPs and primary and secondary air quality standards—remains.

Principal features of the 1990 Amendments include stricter emission limits for cars, provisions designed to slow destruction of the earth's ozone layer, and sections to control acid rain and toxic pollutants. The 1990 Act also provides for compensation to workers displaced by the Act, which is estimated to be $250 million over five years. The estimated costs of the 1990 Act are $20 to 25 billion per year. However, failure to control air pollution would also exact costs in the form of health care, days missed from work, and destruction of lakes, forests, and other property.

*Stricter Vehicle Emissions.* Tailpipe emission levels are set at 0.41 grams per mile for hydrocarbons and 1.0 grams per mile for nitrogen oxide. Many, but not all, cars produced in model year 1994 would have to reduce hydrocarbons by 35 percent and nitrogen oxides by 60 percent from present levels. In the 1996 model year, all new cars would have to meet this standard. Starting in 1992 oil companies would have to offer less polluting gasolines. Also, beginning in 1998 manufacturers have to build auto pollution equipment having a life of 10 years or 100,000 miles. See Table 24.4 for a listing of pollution emissions over the past 30 years.

---

[4]The authors acknowledge reliance on government documents in preparing this segment.

## TABLE 24.4 NATIONAL AIR POLLUTANT EMISSIONS: 1970 TO 1998

[In thousands of tons, except as indicated. PM-10=Particulate matter of less than 10 microns. Methodologies to estimate data for 1970 to 1980 period and 1985 to present emissions differ. Beginning with 1985, the estimates are based on a modified National Acid Precipitation Assessment Program inventory.]

| Year | PM-10 | PM-10, Fugitive Dust[1] | Sulfur Dioxide | Nitrogen Dioxides | Volatile Organic Compounds | Carbon Monoxide | Lead (tons) |
|---|---|---|---|---|---|---|---|
| 1970 | 13,042 | (NA) | 31,161 | 20,928 | 30,982 | 129,444 | 220,869 |
| 1975 | 7,671 | (NA) | 28,011 | 22,632 | 26,079 | 116,757 | 159,659 |
| 1980 | 7,119 | (NA) | 25,905 | 24,384 | 26,336 | 117,434 | 74,153 |
| 1985 | 4,831 | 40,614 | 23,658 | 23,198 | 24,428 | 117,013 | 22,890 |
| 1986 | 4,642 | 46,298 | 22,886 | 22,808 | 23,617 | 111,688 | 14,763 |
| 1987 | 4,758 | 37,711 | 22,661 | 23,068 | 23,470 | 110,798 | 7,681 |
| 1988 | 5,598 | 55,474 | 23,135 | 24,124 | 24,306 | 118,729 | 7,053 |
| 1989 | 4,811 | 48,253 | 23,293 | 23,893 | 22,513 | 106,439 | 5,468 |
| 1990 | 5,057 | 24,905 | 23,660 | 24,049 | 20,936 | 98,523 | 4,975 |
| 1991 | 4,725 | 24,836 | 23,041 | 24,249 | 21,102 | 100,872 | 4,169 |
| 1992 | 4,610 | 24,862 | 22,806 | 24,596 | 20,659 | 97,630 | 3,810 |
| 1993 | 4,528 | 23,478 | 22,466 | 24,961 | 20,868 | 98,160 | 3,916 |
| 1994 | 4,751 | 26,162 | 21,870 | 25,372 | 21,535 | 102,643 | 4,047 |
| 1995 | 4,579 | 22,491 | 19,181 | 24,921 | 20,817 | 93,353 | 3,929 |
| 1996 | 4,732 | 28,309 | 19,121 | 24,676 | 18,736 | 95,479 | 3,899 |
| 1997 | 4,743 | 29,482 | 19,622 | 24,824 | 18,876 | 94,410 | 3,952 |
| 1998 | 4,450 | 30,292 | 19,647 | 24,454 | 17,917 | 89,454 | 3,973 |

NA Not available.[1] Sources such as agricultural tilling, construction, mining and quarrying, unpaved roads, and wind erosion.
*Source: Statistical Abstract of U.S. 2001*

## TABLE 24.5 AIR POLLUTANT EMISSIONS BY POLLUTANT AND SOURCE: 1998

[In thousands of tons, except as indicated]

| SOURCE | Particulates[1] | Sulfur Dioxide | Nitrogen Oxides | Volatile Organic Compounds | Carbon Monoxide | Lead (tons) |
|---|---|---|---|---|---|---|
| **Total Emissions** | **34,741** | **19,647** | **24,454** | **17,917** | **89,454** | **3,973** |
| Fuel combustion, stationary sources | 1,091 | 16,721 | 10,189 | 893 | 5,374 | 503 |
| Electric utilities | 302 | 13,217 | 6,103 | 54 | 417 | 68 |
| Industrial | 245 | 2,895 | 2,969 | 161 | 1,114 | 19 |
| Other fuel combustion | 544 | 609 | 1,117 | 678 | 3,843 | 416 |
| Residential | 432 | 127 | 742 | 654 | 3,699 | 6 |
| Industrial processes | 607 | 1,458 | 786 | 1,417 | 3,624 | 2,327 |
| Chemical and allied product manufacturing | 65 | 299 | 152 | 396 | 1,129 | 175 |
| Metals processing | 171 | 444 | 88 | 75 | 1,495 | 2,098 |
| Petroleum and related industries | 32 | 345 | 138 | 496 | 368 | (NA) |
| Other | 339 | 370 | 408 | 450 | 632 | 54 |
| Solvent utilization | 6 | 1 | 2 | 5,278 | 2 | (NA) |
| Storage and transport | 94 | 3 | 7 | 1,324 | 80 | (NA) |
| Waste disposal and recycling | 310 | 42 | 97 | 433 | 1,154 | 620 |
| Highway vehicles | 257 | 326 | 7,765 | 5,325 | 50,386 | 19 |
| Light-duty gas vehicles and motorcycles | 56 | 130 | 2,849 | 2,832 | 27,039 | 12 |
| Light-duty trucks | 40 | 99 | 1,917 | 2,015 | 18,726 | 7 |
| Heavy-duty gas vehicles | 8 | 11 | 323 | 257 | 3,067 | – |
| Diesels | 152 | 85.3 | 2,676 | 222 | 1,554 | (NA) |
| Off highway[2] | 461 | 1,084 | 5,280 | 2,461 | 19,914 | 503 |
| Miscellaneous[3] | 31,916 | 12 | 328 | 786 | 8,920 | (NA) |

– Represents or rounds to zero. NA Not available. [1]Represents both PM-10 and PM-10 fugitive dust. [2]Includes emissions from farm tractors and other farm machinery, construction equipment, industrial machinery, recreational marine vessels, and small general utility engines such as lawn mowers. [3]Includes emissions such as from forest fires and other kinds of burning, various agricultural activities, fugitive dust from paved and unpaved roads, and other construction and mining activities, and natural sources.

*Source:* U.S. Environmental Protection Agency, *National Air Pollutant Emission Trends*, 1900–1998. EPA–454/R–00–002

*Controls on Ozone Depletion.* Because ozone depletion only came to be recognized as a significant air pollution problem after the 1977 Clean Air Act amendments, no specific sections of prior federal law focused on protecting the atmosphere's ozone layer.

Various chemicals shown to be the cause of ozone depletion—specifically chlorofluorocarbons, hydrochlorofluorocarbons, and carbon tetrachloride—are phased out or banned by the 1990 Act. Chlorofluorocarbons and carbon tetrachloride are phased out through the 1990s and totally banned after the year 2000. A few regulations will require recycling and disposal of such chemicals from refrigeration and air conditioning equipment. Table 24.5 provides a listing of pollutant sources.

*Acid Rain.* For the first time, the 1990 Act adds to the Clean Air Act provisions to curb acid rain. Acid rain was not viewed as a serious problem when the 1977 amendments to the Clean Air Act were passed. Among the harms caused by acid rain are the destruction of lakes as habitats for aquatic life, particularly in the northeastern United States and eastern Canada, and harm to forests. Sources of acid rain have been identified as sulfur dioxide and nitrogen oxide, mainly from coal-burning power plants.

The overall objective of the 1990 Act is to halve present levels of nitrogen oxide and sulfur dioxide. The dates by which this objective would be met are several. By January 1, 1995, sulfur dioxide emissions would be cut 5 million tons annually and 10 million tons annually by the year 2000. Much of the reduction would result from tougher emission standards applied to 111 coal-burning utility plants in more than twenty states. Utilities would also have to cut nitrogen oxide by 2 to 4 million tons yearly within two years after 1990, and further such restrictions would take effect in 1997. These and other greenhouse emission statistics are provided in Table 24.6.

*Limiting Toxic Air Pollutants.* Law prior to the 1990 Act forced the U.S. Environmental Protection Agency (EPA) to protect the public from toxic air pollution with an ample safety margin. However, since 1970 the EPA has regulated only seven toxins found in the air.

The 1990 Act expands the toxic air pollutant list to 189 and forces EPA to list more than 200 categories of hazardous pollutant sources (such as oil refineries) for which air pollution standards would be promulgated. Best control equipment available (BCEA) would have to be installed by most polluters between 1995 and 2003.

The 1990 Act creates a new agency, the Chemical Safety Board, to determine why chemical accidents occur. Also, the act mandates formal safety reviews of industrial plants and would give the public access to these reports.

*Marketable Air Pollution Rights.* The 1990 amendments of the Clean Air Act created a structure that allowed marketable air pollution rights. Recall from the Chapter 19 that anything that meets the three-pronged *Howey* test is legally a "security." In the *Howey* case, cultivated rows of orange trees marketed interstate were "securities." Thus it should come as no surprise that if an air polluter removes more sulfur dioxide than the Clean Air Act requires, the amount by which the polluter "exceeds" the legally required cleanup—called a *credit*—can be sold to another air polluter. Each credit represents one ton of sulfur dioxide. Thus, if a utility company reduces sulfur dioxide emissions by one hundred tons more than it legally has to, it may sell these hundred credits to other air polluters who, for example, cannot meet their sulfur dioxide emission requirements. It is, in essence, a marketable pollution right.

Under the 1990 amendments the marketable pollution rights concept has been thus far applied to sulfur removal only and to slightly more than one hundred power plants around the United States. Each power plant has a sulfur dioxide allowance. If a particular power plant fails to meet its allowance by 1995, then it must pay a fine of $2,000 for every ton of emissions over its allowed level. If a power plant sees that it will not meet its standard, it would pay for the other power plant's credits (assuming they exist), as long as they cost less than $2,000 each, the amount of the fine per ton.

## SOLID WASTE: RESOURCE CONSERVATION AND RECOVERY ACT

In general, waste (or garbage) disposal in the United States is primitive. Our consumption-oriented society yields more than 154 million tons of municipal waste, not counting sewage, each year. Sewage and agriculture runoff are not considered

**TABLE 24.6 EMISSIONS OF GREENHOUSE GASES BY TYPE AND SOURCE: 1990 TO 1999**

[Emission estimates were mandated by Congress through Section 1605(a) of the Energy Policy Act of 1992 (Title XVI). Gases that contain carbon can be measured either in terms of the full molecular weight of the gas or just in terms of their carbon content.]

| TYPE AND SOURCE | UNIT | 1990 | 1994 | 1995 | 1996 | 1997 | 1998 | 1999 |
|---|---|---|---|---|---|---|---|---|
| Carbon dioxide: | | | | | | | | |
|   Carbon content, total[1] | Mil. metric tons | 1,350.5 | 1,422.5 | 1,434.7 | 1,484.1 | 1,505.2 | 1,507.4 | 1,526.8 |
|     Energy sources | Mil. metric tons | 1,325.0 | 1,393.7 | 1,404.7 | 1,453.6 | 1,474.1 | 1,476.3 | 1,495.0 |
| Methane: | | | | | | | | |
|   Gas, total[1] | Mil. metric tons | 31.74 | 31.17 | 31.18 | 30.16 | 30.11 | 29.29 | 28.77 |
|     Energy sources | Mil. metric tons | 11.94 | 11.16 | 11.38 | 10.88 | 11.03 | 10.70 | 10.56 |
|     Landfills | Mil. metric tons | 11.40 | 10.83 | 10.63 | 10.32 | 9.97 | 9.45 | 9.11 |
|     Agricultural sources | Mil. metric tons | 8.29 | 9.05 | 9.03 | 8.83 | 8.98 | 9.00 | 8.96 |
| Nitrous oxide, total[1] | 1,000 metric tons | 1,168 | 1,310 | 1,257 | 1,246 | 1,226 | 1,223 | 1,224 |
|   Agriculture | 1,000 metric tons | 844 | 927 | 859 | 846 | 865 | 874 | 870 |
|   Energy sources | 1,000 metric tons | 211 | 255 | 269 | 266 | 269 | 272 | 279 |
|   Industrial sources | 1,000 metric tons | 96 | 110 | 111 | 116 | 74 | 58 | 57 |
| Chlorofluorocarbons (CFCs) gases | 1,000 metric tons | 202 | 109 | 102 | 67 | 51 | 49 | 41 |
|   CFC-11 | 1,000 metric tons | 54 | 37 | 36 | 27 | 25 | 25 | 24 |
|   CFC-12 | 1,000 metric tons | 113 | 58 | 52 | 36 | 23 | 21 | 14 |
|   CFC-113 | 1,000 metric tons | 26 | 9 | 9 | (Z) | (Z) | (Z) | (Z) |
|   Other CFCs | 1,000 metric tons | 9 | 5 | 5 | 4 | 3 | 3 | 3 |
| Halons | 1,000 metric tons | 2.8 | 2.7 | 2.9 | 3.0 | 3.0 | 3.0 | 3.0 |
| Hydrofluorocarbons: | 1,000 metric tons | | | | | | | |
|   HFC-23 | 1,000 metric tons | 3.0 | 3.0 | 2.0 | 3.0 | 3.0 | 3.4 | 2.6 |
|   HFC-125 | 1,000 metric tons | (Z) | 0.3 | 0.5 | 0.7 | 0.9 | 1.1 | 1.3 |
|   HFC-134a | 1,000 metric tons | 1.0 | 6.3 | 14.3 | 19.0 | 23.5 | 26.9 | 30.3 |
|   HFC-143a | 1,000 metric tons | (Z) | 0.1 | 0.1 | 0.2 | 0.3 | 0.5 | 0.7 |
| Perfluorocarbons: | 1,000 metric tons | 3 | 2 | 2 | 3 | 3 | 3 | 2 |
|   CF-4 | 1,000 metric tons | 3 | 2 | 2 | 2 | 2 | 2 | 2 |
|   C-2 F-6 | 1,000 metric tons | 1 | – | 1 | 1 | 1 | 1 | 1 |
|   C-4 F-10 | 1,000 metric tons | (Z) | (Z) | (Z) | (Z) | (Z) | (Z) | (Z) |
| Sulfur hexafluoride | 1,000 metric tons | 1 | 1 | 2 | 2 | 2 | 2 | 1 |

– Represents or rounds to zero.    Z Less than 500 metric tons.    NA Not available. [1] Includes minor sources not shown separately. [2] Covers principally CFC-11, CFC-12, and CFC-113.

*Source:* U.S. Energy Information Administration, *Emissions of Greenhouse Gases in the United States*, annual.

as solid waste here. Even though technology in many areas has improved, we still commonly use a trash disposal method known for more than hundred years: **open dumping**.

Solid waste disposal was considered a state and local government concern before 1965. In 1965, Congress passed the Solid Waste Disposal Act, the first federal statute to deal with the effect of dumping on the environment. This act gave federal money to states and municipalities for waste disposal research. However, garbage was still viewed as mainly a state and municipal matter.

Congress amended the Solid Waste Disposal Act when it passed the Resource Recovery Act of 1970. This federal law recognized the economic benefits of **recycling** (recovery and reuse of resources from trash and waste). It gave federal money to urban areas with severe solid waste problems.

In the early 1970s, the federal role in solid waste was limited, consisting of five elements:

1. Construction of waste management and resource recovery demonstration projects
2. Technical and financial aid to state agencies' recycling waste management projects
3. National research and development on collection, recovery, recycling, and safe disposal of nonrecoverable waste
4. Federal guidelines (nonbinding suggestions on the proper way to collect, transport, separate, recover, and dispose of solid waste)
5. Occupational training grants

However, because solid waste disposal continued to be viewed as primarily a state and municipal matter, the federal role was limited. Then the roof fell in with several disclosures in the mid-1970s.

- The Hudson River contained massive PCB (toxic oil) contamination.
- Love Canal in Buffalo, New York, was filled with discarded chemicals that threatened the health of hundreds of families living nearby.
- Kepone (a pesticide) dumped at Hopewell, Virginia, into the James River had caused serious human health damage as well as harm to fisheries in the James River and Chesapeake Bay.

These disclosures merely hinted at the secret dumping and disposal of hazardous wastes nationwide that threatened groundwater, surface water, and public health. People built houses on top of buried radioactive waste simply because they were unaware of the presence of hazardous material.

Congress enacted the Toxic Substances Control Act and the Resource Conservation and Recovery Act of 1976 (RCRA) to deal with these problems. RCRA is a federal statute that deals with solid waste problems on a national basis. RCRA tries to control solid waste management practices that pose a danger to public health. It also regulates hazardous and nonhazardous solid wastes. RCRA defines solid wastes to include waste solids, sludges, liquids, and contained gases. Solid and dissolved sewage, irrigation return flows, industrial discharge covered by NPDES permits, and some radioactive wastes are not covered. RCRA defines a *hazardous waste* as one that may cause or significantly contribute to serious illness or death or that poses a substantial threat to human health or the environment if managed improperly.

## GOALS

RCRA has two main goals: to control management of solid waste that would endanger public health or the environment, and to encourage resource conservation and recovery. See Table 24.7 concerning solid waste.

## IMPLEMENTATION

RCRA tries to accomplish its goals in several ways. First, the federal government gives money and know-how to state and municipal governments so they can develop programs to deal with land disposal of solid wastes. Second, it uses cradle-to-grave (from creation to disposal) regulation of hazardous wastes. Third, the act provides for resource recovery and conservation, such as removing

**TABLE 24.7 MUNICIPAL SOLID WASTE GENERATION, RECOVERY, AND DISPOSAL: 1980 TO 1999**

[In millions of tons (151.5 represents 151,500,00), except as indicated. Covers post-consumer residential and commercial solid wastes which comprise the major portion of typical municipal collections. Excludes mining, agricultural and industrial processing, demolition and construction wastes, sewage sludge, and junked autos and obsolete equipment wastes. Based on material-flows estimating procedure and wet weight as generated.]

| ITEM AND MATERIAL | 1980 | 1990 | 1993 | 1994 | 1995 | 1996 | 1997 | 1998 | 1999 |
|---|---|---|---|---|---|---|---|---|---|
| Waste generated | 151.5 | 205.2 | 211.8 | 214.2 | 211.4 | 209.2 | 216.4 | 223.0 | 229.9 |
| Per person per day (lb.) | 3.7 | 4.5 | 4.5 | 4.5 | 4.4 | 4.3 | 4.4 | 4.5 | 4.6 |
| Materials recovered | 14.5 | 33.6 | 43.8 | 50.8 | 54.9 | 57.3 | 59.4 | 61.6 | 63.9 |
| Per person per day (lb.) | 0.35 | 0.7 | 0.9 | 1.1 | 1.1 | 1.2 | 1.2 | 1.3 | 1.3 |
| Combustion for energy recovery | 2.7 | 29.7 | 30.9 | 31.2 | 34.5 | 36.1 | 36.7 | 34.4 | 34.0 |
| Per person per day (lb.) | 0.06 | 0.7 | 0.7 | 0.7 | 0.7 | 0.7 | 0.8 | 0.7 | 0.7 |
| Combustion without energy recovery | 11.0 | 2.2 | 1.6 | 1.3 | 1.0 | (1) | (1) | (1) | (1) |
| Per person per day (lb.) | 0.27 | 0.05 | 0.03 | 0.03 | 0.02 | (1) | (1) | (1) | (1) |
| Landfill, other disposal | 123.3 | 139.7 | 135.5 | 130.9 | 120.9 | 115.8 | 120.4 | 127.1 | 131.9 |
| Per person per day (lb.) | 3.0 | 3.1 | 2.9 | 2.8 | 2.5 | 2.4 | 2.5 | 2.6 | 2.7 |
| Percent distribution of generation | | | | | | | | | |
| Paper and paperboard | 36.1 | 35.4 | 36.6 | 37.7 | 38.6 | 38.1 | 38.5 | 37.7 | 38.1 |
| Glass | 9.9 | 6.4 | 6.4 | 6.2 | 6.1 | 5.9 | 5.5 | 5.6 | 5.5 |
| Metals | 9.6 | 8.1 | 7.5 | 7.6 | 7.5 | 7.7 | 7.7 | 7.6 | 7.8 |
| Plastics | 5.2 | 8.3 | 9.0 | 9.0 | 8.9 | 9.4 | 9.9 | 10.0 | 10.5 |
| Rubber and leather | 2.8 | 2.8 | 2.7 | 2.9 | 2.9 | 3.0 | 3.0 | 3.1 | 2.7 |
| Textiles | 1.7 | 2.8 | 3.2 | 3.4 | 3.5 | 3.7 | 3.8 | 3.9 | 3.9 |
| Wood | 4.4 | 6.0 | 5.8 | 5.3 | 4.9 | 5.2 | 5.3 | 5.3 | 5.3 |
| Food wastes | 8.7 | 10.1 | 10.0 | 10.0 | 10.3 | 10.4 | 10.1 | 11.2 | 10.9 |
| Yard wastes | 18.2 | 17.1 | 15.7 | 14.7 | 14.0 | 13.3 | 12.8 | 12.4 | 12.1 |
| Other wastes | 3.4 | 3.0 | 3.0 | 3.2 | 3.3 | 3.3 | 3.4 | 3.2 | 3.2 |

[1] Combustion without energy recovery is no longer available separately.

*Source:* Franklin Associates, Ltd., Prairie Village, KS, *Characterization of Municipal Solid Waste in the United States: 1998.* Prepared for the U.S. Environmental Protection Agency.

metal beer cans from waste and reusing the metal. Fourth, through regulations the EPA establishes federal standards and a permit program for controlling hazardous wastes. States meeting these standards may run their own hazardous waste control programs. If they do not meet federal standards, the EPA runs the program.

The heart of the hazardous waste control programs is a **manifest system**, which is similar to a permit system. Any entity generating hazardous wastes must get a permit (manifest) to manage it on personal property or to ship it to an EPA-approved treatment, storage, or disposal facility. The idea of the manifest system is that a piece of paper accompanies each hazardous waste as soon as it is created and until it is disposed of. This system lets society know where the hazardous wastes are so that people will not unwittingly build houses on them, cut them, or do anything else with them unknowingly.

Note that the manifest system applies only to hazardous wastes. The manifest system has caused a great deal of controversy. A former EPA official estimated that 750,000 hazardous materials are generated in the United States. There is much paperwork and expense for those generating hazardous waste (mainly the chemical industry), given the paper trail of the manifest system. On the other hand, we are talking about hazardous wastes—things that cause or significantly contribute to serious illness or death or that pose a substantial threat to human health or the environment if improperly managed.

## SANCTIONS

RCRA has criminal and civil penalties. Civil penalties can be as much as $25,000 per day per violation. Criminal penalties include up to one-year prison terms and as much as $25,000 per day fine per offense, or both. One question is whether the EPA will be given enough money to implement RCRA.

The following case shows how both corporations and responsible employees can be criminally liable under RCRA.

## United States v. Johnson & Towers, Inc.
U.S. Court of Appeals (3d Cir.)
741 F.2d 662 (1984)

### Background and Facts

The criminal prosecution in this case arose from the disposal of chemicals at a plant owned by Johnson & Towers in Mount Laurel, New Jersey. In its operations the company, which repairs and overhauls large motor vehicles, uses degreasers and other industrial chemicals that contain chemicals such as methylene chloride and trichlorethylene, classified as "hazardous wastes" under the Resource Conservation and Recovery Act. During the period relevant here, the waste chemicals from cleaning operations were drained into a holding tank and, when the tank was full, pumped into a trench. The trench flowed from the plant property into Parker's Creek, a tributary of the Delaware River. Under RCRA, generators of such waste must obtain a permit for disposal from the Environmental Protection Agency. The EPA had neither issued nor received an application for a permit for Johnson & Towers' operations.

The indictment named as defendants Johnson & Towers and two of its employees, Jack Hopkins, a foreman, and Peter Angel, the service manager in the trucking department. According to the indictment, over a three-day period federal agents saw workers pump waste from the tank into the trench, and on the third day observed toxic chemicals flowing into the creek . . .

The counts under RCRA charged that the defendants "did knowingly treat, store, and dispose of, and did cause to be treated, stored and disposed of hazardous wastes without having obtained a permit . . . in that the defendants discharged, deposited, injected, dumped, spilled, leaked and placed degreasers . . . into the trench. . . . " The indictment alleged that both Angel and Hopkins "managed, supervised and directed a substantial portion of Johnson & Towers' operations . . . including those related to the treatment, storage and disposal of the hazardous wastes and pollutants" and that the chemicals were discharged by "the defendants and others at their discretion." The indictment did not otherwise detail Hopkins' and Angel's activities or responsibilities.

Johnson & Towers pled guilty to the RCRA counts. Hopkins and Angel pled not guilty, and then moved to dismiss counts 2, 3, and 4. The court concluded that the RCRA criminal provision applies only to "owners and operators," i.e., those obligated under the statute to obtain a permit. Since neither Hopkins nor Angel was an "owner" or "operator," the district court granted the motion as to the RCRA charges but held that the individuals could be liable on these three counts under 18 U.S.C. § 2 for aiding and abetting. The court denied the government's motion for reconsideration, and the government appealed to this court under 18 U.S.C. § 3731 (1982).

### Body of Opinion

**Circuit Judge Sloviter.** The permit provision in Section 6925, referred to in Section 6928(d), requires "each person owning or operating a facility for the treatment, storage, or disposal of hazardous waste identified or listed under this subchapter to have a permit" from the EPA.

The parties offer contrary interpretations of Section 6928(d)(2)(A). Defendants consider it an administrative enforcement mechanism, applying only to those who come within Section 6925 and fail to comply; the government reads it as penalizing anyone who handles hazardous waste without a permit or in violation of a permit. Neither party has cited another case, nor have we found one, considering the application of this criminal provision to an individual other than an owner or operator.

. . . Congress enacted RCRA in 1976 as a "cradle-to-grave" regulatory scheme for toxic materials, providing "nationwide protection against the dangers of improper hazardous waste disposal." . . . RCRA was enacted to provide "a multifaceted approach towards solving the problems associated with the 3–4 billion tons of discarded materials generated each year, and the problems resulting from the anticipated 8 percent annual increase in the volume of such waste."

* * *

[4] However, our conclusion that "knowingly" applies to all elements of the offense in Section 6928(d)(2)(A) does not impose on the government as difficult a burden as it fears. On this issue, . . . under certain regulatory statutes requiring "knowing" conduct the government need prove only knowledge of the actions taken and not of the statute forbidding them. . . .

The principle that ignorance of the law is no defense applies whether the law be a statute or a duly promulgated and published regulation. In the context of these proposed 1960 amendments we decline to attribute to Congress the inaccurate view that that Act requires proof of knowledge of the law, as well as the facts, and that it intended to endorse that interpretation by retaining the word "knowingly."

## Judgment and Result

We hold that Section 6928(d)(2)(A) covers employees as well as owners and operators of the facility who knowingly treat, store, or dispose of any hazardous waste, but that the employees can be subject to criminal prosecution only if they knew or should have known that there had been no compliance with the permit requirement of Section 6925.

## Questions

1. Who were the defendants in the case—the corporation and certain employees responsible for handling hazardous wastes?
2. Under what positive law were the defendants charged?
3. Is it a crime to knowingly dump hazardous waste without an RCRA permit obtained from EPA? How could defendants be convicted of knowingly dumping wastes if they did not know the statute existed forbidding such dumping?
4. How could the legal ethics of positive law and natural law react to the result holding both the company and responsible employees liable for dumping the hazardous wastes?
5. Which of the business ethics noted in Chapter 1 is/are in evidence in the case?

## TOXIC SUBSTANCES CONTROL ACT

The Toxic Substances Control Act (TOSCA) is a federal law passed in 1976. As an enabling act, it receives its authority from Congress for an administrative agency (the EPA, in this case) to regulate the manufacture, use, and disposal of toxic substances. TOSCA became law so the public could learn more about chemicals' possible adverse effects on humans as well as on air, water, and natural resources.

TOSCA expressly recognizes that disposing of many human-made chemicals involves unreasonable risks to both natural resources (such as groundwater, where we get much of our drinking water) and humans. TOSCA gives the EPA power to make cradle-to-grave regulations controlling disposal of all toxic organic chemicals now found in groundwater supplies. The EPA has been slow (and is behind) in implementing the waste regulations.

## CONTROL OF TOXIC CHEMICALS

Recall that TOSCA gives EPA the power to regulate chemicals over their entire life cycle (from development through manufacture to disposal). TOSCA orders the EPA to inventory the approximately 55,000 chemicals in interstate commerce. TOSCA next requires chemical manufacturers to notify the EPA of all new chemical substances before they are made, as part of the PMN, or **pre-manufacture notice** requirement. TOSCA also lets the EPA make recordkeeping, testing, and reporting requirements at all stages of toxic chemicals' life (again, the cradle-to-grave part of TOSCA).

Once the EPA has all of the information about toxic chemicals, TOSCA authorizes it to stop the manufacture of new chemicals that present an unreasonable risk to people or the environment, which is done only after the EPA studies the data submitted by industry. This authority represents great regulatory power over the chemical industry. However, the risks are great, because only *toxic* chemicals are at issue. The EPA also has the power under TOSCA to issue temporary limits on chemicals if the EPA has insufficient information to decide whether a chemical presents unreasonable risks.

TOSCA limits the EPA's regulatory power over the chemical industry in one important way: the EPA has the burden of proof to show that a new chemical presents an unreasonable risk to people. In other words, chemicals are presumed safe and nontoxic until the EPA proves otherwise. Tables 24.8 and 24.9 offer some statistics about toxic chemicals and waste.

## CRITICISMS OF **TOSCA**

Criticisms of TOSCA have come from both environmental (proregulatory) and chemical industry (antiregulatory) groups. The chemical industry complains about the red tape, cost, and possible loss of trade secrets because of TOSCA's reporting requirements. Environmental groups complain that the EPA has been slow to regulate. Since TOSCA's passage in 1976, only a few chemical classes have been regulated (including PCBs, chlorofluorocarbons, phthalate esters, chlorinated benzenes, and chloromethane).

Even the EPA has complaints about TOSCA, also based on slowness. EPA officials worry about the staff shortage, which delays putting TOSCA into effect. Also, the EPA complains about industry foot-dragging in supplying information the EPA needs to study the possible toxic effects of chemicals. This problem is particularly troublesome because the burden of showing that chemicals are toxic is on the EPA. Toxins that creep into the water, the air, and the food chain (through fertilizers and insecticides, for example) pose serious a threat of long-term, perhaps irreversible damage to humans and the environment.

## NUCLEAR WASTE POLICY ACT

In 1982 Congress passed the Nuclear Waste Policy Act (NWPA). It provided guidelines under which the federal government would design, construct, and operate nationally at least two high-level waste (HLW) dumps. In addressing what to do with highly toxic waste, the NWPA proposed deep underground injection of HLW.

Through an elaborate process, the NWPA decides which "lucky" states will receive the HLW. The Department of Energy (DOE) names "potentially acceptable sites." Then, within ninety days, DOE must tell the governors and state legislatures of these sites that they are candidates. DOE also must develop regs for HLW disposal and then apply these regs to at least five potentially suitable candidate sites.

In 1983, DOE identified nine potentially acceptable sites (one in Nevada, one in Washington state, two in Texas, two in Utah, one in Louisiana, and two in Mississippi). DOE must then recommend to the president three of the nominated sites for detailed study, but DOE must have a public hearing *before* recommending a site. The president may then approve or disapprove a site but must submit to Congress an endorsement of one site from the three sites recommended by DOE.

The presidentially approved site then becomes *the* site after 60 days unless the affected state submits notice of disapproval to Congress. If such notice is given to Congress, the site is disapproved unless, within 90 days of getting notice, Congress passes a resolution of siting approval.

## TABLE 24.8 TOXIC CHEMICAL RELEASES BY INDUSTRY: 1999

[In millions of pounds (7,754.8 represents 7,754,800,000), except as indicated. "Original Industries" include owners and operators of facilities that are classified within Standard Classification Code groups 20 through 39, have 10 or more full-time employees, and that manufacture, process, or otherwise use any listed toxic chemical in quantities greater than the established threshold in the course of a calendar year are covered and required to report. Beginning in 1998, additional industries (listed below as "New Industries") were required to report.]

| Industries | 1987 SIC1 Code | Total Facilities Number | Total On- and Off-site Releases[2] | Air Emissions | Surface Water Discharges | Surface Impoundments | Other On-site Land Disposal | Total On-site Releases | Off-site Releases Transfers Off-site to Disposal |
|---|---|---|---|---|---|---|---|---|---|
| **Total** | (X) | 22,639 | 7,754.8 | 2,029.4 | 258.9 | 1,231.2 | 3,040.3 | 7,292.6 | 462.2 |
| ORIGINAL INDUSTRIES | | | | | | | | | |
| **Total[3]** | (X) | 20,698 | 2,309.3 | 1,175.1 | 253.6 | 73.8 | 142.5 | 1,951.9 | 357.4 |
| Food and kindred products | 20 | 1,615 | 123.2 | 59.8 | 50.2 | 0.3 | 0.1 | 116.3 | 7.0 |
| Tobacco products | 21 | 23 | 3.7 | 2.8 | 0.2 | – | – | 2.9 | 0.8 |
| Textile mill products | 22 | 241 | 9.8 | 8.5 | 0.2 | 0.1 | 0.1 | 9.1 | 0.7 |
| Apparel and other textile products | 23 | 15 | 0.5 | 0.4 | – | – | – | 0.4 | 0.1 |
| Lumber and wood products | 24 | 830 | 35.2 | 34.1 | 0.1 | – | – | 34.4 | 0.8 |
| Furniture and fixtures | 25 | 352 | 15.3 | 15.2 | – | – | – | 15.2 | 0.1 |
| Paper and allied products | 26 | 438 | 225.6 | 186.0 | 19.1 | 3.2 | 0.3 | 220.4 | 5.2 |
| Printing and publishing | 27 | 213 | 20.7 | 20.5 | – | – | – | 20.6 | 0.1 |
| Chemical and allied products | 28 | 3,759 | 663.4 | 288.2 | 77.1 | 29.1 | 4.2 | 609.3 | 54.2 |
| Petroleum and coal products | 29 | 410 | 69.9 | 48.0 | 15.7 | 0.3 | 0.1 | 67.0 | 2.9 |
| Rubber and misc. plastic products | 30 | 1,831 | 103.5 | 91.6 | – | – | – | 92.2 | 11.3 |
| Leather and leather products | 31 | 72 | 4.4 | 2.2 | 0.1 | – | – | 2.3 | 2.1 |
| Stone, clay, glass products | 32 | 668 | 42.1 | 32.9 | 0.1 | 0.1 | 0.1 | 36.7 | 5.4 |
| Primary metal industries | 33 | 1,912 | 591.1 | 106.6 | 62.5 | 35.9 | 130.4 | 399.9 | 191.2 |
| Fabricated metals products | 34 | 2,846 | 80.4 | 57.3 | 2.4 | – | 0.3 | 60.5 | 19.9 |
| Industrial machinery and equipment | 35 | 1,100 | 15.4 | 10.8 | 0.1 | – | 0.2 | 11.4 | 4.0 |
| Electronic, electric equipment | 36 | 1,167 | 39.4 | 16.9 | 4.4 | – | – | 22.3 | 17.1 |
| Transportation equipment | 37 | 1,295 | 104.0 | 91.7 | 0.2 | – | 0.3 | 92.6 | 11.4 |
| Instruments and related products | 38 | 240 | 10.6 | 8.5 | 1.3 | – | – | 9.8 | 0.7 |
| Miscellaneous | 39 | 307 | 10.2 | 8.8 | – | – | – | 8.9 | 1.3 |
| NEW INDUSTRIES | | | | | | | | | |
| **Total** | (X) | 1,941 | 5,445.5 | 854.3 | 5.3 | 1,157.4 | 2.897.8 | 5,340.8 | 104.8 |
| Metal Mining | 10 | 108 | 3,977.0 | 4.5 | 0.4 | 1,027.3 | 2,892.9 | 3,974.8 | 2.2 |
| Coal mining | 12 | 50 | 11.8 | 1.8 | 0.2 | 2.5 | 0.3 | 11.8 | - |
| Electrical utilities | 49 | 625 | 1,162.5 | 841.9 | 4.5 | 125.4 | 4.6 | 1,104.6 | 58.0 |
| Chemical wholesalers | 5169 | 428 | 2.0 | 1.3 | – | – | – | 1.3 | 0.6 |
| Petroleum bulk terminals | 5171 | 532 | 4.3 | 4.0 | – | – | – | 4.1 | 0.2 |
| RCRA/solvent recovery | 4953/ 7369 | 198 | 288.0 | 0.8 | 0.1 | 2.2 | – | 244.2 | 43.8 |

– Represents or rounds to zero. X Not applicable. [1] Standard industrial Classification, see text, Section 12, Labor Force. Employment, and Earnings. [2] Includes media of release (injection, landfills, ect.), not shown separately. [3] Includes industries with no specific industry identified, not shown separately.
*Source:* U.S. Environmental Protection Agency, *1999 Toxics Release Inventory.*

Several federal agencies regulate nuclear waste disposal. DOE designs, builds, and operates federal nuclear dumps. The NRC licenses them, and the EPA has authority under other federal laws to promulgate regs to protect the general environment from off-site nuclear releases from the site. One such law is the federal Safe Drinking Water Act. Several states and an environmental group argued that the EPA should use its authority under the Safe Drinking Water Act to stop on-site nuclear contamination. *NRDC. v. U.S EPA* deals with the matter.

*The National Resources Defense Council is a private environmental activist group:* **http://www. nrdc.org**

### TABLE 24.9  TOXIC RELEASES BY STATE: 1988 TO 1999

[In millions of pounds (3,213.1 represents 3,213,100,000). Excludes delisted chemicals, chemicals added in 1990, 1991, 1994, and 1995 and aluminum oxide, ammonia, hydrochloric acid, and sulfuric acid.]

| State and Outlying Area | Core Chemicals | | | | | State and Outlying Area | Core Chemicals | | | | |
|---|---|---|---|---|---|---|---|---|---|---|---|
| | 1988 | 1996 | 1997 | 1998 | 1999 | | 1988 | 1996 | 1997 | 1998 | 1999 |
| Total | 3,213.1 | 1.892.1 | 1,904.3 | 1,813.2 | 1,732.5 | MT | 35.6 | 47.2 | 42.6 | 50.4 | 48.8 |
| U.S. total | 3,197.6 | 1,882.9 | 1,895.9 | 1,805.7 | 1,726.2 | NE | 17.1 | 8.8 | 13.9 | 10.2 | 8.9 |
| AL | 111.0 | 90.0 | 80.1 | 67.0 | 63.1 | NV | 2.4 | 3.3 | 4.0 | 3.7 | 4.0 |
| AK | 3.7 | 1.7 | 0.8 | 0.3 | 0.2 | NH | 14.0 | 2.3 | 2.4 | 2.3 | 2.4 |
| AZ | 66.3 | 45.9 | 30.6 | 53.5 | 50.2 | NJ | 48.4 | 12.3 | 13.5 | 11.8 | 13.1 |
| AR | 41.0 | 31.5 | 50.2 | 40.3 | 40.4 | NM | 30.4 | 42.8 | 40.1 | 23.8 | 20.0 |
| CA | 110.3 | 35.5 | 27.9 | 27.3 | 28.1 | NY | 100.9 | 28.2 | 29.1 | 22.7 | 22.9 |
| CO | 15.7 | 3.0 | 2.8 | 3.3 | 3.1 | NC | 124.3 | 63.4 | 55.3 | 49.0 | 45.9 |
| CT | 38.5 | 7.3 | 8.4 | 6.1 | 4.4 | ND | 1.2 | 0.8 | 0.8 | 1.1 | 1.0 |
| DE | 8.7 | 4.9 | 5.9 | 5.9 | 5.3 | OH | 205.8 | 128.6 | 132.0 | 128.4 | 118.3 |
| DC | – | – | – | – | – | OK | 30.5 | 15.3 | 15.4 | 14.1 | 13.5 |
| FL | 33.1 | 34.2 | 31.7 | 30.9 | 31.7 | OR | 21.6 | 23.5 | 23.8 | 28.1 | 25.5 |
| GA | 85.8 | 43.0 | 53.2 | 46.9 | 44.7 | PA | 136.2 | 87.0 | 96.0 | 90.3 | 87.3 |
| HI | 0.8 | 0.4 | 0.3 | 0.3 | 0.3 | RI | 7.8 | 2.3 | 2.1 | 1.6 | 1.2 |
| ID | 7.3 | 13.8 | 12.9 | 12.8 | 14.8 | SC | 66.0 | 48.6 | 52.1 | 49.8 | 57.1 |
| IL | 140.7 | 82.2 | 91.8 | 83.7 | 81.0 | SD | 2.4 | 1.4 | 1.3 | 1.4 | 1.1 |
| IN | 184.5 | 101.1 | 111.8 | 107.1 | 114.6 | TN | 126.8 | 100.0 | 89.9 | 78.1 | 76.6 |
| IA | 43.0 | 19.4 | 20.2 | 25.1 | 25.7 | TX | 322.1 | 186.2 | 179.3 | 172.6 | 168.2 |
| KS | 30.4 | 17.5 | 18.9 | 17.4 | 19.8 | UT | 123.8 | 77.7 | 96.5 | 99.6 | 82.7 |
| KY | 65.7 | 33.3 | 35.1 | 30.7 | 35.9 | VT | 1.7 | 0.4 | 0.3 | 0.2 | 0.3 |
| LA | 129.6 | 105.8 | 93.8 | 92.2 | 77.4 | VA | 112.4 | 39.9 | 41.4 | 39.9 | 39.1 |
| ME | 15.5 | 5.6 | 6.3 | 6.6 | 4.8 | WA | 30.6 | 22.1 | 24.6 | 24.3 | 17.0 |
| MD | 20.2 | 9.3 | 9.8 | 8.8 | 9.1 | WV | 39.7 | 17.6 | 15.3 | 16.3 | 12.0 |
| MA | 32.2 | 7.0 | 6.3 | 6.5 | 5.0 | WI | 62.3 | 33.1 | 33.9 | 33.9 | 31.9 |
| MI | 141.1 | 81.9 | 75.1 | 73.6 | 63.8 | WY | 2.0 | 1.2 | 1.3 | 1.3 | 1.6 |
| MN | 55.9 | 17.2 | 15.6 | 15.0 | 14.5 | Guam | – | – | – | – | |
| MS | 59.7 | 47.1 | 46.4 | 40.8 | 39.8 | Puerto Rico | 12.9 | 7.9 | 7.2 | 6.6 | 5.7 |
| MO | 91.1 | 50.2 | 53.1 | 48.7 | 47.9 | Virgin Island | 2.6 | 1.2 | 1.2 | 0.9 | 0.5 |

– Represents zero
*Source:* U.S. Environmental Protection Agency, *1999 Toxics Release Inventory.*

## Natural Resources Defense Council v. U.S. EPA
U.S. Court of Appeals (First Cir.)
824 F. 2d 1258 (1987)

### Background and Facts

This is a petition to review the standards promulgated by the Environmental Protection Agency (EPA) for the long-term disposal of high-level radioactive waste under the Nuclear Waste Policy Act of 1982, 42 U.S.C. §§ 10101–10226 (1982). The states of Maine and Vermont, and the Natural Resources Defense Council, Conservation Law Foundation of New England, and Environmental Policy Institute were the original petitioners. Later Minnesota and Texas also challenged the same standards in separate proceedings. All suits have been consolidated in this circuit. A coalition of nuclear power utilities has been permitted to intervene.

### Body of Opinion

**Chief Judge Levin H. Campbell.** The challenged standards were written by the EPA to regulate harmful releases into the environment from radioactive waste stored in repositories planned for its disposal. (The standards also regulate releases occurring while the waste is being managed prior to its disposal.)

The waste in question is derived from the fissioning of nuclear fuel in commercial nuclear power plants and in military reactors. Some of the material is first reprocessed so as to recover unfissioned uranium and plutonium. Reprocessing results in a transfer of most of the radioactivity into acidic liquids that are later converted into solid radioactive waste. Some spent nuclear fuel is not reprocessed and itself becomes a waste. Collectively this waste is called high level waste ("HLW"). It is extremely toxic and will maintain its toxicity for thousands of years.

Recognizing the need for repositories within which to dispose safely of the growing amounts of HLW, Congress in 1982 enacted the Nuclear Waste Policy Act (NWPA). The Act provides for a coordinated effort within the federal government to design, construct and operate nationally at least two HLW disposal facilities. Without foreclosing other disposal methods, Congress focused in the NWPA on the creation of repositories located deep underground. These will depend on the surrounding underground rock formations together with engineered barriers, to contain safely the radioactivity from these wastes.

The underground repositories are expected to be constructed using conventional mining techniques in geologic media such as granite, basalt (solidified lava), volcanic tuff (compacted volcanic ash) or salt. The solidified high level waste will be housed in canisters placed in boreholes drilled into the mine floor. When the repository is full, it will be backfilled and sealed.

In the NWPA, Congress prescribed a complex process for selecting the sites of the high level waste repositories. . . . Under this format, DOE in February of 1983 identified nine potentially acceptable sites (a Nevada site in tuff; a Washington site in basalt; two Texas sites in bedded salt; two Utah sites in bedded salt; one Louisiana site in a salt dome; and two Mississippi sites in salt domes).

The Act required DOE to recommend to the President three of the nominated sites for detailed characterization studies. The President may then approve or disapprove a nominated site. In December 1984 DOE tentatively identified five sites for possible detailed site characterization. Three of these sites were formally recommended for detailed site characterization studies (Yucca Mountain site in Nevada; Deaf Smith County site in Texas; and the Hanford site in Washington).

Nominated sites recommended to and approved by the President are then to be characterized by DOE. After conducting the detailed site characterization studies, DOE must make a recommendation to the President concerning the final site approval. Before DOE recommends a site it must hold public hearings, must notify any affected state or Indian tribe, and must prepare an environmental impact statement for each site to be recommended to the President. The President must then submit to Congress an endorsement of one site from the three sites characterized and recommended by DOE. . . .

The site recommended by the President becomes the approval site for the first repository after sixty days, unless the affected state or Indian tribe submits to Congress a notice of disapproval. If such notice of disapproval is received, the site is disapproved unless, during the first ninety days after receipt of the notice, Congress passes a resolution of repository siting approval. The same site approval process is prescribed for the selection of a second federal repository site.

Several federal agencies share responsibility for building, licensing and laying down standards for the HLW repositories. The Department of Energy is to design, build and operate each federally owned repository. However, the Nuclear Regulatory Commission (NRC) has responsibility to license the repositories. Under its licensure

powers, the NRC regulates the construction of the repositories, licenses the receipt and possession of high level radioactive waste at the repositories, and authorizes the closure and decommissioning of repositories.

The EPA also has a major regulatory role. The Act provides that EPA,

> pursuant to authority under other provisions of law, shall, by rule, promulgate generally applicable standards for protection of the general environment from offsite releases from radioactive material in repositories.

The language, "pursuant to authority under other provisions of law," refers to the EPA's responsibility and authority under the Atomic Energy Act of 1954. The Reorganization Plan No. 3 of 1970 (which was the vehicle used by the executive branch to organize the newly formed Environmental Protection Agency) transferred to the EPA certain functions of the Atomic Energy Commission

> to the extent that such functions of the Commission consist of establishing generally applicable environmental standards for the protection of the general environment from radioactive material.

It is these generally applicable HLW environmental standards, recently promulgated by the EPA pursuant to the directive of the NWPA, which we are now called upon to review. DOE must follow these standards when siting, designing, constructing and operating the repositories. The NRC must likewise obey them when licensing the repositories. EPA's standards will also apply to defense-related DOE facilities (not licensed by the NRC) which store and dispose of defense-related waste. . . .

Subpart B, 40 C.F.R. § 191.11–.18 (1986), entitled "Environmental Standards for Disposal," is intended to ensure long-term protection of public health and the environment from releases of radiation *after* the HLW has been stored in the chosen manner. Although this subpart was developed having in mind storage at underground repositories, the standards are said to apply also to any other disposal method that may be chosen.

Subpart B comprises four different types of environmental standards. The first type is the *general containment requirements*. These require that nuclear waste disposal systems be designed to provide a reasonable expectation, based on performance assessment, that the cumulative release of radiation to anywhere in the "accessible environment," for 10,000 years after disposal, shall not exceed certain designated levels.

The term "accessible environment" is defined as the atmosphere; land surfaces; surface waters; oceans; and all of the "lithosphere" that is beyond the "controlled area." The "lithosphere," as defined, includes the entire solid part of the earth below the surface, including any ground water contained within it. The "controlled area" is the surface and underground area (and any ground water found therein) immediately surrounding the repository "that encompasses no more than 100 square kilometers and extends horizontally no more than 5 kilometers in any direction" for the disposed waste.

These definitions taken together show that the general containment requirements limit the total, cumulative release of radiation, for 10,000 years, anywhere in the environment, *outside the controlled area.* Within the controlled area itself, the general containment requirements are inapplicable and, therefore, they place no limits on radiation release. . . .

According to the EPA, the above general containment requirements constitute the principal protection mechanism of the HLW environmental standards. If cumulative releases are within these levels, overall adverse health effects upon the general population will be low. The EPA estimates that the general containment requirements limit population risks from the disposal of these wastes to "no more than the midpoint of the range of estimated risks that future generations would have been exposed to if the uranium ore used to create the wastes had never been mined."

* * *

## IV. Do EPA's Regulations Violate the Safe Drinking Water Act?

Part C of the Safe Drinking Water Act, (1982) (SDWA), indicates that the EPA has a duty to assure that underground sources of drinking water will not be endangered by any underground injection. Petitioners argue here that endangerment of such drinking water is bound to result if HLW is disposed of, underground, under standards no more stringent than the EPA's current HLW regulations. Since violations of the SDWA are inevitable, so petitioners argue, the present regulations are "not in accordance with law" and hence invalid.

To understand this argument we must first look at the SDWA, an Act which preceded the NWPA. The SDWA was enacted in 1974 to assure safe drinking water supplies, protect especially valuable aquifers, and protect drinking water from contamination by the underground injection of waste. The SDWA required the EPA to promulgate standards to protect public health, by setting either (1) maximum containment levels for pollutants in a public water supply, or (2) a treatment technique to reduce the pollutants to an acceptable level if the maximum contaminant level is not economically or technologically attainable.

We conclude that the primary disposal method being considered, underground repositories, would likely constitute an "underground injection" under the SDWA.

* * *

## (2) Do the Regulations under review sanction activities that will "Endanger Drinking Water"?

Part C of the SDWA speaks of the EPA's duty "to assure that underground sources of drinking water will not be *endangered* by any underground injection." [Emphasis supplied.] Assuming, as discussed above, that the planned disposal of HLW in underground repositories amounts to "underground injection," will such injection, if carried out under the EPA's current HLW standards, endanger underground sources of drinking water? We believe the answer is "yes."

As noted, the term "endanger" is defined in the SDWA to include any injection which may result in the presence "in underground water which supplies or can reasonably by expected to supply any public water systems of any contaminant . . . if the presence of such contaminant may result in such system's not complying with any national primary drinking water regulation." 42 U.S.C. § 300h (d)(2). Measured against this definition, the HLW standards permit contamination of most categories of underground water within the so-called controlled area without restriction of any type. More funda-

mentally, they permit water supplies *outside* the controlled area to be contaminated by radiation up to individual exposure levels that exceed the levels allowed in national primary drinking water regulations. It follows that the HLW regulations under review not only do not "assure" the nonendangerment of underground sources of drinking water, but sanction disposal facilities allowing certain levels of endangerment as that term is used in the SDWA.

## Judgment and Result

The Court of Appeals, Levin H. Campbell, Chief Judge, held that (1) because the Agency did not consider the interrelationship of high level waste rules and the Safe Drinking Water Act and thus failed either to reconcile two regulatory standards or to adequately explain divergence, the Agency was arbitrary and capricious in its promulgation of individual protection requirements; (2) the Agency did not provide adequate explanation for selecting 1,000-year design criterion. Petition for review of rules granted in part; rules vacated in part and remanded.

## Questions

1. In the case, does the court believe the EPA took into account the legal requirements under the Safe Drinking Water Act when it regulated nuclear waste?
2. What was the source of the nuclear waste here?
3. One legal ethic involves balancing competing claims. How would you state the competing claims in the preceding case?
4. Recall that at least one Reagan EPA official went to jail for official misconduct. Does the preceding case suggest that the EPA's environmental awareness has improved?
5. Who watches the environment if the EPA does not? Who sued EPA here?
6. The most recent action concerning nuclear waste siting under the Nuclear Waste Policy Act occurred in 2002. President George W. Bush signed a law designating Yucca Mountain in Nevada as the United States' dump for high-level nuclear waste. The site is 90 miles northwest of Las Vegas. The site still needs a license from the Energy Department, which takes at least four years. The target date for opening this site is 2010. Nevada officials—the governor is currently a Republican—promise to sue to challenge the designation, which could add years to the eventual opening of the site.

    Where is the high-level nuclear waste now? It is at numerous power plants and defense sites across the United States. The need to control nuclear waste becomes increasingly important since 9/11.

    The total cost of the nuclear waste storage is expected to be $43 billion over the next century. It is to be paid by taxing nuclear power. More than $3 billion has been spent to date on this storage. It is estimated that the most dangerous radioactive emitters will have decayed by the year 3000, at which time the housings for this waste are projected to leak because of inherent limitations of the housing. By the year 12010 regulators predict the radioactive dosage to farmers in a nearby valley will be 0.007 millirems per year—insignificant. The actual waste containers are expected to corrode by the year 102010. Do you feel safe?

## COMPREHENSIVE ENVIRONMENTAL RESPONSE, COMPENSATION, AND LIABILITY ACT

The United States has estimated 25,000 to 50,000 abandoned hazardous waste dumps. (Professor Frank Popper of Rutgers Law School calls them "LULUs," locally unwanted land uses.) Wastes in these dumps threaten public health and water supplies. To help clean up these dumps, Congress enacted the Comprehensive Environmental Response Compensation and Liability Act of 1980 (CERCLA). Congress originally created a $1.6 billion fund, called the Superfund, made up of industrial and federal appropriations to assist the federal government in cleaning up and containing these dumps. After correcting the environmental degradation at a dump, the government bills the dump's current owners and operators as well as transporters of hazardous wastes to the dump. Such persons are known as potentially responsible parties (PRPs). Court interpretations of CERCLA hold responsible parties strictly liable, that is, liable even if they were not negligent in dumping the hazardous wastes. Hazardous waste sites in each state are listed in Table 24.10.

### FIGURE 24.10 HAZARDOUS WASTE SITES ON THE NATIONAL PRIORITY LIST BY STATE: 2000

[**As of December 31.** Includes both proposed and final sites listed on the National Priorities List for the Superfund program as authorized by the Comprehensive Environmental Response, Compensation, and Liability Act of 1980 and the Superfund Amendments and Reauthorization of 1986.]

– Represents zero. X not applicable.

| STATE AND OUTLYING AREAS | Total Sites | Rank | Percent Distribution | Federal | Nonfederal | STATE AND OUTLYING AREAS | Total Sites | Rank | Percent Distribution | Federal | Nonfederal |
|---|---|---|---|---|---|---|---|---|---|---|---|
| **Total** | **1,292** | **(X)** | **(X)** | **166** | **1,126** | Montana | 14 | 30 | 1.1 | – | 14 |
| **United States** | **1,279** | **(X)** | **100.00** | **165** | **1,114** | Nebraska | 10 | 39 | 0.8 | 1 | 9 |
| Alabama | 15 | 27 | 1.2 | 3 | 12 | Nevada | 1 | 49 | 0.1 | – | 1 |
| Alaska | 7 | 44 | 0.5 | 6 | 1 | New Hampshire | 19 | 20 | 1.5 | 1 | 18 |
| Arizona | 10 | 39 | 0.8 | 3 | 7 | New Jersey | 113 | 1 | 8.8 | 8 | 105 |
| Arkansas | 12 | 32 | 0.9 | – | 12 | New Mexico | 12 | 32 | 0.9 | 1 | 11 |
| California | 99 | 2 | 7.7 | 24 | 75 | New York | 88 | 4 | 6.9 | 4 | 84 |
| Colorado | 17 | 22 | 1.3 | 3 | 14 | North Carolina | 25 | 15 | 2.0 | 2 | 23 |
| Connecticut | 16 | 24 | 1.3 | 1 | 15 | North Dakota | – | 50 | – | – | – |
| Delaware | 17 | 22 | 1.3 | 1 | 16 | Ohio | 35 | 11 | 2.7 | 5 | 30 |
| District of Columbia | 1 | (X) | 0.1 | 1 | – | Oklahoma | 12 | 32 | 0.9 | 1 | 11 |
| Florida | 53 | 6 | 4.1 | 6 | 47 | Oregon | 12 | 32 | 0.9 | 2 | 10 |
| Georgia | 15 | 27 | 1.2 | 2 | 13 | Pennsylvania | 97 | 3 | 7.6 | 6 | 91 |
| Hawaii | 3 | 45 | 0.2 | 2 | 1 | Rhode Island | 12 | 32 | 0.9 | 2 | 10 |
| Idaho | 9 | 41 | 0.7 | 2 | 7 | South Carolina | 25 | 15 | 2.0 | 2 | 23 |
| Illinois | 44 | 8 | 3.4 | 5 | 39 | South Dakota | 2 | 47 | 0.2 | 1 | 1 |
| Indiana | 29 | 14 | 2.3 | – | 29 | Tennessee | 14 | 30 | 1.1 | 4 | 10 |
| Iowa | 16 | 24 | 1.3 | 1 | 15 | Texas | 38 | 10 | 3.0 | 4 | 34 |
| Kansas | 12 | 32 | 0.9 | 2 | 10 | Utah | 20 | 19 | 1.6 | 4 | 16 |
| Kentucky | 15 | 27 | 1.2 | 1 | 14 | Vermont | 8 | 43 | 0.6 | – | 8 |
| Louisiana | 16 | 24 | 1.3 | 1 | 15 | Virginia | 31 | 13 | 2.4 | 11 | 20 |
| Maine | 12 | 32 | 0.9 | 3 | 9 | Washington | 48 | 7 | 3.8 | 14 | 34 |
| Maryland | 18 | 21 | 1.4 | 8 | 10 | West Virginia | 9 | 41 | 0.7 | 2 | 7 |
| Massachusetts | 33 | 12 | 2.6 | 8 | 25 | Wisconsin | 41 | 9 | 3.2 | – | 41 |
| Michigan | 69 | 5 | 5.4 | 1 | 68 | Wyoming | 2 | 48 | 0.2 | 1 | 1 |
| Minnesota | 25 | 15 | 2.0 | 2 | 23 | Guam | 2 | (X) | (X) | 1 | 1 |
| Mississippi | 3 | 45 | 0.2 | – | 3 | Puerto Rico | 9 | (X) | (X) | – | 9 |
| Missouri | 25 | 15 | 2.0 | 3 | 22 | Virgin Islands | 2 | (X) | (X) | – | 2 |

*Source:* U.S. Environmental Protection Agency, *Supplementary Materials: National Priorities List, Proposed Rule*, December 2000.

CERCLA itself does not address the matter of joint and several liability, but court decisions interpreting CERCLA do impose joint and several liability on those partly liable for the hazardous waste dump. Thus, if one hundred persons without a permit each dump one barrel of hazardous wastes at a hazardous waste site, any one of the hundred could be held by the federal government for the entire cleanup of the site. The one who pays the full cleanup amount could then sue the other ninety-nine dumpers for their pro rata share of the cleanup costs, assuming they could be found.

Another problem PRPs face with CERCLA is that they can be held liable for waste dumped before CERCLA was passed. In effect, CERCLA has retroactive impact. Further, CERCLA holds a wide range of persons liable for hazardous waste cleanup including the present site owner, the site owners when the waste was dumped, transporters of the waste, and the operator of the dump even if not the landowner.

A practical way for PRPs to cap their CERCLA liability is found under Section 122 of CERCLA, which creates a site participation agreement for total cleanup liability among PRPs. Such agreements allow similarly situated PRPs to establish a contribution bar to future cleanup liability.

CERCLA generally exempts creditors of the aforementioned liable parties from cleanup liability; but what if a creditor with a mortgage (or other type of security interest) on the dump operator's property has the right to or has exercised management over the dump site operator? Do any of these events cause the creditor to lose the exemption from CERCLA liability and make it liable as an owner or operator? The *Fleet Factors* case held creditors liable when the creditor's involvement in the management process influenced a facility's treatment of hazardous waste. Following the *Fleet* case the EPA tried to "soften" its application to parties such as commercial lenders by promulgating regulations "clarifying" CERCLA's application to creditors. So far, EPA's regulations have been of uncertain comfort to creditors.

The following CERCLA case indicates whether an owner of property on which hazardous waste is dumped can sue transporters and others for all of the cleanup costs.

## Prisco v. A. & D. Carting Corp.
U.S. Court of Appeals (2nd Cir.)
168 F.3d 593 (1999)

### Background and Facts

In the spring of 1987, Thomas and Filomena Prisco, husband and wife, began an attempt to increase the value of their land by leveling a portion of it using as fill waste construction and demolition materials delivered to the site by a variety of business entities. They discovered they could also make substantial sums by permitting others to dispose of waste on their property for a fee. The efforts entangled them with two New York State law enforcement officials who said that they would operate the landfill on the State's behalf. One or both of the officers may have been engaged in an undercover operation designed to obtain information about corruption in the construction and demolition industry. The landfill operation nonetheless was soon shut down by state environmental authorities. Hazardous substances have since been leaching from the Prisco property into the surrounding wetlands.

In 1991, the Priscos filed suit in the U.S. District Court for the Southern District of New York against a host of private and public defendants, asserting causes of action under the Comprehensive Environmental Response, Compensation, and Liability Act (CERCLA) in addition to other legal claims. Sometime between then and trial Thomas Prisco died. . . .

Filomena Prisco continued the suit in her own behalf and as administratrix of his estate. . . . After a simultaneous jury trial on the state claims and bench trial on the federal statutory claims, on October 1, 1997, the district court dismissed her CERCLA claims. She appeals from that judgment.

## Body of Opinion

**Circuit Judge Sack.** CERCLA is a "broad remedial statute . . . enacted to ensure "that those responsible for any damage, environmental harm, or injury from chemical poisons bear the costs of their actions." . . . As a remedial statute, CERCLA should be construed liberally to give effect to its purposes. . . .

CERCLA addresses in particular the costs of responding to the release or threatened release of "hazardous substances," as that term is defined by CERCLA. . . . Towards that end, Section 107, the quantity or concentration of the hazardous substance is not a factor. . . . Congress planned for the 'hazardous substance' definition to include even minimal amounts of pollution. . . . Rather, in order, to make out a prima facie case under § 107, a plaintiff must establish five elements. . . . The plaintiff must prove that:

First, the defendant falls within one of the four categories of potentially responsible parties set forth in § 107. . . . The categories include: 1) the owner and operator of . . . a facility, 2) any person who at the time of disposal of any hazardous substance owned or operated any facility at which such hazardous substances were disposed of, 3) any person who by contract, agreement, or otherwise arranged with a transporter for transport for disposal or treatment, of hazardous substances owned or possessed by such person, by any other party or entity, at any facility or incineration vessel owned or operated by another party or entity and containing such hazardous substances, and 4) any person who accepts or accepted any hazardous substance for transport to disposal or treatment facilities, incineration vessels or sites selected by such persons. . . .

Second, the facility is indeed a "facility" as defined by § 101 (9) of CERCLA. . . .

Third, "there is a release or a threatened release of hazardous substances at the facility." . . .

Fourth, the plaintiff incurred costs in responding to the release or threatened release ("response costs"). . . .

And fifth, the costs incurred conform to the National Contingency Plan. . . .

Once the plaintiff establishes these elements, the defendant is strictly liable for the presence of the hazardous substances unless it succeeds in invoking one of the statutory defenses. . . . It is not a defense that the particular hazardous substance attributable to a specific defendant is not linked to the plaintiff's response costs. . . .

Although not heretofore raised in these proceedings, a serious problem meets Prisco's case at the threshold. Where a party seeking to recover response costs is itself a potentially responsible party within the meaning of § 107 . . . he or she may not bring suit for full cost recovery under § 107 as Prisco has. Such a plaintiff is limited instead to an action for contribution from other potentially responsible parties under CERCLA § 113. . . . Prisco, being the owner at all relevant times of the Prisco landfill, has the characteristics of a potentially responsible party within the meaning of § 107. Accordingly, although the issue appears to have gone unnoticed until now, it seems that Prisco's CERCLA claims should not have proceeded under § 107, but, if at all, only under § 113. . . .

This raises the question whether the dismissal of Prisco's CERCLA claim therefore should be affirmed on the grounds, not argued here or below, that it was improper from its inception or the claim should be construed to be one under § 113 although not pleaded. . . . The question need not be resolved, however. The elements of an action under § 113 are the same as those under § 107. . . . Because we find that the district court correctly determined that Prisco failed to establish the elements of a §107 claim, the same result necessarily would obtain even were we to construe the claim as one for contribution under § 113. . . .

## Judgment and Result

The court of appeals affirmed the district court's dismissal of Prisco's CERCLA claim.

## Questions

1. Can someone who has violated CERCLA bring a CERCLA claim? Against whom and for what?
2. Was enough evidence presented to hold others liable to Prisco for the cleanup here?
3. Who, besides the owner of property onto which hazardous substances are dumped, can be liable for cleanup costs under CERCLA?
4. What are the elements a plaintiff must establish to make a successful CERCLA claim?

## AMENDING CERCLA

There are a number of proposals to amend CERCLA. As of this writing, none has been enacted. Among the proposed amendments are the following: (1) cap liability for transporters and generators at 10 percent of the total cleanup costs of municipal solid waste sites; (2) full repeal of the retroactive liability under CERCLA for multiparty sites; (3) add to the federal amount available for cleanup of hazardous waste sites. These are only some of the proposals. Clearly, these proposals are controversial and some violate the "polluter pays" principle, which is the heart of CERCLA.

## ENDANGERED SPECIES ACT

Dr. David A. Etnier probably never expected that his swimming would popularize an obscure federal law—the Endangered Species Act. Etnier, a University of Tennessee ichthyologist (fish expert), was swimming in the Little Tennessee River (Little T) when he saw a strange fish. It turned out to be a previously unknown perch species *Percina imostoma tanasi*, now popularly called the snail darter.

The Tennessee Valley Authority (TVA), a federally owned corporation, was building a multipurpose dam (called the Tellico Dam) on the Little T. The dam was to control flooding, enhance recreation, promote industrial development, and generate power by increasing the pool size of another dam (within eyesight of the Tellico Dam) about one mile away on the Tennessee River. The Tellico Dam itself does not have any power generators.

As a result of Dr. Etnier's discovering the snail darter, an environmental group sued TVA to stop construction of the Tellico Dam. The legal basis for the environmental group's action was the Endangered Species Act of 1973. The act said that federal money may not be spent on any federal agency project that would wipe a fish, plant, or wild animal species off the face of the earth.

For the Web site to the National Audubon Society, a major private environmental protection group, go to **http://www.audubon.org**

The act authorized the U.S. secretary of the interior to designate those species that were endangered. Once the secretary designates a species as endangered, federal funding of any federal agency project that would extinguish or threaten to extinguish such species in the foreseeable future must end. The act also imposed fines on private parties caught transporting, buying, selling, importing, or exporting endangered species.

The act established a two-tier review process to oversee the "correctness" of the secretary of the interior's designations. The second-tier review committee has the power to exempt a project from the act even if it endangers a species' existence.

If the secretary of the interior designates a species as endangered and the review committees do not reverse this decision, the federal project stops unless either Congress or the courts reverse the secretary's decision. This happened in the snail darter's case. The U.S. Supreme Court upheld the secretary's designation of the snail darter as endangered; but then Congress passed a statute amending the Endangered Species Act by exempting the Tellico Dam from it.

Although the media played up the way the three-inch snail darter stopped the $100-million-plus Tellico Dam project, one point is obscured: At the time of the Tellico lawsuit, TVA had spent about $17 million on the dam structure itself. The remaining $85 million was sunk into planning and land acquisition costs. Some people felt that, had TVA been forced to stop the project and resell the land that it had acquired through condemnation, the appreciated value of the land would have exceeded the $17 million loss on the unused dam. TVA might have lost nothing. This is, of course, only speculation.

One last note about this case: The Tellico Dam was eventually built, and the snail darter survives. Table 24.11 summarizes endangered species statistics.

**TABLE 24.11 THREATENED AND ENDANGERED WILDLIFE AND PLANT SPECIES—NUMBER: 2001**

[**As of August.** Endangered species: One in danger of becoming extinct throughout all or a significant part of its natural range. Threatened species: One likely to become endangered in the foreseeable future.]

– Represents zero

| ITEM | Mammals | Birds | Reptiles | Amphibians | Fishes | Snails | Clams | Crustaceans | Insects | Arachnids | Plants |
|---|---|---|---|---|---|---|---|---|---|---|---|
| Total Listings | 340 | 273 | 115 | 27 | 125 | 32 | 71 | 21 | 46 | 12 | 739 |
| **Endangered** | | | | | | | | | | | |
| **species total** | **314** | **253** | **78** | **18** | **81** | **21** | **63** | **18** | **37** | **12** | **593** |
| United States | 65 | 78 | 14 | 12 | 71 | 21 | 62 | 18 | 35 | 12 | 596 |
| Foreign | 251 | 175 | 64 | 8 | 11 | 1 | 2 | – | 4 | – | 1 |
| **Threatened** | | | | | | | | | | | |
| **species total** | **26** | **20** | **37** | **9** | **44** | **11** | **8** | **3** | **9** | **–** | **146** |
| United States | 9 | 14 | 22 | 9 | 44 | 11 | 8 | 3 | 9 | – | 147 |
| Foreign | 17 | 6 | 15 | 1 | – | – | – | – | – | – | 2 |

*Source:* U.S. Fish and Wildlife Service, *Endangered Species Bulletin*, bimonthly; and http://ecos.fws.gov/tess/html/boxscore.html (accessed May 22, 2001).

## STAGES IN ENVIRONMENTAL LAW

### WINDOW DRESSING

Three discernible stages in U.S. environmental law have taken place in the past forty years. The first stage was the "window dressing" stage. This stage ran from about 1948 (in the case of the Federal Water Pollution Control Act) to the mid-1950s (in the case of federal air pollution control). In this era, Congress recognized the problems of air and water pollution and created "paper remedies"—solutions that sounded good on paper (in the form of statutes) but for various reasons did not work.

### HUE AND CRY

The second stage was the "hue and cry" era. It lasted roughly from 1965 (with passage of the Clean Air Act amendments) until about 1977 (with passage of the Surface Mining Control and Reclamation Act). In the hue-and-cry period, the public awoke to find air, water, and general environmental quality declining. The public saw evidence of environmentally related disease (cancer, emphysema), property damage (faster decay of buildings), and natural resource degradation (injury to lakes and trees from acid rain). People demanded laws to solve such problems. Congress responded the Clean Air Act amendments of 1965 and 1970, NEPA, the 1972 amendments to the Federal Water Pollution Control Act, the Noise Control Act of 1972, the Toxic Substances Control Act (TOSCA), and the Resource Conservation and Recovery Act of 1976 (RCRA). Because virtually all of these laws were enabling acts, they authorized federal agencies (mainly the EPA) to make regulations to deal with environmental problems. The EPA usually, although sometimes slowly, did its duty. The public and businesses soon faced thousands of new regulations.

### HARD LOOK

The flood of federal regulations led to the third and present stage of U.S. environmental law—the "hard-look" era. In the hard-look era, businesses and individuals faced with incredible pollution control costs articulately question environmental control. They demand cost–benefit analysis for statutes and regulations to ensure that such programs are worth as much as or more than they cost. Regulated parties demand to see the data and studies (the so-called development documents) that form the basis for agency regulations. They want to question the design, execution, and technical rigor of the study.

If the basis for the regulations is open to question, why should regulated parties spend billions of dollars to comply with them? In this respect, businesses rightly point to a key legal shortcoming: Business seldom has the right to cross-examine federal agency experts who designed, executed, or drew conclusions from the study that was the factual basis for the regulations. Why should an agency expert responsible for the spending of billions be beyond question? However, agency experts' studies, data, and opinions can be questioned. They are questioned when industry and other regulated parties contact the agency and ask about the study. Agency experts (through agency lawyers) must also answer a reviewing court's questions when industry sues an agency about the regulations. The agency must answer the court's questions, usually prompted by industry, or the regulations are invalidated as arbitrary, capricious, and unreasonable or lacking substantial evidence.

## PRACTICAL EFFECTS

Changes have occurred in environmental laws as a result of the hard-look era. A loosening of regulation on less harmful pollutants and greater control on toxins have taken place. This shift is evident from the 1977 amendments to the Federal Water Pollution Control Act (or FWPCA, or Clean Water Act), which reclassified pollutants into toxins, conventional, and unconventional pollutants. Although toxins receive the BAT (best available treatment), the conventional and nonconventional pollutants meet less stringent controls. If the 1977 amendments to the FWPCA had not occurred, all water pollutants would be subject to the expensive BAT. The 1977 Clean Water Act amendments made water pollution control more practical. The 1987 Clean Water Act amendments add new sanctions to help control water pollution.

Other examples of how the hard look has affected environmental law include development of the bubble policy, emission offsets, and marketable pollution rights in air pollution control. The bubble policy views an entire factory as within a huge bubble. The total amount of air pollution let off by the whole factory is limited; but individual air pollution sources (smokestacks, for example) for the factory may discharge different pollution levels if all outlets together stay within the total pollution level for the whole factory. This practice lets industry control air pollution where it is cheapest and not control so much where it is expensive to do so. Previously, all outlets had to meet the same emission (pollution control) requirements. Current policy, however, provides flexibility and possible cost savings for business. However, policing such an arrangement is more difficult for air pollution inspectors.

One problem business faces is building new plants in areas with bad air quality (so-called nonattainment areas where the ambient air quality standards are not met). **Emission offsets** let a business move into a nonattainment area only if it reduces the amount of pollution in the area by the amount its new source will add, which is called the emission offset policy. Emission offsets can be obtained in at least two ways. If a business already has a pollution source in the nonattainment area, its pollution level can be reduced. The new source may then pollute by as much as the pollution reduction (offset) from the existing source.

Another way a business can build in a nonattainment area is by buying an existing source's rights to pollute (discharge). This practice is now allowed in

Louisville, Kentucky, and a few other parts of the United States. The whole idea of offsets and marketable pollution rights is to maintain air quality while allowing economic development.

The Bush Administration is highly skeptical about the value of environmental regulation. Mr. Andrew Card, a former General Motors lobbyist is the White House chief of staff. The Bush Administration has consistently demanded more data and studies to prove conclusively that all types of environmental regulation is, in fact, needed. The refusal of the U.S. to endorse the Kyoto Treaty is but one illustration of this skepticism.

Although environmental law is far from perfect, it is more refined and developed than at any time in U.S history.

## CHAPTER SUMMARY

The environmental ethic refers to the desire to conserve and use wisely limited natural resources as well as to maintain the ability of the planet earth to sustain human, plant, and animal life.

Among the institutions involved in environmental law are private environmental groups such as the National Resources Defense Council, the Environmental Defense Fund, the Sierra Club, and others. Governmental agencies concerned with environmental protection include the U.S. Environmental Protection Agency, the Department of the Interior, the Department of Defense (particularly the Army Corps of Engineers), the Department of Agriculture, the Department of Transportation, and the various states' departments of environment (sometimes called departments of natural resources).

The National Environmental Policy Act (NEPA) established the Council on Environmental Quality (CEQ) and imposed the requirement that federal agencies prepare environmental impact statements (EISs) before they take certain actions affecting the environment.

Water pollution control is largely governed by the Clean Water Act, a federal law that has been amended several times. The Clean Water Act makes it illegal to discharge a pollutant from a point source without an NPDES permit. For non-point sources of water pollution, the Clean Water Act relies on area-wide waste treatment programs. Civil and criminal sanctions may be brought against violators of the Clean Water Act.

The Clean Air Act tries to control air pollution by regulating stationary and mobile sources of pollution. Among the regulated air pollutants are particulates, sulfur dioxide, ozone, nitrogen oxide, and carbon monoxide. The state implementation plan (SIP) is a major ingredient in air pollution control. Primary air quality standards aim to protect public health, while secondary air quality standards try to protect welfare. In 1990 Congress amended the Clean Air Act by tightening air pollution standards for cars, adding to the protections of the earth's ozone layer. The 1990 amendments also address acid rain and toxic pollutants. The Clean Air Act has both civil and criminal sanctions.

The Resource Conservation and Recovery Act of 1976 (RCRA) uses the manifest system to control hazardous wastes. RCRA also regulates nonhazardous wastes that pose a danger to public health. RCRA has civil and criminal penalties.

Congress enacted the Toxic Substances Control Act (TOSCA) to regulate the manufacture, use, and disposal of toxic substances.

CERCLA, the Comprehensive Environmental Response Compensation and Liability Act, was passed to clean up the thousands of abandoned hazardous waste dumps. Superfund was passed to help the federal government clean up hazardous waste dumps; the government bills the dumps' owners for the costs of cleaning up such dumps. Current owners, operators, and transporters of hazardous wastes to the dump are liable for cleanup of the dump.

Environmental law is increasingly being shaped by international trade. Nations such as India and China are sending inexpensive goods into the United States and competing in international markets often because, the Bush administration asserts, such nations lack environmental protections (and their attendant costs). Consumers seem to ignore environmental protections (as well as employee protections) when they purchase goods in the open market, opting for inexpensive Chinese or Indian-made goods having few environmental or employee protections (and costs), instead of such goods made in nations providing environmental and other legal protections.

---

### ■ Manager's Ethical Dilemma

"It's a NIMBY case," shouted Bob Johnson to his assistant. Bob looked out his factory window at the pickets in front of his plutonium processing plant. The picketers all condemned his plant's waste disposal—process water dumped into a local lake, and plutonium waste buried in a local landfill. The picketers wanted a cleanup of the waste dump and lake. Recently an EPA study revealed excessively high levels of radioactive materials in the dump and lake.

Bob's plant had provided the local population with high-paying white- and blue-collar jobs for more than 20 years. In fact, the city of Hanunder had begged Bob to locate his plant there 40 years ago. Now it was NIMBY (not in my backyard).

The EPA wanted Bob to clean up his prior waste disposal and also to build an expensive state-of-the-art containment for future

plutonium waste disposal if he wanted to continue dumping locally. Bob's original plant met all treatment requirements when it was built as state of the art. However, evidence mounted over the years that then state-of-the-art hazardous waste disposal would be inadequate to contain hazardous wastes over the long term (for example, because of leaks in the containment vessels); and leakage did occur, justifying renewed cleanup efforts.

Bob suddenly got what he thought was a brilliant idea. He had seen on a TV program a Chinese entrepreneur who owned a large piece of land with a deep gorge on it. For a fee, the Chinese entrepreneur would allow persons to dump any kind of waste in it. Discuss the ethical considerations of this scenario.

---

## Discussion Questions

1. Some commentators see nations that have weak environmental protections as realizing economic benefits from pursuing such questionable policies. For example, certain Asian and Central and South American nations have allowed the export of wood from tropical forests, thereby contributing to destruction of tropical rain forests. Such natural resources, which do not have a scarcity value because they have few environmental restrictions on their harvesting, provide a competitive advantage to these emerging nations with a desire for higher living standards for its inhabitants. Suppose that the World Trade Organization was considering an amendment to its trade provisions that allowed nations to bar foreign-made goods if not made under laws as protective as the nation into which they were to be imported. Would you favor or argue against such a change in international trade law? (You may want to review the tuna/dolphin case in Chapter 8.)

2. Many environmental statutes, such as the Clean Air and Clean Water acts, create both civil and criminal liability for violators. Should criminal sanctions be put in environmental statutes? Are environmental offenses violent? Can they cause death or widespread health problems? What should be the test for deciding whether to make an act a crime—its social offensiveness or harm?

3. A leading think tank in Washington, D.C., the Brookings Institution, revealed the results of its study of the Clean Air Act. The study concluded that air quality in the United States had improved, but this improvement was the result of switching from coal to cleaner fuels and the downturn in the nation's economy, and not the result of the Clean Air Act. The Brookings study did note that the act had reduced pollutants from new sources and new cars and trucks. However, the study concluded that existing sources (old factories, cars, and trucks) of pollution are unaffected by the act. The Brookings study made several recommendations for amending the act:

a. Shift the burden for pollution control from new sources to existing sources.

b. Expand the "bubble" and "offset" policies.

c. Encourage marketable discharge licenses and effluent fees.

d. Change pollutants regulated by the national ambient air quality standards (NAAQS) from total suspended particulates (TSP) and sulfur dioxide to fine respirable particulates and acid sulfates.

e. Give states total authority for state implementation plans (SIPs) subject only to EPA's power to reject an SIP within a reasonable time.

Given the Brookings study and recommendations, do you think Congress did enough when it passed the 1990 Clean Air Act Amendments? Is the general direction of the Brookings recommendations to toughen, weaken, fine-tune, or do something else?

4. The Clean Air and Clean Water acts have built on each other. That is, one was passed or amended, and the other copied the ideas used. For example, the 1963 Clean Air Act was based on the 1948 Federal Water Pollution Control Act. Actually, neither was successful. Nonetheless, concepts from one law crept into the other. For example, states were given a role in enforcing the Clean Air Act. They have been given the opportunity to enforce the permit program under the Clean Water Act. Are the problems of air and water pollution similar enough to justify such copying?

5. In late 1980, Congress enacted the Comprehensive Environmental Response, Compensation, and Liability Act of 1980, popularly called the "Superfund Act." It authorized $1.6 billion to clean up abandoned hazardous waste spills and dumps. The bill also authorized the federal government to recover cleanup costs from responsible parties. What industry groups will likely sustain major financial and liability burdens because of the Superfund Act? Is it fair to impose such liability? What legal ethics discussed in Chapter 1 are involved here?

6. The EPA promulgated "Beverage Container Guidelines" (regulations). It described a system for resource conservation recommended to state and local governments. The Resource Conservation and Recovery Act of 1976 (RCRA) requires that executive agencies ensure compliance with EPA's guidelines. The guidelines require all beverage containers sold at federal facilities to be made returnable by requiring a five-cent deposit as an incentive for consumers to return empty bottles for reuse or recycling. Returnable containers need not be refillable. Cans and nonrefillable bottles may be used. Beverages in sealed containers sold on federal facilities must be labeled returnable, and deposits must be refunded to the consumer when containers are returned. Dealers are forbidden to procure beverages in containers from distributors refusing to cooperate in the program. The United States Brewers Association, Inc., asked a U.S. court of appeals to review the EPA's refusal to repeal these guidelines. What was the result? [*United States Ass'n v. EPA*, 600 F.2d 974 (1974)].

7. "NEPA is an environmental Magna Carta." Discuss this statement.

8. Refer to the legal ethics discussed in Chapter 1. Which ethics support environmental law? Which challenge the environmental movement?

9. The state of Ohio got a state court injunction directing William Kovacs to clean up a hazardous waste disposal site. Kovacs did not obey the injunction. Ohio then went to state court and got appointment of a receiver to take possession of Kovacs's property and other assets and put the injunction into effect. The receiver took possession of Kovacs's site but had not completed his task when Kovacs filed a personal bankruptcy petition. To force part of Kovacs's post-bankruptcy income to pay the receiver's tasks, Ohio went to state court to discover Kovacs's income and assets. Kovacs asked the bankruptcy court to stay (stop) Ohio's state court action. The bankruptcy court did so. Ohio then filed a claim in bankruptcy court, asking for a declaration that Kovacs's obligation under the state injunction was not a dischargeable bankruptcy debt (technically, not a "debt" or "liability on a claim"). The bankruptcy court ruled against Ohio, as did the the Sixth Circuit Court of Appeals. What result in the U.S. Supreme Court? [*Ohio v. Kovacs*, 469 U.S. 274, 105 S.Ct. 705, 83 C.Ed. 2d 649 (1985)].

## INFOTRAC KEYWORDS

**Use your InfoTrac password to look up articles on http://www.infotrac-college.com**

Keywords: *environmental impact statements, effluent guidelines, air pollutants, vehicle emissions, ozone depletion, acid rain, solid waste disposal, TSCA.*

For suggested readings, please visit this book's Web site at **http://fisher.westbuslaw.com** (click on "Internet Applications").

# THE CONSTITUTION OF
# THE UNITED STATES OF AMERICA

We the People of the United States, in Order to form a more perfect Union, establish Justice, insure domestic Tranquility, provide for the common defence, promote the general Welfare, and secure the Blessings of Liberty to ourselves and our Posterity, do ordain and establish this Constitution for the United States of America.

## ARTICLE I

### Section 1

All legislative Powers herein granted shall be vested in a Congress of the United States, which shall consist of a Senate and House of Representatives.

### Section 2

The House of Representatives shall be composed of Members chosen every second Year by the People of the several States, and the Electors in each State shall have the Qualifications requisite for Electors of the most numerous Branch of the State Legislature.

No Person shall be a Representative who shall not have attained to the Age of twenty five Years, and been seven Years a Citizen of the United States, and who shall not, when elected, be an Inhabitant of that State in which he shall be chosen.

Representatives and direct Taxes shall be apportioned among the several States which may be included within this Union, according to their respective Numbers, which shall be determined by adding to the whole Number of free Persons, including those bound to Service for a Term of Years, and excluding Indians not taxed, three fifths of all other Persons. The actual Enumeration shall be made within three Years after the first Meeting of the Congress of the United States, and within every subsequent Term of ten Years, in such Manner as they shall by Law direct. The Number of Representatives shall not exceed one for every thirty Thousand, but each State shall have at Least one Representative; and until such enumeration shall be made, the State of New Hampshire shall be entitled to choose three, Massachusetts eight, Rhode Island and Providence Plantations one, Connecticut five, New York six, New Jersey four, Pennsylvania eight, Delaware one, Maryland six, Virginia ten, North Carolina five, South Carolina five, and Georgia three.

When vacancies happen in the Representation from any State, the Executive Authority thereof shall issue Writs of Election to fill such vacancies.

The House of Representatives shall use their Speaker and other Officers; and shall have the sole Power of Impeachment.

### Section 3

The Senate of the United States shall be composed of two Senators from each State, chosen by the Legislature thereof, for six Years; and each Senator shall have one Vote.

Immediately after they shall be assembled in Consequence of the first Election, they shall be divided as equally as may be into three Classes. The Seats of the Senators of the first Class shall be vacated at the Expiration of the second Year, of the second Class at the Expiration of the fourth Year, and of the third Class at the Expiration of the sixth Year, so that one third may be chosen every second Year; and if Vacancies happen by Resignation, or otherwise, during the Recess of the Legislature of any State, the Executive thereof may make temporary Appointments until the next Meeting of the Legislature, which shall then fill such Vacancies.

No Person shall be a Senator who shall not have attained to the Age of thirty Years, and been nine Years a Citizen of the United States, and who shall not, when elected, be an Inhabitant of that State for which he shall be chosen.

The Vice President of the United States shall be President of the Senate, but shall have no Vote, unless they be equally divided.

The Senate shall choose their other Officers, and also a President pro tempore, in the Absence of the Vice President, or when he shall exercise the Office of President of the United States.

The Senate shall have the sole Power to try all Impeachments. When sitting for that Purpose, they shall be on Oath or Affirmation. When the President of the United States is tried the Chief Justice shall preside: And no Person shall be convicted without the Concurrence of two thirds of the Members present.

Judgment in Cases of Impeachment shall not extend further than to removal from Office, and disqualification to hold and enjoy any Office of honor, Trust or Profit under the United States; but the Party convicted shall nevertheless be liable and subject to Indictment, Trial, Judgment and Punishment, according to Law.

## Section 4

The Times, Places and Manner of holding Elections for Senators and Representatives, shall be prescribed in each State by the Legislature thereof; but the Congress may at any time by Law make or alter such Regulations, except as to the Places of choosing Senators.

The Congress shall assemble at least once every Year, and such Meeting shall be on the first Monday in December, unless they shall by Law appoint a different Day.

## Section 5

Each House shall be the Judge of the Elections, Returns and Qualifications of its own Members, and a Majority of each shall constitute a Quorum to do Business; but a smaller Number may adjourn from day to day, and may be authorized to compel the Attendance of absent Members, in such Manner and under such Penalties as each House may provide.

Each House may determine the Rules of its Proceedings, punish its Members for disorderly Behaviour, and, with the Concurrence of two thirds, expel a Member.

Each House shall keep a Journal of its Proceedings, and from time to time publish the same, excepting such Parts as may in their Judgment require Secrecy; and the Yeas and Nays of the Members of either House on any question shall, at the Desire of one fifth of those Present, be entered on the Journal.

Neither House, during the Session of Congress, shall, without the Consent of the other, adjourn for more than three days, nor to any other Place than that in which the two Houses shall be sitting.

## Section 6

The Senators and Representatives shall receive a Compensation for their Services, to be ascertained by Law, and paid out of the Treasury of the United States. They shall in all Cases, except Treason, Felony and Breach of the Peace, be privileged from Arrest during their Attendance at the Session of their respective Houses and in going to and returning from the same; and for any Speech or Debate in either House, they shall not be questioned in any other Place.

No Senator or Representative shall, during the Time for which he was elected, be appointed to any civil Office under the Authority of the United States, which shall have been created, or the Emoluments whereof shall have been increased during such time; and no Person holding any Office under the United States, shall be a Member of either House during his Continuance in Office.

## Section 7

All Bills for raising Revenue shall originate in the House of Representatives; but the Senate may propose or concur with amendments as on other Bills.

Every Bill which shall have passed the House of Representatives and the Senate, shall, before it become a Law, be presented to the President of the United States; If he approve he shall sign it, but if not he shall return it, with his Objections to that House in which it shall have originated, who shall enter the Objections at large on their Journal, and proceed to reconsider it. If after such Reconsideration two thirds of that House shall agree to pass the Bill, it shall be sent, together with the Objections, to the other House, by which it shall likewise be reconsidered, and if approved by two thirds of that House, it shall become a Law. But in all such Cases the Votes of both Houses shall be determined by Yeas and Nays, and the Names of the Persons voting for and against the Bill shall be entered on the Journal of each House respectively. If any Bill shall not be returned by the President within ten Days (Sundays excepted) after it shall have been presented to him, the Same shall be a Law, in like Manner as if he had signed it, unless the Congress by their Adjournment prevent its Return, in which Case it shall not be a Law.

Every Order, Resolution, or Vote to which the Concurrence of the Senate and House of Representa-tives may be necessary (except on a question of Adjournment) shall be presented to the President of the United States; and before the Same shall take Effect, shall be approved by him, or being disapproved by him, shall be repassed by two thirds of the Senate and House of Representatives, according to the Rules and Limitations prescribed in the Case of a Bill.

## Section 8

The Congress shall have Power to lay and collect Taxes, Duties, Imposts and Excises, to pay the Debts and provide for the common Defence and general Welfare of the United States; but all Duties, Imposts and Excises shall be uniform throughout the United States;

To borrow Money on the credit of the United States;

To regulate Commerce with foreign Nations, and among the several States, and with the Indian Tribes;

To establish an uniform Rule of Naturalization, and uniform Laws on the subject of Bankruptcies throughout the United States;

To coin Money, regulate the Value thereof, and of foreign Coin, and fix the Standard of Weights and Measures;

To provide for the Punishment of counterfeiting the Securities and current Coin of the United States;

To establish Post Offices and post Roads;

To promote the Progress of Science and useful Arts, by securing for limited Times to Authors and Inventors the exclusive Right to their respective Writings and Discoveries;

To constitute Tribunals inferior to the supreme Court;

To define and punish Piracies and Felonies committed on the high Seas, and Offences against the Law of Nations;

To declare War, grant Letters of Marque and Reprisal, and make Rules concerning Captures on Land and Water;

To raise and support Armies, but no Appropriation of Money to that Use shall be for a longer Term than two Years;

To provide and maintain a Navy;

To make Rules for the Government and Regulation of the land and naval Forces;

To provide for calling forth the Militia to execute the Laws of the Union, suppress Insurrections and repel Invasions;

To provide for organizing, arming, and disciplining the Militia, and for governing such Part of them as may be employed in the Service of the United States, reserving to the States respectively, the Appointment of the Officers, and the Authority of training the Militia according to the discipline prescribed by Congress;

To exercise exclusive Legislation in all Cases whatsoever, over such District (not exceeding ten Miles square) as may, by Cession of particular States, and the Acceptance of Congress, become the Seat of the Government of the United States, and to exercise like Authority over all Places purchased by the Consent of the Legislature of the State in which the Same shall be, for the Erection of Forts, Magazines, Arsenals, dock-Yards, and other needful Buildings;—And

To make all Laws which shall be necessary and proper for carrying into Execution the foregoing Powers, and all other Powers vested by this Constitution in the Government of the United States, or in any Department or Officer thereof.

## Section 9

The Migration or Importation of such Persons as any of the States now existing shall think proper to admit, shall not be prohibited by the Congress prior to the Year one thousand eight hundred and eight, but a Tax or duty may be imposed on such Importation, not exceeding ten dollars for each Person.

The Privilege of the Writ of Habeas Corpus shall not be suspended, unless when in Cases of Rebellion or Invasion the public Safety may require it.

No Bill of Attainder or ex post facto Law shall be passed.

No Capitation, or other direct, Tax shall be laid, unless in Proportion to the Census or Enumeration herein before directed to be taken.

No Tax or Duty shall be laid on Articles exported from any State.

No Preference shall be given by any Regulation of Commerce or Revenue to the Ports of one State over those of another; nor shall Vessels bound to, or from, one State, be obliged to enter, clear or pay Duties in another.

No Money shall be drawn from the Treasury, but in Consequence of Appropriations made by Law; and a regular Statement and Account of the Receipts and Expenditures of all public Money shall be published from time to time.

No Title of Nobility shall be granted by the United States: And no Person holding any Office of Profit or Trust under them, shall, without the Consent of the Congress, accept of any present, Emolument, Office, or Title, of any kind whatever, from any King, Prince or foreign State.

### Section 10

No State shall enter into any Treaty, Alliance, or Confederation; grant Letters of Marque and Reprisal; coin Money; emit Bills of Credit; make any Thing but gold and silver Coin a Tender in Payment of Debts; pass any Bill of Attainder, ex post facto Law, or Law impairing the Obligation of Contracts, or grant any Title of Nobility.

No State shall, without the Consent of the Congress, lay any Imposts or Duties on Imports or Exports, except what may be absolutely necessary for executing its inspection Laws: and the net Produce of all Duties and Imposts, laid by any State on Imports or Exports, shall be for the Use of the Treasury of the United States; and all such Laws shall be subject to the revision and Control of the Congress.

No State shall, without the Consent of Congress, lay any Duty of Tonnage, keep Troops, or Ships of War in time of Peace, enter into any Agreement or Compact with another State, or with a foreign Power, or engage in War, unless actually invaded, or in such imminent Danger as will not admit of delay.

## ARTICLE II

### Section 1

The executive Power shall be vested in a President of the United States of America. He shall hold his Office during the Term for four Years, and, together with the Vice President, chosen for the same Term, be elected, as follows:

Each State shall appoint, in such Manner as the Legislature thereof may direct, a Number of Electors, equal to the whole Number of Senators and Representatives to which the State may be entitled in the Congress: but no Senator or Representative, or Person holding an Office of Trust or Profit under the United States, shall be appointed an Elector.

The Electors shall meet in their respective States, and vote by Ballot for two Persons, of whom one at least shall not be an Inhabitant of the same State with themselves. And they shall make a List of all the Persons voted for, and of the Number of Votes for each; which List they shall sign and certify, and transmit sealed to the Seat of the Government of the United States, directed to the President of the Senate. The President of the Senate shall, in the Presence of the Senate and House of Representatives, open all the Certificates, and the Votes shall then be counted. The Person having the greatest Number of Votes shall be the President, if such Number be a Majority of the whole Number of Electors appointed; and if there be more than one who have such Majority, and have an equal Number of Votes, then the House of Representatives shall immediately choose by Ballot one of them for President; and if no Person have a Majority, then from the five highest on the List the said House shall in like Manner choose the President. But in choosing the President, the Votes shall be taken by States, the Representation from each State having one Vote; a quorum for this Purpose shall consist of a Member or Members from two thirds of the States, and a Majority of all the States shall be necessary to a Choice. In every Case, after the Choice of the President, the Person having the greater Number of Votes of the Electors shall be the Vice President. But if there should remain two or more who have equal Votes, the Senate shall choose from them by Ballot the Vice President.

The Congress may determine the Time of choosing the Electors, and the Day on which they shall give their Votes; which Day shall be the same throughout the United States.

No Person except a natural born Citizen, or a Citizen of the United States, at the time of the Adoption of this Constitution, shall be eligible to the Office of President; neither shall any Person be eligible to that Office who shall not have attained to the Age of thirty five Years, and been fourteen years a Resident within the United States.

In Case of the Removal of the President from Office, or of his Death, Resignation, or Inability to discharge the Powers and Duties of the said Office, the Same shall devolve on the Vice President, and the Congress may by Law provide for the Case of Removal, Death, Resignation or Inability, both of the President and Vice President, declaring what Officer shall then act as President, and such Officer shall act accordingly, until the Disability be removed, or a President shall be elected.

The President shall, at stated Times, receive for his Services, a Compensation, which shall neither be increased nor diminished during the Period for which he shall have been elected, and he shall not receive within that Period any other Emolument from the United States, or any of them.

Before he enter on the Execution of his Office, he shall take the following Oath or Affirmation:—"I do solemnly swear (or affirm) that I will faithfully execute the Office of President of the United States, and will to the best of my Ability, preserve, protect and defend the Constitution of the United States."

### Section 2

The President shall be Commander in Chief of the Army and Navy of the United States, and of the Militia of the several States, when called into the actual Service of the United States; he may require the Opinion, in writing, of the principal Officer in each of the executive Departments, upon any Subject relating to the Duties of their respective Offices, and he shall have Power to grant Reprieves and Pardons for Offences against the United States, except in Cases of Impeachment.

He shall have Power, by and with the Advice and Consent of the Senate, to make Treaties, provided two thirds of the Senators present concur; and he shall nominate, and by and with the Advice and Consent of the Senate, shall appoint Ambassadors, other public Ministers and Consuls, Judges of the supreme Court, and all other Officers of the United States, whose Appointments are not herein otherwise provided for, and which shall be established by Law: but the Congress may by Law vest the Appointment of such inferior Officers, as they think proper, in the President alone, in the Courts of Law, or in the Heads of Departments.

The President shall have Power to fill up all Vacancies that may happen during the Recess of the Senate, by granting Commissions which shall expire at the End of their next Session.

### Section 3

He shall from time to time give to the Congress Information of the State of the Union, and recommend to their Consideration such Measures as he shall judge necessary and expedient; he may, on extraordinary Occasions, convene both Houses, or either of them, and in Case of Disagreement between them, with Respect to the Time of Adjournment, he may adjourn them to such Time as he shall think proper; he shall receive Ambassadors and other public Ministers; he shall take Care that the Laws be faithfully executed, and shall Commission all the Officers of the United States.

### Section 4

The President, Vice President and all Civil Officers of the United States shall be removed from Office on Impeachment for, and Conviction of, Treason, Bribery, or other high Crimes and Misdemeanors.

## ARTICLE III

### Section 1

The judicial Power of the United States, shall be vested in one supreme Court, and in such inferior Courts as the Congress may from time to time ordain and establish. The Judges, both of the supreme and inferior Courts, shall hold their Offices during good Behaviour, and shall, at stated Times, receive for their Services, a Compensation, which shall not be diminished during their Continuance in Office.

### Section 2

The judicial Power shall extend to all Cases, in Law and Equity, arising under this Constitution, the Laws of the United States, and Treaties made, or which shall be made under their Authority;—to all Cases affecting Ambassadors, other public Ministers and Consuls;—to all Cases of admiralty and maritime Jurisdiction;—to Controversies to which the United States shall be a Party;—to Controversies between two or more States;—between a State and Citizens of another State;—between Citizens of different States;—between Citizens of the same State claiming Lands under Grants of different States, and between a State, or the Citizens thereof, and foreign States, Citizens or Subjects.

In all Cases affecting Ambassadors, other public Ministers and Consuls, and those in which a State shall be a Party, the supreme Court shall have original Jurisdiction. In all the other Cases before mentioned, the supreme Court shall have appellate Jurisdiction, both as to Law and Fact, with such Exceptions, and under such Regulations as the Congress shall make.

The Trial of all Crimes, except in Cases of Impeachment, shall be by Jury; and such Trial shall be held in the State where the said Crimes shall have been committed; but when not committed within any State, the Trial shall be at such Place or Places as the Congress may by Law have directed.

### Section 3

Treason against the United States, shall consist only in levying War against them, or in adhering to their Enemies, giving them Aid and Comfort. No Person shall be convicted of Treason unless on the Testimony of two Witnesses to the same overt Act, or on Confession in open Court.

The Congress shall have Power to declare the Punishment of Treason, but no Attainder of Treason shall work Corruption of Blood or Forfeiture except during the Life of the Person attainted.

## ARTICLE IV

### Section 1

Full Faith and Credit shall be given in each State to the public Acts, Records, and judicial Proceedings of every other State. And the Congress may by general Laws prescribe the Manner in which such Acts, Records and Proceedings shall be proved and the Effect thereof.

### Section 2

The Citizens of each State shall be entitled to all Privileges and Immunities of Citizens in the several States.

A Person charged in any State with Treason, Felony, or other Crime, who shall flee from Justice, and be found in another State, shall on Demand of the executive Authority of the State from which he fled, be delivered up, to be removed to the State having Jurisdiction of the Crime.

No Person held to Service or Labour in one State, under the Laws thereof, escaping into another, shall, in Consequence of any Law or Regulation therein, be discharged from such Service or Labour, but shall be delivered up on Claim of the Party to whom such Service or Labour may be due.

### Section 3

New States may be admitted by the Congress into this Union; but no new State shall be formed or erected within the Jurisdiction of any other State; nor any State be formed by the Junction of two or more States, or Parts of States, without the Consent of the Legislatures of the States concerned as well as of the Congress.

The Congress shall have Power to dispose of and make all needful Rules and Regulations respecting the Territory or other Property belonging to the United States; and nothing in this Constitution shall be so construed as to Prejudice any Claims of the United States, or of any particular State.

### Section 4

The United States shall guarantee to every State in this Union a Republican Form of Government, and shall protect each of them against Invasion; and on Application of the Legislature, or of the Executive (when the Legislature cannot be convened) against domestic Violence.

## ARTICLE V

The Congress, whenever two thirds of both Houses shall deem it necessary, shall propose Amendments to this Constitution, or, on the Application of the Legislatures of two thirds of the several States, shall call a Convention for proposing Amendments, which, in either Case, shall be valid to all Intents and Purposes, as Part of this Constitution, when ratified by the Legislatures of three fourths of the several States, or by Conventions in three fourths thereof, as the one or the other Mode of Ratification may be proposed by the Congress; Provided that no Amendment which may be made prior to the Year One thousand eight hundred and eight shall in any Manner affect the first and fourth Clauses in the Ninth Section of the first Article; and that no State, without its Consent, shall be deprived of its equal Suffrage in the Senate.

## ARTICLE VI

All Debts contracted and Engagements entered into, before the Adoption of this Constitution, shall be as valid against the United States under this Constitution, as under the Confederation.

This Constitution, and the Laws of the United States which shall be made in Pursuance thereof; and all Treaties made, or which shall be made, under the Authority of the United States, shall be the supreme Law of the Land; and the judges in every State shall be bound thereby, any Thing in the Constitution or Laws of any State to the Contrary notwithstanding.

The Senators and Representatives before mentioned, and the Members of the several State Legislatures, and all executive and judicial Officers, both of the United States and of the several States, shall be bound by Oath or Affirmation, to support this Constitution; but no religious Test shall ever be required as a Qualification to any Office or public Trust under the United States.

## ARTICLE VII

The Ratification of the Conventions of nine States, shall be sufficient for the Establishment of this Constitution between the States so ratifying the Same.

## AMENDMENT I [1791]

Congress shall make no law respecting an establishment of religion, or prohibiting the free exercise thereof; or abridging the freedom of speech, or of the press; or the right of the people peaceably to assemble and to petition the Government for a redress of grievances.

## AMENDMENT II [1791]

A well regulated Militia, being necessary to the security of a free State, the right of the people to keep and bear Arms, shall not be infringed.

## AMENDMENT III [1791]

No Soldier shall, in time of peace be quartered in any house, without the consent of the Owner, nor in time of war, but in a manner to be prescribed by law.

## AMENDMENT IV [1791]

The right of the people to be secure in their persons, houses, papers, and effects, against unreasonable searches and seizures, shall not be violated, and no Warrants shall issue, but upon probable cause, supported by Oath or affirmation, and particularly describing the place to be searched, and the persons or things to be seized.

## AMENDMENT V [1791]

No person shall be held to answer for a capital, or otherwise infamous crime, unless on a presentment or indictment of a Grand Jury, except in cases arising in the land or naval forces, or in the Militia, when in actual service in time of War or public danger; nor shall any person be subject for the same offence to be twice put in jeopardy of life or limb; nor shall be compelled in any criminal case to be a witness against himself, nor be deprived of life, liberty, or property, without due process of law; nor shall private property be taken for public use, without just compensation.

## AMENDMENT VI [1791]

In all criminal prosecutions, the accused shall enjoy the right to a speedy and public trial, by an impartial jury of the State and district wherein the crime shall have been committed, which district shall have been previously ascertained by law, and to be informed of the nature and cause of the accusation; to be confronted with the witnesses against him; to have compulsory process for obtaining Witnesses in his favor, and to have Assistance of Counsel for his defence.

## AMENDMENT VII [1791]

In Suits at common law, where the value in controversy shall exceed twenty dollars, the right of trial by jury shall be preserved, and no fact tried by a jury, shall be otherwise reexamined in any Court of the United States, than according to the rules of the common law.

## AMENDMENT VIII [1791]

Excessive bail shall not be required nor excessive fines imposed, nor cruel and unusual punishments inflicted.

## AMENDMENT IX [1791]

The enumeration in the Constitution, of certain rights, shall not be construed to deny or disparage others retained by the people.

## AMENDMENT X [1791]

The powers not delegated to the United States by the Constitution, nor prohibited by it to the States, are reserved to the States respectively, or to the people.

## AMENDMENT XI [1798]

The Judicial power of the United States shall not be construed to extend to any suit in law or equity, commenced or prosecuted against one of the United States by Citizens of another State, or by Citizens or Subjects of any Foreign State.

## AMENDMENT XII [1804]

The Electors shall meet in their respective states and vote by ballot for President and Vice-President, one of whom, at least, shall not be an inhabitant of the same state with themselves; they shall name in their ballots the person voted for as President, and in distinct ballots the person voted for as Vice-President, and they shall make distinct lists of all persons voted for as President, and of all persons voted for as Vice-President, and of the number of votes for each, which lists they shall sign and certify, and transmit sealed to the seat of the government of the United States, directed to the President of the Senate;—The President of the Senate shall, in the presence of the Senate and House of Representatives, open all the certificates and the votes shall then be counted;—The person having the greatest number of votes for President, shall be the President, if such number be a majority of the whole number of Electors appointed; and if no person have such majority, then from the persons having the highest numbers not exceeding three on the list of those voted for as President, the House of Representatives shall choose immediately, by ballot, the President. But in choosing the President, the votes shall be taken by states, the representation from each state having one vote; a quorum for this purpose shall consist of a member or members from two-thirds of the states, and a majority of all the states shall be necessary to a choice. And

if the House of Representatives shall not choose a President whenever the right of choice shall devolve upon them, before the fourth day of March next following, then the Vice-President shall act as President, as in the case of the death or other constitutional disability of the President—The person having the greatest number of votes as Vice-President, shall be the Vice-President, if such number be a majority of the whole number of electors appointed, and if no person have a majority, then from the two highest numbers on the list, the Senate shall choose the Vice-President; a quorum for the purpose shall consist of two-thirds of the whole number of Senators, and a majority of the whole number shall be necessary to a choice. But no person constitutionally ineligible to the office of President shall be eligible to that of Vice-President of the United States.

## AMENDMENT XIII [1865]

### Section 1

Neither slavery nor involuntary servitude, except as punishment for crime whereof the party shall have been duly convicted, shall exist within the United States, or any place subject to their jurisdiction.

### Section 2

Congress shall have power to enforce this article by appropriate legislation.

## AMENDMENT XIV [1868]

### Section 1

All persons born or naturalized in the United States and subject to the jurisdiction thereof, are citizens of the United States and of the State wherein they reside. No State shall make or enforce any law which shall abridge the privileges or immunities of citizens of the United States; nor shall any State deprive any person of life, liberty, or property, without due process of law; nor deny to any person within its jurisdiction the equal protection of the laws.

### Section 2

Representatives shall be apportioned among the several States according to their respective numbers, counting the whole number of persons in each State, excluding Indians not taxed. But when the right to vote at any election for the choice of electors for

President and Vice President of the United States, Representatives in Congress, the Executive and Judicial officers of a State, or the members of the Legislature thereof, is denied to any of the male inhabitants of such State, being twenty-one years of age, and citizens of the United States, or in any way abridged, except for participation in rebellion, or other crime, the basis of representation therein shall be reduced in the proportion which the number of such male citizens shall bear to the whole number of male citizens twenty-one years of age in such State.

### Section 3

No person shall be a Senator or Representative in Congress, or elector of President and Vice President, or hold any office, civil or military, under the United States, or under any State, who, having previously taken an oath, as a member of Congress, or as an officer of the United States, or as a member of any State legislature, or as an executive or judicial officer of any State, to support the Constitution of the United States, shall have engaged in insurrection or rebellion against the same, or given aid or comfort to the enemies thereof. But Congress may by a vote of two-thirds of each House, remove such disability.

### Section 4

The validity of the public debt of the United States, authorized by law, including debts incurred for payment of pensions and bounties for services in suppressing insurrection or rebellion, shall not be questioned. But neither the United States nor any State shall assume or pay any debt or obligation incurred in aid of insurrection or rebellion against the United State, or any claim for the loss or emancipation of any slave; but all such debts, obligations and claims shall be held illegal and void.

### Section 5

The Congress shall have power to enforce, by appropriate legislation, the provisions of this article.

## AMENDMENT XV [1870]

### Section 1

The right of citizens of the United States to vote shall not be denied or abridged by the United States or by any State on account of race, color, or previous condition of servitude.

### Section 2

The Congress shall have power to enforce this article by appropriate legislation.

## AMENDMENT XVI [1913]

The Congress shall have power to lay and collect taxes on incomes, from whatever source derived, without apportionment among the several States, and without regard to any census or enumeration.

## AMENDMENT XVII [1913]

The Senate of the United States shall be composed of two Senators from each State, elected by the people thereof, for six years; and each Senator shall have one vote. The electors in each State shall have the qualifications requisite for electors of the most numerous branch of the State legislatures.

When vacancies happen in the representation of any State in the Senate, the executive authority of such State shall issue writs of election to fill such vacancies: *Provided,* That the legislature of any State may empower the executive thereof to make temporary appointments until the people fill the vacancies by election as the legislature may direct.

This amendment shall not be so construed as to affect the election or term of any Senator chosen before it becomes valid as part of the Constitution.

## AMENDMENT XVIII [1919]

### Section 1

After one year from the ratification of this article the manufacture, sale, or transportation of intoxicating liquors within, the importation thereof into, or the exportation thereof from the United States and all territory subject to the jurisdiction thereof for beverage purposes is hereby prohibited.

### Section 2

The Congress and the several States shall have concurrent power to enforce this article by appropriate legislation.

### Section 3

This article shall be inoperative unless it shall have been ratified as an amendment to the Constitution by the legislatures of the several States, as provided in the Constitution, within seven years from the date of the submission hereof to the States by the Congress.

## AMENDMENT XIX [1920]

The right of citizens of the United States to vote shall not be denied or abridged by the United States or by any State on account of sex.

Congress shall have power to enforce this article by appropriate legislation.

## AMENDMENT XX [1933]

### Section 1

The terms of the President and Vice President shall end at noon on the 20th day of January, and the terms of Senators and Representatives at noon on the 3d day of January, of the years in which such terms would have ended if this article had not been ratified; and the terms of their successors shall then begin.

### Section 2

The Congress shall assemble at least once in every year, and such meeting shall begin at noon on the 3d day of January, unless they shall by law appoint a different day.

### Section 3

If, at the time fixed for the beginning of the term of the President, the President elect shall have died, the Vice President elect shall become President. If the President shall not have been chosen before the time fixed for the beginning of his term, or if the President elect shall have failed to qualify, then the Vice President elect shall act as President until a President shall have qualified; and the Congress may by law provide for the case wherein neither a President elect nor a Vice President elect shall have qualified, declaring who shall then act as President, or the manner in which one who is to act shall be selected, and such person shall act accordingly until a President or Vice President shall have qualified.

### Section 4

The Congress may by law provide for the case of the death of any of the persons from whom the House of Representatives may choose a President whenever the right of choice shall have devolved upon them, and for the case of death of any of the persons from whom the Senate may choose a Vice President whenever the right of choice shall have devolved upon them.

### Section 5

Sections 1 and 2 shall take effect on the 15th day of October following the ratification of this article.

### Section 6

This article shall be inoperative unless it shall have been ratified as an amendment to the Constitution by the legislatures of three-fourths of the several States within seven years from the date of its submission.

## AMENDMENT XXI [1933]

### Section 1

The eighteenth article of amendment to the Constitution of the United States is hereby repealed.

### Section 2

The transportation or importation into any State, Territory, or possession of the United States for delivery or use therein of intoxicating liquors, in violation of the laws thereof, is hereby prohibited.

### Section 3

This article shall be inoperative unless it shall have been ratified as an amendment to the Constitution by conventions in the several states, as provided in the Constitution, within seven years from the date of the submission hereof to the States by the Congress.

## AMENDMENT XXII [1951]

### Section 1

No person shall be elected to the office of the President more than twice, and no person who has held the office of President, or acted as President, for more than two years of a term to which some other person was elected President shall be elected to the office of the President more than once. But this Article shall not apply to any person holding the office of President when this Article was proposed by the Congress, and shall not prevent any person who may be holding the office of President, or acting as President, during the term within which the Article becomes operative from holding the office of President or acting as President during the remainder of such term.

### Section 2

This article shall be inoperative unless it shall have been ratified as an amendment to the Constitution by the legislatures of three-fourths of the several States within seven years from the date of its submission to the States by the Congress.

## AMENDMENT XXIII [1961]

### Section 1

The District constituting the seat of Government of the United States shall appoint in such manner as the Congress may direct:

A number of electors of President and Vice President equal to the whole number of Senators and Representatives in Congress to which the District would be entitled if it were a State, but in no event more than the least populous State; they shall be in addition to those appointed by the States, but they shall be considered, for the purposes of the election of President and Vice President, to be electors appointed by a State; and they shall meet in the District and perform such duties as provided by the twelfth article of amendment.

### Section 2

The Congress shall have power to enforce this article by appropriate legislation.

## AMENDMENT XXIV [1964]

### Section 1

The right of citizens of the United States to vote in any primary or other election for President or Vice President, for electors for President or Vice President, or for Senator or Representative in Congress, shall not be denied or abridged by the United States or any State by reason of failure to pay any poll tax or other tax.

### Section 2

The Congress shall have power to enforce this article by appropriate legislation.

## AMENDMENT XXV [1967]

### Section 1

In case of the removal of the President from office or of his death or resignation, the Vice President shall become President.

### Section 2

Whenever there is a vacancy in the office of the Vice President, the President shall nominate a Vice President who shall take office upon confirmation by a majority vote of both Houses of Congress.

### Section 3

Whenever the President transmits to the President pro tempore of the Senate and the Speaker of the House of Representatives his written declaration that he is unable to discharge the powers and duties of his office, and until he transmits to them a written declaration to the contrary, such powers and duties shall be discharged by the Vice President as Acting President.

### Section 4

Whenever the Vice President and a majority of either the principal officers of the executive departments or of such other body as Congress may by law provide, transmit to the President pro tempore of the Senate and the Speaker of the House of Representatives their written declaration that the President is unable to discharge the powers and duties of his office, the Vice President shall immediately assume the powers and duties of the office as Acting President.

Thereafter, when the President transmits to the President pro tempore of the Senate and the Speaker of the House of Representatives his written declaration that no inability exists, he shall resume the powers and duties of his office unless the Vice President and a majority of either the principal officers of the executive department or of such other body as Congress may by law provide, transmit within four days to the President pro tempore of the

Senate and the Speaker of the House of Representatives their written declaration that the President is unable to discharge the powers and duties of his office. Thereupon Congress shall decide the issue, assembling within forty-eight hours for that purpose if not in session. If the Congress, within twenty-one days after receipt of the latter written declaration, or, if Congress is not in session, within twenty-one days after Congress is required to assemble, determines by two-thirds vote of both Houses that the President is unable to discharge the powers and duties of his office, the Vice President shall continue to discharge the powers and duties of his office, the Vice President shall continue to discharge the same as Acting President; otherwise, the President shall resume the powers and duties of his office.

## AMENDMENT XXVI [1971]

### Section 1

The right of citizens of the United States, who are eighteen years of age or older to vote shall not be denied or abridged by the United States or by any State on account of age.

### Section 2

The Congress shall have power to enforce this article by appropriate legislation.

## AMENDMENT XXVII [1992]

No law, varying compensation for the services of the Senators and Representatives, shall take effect, until an election of Representatives shall have intervened.

# The Sherman Act
## (Excerpts)

## SECTION 1. TRUSTS, ETC., IN RESTRAINT OF TRADE ILLEGAL; PENALTY

Every contract, combination in the form of trust or otherwise, or conspiracy, in restraint of trade or commerce among the several States, or with foreign nations, is declared to be illegal. Every person who shall make any contract or engage in any combination or conspiracy hereby declared to be illegal shall be deemed guilty of a felony, and, on conviction thereof, shall be punished by fine not exceeding one million dollars if a corporation, or, if any other person, one hundred thousand dollars or by imprisonment not exceeding three years, or by both said punishments, in the discretion of the court.

## SECTION 2. MONOPOLIZING TRADE A FELONY; PENALTY

Every person who shall monopolize, or attempt to monopolize, or combine or conspire with any other person or persons, to monopolize any part of the trade or commerce among the several States, or with foreign nations, shall be deemed guilty of a felony, and, on conviction thereof, shall be punished by fine not exceeding one million dollars if a corporation, or, if any other person, one hundred thousand dollars or by imprisonment not exceeding three years, or by both said punishments, in the discretion of the court.

# THE ROBINSON-PATMAN ACT (EXCERPTS)

## SECTION 2. DISCRIMINATION IN PRICE, SERVICES, OR FACILITIES—PRICE; SELECTION OF CUSTOMERS

(a)     It shall be unlawful for any person engaged in commerce, in the course of such commerce, either directly or indirectly, to discriminate in price between different purchasers of commodities of like grade and quality, where either or any of the purchases involved in such discrimination are in commerce, where such commodities are sold for use, consumption, or resale within the United States or any Territory thereof or the District of Columbia or any insular possession or other place under the jurisdiction of the United States, and where the effect of such discrimination may be substantially to lessen competition or tend to create a monopoly in any line of commerce, or to injure, destroy, or prevent competition with any person who either grants or knowingly receives the benefit of such discrimination, or with customers of either of them; *Provided,* That nothing herein contained shall prevent differentials which make only due allowance for differences in the cost of manufacture, sale, or delivery resulting from the differing methods or quantities in which such commodities are to such purchasers sold or delivered: *Provided,* however, That the Federal trade Commission may, after due investigation and hearing to all interested parties, fix and establish quantity limits, and revise the same as it finds necessary, as to particular commodities or classes of commodities, where it finds that available purchasers in greater quantities are so few as to render differentials on account thereof unjustly discriminatory or promotive of monopoly in any line of commerce; and the foregoing shall then not be construed to permit differentials based on differences in quantities greater than those so fixed and established: And *provided further,* That nothing herein contained shall prevent persons engaged in selling goods, wares, or merchandise in commerce from selecting their own customers in bona fide transactions and not in restraint of trade: And *provided further,* That nothing herein contained shall prevent price changes from time to time where in response to changing conditions affecting the market for or the marketability of the goods concerned, such as but not limited to actual or imminent deterioration of perishable goods, obsolescence of seasonal goods, distress sales under court process, or sales in good faith in discontinuance of business in the goods concerned.

## BURDEN OF REBUTTING PRIMA-FACIE CASE OF DISCRIMINATION

(b)     Upon proof being made, at any hearing on a complaint under this section, that there has been discrimination in price or services or facilities furnished, the burden of rebutting the prima-facie case thus made by showing justification shall be upon the person charged with a violation of this section, and unless justification shall be affirmatively shown the Commission is authorized to issue an order terminating the discrimination: *Provided,* however, That nothing herein contained shall prevent a seller rebutting the prima-facie case thus made by showing that his lower price or the furnishing of services or facilities to any purchaser or purchasers was made in good faith to meet an equally low price of a competitor, or the services or facilities furnished by a competitor.

## PAYMENT OR ACCEPTANCE OF COMMISSION, BROKERAGE OR OTHER COMPENSATION

**(c)**     It shall be unlawful for any person engaged in commerce, in the course of such commerce, to pay or grant, or to receive or accept, anything of value as a commission, brokerage, or other compensation, or any allowance or discount in lieu thereof, except for services rendered in connection with the sale or purchase of goods, wares, or merchandise, either to the other party to such transaction or to an agent, representative, or other intermediary therein where such intermediary is acting in fact for or in behalf, or is subject to the direct or indirect control, of any party to such transaction other than the person by whom such compensation is so granted or paid.

## PAYMENT FOR SERVICES OR FACILITIES FOR PROCESSING OR SALE

**(d)**     It shall be unlawful for any person engaged in commerce to pay or contract for the payment of anything of value to or for the benefit of a customer of such person in the course of such commerce as compensation or in consideration for any services or facilities furnished by or through such customer in connection with the processing, handling, sale or offering for sale of any products or commodities manufactured, sold, or offered for sale by such person, unless such payment or consideration is available on proportionally equal terms to all other customers competing in the distribution of such products or commodities.

## FURNISHING SERVICES OR FACILITIES FOR PROCESSING, HANDLING, ETC.

**(e)**     It shall be unlawful for any person to discriminate in favor of one purchaser against another purchaser or purchasers of a commodity bought for resale, with or without processing, by contracting to furnish or furnishing, or by contributing to the furnishing of, any services or facilities connected with the processing, handling, sale, or offering for sale of such commodity so purchased upon terms not accorded to all purchasers on proportionally equal terms.

## KNOWINGLY INDUCING OR RECEIVING DISCRIMINATORY PRICE

**(f)**     It shall be unlawful for any person engaged in commerce, in the course of such commerce, knowingly to induce or receive a discrimination in price which is prohibited by this section.

## SECTION 3. DISCRIMINATION IN REBATES, DISCOUNTS, OR ADVERTISING SERVICE CHARGES; UNDERSELLING IN PARTICULAR LOCALITIES; PENALTIES

It shall be unlawful for any person engaged in commerce, in the course of such commerce, to be a party to, or assist in, any transaction of sale, or contract to sell, which discriminates to his knowledge against competitors of the purchaser, in that, any discount, rebate, allowance, or advertising service charge is granted to the purchaser over and above any discount, rebate, allowance, or advertising service charge available at the time of such transaction to said competitors in respect of a sale of goods of like grade, quality, and quantity; to sell, or contract to sell, goods in any part of the United States at prices lower than those exacted by said person elsewhere in the United States for the purpose of destroying competition, or eliminating a competitor in such part of the United States; or, to sell, or contract to sell, goods at unreasonably low prices for the purpose of destroying competition or eliminating a competitor.

Any person violating any of the provisions of this section shall, upon conviction thereof, be fined not more than $5,000 or imprisoned not more than one year, or both.

## SECTION 402A. SPECIAL LIABILITY OF SELLER OF PRODUCT FOR PHYSICAL HARM TO USER OR CONSUMER

(1) One who sells any product in a defective condition unreasonably dangerous to the user or consumer or to his property is subject to liability for physical harm thereby caused to the ultimate user or consumer, or to his property, if
   (a) the seller is engaged in the business of selling such a product, and
   (b) it is expected to and does reach the user or consumer without substantial change in the condition in which it is sold.

(2) The rule stated in Subsection (1) applies although
   (a) the seller has exercised all possible care in the preparation and sale of his product, and
   (b) the user or consumer has not bought the product from or entered into any contractual relation with the seller.

# UNIFORM COMMERCIAL CODE (SELECTED PROVISIONS)

## SECTION 1-103. SUPPLEMENTARY GENERAL PRINCIPLES OF LAW APPLICABLE

Unless displaced by the particular provisions of this Act, the principles of law and equity, including the law merchant and the law relative to capacity to contract, principal and agent, estoppel, fraud, misrepresentation, duress, coercion, mistake, bankruptcy, or other validating or invalidating cause shall supplement its provisions.

## SECTION 1-201. GENERAL DEFINITIONS

Subject to additional definitions contained in the subsequent Articles of this Act which are applicable to specific Articles or Parts thereof, and unless the context otherwise requires, in this Act:

**(1)** "Action" in the sense of a judicial proceeding includes recoupment, counterclaim, set-off, suit in equity and any other proceedings in which rights are determined.

**(2)** "Aggrieved party" means a party entitled to resort to a remedy.

**(3)** "Agreement" means the bargain of the parties in fact as found in their language or by implication from other circumstances including course of dealing or usage of trade or course of performance as provided in this Act (Sections 1-205 and 2-208). Whether an agreement has legal consequences is determined by the provisions of this Act, if applicable; otherwise by the law of contracts (Section 1-103). (Compare "Contract.")

**(4)** "Bank" means any person engaged in the business of banking.

**(5)** "Bearer" means the person in possession of an instrument, document or title, or certified security payable to bearer or endorsed in blank.

**(6)** "Bill of lading" means a document evidencing the receipt of goods for shipment issued by a person engaged in the business of transporting or forwarding goods, and includes an airbill. "Airbill" means a document serving for air transportation as a bill of lading does for marine or rail transportation, and includes an air consignment note or air waybill.

**(7)** "Branch" includes a separately incorporated foreign branch of a bank.

**(8)** "Burden of establishing" a fact means the burden of persuading the triers of fact that the existence of the fact is more probable than its non-existence.

**(9)** "Buyer in ordinary course of business" means a person who in good faith and without knowledge that the sale to him is in violation of the ownership rights or security interest of a third party in the goods buys in ordinary course from a person in the business of selling goods of that kind but does not include a pawnbroker. All persons who sell minerals or the like (including oil and gas) at wellhead or minehead shall be deemed to be persons in the business of selling goods of that kind. "Buying" may be for cash or by exchange of other property or on secured or unsecured credit and includes receiving goods or documents of title under a preexisting contract for sale but does not include a transfer in bulk or as security for or in total or partial satisfaction of a money debt.

**(10)** "Conspicuous" means A term or clause written so that a reasonable person against whom it is to operate ought to have noticed it. A printed head in capitals (as: NONNEGOTIABLE BILL OF LADING) is conspicuous. Language in the body of a form is "conspicuous." Whether a term or clause is "conspicuous" or not is for decision by the court.

**(11)** "Contract" means the total legal obligation which results from the parties' agreement as affected by this Act and any other applicable rules of law. (Compare "Agreement.")

**(12)** "Creditor" includes a general creditor, a secured creditor, a lien creditor and any representative of creditors, including an assignee for the benefit of creditors, a trustee in bankruptcy, a receiver in equity and an executor or administrator of an insolvent debtor's or assignor's estate.

**(13)** "Defendant" includes a person in the position of defendant in a cross-action or counterclaim.

**(14)** "Delivery" with respect to instruments, documents of title, chattel paper, or certificated securities means voluntary transfer of possession.

**(15)** "Document of title" includes bill of lading, dock warrant, dock receipt, warehouse receipt or order for the delivery of goods, and also any other document which in the regular course of business or financing is treated as adequately evidencing that the person in possession of it is entitled to receive, hold and dispose of the document and the goods it covers. To be a document of title a document must purport to be issued by or addressed to a bailee and purport to cover goods in the bailee's possession which are either identified or are fungible portions of an identified mass.

**(16)** "Fault" means wrongful act, omission or breach.

**(17)** "Fungible" with respect to goods or securities means goods or securities of which any unit is, by nature or usage of trade, the equivalent of any other like unit. Goods which are not fungible shall be deemed fungible for the purposes of this Act to the extent that under a particular agreement or document unlike units are treated as equivalents.

**(18)** "Genuine" means free of forgery or counterfeiting.

**(19)** "Good faith" means honesty in fact in the conduct or transaction concerned.

**(20)** "Holder" means a person who is in possession of a document of title or an instrument or a certificated investment security drawn, issued, or endorsed to him or his orders or to bearer or in blank.

**(21)** "Honor" is to pay or to accept and pay, or where a credit so engages to purchase or discount a draft complying with the terms of the credit.

**(22)** "Insolvency proceedings" includes any assignment for the benefit of creditors or other proceedings intended to liquidate or rehabilitate the estate of the person involved.

**(23)** "Insolvent" means a person who either has ceased to pay his debts in the ordinary course of business or cannot pay his debts as they become due or is insolvent within the meaning of the federal bankruptcy law.

**(24)** "Money" means a medium of exchange authorized or adopted by a domestic or foreign government as a part of its currency.

**(25)** "Notice" of a fact means when a person
   **(a)** has actual knowledge of it; or
   **(b)** has received a notice or notification of it; or
   **(c)** from all the facts and circumstances known to him at the time in question has reason to know that it exists.

    A person "knows" or has "knowledge" of a fact when he has actual knowledge of it. "Discover" or "learn" or a word or phrase of similar import refers to knowledge rather than to reason to know. The time and circumstances under which a notice or notification may cease to be effective are not determined by this Act.

**(26)** A person "notifies" or "gives" a notice or notification to another by taking such steps as may be reasonably required to inform the other in ordinary course whether or not such other actually comes to know of it. A person "receives" a notice or notification when
   **(a)** it comes to his attention; or
   **(b)** it is duly delivered at the place of business through which the contract was made or at any other place held out by him as the place for receipt of such communications.

**(27)** Notice, knowledge or a notice of notification received by an organization is effective for particular transaction from the time when it is brought to the attention of the individual conducting that transaction, and in any event from the time when it would have been brought to his attention if the organization had exercised due diligence. An organization exercises due diligence if it maintains reasonable routines for communicating significant information to the person conducting the transaction and there is reasonable compliance with the routines. Due diligence does not require an individual acting for the organization to communicate information unless such communication is part of his regular duties or unless he has reason to know of the transaction and that the transaction would be materially affected by the information.

**(28)** "Organization" includes a corporation, government or government subdivision or agency, business trust, estate, trust, partnership or association, two or more persons having a joint or common interest, or any other legal or commercial entity.

**(29)** "Party," as distinct from "third party," means a person who has engaged in a transaction or made an agreement within this Act.

**(30)** "Person" includes an individual or an organization (See Section 1-102).

**(31)** "Presumption" or "presumed" means that the trier of fact must find the existence of the fact presumed unless and until evidence is introduced which would support a finding of its nonexistence.

**(32)** "Purchase" includes taking by sale, discount, negotiation, mortgage, pledge, lien, issue, or re-issue, gift or any other voluntary transaction creating an interest in property.

**(33)** "Purchaser" means a person who takes by purchase.

**(34)** "Remedy" means any remedial right to which an aggrieved party is entitled with or without resort to a tribunal.

**(35)** "Representative" includes an agent, an officer of a corporation or association, and a trustee, executor or administrator of an estate, or any other person empowered to act for another.

**(36)** "Rights" includes remedies.

**(37)** "Security interest" means an interest in personal property or fixtures which secures payment or performance of an obligation. The retention or reservation of title by a seller of goods notwithstanding shipment or delivery to the buyer (Section 2-401) is limited in effect to a reservation of a "security interest." The term also includes any interest of a buyer of accounts or chattel paper which is subject to Article 9. The special property interest of a buyer of goods on identification of such goods to a contract for sale under Section 2-401 is not a "security interest," but a buyer may also acquire a "security interest" by complying with Article 9. Unless a lease or consignment is intended as security, reservation of title thereunder is not a "security interest" but a consignment is in any event subject to the provisions on consignment sales (Section 2-326). Whether a lease is intended as security is to be determined by the facts of each case; however, (a) the inclusion of an option to purchase does not of itself make the lease one intended for security, and (b) an agreement that upon compliance with the terms of the lease the lessee shall become or has the option to become the owner of the property for no additional consideration or for a nominal consideration does make the lease one intended for security.

**(38)** "Send" in connection with any writing or notice means to deposit in the mail or deliver for transmission by any other usual means of communication with postage or cost of transmission provided for and properly addressed and in the case of an instrument to an address specified thereon or otherwise agreed, or if there be none to any address reasonable under the circumstances. The receipt of any writing or notice within the time at which it would have arrived if properly sent has the effect of a proper sending.

**(39)** "Signed" includes any symbol executed or adopted by a party with present intention to authenticate a writing.

**(40)** "Surety" includes guarantor.

**(41)** "Telegram" includes message transmitted by radio, teletype, cable, any mechanical method of transmission, or the like.

**(42)** "Term" means that portion of an agreement which relates to a particular matter.

**(43)** "Unauthorized" signature or indorsement means one made without actual, implied or apparent authority and includes a forgery.

**(44)** "Value." Except as otherwise provided with respect to negotiable instruments and bank collections (Sections 3-303, 4-208 and 4-209), a person gives "value" for rights if he acquires them
   **(a)** in return for a binding commitment to extend credit or for the extension of immediately available credit whether or not drawn upon and whether or not a chargeback is provided for in the event of difficulties in collection; or
   **(b)** as security for or in total or partial satisfaction of a pre-existing claim; or
   **(c)** by accepting delivery pursuant to a pre-existing contract for purchase; or

(d) generally in return for any consideration sufficient to support a simple contract.

(45) "Warehouse receipt" means a receipt issued by a person engaged in the business of storing goods for hire.

(46) "Written" or "writing" includes printing, type-writing or any other intentional reduction to tangible form.

## SECTION 1-203. OBLIGATION OF GOOD FAITH

Every contract or duty within this Act imposes an obligation of good faith in its performance or enforcement.

## SECTION 1-205. COURSE OF DEALING AND USAGE OF TRADE

(1) A course of dealing is a sequence of previous conduct between the parties to a particular transaction which is fairly to be regarded as establishing a common basis of understanding for interpreting their expressions and other conduct.

(2) A usage of trade is any practice or method of dealing having such regularity of observance in a place, vocation or trade as to justify an expectation that it will be observed with respect to the transaction in question. The existence and scope of such a usage are to be proved as facts. If it is established that such a usage is embodied in a written trade code or similar writing the interpretation of the writing is for the court.

(3) A course of dealing between parties and any usage of trade in the vocation or trade in which they are engaged or of which they are or should be aware give particular meaning to and supplement or qualify terms of an agreement.

(4) The express terms of an agreement and an applicable course of dealing or usage of trade shall be construed wherever reasonable as consistent with each other; but when such construction is unreasonable express terms control both course of dealing and usage of trade and course of dealing controls usage of trade.

(5) An applicable usage of trade in the place where any part of performance is to occur shall be used in interpreting the agreement as to that part of the performance.

(6) Evidence of a relevant usage of trade offered by one party is not admissible unless and until he has given the other party such notice as the court finds sufficient to prevent unfair surprise to the latter.

## SECTION 2-314. IMPLIED WARRANTY: MERCHANTABILITY; USAGE OF TRADE

(1) Unless excluded or modified (Section 2-316), a warranty that the goods shall be merchantable is implied in a contract for their sale if the seller is a merchant with respect to goods of that kind. Under this section the serving for value of food or drink to be consumed either on the premises or elsewhere is a sale.

(2) Goods to be merchantable must be at least such as
   (a) pass without objection in the trade under the contract description; and
   (b) in the case of fungible goods, are of fair average quality within the description; and
   (c) are fit for the ordinary purposes for which such goods are used; and
   (d) run, within the variations permitted by the agreement, of even kind, quality and quantity within each unit and among all units involved; and
   (e) are adequately contained, packaged, and labeled as the agreement may require; and
   (f) conform to the promises or affirmations of fact made on the container or label if any.

(3) Unless excluded or modified (Section 2-316) other implied warranties may arise from course of dealing or usage of trade.

## SECTION 2-315. IMPLIED WARRANTY: FITNESS FOR PARTICULAR PURPOSE

Where the seller at the time of contracting has reason to know any particular purpose for which the goods are required and that the buyer is relying on the seller's skill of judgment to select or furnish suitable goods, there is unless excluded or modified under the next section an implied warranty that the goods shall be fit for such purpose.

## SECTION 2-302. UNCONSCIONABLE CONTRACT OR CLAUSE

**(1)** If the court as a matter of law finds the contract or any clause of the contract to have been unconscionable at the time it was made the court may refuse to enforce the contract, or it may enforce the remainder of the contract without the unconscionable clause, or it may so limit the application of any unconscionable clause as to avoid any unconscionable result.

**(2)** When it is claimed or appears to the court that the contract or any clause thereof may be unconscionable the parties shall be afforded a reasonable opportunity to present evidence as to its commercial setting, purpose and effect to aid the court in making the determination.

## SECTION 2-313. EXPRESS WARRANTIES BY AFFIRMATION, PROMISE, DESCRIPTION, SAMPLE

**(1)** Express warranties by the seller are created as follows:

    **(a)** Any affirmation of fact or promise made by the seller to the buyer which relates to the goods and becomes part of the basis of the bargain creates an express warranty that the goods shall conform to the affirmation or promise.

    **(b)** Any description of the goods which is made part of the basis of the bargain creates an express warranty that the goods shall conform to the description.

    **(c)** Any sample or model which is made part of the basis of the bargain creates an express warranty that the whole of the goods shall conform to the sample or model.

**(2)** It is not necessary to the creation of an express warranty that the seller use formal words such as "warrant" or "guarantee" or that he have a specific intention to make a warranty, but an affirmation merely of the value of the goods or a statement purporting to be merely the seller's opinion or commendation of the goods does not create a warranty.

## SECTION 2-105. DEFINITIONS: "GOODS"

**(1)** "Goods" means all things (including specially manufactured goods) which are movable at the time of identification of the contract for sale other than the money in which the price is to be paid, investment securities (Article 8) and things in action. "Goods" also includes the unborn young of animals and growing crops and other identified things attached to realty as described in the section on goods to be severed from realty (Section 2-107).

## SECTION 2-107. GOODS TO BE SEVERED FROM REALTY; RECORDING

**(1)** A contract for the sale of minerals or the like (including oil and gas) or a structure or its materials to be removed from realty is a contract for the sale of goods within this Article if they are to be severed by the seller but until severance a purported present sale thereof which is not effective as a transfer of an interest in land is effective only as a contract to sell.

**(2)** A contract for the sale apart from the land of growing crops or other things attached to realty and capable of severance without material harm thereto but not described in subsection (1) or of timber to be cut is a contract for the sale of goods within this Article whether the subject matter is to be severed by the buyer or by the seller even though it forms part of the realty at the time of contracting, and the parties can by identification effect a present sale before severance.

## SECTION 2-202. SCOPE: CERTAIN SECURITY AND OTHER TRANSACTIONS EXCLUDED FROM THIS ARTICLE

Unless the context otherwise requires, this Article applies to transactions in goods: it does not apply to any transaction which, although in the form of an unconditional contract to sell or present sale, is intended to operate only as a security transaction, nor does this Article impair or repeal any statute regulating sales to consumers, farmers or other specified classes of buyers.

## SECTION 2-103. DEFINITIONS AND INDEX OF DEFINITIONS

(1) In this Article unless the context otherwise requires
  (a) "Buyer" means a person who buys or contracts to buy goods.
  (b) "Good faith" in the case of a merchant means honesty in fact and the observance of reasonable commercial standards of fair dealing in the trade.
  (c) "Receipt" of goods means taking physical possession of them.
  (d) "Seller" means a person who sells or contracts to sell goods.

## SECTION 2-104. DEFINITIONS: "MERCHANT"; "BETWEEN MERCHANTS"

(1) "Merchant" means a person who deals in goods of the kind or otherwise by his occupation holds himself out as having knowledge or skill peculiar to the practices or goods involved in the transaction or to whom such knowledge or skill may be attributed by his employment of an agent or broker or other intermediary who by his occupation holds himself out as having such knowledge or skill. . . .
(3) "Between merchants" means in any transaction with respect to which both parties are chargeable with the knowledge or skill of merchants.

## SECTION 2-316. EXCLUSION OR MODIFICATION OF WARRANTIES

(1) Words or conduct relevant to the creation of an express warranty and words or conduct tending to negate or limit warranty shall be construed wherever reasonable as consistent with each other; but subject to the provisions of this Article on parol or extrinsic evidence (Section 2-202) negation or limitation is inoperative to the extent that such construction is unreasonable.
(2) Subject to subsection (3), to exclude or modify the implied warranty of merchantability or any part of it in the language must mention merchantability and in case of a writing must be conspicuous, and to exclude or modify any implied warranty of fitness the exclusion must be by a writing and conspicuous. Language to exclude all implied warranties of fitness is sufficient if it states, for example, that "There are no warranties which extend beyond the description on the face hereof."

(3) Notwithstanding subsection (2)
  (a) unless the circumstances indicate otherwise, all implied warranties are excluded by expressions like "as is," "with all faults," or other language which in common understanding calls the buyer's attention to the exclusion of warranties and makes plain that there is no implied warranty; and
  (b) when the buyer before entering into the contract has examined the goods or the sample or model as fully as he desired or has refused to examine the goods there is no implied warranty with regard to defects which an examination ought in the circumstances to have revealed to him; and
  (c) an implied warranty can also be excluded or modified by course of dealing or course of performance or usage of trade.
(4) Remedies for breach of warranty can be limited in accordance with the provisions of this Article on liquidation or limitation of damages and on contractual modification of remedy (Section 2-718 and 2-719).

## SECTION 2-317. CUMULATION AND CONFLICT OF WARRANTIES EXPRESS OR IMPLIED

Warranties either express or implied shall be construed as consistent with each other and as cumulative, but if such construction is unreasonable the intention of the parties shall determine which warranty is dominant. In ascertaining that intention the following rules apply:
  (a) Exact or technical specifications displace an inconsistent sample or model or general language of description.
  (b) A sample from an existing bulk displaces inconsistent general language of description.
  (c) Express warranties displace inconsistent implied warranties other than an implied warranty of fitness for a particular purpose.

## SECTION 2-318. THIRD-PARTY BENEFICIARIES OF WARRANTIES EXPRESS OR IMPLIED

### Alternative A

A seller's warranty whether express or implied extends to any natural person who is in the family or household of his buyer or who is a guest in his home if it is reasonable to expect that such person may use, consume or be affected by the goods and who is injured in person by breach of the warranty. A seller may not exclude or limit the operation of this section.

### Alternative B

A seller's warranty whether express or implied extends to any natural person who may reasonably be expected to use, consume or be affected by the goods and who is injured in person by breach of the warranty. A seller may not exclude or limit the operation of this section.

### Alternative C

A seller's warranty whether express or implied, extends to any person who may reasonably be expected to use, consume or be affected by the goods and who is injured by breach of the warranty. A seller may not exclude or limit the operation of this section with respect to injury to the person of an individual to whom the warranty extends.

## SECTION 2-714. BUYER'S DAMAGES FOR BREACH IN REGARD TO ACCEPTED GOODS

(1)  Where the buyer has accepted goods and given notification (subsection (3) of Section 2-607) he may recover as damages for any nonconformity of tender the loss resulting in the ordinary course of events from the seller's breach as determined in any manner which is reasonable.

(2)  The measure of damages for breach of warranty is the difference at the time and place of acceptance between the value of the goods accepted and the value they would have had if they had been as warranted, unless special circumstances show proximate damages of a different amount.

(3)  In a proper case any incidental and consequential damages under the next section may also be recovered.

## SECTION 2-715. BUYER'S INCIDENTAL AND CONSEQUENTIAL DAMAGES

(1)  Incidental damages resulting from the seller's breach include expenses reasonably incurred in inspection, receipt, transportation and care and custody of goods rightfully rejected, any commercially reasonable charges, expenses or commissions in connection with effecting cover and any other reasonable expense incident to the delay or other breach.

(2)  Consequential damages resulting from the seller's breach include
   (a)  any loss resulting from general or particular requirements and needs of which the seller at the time of contracting had reason to know and which could not reasonably be prevented by cover or otherwise; and
   (b)  injury to person or property proximately resulting from any breach of warranty.

## SECTION 2-719. CONTRACTUAL MODIFICATION OR LIMITATION OF REMEDY

(1)  Subject to the provisions of subsections (2) and (3) of this section and of the preceding section on liquidation and limitation of damages,
   (a)  the agreement may provide for remedies in addition to or in substitution for those provided in this Article and may limit or alter the measure of damages recoverable under this Article, as by limiting the buyer's remedies to return of the goods and repayment of the price or to repair and replacement of nonconforming goods or parts; and
   (b)  resort to a remedy as provided is optional unless the remedy is expressly agreed to be exclusive, in which case it is the sole remedy.

(2)  Where circumstances cause an exclusive or limited remedy to fail of its essential purpose, remedy may be had as provided in this Act.

(3)  Consequential damages may be limited or excluded unless the limitation or exclusion is unconscionable. Limitation of consequential

damages for injury to the person in the case of consumer goods is prima facie unconscionable but limitation of damages where the loss is commercial is not.

## SECTION 2-725. STATUTE OF LIMITATIONS IN CONTRACTS FOR SALE

**(1)**   An action for breach of any contract for sale must be commenced within four years after the cause of action has accrued. By the original agreement the parties may reduce the period of limitation to not less than one year but may not extend it.

**(2)**   A cause of action accrues when the breach occurs, regardless of the aggrieved party's lack of knowledge of the breach. A breach of warranty occurs when tender of delivery is made, except that where a warranty explicitly extends to future performance of the goods and discovery of the breach must await the time of such performance the cause of action accrues when the breach is or should have been discovered.

**(3)**   Where an action commenced within the time limited by subsection (1) is so terminated as to leave available a remedy by another action for the same breach such other action may be commenced after the expiration of the time limited and within six months after the termination of the first action unless the termination resulted from voluntary discontinuance or from dismissal for failure or neglect to prosecute.

**(4)**   This section does not alter the law on tolling of the statute of limitations nor does it apply to causes of action which have accrued before this Act becomes effective.

# GLOSSARY

**ANPRs** Advance notice of proposed agency rulemakings published in the *Federal Register* warning the public that an agency will soon propose a regulation.

**APA** Administrative Procedure Act; law governing procedures for most federal administrative agencies.

**Abatement Period** Regarding OSHA it refers to a time period OSHA gives an employer to correct OSHA violations.

**Abnormal Use (or Product Misuse)** A product liability defense involving what its name suggests: the plaintiff's misuse of a product.

**Absolute Privilege** A person may make the defamatory remark maliciously or without necessity.

**Abuse of Process** An intentional tort where defendant uses civil or criminal legal procedures for an improper purpose.

**Acceptance** Offeree's manifestation of assent to the terms of an offer made to offeree; forms a contract if made while offer still "alive."

**Accepted Credit Card** As defined by the Truth-in-Lending Act and Regulation—a credit card a person has applied for, received, used, or authorized someone else to use.

**Accountings** Court orders directing the presentation of income and expense records to an authorized party.

**Accredited Persons** Large or sophisticated securities buyers not formally entitled to as much information about a security offering.

**Act Utilitarianism** Maximizing one's happiness even if it means breaking the positive law.

**Actual Notice** Actual contact in person, phone, or letter; actual notice to third persons with whom agent has actually dealt is required when agencies end; distinguished from constructive notice (such as notice in trade journal).

**Adequacy of the Consideration** The general rule that courts look at a contract to see whether each of the parties gave the other enough or a fair amount for what it got from the other party under the contract.

**Adjudicate** Decide at a legal hearing satisfying procedural due process requirements.

**Adjudicatory Hearing** Hearing before a governmental body such as a court or administrative agency

**Adjustment** Word used in labor law to describe a way of settling an unfair labor practice case that basically is an informal settlement.

**Administrative Agency** Nonjudicial, nonlegislative governmental lawmaker, such as the SEC (Securities and Exchange Commission).

**Administrative Hearing** A proceeding somewhat resembling a trial that is held before an administrative agency to determine whether laws enforced by the agency have been violated.

**Administrative Law** Statutes, regulations, rules, and case laws dealing with the general subject of administrative agencies.

**Administrative Penalties** Assessed by the EPA or other regulatory agency for violation of agency rules

**Administrative Quasi-Judicial Agencies** Nonjudicial, nonlegislative government entities with rule-making authority.

**Administrative Regulations** Laws made by government agencies.

**Administrator** A person appointed by a probate judge to administer an estate if the will names no one to be executor or if there is no will.

**Admissions Against Interest** Exception to the hearsay rule of evidence; if a person says or does something against his or her pecuniary or proprietary interests this evidence may be let in at trial even if the person saying or doing it cannot be cross-examined.

**Advance** Money paid to another for services or goods the other has not yet given.

**Adverse Possession** A way to acquire title to realty by openly, hostilely, and continuously holding the property for a statutory period of time.

**Advisory Opinion** In general, a formal opinion issued by a court on a question of law that is not embodied in a concrete case or controversy. In FTC practice, a nonbinding opinion by the Federal Trade Commission issued to parties seeking the FTC's advice on whether a particular business practice violates the laws the FTC enforces.

**Affidavit** A written sworn statement given before someone with the power to administer oaths (such as notary public).

**Affirmative Easement** A right to use someone else's land.

**Agreements to Agree** Not a contract; agreements in which two people decide to form a contract at some future time.

**Air Quality Control Region (AQCR)** The entire United States is divided into AQCRs to help control air pollution.

**Allocative Efficiency** The state of an economy in which resources are placed where they yield the most good (or utility).

**Alternative Dispute Resolution (ADR)** Any means of settling legal disputes without using courts, including conciliation, mediation, and arbitration.

**Ambient Air Quality Standards** The legal requirements for general air quality in the environment.

**Ambulatory** A will may be changed any number of times before the testator dies unless the testator has made the will as a binding contract.

**Anarchy** Lawless society; society where no one has the power to make rules binding all.

**Annotated** Footnotes further explaining something in a text; for example, a code would be annotated to cases interpreting words in the code.

**Annotated Code** A lengthy statute that refers to particular cases interpreting it.

**Annual Percentage Rate of Interest APR** One of two items a creditor must disclose to a debtor under the Truth-in-Lending Act.

**Answer** The document a defendant files with a court after being sued civilly, which "answers" plaintiff's complaint.

**Anti-backsliding** A provision that prevents reissuance of an NPDES permit with less stringent limits than the permit it replaces.

**Antitrust Law** Statutes enacted by Congress to prevent restraint of trade and anticompetitive behavior.

**Apparent Authority** An agent's authority resulting from something the principal does that leads third persons to believe the agent has authority.

**Arbitrary, Capricious, and Unreasonable Test** An evidentiary test used to decide whether certain agency actions are supported by enough facts.

**Arbitration** A way to settle disputes by staying out of court; the disputants hire a third party who makes a decision the parties agree to be bound to.

**Area-Wide Waste Treatment Program** Under federal water pollution control law the way to control nonpoint pollutants (such as general runoff from a field).

**Asset Merger** When two or more companies join together by one's buying the other's (others') assets and the buying company remains in existence while the merged (purchased) company (companies) ceases (cease) to exist.

**Assumed Risk** *see* Assumption of Risk.

**Assumption of Risk** A negligence defense also applicable in some strict liability cases and in many product liability cases. It requires that the plaintiff knowingly accept a certain risk of his or her own free will. An assumption of risk defense can be created by contract. Here, though, the needed voluntariness (because of unequal bargaining power) or knowledge (because of fine print terms) may not be present.

**Attorney at Law** Professional trained in the law who is admitted to practice law in one or more U.S. jurisdictions; usually after passage of bar exam.

**Attorney General** Society's attorney.

**Attorney in Fact** A written agency.

**Autrefois Acquit** A plea in a criminal case that in effect says, "I have already been tried and acquitted for this so leave me alone because the constitution's double jeopardy clause says you should."

**Autrefois Convict** A plea in a criminal case that in effect says, "I have already been tried for this and convicted so leave me alone because the constitution's double jeopardy clause says you should."

**Award** The word describing an arbitrator's decision.

**Bailment** The separation of title and possession to personal, not real, property.

**Bailment for the Sole Benefit of the Bailee** This form of bailment benefits only the borrower.

**Bailment for the Sole Benefit of the Bailor** This form of bailment benefits only the owner of the bailed property.

**Bait Advertising** Businesses advertise goods or services at unusually low prices to attract buyers into the seller's business.

**Balancing Competing Claims** The idea that law is a weighing of competing claims with the heavier prevailing; Roscoe Pound's sociological school of law.

**Barter** A transaction that exchanges goods for other goods, rather than exchanging goods for money.

**Basis of the Bargain Damages** The basic type of contractual recovery. Generally, it is a value of the performance as promised minus the value of the performance as received.

**Beneficence** Doing good deeds.

**Beneficiary** Person(s) holding equitable or beneficial title to property in a trust.

**Best Available Treatment (BAT)** A type of treatment designed to clean water of its pollution. A stricter type of water pollution treatment than BPT.

**Best Conventional Treatment (BCT)** A type of water pollution treatment for conventional pollutants.

**Best Management Practices** Term in environmental law that refers to certain business field techniques that can reduce certain types of pollution (e.g., a tarp over a coal pile can reduce water pollution from rain water runoff from the coal pile).

**Best Practicable Treatment Control (BPT)** A type of treatment designed to clean water of its pollution. An intermediate form of water pollution treatment.

**Beyond a Reasonable Doubt** The test for the amount of evidence the prosecutor must prove in a criminal case to get a conviction.

**Bilateral Contract** A contract formed by each of two parties exchanging promises—"a promise for a promise."

**Bill** A proposed law that has not yet been passed by the legislature nor signed by the chief executive.

**Binding Arbitration** Where a third party, not a court, is selected by parties to a dispute to settle it after hearing both parties' claims and whose decision the parties agree to follow.

**Blue Sky Laws** State laws regulating the sale of securities.

**Body Politic** The society subject to particular government; the people and businesses subject to a rule.

**Bona Fide Occupational Qualification (BFOQ)** A defense that protects defendants from Title VII liability.

**Boulwareism** Term used in labor law where management studies employee demands and makes its best offer at the start of bargaining. It represents a rejection of bargaining given its initial refusal to modify its offer.

**Breach of Duty** The first element of a negligence case; usually, the failure to act as a reasonable person.

**Breach of Warranty of Authority** An agent's breaking his or her duty to third persons by believing to have and claiming to have authority to represent a principal when such authority does not exist.

**Brief** A set of papers containing a lawyer's argument in a lawsuit; also, a way to analyze law cases.

**Bubble Policy** Idea in pollution control that treats an entire facility with several discharge points as one discharge so the various discharge points in the facility can be "netted" so if one discharge point more than satisfies pollution control requirements, it can make up for outlets not meeting standards. An imaginary bubble over an entire factory allows netting for the entire facility.

**Business Ethics** Values used in the business community to determine proper conduct.

**Business Judgment Rule** A rule that holds corporate management harmless from stockholder suits for good faith errors that would injure the corporation.

**Business Trust** A business organized in the form of a trust; similar in many ways to a corporation.

**Buyer in the Ordinary Course of Business (BIOC)** Any entrusting of possession of goods to a merchant who deals in goods of that kind gives the merchant the power to transfer all rights of the entruster to a buyer.

**C**.F.R. *Code of Federal Regulations.*

**Capital Surplus Account** A corporate account that holdings earnings over and above expenses, representing the earnings of the shareholders.

**Case Style** *see* "Style of a Case"

**Categorical Imperative** Kant's ethical idea that we should act in the way that we would want rules to be; similar to the "Golden Rule."

**Causa Mortis** A gift that results when a donor thinks he or she is about to die, makes a gift based on this belief, and then actually dies because of the particular threat of death.

**Cause of Action** A rule of law entitling the plaintiff to recover if certain elements are proven.

**Caveat Emptor** Let the buyer beware.

**Caveat Venditor** Let the seller beware.

**Cease and Desist Orders** Orders from administrative agencies telling someone (such as a business) to stop doing something.

**Cellar-Kefauver Amendment** A federal law passed in 1950 that plugged a loophole in the Clayton Act by outlawing certain asset mergers (certain stock mergers had been forbidden 36 years earlier).

**Chancellor** The "judge" in a chancery (or equity) court.

**Chancery Court** A type of civil court where a case can start; the chancellor (judge) in such a court applies equitable principles (ideas of fairness) to decide the cases.

**Charter** State authorization for someone to act in a certain capacity (for instance, as a corporation).

**Checkoff** A term used in labor law to describe a system for collecting union dues, which involves the employer's deducting the union dues from the employee/union member's check and forwarding this amount to the union; a union security device.

**Churning** A situation that occurs when brokers trade a client's account excessively given the client's investment goals and sophistication.

**Circuit Courts** The basic trial-level courts.

**Civil Disobedience** The idea that people break the positive law when it violates much more important natural law.

**Civil Law** Law that determines rights and duties between private persons; or law of certain European countries relying mainly on codes of law instead of judicial opinions as the main source of law.

**Civil Penalties** Penalties obtained from federal district court involving unfair or deceptive acts or practices where a private party knowingly violates a trade regulation rule defining such acts or practices, or a private party knowingly violates a C&D order involving such acts or practices, even if the order involved some other party.

**Civilization Ethic** The idea that law's frustrating people's basic desires and instincts produces civilization (one of Sigmund Freud's ideas).

**Clayton Act** A federal antitrust law passed in 1914 that addresses several antitrust matters including interlocking directorates, race discrimination, exclusive dealing, tying contracts, requirements contracts, and mergers. The Clayton Act creates only civil, not criminal violations.

**Close Corporation** A corporation whose stock is held by few persons. Often "family" corporations.

**Code** A statute that attempts to cover all law (such as the U.S. code or a state code) or all on a particular subject (such as the Uniform Commercial Code).

**Codes of Federal Regulations (CFR)** A set of federal books organized so that all regulations of a particular agency are together in one (or several) books.

**Commerce Clause** The clause of the U.S. Constitution giving Congress power to regulate commerce among the several states (interstate commerce). The commerce clause is the main constitutional basis for the extensive congressional regulation of U.S. society that exists today. It also is an implicit check on state laws that unduly hinder or burden interstate commerce.

**Commercial Paper** Promissory notes (two-party instruments), drafts and checks (three-party instruments), and certificates of deposit (acknowledgment by a bank of receipt of money with a promise to repay it).

**Commercial Speech** Speech intended to advance the economic interests of the speaker and his or her audience. Advertising is the best example. This sort of speech now receives First Amendment protection, but not as much protection as other forms of First Amendment speech.

**Common Law** Law made by judges when deciding a case not governed by other kinds of law.

**Common Pleas Court** A low-level court with power to try both small civil and criminal cases.

**Community Property** During a marriage, when one spouse acquires property, half of it belongs to the other spouse even if the deed is made out specifically in the name of one spouse.

**Comparable Worth Provisions** Laws that apply only to public employment; they say that relevant government units should not discriminate in pay between female-dominated jobs and male-dominated jobs if those jobs have comparable overall worth to the employer.

**Comparative Fault** Often used as a synonym for comparative negligence. As used here, however, the term refers to a doctrine whereby the plaintiff's recovery is reduced in proportion to his percentage share of the overall fault (not just negligence) causing his injury.

**Comparative Negligence** A modification of contributory negligence in which the fact-finder makes some percentage allocation of fault between plaintiff and defendant, and makes the plaintiff's recovery equal the defendant's percentage share of the plaintiff's losses. Perhaps one-half of the states have instituted comparative negligence. In some states, it will apply only where the defendant is more than fifty percent at fault.

**Compensatory** Something (usually a law) designed to restore one person injured by another.

**Compensatory Damages** Money a lawbreaker must pay to a legally injured person to put him or her in the position he or she was in before legal injury occurred.

**Complaint** Notifies defendant of case and reason for case.

**Complaint Case** A type of lawsuit brought under the Wagner Act in which a claim is made by either an employer or the union that an unfair labor practice has been committed.

**Concealment** A type of fraud in which a defendant misrepresents by covering up or not disclosing a fact he or she has a duty to disclose.

**Conciliation** A situation in which the two disputants get together and work things out between themselves without having anyone else present.

**Conciliation Discussions** Attempts to settle informally a Title VII Civil Rights Act of 1964 case.

**Concurrent Powers** Those powers that both Congress and the states can exercise.

**Concurrent Resolution** Rules legislatures pass to govern their internal workings. Technically they bind on one outside the legislature and thus are not laws.

**Condominium** A way individuals can own the space between the walls of their unit. Owners have equal interest in the common areas of the entire complex.

**Confusion** The commingling of different owners' fungible goods, which are nearly identical in characteristics, such as commodities.

**Conglomerate Merger** When two (or more) companies in unrelated businesses combine with the acquiring company continuing and the acquired company ceasing to exist and becoming part of the acquiring company.

**Consciously Parallel Conduct** An antitrust idea in which oligopolistic competitors who compete in price and other ways knowing that competitors are doing likewise are illegally agreeing to restrain trade.

**Consensual Relations** An arrangement entered into by mutual consent of the parties, but do not necessarily possess all the elements of a contract.

**Consent Decree** A judgment, ruling, or order made by a court or an administrative agency with the consent of the parties. Generally, its terms are the result of a prior agreement between the parties settling the matter before the court or agency.

**Consent Order** As used in Chapter 21, a kind of consent decree in which an alleged violator of a law enforced by the Federal Trade Commission agrees to stop a certain business practice, but does not admit any violation of the law.

**Consequential Damages** Although this term has no good general definition, it refers to those damages, caused by the breach of a contract, that are more remote from the breach than basis of the bargain damages. They include personal injury, property damage, and indirect economic loss (e.g., lost profits) caused by the breach.

**Conservative** When used in modern political/social/economic contexts refers generally to someone who prefers the status quo rather than trying new approaches to deal with problems and situations; refers to someone who prefers individual or private sector solutions to social problems rather than governmental solutions.

**Consideration** In contract situations what one person must give up or give to the person one is contracting with to make the other's promises binding; voluntary relinquishment of a known right bargained for in exchange for another's rights.

**Consignment(s)** Legal arrangement where seller of goods keeps title (ownership) but transfers possession to distributor who agrees to resell them; a type of bailment (separation of title and possession of goods).

**Consolidation** When two companies combine to form a totally new company (neither of the joining companies survives).

**Constitution** Basic law of a society; society's legal framework and basic principles; social contract or compact.

**Constitutional Government** Government limited by law and answerable to the people ruled.

**Constructive Notice** Notice in a newspaper or other media; required when agencies end for third persons with whom agent has not actually dealt.

**Consumer Product** Article customarily produced or distributed for a consumer's use, consumption, or enjoyment in or around a residence or a school, in recreation, or otherwise.

**Consumption Ethic** The social value that says it is good to use up natural resources without regard to long-term social needs.

**Contingent Fee** A lawyer's fee that is based on a percentage of the money the lawyer wins for a client in a civil lawsuit.

**Contract** Agreement between competent parties enforceable in court.

**Contract Bar Rule** A rule of labor law that prevents holding representation election while a union-employer collective bargaining agreement is in effect.

**Contract Clause** A provision in Article 1, section 10 of the U.S. Constitution preventing the states from impairing the obligations of existing contracts, both private and governmental.

**Contracts Contrary to Public Opinion** Contracts that offer some public sense of natural law and, when courts (judges) so decide, will not be enforceable.

**Contributory Infringement** Conduct that occurs when one has a reason to know of a third person's copyright infringement and induces, or causes, or materially contributes to, that person's infringing conduct.

**Contributory Negligence** A negligence defense sometimes applicable in product liability cases generally. It involves the plaintiff's failure to act as a reasonably self-protective person. It is a complete defense no matter how trivial the plaintiff's fault.

**Contributory Pensions** Pensions paid into by both the employer and employees.

**Conversion** An intentional tort involving wrongful interference with the dominion and control by one person of another's personalty. The type of lawsuit one person brings against another if the other steals goods (movables) from him or her.

**Copyright Law** Protects original works of authorship fixed in any tangible medium of expression.

**Corporate Enabling Act** A statute that lets people form a corporation if they follow a certain procedure.

**Corporate Promoter** One who develops a market for corporate stock of a corporation about to be organized. One who organizes corporations and interests others in subscribing to its stock.

**Corporation** A legal, artificial person that is a popular business organizational form.

**Corporation by Estoppel** A court-created doctrine that says that if persons act like corporations even though they are unincorporated and third persons deal with these corporate pretenders, then the third persons may not later challenge the lack of corporateness.

**Corporations for Profit** Corporations that can divide profits among shareholders; however, they do not necessarily have to earn a profit to be so classified.

**Corporations Not for Profit** Corporations that cannot turn over earnings to their members.

**Counterclaim** A legal claim a civil defendant makes against the person suing.

**Counter-offer** An offer made by the offeree back to the original offeror and in response to the original offer; it ends the original offer and is an offer back to the original offeror.

**County Court** Low-level courts that hear disputes involving small amounts of money and other small matters.

**Court of Original Jurisdiction** Court where a case starts.

**Court System** A hierarchy of judges who hear cases and interpret law. The United States has two court systems: state and federal.

**Courts of Record** Courts in which a public official (usually) takes a transcript of what is said in court.

**Coverage Requirement** A federal requirement for employee retirement plans that discourages an employer from merely giving certain employees (often top officers only) retirement contributions but requires some spreading of employer retirement contributions to most employees.

**Credit Card** As defined by the Truth-in-Lending Act and Regulation Z, a single credit device used to buy something on credit.

**Crime** Wrong against society.

**Criminal Conspiracy** Agreement to commit a lawful act in an unlawful way or an unlawful act; often requires some significant step to carry out this agreement.

**Criminal Law** Laws designed to protect social values and which punish violators.

**Criminal Procedure** Steps in a criminal lawsuit; rules telling order of events in criminal lawsuit.

**Criteria Documents** In pollution control law, refers to scientific studies that are the basis for air or water pollution control regulations.

**Cumulative Voting** A way of voting corporate shares that allows minority shareholders (if the minority is large enough) to elect members of the board of directors. Shareholders may cast as many votes for director as they have shares multiplied by the number of directors to be elected; then a shareholder may cumulate or vote all of his or her shares for one (or more) board candidates.

**Curtesy** A man's interest in his wife's property.

**Cybersquatting** Occurs when one person registers an Internet domain name that is anothers trademarked name, or similar name, before the trademark owner registers it as an Internet domain name.

**D**amages Money, property, or human loss that the law permits a person to recover in the form of money from the person(s) injuring him or her.

**Damnum Absque Injuria** Latin for "a loss has occurred but there is no legal way to obtain recovery"; loss without a remedy.

**Debt Collector** Under the Fair Debt Collection Practices Act, anyone other than the creditor or creditor's attorney who tries to collect debts owed to another person.

**Decertification Election** In labor law refers to an election at a unionized employer's plant where unionized employees vote to decide whether to continue having the union represent them.

**Deeds** Documents that transfer ownership to realty.

**Defamation** Oral or written, published untrue statement about another that holds up the person spoken about to ridicule, contempt, or scorn.

**Default Judgment** What the plaintiff wins in civil lawsuit because the defendant fails to answer the complaint within the required time.

**Deferral States** States that have met certain federal requirements entitling them to enforce the Federal Age Discrimination in Employment Act.

**Defined Benefit Plans** Periodic payment into the plan varies so that the benefits ultimately received will be a definite—often indexed—dollar amount.

**Defined Contribution Plans** Periodic payment into the plan is fixed.

**Defined Pension Plans** Pension plans that promise retirees a certain amount when they retire.

**Defunctness** A rule of labor law that says that if a union is a collective bargaining representative but it does not function actively as such, a representation election can be held even though an unexpired collective bargaining agreement exists.

**Del Credere Agent** An agent who sells for a principal and who guarantees to pay the principal if the buyer does not.

**Delivery** Delivery involves the present handing over of control to something from the donor to the donee. Delivery can be either actual (the donor's handing over a ring to the donee) or constructive (the donor's handing over something representing the item being given, such as the keys to a car when one is giving a car).

**Democracy** Government in which the ruled make the rules.

**Demurrer** A defendant's responsive pleading to plaintiff's complaint that, in effect, says plaintiff does not state a cause of action.

**De Novo Trial** New trials, starting from scratch; typically this happens when a case has been tried at an administrative hearing and then is appealed to a trial court.

**Deontology** Ethics; an examination of proper or "right" conduct, moral obligation, and duty.

**Deposition** A document that preserves testimony of witnesses or parties to a lawsuit; the deposition is taken before the trial.

**Derivative Suit** A civil lawsuit where the plaintiff sues on behalf of someone else (who is often unable to sue on its behalf, such as a corporation against its board of directors).

**Deterrence** Discouraging persons who did not commit crimes from community crime by punishing criminals; one of the four basic objectives of criminal law.

**Devises** Realty given by will.

**Dictum (Dicta)** Remarks a judge makes in a legal opinion that are not necessary to decide a case. (Dictum is singular; dicta, plural).

**Direct Emission Standards** Air pollution controls for buildings (plants, businesses, and the like) and other immovables.

**Direct Infringement** Directly copying another's copyrighted material without a defense.

**Directed Verdict** Where a trial judge tells the jury what its verdict will be.

**Discharge** In bankruptcy, the objective of going bankrupt; a discharge is a defense (usually successful) against a creditor's attempting to collect a discharged debt.

**Disclaimer** A term in a contract (often a contract for the sale of goods) by which one party (usually a seller) attempts to prevent the other party from recovering under a particular theory of recovery. If a disclaimer is enforced its effect is to block all recovery under that theory of recovery.

**Disclosure** The requirement that the inventor tell the public how the item is made, how to make it, and the best uses of it.

**Dismissal** Word used in labor law to describe a way of settling an unfair labor practice case by, in effect, "throwing the case out."

**Disparate Impact Theory** A Title VII theory most often used in cases involving a large number of plaintiffs. The plaintiffs must show that the employment practice they are challenging has an adverse impact on the basis of race, color, religion, sex, or national origin. The employer must show that the challenged practice is job related for the position in question and consistent with business necessity. The plaintiffs may show that the employer's legitimate business needs can be advanced by an alternative employment practice that is less discriminatory than the challenged practice.

**Disparate Treatment Theory** A Title VII theory most often used by a single plaintiff or a small number of plaintiffs to allege some isolated instance or instances of discrimination that cannot be proven by direct evidence.

**Dissolution** Selling one's assets and going out of business. In antitrust cases, breaking up a business that restrains trade into several smaller businesses.

**District Attorney** Society's attorney.

**District Courts** Courts hearing cases involving relatively small civil matters, such as a homeowner's breaking a contract with a painter, or criminal matters, such as a bank teller's embezzling $1,500.

**Diversity Cases** *see* Diversity of Citizenship.

**Diversity of Citizenship** A type of federal court jurisdiction that exists because the lawsuit is between people from different states or people *from* a state and citizens of another country.

**Divest** *see* Divestiture.

**Divestiture** In antitrust cases forcing a firm found restraining trade to sell off part of its operations.

**Docket** A list of cases to be tried in a court or other tribunal.

**Domestic Corporation** A corporation organized under the laws of the state one is speaking about.

**Domestic Relations Court** Divorce court (sometimes handles juvenile delinquency matters).

**Dominant Estate** The property enjoying the benefit of an easement.

**Donative Intent** The idea that the gift giver must presently intend to make a gift, not just want to give at some unspecified future time.

**Donee** The person receiving a gift.

**Donor** The giver of the gift.

**Dower** A woman's interest in her husband's property.

**Dual Agency** Where an agent represents both parties to a contract.

**Due Diligence** Individuals sued must meet a standard of care regarding information in their part of the registration statement; if the individuals are experts, such as lawyers, they must meet the diligence of their professions.

**Due Process** A constitutional guarantee, contained in the Fifth and Fourteenth Amendments and thus applicable to both the federal government and the states, that basically requires government to provide fair procedures before it deprives a person of life, liberty, or property. Occasionally, however, due process has been given a substantive meaning and used as the basis for attacking laws regulating social and economic matters.

**Duress** In contract cases such illegal force or the threat of force as deprives a person of his or her free will to decide whether to enter a contract.

**Duress Rule** *see* Duress.

**Duties** When used in connection with the tort of negligence it refers to obligations people automatically have regarding others (such as the duty to be careful).

**Duty of Care** A principle based on common law negligence principles. The elements are negligence, breach of the standard care, proximate cause, and damages.

**Duty to Indemnify** Duty of a principal to pay the agent any losses the agent necessarily incurs while working on the principal's behalf.

**Duty to Reimburse** Duty of a principal to pay an agent for any money the agent has to spend to perform his or her duties for the principal.

**E**PA U.S. Environmental Protection Agency; federal agency whose main job is protecting the environment.

**Easement** A nonpossessory right to use someone else's realty for some purpose.

**Easement Appurtenant** A benefit to another piece of land, which is usually adjacent to the servient estate.

**Easement in Gross** A benefit to a certain person or business, such as a power line easement for a utility.

**Economic Impact Statements** Requirement under 1977 Amendments to the Clean Air Act that forces the EPA to decide the economic costs that will be caused by new Clean Air Act regulations.

**Economic Strikes** Employee strikes motivated by employee economic demands.

**Economic Substantive Due Process** A now-insignificant form of substantive due process that once provided the courts with the ability to strike down forms of economic regulation that interfered with freedom of contract.

**Effluent Guidelines** General water pollution standards for categories of industrial polluters.

**Effluent Limitations** Water pollution limits for particular polluters.

**Election Bar Rule** A rule in labor law that prevents employees from voting on whether to have a union represent them within a certain period after a previous representation election.

**Eminent Domain** The governmental power to condemn property. It must be for public purposes and requires just compensation.

**Emission Offset Policy** Term used in air pollution control law to refer to the idea that new polluters may build in nonattainment areas if they do not increase "net pollution" in the area (they do this by purchasing existing polluters' pollution rights, which is called the emission offset policy).

**Emission Offsets** Concept in pollution control that lets a polluter sell its rights to discharge in a given geographic area to someone else in that same geographic area.

**Employer-Independent Contractor Relationship** In this relationship, the employer does not have the right to control the means by which the independent contractor performs the work. The employer does retain the right to control the end or object of the work.

**En Banc** Term describing rare cases when all judges in a particular court of appeals hear a case; usually courts of appeals have several panels, each of which is made up of three or some other number of judges who decide cases; when a case is important, all judges from all panels of the particular court of appeals sit as judges in the case (this can be as many as seventeen judges).

**Enabling Act** A status that gives an agency authority to propose and promulgate regulations.

**Enabling Statutes** see Enabling Act.

**Enumerated Powers** Those congressional powers listed by Article 1, §8 or some other law making provision of the Constitution.

**Environmental Assessment** A preliminary report private parties (such as businesses) must fill out and turn in to a federal agency before the agency prepares its environmental impact statement.

**Environmental Impact Statement (EIS)** A report that a federal agency must prepare before it does anything major that affects the quality of the human environment.

**Environmental Protection Agency (EPA)** A federal agency that makes law by issuing regulations involving the environment.

**Equal Protection** The requirement that government not deny the "equal protection of the laws," which applies both to the states and the federal government.

**Equitable Remedies** What certain courts (called equity or chancery courts) give to an injured person (such as specific performance) when legal remedies (usually money) are inadequate.

**Equitable Title** A title, also called a beneficial title, to property subject to a trust.

**Equity** Fairness; a type of court that gives equitable remedies.

**Equity Courts** Courts that give equitable remedies (such as injunctions and specific performance) instead of legal remedies; also called *chancery courts*.

**Estate** The land and buildings on the land owned by a person.

**Ethic of Utilitarianism** The need to promote the greatest good for the greatest number.

**Ethical Unity** When ethics of different ethical schools agree on a particular result or solution to a problem.

**Ethics** Refers to the study of what is right, good, or moral conduct in a given set of circumstances; ethics involves the study of clashes of moral values.

**Ex Parte** A legal proceeding where only one party is present (for example, a court hearing where the defendant is present but plaintiff is absent).

**Ex Post Facto Law** Retroactive criminal law that works to the disadvantage of the accused.

**Excited Utterance** A statement sounding as if it were an offer made when one is emotionally aroused by some event, which is not legally regarded as an offer because of the speaker's excited state of mind.

**Exclusive Benefit Rule** A rule under the Employee Retirement Income Security Act that forbids pension assets from being used other than to fund pensions.

**Exclusive Dealing Contract** A business arrangement by which one business agrees to handle only one particular brand of a product as a condition to getting the seller's desirable product.

**Exculpatory Clauses** Contract that clauses excuse someone from liability.

**Executed Contract** Contract that has been performed by both parties.

**Execution** Legal way creditors seize debtor's property to pay debts.

**Executor** A person named in a will to manage and resolve an estate.

**Executory Contract** Formed but unperformed contract.

**Exempt Property** see Exemptions.

**Exempt Securities** Securities that are excused from part or all of the registration process under various federal securities laws (exemptions also exist under state securities laws).

**Exempt Transactions** Certain securities sales that do not have to be fully registered with the Securities and Exchange Commission.

**Exemptions** Laws that prevent creditors from seizing certain property of a debtor. Also, items not available to the partnership when its creditors seek execution against partnership property for partnership debts.

**Experience Rating** A way of deciding what a particular employer's unemployment tax liability is based on the amount of past unemployment for its workers.

**Express Authority** Power a principal spells out for an agent in oral or written words.

**Express Contract** A contract that the parties form by writing or saying their respective promises in words.

**Express Warranty**  A contractual promise arising from a seller's actual words (or, in some cases, from conduct from which a promise can be readily inferred). As a general proposition, express warranties are made openly and voluntarily.

**Extortion**  A felony in which a holder of public office demands property from another by threatening to misuse his or her public office unless the property is given.

**F**OIA Exemptions  The several types of federal agency information that a person may not get by filing an FOIA request.

**FOIA Request**  A request by anyone pursuant to the federal Freedom of Information Act for information a federal agency has in its possession.

**FTC Act**  A federal law passed in 1914 that created the Federal Trade Commission and empowered it to attack unfair competition and various anticompetitive practices.

**FWPCA**  Federal Water Pollution Control Act (also known as the *Clean Water Act*).

**Failing Company Defense**  A defense available to a Clayton Act section 7 defendant; the defense allows a healthy company to merge with a failing company because such a merger is unlikely to hurt competition.

**False Imprisonment**  A type of intentional tort where the defendant unjustifiably confines or restrains the plaintiff for an appreciable period of time.

**False Light**  A type of invasion of privacy; an intentional tort occurring when the defendant makes the plaintiff appear other than how the plaintiff actually is.

**Fault**  Legal idea that someone is not liable unless he/she/it broke a legal duty resulting in harm to someone else.

**Federal Exemptions**  Federal law that prevents certain property of a debtor in bankruptcy from being taken to pay the debtor's creditors.

**Federal Preemption**  A doctrine which makes certain state laws unconstitutional under the Supremacy Clause even though there is no direct verbal clash between state and federal law. The general idea is that congressional action preempted the states from acting within an area staked out by Congress for exclusive federal control.

**Federal Question**  A type of federal court jurisdiction based on the lawsuits involving an interpretation of some federal law.

**Federal Register**  A "newspaper-like" federal publication giving public notice of proposed and promulgated federal regulations, notice of agency meetings, presidential proclamations, and other agency proclamations.

**Federal Register System**  The *U.S. Government Manual*, *Federal Register*, and *Code of Federal Regulations*.

**Federal Reporter**  Set of books containing cases decided by all U.S. Courts of Appeals.

**Federal Supplement**  Set of books containing cases decided by all U.S. Federal District Courts.

**Federal Supremacy**  The doctrine that the Constitution, laws, and treaties of the United States defeat all inconsistent state laws in case of a clash between them.

**Federal Trade Commission Act**  An act establishing the Federal Trade Commission to focus on maintenance of economic competition and consumer protection.

**Federalism**  Government organized so there are dual (two) sovereigns, state and federal, each with its appropriate sphere of operation.

**Fee Simple Absolute**  A type of estate in realty; the estate in realty that confers the greatest number of rights on the holder of the estate.

**Fellow Servant Doctrine**  A legal rule which says that if a worker is injured by a co-worker's negligence or misconduct, the injured employee may not recover from their employer.

**Fellow Servant Rule**  *see* Fellow Servant Doctrine.

**Felony**  A serious crime.

**Feminism**  When used in a legal context the idea that there should be study of the positive law to determine whether women are placed in legally subordinate positions, not given equal employment opportunities, or are legally debilitated from self-actualizing as are their male counterparts.

**Fiduciaries**  Trustees who hold the legal title to the trust res. As such, they have the highest duty of good faith in maintaining the trust. They must avoid conflicts of interest and must account to the trust beneficiaries.

**Fiduciary Duty**  Duty of great faithfulness and confidence to avoid conflicts of interest or any other form of "double dealing."

**Fiduciary Responsibility**  *see* Fiduciary Duty.

**Finance Charge**  One of two items creditors must disclose to debtors under the Truth-in-Lending Act.

**Finder**  A person who locates lost property.

**Firm Offer**  A written offer made by a merchant in which the merchant assures by the offer's terms that the offer will be held open for a definite time up to three months or for a reasonable time up to three months if no definite time is stated, which offer is signed by the merchant; such offers may not be revoked for the term of the offer; such offers are legalized by Article 2-205 of the UCC.

**Five-to-Fifteen Year Graduated Vesting**  A formula for calculating vesting of employer contributions to employee retirement plans.

**Fixed Fee**  A lawyer's fee that is definite and certain in total dollar amount and that does not depend on whether the lawyer wins or loses the lawsuit.

**Fixture**  Property classification denoting personalty attached to realty with the intent of making the personalty permanently part of the realty; fixtures can regain their identity as personalty by the process known as severance.

**Foreign Corporation**  A corporation organized under the laws of a state other than that one is speaking about.

**Formal Complaint**  In connection with the Federal Trade Commission, it refers to the complaint the FTC hands to an alleged FTC Act violator. Also, in civil lawsuits, refers to complaint plaintiff files with court clerk, which is served on defendant.

**Formal Requirements**  The will requirements for witnesses, attestation, signing in the presence of witnesses, and being of a certain age.

**Franchise**  A relationship in which one party (the franchisee) obtains the right to sell goods or services under a marketing plan substantially dictated by another party (the franchisor).

**Franchisee**  The party who sells goods or services under a marketing plan substantially dictated by another party.

**Franchisor** The party who dictates the market plan for the franchisee.

**Frank, Jerome** Legal realist who said law is what trial courts and juries do in fact irrespective of what the positive law is.

**Fraud** An intentional tort occurring where there is misrepresentation of a material fact, knowledge of the misrepresentation by the person misrepresenting, intent to misrepresent, damages sustained by the other person, and the other person reasonably relies on this misrepresentation.

**Fraudulent Conveyance** Transfer of property that in some way misrepresents, such as a debtor's transfer of property to relatives pretending it is sold to them when in fact the relative intends to retransfer the property to the debtor after the creditors leave.

**Freedom of Contract** The idea that people can determine the course of their own lives by making their own contracts unprotected or unassisted by any government agency; this idea is most defensible if people have economic and political equality.

**Freedom of Speech** A constitutional principle, contained in the First Amendment and made applicable to the states through the Fourteenth Amendment, that gives a high degree of protection to "speech" in its many forms.

**Front Pay** Future salary until a Civil Rights Act Title VII plaintiff becomes employed in the rightful place in the workforce.

**Fundamental Rights** Certain rights that, when they are denied by government, are protected by requiring that the strict scrutiny test be met in order for the denial to be constitutional.

**Fungible Goods** Goods that are uniform in size, shape, or nature, such as commodities.

**GATT** General Agreement on Tariffs and Trade. A multiparty treaty among more than 100 nations, designed to lower tariff barriers between member nations.

**Garnishment** A legal way for a creditor to get a debtor's property held by a third person (such as a bank account).

**General Agent** A person who acts in many activities for the benefit of and under the control of another.

**General Duty Standard** An OSHA standard requiring an employer to maintain a generally safe place to work.

**General Jurisdiction** The power of a court to hear all types of lawsuits (for example, will cases, murder cases, breach of contract cases, and others).

**General Partner** A partner with unlimited personal liability in either a conventional partnership or limited partnership.

**Gift** A way to transfer title to property by delivery of the item, donative intent of the giver, and acceptance by the recipient.

**Gift Causa Mortis** A donor, thinking he or she is about to die, makes a gift because of this belief and then actually dies because of the particular threat of death which prompted the gift to be made.

**Golden Parachutes** High benefit severance contracts top management gives itself, particularly when the company becomes the target for a takeover attempt.

**Government Action** Activity of government involving individual rights, which is regulated by the Constitution's individual rights protections, including those found in the First, Fifth, and Fourteenth Amendments.

**Government Manual** A book containing names of all federal agencies and information about them.

**Governmental Corporation** Organization that exists for a social goal rather than a profit motive, such as the Federal Deposit Insurance Corporation.

**Grand Jury** Jury used in criminal law to determine if enough evidence shows probable cause that a crime has been committed and that the person arrested committed it. Grand juries issue "true bills" or "indictments" if they believe the prosecutor has established probable cause or "no true bills" if the prosecutor fails to establish probable cause.

**Gratuitous Agent** A person (agent) who does something for another expecting to receive no pay.

**Grease Payments** Amounts given to persons (often low-level government employees) to induce them to perform their jobs faster.

**Greenhouse Effect** Higher temperatures at the earth's surface caused by increased carbon dioxide.

**Group Boycotts** In antitrust law where competitors agree not to buy from or sell to certain persons; a per se Sherman Act violation.

**HIDC Rule** Rule that an HIDC (holder in due course) of a negotiable instrument takes it free of personal defenses (such as fraud or duress).

**Hart–Scott–Rodino Antitrust Improvement Act** A federal law that, among other things, requires that companies planning to merge notify the U.S. Justice Department and Federal Trade Commission before they merge to get premerger approval.

**Historical School of Law** The idea that positive law reflects long-standing customs.

**Holder in Due Course (HIDC)** Good faith purchaser of a negotiable instrument for value without notice of any defense that would prevent the HIDC from collecting on it.

**Holographic Will** A will in the testator's (testatrix's) handwriting and signed by the testator.

**Homestead Exemption** A debtor's right to keep creditors from taking all or part of the debtor's equity (ownership) in his or her principal residence.

**Horizontal Division of Markets** Where competitors at the same competitive level agree to divide markets to reduce competition; a per se Sherman Act violation.

**Horizontal Mergers** When two (or more) competing corporations combine by asset or stock purchase with the acquired company (companies) ceasing to exist and becoming part of the acquiring company, which continues to exist after the merger.

**Horizontal Price Fixing** Where competitors at the same competitive level agree to fix prices to reduce competition; a per se Sherman Act violation.

**Hostile Tender Offers** Offers to a corporation targeted to be taken over that does not want to be taken over.

**Hot Cargo Contracts** Voluntary agreements between a union and a neutral employer by which the neutral employer agrees to put pressure on the employer with which the union has a dispute.

**Hybrid Rulemakings** A way to make agency regulations, which adds more procedures, such as hearings, to the notice and comment of the informal rulemaking process.

**ICC** The Interstate Commerce Commission; a federal administrative agency.

**Illegal Contracts** Contracts whose formation or performance violates some positive law.

**Immaterial Matter** A matter that the average prudent investor ought to know before buying the security.

**Imminently Hazardous Consumer Product** A product that presents an unreasonable risk of death, serious illness, and severe personal injury.

**Implied** Created by operation of law, often by inference from the relevant facts and circumstances.

**Implied Authority** Power an agent gets as a result of performing necessary activities to carry out the agent's express authority.

**Implied Contract** A contract formed when the parties' actions but not words indicate that they intend to form a contract; contract formed by conduct, not words.

**Implied Powers** Those powers "necessary and proper" for effectuating Congress's inherent or enumerated powers. An example would be the power to regulate intrastate matters affecting interstate commerce.

**Implied Warranty** A warranty arising by operation of law. Implied warranties do not depend on the consent of the party giving the warranty. They contravene "freedom of contract" principles and are usually imposed to protect the buyer.

**Implied Warranty of Fitness for a Particular Purpose** An implied warranty where the seller, at the time of contracting, has reason to know any particular purpose for which the goods are required and that the buyer is relying on the seller's skill or judgment to select or furnish suitable goods, and that the goods are fit for such purpose.

**Implied Warranty of Merchantability** A warranty in Article 2 of the UCC that states that a warranty that the goods shall be merchantable is implied in a contract for their sale if the seller is a merchant with respect to goods of that kind.

**In Pari Delicto** Where two persons are equally culpable or guilty, in which case the law leaves them where it finds them helping neither.

**In Personam Jurisdiction** Power of a court (or other legal authority) over a particular person.

**In Rem Jurisdiction** Power over property ("rem" is Latin for "thing").

**Incapacity** When used in a legal sense it refers to the law's decision that certain people (such as minors, insane people, and drunks) cannot protect themselves so it allows them to escape (avoid) their contracts.

**Incipiency Doctrine** An antitrust rule that says if a merger would start to reduce competition between the merging companies and start to concentrate economic power in an industry, the merger violates section 7 of the Clayton Act.

**Indemnified** Repaid for a loss.

**Independent Constitutional Checks** Limits on congressional power, which exist outside the provision granting Congress power to act in the first place. The Bill of Rights and the Fourteenth Amendment are examples. These limits are the principal checks on congressional lawmaking power today.

**Indictment** The complaint in a criminal lawsuit.

**Indirect Economic Loss** A wide range of economic harm resulting from a product defect or negligence. Examples include lost profits and loss of business goodwill.

**Industry Guides** Nontechnical statements issued by the Federal Trade Commission designed to tell business what is and is not permitted by FTC regulations.

**Inference of Negligence** Case in which plaintiff has proven negligence unless a defendant has some defense.

**Informal Complaints** Used in reference to certain consumer, general public, and business complaints filed with the Federal Trade Commission about a business practice the complainant thinks violates FTC rules and regulations. Different from the formal complaint the FTC hands to an alleged FTC Act violator.

**Information** In criminal procedure the information serves the same purpose as the indictment (the complaint in the criminal lawsuit).

**Infringe** To use property without authorization, including trademarks, patents, copyrights, etc.

**Injunctions** Equity court orders to a person to do or not do something. A type of equitable remedy.

**Injunctive Relief** Enforcement device used by agencies against businesses that are violating agency rules.

**Innocent Misrepresentation** If someone unknowingly states something is a fact when it is not which induces someone else to enter a contract, it is called innocent misrepresentation and is a basis for the party to whom the representation is made to escape the contract in question.

**Integration** A term which when used in connection with employee retirement pensions means that pensions will take into account retirement accounts received from different sources (such as workers' compensation) and thereby reduce the pension coming from one source (such as from a private employer's pension plan).

**Intentional Infliction of Mental Distress** An intentional tort in which defendant knowingly causes plaintiff extreme mental suffering; usually accompanies physical injury although in extreme cases mental distress alone can be recoverable.

**Intentional Torts** Civil wrongs where the defendant has some sort of intent.

**Interbrand Competition** Competition between sellers of different brands of the same type product (for example competition between Ford and Chevrolet dealers).

**Interest in the Partnership** The right to receive profits and surplus from a partnership.

**Intermediate Strict Scrutiny** The sort of equal protection strict scrutiny applying to discrimination based on sex, illegitimacy, and alienage. In gender discrimination cases, it involves the requirement that the challenged law have a substantial relation to the advancement of an important governmental purpose.

**Internal Morality of Law** The idea Professor Lon Fuller posited of eight criteria that positive law must meet to be moral. These items are: there must be rules; rules must be promulgated; rules must be clear; rules should not be retroactive; rules should be noncontradictory; rules should not demand the impossible; rules should not change often; and officials should follow the rules.

**Interpretative Regulations** Rules of administrative agencies that usually take effect as soon as they are made and are not binding as law.

**Interstate Commerce Clause** The portion of Article I, § 8 giving Congress the power to regulate commerce "among the several states." This clause is now probably the single most important source of congressional lawmaking authority.

**Interstate Commerce Commission (ICC)** A federal regulatory agency that makes law by issuing regulations governing interstate commerce.

**Interstitial Lawmaking** Judicial lawmaking by filling gaps in statutes.

**Inter Vivos** Trusts that take effect during the settlor's life.

**Intestate** Dying without a will

**Intrusion Upon Solitude or Seclusion** A type of invasion of privacy; an intentional tort.

**Invasion of Privacy** An intentional tort where defendant does one of four things to the plaintiff (1) invades plaintiff's peace and solitude; (2) holds plaintiff up in a false light; (3) uses plaintiff's name or likeness without authorization; or (4) publicly discloses some private fact about plaintiff.

**Invitations to Negotiate** Statements or actions one party makes trying to induce the other party to make an offer; not an offer.

**Involuntary Bankruptcy** A debtor's being forced into bankruptcy by creditors, against the debtor's will.

**J**oint and Several Liability Liability in which a partner could be forced to pay the entire tort judgment obtained against a copartner who injured others within the scope of the partnership.

**Joint Resolution** A law passed by the legislature, similar in effect to a statute.

**Joint Tenants** Two or more persons who own equal shares in realty at the same time and have the "right of survivorship" feature.

**Judgment Creditor** A person who, when a lawsuit ends, is owed money as a result of the lawsuit.

**Judgment Debtor** A person who, when a lawsuit ends, owes money as a result of the lawsuit.

**Judgment Notwithstanding the Verdict** Where a trial judge, after a jury has given its verdict, gives a judgment different from what the verdict is on the grounds that no reasonable jury could have done what the jury has just done.

**Judgment Proof** When a person is so poor that he or she is not worth suing because a judgment against him or her could not be paid; a person with few if any assets.

**Judicare** A plan for providing legal assistance to members of the public much as medicare provides medical help to the public.

**Judicial Review** The power of courts to declare the idioms of other government bodies unconstitutional.

**Jurisdiction** The power of a court to decide a case.

**Jurisprudence** The study of different legal philosophies (ideas about what law is or is supposed to be).

**Justice of the Peace Courts** Low-level courts dealing with minor civil or criminal matters.

**K**nowing Endangerment When one entity (person or business) knowingly places another person in imminent danger of death or serious bodily injury.

**Knowing Violations** Negligent release of hazardous substances that a person knows or reasonably should have known could cause personal injury or property damage.

**L**LC Limited liability company. A form of business organization combining the "pass-through" advantages of partnerships with respect to federal income taxation (and sometimes state income taxation, too) with the entity and limited liability aspects of the corporate form.

**LLP** Limited liability partnership. A form of business organization, usually of professional partnerships, that limits liability of professional malpractice to the person who commits the malpractice, not to the partnership.

**Laboratory Conditions** Word used in labor law to describe the neutral atmosphere that is supposed to exist when employees vote to decide whether to have a union represent them.

**Laissez Faire** Economy with few, if any, government restrictions on business.

**Law Courts** Courts that give legal remedies (such as money damages) instead of equitable remedies (such as specific performance).

**Law of Large Numbers** The idea that as the number of events (or numbers) increases, the likelihood of unusual things occurring increases.

**Law Merchant** Customs of merchants that came to be included into positive law.

**Lawyers Edition** Set of privately published books containing U.S. Supreme Court decisions in chronological order.

**Lead Agency** Words used in certain environmental law matters where several agencies are involved in a matter, but one fills out an EIS for all agencies involved.

**Leasehold** A temporary possessory interest in real estate; a lease.

**Legal Ethic of Planning** A view of law that uses decision theory to decide what the law should be.

**Legal Fiction** Something the law says exists or is true even though our senses tell us it does not exist; for example, the idea that corporations are people. Legal fictions are created to achieve some desirable social objective such as justice.

**Legal Guardian** Someone a court appoints to manage someone else's (called a "ward") affairs.

**Legal Realist** A person who believes law is what trial judges and juries do even though positive law may require something else.

**Legal Remedies** The usual recovery an injured person receives in a civil lawsuit; damages (money) is the most common legal remedy.

**Legally Void** A contract with serious flaws that cannot be enforced even if it is written.

**Legislative Regulations** Agency regulations that are legally binding; also called substantive regulations.

**Legislative Veto** When a legislature nullifies an agency regulation.

**Liberal** When used in modern political/social/economic contexts refers generally to someone who is inclined to try new approaches to dealing with situations and problems; refers to someone favoring a governmental or socialized approach to solving problems rather than private sector or individual solutions.

**License** The right extended to a person to enter onto another's realty for a limited time and purpose. A patron's sitting in a movie theater is a license.

**Life Estate** A type of estate in realty that lasts as long as the holder of the estate is alive.

**Limited Liability** The idea that a person's financial responsibility for something has limits, said of corporate shareholders with respect to corporate debts.

**Limited Partner** Partner in a limited partnership where liability is limited to a fixed amount.

**Limited Partnership** A partnership formed pursuant to a state statute that requires only one general partner and lets at least one other partner limit liability for limited partnership debts.

**Litigants** Plaintiff(s) and defendant(s) in a lawsuit.

**LLC** Limited liability company. A form of business organization combining the "pass-through" advantages of partnerships with respect to federal income taxation (and sometimes state income taxation, too) with the entity and limited liability aspects of the corporate form.

**Loans** Where creditors give a borrower money (instead of goods) to use for a period of time and charge a fee for this service.

**Lockout** In labor law, the employer's temporary refusal to allow employees to work by locking up the plant.

**Long-Arm Statute** Statutes that let a state get in personam jurisdiction over out-of-staters for certain wrongs committed within the state (usually in such incidents as auto accidents). Also, a law that allows state A's court to reach into another state B and assert personal jurisdiction over one of B's citizens based on some occurrence in state A.

**Lost Property** Personalty that has been unintentionally, involuntarily parted with by the owner.

**M**ailbox Rule Rule of contract law that says acceptance is effective when sent ("put in mailbox") by offeree (not when received by offeror).

**Malingering** False claims of injury or illness to escape work or increase damage recovery from someone.

**Malpractice** Negligence suits brought against professionals such as physicians, lawyers, engineers, architects, veterinarians, and accountants who have not performed their contractual duties to their clients with requisite care.

**Mandamus Orders** Court orders telling someone to do something (such as telling an administrative agency to do a nondiscretionary duty).

**Manifest System** Term used in environmental law to refer to a way to trace hazardous wastes by keeping a paper record (called a "manifest system") of them.

**Marketable Pollution Rights** Idea in pollution control that allows one polluter in a nonattainment air quality area to sell its right to emit pollutants there to someone else in the same area.

**Massachusetts Trust** Business organization form in the form of a trust; similar in many ways to a corporation.

**Master-Servant Relationship** A relationship arising when a person (the "master") employs another person (the "servant") to perform physical tasks not involving the making of contracts with third persons. The tasks are often of a menial sort, such as gardening or cleaning.

**Mediation** Involves using a neutral third party (called a mediator) to hear both sides of a dispute and to communicate between the disputants to get them to compromise.

**Merchant** As defined by UCC section 2-104, a merchant is either a party who regularly deals in goods of the kind sold (e.g., a bicycle manufacturer selling bicycles), or by occupation holds itself out as having knowledge or skill peculiar to the goods involved in the sale (e.g., a heating supply contractor installing a furnace). The UCC often imposes special rules where one or both parties to the transaction are merchants.

**Merger** When two companies combine in such a way that one company continues to exist after the merger.

**Miller-Tydings Act** A federal law passed in 1937 that allowed states to pass laws permitting resale price maintenance without violating a federal antitrust statute. Repealed in 1975.

**Minors** Persons below a certain age set by each state designed to protect young people from making unwise contracts and taking part in other activities society deems is unwise for them.

**Mirror Image** Rule of contract law that says acceptances must conform exactly to the terms of the offer or else the acceptance is ineffective to form a contract.

**Misdemeanor** Insignificant crime.

**Mobile Sources** Term used in air pollution control law to refer to autos and other vehicles that contribute to air pollution.

**Model Business Corporation Act** A model statute drafted by scholars and practitioners in the corporate law area that contains what they think are desirable features for corporate law.

**Model Statutes** Suggested laws that a legislature might pass; often suggested by some organization of scholars or practitioners.

**Monarchy** Government in which only one person makes the rules.

**Monopolies** Economy in which market segments have only one seller.

**Monopolistic Competition** Market in which many sellers compete but in which a particular seller has some distinctive feature to its product or service that gives a limited "monopoly" pricing ability over its competitors.

**Monopoly Power** The ability of a firm to raise prices above the competitive level for a sustained period of time, and to profit by doing so.

**Motion for Summary Judgment** A motion a party to a lawsuit makes that, in effect, says "Because no fact issues, just legal issues, are present, you decide the case without a jury trial, judge."

**Motion to Dismiss** A legal argument a civil defendant makes to cause the judge to "throw a plaintiff's case out of court."

**Multiple-Conscience Problem** A problem with the natural law theory that occurs because natural law means what each person thinks is right and yet each person's idea of "right" could differ from everyone else's, leaving one with no agreement on what is "right" even though all may agree that the "right thing" should be done.

**Municipal Corporations** Cities and towns that have been given charters by the state to govern a geographic area.

**Municipal Courts** Low-level courts dealing with minor civil or criminal matters.

**Mutual Benefit Bailment** A bailment in which both the bailee and bailor benefit.

**N**ational Conference of Commissioners on Uniform State Laws A group of legal scholars who draft suggested laws for states; suggested laws—called model acts—are designed to simplify, make uniform, and modernize the law.

**National Environmental Policy Act (NEPA)** A federal law that tells federal administrative agencies to take environmental factors into account when they decide to do major activities that affect the quality of the human environment.

**Natural Law** What each individual thinks is fair, right, and just.

**Negative Easement** An easement that prevents someone from doing something on one's land, such as stopping the building of a structure if it would block the sunlight to the dominant estate.

**Negligence** A type of tort (civil wrong) that holds a person liable for damages proximately caused by carelessness (conduct not living up to the standard of an ordinary, reasonable, prudent person).

**Negligence *Per Se*** In negligence law, a breach of duty based on the violation of a statute.

**Negotiable Note** A type of negotiable instrument; a signed writing having an unconditional promise to pay a sum certain (exact amount) of money (any country's currency) at an exact date or on demand (when asked) that has certain words (called words of negotiability) implying that the person originally issuing the note intended that person(s) other than the person originally receiving the note could legally come into possession of it.

**Noerr Doctrine** An antitrust idea that allows competitors to join together to petition the government without violating the antitrust laws.

**Noise Emission Limits** Amounts of noise the EPA lets certain products produce.

**Nolo Contendere** A plea of "no contest" in a criminal case that neither admits nor denies the indictment; a type of plea bargain.

**Nominal Damages** Symbolic damages that are a small amount of money a lawbreaker pays to a victim to show a wrong was done but the victim was not harmed.

**Noncontributory Pensions** Retirement plans into which only the employer pays.

**Noncriteria Pollutants** Air pollutants other than the five basic criteria pollutants (ozone, carbon monoxide, sulfur dioxide, particulates, and nitrogen dioxide). The criteria pollutants (plus hydrocarbons) are what the EPA focuses its attention on controlling.

**Nondelegable Duties** Certain duties a master or principal has that, because of various public policy reasons, the master or principal remains liable for even if someone else performs them.

**Nondeterioration Standards** Used in air pollution control to refer to federal standards for clean air areas that exceed air quality standards and that federal law continues to maintain.

**Nondiscretionary Duty** Used in connection with administrative agencies to describe agency duties that must be done and that a court will order an agency to do if it does not do them voluntarily.

**Nonexempt Property** A debtor's property that, according to Bankruptcy Code, may be divided among creditors to discharge debts.

**Nonexistent Principal** A principal that does not legally exist, such as a corporation not yet organized.

**Nonlitigation** Legal work not involving lawsuits.

**Nonobviousness** Requirement under patent law that an item trying to be patented was not readily thought of or apparent to a third party who possessed average skill in the area of endeavor.

**Norms of Conduct** How people act and the effect they have on positive law.

**Norris–LaGuardia Act** A federal labor law that, among other things, removed jurisdiction of federal courts to issue injunctions in labor disputes.

**Nuisance** A type of tort (civil wrong) where someone or something injures or annoys another or his or her property.

**O**SHA Walkaround Privilege Right of an employer and employee subject to OSHA to accompany the OSHA inspector during a plant inspection.

**Obiter Dicta** *see* Dicta.

**Objective Intent** The intent attributed to a person who appears to a reasonable third person to be making an offer to contract.

**Objective Standard** A test of liability based on the defendant's behavior or some other physical fact, and not on what the actor (defendant) thinks.

**Objective Test** Regarding contracts, a test to determine whether a contract exists based on what a reasonable third person would think the people allegedly making the contract have done.

**Objective Theory of Contracts** Way to determine whether a contract exists; the theory says that if a reasonable person would say that two parties appear to have made a contract, a contract exists in the eyes of the law even though the parties did not subjectively intend to form a contract.

**Offensive Use of the Pass-On Theory** A theory of recovering in an antitrust lawsuit where an antitrust plaintiff claims it was damaged by buying goods priced higher because of an "upstream" antitrust violation (someone the plaintiff did not buy directly from) and the plaintiff tries to recover from the "upstream" antitrust violator. This action is not allowed.

**Offer** A definite, communicated expression one party makes to another objectively intending to form a contract stating what the offeror will do and what the offeror expects in return from the offeree.

**Offeree** Person to whom an offer is made.

**Offeror** Person who makes an offer.

**Oligarchy** Government in which a small group makes the rules.

**Ombudspersons** Agency officials who act as inspectors of agencies to ensure that the agencies follow the law.

**Open Dumping** Way to get rid of solid waste by dumping it on land and not covering it.

**Open Meeting Law** A law forcing certain agency meetings to be open to the public. Also called "Sunshine Acts."

**Operation of Law** The idea that the law does something automatically when certain events occur (such as ending an agency when the agent dies).

**Options** Contracts whose subject matter is an offer.

**Ordinances** Laws passed by municipalities (cities and towns).

**Organic Acts** Statutes giving an administrative agency the legal right to exist.

**Orphan Lands** Word used in environmental law to refer to abandoned strip-mined land where no reclamation efforts have been made.

**P**c Professional corporation.

**Paid in Capital Account** Contains the total number of dollars paid into a company by stockholders for stock.

**Paper Remedies** Remedies that theoretically exist ("exist on the pages of the books") but which, as a practical matter, do not exist.

**Parens Patriae** Latin for "parent of the country"; an antitrust doctrine that gives state attorneys general the authority to enforce the Sherman Act.

**Partially Disclosed Principal** Agency where the identity of the agent and fact of agency are known but the principal's identity is unknown.

**Partnership** Two or more persons carrying on as co-owners of a business for profit. A form of business.

**Partnership by Estoppel** Where a person holds out another as a partner, and a third person reasonably relies on this holding out and damages result, the person holding out or permitting another to be held out as a partner is stopped from saying the person held out is not a partner.

**Pass-On Defense** A defense in an antitrust civil lawsuit in which the defendant says that the plaintiff may not recover its antitrust damages because the plaintiff passed on its damages to its customers. This defense is not allowed.

**Pass-On Theory** Antitrust theory that asserts that an antitrust defendant can claim the plaintiff (a direct buyer from an antitrust violator) passed on its antitrust damages to its customers (this defensive use of pass-on is not allowed). Also pass-on may not be used offensively by indirect buyers, one or more steps removed from antitrust violators in the production-distribution chain.

**Patent** A legal monopoly conferred by the government (the patentor) on the private party (patentee). The patent entitles the patentee to exclude anyone else from making, using, or selling the patented item for a period of 20 years from the date of the application.

**Patent License** Permission from a patent holder for another to use the patented item, usually in exchange for royalties.

**Per Se Offenses** Certain antitrust offenses that are so obviously socially harmful that the government does not have to show any particular economic harm to prove its case (harm is presumed).

**Per se rules** Certain antitrust offenses that are so obviously harmful that the government does not have to show any particular economic harm to prove its case.

**Percentage of Disability** A way of paying injured employees covered by workers' compensation when a loss occurs not expressly covered in the workers' comp schedule of recoveries.

**Peremptory Challenges** Challenges to a prospective juror where the challenging lawyer does not have to tell why the prospective juror is excused from jury duty.

**Perfected Security Interest** A creditor's claim on certain property of a debtor where the claim is superior to certain other creditors' claims to the same property.

**Periodic Tenancy** A tenancy created by implication in the case of holdover tenants from whom the landlord accepts rent for a discrete period such as a week or month after the lease has expired.

**Permanent Injunction** A court order telling someone never to do something; punishment for breaking such an injunction is being jailed.

**Personal Injury** Usually bodily harm resulting from negligence or product defeats; includes losses attributable to pain and suffering, mental distress, inconvenience, loss of companionship and consortium, injury to reputation, lost earnings, and so on.

**Personalty** Moveable property such as clothing, vehicles, furniture.

**Philosophical Positivism** The idea that the only real thing in the world is that which can be objectively pointed to, that is, "seeing is believing." Facts and data are evidence of themselves and thus are "real." Distinguished from feelings or ideas.

**Plea Bargain** A deal between the prosecutor and a criminal defendant, often where a guilty defendant pleads guilty to a lesser offense to escape the cost of trial.

**Pleadings** The complaint and answer in a civil lawsuit.

**Pocket Parts** Pamphlets inserted in the back of law books (statute books and case books) to update them with recently made laws.

**Point Sources** Definite points from which any kind of pollutant is discharged into the nation's waters.

**Police Magistrates** Courts that deal with minor legal violations—traffic violations, for example—of both a civil and criminal nature.

**Police Power** The power to regulate for the public health, safety, morals, and welfare. All the states possess this power. For all practical purposes, Congress possesses this power also, especially under the interstate commerce clause.

**Positive Law** Rules laid down by political superiors on political inferiors where there are sanctions (punishments) if the law is broken.

**Powers of Attorney** Written agency under which one person may do future acts for another person.

**Preconstruction Review Mechanism** Term used in air pollution control law to refer to the review that new buildings must go through before they are built to insure they comply with air pollution standards.

**Preempted** Where a federal statue so completely fills or dominates an area of law that the state has no legal power to pass law in the subject matter area.

**Prejudgment Attachment** A creditor's obtaining a legal claim on specific property of the debtor before a lawsuit is held to determine if the debtor in fact owes the creditor anything.

**Prejudgment Garnishment** *see* Prejudgment Wage Garnishment.

**Prejudgment Wage Garnishment** A creditor's obtaining payment from a debtor by obtaining a part of the debtor's weekly wages before a court determines whether the "debtor" owes the creditor anything.

**Pre-Manufacture Notice** Concept in environmental law referring to requirement that chemical makers tell the EPA about new, planned chemicals before they are made.

**Premerger Notification** The notice two companies planning to merge must give the FTC and Justice Department before they merge.

**Preponderance of the Evidence** A test in civil law, which a jury uses to decide whether enough evidence exists to find for the plaintiff.

**Pretreat** When used in connection with water pollution, it refers to certain industrial dischargers' taking some pollutants out of their waste discharge before dumping it in the city sewer.

**Prevention of Significant Deterioration** Term used in air pollution control to mean essentially the same thing as non-deterioration standards (preventing areas with air quality higher than federal law requires from having a drop in air quality to general federal standards).

**Prima Facie Case** A case strong enough to enable the plaintiff to win the suit unless contradicted by persuasive evidence from the defendant.

**Prima Facie Evidence** Enough evidence to get a case before a jury.

**Primary Activities** In labor activities, they are the direct economic weapons: in the case of employees, they use strikes; in the case of employers, they use lockouts.

**Primary Air Quality Standards** When used in connection with air pollution, refers to air pollution control laws designed to protect public health.

**Primary Line Price Discrimination** Involves economic injury to competitors of the discriminating seller; for example, a large manufacturer might finance its low prices in areas where it faces strong competition by charging higher prices in areas where competition is weak.

**Primary Market** The sale of new or just issued securities.

**Primary Rights** Substantive law.

**Principal-Agent Relationship** Occurs when one person (the principal) employs another (the agent) to enter business relations (usually contracts) with third persons

**Privilege** Defense to defamation; basically says that even if defendant's statement about plaintiff is otherwise true certain policy reasons (such as absolute free expression on the floor of the legislature) make defendant's remarks not a basis for a successful defamation suit; some types of privilege are qualified and others are absolute.

**Privity of Contract** Contractual relationship between two parties. If A sells goods to B, who in turn sells the goods to C, both A and B, as well as B and C, are "in" privity of contract, but A and C are not.

**Privity Rule** Rule of sales law that requires a plaintiff buyer to have contracted directly with a defendant seller before certain legal claims (e.g., breach of warranty) can be made against the seller. This rule has been largely abandoned.

**Pro Se** *see* Pro Se Litigant.

**Pro Se Litigant** A party to a lawsuit who does not have a lawyer.

**Probable Cause** Cause to believe a crime was committed and the person arrested committed it. Also the test for a grand jury's issuing an indictment.

**Probate Court** Court that deals with wills and estates.

**Procedural Due Process** A basic requirement of procedural fairness imposed on the federal government and the states by the Fifth and Fourteenth amendments; notice and fair hearing.

**Procedural Law** Rules governing steps in lawsuits or legal matters.

**Procedural Rules** Rules establishing how the legal system, courts, etc. are to operate.

**Procedural Unconscionability** A form of unconscionability involving either the way contract terms are packaged (e.g., fine print), or the factors that made a party enter into a contract (e.g., "sales hype").

**Producer** The creator of a particular trademark in use long enough so that the public associates the mark with the producer.

**Product Liability** Responsibility of manufacturers and sellers for any harm to purchasers of a product or other parties resulting from defective goods.

**Product Market** The market in which a product exists dependent upon the substitutability of other products for that product.

**Product Safety Standards** A standard reasonably necessary to prevent or reduce an unreasonable risk associated with the product, used as an enforcement device by the Consumer Product Safety Commission to promote product safety.

**Productive Efficiency** The ability of an economy to make goods and services in a way that uses the least amount of resources.

**Professional Corporation** A form of business organization reserved for those in the learned professions, which often limits the liability of shareholder professionals in some way.

**Profits** The right to enter someone else's real estate to remove the soil or what the soil produces, such as minerals, crops, or water.

**Promissory Notes** A written promise to pay a sum certain in money (any country's currency) at a future certain date or on demand. It is a two-party document; that is, only two persons—a person promising to pay, called the note's "maker," and a second, called the "payee" are mentioned on the front ("face") of the note.

**Property** The rights one person has regarding other people with respect to something; the rights a person or people have to something.

**Property Damage** Economic loss to property resulting from damage caused by negligence or a defective product.

**Proportionately Liable** Liability of outside directors for losses dependent upon their involvement in the losses.

**Proposed Order** When used in connection with Federal Trade Commission law enforcement, refers to orders the FTC plans to issue in particular cases.

**Proposed Rulemaking** When an agency publishes a regulation in the *Federal Register*, which the agency wants to make binding as law at a future time, unless the public can convince the agency the proposed regulation is unwise.

**Prosecutor** Society's attorney.

**Prospectus** Part of a registration statement that must be given to a securities buyer before or at the sale of certain securities.

**Power of Attorney** Express authority, granted only in writing, to one person to enable him or her to act for another.

**Proximate Cause** A term used to describe the legal issue presented by the degree of proximity or closeness between breach of duty and injury required in a negligence case. In most jurisdictions, it is based on the reasonable foreseeability of the plaintiff's injury having resulted from the defendant's breach.

**Public Function Doctrine** A branch of state action doctrine in which a finding of state action is based on the fact that a private body performs the same functions as a governmental body. A "company town" is an example. The public function doctrine is virtually dead by now.

**Public Law** Law that deals with matters affecting all or a large part of society, such as the Social Security Act, OSHA, and the Clean Water Act.

**Public Nuisance** Conduct or the use of property in a way that annoys or interferes with public rights.

**Public Policy** Refers to desirable goals or conduct.

**Puffing** Seller's talk that is legally only opinion and not fact and therefore may not be the basis for a lawsuit based on fraud.

**Punitive** Used to describe laws that punish. Criminal laws are punitive.

**Punitive (or Exemplary) Damages** Damages imposed on a party as a sort of penalty for particularly egregious behavior. Usually, some sort of recklessness or malicious behavior is required for their imposition. Punitive damages are most common in tort cases.

**Purchase** The most common means of acquiring property, both real and personal.

**Qualified** Said of a foreign corporation once it establishes its corporate existence in a state other than the state of incorporation; once a foreign corporation is qualified in another state, it may do intrastate business there.

**Qualified Employee Retirement Plan** A retirement plan meeting certain federal requirements and which employer contributions to are tax deductible by the employer.

**Qualified Privilege** A right to make defamatory statements limited only by motive and manner in which the remarks are made.

**Quasi in Rem** *see* Quasi in Rem Jurisdiction.

**Quasi in Rem Jurisdiction** Power of a court or other legal authority over a person because the court has physical control over some item of the person's property.

**Quasi-Contract** Contract imposed by a court (judge) on a situation where there actually is no contract but the court wants to avoid unjust enrichment.

**Quid Quo Pro Sexual Harassment** A form of sexual harassment involving some kind of linkage, connection, or trade between the employee's submission to sex-related behavior and tangible job consequences.

**Ratification** Retroactive authority a principal gives someone who, without authority, purports to act for another and whose acts the purported principal fully approves when he or she learns of them.

**Rational Basis Test** The basic equal protection test and the test applied to economic regulation. It requires only that the challenged law have a reasonable relationship with a valid governmental purpose. It is not much of an obstacle to government regulation of the economy.

**Rawls, John** Twentieth-century natural law philosopher who advanced the notion of the "original position" (suppose that you were behind a veil of ignorance and did not know what your status in life or characteristics were; this is the original position and is used to justify positive laws such as affirmative action).

**Real Estate Investment Trust (REIT)** A trust device used to own real estate. A business organization form.

**Real Estate Syndications** Arise when several persons own property. The vehicle for the joint ownership could be a limited partnership, partnership, trust, or corporation.

**Realty** Property classification denoting realty and buildings; immovables.

**Reasonable Person Standard** The basic test used to determine whether a breach of duty has occurred in a negligence case. The defendant's behavior is compared to the way a hypothetical reasonable person would have behaved under the circumstances.

**Recidivism** In criminal law it refers to repeating criminal conduct.

**Reclamation** Word used in environmental law to refer to efforts to restore surface mined land to the condition it was in before it was surface mined.

**Recycling** Reusing something; a conservation measure.

**Red-Herring Prospectus** A prospectus for the sale of securities that has red printing on it and which contains insufficient information to make it an offer or a prospectus.

**Redlining** Where lenders on houses refuse to make loans to borrowers in declining neighborhoods.

**Redress** Compensation given to injured parties or consumers by a business that violated a trade regulation rule.

**Reg-Neg** Regulations that are negotiated. It involves the appointment of a committee by an official of the agency responsible for the rule; the committee meets, shares information relevant to drafting the proposed regulation, comes up with a report, and then submits it to the agency with authority to promulgate it.

**Registered Agent** A person named by corporate organizers on whom process can be served if someone wishes to sue the particular corporation.

**Registers** Files information with the U.S. Patent and Trademark Office concerning a trademark, which limits its use by any other entity.

**Registration Statement** A document that must be filed with the Securities and Exchange Commission before one can offer certain securities for public sale.

**Regulation Z** A regulation promulgated under the Truth-in-Lending Act.

**Regulations** Law made by an administrative agency.

**Regulatory Flexibility Act** A federal statute passed in 1980 that adds certain procedures to help small entities participate in and cope with federal agency rulemaking.

**Regulatory Flexibility Agenda** A list published twice per year by each federal agency telling what regulations it intends to publish in the near future.

**Regulatory Occupational License** A type of permit one needs to do some types of work, where the main purpose of the occupational license is to protect the public from incompetent, unethical persons.

**Rehabilitation** In criminal law it refers to helping criminals become socially valuable members of society. One of the four basic objectives of criminal law.

**Rejection** Unqualified refusal by the offeree communicated to the offeror that the offer is not satisfactory; ends an offer.

**Remedy Limitation** A term in a contract (often a contract for the sale of goods) by which one party (usually a seller) attempts to block the other party's (usually the buyer's) recovery of certain kinds of damages. Remedy limitations are often confused with disclaimers, but differ because they attempt to restrict a party's remedies, not the party's liability under a particular theory of recovery.

**Reporters** Books containing judges' opinions deciding lawsuits.

**Representation Case** A type of lawsuit brought under the Wagner Act in which the employer or union alleges that a particular union should or should not be the collective bargaining representative for an employer.

**Representative Democracy** Form of government wherein the persons ruled elect representatives who make the society's rules.

**Requirements Contract** In a requirements contract, the buyer agrees to purchase all its requirements of a particular commodity from the seller.

**Res** Property in a trust.

**Res Ipsa Loquitur** A way to prove a breach of duty in negligence cases where the accident would not ordinarily have occurred without someone's negligence, and the thing causing the harm is exclusively within the control of the defendant. The doctrine assists the plaintiff because it enables proof of the breach where this would not otherwise be possible yet. Latin for "the thing speaks for itself."

**Res Judicata** Latin for "the matter has already been decided." Said of civil cases where a lawsuit on the matter has already occurred.

**Resale Price Maintenance** Where a manufacturer or distributor refuses to sell goods to a retailer unless the retailer agrees to sell to the public at certain minimum price.

**Rescission** Most often, a contract remedy whereby the court returns the parties to their original precontractual position.

**Respondeat Superior** The employer (superior) must answer for the employee's (agent's or servant's) wrongs committed at work.

**Respondent** The alleged violator.

**Restitution** Returning something to someone else; a type of contract or tort remedy.

**Restraint** Imprisonment of a criminal; one of the four basic objectives of criminal law.

**Retribution** Punishment of a criminal; one of the four basic objectives of criminal law.

**Retrofit Requirement** Term used in environmental law to refer to the idea that when new stricter pollution control requirements take effect, existing products and polluters must "upgrade" to meet them. Failure to impose retrofit requirements in new pollution laws "grandfathers in" existing polluters.

**Revenue-Raising Occupational License** A law whose purpose is to raise money to pay for state government.

**Reverse FOIA Case** A case where someone tries to stop a federal agency from giving information in its possession over to the public because the information is covered by an FOIA exemption.

**Revocation** When an offeror calls back his or her offer; a way to end an offer.

**Right of Survivorship** The idea that the joint tenant who die before other joint tenants loses all interest in the property.

**Right-to-Sue Letter** A procedural requirement in Title VII Civil Rights Act of 1964 cases.

**Risk Spreading** The dispersion of the higher economic risks of such principles as strict liability among all the parties who benefit from such a policy.

**Robinson-Patman Act** Federal antitrust law passed in 1936 which prohibits certain pricing practices.

**Rule Against Perpetuities** A law regarding trusts that limits the length of their existence.

**Rule of 45** A formula for calculating vesting of employer contributions to employee retirement plans.

**Rule of Law** All citizens—the president, governors, members of the Supreme Court, star athletes, and average citizens—must obey the rules.

**Rule of Reason** A rule of law used to interpret section I of the Sherman Antitrust law; to be a crime under section I of the Sherman Act the defendant's conduct must cause an unreasonable restraint of trade; it is not used in per se antitrust cases.

**Rule Utilitarianism** Maximizing one's happiness while still obeying the positive law.

**Rules** Law made by an administrative agency.

**S**ale of Goods Transaction in which the ownership of goods shifts from one party to another in exchange for equivalent consideration, usually money.

**SEC** Securities and Exchange Commission; a major federal administrative agency.

**Savigny** Legal philosopher advancing the historical school of law which emphasizes longstanding custom.

**Schism** A rule of labor law that says if a split in top union officials occurs a representation election can be held even though an unexpired collective bargaining agreement exists.

**Scope of Employment** Limit of one's job.

**Search Warrant** Governmental document entitling government officials to search private property for suspected legal violations or evidence of violations.

**Secondary Boycotts** Any combination of its purpose and effect is to coerce customers, patrons, or suppliers, through fear of loss or bodily harm, to withhold or withdraw their business from an employer the union has a dispute with.

**Secondary Line Price Discrimination** Price discrimination that causes economic injury to competitors of the favored buyer.

**Secondary Market** Old securities bought and sold daily.

**Secondary Rights** Remedies of primary rights (substantive law is broken).

**Secondary Standards** When used in connection with air pollution control, refers to air pollution control laws designed to protect public welfare (such as property and aesthetics).

**Securities and Exchange Commission (SEC)** A major federal administrative agency.

**Self-Insuring** An employer's decision not to hire an insurance company to help it administer losses.

**Service Mark** The equivalent of a trademark for service providers rather than actual goods.

**Servient Estate** Property that is subject to an easement.

**Session Laws** Laws published in the order they were passed by the legislature and before they are in code form.

**Settlement** A way plaintiff and defendant end a lawsuit by reaching an agreement without fully trying the case; a settlement can occur any time in a lawsuit before it otherwise ends.

**Settlor** Person who establishes a trust.

**706 Agencies** State or municipal civil rights agencies which have met legal requirements under section 706 of the Civil Rights Act of 1964.

**Sham Transactions** Matters that appear to be contracts but are not contracts and are made to cheat creditors or the taxing authorities.

**Share Subscriptions** What a corporate promoter sells to persons desiring to invest in stock of a corporation about to be organized.

**Shareholders** People who purchase corporate shares; stockholders.

**Shares** Pieces of a corporation offered for sale to investors.

**Shelf Registration** Registering securities under federal securities laws but not immediately offering them for sale.

**Sherman Antitrust Act** Federal antitrust law enacted in 1890 which outlaws contracts, combinations, or conspiracies in restraint of trade and monopolizing or attempts to monopolize. It makes certain acts both crimes (felonies) and civil treble damage actions.

**Showing of Employee Interest** Word used in federal labor law to describe when enough employees want the National Labor Relations Board to hold a representative election to decide whether a union will represent the employees.

**Simple Resolution** "Housekeeping" rules dealing with running only one house of Congress. Not a law.

**Skip Tracing** Trying to locate debtors.

**Social Compact** Basic legal organization of government, usually contained in a document called a "constitution."

**Social Contract** *see* Social Compact; meanings are identical.

**Social Offers** Statements offering to take part in a social event and are offers but are not legally considered offers in form due in part to the fact that courts do not want to get too involved in individuals' personal affairs and also because a remedy would be difficult to fashion.

**Socialization of Risk** A term used to describe the process whereby the economic risks of certain activities are effectively spread out through society, or socialized. Typically, it involves putting increased legal responsibility (often through strict liability) on the defendant, which then increases its prices to reflect the additional resulting costs. In this way, the economic burden of allowing greater plaintiff recoveries is "spread out" through society.

**Sociological School of Law** The idea that people's conduct shapes the law (Ehrlich's view) or that law is the result of weighing competing claims to see which is heavier (Pound's view).

**Sole Proprietor** One person who owns all of the assets and is solely liable for all of its liabilities. A legal form of business.

**Sovereign** The highest political authority in a society; the state (or government); supreme lawmaker in a society.

**Special Agent** Someone who acts for and under the control of another in a very limited matter (such as an agent hired to do one thing).

**Special 301** A section of the 1988 Trade Act; its purpose is to develop a strategy to protect intellectual property rights and to assume market access for U.S. business.

**Specific Intent Crimes** Crimes in which the intent required is different from the intent to do the act that is the crime (such as "assault with intent to murder").

**Specific Performance** Equity court order to a person to perform a contract exactly as agreed. A kind of equitable remedy.

**Spending Power** Congressional power to spend for the general welfare. This power can be used to regulate by making compliance with certain behavior a condition for getting federal money.

**Stakeholder** Any entity or person affected by the operation of a business; includes stockholders, customers, employees, suppliers, and the community in which the business operate.

**Standards of Performance** Used to describe air pollution control measures for new sources (new plants, buildings, and other sources emitting air pollutants).

**Standing** A question of the plaintiff's proximity to the violation.

**State Action** The requirement that, in order for certain independent constitutional checks to apply, there must be action by a governmental body, state or federal. This doctrine generally frees private bodies from having to obey these constitutional requirements.

**State Blue Book** A book published by each state that explains its government regulations and includes a list of state administrative agencies.

**State Exemptions** Property that cannot be taken by creditors to pay a person's debts because state law does not allow (exempts) it.

**State Implementation Plans (SIPs)** General plans each state has to control air pollution.

**State of Nature** Society in a prelaw, politically unorganized situation; stage of political development before a body politic is formed.

**State Right-to-Work Laws** State laws that allow employees at a unionized employer to refuse to join the union or pay dues.

**State Usury Laws** State laws setting limits on the rate of interest creditors can charge borrowers.

**Statute of Descent** A statutory will the legislature has made for people who die without a will.

**Statute of Frauds** State laws requiring that certain contracts be in writing or evidenced by a writing.

**Statute of Limitations** A period of time within which a particular lawsuit must begin. If suit is not entered within this period, the plaintiff loses his or her right to sue. The applicable time period differs with the particular cause of action the plaintiff is asserting. The period may begin to run at different times depending on the cause of action in question.

**Statute of Repose** A time limitation for the beginning of a suit, which applies to product liability cases. It runs from the time the product is sold to the last party in the chain of distribution not buying for resale. The most common such time period is ten years.

**Statutes** Laws made by legislators.

**Statutory Construction** Judicial lawmaking by filling gaps in statutes.

**Stock Dividend** When a corporation issues a dividend in the form of its own stock and transfers capital from a retained earnings account to a paid-in capital account to reflect this issuance.

**Stock Merger** When two or more companies join together by one's buying the other's (others') shares of stock and the buying company retains existence while the merged (purchased) company (companies) ceases (cease) to exist.

**Stock Proxy** A shareholder's written authorization to someone else to vote the shares.

**Stock Split** When a corporation divides its equity into more parts.

**Stockholders** People who purchase corporate shares; shareholders.

**Straight Bankruptcy** Bankruptcy under Chapter 7 of the federal bankruptcy code; which involves the debtor's turning over nonexempt assets to a bankruptcy trustee, the trustee's selling these assets and paying off creditors to the extent that assets exist, and discharging the debtor of all dischargeable debts.

**Strict Liability** Tort liability without fault. That is, liability imposed irrespective of whether the defendant intended to cause harm, was reckless, or was negligent.

**Strict Liability Criminal Statue** A criminal statute that requires only an act but no intent to commit a crime.

**Strict Scrutiny** An equal protection doctrine generally requiring that governmental classifications be necessary to the advancement of a compelling governmental interest.

**Strike** In labor laws, employees' temporary refusal to work.

**Style (of a Case)** Names of plaintiff(s) and defendant(s) in a lawsuit.

**Subject Matter Jurisdiction** The power of a court or other legal authority to deal with the type of case in question. For example, a probate court may decide the validity of wills but may not try murder cases.

**Subjective Intent** What persons allegedly making a contract think they have done.

**Sublet** When a tenant assigns his or her lease to another tenant.

**Substantial Evidence Test** An evidentiary test used to decide whether certain agency actions are supported by enough facts.

**Substantial Product Hazard** A substantial risk of injury to the public, which may result from the failure to comply with a Consumer Product Safety Commission rule or from a product defect.

**Substantive Due Process** A doctrine according to which certain state or federal substantive laws might be unconstitutional because they interfere with certain protected liberties and cannot be justified by important governmental interests.

**Substantive Law** Laws governing our relationships with other people and things in society; different than procedural law.

**Substantive Regulations** Agency rules that have the effect of law; they must be made in accordance with the Administrative Procedure Act.

**Substantive Rules** Legal rules setting out rights, duties, and standards of behavior applying to the public at large.

**Substantive Unconscionability** A form of unconscionability involving the terms of the contract—specifically, the duties and burdens they impose on the parties.

**Sunset Laws** Laws that cause an administrative agency to end at a certain time.

**Sunshine Exemptions** Certain agency meetings that do not have to be open to the public under open meeting or "sunshine" laws.

**Superior Agent Rule** A rule holding corporate principals liable only for crimes of high-level employees.

**Superior Courts** State courts of general jurisdiction where major civil or criminal lawsuits usually start. These are courts of record with possible jury trials, unlike municipal, justice of the peace, domestic relations, common pleas, juvenile, and probate courts.

**Supremacy Clause** Article VI of the Constitution that establishes the principle of federal supremacy.

*Supreme Court Reporter* A set of privately published books containing U.S. Supreme Court decisions in chronological order.

**Survival Statutes** Statutes that keep a cause of action from dying when the person who has the cause of action dies; for example survival statutes give the dependents of a person killed in an auto accident a claim against the person who killed him or her.

**Suspect Classification** Governmental discrimination based on race or national origin, sex, illegitimacy, and alienage. These classifications all get some form of equal protection strict scrutiny.

**T**aft-Hartley Act A major federal labor law passed in 1947.

**Takings Clause** Part of the Fourteenth Amendment due process provision that states that private property shall not be taken for public use without just compensation.

**Target Corporation** A term used in corporate law to describe a corporation that persons outside the corporation wish to buy, usually by stock purchase.

**Taxing Power** Congressional power to lay and collect taxes. Basically used to raise revenue, this congressional power is also an important regulatory tool.

**Ten-Year Vesting** A formula for calculating vesting of employer contributions to employee retirement plans.

**Tenancy By the Entirety** A specialized form of joint tenancy; the joint tenants must be spouses.

**Tenancy for Years** A lease beginning and ending at a definite time covering a definite period.

**Tenancy in Partnership** Ownership that occurs when business partners own property together; this form of tenancy has the right of survivorship feature.

**Tenant in Partnership** The way partners own partnership property.

**Tenants in Common** The type of ownership that occurs where two or more people have title to an interest in realty.

**Tender Offer** An offer to company shareholders to buy their shares with an eye toward taking over the company.

**Tender Offeror** Someone who makes a tender offer.

**Territorial Market** That region of the country in which a firm can increase its price without drawing in new competitors and without losing sales to competitors outside the region.

**Tertiary Line Price Discrimination** Price discrimination that economic injury to competitors of the favored buyer's buyers.

**Testamentary** A trust that takes effect at the settler's death.

**Testator** The maker of a will.

**Theories of Product Liability Recovery** Legal rules stating the points a plaintiff must prove in order to recover damages from a seller of defective goods.

**Thirty-Day Regulation** Governing Mail-Order Merchandise A Federal Trade Commission regulation that protects consumers buying goods by mail.

**Tied Product** A product one must buy in order to be able to buy another product.

**Title** Property concept used to identify the owner of property.

**Title Documents** Pieces of paper that tell who owns certain types of property, such as vehicles and real estate.

**Titles** Major parts of long statutes.

**Tombstone Ad** A written ad for securities. The ad has black borders (usually) and is not an offer because it does not have enough information. An ad for securities designed to generate public interest in the upcoming offering that is not legally an offer.

**Tort** A civil wrong that is not a breach of contract.

**Trade Fixtures** Such items as signs and counters, which are firmly attached to the realty, and remain the tenant's personal property.

**Trade Regulation Rules** Federal Trade Commission regulations governing various business practices.

**Trade Secrets** Information a person has that is used in business transactions to give advantage over competitors who do not know the information or use it.

**Transferability of Shares** A characteristic of corporate stock that lets a shareholder sell or transfer the stock to someone else.

**Treasury Shares** A corporation's issued shares that it has purchased in the market and holds as an asset.

**Treble Damages** Triple damages.

**Trespass** A type of tort (civil wrong) in which one person unlawfully interferes with another's property or person.

**Trust** Legal way to hold property in which there are two titles; one legal, the other equitable.

**Trustee** Person(s) holding legal title to property in a trust.

**Turbidity** The presence of microscopic particulates in the air.

**Tying Arrangement** *see* Tying Contracts.

**Tying Contracts** In antitrust law, where a business agrees to sell desired goods or services conditioned on the buyer's agreeing to purchase another less desired good or service (this practice often violates the antitrust laws).

**Tying Product** A product that can be bought only if one first buys another product (called a "tied" product).

**U**nannotated Without footnotes explaining the text (said of codes or statutes where no footnotes exist, referring to cases interpreting or refining the code).

**Unannotated Code** A lengthy statute that does not refer to particular cases interpreting it.

**Unauthorized Appropriation** A type of invasion of privacy; an intentional tort occurring when defendant uses plaintiff's name or likeness without permission.

**Unconscionability** An open-ended contract doctrine under which courts refuse to enforce especially one-sided contracts or contract terms.

**Underwriters** Persons who buy securities expecting to resell them to dealers, who in turn resell them to the public.

**Undisclosed Principal** A type of agency relationship where the third person knows neither the fact that an agency exists nor that the person dealt with is an agent nor the principal's identity.

**Undue Influence** Where a trust relationship (although not necessarily a formal trust) exists between two people who make a contract, and the one in whom the other places trust "double-crosses" the trusting person, making the contract to the disadvantage of the trusting party. These are grounds for a court to declare the contract voidable (not enforceable).

**Unenforceable Contracts** Those contracts failing to meet a procedural or formal requirement, making them unenforceable.

**Unfair Labor Practice** A legal wrong that gives rise to a cause of action.

**Uniform Commercial Code** A lengthy state statute covering many aspects of commercial law; mainly covers goods and fixtures; usually does not cover realty, services, or insurance.

**Uniform Guidelines on Employee Selection Procedures (UGESP)** Equal Employment Opportunity Guidelines that help employers comply with federal civil rights laws.

**Uniform Limited Partnership Act** A model statute that permits people to form limited partnerships.

**Unilateral Contract** A contract formed when one party promises something in exchange for the other's act ("a promise for an act").

**United States Reports** A set of books containing cases in chronological order decided by the U.S. Supreme Court; the publisher is U.S. government, which is not noted for its speed in publishing these books.

**Unrestricted, Unreserved Earned Surplus** A requirement that puts limits on dividend declarations by directors.

**U.S. Claims Court** A federal court where people can sue the U.S. government.

**U.S. Court of Appeals** A federal, multi-judge appellate court.

**U.S. Court of International Trade** A federal court with the power to hear cases involving tariff matters.

**Use Immunity** A rule of criminal procedural law that says if the prosecutor gives a criminal suspect immunity from prosecution if the suspect gives the prosecutor information about crimes, the prosecutor will not in any way use that information to convict the person giving the information.

**Useful** To have utility or beneficial use.

**Utilitarian Theory of Law** Bentham's view that law should produce the greatest good for the greatest number.

# Valid Contract A contract that has no legal flaws.

**Vertical Merger** When two (or more) companies at different levels of the production and distribution cycle combine by asset or stock merger so the acquiring company remains in existence and the acquired company ceases to exist by becoming part of the acquiring company.

**Vertical Price Fixing** Where businesses at different levels in the distribution chain agree to price fix; a per se Sherman Act violation.

**Vest** To give someone property rights or the equivalent.

**Vested Benefits** Benefits that are someone's property and that cannot be taken away unless the person is given due process of law.

**Void** Of no legal effect; said of illegal contracts.

**Voidable** In contract matters, a contract that because of some legal flaw can be set aside by at least one of the parties to it.

**Voidable Title** A flawed ownership in property, which allows the holder of the property to pass "good," i.e., flawless, title to good faith purchasers for value without notice of the flaw; this flaw would let another person claim superior title to the property and take it away from the person with the voidable title.

**Voir Dire** The questioning of prospective jurors to see whether they are appropriate to sit on the jury in a particular case.

**Voluntary Bankruptcy** A debtor's entering bankruptcy of his or her own free will.

# Wagner Act The National Labor Relations Act passed in 1935.

**Waiting Period** The period between the filing of a registration statement and the time when the sale of the securities involved can occur.

**Waive** To voluntarily give up a legal right, such as "waive jury trial."

**Waiver-of-Defenses Clause** Used with references to commercial paper referring to words that cause a person signing a note to give up certain defenses they would have had against a person later buying the note.

**Ward** Someone not qualified to manage his or her own affairs (a legal incompetent); also a political subdivision.

**Warnings or Instructions** Product safety standards requiring adequate disclosure to consumers to prevent or reduce any unreasonable risk associated with a product.

**Warrant** Court order, such as arrest warrant.

**Warranty** A contractual promise as to the nature of a thing sold.

**Wheeler-Lea Act** A federal law passed in 1938 that expanded coverage of the Federal Trade Commission Act to allow the FTC to stop unfair competition even if a business were not injured; Wheeler-Lea made it sufficient if a consumer were injured.

**Whipsaw Strikes** Strikes in which unions in a multi employer bargaining unit "play employers off against one another" by striking some but not all employers in the bargaining unit.

**Will** A piece of paper on which a testator indicates the persons who will take his or her property when he or she dies.

**Withdrawal** Words used in labor law to decide a way of settling an unfair labor practice case by, in effect, the complaining party's dropping its complaint.

**Work Environment** Sexual Harassment Sexually related behavior that is so severe or pervasive that it affects work performance and/or creates an intimidating, hostile, or offensive working environment.

**Workers' Compensation** A system of paying workers for damages resulting from job-related injuries, illness, or death; the system abandons fault as a basis for assigning liability for such work-related losses; the employer bears the cost (in the immediate sense) of such losses.

**World Trade Organization** The successor organization to GATT.

**Writ of Execution** A legal device that lets a public official take certain property of a debtor, sell it, and use the proceeds to pay off a debt owed a creditor.

**Wrongful Interference with Contractual Relations** An intentional tort in which a third party knows that two other persons have a contract and knowingly interferes with that contract.

# INDEX